OXFORD REFERENCE

The
Oxford
Paperback
Italian
Dictionary

The Oxford Paperback Italian Dictionary

Italian–English   English–Italian

Italiano–inglese   Inglese–italiano

JOYCE ANDREWS

Oxford   New York

OXFORD UNIVERSITY PRESS

Oxford University Press, Walton Street, Oxford OX2 6DP

Oxford New York Toronto
Delhi Bombay Calcutta Madras Karachi
Petaling Jaya Singapore Hong Kong Tokyo
Nairobi Dar es Salaam Cape Town
Melbourne Auckland

and associated companies in
Berlin Ibadan

Oxford is a trade mark of Oxford University Press

First published 1986
First issued (with corrections) as an Oxford University Press paperback 1989
Reprinted 1989, 1990

British Library Cataloguing in Publication Data
Andrews, Joyce
[The Oxford Italian minidictionary].
The Oxford paperback Italian dictionary:
Italian-English, English-Italian
Italiano-inglese, Inglese-italiano
(Oxford paperback reference).
1. Italian language—Italian & English dictionaries
I. [The Oxford Italian minidictionary]
II. Title
453'.21
ISBN 0–19–282184–9

Library of Congress Cataloging in Publication Data
The Oxford paperback Italian dictionary.
1. Italian language—Dictionaries—English
2. English language—Dictionaries—Italian.
I. Andrews, Joyce
PC1640.094 1988   453'.21   88-1804
ISBN 0–19–282184–9 (pbk.)

Printed in Great Britain by
The Guernsey Press Co. Ltd
Guernsey, Channel Islands

Contents · Indice

Preface

This dictionary is intended for both general and practical use. It provides a comprehensive treatment of the most useful words and expressions in circulation today in the English and Italian languages. I have included idiomatic terms in contemporary usage, and have not excluded technical jargon.

Indicators in brackets mark different uses of the same word and, together with a wide range of style and field labels, guide the user to the appropriate translation.

Common abbreviations, names of countries, and other useful geographical names are included.

English pronunciation is given by means of the International Phonetic Alphabet (see p. xi). It is shown for all headwords and for those derived words whose pronunciation cannot be deduced from that of a headword. The rules for pronunciation of Italian are given on p. x.

I should like to acknowledge the valuable assistance given to me by Dr J. B. Sykes, Emanuela Tandello, and my colleague in lexicography Dr M. Janes. For her constructive suggestions I am indebted to my Italian friend Lia Bodenham. Thanks too to my son Robert Andrews and my daughter Carolyn Forte for comments and criticisms; and, most of all, to my husband Allen Andrews for his constant encouragement and support when words failed me . . .

J.A.

Prefazione

Questo dizionario è stato ideato per uso generale e pratico. Vi offre una trattazione comprensiva dei vocaboli più utili e delle espressioni più aggiornate in uso oggi nella lingua inglese e italiana. Ho incluso i termini più idiomatici che sono entrati a far parte dell'uso corrente, non escludendo il linguaggio tecnico.

Le indicazioni fra parentesi denotano usi differenti dello stesso vocabolo, e con una vasta gamma di definizioni descrittive, conducono a traduzioni diverse secondo il senso in cui una parola identica viene usata.

Sono inclusi abbreviazioni comuni, nomi di paesi e nomi geografici.

La pronuncia inglese è data usando l'Alfabeto Fonetico Internazionale (vedi p. xi). Questo viene indicato in tutti i lemmi e i derivati la cui pronuncia è diversa dal lemma principale. Le regole della pronuncia italiana si trovano a p. x.

Desidero ringraziare il Dr J. B. Sykes, Emanuela Tandello, e il mio collega in lessicografia Dr M. Janes per il loro valido aiuto. Per suggerimenti costruttivi sono grata alla mia amica italiana Lia Bodenham. Sono riconoscente a mio figlio Robert Andrews e mia figlia Carolyn Forte per utilissimi commenti e critiche e, più di tutti, a mio marito Allen Andrews per il suo costante incoraggiamento e sostegno quando mi mancava la parola . . .

J.A.

Introduction

The swung dash ($\sim$) is used to replace a headword or that part of a headword preceding the vertical bar (|). In both English and Italian only irregular plurals are given. As a general rule Italian nouns and adjectives form the plural by replacing the final *o* with *i* and *a* with *e*. The feminine of an Italian adjective is formed by replacing the final *o* with *a*. Nouns and adjectives ending in *e* have the same forms for both masculine and feminine; *e* changes to *i* in the plural (e.g. *grande, grandi*). In the English into Italian section only the masculine form of an Italian adjective is shown. Italian verb tables are given on p. 471.

Proprietary terms

This dictionary includes some words which are, or are asserted to be, proprietary names or trade marks. Their inclusion does not imply that they have acquired for legal purposes a non-proprietary or general significance, nor is any other judgement implied concerning their legal status. In cases where the editor has some evidence that a word is used as a proprietary name or trade mark this is indicated by the letter (*P.*), but no judgement concerning the legal status of such words is made or implied thereby.

Introduzione

Il trattino ondulato (∼) viene usato per sostituire un lemma o la parte di un lemma precedente la barra verticale (|). Sia in inglese che in italiano figurano solamente i plurali irregolari. Il plurale regolare in inglese si forma aggiundendo la lettera *s* al sostantivo singolare, ma si aggiunge *es* quando una parola finisce in *ch*, *sh*, *s*, *ss*, *us*, *x*, o *z* (p.es. *sash*, *sashes*). Nel caso di una parola che finisce in *y* preceduta da una consonante, *y* diventa *ies* (p.es. *baby*, *babies*). Nella sezione inglese-italiano solamente la forma maschile di un aggettivo italiano viene indicata. In generale i verbi regolari inglesi formano il tempo passato e participio passato con l'aggiunta della desinenza *ed* all'infinito (p.es. *last*, *lasted*). Nel caso di verbi che finiscono con *e* muta, questi aggiungono solamente *d* (p.es. *move*, *moved*). Nei verbi che finiscono in *y*, la *y* diventa *i* prima di aggiungere *ed* (p.es. *carry*, *carried*). I verbi irregolari si trovano nella nomenclatura in ordine alfabetico con rimando all'infinito.

Marche depositate

Questo dizionario include alcune parole che sono o asseriscono di essere termini di marca depositata. La loro presenza non denota che hanno acquistato legalmente un significato generale, né si suggerisce alcun altro giudizio riguardo il loro stato legale. In casi in cui il redattore ha evidenza che una parola viene usata come marca depositata, questa viene indicata dalla lettera (*P*.), ma nessun giudizio riguardo lo stato legale di tali parole viene fatto o suggerito.

Pronunciation of Italian

Vowels:

a is broad like *a* in *bath*: **casa**.

e has two sounds: close like *ey* in *they*: **sera**; open like *e* in *egg*: **sette**.

i is like *ee* in *feet*: **venire**.

o has two sounds: close like *o* in *show*: **brodo**; open like *o* in *dog*: **bocca**.

u is like *oo* in *moon*: **luna**.

When two or more vowels come together each vowel is pronounced separately: **buono**; **baia**.

Consonants:

b, d, f, l, m, n, p, t, v are pronounced as in English. When these are double they are sounded distinctly: **bello**.

c before **a, o,** or **u** and before consonants is like *k* in *king*: **cane**.
before **e** or **i** is like *ch* in *church*: **cena**.

ch is also like *k* in *king*: **chiesa**.

g before **a, o,** or **u** is hard like *g* in *got*: **gufo**.
before **e** or **i** is like *j* in *jelly*: **gentile**.

gh is like *gu* in *guilty*: **ghiaccio**.

gl when followed by **a, e, o, u** is like *gl* in *glass*: **gloria**.

gli is like *lli* in *million*: **figlio**.

gn is like *ni* in *onion*: **bagno**.

h is silent.

ng is like *ng* in *finger* (not *singer*): **ringraziare**.

r is pronounced distinctly.

s between two vowels is like *s* in *rose*: **riso**.
at the beginning of a word it is like *s* in *soap*: **sapone**.

sc before *e* or *i* is like *sh* in *shell*: **scienza**.

z sounds like *dz*: **zio**.

The stress is shown by the sign ′ printed after the syllable stressed.

Pronuncia Inglese

Vocali e dittonghi

ɪ	s*i*t	u:	t*oo*	aʊ	n*ow*
i:	s*ee*	ʌ	c*u*p	aʊə	fl*our*
e	w*e*t	ə	*a*go	ɔɪ	c*oi*n
æ	b*a*d	ɜ:	w*o*rk	ɪə	h*ere*
ɑ:	c*a*r	eɪ	m*a*de	eə	h*air*
ɒ	g*o*t	əʊ	h*o*me	ʊə	p*oor*
ɔ:	d*oo*r	aɪ	f*i*ve		
ʊ	p*u*t	aɪə	f*ire*		

Consonanti

p	*p*en	θ	*th*ree	dʒ	pa*ge*
b	*b*oy	ð	*th*is	h	*h*e
t	*t*en	s	*s*peak	m	*m*an
d	*d*ay	z	hi*s*	n	*n*ew
k	*c*oat	ʃ	*sh*ip	ŋ	thi*ng*
g	*g*o	tʃ	mu*ch*	l	*l*eg
f	*f*oot	j	*y*es	r	*r*un
v	*v*erb	ʒ	plea*s*ure	w	*w*et

Nota: ' precede la sillaba accentata.

Abbreviations · Abbreviazioni

English	Abbreviation	Italiano
adjective	*a.*	aggettivo
abbreviation	*abbr.*	abbreviazione
adjectives	*adjs.*	aggettivi
adverb	*adv.*	avverbio
adverbs	*advs.*	avverbi
administration	*admin.*	amministrazione
aeronautics	*aeron.*	aeronautica
American	*Amer.*	americano
anatomy	*anat.*	anatomia
archaeology	*archaeol.*	archeologia
architecture	*archit.*	architettura
definite article	*art. def.*	articolo determinativo
indefinite article	*art. indef.*	articolo indeterminativo
astrology	*astr.*	astrologia
motor car	*auto.*	automobile
auxiliary	*aux.*	ausiliario
biology	*biol.*	biologia
botany	*bot.*	botanica
commerce	*comm.*	commercio
conjunction	*conj.*	congiunzione
conjunctions	*conjs.*	congiunzioni
cookery	*culin.*	cucina
	ecc.	eccetera
electricity	*electr.*	elettricità
et cetera	*etc.*	
feminine	*f.*	femminile
familiar	*fam.*	familiare
figurative	*fig.*	figurato
geography	*geog.*	geografia
geology	*geol.*	geologia
grammar	*gram.*	grammatica
humorous	*hum.*	umoristico
interjection	*int.*	interiezione
interrogative	*inter.*	interrogativo
invariable	*invar.*	invariabile
law	*jurid.*	legge/giuridico
language	*lang.*	lingua
masculine	*m.*	maschile
mathematics	*math.*	matematica
mechanics	*mech.*	meccanica
medicine	*med.*	medicina
military	*mil.*	militare
music	*mus.*	musica
mythology	*myth.*	mitologia

noun	*n.*	sostantivo
nouns	*ns.*	sostantivi
navigation	*naut.*	nautica
oneself	*o.s.*	
proprietary term	*P.*	marca depositata
pejorative	*pej.*	peggiorativo
plural	*pl.*	plurale
politics	*pol.*	politica
possessive	*poss.*	possessivo
past participle	*p.p.*	participio passato
prefix	*pref.*	prefisso
preposition	*prep.*	preposizione
prepositions	*preps.*	preposizioni
present tense	*pres.*	presente
pronoun	*pron.*	pronome
pronouns	*prons.*	pronomi
psychology	*psych.*	psicologia
past tense	*p.t.*	tempo passato
	qcsa.	qualche cosa
	qcno.	qualcuno
reflexive	*r.*	riflessivo
railway	*rail.*	ferrovia
relative pronoun	*rel. pron.*	pronome relativo
religion	*relig.*	religione
singular	*s.*	singolare
school	*schol.*	scuola
slang	*sl.*	gergo
someone	*s.o.*	
something	*sthg.*	
technical	*techn.*	tecnico
theatrical	*theatr.*	teatrale
television	*TV*	televisione
typography	*typ.*	tipografia
university	*univ.*	università
auxiliary verb	*v. aux.*	verbo ausiliare
intransitive verb	*v.i.*	verbo intransitivo
reflexive verb	*v.r.*	verbo riflessivo
transitive verb	*v.t.*	verbo transitivo
transitive and intransitive verb	*v.t./i.*	verbo transitivo e intransitivo

A

a *prep.* (*termine*) to; (*stato in luogo, tempo, età*) at; (*per città grande*) in; (*costo, frequenza*) a, an; (*distributivo*) by. ~ **domani** see you tomorrow. ~ **due** ~ **due** two by two. ~ **piedi** on foot. ~ **venti chilometri da qui** twenty kilometres away.

aba'te *n.m.* abbot.

abbacchia'to *a.* downhearted.

abba'cchio *n.m.* (young) lamb.

abbaglia'nte *a.* dazzling. —*n.m.* headlight.

abbaglia're *v.t.* dazzle. **abba'glio** *n.m.* blunder. **prendere un abbaglio** make a mistake.

abbaia're *v.i.* bark.

abbai'no *n.m.* dormer window.

abbandona'r|e *v.t.* forsake; (*luogo*) leave; (*piani ecc.*) give up. ~si *v.r.* let oneself go. ~si a (*ricordi ecc.*) give oneself up to. **abbando'no** *n.m.* abandoning; (*fig.*) abandon; (*stato*) neglect.

abbassa'r|e *v.t.* lower; (*radio, TV*) turn down. ~si *v.r.* stoop; (*sole ecc.*) sink; (*fig.*) demean oneself. ~e i fari dip the headlights.

abba'sso *adv.* below. —*int.* down with.

abbasta'nza *adv.* enough; (*piuttosto*) rather.

abba'tter|e *v.t.* demolish; (*aereo*) shoot down; (*fig.*) dishearten. ~si *v.r.* (*cadere*) fall; (*fig.*) be discouraged.

abbazi'a *n.f.* abbey.

abbeceda'rio *n.m.* primer.

abbelli'r|e *v.t.* embellish. ~si *v.r.* adorn oneself.

abbevera'r|e *v.t.* water. ~to'io *n.m.* drinking trough.

abbiccì *n.m. invar.* alphabet.

abbie'nte *a.* well-to-do.

abbigliame'nto *n.m.* clothes *pl.*; (*industria*) clothing industry.

abbiglia'r|e *v.t.* dress. ~si *v.r.* dress up.

abbina'r|e *v.t.* combine. ~me'nto *n.m.* combining.

abbindola're *v.t.* cheat.

abboccame'nto *n.m.* interview; (*conversazione*) talk.

abbocca're *v.i.* bite; (*tubi*) join; (*fig.*) swallow the bait.

abboffa'rsi *v.r.* stuff oneself.

abboname'nto *n.m.* subscription; (*ferroviario ecc.*) season-ticket. **fare l'~** take out a subscription. **abbona're** *v.t.* make s.o. a subscriber. **abbona'rsi (a)** *v.r.* subscribe (to); take out a season-ticket (for). **abbona'to, a** *n.m., f.* subscriber.

abbonda'n|te *a.* abundant; (*vestiario*) roomy. ~te di abounding in. ~za *n.f.* abundance.

abbonda're *v.i.* abound.

abborda'bile *a.* (*persona*) approachable; (*prezzo*) reasonable.

abborda're *v.t.* (*nave*) board; (*persona*) approach; (*compito ecc.*) tackle.

abbottona'|re *v.t.* button up. ~tu'ra *n.f.* (row of) buttons.

abbozza're *v.t.* sketch (out). ~ **un sorriso** give a hint of a smile. **abbo'zzo** *n.m.* sketch.

abbraccia're *v.t.* embrace; (*persona*) hug; (*professione*) take up; (*fig.*) include. **abbra'ccio** *n.m.* embrace; hug.

abbrevia'|re *v.t.* shorten; (*ridurre*) curtail. ~zio'ne *n.f.* abbreviation.

abbronza'|re *v.t.* bronze; (*pelle*) tan. ~to *a.* tanned. ~tu'ra *n.f.* sun-tan.

abbrustoli're *v.t.* toast; (*caffè ecc.*) roast.

abbrutime'nto *n.m.* brutalization. **abbruti're** *v.t.* brutalize.

abbuia'rsi *v.r.* darken.

abbuo'no *n.m.* allowance; (*sport*) handicap.

abdica'|re *v.i.* abdicate. ~zio'ne *n.f.* abdication.

aberrazio'ne *n.f.* aberration.

abe'te *n.m.* fir (-tree); (*legno*) fir wood.

abie'tto *a.* despicable.

a'bil|e *a.* able; (*idoneo*) fit; (*intelligente*) clever. ~ità *n.f.* ability; fitness; cleverness. ~me'nte *adv.* ably; cleverly.

abilitazio'ne *n.f.* qualification; (*titolo*) diploma. **abilita'to** *a.* qualified.

abi'sso *n.m.* abyss.

abita'nte *n.m./f.* inhabitant.
abita'|re *v.i.* live. ∾**to** *a.* inhabited; *n.m.* built-up area. ∾**zio'ne** *n.f.* house. **crisi delle** ∾**zioni** housing problem.
a'bito *n.m.* (*da donna*) dress; (*da uomo*) suit.
abitua'l|e *a.* usual, habitual. ∾**me'nte** *adv.* usually.
abitua'r|e *v.t.* accustom. ∾**si a** *v.r.* get used to.
abitu'din|e *n.f.* habit. **d'**∾**e** usually. **per** ∾**e** out of habit. ∾**a'rio, a** *a.* of fixed habits; *n.m.*, *f.* person of fixed habits.
abiura're *v.t.* renounce.
abluzio'ne *n.f.* ablution.
abnegazio'ne *n.f.* self-sacrifice.
aboli'|re *v.t.* abolish; (*legge*) repeal. ∾**zio'ne** *n.f.* abolition; repeal.
abomine'vole *a.* abominable.
abori'geno, a *a.* & *n.m.,f.* aboriginal.
aborri're *v.t.* abhor.
aborti'|re *v.i.* miscarry; (*non naturalmente*) have an abortion. ∾**vo** *a.* abortive. **abo'rto** *n.m.* miscarriage; abortion.
abras|io'ne *n.f.* abrasion. ∾**i'vo** *a.* & *n.m.* abrasive.
abroga'|re *v.t.* repeal. ∾**zio'ne** *n.f.* repeal.
a'bside *n.f.* apse.
abusa're *v.i.* ∾ **di** abuse; (*approfittare*) take advantage of. **abu'so** *n.m.* abuse. **abuso di confidenza** breach of confidence.
abusi'vo *a.* illegal.
a.C. *abbr.* (*di* **avanti Cristo**) BC; Before Christ.
accade'mia *n.f.* academy. **fare dell'**∾ talk to no purpose.
accade'mico, a *a.* academic. —*n.m.*, *f.* academician.
accad|e're *v.i.* happen. **acca'da quel che accada** come what may. ∾**u'to** *n.m.* event.
accalappia're *v.t.* catch; (*fig.*) allure.
accalca'rsi *v.r.* crowd.
accalda'|rsi *v.r.* get overheated; (*fig.*) get excited. ∾**to** *a.* overheated.
accalora'rsi *v.r.* get excited.
accampame'nto *n.m.* camp. **accampa're** *v.t.* camp; (*fig.*) put forth.
accani'me'nto *n.m.* tenacity; (*odio*) rage. **accani'to** *a.* persistent; (*odio*) fierce; (*fig.*) inveterate.
accani'rsi *v.r.* persist; (*infierire*) rage.
acca'nto *adv.* near. ∾ **a** *prep.* next to.

accantona're *v.t.* set aside; (*mil.*) billet.
accaparra|me'nto *n.m.* hoarding; (*comm.*) cornering. **accaparra're** *v.t.* hoard; corner. ∾**to're, ∾tri'ce** *n.m.*, *f.* hoarder.
accapiglia'rsi *v.r.* scuffle; (*litigare*) squabble.
accappato'io *n.m.* bathrobe.
accappona're *v.t.* **fare** ∾ **la pelle di qcno.** make s.o.'s flesh creep.
accarezza're *v.t.* caress; (*fig.*) cherish.
accasa'rsi *v.r.* get married.
accascia'rsi *v.r.* collapse; (*fig.*) lose heart.
accatasta're *v.t.* pile up.
accatto'n|e, a *n.m.,f.* beggar. ∾**a'ggio** *n.m.* begging.
accavalcio'n|e, ∾i *adv.* astride.
accavalla'r|e *v.t.* (*gambe*) cross. ∾**si** *v.r.* pile up; (*fig.*) overlap.
acceca're *v.t.* blind. —*v.i.* go blind.
acce'dere *v.i.* ∾ **a** approach; (*acconsentire*) comply with.
accelera'|re *v.i.* accelerate. —*v.t.* speed up. ∾**re il passo** quicken one's pace. ∾**to're** *n.m.* accelerator. ∾**zio'ne** *n.f.* acceleration.
accelera'to *a.* rapid. —*n.m.* slow train.
acce'nder|e *v.t.* light; (*luce, TV, ecc.*) turn on; (*fig.*) inflame. ∾**si** *v.r.* catch fire; (*illuminarsi*) light up; (*fig.*) become inflamed. **accensio'ne** *n.f.* lighting; (*di motore*) ignition.
accendi'no *n.m.* lighter.
accenna're *v.t.* indicate. —*v.i.* ∾ **a** beckon to; (*fig.*) hint at; (*far l'atto di*) make as if. **acce'nno** *n.m.* gesture; (*con il capo*) nod; (*fig.*) hint.
acce'nt|o *n.m.* accent; (*tonico*) stress. ∾**a're** *v.t.* accent; stress.
accentra'|re *v.t.* centralize. ∾**me'nto** *n.m.* centralizing.
accentua'|re *v.t.* accentuate. ∾**rsi** *v.r.* become more noticeable. ∾**to** *a.* marked.
accerchia'|re *v.t.* surround. ∾**me'nto** *n.m.* surrounding.
accerta're *v.t.* ascertain; (*controllare*) check; (*reddito*) assess.
acce'so *a.* lighted; (*radio, TV, ecc.*) on; (*colore*) bright.
accessi'bile *a.* accessible; (*persona*) approachable; (*spesa*) reasonable.
acce'sso *n.m.* access; (*med., impeto*) fit. **vietato l'**∾ no admittance.

accesso'rio *a.* & *n.m.* accessory; (*pl.,* *rifiniture*) fittings.

acce'tta *n.f.* hatchet.

accetta'|re *v.t.* accept; (*aderire a*) agree to. ∿bile *a.* acceptable. ∿zio'ne *n.f.* acceptance; (*luogo*) reception.

acce'tto *a.* agreeable. **essere bene** ∿ be liked.

accezio'ne *n.f.* meaning.

acchiappa're *v.t.* catch.

acciacca're *v.t.* crush; (*fig.*) prostrate.

accia'cco *n.m.* infirmity; (*pl., afflizioni*) aches and pains.

accia'i|o *n.m.* steel. ∿o **inossidabile** stainless steel. **lana d'**∿o steel wool. ∿eri'a *n.f.* steelworks.

accidenta'le *a.* accidental.

accidenta'to *a.* (*terreno*) uneven.

accide'nte *n.m.* accident; (*med.*) stroke. **accide'nti!** *int.* damn!

acci'dia *n.f.* sloth.

acciglia'|rsi *v.r.* frown. ∿to *a.* frowning.

accin'gersi *v.r.* ∿ **a** be about to.

acciocché *conj.* in order that.

acciottola'|re *v.t.* pave with cobbles. ∿to *n.m.* cobbled paving.

accipi'cchia *int.* good Lord!

acciuffa're *v.t.* catch.

acciu'ga *n.f.* anchovy.

acclama'|re *v.t.* applaud; (*eleggere*) acclaim. ∿zio'ne *n.f.* applause.

acclimata'r|e *v.t.* acclimatize. ∿si *v.r.* get acclimatized.

acclu'|dere *v.t.* enclose. ∿so *a.* enclosed.

accoccola'rsi *v.r.* squat.

accoglie'n|te *a.* welcoming; (*confortevole*) cosy. ∿za *n.f.* welcome.

acco'gliere *v.t.* receive; (*con piacere*) welcome; (*contenere*) hold.

accolla'to *a.* high-necked.

accoltella're *v.t.* knife.

accomiata'r|e *v.t.* dismiss. ∿si *v.r.* ∿si (*da*) take one's leave (of).

accomodame'nto *n.m.* arrangement; (*riparazione*) mending; (*adattamento*) adaptation.

accomoda'nte *a.* accommodating.

accomoda'r|e *v.t.* (*riparare*) mend; (*disporre*) arrange. ∿si *v.r.* make o.s. at home. **si accomodi!** come in!

accompagname'nto *n.m.* accompaniment; (*seguito*) retinue.

accompagna'|re *v.t.* accompany. ∿re **qcno. a casa** see s.o. home. ∿re **qcno. alla porta** show s.o. out. ∿-

to're, ∿**tri'ce** *n.m., f.* companion; (*di comitiva*) escort; (*mus.*) accompanist.

accomuna're *v.t.* pool.

acconcia're *v.t.* arrange.

acconciatu'ra *n.f.* hair-style; (*ornamento*) head-dress.

acco'ncio *a.* proper.

accondisce'ndere *v.i.* ∿ **a** condescend; (*desiderio*) comply with; (*acconsentire*) consent to.

acconsenti're *v.i.* consent.

accontenta'r|e *v.t.* satisfy. ∿si (di) *v.r.* be satisfied (with).

acco'nto *n.m.* instalment. **in** ∿ on account. **lasciare un** ∿ leave a deposit.

accoppia'|re *v.t.* couple; (*animali*) mate. ∿rsi *v.r.* pair off; mate. ∿me'nto *n.m.* coupling; mating.

accora|me'nto *n.m.* grief. ∿to *a.* sorrowful.

accorcia'r|e *v.t.* shorten. ∿si *v.r.* get shorter.

accorda'r|e *v.t.* concede; (*colori ecc.*) match; (*mus.*) tune. ∿si *v.r.* agree.

acco'rdo *n.m.* agreement; (*mus.*) chord; (*armonia*) harmony. **andare d'**∿ get on well. **d'**∿**!** agreed! **essere d'**∿ agree.

acco'rgersi *v.r.* ∿ **di** notice; (*capire*) realize.

accorgime'nto *n.m.* shrewdness; (*espediente*) device.

acco'rrere *v.i.* hasten.

acco'rto *a.* shrewd. **mal** ∿ incautious.

accosta'r|e *v.t.* draw close to; (*persona*) approach; (*porta ecc.*) set ajar. ∿si *v.r.* ∿si **a** come near.

accovaccia'rsi *v.r.* crouch.

accozza'glia *n.f.* jumble; (*di persone*) mob.

accredita're *v.t.* give credit to; (*comm.*) credit.

accre'sc|ere *v.t.* increase. ∿ersi *v.r.* grow larger. ∿ime'nto *n.m.* increase.

accuccia'rsi *v.r.* (*of dogs*) lie down; (*of people*) curl up.

accudi're *v.i.* ∿ (a) attend to.

accumula'|re *v.t.* accumulate. ∿to're *n.m.* accumulator; (*auto.*) battery. ∿zio'ne *n.f.* accumulation.

accura't|o *a.* accurate. ∿e'zza *n.f.* accuracy.

accu's|a *n.f.* accusation; (*legge*) charge. ∿a're *v.t.* accuse; (*legge*) charge; (*un dolore*) complain of. ∿a'to, a *n.m., f.* accused. ∿ato're *n.m.* (*legge*) prosecutor.

ace'rbo *a.* sharp; (*immaturo*) unripe.

a'cero *n.m.* maple.

ace'rrimo *a.* implacable.

ace'to *n.m.* vinegar.

a'cid|o *a.* & *n.m.* acid. ∼ità *n.f.* acidity.

a'cino *n.m.* berry; (*chicco*) grape.

a'cme *n.f.* acme.

a'cne *n.f.* acne.

a'cqua *n.f.* water. ∼ corrente running water. ∼ potabile drinking water. ∼ tonica tonic water. fare ∼ (*naut.*) leak.

acquafo'rte *n.f.* etching.

acqua'io *n.m.* sink.

acqua'rio *n.m.* aquarium; (*astr.*) Aquarius.

acquasantie'ra *n.f.* font.

acqua'tico *a.* aquatic.

acquavi'te *n.f.* brandy.

acquazzo'ne *n.m.* downpour.

acquedo'tto *n.m.* aqueduct.

acquere'llo *n.m.* water-colour.

acquieta're *v.t.* appease; (*dolore*) calm.

acquire'nte *n.m./f.* purchaser.

acquisi're *v.t.* acquire.

acquist|a're *v.t.* purchase; (*ottenere*) acquire. acqui'sto *n.m.* purchase. uscire per ∼i go shopping.

acquitri'no *n.m.* marsh.

acquoli'na *n.f.* far venire l'∼ in bocca a qcno. make s.o.'s mouth water.

acquo'so *a.* watery.

a'cre *a.* acrid; (*fig., suono*) harsh.

acrobazi'a *n.f.* acrobatics *pl.* acro'-bata *n.m./f.* acrobat.

acui're *v.t.* sharpen.

acu'leo *n.m.* sting; (*bot.*) prickle.

acu'me *n.m.* acumen.

acu'stica *n.f.* acoustics *pl.*

acu'to *a.* sharp; (*gram., math., med.*) acute. —*n.m.* (*mus.*) high note.

ad *prep.* = a (*davanti a vocale*).

adagia'r|e *v.t.* lay down. ∼si *v.r.* lie down.

ada'gio *adv.* slowly. —*n.m.* (*mus.*) adagio; (*proverbio*) adage.

adattame'nto *n.m.* adaptation.

adatta'r|e *v.t.* adapt; (*aggiustare*) fit. ∼si *v.r.* adapt oneself.

ada'tto *a.* suitable; (*giusto*) right.

addebita're *v.t.* debit; (*fig.*) blame.

addensa'r|e *v.t.* thicken. ∼si *v.r.* thicken; (*affollarsi*) gather.

addenta're *v.t.* bite.

addentra'rsi *v.r.* penetrate.

adde'ntro *adv.* deeply. essere ∼ in be in on.

addestra'|re *v.t.* train. ∼me'nto *n.m.* training.

adde'tto *a.* assigned. —*n.m.* employee; (*diplomatico*) attaché.

addie'tro *adv.* (*indietro*) back; (*nel passato*) before.

addi'o *n.m.* & *int.* goodbye.

addirittu'ra *adv.* (*direttamente*) immediately; (*assolutamente*) absolutely.

addi'rsi *v.r.* ∼ a suit.

addita're *v.t.* point at o to.

additi'vo *a.* & *n.m.* additive.

addiziona'l|e *a.* additional. ∼me'nte *adv.* additionally.

addiziona're *v.t.* add (up). addizio'ne *n.f.* addition.

addobba're *v.t.* decorate. addo'bbo *n.m.* decoration.

addolci'r|e *v.t.* sweeten; (*colore*) tone down; (*fig.*) soften. ∼si *v.r.* (*fig.*) mellow.

addolora'r|e *v.t.* grieve. ∼si (per) *v.r.* regret.

addo'm|e *n.m.* abdomen. ∼ina'le *a.* abdominal.

addomestica'|re *v.t.* tame. ∼to're *n.m.* tamer.

addormenta'|re *v.t.* put to sleep. ∼rsi *v.r.* go to sleep. ∼to *a.* asleep.

addossa'r|e *v.t.* ∼e a (*appoggiare*) lean against; (*attribuire*) lay on. ∼si *v.r.* (*ammassarsi*) crowd; (*responsabilità ecc.*) shoulder.

addo'sso *adv.* on. ∼ a *prep.* on; (*molto vicino*) on top of.

addu'rre *v.t.* adduce. ∼ esempi give examples.

adegua'r|e *v.t.* adjust. ∼si *v.r.* conform.

adegua'to *a.* adequate; (*conforme*) consistent.

ade'mpiere *v.t.* fulfil.

adere'n|te *a.* adhesive; (*di vestito*) tight. — *n.m./f.* follower. ∼za *n.f.* adhesion. ∼ze *n.pl.* connections.

aderi're *v.i.* ∼ a adhere to; (*richiesta*) agree to.

adesca're *v.t.* bait; (*fig.*) entice.

ades|io'ne *n.f.* adhesion; (*fig.*) agreement. ∼i'vo *a.* adhesive.

ade'sso *adv.* now. da ∼ in poi from now on. per ∼ for the moment.

adiace'nte *a.* adjacent. ∼ a next to.

adibi're *v.t.* ∼ a put to use as.

adira'|rsi *v.r.* get angry. ∼to *a.* angry.

adi're *v.t.* resort to. ∼ **le vie legali** take legal proceedings.

a'dito *n.m.* entrance. **dare** ∼ **a** give rise to.

adocchia're *v.t.* eye; (*con desiderio*) covet.

adolesce'n|te *a.* & *n.m.|f.* adolescent. ∼**za** *n.f.* adolescence.

adombra'r|e *v.t.* darken; (*fig.*) veil. ∼**si** *v.r.* (*offendersi*) take offence.

adopera'r|e *v.t.* use. ∼**si** *v.r.* take trouble.

adora'|re *v.t.* adore. ∼**bile** a. adorable. ∼**zio'ne** *n.f.* adoration.

adorna're *v.t.* adorn.

ado|tta're *v.t.* adopt. ∼**tti'vo** *a.* adoptive. ∼**zio'ne** *n.f.* adoption.

adria'tico *a.* Adriatic. **l'A**∼ *n.m.* the Adriatic.

adula'|re *v.t.* flatter. ∼**to're**, ∼**tri'ce** *n.m.,f.* flatterer. ∼**zio'ne** *n.f.* flattery.

adultera're *v.t.* adulterate.

adulte'rio *n.m.* adultery. **adu'ltero, a** *a.* adulterous; *n.m., f.* adulterer, adulteress.

adu'lto, a *a.* & *n.m.,f.* adult.

aduna'nza *n.f.* assembly.

aduna'|re *v.t.* gather. ∼**ta** *n.f.* (*mil.*) parade.

adu'nco *a.* hooked.

ae'reo *a.* aerial; (*dell'aviazione*) air. —*n.m.* aeroplane.

aero'bic|o *a.* aerobic. ∼**a** *n.f.* aerobics.

aerodina'mic|o *a.* aerodynamic; (*di linea*) streamlined. ∼**a** *n.f.* aerodynamics *s.*

aerona'utica *n.f.* aeronautics *s.*; (*mil.*) Air Force.

aeropla'no *n.m.* aeroplane.

aeropo'rto *n.m.* airport.

aeroso'l *n.m. invar.* aerosol.

a'fa *n.f.* sultriness.

affa'bil|e *a.* affable. ∼**ità** *n.f.* affability.

affaccenda'|rsi *v.r.* busy oneself (**a,** with). ∼**to** *a.* busy.

affaccia'rsi *v.r.* show oneself. ∼ **alla finestra** appear at the window.

affama'|re *v.t.* starve (out). ∼**to** *a.* starving.

affanna'|re *v.t.* leave breathless. ∼**rsi** *v.r.* busy oneself; (*agitarsi*) get worked up. ∼**to** *a.* breathless. **affa'nno** *n.m.* breathlessness; (*fig.*) worry. **essere in affanno per** be anxious about.

affa'r|e *n.m.* matter; (*comm.*) trans-

action, deal. ∼**i** *n.pl.* business. ∼**i'sta** *n.m.|f.* speculator.

affascina'nte *a.* fascinating.

affascina're *v.t.* bewitch; (*fig.*) charm.

affastella're *v.t.* tie up into bundles.

affatica'r|e *v.t.* tire; (*sfinire*) exhaust. ∼**si** *v.r.* tire o.s. out; (*affannarsi*) strive.

affa'tto *adv.* completely. **non** ∼ (not) at all.

afferma'|re *v.t.* affirm; (*sostenere*) assert. ∼**zio'ne** *n.f.* affirmation; assertion; (*successo*) achievement.

afferra'r|e *v.t.* seize; (*capire*) grasp. ∼**e a volo** be quick on the uptake. ∼**si** *v.r.* grasp (at s.o., sthg.).

affetta'|re *v.t.* slice; (*ostentare*) affect. ∼**to** *a.* sliced; affected; *n.m.* sliced meat. ∼**zio'ne** *n.f.* affectation.

affetti'vo *a.* affective.

affe'tto[1] *n.m.* affection. **con** ∼ affectionately.

affe'tto[2] *a.* suffering (**da,** from).

affettuo'so *a.* affectionate.

affeziona'|rsi *v.r.* grow fond of. ∼**to** (**a**) *a.* devoted (to).

affezio'ne *n.f.* affection; (*med.*) ailment.

affianca'r|e *v.t.* put side by side; (*mil.*) flank; (*fig.*) support. ∼**si a qcno.** stand beside s.o.

affiatame'nto *n.m.* harmony.

affiata'rsi *v.r.* get on well together.

affibbia're *v.t.* buckle; (*fig.*, *un colpo*) let fly; (*addossare*) saddle (s.o. with).

affidame'nto *n.m.* confidence. **fare** ∼ **su qcno.** rely on s.o.

affida'r|e *v.t.* entrust. ∼**si** *v.r.* rely (**a,** on).

affievoli'rsi *v.r.* grow weak.

affi'ggere *v.t.* affix.

affila're *v.t.* sharpen.

affilia'r|e *v.t.* affiliate. ∼**si** *v.r.* become affiliated to.

affina're *v.t.* sharpen; (*assottigliare*) make thinner.

affinché *conj.* so that, in order that.

affi'n|e *a.* similar. ∼**ità** *n.f.* affinity.

affiora'|re *v.i.* emerge; (*fig.*) come to light. ∼**me'nto** *n.m.* emergence; (*naut.*) surfacing.

affi'sso *n.m.* bill; (*gram.*) affix.

affittaca'mere *n.m., f. invar.* landlord, landlady.

affitta're *v.t.* (*dare in affitto*) let; (*prendere in affitto*) rent. **affi'tto** *n.m.* rent. **contratto d'affitto** lease.

affli'|ggere *v.t.* torment. ∼**ggersi** *v.r.*

distress o.s. ~**tto** *a.* distressed. ~**tto
da** suffering from. ~**zio'ne** *n.f.* distress; (*fig.*) affliction.

affloscia'rsi *v.r.* become floppy; (*accasciarsi*) flop down.

afflue'n|te *a.* & *n.m.* tributary. ~**za**
n.f. flow; (*di gente*) crowd.

afflui're *v.i.* flow; (*fig.*) pour in.

afflu'sso *n.m.* influx.

affoga're *v.t./i.* drown; (*culin.*) poach.

affolla'|re, ~**rsi** *v.t., v.r.* crowd. ~**to**
a. crowded.

affonda're *v.t./i.* sink.

affossa'r|e *v.t.* ditch. ~**si** *v.r.* grow
hollow.

affranca'|re *v.t.* free; (*lettera*) stamp.
~**rsi** *v.r.* free oneself. ~**tu'ra** *n.f.*
stamping; (*di spedizione*) postage.

affre'sco *n.m.* fresco.

affretta'|re *v.t.* speed up. ~**rsi** *v.r.*
hurry. ~**to** *a.* hasty.

affronta're *v.t.* face; (*il nemico*) confront; (*le spese*) meet.

affro'nto *n.m.* affront.

affumica're *v.t.* fill with smoke;
(*culin.*) smoke.

affusola'|re *v.t.* taper (off). ~**to** *a.*
tapering.

afori'sma *n.m.* aphorism.

afo'so *a.* sultry.

A'fric|a *n.f.* Africa. **a**~**a'no, a** *a.*
& *n.m., f.* African.

afrodisi'aco *a.* & *n.m.* aphrodisiac.

age'nda *n.f.* diary.

age'n|te *n.m.* agent. ~**te di cambio**
stockbroker. ~**te di polizia** policeman. ~**zi'a** *n.f.* agency. ~**zia di
viaggi** travel agency. ~**zia immobiliare** estate agency.

agevola'|re *v.t.* facilitate. ~**zio'ne** *n.f.*
facilitation. **age'vole** *a.* easy; (*di
strada*) smooth.

aggancia're *v.t.* hook up; (*ferrovia*)
couple.

agge'ggio *n.m.* gadget.

aggetti'vo *n.m.* adjective.

agghiaccia'r|e *v.t.* ice; (*fig.*) make
one's blood run cold. ~**si** *v.r.* freeze.

agghinda'r|e *v.t.* (*fam.*) dress up. ~**si**
v.r. (*fam.*) doll oneself up.

aggiorna'|re *v.t.* (*rinviare*) postpone;
(*mettere a giorno*) bring up to date.
~**rsi** *v.r.* get up to date. ~**to** *a.* up-to-
date.

aggira'r|e *v.t.* surround; (*fig., ingannare*) trick. ~**si** *v.r.* hang about. ~**si**

su (*di discorso ecc.*) be about; (*approssimarsi*) be around.

aggiudica'r|e *v.t.* award; (*all'asta*)
knock down. ~**si** *v.r.* win.

aggiu'n|gere *v.t.* add. ~**ta** *n.f.* addition. ~**to** *a.* added; *a.* & *n.m.* (*assistente*) assistant.

aggiusta'r|e *v.t.* mend; (*sistemare*)
settle; (*fam., mettere a posto*) fix. ~**si**
v.r. adapt oneself; (*mettersi in ordine*)
tidy oneself up; (*di tempo*) migliorare;
(*reciproco*) come to an agreement.

agglomera'|to *n.m.* built-up area.
~**me'nto** *n.m.* conglomeration.

aggomitola'r|e *v.t.* wind into a ball.
~**si** *v.r.* curl up.

aggrappa'r|e *v.t.* grasp. ~**si** *v.r.* ~**si**
a cling to.

aggrava'r|e *v.t.* (*appesantire*) weigh
down; (*peggiorare*) make worse. ~**si**
v.r. worsen.

aggrazia'to *a.* graceful.

aggredi're *v.t.* attack.

aggrega'|re *v.t.* add; (*associare a un
gruppo ecc.*) admit. ~**rsi** *v.r.* ~**rsi a**
join. ~**to** *a.* associated; *n.m.* aggregate; (*di case*) block.

aggress|io'ne *n.f.* aggression; (*atto*)
attack. ~**i'vo** *a.* aggressive. ~**o're**
n.m. aggressor; attacker.

aggrinza're, aggrinzi're *v.t.* wrinkle.

aggrotta're *v.t.* ~ **le ciglia** frown.

aggroviglia'r|e *v.t.* tangle. ~**si** *v.r.*
get entangled.

aggruppa'r|e *v.t.* group. ~**si** *v.r.*
gather (together).

agguanta're *v.t.* catch.

aggua'to *n.m.* ambush; (*tranello*) trap.
stare in ~ lie in wait.

agguerri'to *a.* prepared.

agiate'zza *n.f.* comfort. **agia'to** *a.* (*persona*) well off; (*vita*) comfortable.

a'gil|e *a.* agile. ~**ità** *n.f.* agility.

a'gio *n.m.* ease. **mettersi a proprio**
~ make o.s. at home.

agi're *v.i.* act; (*comportarsi*) behave;
(*funzionare*) work. ~ **su** affect.

agita'|re *v.t.* shake; (*mano*) wave; (*fig.,
turbare*) trouble. ~**rsi** *v.r.* toss about;
(*essere inquieto*) be restless; (*di mare*)
get rough. ~**to** *a.* restless; rough.
~**zio'ne** *n.f.* agitation.

a'gli = a + gli.

a'glio *n.m.* garlic.

agne'llo *n.m.* lamb.

agno'stico, a *a.* & *n.m., f.* agnostic.

a'go *n.m.* needle.

agogna're *v.t./i.* yearn for.

agoni'|a *n.f.* agony. **~zza're** *v.i.* be on one's deathbed.

agoni'stic|a *n. f.* athletics *s.* **~o** *a.* sporting.

agopuntu'ra *n.f.* acupuncture.

agorafo'bia *n.f.* agoraphobia.

ago'sto *n.m.* August.

agra'ri|a *n.f.* agriculture. **~o** *a.* agricultural; *n.m.* landowner.

agri'col|o *a.* agricultural. **~to're** *n.m.* farmer. **~tu'ra** *n.f.* agriculture.

agrifo'glio *n.m.* holly.

a'gr|o *a.* sour. **~e'zza** *n.f.* sourness.

agrodo'lce *a.* bitter-sweet; (*culin.*) sweet-and-sour.

agru'me *n.m.* citrus fruit.

aguzza're *v.t.* sharpen; (*la vista*) look hard.

aguzzi'no *n.m.* slave-driver; (*carceriere*) jailer.

a'i = **a** + **i.**

ahimè *int.* alas.

A'ia *n.f.* l'**~** the Hague.

a'ia *n.f.* threshing-floor.

airo'ne *n.m.* heron.

aita'nte *a.* sturdy.

aiuo'la *n.f.* flower-bed.

aiut|a're *v.t.* help. **~a'nte** *n.m.|f.* assistant; *n.m.* (*mil.*) adjutant. **~ante di campo** aide-de-camp. **aiu'to** *n.m.* help, aid; (*assistente*) assistant.

aizza're *v.t.* incite. **~ contro** set on.

al = **a** + **il. a'lla** = **a** + **la. a'lle** = **a** + **le. a'llo** = **a** + **lo.**

a'la *n.f.* wing. **fare ~** make way.

alaba'stro *n.m.* alabaster.

a'lacre *a.* brisk.

ala'no *n.m.* Great Dane.

ala're *n.m.* firedog.

a'lb|a *n.f.* dawn. **~eggia're** *v.i.* dawn.

Alban|i'a *n.f.* Albania. **a~e'se** *a.* & *n.m.|f.* Albanian.

albe'rg|o *n.m.* hotel. **~ato're, ~atri'ce** *n.m.,* *f.* hotel-keeper. **~hie'ro** *a.* hotel.

a'lber|o *n.m.* tree; (*naut.*) mast; (*mech.*) shaft. **~a'to** *a.* wooded; (*di viale*) tree-lined. **~atu'ra** *n.f.* (*naut.*) masts *pl.* **~e'llo** *n.m.* sapling.

albico'cc|a *n.f.* apricot. **~o** *n.m.* apricot-tree.

albi'no *n.m.* albino.

a'lbo *n.m.* register; (*libro ecc.*) album.

a'lbum *n.m.* album.

albu'me *n.m.* albumen.

a'lce *n.m.* elk.

a'lcool *n.m.* alcohol; (*med.*) spirit; (*liquori forti*) spirits *pl.* **darsi all'~**

take to drink. **alcoo'lico** *a.* alcoholic. **~i'smo** *n.m.* alcoholism. **~izza'to, a** *a.* & *n.m.,* *f.* alcoholic.

alco'va *n.f.* alcove.

alcu'n, alcu'no *adjs.* (*s. negativo & inter.*) any; no; (*pl. affermativo*) some. **non ha ~ amico** he hasn't any friends; he has no friends. **~i suoi amici** some of his friends. — *pron.* (*s. negativo riferito a persona*) anybody, anyone; (*pl. affermativo*) some, a few.

ale'tta *n.f.* (*mech.*) fin.

alfabe't|o *n.m.* alphabet. **~ico** *a.* alphabetical.

alfie're *n.m.* standard-bearer; (*mil.*) ensign; (*scacchi*) bishop.

alfi'ne *adv.* eventually, in the end.

a'lga *n.f.* seaweed.

a'lgebra *n.f.* algebra.

Algeri'|a *n.f.* Algeria. **a~no, a** *a.* & *n.m.,* *f.* Algerian.

alia'nte *n.m.* glider.

a'libi *n.m. invar.* alibi.

aliena'|re *v.t.* alienate. **~rsi** *v.r.* become estranged. **~to, a** *a.* alienated; *n.m.,* *f.* lunatic.

alie'no *a.* **~ da** opposed to.

alimenta'|re *v.t.* feed; (*fig.*) foment. —*a.* food. **~ri** *n.pl.* foodstuffs. **~zio'ne** *n.f.* feeding.

alime'nt|o *n.m.* food. **~i** *n.m. pl.* food; (*legge*) alimony.

aliquo'ta *n.f.* share.

alisca'fo *n.m.* hydrofoil.

a'lito *n.m.* breath.

allaccia're *v.t.* tie (up); (*cintura*) fasten; (*scarpe ecc.*) lace up; (*collegare*) link; (*amicizia*) form.

allaga'|re *v.t.* flood. **~me'nto** *n.m.* flooding.

allampana'to *a.* lanky.

allarga're *v.t.* widen; (*aprire*) open; (*vestito ecc.*) let out.

allarm|a're *v.t.* alarm. **~a'nte** *a.* alarming.

alla'rm|e *n.m.* alarm. **~e aereo** air raid warning. **~i'smo** *n.m.* alarmism.

allatta'|re *v.t.* suckle. **~me'nto** *n.m.* suckling.

allea'|nza *n.f.* alliance. **~to, a** *a.* allied; *n.m.,* *f.* ally.

allea'|re *v.t.* unite. **~rsi** *v.r.* form an alliance.

allega'|re[1] *v.t.* (*legge*) allege. **~zio'ne** *n.f.* (*legge*) allegation.

allega'|re[2] *v.t.* (*accludere*) enclose; (*denti*) set on edge. **~to** *a.* enclosed; *n.m.* enclosure.

alleggeri'r|e v.t. lighten; (fig.) allevi-
ate. **~si** v.r. become lighter; (vestirsi
leggero) put on lighter clothes.
allegori'a n.f. allegory. **allego'rico** a.
allegorical.
allegri'a n.f. gaiety. **alle'gro** a. gay;
(di colore) bright; (brillo) tipsy; n.m.
(mus.) allegro.
allena'|re v.t., **~rsi** v.r. train.
~me'nto n.m. training. **~to're** n.m.
trainer.
allenta'r|e v.t. loosen; (fig.) relax. **~si**
v.r. become loose; (mech.) work loose.
allergi'|a n.f. allergy. **alle'rgico** a.
allergic.
allesti're v.t. prepare; (spettacolo)
stage; (naut.) fit out.
alletta're v.t. entice.
alleva'|re v.t. (bambini) bring up; (ani-
mali) breed; (piante) grow. **~me'nto**
n.m. bringing up; breeding; (luogo)
farm; (per piante) nursery. **pollo di**
~mento battery chicken.
allevia're v.t. alleviate; (fig.) lighten.
allibi're v.i. be astounded (at).
allibrato're n.m. bookmaker.
allieta'r|e v.t. gladden. **~si** v.r.
rejoice.
allie'vo, a n.m., f. pupil. —n.m. (mil.)
cadet.
alligato're n.m. alligator.
allinea'|re v.t. line up; (typ.) align;
(econ. ecc.) adjust. **~rsi** v.r. fall into
line. **~me'nto** n.m. lining up; align-
ment.
allo'cco n.m. tawny owl; (fig.) dunce.
allo'dola n.f. (sky)lark.
alloggia're v.t. give lodging to; (mil.)
billet. —v.i. put up; be billeted.
allo'ggio n.m. lodging; billet.
allontana'|re v.t. move away;
(licenziare) dismiss; (pericolo) avert.
~rsi v.r. go away. **~me'nto** n.m.
removal; dismissal.
allo'ra adv. then; (in quel tempo) at
that time; (in tal caso) in that case. **~**
allora just (then). **d'~ in poi** from
then on. **e ~?** what now?; (e con ciò?)
so what? **sino ~** until then.
allorché conj. when.
allo'ro n.m. laurel; (culin.) bay.
a'lluce n.m. big toe.
allucinazio'ne n.f. hallucination.
allu'dere v.i. **~ a** allude to.
allumi'nio n.m. aluminium.
allunga'r|e v.t. lengthen; (stendere)
stretch (out); (diluire) dilute. **~e il**
muso pull a long face. **~si** v.r. grow

longer; (crescere) grow taller; (sdraiarsi) lie down.
allusio'ne n.f. allusion.
alluvio'ne n.f. flood.
almana'cco n.m. almanack.
alme'no adv. at least. **se ~ venisse**
il sole! if only the sun would come
out!
alo'ne n.m. halo.
A'lpi n.f. pl. **le ~** the Alps.
alpini's|mo n.m. mountaineering.
~ta n.m./f. mountaineer.
alpi'no a. Alpine. —n.m. (mil.) Alpino.
alqua'nto a. a certain amount of.
—adv. rather.
a'lt int. stop.
altale'na n.f. swing; (tavola in bilico)
see-saw.
alta're n.m. altar.
altera'|re v.t. alter; (cibo) adulterate;
(falsificare) falsify. **~rsi** v.r. be al-
tered; (cibo) go bad; (arrabbiarsi) get
angry; (di merci) deteriorate. **~zio'ne**
n.f. alteration; (cibo) adulteration.
alte'rco n.m. altercation.
alteri'gia n.f. haughtiness. **alte'ro** a.
haughty.
alterna'|re v.t., **~rsi** v.r. alternate.
~ti'va n.f. alternative. **~ti'vo** a.
alternate. **~to're** n.m. (electr.) alter-
nator.
alte'rn|o a. alternate. **a giorni ~i**
every other day.
alte'zza n.f. height; (di statura) tall-
ness; (profondità) depth; (suono)
pitch; (di tessuto) width; (titolo) High-
ness. **essere all'~ di** be up to.
altezzo'so a. haughty.
altitu'dine n.f. altitude.
a'lt|o a. high; (di statura) tall; (pro-
fondo) deep; (di suono) highpitched;
(di tessuto) wide. —adv. high. **ad ~a**
voce aloud. **in ~o** at the top. **mani**
in ~o! hands up!
altofo'rno n.m. blast-furnace.
altolà int. halt there!
altoloca'to a. highly placed.
altoparla'nte n.m. loudspeaker.
altopia'no n.m. plateau.
altretta'nto a. & pron. as much; (pl.)
as many. —adv. likewise, equally.
buona fortuna! grazie, ~ good luck!
thank you, the same to you.
a'ltri pron. invar. others; (qualcun
altro) someone else.
altrime'nti adv. otherwise.
a'ltro a. other; (un altro) another;
(in più) ancora; (futuro) next.

—pron. other (one); (*chiunque altro*) anybody else. **~ che!** and how! **l'un l'~** one another. **nessun ~** nobody else. **tra l'~** among other things.
altro'nde *adv.* **d'~** on the other hand.
altro've *adv.* elsewhere.
altru'i *a.* other people's. *—n.m.* other people's belongings *pl.*
altrui's|mo *n.m.* altruism. **~ta** *n.m.|f.* altruist.
altu'ra *n.f.* hill.
alu'nno, a *n.m., f.* pupil.
alvea're *n.m.* hive.
alza'ia *n.f.* towpath.
alza'|re *v.t.* raise; (*costruire*) build; (*naut.*) hoist. **~rsi** *v.r.* rise; (*in piedi*) stand up; (*da letto*) get up. **~re le spalle** shrug one's shoulders. **~ta** *n.f.* lifting; (*aumento*) rise; (*da letto*) getting up; (*archit.*) elevation. **~to** *a.* up.
ama'bile *a.* lovable; (*vino*) sweet.
ama'ca *n.f.* hammock.
amalgama'r|e *v.t.,* **~si** *v.r.* amalgamate.
ama'nte *a.* **~ di** fond of. *—n.m.* lover. *—n.f.* mistress.
ama'|re *v.t.* love; (*musica, sport, ecc.*) be fond of, like. **~to, a** *a.* loved; *n.m., f.* beloved.
amare'na *n.f.* sour black cherry.
amare'tto *n.m.* macaroon.
ama'r|o *a.* bitter. *—n.m.* bitterness; (*liquore*) bitters *pl.* **~e'zza** *n.f.* bitterness; (*dolore*) sorrow.
amba'scia *n.f.* (*fig.*) anguish.
ambascia'|ta *n.f.* embassy; (*messaggio*) message. **~to're, ~tri'ce** *n.m.,f.* ambassador, ambassadress.
ambedu'e *a. & pron.* both.
ambide'stro *a.* ambidextrous.
ambie'nt|e *n.m.* environment; (*stanza*) room. **~a'le** *a.* environmental. **~a're** *v.t.* acclimatize; (*personaggio, film, ecc.*) set. **~a'rsi** *v.r.* get acclimatized.
ambi'gu|o *a.* ambiguous; (*di persona*) shady. **~ità** *n.f.* ambiguity; shadiness.
ambi're *v.t.* **~ (a)** aspire (to).
a'mbito *n.m.* ambit.
ambivale'nte *a.* ambivalent.
ambizio'|ne *n.f.* ambition. **~so** *a.* ambitious.
a'mbra *n.f.* amber.
ambula'nte *a.* wandering. **venditore ~** hawker.
ambula'nza *n.f.* ambulance.

ambulato'rio *n.m.* (*di medico*) surgery; (*di ospedale*) outpatients' department.
ame'n|o *a.* pleasant. **~ità** *n.f.* pleasantness; (*facezia*) pleasantry.
Ame'ric|a *n.f.* America. **~a del Sud** South America. **a~a'no, a** *a. & n.m., f.* American.
ameti'sta *n.f.* amethyst.
amici'zi|a *n.f.* friendship. **~e** *n.f. pl.* (*amici*) friends.
ami'c|o, a *n.m., f.* friend. **~o del cuore** bosom friend. **~he'vole** *a.* friendly.
a'mido *n.m.* starch.
ammacca'|re *v.t.* bruise; (*metallo ecc.*) dent. **~tu'ra** *n.f.* bruise; dent.
ammaestra're *v.t.* (*istruire*) teach; (*animale*) train.
ammaina're *v.t.* (*bandiera*) lower; (*vele*) furl.
ammala'|rsi *v.r.* fall ill. **~to, a** *a.* ill; *n.m.,f.* sick person; (*paziente*) patient.
ammalia'|re *v.t.* bewitch. **~to're, ~tri'ce** *n.m., f.* enchanter, enchantress.
amma'nco *n.m.* deficit.
ammanetta're *v.t.* handcuff.
ammara'|re *v.i.* land; (*aeron.*) splash down. **~ggio** *n.m.* splashdown.
ammassa'r|e *v.t.* amass. **~si** *v.r.* crowd together. **amma'sso** *n.m.* mass; (*mucchio*) pile.
ammatti're *v.i.* go mad.
ammazza'r|e *v.t.* kill. **~si** *v.r.* (*suicidarsi*) kill oneself; (*rimanere ucciso*) be killed.
amme'nda *n.f.* amends *pl.*; (*multa*) fine.
amme'sso *p.p. di* **ammettere.** *—conj.* **~ che** supposing that.
amme'ttere *v.t.* admit; (*riconoscere*) acknowledge; (*supporre*) suppose.
ammicca're *v.i.* wink.
amministra'|re *v.t.* administer; (*gestire*) run. **~ti'vo** *a.* administrative. **~to're** *n.m.* administrator; (*di azienda*) manager; (*di società*) director. **~zio'ne** *n.f.* administration; management.
ammira'gli|o *n.m.* admiral. **~a'to** *n.m.* admiralty.
ammira'|re *v.t.* admire. **~to're, ~tri'ce** *n.m., f.* admirer. **~zio'ne** *n.f.* admiration. **ammire'vole** *a.* admirable.
ammissi'bile *a.* admissible.
ammissio'ne *n.f.* admission; (*approvazione*) acknowledgement.
ammobilia're *v.t.* furnish.

ammo'do *a.* proper. —*adv.* properly.

ammoglia'|rsi *v.r.* get married. **~to** *a.* married; *n.m.* married man.

ammolla're *v.t.* (*bagnare*) soak.

ammoni'aca *n.f.* ammonia.

ammoni'|re *v.t.* warn; (*rimproverare*) admonish; (*legge*) caution. **~me'nto** *n.m.* warning; admonishment.

ammonta're *v.i.* **~ a** amount to. —*n.m.* amount.

ammonticchia're *v.t.* heap up.

ammorbidi'r|e *v.t.*, **~si** *v.r.* soften.

ammortizza'|re *v.t.* (*comm.*) redeem; (*mech.*) cushion. **~to're** *n.m.* shock-absorber.

ammoscia'r|e *v.t.* make flabby. **~si** *v.i.* get flabby.

ammucchia'r|e *v.t.*, **~si** *v.r.* pile up.

ammuffi're *v.i.* go mouldy.

ammutina're *v.t.*, **~rsi** *v.r.* mutiny. **~me'nto** *n.m.* mutiny.

ammutoli're *v.i.* become dumb.

amnesi'a *n.f.* amnesia.

amnisti'a *n.f.* amnesty.

a'mo *n.m.* hook; (*fig.*) bait.

amora'le *a.* amoral.

amo'r|e *n.m.* love. **~ proprio** self-respect. **è un ~e** it's a darling. **per ~ di** for the sake of. **~i** *n.m. pl.* love affairs. **~e'vole** *a.* loving.

amo'rfo *a.* shapeless; (*di persona*) colourless.

amoro'so *a.* loving; (*sguardo ecc.*) amorous; (*lettera, relazione*) love.

a'mpi|o *a.* ample; (*largo*) wide; (*vasto*) spacious; (*vestito*) loose; (*gonna*) full. **~e'zza** *n.f.* width; spaciousness; fullness.

ample'sso *n.m.* embrace.

amplifica'|re *v.t.* amplify; (*fig.*) magnify. **~to're** *n.m.* amplifier. **~zio'ne** *n.f.* amplification.

ampo'll|a, **~ie'ra** *ns. f.* cruet.

ampollo'so *a.* pompous.

amputa'|re *v.t.* amputate. **~zio'ne** *n.f.* amputation.

amule'to *n.m.* amulet.

anabbaglia'nt|e *a.* (*auto.*) dipped. **~i** *n.m. pl.* dipped headlights.

anacroni'smo *n.m.* anachronism.

ana'grafe *n.f.* (*ufficio*) registry office; (*registro*) register.

anagra'mma *n.m.* anagram.

analco'lico *a.* non-alcoholic. —*n.m.* soft drink.

analfabe't|a *a.* & *n.m.|f.* illiterate. **~i'smo** *n.m.* illiteracy.

ana'l|isi *n.f. invar.* analysis; (*med.*) test. **~i'sta** *n.m.|f.* analyst.

analizza're *v.t.* analyse; (*med.*) test.

analog|i'a *n.f.* analogy. **ana'logo** *a.* analogous.

a'nanas *n.m. invar.* pineapple.

anarchi'|a *n.f.* anarchy. **ana'rchico, a** *a.* anarchic; *n.m., f.* anarchist. **~smo** *n.m.* anarchism.

anate'ma *n.m.* anathema.

anat|omi'a *n.f.* anatomy. **~o'mico** *a.* anatomical.

a'natra *n.f.* duck.

a'nca *n.f.* hip; (*di animale*) flank.

ancestra'le *a.* ancestral.

a'nche *conj.* also, too; (*persino*) even. **~ se** even if.

anco'ra *adv.* still, yet; (*di nuovo*) again; (*di più*) some more. **~ una volta** once more.

a'ncor|a *n.f.* anchor. **gettare l'~a** cast the anchor. **~a'ggio** *n.m.* anchorage. **~a're** *v.t.* anchor.

andame'nto *n.m.* course.

anda'nte *a.* (*corrente*) current; (*di poco valore*) cheap. —*n.m.* (*mus.*) andante.

anda'|re *v.i.* go; (*confarsi*) suit; (*di misure*) fit; (*funzionare*) work. —*n.m.* going. **a lungo ~re** in the long run. **andiamo!** come on! **la mia macchina non va** my car is not working. **non mi va** I don't like it. **~rsene** go away; (*scomparire*) disappear; (*morire*) die. **~ta** *n.f.* going; (*viaggio*) outward journey. **biglietto di sola ~ta, ~ta e ritorno** single, return ticket. **~tu'ra** *n.f.* walk; (*portamento*) bearing; (*naut.*) tack; (*sport*) pace.

andirivie'ni *n.m. invar.* coming and going.

an'dito *n.m.* passage.

andro'ne *n.m.* entrance.

ane'ddoto *n.m.* anecdote.

anela're *v.t.* **~ a** long for. **ane'lito** *n.m.* longing.

ane'llo *n.m.* ring; (*di catena*) link.

anemi'a *n.f.* anaemia. **ane'mico** *a.* anaemic.

ane'mone *n.m.* anemone.

anest|esi'a *n.f.* anaesthesia. **~esi'sta** *n.m.|f.* anaesthetist. **~e'tico** *a.* & *n.m.* anaesthetic.

anfi'bio *a.* amphibious.

anfitea'tro *n.m.* amphitheatre.

anfra'tto *n.m.* ravine.

a'ngel|o *n.m.* angel. **~o custode** guardian angel. **ange'lico** *a.* angelic.

angheri'a *n.f.* harassment.

anglica'no *a.* Anglican.

anglici'smo *n.m.* Anglicism.

anglo'filo, a *a.* & *n.m.*, *f.* Anglophile.

anglosassone *a.* & *n.m.|f.* Anglo-Saxon.

a'ngol|o *n.m.* corner; (*math.*) angle. **~a're** *a.* angular.

ango'sci|a *n.f.* anguish. **~o'so** *a.* (*disperato*) anguished; (*che dà angoscia*) distressing.

angui'lla *n.f.* eel.

angu'ria *n.f.* water-melon.

angu'sti|a *n.f.* (*ansia*) anxiety; (*penuria*) poverty. **~a're** *v.t.* distress; **~a'rsi (per)** *v.r.* worry (about).

angu'sto *a.* narrow.

a'nice *n.m.* anise; (*culin.*) aniseed.

a'nima *n.f.* soul; (*persona*) person. **non c'era ~ viva** there was not a soul about.

anima'l|e *a.* & *n.m.* animal. **~e'sco** *a.* animal.

anima'|re *v.t.* give life to; (*ravvivare*) enliven; (*incoraggiare*) encourage. **~rsi** *v.r.* come to life; (*accalorarsi*) become animated. **~to** *a.* animate; (*vivace*) animated. **~to're, ~tri'ce** *n.m.*, *f.* leading spirit; (*cinema*) animator. **~zio'ne** *n.f.* animation.

a'nimo *n.m.* (*mente*) mind; (*indole*) disposition; (*cuore*) heart. **perdersi d'~** lose heart.

animo's|o *a.* brave; (*ostile*) hostile. **~ità** *n.f.* animosity.

a'nitra *n.f.* = **anatra**.

annacqua're *v.t.* water down.

annaffia'|re *v.t.* water. **~to'io** *n.m.* watering-can.

anna'li *n.m. pl.* annals.

anna'ta *n.f.* year.

annebbia'|re *v.t.* cloud. **~rsi** *v.r.* cloud (over); (*vista*) dim. **~me'nto** *n.m.* (spreading of) fog.

annega'|re *v.t./i.* drown. **~rsi** *v.r.* drown oneself. **~me'nto** *n.m.* drowning.

anneri'r|e *v.t./i.* blacken. **~si** *v.r.* become black.

anne'ssi *n.m. pl.* outbuildings.

anne'sso *p.p. di* **annettere**. **—a.** attached.

anne'ttere *v.t.* add; (*accludere*) enclose.

annichili're *v.t.* annihilate.

annida'rsi *v.r.* nest.

annienta'|re *v.t.* annihilate. **~rsi** *v.r.* abase oneself. **~me'nto** *n.m.* annihilation.

anniversa'rio *a.* & *n.m.* anniversary. **—n.m.** (*compleanno*) birthday.

a'nno *n.m.* year. **~ bisestile** leap year. **Buon A~!** Happy New Year! **Tommaso ha dieci anni** Thomas is ten (years old).

annoda'r|e *v.t.* knot; (*lacci*) lace up. **~si** *v.r.* become knotted.

annoia'r|e *v.t.* bore; (*recare fastidio*) annoy. **~si** *v.r.* be bored; be annoyed.

annota'|re *v.t.* note down. **~zio'ne** *n.f.* note.

annovera're *v.t.* number.

annua'le *a.* annual.

annua'rio *n.m.* year-book.

annui're *v.i.* nod; (*acconsentire*) agree.

annulla'|re *v.t.* annul; (*comm.*) cancel; (*una legge*) repeal; (*togliere efficacia*) undo. **~me'nto** *n.m.* annulment; cancellation.

annuncia'|re *v.t.* announce; (*preannunciare*) foretell. **~to're, ~tri'ce** *n.m.*, *f.* announcer. **~zio'ne** *n.f.* Annunciation.

annu'nci|o *n.m.* announcement; (*pubblicitario*) advertisement; (*notizia*) news. **~ economici** classified advertisements.

a'nnuo *a.* annual, yearly.

annusa're *v.t.* sniff.

annuvola'r|e *v.t.* cloud. **~si** *v.r.* cloud over.

anomali'a *n.f.* anomaly.

ano'nimo *a.* anonymous.

anorma'l|e *a.* abnormal. **—n.m.|f.** deviant, abnormal person. **~ità** *n.f.* abnormality.

a'nsa *n.f.* handle; (*di fiume*) bend.

ansa're *v.i.* pant.

a'nsi|a, ansietà *ns. f.* anxiety. **~o'so** *a.* anxious.

antagoni's|mo *n.m.* antagonism. **~ta** *n.m.|f.* antagonist.

anta'rtico *a.* & *n.m.* Antarctic.

antecede'nte *a.* preceding.

antefa'tto *n.m.* prior event.

antegue'rra *a.* pre-war. **—n.m.** pre-war period.

antenato, a *n.m.*, *f.* ancestor.

ante'nna *n.f.* (*radio, TV*) aerial; (*di animale*) antenna; (*naut.*) yard.

antepo'rre *v.t.* put before.

antepri'ma *n.f.* preview.

anterio're *a.* front; (*nel tempo*) previous.

antiae'reo *a.* anti-aircraft.

antibio'tico *a.* & *n.m.* antibiotic.

antica'mera *n.f.* ante-room. **far ~** be kept waiting.

antichità *n.f.* antiquity; (*oggetto*) antique.

anticiclo'ne *n.m.* anticyclone.

anticip|a're *v.t.* advance; (*comm.*) pay in advance; (*prevedere*) anticipate; (*prevenire*) forestall. —*v.i.* be early. **~azio'ne** *n.f.* anticipation; (*notizia*) advance news. **anti'cipo** *n.m.* advance; (*caparra*) deposit. **in ~o** early.

anti'c|o *a.* ancient; (*mobile ecc.*) antique; (*vecchio*) old. —*n.m. pl.* **gli antichi** the ancients. **all'~a** old-fashioned. **~ame'nte** *adv.* in ancient times.

anticonceziona'le *a.* & *n.m.* contraceptive.

antico'rpo *n.m.* antibody.

anti'doto *n.m.* antidote.

antieste'tico *a.* ugly.

antige'lo *n.m.* antifreeze.

Anti'lle *n.f. pl.* **le ~** the West Indies.

anti'lope *n.f.* antelope.

antipa'sto *n.m.* hors d'œuvre.

antip|ati'a *n.f.* antipathy. **~a'tico** *a.* unpleasant.

anti'podi *n.m. pl.* antipodes.

antiqua'ri|o, a *n.m.,f.* antique dealer. **~a'to** *n.m.* antique trade.

antiqua'to *a.* antiquated.

antise'ttico *a.* & *n.m.* antiseptic.

anti'tesi *n.f.* antithesis.

antologi'a *n.f.* anthology.

a'ntro *n.m.* cavern.

antrop|ologi'a *n.f.* anthropology. **~o'logo, a** *n.m.,f.* anthropologist.

anula're *n.m.* ring-finger.

a'nzi *conj.* in fact; (*o meglio*) or better still; (*al contrario*) on the contrary.

anzia'n|o, a *a.* old, elderly; (*di grado ecc.*) senior. —*n.m.,f.* elderly person. **~ità** *n.f.* old age; seniority.

anziché *conj.* rather than.

anzitu'tto *adv.* first of all.

apati'a *n.f.* apathy. **apa'tico** *a.* apathetic.

a'pe *n.f.* bee. **nido di api** honeycomb.

aperiti'vo *n.m.* aperitif.

ape'rt|o *a.* open; (*di luogo*) exposed. **all'aria ~a** in the open air.

apertu'ra *n.f.* opening; (*inizio*) beginning; (*ampiezza*) spread; (*di arco*) span; (*fotografia*) aperture.

a'pice *n.m.* apex.

apicolt|u'ra *n.f.* beekeeping. **~o're** *n.m.* beekeeper.

apo'lide *a.* stateless. —*n.m./f.* stateless person.

apoplessi'a *n.f.* apoplexy.

apo'stolo *n.m.* apostle.

apo'strofo *n.m.* apostrophe.

appaga'|re *v.t.* satisfy. **~rsi** *v.r.* **~rsi di** be satisfied with. **~me'nto** *n.m.* fulfilment.

appaia're *v.t.* pair; (*animali*) mate.

appallottola're *v.t.* roll into a ball.

appa'lt|o *n.m.* contract. **dare in ~o** contract for. **~ato're** *n.m.* contractor.

appanna'r|e *v.t.* (*vetro*) mist; (*vista*) dim. **~si** *v.r.* mist over; grow dim.

appara'to *n.m.* apparatus; (*pompa*) display.

apparecchia're *v.t.* prepare. —*v.i.* lay the table.

appare'cchio *n.m.* apparatus; (*congegno*) device; (*radio, TV, ecc.*) set; (*aeroplano*) aircraft.

appare'n|te *a.* apparent. **~za** *n.f.* appearance. **in ~za** apparently.

appari'|re *v.i.* appear; (*sembrare*) look. **~zio'ne** *n.f.* apparition.

apparisce'nte *a.* striking.

appartame'nto *n.m.* flat; apartment (*Amer.*).

apparta'|rsi *v.r.* withdraw. **~to** *a.* secluded.

appartene're *v.i.* belong.

appassiona'|re *v.t.* interest (deeply); (*commuovere*) move. **~rsi** *v.r.* **~rsi a** become interested in. **~to** *a.* passionate. **~to di** (*entusiastico*) fond of.

appassi're *v.i.* wither.

appell|a're *v.t.* call. **~a'rsi** *v.r.* **~arsi a** appeal to. **appe'llo** *n.m.* appeal; (*chiamata per nome*) roll-call. **fare l'~o** call the roll.

appe'na *adv.* just; (*a fatica*) hardly. —*conj.* **(non) ~ (che)** as soon as, no sooner … than.

appe'ndere *v.t.* hang (up).

appendi'c|e *n.f.* appendix. **~i'te** *n.f.* appendicitis.

Appenni'ni *n.m. pl.* **gli ~** the Appennines.

appesanti'r|e *v.t.* weigh down. **~si** *v.r.* become heavy.

appe'so *p.p. di* **appendere.** —*a.* hanging; (*impiccato*) hanged.

appeti't|o *n.m.* appetite. **aver ~o** be hungry. **~o'so** *a.* appetizing; (*fig.*) tempting.

appezzame'nto *n.m.* plot of land.

appiana're *v.t.* level; (*fig.*) smooth.

appiatta'rsi *v.r.* hide oneself.
appiatti'r|e *v.t.* flatten. ~**si** *v.r.* flatten oneself.
appicca're *v.t.* hang (up). ~ **il fuoco a** set fire to.
appiccica'r|e *v.t.* stick. ~**e a** (*fig.*, *appioppare*) palm off on. —*v.i.* be sticky. ~**si** *v.r.* stick together.
appiglia'r|si *v.r.* ~**si a** get hold of; (*fig.*) stick to. **appi'glio** *n.m.* foothold; (*fig.*) pretext.
appioppa're *v.t.* ~ **a** palm off on; (*fam.*, *dare*) give.
appisola'rsi *v.r.* doze off.
applau|di're *v.t./i.* applaud. **appla'uso** *n.m.* applause.
applica'|re *v.t.* apply; (*legge ecc.*) enforce. ~**rsi** *v.r.* apply oneself. ~**bile** *a.* applicable. ~**zio'ne** *n.f.* application; enforcement.
appoggia'r|e *v.t.* put; (*sostenere*) back. ~**si** *v.r.* ~**si a** lean against; (*fig.*) rely on. **appo'ggio** *n.m.* support.
appo'rre *v.t.* affix.
apporta're *v.t.* bring; (*causare*) cause. **appo'rto** *n.m.* contribution.
appo'sito *a.* proper.
appo'sta *adv.* on purpose; (*espressamente*) specially.
apposta'|re *v.t.* lie in wait (for). ~**rsi** *v.r.* lie in wait. ~**me'nto** *n.m.* ambush; (*caccia*) lying in wait.
appre'ndere *v.t.* understand; (*imparare*) learn.
apprendi'sta *n.m./f.* apprentice.
apprens|io'ne *n.f.* apprehension. **essere in** ~**ione per** be anxious about. ~**i'vo** *a.* apprehensive.
appre'sso *adv. & prep.* (*vicino*) near; (*dietro*) behind. **come** ~ as follows.
appresta'r|e *v.t.* prepare. ~**si** *v.r.* get ready.
apprezza'|re *v.t.* appreciate. ~**bile** *a.* appreciable. ~**me'nto** *n.m.* appreciation; (*giudizio*) opinion.
appro'ccio *n.m.* approach.
appr|oda're *v.i.* land; (*fig.*) come to something. ~**o'do** *n.m.* landing; (*luogo*) landing-stage.
approfitta're *v.i.* ~ (**di**) take advantage (of), profit (by).
approfondi'r|e *v.t.* deepen. ~**si** *v.r.* ~**si in** (*fig.*) make a thorough study of.
appropria'|rsi *v.r.* take possession; (*essere adatto*) suit. ~**to** *a.* appropriate.

approssima'|re *v.t.* approach. ~**rsi** *v.r.* draw near.
approssimati'v|o *a.* approximate. ~**ame'nte** *adv.* approximately.
approva'|re *v.t.* approve (of); (*accettare*) accept. ~**zio'ne** *n.f.* approval; acceptance.
approvvigioname'nt|o *n.m.* supplying. ~**i** *n.m. pl.* provisions.
approvvigiona'r|e *v.t.* supply. ~**si** *v.r.* stock up.
appuntame'nto *n.m.* appointment; (*fam.*) date. **fissare un** ~ make an appointment.
appunta'r|e *v.t.* (*annotare*) take notes; (*fissare*) fix; (*con spillo*) pin; (*appuntire*) sharpen. ~**si** *v.r.* ~**si su** be pointed on.
appu'nto[1] *n.m.* note; (*rimprovero*) reproach.
appu'nto[2] *adv.* exactly.
appura're *v.t.* verify.
apribotti'glie *n.m. invar.* bottle-opener.
apri'le *n.m.* April.
apri'r|e *v.t.* open; (*luce, acqua, ecc.*) turn on; (*con chiave*) unlock; (*ferita ecc.*) open up. ~**si** *v.r.* open; (*spaccarsi*) split; (*confidarsi*) confide (**con**, in).
aprisca'tole *n.f. invar.* tin-opener.
a'quila *n.f.* eagle. **non è un'**~! he is no genius!
aquili'no *a.* aquiline.
aquilo'ne *n.m.* (*giocattolo*) kite.
Ara'bia Saudi'ta *n.f.* l'~ Saudi Arabia. **a'rabo, a** *a. & n.m., f.* Arab; *n.m.* (*lingua*) Arabic.
arachi'de *n.f.* peanut.
arago'sta *n.f.* lobster.
ara'ld|ica *n.f.* heraldry. ~**o** *n.m.* herald.
ara'nc|ia *n.f.* orange. ~**e'to** *n.m.* orange grove. ~**ia'ta** *n.f.* orangeade. ~**io** *n.m.* orange-tree; (*colore*) orange.
ara'|re *v.t.* plough. ~**tro** *n.m.* plough.
ara'zzo *n.m.* tapestry.
arbi'tr|io *n.m.* will; (*abuso*) arbitrary act. ~**a'rio** *a.* arbitrary.
a'rbitr|o *n.m.* arbiter; (*sport*) referee; (*tennis, cricket*) umpire. ~**a're** *v.t.* arbitrate; referee; umpire.
arbosce'llo *n.m.* sapling.
arbu'sto *n.m.* shrub.
a'rca *n.f.* ark; (*cassa*) chest.
arca'ico *a.* archaic.
arca'ngelo *n.m.* archangel.
arca'no *a.* mysterious.

arca'ta *n.f.* arch; (*serie di archi*) arcade.

arche|ologi'a *n.f.* archaeology. **∼o'logo, a** *n.m., f.* archaeologist.

archite'tt|o *n.m.* architect. **∼u'ra** *n.f.* architecture.

archi'vio *n.m.* archives *pl.*

arcie're *n.m.* archer.

arci'gno *a.* grim.

arcipe'lago *n.m.* archipelago.

arcive'scovo *n.m.* archbishop.

a'rco *n.m.* arch; (*math.*) arc; (*arma, mus.*) bow.

arcobale'no *n.m.* rainbow.

arcua'to *a.* curved.

arde'nte *a.* burning; (*fig.*) ardent.

a'rdere *v.t./i.* burn.

arde'sia *n.f.* slate.

ardi'|re *v.i.* dare. —*n.m.* daring. **∼to** *a.* daring; (*coraggioso*) bold; (*sfacciato*) impudent.

ardo're *n.m.* (*calore*) heat; (*fig.*) ardour.

a'rduo *a.* arduous; (*ripido*) steep.

a'rea *n.f.* area.

are'na *n.f.* arena; (*sabbia*) sand.

arena'rsi *v.r.* run aground.

a'rgano *n.m.* winch.

arge'nt|o *n.m.* silver. **∼eo** *a.* silvery. **∼eri'a** *n.f.* silver(ware). **∼ie're** *n.m.* silversmith.

argi'lla *n.f.* clay.

a'rgine *n.m.* embankment; (*diga*) dike.

argome'nt|o *n.m.* argument; (*motivo*) reason; (*soggetto*) subject. **∼a're** *v.i.* argue.

argui're *v.t.* deduce.

argu'|to *a.* witty. **∼zia** *n.f.* wit; (*battuta*) witticism.

a'ria *n.f.* air; (*aspetto*) appearance; (*mus.*) tune. **andare all'∼** come to nothing. **corrente d'∼** draught.

arid|o *a.* arid. **∼ità** *n.f.* dryness.

arieggia'|re *v.t.* air. **∼to** *a.* airy.

arie'te *n.m.* ram. **A∼** (*astr.*) Aries.

ari'nga *n.f.* herring.

aristocr|azi'a *n.f.* aristocracy. **∼a'tico, a** *a.* aristocratic; *n.m., f.* aristocrat.

aritme'tica *n.f.* arithmetic.

arlecchi'no *n.m.* Harlequin; (*fig.*) buffoon.

a'rm|a *n.f.* weapon. **∼i** *n.f. pl.* arms; (*forze armate*) (armed) forces. **∼a da fuoco** firearm. **chiamare alle ∼i** call up. **sotto le ∼i** in the army.

arma'dio *n.m.* cupboard; (*guardaroba*) wardrobe.

armamenta'rio *n.m.* tools *pl.*; (*fig.*) paraphernalia *pl.*

armame'nto *n.m.* armament; (*naut.*) fitting out.

arma'|re *v.t.* arm; (*equipaggiare*) fit out; (*archit.*) reinforce. **∼rsi** *v.r.* arm oneself. **∼ta** *n.f.* army; (*flotta*) fleet. **∼to're** *n.m.* shipowner. **∼tu'ra** *n.f.* (*impalcatura*) scaffolding; (*di guerriero*) armour.

armeggia're *v.i.* (*fig.*) manœuvre.

armisti'zio *n.m.* armistice.

armoni'|a *n.f.* harmony. **armo'nico** *a.* harmonic. **∼o'so** *a.* harmonious.

armonizza're *v.t.* harmonize. —*v.i.* match.

arne'se *n.m.* tool; (*oggetto*) thing; (*congegno*) gadget. **male in ∼** in bad condition.

a'rnia *n.f.* beehive.

aro'm|a *n.m.* aroma. **∼i** *n.m. pl.* herbs. **∼a'tico** *a.* aromatic.

a'rpa *n.f.* harp.

arpe'ggio *n.m.* arpeggio.

arpi'a *n.f.* harpy.

arpio'ne *n.m.* hook; (*pesca*) harpoon.

arrabatta'rsi *v.r.* do all one can.

arrabbia'|rsi *v.r.* get angry. **∼to** *a.* angry. **∼tu'ra** *n.f.* rage. **prendersi un'∼tura** get angry.

arraffa're *v.t.* grab.

arrampica'rsi *v.r.* climb (up).

arrangia'|re *v.t.* arrange. **∼rsi** *v.r.* manage. **∼rsi alla meglio** get by. **arra'ngiati!** get on with it! **∼me'nto** *n.m.* arrangement.

arreca're *v.t.* bring; (*causare*) cause.

arreda'|re *v.t.* furnish. **∼me'nto** *n.m.* interior decoration; (*l'arredare*) furnishing; (*mobili ecc.*) furnishings *pl.* **∼to're, ∼tri'ce** *n.m., f.* interior decorator. **arre'do** *n.m.* furnishings *pl.*

arre'ndersi *v.r.* surrender.

arrende'vole *a.* (*persona*) yielding.

arrest|a're *v.t.* arrest; (*fermare*) stop. **∼a'rsi** *v.r.* halt. **arre'sto** *n.m.* stop; (*med., legge*) arrest. **mandato di ∼** warrant.

arretra'|re *v.t./i.* withdraw. **∼to** *a.* behind(hand); (*paese ecc.*) backward. **numero ∼to** (*di rivista*) back number. **∼ti** *n.m. pl.* arrears.

arricchi'|re *v.t.* enrich. **∼rsi** *v.r.* get rich. **∼to, a** *n.m., f.* nouveau riche.

arriccia're *v.t.* curl. **∼ il naso** turn up one's nose.

arri'nga *n.f.* harangue.

arrischia'|re *v.t.* risk. **~rsi** *v.r.* dare. **~to** *a.* risky; (*imprudente*) rash.

arriva'|re *v.i.* arrive. **~re a** (*raggiungere*) reach; (*ridursi*) be reduced to. **~to, a** *a.* successful; *n.m.*, *f.* successful person. **ben ~to!** welcome!

arrivede'rci *int.* goodbye. **~ a domani** see you tomorrow.

arrivi's|mo *n.m.* social climbing. **~ta** *n.m./f.* social climber.

arri'vo *n.m.* arrival; (*sport*) finish.

arroga'n|te *a.* arrogant. **~za** *n.f.* arrogance.

arrossi're *v.i.* blush.

arrosti're *v.t.* roast; (*pane*) toast; (*ai ferri*) grill. **arro'sto** *a. & n.m.* roast.

arrota're *v.t.* sharpen; (*investire*) graze.

arrotola're *v.t.* roll up.

arrotonda'r|e *v.t.* round; (*math. ecc.*) round off. **~si** *v.r.* become round; (*di persona*) become plump.

arrovella'rsi *v.r.* **~ il cervello** rack one's brains.

arroventa'r|e *v.t.* make red-hot. **~si** *v.r.* become red-hot.

arruffa're *v.t.* ruffle; (*fig.*) confuse.

arruggini'|re *v.t.* rust. **~rsi** *v.r.* go rusty. **~to** *a.* rusty.

arruola'|re *v.t./i.*, **~rsi** *v.r.* enlist. **~me'nto** *n.m.* enlistment.

arsena'le *n.m.* arsenal; (*cantiere*) dockyard.

arse'nico *n.m.* arsenic.

a'rs|o *p.p. di* **ardere.** *—a.* burnt; (*arido*) dry. **~u'ra** *n.f.* burning heat; dryness; (*sete*) parching thirst.

a'rte *n.f.* art; (*abilità*) craftsmanship.

artefa'tto *a.* fake.

arte'fice *n.m./f.* craftsman, craftswoman; (*fig.*) author.

arte'ria *n.f.* artery.

a'rtico *a.* arctic.

articola're *a.* articular. *—v.t.* articulate.

arti'colo *n.m.* article. **~ di fondo** leader.

artificia'le *a.* artificial.

artifi'ci|o *n.m.* artifice. **fuochi d'~o** fireworks. **~o'so** *a.* artful.

artigi|ana'to *n.m.* craftsmanship; (*ceto*) craftsmen *pl.* **~a'no, a** *n.m.*, *f.* craftsman, craftswoman.

artigli|eri'a *n.f.* artillery. **~e're** *n.m.* artilleryman.

arti'glio *n.m.* claw; (*fig.*) clutch.

arti'st|a *n.m./f.* artist. **~ico** *a.* artistic.

a'rto *n.m.* limb.

artri'te *n.f.* arthritis.

arzi'llo *a.* sprightly.

asce'lla *n.f.* armpit.

ascende'n|te *a.* ascending. *—n.m.* (*antenato*) ancestor; (*influenza*) ascendancy. **~za** *n.f.* ancestry.

ascensio'ne *n.f.* ascent. **l'A~** the Ascension.

ascenso're *n.m.* lift; elevator (*Amer.*).

asce'sa *n.f.* ascent; (*al trono*) accession.

asce'sso *n.m.* abscess.

asce'ta *n.m./f.* ascetic.

asciugacape'lli *n.m. invar.* hairdrier.

asciugama'no *n.m.* towel.

asciuga'r|e *v.t.* dry. **~si** *v.r.* dry oneself; (*diventare asciutto*) dry up.

asciu'tto *a.* dry; (*magro*) thin. **essere all'~** (*fig.*) be hard up.

ascolta'|re *v.t./i.* listen (to). **~to're**, **~tri'ce** *n.m.*, *f.* listener. **ascolto** *n.m.* listening. **dare ascolto a** pay attention to.

asfa'lt|o *n.m.* asphalt. **~a're** *v.t.* asphalt.

asfi'ssi|a *n.f.* asphyxia. **~a'nte** *a.* asphyxiating.

A'sia *n.f.* Asia. **asia'tico, a** *a. & n.m.*, *f.* Asian.

asi'lo *n.m.* shelter; (*d'infanzia*) nursery school. **~ politico** political asylum.

asimme'trico *a.* asymmetrical.

a'sino *n.m.* donkey; (*fig., persona stupida*) ass.

a'sma *n.f.* asthma.

a'sola *n.f.* buttonhole.

aspa'rago *n.m.* asparagus.

aspe'rgere *v.t.* sprinkle.

asperità *n.f.* harshness; (*di terreno*) roughness.

aspetta'|re *v.t./i.* wait (for); (*con la mente, essere incinta*) expect. **fare ~re qcno.** keep s.o. waiting. **~rsi** *v.r.* expect. **~ti'va** *n.f.* expectation.

aspe'tto[1] *n.m.* appearance; (*punto di vista*) point of view. **di bell'~** goodlooking.

aspe'tto[2] *n.m.* **sala d'~** waiting-room.

aspira'nte *a.* aspiring. *—n.m./f.* candidate.

aspirapo'lvere *n.m. invar.* vacuum cleaner.

aspira're *v.t.* inhale; (*mech.*) suck

in. —*v.i.* ~**re a** aspire to. ~**to're** *n.m.*
exhaust fan. ~**zio'ne** *n.f.* inhalation;
suction; (*ambizione*) ambition.

aspiri'na *n.f.* aspirin.

asporta're *v.t.* take away.

a'spr|o *a.* sour; (*ruvido*) rough; (*di
clima*) severe; (*di suono*) harsh.
~**e'zza** *n.f.* sourness; roughness;
severity; harshness.

assaggia're *v.t.* taste. **assa'ggio** *n.m.*
tasting; (*piccola quantità*) taste.

assa'i *adv.* very; (*moltissimo*) very
much; (*abbastanza*) enough.

assali're *v.t.* attack.

assa'lto *n.m.* attack. **prendere d'~**
storm.

assapora're *v.t.* savour.

assassi'n|o, a *a.* murderous. —*n.m.,
f.* murderer. ~**a're** *v.t.* murder, as-
sassinate, ~**io** *n.m.* murder, assas-
sination.

a'sse *n.f.* board. —*n.m.* (*techn.*) axle;
(*math.*) axis.

asseconda're *v.t.* satisfy; (*favorire*)
support.

assedia're *v.t.* besiege. **asse'dio** *n.m.*
siege.

assegna'|re *v.t.* allot; (*premio*) award.
~**me'nto** *n.m.* allotment. **fare
~mento su** rely on.

asse'gno *n.m.* allowance; (*bancario*)
cheque. ~ **circolare** bank draft. **contro ~** cash on delivery.

assemble'a *n.f.* assembly; (*adunanza*)
gathering.

assembrame'nto *n.m.* gathering.

assenna'to *a.* sensible.

asse'nso *n.m.* assent.

assenta'rsi *v.r.* absent oneself.

asse'n|te *a.* absent; (*distratto*) absent-
minded. —*n.m./f.* absentee. ~**tei'smo**
n.m. absenteeism. ~**za** *n.f.* absence;
(*mancanza*) lack.

asser|i're *v.t.* assert. ~**ti'vo** *a.* assert-
ive.

assesso're *n.m.* councillor.

assesta'|re *v.t.* arrange. ~**re un colpo**
deal a blow. ~**rsi** *v.r.* settle oneself.
~**me'nto** *n.m.* settlement.

asseta'to *a.* thirsty.

asse'tto *n.m.* order; (*naut., aeron.*)
trim.

assicura'|re *v.t.* assure; (*comm.*) in-
sure; (*posta*) register; (*fissare*) secure;
(*accertare*) ensure. ~**rsi** *v.r.* make
sure; insure oneself; (*legarsi*) fasten
oneself. ~**zio'ne** *n.f.* assurance; insurance.

assiderame'nto *n.m.* exposure.

assi'duo *a.* assiduous.

assi'll|o *n.m.* worry. ~**a're** *v.t.*
pester.

assimila'|re *v.t.* assimilate. ~**zio'ne**
n.f. assimilation.

assi'se *n.f. pl.* assizes. **Corte d'Assise**
Court of Assize.

assiste'n|te *n.m./f.* assistant. ~**te so-
ciale** social worker. ~**za** *n.f.* assistance; (*presenza*) presence. ~**za
sociale** social services *pl.*

assistere *v.t.* assist; (*curare*) nurse.
—*v.i.* ~ **a** (*essere presente*) be present
at; (*spettacolo ecc.*) watch.

a'sso *n.m.* ace. **piantare in ~** leave
in the lurch.

associa'r|e *v.t.* join; (*collegare*) associ-
ate. ~**si** *v.r.* join forces; (*comm.*) enter
into partnership. ~**si a** join; (*giornale
ecc.*) subscribe to.

associazio'ne *n.f.* association.

assoggetta're *v.t.* subject.

assola'to *a.* sunny.

assolda're *v.t.* recruit.

asso'lo *n.m.* (*mus.*) solo.

asso'lto *p.p. di* **assolvere**.

assolu't|o *a.* absolute. ~**ame'nte** *adv.*
absolutely.

assoluzio'ne *n.f.* acquittal; (*relig.*) absolution.

asso'lvere *v.t.* perform; (*legge*) acquit;
(*relig.*) absolve.

assomiglia're *v.i.* ~ **a** be like, resemble.

assonna'to *a.* drowsy.

assopi'rsi *v.r.* doze off.

assorbe'nte *a. & n.m.* absorbent.
~ **igienico** sanitary towel. **carta ~**
blotting-paper.

assorbi're *v.t.* absorb.

assorda'|re *v.t.* deafen. ~**nte** *a.* deaf-
ening.

assortime'nto *n.m.* assortment.

assorti'to *a.* assorted; (*di colori, persone*) matched.

asso'rto *a.* engrossed.

assottiglia'r|e *v.t.* make thin; (*aguz-
zare*) sharpen; (*ridurre*) reduce. ~**si**
v.r. grow thin; be reduced.

assuefa'r|e *v.t.* accustom. ~**si a** *v.r.*
get used to.

assu'mere *v.t.* assume; (*impiegato*)
engage. ~ **informazioni** make in-
quiries.

assu'nto *p.p. di* **assumere**. —*n.m.*
task.

assu'rd|o *a.* absurd. **~ità** *n.f.* absurdity.

a'sta *n.f.* pole; (*mech.*) bar; (*comm.*) auction.

aste'mio *a.* abstemious.

asten|e'rsi *v.r.* abstain (**da**, from). **~sio'ne** *n.f.* abstention.

asteri'sco *n.m.* asterisk.

astine'nza *n.f.* abstinence.

a'sti|o *n.m.* rancour. **avere ~o contro qcno.** bear s.o. a grudge. **~o'so** *a.* resentful.

astra'tto *a.* abstract.

a'stro *n.m.* star.

astr|ologi'a *n.f.* astrology. **~o'logo, a** *n.m., f.* astrologer.

astrona'uta *n.m./f.* astronaut.

astrona've *n.f.* spaceship.

astr|onomi'a *n.f.* astronomy. **~ono'-mico** *a.* astronomical. **~o'nomo** *n.m.* astronomer.

astu'ccio *n.m.* case.

astu'|to *a.* shrewd; (*furbo*) cunning. **~zia** *n.f.* shrewdness; (*azione*) trick.

Ate'ne *n.f.* Athens.

a'teo, a *a. & n.m., f.* atheist.

atla'nte *n.m.* atlas.

atla'ntico *a.* Atlantic. **l'(Oceano) A~** the Atlantic (Ocean).

atle't|a *n.m./f.* athlete. **~ica** *n.f.* athletics *s.* **~ico** *a.* athletic.

atmosfe'r|a *n.f.* atmosphere. **~ico** *a.* atmospheric.

a'tomo *n.m.* atom. **ato'mico** *a.* atomic.

a'trio *n.m.* entrance hall.

atro'ce *a.* atrocious; (*terribile*) dreadful.

attaccabotto'ni *n.m./f. invar.* (persistent) bore.

attaccabri'ghe *n.m./f. invar.* troublemaker.

attaccame'nto *n.m.* attachment.

attaccapa'nni *n.m. invar.* (coat-)hanger; (*a muro*) (clothes-)hook.

attacca'r|e *v.t.* attach; (*legare*) tie; (*appendere*) hang; (*contagiare*) pass on; (*assalire*) attack; (*iniziare*) start. —*v.i.* stick; (*diffondersi*) catch on. **~si** *v.r.* cling; (*affezionarsi*) become attached; (*litigare*) quarrel. **atta'cco** *n.m.* attack; (*punto d'unione*) junction.

attarda'rsi *v.r.* stay late; (*indugiare*) linger.

attecchi're *v.i.* take; (*di moda ecc.*) catch on.

atteggiame'nto *n.m.* attitude.

atteggia'r|e *v.t.* assume. **~si** *v.r.* **~si a pose as.**

attende'nte *n.m.* batman.

atte'nder|e *v.t.* wait for. —*v.i.* **~e a** attend to. **~si** *v.r.* expect.

attendi'bile *a.* reliable.

attene'rsi *v.r.* **~ a** stick to.

attenta'|re *v.i.* **~re a** make an attempt on. **~to** *n.m.* (criminal) attempt.

atte'nto *a.* attentive; (*accurato*) careful. **~!** look out! **stare ~** pay attention.

attenua'nte *n.f.* extenuating circumstance.

attenua'r|e *v.t.* attenuate; (*minimizzare*) minimize; (*colori ecc.*) subdue; (*dolore*) calm; (*colpo*) soften. **~si** *v.r.* diminish.

attenzio'ne *n.f.* attention. **~!** mind!

atterra'|ggio *n.m.* landing. **~re** *v.t.* knock down; *v.i.* land.

atterri'r|e *v.t.* terrorize. **~si** *v.r.* be terrified.

atte'sa *n.f.* waiting; (*aspettativa*) expectation. **in ~ di** waiting for. **lista d'~** waiting-list.

atte'so *p.p. di* **attendere**.

attesta'|re *v.t.* state; (*certificare*) certify. **~to** *n.m.* certificate.

a'ttico *n.m.* attic.

atti'guo *a.* adjacent.

attilla'to *a.* (*vestito*) close-fitting; (*elegante*) dressed up.

a'ttimo *n.m.* moment.

attine'nte *a.* **~ a** pertaining to.

atti'ngere *v.t.* draw; (*fig.*) obtain.

attira're *v.t.* attract.

attitu'dine *n.f.* (*disposizione*) aptitude; (*atteggiamento*) attitude.

attiva're *v.t.* activate.

atti'v|o *a.* active; (*comm.*) productive. —*n.m.* assets *pl.* **~ità** *n.f.* activity; (*comm.*) assets *pl.*

attizza'|re *v.t.* poke; (*fig.*) stir up. **~to'io** *n.m.* poker.

a'tt|o *n.m.* act; (*azione*) action; (*comm., legge*) deed; (*certificato*) certificate. **~i** *n.m. pl.* (*di società ecc.*) proceedings *pl.* **fare ~o di presenza** put in an appearance. **mettere in ~o** put into action.

atto'nito *a.* astonished.

attorciglia'r|e *v.t.* twist. **~si** *v.r.* get twisted.

atto're *n.m.* actor.

attornia'r|e *v.t.* surround. **~si** *v.r.* surround oneself.

atto'rno *adv.* around. ~ **a** *pr.p.* around; about.

attrae'nte *a.* attractive.

attra'|rre *v.t.* attract. ~**tti'va** *n.f.* charm. ~**zio'ne** *n.f.* attraction.

attraversa're *v.t.* cross; (*passare*) go through.

attrave'rso *prep.* through; (*obliquamente*) across.

attrezza'|re *v.t.* equip. ~**tu'ra** *n.f.* equipment.

attre'zz|o *n.m.* tool. ~**i** *n.m. pl.* equipment; (*sport*) appliances *pl.*; (*theatr.*) props *pl.*

attribui'r|e *v.t.* attribute. ~**si** *v.r.* ascribe to oneself. ~**si il merito di** claim credit for.

attribu'to *n.m.* attribute.

attri'ce *n.f.* actress.

attri'to *n.m.* friction.

attua'l|e *a.* present; (*di attualità*) topical; (*effettivo*) actual. ~**ità** *n.f.* topicality; (*avvenimento*) news. **programma di** ~**ità** current events programme. ~**me'nte** *adv.* at present.

attua'r|e *v.t.* carry out. ~**si** *v.r.* be realized.

attuti'r|e *v.t.* deaden. ~**e il colpo** soften the blow. ~**si** *v.r.* diminish.

auda'c|e *a.* daring; (*coraggioso*) bold; (*insolente*) audacious; (*sfacciato*) cheeky. ~**ia** *n.f.* boldness; audacity; cheek.

a'udio *n.m.* audio.

audiovisi'vo *a.* audiovisual.

audito'rio *n.m.* auditorium.

audizio'ne *n.f.* audition; (*legge*) hearing.

a'uge *n.m.* height. **essere in** ~ be popular.

augura'r|e *v.t.* wish. ~**si** *v.r.* hope. **augu'rio** *n.m.* wish; (*presagio*) omen. **auguri!** all the best!; (*a Natale*) Happy Christmas!

augu'sto *a.* august.

a'ula *n.f.* classroom; (*università*) lecture-hall; (*sala*) hall.

aum|enta're *v.t./i.* increase. ~**e'nto** *n.m.* increase.

aure'ola *n.f.* halo.

auro'ra *n.f.* dawn.

ausilia're *a. & n.m./f.* auxiliary.

auspi'ci|o *n.m.* omen. ~ *n.m. pl.* (*protezione*) auspices.

auste'r|o *a.* austere. ~**ità** *n.f.* austerity.

Austra'li|a *n.f.* Australia. **a**~**a'no, a** *a. & n.m., f.* Australian.

Au'str|ia *n.f.* Austria. **a**~**i'aco, a** *a. & n.m., f.* Austrian.

autarchi'a *n.f.* autarchy. **auta'rchico** *a.* autarchic.

aute'ntic|o *a.* authentic; (*vero*) true. ~**a're** *v.t.* authenticate. ~**ità** *n.f.* authenticity.

auti'sta *n.m.* driver.

a'uto *n.f. invar.* car.

a'uto- *pref.* self-.

autoambula'nza *n.f.* ambulance.

autobiogr|afi'a *n.f.* autobiography. ~**a'fico** *a.* autobiographical.

a'utobus *n.m. invar.* bus.

autoca'rro *n.m.* lorry.

auto'cr|ate *n.m.* autocrat. ~**a'tico** *a.* autocratic.

auto'grafo *a. & n.m.* autograph.

autoli'nea *n.f.* bus line.

auto'ma *n.m.* robot.

automa'tico *a.* automatic. —*n.m.* (*bottone*) press-stud; (*fucile*) automatic.

autome'zzo *n.m.* motor vehicle.

automo'bil|e *n.f.* (motor) car. ~**i'smo** *n.m.* motoring. ~**i'sta** *n.m./f.* motorist.

autonomi'a *n.f.* autonomy. **auto'nomo** *a.* autonomous.

autopsi'a *n.f.* autopsy.

autora'dio *n.f. invar.* car radio; (*veicolo*) radio car.

au|to're, ~**tri'ce** *n.m., f.* author; (*di pitture*) painter; (*di furto ecc.*) perpetrator. **diritti d'**~**tore** royalties. **quadro d'**~**tore** genuine master.

autore'vole *a.* authoritative; (*che ha influenza*) influential.

autorime'ssa *n.f.* garage.

autorità *n.f.* authority.

autorita'rio *a.* autocratic.

autoritra'tto *n.m.* self-portrait.

autorizza're *v.t.* authorize. ~**zio'ne** *n.f.* authorization.

autoscuo'la *n.f.* driving school.

autosto'p *n.m.* hitch-hiking. **fare l'**~ hitch-hike. ~**pi'sta** *n.m./f.* hitch-hiker.

autostra'da *n.f.* motorway.

autotre'no *n.m.* articulated lorry.

autovei'colo *n.m.* motor vehicle.

autu'nn|o *n.m.* autumn. ~**a'le** *a.* autumn(al).

avambra'ccio *n.m.* forearm.

avangua'rdia *n.f.* vanguard; (*fig.*) avant-garde. **essere all'**~ be in the forefront.

ava'nti *adv.* (*in avanti*) forward; (*davanti*) in front; (*prima*) before. ~!

(*entrate*) come in!; (*suvvia*) come on! va' ~! go ahead! —*a*. (*precedente*) before. ~ a *prep*. before; (*in presenza*) in the presence of. **andare** ~ (*precedere*) go ahead; (*di orologio*) be fast. ~ e **indietro** backwards and forwards.

avanzame'nto *n.m.* progress; (*promozione*) promotion.

avanza'|re *v.i.* advance; (*progredire*) progress; (*essere d'avanzo*) be left (over). —*v.t.* advance; (*superare*) surpass; (*promuovere*) promote. ~rsi *v.r.* advance; (*avvicinarsi*) approach. ~ta *n.f.* advance. ~to *a.* advanced; (*nella notte*) late. **ava'nzo** *n.m.* remainder; (*comm.*) surplus. **avanzi** *n.m. pl.* (*rovine*) remains; (*di cibo*) left-overs.

avari'a *n.f.* damage; (*mech.*) breakdown.

avari'zia *n.f.* avarice. **ava'ro, a** *a.* stingy; *n.m., f.* miser.

ave'na *n.f.* oats *pl.*

ave're *v.t. aux.* have; (*ottenere*) get. ~ **fame/sete/freddo/caldo/sonno** be hungry/thirsty/cold/hot/sleepy. ~ **a che fare con** have to do with. ~ **da fare** be busy. **che hai?** what is the matter with you? **ha avuto il posto** he got the job. **hai fatto tutto?** have you done everything? —*n.m.* (*patrimonio*) property.

avi *n.m. pl.* ancestors.

avia'|to're *n.m.* flyer, aviator. ~zio'ne *n.f.* air force, aviation.

a'vid|o *a.* avid; (*pej.*) greedy. ~ità *n.f.* avidity; greed.

avioge'tto *n.m.* jet.

avoca'do *n.m.* avocado.

avo'rio *n.m.* ivory.

avvale'rsi *v.r.* avail oneself (**of,** di).

avvallame'nto *n.m.* depression.

avvalora're *v.t.* give value to; (*accrescere*) enhance.

avvampa're *v.i.* flare up; (*arrossire*) blush.

avvantaggia'r|e *v.t.* favour. ~si *v.r.* ~si **di** benefit from; (*approfittare*) take advantage of.

avvede'rsi *v.r.* (*accorgersi*) notice; (*capire*) realize.

avvedu'to *a.* shrewd.

avvelena'|re *v.t.* poison. ~me'nto *n.m.* poisoning.

avvene'nte *a.* attractive.

avvenime'nto *n.m.* event.

avveni're[1] *v.i.* happen; (*aver luogo*) take place.

avveni're[2] *n.m.* future.

avventa'rsi *v.r.* fling oneself.

avventa'to *a.* rash.

avve'nto *n.m.* advent; (*relig.*) Advent.

avvento're *n.m.* (regular) customer.

avventu'ra *n.f.* adventure; (*amorosa*) affair.

avventurie'ro, a *n.m., f.* adventurer, adventuress.

avventuro'so *a.* adventurous.

avvera'rsi *v.r.* come true.

avve'rbio *n.m.* adverb.

avversa're *v.t.* oppose.

avversa'rio, a *a.* opposing. —*n.m., f.* opponent.

avversio'ne *n.f.* aversion.

avversità *n.f.* adversity.

avve'rso *a.* (*sfavorevole*) adverse; (*contrario*) averse.

avverte'nz|a *n.f.* (*cura*) care; (*avvertimento*) warning; (*avviso*) notice. ~e *n.f. pl.* (*istruzioni*) instructions.

avvert|ime'nto *n.m.* warning. ~i're *v.t.* warn; (*informare*) inform; (*sentire*) feel.

avvezza'r|e *v.t.* accustom. ~si *v.r.* accustom oneself. **avve'zzo** *a.* **avvezzo a** used to.

avvia'|re *v.t.* start. ~rsi *v.r.* set out. ~me'nto *n.m.* starting; (*comm.*) goodwill. ~to *a.* under way. **bene** ~to thriving.

avvicina'|re *v.t.* bring near; (*persona*) approach. ~rsi *v.r.* come near; approach. ~me'nto *n.m.* approach.

avvil|i're *v.t.* dishearten; (*umiliare*) humiliate. ~rsi *v.r.* lose heart; (*umiliarsi*) humble oneself. ~me'nto *n.m.* despondency; humiliation. ~to *a.* disheartened; humiliated.

avviluppa'r|e *v.t.* envelop. ~si *v.r.* wrap oneself up; (*aggrovigliarsi*) get entangled.

avvinazza'to *a.* drunk.

avvi'nc|ere *v.t.* charm. ~e'nte *a.* charming; (*di libro ecc.*) enthralling.

avvinghia'r|e *v.t.* clutch. ~si *v.r.* cling.

avvisa're *v.t.* inform; (*mettere in guardia*) warn. **avvi'so** *n.m.* notice; (*annuncio*) announcement; (*avvertimento*) warning; (*pubblicitario*) advertisement. **a mio avviso** in my opinion.

avvista're *v.t.* catch sight of.

avvita're *v.t.* screw down *o* in.

avvizzi're *v.i.* wither.

avvoca'to, ~e'ssa *n.m.*, *f.* lawyer; (*fig.*) advocate.

avvo'lger|e *v.t.* wrap (up). **~si** *v.r.* wrap oneself up.

avvolgi'bile *n.m.* roller blind.

avvolto'io *n.m.* vulture.

azale'a *n.f.* azalea.

azie'nda *n.f.* firm. **~ agricola** farm. **~ di soggiorno** tourist bureau.

aziona're *v.t.* operate.

azio'n|e *n.f.* action; (*comm.*) share. **~i'sta** *n.m.|f.* shareholder.

azzanna're *v.t.* seize with the fangs.

azzard|a're *v.t.* risk. **~a'rsi** *v.r.* dare. **~a'to** *a.* risky; (*precipitoso*) rash. **azza'rdo** *n.m.* hazard. **gioco d'azzardo** game of chance.

azzecca're *v.t.* hit; (*fig.*, *indovinare*) guess.

azzuffa'rsi *v.r.* come to blows.

azzu'rro *a.* & *n.m.* blue. **principe ~** Prince Charming.

B

babbe'o *a.* foolish. —*n.m.* idiot.
ba'bbo *n.m.* (*fam.*) dad, daddy. **B~ Natale** Father Christmas.
babbu'ccia *n.f.* slipper.
babilo'nia *n.f.* (*fig.*) bedlam.
babo'rdo *n.m.* (*naut.*) port side.
baca'to *a.* wormeaten.
ba'cca *n.f.* berry.
baccalà *n.m.* stockfish.
bacca'no *n.m.* din.
bacce'llo *n.m.* pod.
bacche'tta *n.f.* rod; (*magica*) wand; (*di direttore d'orchestra*) baton; (*di tamburo*) drumstick.
bache'ca *n.f.* showcase.
bacia'r|e *v.t.* kiss. **~si** *v.r.* kiss (each other). **ba'cio** *n.m.* kiss.
baci'le *n.m.* basin.
bacine'lla *n.f.* (small) basin.
baci'no *n.m.* basin; (*anat.*) pelvis; (*di porto*) dock.
ba'co *n.m.* worm. **~ da seta** silkworm.
bacu'cco *a.* decrepit.
ba'da *n.f.* **tenere qcno. a ~** keep s.o. at bay.
bada're *v.i.* take care (**a**, of); (*fare attenzione*) look out. **bada ai fatti tuoi!** mind your own business! **bada al gradino!** mind the step.
badi'a *n.f.* abbey.
badi'le *n.m.* shovel.
ba'ff|i *n.m. pl.* moustache *s.*; (*di animale*) whiskers. **farsene un ~o** not to give a damn. **ridere sotto i ~i** laugh up one's sleeve. **~u'to** *a.* moustached; whiskered.
baga'gli|o *n.m.* luggage; (*mil.*) kit. **~a'io** *n.m.* (*di treno*) luggage van; (*auto.*) boot.
bagatte'lla *n.f.* trifle; (*mus.*) bagatelle.
baglio're *n.m.* glare; (*improvviso*) flash; (*fig.*) gleam.
bagna'nte *n.m./f.* bather.
bagna'|re *v.t.* wet; (*inzuppare*) soak; (*immergere*) dip; (*innaffiare*) water; (*parte del corpo*) bathe; (*di mare, lago*) wash; (*di fiume*) flow through. **~rsi** *v.r.* get wet; (*al mare ecc.*) bathe. **~to** *a.* wet; soaked.
bagni'no *n.m.* life-guard.
ba'gn|o *n.m.* bath; (*stanza*) bathroom; (*all'aperto*) bathe. **~i** *n.m. pl.* (*stabili-*

mento) baths. **fare il ~o** have a bath; (*nel mare ecc.*) (have a) bathe.
ba'ia *n.f.* bay.
baione'tta *n.f.* bayonet.
balau'stra, balaustra'ta *ns. f.* balustrade.
balbett|a're *v.t./i.* stammer; (*di bambino*) babble. **~i'o** *n.m.* stammering; babble.
balbu'zi|e *n.f.* stutter. **~e'nte** *a.* stuttering; *n.m./f.* stutterer.
balco'ne *n.m.* balcony.
baldacchi'no *n.m.* canopy.
balda'nza *n.f.* boldness. **ba'ldo** *a.* bold.
baldo'ria *n.f.* merrymaking. **far ~** make merry.
bale'na *n.f.* whale.
balena're *v.i.* lighten; (*fig.*) flash. **mi balenò un'idea** an idea flashed through my mind. **bale'no** *n.m.* flash; (*lampo*) lightning. **in un baleno** in a flash.
bale'stra *n.f.* crossbow.
ba'lia *n.f.* wet-nurse.
bali'a *n.f.* **in ~ di** at the mercy of.
ba'lla *n.f.* bale; (*fam., frottola*) tall story.
balla'|re *v.i.* dance. **~ta** *n.f.* ballad. **ba'llo** *n.m.* dance; (*il ballare*) dancing. **essere in ballo** be at stake.
ballerino, a *n.m., f.* (ballet) dancer.
balle'tto *n.m.* ballet.
ballonzola're *v.i.* skip about.
ballotta'ggio *n.m.* second count (of votes).
balnea're *a.* bathing. **stazione ~** seaside resort.
balo'cco *n.m.* toy.
balo'rdo *a.* foolish; (*stordito*) stunned. **tempo ~** nasty weather.
ba'lsamo *n.m.* balsam; (*lenimento*) remedy.
ba'ltico *a.* **Baltic. il (Mar) B~** The Baltic (Sea).
balua'rdo *n.m.* bulwark.
ba'lza *n.f.* crag; (*di abito*) flounce.
balza're *v.i.* bounce; (*saltare*) jump. **ba'lzo** *n.m.* bounce; jump; (*dirupo*) cliff. **dare un balzo** start up. **prendere la palla al balzo** seize an opportunity.

bamba'gia *n.f.* cotton wool; (*cascame*) cotton waste.

bambina'ia *n.f.* nursemaid, nanny.

bambi'no, a *n.m.*, *f.* child. **avere un** ∼ have a baby.

bambo'ccio *n.m.* chubby child; (*sciocco*) simpleton; (*fantoccio*) rag doll.

ba'mbola *n.f.* doll.

bambù *n.m.* bamboo.

bana'l|e *a.* banal. ∼**ità** *n.f.* banality.

bana'n|a *n.f.* banana. ∼**o** *n.m.* banana-tree.

ban'c|a *n.f.* bank. ∼**a'rio, a** *a.* banking; *n.m.*, *f.* bank clerk.

bancare'lla *n.f.* stall.

bancaro'tta *n.f.* bankruptcy. **fare** ∼ go bankrupt.

banche'tto *n.m.* banquet.

banchie're *n.m.* banker.

banchi'na *n.f.* (*naut.*) quay; (*marciapiede*) platform; (*di strada*) path.

ba'nco *n.m.* (*di scuola*) desk; (*di negozio*) counter; (*di officina*) bench; (*di gioco, banca*) bank; (*di mercato*) stall.

bancono'ta *n.f.* banknote.

ba'nda *n.f.* band; (*di delinquenti*) gang. ∼ **d'atterraggio** (*aeron.*) landing strip.

bandie'ra *n.f.* flag.

bandi're *v.t.* banish; (*pubblicare*) publish; (*fig.*) dispense with.

bandi'to *n.m.* bandit.

bandito're *n.m.* town crier; (*di aste*) auctioneer.

ba'ndo *n.m.* proclamation; (*esilio*) banishment.

bar *n.m. invar.* bar.

ba'ra *n.f.* coffin.

bara'cca *n.f.* hut; (*catapecchia*) hovel. **mandare avanti la** ∼ keep the ship afloat.

barao'nda *n.f.* confusion.

bara're *v.i.* cheat.

baratta're *v.t.* barter. **bara'tto** *n.m.* barter.

bara'ttolo *n.m.* jar; (*di latta*) tin.

ba'rb|a *n.f.* beard; (*fam., noia*) bore. **farsi la** ∼**a** shave. **in** ∼**a a** in spite of. ∼**u'to** *a.* bearded.

barbabie'tola *n.f.* beetroot. ∼ **da zucchero** sugar-beet.

ba'rb|aro *a.* barbarous. —*n.m.* barbarian. ∼**a'rico** *a.* barbaric. ∼**a'rie** *n.f.* barbarity.

barbie're *n.m.* barber.

barbo'ne *n.m.* (*vagabondo*) vagrant; (*cane*) poodle.

ba'rca *n.f.* boat. ∼ **a vela** sailing boat. ∼ **da pesca** fishing boat. ∼ **di salvataggio** lifeboat. ∼**io'lo** *n.m.* boatman.

barcamena'rsi *v.r.* manage.

barcolla're *v.i.* stagger.

barcollo'ni *adv.* **camminare** ∼ stagger.

barco'ne *n.m.* barǳe; (*di ponte*) pontoon.

barda're *v.t.* harness; (*hum.*) dress up.

bare'lla *n.f.* stretcher.

bari'le *n.m.* barrel.

bari'sta *n.m./f.* barman, barmaid.

bari'tono *n.m.* baritone.

barlu'me *n.m.* glimmer.

baro'cco *a.* & *n.m.* baroque.

baro'metro *n.m.* barometer.

baro'n|e *n.m.* baron. ∼**e'ssa** *n.f.* baroness.

ba'rra *n.f.* bar; (*lineetta*) line; (*naut.*) tiller.

barrica'|re *v.t.* barricade. ∼**ta** *n.f.* barricade.

barrie'ra *n.f.* barrier; (*stradale*) roadblock. ∼ **razziale** colour bar.

barri'|re *v.i.* trumpet. ∼**to** *n.m.* trumpeting.

baru'ffa *n.f.* scuffle. **far** ∼ quarrel.

barzelle'tta *n.f.* joke.

basa'r|e *v.t.* base. ∼**si** *v.r.* ∼**si su** be based on.

ba'sco *n.m.* (*copricapo*) beret.

ba'se *n.f.* basis; (*fondamento*) foundation; (*mil. ecc.*) base; (*pol.*) rank and file. —*a.* basic. **a** ∼ **di** containing. **in** ∼ **a** on the basis of.

base'tta *n.f.* sideburn.

basi'lica *n.f.* basilica.

basi'lico *n.m.* basil.

ba'ss|o *a.* low; (*di statura*) short; (*acqua*) shallow; (*vile*) vile. —*n.m.* lower part; (*mus.*) bass. **la** ∼**a Italia** southern Italy. ∼**e'zza** *n.f.* lowness; shortness; vileness.

bassofo'ndo *n.m.* (*pl.* **bassifo'ndi**) shallow(s). **bassifondi** *n.m. pl.* (*quartieri poveri*) slums.

bassorilie'vo *n.m.* bas-relief.

basta'rdo, a *a.* bastard, illegitimate; (*di animale*) mongrel. —*n.m.*, *f.* illegitimate child, bastard; mongrel.

basta're *v.i.* be enough; (*durare*) last. **ba'sta!** stop it! **basta che** (*purché*) provided that.

bastime'nto *n.m.* ship.

bastio'ne *n.m.* bastion.

bastona're *v.t.* beat.

basto'ne *n.m.* stick; (*da golf*) club; (*da passeggio*) walking-stick.

bato'sta *n.f.* blow.

batta'gli|a *n.f.* battle; (*lotta*) fight. ~**a're** *v.i.* battle; fight.

batta'glio *n.m.* (*di campana*) clapper; (*di porta*) knocker.

battaglio'ne *n.m.* battalion.

batte'llo *n.m.* boat; (*motonave*) steamer.

batte'nte *n.m.* (*di porta*) wing; (*di finestra*) shutter; (*battaglio*) knocker.

ba'tter|e *v.t.* beat; (*percorrere*) scour; (*grano*) thresh. —*v.i.* (*alla porta*) knock; (*cuore*) beat; (*di ali ecc.*) flap; (*tennis*) serve. ~**e a macchina** type. ~**e gli occhi** blink. ~**e il piede** tap one's foot. ~**e le mani** clap (one's hands). ~**e le ore** strike the hours. ~**si** *v.r.* fight.

batte'ri *n.m. pl.* bacteria.

batteri'a *n.f.* battery; (*mus.*) drums *pl.*

batte'simo *n.m.* baptism, christening.

battezza're *v.t.* baptize, christen.

battibale'no *n.m.* **in un** ~ in a flash.

battibe'cco *n.m.* squabble.

batticuo're *n.m.* palpitation. **mi venne il** ~ I was scared.

battima'no *n.m.* applause.

battipa'nni *n.m. invar.* carpetbeater.

battiste'ro *n.m.* baptistery.

battistra'da *n.m. invar.* outrider; (*di pneumatico*) tread; (*sport*) pacesetter.

ba'ttito *n.m.* (*del cuore*) (heart) beat; (*alle tempie*) throbbing; (*di orologio*) ticking; (*della pioggia*) beating.

battu'ta *n.f.* beat; (*bastonatura*) beating; (*colpo*) knock; (*spiritosaggine*) wisecrack; (*osservazione*) remark; (*mus.*) bar; (*tennis*) service; (*theatr.*) cue; (*dattilografia*) stroke.

batu'ffolo *n.m.* flock.

bau'le *n.m.* trunk.

ba'va *n.f.* dribble; (*di cane ecc.*) slobber. **aver la** ~ **alla bocca** foam at the mouth.

bavagli'no *n.m.* bib.

bava'glio *n.m.* gag.

ba'vero *n.m.* collar.

baza'r *n.m. invar.* bazaar.

bazze'cola *n.f.* trifle.

bazzica're *v.t./i.* haunt.

bea'rsi *v.r.* delight (**di**, in).

beatitu'dine *n.f.* bliss.

bea'to *a.* blissful; (*relig.*) blessed. ~ **te!** lucky you!

bebè *n.m.* baby.

becca'ccia *n.f.* woodcock.

becca'r|e *v.t.* peck; (*fig.*) catch. ~**si** *v.r.* (*litigare*) quarrel.

beccheggia're *v.i.* pitch.

becchi'no *n.m.* grave-digger.

be'cco *n.m.* beak; (*di caffettiera ecc.*) spout.

befa'na *n.f.* Epiphany; (*donna brutta*) old witch.

be'ff|a *n.f.* hoax. **farsi** ~**e di qcno.** mock s.o. ~**a'rdo** *a.* derisory; (*di persona*) mocking. ~**a're** *v.t.* mock. ~**arsi di** *v.r.* make fun of.

be'ga *n.f.* quarrel.

be'ige *a. & n.m.* beige.

bela'|re *v.i.* bleat. ~**to** *n.m.* bleating.

Be'lg|io *n.m.* Belgium. **be'lga** *a. & n.m./f.* Belgian.

belle'zza *n.f.* beauty. **che** ~**!** how lovely!

bellico'so *a.* warlike.

belligera'nte *a. & n.m./f.* belligerent.

bellimbu'sto *n.m.* dandy.

be'llo *a.* beautiful; (*uomo*) handsome; (*di aspetto*) good-looking; (*tempo*) fine. —*n.m.* beauty; (*innamorato*) sweetheart. **bell'e fatto** ready-made. **il** ~ **è che** the funny thing is that. **nel bel mezzo** right in the middle. **questa è bella!** that's a good one! **scamparla bella** have a narrow escape. **sul più** ~ at the crucial point. **un bel niente** absolutely nothing.

be'lva *n.f.* wild beast.

belvede're *n.m. invar.* belvedere.

ben *vedi* **bene.**

benché *conj.* though, although.

be'nd|a *n.f.* bandage; (*per occhi*) blindfold. ~**a're** *v.t.* bandage; blindfold.

be'ne *adv.* well. —*n.m.* good; (*dono*) gift; (*pl., averi*) property. **ben** ~ truly. ~**!** good! **come tu ben sai** as you well know. **lo credo** ~**!** I can well believe it! **non sta** ~ (*non è giusto*) it is not right. **sta|va** ~**!** all right! **star** ~ (*di salute*) be well; (*di stile*) suit. **ti auguro** ~ I wish you well. **ti sta** ~**!** it serves you right! **voler** ~ (**a**) love.

benede'tto *a.* blessed.

benedi'|re *v.t.* bless. ~**zio'ne** *n.f.* blessing.

beneduca'to *a.* well-mannered.

benefat|to're, ~**tri'ce** *n.m., f.* benefactor, benefactress.

benefica're *v.t.* help.

benefice'nza *n.f.* charity.

benefi'ci|o *n.m.* benefit. ~**a're** *v.i.* profit (by). ~**a'rio, a** *a. & n.m., f.*

beneficiary. **bene'fico** *a.* beneficial; (*di beneficenza*) charitable.
beneme'rito *a.* worthy.
bene'ssere *n.m.* well-being.
benesta'nte *a.* well off. —*n.m.*/*f.* well off person.
benesta're *n.m.* consent.
bene'vol|**o** *a.* benevolent. ~**e'nza** *n.f.* benevolence.
beniami'no *n.m.* favourite.
beni'gno *a.* kindly; (*med.*) benign.
beninte'so *adv.* of course.
bensì *conj.* (but) rather.
benvenu'to *a.* & *n.m.* welcome.
benzi'n|**a** *n.f.* petrol. **far ~a** get petrol. ~**a'io** *n.m.* petrol station attendant.
be're *v.t.* drink; (*assorbire*) absorb; (*fig.*) swallow. —*n.m.* drinking; (*bevande*) drinks *pl.*
berli'na *n.f.* (*auto.*) saloon.
Berli'no *n.m.* Berlin.
berno'ccolo *n.m.* bump; (*disposizione*) flair.
berre'tto *n.m.* cap.
bersaglia're *v.t.* batter away.
bersa'glio *n.m.* target.
beste'mmi|**a** *n.f.* swear-word; (*maledizione*) oath; (*sproposito*) blasphemy. ~**a're** *v.i.* swear.
be'sti|**a** *n.f.* animal; (*feroce, persona brutale*) beast; (*persona sciocca*) fool. ~**a'le** *a.* bestial; brutal. ~**alità** *n.f.* bestiality; (*fig.*) nonsense. ~**a'me** *n.m.* livestock.
be'ttola *n.f.* (low) tavern.
betu'lla *n.f.* birch.
beva'nda *n.f.* drink.
bevi|**to're**, ~**tri'ce** *n.m.*, *f.* drinker.
bevu'ta *n.f.* drink.
bevu'to *p.p. di* **bere.**
bia'da *n.f.* fodder.
biancheri'a *n.f.* linen. ~ **personale** underwear.
bia'nco *a.* white; (*di foglio*) blank. —*n.m.* white; blank. **di punto in ~** all of a sudden. **mangiare in ~** eat plain food.
biancospi'no *n.m.* hawthorn.
biasima're *v.t.* blame. **bia'simo** *n.m.* blame.
Bi'bbia *n.f.* Bible.
bibero'n *n.m.* (baby's) bottle.
bi'bita *n.f.* (soft) drink.
bi'blico *a.* biblical.
bibliote'c|**a** *n.f.* library; (*mobile*) bookcase. ~**a'rio, a** *n.m.*, *f.* librarian.
bicarbona'to *n.m.* bicarbonate.

bicchie're *n.m.* glass; (*senza stelo*) tumbler.
bicicle'tta *n.f.* bicycle. **andare in ~** ride a bicycle.
bicolo're *a.* two-coloured.
bidè *n.m.* bidet.
bidello, a *n.m.*, *f.* (school) caretaker.
bido'ne *n.m.* bin; (*fam.*, *truffa*) swindle.
bienna'le *a.* biennial.
bie'tola *n.f.* beet.
bifoca'le *a.* bifocal.
biforca'|**rsi** *v.r.* fork. ~**zio'ne** *n.f.* fork.
bigami'a *n.f.* bigamy. **bi'gamo, a** *a.* bigamous; *n.m.*, *f.* bigamist.
bighell|**ona're** *v.i.* loaf. ~**o'ne** *n.m.* loafer.
bigiotteri'a *n.f.* costume jewellery; (*negozio*) jeweller's.
biglie'tt|**o** *n.m.* ticket; (*lettera breve*) note; (*cartoncino*) card; (*di banca*) banknote. ~**a'io** *n.m.* booking clerk; (*sui treni*) ticket-collector. ~**eri'a** *n.f.* ticket-office; (*ferrovia*) booking-office; (*theatr.*) box-office.
bigodi'no *n.m.* roller.
bigo'tto *n.m.* bigot.
bila'nci|**a** *n.f.* scales *pl.*; (*di orologio, comm.*) balance. **B~a** *n.f.* (*astr.*) Libra. ~**a're** *v.t.* balance; (*fig.*) weigh.
bila'ncio *n.m.* budget; (*comm.*) balance (sheet). **fare il ~** strike the balance.
bi'l|**e** *n.f.* bile; (*fig.*) rage. ~**io'so** *a.* bilious.
bilia'rdo *n.m.* billiards *s.*
bi'lico *n.m.* equilibrium. **in ~** in the balance.
bili'ngue *a.* bilingual.
bilio'ne *n.m.* thousand million.
bimbo, a *n.m.*, *f.* child.
bimensi'le *a.* fortnightly.
bimestra'le *a.* bimonthly.
bina'rio *n.m.* track; (*piattaforma*) platform.
bino'colo *n.m.* binoculars *pl.*
biochi'mica *n.f.* biochemistry.
biografi'a *n.f.* biography. **biogra'fico** *a.* biographic(al). **bio'grafo, a** *n.m.*, *f.* biographer.
biologi'a *n.f.* biology. **biolo'gico** *a.* biological. **bio'logo, a** *m.*, *f.* biologist.
bio'nd|**o** *a.* blond. —*n.m.* fair colour; (*uomo*) fair-haired man. ~**a** *n.f.* blonde.
bi'rb|**a** *n.f.*, **birba'nte** *n.m.* rascal, rogue. ~**o'ne** *a.* wicked.

birichi'no, a *a.* naughty. —*n.m.*, *f.* little devil.

biri'llo *n.m.* skittle.

bi'rr|a *n.f.* beer. ~**eri'a** *n.f.* beerhouse; (*fabbrica*) brewery.

bis *n.m. invar.* encore.

bisa'ccia *n.f.* haversack.

bisbe'tic|a *n.f.* shrew. ~**o** *a.* bad-tempered.

bisb|iglia're *v.t./i.* whisper. ~**i'glio** *n.m.* whisper.

bi'sca *n.f.* gambling-house.

bi'scia *n.f.* snake.

bisco'tto *n.m.* biscuit.

bisessua'le *a.* bisexual.

bisesti'le *a.* **anno** ~ leap year.

bisla'cco *a.* peculiar.

bisno'nno, a *n.m.*, *f.* great-grandfather, great-grandmother.

bis|ogna're *v.i. impersonale* ~**o'gna agire subito** we must act at once. ~**ogna farlo** it is necessary to do it. —*v.i.* (*aver bisogno di*) need. **ho** ~**ogno il tuo aiuto** I need your help. ~**o'gno** *n.m.* need; (*povertà*) poverty. ~**ogno'so** *a.* needy; poor. ~**ognoso di** in need of.

biste'cca *n.f.* steak.

bist|iccia're *v.i.* quarrel. ~**i'ccio** *n.m.* quarrel; (*gioco di parole*) pun.

bi'sturi *n.m.* scalpel.

bito'rzolo *n.m.* lump.

bi'tter *n.m. invar.* (bitter) aperitif.

biva'cco *n.m.* bivouac.

bi'vio *n.m.* crossroad(s); (*di strada*) fork.

bi'zz|a *n.f.* tantrum. **fare le** ~**e** (*di bambini*) play up.

bizza'rr|o *a.* bizarre. ~**i'a** *n.f.* eccentricity.

bizze'ffe *adv.* **a** ~ galore.

blandi're *v.t.* soothe; (*allettare*) flatter.

bla'ndo *a.* mild.

bla'sfemo *a.* blasphemous.

blaso'ne *n.m.* coat of arms.

blaterare *v.i.* blether.

bla'tta *n.f.* cockroach.

ble'so *a.* lisping.

blinda'to *a.* armoured.

blocca'r|e *v.t.* block; (*isolare*) cut off; (*mil.*) blockade; (*comm.*) freeze. ~**si** *v.r.* (*mech.*) jam. **blo'cco** *n.m.* block; blockade; (*dei fitti*) restriction; (*di carta*) pad. **in blocco** (*comm.*) in bulk.

blu *a.* & *n.m.* blue.

blu'sa *n.f.* blouse.

bo'a *n.m.* boa (constrictor); (*sciarpa*) (feather) boa. — *n.f.* (*naut.*) buoy.

boa'to *n.m.* rumbling.

bobi'na *n.f.* spool; (*di film*) reel; (*electr.*) coil.

bo'cc|a *n.f.* mouth. **a** ~**a aperta** (*fig.*) dumbfounded. **in** ~**a al lupo!** good luck! ~**a'ta** *n.f.* (*di fumo*) puff. **prendere una** ~**ata d'aria** get a breath of fresh air.

bocca'cc|ia *n.f.* grimace. **far** ~**e** make faces.

bocca'le *n.m.* jug; (*da birra*) tankard.

bocce'tta *n.f.* small bottle.

boccheggia're *v.i.* gasp.

bocchi'no *n.m.* (cigarette) holder; (*di pipa*, *mus.*) mouthpiece.

bo'cc|ia *n.f.* bottle; (*palla*) bowl. ~**e** *n.f. pl.* (*gioco*) bowls *s.*

boccia'|re *v.t.* (*agli esami*) fail; (*respingere*) reject; (*alle bocce*) hit. ~**tu'ra** *n.f.* failure.

boccio'lo *n.m.* bud.

bocco'ne *n.m.* mouthful; (*piccolo pasto*) snack.

bocco'ni *adv.* face downwards.

bo'ia *n.m.* executioner.

boia'ta *n.f.* (*fam.*) rubbish.

boicotta're *v.t.* boycott.

Boli'vi|a *n.f.* Bolivia. **b**~**a'no, a** *a.* & *n.m.*, *f.* Bolivian.

bole'ro *n.m.* bolero.

bo'lgia *n.f.* (*caos*) bedlam.

bo'lide *n.m.* meteor. **passare come un** ~ flash past like a rocket.

bo'lla *n.f.* bubble; (*pustola*) blister.

bolla're *v.t.* stamp; (*fig.*) brand.

bolle'nte *a.* boiling (hot).

bolle'tta *n.f.* bill. **essere in** ~ be hard up.

bolletti'no *n.m.* bulletin; (*comm.*) list.

bolli'no *n.m.* coupon.

bolli'|re *v.t./i.* boil. ~**to** *n.m.* boiled meat. ~**to're** *n.m.* boiler; (*per l'acqua*) kettle. ~**tu'ra** *n.f.* boiling.

bo'llo *n.m.* stamp.

bollo're *n.m.* boil; (*caldo*) intense heat; (*fig.*) ardour.

bo'mba *n.f.* bomb. **a prova di** ~ bombproof.

bombard|a're *v.t.* shell; (*con aerei*) bomb; (*fig.*) bombard. ~**ame'nto** *n.m.* shelling; bombing; bombardment. ~**amento aereo** air raid. ~**ie're** *n.m.* bomber.

bombe'tta *n.f.* bowler (hat).

bo'mbola *n.f.* cylinder.

bombonie'ra *n.f.* wedding keepsake.

bona'ccia *n.f.* (*naut.*) calm.
bonaccio'ne *a.* good-natured.
bona'rio *a.* kindly.
boni'fic|a *n.f.* land reclamation. ∼a're *v.t.* reclaim.
boni'fico *n.m.* (*comm.*) discount; (*bancario*) transfer.
bontà *n.f.* goodness; (*gentilezza*) kindness.
borbott|a're *v.i.* mumble; (*di stomaco*) rumble. ∼i'o *n.m.* mumbling; rumbling.
bo'rchia *n.f.* stud.
borda'|re *v.t.* border. ∼tu'ra *n.f.* border.
borde'llo *n.m.* brothel; (*fig.*) bedlam.
bo'rdo *n.m.* border; (*estremità*) edge. **a** ∼ (*naut.*) on board.
bordu'ra *n.f.* border.
borga'ta *n.f.* hamlet.
borghe's|e *a.* bourgeois; (*abito*) civilian. **in** ∼**e** in civilian dress; (*di poliziotto*) in plain clothes. ∼i'a *n.f.* middle classes *pl.*
bo'rgo *n.m.* village; (*quartiere*) district.
bo'ri|a *n.f.* conceit. ∼o'so *a.* conceited.
borota'lco *n.m.* talcum powder.
borra'ccia *n.f.* flask.
bo'rs|a *n.f.* bag; (*borsetta*) handbag; (*valori*) Stock Exchange. ∼**a della spesa** shopping bag. ∼**a di studio** scholarship. ∼**aio'lo** *n.m.* pickpocket. ∼**elli'no** *n.m.* purse. ∼**i'sta** *n.m.|f.* (*econ.*) speculator; (*schol.*) scholarship holder.
bosc|o *n.m.* wood. ∼**a'glia** *n.f.* woodlands *pl.* ∼**aio'lo** *n.m.* woodman; (*guardaboschi*) forester. ∼**o'so** *a.* wooded.
bo'ssolo *n.m.* cartridge case.
bota'nic|a *n.f.* botany. ∼**o** *a.* botanical; *n.m.* botanist.
bo'tola *n.f.* trapdoor.
bo'tt|a *n.f.* blow; (*rumore*) bang. **fare a** ∼**e** come to blows.
bo'tte *n.f.* barrel.
botte'g|a *n.f.* shop; (*di artigiano*) workshop. ∼**a'io, a** *n.m., f.* shopkeeper.
botteghi'no *n.m.* (*theatr.*) box-office; (*del lotto*) lottery-shop.
botti'gli|a *n.f.* bottle. **in** ∼**a** bottled. ∼**eri'a** *n.f.* wine shop.
bottino *n.m.* loot; (*mil.*) booty.
bo'tto *n.m.* bang. **di** ∼ all of a sudden.
botto'ne *n.m.* button; (*bot.*) bud.
bovi'n|o *a.* bovine. —∼**i** *n.m. pl.* cattle.

box *n.m.* (*per cavalli*) loose box; (*recinto per bambini*) play-pen.
bo'xe *n.f.* boxing.
bo'zz|a *n.f.* draft; (*typ.*) proof; (*bernoccolo*) bump. ∼**a in colonna** galley (proof). ∼**e'tto** *n.m.* sketch.
bo'zzolo *n.m.* cocoon.
bracca're *v.t.* hunt.
bracce'tto *n.m.* **a** ∼ arm in arm.
braccia'l|e *n.m.* bracelet; (*fascia*) armband. ∼**e'tto** *n.m.* bracelet; (*di orologio*) watch-strap.
braccia'nte *n.m.* day labourer.
bra'ccio *n.m.* (*pl.f.* **braccia**) arm; (*pl.m.* **bracci**) (*di fiume*) arm; (*di mare*) sound. **braccio'lo** *n.m.* (*di sedia*) arm.
bra'cco *n.m.* hound.
bracconie're *n.m.* poacher.
bra'c|e *n.f.* embers *pl.* ∼**ie're** *n.m.* brazier.
bracio'la *n.f.* chop.
bra'm|a *n.f.* longing. ∼**a're** *v.t.* long for.
bra'nca *n.f.* branch; (*artiglio*) claw.
bra'nchia *n.f.* gill.
bra'nco *n.m.* (*di cani*) pack; (*di uccelli, pecore*) flock; (*pej., di persone*) gang.
brancola're *v.i.* grope.
bra'nda *n.f.* camp-bed.
brande'll|o *n.m.* scrap. **a** ∼**i** in tatters.
brandi're *v.t.* brandish.
bra'no *n.m.* piece; (*di libro*) passage.
brasa're *v.t.* braise.
Brasi'l|e *n.m.* Brazil. **b**∼**ia'no, a** *a.* & *n.m., f.* Brazilian.
bra'v|o *a.* good; (*abile*) clever; (*coraggioso*) brave. ∼**o!** well done! ∼**a'ta** *n.f.* bragging. ∼**u'ra** *n.f.* skill.
bre'ccia *n.f.* breach.
brete'll|a *n.f.* shoulder-strap. ∼**e** *n.f. pl.* (*di calzoni*) braces.
bre'v|e *a.* brief, short. **in** ∼**e** briefly. **tra** ∼**e** shortly. ∼**ità** *n.f.* shortness.
breve'tt|o *n.m.* patent; (*attestato*) licence. ∼**a're** *v.t.* patent.
bre'zza *n.f.* breeze.
bri'cco *n.m.* jug.
bricco'n|e *n.m.* blackguard; (*hum.*) rascal. ∼**a'ta** *n.f.* dirty trick.
bri'ciola *n.f.* crumb; (*fig.*) grain.
bri'ciolo *n.m.* fragment.
bri'ga *n.f.* (*fastidio*) trouble; (*lite*) quarrel. **attaccar** ∼ pick a quarrel.
brigadie're *n.m.* (*dei carabinieri*) sergeant.
briga'nte *n.m.* bandit; (*hum.*) rogue.
briga're *v.i.* scheme.

briga'ta *n.f.* brigade; (*gruppo*) group.

bri'glia *n.f.* rein. **a ~ sciolta** at full gallop.

brilla'nte *a.* brilliant; (*scintillante*) sparkling. —*n.m.* diamond.

brilla're *v.i.* shine; (*di metallo*) glitter; (*scintillare*) sparkle.

bri'llo *a.* tipsy.

bri'na *n.f.* hoar-frost.

brinda're *v.i.* toast. **~ a qcno.** drink a toast to s.o.

bri'ndisi *n.m. invar.* toast.

bri'|o *n.m.* vivacity. **~o'so** *a.* vivacious.

brita'nnico *a.* British.

bri'vido *n.m.* shiver; (*di paura ecc.*) shudder; (*di emozione*) thrill.

brizzola'to *a.* (*persona*) going grey; (*capelli*) grizzled.

bro'cca *n.f.* jug.

brocca'to *n.m.* brocade.

bro'ccolo *n.m.* broccoli *s.*

bro'do *n.m.* broth; (*per cucinare*) stock. **~ ristretto** consommé.

broglia'ccio *n.m.* notebook.

bro'glio *n.m.* **~ elettorale** gerrymander.

bronchi'te *n.f.* bronchitis.

bro'ncio *n.m.* sulk. **fare il ~** sulk. **tenere il ~ a** have a grudge against.

brontol|a're *v.i.* grumble; (*di tuono ecc.*) rumble. **~i'o** *n.m.* grumbling; rumbling. **~o'ne, a** *n.m.,f.* grumbler.

bro'nzo *n.m.* bronze.

brossu'ra *n.f.* **edizione in ~** paperback.

bruca're *v.t.* (*di pecora*) graze.

bruciacchia're *v.t.* scorch.

bruciape'lo *adv.* **a ~** point-blank.

bruci|a're *v.t.* burn; (*incendiare*) set fire to. —*v.i.* burn. **~a'to** *a.* burnt; (*fig.*) burnt-out. **~ato're** *n.m.* burner. **~atu'ra** *n.f.* burn. **~o're** *n.m.* burning sensation.

bru'co *n.m.* caterpillar.

bru'folo *n.m.* spot.

brughie'ra *n.f.* heath.

brulica're *v.i.* swarm.

bru'llo *a.* bare.

bru'ma *n.f.* mist.

bru'no *a.* brown; (*di occhi, capelli*) dark.

bru'sco *a.* sharp; (*di persona*) abrupt; (*improvviso*) sudden.

brusi'o *n.m.* buzzing.

brut|a'le *a.* brutal. **~alità** *n.f.* brutality. **bru'to** *a.* & *n.m.* brute.

brutt|o *a.* ugly; (*cattivo*) bad. **~a**

copia rough copy. **~o tiro** dirty trick. **~e'zza** *n.f.* ugliness. **~u'ra** *n.f.* ugly thing.

bu'ca *n.f.* hole; (*avvallamento*) hollow. **~ delle lettere** post-box.

bucane've *n.m. invar.* snowdrop.

buca'r|e *v.t.* make a hole in; (*pungere*) prick; (*biglietti*) punch. —*v.i.* have a puncture. **~si** *v.r.* prick oneself.

buca'to *n.m.* washing.

bu'ccia *n.f.* peel, skin.

bucherella're *v.t.* riddle.

bu'co *n.m.* hole.

bude'llo *n.m.* (*pl.f.* **budella**) bowel.

budi'no *n.m.* pudding.

bu'e *n.m.* (*pl.* **buoi**) ox. **carne di ~** beef.

bu'falo *n.m.* buffalo.

bufe'ra *n.f.* storm; (*di neve*) blizzard.

bu'ffo *a.* funny. —*n.m.* funny thing.

buffo'n|e *n.m.* buffoon. **fare il ~e** play the fool. **~a'ta** *n.f.* (*scherzo*) joke.

bugi'|a *n.f.* lie. **~a pietosa** white lie. **~a'rdo, a** *a.* lying; *n.m.,f.* liar.

bugiga'ttolo *n.m.* cubby-hole.

bu'io *a.* dark. —*n.m.* darkness. **al ~** in the dark. **~ pesto** pitch dark.

bu'lbo *n.m.* bulb; (*dell'occhio*) eyeball.

Bulgari'a *n.f.* Bulgaria. **bu'lgaro, a** *a.* & *n.m.,f.* Bulgarian.

bu'llo *n.m.* bully.

bullo'ne *n.m.* bolt.

buongusta'io, a *n.m.,f.* gourmet.

buo'n|o *a.* good; (*adatto*) fit; (*benevolo*) kind; (*di tempo*) fine. —*n.m.* good; (*tagliando*) voucher; (*titolo*) bond. **~a fortuna** good luck. **~a notte/ sera** good night/evening. **~ compleanno/Natale** happy birthday/ Christmas. **~ giorno** good morning; (*dopo mezzogiorno*) good afternoon. **~ senso** common sense. **di ~'ora** early. **una ~a volta** once and for all.

buontempo'ne, a *n.m., f.* happy-go-lucky person.

buonumo're *n.m.* good temper.

buonusci'ta *n.f.* retirement bonus; (*di dirigente*) golden handshake.

buratti'no *n.m.* puppet.

bu'rbero *a.* surly; (*nei modi*) rough.

bu'rl|a *n.f.* joke. **fare una ~a a** play a trick on. **per ~a** for fun. **~a're** *v.t.* make a fool of. **~a'rsi di** make fun of.

buro'cr|ate *n.m.* bureaucrat. **~a'tico** *a.* bureaucratic. **~azi'a** *n.f.* bureaucracy.

burra'sc|a *n.f.* storm. ∼**o'so** *a.* stormy.

bu'rro *n.m.* butter.

burro'ne *n.m.* ravine.

busca'r|e *v.t.*, ∼**si** *v.r.* catch. ∼**le** (*fam.*) get a hiding.

bussa're *v.t.* knock.

bu'ssola *n.f.* compass. **perdere la** ∼ lose one's bearings.

bu'sta *n.f.* envelope; (*astuccio*) case. ∼ **paga** pay packet.

bustare'lla *n.f.* bribe.

bu'sto *n.m.* bust; (*indumento*) girdle.

butta'r|e *v.t.* throw. ∼ **giù** (*demolire*) knock down; (*inghiottire*) gulp down; (*scritto*) scribble down; (*fam.*, *mettere a cuocere*) put on; (*scoraggiare*) dishearten. ∼**si** *v.r.* throw oneself; (*saltare*) jump.

buttera'to *a.* pock-marked.

buzzu'rro *n.m.* (*fam.*) yokel.

C

cabi′n|a *n.f.* box; (*naut.*, *aeron.*) cabin; (*balneare*) bathing hut. ~**a di pilotaggio** cockpit. ~**a telefonica** telephone booth. ~**a′to** *n.m.* cabin cruiser.

caca′o *n.m.* cocoa.

ca′ccia *n.f.* hunt; (*con fucile*) shooting; (*inseguimento*) chase; (*selvaggina*) game. —*n.m. invar.* (*aeron.*) fighter; (*naut.*) destroyer. **cane da ~** hound. ~**to′re** *n.m.* hunter. ~**tore di frodo** poacher.

cacciabombardie′re *n.m.* fighter bomber.

cacciagio′ne *n.f.* game.

caccia′r|e *v.t.* hunt; (*mandar via*) chase away; (*scacciare*) drive out; (*ficcare*) shove. —*v.i.* go hunting. ~**si** *v.r.* (*nascondersi*) hide; (*andare a finire*) get to.

cacciavi′te *n.m. invar.* screwdriver.

cachet *n.m. invar.* (*med.*) capsule; (*colorante*) colour rinse; (*stile*) cachet.

ca′ctus *n.m. invar.* cactus.

cada′v|ere *n.m.* corpse. ~**e′rico** *a.* (*fig.*) deathly pale.

cade′nte *a.* falling; (*casa*) crumbling; (*persona*) decrepit.

cade′nza *n.f.* cadence; (*ritmo*) rhythm.

cade′re *v.i.* fall; (*capelli ecc.*) fall out; (*capitombolare*) tumble; (*di vestito ecc.*) hang. **~ dal sonno** feel very sleepy. **lasciar ~** drop.

cade′tto *n.m.* cadet.

cadu′ta *n.f.* fall; (*fig.*) downfall.

caffè *n.m. invar.* coffee; (*locale*) café. **~ macchiato** coffee with a dash of milk. ~**lla′tte** *n.m. invar.* white coffee.

caffettie′ra *n.f.* coffee-pot.

cafo′ne, a *n.m.*, *f.* boor.

cagiona′re *v.t.* cause.

cagione′vole *a.* delicate.

caglia′r|e *v.i.*, ~**si** *v.r.* curdle.

ca′gna *n.f.* bitch.

cagna′ra *n.f.* (*fam.*) din.

cagne′sco *a.* **guardare qcno. in ~** scowl at s.o.

ca′la *n.f.* creek.

calabro′ne *n.m.* hornet.

calama′io *n.m.* inkpot.

calama′ro *n.m.* squid.

calami′ta *n.f.* magnet.

calamità *n.f.* calamity.

cala′ndra *n.f.* (*uccello*) lark; (*insetto*) weevil.

cala′r|e *v.i.* come down; (*di vento*) drop; (*diminuire*) fall; (*tramontare*) set. —*v.t.* (*abbassare*) lower; (*nei lavori a maglia*) decrease. ~**si** *v.r.* lower oneself.

ca′lca *n.f.* throng.

calca′gno *n.m.* heel.

calca′re[1] *n.m.* limestone.

calca′re[2] *v.t.* tread; (*premere*) press (down). **~ la mano** exaggerate.

ca′lce[1] *n.f.* lime.

ca′lce[2] *n.m.* **in ~** at the foot of the page.

calcestru′zzo *n.m.* concrete.

calci′na *n.f.* mortar.

ca′lci|o[1] *n.m.* kick; (*sport*) football; (*di arma da fuoco*) butt. ~**a′re** *v.t.* kick. ~**ato′re** *n.m.* footballer.

ca′lcio[2] *n.m.* (*chimica*) calcium.

ca′lco *n.m.* (*con carta*) tracing; (*arte*) cast.

calcola′|re *v.t.* calculate; (*considerare*) consider. ~**to′re**, ~**tri′ce** *a.* calculating; *n.m.* calculator; (*macchina elettronica*) computer.

ca′lcolo *n.m.* calculation; (*med.*) stone.

calda′ia *n.f.* boiler.

caldeggia′re *v.t.* support.

ca′ldo *a.* warm; (*molto caldo*) hot. —*n.m.* heat. **avere ~** be warm *o* hot. **fa ~** it is warm *o* hot.

calenda′rio *n.m.* calendar.

cale′sse *n.m.* gig.

ca′libro *n.m.* calibre; (*strumento*) callipers *pl*.

ca′lice *n.m.* goblet; (*relig.*) chalice.

cali′gine *n.m.* fog; (*industriale*) smog.

calligrafi′a *n.f.* handwriting.

ca′llo *n.m.* corn. **fare il ~ a** become hardened to.

ca′lm|a *n.f.* calm. ~**a′nte** *a.* calming; *n.m.* sedative. ~**a′re** *v.t.* calm (down); (*lenire*) soothe. ~**a′rsi** *v.r.* calm down; (*vento*) drop; (*dolore*) die down. ~**o** *a.* calm.

ca′lo *n.m.* (*comm.*) fall; (*di volume*) shrinkage; (*di peso*) loss.

calo′r|e *n.m.* heat; (*moderato*) warmth. **in ~e** (*di animale*) on heat. ~**o′so** *a.* warm.

calori'a *n.f.* calorie.

calo'scia *n.f.* galosh.

calpesta're *v.t.* trample (down). **vietato ~ l'erba** keep off the grass.

calu'nni|a *n.f.* slander. **~a're** *v.t.* slander.

calva'rio *n.m.* Calvary; (*fig.*) trial.

calvi'zie *n.f.* baldness. **ca'lvo** *a.* bald.

ca'lz|a *n.f.* (*da donna*) stocking; (*da uomo*) sock. **~ama'glia** *n.f.* tights *pl.* **~etto'ne** *n.m.* kneelength woollen sock. **~i'no** *n.m.* sock.

calza'|re *v.t.* (*indossare*) wear; (*mettersi*) put on. —*v.i.* fit. **~tu'ra** *n.f.* footwear.

calzol|a'io *n.m.* shoemaker. **~eri'a** *n.f.* (*negozio*) shoe shop.

calzonci'ni *n.m. pl.* shorts.

calzo'ni *n.m. pl.* trousers; (*sportivi*) slacks; (*alla zuava*) knickerbockers.

camaleo'nte *n.m.* chameleon.

cambia'le *n.f.* bill of exchange.

cambia'|re *v.t./i.* change; (*casa*) move. **~rsi** *v.r.* change. **~re idea** change one's mind. **~re rotta** (*naut.*) alter course. **~me'nto** *n.m.* change.

ca'mbio *n.m.* change; (*comm., scambio*) exchange; (*mech.*) gear. **dare il ~ a qcno.** relieve s.o. **in ~ di** in exchange for.

ca'mera *n.f.* room; (*mobili*) (bedroom) suite; (*foto*) camera. **C~** (*pol., comm.*) Chamber. **~ da letto** bedroom. **C~ dei Comuni** House of Commons.

camera'ta[1] *n.f.* (*dormitorio*) dormitory.

camera't|a[2] *n.m./f.* mate; (*pol.*) comrade. **~i'smo** *n.m.* comradeship.

camerie'r|e *n.m.* manservant; (*di ristorante*) waiter; (*di bordo*) steward. **~a** *n.f.* maid; (*di ristorante*) waitress; (*in albergo*) chamber-maid; (*di bordo*) stewardess.

cameri'no *n.m.* dressing-room.

ca'mice *n.m.* overall.

camice'tta *n.f.* blouse.

cami'cia *n.f.* shirt. **~ da notte** nightdress. **~ di forza** strait-jacket. **uovo in ~** poached egg.

cami'no *n.m.* chimney; (*focolare*) fireplace.

ca'mion *n.m. invar.* lorry. **~e'tta** *n.f.* jeep.

camme'llo *n.m.* camel; (*tessuto*) camel-hair.

ca'mmeo *n.m.* cameo.

camm|ina're *v.i.* walk; (*mech.*) go, work. **~i'no** *n.m.* way. **essere in ~ino** be on the way. **mettersi in ~ino** set out.

camomi'lla *n.f.* camomile.

camo'rra *n.f.* camorra.

camo'scio *n.m.* chamois.

camp'agn|a *n.f.* country; (*paesaggio*) countryside; (*comm., mil.*) campaign. **in ~a** in the country. **~o'lo, a** *a.* rustic; *n.m.,f.* country/man, -woman.

campa'le *a.* field. **giornata ~** (*fig.*) strenuous day.

campa'n|a *n.f.* bell; (*di vetro*) bell-jar. **~e'lla** *n.f.* (*di tenda*) curtain ring.

campane'llo *n.m.* (electric) doorbell; (*cicalino*) buzzer.

campani'le *n.m.* belfry.

campa're *v.i.* live; (*a stento*) get by.

campa'to *a.* **~ in aria** unfounded.

camp|eggia're *v.i.* camp; (*spiccare*) stand out. **~e'ggio** *n.m.* camping; (*terreno*) campsite.

campe'stre *a.* rural.

campiona'ri|o *n.m.* (set of) samples. **fiera ~a** trade fair.

campiona'to *n.m.* championship.

campio'n|e *n.m.* champion; (*comm.*) sample; (*esemplare*) specimen. **~e'ssa** *n.f.* ladies' champion.

ca'mpo *n.m.* field; (*accampamento*) camp. **~ da tennis** tennis court. **~ di golf** golf course.

camposa'nto *n.m.* cemetery.

camuffa'r|e *v.t.* disguise. **~si** *v.r.* disguise oneself.

camu'so *a.* snub-nosed.

Canad|à *n.m.* Canada. **c~e'se** *a.* & *n.m./f.* Canadian.

cana'glia *n.f.* scoundrel; (*plebaglia*) rabble.

cana'le *n.m.* channel; (*artificiale*) canal.

ca'napa *n.f.* hemp.

canari'no *n.m.* canary.

cancella'|re *v.t.* cross out; (*con la gomma*) rub out; (*fig.*) wipe out; (*annullare*) cancel. **~zio'ne** *n.f.* cancellation.

cancelleri'a *n.f.* chancellery; (*articoli per scrivere*) stationery.

cancellie're *n.m.* chancellor; (*di tribunale*) clerk.

cance'llo *n.m.* gate.

cancre'na *n.f.* gangrene.

ca'ncro *n.m.* cancer. **C~** *n.m.* (*astr.*) Cancer.

candeggi'|na *n.f.* bleach. **~a're** *v.t.* bleach.

cande'la *n.f.* candle; (*auto*) sparking plug. **lume di** ~ candle-light.

candela'bro *n.m.* candelabra.

candelie're *n.m.* candlestick.

candida'to, a *n.m., f.* candidate.

ca'ndido *a.* snow-white; (*sincero*) candid; (*puro*) pure.

candi'to *a.* candied.

cando're *n.m.* whiteness; (*fig.*) innocence.

ca'ne *n.m.* dog; (*di arma da fuoco*) cock. ~ **da caccia** hound. ~ **da corsa** greyhound. **un tempo** ~ **foul** weather.

cane'stro *n.m.* basket.

cangia'nte *a.* iridescent. **seta** ~ shot silk.

cangu'ro *n.m.* kangaroo.

cani'le *n.m.* kennel; (*di allevamento*) kennels *pl.*

cani'no *a. & n.m.* canine.

cani'zie *n.f.* white hair.

ca'nna *n.f.* reed; (*da zucchero*) cane; (*di fucile*) barrel; (*bastone*) stick; (*di bicicletta*) crossbar; (*asta*) rod. **povero in** ~ destitute.

canne'lla *n.f.* cinnamon.

canri'bale *n.m.* cannibal.

cannocchia'le *n.m.* telescope.

canno'ne *n.m.* gun; (*fig.*) ace.

cannu'ccia *n.f.* (drinking) straw; (*di pipa*) stem.

cano'a *n.f.* canoe.

ca'none *n.m.* canon; (*affitto*) rent. **equo** ~ fair rents act.

cano'ni|co *n.m.* canon. ~**zza're** *v.t.* canonize.

cano'ro *a.* melodious.

canottie'ra *n.f.* singlet.

cano'tt|o *n.m.* dinghy. ~**a'ggio** *n.m.* rowing. ~**ie're** *n.m.* oarsman.

canova'ccio *n.m.* (*per asciugare*) dish-cloth; (*per spolverare*) duster; (*trama*) plot.

canta'|re *v.t./i.* sing. ~**nte** *n.m./f.* singer.

canterella're *v.t.* sing softly; (*a bocca chiusa*) hum.

ca'ntico *n.m.* hymn.

cantie're *n.m.* yard; (*naut.*) shipyard.

cantile'na *n.f.* singsong; (*ninna-nanna*) lullaby.

canti'na *n.f.* cellar; (*osteria*) wine shop

ca'nt|o[1] *n.m.* singing; (*canzone*) song; (*relig.*) chant; (*poesia*) poem. ~**o're** *n.m.* chorister.

ca'nto[2] *n.m.* (*angolo*) corner; (*lato*)

side. **dal** ~ **mio** for my part. **d'altro** ~ on the other hand.

canto'ne *n.m.* canton; (*angolo*) corner.

cantu'ccio *n.m.* nook.

canu'to *a.* white-haired.

canzona're *v.t.* tease.

canzo'n|e *n.f.* song. ~**e'tta** *n.f.* (*fam.*) pop song. ~**ie're** *n.m.* songbook.

ca'os *n.m.* chaos. **cao'tico** *a.* chaotic.

C.A.P. *abbr. vedi* **codice.**

capa'c|e *a.* able; . (*esperto*) skilled; (*ampio*) capacious. ~**e di** (*disposto a*) capable of. ~**ità** *n.f.* ability; skill; (*capienza*) capacity.

capacita'rsi *v.r.* ~ **(di)** (*rendersi conto*) understand; (*accorgersi*) realize.

capa'nna *n.f.* hut.

capanno'ne *n.m.* shed; (*aeron.*) hangar.

capa'rbio *a.* obstinate.

capa'rra *n.f.* deposit.

capati'na *n.f.* short visit.

cape'll|o *n.m.* hair. ~**i** *n.m. pl.* (*capigliatura*) hair *s.* ~**u'to** *a.* hairy. **cuoio** ~**uto** scalp.

capezza'le *n.m.* bolster; (*fig.*) bedside.

cape'zzolo *n.m.* nipple.

capie'nza *n.f.* capacity.

capigliatu'ra *n.f.* hair.

capi're *v.t.* understand. ~ **male** misunderstand. **si capisce!** naturally!

capita'l|e *a.* (*legge ecc.*) capital; (*principale*) main. —*n.f.* (*città*) capital. —*n.m.* (*comm.*) capital. ~**i'smo** *n.m.* capitalism. ~**i'sta** *n.m./f.* capitalist. ~**izza're** *v.t.* capitalize.

capita'no *n.m.* captain.

capita're *v.i.* (*giungere per caso*) come; turn up (*fam.*); (*accadere*) happen.

capite'llo *n.m.* (*archit.*) capital.

capitola're *v.i.* capitulate.

capi'tolo *n.m.* chapter.

capito'mbolo *n.m.* headlong fall. **fare un** ~ tumble down.

ca'po *n.m.* head; (*chi comanda*) boss (*fam.*); (*di vestiario*) item; (*geog.*) cape; (*in tribù*) chief; (*parte estrema*) top. **a** ~ (*in dettato*) new paragraph. **a** ~**fitto** headlong. **da** ~ over again. **giramento di** ~ dizziness. **lavata di** ~ scolding. **mal di** ~ headache. **in** ~ **a un mese** within a month.

capoba'nda *n.m.* (*mus.*) bandmaster; (*di delinquenti*) ringleader.

capoda'nno *n.m.* New Year's Day.

capolavo'ro *n.m.* masterpiece.

capoli'nea *n.m.* terminus.

capoluo'go *n.m.* main town.

capoma'stro *n.m.* master builder.

capora'le *n.m.* lance-corporal.

caporio'ne *n.m.* ringleader.

capotre'no *n.m.* guard.

capovo'l|gere *v.t.* overturn; (*fig.*) reverse. ∼**gersi** *v.r.* overturn; (*barca*) capsize; (*fig.*) be reversed. ∼**to** *p.p. di* ∼**gere**; *a.* upsidedown.

ca'ppa *n.f.* cloak; (*di camino*) cowl.

cappe'll|a *n.f.* chapel. ∼**a'no** *n.m.* chaplain.

cappe'llo *n.m.* hat. ∼ **a cilindro** top hat.

ca'ppero *n.m.* caper.

cappo'ne *n.m.* capon.

cappo'tto *n.m.* (over)coat.

cappucci'no *n.m.* (*frate*) Capuchin (friar); (*bevanda*) white coffee.

cappu'ccio *n.m.* hood; (*di penna stilografica*) cap.

ca'pr|a *n.f.* goat. ∼**e'tto** *n.m.* kid.

capri'cci|o *n.m.* whim; (*bizzarria*) freak. **fare i** ∼ have tantrums. ∼**o'so** *a.* capricious; (*di bambino*) naughty.

Caprico'rno *n.m.* (*astr.*) Capricorn.

caprio'la *n.f.* somersault.

caprio'lo *n.m.* roe-deer.

ca'pro *n.m.* (billy-)goat. ∼ **espiatorio** scapegoat.

ca'psula *n.f.* capsule; (*di proiettile*) cap; (*di dente*) crown.

capta're *v.t.* (*radio, TV*) pick up; (*ottenere favori*) gain.

carabinie're *n.m.* carabiniere.

cara'ffa *n.f.* carafe.

Cara'ibi *n.m. pl.* Caribbeans. **Mar dei** ∼ Caribbean Sea.

carame'lla *n.f.* sweet; (*monocolo*) monocle.

cara'to *n.m.* carat.

cara'tter|e *n.m.* character; (*caratteristica*) characteristic; (*typ.*) type. **di buon** ∼**e** good-natured. ∼**i'stico, a** *a.* characteristic; (*pittoresco*) quaint; *n.f.* characteristic. ∼**izza're** *v.t.* characterize.

carbo'ne *n.m.* coal.

carbura'nte *n.m.* fuel.

carburato're *n.m.* carburettor.

carca'ssa *n.f.* carcass.

ca'rcer|e *n.m.* prison; (*punizione*) imprisonment. ∼**a'to, a** *n.m., f.* prisoner. ∼**ie're, a** *n.m., f.* gaoler.

carcio'fo *n.m.* artichoke.

cardi'aco *a.* cardiac.

cardina'le *a. & n.m.* cardinal.

ca'rdine *n.m.* hinge.

cardio'log|o *n.m.* heart specialist. ∼**i'a** *n.f.* cardiology.

car'do *n.m.* thistle.

care'na *n.f.* (*naut.*) bottom.

care'nza *n.f.* lack; (*scarsità*) scarcity.

caresti'a *n.f.* famine; (*mancanza*) dearth.

care'zza *n.f.* caress.

ca'ric|a *n.f.* office; (*mil., electr.*) charge. ∼**a're** *v.t.* load; (*mil., electr.*) charge; (*orologio*) wind up.

caricatu'ra *n.f.* caricature.

ca'rico *a.* loaded (**di**, with); (*colore*) dark; (*orologio*) wound (up); (*batteria*) charged. —*n.m.* load; (*di nave*) cargo; (*il caricare*) loading. **a** ∼ **di** (*comm.*) to be charged to; (*persona*) dependent on.

ca'ri|e *n.f.* (tooth) decay. ∼**a'to** *a.* decayed.

cari'no *a.* pretty; (*piacevole*) agreeable.

cari'sm|a *n.m.* charisma. ∼**a'tico** *a.* charismatic.

carit|à *n.f.* charity. **per** ∼! (*come rifiuto*) God forbid! ∼**ate'vole** *a.* charitable.

carnagio'ne *n.f.* complexion.

carna'io *n.m.* (*fig.*) shambles.

carna'le *a.* carnal. **cugino** ∼ first cousin.

ca'rn|e *n.f.* flesh; (*alimento*) meat. ∼**e di manzo/maiale/vitello** beef/pork/veal. ∼**o'so** *a.* fleshy.

carne'fice *n.m.* executioner.

carnefici'na *n.f.* slaughter.

carneva'le *n.m.* carnival.

carni'voro *a.* carnivorous.

ca'r|o, a *a.* dear. ∼**i saluti** kind regards. —*n.m., f.* (*fam.*) dear one.

caro'gna *n.f.* carcass; (*fig.*) rotter.

carose'llo *n.m.* merry-go-round.

caro'ta *n.f.* carrot.

carova'na *n.f.* caravan.

carovi'ta *n.m.* high cost of living.

carpentie're *n.m.* carpenter.

carpi're *v.t.* seize; (*con difficoltà*) extort.

carpo'ne, carpo'ni *advs.* on all fours.

carra'bile *a.* suitable for vehicles.

carra'io *a.* **passo** ∼ driveway.

carreggia'ta *n.f.* roadway. **doppia** ∼ dual carriageway.

carre'llo *n.m.* trolley; (*di macchina da scrivere*) carriage; (*aeron.*) undercarriage; (*cinema, TV*) dolly.

carre'tto *n.m.* cart.

carrie'ra *n.f.* career. **di gran** ~ at full speed. **fare** ~ get on.

carrio'la *n.f.* wheelbarrow.

ca'rro *n.m.* cart. ~ **armato** tank. ~ **funebre** hearse. ~ **merci** truck.

carro'zza *n.f.* carriage; (*ferrovia*) coach.

carrozze'lla *n.f.* (*per bambini*) perambulator, pram (*fam.*); (*per invalidi*) wheelchair.

carrozzeri'a *n.f.* bodywork; (*officina*) car repairer's.

carrozzi'na *n.f.* baby carriage; (*pieghevole*) push-chair.

ca'rta *n.f.* paper; (*da gioco*) card; (*statuto*) charter; (*geog.*) map. ~ **assorbente** blotting-paper. ~ **da lettere** writing-paper. ~ **da parati** wallpaper. ~ **di credito** credit card. ~ **igienica** toilet-paper. ~ **velina** tissue-paper. ~ **vetrata** sandpaper.

cartacarbo'ne *n.f.* carbon paper.

cartape'cora *n.f.* parchment.

cartape'sta *n.f.* papier mâché.

carte'ggio *n.m.* correspondence.

carte'lla *n.f.* (*per documenti ecc.*) briefcase; (*di cartone*) folder; (*di scolaro*) satchel. ~ **clinica** medical record.

cartelli'no *n.m.* (*etichetta*) label; (*dei prezzi*) price-tag; (*di presenza*) time-card. **timbrare il** ~ clock in.

carte'll|o *n.m.* sign; (*pubblicitario*) poster; (*stradale*) road sign; (*comm.*) cartel. ~**o'ne** *n.m.* poster; (*theatr.*) bill.

cartie'ra *n.f.* paper-mill.

cartila'gine *n.f.* cartilage.

carto'ccio *n.m.* paper bag.

cartol|èri'a *n.f.* stationer's (shop). ~**a'io, a** *n.m., f.* stationer.

cartoli'na *n.f.* postcard.

carto'n|e *n.m.* cardboard; (*arte*) cartoon. ~**i animati** cartoons.

cartu'ccia *n.f.* cartridge.

ca'sa *n.f.* house; (*abitazione propria*) home; (*ditta*) firm. **amico di** ~ family friend. **andare a** ~ go home. ~ **dello studente** student hostel. ~ **di cura** nursing home. ~ **popolare** council house. **essere di** ~ be like one of the family. **fatto in** ~ home-made. **padrone di** ~ (*di pensione ecc.*) landlord; (*proprietario*) house owner.

casa'cca *n.f.* military coat; (*giacca*) jacket.

casa'ccio *adv.* **a** ~ at random.

casali'ng|o *a.* domestic; (*fatto in casa*) home-made; (*amante della casa*) home-loving; (*semplice*) homely. ~**a** *n.f.* housewife.

cascamo'rto *n.m.* **fare il** ~ spoon.

casca'|re *v.i.* fall (down). ~**nte** *a.* falling; (*floscio*) flabby. ~**ta** *n.f.* (*di acqua*) waterfall.

casci'na *n.f.* farm building.

ca'sco *n.m.* crash-helmet; (*asciugacapelli*) (hair-)drier.

case'lla *n.f.* pigeon-hole. ~ **postale** post office box.

case'llo *n.m.* (*di autostrada*) tollhouse.

case'rma *n.f.* barracks *pl.*

casi'no *n.m.* (*bordello*) brothel; (*fig., sl., confusione*) racket.

casinò *n.m. invar.* casino.

ca'so *n.m.* chance; (*fatto, circostanza, med., gram.*) case. **a** ~ at random. ~ **mai** if need be. **far** ~ **a** pay attention to. **non far** ~ **a** take no account of. **per** ~ by chance.

casola're *n.m.* farmhouse.

ca'spita *int.* good gracious!

ca'ssa *n.f.* case; (*comm.*) cash; (*luogo di pagamento*) cash desk; (*mobile*) chest. ~ **da morto** coffin. ~ **toracica** chest.

cassafo'rte *n.f.* safe.

cassapa'nca *n.f.* (linen) chest.

casseruo'la *n.f.* saucepan.

casse'tta *n.f.* (small) case; (*per registratore*) cassette. ~ **delle lettere** post-box. ~ **di sicurezza** strong-box. **far buona** ~ (*theatr.*) be good box-office.

casse'tt|o *n.m.* drawer. ~**o'ne** *n.m.* chest of drawers.

cassie're, a *n.m., f.* cashier; (*di banca*) teller.

ca'sta *n.f.* caste.

casta'gn|a *n.f.* chestnut. ~**o** *n.m.* chestnut (-tree).

casta'no *a.* chestnut.

caste'llo *n.m.* castle; (*impalcatura*) scaffold.

cast|iga're *v.t.* punish. ~**i'go** *n.m.* punishment.

ca'st|o *a.* chaste. ~**ità** *n.f.* chastity.

casto'ro *n.m.* beaver.

castra're *v.t.* castrate.

casua'l|e *a.* fortuitous. ~**me'nte** *adv.* by chance.

cataclisma *n.m.* cataclysm.

cataco'mba *n.f.* catacomb.

catafa'lco *n.m.* catafalque.

cata'logo *n.m.* catalogue.

catape'cchia *n.f.* hovel; dump (*fam.*).

catarifrange'nte *n.m.* reflector.

cata'rro *n.m.* catarrh.
cata'sta *n.f.* pile.
cata'sto *n.m.* land register.
cata'str|ofe *n.f.* catastrophe. ∼o'fico *a.* catastrophic(al).
catechi'smo *n.m.* catechism.
categ|ori'a *n.f.* category. ∼o'rico *a.* categorical
cate'n|a *n.f.* chain. ∼e da neve tyre-chains. ∼a'ccio *n.m.* bolt.
catera'tta *n.f.* cataract.
catine'll|a *n.f.* basin. piovere a ∼e pour with rain.
cati'no *n.m.* basin.
catra'me *n.m.* tar.
ca'ttedra *n.f.* (*tavolo di insegnante*) desk; (*incarico nelle università*) chair.
cattedra'le *n.f.* cathedral.
catti'v|o *a.* bad; (*bambino*) naughty; (*mare*) rough. farsi il sangue ∼o get angry. ∼e'ria *n.f.* wickedness; naughtiness; (*azione*) wicked action. fare una ∼eria a qcno. do s.o. an ill turn.
catto'lic|o, a *a.* & *n.m., f.* (Roman) Catholic. ∼e'simo *n.m.* Catholicism.
cattu'r|a *n.f.* capture. ∼a're *v.t.* capture.
cauccíù *n.m.* rubber.
ca'us|a *n.f.* cause; (*legge*) lawsuit. far ∼a a qcno. sue s.o. ∼a're *v.t.* cause.
ca'ustico *a.* caustic.
caute'la *n.f.* caution.
cautela'r|e *v.t.* protect. ∼si *v.r.* take precautions.
ca'uto *a.* cautious.
cauzio'ne *n.f.* security; (*per libertà provvisoria*) bail.
ca'va *n.f.* quarry; (*fig.*) mine.
cavalca'|re *v.t.* ride; (*stare a cavalcioni*) sit astride. ∼ta *n.f.* ride; (*corteo*) cavalcade.
cavalcavi'a *n.m.* flyover.
cavalcio'ni *adv.* a ∼ astride.
cavalie're *n.m.* rider; (*titolo*) knight; (*accompagnatore*) escort; (*al ballo*) partner.
cavaller|i'a *n.f.* chivalry; (*mil.*) cavalry. ∼e'sco *a.* chivalrous.
cavalleri'zzo, a *n.m., f.* horse/man, -woman.
cavalle'tta *n.f.* grasshopper.
cavalle'tto *n.m.* trestle; (*di macchina fotografica*) tripod; (*di pittore*) easel.
cava'llo *n.m.* horse; (*misura di potenza*) horsepower; (*scacchi*) knight; (*dei pantaloni*) crotch. a ∼ on horse-

back. ∼ a dondolo rocking-horse. ferro di ∼ horseshoe.
cavallo'ne *n.m.* (*ondata*) roller.
cava'r|e *v.t.* take out; (*di dosso*) take off. ∼sela get away with it.
cavata'ppi *n.m. invar.* corkscrew.
cave'rn|a *n.f.* cave. ∼o'so *a.* (*di voce*) deep.
cave'zza *n.f.* halter.
ca'via *n.f.* guinea-pig.
cavia'le *n.m.* caviar.
cavi'glia *n.f.* ankle.
cavilla're *v.i.* quibble.
cavità *n.f.* cavity.
ca'vo *a.* hollow. —*n.m.* cavity; (*di metallo*) cable; (*naut.*) rope.
cavolfio're *n.m.* cauliflower.
ca'volo *n.m.* cabbage. ∼ di Bruxelles Brussels sprout.
cazzuo'la *n.f.* trowel.
ce *pron. pers.* (*a noi*) (to) us. —*adv.* there. ∼ ne sono molti there are many.
ce'ce *n.m.* chick-pea.
cecità *n.f.* blindness.
Cecoslova'cc|hia *n.f.* Czechoslovakia. c∼o, a a. & *n.m., f.* Czechoslovak.
ce'd|ere *v.i.* (*arrendersi*) surrender; (*concedere*) yield; (*sprofondare*) subside. —*v.t.* give up; (*proprietà ecc.*) make over. ∼e'vole *a.* (*terreno ecc.*) soft; (*fig.*) yielding.
ce'dola *n.f.* coupon.
ce'dro *n.m.* (*albero*) cedar.
C.E.E. *abbr. vedi* comunità.
ce'ffo *n.m.* (*muso*) snout; (*pej., persona*) mug.
ceffo'ne *n.m.* slap.
cela'r|e *v.t.* conceal. ∼si *v.r.* hide.
celebra'|re *v.t.* celebrate. ∼zio'ne *n.f.* celebration.
ce'lebr|e *a.* famous. ∼ità *n.f.* celebrity.
ce'lere *a.* swift. corso ∼ crash course.
cele'ste *a.* (*divino*) heavenly. *a.* & *n.m.* (*colore*) sky-blue.
ce'lia *n.f.* jest.
ce'lib|e *a.* single. —*n.m.* bachelor. ∼a'to *n.m.* celibacy.
ce'lla *n.f.* cell.
ce'llula *n.f.* cell.
cellulo'sa *n.f.* cellulose.
ce'lt|a *n.m.* Celt. ∼ico *a.* Celtic.
ceme'nt|o *n.m.* cement. ∼o armato reinforced concrete. ∼a're *v.t.* cement.
ce'n|a *n.f.* dinner; (*leggera*) supper. ∼a're *v.i.* dine.

ce'nci|o *n.m.* rag; (*per spolverare*) duster. ∼**o'so** *a.* in rags.

ce'nere *n.f.* ash; (*di carbone ecc.*) cinders.

ce'nno *n.m.* sign; (*col capo*) nod; (*con la mano*) wave; (*allusione*) hint; (*breve resoconto*) mention.

censime'nto *n.m.* census.

cens|o're *n.m.* censor. ∼**u'ra** *n.f.* censorship. ∼**ura're** *v.t.* censor.

centena'rio, a *a.* & *n.m., f.* centenarian. −*n.m.* (*commemorazione*) centenary.

cente'simo *a.* hundredth. −*n.m.* (*di dollaro*) cent. **non avere un** ∼ be penniless.

centi'grado *a.* centigrade.

centi'metro *n.m.* centimetre.

ce'nto *a.* & *n.m.* a *o* one hundred. **per** ∼ per cent.

centra'l|e *a.* central. −*n.f.* (*di società ecc.*) head office. ∼**e elettrica** power station. ∼**e telefonica** (telephone) exchange. ∼**ini'sta** *n.m./f.* operator. ∼**i'no** *n.m.* exchange; (*di albergo ecc.*) switchboard.

centralizza're *v.t.* centralize.

centra're *v.t.* hit the centre (of); (*fissare nel centro*) centre. **ce'ntro** *n.m.* centre.

centri'fuga *n.f.* spin-drier.

centuplica're *v.t.* (*fig.*) multiply.

ce'ppo *n.m.* (*di albero*) stump; (*da ardere*) log; (*fig.*) stock.

ce'r|a *n.f.* wax; (*aspetto*) look. ∼**eo** *a.* waxen.

cerala'cca *n.f.* sealing-wax.

cera'mica *n.f.* (*arte*) ceramics *s.*; (*materia*) pottery; (*oggetto*) piece of pottery.

cerbia'tto *n.m.* fawn.

ce'rca *n.f.* **andare in** ∼ **di** look for.

cerca're *v.t.* look for. −*v.i.* ∼ **di** try to.

ce'rchi|a *n.f.* circle. ∼**a're** *v.t.* encircle. ∼**a'to** *a.* (*di occhi*) black-ringed.

ce'rchio *n.m.* circle; (*giocattolo*) hoop.

cerea'le *n.m.* cereal.

cerebra'le *a.* cerebral.

cerimo'ni|a *n.f.* ceremony. ∼**a'le** *n.m.* ceremonial. ∼**o'so** *a.* ceremonious.

ceri'no *n.m.* (wax) match.

cernie'ra *n.f.* hinge; (*di borsa*) clasp. ∼ **lampo** zip(-fastener).

ce'rnita *n.f.* selection.

ce'ro *n.m.* candle.

cero'ne *n.m.* grease-paint.

cero'tto *n.m.* plaster.

certifica'|to *n.m.* certificate. ∼**re** *v.t.* certify.

ce'rt|o *a.* certain; (*quantità*) some. −*adv.* certainly. ∼**o!** of course! ∼**e'zza** *n.f.* certainty.

certu'ni *pron. pl.* some people.

cerve'llo *n.m.* brain.

ce'rvo *n.m.* deer.

cesella're *v.t.* chisel. **cese'llo** *n.m.* chisel.

ceso'ie *n.f. pl.* shears.

ce'spite *n.m.* source (of income).

cespu'glio *n.m.* bush.

cessa'|re *v.i.* cease. −*v.t.* stop.

ce'sso *n.m.* (*sl.*) lavatory.

ce'st|o *n.m.* basket. ∼**a** *n.f.* (large) basket. ∼**i'no** *n.m.* (small) basket; (*per la carta straccia*) waste-paper basket.

ce'to *n.m.* (social) class.

cetrioli'no *n.m.* gherkin.

cetrio'lo *n.m.* cucumber.

che *pron. rel.* (*persona, soggetto*) who; (*persona, oggetto*) whom; (*cosa*) which, that. −*pron. inter.* what. −*conj.* that. −*a.* (*esclamativo*) what a ... *s.*; what ... *pl.*; (*in espressioni*) how ... **a** ∼ **pensi?** what are you thinking about? ∼ **bello!** how nice! **credo** ∼ **abbia ragione** I think (that) he is right. **dal** ∼ from which. **questo è il ragazzo** ∼ **verrà con te** this is the boy who will come with you.

checché *pron. indef.* whatever.

cherubi'no *n.m.* cherub.

cheta'r|e *v.t.* quieten. ∼**si** *v.r.* quieten down. **che'to** *a.* quiet.

chetiche'lla *adv.* **alla** ∼ silently.

chi *pron. inter.* (*soggetto*) who; (*oggetto*) whom; (*rel., colui che*) he who; (*indef.*) ∼ ... ∼ some ... some; (*poss.*) **di** ∼ whose. ∼ **hai incontrato?** whom did you meet? ∼ **sei?** who are you? **di** ∼ **sono questi libri?** whose books are these?

chia'cchier|a *n.f.* chat; (*pettegolezzo*) gossip. **far quattro** ∼**e** have a chat. ∼**a're** *v.i.* chat; (*far pettegolezzi*) gossip. ∼**o'ne, a** *a.* talkative; *n.m., f.* chatterer.

chiama'|re *v.t.* call; (*far venire*) send for. ∼**rsi** *v.r.* be called. ∼**re alle armi** call up. ∼**ta** *n.f.* call; (*mil.*) call-up. **mi chiamo Roberto** my name is Robert.

chia'r|o *a.* clear; (*luminoso*) bright; (*colore*) light. ∼**e'zza** *n.f.* clarity;

(*limpidezza*) clearness. ~**o're** *n.m.* glimmer.

chiarifica're *v.t.* clarify.

chiari'r|e *v.t.* make clear; (*spiegare*) clear up. ~**si** *v.r.* become clear.

chiarovegge'nte *a.* clear-sighted. —*n.m.|f.* clairvoyant.

chia'ss|o *n.m.* din. ~**o'so** *a.* rowdy.

chia've|e *n.f.* key. ~**e inglese** monkey-wrench. **chiudere a** ~**e** lock. ~**iste'llo** *n.m.* latch.

chia'zz|a *n.f.* stain. ~**a're** *v.t.* stain.

chic *a.* chic.

chi'cco *n.m.* grain; (*di caffè*) bean; (*d'uva*) grape.

chie'der|e *v.t.* ask; (*per avere*) ask for; (*esigere*) demand ~**e l'elemosina** beg. ~**e notizie di** ask after. ~**e scusa** apologize. **chiedo scusa!** I am sorry! ~**si** *v.r.* wonder.

chie'rico *n.m.* cleric.

chie'sa *n.f.* church.

chie'sto *p.p. di* **chiedere**.

chi'glia *n.f.* keel.

chi'lo *n.m.* (*abbr. di* **chilogra'mmo**) kilo, kilogram(me).

chilo'metro *n.m.* kilometre.

chime'ra *n.f.* (*fig.*) illusion.

chi'mic|a *n.f.* chemistry. ~**o, a** *a.* chemical; *n.m., f.* chemist.

chi'na *n.f.* (*declivio*) slope. **inchiostro di** ~ Indian ink.

china'r|e *v.t.* lower. ~**si** *v.r.* stoop. **chi'no** *a.* bent.

chincaglieri'a *n.f.* knick-knacks *pl.*; (*negozio*) gift shop.

chini'no *n.m.* quinine.

chio'ccia *n.f.* sitting hen.

chio'cciola *n.f.* snail. **scala a** ~ spiral staircase.

chio'do *n.m.* nail; (*idea fissa*) obsession. ~ **di garofano** clove.

chio'ma *n.f.* (head of) hair; (*fogliame*) foliage.

chio'sco *n.m.* kiosk; (*per giornali*) news-stand.

chio'stro *n.m.* cloister.

chiroma'n|te *n.m.|f.* palmist. ~**zi'a** *n.f.* palmistry.

chiru'rg|o *n.m.* surgeon. ~**i'a** *n.f.* surgery. ~**ico** *a.* surgical.

chissà *adv.* who knows. ~ **quando arriverà** I wonder when he will arrive.

chita'rr|a *n.f.* guitar. ~**i'sta** *n.m.|f.* guitarist.

chiu'der|e *v.t.* shut, close; (*con la chiave*) lock; (*luce, acqua, ecc.*) turn off

o out; (*per sempre, negozio, fabbrica, ecc.*) close down; (*recingere*) enclose. —*v.i.* shut, close. ~**si** *v.r.* shut; (*di tempo*) cloud over; (*di ferita*) heal over; (*fig.*) withdraw into oneself.

chiu'nque *pron. indef.* anyone, anybody; *pron. rel.* whoever.

chiu'sa *n.f.* enclosure; (*di canale*) lock; (*conclusione*) close.

chiu's|o *p.p. di* **chiudere**. —*a.* shut; (*di tempo*) overcast; (*di persona*) reserved. ~**u'ra** *n.f.* closing; (*mech.*) lock; (*allacciatura*) fastening. ~**ura lampo** zipper.

ci *pron.* (*personale*) us; (*r.*) ourselves; (*reciproco*) each other; (*dimostrativo, di ciò*) about it. **pensaci!** think about it! —*adv.* (*qui*) here; (*lì*) there. ~ **siamo** we are here. ~ **siete?** are you there?

ciaba'tt|a *n.f.* slipper. ~**i'no** *n.m.* cobbler.

cia'lda *n.f.* wafer.

ciambe'lla *n.f.* (*culin.*) ring-shaped cake; (*salvagente*) lifebelt.

ciambella'no *n.m.* chamberlain.

cianfrusa'glie *n.f. pl.* knick-knacks.

cia'o *int.* (*fam.*) (*all'arrivo*) hallo!; (*alla partenza*) bye-bye!

cia'r|la *n.f.* gossip. ~**a're** *v.i.* chat.

ciarlata'no *n.m.* charlatan.

ciascu'no *a. indef.* (*ogni*) every; (*distributivo*) each. —*pron. indef.* everyone, everybody; (*distributivo*) each (one).

ci'b|o *n.m.* food. ~**a're** *v.t.* feed. ~**a'rsi (di)** *v.r.* live (on).

cica'la *n.f.* cicada.

cicale'ccio *n.m.* chattering.

cicali'no *n.m.* buzzer.

cicatri'|ce *n.f.* scar. ~**zza'rsi** *v.r.* heal (up).

ci'cca *n.f.* cigarette end.

cicche'tto *n.m.* (*bicchierino*) nip. **ci'ccia** *n.f.* (*fam.*) fat.

cicero'ne *n.m.* guide.

ciclami'no *n.m.* cyclamen.

cicli's|mo *n.m.* cycling. ~**ta** *n.m.|f.* cyclist.

ci'clo *n.m.* cycle; (*di malattia*) course.

ciclomoto're *n.m.* moped.

ciclo'ne *n.m.* cyclone.

ciclosti'le *n.m.* duplicating machine.

cico'gna *n.f.* stork.

cico'ria *n.f.* chicory.

cie'co, a *a.* blind. —*n.m., f.* blind man/woman.

cie'lo *n.m.* sky; (*relig.*) heaven.

ci'fr|a *n.f.* figure; (*somma*) sum; (*monogramma*) monogram; (*codice*) code. **~a're** *v.t.* embroider with a monogram; code.

ci'glio *n.m.* (*bordo*) edge; (*pl. f.* **ciglia**) (*delle palpebre*) eyelash.

ci'gno *n.m.* swan.

cigol|a're *v.t.* squeak. **~i'o** *n.m.* squeak.

Ci'le *n.m.* Chile. **cile'no, a** *a.* & *n.m., f.* Chilean.

cile'cca *n.f.* far ~ miss.

cilie'gi|a *n.f.* cherry. **~o** *n.m.* cherry (-tree).

cilindra'ta *n.f.* cubic capacity. **macchina di alta** ~ high-powered car.

cili'ndro *n.m.* cylinder; (*cappello*) top hat.

ci'ma *n.f.* top; (*fig., persona*) genius. **da** ~ **a fondo** from top to bottom.

cimenta're *v.t.* put to the test.

ci'mice *n.f.* bug.

ciminie'ra *n.f.* chimney; (*naut.*) funnel.

cimite'ro *n.m.* cemetery.

cimu'rro *n.m.* distemper.

Ci'na *n.f.* China. **cine'se** *a.* & *n.m.|f.* Chinese.

cinegiorna'le *n.m.* news-reel.

ci'ne|ma *n.m. invar.* cinema. **~matografa're** *v.t.* film. **~pre'sa** *n.f.* cine-camera.

cine'tico *a.* kinetic.

ci'ngere *v.t.* (*circondare*) surround.

ci'nghia *n.f.* strap; (*cintura*) belt.

cinghia'le *n.m.* wild boar. **pelle di** ~ pigskin.

cinguett|a're *v.i.* twitter. **~i'o** *n.m.* twittering.

ci'n|ico *a.* cynical. **~i'smo** *n.m.* cynicism.

cinqua'nt|a *a.* & *n.m.* fifty. **~e'nne** *a.* fifty-year-old; *n.m.|f.* fifty-year-old man/woman. **~e'simo** *a.* fiftieth. **~i'na** *n.f.* **una ~ina** about fifty.

ci'nque *a.* & *n.m.* five.

cinquece'nto *a.* five hundred. —*n.m.* **il C~** the sixteenth century.

cinquemi'la *a.* & *n.m.* five thousand.

ci'nto *p.p. di* **cingere.** —*n.m.* belt.

cintu'ra *n.f.* belt. ~ **di salvataggio** lifebelt. ~ **di sicurezza** (*aeron.*) safety belt; (*auto*) seat belt.

ciò *pron.* this, that. ~ **che** what. ~ **nondimeno** nevertheless.

cio'cca *n.f.* lock.

cioccola't|o, a *n.m., f.* chocolate. **~i'no** *n.m.* chocolate.

cioè *adv.* that is.

ciondol|a're *v.i.* dangle. **cio'ndolo** *n.m.* pendant. **~o'ni** *adv.* (*fig.*) hanging about.

cio'tola *n.f.* bowl.

cio'ttolo *n.m.* pebble.

cipo'lla *n.f.* onion; (*bulbo*) bulb.

cipre'sso *n.m.* cypress.

ci'pria *n.f.* (face) powder.

Ci'pro *n.m.* Cyprus. **ciprio'ta** *a.* & *n.m.|f.* Cypriot.

ci'rca *adv.* & *prep.* about.

ci'rco *n.m.* circus.

circola'|re *a.* circular. —*n.f.* circular; (*di metropolitana*) circle line. —*v.i.* circulate. **~zio'ne** *n.f.* circulation; (*traffico*) traffic.

ci'rcolo *n.m.* circle; (*società*) club.

circonci'|dere *v.t.* circumcise. **~sio'ne** *n.f.* circumcision.

circonda're *v.t.* surround.

circonfere'nza *n.f.* circumference.

circonfle'sso *a.* circumflex.

circonvallazio'ne *n.f.* ring road.

circoscri'tto *p.p. di* **circoscrivere.** —*a.* limited.

circoscri'|vere *v.t.* circumscribe. **~zio'ne** *n.f.* area. **~zione elettorale** constituency.

circospe'tto *a.* wary.

circosta'nte *a.* surrounding.

circosta'nza *n.f.* circumstance; (*occasione*) occasion.

circu'ito *n.m.* circuit.

ciste'rna *n.f.* cistern; (*serbatoio*) tank.

ci'sti *n.f.* cyst.

cita'|re *v.t.* (*riportare brani ecc.*) quote; (*come esempio*) cite; (*legge*) summon. **~zio'ne** *n.f.* quotation; summons *s.*

cito'fono *n.m.* entry phone; (*in ufficio, su aereo, ecc.*) intercom.

città *n.f.* town; (*grande*) city.

cittade'lla *n.f.* citadel.

cittadina'nza *n.f.* citizenship; (*popolazione*) citizens *pl.*

cittadi'no, a *n.m., f.* citizen; (*abitante di città*) city dweller.

ciu'ccio *n.m.* (*fam.*) dummy.

ciu'co *n.m.* ass.

ciu'ffo *n.m.* tuft.

ciu'rma *n.f.* (*naut.*) crew.

cive'tt|a *n.f.* owl; (*fig., donna*) flirt. **~a're** *v.i.* flirt. **~eri'a** *n.f.* coquettishness.

ci'vico *a.* civic.

civi'le *a.* civil.

civilizza'|re *v.t.* civilize. **~zio'ne** *n.f.*

civilization. **civiltà** *n.f.* civilization; (*cortesia*) civility.

civi'smo *n.m.* public spirit.

cla'cson *n.m. invar.* hooter.

clamo'r|e *n.m.* clamour. ~o'so *a.* clamorous.

clan *n.m.* clan; (*fig.*) clique.

clandesti'no *a.* clandestine. **movimento** ~ underground movement. **passeggero** ~ stowaway.

clarine'tto *n.m.* clarinet.

cla'sse *n.f.* class.

cla'ssic|o *a.* classic(al). —*n.m.* classic. ~**i'smo** *n.m.* classicism. ~**i'sta** *n.m./f.* classicist.

classi'fic|a *n.f.* classification; (*sport*) results *pl.* ~**a're** *v.t.* classify. ~**a'rsi** *v.r.* be placed. ~**azio'ne** *n.f.* classification.

cla'usola *n.f.* clause.

cla'va *n.f.* club.

clavice'mbalo *n.m.* harpsichord.

clavi'cola *n.f.* collar-bone.

cleme'n|te *a.* merciful; (*tempo*) mild. ~**za** *n.f.* mercy; mildness.

cle'r|o *n.m.* clergy. ~**ica'le** *a.* clerical.

clie'nt|e *n.m./f.* client; (*di negozio*) customer. ~**e'la** *n.f.* customers *pl.*

cli'm|a *n.m.* climate. ~**a'tico** *a.* climatic. **stazione** ~**atica** health resort.

cli'nic|o *a.* clinical. —*n.m.* clinician. ~**a** *n.f.* clinic.

cloa'ca *n.f.* sewer.

clo'ro *n.m.* chlorine.

clorofo'rmio *n.m.* chloroform.

coabita're *v.i.* live together.

coagula'r|e *v.t.*, ~**si** *v.r.* coagulate.

coalizio'ne *n.f.* coalition.

coa'tto *a.* (*legge*) compulsory.

co'bra *n.m. invar.* cobra.

cocai'n|a *n.f.* cocaine. ~**o'mane** *n.m./f.* cocaine addict.

co'cchi|o *n.m.* coach. ~**e're** *n.m.* coachman.

coccine'lla *n.f.* ladybird.

co'ccio *n.m.* earthenware; (*frammento*) fragment.

cocciu't|o *a.* stubborn. ~**a'ggine** *n.f.* stubbornness.

co'cco *n.m.* coconut palm. **noce di** ~ coconut.

coccodri'llo *n.m.* crocodile.

coccola're *v.t.* cuddle.

coce'nte *a.* burning.

coco'mero *n.m.* water-melon.

cocu'zzolo *n.m.* top; (*di testa, cappello*) crown.

co'da *n.f.* tail; (*di abito*) train; (*fila*) queue. **fare la** ~ queue (up).

coda'rdo, a *a.* cowardly. —*n.m.*, *f.* coward.

co'dice *n.m.* code. ~ **della strada** highway code. ~ **di avviamento postale (C.A.P.)** postal code.

codici'llo *n.m.* codicil.

codifica're *v.t.* codify.

coere'n|te *a.* coherent. ~**za** *n.f.* coherence.

coesio'ne *n.f.* cohesion. **coesi'vo** *a.* cohesive.

coesi'stere *v.i.* coexist.

coeta'neo, a *a. & n.m.*, *f.* contemporary.

co'fano *n.m.* (*forziere*) chest; (*auto.*) bonnet.

cogita're *v.i.* ponder.

co'gliere *v.t.* pick; (*sorprendere*) catch; (*afferrare*) seize; (*colpire*) hit.

cogna'to, a *n.m.*, *f.* brother-/ sister-in-law.

cognizio'ne *n.f.* knowledge.

cogno'me *n.m.* surname.

co'i = **con + i**.

coinc|ide'nza *n.f.* coincidence; (*di treno ecc.*) connection. ~**i'dere** *v.i.* coincide.

coinvo'lgere *v.t.* involve.

col = **con + il**.

colà *adv.* there.

cola|bro'do *n.m. invar.* strainer. ~**pa'sta** *n.m. invar.* colander.

cola're *v.t.* strain; (*versare lentamente*) drip. —*v.i.* (*gocciolare*) drip. ~ **a picco** (*naut.*) sink.

cola'ta *n.f.* (*di metallo*) casting; (*di lava*) flow.

colazio'ne *n.f.* (*del mattino*) breakfast; (*di mezzogiorno*) lunch. **far** ~ have breakfast *o* lunch.

cole'i *pron. vedi* **colui.**

cole'ra *n.m.* cholera.

co'lica *n.f.* colic.

coli'no *n.m.* (tea) strainer.

co'lla *n.f.* glue; (*di farina*) paste.

collabora'r|e *v.i.* collaborate. ~**to're**, ~**tri'ce** *n.m.*, *f.* collaborator. ~**zio'ne** *n.f.* collaboration.

colla'na *n.f.* necklace; (*serie*) series.

colla'nt *n.m. invar.* tights *pl.*

colla're *n.m.* collar.

colla'sso *n.m.* collapse.

collauda're *v.t.* test. **colla'udo** *n.m.* test.

co'lle *n.m.* hill.

colle'ga *n.m./f.* colleague.

colleg|ame'nto *n.m.* connection; (*mil.*) liaison; (*radio ecc.*) link. **~a're** *v.t.* connect; link.

colle'gio *n.m.* college; (*convitto*) boarding-school.

co'll|era *n.f.* anger. **~e'rico** *a.* irascible.

colle'tta *n.f.* collection.

collettività *n.f.* community.

colletti'vo *a.* collective. **biglietto ~** group ticket.

colle'tto *n.m.* collar.

collezi|ona're *v.t.* collect. **~o'ne** *n.f.* collection. **~oni'sta** *n.m./f.* collector.

collima're *v.i.* coincide.

colli'na *n.f.* hill.

collisio'ne *n.f.* collision.

co'llo *n.m.* neck; (*pacco*) package. **~ del piede** instep.

colloca'|re *v.t.* place. **~rsi** *v.r.* take one's place. **~me'nto** *n.m.* placing; (*impiego*) employment.

collo'quio *n.m.* conversation; (*udienza ecc.*) interview; (*esame*) oral (exam).

colluttazio'ne *n.f.* scuffle.

colma're *v.t.* fill (to the brim). **~ qcno. di gentilezze** overwhelm s.o. with kindness. **co'lmo** *a.* full; *n.m.* top; (*fig.*) height. **al colmo della disperazione** in the depths of despair. **questo è il colmo!** this is the limit!

colo'mbo, a *n.m., f.* dove.

colo'ni|a[1] *n.f.* colony; (*per bambini*) holiday camp. **~a'le** *a.* colonial. **~zza're** *v.t.* colonize.

colo'nia[2] *n.f.* (**acqua di**) **~** (eau de) Cologne.

colo'nna *n.f.* column. **~ sonora** sound-track.

colonne'llo *n.m.* colonel.

colo'no *n.m.* tenant farmer.

colo'r|e *n.m.* colour. **a ~i** in colour. **di ~e** coloured. **farne di tutti i ~i** get up to all sorts of tricks. **~a'nte** *n.m.* colouring. **~a're** *v.t.* colour.

colori'to *a.* coloured; (*del viso*) rosy. **—n.m.** complexion.

colo'ro *pron. vedi* **colui**.

colo'ss|o *n.m.* colossus. **~a'le** *a.* colossal.

co'lp|a *n.f.* fault; (*biasimo*) blame; (*colpevolezza*) guilt. **dare la ~a a** blame. **essere in ~a** be at fault. **~e'vole** *a.* guilty; *n.m./f.* culprit.

colpi're *v.t.* hit, strike.

co'lpo *n.m.* blow; (*di arma da fuoco*) shot; (*urto*) knock; (*emozione*) shock; (*med., sport*) stroke. **a ~ d'occhio** at a glance. **~ d'aria** chill. **~ di telefono** ring. **~ di testa** (sudden) impulse. **di ~** suddenly. **far ~** make a strong impression.

colte'll|o *n.m.* knife. **~a'ta** *n.f.* stab.

coltiva'|re *v.t.* cultivate. **~to're** *n.m.* farmer. **~zio'ne** *n.f.* farming; (*di piante*) growing.

co'lto *p.p. di* **cogliere**. **—a.** cultured.

co'ltre *n.f.* blanket.

coltu'ra *n.f.* cultivation.

colu'i, *pron. m.s.*, **cole'i**, *pron. f.s.* the one. **colo'ro** *pron. pl.* the ones. **~ che parla** the one who is speaking.

coma *n.m.* coma. **in ~** in a coma.

comandame'nto *n.m.* commandment.

comanda'nte *n.m.* commander; (*naut., aeron.*) captain.

comanda're *v.t.* command; (*mech.*) control. **coma'ndo** *n.m.* command; control.

coma're *n.f.* (*madrina*) godmother.

combacia're *v.i.* fit together.

comba'tt|ere *v.t./i.* fight. **~e'nte** *a.* fighting; *n.m.* combatant. **ex-~ente** ex-serviceman. **~ime'nto** *n.m.* fight; (*mil.*) battle. **fuori ~imento** (*pugilato*) knocked out.

combina'|re *v.t./i.* arrange; (*mettere insieme*) combine; (*fam., fare*) do. **cosa stai ~ndo?** what are you doing? **~rsi** *v.r.* combine; (*mettersi d'accordo*) come to an agreement. **~zio'ne** *n.f.* combination; (*caso*) coincidence; (*biancheria*) combinations *pl*.

combri'ccola *n.f.* gang.

combusti'bile *a.* combustible. **—n.m.** fuel.

combu'tta *n.f.* gang. **in ~** in league.

co'me *adv.* like; (*in qualità di*) as; (*inter., esclamativo*) how; (*che cosa, inter., esclamativo, enfatico*) what. **—conj.** as; (*non appena*) as soon as. **~?** what? **~ sta bene!** how well he looks! **~ stai?** how are you? **~ tu sai** as you know. **fa ~ vuoi** do as you like. **questo vestito è ~ il tuo** this dress is like yours.

come'ta *n.f.* comet.

co'mico *a.* comic(al). **—n.m.** funny side; (*attore*) comedian.

comi'gnolo *n.m.* chimney-pot.

comincia're *v.t./i.* begin, start. **a ~**

da oggi from today. **per ~** to begin with.

comita'to *n.m.* committee.

comiti'va *n.f.* party, group.

comi'zio *n.m.* meeting.

comma'ndo *n.m. invar.* commando.

comme'di|a *n.f.* comedy; (*opera teatrale*) play; (*fig.*) sham. **~a'nte** *n.m.|f.* comedian; (*pej.*) second-rate actor/actress. **~o'grafo, a** *n.m., f.* playwright.

commemora'|re *v.t.* commemorate. **~zio'ne** *n.f.* commemoration.

comment|a're *v.t.* comment (on); (*annotare*) annotate. **~a'rio** *n.m.* commentary. **~ato're, ~atri'ce** *n.m., f.* commentator. **comme'nto** *n.m.* comment.

comme'rci|o *n.m.* commerce; (*attività*) trade; (*affari*) business. **~a'le** *a.* commercial; trading. **~a'nte** *n.m.|f.* trader; (*negoziante*) shopkeeper. **~ante all'ingrosso** wholesaler. **~are in** deal in.

commerciali'sta *n.m.|f.* business consultant; (*contabile*) accountant.

comme'sso, a *p.p. di* **commettere.** —*n.m., f.* shop assistant. **~ viaggiatore** *n.m.* commercial traveller.

commesti'bil|e *a.* edible. **~i** *n.m. pl.* groceries.

comme'ttere *v.t.* commit.

commia'to *n.m.* leave. **prendere ~ da** take leave of.

commisera're *v.t.* commiserate.

commissa'ri|o *n.m.* commissioner; (*sport*) steward; (*membro di commissione*) member of a board. **~a'to** *n.m.* (*mil.*) Service Corps; (*di polizia*) police station.

commissiona'rio *n.m.* commission agent.

commissio'n|e *n.f.* errand; (*comm., comitato, ecc.*) commission. **~i** *n.f. pl.* (*acquisti*) shopping *s.* **fare ~i** go shopping.

committe'nte *n.m.|f.* purchaser.

commo'|sso *p.p. di* **commuovere.** —*a.* moved. **~ve'nte** *a.* moving.

commozio'ne *n.f.* emotion. **~ cerebrale** concussion.

commuo'ver|e *v.t.* touch, move. **~si** *v.r.* be touched.

commuta're *v.t.* change; (*legge*) commute.

comò *n.m. invar.* chest of drawers.

comodi'no *n.m.* bedside table.

co'modo *a.* comfortable; (*conveniente*)

convenient; (*spazioso*) roomy; (*facile*) easy. —*n.m.* comfort; convenience. **fare il proprio ~** do as one pleases. **prendila con ~!** take it easy!

compaesa'no, a *n.m., f.* fellow countryman.

compa'gine *n.f.* (*squadra*) team.

compagni'a *n.f.* company; (*gruppo*) party. **fare ~ a qcno.** keep s.o. company.

compa'gno, a *n.m., f.* companion, mate; (*comm., sport*) partner; (*pol.*) comrade. **~ di scuola** schoolmate.

compara'|re *v.t.* compare. **~bile** *a.* comparable. **~ti'vo** *a. & n.m.* comparative. **~zio'ne** *n.f.* comparison.

compa're *n.m.* (*padrino*) godfather; (*testimone di matrimonio*) witness.

compari're *v.i.* appear; (*spiccare*) stand out.

compa'rso, a *p.p. di* **comparire.** —*n.f.* appearance; (*cinema*) extra.

compartecipazio'ne *n.f.* sharing.

compartime'nto *n.m.* compartment; (*amministrativo*) department.

compassa'to *a.* calm and collected.

compassio'n|e *n.f.* compassion. **aver ~e per** feel pity for. **~e'vole** *a.* compassionate.

compa'sso *n.m.* (pair of) compasses *pl.*

compati'bil|e *a.* (*conciliabile*) compatible; (*scusabile*) excusable. **~ità** *n.f.* compatibility.

compat|ime'nto *n.m.* pity; (*indulgenza*) indulgence. **~i're** *v.t.* pity; (*scusare*) make allowances for.

compatrio'ta *n.m.|f.* compatriot.

compa'tto *a.* compact; (*denso*) dense; (*solido*) solid; (*fig.*) united.

comp|endia're *v.t.* epitomize; (*fare un sunto*) summarize. **~e'ndio** *n.m.* outline; (*sunto*) synopsis; (*libro*) compendium.

compenetra're *v.t.* pervade.

compensa're *v.t.* compensate; (*supplire*) make up for. **compe'nso** *n.m.* compensation; (*retribuzione*) remuneration. **in compenso** (*in cambio*) in return.

co'mper|a *n.f.* purchase. **far ~e** do some shopping.

compete'n|te *a.* competent. **~za** *n.f.* competence.

compe't|ere *v.i.* compete. **~ito're, ~itri'ce** *n.m., f.* competitor. **~izio'ne** *n.f.* competition.

compiace'n|te *a.* complaisant; (*ar-*

rendevole) compliant. ~**za** *n.f.* courtesy.

compiace'|re *v.t./i.* please. ~**rsi** *v.r.* (*congratularsi*) congratulate. ~**rsi di** (*degnarsi*) condescend.

compia'n|gere *v.t.* pity; (*per lutto ecc.*) sympathize with. ~**to** *a.* lamented; *n.m.* grief.

co'mpier|e *v.t.* (*concludere*) complete; (*un delitto*) commit. ~**si** *v.r.* end; (*avverarsi*) come true. ~**e gli anni** have one's birthday.

compi're *v.t.* = **compiere.**

compila're *v.t.* compile.

compita're *v.t.* spell (out).

compi'to *a.* polite.

co'mpito *n.m.* task; (*schol.*) homework.

complea'nno *n.m.* birthday.

compleme'nt|o *n.m.* complement; (*mil.*) draft. ~**o oggetto** direct object. ~**a're** *a.* complementary; (*secondario*) subsidiary.

comple'ss|o *a.* complex; (*difficile*) complicated. —*n.m.* complex; (*di cantanti ecc.*) group. **in** ~**o** on the whole. ~**ità** *n.f.* complexity. ~**i'vo** *a.* comprehensive; (*totale*) total.

comple't|o *a.* complete; (*pieno*) full (up). —*n.m.* (*vestito*) suit; (*insieme di cose*) set. ~**a're** *v.t.* complete.

complica'r|e *v.t.* complicate. ~**si** *v.r.* become complicated.

co'mplice *n.m./f.* accomplice.

complimenta'r|e *v.t.* compliment. ~**si** *v.r.* ~**si con** congratulate.

complime'nt|o *n.m.* compliment. ~**i** *n.m. pl.* (*ossequi*) regards; (*congratulazioni*) congratulations. **far** ~**i** stand on ceremony.

complo'tt|o *n.m.* plot, ~**a're** *v.i.* plot.

compone'nte *a.* & *n.m.* component. —*n.m./f.* member.

componime'nto *n.m.* composition; (*letterario*) work.

compo'r|re *v.t.* compose; (*ordinare*) put in order; (*typ.*) set. ~**si** *v.r.* ~**si di** be made up of.

comportame'nto *n.m.* behaviour.

comporta'r|e *v.t.* involve; (*consentire*) allow. ~**si** *v.r.* behave.

composi|to're, ~**tri'ce** *n.m.*, *f.* composer; (*typ.*) compositor.

composizio'ne *n.f.* composition.

compo'sta *n.f.* stewed fruit.

compo'st|o *p.p. di* **comporre.** —*a.* composed; (*costituito*) comprising.

stai ~**o!** sit straight! ~**e'zza** *n.f.* composure.

compra'|re *v.t.* buy. ~**to're,** ~**tri'ce** *n.m.*, *f.* buyer.

compre'ndere *v.t.* understand; (*includere*) comprise.

comprens|io'ne *n.f.* understanding. ~**i'bile** *a.* understandable. ~**i'vo** *a.* understanding; (*che include*) comprehensive.

compre'so *p.p. di* **comprendere.** —*a.* included.

compre'ssa *n.f.* compress; (*pastiglia*) tablet.

compressio'ne *n.f.* compression.

compre'sso *p.p. di* **comprimere;** *a.* compressed.

compri'mere *v.t.* press; (*reprimere*) repress.

comprome'|sso *p.p. di* **compromettere.** —*n.m.* compromise. ~**ttere** *v.t.* compromise.

comprova're *v.t.* prove.

compu'n|to *a.* contrite. ~**zio'ne** *n.f.* compunction.

computa're *v.t.* calculate. **co'mputo** *n.m.* calculation.

computerizza're *v.t.* computerize.

comput|isteri'a *n.f.* bookkeeping. ~**i'sta** *n.m./f.* bookkeeper.

comuna'le *a.* municipal.

comuna'nza *n.f.* community.

comu'ne *a.* common; (*condiviso*) mutual; (*ordinario*) ordinary. —*n.m.* borough; (*amministrativo*) commune. **fuori del** ~ out of the ordinary.

comunica'|re *v.t.* communicate; (*malattia*) pass on; (*relig.*) administer Communion. ~**rsi** *v.r.* receive Communion. ~**ti'vo** *a.* communicative.

comunica'to *n.m.* communiqué.

comunicazio'ne *n.f.* communication; (*telefonica*) (phone) call. **avere la** ~ get through. **dare la** ~ **a qcno.** put s.o. through.

comunio'ne *n.f.* communion; (*relig.*) (Holy) Communion.

comuni's|mo *n.m.* communism. ~**ta** *a.* & *n.m./f.* communist.

comunità *n.f.* community. **C**~ **Economica Europea (C.E.E.)** European Economic Community (EEC).

comu'nque *conj.* however. —*adv.* anyhow.

con *prep.* with. ~ **mia grande gioia** to my great delight. **è gentile** ~ **tutti** he is kind to everyone.

cona'to *n.m.* ~ **di vomito** retching.

co'nca *n.f.* basin; (*valle*) dell.

concatena're *v.t.* link together.

con'cavo *a.* concave.

conce'dere *v.t.* grant; (*premio*) award; (*ammettere*) admit.

concentra'|re *v.t.*, **~rsi** *v.r.* concentrate. **~me'nto** *n.m.*, **~zio'ne** *n.f.* concentration.

concepi'|re *v.t.* conceive; (*capire*) understand; (*piano ecc.*) devise. **~me'nto** *n.m.* conception.

conce'rnere *v.t.* concern.

concerta'r|e *v.t.* (*mus.*) harmonize; (*organizzare*) arrange. **~si** *v.r.* agree.

conce'rto *n.m.* concert.

concessio'n|e *n.f.* concession. **~a'rio** *n.m.* agent.

conce'sso *p.p. di* **concedere**.

conce'tto *n.m.* concept; (*opinione*) opinion.

concezio'ne *n.f.* conception; (*idea*) concept.

conchi'glia *n.f.* (sea) shell.

co'ncia *n.f.* tanning; (*di tabacco*) curing.

concia'r|e *v.t.* tan; (*tabacco*) cure. **~e qcno. per le feste** give s.o. a good hiding. **~si** *v.r.* (*sporcarsi*) get dirty; (*vestirsi male*) dress badly.

concilia'bolo *n.m.* secret meeting.

concilia'|re *v.t.* reconcile; (*contravvenzione*) settle; (*favorire*) induce. **~rsi** *v.r.* go together; (*mettersi d'accordo*) become reconciled. **~bile** *a.* compatible. **~zio'ne** *n.f.* reconciliation.

conci'lio *n.m.* (*relig.*) council; (*riunione*) assembly.

conci'me *n.m.* manure; (*chimico*) fertilizer.

conci'so *a.* concise.

concita'to *a.* excited.

concittadi'no, a *n.m., f.* fellow citizen.

concla've *n.m.* conclave.

conclu'|dere *v.t.* conclude; (*finire con successo*) achieve. **~dersi** *v.r.* come to an end. **~sio'ne** *n.f.* conclusion. **in ~sione** (*insomma*) in short. **~si'vo** *a.* conclusive. **~so** *p.p. di* **concludere**.

concorda'|nza *n.f.* agreement. **~re** *v.t.* agree; (*gram.*) make agree. **~to** *n.m.* agreement; (*legge, comm.*) arrangement.

conco'rde *a.* in agreement; (*unanime*) unanimous.

conco'rdia *n.f.* concord.

concorre'n|te *a.* concurrent; (*rivale*)

competing. **—***n.m./f.* (*comm., sport*) competitor; (*candidato*) candidate. **~za** *n.f.* competition.

conco'r|rere *v.i.* (*contribuire*) concur; (*andare insieme*) go together; (*competere*) compete. **~so** *p.p. di* **concorrere**; *n.m.* competitior.

concre't|o *a.* concrete. **~a re** *v.t.* (*concludere*) achieve.

concubi'na *n.f.* concubine.

concussio'ne *n.f.* extortion.

conda'nn|a *n.f.* sentence. **pronunziare una ~a** pass a sentence. **~a're** *v.t.* condemn; (*legge*) sentence. **~a'to, a** *n.m., f.* convict.

condensa'|re *v.t.*, **~si** *v.r.* condense. **~zio'ne** *n.f.* condensation.

condi'|re *v.t.* flavour; (*insalata*) dress. **~me'nto** *n.m.* seasoning; dressing.

condiscende'n|te *a.* indulgent; (*pej.*) condescending. **~za** *n.f.* indulgence; condescension.

condivi'dere *v.t.* share.

condiziona'le *a. & n.m.* conditional. **—***n.f.* (*legge*) suspended sentence.

condiziona'|re *v.t.* condition. **~to** *a.* conditional. **aria ~ta** air-conditioning.

condizio'ne *n.f.* condition. **a ~ che** on condition that.

condoglia'nze *n.f. pl.* condolences. **fare le ~ a** offer condolences to.

condomi'nio *n.m.* joint ownership.

condona're *v.t.* remit. **condo'no** *n.m.* remission.

condo'tta *n.f.* conduct., (*circoscrizione di medico*) district; (*di gara ecc.*) management; (*tubazione*) piping.

condo'tto *p.p. di* **condurre**. **—***a.* **medico ~** district doctor. **—***n.m.* pipe; (*anat.*) duct.

conduce'nte *n.m.* driver.

condu'r|re *v.t.* lead; (*veicoli*) drive; (*accompagnare*) take; (*gas, electr., ecc.*) conduct; (*gestire*) run. **~si** *v.r.* behave.

condutto're *n.m.* (*di veicolo*) driver; (*electr.*) conductor.

conduttu'ra *n.f.* duct.

confabula're *v.i.* confabulate.

conf|ace'nte *a.* suitable. **~a'rsi** *v.r.* **~arsi a** suit.

confederazio'ne *n.f.* confederation.

confere'nz|a *n.f.* (*discorso*) lecture; (*congresso*) conference. **~ie're, a** *n.m., f.* lecturer.

conferi're *v.t.* (*donare*) give. —*v.i.* confer.

confe'rm|a *n.f.* confirmation. ~**a're** *v.t.* confirm.

confess|a're *v.t.*, ~**a'rsi** *v.r.* confess. ~**iona'le** *a.* & *n.m.* confessional. ~**io'ne** *n.f.* confession. ~**o're** *n.m.* confessor.

confe'tt|o *n.m.* sugared almond. ~**u'ra** *n.f.* jam.

confezio'n|e *n.f.* manufacture; (*di abiti*) tailoring; (*di pacchi*) packaging. ~**i** *n.m. pl.* clothes. ~**a're** *v.t.* manufacture; (*abiti*) make; (*merci*) package.

conficca'r|e *v.t.* thrust. ~**si** *v.r.* run into.

confid|a're *v.i.* ~**are in** trust. —*v.t.* confide. ~**a'rsi con** confide in. ~**e'nte** *a.* confident; *n.m.*, *f.* confidant.

confide'nz|a *n.f.* confidence; (*familiarità*) familiarity. **prendersi delle** ~**e** take liberties. ~**ia'le** *a.* confidential.

configurazio'ne *n.f.* configuration.

confina'r|e *v.t.* (*relegare*) confine. —*v.i.* ~**e con** border on. ~**si** *v.r.* withdraw.

confi'ne *n.m.* border; (*tra terreni*) boundary.

confi'no *n.m.* political exile.

confisca're *v.t.* confiscate.

conflagrazio'ne *n.f.* conflagration.

confli'tto *n.m.* conflict.

conflue'nza *n.f.* confluence; (*di strade*) junction.

conflui're *v.i.* (*di fiumi*) flow together; (*di strade*) meet.

confo'nder|e *v.t.* confuse; (*turbare*) confound. ~**si** *v.r.* (*mescolarsi*) mingle; (*turbarsi*) become confused.

conforma'r|e *v.t.*, ~**si** *v.r.* conform.

conformazio'ne *n.f.* conformation.

confo'rme *a.* according. ~**me'nte** *adv.* accordingly.

conformi'sta *n.m./f.* conformist.

confort|a're *v.t.* comfort. ~**a'nte** *a.* comforting. ~**e'vole** *a.* (*comodo*) comfortable. **confo'rto** *n.m.* comfort.

confronta're *v.t.* compare. **confro'nto** *n.m.* comparison. **in confronto a** by comparison with. **nei tuoi confronti** towards you.

confusio'ne *n.f.* confusion. **confu'so** *p.p. di* **confondere**; *a.* confused; (*indistinto*) indistinct.

confuta're *v.t.* confute.

congeda'r|e *v.t.* dismiss; (*mil.*) discharge. ~**si** *v.r.* take one's leave. **conge'do** *n.m.* leave; discharge. **essere in congedo** be on leave.

congegna're *v.t.* devise; (*mettere insieme*) assemble. **conge'gno** *n.m.* device.

congela'r|e *v.t.* freeze. ~**me'nto** *n.m.* freezing; (*med.*) frost-bite. ~**to're** *n.m.* freezer.

congenia'le *a.* congenial.

conge'nito *a.* congenital.

congestiona'|re *v.t.* congest. ~**to** *a.* (*traffico*) congested; (*viso*) flushed. **congestio'ne** *n.f.* congestion.

congettu'ra *n.f.* conjecture.

congiu'nger|e *v.t.* join; (*collegare*) connect. ~**si** *v.r.* join.

congiuntivi'te *n.f.* conjunctivitis.

congiunti'vo *n.m.* subjunctive.

congiu'nto *p.p. di* **congiungere**. —*a.* joined. —*n.m.* relative.

congiuntu'ra *n.f.* joint, (*circostanza*) juncture; (*situazione*) situation.

congiunzio'ne *n.f.* (*gram.*) conjunction.

congiu'r|a *n.f.* conspiracy. ~**a're** *v.i.* conspire.

conglomera'to *n.m.* conglomerate; (*fig.*) conglomeration.

congratula'|rsi *v.r.* ~**rsi con qcno. per** congratulate s.o. on. ~**zio'ni** *n.f. pl.* congratulations.

congre'ga *n.f.* band.

congrega'|re *v.t.*, ~**rsi** *v.r.* congregate. ~**zio'ne** *n.f.* congregation.

congre'sso *n.m.* congress.

co'ngruo *a.* proper; (*giusto*) fair.

conguaglia're *v.t.* balance. **congua'glio** *n.m.* balance.

conia're *v.t.* coin.

coni'fera *n.f.* conifer.

coni'glio *n.m.* rabbit.

coniug|a're *v.t.* conjugate. ~**a'rsi** *v.r.* get married. ~**azio'ne** *n.f.* conjugation.

co'niuge *n.m./f.* spouse.

connaziona'le *n.m./f.* compatriot.

connessio'ne *n.f.* connection.

conne'sso *p.p. di* **connettere**.

conne'ttere *v.t.* connect. —*v.i.* think rationally.

connive'nte *a.* conniving.

connota't|o *n.m.* distinguishing feature. ~**i** *n.m. pl.* description.

co'no *n.m.* cone. ~**ico** *a.* conical.

conosce'nte *n.m./f.* acquaintance.

conosce'nza *n.f.* knowledge; (*persona*) acquaintance; (*sensi*) consciousness.

cono'sc|ere *v.t.* know; (*essere a*

conoscenza di) be acquainted with; (*fare la conoscenza di*) meet. ~**ito're**, ~**itri'ce** *n.m.*, *f.* connoisseur. ~**iu'to** *p.p. di* **conoscere**; *a.* well-known.

conqui'st|a *n.f.* conquest. ~**a're** *v.t.* conquer; (*fig.*) win. ~**ato're** *n.m.* conqueror; (*fig.*) lady-killer.

consacra'|re *v.t.* consecrate; (*sacerdote*) ordain. ~**rsi** *v.r.* devote oneself. ~**zio'ne** *n.f.* consecration.

consangui'neo, a *n.m.*, *f.* blood-relation.

consape'vol|e *a.* conscious. ~**e'zza** *n.f.* consciousness.

co'nscio *a.* conscious.

consecuti'vo *a.* consecutive; (*seguente*) next.

conse'gn|a *n.f.* delivery; (*merce*) consignment; (*custodia*) care; (*mil.*, *punizione*) confinement. **pagamento alla** ~**a** cash on delivery. ~**a're** *v.t.* deliver; (*affidare*) give in charge; (*mil.*) confine to barracks.

consegue'n|te *a.* consequent. ~**za** *n.f.* consequence.

consegui're *v.t.* achieve. —*v.i.* follow.

conse'nso *n.m.* consent.

consenti're *v.i.* consent. —*v.t.* allow.

conse'rv|a *n.f.* preserve; (*di frutta*) jam; (*di agrumi*) marmalade. ~**a're** *v.t.* preserve; (*mantenere*) keep. ~**a'rsi** *v.r.* keep. ~**arsi in salute** keep well. ~**azio'ne** *n.f.* preservation.

conserva|to're, ~**tri'ce** *n.m.*, *f.* (*pol.*) conservative.

consider'|are *v.t.* consider; (*stimare*) regard. ~**azio'ne** *n.f.* consideration; regard. ~**e'vole** *a.* considerable.

consigli|a're *v.t.* advise; (*raccomandare*) recommend. ~**a'rsi** *v.r.* ask s.o.'s advice. ~**e're, a're** *n.m.*, *f.* adviser; (*membro di un consiglio*) councillor.

consi'glio *n.m.* advice; (*ente*) council. **consiglio d'amministrazione** board of directors. **Consiglio dei Ministri** Cabinet.

consi'mile *a.* similar.

consiste'n|te *a.* substantial; (*denso*) thick. ~**za** *n.f.* consistency; thickness.

consi'stere *v.i.* ~ **in** consist of.

conso'cio *n.m.* fellow-member.

consola'|re *v.t.* console; (*rallegrare*) cheer. ~**zio'ne** *n.f.* consolation; (*gioia*) joy.

co'nsol|e *n.m.* consul. ~**a're** *a.* consular. ~**a'to** *n.m.* consulate.

consolida'r|e *v.t.*, ~**si** *v.r.* consolidate.

consona'nte *n.f.* consonant.

consona'nza *n.f.* consonance.

conso'rte *n.m.*/*f.* consort.

conso'rzio *n.m.* consortium.

consta're *v.i.* ~ **di** consist of; (*risultare*) appear. **a quanto mi consta** as far as I know. **mi consta che** it appears that.

constata'|re *v.t.* ascertain. ~**zio'ne** *n.f.* observation.

consue't|o *a.* & *n.m.* usual. ~**u'dine** *n.f.* habit; (*usanza*) custom.

consule'n|te *n.m.*/*f.* consultant. ~**za** *n.f.* consultancy.

consulta'|re *v.t.* consult. ~**rsi con** seek the advice of. ~**zio'ne** *n.f.* consultation.

consuma'|re *v.t.* (*usare*) consume; (*logorare abiti ecc.*) wear out; (*legge*) consummate. ~**rsi** *v.r.* consume; wear out; (*struggersi*) pine. ~**to're** *n.m.* consumer. ~**zio'ne** *n.f.* (*bibita*) drink; (*spuntino*) snack. **consu'mo** *n.m.* consumption; wear; (*uso*) use.

consunti'vo *n.m.* (**bilancio**) ~ final statement.

consu'nto *a.* worn-out; (*smunto*) wasted.

conta'bil|e *a.* book-keeping. —*n.m.*/*f.* accountant. ~**ità** *n.f.* accounting. **tenere la** ~**ità** keep the accounts.

contachilo'metri *n.m. invar.* speedometer.

contadi'no, a *n.m.*, *f.* peasant. **il mondo** ~ the farming world.

conta'gi|o *n.m.* infection. ~**a're** *v.t.* infect. ~**o'so** *a.* infectious.

contamina'|re *v.t.* contaminate. ~**zio'ne** *n.f.* contamination.

conta'nt|e *n.m.* cash. **pagare in** ~**i** pay cash.

conta're *v.t.*/*i.* count; (*proporsi*) intend.

contato're *n.m.* meter.

contatta're *v.t.* contact. **conta'tto** *n.m.* contact.

co'nte *n.m.* count.

conte'a *n.f.* (*territorio*) county.

conteggia're *v.t.* put on the bill. —*v.i.* calculate. **conte'ggio** *n.m.* calculation. **conteggio alla rovescia** count-down.

conte'gn|o *n.m.* behaviour; (*atteggiamento*) attitude. ~**o'so** *a.* dignified.

contempla'|re *v.t.* contemplate;

(*fissare*) gaze (at). ~**zio'ne** *n.f.* contemplation.

contempora'neo, a *a.* & *n.m.*, *f.* contemporary.

contende'nte *n.m.|f.* competitor. **conte'ndere** *v.i.* compete; (*litigare*) quarrel. —*v.t.* contend.

conten|e're *v.t.* contain; (*reprimere*) repress. ~**e'rsi** *v.r.* contain oneself. ~**ito're** *n.m.* container.

contenta'r|e *v.t.* please. ~**si** *v.r.* ~**si di** be satisfied with.

conte'nt|o *a.* glad; (*soddisfatto*) contented. ~**e'zza** *n.f.* joy; contentment.

contenu'to *n.m.* contents *pl.*; (*soggetto*) content.

conte'sa *n.f.* disagreement; (*sport*) contest.

conte'so *p.p. di* **contendere.** —*a.* contested.

conte'ssa *n.f.* countess.

contesta're *v.t.* contest; (*legge*) notify.

conte'sto *n.m.* context.

conti'guo *a.* adjacent.

contine'n|te *n.m.* continent. ~**ta'le** *a.* continental. ~**za** *n.f.* continence.

continge'n|te *n.m.* contingent; (*quota*) quota. ~**za** *n.f.* contingency.

conti'nu|o *a.* continuous; (*molto frequente*) continual. **corrente** ~**a** direct current. ~**a're** *v.t./i.* continue; (*riprendere*) resume. ~**azio'ne** *n.f.* continuation. ~**ità** *n.f.* continuity.

co'nt|o *n.m.* account; (*di ristorante ecc.*) bill; (*stima*) consideration. **a** ~**i fatti** all things considered. **far** ~**o di** (*supporre*) suppose; (*proporsi*) intend. **far** ~**o su** rely on. **in fin dei** ~**i** when all is said and done. **per** ~**o di** on behalf of. **per** ~**o proprio** on one's own account.

conto'rcer|e *v.t.* twist. ~**si** *v.r.* twist (about).

contorna're *v.t.* surround.

conto'rno *n.m.* contour; (*culin.*) vegetables *pl.*

contorsio'ne *n.f.* contortion.

conto'rto *p.p. di* **contorcere.** —*a.* twisted.

contrabba'nd|o *n.m.* contraband. ~**ie're, a** *n.m.*, *f.* smuggler.

contracc|ambia're *v.t.* return. ~**a'mbio** *n.m.* return.

contraccetti'vo *n.m.* contraceptive.

contracco'l|po *n.m.* rebound; (*di arma da fuoco*) recoil; (*fig.*) repercussion.

contra'da *n.f.* (*rione*) district.

contradde'tto *p.p. di* **contraddire.**

contraddi'|re *v.t.* contradict. ~**to'rio** *a.* contradictory. ~**zio'ne** *n.f.* contradiction.

contrae'reo *a.* anti-aircraft.

contraffa'|re *v.t.* disguise; (*imitare*) imitate; (*falsificare*) forge. ~**zio'ne** *n.f.* disguising; imitation; forgery.

contra'lto *n.f.* contralto.

contrappe'so *n.m.* counterbalance.

contrappo'rre *v.t.* counter; (*confrontare*) compare.

contra'ri|o *a.* contrary; (*direzione*) opposite; (*sfavorevole*) unfavourable. —*n.m.* contrary; opposite. **al** ~**o** on the contrary. ~**ame'nte** *adv.* contrary (**a**, to). ~**a're** *v.t.* oppose; (*infastidire*) annoy. ~**a'rsi** *v.r.* get annoyed. ~**età** *n.f.* adversity; (*ostacolo*) set-back.

contra'rre *v.t.* contract.

contrasse'gn|o *n.m.* mark. ~**a're** *v.t.* mark.

contra'st|o *n.m.* contrast; (*litigio*) dispute. ~**a're** *v.t.* oppose; (*contestare*) contest; *v.i.* clash.

contratta'cc|o *n.m.* counterattack. ~**a're** *v.t.* counter-attack.

contratta're *v.t./i.* negotiate; (*mercanteggiare*) bargain.

contratte'mpo *n.m.* hitch.

contra'tt|o *p.p. di* **contrarre.** —*n.m.* contract. ~**ua'le** *a.* contractual.

contravvele'no *n.m.* antidote.

contravven|i're *v.i.* contravene. ~**zio'ne** *n.f.* contravention; (*multa*) fine.

contrazio'ne *n.f.* contraction.

contribue'nte *n.m.|f.* contributor; (*del fisco*) taxpayer.

contrib|ui're *v.i.* contribute. ~**u'to** *n.m.* contribution.

contri'to *a.* contrite.

co'ntro *prep.* against. ~ **di me** against me. ~ **il terrorismo** against terrorism. —*n.m.* **il pro e il** ~ the pros and cons *pl.*

controba'ttere *v.t.* counter.

controfigu'ra *n.f.* stand-in.

controfirma're *v.t.* countersign.

controlla'r|e *v.t.* control; (*verificare*) check; (*collaudare*) test. ~**si** *v.r.* have self-control. **contro'llo** *n.m.* control; check; (*med.*) check-up; test. **controllo delle nascite** birth control.

controllo're *n.m.* controller; (*sui treni ecc.*) (ticket) inspector.

controma'no adv. in the wrong direction.

controproduce'nte a. self-defeating.

controse'nso n.m. contradiction in terms.

controspiona'ggio n.m. counter-espionage.

controve'rs|ia n.f. controversy. ~o a. controversial

contuma'cia n.f. default.

conturba're v.t. perturb.

contusio'ne n.f. bruise.

convalesce'n|te a. convalescent. ~za n.f. convalescence.

convalida're v.t. confirm.

conve'gno n.m. meeting; (congresso) congress.

convene'vole a. suitable.

convenie'n|te a. convenient; (prezzo) moderate; (vantagioso) advantageous. ~za n.f. convenience; advantage.

conveni're v.i. (riunirsi) gather; (concordare) agree; (ammettere) admit; (essere opportuno) be suitable. —v.t. agree upon. **ci conviene andare** it is better to go. **non mi conviene** it does not suit me.

conve'nto n.m. convent.

convenu'to a. fixed.

convenzi|ona'le a. conventional. ~o'ne n.f. convention.

conve'rg|ere v.i. converge. ~e'nte a. converging.

conversa'|re v.i. converse. ~zio'ne n.f. conversation.

conversio'ne n.f. conversion.

conve'rso p.p. di **convergere**.

converti'|re v.t. convert. ~rsi v.r. be converted. ~to, a n.m., f. convert.

conve'sso a. convex.

convi'n|cere v.t. convince. ~to a. convinced. ~zio'ne n.f. conviction.

convi't|to n.m. boarding-school. ~to're, ~tri'ce n.m., f. boarder.

convi'vere v.i. live together.

convivia'le a. convivial.

convoca're v.t. convene.

convo'gli|o n.m. convoy; (ferroviario) train. ~a're v.t. convey; (di navi) convoy.

convulsio'ne n.f. convulsion. **convu'lso** a. convulsive; (febbrile) feverish.

coopera'|re v.i. co-operate. ~ti'va n.f. co-operative. ~zio'ne n.f. co-operation.

coordina'|re v.t. co-ordinate ~ta n.f.

(math.) coordinate. ~zio'ne n.f. co-ordination.

cope'rchio n.m. lid; (copertura) cover.

cope'rta n.f. blanket; (copertura) cover; (naut.) deck.

coperti'na n.f. cover; (di libro) dust-jacket.

cope'rto p.p. di **coprire**. —a. covered; (del cielo) overcast. —n.m. (a tavola) place; (prezzo del coperto) cover charge. **al** ~ under cover.

coperto'ne n.m. tarpaulin; (gomma) tyre.

copertu'ra n.f. covering; (comm., econ.) cover.

co'pi|a n.f. copy. **bella/brutta** ~a fair/rough copy. ~a're v.t. copy.

copio'ne n.m. script.

copio'so a. plentiful.

co'ppa n.f. (calice) goblet; (per gelato ecc.) dish; (sport) cup.

co'ppia n.f. couple.

coprifuo'co n.m. curfew.

coprile'tto n.m. bedspread.

copripiumi'no n.m. duvet cover.

copri'r|e v.t. cover; (un suono) drown; (tenere una carica) hold. ~si v.r. (vestirsi) cover up; (fig.) cover oneself; (di cielo) become overcast.

cora'ggi|o n.m. courage; (sfacciataggine) nerve. ~o'so a. courageous.

cora'le a. choral.

cora'llo n.m. coral.

cora'no n.m. Koran.

cora'zza n.f. armour; (di animali) shell.

corazza'ta n.f. battleship.

corbelleri'a n.f. nonsense; (sproposito) blunder.

co'rda n.f. cord; (spago, mus.) string; (fune) rope; (cavo) cable. **essere giù di** ~ be depressed.

cordia'l|e a. cordial. —n.m. (bevanda) cordial. **saluti** ~i best wishes. ~ità n.f. cordiality.

cordo'glio n.m. grief; (lutto) mourning.

cordo'ne n.m. cord; (schieramento) cordon. ~ **ombelicale** umbilical cord.

coreografi'a n.f. choreography. **coreo'grafo, a** n.m., f. choreographer.

coria'ndoli n.m. pl. confetti s.

corica'r|e v.t. put to bed. ~si v.r. go to bed.

corna'cchia n.f. crow.

cornamu'sa n.f. bagpipes pl.

co'rnea n.f. cornea.

corne'tta *n.f.* (*mus.*) cornet; (*del telefono*) receiver.

corne'tto *n.m.* (*panino*) crescent-shaped roll. ~ **acustico** ear-trumpet.

corni'ce *n.f.* frame.

co'rn|o *n.m.* (*pl. f.* **corna**) horn. **fare le** ~**a a qcno.** be unfaithful to s.o. ~**u'to** *a.* horned; *n.m.* (*fam.*, *marito tradito*) cuckold; (*insulto*) bastard.

co'ro *n.m.* chorus; (*relig.*) choir.

coro'n|a *n.f.* crown; (*di fiori*) wreath; (*rosario*) rosary. ~**a're** *v.t.* crown.

corpe'tto *n.m.* bodice.

co'rpo *n.m.* body; (*mil.*, *diplomatico*) corps *invar.* **a** ~ **a** ~ man to man. ~ **insegnante** teaching staff. ~**ra'le** *a.* corporal. **corpo'reo** *a.* bodily.

corporatu'ra *n.f.* build.

corporazio'ne *n.f.* corporation.

corpule'nto *a.* stout.

correda're *v.t.* equip.

corre'd|o *n.m.* (*nuziale*) trousseau. ~**i'no** *n.m.* (*per neonato*) layette.

corre'ggere *v.t.* correct; (*di bevanda*) lace.

corre'nte *a.* running; (*in vigore*) current. —*n.f.* current; (*d'aria*) draught. **essere al** ~ be up to date.

co'rrere *v.i.* run; (*affrettarsi*) hurry; (*sport*) race; (*notizie*) circulate. —*v.t.* run. ~ **dietro** a run after. ~ **un pericolo** be in danger. **lascia** ~! don't bother!

corre'tto *p.p. di* **correggere.** —*a.* correct.

correzio'ne *n.f.* correction. ~ **di bozze** proof-reading.

corrido'io *n.m.* corridor.

corrido're *n.m.* racer; (*a piedi*) runner.

corrie'ra *n.f.* coach.

corrie're *n.m.* courier; (*posta*) mail.

corrige'ndo, a *n.m.,f.* juvenile offender.

corrisponde'n|te *a.* corresponding. —*n.m./f.* correspondent. ~**za** *n.f.* correspondence. **corrispo'ndere** *v.i.* correspond; **corrispondere a** (*contraccambiare*) return; (*di stanza*) communicate.

corrobora're *v.t.* strengthen; (*fig.*) corroborate.

corro'der|e *v.t.*, ~**si** *v.r.* corrode.

corro'mpere *v.t.* corrupt; (*con denaro*) bribe.

corros|io'ne *n.f.* corrosion. ~**i'vo** *a.* corrosive.

corro'so *p.p. di* **corrodere.**

corro'tto *p.p. di* **corrompere.** —*a.* corrupt.

corruccia'|rsi *v.r.* be vexed. ~**to** *a.* upset.

corruga're *v.t.* wrinkle. ~ **la fronte** knit one's brows.

corruzio'ne *n.f.* corruption; (*con denaro*) bribery.

co'rsa *n.f.* running; (*rapida*) dash; (*sport*) race; (*di treno ecc.*) journey. **di gran** ~ in a great hurry. **fare una** ~ run.

corsi'a *n.f.* gangway; (*di ospedale*) ward.

corsi'vo *n.m.* italics *pl.*

co'rso *p.p. di* **correre.** —*n.m.* course; (*strada*) main street; (*comm.*) circulation. **lavori in** ~ work in progress. **nel** ~ **di** during.

co'rte *n.f.* (court)yard; (*legge, regale*) court. **fare la** ~ **a qcno.** court s.o.

corte'ccia *n.f.* bark.

corteggia'|re *v.t.* court. ~**to're** *n.m.* admirer.

corte'o *n.m.* procession.

corte's|e *a.* courteous. ~**i'a** *n.f.* courtesy. **per** ~**ia** please.

cortigia'no, a *n.m.,f.* courtier. —*n.f.* courtesan.

corti'le *n.m.* courtyard.

corti'na *n.f.* curtain; (*schermo*) screen.

co'rt|o *a.* short. **andare per le** ~**e** come straight to the point. **per farla** ~**a** in short.

co'rvo *n.m.* raven.

co'sa *n.f.* thing; (*faccenda*) matter; (*inter.*, *rel.*) (**che**) ~ what. **nessuna** ~ nothing. **ogni** ~ everything. **per prima** ~ first of all. **tante cose** (so) many things; (*augurio*) all the best.

co'scia *n.f.* thigh.

coscie'n|te *a.* conscious. ~**za** *n.f.* conscience; (*consapevolezza*) consciousness.

coscri'|tto *n.m.* conscript. ~**zio'ne** *n.f.* conscription.

così *adv.* so; (*in questo modo*) like this, like that. —*a.* (*tale*) such. —*conj.* (*allora*) so; (*perciò*) therefore. **basta** ~! that will do! **e** ~ **via** and so on. **una** ~ **cara ragazza!** such a nice girl!

cosidde'tto *a.* so-called.

cosme'tico *a.* & *n.m.* cosmetic.

co'sm|o *n.m.* cosmos. ~**ico** *a.* cosmic.

cosmona'uta *n.m./f.* cosmonaut.

cosmopo'lita *a.* cosmopolitan.

cospa'rgere *v.t.* sprinkle; (*disseminare*) scatter.

cospe'tto *n.m.* **al ~ di** in the presence of.

cospi'cuo *a.* conspicuous; (*di somma ecc.*) considerable.

cospira'|re *v.i.* conspire. **~to're, ~tri'ce** *n.m., f.* conspirator. **~zio'ne** *n.f.* conspiracy.

co'sta *n.f.* coast, coastline; (*pendio*) slope; (*anat.*) rib.

costà *adv.* there.

costa'nte *a.* constant. **—***n.f.* constant.

costa're *v.i.* cost. **quanto costa?** how much is it?

costa'ta *n.f.* chop.

costeggia're *v.t.* (*per mare*) coast; (*per terra*) skirt.

coste'i *pron. vedi* **costui.**

costellazio'ne *n.f.* constellation.

costernazio'ne *n.f.* consternation.

costie'r|o *a.* coastal. **~a** *n.f.* stretch of coast.

costipa'to *a.* constipated.

costitui'r|e *v.t.* constitute; (*formare*) form; (*nominare*) appoint. **~si** *v.r.* (*legge*) give oneself up.

costituzio'n|e *n.f.* constitution; (*fondazione*) setting up. **~a'le** *a.* constitutional.

co'sto *n.m.* cost. **ad ogni ~** at all costs. **a nessun ~** on no account.

co'stola *n.f.* rib; (*di libro*) spine.

costole'tta *n.f.* cutlet.

costo'ro *vedi* **costui.**

costo'so *a.* costly.

costre'tto *p.p. di* **costringere.**

costri'|ngere *v.t.* compel; (*stringere*) constrict. **~zio'ne** *n.f.* compulsion; constraint.

costru|i're *v.t.* build, construct. **~zio'ne** *n.f.* building, construction.

costu'i, coste'i, *pl.* **costo'ro** *prons.* (*soggetto*) he, she, *pl.* they; (*complemento*) him, her, *pl.* them.

costu'me *n.m.* (*usanza*) custom; (*condotta*) morals *pl.*; (*indumento*) costume. **~ da bagno** swim-suit.

cote'nna *n.f.* pigskin; (*della pancetta*) rind.

coto'gna *n.f.* quince.

cotole'tta *n.f.* cutlet.

coto'ne *n.m.* cotton. **~ idrofilo** cotton wool.

co'tta *n.f.* (*relig.*) surplice; (*fam., innamoramento*) infatuation. **prendere una ~ per qcno.** have a crush on s.o.

co'ttimo *n.m.* piece-work.

co'tto *p.p. di* **cuocere.** **—***a.* done; (*infatuato*) in love; (*sbronzo*) drunk.

cottu'ra *n.f.* cooking.

cova're *v.t.* hatch; (*una malattia*) sicken for; (*odio*) harbour. **—***v.i.* smoulder.

co'vo *n.m.* den.

covo'ne *n.m.* sheaf.

co'zza *n.f.* mussel.

cozza're *v.i.* **~ contro** bump into.

co'zzo *n.m.* (*fig.*) clash.

cra'mpo *n.m.* cramp.

cra'nio *n.m.* skull.

crate're *n.m.* crater.

crava'tta *n.f.* tie; (*a farfalla*) bow-tie.

crea'nza *n.f.* politeness. **mala ~** bad manners.

crea'|re *v.t.* create; (*causare*) cause. **~ti'vo** *a.* creative. **~to're, ~tri'ce** *n.m., f.* creator. **~zio'ne** *n.f.* creation.

creatu'ra *n.f.* creature; (*bambino*) baby. **povera ~!** poor thing!

crede'nte *n.m./f.* believer.

crede'nza *n.f.* belief; (*comm.*) credit; (*mobile*) sideboard.

credenzia'li *n.f. pl.* credentials.

cre'd|ere *v.t.* believe; (*pensare*) think. **—***v.i.* **~ere in** believe in. **~o di sì** I think so. **non ti ~o** I don't believe you. **~ersi** *v.r.* think o.s. to be. **si ~e uno scrittore** he flatters himself he is a writer. **~i'bile** *a.* credible.

cre'di|to *n.m.* credit; (*stima*) esteem. **comprare a ~to** buy on credit. **~to're, ~tri'ce** *n.m., f.* creditor.

cre'do *n.m. invar.* credo.

cre'dul|o *a.* credulous. **~o'ne, a** *n.m., f.* simpleton.

cre'ma *n.f.* cream; (*di uova e latte*) custard.

crema'|re *v.t.* cremate. **~to'rio** *n.m.* crematorium. **~zio'ne** *n.f.* cremation.

Cremli'no *n.m.* Kremlin.

cre'pa *n.f.* crack. **~tu'ra** *n.f.* crevice.

crepa'ccio *n.m.* cleft; (*di ghiacciaio*) crevasse.

crepacuo're *n.m.* heart-break.

crepape'lle *adv.* **a ~** fit to burst. **ridere a ~** split one's sides with laughter.

crepa'|re *v.i.* crack; (*fam., morire*) kick the bucket. **~re dal ridere/ di salute** burst with laughter/ health.

crepita're *v.i.* crackle.

crepu'scolo *n.m.* twilight.

cresce'ndo *n.m.* crescendo.

cre'sc|ere *v.i.* grow; (*aumentare*) increase. —*v.t.* (*allevare*) bring up; (*aumentare*) raise. ~**ita** *n.f.* growth; increase. ~**iu'to** *p.p. di* crescere.

cre'sim|a *n.f.* confirmation. ~**a're** *v.t.* confirm.

cre'spa *n.f.* (*di vestito*) gather.

cre'spo *a.* (*capelli*) frizzy. —*n.m.* crêpe.

cre'sta *n.f.* crest; (*cima*) peak.

cre'ta *n.f.* clay.

Cre'ta *n.f.* Crete.

creti'no, a *a.* stupid. —*n.m.*, *f.* idiot.

cric *n.m.* jack.

cri'cca *n.f.* gang.

crimina'le *a.* & *n.m.|f.* criminal. **cri'mine** *n.m.* crime.

cri'n|e *n.m.* horsehair. ~**ie'ra** *n.f.* mane.

crinoli'na *n.f.* crinoline.

cri'pta *n.f.* crypt.

crisante'mo *n.m.* chrysanthemum.

cri'si *n.f. invar.* crisis; (*med.*) fit.

cristallizza'r|e *v.t.*, ~**si** *v.r.* crystallize.

crista'llo *n.m.* crystal.

cristia'n|o, a *a.* & *n.m.*, *f.* Christian. ~**e'simo** *n.m.* Christianity.

Cri'sto *n.m.* Christ.

crite'rio *n.m.* criterion; (*buon senso*) (common) sense.

cri'tic|a *n.f.* criticism; (*recensione*) review. ~**a're** *v.t.* criticize. ~**o** *a.* critical; *n.m.* critic; (*recensore*) reviewer.

crive'll|o *n.m.* sieve. ~**a're** *v.t.* riddle (**di,** with).

crocca'nte *a.* crisp.

crocche'tta *n.f.* croquette.

cro'ce *n.f.* cross. **a occhio e** ~ roughly. **fare testa e** ~ spin a coin.

crocevi'a *n.m. invar.* crossroads *s.*

crocia'ta *n.f.* crusade.

croci'cchio *n.m.* crossroads *s.*

crocie'ra *n.f.* cruise.

crocifi'|ggere *v.t.* crucify. ~**ssio'ne** *n.f.* crucifixion. ~**sso** *p.p. di* ~**ggere**; *a.* crucified; *n.m.* crucifix.

crogiola'rsi *v.r.* bask.

crogi(u)o'lo *n.m.* crucible; (*fig.*) melting pot.

crolla're *v.i.* collapse; (*di prezzi*) slump. **cro'llo** *n.m.* collapse; slump.

cro'm|o *n.m.* chrome. ~**a'to** *a.* chromium-plated.

cromoso'ma *n.m.* chromosome.

cro'naca *n.f.* chronicle; (*di giornale*) news; (*TV, radio*) commentary. ~ **nera** crime news.

cro'nico *a.* chronic.

croni'sta *n.m.|f.* reporter.

cronol|ogi'a *n.f.* chronology. ~**o'gico** *a.* chronological.

cronometra'|re *v.t.* time. ~**ggio** *n.m.* timing. **crono'metro** *n.m.* chronometer.

cro'sta *n.f.* crust; (*di formaggio*) rind; (*di ferita*) scab.

crosta'ceo *n.m.* shellfish.

crosta'ta *n.f.* tart.

crosti'no *n.m.* croûton.

cru'cci|o *n.m.* worry. ~**a'rsi** *v.r.* worry.

crucia'le *a.* crucial.

crucive'rba *n.m. invar.* crossword (puzzle).

crude'l|e *a.* cruel. ~**tà** *n.f.* cruelty.

cru'do *a.* raw; (*rigido*) harsh.

crumi'ro *n.m.* blackleg.

cru'sca *n.f.* bran.

crusco'tto *n.m.* dashboard.

Cu'ba *n.f.* Cuba.

cub|o *n.m.* cube. ~**ico** *a.* cubic.

cucca'gna *n.f.* abundance; (*baldoria*) merry-making. **paese della** ~ land of plenty.

cucce'tta *n.f.* (*su un treno*) couchette; (*naut.*) berth.

cucchia'|io *n.m.* spoon. ~**ia'ta** *n.f.* spoonful. ~**i'no** *n.m.* teaspoon, coffee spoon.

cu'ccia *n.f.* dog's bed. **fa la** ~**!** lie down!

cu'cciolo *n.m.* puppy.

cuci'na *n.f.* kitchen; (*il cucinare*) cooking; (*cibo*) food; (*apparecchio*) cooker. **far da** ~ cook. **libro di** ~ cookery book.

cucina're *v.t.* cook.

cuci're *v.t.* sew. **macchina per** ~ sewing-machine.

cucitu'ra *n.f.* seam.

cucu'lo *n.m.* cuckoo.

cu'ffia *n.f.* bonnet; (*da bagno*) bathing-cap; (*ricevitore*) headphones *pl.*

cugi'no, a *n.m.*, *f.* cousin.

cu'i *pron. rel.* (*persone*) who(m), that; (*cose e animali*) which, that. **di** ~ (*persone*) whose; (*cose e animali*) of which. **in** ~ (*dove*) where; (*quando*) when. **per** ~ (*perciò*) therefore.

culina'ria *n.f.* cookery.

cu'll|a *n.f.* cradle. ~**a're** *v.t.* rock.

culmin'a|re *v.i.* culminate. ~**nte** *a.* culminating. **cu'lmine** *n.m.* peak.

cu'lo *n.m.* (*sl.*) bum.
cu'lto *n.m.* cult; (*relig.*) religion; (*adorazione*) worship.
cultu'r|a *n.f.* culture. **~a'le** *a.* cultural.
cumulati'vo *a.* cumulative.
cu'mulo *n.m.* pile; (*mucchio*) heap. (*nuvola*) cumulus.
cu'neo *n.m.* wedge.
cune'tta *n.f.* gutter.
cuo'cere *v.t./i.* cook; (*mattoni ecc.*) bake.
cuo'co, a *n.m., f.* cook.
cuo'io *n.m.* leather. **~ capelluto** scalp.
cuo'r|e *n.m.* heart. **~i** *n.m. pl.* (*carte*) hearts. **nel profondo del ~e** in one's heart of hearts. **persona di buon ~e** kind-hearted person.
cupidi'gia *n.f.* greed.
cu'po *a.* gloomy; (*di suono*) deep.
cu'pola *n.f.* dome.
cu'r|a *n.f.* care; (*amministrazione*) management; (*med.*) treatment. **a ~a di** edited by. **in ~a** under treatment. **~a're** *v.t.* take care of; (*med.*) treat;

(*guarire*) cure; (*testo*) edit. **~a'rsi** *v.r.* take care of oneself; (*med.*) follow a treatment. **~arsi di** (*badare a*) mind.
cura'to *n.m.* parish priest.
cura|to're, ~tri'ce *n.m., f.* trustee; (*di testo*) editor.
cu'ria *n.f.* curia.
curio's|o *a.* curious; (*strano*) odd. **~a're** *v.i.* be curious; (*mettere il naso*) pry (into sthg.). **~ità** *n.f.* curiosity.
cu'rv|a *n.f.* curve; (*stradale*) bend. **~a're** *v.t.* curve; bend; (*il capo*) bow. **~a'rsi** *v.r.* bend. **~o** *a.* curved; (*piegato*) bent.
cusci'n|o *n.m.* cushion; (*guanciale*) pillow. **~e'tto** *n.m.* pad; (*mech.*) bearing. **~etto punta-spilli** pincushion.
cu'spide *n.f.* spire.
custo'de *n.m.* caretaker. **~ giudiziario** official receiver.
custo'dia *n.f.* care; (*legge*) custody; (*astuccio*) case.
custodi're *v.t.* keep; (*badare*) look after.
cu'te *n.f.* skin.
cuti'cola *n.f.* cuticle.

D

da *prep.* (*agente, causa*) by; (*da luogo*) from; (*a luogo*) to; (*in luogo*) at; (*per luogo*) through; (*tempo, durata*) for; (*fin da*) since; (*causale*) with; (*scopo*) as, for; (*come*) like; (*valore*) at. **ho molto ∼ fare** I have much to do. **piange dal dolore** she cries with pain. **qualcosa ∼ mangiare** something to eat. **scritto ∼** written by. **si è fatto ∼ sé** he is a self-made man. **vive ∼ re** he lives like a king.

dabba'sso *adv.* downstairs.

dabbe'ne *a.* honest.

dacca'po *adv.* again; (*dall'inizio*) from the beginning.

dacché *conj.* since.

da'do *n.m.* dice; (*culin.*) (stock) cube.

daffa're *n.m.* work.

da'gli = da + gli. **da'i** = da + i.

da'ino *n.m.* deer; (*pelle*) buckskin.

dal = da + il. **dalla** = da + la. **dalle** = da + le. **dallo** = da + lo.

da'lia *n.f.* dahlia.

d'altro'nde *adv.* on the other hand.

da'ma *n.f.* lady; (*nei balli*) partner; (*gioco*) draughts *s.*

damige'lla *n.f.* (*di sposa*) bridesmaid.

damigia'na *n.f.* demijohn.

dana'ro *n.m.* = denaro.

Danima'rca *n.f.* Denmark. **dane'se** *a.* Danish; *n.m./f.* Dane; *n.m.* (*lingua*) Danish.

danna'|re *v.t.* damn. **far ∼re qcno.** drive s.o. mad. **∼zio'ne** *n.f.* damnation.

danneggia're *v.t.* damage; (*nuocere*) harm.

da'nn|o *n.m.* damage; (*a persona*) harm. **∼o'so** *a.* harmful.

Danu'bio *n.m.* Danube.

da'nz|a *n.f.* dance; (*il danzare*) dancing. **∼a're** *v.i.* dance. **∼ato're, ∼atri'ce** *n.m., f.* dancer.

dappertu'tto *adv.* everywhere.

dappo'co *a.* worthless.

dappre'sso *adv.* (*vicino*) near; (*da vicino*) closely.

dappri'ma *adv.* at first.

da'rdo *n.m.* dart.

da'r|e *v.t.* give; (*produrre*) yield. —*v.i.* **∼e su** give on to. **∼si** *v.r.* **∼si a** give oneself to. **∼si al bere** take to drink.

∼si per vinto give up. **può ∼si** maybe. —*n.m.* (*comm.*) debit.

da'rsena *n.f.* dock.

da't|a *n.f.* date. **∼a're** *v.t.* date. **a ∼are da** as from.

da't|o *a.* given; (*dedito*) addicted. —*n.m.* datum. **∼i** *n.m. pl.* data. **∼o che** since. **∼o're** *n.m.* giver. **∼ore di lavoro** employer.

da'ttero *n.m.* date.

dattilografa're *v.t.* type. **∼i'a** *n.f.* typing. **dattilo'grafo, a** *n.m., f.* typist.

dava'nti *adv.* before; (*dirimpetto*) opposite; (*di fronte*) in front. —*a.* front. —*n.m.* front. **∼ a** *prep.* before, in front of.

davanza'le *n.m.* window sill.

dava'nzo *adv.* more than enough.

davve'ro *adv.* really. **per ∼** in earnest.

da'zio *n.m.* duty; (*ufficio*) customs *pl.*

d.C. *abbr.* (*di dopo Cristo*) AD.

de'a *n.f.* goddess.

debella're *v.t.* defeat.

debilita'|re *v.t.* weaken. **∼nte** *a.* weakening.

de'bi|to *a.* due. —*n.m.* debt. **∼to're, ∼tri'ce** *n.m., f.* debtor.

de'bol|e *a.* weak; (*luce*) dim; (*suono*) faint. —*n.m.* weak point; (*preferenza*) weakness. **∼e'zza** *n.f.* weakness.

deboscia'to *a.* debauched.

debutta're *v.i.* make one's début. **debu'tto** *n.m.* début.

decade'n|te *a.* decadent. **∼za** *n.f.* decline; (*legge*) loss.

decampa're *v.i.* decamp.

deca'no *n.m.* dean.

decanta're *v.t.* (*lodare*) praise.

decapita'|re *v.t.* behead. **∼zio'ne** *n.f.* beheading.

decappotta'bile *a.* convertible.

decedu'to *a.* deceased.

dece'nn|e *a. & n.m./f.* ten-year-old. **∼io** *n.m.* decade.

dece'n|te *a.* decent. **∼za** *n.f.* decency.

dece'sso *n.m.* death. **atto di ∼** death certificate.

deci'der|e *v.t.* decide; (*una questione*) settle. **∼si** *v.r.* make up one's mind.

decifra're *v.t.* decipher; (*documenti cifrati*) decode.

decima'le *a.* decimal.

decima're *v.t.* decimate.
de'cimo *a.* tenth.
deci'na *n.f.* ten. **una** ∼ (*circa dieci*) about ten.
decis|io'ne *n.f.* decision. ∼i'vo *a.* decisive. **deci'so** *p.p. di* **decidere**; *a.* decided.
declama're *v.t./i.* declaim.
declassa're *v.t.* downgrade.
declina'|re *v.t.* decline. —*v.i.* go down; (*tramontare*) set. ∼zio'ne *n.f.* (*gram.*) declension. **decli'no** *n.m.* decline.
decli'vio *n.m.* slope.
deco'll|o *n.m.* take-off. ∼a're *v.i.* take off.
decolora'|re *v.t.* bleach. ∼nte *n.m.* bleach.
decompo'|rre *v.t.*, ∼rsi *v.r.* decompose. ∼sizio'ne *n.f.* decomposition.
decongela're *v.t.* defrost.
decora'|re *v.t.* decorate. ∼ti'vo *a.* decorative. ∼to're, ∼tri'ce *n.m.*, *f.* decorator. ∼zio'ne *n.f.* decoration.
deco'r|o *n.m.* decorum. ∼o'so *a.* dignified.
deco'r|rere *v.i.* run. **a** ∼**rere da domani** starting from tomorrow. ∼**so** *p.p. di* **decorrere**; *n.m.* passing; (*med.*) course.
decre'pito *a.* decrepit.
decre'scere *v.i.* decrease; (*di prezzi*) go down; (*di acque*) subside.
decre't|o *n.m.* decree. ∼a're *v.t.* decree.
de'dalo *n.m.* maze.
de'dic|a *n.f.* dedication. ∼a're *v.t.* dedicate.
de'dito *a.* ∼ **a** given to; (*assorto*) engrossed in; (*vizi*) addicted to.
dedo'tto *p.p. di* **dedurre**.
dedu'|rre *v.t.* deduce; (*sottrarre*) deduct. ∼zio'ne *n.f.* deduction.
defalca're *v.t.* deduct.
defere'n|te *a.* deferential. ∼za *n.f.* deference.
deferi're *v.t.* (*legge*) remit.
defezio'ne *n.f.* defection.
deficie'n|te *a.* (*mancante*) deficient; (*med.*) mentally deficient. —*n.m./f.* mental defective; (*pej.*) half-wit. ∼za *n.f.* deficiency; (*lacuna*) gap; (*med.*) mental deficiency.
de'ficit *n.m. invar.* deficit.
defini'|re *v.t.* define; (*risolvere*) settle. ∼ti'vo *a.* definitive. ∼to *a.* definite. ∼zio'ne *n.f.* definition; settlement.
deflazio'ne *n.f.* deflation.
defle'ttere *v.i.* ∼ **da** deviate from.

deflu'sso *n.m.* downflow; (*di marea*) ebb.
deforma'r|e *v.t.* deform; (*fig.*) distort. ∼si *v.r.* lose its shape. **defo'rme** *a.* deformed. **deformità** *n.f.* deformity.
defrauda're *v.t.* defraud.
defu'nto, a *a.* & *n.m.*, *f.* deceased.
degenera'|re *v.i.* degenerate. ∼to, degene're *adjs.* degenerate.
dege'nte *a.* bedridden. —*n.m./f.* patient.
degli = **di** + **gli**.
degna'r|e *v.t./i.* deign. ∼si *v.r.* condescend.
de'gno *a.* worthy; (*meritevole*) deserving.
degrada'r|e *v.t.* degrade. ∼si *v.r.* lower oneself.
degusta'|re *v.t.* taste. ∼zio'ne *n.f.* tasting.
dei = **di** + **i. del** = **di** + **il**.
dela|to're, ∼**tri'ce** *n.m.*, *f.* (police) informer.
de'lega *n.f.* delegation; (*procura*) proxy.
delega'|re *v.t.* delegate. ∼to *n.m.* delegate. ∼zio'ne *n.f.* delegation.
delete'rio *a.* harmful.
delfi'no *n.m.* dolphin.
delibera're *v.t./i.* deliberate.
delica't|o *a.* delicate; (*salute*) frail; (*suono, colore*) soft. ∼e'zza *n.f.* delicacy; (*fragilità*) frailty; (*tatto*) tact.
delimita're *v.t.* delimit.
delinea'r|e *v.t.* outline. ∼si *v.r.* be outlined; (*fig.*) take shape.
delinque'n|te *n.m./f.* delinquent. ∼za *n.f.* delinquency.
deli'quio *n.m.* swoon.
delira're *v.i.* be delirious. **deli'rio** *n.m.* delirium; (*fig.*) frenzy.
deli'tt|o *n.m.* crime. ∼uo'so *a.* criminal.
deli'zi|a *n.f.* delight. ∼a're *v.t.* delight. ∼o'so *a.* delightful.
de'lla = **di** + **la. de'lle** = **di** + **le. de'llo** = **di** + **lo**.
de'lta *n.m. invar.* delta.
deltapla'no *n.m.* hang-glider.
delu'|dere *v.t.* disappoint. ∼sio'ne *n.f.* disappointment.
dema'gogo *n.m.* demagogue.
demarca're *v.t.* demarcate.
deme'n|te *a.* demented. ∼za *n.f.* madness.
democra'|tico *a.* democratic. ∼zi'a *n.f.* democracy.

democristia'no, a *a.* & *n.m.,f.* Christian Democrat.

demoli'|re *v.t.* demolish. **~zio'ne** *n.f.* demolition.

de'mone *n.m.* demon.

demo'nio *n.m.* demon.

demoralizza're *v.t.* demoralize.

dena'ro *n.m.* money.

denigra're *v.t.* denigrate.

denomina'|re *v.t.* name. **~to're** *n.m.* denominator. **~zio'ne** *n.f.* denomination.

denota're *v.t.* denote.

densità *n.f.* density. **de'nso** *a.* thick, dense.

de'nt|e *n.m.* tooth; (*di forchetta*) prong. **al ~e** (*culin.*) underdone. **~e del giudizio** wisdom tooth. **~a'rio** *a.* dental. **~a'ta** *n.f.* bite. **~ie'ra** *n.f.* denture.

dentifri'cio *n.m.* toothpaste.

denti'sta *n.m.|f.* dentist.

de'ntro *adv.* in, inside; (*in casa*) indoors. **da ~** from within. **qui ~** in here. *—prep.* in, inside; (*di tempo*) within, by. *—n.m.* inside.

denuda'r|e *v.t.* bare. **~si** *v.r.* strip.

denu'nci|a, denu'nzi|a *ns.f.* declaration; (*legge*) charge; (*dei redditi*) (income tax) return. **~a're** *v.t.* denounce; (*dichiarare*) declare; (*accusare*) accuse.

denutri|zio'ne *n.f.* malnutrition. **~i'to** *a.* underfed.

deodora'nte *a.* & *n.m.* deodorant.

deperi'|re *v.i.* waste away. **~bile** *a.* perishable. **~me'nto** *n.m.* wasting away; (*di merci*) deterioration.

depila'|re *v.t.* depilate. **~to'rio** *n.m.* depilatory.

deplor|a're *v.t.* deplore; (*dolersi di*) grieve (over). **~e'vole** *a.* deplorable.

depo'rre *v.t.* put (down); (*armi*) lay down; (*togliere da una carica*) depose; (*testimoniare*) testify.

deporta'|re *v.t.* deport. **~zio'ne** *n.f.* deportation.

deposit|a're *v.t.* deposit; (*lasciare in custodia*) leave; (*in magazzino*) store.

depo'sito *n.m.* deposit; (*luogo*) warehouse; (*mil.*) depot. **~o bagagli** left-luggage office.

deposizio'ne *n.f.* deposition; (*da una carica*) removal.

deprava'|to *a.* depraved. **~re** *v.t.* deprave. **~zio'ne** *n.f.* depravity.

depreca'|re *v.t.* deprecate. **~bile** *a.* deprecable.

depreda're *v.t.* plunder.

depressio'ne *n.f.* depression. **depre'sso** *p.p. di* **deprimere**; *a.* depressed.

deprezza'|re *v.t.* depreciate. **~me'nto** *n.m.* depreciation.

depri'm|ere *v.t.* depress. **~e'nte** *a.* depressing.

depura'|re *v.t.* purify. **~to're** *n.m.* purifier.

deputa'|re *v.t.* delegate. **~to, a** *n.m., f.* deputy, Member of Parliament. **~zio'ne** *n.f.* deputation.

deraglia'|re *v.i.* go off the lines. **far ~re** derail. **~me'nto** *n.m.* derailment.

dereli'tto *a.* derelict.

dereta'no *n.m.* backside, bottom.

deri'|dere *v.t.* deride. **~sio'ne** *n.f.* derision. **~so'rio** *a.* derisory.

deri'va *n.f.* drift. **andare alla ~** drift.

deriva'|re *v.i.* **~re da** (*provenire*) derive from. *—v.t.* derive; (*sviare*) divert. **~zio'ne** *n.f.* derivation; diversion.

deroga're *v.i.* **~ a** depart from.

derra't|a *n.f.* merchandise. **~e alimentari** foodstuffs.

deruba're *v.t.* rob.

descri'tto *p.p. di* **descrivere**.

descri'|vere *v.t.* describe. **~tti'vo** *a.* descriptive. **~zio'ne** *n.f.* description.

dese'rto *a.* uninhabited. *—n.m.* desert.

desiderare *v.t.* wish; (*volere*) want; (*intensamente*) long for; (*bramare*) desire. **lasciare a ~** come short of expectations.

deside'r|io *n.m.* wish; (*brama*) desire; (*intenso*) longing. **~o'so** *a.* desirous; (*bramoso*) longing.

designa're *v.t.* designate; (*fissare*) fix.

desina're *v.i.* dine. *—n.m.* dinner.

desine'nza *n.f.* ending.

desi'stere *v.i.* **~ da** desist from.

desola'|re *v.t.* distress. **~to** desolate; (*spiacente*) sorry. **~zio'ne** *n.f.* desolation.

de'spota *n.m.* despot.

desta'r|e *v.t.* awake. **~si** *v.r.* wake up. **de'sto** *a.* awake.

destina'|re *v.t.* destine; (*nominare*) appoint; (*assegnare*) assign; (*indirizzare*) address. **~zio'ne** *n.f.* destination; (*fig.*) purpose.

desti'no *n.m.* destiny; (*fato*) fate.

destitu|i're *v.t.* dismiss. **~zio'ne** *n.f.* dismissal.

de'stra *n.f.* (*parte*) right; (*mano*) right hand. **prendere a ~** turn right.

destreggia'r|e *v.i.*, **~si** *v.r.* manœuvre.

destre'zza *n.f.* dexterity; (*abilità*) skill.

de'stro *a.* right; (*abile*) skilful.

deten|e're *v.t.* hold; (*tenere prigioniero*) detain. **~u'to, a** *n.m.*, *f.* prisoner. **~zio'ne** *n.f.* detention.

deterge'nte *n.m.* detergent.

deteriora'|re *v.t.*, **~rsi** *v.r.* deteriorate. **~me'nto** *n.m.* deterioration.

determina'|re *v.t.* determine. **~rsi** *v.r.* **~rsi a** resolve to. **~nte** *a.* decisive. **~zio'ne** *n.f.* determination; (*decisione*) decision.

deterre'nte *a.* & *n.m.* deterrent.

detersi'vo *n.m.* detergent.

detesta're *v.t.* detest.

detona're *v.i.* detonate.

detra'rre *v.t.* deduct (**da**, from).

detrime'nto *n.m.* detriment. **a ~ di** detrimental to.

detri'to *n.m.* debris.

dettaglia'nte *n.m.|f.* (*comm.*) retailer.

detta'gli|o *n.m.* detail. **al ~o** (*comm.*) retail. **~a're** *v.t.* detail.

detta'|re *v.t.* dictate. **~to** *n.m.*, **~tu'ra** *n.f.* dictation.

de'tto *a.* said; (*chiamato*) called; (*soprannominato*) nicknamed. **~ fatto** no sooner said than done. **—*n.m.*** saying.

deturpa'|re *v.t.* disfigure. **~zio'ne** *n.f.* disfigurement.

devasta'|re *v.t.* devastate; (*fig.*) ravage. **~zio'ne** *n.f.* devastation; ravages *pl.*

devia'|re *v.i.* deviate. **—*v.t.*** divert. **~zio'ne** *n.f.* deviation; (*stradale*) diversion.

devolu'|to *p.p. di* **devolvere**. **—*a.*** devolved. **~zio'ne** *n.f.* devolution.

devo'lvere *v.t.* devolve.

devo'|to *a.* devout; (*affezionato*) devoted. **~zio'ne** *n.f.* devotion.

di *prep.* of; (*un po'*) some; (*negativo*, *inter.*) any; (*possessivo*) 's; (*scritto da*) by. **~ domenica** on Sundays. **~ sera** in the evening. **dire ~ sì** say yes. **la macchina ~ mia figlia** my daughter's car. **piangere ~ dolore** cry with pain.

diabe't|e *n.m.* diabetes. **~ico, a** *a.* & *n.m.*, *f.* diabetic.

diabo'lico *a.* diabolic(al).

dia'cono *n.m.* deacon.

diade'ma *n.m.* diadem; (*di donna*) tiara.

dia'fano *a.* diaphanous.

diafra'mma *n.m.* diaphragm; (*divisione*) screen.

dia'gnos|i *n.f.* diagnosis. **~tica're** *v.t.* diagnose.

diagona'le *a.* & *n.f.* diagonal.

diagra'mma *n.m.* diagram.

diale'tto *n.m.* dialect.

dia'lisi *n.f.* dialysis.

dia'logo *n.m.* dialogue.

diama'nte *n.m.* diamond.

dia'metro *n.m.* diameter.

dia'mine *int.* **che ~ ...** what on earth ...

diapositi'va *n.f.* transparency; slide.

dia'rio *n.m.* diary.

diarre'a *n.f.* diarrhoea.

dia'volo *n.m.* devil.

diba'tt|ere *v.t.* debate. **~ersi** *v.r.* struggle. **~ito** *n.m.* debate; (*meno formale*) discussion.

dicaste'ro *n.m.* office.

dice'mbre *n.m.* December.

diceri'a *n.f.* rumour.

dichiara'|re *v.t.* declare. **~zio'ne** *n.f.* declaration.

dicianno've *a.* & *n.m.* nineteen.

diciasse'tte *a.* & *n.m.* seventeen.

dicio'tto *a.* & *n.m.* eighteen.

dicitu'ra *n.f.* wording.

dida'ttico *a.* didactic.

die'ci *a.* & *n.m.* ten.

die't|a *n.f.* diet. **essere a ~a** be on a diet. **~i'sta** *n.m.|f.* dietitian.

die'tro *adv.* behind. **—*prep.*** behind; (*dopo*) after. **—*a.*** back; (*di zampe*) hind. **—*n.m.*** back. **le stanze di ~** the back rooms. **le zampe di ~** the hind legs.

difa'tti *adv.* in fact.

dife'n|dere *v.t.* defend. **~si'va** *n.f.* **stare sulla ~siva** be on the defensive. **~si'vo** *a.* defensive. **~so're** *n.m.* defender. **avvocato ~sore** defence counsel.

dife'sa *n.f.* defence.

dife'so *p.p. di* **difendere**.

difett|a're *v.i.* be defective. **~are di** lack. **~i'vo** *a.* defective.

dife'tt|o *n.m.* defect; (*morale*) fault; (*mancanza*) lack. **essere in ~o** be at fault. **~o'so** *a.* defective; faulty.

diffama'|re *v.t.* (*con parole*) slander; (*per iscritto*) libel. **~zio'ne** *n.f.* slander; libel.

differe'n|te *a.* different. **~za** *n.f.* difference. **a ~za di** unlike.

differenzia'|le *a.* & *n.m.* differential. **~re** *v.t.* differentiate. **~rsi da** differ from.

differi're *v.t.* postpone. *—v.i.* be different.

diffi'cile *a.* difficult; (*duro*) hard; (*improbabile*) unlikely. *—n.m.* difficulty.

difficoltà *n.f.* difficulty. **trovarsi in ~** be in trouble.

diffi'da *n.f.* warning.

diffid|a're *v.i.* **~are di** distrust. *—v.t.* warn. **~e'nte** *a.* mistrustful. **~e'nza** *n.f.* mistrust.

diffo'nder|e *v.t.* spread; (*calore, luce, ecc.*) diffuse. **~si** *v.r.* spread.

diffusio'ne *n.f.* diffusion; (*di giornale*) circulation.

diffu'so *p.p. di* **diffondere.**

difila'to *adv.* straight; (*subito*) straightaway.

difteri'te *n.f.* diphtheria.

di'ga *n.f.* dam; (*argine*) dike.

dige|ri're *v.t.* digest. **~stio'ne** *n.f.* digestion. **~sti'vo** *a.* digestive; *n.m.* digestive; (*dopo cena*) liqueur.

digita'le *a.* digital; (*delle dita*) finger. *—n.f.* (*fiore*) foxglove.

digiu'n|o *a.* **essere ~o** have an empty stomach. *—n.m.* fast. **a ~o** on an empty stomach. **~a're** *v.i.* fast.

dignit|à *n.f.* dignity. **~a'rio** *n.m.* dignitary. **~o'so** *a.* dignified.

digressio'ne *n.f.* digression.

digrigna're *v.i.* **~ i denti** grind one's teeth.

dilaga're *v.i.* flood; (*fig.*) spread.

dilania're *v.t.* tear to pieces.

dilapida're *v.t.* squander.

dilata'r|e *v.t.*, **~si** *v.r.* dilate.

dilaziona're *v.t.* delay. **dilazio'ne** *n.f.* delay.

dileggia're *v.t.* mock. **dile'ggio** *n.m.* mockery.

dilegua'r|e *v.t.* disperse. **~si** *v.r.* disappear.

dile'mma *n.m.* dilemma.

diletta'nte *n.m./f.* amateur.

diletta'r|e *v.t.* delight. **~si** *v.r.* **~si di** delight in.

dile'tto, a *a.* beloved. *—n.m.* (*piacere*) delight. *—n.m., f.* (*persona*) beloved.

dilige'n|te *a.* diligent. **~za** *n.f.* diligence; (*carrozza*) stage-coach.

dilui're *v.t.* dilute.

dilunga'r|e *v.t.* prolong. **~si** *v.r.* **~si su** (*argomento*) dwell on.

dilu'vi|o *n.m.* downpour; (*fig.*) flood. **~a're** *v.i.* pour (down).

dimagri're *v.i.* slim.

dimena'r|e *v.t.* wave; (*la coda*) wag. **~si** *v.r.* be agitated.

dimensio'ne *n.f.* dimension; (*misura*) size.

dimentica'|re *v.t.*, **~rsi** *v.r.* forget. **~nza** *n.f.* forgetfulness; (*svista*) oversight.

dime'sso *p.p. di* **dimettere.** *—a.* humble; (*trasandato*) shabby; (*voce*) low.

dimestiche'zza *n.f.* familiarity.

dime'tter|e *v.t.* dismiss; (*da ospedale ecc.*) discharge. **~si** *v.r.* resign.

dimezza're *v.t.* halve.

diminu|i're *v.t./i.* diminish. **~zio'ne** *n.f.* decrease; (*riduzione*) reduction.

diminuti'vo *a.* & *n.m.* diminutive.

dimissio'ni *n.f. pl.* resignation *s.* **dare le ~** resign.

dimo'r|a *n.f.* residence. **~a're** *v.i.* reside.

dimostra'|re *v.t.* demonstrate; (*provare*) prove; (*mostrare*) show. **~rsi** *v.r.* prove (to be). **~nte** *n.m./f.* demonstrator. **~ti'vo** *a.* demonstrative. **~zio'ne** *n.f.* demonstration.

dina'm|ico, a *a.* dynamic. *—n.f.* dynamics *s.* **~i'smo** *n.m.* dynamism.

dinami'te *n.f.* dynamite.

di'namo *n.f. invar.* dynamo.

dina'nzi *adv.* in front. *—prep.* **~ a** in front of.

dinasti'a *n.f.* dynasty.

dinie'go *n.m.* denial.

dinoccola'to *a.* lanky.

dinosa'uro *n.m.* dinosaur.

dinto'rn|o *adv.* around. **~i** *n.m. pl.* outskirts. **nei ~i di** in the vicinity of.

di'o *n.m.* (*pl.* **de'i**) god. **D~** God.

dio'cesi *n.f.* diocese.

dipana're *v.t.* wind into a ball; (*fig.*) unravel.

dipartime'nto *n.m.* department.

dipende'n|te *a.* depending. *—n.m./f.* employee. **~za** *n.f.* dependence; (*edificio*) annexe.

dipe'ndere *v.i.* **~ da** depend on; (*provenire*) derive from.

dipi'nger|e *v.t.* paint; (*descrivere*) describe. **~si** *v.r.* (*truccarsi*) make up.

dipi'nto *p.p. di* **~e**; *a.* painted; *n.m.* painting.

diplo'ma *n.m.* diploma.

diploma'|tico *a.* diplomatic. *—n.m.* diplomat. **~zi'a** *n.f.* diplomacy.

dipo'rto *n.m.* recreation. **imbarcazione da** ~ pleasure craft.

dirada'r|e *v.t.* thin out; (*visite*) make less frequent. ~**si** *v.r.* thin out; (*di nebbia*) clear.

dirama'r|e *v.t.* issue. —*v.i.*, ~**si** *v.r.* branch out; (*diffondersi*) spread.

di're *v.t.* say; (*raccontare, riferire*) tell; (*parlare*) speak. **dir bene di** speak highly of. ~ **di sì** say yes. **mi si dice che** I am told that. **per modo di** ~ as it were.

diretti'ssimo *n.m.* fast train.

diretti'va *n.f.* directive.

dire'tto *p.p. di* **dirigere.** —*a.* direct. ~ **a** (*inteso*) meant for. **essere** ~ **a** be going to. **in diretta** (*trasmissione*) live. —*n.m.* (*treno*) through train.

diret|to're, ~**tri'ce** *n.m., f.* manager, -ess; (*di scuola*) headmaster, -mistress. ~**tore d'orchestra** conductor.

direzio'ne *n.f.* direction; (*di società*) management.

dirige'nte *a.* ruling. —*n.m.|f.* executive; (*pol.*) leader.

diri'ger|e *v.t.* direct; (*orchestra*) conduct; (*impresa*) run. ~**si** *v.r.* ~**si verso** make for.

dirigi'bile *n.m.* airship.

dirimpe'tto *adv.* opposite. —*prep.* ~ **a** facing.

diri'tto[1], **dritto** *adjs.* straight; (*destro*) right. —*advs.* straight. **andare** ~ go straight on. —*ns.m.* right side.

diri'tt|o[2] *n.m.* right; (*legge*) law. ~**i d'autore** royalties.

dirittu'ra *n.f.* straight line.

dirocca'|re *v.t.* demolish. ~**to** *a.* tumbledown.

dirotta'|re *v.t.* alter the course of; (*aereo, abusivamente*) skyjack; (*traffico*) divert. —*v.i.* alter course. ~**to're**, ~**tri'ce** *n.m., f.* skyjacker.

diro'tto *a.* (*pioggia*) pouring; (*pianto*) uncontrollable. **piovere a** ~ rain heavily.

diru'po *n.m.* precipice.

disabita'to *a.* uninhabited.

disabitua'rsi *v.r.* ~ **a** get out of the habit of.

disacco'rdo *n.m.* disagreement.

disadatta'to, a *a.* maladjusted. —*n.m., f.* misfit.

disada'tto *a.* unsuitable.

disado'rno *a.* unadorned.

disa'gi|o *n.m.* discomfort; (*difficoltà*) inconvenience; (*imbarazzo*) embarrassment. ~ *n.m. pl.* (*privazioni*) hardships. **sentirsi a** ~**o** feel uncomfortable. ~**a'to** *a.* poor; (*vita*) hard.

disamora'r|e *v.t.* estrange. ~**si** *v.r.* ~**si di** fall out of love with.

disapprova'|re *v.t.* disapprove (of). ~**zio'ne** *n.f.* disapproval.

disappu'nto *n.m.* disappointment.

disarma're *v.t.|i.* disarm. **disa'rmo** *n.m.* disarmament.

disa'str|o *n.m.* disaster. ~**a'to, a** *a.* devastated; *n.m., f.* victim. ~**o'so** *a.* disastrous.

disatte'n|to *a.* inattentive. ~**zio'ne** *n.f.* inattention; (*svista*) oversight.

disava'nzo *n.m.* deficit.

disavvedu'to *a.* thoughtless.

disavventu'ra *n.f.* misadventure.

disavverte'nza *n.f.* inadvertence.

disbri'g|o *n.m.* dispatch. ~**a're** *v.t.* settle.

disca'pito *n.m.* disadvantage. **a** ~ **di** to the detriment of.

discenden|te *a.* descending. —*n.m.|f.* descendant. ~**za** *n.f.* descent; (*discendenti*) descendants *pl.*

disce'ndere *v.t.|i.* descend; (*dal treno*) get off; (*da cavallo*) dismount; (*sbarcare*) land. ~ **da** (*trarre origine*) be a descendant of.

disce'polo, a *n.m., f.* disciple.

disce'rn|ere *v.t.* discern. ~**ime'nto** *n.m.* discernment.

disce's|a *n.f.* descent; (*pendio*) slope. ~**a in picchiata** (*di aereo*) nosedive. **essere in** ~**a** (*di strada*) go downhill. ~**o** *p.p. di* **discendere.**

dischiu'dere *v.t.* open; (*svelare*) disclose.

disci'nto *a.* scantily dressed.

discio'glier|e *v.t.*, ~**si** *v.r.* dissolve; (*di neve*) thaw; (*fondersi*) melt. **discio'lto** *p.p. di* ~**e.**

discipli'n|a *n.f.* discipline. ~**a're** *a.* disciplinary; *v.t.* discipline.

di'sco *n.m.* disc; (*sport*) discus; (*mus.*) record. ~ **volante** flying saucer. **ernia del** ~ slipped disc.

di'scolo *a.* unruly.

discolpa'r|e *v.t.* clear. ~**si** *v.r.* clear oneself.

discono'scere *v.t.* refuse to acknowledge; (*figlio*) disown.

disconti'nuo *a.* intermittent.

discorda'nte *a.* discordant.

disco'rde *a.* clashing.

disco'rdia *n.f.* discord.

disco'rrere *v.i.* ~ (**di**) talk (about).

disco'rso *p.p. di* **discorrere.** —*n.m.* speech; (*conversazione*) talk.

disco'sto *a.* distant. —*adv.* far away. **stare** ~ stand apart.

discote'ca *n.f.* discothèque; (*raccolta*) record library.

discre'dit|o *n.m.* discredit. ~**a're** *v.t.* discredit.

discrepa'n|za *n.f.* discrepancy. ~**te** *a.* contradictory.

discre'|to *a.* discreet; (*moderato*) moderate; (*abbastanza buono*) fairly good. ~**zio'ne** *n.f.* discretion; (*giudizio*) judgement.

discrimina'|re *v.t.* discriminate. ~**zio'ne** *n.f.* discrimination.

discussio'ne *n.f.* discussion; (*alterco*) argument. **discu'sso** *p.p. di* **discutere.**

discu't|ere *v.t.* discuss; (*formale*) debate; (*litigare*) argue. ~**ere sul prezzo** bargain. ~**i'bile** *a.* debatable; (*gusto*) questionable.

disdegna're *v.t.* disdain. **disde'gno** *n.m.* disdain.

disde'tt|a *n.f.* retraction; (*sfortuna*) bad luck; (*comm.*) cancellation. ~**o** *p.p. di* **disdire.**

disdice'vole *a.* unbecoming.

disdi're *v.t.* retract; (*annullare*) cancel.

disegna'|re *v.t.* draw; (*progettare*) design. ~**to're,** ~**tri'ce** *n.m., f.* designer. **dise'gno** *n.m.* drawing; design.

disereda're *v.t.* disinherit.

diser|ta're *v.t./i.* desert. ~**tare la scuola** stay away from school. ~**to're** *n.m.* deserter. ~**zio'ne** *n.f.* desertion.

disfa'|re *v.t.* undo; (*strappando*) rip open; (*letto*) strip; (*valigie*) unpack; (*smantellare*) take down; (*annientare*) defeat. ~**rsi** *v.r.* fall to pieces; (*sciogliersi*) melt. ~**rsi di** (*liberarsi*) get rid of. ~**rsi in lacrime** dissolve into tears. ~**tta** *n.f.* defeat. ~**tto** *a.* (*fig.*) worn out.

disfatti's|mo *n.m.* defeatism. ~**ta** *n.m./f.* defeatist.

disfunzio'ne *n.f.* disorder.

disge'l|o *n.m.* thaw. ~**a're** *v.t./i.,* ~**arsi** *v.r.* thaw.

disgiu'ngere *v.t.* disconnect.

disgra'zi|a *n.f.* misfortune; (*incidente*) accident; (*sfavore*) disgrace. ~**a'to, a** *a.* unfortunate; *n.m., f.* wretch.

disgrega'r|e *v.t.* break up. ~**si** *v.r.* disintegrate.

disgui'do *n.m.* ~ **postale** mistake in delivery.

disgust|a're *v.t.* disgust. ~**a'rsi** *v.r.* ~**arsi di** be disgusted by. **disgu'sto** *n.m.* disgust. ~**o'so** *a.* disgusting.

disidrata're *v.t.* dehydrate.

disillu'|dere *v.t.* disenchant. ~**sio'ne** *n.f.* disenchantment.

disimballa're *v.t.* unpack.

disimpara're *v.t.* forget.

disimpegna'r|e *v.t.* release; (*compiere*) fulfil; (*oggetto dato in pegno*) redeem. ~**si** *v.r.* disengage oneself; (*cavarsela*) manage.

disinfe|tta're *v.t.* disinfect. ~**tta'nte** *a. & n.m.* disinfectant. ~**zio'ne** *n.f.* disinfection.

disinganna're *v.t.* disabuse.

disintegra'|re *v.t.,* ~**rsi** *v.r.* disintegrate. ~**zio'ne** *n.f.* disintegration.

disinteressa'rsi *v.r.* ~ **di** take no interest in. **disintere'sse** *n.m.* indifference; (*altruismo*) unselfishness.

disinvo'lt|o *a.* natural. ~**u'ra** *n.f.* confidence.

disle'ssia *n.f.* dyslexia.

dislive'llo *n.m.* difference in height; (*fig.*) inequality.

disloca're *v.t.* (*mil.*) post.

dismisu'ra *n.f.* excess. **a** ~ excessively.

disobbliga'rsi *v.r.* return s.o.'s kindness.

disoccupa'|to, a *a.* unemployed. —*n.m., f.* unemployed person. ~**zio'ne** *n.f.* unemployment.

disone'st|o *a.* dishonest. ~**à** *n.f.* dishonesty.

disonora're *v.t.* dishonour. **diso-no're** *n.m.* dishonour.

diso'pra *adv.* above. —*a.* upper. —*n.m.* top.

diso'rdin|e *n.m.* disorder, untidiness; (*sregolatezza*) debauchery. ~**a're** *v.t.* disarrange. ~**a'to** *a.* untidy; (*sregolato*) immoderate.

disorganizza'|re *v.t.* disorganize. ~**to** *a.* disorganized.

disorienta'|re *v.t.* disorientate. ~**rsi** *v.r.* lose one's bearings. ~**to** *a.* (*fig.*) bewildered.

disossa're *v.t.* bone.

diso'tto *adv.* below. —*a.* lower. —*n.m.* bottom.

dispa'ccio *n.m.* dispatch.

dispara'to *a.* disparate.

di'spari *a.* odd, uneven.

disparità *n.f.* disparity.

dispa'rte *adv.* in ~ apart. **stare in** ~ stand aside.

dispendio'so *a.* expensive.

dispe'ns|a *n.f.* pantry; (*distribuzione*) distribution; (*mobile*) cupboard; (*legge*) exemption; (*relig.*) dispensation; (*pubblicazione periodica*) number. ~**a're** *v.t.* distribute; grant a dispensation; (*esentare*) exonerate.

dispera'|re *v.i.* ~**re (di)** despair (of). ~**rsi** *v.r.* despair. ~**to** *a.* desperate. ~**zio'ne** *n.f.* despair.

dispe'r|dere *v.t.*, ~**dersi** *v.r.* scatter, disperse. ~**sio'ne** *n.f.* dispersion; (*di truppe*) dispersal. ~**so** *p.p. di* **disperdere**; *a.* scattered; (*smarrito*) lost; *n.m.* missing soldier.

dispe'tt|o *n.m.* spite. **a** ~**o di** in spite of. **fare un** ~**o a** qcno. spite s.o. ~**o'so** *a.* spiteful.

dispiac|e're *n.m.* upset; (*rammarico*) regret; (*dolore*) sorrow; (*preoccupazione*) worry. —*v.i.* ~**ere a** displease; (*essere spiacente*) be sorry; (*rammaricarsi*) regret; (*essere sgradito*) dislike. **non mi** ~**e** I don't dislike it. **se non ti** ~**e** if you don't mind. ~**iu'to** *a.* upset; (*dolente*) sorry.

disponi'bil|e *a.* available; (*di persona*) free. ~**ità** *n.f.* availability.

dispo'r|re *v.t.* arrange. —*v.i.* dispose; (*stabilire*) order. ~**re di** have at one's disposal. ~**si** *v.r.* (*in fila*) line up.

dispositi'vo *n.m.* device.

disposizio'ne *n.f.* disposition; (*ordine*) order; (*libera disponibilità*) disposal. **dispo'sto** *p.p. di* **disporre**; *a.* ready; (*incline*) disposed. **essere ben disposto verso** be favourably disposed towards.

dispo'tico *a.* despotic.

dispregiati'vo *a.* disparaging.

disprezza're *v.t.* despise. **dispre'zzo** *n.m.* contempt.

di'sput|a *n.f.* dispute. ~**a're** *v.i.* dispute; (*gareggiare*) compete. ~**a'rsi** *v.r.* contend with each other.

dissangua'|re *v.t.*, ~**rsi** *v.r.* bleed. ~**me'nto** *n.m.* loss of blood.

disse|ca're *v.t.* dissect. ~**zio'ne** *n.f.* dissection.

dissecca'r|e *v.t.*, ~**si** *v.r.* dry up.

dissemina're *v.t.* disseminate; (*notizie*) spread.

disse'nso *n.m.* dissent; (*disaccordo*) disagreement.

dissenteri'a *n.f.* dysentery.

dissenti're *v.i.* ~ (**da**) disagree (with).

dissertazio'ne *n.f.* dissertation.

disservi'zio *n.m.* poor service.

dissesta're *v.t.* upset; (*comm.*) damage. **disse'sto** *n.m.* ruin.

disseta're *v.t.* quench s.o.'s thirst. ~**nte** *a.* thirst-quenching.

disside'nte *a.* & *n.m.|f.* dissident.

dissi'dio *n.m.* disagreement.

dissi'mile *a.* unlike, dissimilar.

dissimula're *v.t.* conceal; (*fingere*) dissimulate.

dissipa'|re *v.t.* dissipate; (*sperperare*) squander. ~**to** *a.* dissipated. ~**zio'ne** *n.f.* squandering.

dissocia'r|e *v.t.*, ~**si** *v.r.* dissociate.

disso'lto *p.p. di* **dissolvere**.

dissolu'bile *a.* dissoluble.

dissolu'to *a.* dissolute.

disso'lver|e *v.t.*, ~**si** *v.r.* dissolve; (*disperdere*) dispel.

dissona'nte *a.* dissonant.

dissua|de're *v.t.* dissuade. ~**sio'ne** *n.f.* dissuasion.

distacca'r|e *v.t.* detach; (*sport*) leave behind. ~**si** *v.r.* be detached. **dista'cco** *n.m.* detachment; (*separazione*) separation; (*sport*) lead.

dista'n|te *a.* & *adv.* far away. ~**za** *n.f.* distance.

distanzia're *v.t.* space out; (*sport*) outdistance.

dista're *v.i.* be distant. **quanto dista?** how far is it?

diste'n|dere *v.t.* (*parte del corpo*) stretch (out); (*spiegare*) spread; (*deporre*) lay. ~**dersi** *v.r.* stretch; (*sdraiarsi*) lie down; (*rilassarsi*) relax. ~**sio'ne** *n.f.* stretching; (*rilassamento*) relaxation; (*pol.*) détente. ~**si'vo** *a.* relaxing.

diste'so, a *p.p. di* **distendere**. —*n.f.* expanse.

distill|a're *v.t./i.* distil. ~**eri'a** *n.f.* distillery.

disti'nguer|e *v.t.* distinguish. ~**si** *v.r.* distinguish oneself.

distinti'vo *a.* distinctive. —*n.m.* badge.

disti'nt|o, a *p.p. di* **distinguere**. —*a.* distinct; (*signorile*) distinguished. ~**i saluti** Yours faithfully. ~**a** *n.f.* (*comm.*) list. ~**a di versamento** paying-in slip.

distinzio'ne *n.f.* distinction.

disto'gliere *v.t.* ~ **da** (*allontanare*)

remove from; (*dissuadere*) dissuade from.

disto'lto *p.p. di* **distogliere.**

disto'rcere *v.t.* twist.

distorsio'ne *n.f.* (*med.*) sprain; (*alterazione*) distortion.

distra'|rre *v.t.* distract; (*divertire*) amuse. ~**rsi** *v.r.* (*svagarsi*) amuse oneself. ~**tto** *a.* absent-minded; (*disattento*) inattentive. ~**zio'ne** *n.f.* absent-mindedness; inattention; (*svago*) amusement.

distre'tto *n.m.* district.

distribu'|i're *v.t.* distribute; (*disporre*) arrange; (*carte*) deal. ~**to're** *n.m.* distributor; (*di benzina*) petrol pump; (*automatico*) slot-machine. ~**zio'ne** *n.f.* distribution.

districa're *v.t.* disentangle.

distru'|ggere *v.t.* destroy. ~**tti'vo** *a.* destructive. ~**tto** *p.p. di* ~**ggere**; *a.* destroyed. **un uomo** ~**tto** a broken man. ~**zio'ne** *n.f.* destruction.

disturba'r|e *v.t.* disturb; (*sconvolgere*) upset. ~**si** *v.r.* trouble oneself. **disturbo** *n.m.* bother; (*indisposizione*) trouble; (*radio, TV*) interference. **disturbi** *n.m. pl.* (*radio, TV*) static *s.*

disubbidi'|re *v.i.* ~**re a** disobey. ~**e'nte** *a.* disobedient. ~**e'nza** *n.f.* disobedience.

disugua'le *a.* unequal; (*irregolare*) irregular.

disuma'no *a.* inhuman.

disuni're *v.t.* divide.

disu'so *n.m.* disuse.

dita'le *n.m.* thimble.

di't|o *n.m.* (*pl.f.* **dita**) finger; (*del piede*) toe. ~**a'ta** *n.f.* finger-mark.

di'tta *n.f.* firm.

ditta'fono *n.m.* dictaphone.

dittat|o're *n.m.* dictator. ~**u'ra** *n.f.* dictatorship.

ditto'ngo *n.m.* diphthong.

diu'rno *a.* daytime. **spettacolo** ~ matinée.

divaga'|re *v.i.* digress. ~**zio'ne** *n.f.* digression.

divampa're *v.i.* burst into flames.

diva'no *n.m.* settee, sofa.

divarica're *v.t.* open (out); (*gambe*) straddle.

diva'rio *n.m.* discrepancy.

diven|i're *v.i.* = **diventare.** ~**u'to** *p.p. di* ~**ire.**

diventa're *v.i.* become; (*lentamente*) grow; (*rapidamente*) turn.

dive'rbio *n.m.* squabble.

dive'rg|ere *v.i.* diverge. ~**e'nte** divergent. ~**e'nza** *n.f.* divergence.

diversifica're *v.t.* diversify.

divers|io'ne *n.f.*, ~**i'vo** *n.m.* diversion.

dive'rs|o *a.* different. ~**i** *pl.* (*parecchi*) several; *pron.* several (people). ~**ità** *n.f.* difference.

divert|i're *v.t.* amuse. ~**i'rsi** *v.r.* enjoy oneself. ~**e'nte** *a.* amusing. ~**ime'nto** *n.m.* amusement; (*passatempo*) pastime.

divide'ndo *n.m.* dividend.

divi'der|e *v.t.* divide; (*condividere*) share. ~**si** *v.r.* (*separarsi*) separate.

divie'to *n.m.* prohibition. ~ **di sosta** no parking.

divina'|re *v.t.* divine. ~**to're** *n.m.* diviner.

divincola'rsi *v.r.* wriggle.

divi'n|o *a.* divine. ~**ità** *n.f.* divinity.

divi'sa *n.f.* uniform; (*comm.*) currency.

divis|io'ne *n.f.* division. ~**o're** *n.m.* divisor. ~**o'rio** *a.* dividing.

divi'so *p.p. di* **dividere.**

di'v|o, a *n.m.,f.* star. ~**i'smo** *n.m.* star cult.

divora'r|e *v.t.* devour. ~**si** *v.r.* ~**si da** be consumed with.

divo'rzi|o *n.m.* divorce. ~**a're** *v.i.* divorce. ~**a'to, a** *n.m.,f.* divorcee.

divulga'r|e *v.t.* divulge; (*rendere popolare*) popularize. ~**si** *v.r.* spread.

diziona'rio *n.m.* dictionary.

dizio'ne *n.f.* diction.

do *n.m.* (*mus.*) doh.

do'ccia *n.f.* shower; (*grondaia*) gutter.

doce'n|te *a.* teaching. — *n.m.,f.* teacher; (*di università*) lecturer. ~**za** *n.f.* university teacher's qualification.

do'cile *a.* docile.

documenta'r|e *v.t.* document. ~**si** *v.r.* ~**si (su)** gather information (about).

docume'nt|o *n.m.* document. ~**a'rio** *a. & n.m.* documentary. ~**azio'ne** *n.f.* documentation.

do'dic|i *a. & n.m.* twelve. ~**e'simo** *a. & n.m.* twelfth.

doga'n|a *n.f.* customs *pl.*; (*dazio*) duty. ~**a'le** *a.* customs. ~**ie're** *n.m.* customs officer.

do'glie *n.f. pl.* labour pains.

do'gm|a *n.m.* dogma. ~**a'tico** *a.* dogmatic.

do'lc|e *a.* sweet; (*clima*) mild; (*voce, fonetica*) soft; (*acqua*) fresh. — *n.m.*

sweet; (*torta*) cake. ⁓e′zza *n.f.* sweetness; mildness; softness. ⁓iu′mi *n.m. pl.* sweets.

dolcifica′nte *n.m.* sweetener.

dole′|re *v.i.* ache, hurt; (*dispiacere*) regret. ⁓rsi *v.r.* regret; (*protestare*) complain. ⁓rsi di be sorry for. ⁓nte *a.* painful; (*spiacente*) sorry.

do′llaro *n.m.* dollar.

do′l|o *n.m.* (*legge*) malice; (*truffa*) fraud. ⁓o′so malicious.

Dolomi′ti *n.f. pl.* le ⁓ the Dolomites.

dolo′r|e *n.m.* pain; (*morale*) sorrow. ⁓o′so *a.* painful; sad.

doma′nd|a *n.f.* question; (*richiesta*) request; (*scritta*) application; (*comm.*) demand. **fare una** ⁓a (a qcno.) ask (s.o.) a question. ⁓a′re *v.t.* ask; (*esigere*) demand. ⁓are qcsa. a qcno. ask s.o. for sthg. ⁓a′rsi *v.r.* wonder.

doma′ni *adv.* tomorrow. —*n.m.* il ⁓ the future.

doma′|re *v.t.* tame. ⁓to′re *n.m.* tamer.

domatti′na *adv.* tomorrow morning.

dome′nic|a *n.f.* Sunday. di ⁓a on Sundays. ⁓a′le *a.* Sunday.

dome′stico, a *a.* domestic. —*n.m.* servant. —*n.f.* maid.

domici′li|o *n.m.* domicile; (*abitazione*) home. ⁓a′rsi *v.r.* settle.

domina′|re *v.t.* dominate; (*controllare*) control. —*v.i.* rule over; (*prevalere*) be dominant. ⁓rsi *v.r.* control oneself. ⁓zio′ne *n.f.* domination.

domi′nio *n.m.* dominion.

don′a|re *v.t.* give. —*v.i.* ⁓re a (*giovare esteticamente*) suit. ⁓to′re, ⁓tri′ce *n.m., f.* donor. ⁓zio′ne *n.f.* donation.

do′no *n.m.* gift.

dondol|a′re *v.t.* swing; (*cullare*) rock. —*v.i.* sway. ⁓a′rsi *v.r.* swing. ⁓i′o *n.m.* rocking. **do′ndolo** *n.m.* swing. **cavallo/ sedia a dondolo** rocking-horse/ chair.

do′nn|a *n.f.* woman. ⁓a di servizio domestic help.

donnaio′lo *n.m.* philanderer.

do′nnola *n.f.* weasel.

donze′lla *n.f.* maiden.

do′po *prep.* after; (*a partire da*) since. —*adv.* after, afterwards; (*più tardi*) later; (*in seguito*) later on. ⁓ di me after me.

dopodoma′ni *adv.* the day after tomorrow.

dopogue′rra *n.m. invar.* post-war period.

doposcì *a. & n.m. invar.* après-ski.

doposcuo′la *n.m. invar.* after-school activities *pl.*

dopotu′tto *adv.* after all.

doppia′|ggio *n.m.* dubbing. ⁓re *v.t.* (*naut.*) double; (*sport*) lap; (*cinema*) dub.

do′ppio *a. & adv.* double. —*n.m.* double, twice the quantity; (*tennis*) doubles *pl.*

doppio′ne *n.m.* duplicate.

doppiope′tto *a.* double-breasted.

dora′|re *v.t.* gild; (*culin.*) brown. ⁓to *a.* gilt; (*color oro*) golden. ⁓tu′ra *n.f.* gilding.

dormicchia′re *v.i.* doze.

dormiglio′ne, a *n.m., f.* sleepyhead.

dormi′|re *v.i.* sleep; (*essere addormentato*) be asleep; (*fig.*) be dormant. ⁓ta *n.f.* good sleep. ⁓ti′na *n.f.* nap.

dormito′rio *n.m.* dormitory.

dormive′glia *n.m.* **essere in** ⁓ be half asleep.

do′rs|o *n.m.* back; (*di libro*) spine. a ⁓o di cavallo on horseback. ⁓a′le *a.* dorsal; *n.f.* (*di monte*) ridge.

dosa′re *v.t.* dose. ⁓ le parole weigh one's words. **do′se** *n.f.* dose. **dose eccessiva** overdose. **in buona dose** (*fig.*) in good measure.

do′sso *n.m.* (*dorso*) back. **levarsi di** ⁓ gli abiti take off one's clothes.

dota′|re *v.t.* endow; (*di accessori*) equip. ⁓to *a.* (*di persona*) gifted; (*fornito*) equipped.

do′te *n.f.* dowry; (*qualità*) gift.

do′tto *a.* learned. —*n.m.* scholar; (*anat.*) duct.

dottora′to *n.m.* doctorate.

dotto′r|e, ⁓e′ssa *n.m., f.* doctor.

dottri′na *n.f.* doctrine.

do′ve *adv.* where. di ⁓ sei? where do you come from. fin ⁓? how far? per ⁓? which way?

dove′r|e *n.m.* duty. **per** ⁓e out of duty. —*v.i.* (*obbligo*) have to, must; (*inter., neg.*) need. **devo andare** I have to go. **devo venire anch′io?** need I come too? **non devi farlo se non ne hai voglia** you needn't do it if you don't want to. —*v.t.* (*essere debitore di*) owe. ⁓o′so *a.* right and proper.

dovu′nque *adv.* (*dappertutto*) everywhere; (*in qualsiasi luogo*) anywhere. —*conj.* wherever.

dovu′to *a.* due; (*debito*) proper.

dozzi′na *n.f.* dozen.

dozzina′le *a.* cheap.

draga're *v.t.* dredge.
dra'go *n.m.* dragon.
dragoncello *n.m.* tarragon.
dra'mm|a *n.m.* drama. **∼a'tico** *a.* dramatic. **∼atizza're** *v.t.* dramatize. **∼atu'rgo** *n.m.* playwright.
drappe'ggi|o *n.m.* drapery. **∼a're** *v.t.* drape.
drappe'llo *n.m.* (*mil.*) squad; (*gruppo*) band.
drapperi'a *n.f.* drapery.
dra'stico *a.* drastic.
drena'|ggio *n.m.* drainage. **∼re** *v.t.* drain.
dri'tta *n.f.* (*mano destra*) right hand.
dri'tto *a.* = **diritto**¹.
drizza'r|e *v.t.* straighten; (*rizzare*) prick up. **∼si** *v.r.* straighten (up); (*alzarsi*) raise.
dro'g|a *n.f.* drug. **∼a're** *v.t.* drug. **∼a'rsi** *v.r.* take drugs. **∼a'to, a** *n.m.,f.* drug addict.
drogh|eri'a *n.f.* grocery. **∼ie're, a** *n.m.,f.* grocer.
dromeda'rio *n.m.* dromedary.
du'bbio *a.* doubtful; (*ambiguo*) dubious. **—***n.m.* doubt; (*sospetto*) suspicion. **mettere in ∼** doubt.

dubita'|re *v.i.* doubt; (*diffidare*) mistrust. **∼ti'vo** *a.* (*ambiguo*) ambiguous.
du'c|a, ∼he'ssa *n.m.,f.* duke, duchess.
du'e *a.* & *n.m.* two.
duece'nto *a.* & *n.m.* two hundred.
due'llo *n.m.* duel.
duemi'la *a.* & *n.m.* two thousand.
due'tto *n.m.* duet.
du'na *n.f.* dune.
du'nque *conj.* therefore; (*allora*) well (then).
duo'mo *n.m.* cathedral.
du'plex *n.m.* (*telefono*) party line.
duplica're *v.t.* duplicate.
du'plice *a.* double. **in ∼** in duplicate.
dura'nte *prep.* during.
dur|a're *v.i.* last; (*di cibo*) keep; (*resistere*) hold out. **∼a'ta** *n.f.* duration. **∼atu'ro, ∼e'vole** *adjs.* lasting.
du'r|o *a.* hard; (*difficile, resistente, di carne*) tough; (*voce*) harsh; (*pane*) stale. **—***n.m.* (*difficoltà*) difficulty; (*persona*) tough person. **∼e'zza** *n.f.* hardness; toughness; harshness.
duro'ne *n.m.* hardened skin.

E

e, ed *conjs.* and.
e'ban|o *n.m.* ebony. ~i'sta *n.m.* cabinet-maker.
ebbe'ne *conj.* well (then).
e'bbr|o *a.* inebriated. ~o di gioia mad with joy. ~e'zza *n.f.* inebriation.
e'bete *a.* stupid.
ebollizio'ne *n.f.* boiling.
ebr|e'o, a *a.* Jewish. —*n.m., f.* Jew, Jewess. ~a'ico *a.* Hebrew; *n.m.* (*lingua*) Hebrew.
ecc. *adv.* (*abbr. di* eccetera) etc.
eccede'nza *n.f.* excess; (*d'avanzo*) surplus. ecce'dere *v.t.* exceed; *v.i.* go too far. eccedere nel mangiare overeat.
eccelle'n|te *a.* excellent. ~za *n.f.* excellence; (*titolo*) Excellency.
ecce'llere *v.i.* excel.
ecce'ntric|o, a *a.* & *n.m., f.* eccentric. ~ità *n.f.* eccentricity.
eccessi'vo *a.* excessive.
ecce'ss|o *n.m.* excess. andare agli ~i go to extremes. dare in ~i fly into a temper.
ecce'tera *adv.* et cetera.
ecce'tto *prep.* except. ~ che (*a meno che*) unless.
eccettua're *v.t.* except.
ecceziona'le *a.* exceptional.
eccezio'ne *n.f.* exception. a ~ di with the exception of.
eccita'|re *v.t.* excite. ~rsi *v.r.* get excited. ~me'nto, *n.m.*, ~zio'ne *n.f.* excitement. ~nte *a.* exciting; *n.m.* stimulant.
ecclesia'stico *a.* ecclesiastical. —*n.m.* priest.
e'cco *adv.* (*qui*) here; (*là*) there; (*int., proprio così*) exactly! ~ la tua borsa here is your bag. ~ (lì) mio figlio there is my son. ~mi here I am. ~ tutto that is all.
ecco'me *adv.* & *int.* and how!
echeggia're *v.i.* echo; (*di luogo*) resound.
ecli'ssi *n.f. invar.* eclipse.
e'co *n.m./f.* (*pl. m.* echi) echo.
ecologi'a *n.f.* ecology.
econom|i'a *n.f.* economy; (*scienza*) economics *s.* fare ~ia economize. econo'mico *a.* economic; (*a buon prezzo*) cheap. ~i'sta *n.m./f.* economist. ~izza're *v.t./i.* economize. eco'-

nomo, a *a.* thrifty; *n.m., f.* (*di collegio*) bursar.
ed *conj. vedi* e.
e'dera *n.f.* ivy.
edi'cola *n.f.* (newspaper) kiosk.
edifica'|re *v.t.* build; (*indurre al bene*) edify. ~nte *a.* edifying.
edifi'cio *n.m.* building; (*fig.*) structure.
e'dil|e *a.* building. ~i'zio, a *a.* building; *n.f.* building trade.
edi|to're, ~tri'ce *a.* publishing. —*n.m., f.* publisher; (*curatore*) editor. ~to'ria *n.f.* publishing. ~toria'le *a.* publishing; *n.m.* leader.
edizio'ne *n.f.* edition; (*di manifestazione*) performance.
educa'|re *v.t.* educate; (*allevare*) bring up. ~to *a.* polite. ~zio'ne *n.f.* education; (*buone maniere*) (good) manners *pl.*
effemina'to *a.* effeminate.
effervesce'nte *a.* effervescent; (*frizzante*) fizzy.
effetti'vo *a.* actual; (*efficace*) effective; (*di personale*) permanent; (*mil.*) regular. —*n.m.* (*somma totale*) sum total.
effe'tt|o *n.m.* effect; (*impressione*) impression. in ~i in fact. ~ua're *v.t.* effect. ~ua'rsi *v.r.* take place.
effica'c|e *a.* effective. ~ia *n.f.* effectiveness.
efficie'n|te *a.* efficient. ~za *n.f.* efficiency.
effi'gie *n.f.* effigy.
effi'mero *a.* ephemeral.
efflu'sso *n.m.* outflow.
effus|io'ne *n.f.* effusion. ~i'vo *a.* gushing.
Ege'o *n.m.* l'~ the Aegean (Sea).
Egi'tto *n.m.* Egypt. egizia'no, a *a.* & *n.m., f.* Egyptian.
e'gli *pron.* he. ~ stesso he himself.
egoce'ntrico, a *a.* egocentric. —*n.m. f.* egocentric person.
egoi's|mo *n.m.* selfishness. ~ta *a.* selfish; *n.m./f.* selfish person.
egre'gio *a.* distinguished. E~ Signore Dear Sir.
egualita'rio *a.* & *n.m.* egalitarian.
elabora'|re *v.t.* elaborate; (*dati*) process. ~zio'ne *n.f.* elaboration; processing.

elargi're *v.t.* lavish.

ela'stic|o *a.* elastic. −*n.m.* elastic; (*fascia*) rubber band. ~ità *n.f.* elasticity.

elefa'nte *n.m.* elephant.

elega'n|te *a.* elegant. ~za *n.f.* elegance.

ele'gg|ere *v.t.* elect. ~i'bile *a.* eligible.

elegi'a *n.f.* elegy.

elementa're *a.* elementary. **scuola** ~ primary school.

eleme'nt|o *n.m.* element. ~i *n.m. pl.* (*fatti*) data; (*rudimenti*) elements.

elemo'sin|a *n.f.* alms *pl.*, charity. **chiedere l'**~a beg. **vivere d'**~a live on charity. ~a're *v.t./i.* beg.

ele'nc|o *n.m.* list. ~o **telefonico** telephone directory. ~a're *v.t.* list.

ele'tto, a *p.p. di* **eleggere.** −*a.* chosen; (*di pregio*) select. −*n.m.,f.* (*nominato*) elected member.

elet|to're, ~tri'ce *n.m.,f.* voter. ~tora'le *a.* electoral. ~tora'to *n.m.* electorate.

elettric|ità *n.f.* electricity. ~i'sta *n.m.* electrician. **ele'ttrico** *a.* electric.

elettri|fica're *v.t.,* ~zza're *v.t.* electrify.

ele'ttrodo *n.m.* electrode.

elettrodome'stico *n.m.* (electrical) household appliance.

elettro'ne *n.m.* electron.

elettro'nico, a *a.* electronic. −*n.f.* electronics *s.*

elettrotre'no *n.m.* electric train.

eleva'|re *v.t.* raise; (*promuovere*) promote; (*erigere*) erect. ~rsi *v.r.* rise; (*di edificio*) stand. ~zio'ne *n.f.* elevation.

elezio'ne *n.f.* election.

e'lica *n.f.* propeller.

elico'ttero *n.m.* helicopter.

elimina'|re *v.t.* eliminate. ~to'ria *n.f.* (*sport*) preliminary heat.

elipo'rto *n.m.* heliport.

e'lla *pron.* she.

elme'tto *n.m.* helmet.

elo'gi|o *n.m.* praise; (*discorso, scritto*) eulogy. ~a're *v.t.* praise.

eloque'n|te *a.* eloquent. ~za *n.f.* eloquence.

elu'|dere *v.t.* elude. ~si'vo *a.* elusive.

emacia'to *a.* emaciated.

emana'|re *v.t.* give off; (*una legge*) pass. −*v.i.* emanate. ~zio'ne *n.f.* giving off; (*di legge*) enactment.

emancipa'|re *v.t.* emancipate. ~rsi *v.r.* become emancipated. ~to *a.* emancipated. ~zio'ne *n.f.* emancipation.

emble'ma *n.m.* emblem.

embrio'ne *n.m.* embryo.

emenda'|re *v.t.* amend. ~me'nto *n.m.* amendment.

emerge'nte *a.* emergent.

emerge'nza *n.f.* emergency. **in caso di** ~ in an emergency.

eme'rgere *v.i.* emerge; (*di sottomarino*) surface; (*distinguersi*) stand out.

eme'rso *p.p. di* **emergere.**

eme'sso *p.p. di* **emettere.**

eme'ttere *v.t.* emit; (*voce*) utter; (*luce, suono*) give out; (*grido*) let out; (*mettere in circolazione*) issue.

emicra'nia *n.f.* migraine.

emigra'|re *v.i.* emigrate. ~zio'ne *n.f.* emigration.

emine'n|te *a.* eminent. ~za *n.f.* eminence.

emisfe'ro *n.m.* hemisphere.

emissa'rio *n.m.* emissary.

emissio'ne *n.f.* emission; (*di denaro*) issue; (*trasmissione*) broadcast.

emitte'nte *a.* issuing; (*trasmittente*) broadcasting. −*n.f.* (*radio*) transmitter.

emorragi'a *n.f.* haemorrhage.

emoti'vo *a.* emotional.

emoziona'|nte *a.* exciting; (*commovente*) moving. ~re *v.t.* excite; move. ~rsi *v.r.* become excited; be moved. ~to *a.* excited; moved. **emozio'ne** *n.f.* emotion; (*agitazione*) excitement.

e'mpio *a.* ungodly; (*spietato*) pitiless; (*malvagio*) wicked.

empi're *v.t.* fill (up).

empo'rio *n.m.* emporium; (*negozio*) general store.

emula're *v.t.* emulate.

emulsio'ne *n.f.* emulsion.

enci'clica *n.f.* encyclical.

enciclopedi'a *n.f.* encyclopaedia.

encomia're *v.t.* commend. **enco'mio** *n.m.* commendation.

endoveno'so *a.* intravenous.

energi'a *n.f.* energy. **ene'rgico** *a.* energetic; (*efficace*) strong.

e'nfasi *n.f.* emphasis. **enfa'tico** *a.* emphatic.

eni'gm|a *n.m.* enigma. ~a'tico *a.* enigmatic. ~i'stica *n.f.* puzzles *pl.*

E.N.I.T. *abbr.* (*di* **Ente Nazionale Italiano per il Turismo**) Italian State Tourist Office.

enne'simo *a.* (*math.*) nth; umpteenth (*fam.*).

eno'rm|e *a.* enormous. ~ità *n.f.* enormity; (*assurdità*) absurdity.

e'nte *n.m.* board; (*società*) company; (*filosofia*) being.

entità *n.f.* (*filosofia*) entity; (*gravità*) seriousness; (*dimensione*) extent.

entra'mbi *a. pl. & pron.* both.

entra'|re *v.i.* go in, enter. ~**re in** go into; (*stare, trovar posto*) fit into; (*arruolarsi*) join. ~**rci** (*avere a che fare*) have to do with. **tu che c'entri?** what has it got to do with you? ~**ta** *n.f.* entry, entrance. ~**te** (*n.f. pl., comm.*) takings; (*reddito*) income *s.*

e'ntro *prep.* (*tempo*) within.

entusiasma'r|e *v.t.* arouse enthusiasm in. ~**si** (**per**) *v.r.* be enthusiastic (about). **entusia'smo** *n.m.* enthusiasm. **entusia'sta** *a.* enthusiastic; *n.m.|f.* enthusiast. **entusia'stico** *a.* enthusiastic.

enumera'|re *v.t.* enumerate. ~**zio'ne** *n.f.* enumeration.

enuncia'|re *v.t.* enunciate. ~**zio'ne** *n.f.* enunciation.

e'pico *a.* epic.

epidemi'a *n.f.* epidemic.

Epifani'a *n.f.* Epiphany.

epigra'mma *n.m.* epigram.

epil|essi'a *n.f.* epilepsy. ~**e'ttico, a** *a. & n.m., f.* epileptic.

epi'logo *n.m.* epilogue.

episo'dio *n.m.* episode.

epi'stola *n.f.* epistle.

epita'ffio *n.m.* epitaph.

epi'teto *n.m.* epithet.

e'poca *n.f.* age; (*periodo*) period. **a quell'**~ in those days.

eppu're *conj.* (and) yet.

epura're *v.t.* purge.

equa'nime *a.* level-headed; (*imparziale*) impartial.

equato're *n.m.* equator.

equazio'ne *n.f.* equation.

eque'stre *a.* equestrian. **circo** ~ circus.

equila'tero *a.* equilateral.

equilibra'|re *v.t.* balance. ~**to** *a.* (*persona*) well-balanced. **equili'brio** *n.m.* balance; (*buon senso*) common sense; (*di bilancia*) equilibrium.

equi'no *a.* horse.

equino'zio *n.m.* equinox.

equipa'ggi|o *n.m.* crew. ~**a're** *v.t.* equip; (*di persone*) man.

equipara're *v.t.* make equal.

equità *n.f.* equity.

equitazio'ne *n.f.* riding.

equivale'n|te *a. & n.m.* equivalent. ~**za** *n.f.* equivalence.

equi'voc|o *a.* equivocal; (*sospetto*) suspicious. **un tipo** ~**o** a shady character. —*n.m.* misunderstanding. ~**a're** *v.i.* misunderstand.

e'quo *a.* fair, just.

e'ra *n.f.* era.

e'rb|a *n.f.* grass; (*aromatica, medicinale*) herb. ~**a'ccia** *n.f.* weed. ~**a'ceo** *a.* herbaceous. ~**o'so** *a.* grassy.

ere'd|e *n.m.|f.* heir, heiress. ~**ità** *n.f.* inheritance; (*biol.*) heredity. ~**ita're** *v.t.* inherit. ~**ita'rio** *a.* hereditary.

eremi'ta *n.m.* hermit.

eresi'a *n.f.* heresy. **ere'tico, a** *a.* heretical; *n.m., f.* heretic.

ere'|tto *p.p. di* **erigere**. —*a.* erect. ~**zio'ne** *n.f.* erection; (*costruzione*) building.

erga'stolo *n.m.* life sentence; (*luogo*) prison.

e'rica *n.f.* heather.

eri'ger|e *v.t.* erect. ~**si** *v.r.* set oneself up.

ermelli'no *n.m.* ermine.

erme'tico *a.* hermetic; (*a tenuta d'aria*) airtight.

e'rnia *n.f.* hernia.

ero'dere *v.i.* erode.

ero'|e *n.m.* hero. ~**ico** *a.* heroic. ~**i'smo** *n.m.* heroism.

eroga're *v.t.* distribute; (*fornire*) supply.

eroi'na *n.f.* heroine; (*droga*) heroin.

erosio'ne *n.f.* erosion.

ero't|ico *a.* erotic. ~**i'smo** *n.m.* eroticism.

e'rpice *n.m.* harrow.

erra'|re *v.i.* (*vagare*) wander; (*sbagliare*) err, be mistaken. ~**nte** *a.* wandering.

erra'tico *a.* erratic.

erro're *n.m.* error, mistake; (*di stampa*) misprint. **essere in** ~ be wrong.

e'rta *n.f.* steep slope. **stare all'**~ be on the alert.

erudi'|rsi *v.r.* get educated. ~**to** *a.* learned.

erutta're *v.t.* (*di vulcano*) erupt. —*v.i.* (*ruttare*) belch.

eruzio'ne *n.f.* eruption; (*med.*) rash.

esacerba're *v.t.* exacerbate.

esagera'|re *v.t./i.* exaggerate. ~**to** *a.* exaggerated. ~**zio'ne** *n.f.* exaggeration.

esa'gono *n.m.* hexagon.

esala're *v.t./i.* exhale.

esalta'|re *v.t.* exalt; (*entusiasmare*)

elate. ~to a. (fanatic) fanatical; n.m. fanatic.

esa'me n.m. examination; exam (fam.). dare un ~ take an exam. ~ del sangue blood test.

esamina're v.t. examine.

esa'nime a. lifeless.

esaspera'|re v.t. exasperate. ~rsi v.r. become exasperated. ~zio'ne n.f. exasperation.

esa'tt|o p.p. di esigere. —a. exact; (di ore) sharp; (puntuale) punctual. ~e'zza n.f. exactness; punctuality; (precisione) precision.

esatto're n.m. collector.

esaudi're v.t. grant; (speranze) fulfil.

esauri're v.t. exhaust. ~rsi v.r. exhaust oneself; (di merci ecc.) run out. ~to a. exhausted; (di merci) sold out; (di libro) out of print. esa'usto a. exhausted.

e'sca n.f. bait; (per fuoco) tinder.

escandesce'nz|a n.f. outburst. dare in ~e lose one's temper.

esclama'|re v.i. exclaim. ~ti'vo a. exclamatory. punto ~tivo exclamation mark. ~zio'ne n.f. exclamation.

esclu'|dere v.t. exclude. ~sio'ne n.f. exclusion.

esclusi'vo, a a. exclusive. —n.f. sole right.

esclu'so p.p. di escludere.

escogita're v.t. contrive.

escreme'nto n.m. excrement.

escursio'ne n.f. excursion; (scorreria) raid; (di temperatura) range.

esecra'|re v.t. abhor. ~bile a. abominable.

esecuti'vo a. & n.m. executive.

esecu|to're, ~tri'ce n.m.,f. executor; (mus.) performer. ~zio'ne n.f. execution; (mus.) performance.

esegui're v.t. carry out; (legge) execute; (mus.) perform.

ese'mp|io n.m. example. dare l'~io a qcno. set s.o. an example. ~la're a. exemplary; n.m. specimen. ~lifica're v.t. exemplify.

esenta'r|e v.t. exempt. ~si v.r. ~si (da) free oneself (from). ese'nte a. exempt. esente da imposta duty-free.

ese'quie n.f. pl. funeral rites.

eserce'nte n.m.|f. shopkeeper.

esercita'|re v.t. exercise; (addestrare) train; (fare uso di) exert; (professione)

practise. ~rsi v.r. practise. ~zio'ne n.f. exercise; (mil.) drill.

ese'rcito n.m. army.

eserci'zio n.m. exercise; (pratica) practice; (comm.) financial year; (azienda) business.

esibi'|re v.t. exhibit; (documenti) produce. ~rsi v.r. exhibit oneself; (theatr.) perform; (fig.) show off. ~zio'ne n.f. exhibition; production; performance.

esige'n|te a. exacting; (pignolo) fastidious. ~za n.f. demand; (bisogno) need. esi'gere v.t. demand; (riscuotere) collect.

esi'guo a. meagre.

esilara'|re v.t. exhilarate. ~nte a. exhilarating.

e'sile a. slender; (voce) thin.

esi'li|o n.m. exile. ~a're v.t. exile. ~a'rsi v.r. go into exile. ~a'to, a a. exiled; n.m.,f. exile.

esi'mer|e v.t. release. ~si v.r. ~si da get out of.

esi'mio a. distinguished.

esistenzia'l|e a. existential. ~i'smo n.m. existentialism.

esi'st|ere v.i. exist. ~e'nte a. existing. ~e'nza n.f. existence.

esita'|re v.i. hesitate. ~nte a. hesitating; (di voce) faltering. ~zio'ne n.f. hesitation.

e'sito n.m. result.

e'sodo n.m. exodus.

esonera're v.t. exempt. eso'nero n.m. exemption.

esorbita'nte a. exorbitant.

esorcizza're v.t. exorcise.

eso'rdio n.m. début.

esorta're v.t. (pregare) beg; (incitare) urge.

esote'rico a. esoteric.

eso'tico a. exotic.

espa'n|dere v.t. expand; (diffondere) spread (out). ~dersi v.r. expand; (diffondersi) extend. ~sio'ne n.f. expansion. ~si'vo a. expansive.

espatria're v.i. leave one's country.

espedie'nt|e n.m. expedient. vivere di ~i live by one's wits.

espe'llere v.t. expel.

esperie'nza n.f. experience. parlare per ~ speak from experience.

esperime'nto n.m. experiment.

espe'rto, a a. & n.m.,f. expert.

espia'|re v.t. atone for. ~to'rio a. expiatory.

espira're v.t.|i. breathe out.

esplica're v.t. carry on.

espli'cito *a.* explicit.

esplo'dere *v.i.* explode. —*v.t.* fire.

esplora'|re *v.t.* explore. ~**to're**, ~**tri'ce** *n.m.*, *f.* explorer. **giovane** ~**tore** boy scout. ~**zio'ne** *n.f.* exploration.

esplos|io'ne *n.f.* explosion. ~**i'vo** *a.* & *n.m.* explosive.

espone'nte *n.m.* exponent.

espo'rre *v.t.* expose; (*merci*) display; (*spiegare*) expound; (*quadri ecc.*) exhibit.

esporta'|re *v.t.* export. ~**to're**, ~**tri'ce** *n.m.*, *f.* exporter. ~**zio'ne** *n.f.* export.

esposizio'ne *n.f.* (*mostra*) exhibition; (*in vetrina*) display; (*spiegazione ecc.*) exposition; (*posizione, fotografia*) exposure.

espo'sto *p.p. di* **esporre**. —*a.* exposed. ~ **a** (*rivolto*) facing. —*n.m.* (*legge ecc.*) statement.

espress|io'ne *n.f.* expression. ~**i'vo** *a.* expressive.

espre'sso *p.p. di* **esprimere**. —*a.* express. —*n.m.* (*lettera*) express letter; (*treno*) express train; (*caffè*) espresso.

espri'mer|e *v.t.* express. ~**si** *v.r.* express oneself.

espropria're *v.t.* dispossess.

espulsio'ne *n.f.* expulsion. **espu'lso** *p.p. di* **espellere**.

esse'nz|a *n.f.* essence. ~**ia'le** *a.* essential; *n.m.* important thing.

e'ssere *v.i.* be. —*v. aux.* have, be. **che ora è? sono le dieci** what time is it? it is ten o'clock. **chi è? sono io** who is it? it is me. **ci siamo** here we are. **è stato detto che** it has been said that. **siete in due** there are two of you. ~ **da** (*convenire*) be worthy of. ~ **di** (*provenire*) be from. ~ **per** be in favour of. —*n.m.* being.

e'sso, a *pron.* he, she; (*cosa, animale*) it.

est *n.m.* east.

e'stasi *n.f.* ecstasy. **andare in** ~ **per** go into raptures over. ~**a're** *v.t.* enrapture.

esta'te *n.f.* summer.

esta'tico *a.* ecstatic.

este'n|dere *v.t.* extend. ~**dersi** *v.r.* spread; (*allungarsi*) stretch. ~**sio'ne** *n.f.* extention; (*ampiezza*) expanse; (*mus.*) range. ~**si'vo** *a.* extensive.

estenua'|re *v.t.* wear out. ~**rsi** *v.r.* wear oneself out. ~**nte** *a.* exhausting.

esterio're *a.* & *n.m.* exterior.

este'rno *a.* external. —*n.m.* (*allievo*) day-boy; (*archit.*) exterior; (*scala*) outside.

e'stero *a.* foreign. —*n.m.* foreign countries. **all'**~ abroad.

esterrefa'tto *a.* horrified.

este'so *p.p. di* **estendere**. —*a.* extensive; (*diffuso*) widespread.

este't|ico, a *a.* aesthetic. —*n.f.* aesthetics *s.* ~**i'sta** *n.f.* beautician.

e'stimo *n.m.* estimate.

esti'n|guere *v.t.* extinguish. ~**guersi** *v.r.* die out. ~**to** *p.p. di* **estinguere**; *n.m.* (the) deceased. ~**to're** *n.m.* (fire) extinguisher. ~**zio'ne** *n.f.* extinction; (*di incendio*) putting out.

estirpa'|re *v.t.* uproot; (*dente*) extract. ~**zio'ne** *n.f.* eradication; extraction.

esti'vo *a.* summer.

esto'r|cere *v.t.* extort. ~**sio'ne** *n.f.* extortion. ~**to** *p.p. di* ~**cere**.

estradizio'ne *n.f.* extradition.

estra'neo, a *a.* extraneous; (*straniero*) foreign. —*n.m.*, *f.* stranger.

estrania'r|e *v.t.* estrange. ~**si** *v.r.* become estranged.

estra'|rre *v.t.* extract; (*sorteggiare*) draw. ~**tto** *p.p. di* ~**rre**; *n.m.* extract; (*brano*) excerpt; (*documento*) abstract. ~**tto conto** statement (of account). ~**zio'ne** *n.f.* extraction; (*a sorte*) draw.

estremi'sta *n.m.|f.* extremist.

estremità *n.f.* extremity. —*n.f. pl.* (*anat.*) extremities.

estre'm|o *a.* & *n.m.* extreme. **essere agli** ~**i** be at the end of one's tether. **l'E**~ **Oriente** the Far East. **misure** ~**e** drastic measures.

e'str|o *n.m.* talent; (*capriccio*) whim. ~**o'so** *a.* gifted; (*capriccioso*) unpredictable; (*lunatico*) moody.

estrove'rso *a.* extroverted. —*n.m.* extrovert.

estua'rio *n.m.* estuary.

esube'ra'n|te *a.* exuberant. ~**za** *n.f.* exuberance.

e'sule *n.m.|f.* exile.

esulta'|re *v.i.* rejoice. ~**nza** *n.f.* exultation.

esuma're *v.t.* exhume.

età *n.f.* age. **raggiungere la maggiore** ~ come of age. **un uomo di mezz'**~ a middle-aged man.

e'tere *n.m.* ether. **ete'reo** *a.* ethereal.

ete'rn|o *a.* eternal. ~**ità** *n.f.* eternity.

eteroge'neo *a.* heterogeneous.

e'tic|a *n.f.* ethics *s.* ~**o** *a.* ethical.

etiche'tta[1] *n.f.* label; (*con il prezzo*) price-tag.
etiche'tta[2] *n.f.* (*cerimoniale*) etiquette.
etimologi'a *n.f.* etymology.
Etio'pia *n.f.* Ethiopia.
e'tnico *a.* ethnic(al).
etru'sco *a.* & *n.m.* Etruscan.
e'ttaro *n.m.* hectare.
e'tto, ettogra'mmo *ns.m.* hectogram(me).
eucali'pto *n.m.* eucalyptus.
eucaristi'a *n.f.* Eucharist.
eufemi'smo *n.m.* euphemism.
eufori'a *n.f.* elation; (*med.*) euphoria. **eufo'rico** *a.* elated; euphoric.
Euro'pa *n.f.* Europe. **europe'o, a** *a.* & *n.m.,f.* European.
eutana'sia *n.f.* euthanasia.
evacua'|re *v.t.* evacuate. ∼**zio'ne** *n.f.* evacuation.
eva'dere *v.t.* evade; (*sbrigare*) deal with. −*v.i.* ∼ **da** escape from.
evanesce'nte *a.* vanishing.
evange'l|ico *a.* evangelical. ∼**i'sta** *n.m.* evangelist ∼**o** *n.m.* = **vangelo.**
evapora'|re *v.i.* evaporate. ∼**zio'ne** *n.f.* evaporation.
evasio'ne *n.f.* escape; (*fiscale*) evasion; (*fig.*) escapism.

evasi'vo *a.* evasive.
eva'so *p.p. di* **evadere.** −*n.m.* fugitive.
evenie'nza *n.f.* eventuality.
eve'nto *n.m.* event.
eventua'l|e *a.* possible. ∼**ità** *n.f.* eventuality.
evide'n|te *a.* evident. **è** ∼**te che** it is obvious that. ∼**za** *n.f.* evidence. **mettere in** ∼**za** emphasize. **mettersi in** ∼**za** make oneself conspicuous.
evidenzia're *v.t.* give prominence to.
evita're *v.t.* avoid; (*risparmiare*) spare.
e'vo *n.m.* age.
evoca're *v.t.* evoke.
evolu't|o *p.p. di* **evolvere.** −*a.* evolved; (*progredito*) progressive. **una donna** ∼**a** a modern woman.
evoluzio'ne *n.f.* evolution.
evo'lver|e *v.t.* develop. ∼**si** *v.r.* evolve.
evvi'va *int.* hurray. ∼ **il Papa!** long live the Pope! **gridare** ∼ cheer.
ex *pref.* ex-, former.
extra *a.* extra; (*speciale*) special. −*n.m.* extra.
extraconiuga'le *a.* extramarital.
extrauniversita'rio *a.* extramural.

F

fa¹ *n.m. invar.* (*mus.*) fah.

fa² *adv.* ago. **due mesi** ~ two months ago.

fa'bbric|a *n.f.* factory. **~a'nte** *n.m.* manufacturer. **~a're** *v.t.* build; (*produrre*) manufacture; (*fig., inventare*) fabricate. **~a'to** *n.m.* building. **~azio'ne** *n.f.* manufacturing; (*costruzione*) building.

fa'bbro *n.m.* blacksmith.

facce'nd|a *n.f.* matter. **~e** *n.f. pl.* (*lavori domestici*) housework *s.*

facchi'n|o *n.m.* porter. **~a'ggio** *n.m.* porterage.

fa'ccia *n.f.* face. ~ **tosta** cheek. **voltar** ~ change sides.

faccia'ta *n.f.* façade; (*pagina*) page.

face'|to *a.* facetious. **~zia** *n.f.* pleasantry.

fachi'ro *n.m.* fakir.

fa'cil|e *a.* easy; (*probabile*) likely. **~e a** ready to. **~ità** *n.f.* ease; (*disposizione*) aptitude. **~ita're** *v.t.* facilitate. **~itazio'ne** *n.f.* facility. **~itazioni** *n.f. pl.* special terms.

facinoro'so *a.* violent.

facoltà *n.f.* faculty; (*potere*) power.

facoltati'v|o *a.* optional. **fermata ~a** request stop.

facolto'so *a.* wealthy.

fa'ggio *n.m.* beech.

fagia'no *n.m.* pheasant.

fagio'l|o *n.m.* bean. **~i'no** *n.m.* French bean.

fago'tto *n.m.* bundle; (*mus.*) bassoon.

fa'lc|e *n.f.* scythe. **~e'tto** *n.m.* sickle. **~ia're** *v.t.* cut; (*fig.*) mow down. **~iatri'ce** *n.f.* (lawn-)mower.

fa'lco *n.m.* hawk.

falco'ne *n.m.* falcon.

fa'lda *n.f.* stratum; (*di neve*) flake; (*di cappello*) brim; (*pendio*) slope.

falegna'me *n.m.* carpenter. **~ri'a** *n.f.* carpentry.

fa'lla *n.f.* leak.

falla'ce *a.* deceptive.

fallime'nto *n.m.* (*comm.*) bankruptcy; (*fig.*) failure. **falli're** *v.i.* (*comm.*) go bankrupt; (*fig.*) fail. **—v.t.** (*colpo*) miss. **falli'to** *a.* unsuccessful; *a.* & *n.m.* bankrupt.

fa'llo *n.m.* fault; (*errore*) mistake; (*imperfezione*) flaw. **senza ~** without fail.

falò *n.m.* bonfire.

fals|a're *v.t.* alter; (*falsificare*) falsify. **~a'rio** *n.m.* forger; (*di documenti*) counterfeiter. **~ifica're** *v.t.* fake; (*contraffare*) forge.

fa'ls|o *a.* false; (*sbagliato*) wrong; (*di opera d'arte ecc.*) fake. **—n.m.** forgery. **giurare il ~o** commit perjury. **~ità** *n.f.* falseness.

fa'ma *n.f.* fame; (*reputazione*) reputation.

fa'm|e *n.f.* hunger. **aver ~e** be hungry. **~e'lico** *a.* ravenous.

famigera'to *a.* infamous.

fami'glia *n.f.* family.

familia'r|e *a.* family; (*ben noto*) familiar; (*senza cerimonie*) informal. **—n.m.** relative. **~ità** *n.f.* familiarity; informality. **~izza'rsi** *v.r.* become familiar (with).

famo'so *a.* famous.

fana'le *n.m.* lamp; (*di auto ecc.*) light.

fana'tico, a *a.* fanatical. **—n.m., f.** fanatic.

fanciu'll|o, a *n.m., f.* young boy, young girl. **~e'zza** *n.f.* childhood.

fando'ni|a *n.f.* lie. **~e!** nonsense!

fanfa'ra *n.f.* fanfare; (*complesso*) brass band.

fa'ng|o *n.m.* mud. **~o'so** *a.* muddy.

fannullo'ne, a *n.m., f.* idler.

fantascie'nza *n.f.* science fiction.

fantasi'a *n.f.* fantasy; (*immaginazione*) imagination; (*capriccio*) fancy; (*di tessuto*) pattern.

fanta'sma *n.m.* ghost.

fantastic|a're *v.i.* day-dream. **~heri'a** *n.f.* day-dream.

fanta'stico *a.* fantastic. **~!** great!

fa'nte *n.m.* infantryman; (*carte*) jack. **~ri'a** *n.m.* infantry.

fanti'no *n.m.* jockey.

fanto'ccio *n.m.* puppet.

farabu'tto *n.m.* rogue.

farci're *v.t.* stuff.

farde'llo *n.m.* bundle; (*fig.*) burden.

fa're *v.t./i.* do; (*creare, produrre, ecc.*) make; (*essere*) be; (*praticare*) go in for; (*fare la parte di*) play; (*trascorrere*) spend. **~ da** act as. **~ in modo di** try and. **~ l'insegnante** be a teacher. **~ per** be about to. **~ vedere** show. **fammi parlare** let me speak. **niente**

a che ~ con nothing to do with. **non c'è niente da** ~ there is nothing doing. **non fa niente** it does not matter. **strada facendo** on the way. **farcela** (*riuscire*) manage. **farsi** *v.r.* (*diventare*) become. **farsi avanti** step forward. **farsi coraggio** take heart. **farsi i fatti propri** mind one's own business. **farsi male** hurt oneself. **farsi strada** (*aver successo*) make one's way in the world. —*n.m.* manner. **ho molto da** ~ I am very busy. **sul far del giorno** at daybreak.

farfa'lla *n.f.* butterfly.

fari'n|a *n.f.* flour. ~**a'cei** *n.m. pl.* starchy food *s.*

fari'nge *n.f.* pharynx.

farmac|i'a *n.f.* pharmacy; (*negozio*) chemist's (shop). ~**e'utico** *a.* pharmaceutical. ~**i'sta** *n.m./f.* chemist.

fa'rmaco *n.m.* drug.

fa'ro *n.m.* lighthouse; (*aeron.*) beacon; (*auto*) headlight.

fa'rsa *n.f.* farce.

fa'sci|a *n.f.* band; (*ufficiale*) sash; (*benda*) bandage. ~**a're** *v.t.* bandage. ~**atu'ra** *n.f.* dressing.

fasci'colo *n.m.* file; (*di rivista*) issue; (*libretto*) booklet.

fa'scino *n.m.* fascination.

fa'scio *n.m.* bundle; (*di fiori*) bunch.

fasci'smo *n.m.* fascism.

fa'se *n.f.* phase.

fasti'di|o *n.m.* nuisance; (*scomodo*) inconvenience. ~ *n.m. pl.* (*preoccupazioni*) worries; (*disturbi*) troubles. **dar** ~**o a qcno.** bother s.o. ~**o'so** *a.* tiresome.

fa'st|o *n.m.* pomp. ~**o'so** *a.* sumptious.

fasu'llo *a.* bogus; (*di persona*) inept.

fa'ta *n.f.* fairy.

fata'l|e *a.* fatal; (*inevitabile*) fated. ~**i'sta** *n.m./f.* fatalist. ~**ità** *n.f.* fate; (*caso sfortunato*) misfortune.

fati'c|a *n.f.* effort; (*lavoro faticoso*) hard work; (*stanchezza*) fatigue. **a** ~**a** with great difficulty. ~**a're** *v.i.* toil. ~**are a** (*stentare*) find it difficult to. ~**a'ta** *n.f.* effort; (*sfacchinata*) grind. ~**o'so** *a.* tiring; difficult.

fa'to *n.m.* fate.

fatte'zze *n.f. pl.* features.

fatti'vo *a.* effective; (*attivo*) active.

fa'tt|o *p.p. di* fare. —*a.* done, made. ~**o a mano/in casa** handmade/home-made. —*n.m.* fact; (*azione*) action; (*avvenimento*) event. **bada ai** ~**i tuoi!** mind your own

business. **sa il** ~**o suo** he knows his business.

fatto'r|e *n.m.* (*causa, math.*) factor; (*di fattoria*) farm manager. ~**i'a** *n.f.* farm; (*casa*) farmhouse.

fattori'no *n.m.* messenger (boy).

fattu'r|a *n.f.* (*stile*) cut; (*lavorazione*) workmanship; (*comm.*) invoice. ~**a're** *v.t.* invoice; (*adulterare*) adulterate.

fa'tuo *a.* fatuous.

fa'una *n.f.* fauna.

fa'usto *a.* propitious.

fauto're *n.m.* supporter.

fa'va *n.f.* broad bean.

fave'lla *n.f.* speech.

favi'lla *n.f.* spark.

fa'vol|a *n.f.* fable; (*fiaba*) story; (*frottola*) tall story; (*oggetto di pettegolezzi*) laughing-stock. ~**o'so** *a.* fabulous.

favo'r|e *n.m.* favour. **essere a** ~**e di** be in favour of. **per** ~**e** please. ~**e'vole** favourable.

favori'|re *v.t.* favour; (*promuovere*) promote. **vuol** ~**re?** (*accettare*) will you have some?; (*entrare*) will you come in? ~**to, a** *a. & n.m., f.* favourite.

fazio'ne *n.f.* faction.

fazzole'tto *n.m.* handkerchief; (*da testa*) headscarf.

febbra'io *n.m.* February.

fe'bbr|e *n.f.* fever. **avere la** ~**e** have o run a temperature. ~**e da fieno** hay fever. ~**i'le** *a.* feverish.

fe'ccia *n.f.* dregs *pl.*

fe'cola *n.f.* potato flour.

feconda'|re *v.t.* fertilize. ~**to're** *n.m.* fertilizer. ~**zio'ne** *n.f.* fertilization. ~**zione artificiale** artificial insemination. **feco'ndo** *a.* fertile.

fe'd|e *n.f.* faith; (*fiducia*) trust; (*anello*) wedding-ring; (*certificato*) certificate. ~**e'le** *a.* faithful; *n.m./f.* believer; (*seguace*) follower. ~**eltà** *n.f.* faithfulness. **alta** ~**eltà** high fidelity.

fe'dera *n.f.* pillowcase.

federa'|le *a.* federal. ~**zio'ne** *n.f.* federation.

fe'gato *n.m.* liver; (*fig.*) guts *pl.*

fe'lce *n.f.* fern.

feli'c|e *a.* happy; (*fortunato*) lucky. ~**ità** *n.f.* happiness.

felicita'|rsi *v.r.* ~**rsi con** congratulate. ~**zio'ni** *n.m. pl.* congratulations.

feli'no *a.* feline.

felpa'to *a.* plushy.

fe'ltro *n.m.* felt; (*cappello*) felt hat.

fe'mmin|a *n.f.* female; (*donna*) woman; (*bambina*) girl. ∼**i'le** *a.* feminine; (*sesso*) female; *n.m.* feminine. ∼**ilità** *n.f.* femininity.

fe'nd|ere *v.t.* split; (*spaccare*) break (up). ∼**itu'ra** *n.f.* split.

feno'men|o *n.m.* phenomenon. ∼**a'le** *a.* phenomenal.

fe'retro *n.m.* coffin.

fe'ri|e *n.f. pl.* holidays; (*di università, tribunale, ecc.*) vacation *s.* ∼**a'le** *a.* weekday. **giorno** ∼**ale** weekday.

feri'|re *v.t.* wound; (*produrre lesioni a*) injure; (*fig.*) hurt. ∼**ta** *n.f.* wound; injury. ∼**to** *a.* wounded; *n.m.* wounded person; (*mil.*) casualty.

fe'rma *n.f.* (*mil.*) (period of) service.

fermaca'rte *n.m. invar.* paperweight.

ferma'glio *n.m.* clasp; (*spilla*) brooch; (*per capelli*) hair-grip.

ferma'|re *v.t.* stop; (*fissare*) fix; (*legge*) detain. –*v.i.* stop. ∼**rsi** *v.r.* stop. ∼**ta** *n.f.* stop. ∼**ta dell'autobus** bus-stop.

ferme'nt|o *n.m.* ferment; (*lievito*) yeast. ∼**a're** *v.i.* ferment.

fe'rm|o *a.* still; (*veicolo*) stationary; (*stabile*) steady; (*orologio*) not working. –*n.m.* (*legge*) detention; (*mech.*) catch. ∼**e'zza** *n.f.* firmness; steadiness.

fero'c|e *a.* ferocious; (*bestia*) wild. ∼**ia** *n.f.* ferocity.

ferrago'sto *n.m.* Assumption Day; (*periodo*) August holidays *pl.*

ferrame'nta *n.f. pl.* ironmongery *s.* **negozio di** ∼ (*anche*) hardware shop.

ferra're *v.t.* (*cavallo*) shoe.

fe'rr|o *n.m.* iron; (*attrezzo*) tool; (*di chirurgo*) instrument. **bistecca ai** ∼**i** grilled steak. ∼**o battuto** wrought iron. ∼**o da calza** knitting needle. ∼**o di cavallo** horseshoe. **filo di** ∼**o** (steel) wire. ∼**eo** *a.* iron.

ferrovi'|a *n.f.* railway. ∼**a'rio** *a.* railway. ∼**e're** *n.m.* railwayman.

fe'rtil|e *a.* fertile. ∼**ità** *n.f.* fertility. ∼**izza'nte** *n.m.* fertilizer. ∼**izza-zio'ne** *n.f.* fertilization.

ferve'nte *a.* blazing; (*fig.*) fervent.

fe'rvid|o *a.* fervent. ∼**i auguri** best wishes.

fervo're *n.m.* fervour.

fe'ss|o *p.p. di* **fendere.** –*a.* cracked; (*sciocco*) foolish. –*n.m.* (*idiota*) fool. ∼**eri'a** *n.f.* nonsense.

fessu'ra *n.f.* crack; (*per gettone ecc.*) slot.

fe'st|a *n.f.* feast; (*giorno festivo*) holiday; (*onomastico*) name day; (*compleanno*) birthday; (*ricevimento*) party; (*fig.*) joy. **fare** ∼**a a qcno.** welcome s.o. ∼**i'no** *n.m.* party.

festeggia'|re *v.t.* celebrate; (*accogliere festosamente*) give a hearty welcome to. ∼**me'nto** *n.m.* celebration; (*manifestazione*) festivity.

festi'vo *a.* holiday; (*lieto*) festive.

festo'so *a.* merry.

fete'nte *a.* stinking; (*fig.*) revolting.

feti'ccio *n.m.* fetish.

fe'to *n.m.* foetus.

feto're *n.m.* stench.

fe'tta *n.f.* slice.

fettu'ccia *n.f.* tape.

fe'ud|o *n.m.* feud. ∼**a'le** *a.* feudal.

fia'ba *n.f.* fairy-tale.

fia'cc|a *n.f.* weariness; (*indolenza*) laziness. ∼**a're** *v.t.* weaken. ∼**o** *a.* weak; (*indolente*) slack.

fia'ccola *n.f.* torch.

fia'la *n.f.* phial.

fia'mm|a *n.f.* flame; (*naut.*) pennant. ∼**a'nte** *a.* flaming. ∼**a'ta** *n.f.* blaze.

fiammeggia're *v.i.* blaze.

fiammi'fero *n.m.* match.

fiammi'ngo, a *a.* Flemish. –*n.m., f.* Fleming. –*n.m.* (*lingua*) Flemish; (*uccello*) flamingo.

fiancheggia're *v.t.* border; (*fig.*) support.

fia'nco *n.m.* side; (*di persona*) hip; (*di animale*) flank; (*mil.*) wing. **al mio** ∼ by my side.

fia'sco *n.m.* flask; (*fig.*) fiasco. **fare** ∼ be a fiasco.

fia't|o *n.m.* breath; (*vigore*) stamina. **strumenti a** ∼**o** wind instruments. ∼**a're** *v.i.* breathe; (*parlare*) say a word.

fi'bbia *n.f.* buckle.

fi'br|a *n.f.* fibre. ∼**e** *n.f. pl.* roughage.

ficca'r|e *v.t.* thrust; (*un chiodo ecc.*) drive; (*fam., mettere*) put. ∼**si** *v.r.* thrust oneself. ∼**si nei guai** get o.s. into trouble.

fi'co *n.m.* (*albero*) fig-tree; (*frutto*) fig. ∼ **d'India** prickly pear.

fidanz|ame'nto *n.m.* engagement. ∼**a'rsi** *v.r.* become engaged. ∼**a'to, a** *n.m., f.* fiancé, fiancée.

fida'|rsi *v.r.* ∼**rsi di** trust; (*osare*) dare. ∼**to** *a.* trustworthy.

fi'do *n.m.* devoted follower; (*comm.*) credit.

fidu'ci|a *n.f.* confidence. **degno di** ∼**a**

trustworthy. **persona di** ~a reliable person. ~o'so *a.* trustful.

fie'le *n.m.* bile.

fieni'le *n.m.* barn.

fie'no *n.m.* hay.

fie'ra *n.f.* fair.

fie'r|o *a.* (*audace*) bold; (*feroce*) fierce; (*orgoglioso*) proud. ~e'zza *n.f.* boldness; fierceness; pride.

fie'vole *a.* faint; (*di luce*) dim.

fi'f|a *n.f.* (*fam.*) funk. **aver** ~a be afraid. ~o'ne, a *n.m., f.* (*fam.*) coward.

figlia'stro, a *n.m., f.* stepson, stepdaughter.

fi'glio, a *n.m., f.* son, daughter; (*generico*) child. ~ **di papà** spoilt young man.

figlio'ccio, a *n.m., f.* godson, goddaughter.

figlio'|lo, a *n.m., f.* boy, girl. ~la'nza *n.f.* offspring.

figu'ra *n.f.* figure; (*aspetto esteriore*) shape; (*illustrazione*) illustration. **far bella** ~ cut a fine figure.

figura'|re *v.t.* represent; (*simboleggiare*) symbolize; (*immaginare*) imagine. —*v.i.* (*far figura*) cut a fine figure. **figu'rati!** imagine that! ~ti'vo *a.* figurative.

figurini'sta *n.m./f.* dress designer.

fi'la *n.f.* line; (*di soldati ecc.*) file; (*di oggetti*) row; (*coda*) queue. **di** ~ in succession. **fare la** ~ queue (up).

filame'nto *n.m.* filament.

filantropi'a *n.f.* philanthropy. **fila'ntropo, a** *n.m., f.* philanthropist.

fila'|re *v.t.* spin; (*naut.*) pay out. —*v.i.* (*andarsene*) run away; (*procedere*) go; (*liquido*) trickle. ~re con (*fam., amoreggiare*) go out with. ~re dritto toe the line. ~to're, ~tri'ce *n.m., f.* spinner.

filastro'cca *n.f.* rigmarole; (*per bambini*) nursery rhyme.

filate'li|a *n.f.* philately. ~co, a *n.m., f.* philatelist.

fila't|o *a.* spun; (*ininterrotto*) running. —*n.m.* yarn. ~u'ra *n.f.* spinning; (*filanda*) spinning mill.

file'tto *n.m.* (*bordo*) border; (*di vite*) thread; (*culin.*) fillet.

filia'le *a.* filial. —*n.f.* (*comm.*) branch.

filibustie're *n.m.* scoundrel.

filigra'na *n.f.* filigree; (*su carta*) watermark.

film *n.m. invar.* film. ~ **a lungo me-**

traggio feature film. ~ **giallo** thriller. ~a're *v.t.* film.

fi'lo *n.m.* thread; (*tessile*) yarn; (*metallico*) wire; (*di lama*) edge; (*venatura*) grain; (*di perle*) string; (*d'erba*) blade. **con un** ~ **di voce** in a whisper. ~ **spinato** barbed wire. **per** ~ **e per segno** in detail.

fi'lobus *n.m. invar.* trolleybus.

filodiffusio'ne *n.f.* rediffusion.

filo'ne *n.m.* vein; (*di pane*) French bread.

filosofi'a *n.f.* philosophy. **filo'sofo, a** *n.m., f.* philosopher.

filtra're *v.t.* filter. **fi'ltro** *n.m.* filter.

fi'lza *n.f.* string.

fina'l|e *a.* final. —*n.m.* end. —*n.f.* (*sport*) final. ~i'sta *n.m./f.* finalist. ~ità *n.f.* finality; (*scopo*) aim.

finalme'nte *adv.* at last; (*in ultimo*) finally.

fina'nz|a *n.f.* finance. ~ia'rio *a.* financial. ~ie're *n.m.* financier; (*guardia di finanza*) customs officer.

finché *conj.* until; (*per tutto il tempo che*) as long as.

fi'n|e *a.* fine; (*sottile*) thin; (*udito, vista*) keen; (*raffinato*) refined. —*n.f.* end. **alla fin** ~e after all. **senza** ~e endless. —*n.m.* aim; (*esito*) conclusion. ~e'zza *n.f.* fineness; thinness; refinement.

fine'str|a *n.f.* window. ~i'no *n.m.* (*di treno, auto*) window.

fi'nger|e *v.t.* pretend; (*affetto ecc.*) feign. ~si *v.r.* pretend to be.

finime'nti *n.m. pl.* harness *s.*

finimo'ndo *n.m.* end of the world; (*fig.*) pandemonium.

fini'|re *v.t./i.* finish, end; (*smettere*) stop; (*diventare, andare a finire*) end up. ~scila! stop it! ~to *a.* finished; (*abile*) accomplished. ~tu'ra *n.f.* finish.

Finla'nd|ia *n.f.* Finland. **f~e'se** *a.* Finnish; *n.m./f.* Finn; *n.m.* (*lingua*) Finnish.

fi'no[1] (a) *prep.* till, until, up to; (*spazio*) as far as. ~ **all'ultimo** to the last. **fin da** (*tempo*) since; (*spazio*) from. **fin qui** as far as here. **fin troppo** too much.

fi'no[2] *a.* fine; (*acuto*) subtle; (*puro*) pure.

fino'cchio *n.m.* fennel; (*fam., omosessuale*) queer.

fino'ra *adv.* so far, up till now.

fi'nt|o, a *p.p. di* **fingere.** —*a.* false;

(*artificiale*) artificial. —*n.f.* pretence; (*sport*) feint. **far ~a di** pretend to.
finzio'ne *n.f.* pretence.
fio'cc|o *n.m.* bow; (*di neve*) flake; (*nappa*) tassel. **coi ~hi** (*fig.*) excellent.
fio'cina *n.f.* harpoon.
fio'co *a.* weak.
fio'nda *n.f.* catapult.
fiordali'so *n.m.* cornflower.
fio'rdo *n.m.* fiord.
fio'r|e *n.m.* flower; (*parte scelta*) cream. **~i** *n.m. pl.* (*carte*) clubs. **a ~ d'acqua** on the surface of the water. **a ~i** flowered. **~ di** (*abbondanza*) a lot of. **~a'io, a** *n.m.*, *f.* florist.
fiorenti'no *a.* Florentine.
fiore'tto *n.m.* (*scherma*) foil; (*piccola rinuncia*) act of mortification.
fiori're *v.i.* flower; (*albero*) blossom; (*fig.*) flourish.
fio'tto *n.m.* gush.
Fire'nze *n.f.* Florence.
fi'rm|a *n.f.* signature; (*nome*) name. **~a're** *v.t.* sign.
firmame'nto *n.m.* firmament.
fisarmo'nica *n.f.* accordion.
fi'schi|o *n.m.* whistle. **~a're** *v.i.* whistle. —*v.t.* whistle; (*in segno di disapprovazione*) boo. **~etti'o** *n.m.* whistling. **~e'tto** *n.m.* whistle.
fi'sc|o *n.m.* treasury; (*tasse*) taxation. **~a'le** *a.* fiscal.
fi'sic|o, a *a.* physical. —*n.m.*, *f.* physicist. —*n.m.* physique. —*n.f.* physics *s.*
fi'sima *n.f.* whim.
fisiol|ogi'a *n.f.* physiology. **~o'gico** *a.* physiological. **fisio'logo, a** *n.m.*, *f.* physiologist.
fisionomi'a *n.f.* physiognomy; (*volto*) face.
fisioterapi'|a *n.f.* physiotherapy. **~sta** *n.m.*/*f.* physiotherapist.
fissa'r|e *v.t.* fix, fasten; (*guardare fissamente*) stare (at); (*prenotare*) reserve. **~si** *v.r.* be fixed. **~si su** (*ostinarsi*) fix one's mind on. **fi'sso** *a.* fixed. **un lavoro fisso** a regular job.
fissazio'ne *n.f.* fixation.
fi'tta *n.f.* sharp pain.
fitti'zio *a.* fictitious.
fi'tto¹ *a.* thick. **a capo ~** headlong. **~ di** full of. —*n.m.* depth.
fitto² *n.m.* (*affitto*) rent. **dare a ~** let. **prendere a ~** rent; (*noleggiare*) hire.
fiu'm|e *n.m.* river; (*fig.*) stream. **~a'na** *n.f.* swollen river; (*fig.*) stream.

fiuta're *v.t.* smell. **fiu'to** *n.m.* (sense of) smell; (*fig.*) nose.
fla'ccido *a.* flabby.
flaco'ne *n.m.* bottle.
flage'llo *n.m.* scourge.
flagra'nte *a.* flagrant. **in ~** in the act.
flane'lla *n.f.* flannel.
flatule'nza *n.f.* flatulence.
fla'uto *n.m.* flute.
fle'bile *a.* feeble.
fle'mm|a *n.f.* calm; (*med.*) phlegm. **~a'tico** *a.* phlegmatic.
flessi'bil|e *a.* flexible. **~ità** *n.f.* flexibility.
fle'sso *p.p. di* **flettere**.
flessuo'so *a.* supple.
fle'ttere *v.t.* bend.
flo'ra *n.f.* flora.
flo'rido *a.* flourishing.
flo'scio *a.* limp; (*flaccido*) flabby.
flo'tt|a *n.f.* fleet. **~i'glia** *n.f.* flotilla.
flue'nte *a.* fluent.
flu'ido *n.m.* fluid.
flui're *v.i.* flow.
fluoresce'n|te *a.* fluorescent. **~za** *n.f.* fluorescence.
fluo'ro *n.m.* fluorine.
fluoru'ro *n.m.* fluoride.
flu'sso *n.m.* flow; (*del mare*) flood (-tide). **~ e riflusso** ebb and flow.
fluttua'|re *v.i.* rise and fall; (*fig.*) fluctuate. **~nte** *a.* fluctuating.
fluvia'le *a.* river.
fobi'a *n.f.* phobia.
fo'ca *n.f.* seal.
foca'ccia *n.f.* flat cake.
fo'ce *n.f.* mouth.
fochi'sta *n.m.* stoker.
focola'io *n.m.* (*med.*) focus; (*fig.*) centre.
focola're *n.m.* hearth; (*caminetto*) fireplace.
foco'so *a.* fiery.
fo'der|a *n.f.* lining; (*di libro*) dust-jacket; (*di poltrona ecc.*) loose cover. **~a're** *v.t.* line; cover. **~o** *n.m.* sheath.
fo'ga *n.f.* impetuosity.
fo'ggi|a *n.f.* fashion; (*maniera*) manner; (*forma*) shape. **~a're** *v.t.* mould.
fo'gli|a *n.f.* leaf; (*di metallo*) foil. **~a'me** *n.m.* foliage.
fo'glio *n.m.* sheet; (*pagina*) leaf.
fo'gna *n.f.* drain. **~tu'ra** *n.f.* drainage.
fola'ta *n.f.* gust.
folclo're *n.m.* folklore.
folgora're *v.i.* (*splendere*) shine. —*v.t.* (*con un fulmine*) strike.
fo'lla *n.f.* crowd.

fo'll|e *a.* mad. **in ~e** (*auto*) in neutral. **~i'a** *n.f.* madness.

folle'tto *n.m.* elf.

fo'lto *a.* thick.

fomenta're *v.t.* stir up.

fonda'|re *v.t.* found. **~me'nto** *n.m.* (*pl. f.* **~menta**) foundation. **~zio'ne** *n.f.* foundation.

fo'nder|e *v.t./i.* melt; (*colori*) blend. **~si** *v.r.* melt; (*comm.*) merge. **~i'a** *n.f.* foundry.

fo'nd|o *a.* deep *—n.m.* bottom; (*fine*) end; (*sfondo*) background; (*indole*) nature; (*somma di denaro*) fund; (*feccia*) dregs *pl.* **~i** *n.m. pl.* (*denaro*) funds; (*di caffè*) grounds. **andare a ~o** (*nave*) sink. **da cima a ~o** from beginning to end. **in ~o in ~o** after all.

fone'tic|a *n.f.* phonetics *s.* **~o** *a.* phonetic.

fonta'na *n.f.* fountain.

fo'nte *n.f.* spring; (*fig.*) source. *—n.m.* font.

fora'ggio *n.m.* forage.

fora're *v.t.* pierce; (*biglietto*) punch. *—v.i.* puncture.

fo'rbici *n.f. pl.* scissors.

fo'rca *n.f.* fork; (*patibolo*) gallows *pl.*

force'lla *n.f.* fork; (*per capelli*) (large) hairpin.

forche'tta *n.f.* fork.

forci'na *n.f.* hairpin.

fo'rcipe *n.m.* forceps *pl.*

fore'sta *n.f.* forest.

forest|ie'ro, a *a.* foreign. *—n.m., f.* foreigner. **~eri'a** *n.f.* guest-rooms *pl.*

fo'rfora *n.f.* dandruff.

fo'rgi|a *n.f.* forge. **~a're** *v.t.* forge.

fo'rm|a *n.f.* form; (*sagoma*) shape; (*culin.*) mould; (*da calzolaio*) last. **essere in ~a** be in good form. **~e** *n.f. pl.* (*del corpo*) figure *s.* **le ~e** (*convenzioni*) appearances. **~a're** *v.t.* form; shape. **~a'rsi** *v.r.* form; take shape; (*svilupparsi*) develop. **~a'to** *n.m.* size; (*di libro*) format. **~azio'ne** *n.f.* formation. **~o'so** *a.* shapely; (*di donna*) buxom.

forma'gg|io *n.m.* cheese. **~i'no** *n.m.* processed cheese.

forma'l|e *a.* formal. **~ità** *n.f.* formality.

formi'c|a *n.f.* ant. **~a'io** *n.m.* anthill.

formicol|a're *v.i.* (*di braccio ecc.*) tingle. **~are di** be swarming with. **mi formi'cola la mano** I have pins and needles in my hand. **~i'o** *n.m.* swarming; pins and needles *pl.*

formida'bile *a.* formidable; (*tremendo*) tremendous.

fo'rmula *n.f.* formula.

formula're *v.t.* formulate; (*esprimere*) express.

forna'ce *n.f.* furnace; (*per laterizi*) kiln.

forne'llo *n.m.* stove; (*di pipa*) bowl.

forni'|re *v.t.* **~re di** supply with. **~to're** *n.m.* supplier.

fo'rn|o *n.m.* oven; (*panetteria*) bakery. **~a'io** *n.m.* baker.

fo'ro *n.m.* hole; (*storia romana*) forum; (*tribunale*) (law) court.

fo'rse *adv.* perhaps, maybe. **essere in ~** be in doubt.

forsenna'to, a *a.* mad. *—n.m., f.* madman, madwoman.

fo'rte *a.* strong; (*colore*) bright; (*suono*) loud; (*resistente*) tough; (*spesa*) considerable; (*dolore*) severe; (*grande*) large. *—adv.* strongly; loudly; (*velocemente*) fast. *—n.m.* (*fortezza*) fort; (*specialità*) strong point.

forte'zza *n.f.* fortress; (*forza morale*) fortitude.

fortifica're *v.t.* fortify.

fortu'ito *a.* fortuitous. **incontro ~** chance encounter.

fortu'n|a *n.f.* fortune; (*successo*) success; (*buona sorte*) luck. **atterraggio di ~a** forced landing. **aver ~a** be lucky. **di ~a** makeshift. **per ~a** luckily. **~a'to** *a.* lucky, fortunate; (*impresa*) successful.

foru'ncolo *n.m.* pimple; (*grosso*) boil.

fo'rz|a *n.f.* strength; (*potenza*) power; (*fisica*) force. **a ~a di** by dint of. **con ~a** hard. **~a!** come on! **~a di volontà** will-power. **~a maggiore** circumstances beyond one's control. **la ~a pubblica** the police. **le ~e armate** the armed forces. **per ~a** against one's will; (*naturalmente*) of course. **~a're** *v.t.* force; (*scassare*) break open; (*sforzare*) strain. **~a'to** *a.* forced; strained; *n.m.* convict.

forzie're *n.m.* coffer.

foschi'a *n.f.* haze.

fo'sco *a.* dark.

fosfa'to *n.m.* phosphate.

fo'sforo *n.m.* phosphorus.

fo'ssa *n.f.* pit; (*tomba*) grave. **~ biologica** cesspool.

fossa'to *n.m.* (*di fortificazione*) moat.

fosse'tta *n.f.* dimple.

fo'ssile *n.m.* fossil.

fo'sso *n.m.* ditch; (*mil.*) trench.

fo'to *n.f. invar. (fam.)* photo. **fare delle** ~ take some snaps.

fotoco'pi|a *n.f.* photocopy. ~**a're** *v.t.* photocopy.

fotoge'nico *a.* photogenic.

foto'graf|o, a *n.m., f.* photographer. ~**a're** *v.t.* photograph. ~**i'a** *n.f. (arte)* photography; *(immagine)* photograph. **fotogra'fico** *a.* photographic. **macchina fotografica** camera.

fra *prep. (di due cose o persone)* between; *(più di due)* among(st); *(attraverso luogo)* through; *(tempo, distanza)* within, in. ~ **breve** soon. ~ **l'altro** furthermore.

fracassa'r|e *v.t.* smash. ~**si** *v.r.* shatter. **fraca'sso** *n.m.* din; *(di cose che cadono)* crash.

fra'dicio *a. (bagnato)* soaked; *(guasto)* rotten. **ubriaco** ~ dead drunk.

fra'gil|e *a.* fragile; *(fig.)* frail. ~**ità** *n.f.* fragility; frailty.

fra'gola *n.f.* strawberry.

frago'r|e *n.m.* uproar; *(di cose rotte)* clatter; *(di tuono)* rumble. ~**o'so** *a.* uproarious; rumbling; *(di suono)* clanging.

fragra'n|te *a.* fragrant. ~**za** *n.f.* fragrance.

frainte'|ndere *v.t.* misunderstand. ~**so** *p.p. di* ~**ndere.**

framme'nt|o *n.m.* fragment. ~**a'rio** *a.* fragmentary.

fra'n|a *n.f.* landslide. ~**a're** *v.i.* slide down. ~**o'so** *a.* subject to landslides.

Fra'nc|ia *n.f.* France. **f~e'se** *a.* French; *n.m.|f.* Frenchman/ woman; *n.m. (lingua)* French.

fra'nc|o¹ *a.* frank; *(comm.)* free. **farla** ~**a** get away with sth. **parlare** ~**o** speak openly. ~**he'zza** *n.f.* frankness; openness.

fra'nco² *n.m. (moneta)* franc.

francobo'llo *n.m.* stamp.

frange'nte *n.m.* breaker; *(fig., momento difficile)* crisis.

fra'ngia *n.f.* fringe.

frantuma'r|e *v.t.,* ~**si** *v.r.* shatter. **frantu'mi** *n.m. pl.* splinters.

frappo'r|re *v.t.* interpose. ~**si** *v.r.* intervene.

fra'sca *n.f. (leafy)* branch.

fra's|e *n.f.* sentence; *(espressione)* phrase. ~**e fatta** cliché. ~**a'rio** *n.m.* vocabulary.

fra'ssino *n.m.* ash (-tree).

frastaglia're *v.t.* indent.

frastuo'no *n.m.* racket.

fra'te *n.m.* friar; *(monaco)* monk.

fratella'nza *n.f.* brotherhood.

frate'll|o *n.m.* brother. ~**a'stro** *n.m.* half-brother.

frate'rno *a.* brotherly.

fratta'glie *n.f. pl. (di pollo ecc.)* giblets.

fratta'nto *adv.* in the meantime.

fratte'mpo *n.m.* **nel** ~ meanwhile.

frattu'r|a *n.f.* fracture. ~**a're** *v.t.,* ~**a'rsi** *v.r.* break.

fraudole'nto *a.* fraudulent.

frazio'ne *n.f.* fraction; *(borgata)* hamlet.

fre'cci|a *n.f.* arrow; *(auto.)* indicator. ~**a'ta** *n.f. (osservazione pungente)* cutting remark.

fredda're *v.t. (uccidere)* kill.

fre'dd|o *a. & n.m.* cold. **aver** ~**o** be cold. ~**e'zza** *n.f.* coldness. ~**olo'so** *a.* sensitive to cold.

freddu'ra *n.f.* pun.

frega'|re *v.t.* rub; *(fam., truffare)* cheat; *(fam., rubare)* swipe. ~**rsene** *(fam.)* not to give a damn. **me ne frego!** I don't give a damn! ~**ta** *n.f.* rub. ~**tu'ra** *n.f. (truffa)* swindle.

fre'gio *n.m. (archit.)* frieze; *(ornamento)* decoration.

fre'm|ere *v.i.* quiver; *(tremare)* tremble. ~**e'nte** *a.* quivering; trembling. ~**ito** *n.m.* quiver; *(brivido)* shudder.

frena'|re *v.t.* brake; *(fig.)* restrain. —*v.i.* put on the brakes. ~**rsi** *v.r.* check oneself. ~**ta** *n.f.* **fare una** ~**ta** brake.

frenesi'a *n.f.* frenzy; *(desiderio smodato)* craze. **frene'tico** *a.* frenzied.

fre'no *n.m.* brake; *(fig.)* check. **togliere il** ~ release the brake. **usare il** ~ apply the brake.

frequenta're *v.t.* frequent; *(scuola ecc.)* attend; *(persone)* mix with.

freque'n|te *a.* frequent. **di** ~**te** frequently. ~**za** *n.f.* frequency; *(assiduità)* attendance.

fre'sc|o *a.* fresh; *(di temperatura)* cool. **stai** ~**o!** not on your life! —*n.m.* coolness; freshness. **far** ~**o** be cool. ~**he'zza** *n.f.* freshness.

fre'tt|a *n.f.* hurry, haste. **aver** ~**a** be in a hurry. **far** ~**a a qcno.** hurry s.o. **in** ~**a e furia** in a great hurry. ~**olo'so** *a.* hasty.

fria'bile *a.* friable; *(pasta)* crumbly.

fri'ggere *v.t.* fry. —*v.i.* sizzle; *(fig.)* fret.

fri'gid|o *a.* frigid. ~**ità** *n.f.* frigidity.

fri'go *n.m.* fridge.

frigori'fero *a.* refrigerating. —*n.m.* refrigerator.

fringue'llo *n.m.* chaffinch.

fritta'ta *n.f.* omelette.

fritte'lla *n.f.* fritter; (*fam., macchia d'unto*) grease stain.

fri'tt|o *p.p. di* **friggere.** —*a.* fried. —*n.m.* fried food. ~**o misto** mixed fry. ~**u'ra** *n.f.* (*pietanza*) fried dish.

fri'vol|o *a.* frivolous. ~**e'zza** *n.f.* frivolity.

frizio'n|e *n.f.* friction; (*mech.*) clutch; (*di pelle*) rub. ~**a're** *v.t.* rub.

frizza'nte *a.* fizzy; (*di vino*) sparkling; (*di aria*) bracing.

fri'zzo *n.m.* gibe.

fro'd|e *n.f.* fraud. ~**e fiscale** tax evasion. ~**a're** *v.t.* defraud.

fro'll|o *a.* tender; (*di selvaggina*) high; (*persona*) spineless. **pasta** ~**a** short (crust) pastry.

fro'nd|a *n.f.* (leafy) branch; (*fig.*) rebellion. ~**o'so** *a.* leafy.

fronta'le *a.* frontal; (*scontro*) head-on.

fro'nte *n.f.* forehead; (*di edificio*) front. —*n.m.* (*mil., pol.*) front. **di** ~ facing. **di** ~ **a** opposite; (*a paragone*) compared with. **far** ~ **a** face.

fronteggia're *v.t.* face.

frontie'ra *n.f.* frontier.

fro'nzolo *n.m.* frill.

fro'tta *n.f.* swarm; (*di animali*) flock.

fro'ttol|a *n.f.* fib. ~**e** *n.f. pl.* nonsense *s.*

fruga'le *a.* frugal.

fruga're *v.i.* rummage. —*v.t.* search.

frull|a're *v.t.* (*culin.*) whisk. —*v.i.* (*di ali*) whirr. ~**ato're** *n.m.* (electric) mixer. ~**i'no** *n.m.* whisk.

frume'nto *n.m.* wheat.

frusci'|o *n.m.* rustle; (*radio, giradischi*) ground noise; (*di acque*) murmur. ~**a're** *v.i.* rustle.

fru'st|a *n.f.* whip; (*frullino*) whisk. ~**a're** *v.t.* whip. ~**a'ta** *n.f.* lash. ~**i'no** *n.m.* riding crop.

frustra'|re *v.t.* frustrate. ~**zio'ne** *n.f.* frustration.

fru'tt|a *n.f.* fruit; (*portata*) dessert. ~**a're** *v.i.* bear fruit; *v.t.* yield. ~**e'to** *n.m.* orchard. ~**ive'ndolo, a** *n.m., f.* greengrocer. ~**o** *n.m.* fruit; (*fig.*) result. ~**i di mare** seafood *s.*

fu *a.* (*defunto*) late. **il** ~ **signor Rossi** the late Mr Rossi.

fuci'l|e *n.m.* gun; (*carabina*) rifle. ~**a're** shoot. ~**a'ta** *n.f.* shot.

fuci'na *n.f.* forge.

fu'csia *n.f.* fuchsia.

fu'ga *n.f.* escape; (*perdita*) leak; (*mus.*) fugue. **darsi alla** ~ take to flight. ~ **di gradini** flight of steps.

fuga'ce *a.* fleeting.

fugge'vole *a.* short-lived.

fuggia'sco, a *n.m., f.* fugitive.

fuggifu'ggi *n.m.* stampede.

fuggi'|re *v.i.* flee; (*di innamorati*) elope; (*fig.*) fly. ~**ti'vo, a** *n.m., f.* fugitive.

fu'lcro *n.m.* fulcrum.

fulge'nte *a.* shining.

fulgo're *n.m.* splendour.

fuli'ggine *n.f.* soot.

fulmina'r|e *v.t.* strike by lightning; (*con scarica elettrica*) electrocute. ~**si** *v.r.* burn out.

fu'lm|ine *n.m.* lightning. ~**i'neo** *a.* rapid.

fumaio'lo *n.m.* funnel; (*di casa*) chimney.

fuma'|re *v.t./i.* smoke; (*in ebollizione*) steam. ~**to're,** ~**tri'ce** *n.m., f.* smoker. **fu'mo** *n.m.* smoke; (*vapore*) steam; (*fig.*) hot air. **andare in fumo** vanish.

fume'tt|o *n.m.* comic strip. ~**i** *n.m. pl.* comics.

funa'mbolo, a *n.m., f.* tightrope walker.

fu'ne *n.f.* rope; (*cavo*) cable.

fu'nebre *a.* funeral; (*cupo*) gloomy.

funera'le *n.m.* funeral.

fune'sto *a.* sad.

fu'ngere *v.i.* ~ **da** act as.

fu'ngo *n.m.* mushroom; (*bot., med.*) fungus.

funicola're *n.f.* funicular (railway).

funivi'a *n.f.* cableway.

funziona'|re *v.i.* work, function. ~ **re da** (*fungere da*) act as. ~**le** *a.* functional. ~**me'nto** *n.m.* functioning.

funziona'rio *n.m.* official.

funzio'ne *n.f.* function; (*carica*) office; (*relig.*) service. **entrare in** ~ take up office.

fuo'c|o *n.m.* fire; (*fisica, fotografia*) focus. **far** ~**o** fire. ~**hi d'artificio** fireworks. **prendere** ~**o** catch fire.

fuorché *prep.* except.

fuo'ri *adv.* out; (*all'esterno*) outside; (*all'aperto*) outdoors. **andare di** ~ (*traboccare*) spill over. **essere** ~ **di sé** be beside oneself. **essere in** ~ (*sporgere*) stick out. ~ **luogo** (*inopportuno*) out of place. ~ **mano** out of

the way. ~ **moda** old-fashioned. ~
questione out of the question. —*n.m.*
outside.

fuoribo'rdo *n.m.* speedboat (with outboard motor).

fuoricla'sse *n.m.|f. invar.* champion.

fuorigio'co *n.m. & adv.* offside.

fuorile'gge *n.m.|f.* outlaw.

fuorise'rie *a.* custom-made. —*n.f.*
custom-built model.

fuorusci'to, a *n.m., f.* exile.

fuorvia're *v.t.* lead astray. —*v.i.* go
astray.

fu'rb|o *a.* cunning; (*intelligente*)
clever; (*astuto*) shrewd. **~eri'a** *n.f.*
cunning.

fure'nte *a.* furious.

furfa'nte *n.m.* scoundrel.

furgo'n|e *n.m.* van. **~ci'no** *n.m.* deliv-
ery van.

fu'ri|a *n.f.* fury; (*fretta*) haste. **a ~a
di** by dint of. **~bo'ndo, ~o'so** *adjs.*
furious.

furo're *n.m.* fury; (*veemenza*) frenzy.
far ~ be all the rage.

furoreggia're *v.i.* be a great success.

furti'vo *a.* furtive.

fu'rto *n.m.* theft; (*con scasso*) burglary.
commettere un ~ steal.

fu'sa *n.f. pl.* **fare le ~** purr.

fusce'llo *n.m.* (*di legno*) twig; (*di paglia*) straw.

fusi'bile *n.m.* fuse.

fusio'ne *n.f.* fusion; (*comm.*) merger.

fu'so *p.p. di* **fondere.** —*a.* melted.
—*n.m.* spindle. **a ~** spindle-shaped.
~ orario time zone.

fusolie'ra *n.f.* fuselage.

fu'sto *n.m.* stem; (*tronco*) trunk; (*recipiente di metallo*) drum; (*di legno*)
barrel.

fu'tile *a.* futile.

futu'r|o *a. & n.m.* future. **~i'sta**
n.m.|f. futurist.

G

gabba'r|e *v.t.* cheat. **∼si** *v.r.* **∼si di** make fun of.

ga'bbia *n.f.* cage; (*da imballaggio*) crate. **∼ degli imputati** dock. **mettere in ∼** (*fam.*) put in jail.

gabbia'no *n.m.* (sea)gull.

gabine'tto *n.m.* (*di medico*) consulting room; (*pol.*) cabinet; (*toletta*) lavatory; (*laboratorio*) laboratory.

ga'ffe *n.f.* blunder.

gaglia'rdo *a.* vigorous.

ga'i|o *a.* gay; (*di colore*) bright. **∼e'zza** *n.f.* gaiety.

ga'la *n.f.* gala.

gala'nte *a.* gallant. **∼ri'a** *n.f.* gallantry.

galantuo'm|o *n.m.* (*pl.* **∼ini**) gentleman.

gala'ssia *n.f.* galaxy.

galate'o *n.m.* (good) manners *pl.*; (*trattato*) book of etiquette.

galeo'tto *n.m.* (*rematore*) galley-slave; (*condannato*) convict.

gale'ra *n.f.* (*fam.*) prison.

ga'lla *n.f.* (*bot.*) gall. **a ∼** *adv.* afloat. **venire a ∼** surface.

galleggia'|re *v.i.* float. **∼nte** *a.* floating; *n.m.* craft; (*boa*) float.

galleri'a *n.f.* (*traforo*) tunnel; (*d'arte*) gallery; (*theatr.*) circle; (*arcata*) arcade.

Gall|es *n.m.* Wales. **g∼e'se** *a.* welsh; *n.m./f.* Welshman, -woman; *n.m.* (*lingua*) Welsh.

galli'na *n.f.* hen.

galli'smo *n.m.* machismo.

ga'll|o *n.m.* cock. **∼e'tto** *n.m.* cockerel.

gallo'ne *n.m.* braid; (*misura*) gallon.

galoppa're *v.i.* gallop. **galo'ppo** *n.m.* gallop. **al galoppo** at a gallop.

galvanizza're *v.t.* galvanize.

ga'mb|a *n.f.* leg; (*di lettera*) stem. **a quattro ∼e** on all fours. **darsela a ∼e** take to one's heels. **essere in ∼a** (*essere forte*) be strong; (*capace*) be smart.

gamba'le *n.m.* legging.

ga'mber|o *n.m.* prawn; (*di fiume*) crayfish. **∼e'tto** *n.m.* shrimp.

ga'mbo *n.m.* stem; (*di pianta*) stalk.

ga'mma *n.f.* (*mus.*) scale; (*fig.*) range.

gana'scia *n.f.* jaw.

ga'ncio *n.m.* hook.

ga'ngher|o *n.m.* hinge. **uscire dai ∼i** (*fig.*) get into a rage.

ga'ra *n.f.* competition; (*di velocità*) race. **fare a ∼** compete.

gara'ge *n.m.* garage.

garanti're *v.t.* guarantee; (*rendersi garante*) vouch for; (*assicurare*) assure. **gara'nte** *n.m./f.* guarantor.

garanzi'a *n.f.* guarantee.

garba're *v.i.* like. **non mi garba** I don't like it.

ga'rb|o *n.m.* courtesy; (*grazia*) grace. **con ∼o** graciously. **∼a'to** *a.* courteous.

garbu'glio *n.m.* muddle.

gareggia're *v.i.* compete.

gargari'sm|o *n.m.* gargle. **fare i ∼i** gargle.

garo'fano *n.m.* carnation. **chiodo di ∼** clove.

garri're *v.i.* chirp.

ga'rrulo *a.* garrulous.

ga'rza *n.f.* gauze.

garzo'ne *n.m.* boy. **∼ di stalla** stableboy.

gas *n.m. invar.* gas. **dare ∼** (*auto.*) accelerate.

gaso'lio *n.m.* diesel oil.

gassa're *v.t.* aerate; (*uccidere col gas*) gas.

gasso'so, a *a.* gassy. **—***n.f.* lemonade.

ga'strico *a.* gastric.

gastron|omi'a *n.f.* gastronomy. **∼o'mico** *a.* gastronomic(al).

ga'tt|o, a *n.m., f.* cat. **∼i'no, a** *n.m., f.* kitten.

gattopa'rdo *n.m.* leopard.

gaude'nte *a.* pleasure-loving.

gave'tta *n.f.* mess tin.

ga'zza *n.f.* magpie.

gazze'lla *n.f.* gazelle.

gazze'tta *n.f.* gazette.

gela'|re *v.t./i.* freeze. **∼ta** *n.f.* frost.

gelati'na *n.f.* gelatine; (*dolce*) jelly.

gela't|o *a.* frozen. **—***n.m.* ice-cream. **∼eri'a** *n.f.* ice-cream parlour.

ge'lido *a.* freezing.

ge'lo *n.m.* (*freddo intenso*) intense cold; (*brina*) frost; (*fig.*) chill.

gelo'ne *n.m.* chilblain.

gelosi'a *n.f.* jealousy; (*persiana*) shutter. **gelo'so** *a.* jealous.

ge′lso *n.m.* mulberry(-tree).

gelsomi′no *n.m.* jasmine.

geme′ll|o, a *a.* & *n.m.*, *f.* twin; (*di polsino*) cuff-link. **G~i** *n.m. pl.* (*astr.*) Gemini *s.*

ge′m|ere *v.i.* groan; (*tubare*) coo. **~ito** *n.m.* groan.

ge′mma *n.f.* gem; (*bot.*) bud.

ge′ne *n.m.* gene.

genealogi′a *n.f.* genealogy.

genera′l|e[1] *a.* general. **spese ~i** overheads. **~ità** *n.f. pl.* (*dati personali*) particulars. **~izza′re** *v.t.* generalize.

genera′le[2] *n.m.* (*mil.*) general.

genera′|re *v.t.* give birth (to); (*causare*) breed; (*techn.*) generate. **~to′re** *n.m.* (*techn.*) generator. **~zio′ne** *n.f.* generation.

ge′ner|e *n.m.* kind; (*biol.*) genus; (*gram.*) gender; (*prodotto*) product. **~i alimentari** provisions. **il ~e umano** mankind. **in ~e** generally.

gene′rico *a.* generic. **medico ~** general practitioner.

ge′nero *n.m.* son-in-law.

genero′s|o *a.* generous. **~ità** *n.f.* generosity.

ge′nesi *n.f.* genesis.

gene′tico, a *a.* genetic. **—***n.f.* genetics *s.*

gengi′va *n.f.* gum.

genia′le *a.* ingenious; (*congeniale*) congenial.

ge′nio *n.m.* genius. **andare a ~** be to one's taste.

genita′l|e *a.* genital. **~i** *n.m. pl.* genitals.

genito′r|e *n.m.* father. **~i** *n.m. pl.* parents.

genna′io *n.m.* January.

Ge′nova *n.f.* Genoa.

genta′glia *n.f.* rabble.

ge′nte *n.f.* people *pl.*

genti′l|e *a.* kind; (*cortese*) polite. **G~e Signore** Dear Sir. **~do′nna** *n.f.* gentlewoman. **~e′zza** *n.f.* kindness; politeness. **per ~ezza** (*per favore*) please. **~uo′mo** (*pl.* **~uo′mini**) *n.m.* gentleman.

genuflessio′ne *n.f.* genuflection.

genui′no *a.* genuine.

geogr|afi′a *n.f.* geography. **~a′fico** *a.* geographical.

geol|ogi′a *n.f.* geology. **~o′gico** *a.* geological.

geo′metra *n.m./f.* surveyor.

geom|etri′a *n.f.* geometry. **~e′trico** *a.* geometric(al).

gera′nio *n.m.* geranium.

gerarchi′a *n.f.* hierarchy.

gere′nte *n.m.* manager. **—***n.f.* manageress.

ge′rgo *n.m.* jargon.

geriatri′a *n.f.* geriatrics *s.*

Germa′nia *n.f.* Germany.

ge′rme *n.m.* germ.

germoglia′re *v.i.* sprout. **germo′glio** *n.m.* sprout.

gerogli′fico *n.m.* hieroglyph.

ge′sso *n.m.* chalk; (*med.*, *scultura*) plaster.

gestazio′ne *n.f.* gestation.

gesticola′re *v.i.* gesticulate.

gestio′ne *n.f.* management. **gesti′re** *v.i.* manage. **gesto′re** *n.m.* manager.

ge′sto *n.m.* gesture; (*azione*) (*pl. f.* **gesta**) deed.

Gesù *n.m.* Jesus.

gesui′ta *n.m.* Jesuit.

getta′|re *v.t.* throw; (*scagliare*) fling; (*emettere*) spout; (*techn.*, *fig.*) cast. **~rsi** *v.r.* throw oneself. **~rsi in** (*di fiume*) flow into. **~ta** *n.f.* throw; casting.

ge′tto *n.m.* throw; (*di liquidi, gas*) jet. **a ~ continuo** in a continuous stream. **di ~** straight off.

getto′ne *n.m.* token; (*per giochi*) counter.

ghermi′re *v.t.* seize.

ghe′tto *n.m.* ghetto.

ghiaccia′|o *n.m.* glacier.

ghiaccia′|re *v.t./i.* freeze. **~to** *a.* frozen; (*freddissimo*) ice-cold.

ghia′ccio *n.m.* ice.

ghiaccio′lo *n.m.* icicle; (*gelato*) ice lolly.

ghia′ia *n.f.* gravel.

ghia′nda *n.f.* acorn.

ghia′ndola *n.f.* gland.

ghigliotti′na *n.f.* guillotine.

ghigna′re *v.i.* sneer. **ghi′gno** *n.m.* sneer.

ghio′tt|o *a.* greedy; (*appetitoso*) appetizing. **~o′ne, a** *n.m.*, *f.* glutton.

ghiribi′zzo *n.m.* whim.

ghirigo′ro *n.m.* flourish.

ghirla′nda *n.f.* (*corona*) wreath; (*di fiori*) garland.

ghi′ro *n.m.* dormouse.

ghi′sa *n.f.* cast iron.

già *adv.* already; (*un tempo*) formerly; **~!** indeed! **~ da ieri** since yesterday.

gia′cca *n.f.* jacket. **~ a vento** windcheater.

giacché *conj.* since.

giace're v.i. lie.
giaci'glio n.m. pallet.
giacime'nto n.m. deposit.
giaci'nto n.m. hyacinth.
gia'da n.f. jade.
giaggio'lo n.m. iris.
giagua'ro n.m. jaguar.
gia'll|o a. & n.m. yellow. libro ∼o thriller. ∼a'stro a. yellowish.
giamma'i adv. never.
Giappo'n|e n.m. Japan. g∼e'se a. & n.m.|f. Japanese.
gia'ra n.f. jar.
giardi'n|o n.m. garden. ∼o d'infanzia kindergarten. ∼o pensile roof-garden. ∼a'ggio n.m. gardening. ∼ie're, a n.m., f. gardener; n.f. (automobile) estate car; (sottaceti) pickles pl.
giarrettie'ra n.f. garter.
giavello'tto n.m. javelin.
giga'nt|e n.m. giant. ∼e'ssa n.f. giantess. ∼e, ∼e'sco adjs. gigantic.
gi'glio n.m. lily.
gilè n.m. invar. waistcoat.
gin n.m. gin.
ginca'na n.f. gymkhana.
ginec|ologi'a n.f. gynaecology. ∼o'logo, a n.m., f. gynaecologist.
gine'pro n.m. juniper.
gine'stra n.f. broom.
gingilla'rsi v.r. fiddle; (perder tempo) potter. gingi'llo n.m. plaything; (ninnolo) knick-knack.
ginna'sio n.m. (scuola) grammar school.
ginna'st|ica n.f. gymnastics; (da camera) exercises pl. ∼a n.m.|f. gymnast.
gino'cchi|o n.m. (pl. m. ginocchi o f. ginocchia) knee. in ∼o on one's knees. ∼o'ni adv. kneeling.
gioca'|re v.t./i. play; (giocherellare) toy; (d'azzardo) gamble; (puntare) stake. ∼to're, ∼tri'ce n.m., f. player; gambler.
gioca'ttolo n.m. toy.
giocherella're v.i. toy; (nervosamente) fiddle.
gio'co n.m. game; (di bambini, techn.) play; (d'azzardo) gambling; (scherzo) joke; (insieme di pezzi ecc.) set. essere in ∼ be at stake. fare il doppio ∼ con qcno. double-cross s.o.
gioco'ndo a. cheerful.
gioco'so a. playful.
gioga'ia n.f. (geog.) mountain range.
gio'go n.m. yoke.

gio'i|a n.f. joy; (gioiello) jewel. ∼o'so a. joyous.
gioie'll|o n.m. jewel. ∼eri'a n.f. jeweller's (shop). ∼ie're, a n.m., f. jeweller.
gioi're v.i. ∼ (per) rejoice (at).
Giorda'nia n.f. Jordan.
giorna'l|e n.m. (news)paper; (diario) journal. ∼e di bordo log-book. ∼e radio news bulletin. ∼a'io, a n.m., f. newsagent.
giornalie'ro a. daily.
giornali's|mo n.m. journalism. ∼ta n.m.|f. journalist.
giorna'ta n.f. day. in ∼ today. vivere alla ∼ live from hand to mouth.
gio'rno n.m. day. al ∼ per day. al ∼ d'oggi nowadays. di ∼ by day. in pieno ∼ in broad daylight. un ∼ sì, un ∼ no every other day.
gio'stra n.f. merry-go-round; (torneo) tournament.
gio'van|e a. young; (giovanile) youthful. —n.m. youth, young man. —n.f. girl, young woman. ∼i'le a. youthful. ∼o'tto n.m. young man.
giova'r|e v.i. ∼e a be useful to; (far bene) be good for. ∼si v.r. ∼si di avail oneself of.
giovedì n.m. Thursday. di ∼ on Thursdays.
gioventù n.f. youth; (i giovani) young people pl.
giovia'le a. jovial.
giovine'zza n.f. youth.
giradi'schi n.m. invar. record-player.
gira'ffa n.f. giraffe.
gira'ndola n.f. (fuoco d'artificio) Catherine wheel; (giocattolo) windmill; (banderuola) weathercock.
gira'|re v.t. turn; (andare intorno, visitare) go round; (comm.) endorse; (cinema) shoot. —v.i. turn; (di aerei, uccelli) circle; (andare in giro) wander. ∼rsi v.r. turn (round). mi gira la testa I feel dizzy. ∼ta n.f. turn; (comm.) endorsement; (in macchina ecc.) ride.
girarro'sto n.m. spit.
giraso'le n.m. sunflower.
giravo'lta n.f. spin; (fig.) change of front.
gire'llo n.m. (per bambini) babywalker; (culin., carne) silverside.
gire'vole a. revolving. ponte ∼ swing bridge.
giri'no n.m. tadpole.
gi'ro n.m. turn; (circolo) circle; (percorso) round; (viaggio) tour; (passeg-

giata) short walk; (*in macchina*) drive; (*in bicicletta*) ride; (*circolazione di denaro*) circulation. ∼ **della manica** armhole. ∼ **d'affari** (*comm.*) turnover. **prendere in** ∼ **qcno.** take s.o. for a ride.

gironzola're *v.i.* stroll about.

girosco'pio *n.m.* gyroscope.

girovaga're *v.i.* wander about. **giro'vago** *n.m.* wanderer.

gi't|a *n.f.* trip. **andare in** ∼**a** go on a trip. ∼**a'nte** *n.m.|f.* tripper.

giù *adv.* down; (*sotto*) below; (*dabbasso*) downstairs. **a testa in** ∼ (*a capofitto*) headlong. **essere** ∼ (*di morale*) be depressed; (*di salute*) be run down. ∼ **di lì** (*su per giù*) more or less.

giu'bb|a *n.f.* jacket; (*mil.*) tunic. ∼**o'tto** *n.m.* jerkin.

giubila'|re *v.i.* rejoice. ∼**nte** *a.* jubilant. **giu'bilo** *n.m.* rejoicing.

giu'dic|e *n.m.* judge. ∼**e conciliatore** justice of the peace. ∼**a're** *v.t.* judge; (*ritenere*) consider.

giudi'zi|o *n.m.* judgement; (*legge*) judgment; (*opinione*) opinion; (*senno*) wisdom; (*processo*) trial; (*sentenza*) sentence. **mettere** ∼**o** become wise. ∼**o'so** *a.* sensible.

giu'gno *n.m.* June.

giume'nta *n.f.* mare.

giu'nco *n.m.* reed.

giu'ngere *v.i.* arrive. ∼ **a** (*riuscire*) succeed in. −*v.t.* (*unire*) join.

giu'ngla *n.f.* jungle.

giu'nta *n.f.* addition; (*mil.*) junta. **per** ∼ in addition.

giunt|a're *v.t.* (*con cucitura*) sew together. ∼**u'ra** *n.f.* joint.

giu'nto *p.p.* *di* **giungere.** −*n.m.* (*mech.*) joint.

giuoca're, giuo'co = **giocare, gioco.**

giura'|re *v.t./i.* swear. ∼**me'nto** *n.m.* oath. **prestare** ∼**mento** take the oath. ∼**to, a** *a.* sworn; *n.m, f.* juror.

giuri'a *n.f.* jury.

giuri'dico *a.* legal.

giurisdizio'ne *n.f.* jurisdiction.

giurisprude'nza *n.f.* jurisprudence.

giustifica'|re *v.t.* justify. ∼**zio'ne** *n.f.* justification.

giusti'zi|a *n.f.* justice. ∼**a're** *v.t.* execute. ∼**e're** *n.m.* executioner.

giu'sto *a.* just, fair; (*adatto*) right; (*esatto*) exact. −*n.m.* (*uomo retto*) just man; (*cosa giusta*) right. −*adv.* exactly. ∼ **ora** just now.

glacia'le *a.* glacial.

gladio'lo *n.m.* gladiolus.

gla'ss|a *n.f.* (*culin.*) icing. ∼**a're** *v.t.* ice.

gli *art. def. m. pl.* the. −*pron.* (*a lui*) (to) him; (*a esso*) (to) it; (*fam., loro, a loro*) (to) them.

gliceri'na *n.f.* glycerine.

glie'|lo *pron. composto* (*a lui*) (to) him. ∼**la** (*a lei*) (to) her. ∼**li, **∼**le** (*a loro*) (to) them; (*a Lei, forma di cortesia*) (to) you. ∼**ne** (*di ciò*) (of) it. ∼**lo prestai** I lent it to him. ∼**ne diedi un po'** I gave him some.

globa'le *a.* global; (*fig.*) overall.

glo'bo *n.m.* globe.

glo'bulo *n.m.* globule; (*med.*) corpuscle.

glo'ri|a *n.f.* glory. ∼**a'rsi** *v.r.* ∼**arsi di** be proud of. ∼**fica're** *v.t.* glorify. ∼**o'so** *a.* glorious.

glossa'rio *n.m.* glossary.

gluco'sio *n.m.* glucose.

gno'mo *n.m.* gnome.

go'bb|a *n.f.* hump. ∼**o, a** *a.* hunchbacked; *n.m., f.* hunchback.

go'cci|a *n.f.* drop; (*di sudore*) bead. ∼**ola're** *v.i.* drip. ∼**oli'o** *n.m.* dripping.

gode'r|e *v.t./i.* enjoy. ∼**sela** have a good time. **godime'nto** *n.m.* enjoyment.

go'ffo *a.* awkward.

go'la *n.f.* throat; (*ingordigia*) gluttony; (*geog.*) gorge; (*di camino*) flue. **avere mal di** ∼ have a sore throat. **far** ∼ **a qcno.** tempt s.o.

golf *n.m. invar.* jersey; (*sport*) golf.

go'lfo *n.m.* gulf.

golo's|o *a.* greedy. ∼**ità** *n.f.* greediness.

go'mit|o *n.m.* elbow. ∼**a'ta** *n.f.* nudge.

gomi'tolo *n.m.* ball.

go'mma *n.f.* rubber; (*colla*) gum; (*pneumatico*) tyre. ∼**piu'ma** *n.f.* foam rubber.

go'ndol|a *n.f.* gondola. ∼**ie're** *n.m.* gondolier.

gonfalo'ne *n.m.* banner.

gonfia'r|e *v.i.* swell. −*v.t.* blow up; (*pneumatico*) pump up; (*esagerare*) exaggerate. ∼**si** *v.r.* swell; (*di acque*) rise. **go'nfio** *a.* swollen; (*di pneumatico*) inflated. **a gonfie vele** splendidly. **gonfio're** *n.m.* swelling.

gongola'|re *v.i.* be overjoyed. ∼**nte** *a.* overjoyed.

go'nna *n.f.* skirt.

go'nzo *n.m.* simpleton.

gorgheggia're *v.i.* warble. **gorghe'ggio** *n.m.* warble.

go'rgo *n.m.* whirlpool.

gorgoglia're *v.i.* gurgle.

gori'lla *n.m. invar.* gorilla.

go'ta *n.f.* cheek.

go'tico *a. & n.m.* Gothic.

go'tta *n.f.* gout.

governa'|re *v.t.* govern; (*dominare*) rule; (*dirigere*) manage; (*curare*) look after. **~ti'vo** *a.* government. **~to're** *n.m.* governor.

gove'rno *n.m.* government; (*dominio*) rule. **~ della casa** housekeeping.

gozzovi'glia *n.f.* revelry.

gracchia're *v.i.* caw.

gracida're *v.i.* croak.

gra'cile *a.* delicate.

grada'sso *n.m.* braggart.

gradazio'ne *n.f.* gradation. **~ alcoolica** alcohol(ic) content.

grade'vole *a.* agreeable.

gradie'nte *n.m.* gradient.

gradime'nto *n.m.* liking. **indice di ~** (*radio, TV*) popularity rating.

gradina'ta *n.f.* flight of steps; (*di stadio, teatro*) tiers *pl.*

gradi'no *n.m.* step.

gradi'|re *v.t.* like; (*desiderare*) wish. **~to** *a.* pleasant; (*bene accetto*) welcome.

gra'do *n.m.* degree; (*rango*) rank. **di buon ~** willingly. **essere in ~ di fare** be in a position to do.

gradua'le *a.* gradual.

gradua'|re *v.t.* graduate. **~to** *a.* graded; (*provvisto di scàla graduata*) graduated; *n.m.* (*mil.*) noncommissioned officer. **~to'ria** *n.f.* list. **~zio'ne** *n.f.* graduation.

gra'ff|a *n.f.* clip; (*segno grafico*) brace. **~e'tta** *n.f.* staple.

graffia'|re *v.t.* scratch. **~tu'ra** *n.f.* scratch. **gra'ffio** *n.m.* scratch.

grafi'a *n.f.* (hand)writing; (*ortografia*) spelling.

gra'fico *a.* graphic. *—n.m.* graph; (*persona*) graphic designer. *—n.f.* graphics *s.*

grama'glie *n.f. pl.* widow's weeds.

grami'gna *n.f.* weed.

gramma'tic|a *n.f.* grammar. **~a'le** *a.* grammatical.

gra'mmo *n.m.* gram(me).

grammo'fono *n.m.* gramophone.

gran *a. vedi* **grande.**

gra'na *n.f.* grain; (*formaggio*) parme-

san; (*fam., seccatura*) trouble; (*sl., denaro*) money.

grana'io *n.m.* barn.

grana'ta *n.f.* (*mil.*) grenade; (*frutto*) pomegranate.

granatie're *n.m.* (*mil.*) grenadier.

grana'to *n.m.* garnet.

Gran Breta'gna *n.f.* Great Britain.

gra'nchio *n.m.* crab; (*fig., errore*) blunder. **prendere un ~** make a blunder.

grandangola're *n.m.* wide-angle lens.

gra'nde *qualche volta* **gran** *a.* (*ampio*) large; (*grosso*) big; (*largo*) wide; (*fig., senso morale*) great; (*grandioso*) grand. **con mia ~ meraviglia** much to my astonishment. **fa un gran caldo** it is very hot. **in ~** on a large scale. **in gran parte** to a great extent. **non è un gran che** it is nothing much. **un gran ballo** a grand ball. *—n.m.|f.* (*persona adulta*) grown-up; (*persona eminente*) great man/woman.

grandeggia're *v.i.* **~ su** tower over; (*darsi arie*) show off.

grande'zza *n.f.* greatness; (*ampiezza*) largeness; (*larghezza*) width, breadth; (*dimensione*) size; (*fasto*) grandeur; (*prodigalità*) lavishness.

gra'ndin|e *n.f.* hail. **~a're** *v.i.* hail. **~a** it is hailing.

grandio'|s|o *a.* grand. **~ità** *n.f.* grandeur.

grandu'ca *n.m.* grand duke.

grane'llo *n.m.* grain; (*di frutta*) pip.

grani'ta *n.f.* crushed ice drink.

grani'to *n.m.* granite.

gra'no *n.m.* grain; (*frumento*) wheat; (*di collana*) bead.

grantu'rco *n.m.* maize.

gra'nulo *n.m.* granule.

gra'ppa *n.f.* grappa; (*morsa*) cramp.

gra'ppolo *n.m.* bunch.

gra'ss|o *a.* fat; (*di cibo*) fatty; (*unto*) greasy; (*terreno*) rich; (*grossolano*) coarse. *—n.m.* fat; (*sostanza*) grease. **~e'zza** *n.f.* fatness; greasiness. **~o'ccio** *a.* plump.

gra't|a *n.f.* grating. **~e'lla, ~i'cola** *ns.f.* (*culin.*) grill.

grati'ccio *n.m.* (*per piante*) trellis; (*stuoia*) rush matting.

grati'fica *n.f.* bonus.

gra'tis *adv.* free.

gra't|o *a.* grateful; (*gradito*) pleasant. **~itu'dine** *n.f.* gratitude.

grattaca'po *n.m.* trouble.

grattacie'lo *n.m.* skyscraper.

gratta'r|e *v.t.* scratch; (*raschiare*) scrape; (*grattugiare*) grate; (*fam.*, *rubare*) pinch. *—v.i.* grate. **~si** *v.r.* scratch oneself.

grattu'gi|a *n.f.* grater. **~a're** *v.t.* grate.

gratu'ito *a.* free (of charge); (*ingiustificato*) gratuitous.

grava're *v.t.* burden. *—v.i.* **~ su** weigh on.

gra'v|e *a.* (*pesante*) heavy; (*serio*) grave; (*difficile*) hard; (*di voce, suono*) low; (*fonetica*) grave. **essere ~e** (*gravemente ammalato*) be seriously ill. **~ità** *n.f.* seriousness; (*fisica*) gravity.

gravida'nza *n.f.* pregnancy. **gra'vido** *a.* pregnant.

gravita're *v.i.* gravitate.

gravo'so *a.* onerous.

gra'zi|a *n.f.* grace; (*favore*) favour; (*legge*) pardon. **~a're** *v.t.* pardon.

gra'zie *int.* thank you!, thanks! **~ mille!** many thanks!

grazio'so *a.* charming; (*carino*) pretty.

Gre'c|ia *n.f.* Greece. **g~o, a** *a.* & *n.m.*, *f.* Greek.

grega'rio *a.* gregarious. *—n.m.* (*ciclismo*) supporting rider.

gre'gge *n.m.* flock; (*di bovini*) herd.

gre'ggio *a.* raw. *—n.m.* (*petrolio*) crude (oil).

grembia'le, grembiu'le *ns.m.* apron.

gre'mbo *n.m.* lap; (*utero*) womb; (*fig.*) bosom.

gremi'|re *v.t.* pack. **~rsi** *v.r.* **~rsi** (**di**) become crowded (with). **~to** *a.* packed.

gre'tto *a.* stingy; (*di vedute ristrette*) narrow-minded.

gre've *a.* heavy.

gre'zzo *a.* = **greggio.**

grida're *v.i.* shout, cry (out); (*strillare*) scream. *—v.t.* shout (for), cry (for). **gri'do** *n.m.* (*pl. m.* **gridi** *o f.* **grida**) shout, cry; scream; (*di animale*) cry. **l'ultimo grido** the latest fashion. **scrittore di grido** celebrated writer.

gri'gio *a.* & *n.m.* grey.

gri'glia *n.f.* grill. **alla ~** grilled.

grille'tto *n.m.* trigger.

gri'llo *n.m.* cricket; (*fig.*, *capriccio*) whim.

grimalde'llo *n.m.* picklock.

gri'nfia *n.f.* (*fig.*) clutch.

gri'nta *n.f.* grim face; (*coraggio*) guts *pl.*

gri'nza *n.f.* wrinkle; (*di stoffa*) crease.

grippa're *v.i.* (*mech.*) seize.

grissi'no *n.m.* bread-stick.

gro'nda *n.f.* eaves *pl.*

gronda'ia *n.f.* gutter.

gronda're *v.i.* pour; (*essere bagnato fradicio*) be dripping wet.

gro'ppa *n.f.* back.

gro'ppo *n.m.* knot. **avere un ~ alla gola** have a lump in one's throat.

gro'ssa *n.f.* (*comm.*) gross.

grossi'sta *n.m.|f.* wholesaler.

gro'ss|o *a.* big, large; (*spesso*) thick; (*grossolano*) coarse; (*grave*) serious. *—n.m.* big part; (*massa*) bulk. **farla ~a** do a stupid thing. **un pezzo ~o** a big shot (*sl.*). **~e'zza** *n.f.* size; (*spessore*) thickness.

grossola'no *a.* coarse.

gro'tta *n.f.* cave, grotto.

grotte'sco *a.* & *n.m.* grotesque.

grovie'ra *n.m.|f.* gruyère.

grovi'glio *n.m.* tangle; (*fig.*) muddle.

gru *n.f. invar.* crane.

gru'ccia *n.f.* crutch; (*per vestito*) hanger.

grugni'|re *v.i.* grunt. **~to** *n.m.* grunt.

gru'gno *n.m.* snout.

gru'llo *a.* silly.

gru'mo *n.m.* clot; (*di farina ecc.*) lump.

gru'ppo *n.m.* group; (*comitiva*) party.

gru'zzolo *n.m.* nest-egg.

guadagna're *v.t.* earn; (*tempo, forza, ecc.*) gain. **guada'gno** *n.m.* gain; (*profitto*) profit; (*entrate*) earnings *pl.*

gua'do *n.m.* ford. **passare a ~** ford.

guai'na *n.f.* sheath; (*busto*) girdle.

gua'io *n.m.* trouble. **che ~!** what a nuisance! **essere nei guai** be in a fix. **guai a te se lo tocchi!** don't you dare touch it!

guai'|re *v.i.* yelp. **~to** *n.m.* yelp.

gua'ncia *n.f.* cheek.

guancia'le *n.m.* pillow.

gua'nto *n.m.* glove.

guardabo'schi *n.m. invar.* forester.

guardaca'ccia *n.m. invar.* gamekeeper.

guardaco'ste *n.m. invar.* coastguard.

guardali'nee *n.m. invar.* (*sport*) linesman.

guarda'r|e *v.t.* look at; (*osservare*) watch; (*badare a*) look after; (*dare su*) look out on. *—v.i.* look; (*essere orientato verso*) face. **~si** *v.r.* look at oneself. **~si da** beware of; (*astenersi*) refrain from.

guardaro'b|a *n.m. invar.* wardrobe; (*di locale pubblico*) cloakroom. **∼ie're, a** *n.m.*, *f.* cloakroom attendant.

gua'rdia *n.f.* guard; (*poliziotto*) policeman; (*vigilanza*) watch. **essere di ∼** be on guard; (*di medico*) be on duty. **fare la ∼ a** keep guard over. **mettere in ∼ qcno.** warn s.o. **stare in ∼** be on one's guard.

guardia'no, a *n.m.*, *f.* caretaker. **∼ notturno** night watchman.

guardi'ngo *a.* cautious.

guardio'la *n.f.* gatekeeper's lodge.

guari'|re *v.t.* cure. —*v.i.* recover; (*di ferita*) heal (up). **∼gio'ne** *n.f.* recovery. **∼to're** *n.m.* healer.

guarnigio'ne *n.f.* garrison.

guarni'|re *v.t.* trim; (*culin.*) garnish. **∼zio'ne** *n.f.* trimming; garnish; (*mech.*) gasket.

guastafe'ste *n.m.*|*f. invar.* spoil-sport.

guasta'r|e *v.t.* spoil; (*rovinare*) ruin; (*meccanismo*) break. **∼si** *v.r.* spoil; (*andare a male*) go bad; (*tempo*) change for the worse; (*meccanismo*) break down. **gua'sto** *a.* (*di meccanismo*) out of order; (*andato a male*) bad; (*dente*) decayed; *n.m.* breakdown; (*danno*) damage.

gua'zza *n.f.* (heavy) dew.

guazzabu'glio *n.m.* muddle.

guazza're *v.i.* wallow. **gua'zzo** *n.m.* puddle; (*pittura*) gouache.

gue'rcio *a.* cross-eyed.

gue'rr|a *n.f.* war; (*tecnica bellica*) warfare. **∼afonda'io** *n.m.* warmonger. **∼eggia're** *v.i.* wage war. **∼e'sco** *a.* (*di guerra*) war; (*bellicoso*) warlike. **∼ie'ro** *n.m.* warrior.

guerri'gli|a *n.f.* guerrilla warfare. **∼e'ro, a** *n.m.*, *f.* guerrilla.

gu'fo *n.m.* owl.

gu'glia *n.f.* spire.

gui'd|a *n.f.* guide; (*direzione*) guidance; (*comando*) leadership; (*auto.*) driving; (*tappeto*) runner. **∼a a destra/sinistra** right-/left-hand drive. **∼a're** *v.t.* guide; lead; drive; (*una nave*) steer. **∼ato're** *n.m.* driver.

guinza'glio *n.m.* leash.

gui'sa *n.f.* manner. **a ∼ di** like.

guizza're *v.i.* dart; (*di luce*) flash. **gui'zzo** *n.m.* dart; flash.

gu'scio *n.m.* shell.

gu'st|o *n.m.* taste; (*piacere*) liking. **mangiare di ∼o** eat heartily. **∼a're** *v.t.* taste; *v.i.* like. **∼o'so** *a.* tasty; (*fig.*) delightful.

guttura'le *a.* guttural.

H

habituè *n.m.*|*f.* regular (customer).

handicappa're *v.t.* handicap.

ha'rem *n.m. invar.* harem.

ha'scisc *n.m.* hashish.

I

i *art. def. m. pl.* the.
ia'to *n.m.* hiatus.
iberna'|re *v.i.* hibernate. ∼**zio'ne** *n.f.* hibernation.
ibi'sco *n.m.* hibiscus.
i'brido *a.* & *n.m.* hybrid.
ico'na *n.f.* icon.
Iddi'o *n.m.* God.
ide'a *n.f.* idea; (*opinione*) opinion; (*ideale*) ideal. **cambiare** ∼ change one's mind. **neanche per** ∼! not on your life!
idea'l|e *a.* & *n.m.* ideal. ∼**i'sta** *n.m.|f.* idealist. ∼**izza're** *v.t.* idealize.
idea're *v.t.* conceive.
i'dem *adv.* the same.
ide'ntico *a.* identical.
identifica'|re *v.t.* identify. ∼**zio'ne** *n.f.* identification.
identità *n.f.* identity.
ideol|ogi'a *n.f.* ideology. ∼**o'gico** *a.* ideologic(al).
idi'lli|o *n.m.* idyll. ∼**co** *a.* idyllic.
idio'm|a *n.m.* idiom. ∼**a'tico** *a.* idiomatic.
idiosincrasi'a *n.f.* idiosyncrasy.
idio'ta *a.* idiotic. —*n.m.|f.* idiot.
idioti'smo *n.m.* idiom; (*med.*) idiocy.
idolatra're *v.t.* worship.
i'dol|o *n.m.* idol. ∼**eggia're** *v.t.* idolize.
ido'ne|o *a.* ∼**o a** suitable for; (*mil.*) fit for. ∼**ità** *n.f.* suitability; fitness. **esame di** ∼**ità** qualifying examination.
idra'nte *n.m.* hydrant.
idrata'|re *v.t.* hydrate; (*cosmetica*) moisturize. **crema** ∼**nte** moisturizing cream.
idra'ulico *a.* hydraulic. —*n.m.* plumber.
idroele'ttrico *a.* hydroelectric.
idro'filo *a. vedi* **cotone.**
idrofobi'a *n.f.* rabies *s.* **idro'fobo** *a.* rabid; (*fig.*) furious.
idro'geno *n.m.* hydrogen.
idropla'no *n.m.* hydroplane.
idrosca'lo *n.m.* seaplane basin.
idrovola'nte *n.m.* seaplane.
ie'lla *n.f.* evil eye.
ie'na *n.f.* hyena.

ie'ri *adv.* yesterday. ∼ **l'altro, l'altro** ∼ the day before yesterday.
iettatu'ra *n.f.* (*sfortuna*) bad luck.
igie'n|e *n.f.* hygiene. ∼**ico** *a.* hygienic(al). ∼**i'sta** *n.m.|f.* hygienist.
igna'ro *a.* unaware.
igno'bile *a.* base; (*non onorevole*) dishonourable.
ignomi'nia *n.f.* disgrace.
ignora'n|te *a.* ignorant. —*n.m.|f.* ignoramus. ∼**za** *n.f.* ignorance.
ignora're *v.t.* (*non sapere*) be unaware of; (*trascurare*) ignore.
igno'to *a.* unknown.
il *art. def. m. s.* the.
i'lar|e *a.* merry. ∼**ità** *n.f.* hilarity.
illanguidi're *v.i.* languish.
ille'cito *a.* illicit.
illega'le *a.* illegal.
illeggi'bile *a.* illegible.
illegi'ttim|o *a.* illegitimate. ∼**ità** *n.f.* illegitimacy.
ille'so *a.* unhurt.
illettera'to, a *a.* & *n.m., f.* illiterate.
illiba'to *a.* chaste.
illimita'to *a.* unlimited.
illividi're *v.t.* bruise. —*v.i.* (*per rabbia*) turn livid.
illo'gico *a.* illogical.
illu'der|e *v.t.* deceive. ∼**si** *v.r.* deceive oneself.
illumina'|re *v.t.* illuminate; (*fig.*) enlighten. ∼**re a giorno** floodlight. ∼**rsi** *v.r.* light up. ∼**zio'ne** *n.f.* lighting; (*fig.*) enlightenment.
illusio'n|e *n.f.* illusion. **farsi** ∼**i** delude oneself.
illusioni's|mo *n.m.* conjuring. ∼**ta** *n.m.|f.* conjurer.
illu'so, a *p.p. di* **illudere.** —*a.* deluded. —*n.m., f.* day-dreamer.
illustra'|re *v.t.* illustrate. ∼**ti'vo** *a.* illustrative. ∼**to're** *n.m.* illustrator. ∼**zio'ne** *n.f.* illustration.
illu'stre *a.* distinguished.
imbacucca'r|e *v.t.* ∼**si** *v.r.* wrap up.
imballa'|re *v.t.* pack; (*auto.*) race. ∼**ggio** *n.m.* packing.
imbalsama're *v.t.* embalm.
imbandiera're *v.t.* deck with flags.
imbandi're *v.t.* ∼ **la tavola** lay the table (sumptuously).
imbarazza'|re *v.t.* embarrass; (*ostaco-*

lare) encumber. ~nte *a.* embarrassing. **imbara'zzo** *n.m.* embarrassment; (*ostacolo*) hindrance. **imbarazzo di stomaco** indigestion. **trarre qcno. d'imbarazzo** help s.o. out of a difficulty.

imbarcade'ro *n.m.* landing-stage.

imbarca'r|e *v.t.* embark. ~si *v.r.* go on board. **imba'rco** *n.m.* embarkation; (*banchina*) landing-stage.

imbarcazio'ne *n.f.* boat. ~ **di salvataggio** lifeboat.

imbasti'|re *v.t.* tack; (*fig.*) sketch. ~tu'ra *n.f.* basting.

imba'ttersi *v.r.* ~ **in** run into.

imbatti'bile *a.* unbeatable.

imbavaglia're *v.t.* gag.

imbecca'|re *v.t.* (*uccelli*) feed. ~ta *n.f.* (*theatr.*) prompt.

imbeci'lle *a.* stupid. —*n.m.|f.* (*med.*) imbecile.

imbelletta'rsi *v.r.* make oneself up.

imbelli're *v.t.* embellish.

imbe'rbe *a.* beardless; (*fig.*) inexperienced.

imbestiali'r|e *v.i.*, ~si *v.r.* fly into a rage.

imbe'ver|e *v.t.* imbue (**di**, with). ~si *v.r.* absorb.

imbianca're *v.t.* whiten. —*v.i.* turn white.

imbianchi'no *n.m.* (house) painter.

imbizzarrir|e *v.i.*, ~si *v.r.* become restless.

imbocca'|re *v.t.* feed; (*entrare*) enter; (*fig.*) prompt. ~tu'ra *n.f.* opening; (*ingresso*) entrance. **imbo'cco** *n.m.* entrance.

imbosca'r|e *v.t.* hide. ~si *v.r.* (*mil.*) shirk military service.

imbosca'ta *n.f.* ambush.

imbottiglia're *v.t.* bottle. ~si *v.r.* get caught in a traffic jam.

imbotti'|re *v.t.* stuff; (*giacca*) pad; (*panino*) fill. ~tu'ra *n.f.* stuffing; padding; filling.

imbotti'ta *n.f.* quilt.

imbratta'r|e *v.t.* soil. ~si *v.r.* dirty oneself.

imbriglia're *v.t.* bridle.

imbrocca'r|e *v.t.* hit. ~la giusta hit the nail on the head.

imbroglia'r|e *v.t.* muddle; (*raggirare*) cheat. ~si *v.r.* get tangled; (*confondersi*) get confused. **imbro'glio** *n.m.* tangle; (*pasticcio*) mess; (*inganno*) trick. **imbroglio'ne, a** *n.m., f.* cheat.

imbroncia'|re *v.i.*, ~rsi *v.r.* sulk. ~to *a.* sulky.

imbruni're *v.i.* get dark. **all'~** at dusk.

imbrutti're *v.t.* make ugly. —*v.i.* become ugly.

imbuca're *v.t.* post.

imburra're *v.t.* butter.

imbu'to *n.m.* funnel.

imita'|re *v.t.* imitate. ~zio'ne *n.f.* imitation.

immacola'to *a.* spotless.

immagazzina're *v.t.* store.

immagina'|re *v.t.* imagine; (*supporre*) suppose. ~rio *a.* imaginary. ~zio'ne *n.f.* imagination.

imma'gine *n.f.* image; (*rappresentazione, idea*) picture.

immanca'bile *a.* unfailing.

imma'ne *a.* huge.

immangia'bile *a.* uneatable.

immatricola'|re *v.t.* register. ~rsi *v.r.* (*studente*) matriculate. ~zio'ne *n.f.* registration; matriculation.

immatu'ro *a.* unripe; (*persona*) immature.

immedesima'rsi *v.r.* ~ **in** identify oneself with.

immedia'|t|o *a.* immediate. ~ame'nte *adv.* immediately.

immemora'bile *a.* immemorial.

imme'more *a.* oblivious.

imme'ns|o *a.* immense. ~ità *n.f.* immensity.

immensura'bile *a.* immeasurable.

imme'rger|e *v.t.* immerse. ~si *v.r.* plunge; (*sommergibile*) dive. ~si **in** immerse oneself in.

immerit|a'to *a.* undeserved. ~e'vole *a.* undeserving.

immersio'ne *n.f.* immersion; (*di sommergibile*) dive.

imme'rso *p.p. di* **immergere**.

immigra'|nte *a.* & *n.m.|f.* immigrant. ~re *v.i.* immigrate. ~to, a *n.m., f.* immigrant. ~zio'ne *n.f.* immigration.

immine'n|te *a.* imminent. ~za *n.f.* imminence.

immischia'r|e *v.t.* involve. ~si *v.r.* ~si **in** meddle in.

immissa'rio *n.m.* tributary.

immissio'ne *n.f.* insertion.

immo'bil|e *a.* motionless. ~ità *n.f.* immobility. ~izza're *v.t.* immobilize; (*comm.*) tie up.

immo'bili *n.m. pl.* real estate *s.* ~a're *a.* società ~are building society.

immodera'to *a.* immoderate.

immode'sto *a.* immodest.

immola're *v.t.* sacrifice.

immondi'zia *n.f.* filth; (*spazzatura*) rubbish. **immo'ndo** *a.* filthy.

immora'l|e *a.* immoral. ∼**ità** *n.f.* immorality.

immorta'l|e *a.* immortal. ∼**a're** *v.t.* immortalize.

immo'to *a.* motionless.

immu'n|e *a.* exempt; (*med.*) immune. ∼**ità** *n.f.* immunity. ∼**izza're** *v.t.* immunize. ∼**izzazio'ne** *n.f.* immunization.

immuta'|bile *a.* unchangeable. ∼**to** *a.* unchanging.

impacchetta're *v.t.* parcel up.

impaccia'|re *v.t.* hamper; (*disturbare*) inconvenience; (*imbarazzare*) embarrass. ∼**to** *a.* embarrassed; (*goffo*) awkward. **impa'ccio** *n.m.* embarrassment; (*ostacolo*) hindrance; (*situazione difficile*) awkward situation.

impa'cco *n.m.* compress.

impadroni'rsi *v.r.* ∼ **di** take possession of; (*fig.*, *imparare*) master.

impaga'bile *a.* priceless.

impaglia'|re *v.t.* cover with straw. ∼**tu'ra** *n.f.* straw covering.

impala'|re *v.t.* impale. ∼**to** *a.* (*fig.*) stiff.

impalcatu'ra *n.f.* scaffolding; (*fig.*) structure.

impallidi're *v.i.* turn pale.

impana're *v.t.* (*culin.*) roll in breadcrumbs.

impantana'rsi *v.r.* get bogged down.

impappina'rsi *v.r.* falter.

impara're *v.t.* learn. ∼ **a memoria** learn by heart.

impareggia'bile *a.* incomparable.

imparenta'rsi *v.r.* ∼ **con** become related to.

i'mpari *a.* unequal; (*dispari*) odd.

imparti're *v.t.* impart.

imparzia'l|e *a.* impartial. ∼**ità** *n.f.* impartiality.

impassi'bile *a.* impassive.

impasta'|re *v.t.* (*culin.*) knead; (*colori*) blend. ∼**tu'ra** *n.f.* kneading. **impa'sto** *n.m.* (*culin.*) dough; (*miscuglio*) mixture.

impasticcia're *v.t.* make a mess (of).

impa'tto *n.m.* impact.

impauri'r|e *v.t.* frighten. ∼**si** *v.r.* become frightened.

impa'vido *a.* fearless.

impazie'n|te *a.* impatient. ∼**ti'rsi** *v.r.* lose patience. ∼**za** *n.f.* impatience.

impazza'ta *n.f.* **all'**∼ at breakneck speed.

impazzi're *v.i.* go mad. **far** ∼ **qcno.** drive s.o. mad. ∼ **per** be crazy about.

impecca'bile *a.* impeccable.

impedi'|re *v.t.* ∼**re di** prevent from; (*impacciare*) hinder; (*ostruire*) obstruct. ∼**me'nto** *n.m.* hindrance; (*ostacolo*) obstacle.

impegna'|re *v.t.* (*dare in pegno*) pawn; (*vincolare*) bind; (*prenotare*) reserve; (*assorbire*) take up. ∼**rsi** *v.r.* ∼**rsi a** engage oneself in; (*dedicarsi*) devote oneself to. ∼**ti'vo** *a.* binding; (*lavoro*) demanding. ∼**to** *a.* engaged.

impe'gno *n.m.* engagement, (*comm.*) commitment; (*zelo*) care.

impelle'nte *a.* pressing.

impenetra'bile *a.* impenetrable.

impenite'nte *a.* unrepentant.

impenna'rsi *v.r.* (*di cavallo*) rear; (*fig.*) bristle.

impensa'to *a.* unexpected.

impensieri'r|e *v.t.*, ∼**si** *v.r.* worry.

impera're *v.i.* reign.

imperati'vo *a.* & *n.m.* imperative.

impera|to're, ∼**tri'ce** *n.m.*, *f.* emperor, empress.

impercetti'bile *a.* imperceptible.

imperdona'bile *a.* unforgivable.

imperfe'|tto *a.* & *n.m.* imperfect. ∼**zio'ne** *n.f.* imperfection.

imperia'l|e *a.* imperial. ∼**i'smo** *n.m.* imperialism.

imperio'so *a.* imperious; (*impellente*) urgent.

imperi'zia *n.f.* lack of skill.

impermali'r|e *v.t.* annoy. ∼**si** *v.r.* take offence.

impermea'bile *a.* waterproof. —*n.m.* raincoat.

impernia're *v.t.* pivot; (*fondare*) base.

impe'ro *n.m.* empire; (*potere*) rule.

imperscruta'bile *a.* inscrutable.

impersona'le *a.* impersonal.

impersona're *v.t.* personify; (*interpretare*) act (the part of).

imperte'rrito *a.* undaunted.

impertine'n|te *a.* impertinent. ∼**za** *n.f.* impertinence.

imperturba'|bile *a.* imperturbable. ∼**to** *a.* unperturbed.

imperversa're *v.i.* rage.

impe'rvio *a.* inaccessible.

i'mpet|o *n.m.* impetus; (*impulso*) im-

pulse; (*slancio*) transport. ~**uo'so** *a.*
impetuous; (*del vento*) blustering.
impetti'to *a.* stiff.
impianta're *v.t.* set up; (*fondare*)
found.
impia'nto *n.m.* plant; (*sistema*) system; (*l'impiantare*) installation.
impia'str|o *n.m.* poultice; (*persona
noiosa*) bore. ~**a're** *v.t.* plaster.
impicca'r|e *v.t.* hang. ~**si** *v.r.* hang
oneself.
impiccia'r|e *v.t.* encumber. ~**si** *v.r.*
meddle. **impi'ccio** *n.m.* hindrance;
(*seccatura*) bother.
impiega'|re *v.t.* employ; (*usare*) use;
(*tempo, denaro*) spend; (*comm.*) invest. ~**rsi** *v.r.* get (oneself) a job. ~**to**,
a *n.m.*, *f.* employee. **impie'go** *n.m.*
employment; (*posto*) job; (*comm.*)
investment.
impietosi'r|e *v.t.* move to pity. ~**si**
v.r. be moved to pity.
impietri'to *a.* petrified.
impiglia'r|e *v.t.* entangle. ~**si** *v.r.* get
entangled.
impigri'r|e *v.t.* make lazy. ~**si** *v.r.*
become lazy.
impiomba'|re *v.t.* (*sigillare*) seal
(with lead); (*dente*) fill. ~**tu'ra** *n.f.*
sealing (with lead); filling.
implaca'bile *a.* implacable.
implica'|re *v.t.* implicate; (*sottinten-
dere*) imply. ~**rsi** *v.r.* become involved. ~**zio'ne** *n.f.* implication.
impli'cito *a.* implicit.
implora'|re *v.t.* implore. ~**zio'ne** *n.f.*
entreaty.
impoltroni'r|e *v.t.* make lazy. ~**si** *v.r.*
become lazy.
impolvera'|re *v.t.* cover with dust.
~**rsi** *v.r.* get covered with dust. ~**to**
a. dusty.
impondera'bile *a.* imponderable.
impone'n|te *a.* imposing. ~**za** *n.f.* im-
pressiveness.
imponi'bile *a.* taxable. —*n.m.* taxable
income.
impopola'r|e *a.* unpopular. ~**ità** *n.f.*
unpopularity.
imporpora'rsi *v.r.* turn red.
impo'r|re *v.t.* impose; (*ordinare*) or-
der. ~**si** *v.r.* impose oneself; (*aver
successo*) be successful. ~**si di** (*prefig-
gersi*) set oneself the task of.
importa'n|te *a.* important. —*n.m.* im-
portant thing. ~**za** *n.f.* importance.
importa'|re *v.t.* (*comm.*) import; (*com-
portare*) cause. —*v.i.* matter; (*essere*

necessario) be necessary. **non importa!** it doesn't matter! **non me ne
importa niente!** I couldn't care less!
~**zio'ne** *n.f.* importation; (*merce im-
portata*) import.
impo'rto *n.m.* amount.
importu'n|o *a.* troublesome; (*inop-
portuno*) untimely. ~**a're** *v.t.* pester.
imposizio'ne *n.f.* imposition; (*imposta*) tax.
impossessa'rsi *v.r.* ~ **di** seize.
impossi'bil|e *a.* impossible. —*n.m.*
fare l'~e do all one can. ~**ità** *n.f.*
impossibility.
impo'sta[1] *n.f.* tax. ~ **sul reddito** income tax. ~ **sul valore aggiunto
(I.V.A.)** value added tax (V.A.T.).
impo'sta[2] *n.f.* (*di finestra*) shutter.
impo'sto *p.p. di* **imporre**.
imposta'|re *v.t.* (*progettare*) plan; (*ba-
sare*) base; (*mus.*) pitch; (*imbucare*)
post. ~**zio'ne** *n.f.* planning; pitching.
impo'sto're, a *n.m.*, *f.* impostor.
impote'n|te *a.* powerless; (*med.*) im-
potent. ~**za** *n.f.* powerlessness; impo-
tence.
impoveri'r|e *v.t.* impoverish. ~**si** *v.r.*
become poor.
impratica'bile *a.* impracticable;
(*strada*) impassable.
impratichi'r|e *v.t.* train. ~**si** *v.r.* ~**si
in** *o* a get practice in.
impreca'|re *v.i.* curse. ~**zio'ne** *n.f.*
curse.
impreci's|o *a.* inaccurate. ~**io'ne** *n.f.*
inaccuracy.
impregna're *v.t.* impregnate; (*imbevere*) soak; (*fig.*) imbue.
imprendito're *n.m.* entrepreneur;
(*appaltatore*) contractor.
imprepara'to *a.* unprepared.
impre'sa *n.f.* undertaking; (*gesta*) exploit; (*azienda*) firm; (*appalto*) contract.
impresa'rio *n.m.* impresario; (*appaltatore*) contractor.
imprescindi'bile *a.* inescapable.
impressiona'|re *v.t.* impress; (*spa-
ventare*) frighten; (*foto*) expose. ~**rsi**
v.r. be affected; be frightened. ~**nte** *a.*
impressive; (*spaventoso*) frightening.
impressio'ne *n.f.* impression; (*sensazione*) sensation; (*impronta*) mark.
impressioni's|ta *n.m.|f.* impression-
ist. ~**mo** *n.m.* impressionism.
impre'sso *p.p. di* **imprimere**. —*a.*
printed.
impresta're *v.t.* lend.

imprevedi'bile *a.* unforeseeable.
imprevide'nte *a.* improvident.
imprevi'st|o *a.* unforeseen. −*n.m.* unforeseen event. **salvo** ∼**i** all being well.
imprigiona'|re *v.t.* imprison. ∼**me'nto** *n.m.* imprisonment.
impri'mere *v.t.* impress; (*stampare*) print; (*comunicare*) impart.
improba'bil|e *a.* unlikely, improbable. ∼**ità** *n.f.* improbability.
improdutti'vo *a.* unproductive.
impro'nta *n.f.* impression; (*fig.*) mark. ∼ **del piede** footprint. ∼ **digitale** fingerprint.
imprope'ri|o *n.m.* insult. −*n.m. pl.* abuse *s.*
impro'prio *a.* improper.
improvvis|a're *v.t./i.* improvise. ∼**a'rsi** *v.r.* turn oneself into (a). ∼**a'ta** *n.f.* surprise.
improvvi'so *a.* sudden. **all'**∼**o** unexpectedly. ∼**a'mente** *adv.* suddenly.
imprude'n|te *a.* imprudent. ∼**za** *n.f.* imprudence.
impude'n|te *a.* impudent. ∼**za** *n.f.* impudence.
impudi'c|o *a.* immodest. ∼**i'zia** *n.f.* immodesty.
impugna'|re *v.t.* grasp; (*legge*) contest. ∼**tu'ra** *n.f.* grip; (*manico*) handle.
impulsi'v|o *a.* impulsive. ∼**ità** *n.f.* impulsiveness. **impu'lso** *n.m.* impulse.
impuni'to *a.* unpunished.
impunta'rsi *v.r.* dig one's heels in.
impuntu'ra *n.f.* stitching.
impu'r|o *a.* impure. ∼**ità** *n.f.* impurity.
imputa'|re *v.t.* attribute; (*accusare*) charge. ∼**to, a** *n.m.*, *f.* accused. ∼**zio'ne** *n.f.* charge.
imputridi'|re *v.i.* rot.
in *prep.* (*stato in luogo*) in, at; (*su*) on; (*dentro*) within; (*moto a luogo*) to; (*mezzo*) by; (*verso l'interno*) into. **alzarsi** ∼ **piedi** stand up. **di giorno** ∼ **giorno** from day to day. ∼ **alto** up there. **se fossi** ∼ **te** if I were you. **siamo** ∼ **sette** there are seven of us.
ina'bil|e *a.* incapable; (*fisicamente*) unfit. ∼**ità** *n.f.* incapacity.
inabita'bile *a.* uninhabitable.
inaccessi'bile *a.* inaccessible; (*di persona*) unapproachable.
inaccetta'bile *a.* unacceptable.

inacerbi'r|e *v.t.* embitter. ∼**si** *v.r.* grow bitter.
inacidi'r|e *v.t.* turn sour. ∼**si** *v.r.* go sour.
inada'tto *a.* unsuitable.
inadegua'to *a.* inadequate.
inadempie'nte *n.m./f.* defaulter.
inafferra'bile *a.* elusive.
inala'|re *v.t.* inhale. ∼**to're** *n.m.* inhaler. ∼**zio'ne** *n.f.* inhalation.
inalbera'r|e *v.t.* hoist. ∼**si** *v.r.* (*di cavallo*) rear (up); (*adirarsi*) lose one's temper.
inaltera'|bile *a.* unchangeable; (*di colore*) fast. ∼**to** *a.* unchanged.
inamida'|re *v.t.* starch. ∼**to** *a.* starched.
inammissi'bile *a.* inadmissible.
inanima'to *a.* inanimate; (*senza vita*) lifeless.
inanità *n.f.* uselessness.
inappaga'bile *a.* unsatisfiable.
inappella'bile *a.* final.
inappete'nza *n.f.* lack of appetite.
inapplica'bile *a.* inapplicable.
inappunta'bile *a.* faultless.
inarca're *v.t.* arch; (*sopracciglia*) raise.
inaridi'r|e *v.t.* parch. ∼**si** *v.r.* dry up.
inarticola'to *a.* inarticulate.
inaspetta'to *a.* unexpected.
inaspri'r|e *v.t.* embitter. ∼**si** *v.r.* become embittered.
inattacca'bile *a.* unassailable; (*irreprensibile*) irreproachable.
inattendi'bile *a.* unreliable.
inatte'so *a.* unexpected.
inatti'v|o *a.* inactive. ∼**ità** *n.f.* inactivity.
inattua'bile *a.* impracticable.
inaudi'to *a.* unheard of.
inaugura'|re *v.t.* inaugurate; (*mostra*) open; (*statua*) unveil. ∼**le** *a.* inaugural. **viaggio** ∼**le** maiden voyage. ∼**zio'ne** *n.f.* inauguration; opening; unveiling.
inavvedu'to *a.* inadvertent; (*sbadato*) careless.
inavverte'nza *n.f.* inadvertence.
incaglia'r|e *v.i.* ground. −*v.t.* hinder. ∼**si** *v.r.* run aground. **inca'glio** *n.m.* running aground; (*fig.*) obstacle.
incalcola'bile *a.* incalculable.
incalli'|rsi *v.r.* grow callous. ∼**to** *a.* callous; (*fig.*) inveterate.
incalza're *v.t.* pursue; (*fig.*) press.
incamera're *v.t.* appropriate.

incammina'r|e v.t. get going. ~si v.r. set out.

incanala're v.t. canalize; (fig.) direct.

incancella'bile a. indelible.

incandesce'n|te a. incandescent. ~za n.f. incandescence.

incant|a're v.t. enchant. ~a'rsi v.r. stand spellbound; (incepparsi) jam. ~ato're, ~atri'ce n.m.,f. enchanter, enchantress. ~e'vole a. enchanting.

incante'simo n.m. spell.

inca'nto n.m. enchantment; (fig.) delight; (asta) auction. **come per ~** as if by magic.

incantuccia'rsi v.r. hide in a corner.

incanuti'|re v.i. turn white. ~to a. white.

incapa'c|e a. incapable. ~ità n.f. inability.

incaponi'rsi v.r. be set.

incappa're v.i. ~ **in** run into.

incappuccia'rsi v.r. wrap up.

incapriccia'rsi v.r. ~ **di** take a fancy to.

incapsula're v.t. seal; (dente) crown.

incarcera'|re v.t. imprison. ~zio'ne n.f. imprisonment.

incarica'|re v.t. charge. ~rsi v.r. take upon oneself. **me ne incarico io** I will see to it. ~to, a a. in charge; n.m.,f. representative. **inca'rico** n.m. charge. **per incarico di** on behalf of.

incarna'|re v.t. embody. ~rsi v.r. become incarnate. ~zio'ne n.f. incarnation.

incartame'nto n.m. documents pl.

incartapecori'r|e v.i., ~si v.r. shrivel (up).

incarta're v.t. wrap (in paper).

incassa'|re v.t. pack (in a case); (mech.) embed; (incastonare) set; (riscuotere) cash; (pugilato) take (a blow). ~to a. set; (di fiume) deeply embanked. **inca'sso** n.m. collection; (introito) takings pl.

incastona'|re v.t. set. ~tu'ra n.f. setting.

incastra'r|e v.t. fit in. ~si v.r. fit (into). **inca'stro** n.m. joint.

incatena're v.t. chain.

incatrama're v.t. tar.

inca'uto a. imprudent.

incava'|re v.t. hollow out. ~to a. hollow. ~tu'ra n.f. hollow. **inca'vo** n.m. hollow; (scanalatura) groove.

incendia'r|e v.t. set fire to. ~si v.r. catch fire. ~io, a a. incendiary; n.m., f. arsonist. **ince'ndio** n.m. fire.

inceneri'r|e v.t. burn to ashes; (cremare) cremate. ~si v.r. be burnt to ashes.

ince'nso n.m. incense.

incensura'to a. blameless. **essere ~** (legge) have a clean record.

incenti'vo n.m. incentive.

inceppa'r|e v.t. block; (fig.) hamper. ~si v.r. jam.

incera'ta n.f. oilcloth.

ince'rt|o a. uncertain. —n.m. uncertainty. ~e'zza n.f. uncertainty.

incespica're v.i. stumble.

incessa'nte a. unceasing.

ince'st|o n.m. incest. ~uo'so a. incestuous.

ince'tta n.f. buying up.

inchie'sta n.f. investigation. **fare un'~** conduct an inquiry.

inchina'r|e v.t., ~si v.r. bow. **inchi'no** n.m. bow; (di donna) curtsy.

inchioda're v.t. nail (down).

inchio'stro n.m. ink.

inciampa're v.i. stumble. ~ **in** (imbattersi) run into. **incia'mpo** n.m. hindrance. **essere d'inciampo a qcno.** hinder s.o.

incidenta'le a. incidental.

inciden|te n.m. (episodio) incident; (infortunio) accident. ~za n.f. incidence.

inci'dere v.t. cut (into); (arte) engrave; (registrare) record. —v.i. ~ **su** (gravare) weigh upon.

inci'nta a. pregnant.

incipie'nte a. incipient.

incipria're v.t. powder.

inci'rca adv. **all'~** more or less.

incisio'ne n.f. incision; (arte) engraving; (acquaforte) etching; (registrazione) recording.

incisi'vo a. incisive. —n.m. (dente) incisor.

inci'so n.m. **per ~** incidentally.

incita're v.t. incite.

incivi'le a. uncivilized; (maleducato) impolite.

incivili'r|e v.t. civilize. ~si v.r. become civilized.

incleme'n|te a. harsh. ~za n.f. harshness.

inclina'|re v.t. incline. —v.i. ~**re a** be inclined to. ~to a. tilted; (terreno) sloping. ~zio'ne n.f. slope, inclination. **incli'ne** a. inclined.

inclu'|dere v.t. include; (allegare) enclose. ~sio'ne n.f. inclusion. ~si'vo *a.* inclusive. ~**so** *p.p. di* ~**dere;** *a.* included; enclosed.

incoere'n|te *a.* incoherent; (*contraddittorio*) inconsistent. ~**za** *n.f.* incoherence; inconsistency.

inco'gnito *a.* unknown. —*n.m.* **in** ~ incognito.

incolla're *v.t.* stick; (*con colla liquida*) glue.

incolleri'|rsi *v.r.* lose one's temper. ~**to** *a.* enraged.

incolonna're *v.t.* line up.

incolo're *a.* colourless.

incolpa're *v.t.* blame.

inco'lto *a.* uncultivated; (*persona*) uneducated.

inco'lume *a.* unhurt.

inco'mb|ere *v.i.* ~**ere su** hang over. ~**ere a** (*spettare*) be incumbent on. ~**e'nte** *a.* impending. ~**e'nza** *n.f.* task.

incombusti'ble *a.* non-flammable.

incomincia're *v.t./i.* begin, start.

incomoda'r|e *v.t.* inconvenience. ~**si** *v.r.* trouble. **inco'modo** *a.* uncomfortable; (*inopportuno*) inconvenient; *n.m.* inconvenience.

incompara'bile *a.* incomparable.

incompati'bil|e *a.* incompatible. ~**ità** *n.f.* incompatibility.

incompete'n|te *a.* incompetent. ~**za** *n.f.* incompetence.

incompiu'to *a.* unfinished.

incomple'to *a.* incomplete.

incomprensi'bile *a.* incomprehensible.

incomprensio'ne *n.f.* lack of understanding. **incompre'so** *a.* misunderstood.

inconcepi'bile *a.* inconceivable.

inconcilia'bile *a.* irreconcilable.

inconclude'nte *a.* inconclusive; (*persona*) ineffectual.

incondiziona'to *a.* unconditional.

inconfondi'bile *a.* unmistakable.

inconfuta'bile *a.* irrefutable.

incongrue'nte *a.* inconsistent.

inco'ngruo *a.* inadequate.

inconsape'vole *a.* unaware; (*inconscio*) unconscious.

inco'nscio *a.* & *n.m.* (*psych.*) unconscious.

inconsegue'nte *a.* inconsequent.

inconsidera'bile *a.* negligible.

inconsidera'to *a.* inconsiderate.

inconsiste'nte *a.* insubstantial; (*notizia ecc.*) unfounded.

inconsola'bile *a.* inconsolable.

inconsue'to *a.* unusual.

inconsu'lto *a.* rash.

incontamina'to *a.* uncontaminated.

inconteni'bile *a.* irrepressible.

incontenta'bile *a.* insatiable; (*esigente*) hard to please.

incontesta'bile *a.* indisputable.

incontine'n|te *a.* incontinent. ~**za** *n.f.* incontinence.

incontra'r|e *v.t.* meet; (*difficoltà*) meet with. —*v.i.* (*aver successo*) be successful. ~**si** *v.r.* meet. **inco'ntro** *n.m.* meeting; (*sport*) match; *prep.* **incontro (a)** towards.

incontrasta'bile *a.* incontrovertible.

inconvenie'nte *a.* unseemly. —*n.m.* drawback.

incoraggia'|re *v.t.* encourage. ~**me'nto** *n.m.* encouragement. ~**nte** *a.* encouraging.

incorda'|re *v.t.* (*mus.*) string. ~**tu'ra** *n.f.* stringing.

incornicia'|re *v.t.* frame. ~**tu'ra** *n.f.* framing.

incorona'|re *v.t.* crown. ~**zio'ne** *n.f.* coronation.

incorpora'r|e *v.t.* incorporate; (*mescolare*) blend. ~**si** *v.r.* blend; (*di territori*) merge.

incorreggi'bile *a.* incorrigible.

inco'rrere *v.i.* ~ **in** incur. ~ **nel pericolo** run into danger.

incorrutti'bile *a.* incorruptible.

incoscie'n|te *a.* unconscious; (*irresponsabile*) reckless. —*n.m.|f.* irresponsible person. ~**za** *n.f.* unconsciousness; recklessness.

incosta'n|te *a.* changeable; (*di persona*) fickle. ~**za** *n.f.* inconstancy; fickleness.

incostituziona'le *a.* unconstitutional.

incredi'bile *a.* unbelievable.

incre'dulo *a.* incredulous.

increme'nt|o *n.m.* increase. ~**a're** *v.t.* increase; (*intensificare*) step up.

increscio'so *a.* regrettable.

increspa'r|e *v.t.* ruffle. ~**si** *v.r.* (*acqua*) ripple; (*pelle*) wrinkle; (*capelli*) go frizzy.

incrimina're *v.t.* incriminate.

incrina'|re *v.t.*, ~**rsi** *v.r.* crack. ~**tu'ra** *n.f.* crack.

incrocia'r|e *v.t.* cross. —*v.i.* (*naut., aeron.*) cruise. ~**si** *v.r.* cross. **incro'cio** *n.m.* crossing; (*di strade*) crossroads *s.*

incrociato're *n.m.* cruiser.

incrolla'bile *a.* indestructible.

incrosta're *v.t.* encrust.

incuba|zio'ne *n.f.* incubation. ∼-**tri'ce** *n.f.* incubator.

i'ncubo *n.m.* nightmare.

incu'dine *n.f.* anvil.

inculca're *v.t.* inculcate.

incunea're *v.t.* wedge.

incura'bile *a.* incurable.

incura'nte *a.* careless.

incuriosi'r|e *v.t.* make curious. ∼**si** *v.r.* become curious.

incursio'ne *n.f.* raid.

incurva'|re *v.t.*, ∼**rsi** *v.r.* bend. ∼**me'nto** *n.m.*, ∼**tu'ra** *n.f.* bending.

incu'sso *p.p. di* **incutere**.

incustodi'to *a.* unguarded.

incu'tere *v.t.* arouse. ∼ **spavento a qcno.** strike fear into s.o.

i'ndaco *n.m.* indigo.

indaffara'to *a.* busy.

indaga're *v.t.* investigate.

inda'gine *n.f.* investigation.

indebita'r|e *v.t.* get into debt. ∼**si** *v.r.* run up debts.

inde'bito *a.* undue.

indeboli'r|e *v.t.*, ∼**si** *v.r.* weaken.

indece'n|te *a.* indecent. ∼**za** *n.f.* indecency; (*vergogna*) disgrace.

indecifra'bile *a.* indecipherable.

indeci's|o *a.* undecided. ∼**io'ne** *n.f.* indecision.

indefe'sso *a.* tireless.

indefini'|bile *a.* indefinable. ∼**to** *a.* indefinite.

inde'gno *a.* unworthy.

indele'bile *a.* indelible.

indelica't|o *a.* indiscreet; (*grossolano*) indelicate. ∼**e'zza** *n.f.* indelicacy; (*azione*) tactless act.

indemonia'to *a.* possessed.

inde'nn|e *a.* undamaged. ∼**ità** *n.f.* allowance. ∼**ità di trasferta** travelling allowance. ∼**izza're** *v.t.* indemnify. ∼**i'zzo** *n.m.* indemnity.

inderoga'bile *a.* binding.

indescrivi'bile *a.* indescribable.

indesidera'bile *a.* undesirable.

indetermina'|to *a.* indeterminate. ∼**bile** *a.* indeterminable.

i'ndi *adv.* then.

I'ndi|a *n.f.* India. **i∼a'no, a a. & *n.m.*,** *f.* Indian. **in fila i∼ana** in single file.

indiavola'to *a.* possessed; (*vivace*) wild.

indica'r|e *v.t.* show, indicate; (*col dito*) point at; (*far notare*) point out; (*consigliare*) advise. ∼**ti'vo** *a.* indicative;

n.m. (*gram.*) indicative. ∼**to're** *n.m.* indicator; (*techn.*) gauge; (*prontuario*) directory. ∼**zio'ne** *n.f.* indication; (*istruzione*) direction.

i'ndice *n.m.* (*dito*) forefinger; (*lancetta*) pointer; (*di libro, statistica*) index.

indici'bile *a.* inexpressible.

indietreggia're *v.i.* draw back; (*mil.*) retreat.

indie'tro *adv.* back, behind. **all'**∼ backwards. **avanti e** ∼ back and forth. **essere** ∼ be behind; (*mentalmente*) be backward; (*con pagamenti*) be in arrear(s); (*di orologio*) be slow. **fare marcia** ∼ reverse. **rimandare** ∼ send back. **rimanere** ∼ be left behind. **torna** ∼**!** come back!

indife'so *a.* undefended; (*inerme*) helpless.

indiffere'n|te *a.* indifferent. **mi è** ∼**te** it is all the same to me. ∼**za** *n.f.* indifference.

indi'geno, a *a.* indigenous. —*n.m., f.* native.

indige'n|te *a.* needy. ∼**za** *n.f.* poverty.

indigestio'ne *n.f.* indigestion. **indige'sto** *a.* indigestible.

indigna'|re *v.t.* make indignant. ∼**rsi** *v.r.* be indignant. ∼**to** *a.* indignant. ∼**zio'ne** *n.f.* indignation.

indimentica'bile *a.* unforgettable.

indipende'n|te *a.* independent. ∼**za** *n.f.* independence.

indire'tto *a.* indirect.

indirizza'r|e *v.t.* address; (*mandare*) send; (*dirigere*) direct. ∼**si** *v.r.* direct one's steps. **indiri'zzo** *n.m.* address; (*direzione*) direction.

indiscipli'n|a *n.f.* lack of discipline. ∼**a'to** *a.* undisciplined.

indiscre'|to *a.* indiscreet. ∼**zio'ne** *n.f.* indiscretion.

indiscrimina'to *a.* indiscriminate.

indiscu'|sso *a.* unquestioned. ∼**ti'bile** *a.* unquestionable.

indispensa'bile *a.* indispensable.

indispetti'r|e *v.t.* irritate. ∼**si** *v.r.* get irritated.

indispo'|rre *v.t.* antagonize.

indispo's|to *p.p. di* **indisporre**. —*a.* indisposed. ∼**izio'ne** *n.f.* indisposition.

indissolu'bile *a.* indissoluble.

indisti'nto *a.* indistinct.

indistrutti'bile *a.* indestructible.

indisturba'to *a.* undisturbed.

indi'via *n.f.* endive.

individua'|le *a.* individual. **~li'sta** *n.m./f.* individualist. **~lità** *n.f.* individuality. **~re** *v.t.* individualize; (*localizzare*) locate; (*riconoscere*) single out.

indivi'duo *n.m.* individual.

indivi'so *a.* undivided.

indizia'|re *v.t.* throw suspicion on. **~to, a** *a.* suspected; *n.m., f.* suspect.

indi'zio *n.m.* sign; (*legge*) circumstantial evidence.

i'ndole *n.f.* nature.

indole'n|te *a.* indolent. **~za** *n.f.* indolence.

indolenzi'to *a.* aching.

indolo're *a.* painless.

indoma'bile *a.* untameable.

indoma'ni *n.m.* l'**~** the following day.

indo'mito *a.* indomitable.

Indone'sia *n.f.* Indonesia.

indora're *v.t.* gild.

indossa'|re *v.t.* wear; (*mettere addosso*) put on, **~to're**, **~tri'ce** *n.m., f.* model.

indo'tto *p.p. di* **indurre**

indottrina're *v.t.* indoctrinate.

indovin|a're *v.t.* guess; (*predire*) foretell. **~a'to** *a.* successful; (*scelta*) well-chosen. **~e'llo** *n.m.* riddle. **indovi'no, a** *n.m., f.* fortune-teller.

indu'bbi|o *a.* undoubted. **~ame'nte** *adv.* undoubtedly.

indugia'r|e *v.i.*, **~si** *v.r.* linger. **indu'gio** *n.m.* delay.

indulge'n|te *a.* indulgent. **~za** *n.f.* indulgence.

indu'l|gere *v.i.* **~gere a** indulge in. **~to** *p.p. di* **indulgere**; *n.m.* (*legge*) pardon.

indume'nt|o *n.m.* garment. **~i** *n.m. pl.* clothes.

induri'|re *v.t.*, **~rsi** *v.r.* harden. **~me'nto** *n.m.* hardening.

indu'rre *v.t.* induce.

indu'stri|a *n.f.* industry. **~a'le** *a.* industrial; *n.m.* industrialist. **~alizza're** *v.t.* industrialize. **~alizzazio'ne** *n.f.* industrialization.

industria'rsi *v.r.* do one's best.

industrio'so *a.* industrious.

induzio'ne *n.f.* induction.

inebeti'to *a.* stunned.

inebria'r|e *v.t.* intoxicate. **~si** *v.r.* become inebriated.

ineccepi'bile *a.* unexceptionable.

ine'dia *n.f.* starvation.

ine'dito *a.* unpublished.

ineduca'to *a.* impolite.

ineffa'bile *a.* inexpressible.

ineffettua'bile *a.* impracticable.

ineffica'ce *a.* ineffective.

inefficie'nte *a.* inefficient.

inegua'le *a.* unequal; (*di superficie*) uneven.

inere'nte *a.* **~ a** concerning.

ine'rme *a.* unarmed.

inerpica'rsi *v.r.* **~ (su)** clamber (up).

ine'r|te *a.* inactive. **~zia** *n.f.* inactivity.

inesa'tto *a.* inaccurate; (*erroneo*) incorrect; (*non riscosso*) uncollected.

inesauri'bile *a.* inexhaustible.

inesegui'bile *a.* impracticable.

inesiste'nte *a.* non-existent.

inesora'bile *a.* inexorable.

inesp|erie'nza *n.f.* inexperience. **~e'rto** *a.* inexperienced.

inesplica'bile *a.* inexplicable.

inesplo'so *a.* unexploded.

inesprimi'bile *a.* inexpressible.

inestima'bile *a.* inestimable.

ine'tto *a.* inept. **~ a** unsuited to.

inevita'bile *a.* inevitable.

ine'zia *n.f.* trifle.

infagotta'r|e *v.t.* wrap up. **~si** *v.r.* wrap (oneself) up.

infalli'bile *a.* infallible.

infama'|re *v.t.* defame. **~to'rio** *a.* defamatory.

infa'm|e *a.* infamous; (*fam., terribile*) awful. **~ia** *n.f.* infamy.

infanga'rsi *v.r.* get muddy.

infanti'le *a.* babyish; (*med.*) infantile.

infa'nzia *n.f.* childhood; (*bambini*) children *pl.* **prima ~** infancy.

infarina'|re *v.t.* flour. **~re di** sprinkle with. **~tu'ra** *n.f.* (*fig.*) smattering.

infa'rto *n.m.* coronary.

infastidi'r|e *v.t.* irritate. **~si** *v.r.* get irritated.

infatica'bile *a.* untiring.

infa'tti *conj.* as a matter of fact; (*veramente*) indeed.

infatua'|rsi *v.r.* **~rsi (di)** become infatuated (with) **~zio'ne** *n.f.* infatuation.

infa'usto *a.* ill-omened.

infeco'ndo *a.* infertile.

infede'l|e *a.* unfaithful. **~tà** *n.f.* unfaithfulness.

infeli'c|e *a.* unhappy; (*inappropriato*) unfortunate; (*cattivo*) bad. **~ità** *n.f.* unhappiness.

inferio'r|e *a.* (*più basso*) lower; (*qua-*

lità) inferior. —*n.m.|f.* inferior. ∼**ità**
n.f. inferiority.
infermeri'a *n.f.* infirmary; (*di nave*)
sick-bay.
infermie're, a *n.m., f.* nurse.
infe'rm|o, a *a.* sick. —*n.m., f.* invalid.
∼**ità** *n.f.* sickness.
infe'rn|o *n.m.* hell. ∼**a'le** *a.* infernal,
hellish.
inferoci'rsi *v.r.* become fierce.
inferria'ta *n.f.* grating.
infervora'r|e *v.t.* arouse enthusiasm
in. ∼**si** *v.r.* get excited.
infesta're *v.t.* infest.
infett|a're *v.t.* infect. ∼**a'rsi** *v.r.* be-
come infected. ∼**i'vo** *a.* infectious.
infe'tto *a.* infected. **infezio'ne** *n.f.*
infection.
infiacchi'r|e *v.t./i.,* ∼**si** *v.r.* weaken.
infiamma'bile *a.* (in)flammable.
infiamma'|re *v.t.* set on fire; (*fig.,
med.*) inflame. ∼**rsi** *v.r.* catch fire;
(*med.*) become inflamed. ∼**zio'ne**
n.f. (*med.*) inflammation.
infiasca're *v.t.* put into flasks.
infi'do *a.* treacherous.
infi'gger|e *v.t.* drive. ∼**si** *v.r.* ∼**si in**
penetrate.
infila'r|e *v.t.* thread; (*mettere*) insert;
(*indossare*) put on; (*imboccare una
strada*) take. ∼**si** *v.r.* (*vestito*) slip on;
(*introdursi*) slip into.
infiltra'|rsi *v.r.* infiltrate. ∼**zio'ne**
n.f. infiltration.
infilza're *v.t.* pierce; (*infilare*) string;
(*conficcare*) stick.
i'nfimo *a.* lowest.
infi'ne *adv.* finally; (*insomma*) in
short.
infini'to *a.* infinite; (*gram.*) infinitive. —*n.m.* infinite; (*gram.*) infinitive; (*math.*) infinity. **all'**∼ endlessly.
infinocchia're *v.t.* (*fam.*) hoodwink.
infischia'rsi *v.r.* ∼ **di** not to care
about. **me ne infischio** (*fam.*) I
couldn't care less.
infi'sso *p.p. di* **infiggere.** —*n.m.*
fixture; (*di porta, finestra*) frame.
infitti'r|e *v.t./i.,* ∼**si** *v.r.* thicken.
inflazio'ne *n.f.* inflation.
inflessi'bile *a.* inflexible.
inflessio'ne *n.f.* inflexion.
infli'|ggere *v.t.* inflict. ∼**tto** *p.p. di*
infliggere.
influe'n|te *a.* influential. ∼**za** *n.f.* infl-
uence; (*med.*) influenza. ∼**za're** *v.t.*
influence.
influi're *v.i.* ∼ **su** influence.

influ'sso *n.m.* influence.
infoca'rsi *v.r.* get hot.
infolti're *v.t./i.* thicken.
infonda'to *a.* unfounded.
info'ndere *v.t.* infuse.
inforca're *v.t.* get on; (*occhiali*) put
on.
informa'le *a.* informal.
informa'|re *v.t.* inform. ∼**rsi** *v.r.*
∼**rsi (di)** inquire (about). ∼**ti'vo** *a.*
informative. ∼**to're** *n.m.* informer.
∼**zio'ne** *n.f.* information (*solo s.*).
info'rme *a.* shapeless.
inforna're *v.t.* put into the oven.
infortu'nio *n.m.* accident.
infossa'|rsi *v.r.* sink; (*di guance, oc-
chi*) become hollow. ∼**to** *a.* sunken,
hollow.
infradicia'rsi *v.r.* get drenched; (*diventare marcio*) rot.
infra'ng|ere *v.t.* break; (*in mille pezzi*)
shatter. ∼**ersi** *v.r.* break. ∼**i'bile** *a.*
unbreakable.
infra'nto *p.p. di* **infrangere.** —*a.*
shattered.
infraro'sso *a.* infra-red.
infrastruttu'ra *n.f.* infrastructure.
infrazio'ne *n.f.* infringement.
infreddatu'ra *n.f.* cold.
infreddoli'|rsi *v.r.* feel cold. ∼**to**
a. cold.
infreque'nte *a.* infrequent.
infruttuo'so *a.* fruitless.
infuo'ri *adv.* **all'**∼ outwards. **all'**∼
di except.
infuria'r|e *v.i.* rage. ∼**si** *v.r.* fly into
a rage.
infusio'ne *n.f.* infusion. **infu'so** *p.p.
di* **infondere;** *n.m.* infusion.
ingabbia're *v.t.* cage.
ingaggia're *v.t.* engage; (*calciatori
ecc.*) sign on. **inga'ggio** *n.m.* engagement; signing on.
ingann|a're *v.t.* deceive; (*essere infe-
dele a*) be unfaithful to. ∼**a'rsi** *v.r.*
deceive oneself. **se non m'inganno**
if I am not mistaken. ∼**e'vole** *a.* deceptive. **inga'nno** *n.m.* deceit; (*frode*)
fraud.
ingarbuglia'r|e *v.t.* entangle; (*confon-
dere*) confuse. ∼**si** *v.r.* get entangled;
become confused.
ingegna'rsi *v.r.* do one's best. ∼ **per
vivere** try to scrape a living.
ingegne'r|e *n.m.* engineer. ∼**i'a** *n.f.*
engineering.
inge'gn|o *n.m.* brains *pl.*; (*genio*)

genius; (*abilità*) ingenuity. ∼o'so *a.* ingenious.

ingelosi'r|e *v.t.* make jealous. ∼si *v.r.* become jealous.

inge'nte *a.* huge.

inge'nu|o *a.* ingenuous; (*credulone*) naïve. ∼ità *n.f.* ingenuousness.

ingeri'r|e *v.t.* swallow. ∼si *v.r.* interfere.

ingessa'|re *v.t.* put in plaster. ∼tu'ra *n.f.* plaster.

Inghilte'rra *n.f.* England.

inghiotti're *v.t.* swallow.

ingialli'r|e *v.i.*, ∼si *v.r.* turn yellow.

ingiganti'r|e *v.t.* magnify. −*v.i.*, ∼si *v.r.* become gigantic.

inginocchia'rsi *v.r.* kneel (down).

ingiù *adv.* down. all'∼ downwards.

ingiu'n|gere *v.t.* order. ∼zio'ne *n.f.* injunction.

ingiu'ri|a *n.f.* insult; (*torto*) wrong. ∼a're *v.t.* insult; wrong. ∼o'so *a.* insulting.

ingiu'st|o *a.* unjust. ∼i'zia *n.f.* injustice.

ingle'se *a.* English. −*n.m./f.* Englishman/woman. −*n.m.* (*lingua*) English.

ingoia're *v.t.* swallow.

ingolfa'rsi *v.r.* (*fig.*) get involved; (*di motore*) flood.

ingombra'|re *v.t.* encumber; (*stanza*) clutter up. ∼nte *a.* cumbersome. **ingo'mbro** *n.m.* encumbrance. **essere d'ingombro** be in the way.

ingo'rd|o *a.* greedy. ∼i'gia *n.f.* greed.

ingorga'r|e *v.t.* block. ∼si *v.r.* be blocked (up). **ingo'rgo** *n.m.* blockage; (*del traffico*) jam.

ingozza're *v.t.* gobble up; (*nutrire eccessivamente*) stuff.

ingrana'|re *v.t.* engage. −*v.i.* be in gear. ∼ggio *n.m.* gear; (*fig.*) mechanism.

ingrandi'|re *v.t.* enlarge; (*esagerare*) magnify. ∼rsi *v.r.* become larger; (*aumentare*) increase. ∼me'nto *n.m.* enlargement. **lente d'∼mento** magnifying glass.

ingrassa'r|e *v.t.* fatten (up); (*mech.*) grease. −*v.i.*, ∼si *v.r.* put on weight.

ingra't|o *a.* ungrateful; (*sgradevole*) thankless. ∼itu'dine *n.f.* ingratitude.

ingrazia'r|e *v.t.*, ∼si *v.r.* ingratiate oneself (with).

ingredie'nte *n.m.* ingredient.

ingre'sso *n.m.* entrance; (*accesso*) admittance; (*sala*) hall.

ingrossa'r|e *v.t.* make big; (*gonfiare*) swell. −*v.i.*, ∼si *v.r.* grow big; swell.

ingro'sso *adv.* all'∼ wholesale; (*pressappoco*) roughly.

inguaia'r|e *v.t.*, ∼si *v.r.* get into trouble.

ingualci'bile *a.* crease-resistant.

inguari'bile *a.* incurable.

i'nguine *n.m.* groin.

inibi'|re *v.t.* inhibit; (*vietare*) forbid. ∼to *a.* inhibited. ∼zio'ne *n.f.* inhibition.

inietta'r|e *v.t.* inject. ∼si di sangue (*occhi*) become bloodshot.

iniezio'ne *n.f.* injection.

inimic|a'rsi *v.r.* become enemies. ∼i'zia *n.f.* enmity.

ininterro'tto *a.* continuous.

iniquità *n.f.* iniquity. **ini'quo** *a.* iniquitous.

inizia'le *a.* & *n.f.* initial.

inizia're *v.t./i.* begin; (*introdurre*) initiate; (*avviare*) open. **ini'zio** *n.m.* beginning. **dare inizio a** start.

iniziati'va *n.f.* initiative.

innaffia'|re *v.t.* water. ∼to'io *n.m.* watering-can.

innalza'r|e *v.t.* raise; (*erigere*) erect. ∼si *v.r.* rise.

innamora'|re *v.t.* charm. ∼rsi *v.r.* ∼rsi (di) fall in love (with). ∼to *a.* in love; *n.m.* lover.

innanzi *adv.* (*stato in luogo*) in front; (*di tempo*) ahead; (*avanti*) forward; (*prima*) before. **d'ora** ∼ from now on. −*prep.* (*prima*) before. ∼ a in front of. ∼ **tutto** in the first place.

inna'to *a.* innate.

innatura'le *a.* unnatural.

innega'bile *a.* undeniable.

inneggia're *v.i.* praise.

innervosi'r|e *v.t.* make nervous. ∼si *v.r.* get irritated.

innesca're *v.t.* prime. **inne'sco** *n.m.* primer.

innesta're *v.t.* graft; (*mech.*) engage; (*inserire*) insert. **inne'sto** *n.m.* graft; (*mech.*) clutch; (*electr.*) connection.

i'nno *n.m.* hymn. ∼ **nazionale** national anthem.

innoce'n|te *a.* innocent. ∼za *n.f.* innocence.

inno'cuo *a.* innocuous.

innova'|re *v.t.* make changes (in). ∼zio'ne *n.f.* innovation.

innumere'vole *a.* innumerable.

inocula'|re *v.t.* inoculate. ∼zio'ne *n.f.* inoculation.

inodo'ro *a.* odourless.

inoltra'r|e *v.t.* forward. ~**si** *v.r.* advance.

ino'ltre *adv.* besides.

inonda'|re *v.t.* flood. ~**zio'ne** *n.f.* flood.

inopero'so *a.* inactive.

inopportu'no *a.* untimely.

inorga'nico *a.* inorganic.

inorgogli'r|e *v.t.* make proud. ~**si** *v.r.* become proud.

inorridi're *v.t.* horrify. —*v.i.* be horrified.

inospita'le *a.* inhospitable.

inosserva'to *a.* unobserved; (*non rispettato*) disregarded.

inossida'bile *a.* stainless.

inquadra'|re *v.t.* frame; (*fig.*) set. ~**rsi** *v.r.* fit into. ~**tu'ra** *n.f.* framing.

inquieta'r|e *v.t.* worry. ~**si** get worried; (*impazientirsi*) get cross. **inquie'to** *a.* restless; (*preoccupato*) worried. **inquietu'dine** *n.f.* anxiety.

inquili'no, a *n.m., f.* tenant.

inquina'|re *v.t.* pollute. ~**me'nto** *n.m.* pollution.

inquisi'|re *v.t./i.* investigate. ~**to're**, ~**tri'ce** *a.* inquiring; *n.m., f.* inquisitor. ~**zio'ne** *n.f.* inquisition.

insala't|a *n.f.* salad. ~**ie'ra** *n.f.* salad bowl.

insalu'bre *a.* unhealthy.

insana'bile *a.* incurable.

insanguina'|re *v.t.* stain with blood. ~**to** *a.* bloody.

insa'nia *n.f.* madness.

insapona're *v.t.* soap.

insapori're *v.t.* flavour.

insapu'ta *n.f.* **all'~ di** unknown to.

insazia'bile *a.* insatiable.

inscena're *v.t.* stage.

inscruta'bile *a.* inscrutable.

insedia'r|e *v.t.* install. ~**si** *v.r.* install oneself.

inse'gna *n.f.* sign; (*bandiera*) flag; (*decorazione*) decoration; (*emblema*) insignia *pl.*

insegna'|re *v.t./i.* teach. ~**me'nto** *n.m.* teaching. ~**nte** *a.* teaching; *n.m./f.* teacher.

insegui'|re *v.t.* pursue. ~**me'nto** *n.m.* pursuit. ~**to're**, ~**tri'ce** *n.m., f.* pursuer.

inselvatichi'r|e *v.t.* make wild. —*v.i.*, ~**si** *v.r.* grow wild.

insemina'|re *v.t.* inseminate. ~**zio'ne** *n.f.* insemination.

insenatu'ra *n.f.* inlet.

insensa'to *a.* senseless; (*folle*) crazy.

insensi'bile *a.* insensible; (*che non sente*) insensitive.

insepara'bile *a.* inseparable.

inseri'r|e *v.t.* insert; (*electr.*) connect. ~**si** *v.r.* ~**si in** get into.

inse'rto *n.m.* file; (*in un film ecc.*) insert.

inservie'nte *n.m.* attendant.

inserzio'ne *n.f.* insertion; (*avviso*) advertisement.

insettici'da *n.m.* insecticide.

inse'tto *n.m.* insect.

insicu'r|o *a.* insecure. ~**e'zza** *n.f.* insecurity.

insi'di|a *n.f.* trick; (*tranello*) snare. ~**a're** *v.t./i.* lay a trap for. ~**o'so** *a.* insidious.

insie'me *adv.* together; (*contemporaneamente*) at the same time. ~ **a** *prep.* (together) with. —*n.m.* whole; (*completo*) outfit; (*theatr.*) ensemble. **nell'~** as a whole. **tutto ~** (*in una volta*) at one go.

insi'gne *a.* famous.

insignifica'nte *a.* insignificant.

insigni're *v.t.* decorate.

insince'ro *a.* insincere.

insindaca'bile *a.* final.

insinua'|re *v.t.* insinuate. ~**rsi** *v.r.* penetrate. ~**rsi in** (*fig.*) creep into. ~**nte** *a.* insinuating. ~**zio'ne** *n.f.* insinuation.

insi'pido *a.* insipid.

insi'st|ere *v.i.* insist; (*perseverare*) persevere. ~**e'nte** *a.* insistent. ~**e'nza** *n.f.* insistence.

insoddisfa'tto *a.* unsatisfied; (*scontento*) dissatisfied.

insoffere'n|te *a.* intolerant. ~**za** *n.f.* intolerance.

insolazio'ne *n.f.* sunstroke.

insole'n|te *a.* rude, insolent. ~**za** *n.f.* rudeness, insolence.

inso'lito *a.* unusual.

insolu'bile *a.* insoluble.

insolu'to *a.* unsolved; (*non pagato*) unpaid.

insolvi'bile *a.* insolvent.

inso'mma *adv.* in short; (*int.*) well!

inso'nn|ia *n.f.* insomnia. ~**e** *a.* sleepless.

insonnoli'to *a.* sleepy.

insopporta'bile *a.* unbearable.

inso'r|gere *v.i.* revolt; (*sorgere*) arise. ~**to** *p.p. di* ~**gere**; *a.* rebellious; *n.m.* rebel.

insospetti'r|e v.t. make suspicious. —v.i., ~si v.r. become suspicious.

insosteni'bile a. untenable; (insopportabile) unbearable.

insostitui'bile a. irreplaceable.

insozza're v.t. soil.

inspera'to a. unhoped-for.

inspiega'bile a. inexplicable.

inspira're v.t. breathe in.

insta'bile a. unstable; (variabile) unsettled.

installa'|re v.t. install. ~rsi v.r. settle in. ~zio'ne n.f. installation.

instanca'bile a. untiring.

instaura'|re v.t. found. ~zio'ne n.f. foundation.

instrada're v.t. direct.

insubordinazio'ne n.f. insubordination.

insucce'sso n.m. failure.

insudicia'r|e v.t. dirty. ~si v.r. get dirty.

insufficie'n|te a. insufficient; (non adatto) inadequate. ~za n.f. insufficiency; inadequacy.

insula're a. insular.

insuli'na n.f. insulin.

insu'lso a. insipid; (sciocco) silly.

insu'lt|o n.m. insult. ~a're v.t. insult.

insupera'bile a. insuperable.

insurrezio'ne n.f. insurrection.

insussiste'nte a. groundless.

intacca're v.t. nick; (corrodere) corrode; (un capitale) draw on; (danneggiare) damage.

intaglia're v.t. carve. **inta'glio** n.m. carving.

intangi'ble a. untouchable.

inta'nto adv. meanwhile; (per ora) for the moment; (anzitutto) first of all. ~ che while.

intarsia're v.t. inlay. **inta'rsio** n.m. inlay.

intasa'r|e v.t. clog; (produrre un ingorgo) block. ~si v.r. become blocked.

intasca're v.t. pocket.

inta'tto a. intact.

intavola're v.t. start.

integra'|le a. whole. **edizione** ~le unabridged edition. **pane** ~le wholemeal bread. ~nte a. integral. **i'ntegro** a. complete; (retto) upright.

integra'|re v.t. integrate; (aggiungere) supplement. ~rsi v.r. integrate. ~zio'ne n.f. integration.

integrità n.f. integrity.

intelaiatu'ra n.f. framework.

intelle'tt|o n.m. intellect. ~ua'le a. & n.m.|f. intellectual.

intellige'n|te a. intelligent. ~za n.f. intelligence.

intelligi'bile a. intelligible.

intempera'nza n.f. intemperance.

intempe'rie n.f. pl. bad weather s.

intempesti'vo a. untimely.

intende'n|te n.m. superintendent. ~za n.f. ~za di finanza inland revenue office.

inte'nder|e v.t. (comprendere) understand; (udire) hear; (avere intenzione) intend; (significare) mean. ~si v.r. (capirsi) understand each other. ~si di (essere esperto) have a good knowledge of. ~sela con have an understanding with. **intendime'nto** n.m. understanding; (intenzione) intention.

intendi'|to're, ~tri'ce n.m., f. connoisseur.

inteneri'r|e v.t. soften; (commuovere) touch. ~si v.r. be touched.

intensifica'r|e v.t., ~si v.r. intensify.

inte'ns|o a. intense. ~ità n.f. intensity. ~i'vo a. intensive.

inte'nto a. intent (a, on). —n.m. purpose.

intenzio'n|e n.f. intention. **senza** ~e unintentionally. ~a'le a. intentional.

intercala're[1] n.m. mannerism.

intercala're[2] v.t. insert.

interce'|dere v.i. intercede. ~ssio'ne n.f. intercession.

intercetta're v.t. intercept; (telefono) tap.

interco'rrere v.i. (di tempo) elapse; (esistere) exist.

interde'tto p.p. di interdire. —a. astonished; (proibito) forbidden. —n.m. (relig.) interdict.

interdi'|re v.t. forbid. ~zio'ne n.f. prohibition.

interessa'|re v.t. interest; (riguardare) concern. —v.i. ~re a matter to. ~rsi v.r. ~rsi (a) take an interest (in). ~rsi di take care of. ~me'nto n.m. interest. ~nte a. interesting. **essere in stato** ~nte be pregnant.

intere'sse n.m. interest.

interfer|i're v.i. interfere. ~e'nza n.f. interference.

interiezio'ne n.f. interjection.

interi'no n.m. (medico) locum (doctor).

interio'ra n.f. pl. entrails.

interio're a. interior.

interlu'dio *n.m.* interlude.

intermedia'rio, a *a.* & *n.m.*, *f.* intermediary.

interme'zzo *n.m.* (*theatr.*, *mus.*) intermezzo.

intermina'bile *a.* interminable.

intermissio'ne *n.f.* intermission.

intermitte'nte *a.* intermittent.

interna'|re *v.t.* intern; (*in manicomio*) commit (to a mental institution). ~**me'nto** *n.m.* internment; committal.

internaziona'le *a.* international.

inte'rn|o *a.* internal; (*geog.*) inland; (*interiore*) inner. **alunno** ~**o** boarder. —*n.m.* interior; (*di condominio*) flat; (*telefono*) extension. ~**i** *n.m. pl.* (*cinema*) interior shots. **all'**~**o** inside.

inte'ro *a.* whole, entire; (*intatto*) intact; (*completo*) complete. **per** ~ in full.

interpella're *v.t.* consult.

interpo'r|re *v.t.* interpose. ~**si** *v.r.* come between.

interpreta'|re *v.t.* interpret. ~**zio'ne** *n.f.* interpretation. **inte'rprete** *n.m.|f.* interpreter; (*mus.*) performer.

interra're *v.t.* (*seppellire*) bury.

interroga'|re *v.t.* question; (*schol.*) test. ~**ti'vo** *a.* interrogative; (*sguardo*) questioning; *n.m.* question. **punto** ~**tivo** question mark. ~**to'rio** *a.* & *n.m.* questioning. ~**zio'ne** *n.f.* question; (*schol.*) oral test.

interro'mper|e *v.t.* interrupt; (*sospendere*) stop; (*collegamento*) cut off. ~**si** *v.r.* break off.

interrutto're *n.m.* switch.

interruzio'ne *n.f.* interruption.

interseca'r|e *v.t.*, ~**si** *v.r.* intersect.

interurba'n|o *a.* inter-city. **telefonata** ~**a** trunk-call.

interva'llo *n.m.* interval; (*spazio*) space.

interveni're *v.i.* intervene; (*med.*, *operare*) operate. ~ **a** take part in. **interve'nto** *n.m.* intervention; (*presenza*) presence; (*chirurgico*) operation.

intervi'st|a *n.f.* interview. ~**a're** *v.t.* interview.

inte's|o, a *p.p. di* **intendere.** —*a.* understood. —*n.f.* understanding. ~**i!** agreed! ~**o a** meant to. **non darsi per** ~**o** refuse to understand.

intesta'|re *v.t.* head; (*comm.*) register. ~**rsi** *v.r.* ~**rsi a** take it into one's

head to. ~**zio'ne** *n.f.* heading; (*su carta da lettere*) letterhead.

intesti'no *a.* (*lotte*) internal. —*n.m.* intestine.

intima'|re *v.t.* order. ~**zio'ne** *n.f.* order.

intimidi'r|e *v.t.* intimidate. ~**si** *v.r.* become shy.

i'ntimo *a.* intimate; (*interno*) innermost. —*n.m.* (*amico*) intimate friend; (*dell'animo*) heart.

intimori'r|e *v.t.* frighten. ~**si** *v.r.* get frightened.

inti'ngere *v.t.* dip.

inti'ngolo *n.m.* sauce; (*pietanza*) stew.

intirizzi'r|e *v.t.* numb. ~**si** *v.r.* grow numb.

intitola're *v.t.* entitle; (*dedicare*) dedicate.

intollera'|bile *a.* intolerable. ~**nte** *a.* intolerant.

into'nac|o *n.m.* plaster. ~**a're** *v.t.* plaster.

intona'|re *v.t.* start to sing; (*strumento*) tune; (*accordare*) match. ~**rsi** *v.r.* match. ~**zio'ne** *n.f.* intonation; tuning.

intonti're *v.t.* daze. —*v.i.* be dazed.

into'pp|o *n.m.* obstacle. ~**a're** *v.i.* ~**are in** run into.

into'rno *adv.* around. ~ **a** *prep.* around; (*circa*) about.

intorpidi'r|e *v.t.* numb. ~**si** *v.r.* become numb.

intossica'|re *v.t.* poison. ~**rsi** *v.r.* be poisoned. ~**zio'ne** *n.f.* poisoning.

intralcia're *v.t.* hamper.

intralla'zzo *n.m.* racket.

intransige'nte *a.* uncompromising.

intransiti'vo *a.* intransitive.

intraprende'nte *a.* enterprising.

intrapre'ndere *v.t.* undertake.

intratta'bile *a.* intractable.

intrattene'r|e *v.t.* entertain. ~**si** *v.r.* linger.

intravede're *v.t.* catch a glimpse of; (*presagire*) foresee.

intreccia'r|e *v.t.* plait. ~**si** *v.r.* intertwine. ~**e le mani** clasp one's hands.

intre'ccio *n.m.* (*trama*) plot.

intre'pido *a.* intrepid.

intriga'|re *v.t.* entangle. —*v.i.* intrigue. ~**rsi** *v.r.* meddle. ~**nte** *a.* intriguing. **intri'go** *n.m.* plot. **intrighi** *n.m. pl.* intrigue *s*.

intri'nseco *a.* intrinsic.

intri'so *a.* ~ **(di)** soaked (in).

introdu'|rre *v.t.* introduce; (*inserire*)

insert; (*far entrare*) show in. ∼**rsi** *v.r.*
get into. ∼**zio'ne** *n.f.* introduction.
intro'ito *n.m.* income; (*incasso*)
takings *pl.*
introme'tter|e *v.t.* introduce. ∼**si** *v.r.*
interfere; (*interporsi*) intervene.
intromissio'ne *n.f.* intervention.
introve'rso *a.* introverted. −*n.m.* introvert.
intrufola'rsi *v.r.* sneak in.
intru'glio *n.m.* concoction.
intrusio'ne *n.f.* intrusion. **intru'so, a**
n.m., f. intruder.
intui'|re *v.t.* perceive. ∼**ti'vo** *a.* intuit-
ive. **intu'ito** *n.m.* intuition.
inuma'no *a.* inhuman.
inumidi'r|e *v.t.* dampen; (*labbra*)
moisten. ∼**si** *v.r.* become damp.
inu'til|e *a.* useless; (*superfluo*) un-
necessary. ∼**ità** *n.f.* uselessness.
inva'd|ere *v.t.* invade; (*affollare*)
overrun. ∼**e'nte** *a.* intrusive.
invaghi'rsi *v.r.* take a fancy (**di**, to).
inva'lid|o, a *a.* invalid; (*handicap-
pato*) disabled. −*n.m., f.* disabled person. ∼**ità** *n.f.* disability; (*legge*)
invalidity.
inva'no *adv.* in vain.
invaria'|bile *a.* invariable. ∼**to** *a.* un-
changed.
invas|io'ne *n.f.* invasion. ∼**o're** *a.*
invading; *n.m.* invader.
inva'so *p.p. di* **invadere**.
invecchia're *v.t.* age. −*v.i.* grow old.
inve'ce *adv.* instead; (*anzi*) on the
contrary; (*mentre*) whereas. ∼ **di**
prep. instead of.
invei're *v.i.* ∼ **contro** rail against.
inven|ta're *v.t.* invent. ∼**ti'vo, a** *a.*
inventive; *n.f.* inventiveness. ∼**to're**
n.m. inventor. ∼**zio'ne** *n.f.* invention.
inventa'rio *n.m.* inventory.
inve'rn|o *n.m.* winter. ∼**a'le** *a.*
wintry.
inverosi'mile *a.* improbable.
inversio'ne *n.f.* inversion; (*mech.*) re-
versal. **inve'rso** *a.* inverse; (*opposto*)
opposite; *n.m.* opposite.
invertebra'to *a. & n.m.* invertebrate.
inverti'|re *v.t.* reverse; (*capovolgere*)
turn upside down. ∼**to, a** *n.m., f.*
homosexual.
investiga'|re *v.t.* investigate. ∼**to're**
n.m. investigator. ∼**zio'ne** *n.f.* investigation.
investi'|re *v.t.* invest; (*urtare*) collide
with; (*travolgere*) run over. ∼**re**
qcno. di invest s.o. with. ∼**me'nto**

n.m. investment; (*incidente*) crash.
∼**tu'ra** *n.f.* investiture.
invetera'to *a.* inveterate.
invetti'va *n.f.* invective.
invia're *v.t.* send. **invi'o** *n.m.* dispatch.
invia'to, a *n.m., f.* envoy; (*di giornale*)
correspondent.
invidi|a're *v.t.* envy. **invi'dia** *n.f.*
envy. ∼**o'so a.** envious.
invigori'r|e *v.t.* invigorate. ∼**si** *v.r.*
become strong.
invinci'bile *a.* invincible.
inviola'bile *a.* inviolable.
inviperi'|rsi *v.r.* get nasty. ∼**to** *a.*
furious.
invisi'bil|e *a.* invisible. ∼**ità** *n.f.* in-
visibility.
invita'|re *v.t.* invite. ∼**to, a** *n.m., f.*
guest. **invi'to** *n.m.* invitation.
invoca'|re *v.t.* invoke; (*implorare*)
beg. ∼**zio'ne** *n.f.* invocation.
invoglia'r|e *v.t.* tempt; (*indurre*) in-
duce. ∼**si** *v.r.* ∼**si di** take a fancy to.
involonta'rio *a.* involuntary.
involti'no *n.m.* (*culin.*) meat olive.
invo'lto *n.m.* parcel; (*fagotto*) bundle.
invo'lucro *n.m.* wrapping.
involu'to *a.* involved.
invulnera'bile *a.* invulnerable.
inzacchera're *v.t.* splash with mud.
inzuppa'r|e *v.t.* soak. ∼**si** *v.r.* get
soaked.
i'o *pron.* I. −*n.m.* **l'**∼ the ego. ∼ **stesso**
I myself.
io'dio *n.m.* iodine.
io'ne *n.m.* ion.
Io'nio *n.m.* **lo** ∼ the Ionian (Sea).
ipersensi'bile *a.* hypersensitive.
ipertensio'ne *n.f.* high blood pressure.
ipno'|si *n.f.* hypnosis. ∼**tico** *a.* hyp-
notic. ∼**ti'smo** *n.m.* hypnotism. ∼**tiz-
za're** *v.t.* hypnotize.
ipocondri'aco, a *a. & n.m., f.* hypochondriac.
ipocrisi'a *n.f.* hypocrisy. **ipo'crita** *a.*
hypocritical; *n.m./f.* hypocrite.
ipote'c|a *n.f.* mortgage. ∼**a're** *v.t.*
mortgage.
ipo't|esi *n.f. invar.* hypothesis. ∼**e'-
tico** *a.* hypothetical.
i'ppico, a *a.* horse. −*n.f.* riding.
ippocasta'no *n.m.* horse-chestnut.
ippo'dromo *n.m.* racecourse.
ippopo'tamo *n.m.* hippopotamus.
i'r|a *n.f.* anger. ∼**a'to** *a.* angry.
irasci'bile *a.* irascible.

i'ride *n.f.* (*anat.*) iris; (*arcobaleno*) rainbow.

Irla'nd|a *n.f.* Ireland. **i~e'se** *a.* Irish; *n.m.*, *f.* Irishman/woman.

ironi'a *n.f.* irony. **iro'nico** *a.* ironic(al).

irradia'|re *v.t./i.* radiate. **~zio'ne** *n.f.* radiation.

irragione'vole *a.* unreasonable; (*assurdo*) absurd.

irraziona'le *a.* irrational.

irrea'l|e *a.* unreal. **~tà** *n.f.* unreality.

irrealizza'bile *a.* unattainable.

irreconcilia'bile *a.* irreconcilable.

irrecusa'bile *a.* incontrovertible.

irrefuta'bile *a.* irrefutable.

irregola'r|e *a.* irregular. **~ità** *n.f.* irregularity.

irremovi'bile *a.* (*fig.*) adamant.

irrepara'bile *a.* irreparable.

irreperi'bile *a.* untraceable.

irreprensi'bile *a.* irreproachable.

irreprimi'bile *a.* irrepressible.

irrequie'to *a.* restless.

irresisti'bile *a.* irresistible.

irresolu'to *a.* irresolute.

irresponsa'bile *a.* irresponsible.

irrevoca'bile *a.* irrevocable.

irriconosci'bile *a.* unrecognizable.

irriduci'bile *a.* irreducible.

irriga'|re *v.t.* irrigate; (*fiume*) flow through. **~zio'ne** *n.f.* irrigation.

irrigidi'r|e *v.t.*, **~si** *v.r.* stiffen.

irriso'rio *a.* derisive; (*insignificante*) ridiculous.

irrita'|re *v.t.* irritate. **~rsi** *v.r.* get annoyed. **~bile** *a.* irritable. **~zio'ne** *n.f.* irritation.

irrobusti'r|e *v.t.* fortify. **~si** *v.r.* get stronger.

irro'mpere *v.i.* burst (**in**, into).

irrora're *v.t.* sprinkle.

irrue'nte *a.* impetuous.

irruzio'ne *n.f.* irruption. **fare ~ in** break into.

irsu'to *a.* shaggy.

i'rto *a.* bristly.

iscri'tto, a *p.p. di* **iscrivere**. **—***a.* registered. **—***n.m.*, *f.* member. **per ~ in writing**.

iscri'ver|e *v.t.* register. **~si** *v.r.* **~si a** (*scuola*) register, enrol at; (*circolo ecc.*) join. **iscrizio'ne** *n.f.* registration; (*epigrafe*) inscription.

Isla'nd|a *n.f.* Iceland. **i~e'se** *a.* Icelandic; *n.m.*/*f.* Icelander.

i'sol|a *n.f.* island. **~a pedonale** traffic island. **le ~e britanniche** the British Isles. **~a'no, a** *a.* insular; *n.m.*, *f.* islander.

isola'nte *a.* insulating. **—***n.m.* insulator.

isola'|re *v.t.* isolate; (*mech.*, *electr.*) insulate; (*acusticamente*) soundproof. **~to** *a.* isolated; *n.m.* (*di appartamenti*) block.

ispessi'r|e *v.t.*, **~si** *v.r.* thicken.

ispetto'r|e *n.m.* inspector. **~a'to** *n.m.* inspectorate.

ispezio'n|e *n.f.* inspection. **~a're** *v.t.* inspect.

i'spido *a.* bristly.

ispira'|re *v.t.* inspire. **~rsi** *v.r.* be inspired. **~zio'ne** *n.f.* inspiration.

Israe'l|e *n.m.* Israel. **i~ia'no, a** *a.* & *n.m.*, *f.* Israeli.

issa're *v.t.* hoist.

istanta'neo, a *a.* instantaneous. **—***n.f.* snapshot.

ista'nte *n.m.* instant. **all'~** instantly.

ista'nza *n.f.* petition.

iste'r|ico *a.* hysterical. **attacco ~ico** hysterics *pl.* **~i'smo** *n.m.* hysteria.

istiga'|re *v.t.* instigate. **~re qcno. al male** incite s.o. to evil. **~to're, ~tri'ce** *n.m.*, *f.* instigator. **~zio'ne** *n.f.* instigation.

istinti'vo *a.* instinctive. **isti'nto** *n.m.* instinct.

istitui're *v.t.* institute; (*dare avvio*) initiate.

istitu'|to *n.m.* institute. **~to di bellezza** beauty salon. **~zio'ne** *n.f.* institution.

i'stmo *n.m.* isthmus.

i'strice *n.m.* porcupine.

istrio'ne *n.m.* clown; (*theatr.*, *sl.*) ham.

istru'i|re *v.t.* instruct; (*addestrare*) train; (*informare*) inform; (*legge*) prepare. **~tti'vo** *a.* instructive. **~tto're, -ttri'ce** *n.m.*, *f.* instructor. **giudice ~ttore** examining magistrate. **~tto'ria** *n.f.* (*legge*) investigation. **~zio'ne** *n.f.* education, instruction. **~zioni** *n.f. pl.* (*indicazioni*) instructions.

Ita'li|a *n.f.* Italy. **i~a'no, a** *a.* & *n.m.*, *f.* Italian.

itinera'rio *n.m.* itinerary.

itteri'zia *n.f.* jaundice.

i'ttico *a.* fishing.

I.V.A. *abbr. vedi* **imposta**.

J

jazz *n.m.* jazz.
jo'lly *n.m.* (*carta da gioco*) joker.
Jugosla'v|ia *n.f.* Yugoslavia. **j~o, a**
  a. & *n.m.*, *f.* Yugoslav(ian).

ju'ta *n.f.* jute.

L

la *art. def. f. s.* the. —*pron. (oggetto, riferito a persona)* her; *(riferito a cosa)* it; *(forma di cortesia)* you. —*n.m. invar. (mus.)* lah.

là *adv.* there. **di** ~ *(in quel luogo)* in there; *(da quella parte)* that way. **eccolo** ~! there he is! **farsi più in** ~ *(far largo)* make way. ~ **dentro** in there. ~ **fuori** out there. **(ma) va** ~! come off it! **più in** ~ *(nel tempo)* later on; *(nello spazio)* further on.

la'bbro *n.m. (pl. f. anat.* **labbra**) lip.

labiri'nto *n.m.* labyrinth; *(di sentieri ecc.)* maze.

laborato'rio *n.m.* laboratory; *(di negozio, officina, ecc.)* workshop.

laborio'so *a. (operoso)* industrious; *(faticoso)* laborious.

laburi'sta *a.* Labour. —*n.m./f.* member of the Labour Party.

la'cc|a *n.f.* lacquer. ~**a're** *v.t.* lacquer.

la'ccio *n.m.* noose; *(lazo)* lasso; *(trappola)* snare; *(stringa)* lace.

lacera'r|e *v.t.* lacerate; *(strappare)* tear. ~**si** *v.r.* tear. **la'cero** *a.* torn; *(cencioso)* ragged.

laco'nico *a.* laconic.

la'crim|a *n.f.* tear; *(goccia)* drop. ~**a're** *v.i.* weep. ~**o'geno** *a.* **gas** ~**o'geno** tear gas. ~**o'so** *a.* tearful.

lacu'na *n.f.* gap.

la'dr|o, a *n.m., f.* thief. ~**oci'nio** *n.m.* theft. ~**u'ncolo** *n.m.* petty thief.

laggiù *adv.* down there; *(lontano)* over there.

lagna'|rsi *v.r.* moan. ~**rsi di** complain about. ~**nza** *n.f.* complaint.

la'go *n.m.* lake.

lagu'na *n.f.* lagoon.

la'ico, a *a.* lay; *(vita)* secular. —*n.m., f.* layman/woman.

la'ma *n.f.* blade. —*n.m. invar. (animale)* llama.

lambicca'r|e *v.t.* distil. ~**si il cervello** rack one's brains.

lambi're *v.t.* lap.

lament|a're *v.t.* lament. ~**a'rsi** *v.r.* moan. ~**arsi di** *(lagnarsi)* complain about. ~**e'la** *n.f.* complaint. ~**e'vole** *a.* mournful; *(pietoso)* pitiful. **lame'nto** *n.m.* moan.

lame'tta *n.f.* (razor)blade.

lamie'ra *n.f.* sheet metal.

la'min|a *n.f.* foil. ~**a d'oro** gold leaf. ~**a're** *v.t.* laminate. ~**a'to** *a.* laminated; *n.m.* laminate; *(tessuto)* lamé.

la'mpad|a *n.f.* lamp. ~**a a pila** torch. ~**i'na** *n.f.* light bulb.

lampada'rio *n.m.* chandelier.

lampa'nte *a.* clear.

lampeggia'|re *v.i.* flash; *(di lampi)* lighten. ~**to're** *n.m. (auto)* indicator.

lampio'ne *n.m.* street lamp.

la'mp|o *n.m.* flash of lightning; *(di luce, fig.)* flash. ~**i** *n.m. pl.* lightning *s.* **cerniera** ~**o** zip (fastener).

lampo'ne *n.m.* raspberry.

la'n|a *n.f.* wool. **di** ~**a** woollen. ~**a d'acciaio** steel wool. ~**a vergine** new wool. ~**o'so** *a.* woolly.

lance'tta *n.f.* pointer; *(di orologio)* hand.

la'ncia *n.f. (arma)* lance; *(naut.)* launch.

lanciafia'mme *n.m. invar.* flame-thrower.

lancia'r|e *v.t.* throw; *(da un aereo)* drop; *(missile, prodotto)* launch. ~**si** *v.r.* fling oneself; *(intraprendere)* launch out. **la'ncio** *n.m.* throwing; drop; launching.

lancina'nte *a.* piercing.

la'nda *n.f.* heath.

la'nguido *a.* languid; *(debole)* feeble.

langui're *v.i.* languish; *(indebolirsi)* flag.

languo're *n.m.* languor.

lanie'r|o *a.* wool. **industria** ~**a** wool industry.

lanifi'cio *n.m.* woollen mill.

lante'rna *n.f.* lantern; *(faro)* lighthouse.

lanu'gine *n.f.* down.

lapida're *v.t.* stone.

la'pide *n.f.* tombstone; *(commemorativa)* memorial tablet.

la'pis *n.m. invar.* pencil.

lappa're *v.i.* lap.

la'rdo *n.m.* lard.

largheggia're *v.i.* ~ **in** be free with.

larghe'zza *n.f.* width, breadth; *(fig.)* liberality. ~ **di vedute** broadmindedness.

largi're *v.t.* lavish.

la'rgo *a.* wide; *(ampio)* broad; *(abito)* loose; *(liberale)* liberal. —*n.m.* width.

andare al ~ (*naut.*) take to the open sea. **fare** ~ make room. **farsi** ~ make one's way.

la'rice *n.m.* larch.

lari'ng|e *n.f.* larynx. ~**i'te** *n.f.* laryngitis.

la'rva *n.f.* larva; (*persona emaciata*) shadow.

lasciapassa're *n.m. invar.* pass.

lascia'r|e *v.t.* leave; (*rinunciare*) give up; (*rimetterci*) lose; (*mollare*) let go; (*concedere*) let. **lascia andare!** forget it! ~**e di** (*smettere*) stop. ~**si** *v.r.* let oneself; (*reciproco*) leave each other.

la'scito *n.m.* legacy.

lasci'vo *a.* lascivious.

la'ser *a. & n.m. invar.* **(raggio)**~ laser (beam).

lassati'vo *a. & n.m.* laxative.

la'sso *n.m.* (*periodo*) lapse.

lassù *adv.* up there.

la'stra *n.f.* slab; (*di ghiaccio*) sheet; (*di metallo, foto*) plate; (*radiografia*) X-ray (plate).

lastrica'|re *v.t.* pave. ~**to, la'strico** *ns.m.* pavement.

late'nte *a.* latent.

latera'le *a.* lateral. **via** ~ side street. —*n.m.* (*calcio*) half.

lateri'zi *n.m. pl.* bricks.

latifo'ndo *n.m.* (large) estate.

lati'no *a. & n.m.* Latin.

latita'n|te *a.* in hiding. —*n.m./f.* fugitive (from justice). ~**za** *n.f.* **darsi alla** ~**za** go into hiding.

latitu'dine *n.f.* latitude.

la'to *a.* (*ampio*) broad. —*n.m.* side; (*aspetto*) aspect. **a** ~ **di** beside. **dal** ~ **mio** (*punto di vista*) for my part. **d'altro** ~ (*fig.*) on the other hand.

lato're *n.m.* bearer.

latra'|re *v.i.* bark. ~**to** *n.m.* barking.

la'tta *n.f.* tin, can.

latta'io, a *n.m., f.* milkman, dairymaid.

latta'nte *a.* breast-fed. —*n.m./f.* suckling.

la'tt|e *n.m.* milk. ~**e acido** sour milk. ~ **scremato** skimmed milk. ~**eo** *a.* milky. ~**eri'a** *n.f.* dairy. ~**ici'ni** *n.m. pl.* dairy products. ~**ie'ra** *n.f.* milk jug.

lattuga *n.f.* lettuce.

la'ure|a *n.f.* degree. ~**a'ndo, a** *n.m., f.* final-year student. ~**a're** *v.t.* confer a degree on. ~**a'rsi** *v.r.* graduate. ~**a'to, a** *a. & n.m., f.* graduate.

la'uro *n.m.* laurel.

la'uto *a.* lavish. **guadagno** ~ handsome profit.

la'va *n.f.* lava.

lava'bo *n.m.* wash-basin.

lava'ggio *n.m.* washing. ~ **del cervello** brainwashing.

lava'gna *n.f.* (*min.*) slate; (*schol.*) blackboard.

lava'nd|a *n.f.* wash; (*bot.*) lavender. ~**a'ia** *n.f.* washerwoman. ~**eri'a** *n.f.* laundry. ~**eria automatica** launderette.

lavandi'no *n.m.* sink.

lavapia'tti *n.m./f.* dishwasher.

lava'|re *v.t.*, ~**rsi** *v.r.* wash. ~**re a secco** dry-clean. ~**re i piatti** wash up. ~**bile** *a.* washable. ~**ta** *n.f.* wash. ~**ta di capo** (*fig.*) scolding.

lavase'cco *n.m./f. invar.* dry-cleaner's.

lavato'io *n.m.* wash-house.

lavatri'ce *n.f.* washing-machine.

lavora'nte *n.m./f.* worker.

lavora'|re *v.i.* work; (*fare affari*) do business. —*v.t.* work; (*pasta ecc.*) knead; (*la terra*) till. ~**re a maglia** knit. ~**ti'vo** *a.* working. ~**to're, ~tri'ce** *n.m., f.* worker; *a.* working. ~**zio'ne** *n.f.* manufacture; (*produzione*) production; (*fattura*) workmanship; (*del terreno*) cultivation.

lavori'o *n.m.* intense activity.

lavo'r|o *n.m.* work; (*faticoso, sociale*) labour; (*impiego*) job; (*theatr.*) play. ~**i di casa** housework. ~**i forzati** hard labour.

lazzaro'ne *n.m.* rascal.

le *art. def. f. pl.* the. —*pron.* (*oggetto*) them; (*a lei*) to her; (*forma di cortesia*) to you.

lea'l|e *a.* loyal; (*fedele*) faithful. ~**tà** *n.f.* loyalty; faithfulness.

le'bbra *n.f.* leprosy.

le'cca le'cca *n.m. invar.* lollipop.

leccapie'di *n.m./f. invar.* (*pej.*) toady.

lecca'|re *v.t.* lick; (*fig.*) flatter. ~**rsi** *v.r.* lick. ~**ta** *n.f.* lick.

leccorni'a *n.f.* delicacy.

le'cito *a.* lawful; (*permesso*) permissible.

le'dere *v.t.* damage; (*med.*) injure.

le'ga *n.f.* league; (*di metalli*) alloy. **far** ~ **con qcno.** take up with s.o.

lega'ccio *n.m.* string.

lega'l|e *a.* legal. —*n.m.* lawyer. ~**ità** *n.f.* legality. ~**izza're** *v.t.* authenticate; (*rendere legale*) legalize.

lega'me *n.m.* tie; (*amoroso*) liaison; (*connessione*) link.

legame'nto *n.m.* ligament.

lega'r|e *v.t.* tie (up); (*unire, rilegare*) bind; (*metalli*) alloy; (*connettere*) connect. —*v.i.* (*far lega*) get on well. ~**si** *v.r.* bind oneself. ~**si a qcno.** become attached to s.o.

lega'to *n.m.* legacy; (*relig.*) legate.

legatu'ra *n.f.* tying; (*mus.*) ligature; (*di libro*) binding.

legazio'ne *n.f.* legation.

le'gge *n.f.* law; (*parlamentare*) act.

legge'nd|a *n.f.* legend. ~**a'rio** *a.* legendary.

le'ggere *v.t./i.* read.

legge'r|o *a.* light; (*di bevanda*) weak; (*lieve*) slight; (*frivolo*) frivolous; (*incostante*) fickle. **alla ~a** frivolously. ~**e'zza** *n.f.* lightness; frivolity; fickleness.

leggia'dr|o *a.* graceful. ~**i'a** *n.f.* gracefulness.

leggi'bile *a.* (*scrittura*) legible; (*stile*) readable.

le'ggio *n.m.* reading-desk; (*mus.*) music stand.

legio'n|e *n.f.* legion. ~**a'rio** *n.m.* legionary.

legisla|tu'ra *n.f.* legislature. ~**ti'vo** *a.* legislative. ~**to're** *n.m.* legislator. ~**zio'ne** *n.f.* legislation.

legi'ttim|o *a.* legitimate; (*giusto*) proper. ~**ità** *n.f.* legitimacy.

le'gn|o *n.m.* wood. **di ~o** wooden. ~**o compensato** plywood. ~**a** *n.f.* firewood. ~**a'me** *n.m.* timber.

legu'm|e *n.m.* pod. ~**i** *n.m. pl.* (*culin.*) vegetables.

le'i *pron.* (*soggetto*) she; (*oggetto*) her. **Lei** (*forma di cortesia*) you.

le'mbo *n.m.* edge; (*di terra*) strip.

le'mma *n.m.* headword.

le'na *n.f.* vigour.

leni're *v.t.* soothe.

le'nt|e *n.f.* lens. ~**i** *n.f. pl.* (*occhiali*) spectacles. ~**e d'ingrandimento** magnifying glass.

lenti'cchia *n.f.* lentil.

lenti'ggine *n.f.* freckle.

le'nto *a.* slow; (*allentato*) slack; (*abito*) loose.

le'nza *n.f.* fishing-line.

lenzuo'l|o *n.m.* sheet. ~**a** *n.f. pl.* (pair of) sheets.

leo'ne *n.m.* lion; (*astr.*) Leo.

leopa'rdo *n.m.* leopard.

le'pre *n.f.* hare.

le'sbica *n.f.* lesbian.

lesina're *v.t.* grudge. —*v.i.* be stingy.

lesio'n|e *n.f.* lesion; (*danno*) damage. ~**a're** *v.t.* damage.

le'so *p.p. di* **ledere.** —*a.* injured.

lessa're *v.t.* boil. **le'sso** *a.* boiled; *n.m.* boiled meat.

le'ssico *n.m.* vocabulary.

le'sto *a.* quick; (*di mente*) sharp. ~ **di mano** light-fingered.

leta'le *a.* lethal.

letama'io *n.m.* dunghill. **leta'me** *n.m.* dung.

leta'rg|o *n.m.* lethargy; (*di animali*) hibernation. ~**ico** *a.* lethargic.

leti'zia *n.f.* joy.

le'tter|a *n.f.* letter. ~**e** *n.f. pl.* (*letteratura*) literature *s.*; (*univ.*) Arts. **alla ~a** literally. **dottore in ~e** Bachelor of Arts (*abbr.* B.A.). ~**a'le** *a.* literal.

letter|atu'ra *n.f.* literature. ~**a'rio** *a.* literary. ~**a'to** *a.* well-read.

letti'ga *n.f.* stretcher.

le'tto *n.m.* bed. ~ **a castello** bunkbed. ~ **a una piazza** single bed. ~ **matrimoniale** double bed.

let|to're, ~**tri'ce** *n.m., f.* reader; (*univ.*) language assistant.

lettu'ra *n.f.* reading.

leucemi'a *n.f.* leukaemia.

le'va *n.f.* lever; (*mil.*) call-up. **far ~** lever. ~ **del cambio** gear lever.

leva'nte *n.m.* East; (*vento*) east wind.

leva'|re *v.t.* (*alzare*) raise; (*togliere*) take away; (*rimuovere*) take off; (*estrarre*) pull out. ~**rsi** *v.r.* rise; (*da letto*) get up; (*allontanarsi*) get out of. ~**ta** *n.f.* rising; (*di posta*) collection.

levato'io *a.* **ponte ~** drawbridge.

levatri'ce *n.f.* midwife.

levatu'ra *n.f.* intelligence.

leviga're *v.t.* smooth; (*con carta vetro*) rub down.

levrie'ro *n.m.* greyhound.

lezio'ne *n.f.* lesson; (*univ.*) lecture; (*rimprovero*) rebuke.

li *pron. pl.* (*oggetto*) them.

lì *adv.* there. **fin ~** as far as there. **giù di ~** thereabouts. ~ **per ~** there and then.

Liba'no *n.m.* Lebanon.

li'bbra *n.f.* (*peso*) pound.

libe'ccio *n.m.* south-west wind.

libe'llula *n.f.* dragon-fly.

libera'le *a.* & *n.m./f.* liberal.

libera'|re *v.t.* free; (*prigioniero*) release; (*salvare*) rescue. ~**rsi** *v.r.* ~**rsi di** get rid of. ~**to're,** ~**tri'ce** *a.*

liberating; *n.m., f.* liberator. ~**zio'ne** *n.f.* liberation.

li'ber|o *a.* free; (*strada*) clear. ~**o do-cente** qualified university lecturer. ~**o professionista** self-employed person. ~**tà** *n.f.* freedom; (*di prigioniero*) release; ~**tà** *n.f. pl.* (*licenza*) liberties. ~**tà provvisoria** (*legge*) bail.

liberti'no *n.m.* libertine.

Li'bi|a *n.f.* Libya. l~**co, a** *a. & n.m., f.* Libyan.

libi'din|e *n.f.* lust. ~**o'so** *a.* lustful.

libi'do *n.f.* libido.

libra'rsi *v.r.* hover.

libreri'a *n.f.* (*biblioteca*) library; (*negozio*) bookshop; (*mobile*) bookcase.

libre'tto *n.m.* booklet; (*mus.*) libretto. ~ **di circolazione** log-book.

li'br|o *n.m.* book. ~**o paga** wages book. ~**a'io** *n.m.* bookseller.

lice'nza *n.f.* licence; (*permesso*) permission; (*mil.*) leave; (*schol.*) school-leaving certificate. **essere in** ~ be on leave.

licenzia'|re *v.t.* dismiss, sack (*fam.*); (*conferire un diploma*) grant a diploma. ~**rsi** *v.r.* (*da un impiego*) resign; (*accomiatarsi*) take one's leave. ~**me'nto** *n.m.* dismissal.

licenzio'so *a.* licentious.

lice'o *n.m.* high *o* secondary school.

licitazio'ne *n.f.* (*offerta all'asta*) bid.

li'do *n.m.* beach.

lie'to *a.* glad. ~ **evento** happy event. **molto** ~! (*nelle presentazioni*) how do you do?

lie've *a.* light; (*debole*) faint; (*trascurabile*) slight.

lie'vit|o *n.m.* yeast. ~**o in polvere** baking powder. ~**a're** *v.i.* rise; *v.t.* leaven.

li'gio *a.* faithful.

ligna'ggio *n.m.* lineage.

li'lla *n.f.* (*bot.*) lilac. —*n.m.* (*colore*) lilac.

li'm|a *n.f.* file. ~**a're** *v.t.* file. ~**e'tta** *n.f.* nail-file.

limaccio'so *a.* slimy.

li'mbo *n.m.* limbo.

limita'|re *n.m.* threshold. —*v.t.* limit. ~**ti'vo** *a.* limiting. ~**to** *a.* limited. ~**zio'ne** *n.f.* limitation.

li'mite *n.m.* limit; (*confine*) boundary.

limo'n|e *n.m.* lemon; (*albero*) lemon tree. ~**a'ta** *n.f.* lemonade.

li'mpido *a.* clear; (*di acqua, occhi*) limpid.

li'nce *n.f.* lynx.

lincia're *v.t.* lynch.

li'ndo *a.* neat; (*pulito*) clean.

li'nea *n.f.* line; (*figura*) figure. **in** ~ **d'aria** as the crow flies. **in** ~ **di massima** as a rule. **mettersi in** ~ line up. **nave di** ~ liner.

lineame'nti *n.m. pl.* features.

linea're *a.* linear.

linee'tta *n.f.* (*tratto lungo*) dash; (*d'unione*) hyphen.

lingo'tto *n.m.* ingot.

li'ngua *n.f.* tongue; (*linguaggio*) language.

lingua'ggio *n.m.* language.

lingue'tta *n.f.* (*di scarpa*) tongue; (*di strumento*) reed; (*di busta*) flap.

lingui'st|a *n.m., f.* linguist. ~**ico, a** *a.* linguistic; *n.f.* linguistics *s.*

linime'nto *n.m.* liniment.

li'no *n.m.* (*bot.*) flax; (*tessuto*) linen.

lino'leum *n.m.* linoleum.

liquefa'r|e *v.t.*, ~**si** *v.r.* liquefy; (*sciogliersi*) melt.

liquida'|re *v.t.* liquidate; (*conto*) settle; (*merce*) clear. ~**zio'ne** *n.f.* liquidation; (*di conti*) settling; (*di merce*) (clearance) sale.

li'quido *a. & n.m.* liquid.

liquiri'zia *n.f.* liquorice.

liquo'r|e *n.m.* liqueur. ~**i** *n.m. pl.* (*bevande alcooliche*) liquors.

li'ra *n.f.* lira; (*mus.*) lyre.

li'rico, a *a.* lyric(al). —*n.f.* lyric poetry; (*mus.*) opera.

li'sca *n.f.* fishbone.

liscia're *v.t.* smooth; (*accarezzare*) stroke. **li'scio** *a.* smooth; (*capelli*) straight; (*liquore*) neat. **passarla liscia** get away with it.

li'so *a.* worn (out).

li'st|a *n.f.* list; (*striscia*) strip. ~**a elettorale** electoral register. ~**a're** *v.t.* border. ~**i'no** *n.m.* list.

litani'a *n.f.* litany.

li'te *n.f.* quarrel; (*baruffa*) row; (*legge*) lawsuit.

litiga're *v.i.* quarrel; (*legge*) litigate. **liti'gio** *n.m.* quarrel. **litigio'so** *a.* quarrelsome.

litografi'a *n.f.* (*procedimento*) lithography; (*stampa*) lithograph.

litora'le *a.* coastal. —*n.m.* coast.

li'tro *n.m.* litre.

liturgi'a *n.f.* liturgy.

liu'to *n.m.* lute.

live'lla *n.f.* level. ~ **a bolla d'aria** spirit level.

live'll|o *n.m.* level. **passaggio a ~o** level crossing. **~a're** *v.t.* level. **~a'rsi** *v.r.* become level.

li'vido *a.* livid. —*n.m.* bruise.

livo're *n.m.* envy.

Livo'rno *n.f.* Leghorn.

livre'a *n.f.* livery.

li'zza *n.f.* lists *pl.*

lo *art. def. m. s.* the. —*pron.* (*riferito a persona*) him; (*riferito a cosa*) it. **non ~ so** I don't know (it).

lo'bo *n.m.* lobe.

loca'l|e *a.* local. —*n.m.* (*stanza*) room; **~i** *n.m. pl.* (*edifici*) premises. **~e** notturno night-club. **~ità** *n.f.* locality.

localizza're *v.t.* localize; (*determinare un luogo*) locate.

loca'nd|a *n.f.* inn. **~ie're, a** *n.m., f.* innkeeper.

loca|ta'rio, a *n.m., f.* tenant. **~to're, ~tri'ce** *n.m., f.* landlord/lady. **~zio'ne** *n.f.* tenancy.

locomo|ti'va *n.f.* locomotive. **~zio'ne** *n.f.* locomotion. **mezzi di ~zione** means of transport.

locu'sta *n.f.* locust.

locuzio'ne *n.f.* expression.

lod|a're *v.t.* praise. **lo'de** *n.f.* praise. **laurea con lode** first-class degree. **~e'vole** *a.* praiseworthy.

lo'dola *n.f.* lark.

logari'tmo *n.m.* logarithm.

lo'ggia *n.f.* loggia; (*massonica*) lodge.

loggio'ne *n.m.* gallery.

lo'gic|a *n.f.* logic. **~o** *a.* logical.

logi'stica *n.f.* logistics *s.*

logora'|re *v.t.* wear out; (*sciupare*) waste. **~rsi** *v.r.* wear (oneself) out.

logori'o *n.m.* wear and tear. **lo'goro** *a.* worn-out.

lomba'ggine *n.f.* lumbago.

Lombardi'a *n.f.* Lombardy.

lomba'ta *n.f.* loin. **lo'mbo** *n.m.* (*anat.*) loin.

lombri'co *n.m.* earthworm.

Lo'ndra *n.f.* London.

longe'v|o *a.* long-lived. **~ità** *n.f.* longevity.

longitu'dine *n.f.* longitude.

lonta'n|o *a.* far; (*distante*) distant; (*nel tempo*) far-off; (*vago*) vague; (*assente*) absent. **più ~o** further. —*adv.* far (away). **da ~o** from a distance. **tenersi ~o da** keep away from. **~a'nza** *n.f.* distance; (*separazione*) separation. **~ame'nte** *adv.* distantly.

neanche ~amente not for a moment.

lo'ntra *n.f.* otter.

loqua'ce *a.* talkative.

lo'rd|o *a.* dirty; (*peso*) gross. **~u'ra** *n.f.* dirt.

lo'ro *pron. pl.* (*soggetto*) they; (*oggetto*) them. **L~** (*forma di cortesia*) you. **da ~** (*da soli*) by themselves. **sta a ~** it is up to them. —*a. & pron. poss.* their, theirs; (*loro proprio*) their own. **L~** (*forma di cortesia*) your, yours.

lo'sco *a.* suspicious.

lo'to *n.m.* lotus.

lo'tt|a *n.f.* struggle; (*contrasto*) conflict; (*sport*) wrestling. **~a're** *v.i.* struggle; fight; wrestle. **~ato're** *n.m.* wrestler.

lotteri'a *n.f.* lottery.

lo'tto *n.m.* (*state*) lottery; (*porzione*) lot; (*di terreno*) plot.

lozio'ne *n.f.* lotion.

lubrifica'|re *v.t.* lubricate. **~nte** *a.* lubricating; *n.m.* lubricant.

lucche'tto *n.m.* padlock.

luccica'|re *v.i.* sparkle. **~nte** *a.* sparkling. **luccichi'o** *n.m.* sparkle.

lu'ccio *n.m.* pike.

lu'cciola *n.f.* glow-worm.

lu'c|e *n.f.* light. **far ~e su** shed light on. **~e della luna** moonlight. **~e del sole** sunlight. **~e'nte** *a.* shining. **~ente'zza** *n.f.* shine.

luce'rna *n.f.* oil-lamp.

lucerna'rio *n.m.* skylight.

luce'rtola *n.f.* lizard.

lucida'|re *v.t.* polish. **~tri'ce** *n.f.* (floor-) polisher. **lu'cido** *a.* shiny; (*chiaro*) clear; (*fig.*) lucid; *n.m.* shine; (*vernice, smalto*) polish.

luci'gnolo *n.m.* wick.

lucrati'vo *a.* lucrative. **lu'cro** *n.m.* lucre.

ludi'brio *n.m.* (*zimbello*) laughing-stock.

lu'glio *n.m.* July.

lu'gubre *a.* gloomy.

lu'i *pron.* (*soggetto*) he; (*oggetto*) him. **~ stesso** he himself.

luma'ca *n.f.* snail.

lu'me *n.m.* lamp; (*luce*) light.

lumino'so *a.* luminous; (*stanza, cielo, ecc.*) bright.

lu'n|a *n.f.* moon. **chiaro di ~a** moonlight. **~a di miele** honeymoon. **~a're** *a.* lunar. **~a'tico** *a.* moody.

luna'rio *n.m.* almanac. **sbarcare il ~** make both ends meet.

lunedì *n.m.* Monday. **di** ∼ on Mondays.

lu'ngi *adv.* far.

lungimira'nte *a.* far-seeing.

lu'ng|o *a.* long; (*diluito*) weak; (*lento*) slow. —*n.m.* length. —*prep.* (*durante*) throughout; (*per la lunghezza di*) along. **a** ∼**o andare** in the long run. **di gran** ∼**a** by far. **saperla** ∼**a** be shrewd. ∼**a'ggine** *n.f.* slowness. ∼**he'zza** *n.f.* length. ∼**hezza d'onda** wavelength.

lungoma're *n.m.* sea front.

luno'tto *n.m.* rear window.

luo'go *n.m.* place; (*punto preciso*) spot; (*passo d'autore*) passage. **aver** ∼ take place. **dar** ∼ **a** give rise to. **fuori** ∼ out of place. **usanze del** ∼ local customs.

luogotene'nte *n.m.* (*mil.*) lieutenant.

lupa'ra *n.f.* sawn-off shotgun.

lu'po *n.m.* wolf.

lu'ppolo *n.m.* hop.

lu'rid|o *a.* filthy. ∼**u'me** *n.m.* filth.

lusi'ng|a *n.f.* flattery. ∼**a're** *v.t.* flatter. ∼**a'rsi** *v.r.* flatter oneself; (*illudersi*) fool oneself. ∼**hie'ro** *a.* flattering.

lussa'r|e *v.t.*, ∼**si** *v.r.* dislocate.

Lussembu'rgo *n.m.* Luxembourg.

lu'ss|o *n.m.* luxury. **di** ∼**o** luxury. ∼**uo'so** *a.* luxurious.

lussureggia'nte *a.* luxuriant.

lussu'ria *n.f.* lust.

lustrascarpe *n.m./f.* *invar.* shoeblack.

lustri'no *n.m.* sequin.

lu'str|o *a.* shiny. —*n.m.* sheen; (*fig.*) prestige; (*quinquennio*) five-year period. ∼**a're** *v.t.* polish.

lu'tt|o *n.m.* mourning. ∼**o stretto** deep mourning. ∼**uo'so** *a.* mournful.

M

ma *conj.* but; (*eppure*) yet. ∼ **davvero?** really? ∼ **sì!** indeed!

ma'cabro *a.* macabre.

macché *int.* of course not!

macchero'ni *n.m. pl.* macaroni *s.*

ma'cchia[1] *n.f.* stain; (*di diverso colore*) spot; (*piccola*) speck. **senza** ∼ spotless. ∼**a're** *v.t.*, ∼**a'rsi** *v.r.* stain.

macchia[2] *n.f.* (*boscaglia*) scrub. **darsi alla** ∼ take to the woods.

ma'cchin|a *n.f.* machine; (*motore*) engine; (*automobile*) car. ∼**a da scrivere** typewriter. ∼**a fotografica** camera. ∼**a'rio** *n.m.* machinery.

macchina're *v.t.* plot.

macchini'sta *n.m.* (*ferrovia*) engine-driver; (*naut.*) engineer; (*theatr.*) stage-hand.

macchino'so *a.* complicated.

macedo'nia *n.f.* fruit salad.

macell|a're *v.t.* slaughter. ∼**a'io** *n.m.* butcher. ∼**eri'a** *n.f.* butcher's (shop).

mace'llo *n.m.* (*mattatoio*) slaughterhouse; (*fig.*) a shambles *s.*

macera'r|e *v.t.* macerate; (*fig.*) distress. ∼**si** *v.r.* be consumed.

mace'rie *n.f. pl.* rubble *s.*; (*rottami*) debris *s.*

maci'gno *n.m.* boulder.

macile'nto *a.* emaciated.

ma'cina *n.f.* millstone.

macinacaffè *n.m. invar.* coffee-mill.

macinape'pe *n.m. invar.* pepper-mill.

macina'|re *v.t.* mill. ∼**to** *a.* ground; *n.m.* (*carne*) mince.

macini'no *n.m.* mill; (*hum.*, *macchina vecchia*) old crock.

maciulla're *v.t.* (*stritolare*) crush.

macrobio'tico *a.* macrobiotic.

mada'm|a *n.f.* (*hum.*) madam.

ma'dido *a.* ∼ **di** moist with.

Mado'nna *n.f.* Our Lady.

madorna'le *a.* gross.

ma'dr|e *n.f.* mother. ∼**i'na** *n.f.* godmother.

madrepe'rla *n.f.* mother-of-pearl.

madriga'le *n.m.* madrigal.

maest|à *n.f.* majesty. ∼**o'so** *a.* majestic.

maestra'le *n.m.* north-west wind.

maestra'nza *n.f.* workers *pl.*

maestri'a *n.f.* mastery.

mae'stro, a *n.m.*, *f.* teacher. —*n.m.*

master; (*mus.*) maestro. —*a.* (*principale*) chief; (*di grande abilità*) skilful.

ma'fi|a *n.f.* Mafia. ∼**o'so** *a.* of the Mafia; *n.m.* member of the Mafia.

ma'ga *n.f.* sorceress.

maga'gna *n.f.* fault.

maga'ri *adv.* (*forse*) perhaps. —*int.* rather! —*conj.* (*anche se*) even if; (*volesse il cielo che*) if only.

magazzi'no *n.m.* warehouse; (*emporio*) shop.

ma'ggio *n.m.* May.

maggiora'na *n.f.* marjoram.

maggiora'nza *n.f.* majority.

maggiora're *v.t.* increase.

maggiordo'mo *n.m.* butler.

maggio'r|e *a.* (*comparativo*, *più grande*) greater, bigger, larger; (*di età*) older; (*di grado superiore*) senior; (*mil.*, *mus.*, *ecc.*) major; (*superlativo*) (the) greatest, (the) biggest, (the) largest; (*di età*) (the) oldest; (*di primaria importanza*) (the) major. —*n.m.*|*f.* (*di grado*) superior; (*di età*) oldest. —*n.m.* (*mil.*) major; (*aeron.*) squadron leader. **la** ∼ **parte** the majority. ∼**e'nne** *a.* of age; *n.m.*|*f.* adult. ∼**me'nte** *adv.* (all) the more; (*più di tutto*) most.

Ma'gi *n.m. pl.* **i re** ∼ the Magi.

magi'a *n.f.* magic. **ma'gico** *a.* magic.

magiste'ro *n.m.* (*insegnamento*) teaching; (*maestria*) skill. **facoltà di** ∼ arts faculty.

magistra'le *a.* magisterial. **istituto** ∼ teachers' training college.

magistra't|o *n.m.* magistrate. ∼**u'ra** *n.f.* magistrature. **la** ∼**ura** the Bench.

ma'gli|a *n.f.* stitch; (*lavoro ai ferri*) knitting; (*tessuto*) jersey; (*di rete*) mesh; (*di catena*) link; (*indumento*) vest. ∼**eri'a** *n.f.* knitwear. ∼**fi'cio** *n.m.* knitwear factory.

ma'glio *n.m.* mallet.

maglio'ne *n.m.* sweater.

magna'nimo *a.* magnanimous.

magna'te *n.m.* magnate.

magne'sia *n.f.* magnesia.

magne'sio *n.m.* magnesium.

magne't|e *n.m.* magnet. ∼**ico** *a.* magnetic. ∼**i'smo** *n.m.* magnetism.

magneto'fono *n.m.* tape recorder.

magni'fic|o *a.* magnificent; (*generoso*)

munificent. **~e'nza** *n.f.* magnificence; munificence.

magno'lia *n.f.* magnolia.

ma'go *n.m.* magician.

ma'gr|o *a.* thin; (*carne*) lean; (*scarso*) meagre.

ma'i *adv.* never; (*inter., talvolta*) ever. **caso ~** if anything. **caso ~ tornasse** in case he comes back. **come ~?** why? **cosa ~?** what on earth? **~ più** never again. **più che ~** more than ever. **quando ~?** whenever? **quasi ~** hardly ever.

maia'le *n.m.* pig; (*carne*) pork.

maione'se *n.f.* mayonnaise.

ma'is *n.m. invar.* maize.

maiu'scolo, a *a.* capital. —*n.f.* capital letter.

mal *vedi* **male.**

malacco'rto *a.* unwise.

malafe'de *n.f.* bad faith.

malaffa're *n.m.* **gente di ~** shady characters *pl.*

malali'ngua *n.f.* backbiter.

malanda'to *a.* in bad shape; (*di salute*) in poor health.

malandri'no *n.m.* scoundrel. —*a.* crooked.

mala'nimo *n.m.* ill will.

mala'nno *n.m.* misfortune; (*malattia*) ailment. **prendersi un ~** get ill.

malape'na *adv.* **a ~** hardly.

mala'ria *n.f.* malaria.

mala't|o, a *a.* ill, sick; (*di pianta*) diseased. —*n.m., f.* sick person. **~i'ccio** *a.* sickly. **~ti'a** *n.f.* illness, sickness; (*infettiva*) disease.

malaugu'rio *n.m.* bad *o* ill omen.

malavi'ta *n.f.* underworld.

malavo'glia *n.f.* unwillingness. **di ~** unwillingly.

malcapita'to *a.* wretched.

malco'ncio *a.* battered.

malconte'nto *n.m.* discontent.

malcostu'me *n.m.* immorality.

malde'stro *a.* awkward; (*inesperto*) inexperienced.

maldice'n|te *a.* slanderous. **~za** *n.f.* slander.

maldispo'sto *a.* ill-disposed.

ma'le *adv.* badly. **andare a ~** go bad. **star ~** be ill; (*vestito ecc.*) not to suit. —*n.m.* evil; (*dolore*) pain; (*malattia*) illness; (*danno*) harm. **mal di gola** sore throat. **mal di testa** headache. **non c'è ~!** pretty well!

malede'tto *a.* cursed; (*orribile*) awful.

maledi'|re *v.t.* curse. **~zio'ne** *n.f.* curse. **~zione!** damn!

maleduca'to *a.* ill-mannered.

malefi'cio *n.m.* witchcraft.

male'fico *a.* (*azione*) evil; (*nocivo*) harmful.

male'ssere *n.m.* indisposition; (*fig.*) uneasiness.

male'volo *a.* malevolent.

malfama'to *a.* of ill repute.

malfa'tto *a.* badly done; (*malformato*) ill-shaped.

malfatto're *n.m.* wrongdoer.

malfe'rmo *a.* unsteady; (*di salute*) poor.

malforma'|to *a.* misshapen. **~zio'ne** *n.f.* malformation.

malga'rbo *n.m.* rudeness.

malgove'rno *n.m.* misgovernment.

malgra'do *prep.* in spite of. —*conj.* although.

mali'a *n.f.* spell.

mali'gn|o *a.* malicious; (*perfido*) evil; (*med.*) malignant. **~a're** *v.i.* malign. **~ità** *n.f.* malice; malignancy.

malinc|oni'a *n.f.* melancholy. **~o'nico** *a.* melancholy.

malincuo're *adv.* **a ~** unwillingly.

malintenziona'to *a.* ill-intentioned.

malinte'so *a.* mistaken. —*n.m.* misunderstanding.

mali'zi|a *n.f.* malice; (*astuzia*) cunning; (*espediente*) trick. **~o'so** *a.* malicious; (*birichino*) mischievous.

mallea'bile *a.* malleable.

malmena're *v.t.* ill-treat.

malme'sso *a.* (*vestito male*) shabbily dressed; (*di casa*) poorly furnished.

malnutri'|to *a.,* undernourished. **~zio'ne** *n.f.* malnutrition.

malo'cchio *n.m.* evil eye.

malo'ra *n.f.* ruin. **andare in ~** go to ruin.

malo're *n.m.* illness. **essere colto da ~** be suddenly taken ill.

malsa'no *a.* unhealthy.

malsicu'ro *a.* unsafe; (*incerto*) uncertain.

ma'lta *n.f.* mortar.

malte'mpo *n.m.* bad weather.

ma'lto *n.m.* malt.

maltratta'|re *v.t.* ill-treat. **~me'nto** *n.m.* ill-treatment.

malumo're *n.m.* bad mood. **di ~** in a bad mood.

malva'gi|o *a.* wicked. **~tà** *n.f.* wickedness.

malversazio'ne *n.f.* embezzlement.

malvi'sto *a.* ~ **(da)** unpopular (with).

malvive'nte *n.m.* criminal.

malvolentie'ri *adv.* unwillingly.

malvole're *n.m.* ill will. —*v.t.* **farsi** ~ make oneself disliked. **prendere a** ~ **qcno.** take a dislike to s.o.

ma'mma *n.f.* mummy, mum. ~ **mia!** good gracious!

mamme'lla *n.f.* breast.

mammi'fero *n.m.* mammal.

ma'mmola *n.f.* violet.

mana'ta *n.f.* (*colpo*) slap.

ma'nca *n.f.* *vedi* **manco.**

manca'nza *n.f.* lack; (*assenza*) absence; (*insufficienza*) shortage; (*fallo*) fault; (*imperfezione*) defect. **in** ~ **d'altro** failing all else. **sento la sua** ~ I miss him.

manca're *v.i.* lack; (*essere assente*) be absent; (*sentire la mancanza di*) miss; (*venir meno*) fail. —*v.t.* miss. ~ **a** (*promessa*) fail to keep. ~ **di** be lacking in. **poco mancò che non cadde** he nearly fell. **sentirsi** ~ feel faint.

manche'vole *a.* defective.

ma'ncia *n.f.* tip.

mancia'ta *n.f.* handful.

manci'no *a.* left-handed.

ma'nco, a *a.* left. —*n.f.* left hand. —*adv.* (*nemmeno*) not even.

manda're *v.t.* send; (*emettere*) give off; (*suono*) utter. ~ **a chiamare** send for. ~ **avanti la casa** run the house. ~ **giù** (*ingoiare*) swallow.

mandari'no *n.m.* (*bot.*) mandarin(e); tangerine.

manda'ta *n.f.* consignment; (*di serratura*) turn.

manda'to *n.m.* (*incarico*) mandate; (*legge*) warrant; (*di pagamento*) money order.

mandi'bola *n.f.* jaw.

mandoli'no *n.m.* mandolin.

ma'ndorl|a *n.f.* almond. ~**o** *n.m.* almond(-tree).

ma'ndria *n.f.* herd.

manegg|ia're *v.t.* handle. ~**e'vole** *a.* easy to handle. **mane'ggio** *n.m.* handling; (*intrigo*) plot; (*scuola di equitazione*) riding school.

mane'sco *a.* quick with one's fists.

mane'tt|a *n.f.* hand lever. ~**e** *n.f. pl.* handcuffs.

mangane'llo *n.m.* truncheon.

mangane'se *n.m.* manganese.

ma'ngano *n.m.* mangle.

mangeri'a *n.f.* illicit profit.

mangia'r|e *v.t./i.* eat; (*consumare*)

eat up; (*corrodere*) eat away; (*scacchi, carte, ecc.*) take. —*n.m.* eating; (*cibo*) food; (*pasto*) meal. ~**si le parole** mumble. ~**si le unghie** bite one's nails.

mangi'me *n.m.* fodder.

ma'ngo *n.m.* mango.

mani'a *n.f.* mania. ~**co, a** *a.* maniacal; *n.m., f.* maniac.

ma'nica *n.f.* sleeve; (*gruppo*) band.

Ma'nica *n.f.* **la** ~ the (English) Channel.

manichi'no *n.m.* (*da sarto, vetrina*) dummy.

ma'nico *n.m.* handle; (*mus.*) neck.

manico'mio *n.m.* mental home.

manico'tto *n.m.* muff; (*mech.*) sleeve.

manicu're *n.m. invar.* manicure. —*n.m./f. invar.* (*persona*) manicurist.

manie'r|a *n.f.* manner. **in** ~**a che** so that. ~**a'to** *a.* affected; (*di stile*) mannered. ~**i'smo** *n.m.* mannerism.

manie'ro *n.m.* manor.

manifattu'ra *n.f.* manufacture; (*fabbrica*) factory.

manifesta'|re *v.t.* show; (*esprimere*) express. —*v.i.* demonstrate. ~**rsi** *v.r.* show oneself. ~**zio'ne** *n.f.* show; expression; (*sintomo*) manifestation; (*dimostrazione pubblica*) demonstration.

manife'sto *a.* evident. —*n.m.* poster; (*dichiarazione pubblica*) manifesto.

mani'glia *n.f.* handle; (*sostegno, in autobus ecc.*) strap.

manipola'|re *v.t.* handle; (*alterare*) adulterate; (*fig.*) manipulate. ~**zio'ne** *n.f.* handling; adulteration; manipulation.

manisca'lco *n.m.* smith.

manna'ia *n.f.* (*scure*) axe; (*da macellaio*) cleaver.

manna'ro *a.* **lupo** ~ werewolf.

ma'no *n.f.* hand; (*strato di vernice ecc.*) coat. **a portata di** ~ within reach. **essere alla** ~ be informal. **fuori** ~ out of the way. **man** ~ little by little. **man** ~ **che** as. **sotto** ~ (*in segreto*) on the sly.

manodo'pera *n.f.* labour.

mano'metro *n.m.* gauge.

manome'ttere *v.t.* tamper with; (*violare*) violate.

mano'pola *n.f.* (*di apparecchio*) knob; (*guanto*) mitten.

manoscri'tto *a.* handwritten. —*n.m.* manuscript.

manova'le *n.m.* labourer.

manove'lla *n.f.* handle; (*techn.*) crank.

mano'vr|a *n.f.* manœuvre; (*ferrovia*) shunting. ~a're *v.t.* (*azionare*) operate; *v.t./i.* (*fig.*) manœuvre.

manrove'scio *n.m.* (back-handed) slap.

mansa'rda *n.f.* attic.

mansio'ne *n.f.* task; (*dovere*) duty.

mansue'to *a.* meek; (*di animale*) docile.

mante'llo *n.m.* cloak; (*soprabito, di animale*) coat; (*di neve*) mantle.

mantene'r|e *v.t.* (*conservare*) keep; (*in buono stato, sostentare*) maintain. ~si *v.r.* keep oneself. **mantenime'nto** *n.m.* maintenance.

ma'ntice *n.m.* bellows *pl.*; (*di automobile*) hood.

ma'nto *n.m.* cloak; (*coltre*) mantle.

mantova'na *n.f.* pelmet.

manua'le *a.* & *n.m.* manual.

manu'brio *n.m.* handle; (*di bicicletta*) handlebars *pl.*; (*per ginnastica*) dumb-bell.

manufa'tto *a.* manufactured.

manutenzio'ne *n.f.* maintenance.

ma'nzo *n.m.* steer; (*carne*) beef.

maometta'no *a.* & *n.m.* Muslim.

ma'ppa *n.f.* map.

mappamo'ndo *n.m.* globe.

marache'lla *n.f.* prank.

maragià *n.m.* maharaja(h).

mara'sma *n.m.* (*fig.*) decline.

marato'na *n.f.* marathon.

ma'rc|a *n.f.* mark; (*comm.*) brand; (*fabbricazione*) make; (*scontrino*) check. ~a da bollo revenue stamp. ~a're *v.t.* mark; (*sport*) score.

marche'se, a *n.m., f.* marquis, marchioness.

marchia're *v.t.* brand. **ma'rchio** *n.m.* brand. **marchio di fabbrica** trademark.

ma'rci|a *n.f.* march; (*auto.*) gear. ~a indietro reverse gear. mettere in ~a get into gear. mettersi in ~a start off. ~a're *v.t.* march; (*funzionare*) go.

marciapie'de *n.m.* pavement; (*di stazione*) platform.

ma'rc|io *a.* rotten. —*n.m.* (*fig.*) corruption. ~i're *v.i.* go bad, rot.

ma'rco *n.m.* (*moneta*) mark.

ma'r|e *n.m.* sea; (*luogo di mare*) seaside. essere in alto ~e (*fig.*) not to know which way to turn. ~eggia'ta *n.f.* (sea) storm. ~i'no *a.* sea, marine.

mare'a *n.f.* tide.

marescia'llo *n.m.* (*ufficiale*) marshal; (*sottufficiale*) warrant-officer.

margari'na *n.f.* margarine.

margheri't|a *n.f.* marguerite. ~i'na *n.f.* daisy.

margina'le *a.* marginal.

ma'rgine *n.m.* margin; (*orlo*) brink; (*bordo*) border.

mari'na *n.f.* navy; (*costa*) sea-shore; (*quadro*) seascape. ~ mercantile merchant navy.

marina'io *n.m.* sailor.

marina'|re *v.t.* marinate. ~re la scuola play truant. ~ta *n.f.* marinade.

marione'tta *n.f.* puppet.

marita'|re *v.t.* marry. ~rsi *v.r.* get married. ~le *a.* marital.

mari'to *n.m.* husband.

mari'ttimo *a.* maritime.

marma'glia *n.f.* rabble.

marmella'ta *n.f.* jam; (*di agrumi*) marmalade.

marmi'tta *n.f.* pot; (*auto*) silencer.

ma'rmo *n.m.* marble.

marmo'cchio *n.m.* (*fam.*) brat.

marmo'tta *n.f.* marmot.

Maro'cco *n.m.* Morocco.

ma'rra *n.f.* hoe.

marro'ne *a.* brown. —*n.m.* maroon.

marsi'na *n.f.* tails *pl.*

martedì *n.m.* Tuesday. di ~ on Tuesdays. ~ grasso Shrove Tuesday.

martella're *v.t.* hammer. —*v.i.* throb. **marte'llo** *n.m.* hammer; (*di battente*) knocker.

martine'tto *n.m.* jack.

ma'rt|ire *n.m./f.* martyr. ~i'rio *n.m.* martyrdom.

ma'rtora *n.f.* marten.

martoria're *v.t.* torment.

marxi's|mo *n.m.* Marxism. ~ta *a.* & *n.m./f.* Marxist.

marzapa'ne *n.m.* marzipan.

marzia'le *a.* martial.

ma'rzo *n.m.* March.

mascalzo'ne *n.m.* rascal.

masce'lla *n.f.* jaw.

ma'scher|a *n.f.* mask; (*costume*) fancy dress; (*cinema, theatr.*) usher *m.*, usherette *f.*; (*personaggio della commedia dell'arte*) stock character. ~ame'nto *n.m.* masking; (*mil.*) camouflage. ~a're *v.t.* mask; camouflage. ~a'rsi *v.r.* put on a mask. ~arsi da dress up as. ~a'ta *n.f.* masquerade.

maschi′le *a.* masculine; (*sesso*) male. —*n.m.* masculine (gender).

maschili′sta *a.* sexist.

ma′sc|hio *a.* male; (*virile*) manly. —*n.m.* male; (*figlio*) son. ～oli′no *a.* masculine.

maschi′sta *n.m.* macho.

masco′tte *n.f. invar.* mascot.

masochi′s|mo *n.m.* masochism. ～ta *a. & n.m./f.* masochist.

ma′ssa *n.f.* mass; (*electr.*) earth. **comunicazioni di** ～ (mass) media.

massacra′|re *v.t.* massacre. ～nte *a.* gruelling. **massa′cro** *n.m.* massacre; (*fig.*) mess.

massaggia′re *v.t.* massage. **massa′ggio** *n.m.* massage.

massa′ia *n.f.* housewife.

masseri′a *n.f.* farm.

masseri′zie *n.f. pl.* household effects.

massi′ccio *a.* massive; (*oro ecc.*) solid; (*corporatura*) heavy. —*n.m.* massif.

ma′ssima *n.f.* maxim; (*detto*) saying; (*di temperatura*) maximum. **in linea di** ～ as a rule.

ma′ssimo *a.* (the) greatest, (the) maximum. —*n.m.* (the) most, (the) maximum. **al** ～ at (the) most.

ma′sso *n.m.* rock.

masso′ne *n.m.* Freemason. ～ri′a *n.f.* Freemasonry.

mastica′re *v.t.* chew.

ma′stice *n.m.* mastic; (*per vetri*) putty.

masti′no *n.m.* mastiff.

mastodo′ntico *a.* gigantic.

ma′stro *n.m.* master. **libro** ～ ledger.

masturb|azio′ne *n.f.* masturbation. ～a′rsi *v.r.* masturbate.

mata′ssa *n.f.* skein.

matema′tic|a *n.f.* mathematics *s.* ～o, a *a.* mathematical; *n.m., f.* mathematician.

matera′sso *n.m.* mattress.

mate′ria *n.f.* matter; (*materiale*) material; (*di studio*) subject.

materia′le *a.* material; (*grossolano*) coarse. —*n.m.* material.

materiali′s|mo *n.m.* materialism. ～ta *a.* materialistic(al); *n.m./f.* materialist.

mate′rn|o *a.* maternal. **lingua** ～a mother tongue. ～ità *n.f.* motherhood. **ospedale di** ～ità maternity hospital.

mati′ta *n.f.* pencil.

matri′ce *n.f.* matrix; (*comm.*) counterfoil.

matri′cola *n.f.* (*registro*) register; (*univ.*) freshman.

matri′gna *n.f.* stepmother.

matrimo′ni|o *n.m.* marriage; (*cerimonia*) wedding. ～a′le *a.* matrimonial. **vita** ～ale married life.

matro′na *n.f.* matron.

mattacchio′ne, a *n.m., f.* rascal.

mattato′io *n.m.* slaughterhouse.

mattare′llo *n.m.* rolling-pin.

matti′n|o, a *n.m., f.* morning. ～a′ta *n.f.* morning; (*theatr.*) matinée. ～ie′ro *a.* **essere** ～iero be an early riser.

ma′tt|o, a *a.* mad, crazy (*fam.*); (*med.*) insane; (*falso*) false; (*opaco*) matt. —*n.m., f.* madman/woman. **avere una voglia** ～a **di** be dying for.

matto′ne *n.m.* brick.

matto′nella *n.f.* tile.

matura′re *v.t.* ripen.

maturità *n.f.* maturity; (*schol.*) school-leaving certificate. **matu′ro** *a.* mature; (*frutto*) ripe.

matu′sa *n.m.* old fogy.

mausole′o *n.m.* mausoleum.

ma′zz|a *n.f.* club; (*martello*) hammer; (*da baseball, cricket*) bat. ～a′ta *n.f.* blow.

ma′zzo *n.m.* bunch; (*carte da gioco*) pack.

me *pron.* me; (*me stesso*) myself. **fai come** ～ do as I do. **secondo** ～ in my opinion.

mea′ndro *n.m.* meander.

M.E.C. *abbr.* (*di Mercato Comune Europeo*) EEC.

mecca′n|ico *a.* mechanical. —*n.m.* mechanic. ～ica *n.f.* mechanics *s.* ～i′smo *n.m.* mechanism.

meda′gli|a *n.f.* medal. ～o′ne *n.m.* medallion; (*gioiello*) locket.

mede′simo *a.* same.

me′di|a *n.f.* average; (*schol.*) average mark; (*math.*) mean. ～o *a.* average; (*punto*) middle; (*statura*) medium. **scuola** ～a secondary school. ～o *n.m.* (*dito*) middle finger.

media′no *a.* median; (*intermedio*) middle; (*medio*) mean. —*n.m.* (*calcio*) half-back.

media′nte *prep.* by.

media|to′re, ～tri′ce *n.m., f.* mediator; (*comm.*) middleman. ～zio′ne *n.f.* mediation.

medica′|re *v.t.* treat; (*ferita*) dress. ～me′nto *n.m.* medicine. ～zio′ne *n.f.* medication; dressing.

medic|i'na *n.f.* medicine. **~ina legale** forensic medicine. **~ina'le** *a.* medicinal; *n.m.* medicine.

me'dic|o *a.* medical. —*n.m.* doctor. **~o generico** general practitioner.

medio'cre *a.* mediocre; (*scadente*) poor.

medi|oe'vo *n.m.* Middle Ages *pl.* **~o-va'le** *a.* medieval.

medita'|re *v.t.* meditate; (*progettare*) plan. —*v.i.* meditate. **~zio'ne** *n.f.* meditation.

mediterra'neo *a.* mediterranean. **il (mare) M~** the Mediterranean (Sea).

medu'sa *n.f.* jellyfish.

mega'fono *n.m.* megaphone.

mege'ra *n.f.* hag.

me'glio *adv.* better. —*a.* better; (*superlativo*) best. —*n.m./f.* (the) best. **avere la ~ (su)** have the better (of). **fare del proprio ~** do one's best.

me'l|a *n.f.* apple. **~a cotogna** quince. **~o** *n.m.* apple(-tree).

melagra'na *n.f.* pomegranate.

melanza'na *n.f.* aubergine.

mela'ssa *n.f.* molasses *s.*

melli'fluo *a.* honeyed.

me'lma *n.f.* slime.

melodi'|a *n.f.* melody. **melo'dico** *a.* melodic. **~o'so** *a.* melodious.

melodra'mm|a *n.m.* melodrama. **~a'tico** *a.* melodramatic.

melo'ne *n.m.* melon.

membra'na *n.f.* membrane.

me'mbro *n.m.* member; (*pl. f.* **membra,** *anat.*) limb.

memora'bile *a.* memorable.

me'more *a.* mindful; (*riconoscente*) grateful.

memo'ri|a *n.f.* memory; (*oggetto ricordo*) souvenir. **~e** *n.f. pl.* (*biografiche*) memoirs. **imparare a ~a** learn by heart. **~zza're** *v.t.* memorize.

memoria'le *n.m.* memorial.

menadi'to *adv.* **a ~** perfectly.

mena're *v.t.* lead; (*picchiare*) hit. **~ la coda** (*cane*) wag its tail.

mendica'|nte *n.m./f.* beggar. **~re** *v.t./i.* beg.

me'no *adv.* less; (*superlativo*) (the) least; (*fra due*) (the) less; (*math.*) minus. —*a.* less; (*persone ecc.*) fewer. —*n.* (the) least. —*prep.* (*tranne*) except (for). **a ~ che** *conj.* unless. **fare a ~ di** (*privarsi*) do without. **fare a ~ di fare** (*inevitabile*) cannot help doing. **il ~ possibile** as little as possible. **~ male!** thank goodness!

per lo ~ at least. **sempre ~** less and less. **sono le tre ~ un quarto** it is a quarter to three. **venir ~** (*svenire*) faint.

menoma're *v.t.* lessen; (*danneggiare*) maim.

menopa'usa *n.f.* menopause.

me'nsa *n.f.* table; (*mil.*) mess; (*schol., univ.*) refectory.

mensi'le *a.* monthly. —*n.m.* (*stipendio*) (monthly) salary; (*rivista*) monthly.

me'nsola *n.f.* bracket; (*scaffale*) shelf.

me'nta *n.f.* mint. **~ peperita** peppermint.

menta'l|e *a.* mental. **~ità** *n.f.* mentality.

me'nte *n.f.* mind. **a ~ fredda** in cold blood. **saltare in ~** come into one's head. **venire in ~ a qcno.** cross s.o.'s mind.

menti're *v.i.* lie.

me'nto *n.m.* chin.

me'ntre *conj.* (*temporale*) while; (*invece*) whereas.

menziona're *v.t.* mention. **menzio'ne** *n.f.* mention.

menzo'gna *n.f.* lie.

meravi'gli|a *n.f.* wonder. **a ~a** marvellously. **che ~a!** how wonderful! **con mia grande ~a** to my amazement. **mi fa ~a** che I am surprised that. **~a're** *v.t.* surprise. **~a'rsi** *v.r.* **~arsi (di)** marvel (at). **~o'so** *a.* marvellous, wonderful.

merca'n|te *n.m.* merchant. **~te di bestiame** cattle dealer. **~teggia're** *v.t.* trade; (*sul prezzo*) bargain. **~zi'a** *n.f.* merchandise, goods *pl.*

mercanti'le *a.* mercantile. —*n.m.* merchant ship.

merca'to *n.m.* market. **M~ Comune (Europeo)** (European) Common Market. **a buon ~** *adv.* cheaply; *a.* cheap.

me'rce *n.f.* goods *pl.*

mercè *n.f.* mercy.

mercena'rio *a. & n.m.* mercenary.

merceri'a *n.f.* haberdashery; (*negozio*) haberdasher's.

mercoledì *n.m.* Wednesday. **di ~ on** Wednesdays. **~ delle Ceneri** Ash Wednesday.

mercu'rio *n.m.* mercury.

mere'nda *n.f.* snack.

meridia'n|o *a.* midday. —*n.m.* meridian. **~a** *n.f.* sundial.

meridiona'le *a.* southern. —*n.m.|f.* southerner. **meridio'ne** *n.m.* south.

meri'nga *n.f.* meringue.

me'rit|o *n.m.* merit; (*valore*) worth. **in ∼o a** as to. **per ∼o di** thanks to. **∼a're** *v.t.* deserve. **∼e'vole** *a.* deserving; worthy. **∼o'rio** *a.* meritorious.

merle'tto *n.m.* lace.

me'rlo *n.m.* blackbird; (*fig.*, *stupido*) simpleton.

merlu'zzo *n.m.* cod.

meschi'n|o *a.* wretched; (*gretto*) mean. —*n.m.* wretch. **∼eri'a** *n.f.* meanness.

me'scita *n.f.* wine shop.

mescola'|re *v.t.* mix; (*carte*) shuffle; (*confondere*) mix up; (*tè, tabacco, ecc.*) blend. **∼rsi** *v.r.* mix; (*immischiarsi*) meddle. **∼nza** *n.f.* mixture.

me'se *n.m.* month.

me'ss|a[1] *n.f.* Mass. **∼a'le** *n.m.* missal.

me'ssa[2] *n.f.* (*il mettere*) putting. **∼ in moto** (*auto*) starting. **∼ in piega** (*di capelli*) set.

messagge'ro *n.m.* messenger. **messa'ggio** *n.m.* message.

me'sse *n.f.* harvest.

Messi'a *n.m.* Messiah.

Me'ssic|o *n.m.* Mexico. **m∼a'no, a** *a* & *n.m., f.* Mexican.

messinsce'na *n.f.* staging; (*fig.*) act.

me'sso *p.p. di* **mettere**. —*n.m.* messenger.

mestie're *n.m.* trade; (*lavoro*) job. **essere del ∼** be an expert.

me'sto *a.* sad.

me'stolo *n.m.* ladle.

mestruazio'ne *n.f.* menstruation.

me'ta *n.f.* destination; (*fig.*) aim.

metà *n.f.* half; (*centro*) middle. **a ∼ strada** half-way. **fare a ∼ con qcno.** go halves with s.o.

metabo'lismo *n.m.* metabolism.

meta'fora *n.f.* metaphor.

meta'll|o *n.m.* metal. **∼ico** *a.* metallic. **∼urgi'a** *n.f.* metallurgy.

metamo'rfosi *n.f.* metamorphosis.

meta'no *n.m.* methane.

mete'or|a *n.f.* meteor. **∼i'te** *n.m.* meteorite.

meteorolo'g|ico *a.* meteorological. **∼i'a** *n.f.* meteorology.

meti'ccio, a *n.m., f.* half-caste.

meticolo'so *a.* meticulous.

me't|odo *n.m.* method. **∼o'dico** *a.* methodical.

me'tr|o *n.m.* metre; (*nastro*) tape measure. **∼a'ggio** *n.m.* length (in

metres). **∼ico, a** *a.* metric; (*poesia*) metrical; *n.f.* metrics *s.*

metro'poli *n.f. invar.* metropolis.

metropolita'n|a *n.f.* underground. **∼o** *a.* metropolitan; *n.m.* (*vigile urbano*) traffic warden.

me'tter|e *v.t.* put; (*impiegare*) take; (*indossare*) put on; (*supporre*) suppose; (*causare*) cause. **∼e da parte** set aside. **∼e fiducia** inspire trust. **∼e in guardia** warn. **∼e in mostra** display. **∼e in vendita** put up for sale. **∼e paura a** frighten. **∼e su casa** set up house. **∼si** *v.r.* put oneself; (*indossare*) put on; (*diventare*) turn out. **∼si a** start to. **∼si a letto** go to bed. **∼si a proprio agio** make oneself at home. **∼si a sedere** sit down.

mezza'dro *n.m.* share-cropper.

mezzalu'na *n.f.* half moon; (*simbolo islamico*) crescent; (*coltello*) mincing knife.

mezzani'no *n.m.* mezzanine.

mezza'no, a *a.* middle. —*n.m., f.* (*mediatore*) go-between; (*ruffiano*) pimp.

mezzano'tte *n.f.* midnight.

me'zz|o, a *a.* half. **∼o bicchiere** half a glass. —*adv.* (*a metà*) half. —*n.m.* (*metà*) half; (*centro*) middle; (*per raggiungere un fine*) means *s.* **∼i** *n.m. pl.* (*denaro*) means. —*n.f.* (*mezz'ora*) half-hour. **è la ∼a** it is half past twelve. **sono le quattro e ∼a** it is half past four. **trovare una via di ∼o** find a way out.

mezzogio'rno *n.m.* midday; (*sud*) South. **il M∼** Southern Italy.

mi *pron.* me; (*r.*) myself. —*n.m.* (*mus.*) me.

miagol|a're *v.i.* mew. **∼i'o** *n.m.* mewing.

mi'ca[1] *n.f.* (*min.*) mica.

mi'ca[2] *adv.* (*fam., neg.*) at all. (*per caso*) by any chance. **hai ∼ visto Paolo?** have you seen Paul, by any chance? **non è ∼ bello** it is not nice at all.

mi'ccia *n.f.* fuse.

micidia'le *a.* deadly.

mi'cio *n.m.* pussy-cat.

mi'crobo *n.m.* microbe.

microfi'lm *n.m.* microfilm.

micro'fono *n.m.* microphone.

microsco'pi|o *n.m.* microscope. **∼co** *a.* microscopic.

microso'lco *n.m.* (*disco*) long-playing record.

mido'llo *n.m.* (*pl. f.* **midolla**, *anat.*) marrow.

mi'e, mie'i *vedi* mio.

mie'le *n.m.* honey.

mie't|ere *v.t.* reap. ~**itri'ce** *n.f.* (*mech.*) harvester. ~**itu'ra** *n.f.* harvest.

miglia'i|o *n.m.* (*pl. f.* ~**a**) thousand. **a** ~**a** in thousands.

mi'glio *n.m.* (*bot.*) millet; (*pl.f.* **miglia**, *misura*) mile.

migliora'|re *v.t./i.* improve. ~**me'nto** *n.m.* improvement.

miglio're *a.* better; (*superlativo*) the best. —*n.m.* **il** ~ the best.

mi'gnolo *n.m.* little finger; (*del piede*) little toe.

migra'|re *v.i.* migrate. ~**zio'ne** *n.f.* migration.

mi'la *vedi* mille.

Mila'no *n.f.* Milan.

milia'rd|o *n.m.* thousand million(s). ~**a'rio, a** *n.m., f.* millionaire.

milia're *a.* **pietra** ~ milestone.

milio'n|e *n.m.* million. ~**a'rio, a** *n.m., f.* millionaire, millionairess.

milita'nte *a. & n.m.|f.* militant.

milita're *v.i.* serve (in the army); (*fig.*) support. —*a.* military. —*n.m.* soldier.

mi'l|ite *n.m.* soldier. ~**i'zia** *n.f.* militia.

millanta|to're, ~**tri'ce** *n.m., f.* boaster.

mi'll|e *a. & n.m.* (*pl.* **mila**) a thousand. ~**e grazie!** thanks a lot! ~**e'simo** *a. & n.m.* thousandth.

millefo'glie *n.m.* (*bot.*) milfoil; (*culin.*) millefeuilles.

mille'nnio *n.m.* millennium.

millepie'di *n.m. invar.* centipede.

milligra'mmo *n.m.* milligram.

milli'metro *n.m.* millimetre.

mi'lza *n.f.* spleen.

mimetizza'r|e *v.t.,* ~**si** *v.r.* camouflage.

mi'm|ica *n.f.* mime. ~**ico** *a.* mimic. ~**o** *n.m.* mime.

mimo'sa *n.f.* mimosa.

mi'n|a *n.f.* mine; (*di matita*) lead. ~**a're** *v.t.* mine; (*fig.*) undermine.

mina'cci|a *n.f.* threat. ~**a're** *v.t.* threaten. ~**o'so** *a.* threatening.

minato're *n.m.* miner.

minera'l|e *a. & n.m.* mineral. ~**ogi'a** *n.f.* mineralogy.

minera'rio *a.* mining.

mine'str|a *n.f.* soup. ~**o'ne** *n.m.* vegetable soup.

mingherli'no *a.* skinny.

miniatu'ra *n.f.* miniature.

minie'ra *n.f.* mine.

minigo'nna *n.f.* miniskirt.

mi'nimo *a.* least, slightest; (*il più basso*) lowest. —*n.m.* minimum. **girare al** ~ (*auto.*) idle.

ministe'ro *n.m.* ministry; (*governo*) government.

mini'stro *n.m.* minister. **M**~ **del Tesoro** Chancellor of the Exchequer.

minora'nza *n.f.* minority.

minora'to, a *a.* disabled. —*n.m., f.* disabled person.

mino'r|e *a.* less; (*più piccolo*) smaller; (*più breve*) shorter; (*più basso*) lower; (*di età*) younger; (*meno importante*) minor; (*superlativo*) (the) least; (the) smallest; (the) shortest; (the) lowest; (the) youngest. —*n.m.|f.* youngest; (*tra due*) younger; (*legge*) minor. ~**e'nne** *a.* under age; *n.m.|f.* minor.

minue'tto *n.m.* minuet.

minu'scolo, a *a.* tiny. —*n.f.* small letter.

minu'ta *n.f.* rough copy.

minu'to[1] *a.* minute. **al** ~ (*comm.*) retail.

minu'to[2] *n.m.* (*di tempo*) minute. **spaccare il** ~ be dead on time.

minu'zi|a *n.f.* trifle. ~**o'so** *a.* detailed; (*di persona*) meticulous.

mi'o, a *a.* (*pl.* **mie'i, mi'e**) my. **un** ~ **amico** a friend of mine. —*pron.* mine. **i miei** my family.

mi'op|e *a.* short-sighted. ~**i'a** *n.f.* short-sightedness.

mi'r|a *n.f.* aim; (*bersaglio*) target. ~**a're** *v.i.* (take) aim. ~**a'rsi** *v.r.* (*guardarsi*) look at oneself.

mira'bile *a.* admirable.

mira'col|o *n.m.* miracle. ~**o'so** *a.* miraculous.

mira'ggio *n.m.* mirage.

miri'no *n.m.* sight; (*foto*) viewfinder.

mirti'llo *n.m.* blueberry.

mi'rto *n.m.* myrtle.

misa'ntropo, a *n.m., f.* misanthropist.

misce'la *n.f.* mixture; (*di caffè, tabacco, ecc.*) blend.

miscella'nea *n.f.* miscellany.

mi'schia *n.f.* scuffle.

mischia'r|e *v.t.* mix; (*carte da gioco*) shuffle. ~**si** *v.r.* mix; (*immischiarsi*) interfere.

miscu'glio *n.m.* mixture; (*fig.*) medley.

misera'bile *a.* miserable.

mise'ri|a *n.f.* poverty; (*infelicità*) misery; (*inezia*) trifle. **~e** *n.f. pl.* (*disgrazie*) misfortunes. **mi'sero** *a.* (*miserabile*) wretched; (*povero*) poor; (*scarso*) paltry.

miserico'rdia *n.f.* mercy.

misfa'tto *n.m.* misdeed.

miso'gino *n.m.* misogynist.

mi'ssile *n.m.* missile.

missio'n|e *n.f.* mission. **~a'rio, a** *n.m., f.* missionary.

miste'r|o *n.m.* mystery. **~io'so** *a.* mysterious.

mi'stico, a *a.* mystic(al). —*n.m.* mystic. —*n.f.* mysticism.

mistifica're *v.t.* mystify; (*ingannare*) deceive.

mi'st|o *a.* mixed. **scuola ~a** co-educational school. —*n.m.* mixture.

misu'r|a *n.f.* measure; (*dimensione*) measurement; (*taglia*) size; (*limite*) limit. **~a're** *v.t.* measure; (*indumenti*) try on; (*limitare*) limit. **~a'rsi** *v.r.* **~arsi con** (*gareggiare*) compete with. **~a'to** *a.* measured.

mi'te *a.* mild; (*di prezzo*) moderate.

mitiga'r|e *v.t.* mitigate. **~si** *v.r.* calm down; (*di clima*) become mild.

mi'to *n.m.* myth. **~logi'a** *n.f.* mythology.

mi'tra *n.f.* (*relig.*) mitre. —*n.m. invar.* (*mil.*) machine-gun.

mitragliatri'ce *n.f.* machine-gun.

mitte'nte *n.m./f.* sender.

mo'bil|e¹ *a.* mobile; (*volubile*) fickle; (*che si può muovere*) movable. **beni ~i** personal estate. **squadra ~e** flying squad. **~ità** *n.f.* mobility.

mo'bil|e² *n.m.* piece of furniture. **~i** *n.m. pl.* furniture *s.* **mobi'lia** *n.f.* furniture.

mobilita'|re *v.t.* mobilize. **~zio'ne** *n.f.* mobilization.

mocassi'no *n.m.* moccasin.

moccio'so, a *n.m., f.* brat.

mo'ccolo *n.m.* (*di candela*) candle-end.

mo'da *n.f.* fashion. **di ~** in fashion.

modalità *n.f.* formality.

mode'll|a *n.f.* model. **~a're** *v.t.* model. **~a'rsi** *v.r.* model oneself. **~o** *n.m.* model; (*stampo*) mould; (*di carta*) pattern.

modera'|re *v.t.* moderate; (*diminuire*) reduce. **~rsi** *v.r.* control oneself. **~to** *a.* moderate. **~zio'ne** *n.f.* moderation.

mode'rn|o *a.* modern. **~izza're** *v.t.* modernize.

mode'st|o *a.* modest. **~ia** *n.f.* modesty.

mo'dico *a.* reasonable.

modi'fic|a *n.f.* modification. **~a're** *v.t.* modify.

mo'do *n.m.* way; (*garbo*) manners *pl.*; (*occasione*) chance; (*gram.*) mood. **ad ogni ~** anyhow. **di ~ che** so that. **fare in ~ di** try to. **in che ~** (*inter.*) how. **in qualche ~** somehow. **in questo ~** like this. **~ di dire** idiom. **per ~ di dire** so to speak.

modula'|re *v.t.* modulate. **~zio'ne** *n.f.* modulation.

mo'dulo *n.m.* form; (*lunare, di comando*) module.

mo'gano *n.m.* mahogany.

mo'gio *a.* dejected.

mo'glie *n.f.* wife.

moi'ne *n.f. pl.* blandishments.

mo'la *n.f.* millstone; (*mech.*) grindstone.

mola're *n.m.* molar.

mo'le *n.f.* mass; (*dimensione*) size.

mole'cola *n.f.* molecule.

molesta're *v.t.* bother; (*più forte*) molest. **mole'stia** *n.f.* nuisance. **mole'sto** *a.* bothersome.

mo'll|a *n.f.* spring. **~e** *n.f. pl.* tongs.

molla're *v.t.* let go; (*naut.*) cast off. —*v.i.* cease.

mo'll|e *a.* soft; (*di corpo*) flabby; (*rilassato*) loose; (*bagnato*) wet. **~e'zza** *n.f.* softness; flabbiness; looseness. **~e'zze** *n.f. pl.* (*fig.*) luxury.

molle'tt|a *n.f.* (*per capelli*) hair-grip; (*per bucato*) clothes-peg. **~e** *n.f. pl.* (*per ghiaccio ecc.*) tongs.

molli'ca *n.f.* crumb.

mollu'sco *n.m.* mollusc.

mo'lo *n.m.* pier; (*banchina*) dock.

molte'plic|e *a.* manifold; (*numeroso*) numerous. **~ità** *n.f.* multiplicity.

moltiplica'|re *v.t.,* **~rsi** *v.r.* multiply. **~to're** *n.m.* multiplier. **~tri'ce** *n.f.* calculating machine. **~zio'ne** *n.f.* multiplication.

moltitu'dine *n.f.* multitude.

mo'lt|o *a.* much (*pl.* many), a lot (of); (*di tempo*) long, a long time, a lot of time. —*adv.* very much, a lot. —*pron.* a lot.

mome'nt|o *n.m.* moment. **a ~i** (*a volte*) sometimes; (*fra un momento*) in a moment. **dal ~o che** since. **per il ~o** for the time being. **~a'neo** *a.* momentary.

mo'nac|a *n.f.* nun. **~o** *n.m.* monk.

Mo'naco *n.m.* Monaco. —*n.f.* (*di Baviera*) Munich.

mona'rc|a *n.m.* monarch. ∼**hi'a** *n.f.* monarchy. ∼**hico, a** *a.* monarchic; *n.m.*, *f.* monarchist.

monaste'ro *n.m.* (*di monaci*) monastery; (*di monache*) convent. **mona'stico** *a.* monastic.

mo'nco *a.* maimed. ∼ **di un braccio** one-armed.

monda'n|o *a.* worldly. **vita** ∼**a** social life.

monda're *v.t.* (*sbucciare*) peel; (*piselli*) shell; (*pulire*) clean.

monde'zz|a *n.f.* (*immondizia*) rubbish. ∼**a'io** *n.m.* (*luogo sozzo*) pigsty.

mo'nd|o *n.m.* world. **il bel** ∼**o** fashionable society. **un** ∼**o** (*molto*) a lot. ∼**ia'le** *a.* world. **di fama** ∼**iale** world-famous.

mone'll|o, a *n.m.*, *f.* urchin. ∼**eri'a** *n.f.* prank.

mone't|a *n.f.* coin; (*denaro*) money; (*denaro spicciolo*) change. ∼**a estera** foreign currency. ∼**a legale** legal tender. ∼**a'rio** *a.* monetary.

mongolo'ide *a.* & *n.m./f.* (*med.*) mongol.

moni'le *n.m.* jewel.

mo'nito *n.m.* warning.

monito're *n.m.* monitor.

mono'colo *n.m.* monocle.

monocolo're *a.* (*pol.*) one-party.

monogra'mma *n.m.* monogram.

mono'logo *n.m.* monologue.

monopa'ttino *n.m.* (child's) scooter.

monopla'no *n.m.* monoplane.

monopo'li|o *n.m.* monopoly. ∼**zza're** *v.t.* monopolize.

monosi'll|abo *n.m.* monosyllable. ∼**a'bico** *a.* monosyllabic.

mono'ton|o *a.* monotonous. ∼**i'a** *n.f.* monotony.

monsigno're *n.m.* monsignor.

monso'ne *n.m.* monsoon.

montaca'richi *n.m. invar.* hoist.

monta'ggio *n.m.* (*mech.*) assembly; (*cinema*) editing.

monta'gn|a *n.f.* mountain; (*zona*) mountains *pl.* ∼**e russe** big dipper. ∼**o'so** *a.* mountainous.

montana'ro, a *n.m.*, *f.* highlander.

monta'no *a.* mountain.

monta'|re *v.t./i.* mount; (*veicolo*) get on; (*aumentare*) rise; (*mech.*) assemble; (*quadro*) frame; (*culin.*) whip; (*fig.*) blow up. ∼**rsi la testa** become swollen-headed. ∼**tu'ra** *n.f.* (*mech.*)

assembling; (*di occhiali*) frame; (*di gioiello*) mounting; (*fig.*) exaggeration.

mo'nt|e *n.m.* mount. **a** ∼**e** upstream. **andare a** ∼**e** come to nothing. ∼**e di pietà** pawnshop. ∼**uo'so** *a.* mountainous.

monto'ne *n.m.* ram. **carne di** ∼ mutton.

monume'nt|o *n.m.* monument. ∼**a'le** *a.* monumental.

moque'tte *n.f.* (*tappeto*) fitted carpet.

mo'ra *n.f.* (*del gelso*) mulberry; (*del rovo*) blackberry.

mora'l|e *a.* moral. —*n.f.* morals *pl.*; (*insegnamento morale*) moral. —*n.m.* morale. ∼**i'sta** *n.m./f.* moralist. ∼**ità** *n.f.* morality; (*condotta*) morals *pl.* ∼**izza're** *v.t./i.* moralize.

mo'rbid|o *a.* soft. ∼**e'zza** *n.f.* softness.

morbi'llo *n.m.* measles *s.*

mo'rbo *n.m.* disease.

morbo'so *a.* morbid.

mo'rchia *n.f.* sludge.

morda'ce *a.* cutting.

mo'rd|ere *v.t.* bite; (*corrodere*) bite into. ∼**e'nte** *a.* biting.

morfi'n|a *n.f.* morphine. ∼**o'mane** *n.m./f.* morphine addict.

moribo'ndo *a.* dying.

morigera'to *a.* moderate.

mori're *v.i.* die; (*fig.*) die out. **fa un freddo da** ∼ it is bitterly cold. ∼ **di noia** be bored to death.

mormor|a're *v.t./i.* murmur; (*brontolare*) mutter. ∼**i'o** *n.m.* murmuring; (*lamentela*) grumbling.

mo'ro *a.* dark. —*n.m.* Moor; (*negro*) black.

moro'so *a.* in arrears.

mo'rs|a *n.f.* vice. ∼**e'tto** *n.m.* clamp.

morsica're *v.t.* bite.

mo'rso *n.m.* bite; (*di insetto*) sting; (*boccone*) morsel; (*di briglia*) bit.

morta'io *n.m.* mortar.

mo'rt|e *n.f.* death. ∼**a'le** *a.* mortal; (*simile a morte*) deadly. ∼**alità** *n.f.* mortality.

mortifica'|re *v.t.* mortify. ∼**rsi** *v.r.* feel mortified. ∼**zio'ne** *n.f.* mortification.

mo'rt|o, a *p.p. di* **morire.** —*a.* dead. —*n.m.*, *f.* dead man/woman. **natura** ∼**a** still life. **stanco** ∼**o** dead tired.

morto'rio *n.m.* funeral.

mosa'ico *n.m.* mosaic.

mo'sca *n.f.* fly. ∼ **cieca** blind-man's buff.

Mo'sca *n.f.* Moscow.
mosca't|o *a.* muscat. —*n.m.* muscatel.
noce ~a nutmeg.
mosceri'no *n.m.* midge.
mosche'a *n.f.* mosque.
moschetta'to *a.* speckled.
moschettie're *n.m.* musketeer.
mosche'tto *n.m.* musket.
mo'scio *a.* flaccid; (*fig.*) lifeless.
mosco'ne *n.m.* bluebottle; (*barca*)
pedalo.
mo'ssa *n.f.* movement; (*passo*) move.
mo'sso *p.p. di* **muovere**. —*a.* (*mare*)
rough; (*capelli*) wavy.
mosta'rda *n.f.* mustard.
mo'str|a *n.f.* show; (*d'arte*) exhibition.
far ~a di pretend. in ~a on show.
mettersi in ~a make oneself conspicuous. ~a're *v.t.* show; (*indicare*)
point out. ~are di (*sembrare*) seem;
(*fingere*) pretend. ~a'rsi *v.r.* show
oneself; (*apparire*) appear.
mo'str|o *n.m.* monster. ~uo'so *a.*
monstrous.
motiva'|re *v.t.* cause; (*legge*) justify.
~zio'ne *n.f.* motivation; justification.
moti'vo reason; (*movente*) motive;
(*mus.*, *lit.*) theme; (*disegno*) motif.
mo'to *n.m.* motion; (*esercizio*) exercise; (*gesto*) movement; (*sommossa*)
rising. —*n.f. invar.* (*motocicletta*) motor bike. mettere in ~ (*motore*) start
(the engine).
motocicl|e'tta *n.f.* motor cycle. ~i'-
sta *n.m./f.* motor-cyclist.
moto'r|e *a.* motor. —*n.m.* motor, en-
gine. ~e'tta *n.f.* motor scooter. ~i'no
n.m. moped. ~ino d'avviamento
starter. ~izza'to *a.* (*mil.*) motorized.
motosca'fo *n.m.* motorboat.
motri'ce *n.f.* engine.
motte'ggi|o *n.m.* banter. ~a're *v.i.*
jest.
mo'tto *n.m.* motto; (*facezia*) witticism;
(*massima*) saying.
move'nte *n.m.* motive.
movime'nt|o *n.m.* movement. essere
sempre in ~o be always on the go.
~a're *v.t.* enliven. ~a'to *a.* lively.
mozio'ne *n.f.* motion.
mozza're *v.t.* cut off; (*coda*) dock. ~
il fiato a qcno. take s.o.'s breath
away.
mozzico'ne *n.m.* stub.
mo'zzo *n.m.* (*mech.*) hub; (*naut.*) ship's
boy.
mu'cca *n.f.* cow.

mu'cchio *n.m.* heap, pile. un ~ di
(*fig.*) lots of.
mu'co *n.m.* mucus.
mu'ff|a *n.f.* mould. fare la ~a become
mouldy. ~i're *v.i.* go mouldy.
muggi'|re *v.i.* low; (*vento*) roar. ~to
n.m. bellow; roar.
mughe'tto *n.m.* lily of the valley.
mugna'io *n.m.* miller.
mugola're *v.i.* howl; (*persona*) moan.
mulina're *v.i.* whirl.
muline'llo *n.m.* (*d'acqua*) whirlpool;
(*di vento*) eddy.
muli'no *n.m.* mill. ~ a vento windmill.
mu'lo *n.m.* mule.
mu'lt|a *n.f.* fine. ~a're *v.t.* fine.
multicolo're *a.* multicoloured.
mu'ltiplo *a. & n.m.* multiple.
mu'mmia *n.f.* mummy.
mu'ngere *v.t.* milk.
munici'p|io *n.m.* town hall. ~a'le *a.*
municipal.
muni're *v.t.* fortify. ~ di (*provvedere*)
supply with.
munizio'ni *n.f. pl.* ammunition *s.*
mu'nto *p.p. di* **mungere**.
muo'ver|e *v.t./i.* move; (*suscitare*)
arouse. ~si *v.r.* move. **muoviti!**
hurry up!
mura'glia *n.f.* wall.
murato're *n.m.* bricklayer.
mu'r|o *n.m.* wall. ~a *n.f. pl.* (*cinta di
città*) walls. a ~o (*armadio*) built-in.
~o del suono sound barrier. ~a'le
a. mural. ~a're *v.t.* wall up.
mu'schio *n.m.* (*bot.*) moss.
mu'scol|o *n.m.* muscle. ~a're *a.* mus-
cular.
muse'o *n.m.* museum.
museruo'la *n.f.* muzzle.
mu'sic|a *n.f.* music. ~a'le *a.* musical.
~i'sta *n.m./f.* musician.
mu's|o *n.m.* muzzle; (*di persona, hum.,
pej.*) mug. fare il ~o sulk. ~o'ne, a
n.m., f. sulky person.
mu'ssola *n.f.* muslin.
mu'ta *n.f.* (*cambio*) change; (*di penne*)
moult; (*di cani*) pack; (*per immersione
subacquea*) (rubber) suit.
muta'nde *n.f. pl.* pants; (*da donna*)
knickers.
mut|a're *v.t.* change. ~ame'nto *n.m.*
change. ~e'vole *a.* changeable.
mutila'|re *v.t.* mutilate. ~to, a
n.m., f. disabled person. ~zio'ne *n.f.*
mutilation.
mu't|o *a.* dumb; (*silenzioso*) silent;

(*fonetica*) mute. ~**i'smo** *n.m.* dumbness; (*fig.*) obstinate silence.
mu'tua *n.f.* **(cassa)** ~ sickness benefit fund.

mu'tuo[1] *a.* mutual.
mu'tuo[2] *n.m.* loan. **fare un** ~ take out a mortgage.

N

na'cchera *n.f.* castanet.

na'fta *n.f.* naphtha; (*per motori*) diesel oil.

na'ia *n.f.* cobra.

na'ilon *n.m.* nylon.

na'nna *n.f.* (*sl.*, *infantile*) bye-byes. **fare la ~** sleep.

na'no, a *a. & n.m., f.* dwarf.

Na'pol|i *n.f.* Naples. **n~eta'no, a** *a. & n.m., f.* Neapolitan.

na'ppa *n.f.* tassel.

narci'so *n.m.* narcissus.

narco'si *n.f.* general anaesthesia.

narco'tico *a. & n.m.* narcotic.

nari'ce *n.f.* nostril.

narra'|re *v.t.* tell. **~ti'vo, a** *a.* narrative; *n.f.* fiction. **~to're, ~tri'ce** *n.m., f.* narrator. **~zio'ne** *n.f.* narration; (*racconto*) story.

na'sc|ere *v.i.* (*venire al mondo*) be born; (*germogliare*) sprout; (*sorgere*) rise. **~ere da** (*fig.*) arise from. **~ita** *n.f.* birth.

nasco'nd|ere *v.t.*, **~ersi** *v.r.* hide. **~i'glio** *n.m.* hiding-place. **~i'no** *n.m.* hide-and-seek. **nasco'sto** *p.p. di* **~ere**; *a.* hidden. **di nascosto** secretly.

nase'llo *n.m.* (*pesce*) hake.

na's|o *n.m.* nose. **~a'le** *a.* nasal.

na'stro *n.m.* ribbon; (*di registratore ecc.*) tape. **~ trasportatore** conveyor belt.

nastu'rzio *n.m.* nasturtium.

nata'l|e *a.* birth. **N~e** *n.m.* Christmas. **~ità** *n.f.* (number of) births. **~i'zio** *a.* (*del Natale*) Christmas; (*di nascita*) of one's birth.

nata'nte *a.* floating. *—n.m.* craft.

na'tica *n.f.* buttock.

nati'o *a.* native.

Nativ|tà *n.f.* Nativity.

nati'vo, a *a. & n.m., f.* native.

na't|o *p.p. di* nascere. *—a.* born. **uno scrittore ~o** a born writer. **~a Rossi** née Rossi.

natu'ra *n.f.* nature. **~ morta** still life. **pagare in ~** pay in kind.

natura'l|e *a.* natural. **~e'zza** *n.f.* naturalness. **~i'sta** *n.m./f.* naturalist. **~me'nte** *adv.* naturally.

naturalizza're *v.t.* naturalize.

naufraga're *v.i.* be wrecked; (*di per-*

sona) be shipwrecked. **naufra'gio** *n.m.* shipwreck; (*fig.*) wreck. **na'ufrago, a** *n.m., f.* survivor.

na'use|a *n.f.* nausea. **~abo'ndo** *a.* nauseating. **~a're** *v.t.* nauseate.

na'utico, a *a.* nautical. *—n.f.* navigation.

nava'ta *n.f.* (*centrale*) nave; (*laterale*) aisle.

na'v|e *n.f.* ship. **~e cisterna** tanker. **~e da carico** cargo boat. **~e da guerra** warship. **~e spaziale** spaceship. **~e traghetto** ferry. **~a'le** *a.* naval.

nave'tta *n.f.* shuttle.

naviga'|re *v.i.* sail. **~bile** *a.* navigable. **~zio'ne** *n.f.* navigation.

navi'glio *n.m.* fleet; (*canale*) canal.

naziona'l|e *a.* national. *—n.f.* (*sport*) national team. **~i'smo** *n.m.* nationalism. **~ità** *n.f.* nationality. **~izza're** *v.t.* nationalize.

nazio'ne *n.f.* nation.

né *conj.* (*neppure, neanche*) neither, nor; (*con altra negazione*) either, or. **~ tu ~ io vogliamo andare** neither you nor I want to go. **non vuole ~ mangiare ~ bere** he doesn't want either food or drink.

ne *pron.* about, of him/her/it/them; (*partitivo*) some; (*neg.*, *inter.*) any. *—adv.* (*moto da luogo*) from here, from there; (*pleonastico*) **me ~ vado** I am going. **~ ho** I have some. **~ sono contento** I am glad about it. **non ~ ho** I haven't any.

nea'nche *adv.* (*neppure*) not even; (*senza neppure*) without even. *—conj.* (*e neppure*) neither . . . nor. **~ per sogno!** not on your life! **non parlo il tedesco, e lui ~** I don't speak German, neither can he *o* and he cannot either.

ne'bbi|a *n.f.* fog. **~o'so** *a.* foggy.

necessa'ri|o *a.* necessary. **~ame'nte** *adv.* necessarily.

necessit|à *n.f.* necessity; (*bisogno*) need. **~a're** *v.t.* necessitate; *v.i.* need; (*essere necessario*) be necessary.

necrolo'gio *n.m.* obituary (notice).

necroscopi'a *n.f.* post-mortem (examination).

nefa'ndo *a.* wicked.

nefasto

120 nocivo

nefa'sto *a.* ill-omened.
nega'|re *v.t.* deny; (*rifiutare*) refuse.
~**ti'vo, a** *a.* negative; *n.f.* negative.
~**zio'ne** *n.f.* negation; (*diniego*) denial; (*gram.*) negative.
negle'tto *a.* neglected.
ne'gli *prep. vedi* **nei**.
neglige'n|te *a.* negligent. ~**za** *n.f.* negligence.
negozia'|re *v.t.* negotiate. —*v.i.* ~**re** in trade in. ~**bile** *a.* negotiable.
nego'zi|o *n.m.* shop. ~**a'nte** *n.m./f.* dealer; (*bottegaio*) shopkeeper.
ne'gro, a *a.* & *n.m., f.* Negro.
ne'i *prep.* = in + i. **ne'gli** = in + gli. **nel** = in + il. **ne'lla** = in + la. **ne'lle** = in + le. **ne'llo** = in + lo.
ne'mbo *n.m.* nimbus.
nem'ico, a *a.* hostile. —*n.m.,f.* enemy.
nemme'no *adv.* & *conj.* = **neanche**.
ne'nia *n.f.* dirge.
ne'o *n.m.* mole; (*applicato*) beauty spot.
ne'o... *pref.* neo....
neoli'tico *a.* Neolithic.
ne'on *n.m.* neon.
neona'to, a *a.* newborn. —*n.m., f.* newborn baby.
neozelande'se *a.* New Zealand. —*n.m./f.* New Zealander.
neppu're *adv.* & *conj.* = **neanche**.
ne'rb|o *n.m.* lash; (*fig.*) backbone. ~**o-ru'to** *a.* brawny.
nere'tto *n.m.* (*typ.*) bold type.
ne'ro *a.* & *n.m.* black.
nervatu'ra *n.f.* nerves *pl.*; (*bot.*) veining; (*di libro*) band.
ne'rv|o *n.m.* nerve; (*bot.*) vein. **avere i** ~**i** be bad-tempered. **dare ai** ~**i a qcno.** get on s.o.'s nerves. ~**o'so** *a.* nervous; (*irritabile*) bad-tempered. **avere il** ~**oso** be irritable. **esaurimento** ~**oso** nervous breakdown.
ne'spol|a *n.f.* medlar. ~**o** *n.m.* medlar(-tree).
nessu'n|o *a.* no; (*inter., neg.*) any. —*pron.* (*riferto a persone*) nobody, no one; (*riferito a cose, animali*) none; (*qualcuno*) anyone, anybody; (*qualcosa*) anything. **c'è** ~**o?** anybody there? **in** ~ **luogo** nowhere. **in** ~ **modo** on no account. ~**a cosa** nothing. ~**a notizia?** any news? **non ha** ~ **valore** it hasn't any value *o* it has no value.
ne'ttare *n.m.* nectar.
ne'tt|o *a.* clean; (*chiaro*) clear; (*comm.*)

net. ~**a're** *v.t.* clean. ~**e'zza** *n.f.* cleanliness.
netturbi'no *n.m.* dustman.
neurologi'a *n.f.* neurology.
neutra'l|e *a.* & *n.m.* neutral. ~**ità** *n.f.* neutrality. ~**izza're** *v.t.* neutralize.
ne'utro *a.* neutral; (*gram.*) neuter; *n.m.* (*gram.*) neuter.
neutro'ne *n.m.* neutron.
neva'io *n.m.* snow-field.
ne'v|e *n.f.* snow. ~**ica're** *v.i.* snow. ~**ica'ta** *n.f.* snowfall. ~**i'schio** *n.m.* sleet. ~**o'so** *a.* snowy.
nevralgi'a *n.f.* neuralgia.
nevro'si *n.f.* neurosis.
ni'bbio *n.m.* kite.
ni'cchia *n.f.* niche.
nicchia're *v.i.* shilly-shally.
ni'chel *n.m.* nickel.
nicoti'na *n.f.* nicotine.
nidia'ta *n.f.* brood.
ni'do *n.m.* nest; (*giardino d'infanzia*) crèche.
nie'nte *pron.* nothing; (*inter., con altro neg.*) anything. **di** ~**!** (*dopo 'grazie'*) don't mention it! **non fa** ~ (*non importa*) it doesn't matter. **non serve a** ~ it is no use. **vuoi** ~**?** do you want anything?
nientedime'no, nienteme'no *advs.* ~ **che** no less than. —*int.* fancy that!
ni'nfa *n.f.* nymph.
ni'nfea *n.f.* water-lily.
ninnana'nna *n.f.* lullaby.
ni'nnolo *n.m.* plaything; (*fronzolo*) knick-knack.
nipo'te *n.m./f.* (*di zii*) nephew/ niece; (*di nonni*) grand/child, -son *m.*, -daughter *f.*
ni'tido *a.* neat; (*chiaro*) clear.
nitra'to *n.m.* nitrate.
ni'trico *a.* nitric.
nitri'|re *v.i.* neigh. ~**to** *n.m.* (*di cavallo*) neigh.
ni'veo *a.* snow-white.
no *adv.* no; (*con adv.* & *conj.*) not. **credo di** ~ I don't think so. **perché** ~**?** why not?
no'bil|e *a.* noble. —*n.m./f.* noble, nobleman/woman. ~**ia're** *a.* noble. ~**tà** *n.f.* nobility.
no'cca *n.f.* knuckle.
noccio'l|a *n.f.* hazel-nut. ~**o** *n.m.* (*albero*) hazel.
no'cciolo *n.m.* stone; (*fig.*) heart.
no'ce *n.f.* walnut. —*n.m.* (*albero, legno*) walnut. ~ **moscata** nutmeg.
noci'vo *a.* harmful.

no'd|o *n.m.* knot; (*fig.*) lump. **~o'so** *a.* knotty.

no'i *pron.* (*soggetto*) we; (*oggetto*) us. **vieni con ~** come with us.

no'i|a *n.f.* boredom; (*fastidio*) bother. **dar ~a** annoy. **~o'so** *a.* boring; (*fastidioso*) tiresome.

noia'ltri *pron.* we.

noleggia're *v.t.* hire; (*dare a noleggio*) hire out; (*nave, aereo*) charter. **no-le'ggio** *n.m.* hire; charter. **no'lo** *n.m.* hire; (*naut.*) freight.

no'made *a.* nomadic. **—*n.m.|f.* nomad.

no'm|e *n.m.* name; (*gram.*) noun. **a ~e di** in the name of. **di ~e** by name. **~e di famiglia** surname. **~i'gnolo** *n.m.* nickname.

no'mina *n.f.* appointment.

nomina'le *a.* nominal; (*gram.*) noun.

nomina're *v.t.* name; (*menzionare*) mention; (*eleggere*) appoint.

nominati'vo *a.* nominative; (*comm.*) registered. **—*n.m.* nominative; (*nome*) name.

non *adv.* not. **~ c'è di che** not at all. **Emma ~ ha figli** Emma has no children.

nonché *conj.* (*tanto meno*) let alone; (*e anche*) as well as.

noncura'n|te *a.* nonchalant. **~za** *n.f.* nonchalance.

nondime'no *conj.* nevertheless.

no'nn|o, a *n.m., f.* grandfather, grandmother; grandpa, granny (*fam.*). **~i** *n.m. pl.* grandparents.

nonnu'lla *n.m. invar.* trifle.

no'no *a. & n.m.* ninth.

nonosta'nte *prep.* in spite of. **—*conj.* although.

nontiscordardimè *n.m. invar.* forget-me-not.

nord *n.m.* north. **del ~** northern. **no'rdico** *a.* northern.

no'rma *n.f.* rule; (*istruzione*) instruction. **a ~ di legge** according to law.

norma'l|e *a.* normal. **~ità** *n.f.* normality. **~izza're** *v.t.* normalize. **~me'nte** *adv.* normally.

Norve'g|ia *n.f.* Norway. **n~e'se** *a. & n.m.|f.* Norwegian.

nostalgi'a *n.f.* (*di casa, patria*) homesickness; (*del passato*) nostalgia. **aver ~** be homesick. **nosta'lgico** *a.* nostalgic; (*di persona*) homesick.

nostra'no *a.* local; (*fatto in casa*) home-made.

no'stro *a.* our; (*nostro proprio*) our own. **—*pron.* ours. **un ~ amico** a friend of ours.

no't|a *n.f.* (*segno*) sign; (*comunicazione, commento, mus.*) note; (*conto*) bill; (*lista*) list. **degno di ~a** noteworthy. **~e caratteristiche** distinguishing marks.

nota'bile *a. & n.m.* notable.

nota'io *n.m.* notary.

nota'|re *v.t.* (*segnare*) mark; (*annotare*) note (down); (*osservare*) notice. **far ~re qcsa.** point sthg. out. **farsi ~re** draw attention to oneself. **~zio'ne** *n.f.* marking; notation.

note'vole *a.* (*degno di nota*) remarkable; (*grande*) considerable.

notifica're *v.t.* notify; (*comm.*) advise. **noti'fica, notificazio'ne** *ns.f.* notification.

noti'zi|a *n.f.* (piece of) news *s.*; (*informazione*) information. **~a'rio** *n.m.* news *s.*

no'to *a.* (well-)known.

noto'ri|o *a.* well-known; (*pej.*) notorious. **~età** *n.f.* notoriety.

notta'mbulo *n.m.* night-bird.

notta'ta *n.f.* night. **far ~** stay up all night.

no'tt|e *n.f.* night. **di ~e** at night. **~e bianca** sleepless night. **peggio che andar di ~e** worse than ever. **~u'rno** *a.* nocturnal; (*servizio ecc.*) night.

nova'nt|a *a. & n.m.* ninety. **~e'simo** *a.* ninetieth. **~i'na** *n.f.* about ninety.

no've *a. & n.m.* nine.

novece'nto *a. & n.m.* nine hundred. **il N~** the twentieth century.

nove'll|a *n.f.* short story. **~ie're** *n.m.* short-story writer.

nove'll|o a. new. **~i'no, a** *a.* inexperienced; *n.m., f.* novice.

nove'mbre *n.m.* November.

novità *n.f.* novelty; (*notizie*) news *s.* **l'ultima ~** (*di moda*) the latest fashion.

novizia'to *n.m.* (*relig.*) novitiate; (*tirocinio*) apprenticeship.

nozio'n|e *n.f.* notion. **~i** *n.f. pl.* rudiments.

no'zze *n.f. pl.* marriage *s.*; (*cerimonia*) wedding *s.*

nu'b|e *n.f.* cloud. **~ifra'gio** *n.m.* cloudburst.

nu'bile *a.* unmarried. **—*n.f.* unmarried woman.

nu'ca *n.f.* nape.

nu'cle|o *n.m.* nucleus; (*unità*) unit.
~**a're** *a.* nuclear.
nu'd|o *a.* naked; (*spoglio*) bare.
~**i'smo** *n.m.* nudism. ~**i'sta** *n.m./f.*
nudist. ~**ità** *n.f.* nakedness; nudity.
nu'll|a *pron.* = **niente.** ~**o** *a.* (*legge*)
null (and void). ~**ità** *n.f.* (*persona*)
nonentity.
nullao'sta *n.m.* permit.
numera'le *a.* & *n.m.* numeral.
numera'|re *v.t.* number. ~**zio'ne** *n.f.*
numbering.
nu'm|ero *n.m.* number; (*romano,
arabo*) numeral; (*di scarpe ecc.*) size.
~**e'rico** *a.* numerical. ~**ero'so** *a.*
numerous.

nu'nzio *n.m.* nuncio.
nuo'cere *v.i.* ~ **a** harm.
nuo'ra *n.f.* daughter-in-law.
nuota'|re *v.i.* swim; (*fig.*) wallow.
~**to're,** ~**tri'ce** *n.m.,* *f.* swimmer.
nuo'to *n.m.* swimming.
nuov|o, a *a.* new. —*n.f.* (*notizia*)
news *s.* **di** ~**o,** ~**ame'nte** *advs.*
again.
nutri'|re *v.t.* nourish; (*sentimenti*)
harbour. ~**me'nto** *n.m.* nourishment. ~**e'nte,** ~**ti'vo** *adjs.* nourish-
ing. ~**zio'ne** nutrition.
nu'vol|a *n.f.* cloud. ~**o'so** *a.* cloudy.
nuzia'le *a.* nuptial. **pranzo** ~ wedding breakfast.

O

o *conj.* or. ~ l'uno ~ l'altro either.
o'asi *n.f. invar.* oasis.
obbedie'nte *vedi* ubbidiente.
obbliga'|re *v.t.* force, oblige. ~rsi *v.r.*
~rsi a undertake to. ~to *a.* obliged.
~to'rio *a.* compulsory. ~zio'ne *n.f.*
obligation; (*comm.*) bond. o'bbligo
n.m. obligation; (*dovere*) duty. avere
obblighi verso be under an obligation to. d'obbligo obligatory.
obbro'brio *n.m.* disgrace.
obera're *v.t.* overburden.
obe's|o *a.* obese. ~ità *n.f.* obesity.
obietta're *v.t.* object.
obietti'v|o *a.* objective; (*imparziale*)
unbiased. —*n.m.* objective; (*scopo*) object. ~ità *n.f.* objectivity.
obie|tto're *n.m.* objector. ~ttore di
coscienza conscientious objector.
~zio'ne *n.f.* objection.
obito'rio *n.m.* mortuary.
obli'o *n.m.* oblivion.
obli'quo *a.* oblique; (*fig.*) underhand.
oblitera're *v.t.* obliterate.
oblò *n.m.* porthole.
oblu'ngo *a.* oblong.
o'boe *n.m.* oboe.
obsole'|to *a.* obsolete. ~sce'nza *n.f.*
obsolescence.
o'ca *n.f.* (*pl.* o'che) goose.
occasio'ne *n.f.* occasion; (*buon affare*)
bargain; (*motivo*) cause.
occhia'i|a *n.f.* eye socket. ~e *n.f. pl.*
shadows (under the eyes).
occhia'li *n.m. pl.* glasses, spectacles.
~ da sole sun-glasses.
occhia'ta *n.f.* look. dare un'~ a have
a look at.
occhieggia're *v.t.* ogle. —*v.i.* (*far ca-
polino*) peep.
occhie'llo *n.m.* buttonhole; (*asola*)
eyelet.
o'cchi|o *n.m.* eye. a quattr'~ in confi-
dence. a vista d'~o within sight.
tenere d'~o qcno. keep an eye on
s.o.
occhioli'no *n.m.* fare l'~ a qcno.
wink at s.o.
occide'nt|e *n.m.* west. ~a'le *a.* west-
ern; *n.m.|f.* westerner.
occlu'|dere *v.t.* obstruct. ~sio'ne *n.f.*
occlusion.
occorre'n|te *a.* necessary. —*n.m.* the

necessary. ~za *n.f.* need. all'~za if
need be.
occo'rrere *v.i.* be necessary. non occorre farlo there is no need to do it.
occulta're *v.t.* hide. occu'lto *a.* hidden; (*magico*) occult.
occupa'|re *v.t.* occupy; (*tempo*) spend.
~rsi *v.r.* occupy oneself. (*trovare lavoro*) find a job. ~rsi di (*badare*) look
after. o'ccupati dei fatti tuoi! mind
your own business! ~to *a.* engaged;
(*di persona*) busy. casa ~ta (*alloggio
abusivo*) squat. ~nte *n.m.|f.* occupier;
(*abusivo*) squatter. ~zio'ne *n.f.* occupation; (*di edificio, per protesta*) sit-
in; (*abusiva*) squatting.
oce'ano *n.m.* ocean.
o'cra *n.f.* ochre.
ocula're *a.* ocular.
oculi'sta *n.m.|f.* oculist.
o'de *n.f.* ode.
odi|a're *v.t.* hate. o'dio *n.m.* hatred.
~o'so *a.* hateful.
odie'rno *a.* of today; (*attuale*) present.
odora'|re *v.t.* smell; (*profumare*) per-
fume. —*v.i.* ~re di smell of. ~to *n.m.*
sense of smell. odo're *n.m.* smell;
(*profumo*) scent. odori *n.m. pl.* (*culin.*) herbs. odoro'so *a.* fragrant.
offe'nder|e *v.t.* offend; (*violare*) break;
(*ferire*) injure. ~si *v.r.* take offence.
offe'r|ta *n.f.* offer; (*donazione*) do-
nation; (*econ.*) supply; (*nelle aste*) bid.
~e'nte *n.m.|f.* offerer; bidder. ~to
p.p. di offrire.
offe'|sa *n.f.* offence. ~nsi'vo, a *a.*
offensive; *n.f.* offensive. ~nso're *n.m.*
offender. ~so *p.p. di* offendere; *a.*
offended.
officia're *v.t.* officiate.
offici'na *n.f.* workshop. capo di ~
foreman.
offri'r|e *v.t.* offer. ~si *v.r.* offer one-
self; (*occasione*) present itself.
offusca'r|e *v.t.*, ~si *v.r.* darken.
ofta'lmico *a.* ophthalmic.
oggetti'v|o *a.* objective. ~ità *n.f.* ob-
jectivity.
ogge'tto *n.m.* object; (*argomento*) subject.
o'ggi *adv.* & *n.m.* today; (*al giorno
d'oggi*) nowadays. da ~ in poi from
today on. ~ a otto a week today.

oggigio'rno *adv.* nowadays.

ogi'va *n.f.* (*mil.*) warhead.

o'gni *a.* every; (*ciascuno*) each; (*tutti*) all; (*qualsiasi*) any. **ad ~ costo** at any cost. **ad ~ modo** anyway. **~ ben di Dio** all sorts of good things. **~ cosa** everything. **~ tanto** now and then.

ognu'no *pron.* everyone, everybody.

oh *int.* oh!

ohimè *int.* oh dear!

Ola'nd|a *n.f.* Holland. **o~e'se** *a.* & *n.m.* Dutch; *n.m./f.* Dutchman/ woman.

olea't|o *a.* oiled. **carta ~a** grease-proof paper.

oleodo'tto *n.m.* oil pipeline.

oleo'so *a.* oily.

olfa'tto *n.m.* sense of smell.

olimpi'adi *n.f. pl.* Olympic games. **oli'mpico** *a.* Olympic.

o'li|o *n.m.* oil. **~o d'oliva** olive oil. **sott'~o** in oil. **~a're** *v.t.* oil. **~e'ra** *n.f.* cruet.

oli'v|a *n.f.* olive. **~a'stro** *a.* olive. **~e'to** *n.m.* olive grove. **~o** *n.m.* olive tree.

o'lmo *n.m.* elm.

oltraggia're *v.t.* offend. **oltra'ggio** *n.m.* offence.

oltra'nza *n.f.* **ad ~** to the bitter end.

o'ltre *adv.* (*di luogo*) further; (*di tempo*) longer. *—prep.* (*di luogo*) over; (*di tempo*) later than; (*più di*) more than; (*in aggiunta*) besides. **~ a** (*eccetto*) except.

oltrema're *adv.* overseas.

oltrepassa're *v.t.* go beyond; (*eccedere*) exceed.

oma'ggio *n.m.* homage; (*dono*) gift. **omaggi** *n.m. pl.* (*saluti*) respects.

ombeli'c|o *n.m.* navel. **~a'le** *a.* umbilical.

o'mbr|a *n.f.* (*zona*) shade; (*immagine oscura*) shadow. **~eggia're** *v.t.* shade. **~o'so** *a.* shady; (*di cavallo*) skittish.

ombre'll|o *n.m.* umbrella. **~o'ne** *n.m.* beach umbrella.

ombre'tto *n.m.* eye-shadow.

ome'lia *n.f.* homily.

omeop|ati'a *n.f.* homoeopathy. **~a'tico** *a.* homoeopathic; *n.m.* homoeo-path.

ome'sso *p.p. di* **omettere.**

ome'ttere *v.t.* omit.

omici'd|a *a.* murderous. *—n.m./f.* murderer. **~io** *n.m.* murder.

omissio'ne *n.f.* omission.

omogeneizza'to *a.* homogenized.

omoge'neo *a.* homogeneous.

omologa're *v.t.* approve. **fare ~ un testamento** prove a will.

omosessua'l|e *a.* & *n.m./f.* homosexual. **~ità** *n.f.* homosexuality.

o'ncia *n.f.* ounce.

o'nd|a *n.f.* wave. **andare in ~a** (*radio*) be broadcast. **~a'ta** *n.f.* wave. **a ~ate** in waves.

o'nde *conj.* so that. *—pron.* whereby.

ondeggia're *v.i.* wave; (*di barca*) roll.

ondula|to'rio *a.* undulating. **~zio'ne** *n.f.* undulation; (*di capelli*) wave.

o'ner|e *n.m.* burden. **~o'so** *a.* onerous.

one'st|o *a.* honest; (*giusto*) just. **~à** *n.f.* honesty; (*rettitudine*) integrity.

o'nice *n.f.* onyx.

onnipote'nte *a.* omnipotent.

onniscie'nte *a.* omniscient.

onoma'stico *n.m.* name-day.

onora'rio *a.* honorary. *—n.m.* fee.

ono'r|e *n.m.* honour. **fare ~e a** (*pranzo*) do justice to. **farsi ~e in** excel in. **~a'bile** *a.* honourable. **~a're** *v.t.* honour; **~a'rsi** *v.r.* **~arsi di** be proud of. **~e'vole** *a.* honourable; *n.m.* Member of Parliament. **~i'fico** *a.* honorary.

onorifice'nza *n.f.* honour; (*decorazione*) decoration.

o'nta *n.f.* shame.

O.N.U. *abbr.* (*di* **Organizzazione delle Nazioni Unite**) UN.

opa'co *a.* opaque; (*di colori ecc.*) dull.

opa'le *n.f.* opal.

o'pera *n.f.* (*lavoro*) work; (*azione*) deed; (*mus.*) opera; (*ente*) institution.

opera'io, a *a.* working. *—n.m., f.* worker.

opera'|re *v.t.* operate; (*med.*) operate on. *—v.i.* operate; (*agire*) work. **~ti'vo, a** *a.* **~to'rio** *adjs.* operating. **~to're, ~tri'ce** *n.m., f.* operator; (*TV*) cameraman. **~zio'ne** *n.f.* operation; (*comm.*) transaction.

opere'tta *n.f.* operetta.

opero'so *a.* industrious.

opifi'cio *n.m.* factory.

opinio'ne *n.f.* opinion.

o'ppio *n.m.* opium.

oppone'nte *a.* opposing. *—n.m./f.* opponent.

oppo'r|re *v.t.* oppose; (*obiettare*) object. **~re resistenza** offer resistance. **~si** *v.r.* **~si a** oppose.

opport|unità *n.f.* opportunity; (*l'essere opportuno*) timeliness. **~u'no** *a.*

opportune. ~uni'sta *n.m./f.* opportunist.

opposi|zio'ne *n.f.* opposition. ~to're *n.m.* opposer.

oppo'sto *p.p. di* opporre. —*a.* opposite; (*contrario*) opposed. —*n.m.* opposite. all'~ on the contrary.

oppress|io'ne *n.f.* oppression. ~i'vo *a.* oppressive. oppre'sso *p.p. di* opprimere; *a.* oppressed. ~o're *n.m.* oppressor.

oppri'mere *v.t.* oppress; (*gravare*) weigh down.

oppu're *conj.* or (else).

opta're *v.i.* opt.

opule'n|to *a.* opulent. ~za *n.f.* opulence.

opu'scolo *n.m.* booklet; (*pubblicitario*) brochure.

opzio'ne *n.f.* option.

o'ra[1] *n.f.* hour; (*di tempo*) time. di buon'~ early. che ~ è? what time is it? mezz'~ half an hour. non vedo l'~ di vederti I can't wait to see you. ~ di punta rush-hour.

o'ra[2] *adv.* now; (*tra poco*) presently. —*conj.* (*dunque*) now (then).

ora'colo *n.m.* oracle.

o'rafo *n.m.* goldsmith.

ora'le *a. & n.m.* oral.

orama'i *adv.* = ormai.

ora'rio *a.* time; (*all'ora*) per hour. —*n.m.* time; (*tabella dell'orario*) timetable. essere in ~ be on time. in senso ~ clockwise.

ora|to're, ~tri'ce *n.m., f.* speaker.

orato'rio, a *a.* oratorical. —*n.m.* (*mus.*) oratorio. —*n.m., f.* oratory.

orazio'ne *n.f.* (*relig.*) prayer.

orbe'ne *conj.* well.

o'rbita *n.f.* orbit; (*anat.*) (eye-) socket.

orche'str|a *n.f.* orchestra. ~a'le *a.* orchestral; *n.m./f.* member of an orchestra. ~a're *v.t.* orchestrate.

orchide'a *n.f.* orchid.

o'rco *n.m.* ogre.

o'rda *n.f.* horde.

ordi'gno *n.m.* device; (*arnese*) tool. ~ esplosivo booby trap.

ordina'le *a. & n.m.* ordinal.

ordiname'nto *n.m.* order; (*leggi*) rules *pl.*

ordina'nza *n.f.* (*mil.*) order; (*attendente*) batman, orderly.

ordina'|re *v.t.* (*sistemare*) arrange; (*comandare*) order; (*prescrivere*) prescribe; (*relig.*) ordain. ~to *a.* (*in ordine*) tidy.

ordina'rio *a.* ordinary; (*grossolano*) common. —*n.m.* ordinary; (*univ.*) professor.

o'rdin|e *n.m.* order. di prim'~e first-class. ~i sacri Holy Orders. parola d'~e password.

ordi're *v.t.* (*tramare*) plot.

ore'cch|io *n.m.* (*pl./f.* ~ie) ear. ~i'no *n.m.* ear-ring.

orecchio'ni *n.m. pl.* (*med.*) mumps *s.*

ore'fice *n.m.* jeweller. ~ri'a *n.f.* (*arte*) goldsmith's art; (*negozio*) goldsmith's (shop).

o'rfano, a *a.* orphan. —*n.m., f.* orphan. ~tro'fio *n.m.* orphanage.

organe'tto *n.m.* barrel-organ; (*a bocca*) mouth-organ; (*fisarmonica*) accordion.

orga'nico *a.* organic. —*n.m.* personnel.

organi'smo *n.m.* organism.

organizza'|re *v.t.* organize. ~rsi *v.r.* get organized. ~to're, ~tri'ce *n.m., f.* organizer. ~zio'ne *n.f.* organization.

o'rgan|o *n.m.* organ. ~i'sta *n.m./f.* organist.

orga'smo *n.m.* orgasm; (*fig.*) agitation.

o'rgia *n.f.* orgy.

orgo'gli|o *n.m.* pride. ~o'so *a.* proud.

orienta'|re *v.t.* orientate. ~rsi *v.r.* find one's bearings; (*tendere*) tend. ~me'nto *n.m.* orientation. perdere l'~mento lose one's bearings.

orie'nt|e *n.m.* east. ~a'le *a.* eastern, oriental.

ori'gano *n.m.* oregano.

ori'gin|e *n.f.* origin. aver ~e da originate from. dare ~e a give rise to. ~a'le *a.* original; (*eccentrico*) odd; *n.m.* original. ~alità *n.f.* originality. ~a're *v.t./i.* originate. ~a'rio *a.* (*nativo*) native.

origlia're *v.i.* eavesdrop.

ori'n|a *n.f.* urine. ~a'le *n.m.* chamber-pot. ~a're *v.i.* urinate.

oriu'ndo *a.* native.

orizzonta'le *a.* horizontal.

orizzonta're *v.t.* = orientare.

orizzo'nte *n.m.* horizon.

orla'|re *v.t.* hem. ~tu'ra *n.f.* hem. o'rlo *n.m.* edge; (*di vestito ecc.*) hem.

o'rma *n.f.* track; (*di piede*) footprint; (*impronta*) mark.

orma'i *adv.* by now; (*passato*) by then; (*quasi*) almost.

ormeggia're *v.t.* moor. orme'ggio *n.m.* mooring.

ormo'ne *n.m.* hormone.

orname'nt|o *n.m.* ornament. **∼a'le** *a.* ornamental.

orna'|re *v.t.* decorate. **∼rsi** *v.r.* deck oneself. **∼to** *a.* adorned; (*di stile*) ornate.

ornitologi'a *n.f.* ornithology.

o'ro *n.m.* gold. **d'∼** gold; (*fig.*) golden.

orolo'gi|o *n.m.* (*portatile*) watch; (*da tavolo, muro, ecc.*) clock. **∼o da polso** wrist-watch. **∼o a carica automatica** self-winding watch. **∼o a sveglia** alarm clock. **∼a'io** *n.m.* watchmaker.

oro'scopo *n.m.* horoscope.

orre'ndo *a.* awful.

orri'bile *a.* horrible.

orripila'nte *a.* horrifying.

orro're *n.m.* horror. **avere qcsa. in ∼** hate sthg.

o'rs|o *n.m.* bear. **∼acchio'tto** *n.m.* teddy bear.

orsù *int.* come on!

orta'ggio *n.m.* vegetable.

orte'nsia *n.f.* hydrangea.

orti'c|a *n.f.* nettle. **∼a'ria** *n.f.* nettle-rash.

orticoltu'ra *n.f.* horticulture.

o'rto *n.m.* kitchen garden. **∼la'no** *n.m.* market gardener.

ortodo'sso *a.* orthodox.

ortografi'a *n.f.* spelling.

ortope'd|ico *a.* orthopaedic. *−n.m.* orthopaedist. **∼i'a** *n.f.* orthopaedics *s.*

orzaio'lo *n.m.* sty.

orza'ta *n.f.* barley-water.

osa're *v.t.*/*i.* dare; (*avere audacia*) be daring.

osce'n|o *a.* obscene. **∼ità** *n.f.* obscenity.

oscilla'|re *v.i.* swing; (*di prezzi ecc.*) fluctuate; (*techn.*) oscillate. **∼zio'ne** *n.f.* swinging; fluctuation; oscillation.

oscura'|re *v.t.* darken; (*fig.*) obscure. **∼rsi** *v.r.* get dark. **∼me'nto** *n.m.* darkening; (*totale*) black-out. **oscu'ro** *a.* dark; (*triste*) gloomy; (*incomprensibile*) obscure.

ospeda'le *n.m.* hospital.

o'spit|e *n.m.*/*f.* (*chi ospita*) host/ hostess; (*chi viene ospitato*) guest. **∼a'le** *a.* hospitable. **∼alità** *n.f.* hospitality. **∼a're** *v.t.* give hospitality to.

ospi'zio *n.m.* hospice; (*per vecchi*) home.

osse'qu|io *n.m.* homage. **∼i** *n.m. pl.* respects. **∼ia're** *v.t.* pay one's respects to. **∼e'nte** *a.* deferential.

∼ente alla legge law-abiding. **∼io'so** *a.* obsequious.

osserva'|re *v.t.* observe; (*notare*) notice; (*ordine, silenzio*) keep. **∼nza** *n.f.* observance. **∼to're, ∼tri'ce** *n.m., f.* observer. **∼to'rio** *n.m.* (*astr.*) observatory; (*mil.*) observation post. **∼zio'ne** *n.f.* observation; (*rimprovero*) reproach.

ossess|iona're *v.t.* obsess. **∼io'ne** *n.f.* obsession. **∼i'vo** *a.* obsessive. **osse'sso** *a.* obsessed.

ossi'a *conj.* that is.

ossida'r|e *v.t.*, **∼si** *v.r.* oxidize.

o'ssido *n.m.* oxide. **∼ di carbonio** carbon monoxide.

ossi'gen|o *n.m.* oxygen. **∼a're** *v.t.* oxygenate; (*decolorare*) bleach.

o'ss|o *n.m.* (*anat., pl. f.* **ossa**) bone. **∼atu'ra** *n.f.* bone structure. **∼eo, ∼u'to** *adjs.* bony.

ossobu'co *n.m.* marrowbone.

ostacola're *v.t.* hinder; (*ostruire*) obstruct.

osta'colo *n.m.* obstacle; (*sport*) hurdle.

osta'ggio *n.m.* hostage.

o'st|e *n.m.*, **∼e'ssa** *n.f.* innkeeper.

oste'llo *n.m.* **∼ della gioventù** youth hostel.

ostenta'|re *v.t.* show off. **∼zio'ne** *n.f.* ostentation.

osteri'a *n.f.* inn.

oste'trico, a *a.* obstetric. *−n.m., f.* obstetrician.

o'stia *n.f.* host; (*cialda*) wafer.

osti'l|e *a.* hostile. **∼ità** *n.f.* hostility.

ostina'|to *a.* obstinate. **∼rsi** *v.r.* **∼rsi (a)** persist (in). **∼zio'ne** *n.f.* obstinacy.

ostraci'smo *n.m.* ostracism.

o'strica *n.f.* oyster.

ostru|i're *v.t.* obstruct. **∼zio'ne** *n.f.* obstruction.

o'tre *n.m.* leather bottle.

otta'gon|o *n.m.* octagon. **∼a'le** *a.* octagonal.

otta'nt|a *a. & n.m.* eighty. **∼e'nne** *a.* eighty-year-old. **∼e'simo** *a.* eightieth. **∼i'na** *n.f.* about eighty.

otta'vo, a *a.* eighth. *−n.f.* octave.

ottene're *v.t.* obtain; (*più comune*) get; (*conseguire*) achieve.

o'ttico, a *a.* optic(al). *−n.m.* optician. *−n.f.* (*scienza*) optics *s.*; (*di lenti ecc.*) optics *pl*

ottimi's|ta *n.m.*/*f.* optimist. **∼mo** *n.m.* optimism.

o'ttim|o *a.* very good. **~ame'nte** *adv.* very well.

o'tto *a.* & *n.m.* eight.

otto'bre *n.m.* October.

ottoce'nto *a.* & *n.m.* eight hundred. **l'O~** the nineteenth century.

otto'ne *n.m.* brass.

ottuagena'rio, a *a.* & *n.m.*, *f.* octogenarian.

ottu'ndere *v.t.* blunt.

ottura'|re *v.t.* stop. **~rsi** *v.r.* clog. **~to're** *n.m.* (*foto*) shutter. **~zio'ne** *n.f.* stopping.

ottu'so *p.p. di* **ottundere.** —*a.* obtuse.

ova'ia *n.f.* ovary.

ova'le *a.* & *n.m.* oval.

ova'tta *n.f.* cotton wool.

ovazio'ne *n.f.* ovation.

o've *adv.* where.

o'vest *n.m.* west.

ovi'le *n.m.* sheep-fold.

ovi'no *a.* sheep.

ovulazio'ne *n.f.* ovulation.

ovve'ro *conj.* or; (*cioè*) that is.

o'vvi|o *a.* obvious. **~ ame'nte** *adv.* obviously.

o'zi|o *n.m.* idleness. **stare in ~o** idle about. **~a're** *v.i.* idle. **~o'so** *a.* idle.

ozo'no *n.m.* ozone.

P

paca'|re *v.t.* quieten. **~to** *a.* quiet.

pacche'tto *n.m.* packet.

pa'cchia *n.f.* (*fam., situazione*) bed of roses.

pacchia'no *a.* garish.

pa'cco *n.m.* parcel; (*involto*) bundle.

pa'ce *n.f.* peace.

pacifica're *v.t.* reconcile; (*mettere pace*) pacify.

paci'fico *a.* pacific; (*calmo*) peaceful. **il P~** *n.m.* the Pacific.

pacifi's|ta *n.m./f.* pacifist. **~mo** *n.m.* pacifism.

pada'n|o *a.* **pianura ~a** Po valley.

pade'lla *n.f.* frying-pan; (*per malati*) bedpan.

padiglio'ne *n.m.* pavilion.

pa'dr|e *n.m.* father. **~i** *n.m. pl.* (*antenati*) forefathers. **~ete'rno** *n.m.* God Almighty. **~i'no** *n.m.* godfather.

padrona'nza *n.f.* mastery. **~ di sé** self-control.

padro'ne, a *n.m., f.* master, mistress; (*datore di lavoro*) boss; (*proprietario*) owner. **~ di casa** (*di inquilini*) landlord. **~ggia're** *v.t.* master.

paesa'ggio *n.m.* scenery; (*dipinto*) landscape.

pae's|e *n.m.* (*nazione*) country; (*territorio*) land; (*villaggio*) village. **~a'no, a** *a.* country; *n.m., f.* villager.

paffu'to *a.* plump.

pa'g|a *n.f.* pay, wages *pl.* **~ame'nto** *n.m.* payment. **~a're** *v.t.* pay; (*offrire*) stand.

paga'no, a *a. & n.m., f.* pagan.

page'lla *n.f.* (school) report.

pa'ggio *n.m.* page(-boy).

pa'gina *n.f.* page.

pa'glia *n.f.* straw.

pagliacce'tto *n.m.* (*per bambini*) rompers *pl.*

paglia'ccio *n.m.* clown.

paglie'tta *n.f.* (*cappello*) boater; (*per pentole*) steel wool.

pagliu'zza *n.f.* small straw; (*di metallo*) particle.

pagno'tta *n.f.* (round) loaf.

pago'da *n.f.* pagoda.

pa'io *n.m.* (*pl. f.* **paia**) pair. **un ~** (*circa due*) a couple.

pa'l|a *n.f.* shovel; (*di remo, elica*) blade; (*di ruota*) paddle. **~e'tta** *n.f.* spade; (*per focolare*) shovel.

pala'to *n.m.* palate.

pala'zzo *n.m.* palace; (*edificio*) building. **~ di giustizia** Law Courts.

pa'lco *n.m.* (*pedana*) platform; (*theatr.*) box.

palcosce'nico *n.m.* stage.

palesa'r|e *v.t.* disclose. **~si** *v.r.* reveal oneself. **pale'se** *a.* evident.

Palesti'na *n.f.* Palestine.

pale'stra *n.f.* gymnasium; (*ginnastica*) gymnastics *pl.*

pa'lio *n.m.* (*premio*) prize. **il P~** horse-race held at Siena.

palizza'ta *n.f.* fence.

pa'll|a *n.f.* ball; (*proiettile*) bullet. **~acane'stro** *n.f.* basketball. **~anuo'to** *n.f.* water polo. **~avo'lo** *n.f.* volleyball. **~i'na** *n.f.* (*di vetro*) marble.

palleggia're *v.i.* (*calcio*) dribble; (*tennis*) knock up.

palliati'vo *n.m.* palliative.

pa'llido *a.* pale.

pallo'n|e *n.m.* ball; (*calcio*) football; (*aerostato*) balloon. **~ci'no** *n.m.* balloon; (*lanterna*) Chinese lantern.

pallo're *n.m.* pallor.

pallo'ttola *n.f.* pellet; (*proiettile*) bullet.

pa'lma *n.f.* (*bot.*) palm.

pa'lmo *n.m.* (*anat.*) palm. **restare con un ~ di naso** feel disappointed.

pa'lo *n.m.* pole; (*di sostegno*) stake.

palomba'ro *n.m.* diver.

palpa're *v.t.* feel.

pa'lpebra *n.f.* eyelid.

palpita'|re *v.i.* throb; (*fremere*) quiver. **~zio'ne** *n.f.* palpitation. **pa'lpito** *n.m.* throb; (*del cuore*) beat.

paltò *n.m. invar.* overcoat.

palu'd|e *n.f.* marsh. **~o'so** *a.* marshy.

palu'stre *a.* marshy.

pa'mpino *n.m.* vine leaf.

panace'a *n.f.* panacea.

pa'nc|a *n.f.* bench. **~hi'na** *n.f.* garden seat. **~o'ne** *n.m.* work-bench.

pance'tta *n.f.* (*culin.*) bacon.

panche'tto *n.m.* (foot)stool.

pa'ncia *n.f.* belly; tummy (*fam.*). **mal di ~** stomach-ache.

pancio'tto *n.m.* waistcoat.

pandemo'nio *n.m.* pandemonium.

pa′n|e *n.m.* bread; *(forma di pane)* loaf. **~ grattato** breadcrumbs *pl.* **~ tostato** toast. **~etteri′a** *n.f.* bakery; *(negozio)* baker's (shop). **~ettie′re, a** *n.m., f.* baker.

pa′nfilo *n.m.* yacht.

pa′nico *n.m.* panic.

panie′re *n.m.* basket; *(cesta)* hamper.

panifi′cio *n.m.* bakery; *(negozio)* baker's (shop).

pani′no *n.m.* (bread) roll. **~ imbottito** sandwich.

pa′nna[1] *n.f.* cream.

pa′nna[2] *n.f.* (*mech.*) breakdown.

panne′llo *n.m.* panel.

pa′nn|o *n.m.* cloth. **~i** *n.m. pl.* *(abiti)* clothes. **~oli′no** *n.m.* *(per bambini)* nappy.

panno′cchia *n.f.* *(di granoturco)* cob.

panora′m|a *n.m.* panorama. **~ico** *a.* panoramic.

pantalo′ni *n.m. pl.* trousers.

panta′no *n.m.* bog.

pante′ra *n.f.* panther.

panto′fola *n.f.* slipper.

pantomi′ma *n.f.* pantomime.

panza′na *n.f.* fib.

paona′zzo *a.* purple.

papà *n.m. invar.* dad(dy).

pa′p|a *n.m.* Pope. **~a′le** *a.* papal. **~′to** *n.m.* papacy.

papali′na *n.f.* skull-cap.

papa′vero *n.m.* poppy.

pa′pero, a *n.m., f.* gosling. **—n.f.** *(errore)* blunder.

papi′ro *n.m.* papyrus.

pa′ppa *n.f.* *(per bambini)* pap.

pappaga′llo *n.m.* parrot; *(fig., donnaiolo)* wolf.

pappago′rgia *n.f.* double chin.

pa′ra *n.f.* **suole di ~** crêpe soles.

para′bola *n.f.* parable.

parabre′zza *n.m. invar.* windscreen.

paracadu′t|e *n.m. invar.* parachute. **~i′sta** *n.m./f.* parachutist.

paraca′rro *n.m.* kerbstone.

paradi′so *n.m.* paradise.

parado′ss|o *n.m.* paradox. **~a′le** *a.* paradoxical.

parafa′ngo *n.m.* mudguard.

paraffi′na *n.f.* paraffin.

para′fras|i *n.f. invar.* paraphrase. **~a′re** *v.t.* paraphrase.

parafu′lmine *n.m.* lightning-conductor.

parafuo′co *n.m.* fire-screen.

para′ggi *n.m. pl.* neighbourhood *s.*

parago′n|e *n.m.* comparison. **a ~e di** in comparison with. **~a′re** *v.t.* compare.

para′grafo *n.m.* paragraph.

para′l|isi *n.f. invar.* paralysis. **~i′tico, a** *a. & n.m., f.* paralytic. **~izza′re** *v.t.* paralyse.

paralle′l|o, a *a. & n.m.* parallel. **—n.f.** parallel (line). **~e** *n.f. pl.* parallel bars.

paralu′me *n.m.* lampshade.

parame′nto *n.m.* hangings *pl.*

para′metro *n.m.* parameter.

parano′i|a *n.f.* paranoia. **~co, a** *a. & n.m., f.* paranoiac.

parao′cchi *n.m. pl.* blinkers.

parape′tto *n.m.* parapet.

parapi′glia *n.m.* turmoil.

paraple′gico, a *a. & n.m., f.* paraplegic.

para′r|e *v.t.* *(addobbare)* adorn; *(riparare)* shield; *(difendersi da)* ward off. **—v.i.** *(mirare)* lead up to. **~si** *v.r.* *(abbigliarsi)* dress up; *(apparire)* appear.

paraso′le *n.m. invar.* parasol.

parassi′ta *a.* parasitic. **—n.m./f.** parasite.

parastata′le *a.* government-controlled.

para′ta *n.f.* parade; *(calcio)* save.

parau′rti *n.m. invar.* *(auto)* bumper.

parave′nto *n.m.* screen.

parce′lla *n.f.* bill.

parch|eggia′re *v.t.* park. **~e′ggio** *n.m.* parking; *(posteggio)* car-park.

parchi′metro *n.m.* parking-meter.

pa′rco[1] *a.* sparing; *(moderato)* moderate.

pa′rco[2] *n.m.* park. **~ di divertimenti** fun-fair.

pare′cchi|o *a.* quite a lot of. **~ pl.** a good many. **—pron.** quite a lot. **~ pl.** several. **—adv.** rather; *(parecchio tempo)* quite a time.

pare′ggi|o *n.m.* (*comm.*) balance; *(sport)* draw. **~a′re** *v.t.* level; *(eguagliare)* equal; *(comm.)* balance; *v.i.* draw.

pare′nt|e *n.m./f.* relative. **~a′do** *n.m.*, **~e′la** *n.f.* relatives *pl.*; *(vincolo di sangue)* relationship.

pare′ntesi *n.f. invar.* parenthesis; *(segno grafico)* bracket.

pare′re[1] *n.m.* opinion. **a mio ~** in my opinion.

pare′re[2] *v.i.* seem; *(pensare)* think. **che te ne pare?** what do you think of it? **pare di sì** it seems so.

pare'te *n.f.* wall.

pa'ri *a.* equal; (*di numero*) even. **andare di** ~ **passo** keep pace. **essere** ~ be quits. —*n.m.|f.* equal, peer. —*n.m.* (*titolo nobiliare*) peer. ~**tà** *n.f.* equality.

Pari'gi *n.f.* Paris.

pari'glia *n.f.* pair.

parlame'nt|o *n.m.* Parliament. ~**a're** *a.* parliamentary; *n.m.|f.* Member of Parliament; *v.i.* discuss.

parlanti'na *n.f.* loquacity.

parla'|re *v.t.|i.* speak, talk. ~**to're**, ~**tri'ce** *n.m.,f.* speaker. ~**to'rio** *n.m.* parlour.

parmigia'no *n.m.* Parmesan.

parodi'a *n.f.* parody.

paro'l|a *n.f.* word; (*facoltà*) speech. **è una** ~**a!** it is easier said than done! ~**e incrociate** crossword puzzle *s.* **rivolgere la** ~**a** a address. ~**a'ccia** *n.f.* swear-word.

parossi'smo *n.m.* paroxysm.

pa'rr|oco *n.m.* parish priest. ~**o'cchia** *n.f.* parish. ~**occhia'no, a** *n.m.,f.* parishioner.

parru'cca *n.f.* wig.

parrucchie're, a *n.m.,f.* hairdresser.

parsimo'ni|a *n.f.* thrift. ~**o'so** *a.* thrifty.

pa'rso *p.p. di* **parere.**

pa'rte *n.f.* part; (*lato*) side; (*partito*) party; (*porzione*) share. **a** ~ apart (from). **d'altra** ~ on the other hand. **da** ~ aside; (*in disparte*) to one side. **da** ~ **di** from. **è gentile da** ~ **tua** it is kind of you. **fare una brutta** ~ **a** qcno. behave badly towards s.o.

partecipa'|re *v.i.* ~**re** a participate in; (*condividere*) share in. ~**zio'ne** *n.f.* participation; (*annuncio*) announcement; (*comm.*) sharing. **parte-'cipe** *a.* participating.

parteggia're *v.i.* ~ **per** side with.

parte'nza *n.f.* departure; (*sport*) start. **in** ~ **per** leaving for.

partice'lla *n.f.* particle.

partici'pio *n.m.* participle.

particola'r|e *a.* particular; (*privato*) private. —*n.m.* particular. ~**eggia're** *v.t.* detail. ~**ità** *n.f.* particularity.

partigia'no, a, *a. & n.m.,f.* partisan.

parti're *v.i.* leave; (*aver inizio*) start. **a** ~ **da** (beginning) from.

parti'ta *n.f.* game; (*incontro*) match; (*comm.*) lot; (*contabilità*) entry.

parti'to *n.m.* party; (*scelta*) choice; (*occasione di matrimonio*) match.

pa'rto *n.m.* (child)birth; (*med.*) delivery. ~**ri're** *v.t.* give birth to.

parve'nza *n.f.* appearance.

parzia'le *a.* partial.

pa'sc|ere *v.t.* graze; (*fig.*) feed. ~**iu'to** *p.p. di* ~**ere.**

pascola're *v.t.* graze. **pa'scolo** *n.m.* pasture.

Pa'squ|a *n.f.* Easter. **p**~**a'le** *a.* Easter.

passa'bile *a.* passable.

passa'ggio *n.m.* passage; (*traversata*) crossing; (*sport*) pass; (*su veicolo*) lift. **essere di** ~ be passing through. ~ **pedonale** pedestrian crossing.

passa'nte *n.m.|f.* passer-by. —*n.m.* (*di cintura*) loop.

passapo'rto *n.m.* passport.

passa're *v.i.* pass; (*attraversare*) pass through; (*far visita*) call (on); (*andare*) go; (*essere approvato*) be passed; (*al telefono*) put through. —*v.t.* (*far scorrere*) pass over; (*sopportare*) go through; (*culin.*) strain. ~ **di moda** go out of fashion. ~ **in rivista** review. **passarsela bene** be well off.

passa'ta *n.f.* (*di vernice*) coat; (*spolverata*) dusting; (*occhiata*) look.

passate'mpo *n.m.* pastime.

passa'to *a.* past. **l'anno** ~ last year. —*n.m.* past; (*culin.*) purée; (*gram.*) past tense. ~ **prossimo** (*gram.*) present perfect. ~ **remoto** (*gram.*) (simple) past.

passato'ia *n.f.* runner.

passegge'ro, a *a.* passing. —*n.m., f.* passenger.

passeggia'|re *v.i.* walk, stroll. ~**ta** *n.f.* walk, stroll; (*luogo*) public walk. **fare una** ~**ta** go for a walk. **passe'ggio** *n.m.* walk; (*luogo*) promenade.

passere'lla *n.f.* gangway; (*aeron.*) catwalk.

pa'ssero *n.m.* sparrow.

passi'bile *a.* ~ **di** liable to.

passio'n|e *n.f.* passion. ~**a'le** *a.* passionate.

passi'vo *a.* passive. —*n.m.* passive; (*comm.*) liabilities *pl.*

pa'ss|o *n.m.* step; (*orma*) footprint; (*andatura*) pace; (*brano*) passage; (*valico*) pass. **a due** ~**i da qui** a stone's throw away. **a** ~**o d'uomo** at working pace. **fare due** ~**i** go for a stroll.

pa'st|a *n.f.* (*impasto per pane ecc.*) dough; (*per dolci, pasticcino*) pastry; (*alimentare*) pasta; (*massa molle*) paste; (*fig.*) nature. ~**e'lla** *n.f.* batter. ~**ifi'cio** *n.m.* pasta factory.

paste'llo *n.m.* pastel.

pasti'cca *n.f.* pastille.

pasticc|eri'a *n.f.* confectioner's (shop); (*pasticcini*) pastries *pl.*; (*arte*) confectionery. ~ie're, a *n.m.*, *f* confectioner.

pasti'cci|o *n.m.* (*culin.*) pie; (*lavoro disordinato*) mess. **mettersi nei** ~ get into trouble. ~a're *v.t./i.* make a mess (of). ~o'ne, a *n.m.*, *f.* bungler.

pasti'glia *n.f.* lozenge.

pa'sto *n.m.* meal.

pastora'le *a.* pastoral.

pasto're *n.m.* shepherd; (*relig.*) pastor.

pastorizza're *v.t.* pasteurize.

pasto'so *a.* doughy; (*fig.*) mellow.

pastra'no *n.m.* overcoat.

pastu'ra *n.f.* pasture.

pata'cca *n.f.* (*macchia*) stain.

pata't|a *n.f.* potato. ~e fritte chips. ~i'ne *n.f. pl.* (potato) crisps.

patatra'c *n.m.* (*crollo*) crash.

pate'lla *n.f.* limpet.

pate'ma *n.m.* anxiety.

pate'nte *n.f.* licence. ~ di guida driving licence.

paterna'le *n.f.* scolding.

pate'rn|o *a.* paternal; (*affetto ecc.*) fatherly. ~ità *n.f.* paternity.

pate'tico *a.* pathetic.

pa'thos *n.m.* pathos.

pati'bolo *n.m.* gallows *s.*

pa'tina *n.f.* patina; (*sulla lingua*) coating.

pati'|re *v.t./i.* suffer. ~to, a *a.* suffering; *n.m.*, *f.* fan.

patol|ogi'a *n.f.* pathology. ~o'gico *a.* pathological.

pa'tria *n.f.* native land.

patria'rca *n.m.* patriarch.

patri'gno *n.m.* stepfather.

patrimo'nio *n.m.* estate.

patrio't|a *n.m./f.* patriot. ~tico *a.* patriotic. ~ti'smo *n.m.* patriotism.

patri'zio, a *a.* & *n.m.*, *f.* patrician.

patroci'n|io *n.m.* support. ~io gratuito legal aid. ~a're *v.t.* support.

patrona'to *n.m.* patronage.

patro'no *n.m.* (*relig.*) patron saint; (*legge*) counsel.

pa'tta¹ *n.f.* (*di tasca*) flap.

pa'tta² *n.f.* (*pareggio*) draw.

patteggia're *v.t./i.* negotiate.

pattina'|re *v.i.* skate. ~ggio *n.m.* skating. ~to're, ~tri'ce *n.m.*, *f.* skater. **pa'ttino** *n.m.* skate; (*aeron.*) skid. **pattino a rotelle** roller-skate.

pa'tto *n.m.* pact; (*condizione*) term. a ~ che on condition that.

pattu'glia *n.f.* patrol.

pattui're *v.t.* negotiate.

pattumie'ra *n.f.* dustbin.

pau'r|a *n.f.* fear; (*spavento*) fright. aver ~a be afraid. mettere ~a a frighten. ~o'so *a.* (*che fa paura*) frightful; (*che ha paura*) fearful.

pa'usa *n.f.* pause; (*nel lavoro*) break.

pa'vido *a.* timid.

pavime'nt|o *n.m.* floor. ~a're *v.t.* (*strada*) pave.

pavo'ne *n.m.* peacock. ~ggia'rsi *v.r.* show off.

pazie'n|te *a.* & *n.m./f.* patient. ~ta're *v.i.* be patient. ~za *n.f.* patience.

pazz|i'a *n.f.* madness; (*azione*) (act of) folly. ~e'sco *a.* foolish. **pa'zzo, a** *a.* mad; (*fig.*) foolish; *n.m.*, *f.* mad/man, -woman. **essere pazzo per** be crazy about. **pazzo di gioia** mad with joy.

pe'cca *n.f.* fault.

pecca'|re *v.i.* sin. ~mino'so *a.* sinful. ~to *n.m.* sin. che ~to! what a pity! ~to're, ~tri'ce *n.m.*, *f.* sinner.

pe'ce *n.f.* pitch.

pecor|a *n.f.* sheep. ~a'io *n.m.* shepherd. ~i'no *n.m.* (*formaggio*) sheep's milk cheese.

peculia're *a.* ~ di peculiar to.

pecunia'rio *a.* money.

peda'ggio *n.m.* toll.

pedagogi'a *n.f.* pedagogy.

peda'l|e *n.m.* pedal. ~a're *v.i.* pedal.

peda'na *n.f.* rug; (*sport*) spring-board.

peda'nte *a.* pedantic.

peda'ta *n.f.* (*calcio*) kick; (*impronta*) footprint.

pedera'sta *n.m.* pederast.

pede'stre *a.* pedestrian.

pedia'tr|a *n.m./f.* paediatrician. ~i'a *n.f.* paediatrics *s.*

pedicu're *n.m./f. invar.* chiropodist; *n.m.* (*cura dei piedi*) pedicure.

pedi'na *n.f.* (*alla dama*) piece; (*agli scacchi*) pawn.

pedina're *v.t.* shadow.

pedona'le *a.* pedestrian. **pedo'ne, a** *n.m.*, *f.* pedestrian.

pe'ggi|o *adv.* worse. —*a.* worse; (*superlativo*) (the) worst. —*n.m./f.* (the) worst. alla ~o at (the) worst. avere la ~o get the worst of it. ~o per te! so much the worse for you! ~o're *a.* worse; (*superlativo*) (the) worst.

peggiora'|re *v.t./i.* worsen. **~me'nto** *n.m.* worsening. **~ti'vo** *a.* pejorative.

pe'gno *n.m.* pledge; (*nei giochi di società*) forfeit; (*fig.*) token.

pela'|re *v.t.* (*spennare*) pluck; (*spellare*) skin; (*sbucciare*) peel; (*fig.*) fleece. **~rsi** *v.r.* lose one's hair. **~to** *a.* bald.

pe'll|e *n.f.* skin; (*cuoio*) leather; (*buccia*) peel. **avere la ~e d'oca** have goose-flesh. **~a'me** *n.m.* skins *pl.* **~etteri'a** *n.f.* leather goods *pl.*

pellegr|ina'ggio *n.m.* pilgrimage. **~i'no, a** *n.m., f.* pilgrim.

pellero'ssa *n.m./f.* Red Indian.

pellica'no *n.m.* pelican.

pelli'cc|ia *n.f.* fur; (*indumento*) fur coat. **~eri'a** *n.f.* furrier's (shop). **~ia'io, a** *n.m., f.* furrier.

pelli'cola *n.f.* (thin) skin; (*foto, cinema*) film. **~ trasparente** cling film.

pe'l|o *n.m.* hair; (*mantello*) coat; (*di tessuto*) pile. **cavarsela per un ~o** have a narrow escape. **~o'so** *a.* hairy. **~u'ria** *n.f.* down.

pe'ltro *n.m.* pewter.

pe'n|a *n.f.* (*punizione*) punishment; (*sofferenza*) pain; (*dispiacere*) sorrow; (*disturbo*) trouble. **a mala ~a** hardly. **mi fa ~a** I pity him. **vale la ~a andare** it is worth while going. **~a'le** *a.* criminal. **~alità** *n.f.* penalty. **~alizza're** *v.t.* penalize. **~a're** *v.i.* suffer; (*faticare*) find it difficult. **~o'so** *a.* painful.

pende'n|te *a.* hanging; (*comm.*) outstanding. *—n.m.* (*ciondolo*) pendant. **~za** *n.f.* slope; (*comm.*) outstanding account.

pe'ndere *v.i.* hang; (*di superficie*) slope; (*essere inclinato*) lean; (*fig.*) hang over.

pendi'o *n.m.* slope.

pe'ndol|o *n.m.* pendulum. **orologio a ~o** pendulum clock. **~a're** *a.* pendulum; *n.m./f.* commuter.

pe'ne *n.m.* penis.

penetra'|re *v.t./i.* penetrate; (*trafiggere*) pierce; (*entrare furtivamente*) steal in. **~nte** *a.* penetrating; piercing.

penicilli'na *n.f.* penicillin.

peni'sola *n.f.* peninsula.

penite'n|te *a. & n.m./f.* penitent. **~za** *n.f.* penitence; (*punizione*) penance. **~zia'rio** *n.m.* penitentiary.

pe'nna *n.f.* (*da scrivere*) pen; (*di uccello*) feather. **~ a feltro** felt-tipped pen. **~ a sfera** ball-point pen. **~ stilografica** fountain-pen.

penna'cchio *n.m.* plume.

penne'll|o *n.m.* brush. **a ~o** (*a perfezione*) perfectly. **~a're** *v.t.* paint.

penni'no *n.m.* nib.

penno'ne *n.m.* pennon.

peno'mbra *n.f.* half-light.

pensa'|re *v.t./i.* think. **~re a** think of; (*badare*) see to. **pensa ai fatti tuoi!** mind your own business! **penso di sì** I think so. **~ta** *n.f.* idea.

pensie'r|o *n.m.* thought; (*mente*) mind; (*preoccupazione*) worry. **stare in ~o per** be anxious about. **~o'so** *a.* pensive.

pe'nsile *a.* hanging. **giardino ~** roof-garden.

pensio'n|e *n.f.* pension; (*albergo*) boarding-house; (*vitto e alloggio*) board and lodging. **~a'nte** *n.m./f.* boarder; (*ospite pagante*) lodger. **~a'to, a** *n.m., f.* pensioner.

penso'so *a.* pensive.

penta'gono *n.m.* pentagon.

Penteco'ste *n.f.* Whitsun.

penti'|rsi *v.r.* **~rsi di** repent of; (*rammaricarsi*) regret. **~me'nto** *n.m.* repentance.

pe'ntola *n.f.* saucepan. **~ a pressione** pressure cooker.

penu'ltimo *a.* last but one.

penu'ria *n.f.* shortage.

penzol|a're *v.i.* dangle. **~o'ni** *adv.* dangling.

peo'nia *n.f.* peony.

pe'p|e *n.m.* pepper. **grano di ~e** peppercorn. **~a'to** *a.* peppery.

pepero'ne *n.m.* pepper.

pepi'ta *n.f.* nugget.

per *prep.* for; (*attraverso*) through; (*stato in luogo*) in, on; (*distributivo*) per; (*mezzo, entro*) by; (*in qualità di*) as. **~ il momento** for the time being. **~ la fine del mese** by the end of the month. **~ terra** on the floor. **stare ~** be about to. **uno ~ uno** one by one. **venti ~ cento** twenty per cent. *—conj.* (in order) to; (*per quanto*) however.

pe'r|a *n.f.* pear. **~o** *n.m.* pear-tree.

percentua'le *n.f.* percentage.

percepi'|re *v.t.* perceive; (*riscuotere*) cash. **~bile** *a.* perceivable.

perce|tti'bile *a.* perceptible. **~zio'ne** *n.f.* perception.

perché *conj.* (*inter.*) why; (*causale*)

because; (*affinché*) so that; (*consecutivo*) for.

perciò *conj.* so.

perco'rrere *v.t.* (*distanza*) cover; (*viaggiare*) travel.

perco'rso *p.p. di* **percorrere.** —*n.m.* (*tragitto*) course; (*distanza*) distance; (*viaggio*) journey.

perco'ssa *n.f.* blow.

perco'sso *p.p. di* **percuotere.**

percuo'tere *v.t.* strike.

percussio'ne *n.f.* percussion.

pe'rder|e *v.t.* lose; (*sprecare*) waste; (*non prendere*) miss. —*v.i.* (*di recipiente*) leak. ~**si** *v.r.* get lost; (*reciproco*) lose touch. **lascia** ~**e!** forget it!

perdigio'rno *n.m.|f. invar.* idler.

pe'rdit|a *n.f.* loss; (*spreco*) waste; (*falla*) leak. **a** ~**a d'occhio** as far as the eye can see. ~**e'mpo** *n.m.* waste of time.

perdona're *v.t.* forgive; (*scusare*) excuse. **perdo'no** *n.m.* forgiveness; (*legge*) pardon.

perdura're *v.i.* last; (*perseverare*) persist.

perdu't|o *p.p. di* **perdere.** —*a.* lost; (*rovinato*) ruined. ~**ame'nte** *adv.* hopelessly.

peregrina're *v.i.* wander.

pere'nne *a.* everlasting; (*bot.*) perennial.

perento'rio *a.* peremptory.

perfe'tto *a.* perfect. —*n.m.* (*gram.*) perfect (tense).

perfezio'n|e *n.f.* perfection. ~**a're** *v.t.* perfect; (*migliorare*) improve. ~**a'rsi** *v.r.* improve oneself; (*specializzarsi*) specialize.

pe'rf|ido *a.* treacherous; (*malvagio*) perverse. ~**i'dia** *n.f.* wickedness.

perfi'no *adv.* even.

perfora're *v.t.* pierce; (*schede*) punch; (*mech.*) drill. ~**to're**, ~**tri'ce** *n.m.,f.* punch-card operator; *n.m.* perforator. ~**zio'ne** *n.f.* perforation; (*di schede*) punching.

pergame'na *n.f.* parchment.

pe'rgola *n.f.* pergola.

peri'col|o *n.m.* danger; (*rischio*) risk. **mettere in** ~**o** endanger. ~**a'nte** *a.* precarious. ~**o'so** *a.* dangerous.

periferi'a *n.f.* suburbs *pl.*

peri'frasi *n.f. invar.* circumlocution.

peri'metro *n.m.* perimeter.

peri'|odo *n.m.* period. ~**o'dico** *a.* & *n.m.* periodical.

peripezi'e *n.f. pl.* misadventures.

peri're *v.i.* perish.

perisco'pio *n.m.* periscope.

peri'|to, a *a.* skilled. —*n.m.,f.* expert. ~**zia** *n.f.* skill; (*valutazione*) survey.

pe'rl|a *n.f.* pearl. ~**i'na** *n.f.* bead.

perlustra're|re *v.t.* patrol. ~**zio'ne** *n.f.* patrol.

permalo'so *a.* touchy.

permane'n|te *a.* permanent. —*n.f.* permanent wave. ~**za** *n.f.* permanence; (*soggiorno*) stay.

permane're *v.i.* remain.

permea're *v.t.* permeate.

perme'sso *p.p. di* **permettere.** —*n.m.* permission; (*autorizzazione*) permit; (*mil.*) leave. **(è)** ~**?** (*posso entrare?*) may I come in?; (*posso passare?*) excuse me.

perme'ttere *v.t.* allow, permit.

permissi'vo *a.* permissive.

permutazio'ne *n.f.* exchange; (*math.*) permutation.

perna'cchia *n.f.* (*sl.*) raspberry (*sl.*).

perni'ce *n.f.* partridge.

pernicio'so *a.* pernicious.

pe'rno *n.m.* pivot.

pernotta're *v.i.* stay overnight.

però *conj.* but; (*tuttavia*) however.

perora're *v.t.* plead.

perpendi'col|o *n.m.* plumb-line. **a** ~**o** vertically. ~**a're** *a.* & *n.f.* perpendicular.

perpetra're *v.t.* perpetrate.

perpetua're *v.t.* perpetuate. **perpe'tuo** *a.* perpetual.

perple'sso *a.* perplexed.

perquisi'|re *v.t.* search. ~**zio'ne** *n.f.* search.

persecu|to're, ~**tri'ce** *n.m., f.* persecutor. ~**zio'ne** *n.f.* persecution.

persegui're *v.t.* pursue.

perseguita're *v.t.* persecute.

persevera'|nte *a.* persevering. ~**nza** *n.f.* perseverance. ~**re** *v.i.* persevere.

Pe'rsi|a *n.f.* Persia. **p**~**a'no, a** *a.* & *n.m., f.* Persian; *n.f.* (*di finestra*) shutter. **pe'rsico** *a.* Persian.

persi'no *adv.* = **perfino.**

persiste'n|te *a.* persistent. ~**za** *n.f.* persistence. **persi'stere** *v.i.* persist.

pe'rso *p.p. di* **perdere.** —*a.* lost. **a tempo** ~ in one's spare time.

perso'n|a *n.f.* person; (*un tale*) somebody; (*inter. o neg.*) anybody. ~**e** *n.f. pl.* people. **di, in** ~**a** personally. **per** ~**a** a head.

persona'ggio *n.m.* (*persona di*

riguardo) personality; (*theatr. ecc.*) character.

persona'le *a.* personal.—*n.m.* staff.

personalità *n.f.* personality.

personifica'|re *v.t.* personify. ~**zio'ne** *n.f.* personification.

perspica'c|e *a.* shrewd. ~**ia** *n.f.* shrewdness.

persua|de're *v.t.* persuade. ~**sio'ne** *n.f.* persuasion. ~**si'vo** *a.* persuasive. **persua'so** *p.p. di* ~**dere.**

perta'nto *conj.* therefore.

pe'rtica *n.f.* pole.

pertina'ce *a.* pertinacious.

pertine'nte *a.* relevant.

perto'sse *n.f.* whooping cough.

perturba'|re *v.t.* perturb. ~**rsi** *v.r.* be perturbed. ~**zio'ne** *n.f.* disturbance.

perva'|dere *v.t.* pervade. ~**so** *p.p. di* ~**dere.**

perveni're *v.i.* reach.

perve'rs|o *a.* perverse. ~**io'ne** *n.f.* perversion.

perverti'|re *v.t.* pervert. ~**to** *a.* perverted; *n.m.* pervert.

p. es. *abbr.* (*di* **per esempio**) e.g.

pesa'nte *a.* heavy.

pesa're *v.t./i.* weigh. ~ **su** (*fig.*) lie heavy on. **pesa** *n.f.* weighing.

pe'sc|a[1] *n.f.* (*frutto*) peach. ~**o** *n.m.* peach-tree.

pe'sc|a[2] *n.f.* fishing. **andare a** ~**a** go fishing. ~**a're** *v.t.* fish (for); (*trovare*) fish out. ~**ato're** *n.m.* fisherman.

pe'sc|e *n.m.* fish. ~**e d'aprile** April Fool. **P**~**i** (*astr.*) Pisces.

pesceca'ne *n.m.* shark.

peschere'ccio *n.m.* fishing boat.

pesc|heri'a *n.f.* fishmonger's (shop). ~**ive'ndolo** *n.m.* fishmonger.

peschie'ra *n.f.* fish-pond.

pe'so *n.m.* weight.

pessimi's|mo *n.m.* pessimism. ~**ta** *n.m./f.* pessimist.

pe'ssimo *a.* very bad.

pesta're *v.t.* tread on; (*schiacciare*) crush; (*picchiare*) beat.

pe'ste *n.f.* plague; (*persona*) pest.

peste'llo *n.m.* pestle.

pestile'nza *n.f.* pestilence; (*fetore*) stench.

pe'sto *a.* ground. —*n.m.* basil and garlic sauce. **buio** ~ pitch dark. **occhio** ~ black eye.

pe'talo *n.m.* petal.

peta'rdo *n.m.* banger.

petizio'ne *n.f.* petition.

petro'l|io *n.m.* oil; (*per lampada*) par-

affin. ~**ie'ra** *n.f.* (oil) tanker. ~**i'fero** *a.* oil-bearing.

pette'gol|o, a *a.* gossipy. —*n.m., f.* gossip. ~**a're** *v.i.* gossip. ~**e'zzo** *n.m.* gossip. **far** ~**ezzi** gossip.

pe'ttin|e *n.m.* comb. ~**a're** *v.t.* comb. ~**a'rsi** *v.r.* comb one's hair. ~**atu'ra** *n.f.* combing; (*acconciatura*) hair-style.

pettiro'sso *n.m.* robin.

pe'tto *n.m.* chest; (*seno*) breast. **a doppio** ~ double-breasted. ~**ru'to** *a.* full-breasted.

pettori'na *n.f.* bib.

petula'nte *a.* impertinent.

pe'zza *n.f.* cloth; (*toppa*) patch; (*rotolo di tessuto*) roll.

pezze'nte *n.m./f.* tramp; (*avaro*) miser.

pe'zzo *n.m.* piece; (*parte*) part. ~ **grosso** bigwig. **un bel** ~ **d'uomo** a fine figure of a man. **un** ~ (*di tempo*) some time; (*di spazio*) a long way.

piace'|re *n.m.* pleasure; (*favore*) favour. **a** ~**re** at will. **per** ~**re!** please! ~**re!** (*nelle presentazioni*) pleased to meet you! —*v.i.* like; (*far piacere*) please. **faccio come mi pare e piace** I do as I please. **ti piace?** do you like it? ~**nte** *a.* attractive. ~**vole** *a.* pleasant.

pia'ga *n.f.* sore; (*fig.*) scourge.

piagniste'o *n.m.* whining.

piagnucola're *v.i.* whimper.

pia'll|a *n.f.* plane. ~**a're** *v.t.* plane.

pia'na *n.f.* (*pianura*) plane.

pianeggia'|re *v.t.* level. ~**nte** *a.* level.

pianero'ttolo *n.m.* landing.

piane'ta *n.m.* planet.

pia'ngere *v.i.* weep, cry. —*v.t.* (*lamentare*) lament; (*per un lutto*) mourn.

pianifica'|re *v.t.* plan. ~**zio'ne** *n.f.* planning.

pia'n|o *a.* flat; (*a livello*) flush; (*regolare*) smooth; (*facile*) easy. —*adv.* slow; (*con cautela*) gently. **andarci** ~**o** go carefully. —*n.m.* plain; (*di edificio*) floor; (*livello*) plane; (*progetto*) plan; (*mus.*) piano. **di primo** ~**o** first-rate. ~**o di studi** syllabus. ~**o regolatore** town plan. ~**i'sta** *n.m./f.* (*mus.*) pianist.

pianofo'rte *n.m.* piano.

pia'nt|a *n.f.* plant; (*del piede*) sole; (*disegno*) plan. **di sana** ~**a** (*totalmente*) entirely. ~**a stradale** road map. ~**a're** *v.t.* plant; (*conficcare*) drive; (*fam., abbandonare*) leave. ~**a'rsi** *v.r.* plant oneself; (*fam., lasci-*

arsi) leave each other. ∼**ala!** (*fam.*) stop it!

pianta|gio'ne *n.f.* plantation. ∼**to're** *n.m.* planter.

pianterre'no *n.m.* ground floor.

pia'nto *p.p. di* **piangere.** —*n.m.* weeping; (*lacrime*) tears *pl.*

piant|ona're *v.t.* guard. ∼**o'ne** *n.m.* orderly.

pianu'ra *n.f.* plain.

pia'stra *n.f.* plate; (*lastra*) slab.

piastre'lla *n.f.* tile.

piastri'na *n.f.* (*mil.*) identity disc.

piattafo'rma *n.f.* platform.

pia'tt|o *a.* flat. —*n.m.* plate; (*da portata, vivanda*) dish; (*portata*) course; (*parte piatta*) flat; (*di grammofono*) turntable. ∼**i** *n.m. pl.* (*mus.*) cymbals. ∼**o fondo** soup plate.

pia'zz|a *n.f.* square; (*comm.*) market. **far** ∼**a pulita** make a clean sweep. ∼**afo'rte** *n.f.* stronghold. ∼**a'le** *n.m.* large square.

piazza'r|e *v.t.* place. ∼**si** *v.r.* (*sport*) be placed.

piazzi'sta *n.m.* salesman.

pi'cc|a *n.f.* pike; (*puntiglio*) spite. ∼**he** *n.f. pl.* (*carte*) spades.

picca'nte *a.* hot; (*pungente*) sharp; (*salace*) spicy.

picca'rsi *v.r.* (*risentirsi*) take offence.

picchetta're *v.t.* stake; (*di scioperanti*) picket. **picche'tto** *n.m.* picket.

picchia'|re *v.t.* beat, hit. —*v.i.* (*bussare*) knock; (*aeron.*) nosedive. ∼**ta** *n.f.* beating; nosedive.

picchietta're *v.t.* tap; (*punteggiare*) spot.

pi'cchio *n.m.* woodpecker.

picci'no *a.* tiny; (*gretto*) mean; (*di poca importanza*) petty.

piccio'ne *n.m.* pigeon.

pi'cco *n.m.* peak. **a** ∼ vertically.

pi'ccolo, *a a.* small, little, (*di età*) young; (*di statura*) short; (*gretto*) petty. —*n.m.,f.* child, little one. **da** ∼ as a child.

picco'ne *n.m.* pickaxe.

pido'cchio *n.m.* louse.

pie'd|e *n.m.* foot. **a** ∼**i** on foot. **a** ∼**i nudi** barefoot. **in** ∼**i** standing. **in punta di** ∼**i** on tiptoe. **prendere** ∼**e** (*fig.*) gain ground.

piedista'llo *n.m.* pedestal.

pie'g|a *n.f.* (*piegatura*) fold; (*di gonna*) pleat; (*di pantaloni*) crease; (*grinza*) wrinkle; (*andamento*) turn. ∼**a're** *v.t.* fold; (*flettere*) bend; *v.i.* bend. ∼**a'rsi** *v.r.* bend. ∼**arsi a** (*fig.*) yield to. ∼**atu'ra** *n.f.* folding. ∼**hetta're** *v.t.* pleat. ∼**he'vole** *a.* pliable; (*docile*) yielding; (*tavolo*) folding.

pie'n|o, a *a.* full; (*massiccio*) solid. —*n.m.* (*colmo*) height; (*carico*) full load. —*n.f.* (*di fiume*) flood; (*folla*) crowd. **in** ∼**a estate** in the middle of summer. **in** ∼**o** (*completamente*) fully. **in** ∼**o giorno** in broad daylight. ∼**o zeppo** full up.

piet|à *n.f.* pity; (*misericordia*) mercy. **senza** ∼**à** pitiless. ∼**o'so** *a.* pitiful, merciful.

pieta'nza *n.f.* dish.

pie'tr|a *n.f.* stone. ∼**a'me** *n.m.* stones *pl.* ∼**ifica're** *v.t.* petrify. ∼**i'na** *n.f.* (*di accendino*) flint. ∼**o'so** *a.* stony.

pi'ffero *n.m.* fife.

piga'ma *n.m.* pyjamas *pl.*

pigia'|re *v.t.* press. ∼**tri'ce** *n.f.* winepress.

pigio'ne *n.f.* rent. **dare/prendere a** ∼ let/rent.

piglia're *v.t.* = **prendere.**

pi'glio *n.m.* look.

pigme'nto *n.m.* pigment.

pigme'o, a *a. & n.m.,f.* pygmy.

pi'gna *n.f.* cone.

pigno'lo *a.* pedantic.

pignora'|re *v.t.* distrain upon. ∼**me'nto** *n.m.* distraint.

pigol|a're *v.i.* chirp. ∼**i'o** *n.m.* chirping.

pi'gr|o *a.* lazy. ∼**i'zia** *n.f.* laziness.

pi'la *n.f.* pile; (*electr.*) battery; (*fam., lampadina tascabile*) torch; (*vasca*) basin.

pila'stro *n.m.* pillar.

pi'llola *n.f.* pill.

pilo'ne *n.m.* pylon; (*di ponte*) pier.

pilo't|a *n.m./f.* pilot. —*n.m.* (*auto.*) driver. ∼**a're** *v.t.* pilot.

pinacote'ca *n.f.* picture-gallery.

pine'ta *n.f.* pine-wood.

ping-po'ng *n.m.* table tennis.

pi'ngu|e *a.* fat. ∼**e'dine** *n.f.* fatness.

pingui'no *n.m.* penguin.

pi'nna *n.f.* fin; (*per nuotare*) flipper.

pinna'colo *n.m.* pinnacle.

pi'n|o *n.m.* pine(-tree). ∼**o'lo** *n.m.* pine kernel.

pi'nta *n.f.* pint.

pi'nz|a *n.f.* pliers *pl.*; (*med.*) forceps *pl.* ∼**e'tta** *n.f.* tweezers *pl.*

pi'o *a.* pious; (*benefico*) charitable.

pio'ggia *n.f.* rain.

piomba'|re *v.i.* fall heavily. ∼**re su**

fall upon. —*v.t.* (*dente*) fill. ~**tu'ra**
n.f. (*di dente*) filling.

piombi'no *n.m.* (*sigillo*) (lead) seal;
(*nell'edilizia*) plummet.

pio'mbo *n.m.* lead; (*sigillo*) (lead) seal.
a ~ plumb.

pionie're, a *n.m., f.* pioneer.

pio'ppo *n.m.* poplar.

pio'v|ere *v.i.* rain. ~**ere a dirotto**
rain in torrents. ~**iggina're** *v.i.*
drizzle. ~**o'so** *a.* rainy.

pi'pa *n.f.* pipe.

pipistre'llo *n.m.* bat.

pira'mide *n.f.* pyramid.

pira't|a *n.m.* pirate. ~**a della strada**
road-hog. ~**eri'a** *n.f.* piracy.

piroe'tta *n.f.* pirouette.

piro'filo *a.* heat-resistant.

piro'scafo *n.m.* steamer. ~ **di linea**
liner.

pisci'na *n.f.* swimming-pool.

pise'llo *n.m.* pea.

pisoli'no *n.m.* nap.

pi'sta *n.f.* track; (*aeron.*) runway;
(*orma*) footprint.

pista'cchio *n.m.* pistachio.

pisto'la *n.f.* pistol; (*per spruzzare*)
spray-gun.

pisto'ne *n.m.* piston.

pito'cco *n.m.* miser.

pito'ne *n.m.* python.

pit|to're, ~**tri'ce** *n.m., f.* painter.

pittore'sco *a.* picturesque.

pitto'rico *a.* pictorial.

pittu'r|a *n.f.* painting. ~**a're** *v.t.*
paint.

più *adv.* more; (*superlativo*) most;
(*math.*) plus; (*davanti a aggettivo
breve*) ...er; (*superlativo*) ...est. ~
caro dearer. **il** ~ **caro** the dearest;
(*in frasi neg.*) **non** ~ no more; (*di
tempo*) no longer. —*a.* more; (*superlativo*) the most; (*alcuni*) several. —*n.m.*
most; (*math.*) plus sign. **al** ~ **presto**
as soon as possible. **i** ~ the majority.
mai ~! never again! ~ **di** more than.
sempre ~ more and more.

piuccheperfe'tto *n.m.* pluperfect.

piu'm|a *n.f.* feather. ~**a'ggio** *n.m.* plu-
mage. ~**i'no** *n.m.* (*di cigni*) down;
(*copriletto*) eiderdown; (*per cipria*)
powder-puff; (*per spolverare*) feather
duster. ~**o'ne** *n.m.* duvet.

piutto'sto *adv.* rather; (*invece*)
instead.

pi'zz|a *n.f.* pizza. ~**eri'a** *n.f.* pizza res-
taurant.

pizzic|a'gnolo, a *n.m., f.* delicatessen

seller. ~**heri'a** *n.f.* delicatessen
(shop).

pizzic|a're *v.t.* pinch; (*pungere*) sting;
(*di sapore*) taste sharp; (*mus.*)
pluck. —*v.i.* tingle; (*cibo*) be spicy.
pi'zzico, ~**o'tto** *ns.m.* pinch.

pi'zzo *n.m.* lace; (*di montagna*) peak.

placa'r|e *v.t.* placate. ~**si** *v.r.* calm
down.

pla'cc|a *n.f.* plate; (*commemorativa*)
plaque; (*med.*) patch. ~**a're** *v.t.* plate.
~**ato in argento** silver-plated. ~**a-
tu'ra** *n.f.* plating.

pla'cido *a.* placid.

plagia're *v.t.* plagiarize. **pla'gio** *n.m.*
plagiarism.

plana're *v.i.* glide.

pla'ncia *n.f.* (*naut.*) bridge.

planeta'rio *a.* planetary. —*n.m.* plan-
etarium.

plasma're *v.t.* mould.

pla'stic|a *n.f.* (*arte*) plastic art; (*med.*)
plastic surgery; (*materia*) plastic. ~**o**
a. plastic; *n.m.* plastic model.

pla'tano *n.m.* plane(-tree).

plate'a *n.f.* stalls *pl.*

pla'tino *n.m.* platinum.

plato'nico *a.* platonic.

plausi'bile *a.* plausible.

ple'b|e *n.f.* common people. ~**a'glia**
n.f. (*pej.*) mob. ~**e'o, a** *a.* & *n.m., f.*
plebeian.

plebisci'to *n.m.* plebiscite.

plenilu'nio *n.m.* full moon.

ple'ttro *n.m.* plectrum.

pleuri'te *n.f.* pleurisy.

pli'co *n.m.* packet. **in** ~ **a parte** under
separate cover.

ploto'ne *n.m.* platoon. ~ **d'esecuzione** firing-squad.

plu'mbeo *a.* leaden.

plura'l|e *a.* & *n.m.* plural. **al** ~**e** in
the plural. ~**ità** *n.f.* (*maggioranza*)
majority.

plutocra'|tico *a.* plutocratic. ~**zi'a**
n.f. plutocracy.

pluto'nio *n.m.* plutonium.

pluvia'le *a.* rain.

pneuma'tico *a.* pneumatic. —*n.m.*
tyre.

po' *vedi* **poco**.

po'c|o *a.* little; (*di tempo*) short. ~**hi**
pl. few; (*alcuni*) a few. —*pron.* (a)
little. ~**hi** *pl.* few. —*n.m.* little. —*adv.*
little; not much. **a** ~**o a** ~**o** little
by little. **fra** ~**o** soon. **parla** ~**o** he
doesn't speak much. **per** ~**o** (*a poco
prezzo*) cheap; (*quasi*) nearly. ~**o fa**

a short time ago. **un bel po'** quite a lot. **un po' di** a little, some; (*inter.*) any. **un ~o di buono** a good-for-nothing.

pode're *n.m.* farm.

podero'so *a.* powerful.

po'dio *n.m.* dais; (*mus.*) podium.

podi's|mo *n.m.* walking. **~ta** *n.m./f.* walker.

poe'ma *n.m.* poem.

poesi'a *n.f.* poetry; (*componimento*) poem.

poe't|a *n.m.* poet. **~e'ssa** *n.f.* poetess. **~ico** *a.* poetic(al).

poggia'|re *v.t.* lean; (*posare*) place. *—v.i.* **~re su** be based on. **~te'sta** *n.m. invar.* head-rest.

po'ggio *n.m.* hillock.

po'i *adv.* (*dopo*) then; (*più tardi*) later (on); (*finalmente*) finally. **d'ora in ~** from now on.

poiché *conj.* since.

po'ker *n.m.* poker.

pola'cco, a *a.* Polish. *—n.m.,f.* Pole.

polarizza're *v.t.* polarize.

po'lca *n.f.* polka.

pole'mi|ca *n.f.* controversy. **~co** *a.* polemic(al). **~zza're** *v.i.* engage in controversy.

policli'nico *n.m.* general hospital.

poli'gam|o *a.* polygamous. **~i'a** *n.f.* polygamy.

poli'gono *n.m.* polygon.

polio(mieli'te) *n.f.* polio(myelitis).

po'lipo *n.m.* polyp.

polistiro'lo *n.m.* polystyrene.

polite'cnico *n.m.* polytechnic.

poli'tic|a *n.f.* politics *s.*; (*linea di condotta*) policy. **~o, a** *a.* political; *n.m., f.* politician.

polizi'|a *n.f.* police. **~e'sco** *a.* police. **~o'tto** *n.m.* policeman.

po'lizza *n.f.* policy. **~ di pegno** pawn-ticket.

po'llice *n.m.* thumb.

po'lline *n.m.* pollen.

po'll|o *n.m.* chicken. **~a'io** *n.m.* fowl-run. **~a'me** *n.m.* poultry. **~a'stro** *n.m.* cockerel. **~ive'ndolo, a** *n.m., f.* poulterer.

polmo'n|e *n.m.* lung. **~i'te** *n.f.* pneumonia.

po'lo *n.m.* pole; (*sport*) polo.

Polo'nia *n.f.* Poland.

po'lpa *n.f.* pulp.

polpa'ccio *n.m.* calf.

polpastre'llo *n.m.* fingertip.

polpe'tt|a *n.f.* meatball. **~o'ne** *n.m.* meat loaf.

po'lpo *n.m.* octopus.

polpo'so *a.* fleshy.

polsi'no *n.m.* cuff.

po'lso *n.m.* pulse; (*anat.*) wrist; (*fig.*) strength.

polti'glia *n.f.* mush; (*da impiastro*) poultice.

poltri're *v.i.* lie around.

poltro'na *n.f.* armchair; (*theatr.*) stall.

poltro'ne *a.* lazy.

po'lver|e *n.f.* dust; (*sostanza polverizzata*) powder. **in ~e** powdered. **~izza're** *v.t.* pulverize; (*nebulizzare*) atomize. **~o'ne** *n.m.* cloud of dust. **~o'so** *a.* dusty.

poma'ta *n.f.* ointment.

pome'llo *n.m.* knob.

pomeridia'n|o *a.* afternoon. **alle tre ~e** at three p.m.

pomeri'ggio *n.m.* afternoon.

po'mice *n.f.* pumice.

po'mo *n.m.* apple; (*oggetto*) knob.

pomodo'ro *n.m.* tomato.

po'mp|a *n.f.* pump; (*sfarzo*) pomp. **~e funebri** (*funzione*) funeral. **~a're** *v.t.* pump (out); (*gonfiare d'aria*) pump (up).

pompo'so *a.* pompous.

pompe'lmo *n.m.* grapefruit.

pompie'r|e *n.m.* fireman. **i ~i** the fire brigade.

pondera're *v.t.* ponder.

pondero'so *a.* ponderous.

pone'nte *n.m.* west.

po'nte *n.m.* bridge; (*naut.*) deck; (*impalcatura*) scaffolding. **fare il ~** (*fig.*) have an extra long weekend. **~ leva-toio** drawbridge.

ponte'fice *n.m.* pontiff.

pontif|ica're *v.i.* pontificate. **~ica'to** *n.m.* pontificate. **~i'cio** *a.* papal.

ponti'le *n.m.* jetty.

popola'|re *a.* popular; (*comune*) common. *—v.t.* populate. **~rsi** *v.r.* get crowded. **~rità** *n.f.* popularity.

popola'no *a.* of the (common) people.

po'pol|o *n.m.* people. **~azio'ne** *n.f.* population. **~o'so** *a.* populous.

po'ppa *n.f.* (*naut.*) stern; (*mammella*) breast. **a ~** astern.

poppa'|re *v.t.* suck. **~ta** *n.f.* (*pasto*) feed. **~to'io** *n.m.* (feeding-)bottle.

porcella'na *n.f.* china.

porcelli'no *n.m.* piglet. **~ d'India** guinea-pig.

porcheri'a *n.f.* dirt; (*fam.*, *robaccia*) rubbish.

po'rc|o *n.m.* pig; (*carne*) pork. ~**i'le** *n.m.* pigsty. ~**i'no** *a.* pig; *n.m.* (*fungo*) (edible) mushroom.

porcospi'no *n.m.* porcupine.

po'rgere *v.t.* give; (*offrire*) offer.

pornogr|afi'a *n.f.* pornography. ~**a'fico** *a.* pornographic.

po'r|o *n.m.* pore. ~**o'so** *a.* porous.

po'rpora *n.f.* purple.

po'r|re *v.t.* put; (*collocare*) place; (*supporre*) suppose. **ponia'mo il caso che** let us suppose that. ~**si** *v.r.* put oneself. ~**si a sedere** sit down. ~**si in cammino** set out.

po'rro *n.m.* (*bot.*) leek; (*verruca*) wart.

po'rt|a *n.f.* door; (*sport*) goal; (*di città*) gate. ~**ie'ra** *n.f.* door; (*tendaggio*) door curtain.

portabaga'gli *n.m. invar.* (*facchino*) porter; (*di treno ecc.*) luggage-rack.

portabandie'ra *n.m. invar.* standard-bearer.

portace'nere *n.m. invar.* ashtray.

portachia'vi *n.m. invar.* key-ring.

portaci'pria *n.m. invar.* compact.

portae'rei *n.f. invar.* aircraft-carrier.

portafine'stra *n.f.* French window.

portafo'glio *n.m.* wallet; (*per documenti*) portfolio.

portafortu'na *n.m. invar.* mascot; (*amuleto*) amulet.

portagio'ie *n.m. invar.* jewel-case.

porta'le *n.m.* portal.

portame'nto *n.m.* carriage; (*condotta*) behaviour.

porta'nte *a.* bearing.

portanti'na *n.f.* sedan-chair.

porta'|re *v.t.* (*vicino*) bring; (*lontano*) take; (*andare a prendere*) fetch; (*sorreggere, math.*) carry; (*condurre*) lead; (*indossare*) wear; (*avere*) bear. ~**rsi** *v.r.* (*trasferirsi*) move; (*comportarsi*) behave. ~**tile** *a.* portable. ~**to're**, ~**tri'ce** *n.m., f.* bearer.

portasigare'tte *n.m. invar.* cigarette-case.

portaspi'lli *n.m. invar.* pincushion.

porta'ta *n.f.* (*di pranzo*) course; (*auto.*) carrying capacity; (*fig.*) range. **a** ~ **di mano** within reach.

porta'to *a.* ~ **a** inclined to.

portauo'vo *n.m. invar.* egg-cup.

portavo'ce *n.m./f. invar.* spokes/-man, -woman.

porte'nto *n.m.* marvel; (*persona dotata*) prodigy.

po'rtico *n.m.* portico.

portie're *n.m.* porter; (*sport*) goal-keeper.

portin|a'io, a *n.m., f.* porter. ~**eri'a** *n.f.* porter's lodge.

po'rto *p.p. di* **porgere.** —*n.m.* harbour; (*complesso*) port; (*vino*) port (wine); (*spesa di trasporto*) carriage.

Portog|a'llo *n.m.* Portugal. **p~he'se** *a.* & *n.m./f.* Portuguese.

porto'ne *n.m.* main door.

porzio'ne *n.f.* portion.

po's|a *n.f.* laying; (*riposo*) rest; (*foto*) exposure; (*atteggiamento*) pose. ~**a're** *v.t.* put (down); *v.i.* (*poggiare*) rest; (*per un ritratto*) pose. ~**a'rsi** *v.r.* alight; (*sostare*) rest.

posa't|a *n.f.* piece of cutlery. ~**e** *n.f. pl.* cutlery *s.*

posa'to *a.* sedate.

poscri'tto *n.m.* postscript.

positi'vo *a.* positive.

posizio'ne *n.f.* position.

pospo'|rre *v.t.* place after; (*posticipare*) postpone. ~**sto** *p.p. di* ~**rre.**

possed|e're *v.t.* possess, own. ~**ime'nto** *n.m.* possession; (*proprietà*) estate.

possessi'vo *a.* possessive.

posse'ss|o *n.m.* ownership. ~**o're** *n.m.* owner.

possi'bil|e *a.* possible. —*n.m.* **fare (tutto) il** ~**e** do one's best. ~**ità** *n.f.* possibility; (*occasione*) chance; *n.f. pl.* (*mezzi*) means.

posside'nte *n.m./f.* land-owner.

po'st|a *n.f.* post, mail; (*ufficio postale*) post office; (*al gioco*) stake. **spese di** ~**a** postage. ~**a'le** *a.* postal. ~**i'no** *n.m.* postman.

posteggia're *v.t./i.* park. **poste'ggio** *n.m.* car-park; (*di taxi*) taxi-rank.

po'ster|i *n.m. pl.* descendants. ~**ità** *n.f.* posterity.

posterio're *a.* posterior. —*n.m.* (*fam.*) behind.

posti'ccio *a.* artificial. —*n.m.* hairpiece.

posticipa're *v.t.* postpone.

posti'lla *n.f.* footnote.

po'sto *p.p. di* **porre.** —*n.m.* place; (*spazio*) room; (*impiego*) job; (*mil.*) post; (*sedile*) seat. **a/fuori** ~ in/out of place.

po'stumo *a.* posthumous.

pota'bile *a.* drinkable. **acqua** ~ drinking water.

pota're *v.t.* prune.

pota'ssio *n.m.* potassium.

pote'n|te *a.* powerful; (*efficace*) potent. **~za** *n.f.* power; potency.

potenzia'le *a. & n.m.* potential.

pote're *n.m.* power. **al ~** in power. —*v.t.* can, be able; (*per chiedere o dare il permesso, augurale, essere probabile*) may. **che tu possa essere felice!** may you be happy! **posso entrare?** may I come in? **posso fare qualche cosa?** can I do something? **può darsi** perhaps. **spero di poter venire** I hope to be able to come.

potestà *n.f.* power.

po'ver|o, a *a.* poor; (*semplice*) plain. —*n.m., f.* poor man/woman. **i ~i** the poor. **~tà** *n.f.* poverty.

pozio'ne *n.f.* potion.

po'zz|a *n.f.* pool. **~a'nghera** *n.f.* puddle.

po'zzo *n.m.* well; (*minerario*) pit. **~ petrolifero** oil-well.

pramma'tica *n.f.* **essere di ~** be customary.

pranza're *v.i.* dine; (*a mezzogiorno*) lunch. **pra'nzo** *n.m.* dinner; lunch.

pra'tic|a *n.f.* practice; (*addestramento*) training; (*documento*) paper. **~a'bile** *a.* practicable. **~a'nte** *n.m./f.* apprentice; (*relig.*) (regular) churchgoer. **~a're** *v.t.* practise; (*frequentare*) associate with; (*fare*) make. **~o** *a.* practical; (*esperto*) experienced.

pra't|o *n.m.* meadow; (*di giardino*) lawn. **~eri'a** *n.f.* grassland.

prea'mbolo *n.m.* preamble.

preavvi's|o *n.m.* warning. **~a're** *v.t.* forewarn.

preca'rio *a.* precarious.

precauzio'ne *n.f.* precaution. (*cautela*) care.

precede'n|te *a.* previous. —*n.m.* precedent.

prece'd|ere *v.t.* precede. **~e'nza** *n.f.* precedence; (*di veicoli*) right of way.

prece'tt|o *n.m.* precept. **~o're** *n.m.* tutor.

precipit|a're *v.t.* precipitate. —*v.i.* fall headlong. **~a'rsi** *v.r.* (*gettarsi*) throw oneself; (*affrettarsi*) rush. **~o'so** *a.* hasty; (*avventato*) reckless.

precipi'zio *n.m.* precipice. **a ~** headlong.

precisa're *v.t.* specify.

precisio'ne *n.f.* precision. **preci'so** *a.* precise; (*di ore*) sharp.

preclu'|dere *v.t.* preclude. **~so** *p.p. di* **~dere.**

preco'ce *a.* precocious; (*prematuro*) premature.

preconce'tto *a.* preconceived. —*n.m.* prejudice.

precurso're *n.m.* forerunner.

pre'd|a *n.f.* prey; (*bottino*) booty. **essere in ~a a** be overwhelmed with. **~a're** *v.t.* plunder. **~ato're** *n.m.* predator.

predecesso're *n.m./f.* predecessor.

prede'lla *n.f.* platform.

predestina're *v.t.* predestine.

prede'tto *p.p. di* **predire.**

pre'dic|a *n.f.* sermon; (*fig.*) lecture. **~a're** *v.t.* preach.

predica'to *n.m.* predicate.

predile'|tto, a *p.p. di* **prediligere.** —*a.* favourite. —*n.m., f.* pet. **~zio'ne** *n.f.* predilection.

predili'gere *v.t.* prefer.

predi'|re *v.t.* foretell. **~zio'ne** *n.f.* prediction.

predispo'|rre *v.t.* arrange. **~sizio'ne** (*inclinazione*) *n.f.* inclination. **~sto** *p.p. di* **~rre.**

predomina'|nte *a.* predominant. **~re** *v.i.* predominate. **predomi'nio** *n.m.* predominance.

predo'ne *n.m.* robber.

prefabbrica'to *a.* prefabricated.

prefazio'ne *n.f.* preface.

prefere'nz|a *n.f.* preference. **~ia'le** *a.* preferential.

preferi'|re *v.t.* prefer. **~to** *a.* favourite.

prefe'tt|o *n.m.* prefect. **~u'ra** *n.f.* prefecture.

prefi'gger|e *v.t.* fix beforehand. **~si** *v.r.* be determined.

prefi'sso *p.p. di* **prefiggere.** —*n.m.* prefix; (*al telefono*) (dialling) code.

prega're *v.t./i.* pray; (*supplicare*) beg. **farsi ~** need persuading.

prege'vole *a.* valuable.

preghie'ra *n.f.* prayer; (*richiesta*) request.

pregia'|re *v.t.* esteem. **~rsi** *v.r.* **~rsi di** take pleasure in. **~to** *a.* esteemed; (*prezioso*) valuable. **pre'gio** *n.m.* esteem; (*valore*) value.

pregiudica'|re *v.t.* prejudice; (*danneggiare*) harm. **~to** *a.* prejudiced; *n.m.* (*legge*) previous offender.

pregiudi'zio *n.m.* prejudice; (*danno*) detriment.

pre'gno *a.* pregnant; (*pieno*) full.

pre'go *int.* (*non c'è di che*) don't

mention it!; (*per favore*) please. ~? I beg your pardon?

pregusta're *v.t.* look forward to.

preisto'rico *a.* prehistoric(al).

prela'to *n.m.* prelate.

preleva'|re *v.t.* (*denaro*) draw out; (*merci*) collect; (*med.*) take. ~me'nto *n.m.* drawing.

prelimina'r|e *a.* preliminary. ~i *n.m. pl.* preliminaries.

prelu'dio *n.m.* prelude.

prematu'ro *a.* premature.

premedita'|re *v.t.* premeditate. ~zio'ne *n.f.* premeditation.

pre'mere *v.t.* press. —*v.i.* ~ a (*importare*) matter to. **mi preme sapere** I need to know.

preme'ssa *n.f.* introduction.

preme'|ttere *v.t.* put forward; (*mettere prima*) put before. ~sso *p.p. di* ~ttere. ~sso che granted that.

premia'|re *v.t.* give a prize to; (*ricompensare*) reward. ~zio'ne *n.f.* prize giving. **pre'mio** *n.m.* prize; reward; (*comm.*) premium.

premine'nte *a.* pre-eminent.

premonizio'ne *n.f.* premonition.

premuni'r|e *v.t.* fortify. ~si *v.r.* take protective measures. ~si di provide oneself with.

premu'r|a *n.f.* (*fretta*) hurry; (*cura*) care. ~o'so *a.* thoughtful.

prenata'le *a.* antenatal.

pre'nder|e *v.t.* take; (*afferrare*) seize; (*andare a prendere*) fetch; (*acchiappare, contrarre*) catch; (*cibo, bevanda*) have; (*far pagare*) charge; (*assumere*) take on; (*ottenere*) get; (*occupare*) take up. —*v.i.* (*voltare*) turn; (*attecchire*) take root; (*rapprendersi*) set. ~si *v.r.* (*azzuffarsi*) ~si a pugni come to blows. ~e informazioni make inquiries. ~e qcno. in giro pull s.o.'s leg. ~sela get upset.

prendiso'le *n.m.* sun-suit.

prenota'|re *v.t.* book. ~zio'ne *n.f.* booking.

preoccupa'|re *v.t.* worry. ~rsi *v.r.* ~rsi (di) worry (about). ~zio'ne *n.f.* worry; (*apprensione*) concern.

prepara'|re *v.t.* prepare. ~rsi *v.r.* get ready. ~ti'vi *n.m. pl.* preparations. ~to *n.m.* (*prodotto*) preparation. ~to'rio *a.* preparatory. ~zio'ne *n.f.* preparation.

prepondera'n|te *a.* predominant. ~za *n.f.* prevalence.

prepo'rre *v.t.* place before.

preposizio'ne *n.f.* preposition.

prepo'sto *p.p. di* **preporre.**

prepote'n|te *a.* overbearing. —*n.m.|f.* bully. ~za *n.f.* high-handedness.

prerogati'va *n.f.* prerogative.

pre's|a *n.f.* taking; (*conquista*) capture; (*stretta*) hold; (*di cemento ecc.*) setting; (*electr.*) socket; (*pizzico*) pinch. **essere alle** ~e con be struggling with. **macchina da** ~a cine camera. ~a in giro leg-pull.

presa'gio *n.m.* omen.

presagi're *v.t.* foretell.

pre'sbite *a.* long-sighted.

presbite'ri|o *n.m.* presbytery. ~a'no, a *a. & n.m., f.* Presbyterian.

presci'ndere *v.i.* leave aside. a ~ da apart from.

prescri'|vere *v.t.* prescribe. ~tto *p.p. di* ~vere. ~zio'ne *n.f.* prescription; (*norma*) rule.

presenta'|re *v.t.* present; (*far conoscere*) introduce; (*inoltrare*) submit. ~rsi *v.r.* present oneself; introduce oneself; (*occasione*) occur. ~to're, ~tri'ce *n.m., f.* presenter; (*di notizie*) announcer. ~zio'ne *n.f.* presentation; introduction.

prese'nt|e *a.* present; (*attuale*) current; (*questo*) this. —*n.m.* present. i ~i those present. **aver** ~e remember.

presentime'nto *n.m.* foreboding.

prese'nza *n.f.* presence; (*aspetto*) appearance.

prese'p|e, ~io *ns.m.* crib.

preserva'|re *v.t.* preserve. ~ti'vo *n.m.* contraceptive. ~zio'ne *n.f.* preservation.

pre'side *n.m.|f.* head/master, -mistress; (*univ.*) dean.

preside'n|te *n.m.* president; (*di assemblea*) chairman. ~za *n.f.* presidency; chairmanship. ~zia'le *a.* presidential.

presidia're *v.t.* garrison. **presi'dio** *n.m.* garrison.

presie'dere *v.t.i.|i.* ~ a preside over.

pre'so *p.p. di* **prendere.**

pre'ssa *n.f.* crowd; (*mech.*) press.

pressappo'co *adv.* about.

pressa'|re *v.t.* press. ~nte *a.* urgent.

pressio'ne *n.f.* pressure. **far** ~ su put pressure on.

pre'ss|o *adv.* nearby. —*prep.* near; (*a casa di*) with; (*negli indirizzi*) care of (*abbr.* c/o). ~i *n.m. pl.* neighbourhood.

pressurizza're *v.t.* pressurize.

presta'nte *a.* good-looking.

presta'r|e *v.t.* lend. ∼**si** *v.r.* lend oneself.

prestigia|to're, ∼**tri'ce** *n.m., f.* conjurer.

presti'gio *n.m.* prestige. **gioco di** ∼ conjuring trick.

pre'stito *n.m.* loan. **dare in** ∼ lend. **prendere in** ∼ borrow.

pre'sto *adv.* soon; (*di buon'ora*) early; (*in fretta*) quickly. **a** ∼ see you soon. **al più** ∼ as soon as possible. ∼ **o tardi** sooner or later.

presu'mere *v.t.* presume; (*credere*) think.

presun|tuo'so *a.* presumptuous. ∼**zio'ne** *n.f.* presumption.

presuppo'rre *v.t.* suppose.

pre'te *n.m.* priest.

pretende'nte *n.m./f.* pretender. —*n.m.* (*corteggiatore*) suitor.

prete'n|dere *v.t.* (*sostenere*) claim; (*esigere*) demand. —*v.i.* ∼**dere a** claim to. ∼**sio'ne** *n.f.* pretension. ∼**zio'so** *a.* pretentious.

prete's|a *n.f.* pretension; (*esigenza*) claim. **senza** ∼**e** unpretentious. ∼**o** *p.p. di* **pretendere**.

prete'sto *n.m.* pretext.

pret|o're *n.m.* magistrate. ∼**u'ra** *n.f.* magistrate's court.

pre'tto *a.* pure.

prevale'|nte *a.* prevalent. ∼**nza** *n.f.* prevalence. ∼**re** *v.i.* prevail.

preva'lso *p.p. di* **prevalere**.

prevede're *v.t.* foresee; (*di legge ecc.*) provide for.

preveni're *v.t.* precede; (*evitare*) prevent; (*avvertire*) forewarn.

preventi'v|o *a.* preventive. —*n.m.* (*comm.*) estimate. ∼**a're** *v.t.* estimate.

prevenu'to *a.* forewarned; (*mal disposto*) prejudiced.

prevenzio'ne *n.f.* prevention; (*preconcetto*) prejudice.

provide'n|te *a.* provident. ∼**za** *n.f.* foresight. ∼**za sociale** social security.

previsio'ne *n.f.* forecast. **in** ∼ **di** in anticipation of.

previ'sto *p.p. di* **prevedere**. —*a.* foreseen.

prezio'so *a.* precious.

prezze'molo *n.m.* parsley.

pre'zzo *n.m.* price.

prigio'n|e *n.f.* prison; (*pena*) imprisonment. ∼**i'a** *n.f.* imprisonment.

∼**ie'ro, a** *a.* imprisoned; *n.m., f.* prisoner.

pri'ma *adv.* before; (*più presto*) earlier; (*in anticipo*) beforehand; (*in primo luogo*) first; (*un tempo*) once. ∼ **di** *prep.* before. ∼ **che** *conj.* before. —*n.f. vedi* **primo**.

prima'rio *a.* primary; (*principale*) principal.

prima'te *n.m.* primate.

prima'to *n.m.* supremacy; (*sport*) record.

primave'r|a *n.f.* spring. ∼**i'le** *a.* spring.

primeggia're *v.i.* excel.

primiti'vo *a.* primitive; (*originario*) original.

primi'zie *n.f. pl.* early produce *s.*

pri'm|o, a *a.* first; (*precedente di due*) former; (*iniziale*) early; (*migliore*) best. —*n.m.* (the) first. ∼**i** *n.m. pl.* (*i primi giorni*) the beginning. —*n.f.* first class; (*theatr.*) first night; (*auto.*) first (gear). **di** ∼**o piano** first-rate. **in** ∼**o piano** in the foreground. **in un** ∼**o tempo** at first. ∼**a copia** master copy.

primoge'nito, a *a. & n.m., f.* firstborn.

primordia'le *a.* primordial.

pri'mula *n.f.* primrose.

principa'le *a.* main. —*n.m.* head; (*fam.*) boss.

pri'ncip|e *n.m.* prince. ∼**e ereditario** crown prince. ∼**a'to** *n.m.* principality. ∼**e'sco** *a.* princely. ∼**e'ssa** *n.f.* princess.

princi'pi|o *n.m.* beginning; (*concetto*) principle; (*causa*) cause. ∼**a'nte** *n.m./f.* beginner. ∼**a're** *v.t./i.* begin, start.

prio're *n.m.* prior.

priorità *n.f.* priority.

pri'sma *n.m.* prism.

priva'|re *v.t.* deprive. ∼**rsi** *v.r.* deprive oneself. ∼**zio'ne** *n.f.* deprivation.

privati'va *n.f.* monopoly.

priva'to, a *a.* private. —*n.m., f.* private citizen.

privilegia're *v.t.* grant s.o. a privilege. **privile'gio** *n.m.* privilege.

pri'vo *a.* ∼ **di** devoid of; (*mancante*) lacking in.

pro *prep.* for. —*n.m.* advantage. **a che** ∼**?** what for? **il** ∼ **e il contro** the pros and cons.

probabile

142

proba'bil|e *a.* probable. **~ità** *n.f.* probability.

probità *n.f.* integrity.

proble'm|a *n.m.* problem. **~a'tico** *a.* problematic.

probo'scide *n.f.* trunk.

procaccia'r|e *v.t.*, **~si** *v.r.* obtain.

proca'ce *a.* impudent.

proce'd|ere *v.i.* proceed; (*iniziare*) start. **~ere contro** (*legge*) start legal proceedings against. **~ime'nto** *n.m.* process; (*legge*) proceedings *pl.* **~u'ra** *n.f.* procedure.

processio'ne *n.f.* procession.

proce'ss|o *n.m.* process; (*legge*) trial. **~a're** *v.t.* (*legge*) try.

proci'nto *n.m.* **essere in ~ di** be about to.

procla'm|a *n.m.* proclamation. **~a're** *v.t.* proclaim. **~azio'ne** *n.f.* proclamation.

procrastina'|re *v.t.* procrastinate. **~zio'ne** *n.f.* procrastination.

procrea're *v.t.* procreate. **~zio'ne** *n.f.* procreation.

procu'ra *n.f.* power of attorney. **per ~** by proxy. **~to're** *n.m.* attorney.

procura're *v.t./i.* procure; (*causare*) cause; (*cercare*) try.

pro'd|e *a.* brave. **~e'zza** *n.f.* bravery.

prodiga'r|e *v.t.* lavish. **~si** *v.r.* do one's best.

prodi'gi|o *n.m.* prodigy. **~o'so** *a.* prodigious.

pro'digo *a.* prodigal.

prodo'tt|o *p.p. di* **produrre**. *—n.m.* product. **~i agricoli** farm produce *s.* **~o derivato** by-product.

produ'|rre *v.t.* produce. **~rsi** *v.r.* (*di attore*) play; (*accadere*) happen. **~tti'vo** *a.* productive. **~tto're, ~ttri-'ce** *n.m., f.* producer. **~zio'ne** *n.f.* production.

profana'|re *v.t.* desecrate. **~zio'ne** *n.f.* desecration. **profa'no** *a.* profane.

proferi're *v.t.* utter.

professa're *v.t.* profess; (*professione*) practise.

professio'n|e *n.f.* profession. **~a'le** *a.* professional. **~i'sta** *n.m./f.* professional man/woman.

professo'r|e *n.m.* **~e'ssa** *n.f.* (*schol.*) teacher; (*univ.*) lecturer; (*titolare di cattedra*) professor.

profe'|ta *n.m.* prophet. **~tico** *a.* prophetic. **~tizza're** *v.t.* prophesy. **~zi'a** *n.f.* prophecy.

profi'cuo *a.* profitable.

profila'r|e *v.t.* outline; (*ornare*) border; (*aeron.*) streamline. **~si** *v.r.* stand out.

profi'lo *n.m.* profile; (*breve studio*) outline.

profi'tt|o *n.m.* profit; (*vantaggio*) advantage. **~a're** *v.i.* **~are di** (*avvantaggiarsi*) profit by; (*approfittare*) take advantage of.

profo'ndere *v.t.* (*lodi*) lavish; (*denaro*) squander.

profo'nd|o *a.* deep; (*fig.*) profound. **~ità** *n.f.* depth.

pro'fugo, **a** *n.m., f.* refugee.

profu'm|o *n.m.* perfume, scent. **~a're** *v.t.* perfume. **~a'rsi** *v.r.* put on scent. **~eri'a** *n.f.* perfumery.

profusio'ne *n.f.* profusion. **a ~ in** profusion. **profu'so** *p.p. di* **profondere**; *a.* profuse.

proge'nie *n.f.* progeny.

progetta're *v.t.* plan. **proge'tto** *n.m.* project. **progetto di legge** bill.

progra'mm|a *n.m.* programme; (*computer*) program. **~a scolastico** syllabus. **~a're** *v.t.* programme; (*computer*) program. **~ato're, ~atri-'ce** *n.m., f.* computer programmer. **~azio'ne** *n.f.* programming.

progredi're *v.i.* (make) progress.

progre'ss|o *n.m.* progress. **~io'ne** *n.f.* progression. **~i'vo** *a.* progressive.

proibi'|re *v.t.* forbid. **~ti'vo** *a.* prohibitive. **~to** *a.* forbidden. **~zio'ne** *n.f.* prohibition.

proie'tta're *v.t.* project. **~tto're** *n.m.* projector. **~zio'ne** *n.f.* projection.

proie'ttile *n.m.* bullet.

pro'le *n.f.* offspring.

proleta'ri|o *a. & n.m.* proletarian. **~a'to** *n.m.* proletariat.

prolifera're *v.i.* proliferate. **proli'fico** *a.* prolific.

proli'sso *a.* verbose.

pro'logo *n.m.* prologue.

prolu'nga *n.f.* (*electr.*) extension.

prolunga'r|e *v.t.* prolong; (*allungare*) lengthen. **~si** *v.r.* continue. **~si su** (*dilungarsi*) dwell upon.

promemo'ria *n.m.* memorandum.

prome'|ssa *n.f.* promise. **~sso** *p.p. di* **~ttere**. **~ttere** *v.t./i.* promise.

promine'n|te *a.* prominent. **~za** *n.f.* prominence.

promi'scu|o *a.* promiscuous. **~ità** *n.f.* promiscuity.

promonto'rio *n.m.* promontory.

promo'sso *p.p. di* **promuovere**.

promo|zio'ne *n.f.* promotion. **~to're** *n.m.* promoter.

promulga're *v.t.* promulgate.

promuo'vere *v.t.* promote.

pronipo'te *n.m.|f.* (*di bisnonno*) great-grandson / granddaughter; (*di prozio*) great-nephew/niece.

prono'me *n.m.* pronoun.

pronostica're *v.t.* predict.

pro'nt|o *a.* ready; (*rapido*) quick. **~o!** (*telefono*) hallo! **~o soccorso** first aid. **~e'zza** *n.f.* readiness; quickness.

prontua'rio *n.m.* handbook.

pronu'ncia *ecc.* = **pronunzia** *ecc.*

pronu'nzi|a *n.f.* pronunciation. **~a're** *v.t.* pronounce; (*dire*) utter. **~a'to** *a.* pronounced; (*prominente*) prominent.

propaga'nda *n.f.* propaganda.

propaga're *v.t.* propagate. **~rsi** *v.r.* spread. **~zio'ne** *n.f.* propagation.

prope'n|dere *v.i.* **~dere per** be in favour of. **~sio'ne** *n.f.* inclination. **~so** *p.p. di* **~dere**.

propina're *v.t.* administer.

propi'zio *a.* favourable.

proponime'nto *n.m.* resolution.

propo'r|re *v.t.* propose; (*suggerire*) suggest. **~si** *v.r.* **~si di** intend to.

proporzio'n|e *n.f.* proportion. **~a'le** *a.* proportional. **~a're** *v.t.* proportion. **~a'to** *a.* proportioned.

propo'sito *n.m.* purpose. **a ~** by the way. **a ~ di** with regard to. **di ~** (*apposta*) on purpose.

proposizio'ne *n.f.* clause; (*gram.*) sentence.

propo'st|a *n.f.* proposal. **~o** *p.p. di* **proporre**.

propriet|à *n.f.* property; (*diritto*) ownership; (*correttezza*) propriety. **~a'-rio, a** *n.m., f.* owner.

pro'prio *a.* one's (own); (*caratteristico*) typical; (*appropriato*) proper. —*adv.* just; (*veramente*) really; (*affatto*) not … at all. —*pron.* one's own. —*n.m.* one's (own). **lavorare in ~** work on one's own account.

propuls|io'ne *n.f.* propulsion. **~o're** *n.m.* propeller.

pro'rog|a *n.f.* extension. **~a're** *v.t.* extend.

proro'mpere *v.i.* burst out.

pro's|a *n.f.* prose. **~a'ico** *a.* prosaic.

proscio'|gliere *v.t.* release; (*legge*) acquit. **~lto** *p.p. di* **~gliere**.

prosciuga're *v.t.* dry up; (*bonificare*) reclaim.

prosciu'tto *n.m.* ham.

proscri'|tto *p.p. di* **~vere**. —*n.m.* exile. **~vere** *v.t.* banish.

prosecuzio'ne *n.f.* continuation.

prosegui'|re *v.t.* continue. —*v.i.* go on. **~me'nto** *n.m.* continuation.

prosper|a're *v.i.* prosper. **~ità** *n.f.* prosperity. **pro'spero** *a.* prosperous; (*favorevole*) favourable. **~o'so** *a.* flourishing; (*ragazza*) buxom.

prospetta'r|e *v.t.* show. **~si** *v.r.* seem.

prospetti'va *n.f.* perspective; (*panorama*) view; (*fig.*) prospect.

prospe'tto *n.m.* (*vista*) view; (*facciata*) façade; (*tabella*) table.

prospicie'nte *a.* facing.

pro'ssim|o *a.* near; (*seguente*) next; (*molto vicino*) close. —*n.m.* neighbour. **~ame'nte** *adv.* soon. **~ità** *n.f.* proximity.

prostitu'|ta *n.f.* prostitute. **~zio'ne** *n.f.* prostitution.

prostra'|re *v.t.* prostrate. **~rsi** *v.r.* prostrate oneself. **~to** *a.* prostrate.

protagoni'sta *n.m.|f.* protagonist.

prote'|ggere *v.t.* protect; (*favorire*) favour. **~tti'vo** *a.* protective. **~tto** *p.p. di* **~ggere**. **~tto're, ~ttri'ce** *n.m., f.* protector; (*sostenitore*) patron. **~zio'ne** *n.f.* protection.

protei'na *n.f.* protein.

prote'nder|e *v.t.* stretch out. **~si** *v.r.* (*in avanti*) lean out. **prote'so** *p.p. di* **~e**.

prote'st|a *n.f.* protest; (*dichiarazione*) protestation. **~a're** *v.t.|i.* protest.

protesta'nte *a. & n.m.|f.* Protestant.

protoco'll|o *n.m.* protocol; (*registro*) register. **carta ~o** official stamped paper. **~a're** *a.* protocol; *v.t.* register.

prototi'po *n.m.* prototype.

protra'|rre *v.t.* protract; (*differire*) postpone. **~tto** *p.p. di* **~rre**.

protuberan|te *a.* protuberant. **~za** *n.f.* protuberance.

pro'v|a *n.f.* test; (*dimostrazione*) proof; (*tentativo*) try; (*di abito*) fitting; (*theatr.*) rehearsal; (*bozza*) proof. **~a're** *v.t.* test; (*dimostrare*) prove; (*tentare*) try; (*abiti ecc.*) try on; (*sentire*) feel; (*theatr.*) rehearse. **~a'rsi** *v.r.* try.

proven|ie'nza *n.f.* origin. **~i're** *v.i.* **~ire da** come from. **~u'to** *p.p. di* **~ire**.

prove'nto *n.m.* proceeds *pl.*

prove'rbio *n.m.* proverb.

prove'tta *n.f.* test-tube.

prove'tto *a.* skilled.

provi'nci|a *n.f.* province. ~**a'le** *a.* provincial.

provi'no *n.m.* specimen; (*cinema*) screen test.

provoca'|re *v.t.* provoke; (*causare*) cause. ~**nte** *a.* provocative. ~**zio'ne** *n.f.* provocation.

provved|e're *v.t.* provide; (*disporre*) prepare. —*v.i.* ~**ere (a)** provide (for). ~**ime'nto** *n.m.* measure; (*previdenza*) precaution.

provvide'nz|a *n.f.* providence. ~**ia'le** *a.* providential.

provvigio'ne *n.f.* (*comm.*) commission.

provviso'rio *a.* provisional.

provvi'sta *n.f.* supply.

prozi'o, a *n.m., f.* great-uncle/aunt.

pru'a *n.f.* prow.

prude'n|te *a.* prudent. ~**za** *n.f.* prudence. ~**zia'le** *a.* prudential.

pru'dere *v.i.* itch.

pru'gn|a *n.f.* plum. ~**a secca** prune. ~**o** *n.m.* plum(-tree).

pruri'|to *n.m.* itch. ~**gino'so** *a.* itchy.

pseudo'nimo *n.m.* pseudonym.

psicana'l|isi *n.f.* psychoanalysis. ~**i'sta** *n.m.|f.* psychoanalyst. ~**izza're** *v.t.* psychoanalyse.

psi'che *n.f.* psyche.

psichia'tr|a *n.m.|f.* psychiatrist. ~**i'a** *n.f.* psychiatry.

psico'l|ogo, a *n.m., f.* psychologist. ~**ogi'a** *n.f.* psychology. ~**o'gico** *a.* psychological.

psicopa'tico, a *a.* psychopathic. —*n.m., f.* psychopath.

PT *abbr.* (*di* **Posta e Telegrafi**) PO.

pubblica'|re *v.t.* publish. ~**zio'ne** *n.f.* publication. ~**zioni** *n.f. pl.* (*di matrimonio*) banns.

pubblici'sta *n.m.|f.* (*giornalismo*) correspondent.

publicit|à *n.f.* publicity; (*comm.*) advertising. ~**a'rio** *a.* advertising.

pu'bblic|o *a.* public. —*n.m.* public; (*spettatori*) audience. **P~a Sicurezza** Police. ~**o ufficiale** civil servant. **scuola** ~**a** state school.

pu'be *n.m.* pubis.

pubertà *n.f.* puberty.

pu'd|ico *a.* modest. ~**o're** *n.m.* modesty.

pueri'le *a.* childish; (*pej.*) puerile.

pu'gil|e *n.m.* boxer. ~**a'to** *n.m.* boxing.

pugna'l|e *n.m.* dagger. ~**a're** *v.t.* stab. ~**a'ta** *n.f.* stab.

pu'gno *n.m.* fist; (*colpo*) punch; (*manciata*) fistful.

pu'lce *n.f.* flea.

pulci'no *n.m.* chick.

pule'dro, a *n.m., f.* colt, filly.

puli'|re *v.t.* clean. ~**re a secco** dry-clean. ~**to a.** clean. ~**tu'ra** *n.f.* cleaning. ~**zi'a** *n.f.* (*il pulire*) cleaning; (*l'essere pulito*) cleanliness.

pu'llman *n.m. invar.* coach.

pulmi'no *n.m.* minibus.

pu'lpito *n.m.* pulpit.

pulsa'nte *n.m.* (*electr.*) push-button.

pulsa'|re *v.i.* pulsate. ~**zio'ne** *n.f.* pulsation.

pulvi'scolo *n.m.* dust.

pu'ma *n.m. invar.* puma.

pu'ng|ere *v.t.* prick; (*di insetto*) sting. ~**e'nte** *a.* prickly; stinging; (*di odore ecc.*) sharp. ~**iglio'ne** *n.m.* sting.

puni'|re *v.t.* punish. ~**ti'vo** *a.* punitive. ~**zio'ne** *n.f.* punishment.

pu'nta *n.f.* point; (*estremità*) tip; (*di monte*) peak; (*un po'*) pinch.

punta're *v.t.* point; (*spingere con forza*) push; (*scommettere*) bet. —*v.i.* ~ **su** (*fig.*) rely on. ~ **verso** (*dirigersi*) head for.

punta't|a *n.f.* (*di una storia*) instalment; (*al gioco*) stake; (*breve visita*) flying visit. **a** ~**e** (*romanzo*) in instalments.

punteggia'|re *v.t.* dot; (*gram.*) punctuate. ~**tu'ra** *n.f.* punctuation.

punte'ggio *n.m.* score.

puntella're *v.t.* prop. **punte'llo** *n.m.* prop.

punti'glio *n.m.* spite; (*ostinazione*) obstinacy.

punti'na *n.f.* (*da disegno*) drawing pin; (*di giradischi*) stylus.

punti'no *n.m.* dot. **a** ~ perfectly.

pu'nt|o *n.m.* point; (*luogo*) spot; (*schol.*) mark; (*nel cucito*) stitch; (*nella punteggiatura*) full stop. **di** ~**o in bianco** all of a sudden. **due** ~**i** colon. **in** ~**o** sharp. **mettere a** ~**o** put right; (*motore*) tune up. ~**o di riferimento** landmark. ~**o esclamativo/interrogativo** exclamation/question mark. ~**o e virgola** semicolon.

puntua'l|e *a.* punctual. ~**ità** *n.f.* punctuality.

puntu'ra *n.f.* (*di insetto*) sting; (*di ago ecc.*) prick; (*med.*) puncture; (*iniezione*) injection; (*fitta*) stabbing pain.

punzecchia're *v.t.* prick; (*fig.*) tease.

punzo'ne *n.m.* punch.

pu'p|a *n.f.* doll. ~**a'zzo** *n.m.* puppet.

pupi'llo, a *n.m., f.* ward. —*n.f.* (*anat.*) pupil.

purché *conj.* provided.

pu're *adv.* too, also; (*concessivo*) **fate** ~**!** please do! —*conj.* (*tuttavia*) yet; (*anche se*) even if. **pur di** just to.

puré *n.m.* purée. ~ **di patate** mashed potatoes.

pu'rg|a *n.f.* purge. ~**a'nte** *n.m.* laxative. ~**a're** *v.t.* purge.

purgato'rio *n.m.* purgatory.

purita'no, a *a.* & *n.m., f.* Puritan.

pu'r|o *a.* pure; (*vino ecc.*) undiluted.

~**e'zza** *n.f.* purity. ~**ifica're** *v.t.* purify.

purosa'ngue *a.* & *n.m.* thoroughbred.

purtro'ppo *adv.* unfortunately.

pus *n.m.* pus.

pusilla'nime *a.* cowardly.

pu'stola *n.f.* pimple.

putife'rio *n.m.* uproar.

putrefa'r|e *v.i.* ~**si** *v.r.* putrefy.

pu'trido *a.* putrid.

putta'na *n.f.* whore.

pu'zza *n.f.* = **puzzo**.

pu'zz|o *n.m.* stink, bad smell. ~**a're** *v.i.* stink, smell (bad). ~**ole'nte** *a.* stinking.

pu'zzola *n.f.* polecat.

Q

qua *adv.* here. **da un anno in ∼** for the last year (or so). **da quando in ∼?** since when? **di ∼** this way. **di ∼ di** on this side of.

quade'rno *n.m.* exercise book; (*per appunti*) notebook.

quadra'ngolo *n.m.* quadrangle.

quadra'nte *n.m.* quadrant; (*di orologio*) dial.

quadra'|re *v.t.* square; (*contabilità*) balance. —*v.i.* fit in. **∼to** *a.* square; (*equilibrato*) level-headed; *n.m.* square; (*pugilato*) ring.

quadre'tt|o *n.m.* (*piccolo quadro*) small picture. **a ∼i** (*tessuto*) check. **∼a'to** *a.* squared; check.

quadrifo'glio *n.m.* four-leaf clover.

qua'dr|o *n.m.* picture, painting; (*quadrato*) square; (*vista*) sight; (*tabella*) table; (*theatr.*) scene. **∼i** *n.m. pl.* (*carte*) diamonds.

quadru'pede *n.m.* quadruped.

quadruplica're *v.t.* quadruple. **qua'-druplo** *a. & n.m.* quadruple.

quaggiù *adv.* down here.

qua'glia *n.f.* quail.

qua'lche *a.* some; (*alcuni*) a few; (*inter.*) any. **hai ∼ libro italiano?** have you any Italian books? **in ∼ modo** somehow. **in ∼ posto** somewhere. **∼ cosa = qualcosa.**

qualco's|a *pron.* something; (*inter.*) anything. **∼a'ltro** something else; anything else.

qualcu'no *pron.* someone, somebody; (*inter.*) anyone, anybody; (*alcuni*) some.

qua'le *a.* (*indeterminato*) what; (*limitato*) which; (*come*) (just) as. —*pron.* (*soggetto, riferito a persone*) who, that; (*riferito ad animali o cose*) that, which; (*oggetto, con prep.*) whom; (*cosa*) which; (*possessivo*) whose. —*adv.* (*come*) as.

quali'fic|a *n.f.* qualification; (*titolo*) title. **∼a're** *v.t.* qualify; (*definire*) define. **∼a'rsi** *v.r.* be placed. **∼ati'vo** *a.* qualifying. **∼azio'ne** *n.f.* qualification.

qualità *n.f.* quality; (*specie*) kind. **in ∼ di** in one's capacity as.

qualo'ra *conj.* in case.

qualsi'asi, qualu'nque *adjs.* any;

(*quale che sia*) whatever; (*ordinario*) ordinary.

qua'ndo *conj. & adv.* when. **da ∼** since. **da ∼?** since when?

quantità *n.f.* quantity; (*gran numero*) **una ∼ di** a great deal of.

qua'nt|o *a.* (*inter.*) how much; (*quantità*) how many; (*excl.*) what a lot of; (*di tempo*) how long; (*rel.*) as much ... as, as many ... as. —*pron.* (*rel., tutti coloro che*) (all) those who; (*in correlazione con 'tanto'*) as much as, as many as; (*quello che*) what. —*adv.* how (*con a. o adv.*); how much (*con v.*); (*rel.*) as much as. **in ∼o** (*in qualità di*) as; (*poiché*) since. **in ∼o a me** as far as I am concerned. **per ∼o** however. **per ∼o io sappia** as far as I know. **∼i anni hai?** how old are you? **∼o a** as for. **∼o è bello!** how nice! **∼o prima** (*presto*) soon; (*al più presto*) as soon as possible.

quantu'nque *conj.* although.

quara'nt|a *a. & n.m.* forty. **∼e'simo** *a. & n.m.* fortieth. **∼i'na** *n.f.* **una ∼ina** about forty.

quarante'na *n.f.* quarantine.

quare'sima *n.f.* lent.

quarte'tto *n.m.* quartet.

quartie're *n.m.* district; (*mil.*) quarters *pl.* **∼ generale** headquarters.

qua'rto *a.* fourth. —*n.m.* fourth; (*quarta parte*) quarter. **le sette e un ∼** a quarter past seven.

qua'rzo *n.m.* quartz.

qua'si *adv.* almost, nearly. **∼ mai** hardly ever. —*conj.* (*come se*) as if.

quassù *adv.* up here.

qua'tto *a.* crouching; (*silenzioso*) silent. **starsene ∼** keep very quiet.

quatto'rdici *a. & n.m.* fourteen.

quattri'ni *n.m. pl.* money *s.*

qua'ttr|o *a. & n.m.* four. **∼oce'nto** *a. & n.m.* four hundred. **il Q∼ocento** the fifteenth century. **∼omi'la** *a. & n.m.* four thousand.

quattro'cchi *adv.* **a ∼** face to face.

que'll|o *a.* that; **∼i** *pl.* those. —*pron.* that (one), **∼i** *pl.* those (ones); (*riferito a cosa*) the one; (*egli, ella*) he, she. **∼o che** (*ciò che*) what.

que'rcia *n.f.* oak.

quere'l|a *n.f.* (legal) action. ∼**a're** *v.t.*
bring an action against.

quesi'to *n.m.* question.

questiona'rio *n.m.* questionnaire.

questio'n|e *n.f.* question; (*faccenda*)
matter; (*litigio*) quarrel. **in** ∼**e** in
doubt. ∼**a're** *v.i.* dispute.

que'st|o *a.* this, ∼**i** *pl.* these. —*pron.*
this (one), ∼**i** *pl.* these (ones). **per** ∼**o**
for this reason. **quest'oggi** today.

quest|o're *n.m.* chief of police. ∼**u'ra**
n.f. police headquarters *pl.*

qui *adv.* here. **da** ∼ **in poi** from now
on. **fin** ∼ (*di tempo*) up till now.

quieta'nza *n.f.* receipt.

quie't|e *n.f.* quiet. ∼**a're** *v.t.* calm.
∼**a'rsi** *v.r.* quieten down. ∼**o** *a.* quiet.

qui'ndi *adv.* then. —*conj.* therefore.

qui'ndic|i *a.* & *n.m.* fifteen. ∼**i'na** *n.f.*
una ∼**ina** about fifteen. **una** ∼**ina**
di giorni a fortnight.

quinque'nnio *n.m.* (period of) five
years.

qui'nte *n.f. pl.* (*theatr.*) wings.

quinta'le *n.m.* a hundred kilograms.

quinte'tto *n.m.* quintet.

qui'nto *a.* fifth.

quo't|a *n.f.* quota; (*rata*) instalment;
(*altitudine*) height; (*ippica*) odds *pl.*
∼**a're** *v.t.* (*comm.*) quote. ∼**azio'ne**
n.f. quotation.

quotidia'no *a.* daily; (*ordinario*)
everyday. —*n.m.* daily (paper).

quozie'nte *n.m.* quotient. ∼ **d'intel-**
ligenza intelligence quotient, IQ.

R

raba'rbaro *n.m.* rhubarb.
ra'bbi|a *n.f.* rage; (*ira*) anger; (*med.*) rabies *s.* **che ∼a!** what a nuisance! **mi fa ∼a** it makes me angry. **∼o'so** *a.* hot-tempered; (*med.*) rabid; (*violento*) violent.
rabbi'no *n.m.* rabbi.
rabboni'r|e *v.t.* pacify. **∼si** *v.r.* calm down.
rabbrividi're *v.i.* shudder; (*di freddo*) shiver.
rabbuia'rsi *v.r.* become dark.
raccapezza'r|e *v.t.* put together. **∼si** *v.r.* see one's way ahead.
raccapriccia'nte *a.* horrifying.
raccattapa'lle *n.m.* ballboy.
raccatta're *v.t.* pick up.
racche'tta *n.f.* racket.
ra'cchio *a.* (*fam.*) ugly.
racchiu'dere *v.t.* contain.
racco'gli|ere *v.t.* pick; (*da terra*) pick up; (*mietere*) harvest; (*collezionare*) collect; (*radunare*) gather; (*voti ecc.*) win; (*dare asilo*) take in. **∼ersi** *v.r.* gather; (*concentrarsi*) collect one's thoughts. **∼me'nto** *n.m.* concentration. **∼to're**, **∼tri'ce** *n.m.*, *f.* collector.
racco'lto, a *p.p. di* **∼gliere.** *—a.* (*intimo*) cosy; (*concentrato*) engrossed. *—n.m.* (*mietitura*) harvest. *—n.f.* collection; harvesting; (*adunata*) gathering.
raccomanda'|re *v.t.* recommend; (*affidare*) entrust; (*lettera*) register. **∼rsi** *v.r.* (*implorare*) beg. **∼ta** *n.f.* registered letter. **∼zio'ne** *n.f.* recommendation.
raccomoda're *v.t.* repair.
racconta're *v.t.* tell. **racco'nto** *n.m.* story.
raccorcia're *v.t.* shorten.
raccorda're *v.t.* join. **racco'rdo** *n.m.* connection. **raccordo anulare** ring road.
rachi'tico *a.* rickety.
racimola're *v.t.* scrape together.
ra'dar *n.m.* radar.
raddensa'r|e *v.t.*, **∼si** *v.r.* thicken.
raddolci'r|e *v.t.* sweeten; (*fig.*) soften. **∼si** *v.r.* become milder.
raddoppia're *v.t.* double.
raddrizza're *v.t.* straighten.

ra'der|e *v.t.* shave; (*abbattere*) raze. **∼si** *v.r.* shave (oneself).
radia'le *a.* radial.
radia're *v.t.* strike off.
radiato're *n.m.* radiator.
radiazio'ne *n.f.* (*fisica*) radiation.
radica'le *a.* radical. *—n.m.* (*gram.*) root; (*pol.*) radical.
radi'cchio *n.m.* chicory.
radi'ce *n.f.* root.
ra'dio *n.f. invar.* radio. *—n.m.* (*chimica*) radium. **∼attività** *n.f.* radioactivity. **∼atti'vo** *a.* radioactive. **∼diffusio'ne** *n.f.* broadcasting. **∼grafa're** *v.t.* X-ray. **∼grafi'a** *n.f.* X-ray photograph; (*radiologia*) radiography. **∼terapi'a** *n.f.* radiotherapy.
radio'so *a.* radiant.
ra'do *a.* sparse; (*non frequente*) rare. **di ∼** seldom.
raduna'r|e *v.t.*, **∼si** *v.r.* gather (together). **radu'no** *n.m.* meeting; (*sport*) rally.
radu'ra *n.f.* clearing.
ra'fano *n.m.* horse-radish.
raffe'rmo *a.* stale.
ra'ffica *n.f.* gust; (*di armi da fuoco*) burst.
raffigura're *v.t.* represent.
raffin|a're *v.t.* refine. **∼ate'zza** *n.f.* refinement. **∼a'to** *a.* refined. **∼eri'a** *n.f.* refinery.
rafforza're *v.t.* reinforce.
raffredd|a're *v.t.* cool. **∼a'rsi** *v.r.* get cold; (*prendere un raffreddore*) catch a cold. **∼o're** *n.m.* cold.
raffro'nto *n.m.* comparison.
ra'fia *n.f.* raffia.
raga'zzo, a *n.m.*, *f.* boy, girl; (*fidanzato, a*) boyfriend, girlfriend.
raggia'nte *a.* radiant.
ra'ggio *n.m.* ray; (*math.*) radius; (*di ruota*) spoke.
raggira're *v.t.* trick. **raggi'ro** *n.m.* trick.
raggiu'ngere *v.t.* reach; (*conseguire*) achieve.
raggomitola'rsi *v.r.* curl up.
raggranella're *v.t.* scrape together.
raggrinza'r|e *v.t.* wrinkle. **∼si** *v.r.* become wrinkled.
raggruppa're *v.t.* group (together).

ragguaglia're *v.t.* compare; (*informare*) inform. **raggua'glio** *n.m.* comparison; information.

ragguarde'vole *a.* considerable.

ra'gia *n.f.* resin. **acqua** ~ turpentine.

ragiona'|re *v.i.* reason; (*discutere*) discuss. ~**me'nto** *n.m.* reasoning; (*discussione*) discussion.

ragio'n|e *n.f.* reason; (*ciò che è giusto*) right. **a** ~**e o a torto** rightly or wrongly. **aver** ~**e** be right. **perdere la** ~**e** go out of one's mind. ~**e'vole** *a.* reasonable.

ragion|eri'a *n.f.* accountancy. ~**ie're, a** *n.m., f.* accountant.

raglia're *v.i.* bray.

ragnate'la *n.f.* cobweb.

ra'gno *n.m.* spider.

RAI *abbr.* (*di* **Radio Audizione Italiana**).

ragù *n.m.* meat sauce.

rallegra'|re *v.t.* gladden. ~**rsi** *v.r.* rejoice. ~**rsi con qcno.** congratulate s.o. ~**me'nti** *n.m. pl.* congratulations.

rallenta'|re *v.t.* slow down; (*allentare*) slacken. ~**rsi** *v.r.* ease (off). ~**me'nto** *n.m.* slowing down.

ramanzi'na *n.f.* reprimand.

ra'me *n.m.* copper.

ramifica'|re *v.i.*, ~**rsi** *v.r.* branch out. ~**zio'ne** *n.f.* ramification.

ramm|arica'rsi *v.r.* ~ (**di**) regret; (*lamentarsi*) complain (about). ~**a'rico** *n.m.* regret.

rammenda're *v.t.* darn. **ramme'ndo** *n.m.* darning.

rammenta'r|e *v.t.* remember; (*richiamare alla memoria*) remind. ~**si** *v.r.* remember.

rammolli'r|e *v.t.* soften. ~**si** *v.r.* become soft.

ra'mo *n.m.* branch. ~**sce'llo** *n.m.* twig.

ra'mpa *n.f.* (*di scale*) flight. ~ **di lancio** launching pad.

rampica'nte *a.* climbing. —*n.m.* (*bot.*) creeper.

rampi'no *n.m.* hook; (*fig.*) pretext.

rampo'llo *n.m.* (*hum.*) child.

rampo'ne *n.m.* harpoon.

ra'na *n.f.* frog. **uomo** ~ frogman.

ra'ncido *a.* rancid.

ranco're *n.m.* resentment.

randa'gio *a.* stray.

rande'llo *n.m.* club.

ra'ngo *n.m.* rank.

rannicchia'rsi *v.r.* huddle up.

rannuvola'rsi *v.r.* cloud over.

rano'cchio *n.m.* frog.

ra'ntolo *n.m.* wheeze; (*di moribondo*) death-rattle.

ra'pa *n.f.* turnip.

rapa'ce *a.* rapacious; (*uccello*) predatory.

rapa're *v.t.* crop.

ra'pido, a *a.* swift. —*n.m.* (*di treno*) express train. —*n.f.* rapid.

rapi'n|a *n.f.* robbery. ~**a a mano armata** armed robbery. ~**a're** *v.t.* rob. ~**ato're** *n.m.* robber.

rapi'|re *v.t.* abduct; (*a scopo di riscatto*) kidnap; (*estasiare*) ravish. ~**to're**, ~**tri'ce** *n.m., f.* kidnapper.

rappacifica'r|e *v.t.* pacify. ~**si** *v.r.* (*reciproco*) make it up.

rappezza're *v.t.* patch up. **rappe'zzo** *n.m.* patch.

rappo'rt|o *n.m.* report; (*connessione*) relation; (*legame*) relationship; (*math., techn.*) ratio. ~**i** *n.m. pl.* relationship *s.* ~**i sessuali** sexual intercourse *s.* ~**a're** *v.t.* report; (*disegno*) reproduce.

rappre'ndersi *v.r.* set; (*di latte*) curdle.

rappresa'glia *n.f.* reprisal.

rappresenta'n|te *n.m./f.* representative. ~**za** *n.f.* delegation; (*comm.*) agency. **spese di** ~**za** entertainment expenses.

rappresenta'|re *v.t.* represent; (*theatr.*) perform. ~**ti'vo** *a.* representative. ~**zio'ne** *n.f.* representation; (*spettacolo*) performance.

rappre'so *p.p. di* **rapprendersi.**

rapsodi'a *n.f.* rhapsody.

rarefa'r|e *v.t.*, ~**si** *v.r.* rarefy.

ra'r|o a. rare. ~**ame'nte** *adv.* rarely. ~**ità** *n.f.* rarity.

rasa'r|e *v.t.* shave; (*siepe ecc.*) trim. ~**si** *v.r.* shave.

raschia'|re *v.t.* scrape (off). ~**rsi la gola** clear one's throat. ~**me'nto** *n.m.* (*med.*) curettage.

rasenta're *v.t.* go close to. **rase'nte** *adv. & prep.* (very) close (to).

ra'so *p.p. di* **radere.** —*a.* smooth; (*colmo*) full (to the brim); (*di barba*) close-cropped. —*n.m.* satin. ~ **terra** close to the ground. **un cucchiaio** ~ a level spoonful.

raso'io *n.m.* razor.

rasse'gna *n.f.* review; (*esame*) survey; (*mostra*) exhibition. **passare in** ~ (*mil.*) inspect.

rassegna'|re *v.t.* resign. **~rsi** *v.r.* resign oneself. **~zio'ne** *n.f.* resignation.

rasserena'r|e *v.t.* clear; (*fig.*) cheer (s.o.) up. **~si** *v.r.* become clear; (*fig.*) cheer up.

rassetta're *v.t.* tidy up; (*riparare*) mend.

rassicura're *v.t.* reassure.

rassoda're *v.t.* harden; (*fig.*) strengthen.

rassomiglia'|re *v.i.* **~** a resemble. **~nza** *n.f.* resemblance.

rastrella're *v.t.* rake; (*perlustrare*) comb. **rastre'llo** *n.m.* rake.

rastrellie'ra *n.f.* rack; (*scolapiatti*) plate-rack.

ra't|a *n.f.* instalment. **pagare a ~e** pay by instalments. **~ea're**, **~eizza're** *vs.t.* divide into instalments.

ra'tto *n.m.* abduction; (*roditore*) rat.

ratto'pp|o *n.m.* patch. **~a're** *v.t.* patch.

rattrappi'r|e *v.t.* make stiff. **~si** *v.r.* become stiff.

rattrista'r|e *v.t.* sadden. **~si** *v.r.* become sad.

rauce'dine *n.f.* hoarseness. **ra'uco** *a.* hoarse.

ravane'llo *n.m.* radish.

ravvede'rsi *v.r.* mend one's ways.

ravvicina'r|e *v.t.* bring closer. **~si** *v.r.* be reconciled.

ravvisa're *v.t.* recognize.

ravviva'r|e *v.t.* revive; (*fig.*) brighten up. **~si** *v.r.* revive.

razioci'nio *n.m.* reasoning; (*buon senso*) common sense.

raziona'le *a.* rational.

raziona're *v.t.* ration. **razio'ne** *n.f.* ration.

ra'zza *n.f.* race; (*di cani ecc.*) breed; (*genere*) kind. **che ~ di idiota!** (*fam.*) what an idiot!

razzi'a *n.f.* raid.

razz|ia'le *a.* racial. **~i'smo** *n.m.* racism. **~i'sta** *a.* & *n.m./f.* racist.

ra'zzo *n.m.* rocket.

razzola're *v.i.* (*di polli*) scratch about.

re *n.m. invar.* king; (*mus.*) ray.

reagi're *v.i.* react.

rea'l|e *a.* (*di re*) royal; (*vero*) real. **~i'smo** *n.m.* realism. **~i'sta** *n.m./f.* royalist; realist. **~i'stico** *a.* realistic. **~me'nte** *adv.* really.

realizza'r|e *v.t.* (*attuare*) carry out; (*comm.*) make; (*fig.*) realize. **~rsi** *v.r.* come true. **~zio'ne** *n.f.* realization.

realtà *n.f.* reality.

rea'to *n.m.* crime.

reatto're *n.m.* reactor; (*aeron.*) jet (aircraft).

reaziona'rio, a *a.* & *n.m., f.* reactionary.

reazio'ne *n.f.* reaction.

re'bbio *n.m.* prong.

reca'pit|o *n.m.* address; (*consegna*) delivery. **~a're** *v.t.* deliver.

reca'r|e *v.t.* bear; (*produrre*) cause. **~si** *v.r.* go.

rece'dere *v.i.* recede; (*fig.*) give up.

recens|io'ne *n.f.* review. **~i're** *v.t.* review. **~o're**, a *n.m., f.* reviewer.

rece'nte *a.* recent. **di ~** recently.

recessio'ne *n.f.* recession.

rece'sso *n.m.* recess.

reci'dere *v.t.* cut (off).

recidi'vo, a *a.* relapsing. **—***n.m., f.* recidivist.

reci'nto *n.m.* enclosure; (*per animali*) pen; (*per bambini*) play-pen.

recipie'nte *n.m.* container.

reci'proco *a.* reciprocal.

reci'so *p.p. di* **recidere**. **—***a.* (*risoluto*) definite.

re'cit|a *n.f.* performance. **~a're** *v.t.* recite; (*theatr.*) act; (*ruolo*) play. **~azio'ne** *n.f.* recitation; (*theatr.*) acting.

reclama're *v.i.* protest. **—***v.t.* claim.

récla'me *n.f. invar.* advertising; (*avviso pubblicitario*) advertisement.

recla'mo *n.m.* complaint.

reclina're *v.t.* recline.

reclu's|o, a *a.* secluded. **—***n.m., f.* prisoner. **~io'ne** *n.f.* imprisonment.

re'clut|a *n.f.* recruit. **~a're** *v.t.* recruit.

reco'ndito *a.* secluded; (*intimo*) secret.

recrimina'|re *v.i.* recriminate. **~zio'ne** *n.f.* recrimination.

redargui're *v.t.* rebuke.

reda'tto *p.p. di* **redigere**.

reda|tto're, ~ttri'ce *n.m., f.* editor; (*di giornale*) writer. **~zio'ne** *n.f.* (*ufficio*) editorial office; (*di giornale*) editing.

redditi'zio *a.* profitable.

re'ddito *n.m.* income.

rede'n|to *p.p. di* **redimere**. **~to're** *n.m.* redeemer. **~zio'ne** *n.f.* redemption.

redi'gere *v.t.* write; (*documento*) draw up.

redi'mere *v.t.* redeem.

re'dini *n.f. pl.* reins.

redivi'vo *a.* restored to life.

re′duce *a.* ~ **da** returned from. —*n.m.|f.* survivor.

refere′ndum *n.m. invar.* referendum.

refere′nza *n.f.* reference.

refetto′rio *n.m.* refectory.

refratta′rio *a.* refractory. **essere** ~ **a** have no aptitude for.

refrigera′|re *v.t.* refrigerate. ~**zio′ne** *n.f.* refrigeration.

regala′re *v.t.* give. **rega′lo** *n.m.* present, gift.

rega′le *a.* regal.

rega′ta *n.f.* regatta.

regge′n|te *n.m.|f.* regent. ~**za** *n.f.* regency.

re′gger|e *v.t.* (*sorreggere*) bear; (*tenere in mano*) hold; (*dirigere*) run; (*governare*) govern; (*gram.*) take. —*v.i.* (*resistere*) hold out; (*durare*) last; (*fig.*) stand. ~**si** *v.r.* stand.

re′ggia *n.f.* royal palace.

reggica′lze *n.m. invar.* suspender belt.

reggime′nto *n.m.* regiment.

reggipe′tto, reggise′no *ns.m.* brassière; (*abbr.*) bra.

regi′a *n.f.* (*cinema*) direction; (*theatr.*) production.

regi′me *n.m.* regime; (*dieta*) diet; (*mech.*) speed.

regi′na *n.f.* queen.

re′gio *a.* royal.

regio′n|e *n.f.* region. ~**a′le** *a.* regional.

regi′sta *n.m.|f.* (*cinema*) director; (*theatr., TV*) producer.

registra′|re *v.t.* register; (*comm.*) enter; (*incidere su nastro*) tape; (*su disco*) record. ~**to′re** *n.m.* recorder; (*magnetofono*) tape-recorder. ~**tore di cassa** cash register. ~**zio′ne** *n.f.* registration; (*comm.*) entry; (*di programma*) recording.

regi′stro *n.m.* register; (*ufficio*) registry.

re′gn|o *n.m.* kingdom; (*sovranità*) reign. ~**a′re** *v.i.* reign.

re′gol|a *n.f.* rule. **in** ~**a** in order. ~**ame′nto** *n.m.* regulation; (*comm.*) settlement. ~**a′re** *a.* regular; *v.t.* regulate; (*sistemare*) settle. ~**a′rsi** *v.r.* (*agire*) act; (*moderarsi*) control oneself. ~**arità** *n.f.* regularity.

re′golo *n.m.* ruler. ~ **calcolatore** slide-rule.

regress|io′ne *n.f.* regression. ~**i′vo** *a.* regressive.

reintegra′re *v.t.* restore.

relati′v|o *a.* relative. ~**ità** *n.f.* relativity.

relazio′ne *n.f.* relation(ship); (*rapporto amoroso*) (love) affair; (*resoconto*) report.

relega′re *v.t.* relegate.

religio′|ne *n.f.* religion. ~**so, a** *a.* religious; *n.m., f.* monk, nun.

reli′quia *n.f.* relic.

reli′tto *n.m.* wreck.

rema′|re *v.i.* row. ~**to′re**, ~**tri′ce** *n.m., f.* rower. **re′mo** *n.m.* oar.

reminisce′nza *n.f.* reminiscence.

remiss|io′ne *n.f.* remission; (*sottomissione*) submissiveness. ~**i′vo** *a.* submissive.

remo′to *a.* remote. **passato** ~ past tense.

re′na *n.f.* sand.

re′nder|e *v.t.* (*restituire*) return; (*esprimere*) render; (*fruttare*) yield; (*far diventare*) make. ~**si** *v.r.* become. ~**si conto di qcsa.** realize sthg. ~**si utile** make oneself useful.

rendico′nto *n.m.* report.

rendime′nto *n.m.* rendering; (*produzione*) yield.

re′ndita *n.f.* income; (*dello Stato*) revenue.

re′ne *n.m.* kidney.

re′ni *n.f. pl.* (*schiena*) back *s.*

re′nna *n.f.* reindeer (*pl. invar.*); (*pelle*) buckskin.

Re′no *n.m.* Rhine.

re′o, a *a.* guilty. —*n.m., f.* offender.

repa′rto *n.m.* department; (*mil.*) unit.

repelle′nte *a.* repulsive.

repenta′glio *n.m.* **mettere a** ~ risk.

repenti′no *a.* sudden.

reperi′bile *a.* available.

reperto′rio *n.m.* repertory; (*elenco*) index.

re′plic|a *n.f.* reply; (*obiezione*) objection; (*copia*) replica; (*theatr.*) repeat performance. ~**a′re** *v.t.* reply; repeat.

repress|io′ne *n.f.* repression. ~**i′vo** *a.* repressive. **repre′sso** *p.p. di* **reprimere**.

repri′mere *v.t.* repress.

re′probo *a.* reprobate.

repu′bblic|a *n.f.* republic. ~**a′no, a** *a. & n.m., f.* republican.

reputa′re *v.t.* consider.

reputazio′ne *n.f.* reputation.

re′quie *n.f.* rest.

requisi′|re *v.t.* requisition. ~**zio′ne** *n.f.* requisition.

requisi′to *n.m.* requirement.

re'sa *n.f.* surrender; (*comm.*) rendering.

resci'ndere *v.t.* cancel.

reside'n|te *a.* & *n.m./f.* resident. **∼za** *n.f.* residence; (*soggiorno*) stay. **∼zia- 'le** *a.* residential.

resi'duo *a.* residual. *—n.m.* remainder.

resilie'n|te *a.* resilient. **∼za** *n.f.* resilience.

re'sina *n.f.* resin.

resi'st|ere *v.i.* **∼ere (a)** resist; (*reggere la prova contro*) be proof against. **∼e'nte** *a.* resistant. **∼e'nza** *n.f.* resistance.

re'so *p.p. di* **rendere.**

resoco'nto *n.m.* report.

respi'ng|ere *v.t.* repel; (*rifiutare*) reject; (*bocciare*) fail. **∼e'nte** *n.m.* (*ferrovia*) buffer. **respi'nto** *p.p. di* **∼ere.**

respira'|re *v.t./i.* breathe. **∼to're** *n.m.* respirator. **∼to'rio** *a.* respiratory. **∼zio'ne** *n.f.* breathing; (*med.*) respiration. **respi'ro** *n.m.* breath; (*il respirare*) breathing; (*fig.*) respite.

responsa'bil|e *a.* responsible. **∼e di** responsible for. **∼ità** *n.f.* responsibility; (*legge*) liability.

respo'nso *n.m.* response.

re'ssa *n.f.* crowd.

resta're *v.i.* = **rimanere.**

restaura'|re *v.t.* restore. **∼zio'ne** *n.f.* restoration. **resta'uro** *n.m.* (*riparazione*) repair.

resti'o *a.* restive. **∼ a** reluctant to.

restitu|i're *v.t.* return; (*reintegrare*) restore. **∼zio'ne** *n.f.* restitution.

re'st|o *n.m.* remainder; (*saldo*) balance; (*denaro*) change. **∼i** *n.m. pl.* (*avanzi*) remains. **del ∼o** besides.

restri'nger|e *v.t.* contract; (*vestiti*) take in; (*limitare*) restrict; (*stoffa*) shrink. **∼si** *v.r.* contract; (*farsi più vicini*) close up. (*stoffa*) shrink. **restrizio'ne** *n.f.* restriction.

reta'ta *n.f.* round-up.

re'te *n.f.* net; (*sistema*) network; (*fig.*) trap; (*per la spesa*) string bag.

retice'n|te *a.* reticent. **∼za** *n.f.* reticence.

reticola'to *n.m.* grid; (*rete metallica*) wire netting.

re'tina *n.f.* retina.

reto'rico, a *a.* rhetorical. *—n.f.* rhetoric.

retribu|i're *v.t.* remunerate. **∼zio'ne** *n.f.* remuneration.

re'tro *adv.* behind. **vedi ∼** please turn over. *—n.m. invar.* back.

retroce'dere *v.i.* retreat. *—v.t.* (*mil.*) demote; (*sport*) relegate.

retrodata're *v.t.* backdate.

retro'grado *a.* retrograde; (*fig.*) oldfashioned; (*pol.*) reactionary.

retrogua'rdia *n.f.* (*mil.*) rearguard.

retroma'rcia *n.f.* reverse (gear).

retrosce'na *n.m.* (*theatr.*) backstage; (*fig.*) intrigue.

retrospetti'vo *a.* retrospective.

retrosta'nte *a.* at the back.

retrovi'so're *n.m.* rear mirror.

re'tta[1] *n.f.* (*math.*) straight line; (*pagamento*) fee.

re'tta[2] *n.f.* **dar ∼ a** pay attention to.

retta'ngol|o *a.* right-angled. *—n.m.* rectangle. **∼a're** *a.* rectangular.

retti'fic|a *n.f.* rectification. **∼a're** *v.t.* rectify.

re'ttile *n.m.* reptile.

rettili'neo *a.* rectilinear; (*retto*) upright.

rettitu'dine *n.f.* rectitude.

re'tto *p.p. di* **reggere.** *—a.* straight; (*fig.*) upright; (*giusto*) correct. **angolo ∼** right angle.

retto're *n.m.* rector; (*univ.*) chancellor.

reumati'smo *n.m.* rheumatism.

revere'ndo *a.* reverend.

reversi'bile *a.* reversible.

revisio'n|e *n.f.* revision; (*comm.*) audit; (*mech.*) overhaul. **∼a're** *v.t.* revise; audit; overhaul. **reviso're** *n.m.* (*di conti*) auditor; (*di bozze*) proofreader.

re'voc|a *n.f.* repeal. **∼a're** *v.t.* repeal.

riabilita'|re *v.t.* rehabilitate. **∼zio'ne** *n.f.* rehabilitation.

riacquista're *v.t.* (*recuperare*) recover.

riallaccia're *v.t.* (*riprendere*) renew.

rialza're *v.t.* raise. *—v.i.* rise. **ria'lzo** *n.m.* rise.

rianima're *v.t.* (*med.*) resuscitate; (*ravvivare*) cheer up. **∼si** *v.r.* recover consciousness; cheer up.

riapertu'ra *n.f.* reopening.

riapri'r|e *v.t.*, **∼si** *v.r.* reopen.

ria'rmo *n.m.* rearmament.

riassu'mere *v.t.* (*impiegato*) take on again; (*ricapitolare*) resume.

riassu'nto *p.p. di* **riassumere.** *—n.m.* summary.

riave'r|e *v.t.* have again; (*ricuperare*) have back. **∼si** *v.r.* recover.

ribadi're v.t. (confermare) reaffirm.

riba'lt|a n.f. flap; (theatr.) footlights pl.; (fig.) limelight.

ribalta'|re v.t./i., ∼rsi v.r. tip over. (naut.) capsize. ∼bile a. tip-up.

ribassa're v.t. lower. —v.i. fall. **riba'sso** n.m. fall; (sconto) discount.

riba'ttere v.t. return; (controbattere) confute.

ribell|a'rsi v.r. rebel. **ribe'lle** a. rebellious; n.m./f. rebel. ∼io'ne n.f. rebellion.

ri'bes n.m. invar. (rosso) redcurrant; (nero) blackcurrant.

ribolli're v.i. (fermentare) ferment; (fig.) seethe.

ribre'zzo n.m. disgust. far ∼ (a) disgust.

ributta'nte a. repugnant.

ricad|e're v.i. fall back; (nel peccato ecc.) lapse; (pendere) hang (down). ∼ere su (riversarsi) fall on. ∼u'ta n.f. relapse.

ricalca're v.t. trace.

ricalcitra'nte a. recalcitrant.

ricama're v.t. embroider. **rica'mo** n.m. embroidery.

ricambia're v.t. repay. **rica'mbio** n.m. replacement; (biol.) metabolism. **pezzo di ricambio** spare part.

ricapitola'|re v.t. sum up. ∼zio'ne n.f. summing-up.

ricatta'|re v.t. blackmail. ∼to're, ∼tri'ce n.m., f. blackmailer. **rica'tto** n.m. blackmail.

ricava're v.t. get; (ottenere) obtain; (dedurre) draw. **rica'vo** n.m. proceeds pl.

ricche'zz|a n.f. wealth; (fig.) richness. ∼e n.f. pl. riches.

ri'ccio a. curly. —n.m. (animale) hedgehog. ∼ di mare sea-urchin. ∼lo n.m. curl. ∼lu'to a. curly.

ri'cco, a a. rich. —n.m., f. rich man/woman.

rice'rc|a n.f. search; (indagine) investigation; (scientifica) research. ∼a're v.t. search (for); investigate. ∼a'to a. sought-after; (raffinato) refined; (affettato) affected; n.m. (polizia) wanted man.

rice'tta n.f. (med.) prescription; (culin.) recipe.

rice'v|ere v.t. receive; (dare il benvenuto) welcome; (di albergo) accommodate. ∼ime'nto n.m. receiving; (accoglienza) welcome; (trattenimento) reception.

ricevito're n.m. receiver.

ricevu'ta n.f. receipt.

ricezio'ne n.f. (radio, TV) reception.

richiama're v.t. (al telefono) call back; (far tornare) recall; (rimproverare) rebuke; (attirare) draw. ∼ alla mente call to mind. **richia'mo** n.m. recall; (attrazione) call.

richie'dere v.t. ask (again) for; (volere) request.

richie'sta n.f. request; (comm.) demand.

ri'cino n.m. olio di ∼ castor oil.

ricognizio'ne n.f. (mil.) reconnaissance.

rico'lm|o a. full. ∼a're v.t. fill to the brim.

ricomincia're v.t./i. start again.

ricompari're v.i. reappear.

ricompe'ns|a n.f. reward. ∼a're v.t. reward.

ricompo'r|re v.t. (riscrivere) rewrite; (ricostruire) reform; (typ.) reset. ∼si v.r. regain one's composure.

riconcilia'|re v.t. reconcile. ∼rsi v.r. be reconciled. ∼zio'ne n. reconciliation.

riconosce'n|te a. grateful. ∼za n.f. gratitude.

ricono'sc|ere v.t. recognize; (ammettere) acknowledge. ∼ime'nto n.m. recognition; acknowledgement.

ricopri're v.t. re-cover; (rivestire) coat; (carica) hold.

ricorda'r|e v.t. remember; (richiamare alla memoria) recall; (far ricordare) remind; (rassomigliare) look like. ∼si v.r. ∼si (di) remember.

rico'rd|o n.m. memory; (oggetto) memento; (di viaggio) souvenir. ∼i n.m. pl. (memorie) memoirs.

rico'rr|ere v.i. recur; (accadere) occur; (di data) fall. ∼ere a apply to. ∼e'nte a. recurrent. ∼e'nza n.f. recurrence; (anniversario) anniversary.

rico'rso p.p. di ricorrere. —n.m. recourse; (legge) appeal.

ricostitue'nte n.m. tonic.

ricostitui're v.t. re-establish.

ricostru'|ire v.t. reconstruct. ∼zio'ne n.f. reconstruction.

ricovera're v.t. give shelter to. **rico'vero** n.m. shelter; (ospizio) home.

ricrea'r|e v.t. re-create; (ristorare) restore. ∼si v.r. amuse oneself.

ricreazio'ne n.f. recreation; (schol.) break.

ricre'dersi *v.r.* change one's mind.

ricupera're *v.t.* recover. ∼ **il tempo perduto** make up for lost time. **ricu'pero** *n.m.* recovery; (*salvataggio*) rescue.

ricu'rvo *a.* bent.

ricusa're *v.t.* refuse.

ridacchia're *v.i.* giggle.

rida're *v.t.* give back.

ri'd|ere *v.i.* laugh. ∼**ere di** (*deridere*) laugh at. ∼**e'nte** *a.* (*piacevole*) pleasant.

ride'tto *p.p. di* **ridire.**

ridi'colo *a.* ridiculous.

ridimensiona're *v.t.* reshape; (*fig.*) see in the right perspective.

ridi're *v.t.* repeat; (*criticare*) find fault (with).

ridonda'nte *a.* redundant.

rido'tto *p.p. di* **ridurre.** —*n.m.* (*theatr.*) foyer.

ridu'|rre *v.t.* reduce; (*adattare un romanzo ecc.*) adapt. ∼**rsi** *v.r.* ∼**rsi (a)** be reduced (to). ∼**zio'ne** *n.f.* reduction; adaptation.

riempi'|re *v.t.* fill (up); (*moduli ecc.*) fill in. ∼**rsi** *v.r.* fill (up). ∼**ti'vo** *a.* filling; *n.m.* filler.

rientra'nza *n.f.* recess.

rientra're *v.i.* go/come back in; (*tornare*) return; (*piegare indentro*) recede. ∼ **in** (*far parte*) fall within. **rie'ntro** *n.m.* return; (*di astronave*) re-entry.

riepiloga're *v.t.* recapitulate.

rifa'|re *v.t.* do again; (*riparare*) repair; (*imitare*) imitate. ∼**rsi** *v.r.* (*rimettersi*) recover; (*vendicarsi*) get even. ∼**rsi di** make up for. ∼**tto** *p.p. di* ∼**re.**

riferime'nto *n.m.* reference.

riferi'r|e *v.t.* report. ∼**e a** attribute to. —*v.i.* make a report. ∼**si** *v.r.* ∼**si a** refer to.

rifila're *v.t.* (*tagliare a filo*) trim.

rifini'|re *v.t.* finish off. ∼**tu'ra** *n.f.* finish.

rifiori're *v.i.* blossom again; (*fig.*) flourish again.

rifiuta're *v.t.* refuse. **rifiu'to** *n.m.* refusal. **rifiuti** *n.m. pl.* (*immondizie*) rubbish *s.*

rifless|io'ne *n.f.* reflection; (*osservazione*) remark. ∼**i'vo** *a.* thoughtful; (*gram.*) reflexive.

rifle'sso *p.p. di* **riflettere.** —*n.m.* (*luce*) reflection; (*med.*) reflex. **per** ∼ indirectly.

rifle'tter|e *v.t.* reflect. —*v.i.* think over. ∼**si** *v.r.* be reflected.

rifletto're *n.m.* reflector; (*proiettore*) searchlight.

riflu'sso *n.m.* ebb.

rifocilla'r|e *v.t.* restore. ∼**si** *v.r.* restore oneself.

rifo'ndere *v.t.* (*rimborsare*) refund.

rifo'rm|a *n.f.* reform; (*mil.*) exemption on medical grounds. ∼**a're** *v.t.* reform; (*migliorare*) reform; (*mil.*) declare unfit for military service. ∼**ato'rio** *n.m.* reformatory. ∼**ato're,** ∼**atri'ce** *n.m., f.* reformer.

rifornime'nto *n.m.* supply; (*scorta*) stock; (*di combustibile*) refuelling. **stazione di** ∼ petrol station.

riforni'r|e *v.t.* ∼**e di** provide with. ∼**si** *v.r.* ∼**si (di)** (*far provvista*) stock up (with).

rifra'|ngere *v.t.* refract. ∼**tto** *p.p. di* ∼**ngere.** ∼**zio'ne** *n.f.* refraction.

rifuggi're *v.i.* escape again. ∼ **da** (*fig.*) shun.

rifu'gi|o *n.m.* shelter. ∼**a'rsi** *v.r.* take refuge. ∼**a'to, a** *n.m., f.* refugee.

rifu'lgere *v.i.* shine brightly.

ri'g|a *n.f.* line; (*fila*) row; (*striscia*) stripe; (*scriminatura*) parting; (*regolo*) rule. **a** ∼**he** (*stoffa*) striped; (*quaderno*) ruled. **mettersi in** ∼**a** line up. ∼**a're** *v.t.* (*foglio*) rule; *v.i.* ∼**are dritto** behave well.

riga'gnolo *n.m.* rivulet.

rigattie're *n.m.* junk dealer.

rigenera're *v.t.* regenerate.

rigetta're *v.t.* (*gettare indietro*) throw back; (*respingere*) reject; (*vomitare*) throw up. **rige'tto** *n.m.* rejection.

ri'gid|o *a.* rigid; (*freddo*) severe; (*severo*) strict. ∼**ità** *n.f.* rigidity; severity; strictness.

rigira'r|e *v.t.* turn again; (*ripercorrere*) go round. —*v.i.* walk about. ∼**si** *v.r.* turn round; (*nel letto*) turn over. **rigi'ro** *n.m.* (*imbroglio*) trick.

ri'go *n.m.* line; (*mus.*) staff.

rigo'gli|o *n.m.* bloom. ∼**o'so** *a.* luxuriant.

rigo'nfio *a.* swollen.

rigo'r|e *n.m.* rigours *pl.* **a** ∼**e** strictly speaking. **calcio di** ∼**e** penalty (kick). **essere di** ∼**e** be compulsory. ∼**o'so** *a.* (*severo*) strict; (*scrupoloso*) rigorous.

rigoverna're *v.t.* wash up.

riguarda'r|e *v.t.* look at again; (*considerare*) regard; (*concernere*) concern. ∼**si** *v.r.* take care of oneself.

rigua'rdo *n.m.* care; (*considerazione*) consideration. **nei riguardi di** towards. **riguardo a** with regard to.

rigurgita'nte *a.* ~ **di** swarming with.

rilascia'r|e *v.t.* (*concedere*) grant; (*liberare*) release; (*documento*) issue. ~**si** *v.r.* relax. **rila'scio** *n.m.* release; issue.

rilassa'r|e *v.t.*, ~**si** *v.r.* relax.

rilega'|re *v.t.* (*libro*) bind. ~**to** *a.* bound. ~**tu'ra** *n.f.* binding.

rile'ggere *v.t.* reread.

rile'nto *adv.* **a** ~ slowly.

rileva'nte *a.* remarkable.

rileva'|re *v.t.* (*trarre*) get; (*mettere in evidenza*) point out; (*notare*) notice; (*topografia*) survey; (*comm.*) take over; (*mil.*) relieve. ~**me'nto** *n.m.* survey.

rilie'vo *n.m.* relief; (*geog.*) elevation; (*topografia*) survey; (*importanza*) importance; (*osservazione*) remark. **mettere in** ~ **qcsa.** point sthg. out.

riluce'nte *a.* resplendent.

rilutta'n|te *a.* reluctant. ~**za** *n.f.* reluctance.

ri'm|a *n.f.* rhyme. ~**a're** *v.t./i.* rhyme.

rimanda're *v.t.* (*mandare indietro*) send back; (*posporre*) postpone; (*far ridare un esame*) make s.o. repeat an examination. **rima'ndo** *n.m.* return; postponement; (*in un libro*) cross-reference.

rimane'|re *v.i.* stay, remain; (*essere d'avanzo*) be left; (*venirsi a trovare*) be; (*restare stupito*) be astonished; (*restare d'accordo*) agree. ~**nte** *a.* remaining; *n.m.* remainder. ~**nza** *n.f.* remainder. ~**nze** *n.f. pl.* remnants.

rimarche'vole *a.* remarkable.

rimargina'r|e *v.t.*, ~**si** *v.r.* heal.

rima'sto *p.p. di* **rimanere**.

rimasu'gli *n.m. pl.* (*di cibo*) left-overs.

rimbalza're *v.i.* rebound; (*di proiettile*) ricochet. **far** ~ bounce. **rimba'lzo** *n.m.* rebound; ricochet.

rimbambi'|re *v.i.* be in one's dotage. ~**to** *a.* in one's dotage.

rimbecca're *v.i.* retort.

rimbocca're *v.t.* turn up; (*maniche*) roll up; (*coperte*) tuck in.

rimbomba're *v.i.* resound.

rimborsa're *v.t.* reimburse. **rimbo'rso** *n.m.* repayment.

rimbrotta're *v.t.* reproach. **rimbro'tto** *n.m.* reproach.

rimedia're *v.i.* ~ **a** remedy. —*v.t.*

(*procurare*) scrape up. **rime'dio** *n.m.* remedy.

rimescola're *v.t.* mix (up); (*carte*) shuffle; (*rivangare*) rake up. **mi fa** ~ **il sangue** it makes my blood boil.

rime'ssa *n.f.* (*locale per veicoli*) garage; (*per aerei*) hangar; (*per autobus*) depot; (*di denaro*) remittance; (*di merci*) consignment.

rime'sso *p.p. di* **rimettere**.

rime'tter|e *v.t.* (*a posto*) put back; (*restituire*) return; (*affidare*) entrust; (*perdonare*) remit; (*rimandare*) put off; (*vomitare*) bring up. ~**ci** (*fam.*, *perdere*) lose. ~**si** *v.r.* start again; (*ristabilirsi*) recover; (*di tempo*) clear up.

rimoderna're *v.t.* modernize.

rimonta're *v.t.* (*risalire*) go up; (*mech.*) reassemble. —*v.i.* remount. ~ **a** (*risalire*) go back to.

rimorchia'|re *v.t.* tow. ~**to're** *n.m.* tug(boat). **rimo'rchio** *n.m.* tow; (*veicolo*) trailer.

rimo'rso *n.m.* remorse.

rimostra'nza *n.f.* complaint.

rimovi'bile *a.* removable.

rimozio'ne *n.f.* removal; (*da un incarico*) dismissal.

rimpa'sto *n.m.* (*pol.*) reshuffle.

rimpatria're *v.t./i.* repatriate. **rimpa'trio** *n.m.* repatriation.

rimpia'n|gere *v.t.* regret. ~**to** *p.p. di* ~**gere**; *n.m.* regret.

rimpinza'r|e *v.t.* ~**e di** stuff with. ~**si** *v.r.* stuff oneself.

rimprovera're *v.t.* reproach. **rimpro'vero** *n.m.* reproach.

rimugina're *v.t.* (*fig.*) ~ **su** brood over.

rimunera'|re *v.t.* remunerate. ~**zio'ne** *n.f.* remuneration.

rimuo'vere *v.t.* remove.

Rinascime'nto *n.m.* Renaissance.

rina'scita *n.f.* rebirth.

rincalza're *v.t.* (*sostenere*) support; (*rimboccare*) tuck in. **rinca'lzo** *n.m.* support. **rincalzi** *n.m. pl.* (*mil.*) reserves.

rincantuccia'rsi *v.r.* hide oneself (in a corner).

rincara're *v.t.* increase (the price of). —*v.i.* become dearer.

rincasa're *v.i.* return home.

rinchiu'der|e *v.t.* shut up. ~**si** *v.r.* shut oneself up.

rinco'r|rere *v.t.* run after. ~**so** *p.p. di* ~**rere**.

rinco'rsa *n.f.* run-up.

rincre'sc|ere *v.i.* regret; (*dispiacere*) mind. **se non ti** ~**e** if you don't mind. ~**ime'nto** *n.m.* regret. ~**iu'to** *p.p. di* ~**ere.**

rincula're *v.i.* (*arma*) recoil; (*di cavallo*) shy.

rincuora'r|e *v.t.* encourage. ~**si** *v.r.* take heart.

rinfaccia're *v.t.* throw in someone's face.

rinforza'r|e *v.t.* strengthen; (*rendere più saldo*) reinforce. ~**si** *v.r.* become stronger. **rinfo'rzo** *n.m.* reinforcement; (*fig.*) support.

rinfranca're *v.t.* reassure.

rinfresca'r|e *v.t.* cool; (*rinnovare*) freshen up. —*v.i.* get cooler. ~**si** *v.r.* freshen (oneself) up. **rinfre'sco** *n.m.* light refreshment; (*ricevimento*) party.

rinfu'sa *n.f.* **alla** ~ at random.

ringhia're *v.i.* snarl.

ringhie'ra *n.f.* railing; (*di scala*) banisters *pl.*

ringiovani're *v.t.* make someone look younger. —*v.i.* get young again.

ringrazia'|re *v.t.* thank. ~**me'nto** *n.m.* thanks *pl.*

rinnega'|re *v.t.* disown. ~**to, a** *n.m., f.* renegade.

rinnova'|re *v.t.* renew. ~**rsi** *v.r.* be renewed; (*ripetersi*) happen again. ~**me'nto** *n.m.* renovation. **rinno'vo** *n.m.* renewal.

rinocero'nte *n.m.* rhinoceros.

rinoma'to *a.* renowned.

rinsalda're *v.t.* consolidate.

rinsavi're *v.i.* recover one's wits.

rintana'rsi *v.r.* hide oneself.

rint|occa're *v.i.* (*di campana*) toll; (*di orologio*) strike. ~**o'cco** *n.m.* toll; stroke.

rintraccia're *v.t.* trace.

rintrona're *v.t.* stun. —*v.i.* boom.

rintuzza're *v.t.* blunt; (*ribattere*) retort; (*reprimere*) repress.

rinu'ncia = **rinunzia.**

rinu'nzi|a *n.f.* renunciation. ~**a're** *v.i.* ~**are (a)** renounce, give up.

rinveni're *v.t.* find. —*v.i.* (*riprendere i sensi*) come round; (*ridiventare fresco*) revive.

rinvia're *v.t.* put off; (*mandare indietro*) return. **rinvi'o** *n.m.* putting off; return.

rinvigori're *v.t.* strengthen.

rio'n|e *n.m.* district. ~**a'le** *a.* local.

riordina're *v.t.* tidy (up); (*riorganizzare*) reorganize.

riorganizza're *v.t.* reorganize.

ripaga're *v.t.* repay.

ripara'|re *v.t.* (*proteggere*) shelter, protect; (*aggiustare*) repair; (*porre rimedio*) remedy. —*v.i.* ~**re a** make up for. ~**rsi** *v.r.* take shelter. ~**zio'ne** *n.f.* repair; (*fig.*) reparation. **ripa'ro** *n.m.* shelter; (*rimedio*) remedy.

riparti'|re *v.t.* (*dividere*) divide. —*v.i.* leave again. ~**zio'ne** *n.f.* division.

ripassa're *v.t.* (*rivedere*) revise. —*v.i.* pass again.

ripensa're *v.i.* think again; (*cambiare idea*) change one's mind.

riperco'sso *p.p. di* **ripercuotere.**

ripercuo'ter|e *v.t.* strike again. ~**si** *v.r.* (*suono*) reverberate.

ripercussio'ne *n.f.* repercussion.

ripe't|ere *v.t.* repeat. ~**izio'ne** *n.f.* repetition; (*di lezione*) revision; (*lezione privata*) private lesson. ~**uta-me'nte** *adv.* repeatedly.

ripia'no *n.m.* (*di scaffale*) shelf; (*terreno pianeggiante*) terrace.

ripi'cco *n.m.* spite.

ri'pido *a.* steep.

ripiega'r|e *v.t.* refold; (*abbassare*) lower. —*v.i.* (*indietreggiare*) retreat. ~**si** *v.r.* bend (down). **ripie'go** *n.m.* expedient; (*via d'uscita*) way out.

ripie'no *a.* full; (*culin.*) stuffed. —*n.m.* filling; stuffing.

ripo'rre *v.t.* put back; (*mettere da parte*) put away; (*collocare*) place.

riporta'r|e *v.t.* (*restituire*) bring/ take back; (*riferire*) report; (*subire*) suffer; (*math.*) carry; (*disegno*) transfer. ~**si** *v.r.* go back; (*riferirsi*) refer.

riposa'r|e *v.i.* rest. —*v.t.* put back. ~**si** *v.r.* rest. **ripo'so** *n.m.* rest. **andare a riposo** retire. **riposo!** (*mil.*) at ease!

riposti'glio *n.m.* hiding-place.

ripo'sto *p.p. di* **riporre.**

ripre'nder|e *v.t.* take again; (*prendere indietro*) take back; (*riconquistare*) recapture; (*ricuperare*) recover; (*ricominciare*) resume; (*rimproverare*) reprimand; (*cucitura*) take in; (*cinema*) shoot. ~**si** *v.r.* recover; (*correggersi*) correct oneself.

ripre's|a *n.f.* resumption; (*ricupero*) recovery; (*theatr.*) revival; (*cinema*) shot; (*auto*) acceleration; (*mus.*) repeat. ~**o** *p.p. di* **riprendere.**

ripristina're *v.t.* restore.

riprodo'tto *p.p. di* **riprodurre.**

riprodu'|rre *v.t.*, **~rsi** *v.r.* reproduce. **~tti'vo** *a.* reproductive. **~zio'ne** *n.f.* reproduction.

riprome'ttersi *v.r.* (*intendere*) intend.

ripudia're *v.t.* repudiate.

ripugna'|re *v.i.* disgust. **~nte** *a.* repugnant. **~nza** *n.f.* disgust.

ripuli're *v.t.* clean (up); (*fig.*) polish.

ripuls|io'ne *n.f.* repulsion. **~i'vo** *a.* repulsive.

riqua'dro *n.m.* square; (*pannello*) panel.

risa'cca *n.f.* undertow.

risa'ia *n.f.* rice field.

risali're *v.t.* go back up. —*v.i.* **~ a** (*nel tempo*) go back to.

risalta're *v.i.* (*emergere*) stand out. **risa'lto** *n.m.* prominence; (*rilievo*) relief.

risana're *v.t.* heal; (*bonificare*) reclaim.

risape're *v.t.* come to know.

risarci'|re *v.t.* indemnify. **~me'nto** *n.m.* compensation.

risa'ta *n.f.* laugh.

riscalda'|re *v.t.* heat; (*persona*) warm. **~rsi** *v.r.* warm up. **~me'nto** *n.m.* heating.

riscatta'r|e *v.t.* ransom. **~si** *v.r.* redeem oneself. **risca'tto** *n.m.* ransom; redemption.

rischiara'r|e *v.t.* light up; (*colore*) brighten. **~si** *v.r.* light up; (*di cielo*) clear up.

rischi|a're *v.t.* risk. —*v.i.* run the risk. **ri'schio** *n.m.* risk. **~o'so** *a.* risky.

risciacqua're *v.t.* rinse.

riscontra're *v.t.* (*confrontare*) compare; (*verificare*) check; (*rilevare*) find. **risco'ntro** *n.m.* comparison; check; (*comm., risposta*) reply.

risco'ssa *n.f.* revolt; (*riconquista*) recovery.

riscossio'ne *n.f.* collection.

risco'sso *p.p. di* **riscuotere**.

riscuo'ter|e *v.t.* shake; (*percepire*) draw; (*ottenere*) gain. **~si** *v.r.* rouse oneself.

risenti'|re *v.t.* (*provare*) feel. —*v.i.* **~re di** feel the effect of. **~rsi** *v.r.* (*offendersi*) take offence. **~to** *a.* resentful.

rise'rbo *n.m.* reserve.

rise'rv|a *n.f.* reserve; (*di caccia, pesca*) preserve. **~a're** *v.t.* reserve. **~a'rsi** (*ripromettersi*) intend. **~ate'zza** *n.f.* reserve. **~a'to** *a.* reserved.

risie'dere *v.i.* **~ a** reside in.

ri'sma *n.f.* ream; (*fig.*) kind.

ri'so¹ *p.p. di* **ridere**. —*n.m.* (*pl.f.* **risa**) laughter; (*singolo*) laugh. **~li'no** *n.m.* giggle.

ri'so² *n.m.* (*cereale*) rice.

riso'lto *p.p. di* **risolvere**.

risolu't|o *a.* resolute. **~e'zza** *n.f.* determination.

risoluzio'ne *n.f.* resolution.

riso'lver|e *v.t.* resolve; (*math.*) solve. **~si** *v.r.* (*decidersi*) decide. **~si in** turn into.

risona'|nza *n.f.* resonance. **aver ~nza** (*fig.*) arouse great interest. **~re** *v.i.* resound.

riso'rg|ere *v.i.* rise again; (*tornare in vita*) come back to life. **~ime'nto** *n.m.* revival; (*storia*) Risorgimento.

riso'rsa *n.f.* resource; (*espediente*) resort.

riso'rto *p.p. di* **risorgere**.

risparmia're *v.t.* save; (*salvare*) spare. **rispa'rmio** *n.m.* saving.

rispecchia're *v.t.* reflect.

rispetta'|re *v.t.* respect. **farsi ~re** command respect. **~bile** *a.* respectable.

rispetti'vo *a.* respective.

rispe'tt|o *n.m.* respect. **~o a** as regards; (*in paragone a*) compared to. **~o'so** *a.* respectful.

risple'nd|ere *v.i.* shine. **~e'nte** *a.* shining.

risponde'n|te *a.* **~te a** in keeping with. **~za** *n.f.* correspondence.

rispo'ndere *v.i.* answer; (*rimbeccare*) answer back; (*obbedire*) respond. **~ a** reply to. **~ di** (*rendersi responsabile*) answer for.

rispo'st|a *n.f.* answer, reply. **~o** *p.p. di* **rispondere**.

ri'ssa *n.f.* brawl.

ristabili'r|e *v.t.* re-establish. **~si** *v.r.* (*in salute*) recover.

ristagna're *v.i.* stagnate; (*di sangue*) coagulate. **rista'gno** *n.m.* stagnation.

rista'mp|a *n.f.* reprinting. **~a're** *v.t.* reprint.

ristora'nte *n.m.* restaurant.

ristora'r|e *v.t.* refresh. **~si** *v.r.* refresh oneself. **risto'ro** *n.m.* refreshment; (*sollievo*) relief.

ristre'tt|o *p.p. di* **restringere**. —*a.* narrow; (*condensato*) condensed; (*limitato*) restricted. **di idee ~e** narrow-minded. **~e'zza** *n.f.* narrowness; (*povertà*) poverty. **vivere in ~ezze** live in straitened circumstances.

risucchia're *v.t.* suck in. **risu'cchio** *n.m.* whirlpool; (*di corrente*) undertow.

risulta'|re *v.i.* result; (*riuscire*) turn out. **∼to** *n.m.* result.

risurrezio'ne *n.f.* resurrection.

risuscita're *v.t.* resuscitate; (*fig.*) revive. —*v.i.* return to life.

risve'gli|o *n.m.* waking up; (*fig.*) revival. **∼a'rsi** *v.r.* wake (up).

risvo'lto *n.m.* (*di giacca*) lapel; (*di pantaloni*) turn-up; (*di manica*) cuff; (*di tasca*) flap; (*di libro*) inside cover.

ritaglia're *v.t.* cut out. **rita'glio** *n.m.* cutting; (*di stoffa*) scrap.

rita'rd|o *n.m.* delay. **essere in ∼o** be late. **∼a're** *v.i.* be late; (*di orologio*) be slow; *v.t.* delay; (*differire*) postpone. **∼ata'rio, a** *n.m., f.* late-comer.

rite'gno *n.m.* reserve.

riten|e're *v.t.* retain; (*somma*) deduct; (*credere*) believe. **∼u'ta** *n.f.* (*sul salario*) deduction. **∼zio'ne** *n.f.* (*med.*) retention.

ritira'|re *v.t.* withdraw; (*riscuotere*) draw; (*pacco*) collect. **∼rsi** *v.r.* withdraw; (*tornare a casa*) come/go home; (*dal lavoro*) retire; (*di marea*) recede. **∼ta** *n.f.* retreat. **riti'ro** *n.m.* withdrawal; (*luogo appartato*) retreat; (*dal lavoro*) retirement.

ri'tm|o *n.m.* rhythm. **∼ico** *a.* rhythmic(al).

ri'to *n.m.* rite. **di ∼** customary.

ritocca're *v.t.* (*correggere*) touch up. **rito'cco** *n.m.* retouch.

ritorna're *v.i.* return; (*andare/venire indietro*) go/come back; (*ricorrere*) recur; (*ridiventare*) become again. —*v.t.* (*restituire*) return. **rito'rno** *n.m.* return.

ritorne'llo *n.m.* refrain.

ritra'rre *v.t.* (*ritirare*) withdraw; (*distogliere*) turn away; (*ricavare*) derive; (*rappresentare*) portray.

ritra|tta're *v.t.* (*ritirare*) retract. **∼zio'ne** *n.f.* retraction.

ritra'tto *p.p. di* **ritrarre**. —*n.m.* portrait.

ritro'so *a.* backward; (*timido*) shy. **a ∼** backwards. **∼ a** reluctant to.

ritrova'r|e *v.t.* find (again); (*salute*) regain. **∼si** *v.r.* meet (again); (*capitare*) find oneself; (*raccapezzarsi*) see one's way. **ritro'vo** *n.m.* meeting-place; (*notturno*) night-club.

ri'tto *a.* upright; (*diritto*) straight.

ritua'le *a. & n.m.* ritual.

riunio'ne *n.f.* meeting; (*fra amici*) reunion.

riuni'r|e *v.t.* (*unire*) join together; (*radunare*) gather. **∼si** *v.r.* be reunited; (*adunarsi*) meet.

riusci'|re *v.i.* (*aver successo*) succeed; (*essere capace*) be able; (*aver esito*) turn out. **∼ta** *n.f.* (*esito*) result; (*successo*) success.

ri'va *n.f.* (*di mare, lago*) shore; (*di fiume*) bank.

riva'l|e *n.m./f.* rival. **∼ità** *n.f.* rivalry.

rivanga're *v.t.* dig up again.

rivede're *v.t.* see again; (*verificare*) check.

rivela'|re *v.t.* reveal. **∼rsi** *v.r.* (*dimostrarsi*) turn out. **∼to're** *a.* revealing; *n.m.* (*techn.*) detector. **∼zio'ne** *n.f.* revelation.

rivendica're *v.t.* claim.

rive'ndi|ta *n.f.* (*negozio*) shop. **∼to're, ∼tri'ce** *n.m., f.* retailer.

riverbera're *v.t.* reverberate. **rive'rbero** *n.m.* reverberation; (*bagliore*) glare.

rivere'nza *n.f.* reverence; (*inchino*) curtsy.

riveri're *v.t.* respect; (*ossequiare*) pay one's respects to.

riversa'r|e *v.t.* pour. **∼si** *v.r.* (*di fiume*) flow.

riversi'bile *a.* reversible.

rivesti'|re *v.t.* (*rifornire di abiti*) clothe; (*ricoprire*) cover; (*internamente*) line; (*carica*) hold. **∼rsi** *v.r.* dress oneself again. **∼me'nto** *n.m.* covering.

rivie'ra *n.f.* coast. **la ∼ ligure** the Italian Riviera.

rivi'ncita *n.f.* (*sport*) return match; (*vendetta*) revenge.

rivissu'to *p.p. di* **rivivere**.

rivi'sta *n.f.* review; (*pubblicazione*) magazine; (*theatr.*) revue.

rivi'vere *v.i.* come to life again; (*riprendere le forze*) revive. —*v.t.* relive.

ri'vo *n.m.* brook.

rivo'lger|e *v.t.* turn; (*indirizzare*) address. **∼ e da** (*distogliere*) turn away from. **∼si** *v.r.* turn round. **∼si a** (*indirizzarsi*) turn to.

rivo'lta *n.f.* revolt.

rivolta'r|e *v.t.* turn (over); (*mettendo l'interno verso l'esterno*) turn inside out; (*sconvolgere*) upset. **∼si** *v.r.* (*ribellarsi*) revolt.

rivolte'lla *n.f.* revolver.

rivo'lto *p.p. di* **rivolgere**.

rivoluzio'n|e *n.f.* revolution. ~a're
v.t. revolutionize. ~a'rio, a *a.* &
n.m., f. revolutionary.

rizza'r|e *v.t.* raise; (*innalzare*) erect.
~si *v.r.* stand up; (*capelli*) stand on
end.

ro'ba *n.f.* stuff; (*personale*) belongings
pl.; (*faccenda*) matter. ~ **da matti!**
sheer lunacy!

roba'ccia *n.f.* rubbish.

robu'st|o *a.* sturdy; (*forte*) strong.
~e'zza *n.f.* sturdiness; strength.

ro'cca *n.f.* fortress. ~fo'rte *n.f.*
stronghold.

rocche'tto *n.m.* reel.

ro'ccia *n.f.* rock.

roda'|ggio *n.m.* running in. **in** ~ggio
running in. ~re *v.t.* run in.

ro'd|ere *v.t.* gnaw; (*corrodere*) cor-
rode. ~ersi *v.r.* ~ersi di (*logorarsi*)
be consumed with. ~ito're *n.m.*
rodent.

rodode'ndro *n.m.* rhododendron.

ro'gna *n.f.* scabies *s.*; (*fig.*) nuisance.

rogno'ne *n.m.* kidney.

ro'go *n.m.* (*supplizio*) stake; (*per ca-
daveri*) pyre.

Ro'm|a *n.f.* Rome. r~a'nico *a.* Ro-
mar.esque. r~a'no, a *a.* & *n.m., f.*
Roman.

Romani'a *n.f.* Romania.

roma'ntic|o *a.* romantic. ~i'smo *n.m.*
romanticism.

roma'nza *n.f.* romance.

roma'nz|o *a.* Romance. —*n.m.* novel;
(*storia incredibile romantica*) romance. ~o d'appendice serial story.
~o giallo thriller. ~e'sco *a.* (*strava-
gante*) wild. ~ie're *n.m.* novelist.

ro'mbo *n.m.* rumble; (*math.*) rhom-
bus; (*pesce*) turbot.

ro'mper|e *v.t.* break; (*interrompere*)
break off. —*v.i.* break. ~si *v.r.* break;
(*scoppiare*) burst.

rompica'po *n.m.* nuisance; (*indovi-
nello*) puzzle.

rompico'llo *n.m.* daredevil. **a** ~ at
breakneck speed.

rompighia'ccio *n.m.* ice-breaker.

rompisca'tole *n.m./f.* invar. (*fam.*)
pest.

ro'nda *n.f.* rounds *pl.*

ronde'lla *n.f.* washer.

ro'ndine *n.f.* swallow.

rondo'ne *n.m.* swift.

ronz|a're *v.i.* buzz. ~i'o *n.m.* buzz.

ronzi'no *n.m.* jade.

ro's|a *n.f.* rose. —*a.* & *n.m.* (*colore*)

pink. ~a'io *n.m.* rose-bush. ~a'to *a.*
rosy; *n.m.* (*vino*) rosé (wine). ~eo *a.*
pink.

rose'tta *n.f.* (*coccarda*) rosette; (*mech.*)
washer.

rosa'rio *n.m.* rosary.

rosicchia're *v.t.* nibble; (*rodere*)
gnaw.

rosmari'no *n.m.* rosemary.

ro'so *p.p. di* rodere.

rosola're *v.t.* brown.

rosoli'a *n.f.* German measles.

roso'ne *n.m.* rosette; (*apertura*) rose-
window.

ro'spo *n.m.* toad.

rosse'tto *n.m.* (*per labbra*) lipstick;
(*per guance*) rouge.

ro'ss|o *a.* & *n.m.* red. ~o d'uovo (egg)
yolk. ~o're *n.m.* redness; (*della pelle*)
flush.

rosticceri'a *n.f.* rôtisserie.

ro'stro *n.m.* rostrum; (*becco*) bill.

rota'bile *a.* carriageable.

rota'ia *n.f.* rail; (*solco*) rut.

rota'|re *v.t./i.* rotate. ~zio'ne *n.f.* ro-
tation.

rotea're *v.t./i.* roll.

rote'lla *n.f.* small wheel; (*di mobile*)
castor.

rotola'r|e *v.t./i.* roll. ~si *v.r.* roll
(about). ~o'tolo *n.m.* roll. andare a
rotoli go to rack and ruin.

roto'ndo, a *a.* round. —*n.f.* (*spiazzo*)
terrace.

roto're *n.m.* rotor.

ro'tta[1] *n.f.* (*naut., aeron.*) course. **far
~ per** be bound for. **fuori ~** off
course.

ro'tta[2] *n.f.* (*sconfitta*) rout; (*fig.*) break.
a ~ di collo at breakneck speed.
essere in ~ con be on bad terms
with.

rotta'me *n.m.* scrap; (*fig.*) wreck.

ro'tt|o *p.p. di* rompere. —*a.* broken;
(*stracciato*) torn. ~i *n.m. pl.* (*spiccioli*)
(small) change *s.*

rottu'ra *n.f.* break.

rove'nte *a.* scorching.

rovescia'r|e *v.t.* (*buttare a terra*) up-
set; (*sottosopra*) turn upside-down;
(*rivoltare*) turn inside out; (*liquido,
accidentalmente*) spill; (*governo*) overthrow; (*situazione*) reverse. ~si *v.r.*
(*capovolgersi*) overturn; (*riversarsi*)
pour.

rove'sci|o *a.* (*contrario*) reverse; (*ri-
verso*) supine. **alla** ~a (*capovolto*) upside-down; (*con l'interno all'esterno*)

inside out. —*n.m.* reverse; (*di pioggia*) downpour; (*tennis*) backhand.

rovi'n|a *n.f.* ruin; (*crollo*) collapse. **~a're** *v.t.* ruin; (*guastare*) spoil; *v.i.* crash. **~o'so** *a.* ruinous.

rovista're *v.t.* ransack.

ro'vo *n.m.* bramble.

ro'zzo *a.* rough.

ru'ba *n.f.* **andare a ~** sell like hot cakes.

rubacchia're *v.t.* pilfer.

ruba're *v.t.* steal.

rubine'tto *n.m.* tap.

rubi'no *n.m.* ruby.

ru'brica *n.f.* (*in giornale*) column; (*quaderno con indice*) address book.

ru'de *a.* rough.

ru'dere *n.m.* ruin.

rudim|enta'le *a.* rudimentary. **~e'n-ti** *n.m. pl.* rudiments.

ruffia'no, a *n.m.* pimp. —*n.f.* procuress.

ru'g|a *n.f.* wrinkle. **~o'so** *a.* wrinkled.

ru'ggine *n.f.* rust. **fare la ~** go rusty.

ruggi'|re *v.i.* roar. **~to** *n.m.* roar.

rugia'da *n.f.* dew.

rull|a're *v.i.* roll; (*aeron.*) taxi. **~i'o** *n.m.* rolling; taxiing.

ru'llo *n.m.* roll; (*techn.*) roller.

rum *n.m.* rum.

rume'no, a *a.* & *n.m., f.* Romanian.

rumina're *v.t.* ruminate.

rumo'r|e *n.m.* noise; (*fig.*) rumour. **~eggia're** *v.i.* rumble. **~o'so** *a.* noisy; (*sonoro*) loud.

ruo'lo *n.m.* roll; (*theatr.*) role. **di ~** on the staff.

ruo'ta *n.f.* wheel. **~ di scorta** spare wheel.

ru'pe *n.f.* cliff.

rura'le *a.* rural.

rusce'llo *n.m.* stream.

ru'spa *n.f.* bulldozer.

russa're *v.i.* snore.

Ru'ss|ia *n.f.* Russia. **r~o, a** *a.* & *n.m., f.* Russian.

rustico *a.* rural; (*di carattere*) rough.

rutta're *v.i.* belch. **ru'tto** *n.m.* belch.

ru'vido *a.* coarse.

ruzzol|a're *v.i.* tumble down. **~o'ne** *n.m.* tumble. **cadere a ~oni** tumble down.

S

sa'bato *n.m.* Saturday. **di** ~ on Saturdays.

sa'bbi|a *n.f.* sand. ~**e mobili** quicksand *s.* ~**o'so** *a.* sandy.

sabota'|ggio *n.m.* sabotage. ~**re** *v.t.* sabotage.

sa'cca *n.f.* bag; (*zaino*) kitbag. ~ **da viaggio** travelling-bag.

saccari'na *n.f.* saccharin.

sacce'nte *a.* pretentious. —*n.m./f.* know-all.

sacche'ggi|o *n.m.* sack. ~**a're** *v.t.* sack.

sacche'tto *n.m.* (plastic *o* paper) bag.

sa'cco *n.m.* sack; (*anat.*) sac. **mettere nel** ~ (*fig.*) swindle. ~ **a pelo** sleeping-bag. **un** ~ (*moltissimo*) a lot. **un** ~ **di** (*gran quantità*) lots of.

sacerdo'|te *n.m.* priest. ~**zio** *n.m.* priesthood.

sacrame'nto *n.m.* sacrament.

sacrifica'r|e *v.t.* sacrifice. ~**si** *v.r.* sacrifice oneself. **sacrifi'cio** *n.m.* sacrifice.

sacrile'gio *n.m.* sacrilege.

sa'cro *a.* sacred. ~**sa'nto** *a.* sacrosanct.

sa'd|ico, a *a.* sadistic. —*n.m., f.* sadist. ~**i'smo** *n.m.* sadism.

sae'tta *n.f.* arrow; (*fulmine*) thunderbolt.

safa'ri *n.m. invar.* safari.

saga'ce *a.* shrewd.

sa'ggi|o[1] *n.m.* (*scritto*) essay; (*prova*) proof; (*di metallo*) assay; (*campione*) sample; (*esempio*) example. ~**a're** *v.t.* test.

sa'ggi|o[2] *a.* wise. —*n.m.* (*persona*) sage. ~**e'zza** *n.f.* wisdom.

Sagitta'rio *n.m.* (*astr.*) Sagittarius.

sa'goma *n.f.* shape; (*profilo*) outline. **che** ~**!** (*fam.*) what a character!

sa'gra *n.f.* festival.

sagrest|i'a *n.f.* sacristy. ~**a'no** *n.m.* sacristan.

sa'la *n.f.* hall; (*stanza*) room. ~ **da ballo** ballroom. ~ **operatoria** operating-theatre.

sala'ce *a.* salacious.

sala'me *n.m.* salami.

salamo'ia *n.f.* brine.

sala'rio *n.m.* wages *pl.*

salda'|re *v.t.* solder; (*congiungere*) join; (*pagare*) settle; (*fig.*) consolidate. ~**tu'ra** *n.f.* soldering.

sa'ldo *a.* firm. —*n.m.* (*di conto*) settlement; (*svendita*) sale; (*comm.*) balance.

sa'l|e *n.m.* salt. ~**a're** *v.t.* salt. ~**ati'no** *n.m.* cracker. ~**a'to** *a.* salty; (*costoso*) dear. ~**ie'ra** *n.f.* salt-cellar.

sa'lice *n.m.* willow. ~ **piangente** weeping willow.

salie'nte *a.* outstanding.

sali'na *n.f.* salt-works *s.*

sali're *v.i.* go/come up; (*levarsi*) rise; (*su treno ecc.*) get on; (*in macchina*) get in. —*v.t.* go/come up.

sali'ta *n.f.* climb; (*aumento*) rise. **in** ~ *a.* & *adv.* uphill.

sali'va *n.f.* saliva.

sa'lma *n.f.* corpse.

sa'lmo *n.m.* psalm.

salmo'ne *n.m.* salmon.

salo'ne *n.m.* (large) hall; (*salotto*) reception-room.

salo'tto *n.m.* drawing-room; (*soggiorno*) sitting-room; (*mobili*) drawing-room suite.

salpa're *v.i.* sail. ~ **l'ancora** weigh anchor.

sa'ls|a *n.f.* sauce. ~**ie'ra** *n.f.* sauceboat.

salse'dine *n.f.* saltiness.

salsi'ccia *n.f.* sausage.

salta're *v.i.* jump; (*balzare*) leap; (*esplodere*) blow (up). —*v.t.* jump (over); (*sorvolare*) skip; (*culin.*) sauté. **saltar fuori** spring from nowhere.

saltella're *v.i.* hop; (*di gioia*) prance.

saltimba'nco *n.m.* acrobat.

sa'lto *n.m.* jump; (*balzo*) leap; (*dislivello*) drop. **fare un** ~ **da** (*visitare*) drop in on. **in un** ~ (*fig.*) in a jiffy.

saltua'rio *a.* desultory. **lavoro** ~ casual work.

salu'bre *a.* healthy.

salumeri'a *n.f.* delicatessen. **salu'mi** *n.m. pl.* cold cuts.

salu't|e *n.f.* health. **in perfetta** ~**e** healthy. ~**e!** (*dopo uno starnuto*) bless you!; (*a un brindisi*) cheers! ~**a're** *a.* healthy.

salu't|o *n.m.* greeting; (*di addio*) goodbye; (*mil.*) salute. ~**i** *n.m. pl.* (*ossequi*) regards. ~**a're** *v.t.* greet; (*congedan-*

dosi) say goodbye to; (*portare i saluti a*) give one's regards to; (*mil.*) salute.
sa'lva *n.f.* salvo.
salvacondo'tto *n.m.* safe conduct.
salvadana'io *n.m.* money-box.
salvage'nte *n.m.* lifebelt; (*a giubbotto*) life-jacket.
salvaguarda're *v.t.* safeguard.
salva'|re *v.t.* save; (*proteggere*) protect. **~rsi** *v.r.* save oneself. **~ta'ggio** *n.m.* rescue; (*naut.*) salvage. **battello di ~taggio** lifeboat. **~to're**, **~tri'ce** *n.m., f.* saviour. **~zio'ne** *n.f.* salvation.
salvezza *n.f.* (*sicurezza*) safety.
sa'lvia *n.f.* sage.
salvie'tta *n.f.* serviette.
sa'lvo *a.* safe. —*prep.* except (for). **~ che** *conj.* (*a meno che*) unless; (*eccetto che*) except that.
samarita'no, a *a. & n.m., f.* Samaritan.
sambu'co *n.m.* elder.
sanato'rio *n.m.* sanatorium.
sanci're *v.t.* sanction.
sa'ndalo *n.m.* sandal; (*bot.*) sandalwood.
sa'ngu|e *n.m.* blood. **a ~e freddo** in cold blood. **al ~e** (*di carne*) underdone. **farsi cattivo ~e per** worry about. **occhi iniettati di ~e** bloodshot eyes. **spargimento di ~e** bloodshed. **~i'gno** *a.* blood. **~ina're** *v.i.* bleed. **~ino'so** *a.* bloody.
sanguisu'ga *n.f.* leech.
sa'n|o *a.* sound; (*salutare*) healthy. **di ~a pianta** completely. **~o di mente** sane. **~a're** *v.t.* heal. **~ità** *n.f.* soundness; health. **~ità mentale** sanity. **~ita'rio** *a.* sanitary. **Servizio ~ita-rio** National Health Service.
santifica're *v.t.* sanctify.
sa'nto *a.* holy; (*seguito da nome proprio, spesso abbr. in* **San**) saint (*abbr.* St.). —*n.m.* saint (*abbr.* S. *o* St.).
santua'rio *n.m.* sanctuary.
sanzio'n|e *n.f.* sanction. **~a're** *v.t.* sanction.
sape're *v.t.* know; (*essere capace di*) can; (*venire a sapere*) hear. —*v.i.* **~ di** (*aver sapore*) taste of; (*aver odore*) smell of. —*n.m.* knowledge.
sapie'n|te *a.* wise. —*n.m.* (*uomo colto*) sage. **~za** *n.f.* wisdom.
sapo'n|e *n.m.* soap. **~e'tta** *n.f.* bar of soap.
sapo'r|e *n.m.* taste. **~i'to** *a.* tasty; (*piccante*) spicy.

saracine'sca *n.f.* shutter.
sarca's|mo *n.m.* sarcasm. **~tico** *a.* sarcastic.
Sardegna *n.f.* Sardinia. **sa'rdo, a** *a. & n.m., f.* Sardinian.
sardi'na *n.f.* sardine.
sardo'nico *a.* sardonic.
sa'rto, a *n.m., f.* tailor, dressmaker. **~ri'a** *n.f.* tailor's (shop), dressmaker's (shop); (*arte*) couture.
sa'ss|o *n.m.* stone; (*ciottolo*) pebble. **~o'so** *a.* stony.
sasso'fono *n.m.* saxophone.
Sa'tana *n.m.* Satan. **sata'nico** *a.* satanic.
sate'llite *a. & n.m.* satellite.
sa't|ira *n.f.* satire. **~i'rico** *a.* satiric(al).
satura'|re *v.t.* saturate. **~zio'ne** *n.f.* saturation. **sa'turo** *a.* saturated; (*pieno*) full.
sa'una *n.f.* sauna.
savoia'rdo *n.m.* (*biscotto*) sponge finger.
sazia'r|e *v.t.* satiate. **~si** *v.r.* satisfy one's appetite. **~si di** (*fig.*) grow tired of.
sa'zi|o *a.* satiated; (*stufo*) tired. **~età** *n.f.* **mangiare a ~età** eat one's fill.
sbaciucchia'r|e *v.t.*, **~si** *v.r.* kiss over and over again.
sbada't|o *a.* careless. **~a'ggine** *n.f.* carelessness.
sbadi'gli|o *n.m.* yawn. **~a're** *v.i.* yawn.
sba'f|o *n.m.* sponging. **a ~o** (*gratis*) without paying. **~a're** *v.t.* sponge.
sba'gli|o *n.m.* mistake. **per ~o** by mistake. **~a're** *v.t./i.* make a mistake; (*aver torto*) be wrong. **~are strada** take the wrong way. **~a'rsi** *v.r.* be mistaken.
sballa'|re *v.t.* unpack. **~to** *a.* (*squilibrato*) unbalanced.
sballotta're *v.t.* toss about.
sbalordi'|re *v.t.* stun. —*v.i.* be stunned. **~ti'vo** *a.* amazing.
sbalza're *v.t.* throw; (*da una carica*) dismiss. —*v.i.* bounce; (*saltare*) leap.
sba'lzo *n.m.* bounce; (*sussulto*) jolt; (*di temperatura*) sudden change. **a sbalzi** in spurts. **a sbalzo** (*lavoro a rilievo*) embossed.
sbanda'|re *v.t.* disband. —*v.i.* (*auto.*) skid; (*naut.*) list. **~rsi** *v.r.* (*disperdersi*) disperse. **~ta** *n.f.* skid; list. **prendere una ~ta per** get a crush on.
sbandiera're *v.t.* wave; (*fig.*) display.

sbaraglia're *v.t.* rout. **sbara'glio** *n.m.* rout. **mettere allo sbaraglio** endanger.

sbarazza'r|e *v.t.* clear. ∼**si** *v.r.* ∼**si di** get rid of.

sbarazzi'no, a *a.* mischievous. —*n.m., f.* scamp.

sbarba'r|e *v.t.*, ∼**si** *v.r.* shave.

sbarca're *v.t./i.* disembark. **sba'rco** *n.m.* landing; (*di merci*) unloading.

sba'rr|a *n.f.* bar; (*di passaggio a livello*) barrier. ∼**ame'nto** *n.m.* barricade. ∼**a're** *v.t.* bar; (*ostruire*) block; (*assegno*) cross; (*spalancare*) open wide.

sba'tt|ere *v.t.* bang; (*porta*) slam; (*urtare*) knock; (*culin.*) beat. —*v.i.* bang; slam; (*di ali, vele, ecc.*) flap. ∼**u'to** *a.* tossed; beaten; (*fig.*) run down.

sbava're *v.i.* dribble; (*colore*) smear.

sbellica'rsi *v.r.* ∼ **dalle risa** split one's sides (with laughter).

sbiadi'|re *v.t./i.*, ∼**rsi** *v.r.* fade. ∼**to** *a.* faded; (*fig.*) colourless.

sbianca'r|e *v.t./i.*, ∼**si** *v.r.* whiten.

sbie'co *a.* slanting. **di** ∼ on the slant. **guardare qcno. di** ∼ look askance at s.o. **tagliare di** ∼ cut on the bias.

sbigotti'r|e *v.t.* dismay. —*v.i.*, ∼**si** *v.r.* be dismayed.

sbilancia'r|e *v.t.* unbalance. —*v.i.* (*perdere l'equilibrio*) overbalance. ∼**si** *v.r.* lose one's balance. **sbila'ncio** *n.m.* lack of balance; (*comm.*) deficit.

sbircia'|re *v.t.* cast sidelong glances at. ∼**ta** *n.f.* (furtive) glance.

sbi'rro *n.m.* (*pej.*) policeman.

sbizzarri'rsi *v.r.* satisfy one's whims.

sblocca're *v.t.* unblock; (*mech.*) release; (*prezzi*) decontrol.

sbocca're *v.i.* ∼ **in** (*fiume*) flow into; (*strada*) lead to; (*folla*) pour into. **sbo'cco** *n.m.* flowing; (*foce*) mouth; (*comm.*) outlet.

sboccia're *v.i.* blossom.

sbo'rnia *n.f.* **prendere una** ∼ get drunk.

sborsa're *v.t.* pay.

sbotta're *v.i.* burst out.

sbottona're *v.t.* unbutton.

sbozza're *v.t.* outline. **sbo'zzo** *n.m.* outline.

sbraca'rsi *v.r.* undo one's belt. ∼ **dalle risate** (*fam.*) split one's sides with laughter.

sbraccia'to *a.* bare-armed; (*abito*) sleeveless.

sbraita're *v.i.* bawl.

sbrana're *v.t.* tear to pieces.

sbriciola'r|e *v.t.*, ∼**si** *v.r.* crumble.

sbriga'|re *v.t.* expedite; (*occuparsi*) attend to. ∼**rsi** *v.r.* be quick. ∼**ti'vo** *a.* quick.

sbriglia'|re *v.t.* unbridle. ∼**te'zza** *n.f.* unruliness.

sbrindella'|re *v.t.* tear to shreds. ∼**to** *a.* in rags.

sbrodola're *v.t.* stain.

sbroglia're *v.t.* disentangle.

sbro'nzo *a.* (*fam.*) tight.

sbuca're *v.i.* come out.

sbuccia'r|e *v.t.* peel; (*piselli*) shell. ∼**si** *v.r.* graze oneself.

sbudella'rsi *v.r.* ∼ **dal ridere** split one's sides with laughter.

sbuffa're *v.i.* snort; (*per impazienza*) fume. —*v.t.* puff. **sbu'ffo** *n.m.* puff.

sca'bbia *n.f.* scabies *s.*

sca'br|o *a.* rough. ∼**o'so** *a.* (*fig.*) difficult.

scaccia're *v.t.* chase away.

sca'cc|o *n.m.* check. ∼**hi** *n.m. pl.* (*gioco*) chess *s.*; (*pezzi*) chessmen. **dare** ∼**o matto** checkmate. ∼**hie'ra** *n.f.* chess-board.

scade'nte *a.* shoddy.

scade'|nza *n.f.* (*di contratto*) expiry; (*comm.*) maturity. **a breve/lunga** ∼**nza** short-/long-term. ∼**re** *v.i.* expire; (*valore*) decline; (*debito*) be due.

scafa'ndro *n.m.* diving-suit; (*di astronauta*) spacesuit.

scaffa'le *n.m.* shelf.

sca'fo *n.m.* hull.

scagiona're *v.t.* exonerate.

sca'glia *n.f.* scale; (*di sapone*) flake; (*scheggia*) chip.

scaglia'r|e *v.t.* fling. ∼**si** *v.r.* fling oneself. ∼**si contro** (*fig.*) rail against.

scagli|ona're *v.t.* (*fig.*) space out. ∼**o'ne** *n.m.* echelon; (*di monte*) terrace.

sca'l|a *n.f.* staircase; (*portatile*) ladder; (*mus., misura, fig.*) scale. ∼**a a chiocciola** spiral staircase. ∼**a mobile** escalator; (*dei salari*) cost of living index. ∼**e** *n.f. pl.* stairs.

scala'|re *v.t.* climb; (*ridurre*) scale down. ∼**ta** *n.f.* climbing. ∼**to're**, ∼**tri'ce** *n.m., f.* climber.

scalcina'to *a.* shabby.

scaldaba'gno *n.m.* water-heater.

scaldamu'scoli *n.m. invar.* leg-warmer.

scalda'r|e *v.t.* heat. ∼**si** *v.r.* warm up; (*eccitarsi*) get excited.

scalfi'|re *v.t.* graze. **∼ttu'ra** *n.f.* scratch.

scali'n|o *n.m.* step; (*di scala a pioli*) rung. **∼a'ta** *n.f.* flight of steps.

scalmana'rsi *v.r.* get worked up.

sca'lo *n.m.* slipway; (*aeron., naut.*) port of call. **fare ∼ a** call at; (*aeron.*) land at.

scalo'gna *n.f.* bad luck.

scaloppi'na *n.f.* escalope.

scalpe'll|o *n.m.* chisel. **∼a're** *v.t.* chisel.

scalpo're *n.m.* noise. **far ∼** (*fig.*) cause a sensation.

sca'ltr|o *a.* shrewd. **∼e'zza** *n.f.* shrewdness. **∼i'rsi** *v.r.* become shrewd.

scalza're *v.t.* (*albero*) bare the roots of; (*fig.*) undermine; (*da una carica*) oust.

sca'lzo *a. & adv.* barefoot.

scambia're *v.t.* exchange; (*per errore*) mistake. **sca'mbio** *n.m.* exchange; (*comm.*) trade.

scambie'vole *a.* reciprocal.

scampagna'ta *n.f.* trip to the country.

scampana're *v.t.* chime.

scampana'to *a.* (*gonna*) flared.

scampanella'ta *n.f.* (loud) ring.

scampa'r|e *v.t.* save; (*evitare*) escape. **∼la bella** have a lucky escape. **sca'mpo** *n.m.* escape.

sca'mpolo *n.m.* remnant.

scanalatu'ra *n.f.* groove.

scandaglia're *v.t.* sound.

scandal|izza're *v.t.* scandalize. **∼izza'rsi** *v.r.* be scandalized. **sca'ndalo** *n.m.* scandal. **∼o'so** *a.* scandalous.

Scand|ina'via *n.f.* Scandinavia. **s∼i'navo, a** *a. & n.m., f.* Scandinavian.

scandi're *v.t.* (*verso*) scan; (*parole*) pronounce clearly.

scanna're *v.t.* slaughter.

scansafati'che *n.m./f. invar.* lazy-bones *s.*

scansa'r|e *v.t.* shift; (*evitare*) avoid. **∼si** *v.r.* get out of the way. **sca'nso** *n.m.* **a scanso di** in order to avoid.

scansi'a *n.f.* shelves *pl.*

scantina'to *n.m.* basement.

scantona're *v.i.* turn the corner; (*svignarsela*) sneak off.

scapaccio'ne *n.m.* smack.

scapestra'to *a.* dissolute.

sca'pito *n.m.* loss. **a ∼ di** to the detriment of.

sca'pola *n.f.* shoulder-blade.

sca'polo *n.m.* bachelor.

scappame'nto *n.m.* (*auto*) exhaust.

scappa'|re *v.i.* escape; (*andare in fretta*) dash (off); (*sfuggire*) slip. **∼ta** *n.f.* short visit. **∼te'lla** *n.f.* escapade. **∼to'ia** *n.f.* way out.

scappello'tto *n.m.* cuff.

scarabo'cchi|o *n.m.* scribble. **∼a're** *v.t.* scribble.

scarafa'ggio *n.m.* cockroach.

scaramu'ccia *n.f.* skirmish.

scaraventa're *v.t.* hurl.

scarcera're *v.t.* release (from prison).

scardina're *v.t.* unhinge.

sca'ric|a *n.f.* discharge; (*di arma da fuoco*) volley; (*fig.*) shower. **∼a're** *v.t.* discharge; (*arma, merci*) unload; (*fig.*) unburden. **∼a'rsi** *v.r.* (*di fiume*) flow; (*orologio, batteria*) run down; (*fig.*) unwind. **∼ato're** *n.m.* loader; (*di porto*) docker. **∼o** *a.* unloaded; (*vuoto*) empty; (*orologio*) run down; (*batteria*) flat; (*fig.*) untroubled; *n.m.* unloading; (*di rifiuti*) dumping; (*luogo*) (rubbish) dump; (*auto.*) exhaust; (*idraulico*) drain.

scarlatti'na *n.f.* scarlet fever.

scarla'tto *a.* scarlet.

sca'rno *a.* thin.

sca'rpa *n.f.* shoe.

scarpa'ta *n.f.* slope.

scarseggia're *v.i.* be scarce. **∼ di** (*mancare*) be short of.

sca'rs|o *a.* scarce; (*manchevole*) short. **∼e'zza** *n.f.* scarcity; shortage.

scartame'nto *n.m.* (*ferrovia*) gauge. **∼ ridotto** narrow gauge.

scarta're *v.t.* discard; (*pacco*) unwrap; (*respingere*) reject. —*v.i.* (*deviare*) swerve. **sca'rto** *n.m.* discard; (*rottame*) scrap.

scassa're *v.t.* break. **sca'sso** *n.m.* (*furto*) house-breaking.

scassina're *v.t.* force open.

scatena'r|e *v.t.* (*fig.*) stir up. **∼si** *v.r.* (*fig.*) break out.

sca'tola *n.f.* box; (*di latta*) tin.

scatta're *v.i.* go off; (*balzare*) spring up; (*adirarsi*) lose one's temper; (*foto*) take. **sca'tto** *n.m.* (*balzo*) spring; (*d'ira*) outburst; (*di telefono*) unit; (*dispositivo*) release. **a scatti** jerkily. **di scatto** suddenly.

scaturi're *v.i.* spring.

scavalca're *v.t.* jump over.

scava're *v.t.* dig (up); (*città sepolta*) excavate. **sca'vo** *n.m.* excavation.

sce'gliere *v.t.* choose.

scei'cco *n.m.* sheikh.

scellera'to *a.* wicked.

scelli'no *n.m.* shilling.

sce'lt|a *n.f.* choice. ~o *p.p. di* **sceglie-re**; *a.* select; (*merce ecc.*) choice.

scema're *v.t./i.* diminish.

sce'mo *a.* silly.

sce'mpio *n.m.* havoc. **fare** ~ **di** play havoc with.

sce'n|a *n.f.* scene; (*palcoscenico*) stage. **entrare in** ~**a** (*TV*) go/come on set; (*fig.*) enter the scene. ~**ico** *a.* scenic.

scena'rio *n.m.* scenery.

scena'ta *n.f.* row, scene.

sce'ndere *v.i.* go/come down; (*da vei-colo*) get off; (*da strada*) run down; (*di astri*) sink; (*di notte*) fall; (*diminuire*) drop; (*di fiume*) rise; (*discendere*) de-scend. —*v.t.* go/ come down; descend.

sceneggia're *v.t.* dramatize.

scervella'rsi *v.r.* rack one's brains.

scervella'to *a.* brainless.

sce'so *p.p. di* **scendere**.

sce'ttic|o, a *a.* sceptical. —*n.m., f.* sceptic. ~**i'smo** *n.m.* scepticism.

sce'ttro *n.m.* sceptre.

sche'd|a *n.f.* (index) card. ~**a eletto-rale** ballot-paper. ~**a perforata** punch card. ~**a're** *v.t.* file. ~**a'rio** *n.m.* file; (*mobile*) filing cabinet.

sche'ggia *n.f.* splinter.

sche'letro *n.m.* skeleton.

sche'ma *n.m.* scheme; (*abbozzo*) out-line.

sche'rma *n.f.* fencing.

scherma'glia *n.f.* skirmish.

schermi'rsi *v.r.* protect oneself.

sche'rmo *n.m.* screen.

scherni're *v.t.* mock. **sche'rno** *n.m.* mockery.

sche'rz|o *n.m.* joke; (*trucco*) trick; (*effetto*) play; (*mus.*) scherzo. **fare uno** ~**o a qcno.** play a joke on s.o. **per** ~**o** for fun. **stare allo** ~**o** take a joke. ~**a're** *v.i.* joke; (*giocare*) play. ~**o'so** *a.* playful.

schiacciano'ci *n.m. invar.* nut-crackers *pl.*

schiaccia're *v.t.* crush; (*noce*) crack.

schiaffeggia're *v.t.* slap. **schia'ffo** *n.m.* slap.

schiama'zz|o *n.m.* din. ~**a're** *v.i.* make a racket; (*di galline*) cackle.

schianta'r|e *v.t.* break. ~**si** *v.r.* crash. **schia'nto** *n.m.* crash; (*dolore*) pang.

schiari'r|e *v.t.* clear; (*sbiadire*) fade. —*v.i.*, ~**si** *v.r.* brighten (up). ~**si la gola** clear one's throat.

schia'v|o, a *n.m., f.* slave. ~**itù** *n.f.* slavery.

schie'n|a *n.f.* back. ~**a'le** *n.m.* (*di sedia*) back.

schie'r|a *n.f.* (*mil.*) rank; (*moltitudine*) crowd. ~**ame'nto** *n.m.* lining up. ~**a're** *v.t.* draw up. ~**a'rsi** *v.r.* draw up. ~**arsi con** (*parteggiare*) side with.

schie'tto *a.* frank; (*puro*) pure.

schi'f|o *n.m.* disgust. **mi fa** ~**o** it makes me sick. ~**o'so** *a.* disgusting.

schiocca're *v.t.* crack; (*dita*) snap.

schiu'der|e *v.t.*, ~**si** *v.r.* open.

schiu'm|a *n.f.* foam; (*di sapone*) lather; (*feccia*) scum. ~**a're** *v.t.* skim; *v.i.* foam.

schiu'so *p.p. di* **schiudere**.

schiva're *v.t.* avoid. **schi'vo** *a.* bash-ful.

schizofre'nico *a.* schizophrenic.

schizza're *v.t.* squirt; (*inzaccherare*) splash; (*abbozzare*) sketch. —*v.i.* spurt. **schi'zzo** *n.m.* squirt; splash; sketch.

schizzino'so *a.* squeamish.

sci *n.m.* ski; (*sport*) skiing. ~**a're** *v.i.* ski. ~**ato're**, ~**atri'ce** *n.m., f.* skier.

sci'a *n.f.* wake; (*di fumo ecc.*) trail.

scia'bola *n.f.* sabre.

sciaca'llo *n.m.* jackal.

sciacqua're *v.t.* rinse. **scia'cquo** *n.m.* mouthwash.

sciagu'r|a *n.f.* disaster. ~**a'to** *a.* un-fortunate; (*scellerato*) wicked.

scialacqua're *v.t.* squander.

sciala're *v.i.* spend recklessly.

scia'lbo *a.* pale; (*fig.*) dull.

scia'lle *n.m.* shawl.

scialu'ppa *n.f.* dinghy. ~ **di salva-taggio** lifeboat.

scia'me *n.m.* swarm.

scia'nca'to *a.* lame.

scia'rpa *n.f.* scarf.

scia'tt|o *a.* slovenly; (*di stile*) careless. ~**o'ne, a** *n.m., f.* slovenly person.

scienti'fico *a.* scientific.

scie'nz|a *n.f.* science; (*sapere*) know-ledge. ~**ia'to, a** *n.m., f.* scientist.

sci'mmi|a *n.f.* monkey. ~**otta're** *v.t.* ape.

scimpanzé *n.m. invar.* chimpanzee.

scimuni'to *a.* idiotic.

sci'nder|e *v.t.*, ~**si** *v.r.* split.

scinti'll|a *n.f.* spark. ~**a'nte** *a.* spark-ling. ~**a're** *v.i.* sparkle.

sciocche'zza *n.f.* foolishness; (*assur-dità*) nonsense. **scio'cco** *a.* foolish.

scio'glier|e *v.t.* untie; (*disfare*) undo; (*liberare*) release; (*liquefare*) melt; (*nell'acqua, contratto, ecc.*) dissolve; (*muscoli*) loosen up. ∼**si** *v.r.* release oneself; melt; be dissolved.

scioglili'ngua *n.m. invar.* tongue-twister.

scio'lt|o *p.p. di* **sciogliere.** —*a.* loose; (*agile*) agile; (*disinvolto*) easy. **versi** ∼**i** blank verse *s.* ∼**e'zza** *n.f.* agility; (*disinvoltura*) ease.

scio'per|o *n.m.* strike. ∼**o a singhiozzo** on-off strike. ∼**o bianco** work-to-rule. ∼**a'nte** *n.m.|f.* striker. ∼**a're** *v.i.* go on strike.

scipi'to *a.* insipid.

scippa're *v.t.* (*fam.*) snatch. **sci'ppo** *n.m.* (*fam.*) bag-snatching.

sciro'cco *n.m.* sirocco.

sciro'ppo *n.m.* syrup.

sci'sma *n.m.* schism.

scissio'ne *n.f.* division.

sci'sso *p.p. di* **scindere.**

sciup|a're *v.t.* spoil; (*sperperare*) waste. ∼**a'rsi** *v.r.* get spoiled; (*deperire*) wear oneself out. ∼**i'o** *n.m.* waste.

scivola're *v.i.* slide; (*involontariamente*) slip. **sci'volo** *n.m.* slide; (*techn.*) chute.

sclero'si *n.f.* sclerosis.

scocca're *v.t.* shoot. —*v.i.* shoot out; (*ora*) strike.

scoccia're *v.t.* (*dare noia a*) bother. ∼**rsi** *v.r.* be bothered. ∼**to're,** ∼**tri'ce** *n.m.,f.* bore. ∼**tu'ra** *n.f.* nuisance.

scode'lla *n.f.* bowl.

scodinzola're *v.i.* wag its tail.

sco'gli|o *n.m.* rock. ∼**e'ra** *n.f.* cliff; (*a fior d'acqua*) reef.

scoia'ttolo *n.m.* squirrel.

scola're *v.t.* drain; (*pasta, verdura*) strain. —*v.i.* drip. **sco'lo** *n.m.* drainage.

scola'|ro, a *n.m.,f.* schoolboy, schoolgirl. ∼**re'sca** *n.f.* pupils *pl.* ∼**stico** *a.* school.

scolla'|re *v.t.* (*abito*) cut away the neck of; (*staccare*) unstick. ∼**to** *a.* (*di abito*) low-necked. ∼**tu'ra** *n.f.* neckline.

scolori'|re *v.t.,* ∼**si** *v.r.* fade.

scolpi're *v.t.* carve; (*imprimere*) engrave.

scombina're *v.t.* upset.

scombussola're *v.t.* muddle up.

scomme'ss|a *n.f.* bet. ∼**o** *p.p. di* **scommettere.**

scomme'ttere *v.t.* bet.

scomoda'r|e *v.t.,* ∼**si** *v.r.* trouble.

sco'mod|o *a.* uncomfortable. —*n.m.* trouble. ∼**ità** *n.f.* discomfort.

scompagina're *v.t.* disarrange; (*typ.*) break up.

scomp|ari're *v.i.* disappear. ∼**a'rsa** *n.f.* disappearance. ∼**a'rso** *p.p. di* ∼**arire.**

scompartime'nto *n.m.* compartment.

scomp|iglia're *v.t.* disarrange. ∼**i'glio** *n.m.* confusion.

scompo'|rre *v.t.* take to pieces. ∼**rsi** *v.r.* lose one's calm. ∼**sto** *p.p. di* ∼**rre;** *a.* (*sguaiato*) unseemly; (*disordinato*) untidy.

scomu'nic|a *n.f.* excommunication. ∼**a're** *v.t.* excommunicate.

sconcerta're *v.t.* disconcert; (*rendere perplesso*) puzzle.

sco'ncio *a.* indecent. —*n.m.* disgrace.

sconclusiona'to *a.* incoherent.

ssconcorda'nte *a.* discordant.

scondi'to *a.* unseasoned.

sconfessa're *v.t.* disown.

sconfi'ggere *v.t.* defeat.

sconfina're *v.i.* cross the border; (*in proprietà privata*) trespass.

sconfina'to *a.* unlimited.

sconfi'tt|a *n.f.* defeat. ∼**o** *p.p. di* **sconfiggere.**

sconfo'rto *n.m.* dejection.

scongi|ura're *v.t.* beseech; (*evitare*) avert. ∼**u'ro** *n.m.* entreaty; (*esorcismo*) exorcism.

sconne'sso *p.p. di* **sconnettere.** —*a.* (*fig.*) incoherent.

sconne'ttere *v.t.* (*non connettere*) wander.

sconosciu'to, a *a.* unknown. —*n.m., f.* stranger.

sconquassa're *v.t.* smash; (*sconvolgere*) upset.

sconsidera'to *a.* inconsiderate.

sconsiglia'|re *v.t.* advise against. ∼**bile** *a.* inadvisable.

sconsola'to *a.* disconsolate.

sconta're *v.t.* discount; (*dedurre*) deduct; (*pagare*) pay off; (*pena*) serve. **sco'nto** *n.m.* discount.

sconta'to *a.* (*previsto*) expected. **dare per** ∼ take it for granted.

sconte'nto *a.* displeased. —*n.m.* discontent.

scontra'rsi *v.r.* clash; (*urtare violentemente*) collide. **sco'ntro** *n.m.* clash; collision.

scontri'no *n.m.* ticket.

scontro'so *a.* unsociable.

sconvenie'nte *a.* unprofitable; (*scorretto*) unseemly.

sconvo'l|gere *v.t.* upset; (*mettere in disordine*) disarrange. **~gime'nto** *n.m.* upheaval. **~to** *p.p. di* **~gere**; *a.* distraught.

sco'p|a *n.f.* broom. **~a're** *v.t.* sweep.

scoperchia're *v.t.* uncover.

scope'rta *n.f.* discovery.

scope'rto *p.p. di* **scoprire**. —*a.* uncovered; (*senza riparo*) exposed; (*conto*) overdrawn; (*spoglio*) bare.

sco'po *n.m.* aim. **a ~ di** for the sake of. **allo ~ di** in order to.

scoppia're *v.i.* burst; (*fig.*) break out.

sco'ppio *n.m.* burst; (*di guerra*) outbreak; (*esplosione*) explosion.

scoppietta're *v.i.* crackle.

scopri're *v.t.* discover; (*togliere la copertura a*) uncover; (*statua*) unveil.

scoraggia'|re *v.t.* discourage. **~rsi** *v.r.* lose heart. **~nte** *a.* discouraging.

scorbu'tico *a.* peevish.

scorbuto *n.m.* scurvy.

scorciato'ia *n.f.* short cut.

sco'rcio *n.m.* (*di tempo*) short period.

scorda'r|e *v.t.*, **~si** *v.r.* forget.

sco'rgere *v.t.* make out; (*notare*) notice.

sco'rno *n.m.* disgrace.

scorpaccia'ta *n.f.* bellyful. **fare una ~ di** stuff oneself with.

scorpio'ne *n.m.* scorpion; (*astr.*) Scorpio.

scorrazza're *v.i.* run about.

sco'rr|ere *v.t.* (*dare un'occhiata*) glance through. —*v.i.* run; (*scivolare*) slide; (*fluire*) flow. **~e'vole** *a.* **porta ~evole** sliding door.

scorreri'a *n.f.* raid.

scorre'tt|o *a.* incorrect; (*sconveniente*) improper. **~e'zza** *n.f.* (*mancanza di educazione*) bad manners *pl*.

scorriba'nda *n.f.* raid; (*fig.*) excursion.

sco'rsa *n.f.* glance.

sco'rso *p.p. di* **scorrere**. —*a.* last.

scorso'io *a.* **nodo ~** noose.

sco'rt|a *n.f.* escort; (*provvista*) supply. **~a're** *v.t.* escort.

scorte's|e *a.* discourteous. **~i'a** *n.f.* discourtesy.

scortica'|re *v.t.* skin. **~tu'ra** *n.f.* graze.

sco'rto *p.p. di* **scorgere**.

sco'rza *n.f.* peel; (*crosta*) crust; (*corteccia*) bark.

scosce'so *a.* steep.

sco'sso, a *p.p. di* **scuotere**. —*a.* shaken; (*sconvolto*) upset. —*n.f.* shake; (*electr.*, *fig.*) shock.

scosta'|re *v.t.* shift. **~rsi** *v.r.* stand aside. **~nte** *a.* off-putting (*fam.*).

scostuma'to *a.* dissolute; (*maleducato*) ill-mannered.

scotta'|re *v.t.* scald. —*v.i.* burn; (*bevanda*) be (too) hot. **~nte** *a.* (*argomento*) dangerous. **~tu'ra** *n.f.* burn; (*da liquido*) scald.

sco'tto *a.* overcooked.

scova're *v.t.* (*scoprire*) discover.

Sco'z|ia *n.f.* Scotland. **s~ze'se** *a.* Scottish; *n.m./f.* Scot.

screanza'to *a.* rude.

scredita're *v.t.* discredit.

screma're *v.t.* skim.

screpola|re *v.t.*, **~rsi** *v.r.* crack. **~to** *a.* (*labbra*) chapped. **~tu'ra** *n.f.* crack.

screzia'to *a.* speckled.

scre'zio *n.m.* disagreement.

scribacch|ia're *v.t.* scribble. **~i'no, a** *n.m.*, *f.* scribbler.

scricchiol|a're *v.i.* creak. **~i'o** *n.m.* creaking.

scri'cciolo *n.m.* wren.

scri'gno *n.m.* casket.

scriminatu'ra *n.f.* parting.

scri'tto, a *p.p. di* **scrivere**. —*a.* written. —*n.m.* writing; (*lettera*) letter. —*n.f.* inscription.

scritto'io *n.m.* writing-desk.

scrit|to're, ~tri'ce *n.m.*, *f.* writer.

scrittu'ra *n.f.* writing; (*relig.*) scripture.

scrittura're *v.t.* engage.

scrivani'a *n.f.* desk.

scri'vere *v.t.* write; (*descrivere*) write about. **~ a macchina** type.

scrocc|a're *v.t.* **~are a** sponge on. **~o'ne, a** *n.m.*, *f.* sponger.

scro'fa *n.f.* sow.

scrolla're *v.t.* shake. **~ le spalle** shrug one's shoulders.

scroscia're *v.i.* roar; (*pioggia*) pelt (down). **scro'scio** *n.m.* roar; pelting; (*di applausi*) burst.

scrosta'r|e *v.t.* scrape. **~si** *v.r.* peel off.

scru'pol|o *n.m.* scruple; (*diligenza*) care. **~o'so** *a.* scrupulous.

scruta'|re *v.t.* scan; (*indagare*) search. **~to're** *n.m.* (*alle elezioni*) returning officer.

scrut|ina're *v.t.* scrutinize. **~i'nio**

n.m. (*di voti alle elezioni*) poll; (*schol.*) assessment of progress.

scuci're *v.t.* unstitch.

scuderi'a *n.f.* stable.

scudie'ro *n.m.* squire; (*di corte*) equerry.

scudiscia're *v.t.* lash. ~**ta** *n.f.* lash.

scu'do *n.m.* shield.

scugni'zzo *n.m.* (street) urchin.

sculaccia'|re *v.t.* spank. ~**ta** *n.f.* spanking.

scul|to're, ~**tri'ce** *n.m.*, *f.* sculptor. ~**tu'ra** *n.f.* sculpture.

scuo'la *n.f.* school. ~ **elementare /media** primary/secondary school.

scuo'ter|e *v.t.* shake. ~**si** *v.r.* (*destarsi*) rouse oneself. ~**si di dosso** shake off.

scu're *n.f.* axe.

scu'r|o *a.* dark. —*n.m.* darkness; (*imposta*) shutter. ~**i're** *v.t./i.* darken.

scu'rrile *a.* scurrilous.

scu's|a *n.f.* excuse; (*giustificazione*) apology. **chiedere** ~**a** apologize. **chiedo** ~**a!** I am sorry! ~**a're** *v.t.* excuse. ~**a'rsi** *v.r.* ~**arsi (di)** apologize (for).

sdebita'rsi *v.r.* (*disobbligarsi*) repay a kindness.

sde'gn|o *n.m.* disdain. ~**a're** *v.t.* despise. ~**a'rsi** *v.r.* get angry. ~**a'to** *a.* indignant. ~**o'so** *a.* disdainful.

sdenta'to *a.* toothless.

sdolcina'to *a.* mawkish; (*fam.*) sloppy.

sdoppia're *v.t.* halve.

sdraia'rsi *v.r.* lie down.

sdra'io *n.m.* **sedia a** ~ deck-chair.

sdrucciol|a're *v.i.* slither. ~**e'vole** *a.* slippery.

se *conj.* if; (*dubitativo*) whether; ~ **mai** (*caso mai*) in case; (*in tal caso*) if necessary. ~ **no** or else. ~ **non altro** at least. ~ **pure** (*sebbene*) even though.

sé *pron.* one(self); (*lui*) him(self); (*lei*) her(self); (*esso*, *essa*) it(self); (*loro*) them(selves).

sebbe'ne *conj.* although.

secca'|re *v.t.* dry; (*importunare*) annoy. —*v.i.* dry up. ~**rsi** *v.r.* dry up; get annoyed; (*annoiarsi*) get bored. ~**to're** *n.m.* nuisance. ~**tu'ra** *n.f.* bother.

se'cchi|o *n.m.* pail. ~**e'llo** *n.m.* bucket.

se'cco, a *a.* dry; (*dissecato*) dried; (*magro*) thin; (*brusco*) curt; (*preciso*)

sharp. —*n.m.* (*siccità*) drought. —*n.f.* shoal. **lavare a** ~ dry-clean. **nave in** ~ ship aground.

secola're *a.* age-old; (*laico*) secular.

se'colo *n.m.* century; (*epoca*) age.

seco'ndo, a *a.* second. —*n.m.* second; (*secondo piatto*) main course. —*n.f.* (*schol.*, *ferrovia*) second class; (*auto.*) second gear. —*prep.* according to. ~ **me** in my opinion.

secrezio'ne *n.f.* secretion.

se'dano *n.m.* celery.

sedati'vo *a.* & *n.m.* sedative.

se'de *n.f.* seat; (*centro*) centre; (*relig.*) see; (*comm.*) registered office.

sedenta'rio *a.* sedentary.

sede'r|e *v.i.* sit. ~**si** *v.r.* sit down. —*n.m.* (*deretano*) bottom.

se'dia *n.f.* chair.

sedice'nte *a.* self-styled.

se'dici *a.* & *n.m.* sixteen.

sedi'le *n.m.* seat; (*panchina*) bench.

sedime'nto *n.m.* sediment.

sedizio'|ne *n.f.* sedition. ~**so** *a.* seditious.

sedo'tto *p.p. di* **sedurre.**

seduce'nte *a.* seductive; (*allettante*) enticing.

sedu'|rre *v.t.* seduce. ~**zio'ne** *n.f.* seduction.

sedu'ta *n.f.* session; (*di posa*) sitting.

se'g|a *n.f.* saw. ~**a're** *v.t.* saw. ~**atu'ra** *n.f.* sawdust.

se'gala *n.f.* rye.

se'ggio *n.m.* seat. ~ **elettorale** polling station.

seggiolo'ne *n.m.* (*per bambini*) high chair.

seggiovi'a *n.f.* chair-lift.

segheri'a *n.f.* sawmill.

segme'nto *n.m.* segment.

segna'l|e *n.m.* signal; (*stradale*) sign. ~**a're** *v.t.* signal; (*annunciare*) announce; (*indicare*) point out. ~**a'rsi** *v.r.* distinguish oneself. ~**e'tica** *n.f.* signals *pl.* ~**etica stradale** road signs *pl.*

segnali'bro *n.m.* book-mark.

segna'r|e *v.t.* mark; (*prendere nota*) note; (*indicare*) indicate; (*sport*) score. ~**si** *v.r.* cross oneself. **se'gno** *n.m.* sign; (*traccia*, *limite*) mark; (*bersaglio*) target. **far segno** (*col capo*) nod; (*con la mano*) beckon.

segrega'|re *v.t.* segregate. ~ **zio'ne** *n.f.* segregation.

segreta'rio, a *n.m.*, *f.* secretary. ~ **comunale** town clerk.

segreteri'a *n.f.* (*ufficio*) (administrative) office; (*segretariato*) secretariat. ∼ **telefonica** telephone answering-machine.

segre't|o *a.* & *n.m.* secret. ∼e'zza *n.f.* secrecy.

segua'ce *n.m.|f.* follower.

segue'nte *a.* following; (*futuro*) next.

segui're *v.t.|i.* follow; (*continuare*) continue.

se'guit|o *n.m.* retinue; (*sequela*) series; (*continuazione*) continuation. **di** ∼**o** in succession. **in** ∼**o** later on. **in** ∼**o a** owing to. ∼**a're** *v.t.|i.* continue.

se'i *a.* & *n.m.* six.

seice'nto *a.* & *n.m.* six hundred. **il S**∼ the seventeenth century.

seimi'la *a.* & *n.m.* six thousand.

selcia'to *n.m.* pavement.

seletti'vo *a.* selective.

selezio'n|e *n.f.* selection. ∼**a're** *v.t.* select.

se'll|a *n.f.* saddle. ∼**a're** *v.t.* saddle.

se'lva *n.f.* forest.

selvaggi'na *n.f.* game.

selva'ggio, a *a.* wild; (*primitivo*) savage. —*n.m., f.* savage.

selva'tico *a.* wild.

sema'foro *n.m.* traffic-lights *pl.*

sema'ntica *n.f.* semantics *s.*

sembra're *v.i.* seem; (*assomigliare*) look like. **che te ne sembra?** what do you think of it?

se'me *n.m.* seed; (*sperma*) semen.

seme'stre *n.m.* half-year.

semice'rchio *n.m.* semicircle.

semifina'le *n.f.* semifinal.

semina're *v.t.* sow. **se'mina** *n.f.* sowing.

semina'rio *n.m.* seminar; (*relig.*) seminary.

seminterra'to *n.m.* basement.

semi'tico *a.* Semitic.

se'mola *n.f.* bran.

semoli'no *n.m.* semolina.

se'mpli|ce *a.* simple. **in parole** ∼**ci** in plain words. ∼**cio'tto, a** *n.m., f.* simpleton. ∼**cità** *n.f.* simplicity. ∼**fica're** *v.t.* simplify.

se'mpre *adv.* always; (*ancora*) still. **per** ∼ for ever. ∼ **più** more and more.

sempreve'rde *a.* & *n.m.* evergreen.

se'nape *n.f.* mustard.

sena't|o *n.m.* senate. ∼**o're** *n.m.* senator.

seni'l|e *a.* senile. ∼**ità** *n.f.* senility.

se'nno *n.m.* sense.

se'no *n.m.* (*petto*) breast; (*anat.*) sinus.

sensa'le *n.m.* broker.

sensazio'n|e *n.f.* sensation. ∼**a'le** *a.* sensational.

sensi'bil|e *a.* sensitive; (*notevole*) considerable. ∼**ità** *n.f.* sensitivity.

se'ns|o *n.m.* sense; (*significato*) meaning. **far** ∼**o a qcno.** make someone shudder. **in** ∼**o orario/ antiorario** clockwise/anticlockwise. **perdere i** ∼**i** lose consciousness. ∼**o unico** (*strada*) one-way. ∼**a'to** *a.* sensible.

sensua'l|e *a.* sensual. ∼**ità** *n.f.* sensuality.

sente'nz|a *n.f.* sentence; (*massima*) saying. ∼**ia're** *v.i.* (*legge*) pass judgment.

sentie'ro *n.m.* path.

sentime'nt|o *n.m.* feeling. ∼**a'le** *a.* sentimental.

sentine'lla *n.f.* sentry.

senti'r|e *v.t.* feel; (*udire*) hear; (*ascoltare*) listen; (*gustare*) taste; (*odorare*) smell. —*v.i.* feel; hear; taste of; smell of. ∼**si** feel. ∼**si di fare qcsa.** feel like doing sthg.

senti'to *a.* (*sincero*) sincere. **per** ∼ **dire** by hearsay.

sento're *n.m.* inkling.

se'nza *prep.* without. **senz'altro** certainly. ∼ **dubbio** no doubt. ∼ **fine** endless. ∼ **un soldo** penniless.

separa'|re *v.t.* separate. ∼**rsi** *v.r.* separate; (*amici*) part. ∼**zio'ne** *n.f.* separation.

sepo'lcro *n.m.* sepulchre.

sepo'lto *p.p. di* **seppellire.**

sepoltu'ra *n.f.* burial.

seppelli're *v.t.* bury.

se'ppia *n.f.* cuttle fish. **nero di** ∼ sepia.

seque'la *n.f.* succession.

seque'nza *n.f.* sequence.

sequestra're *v.t.* (*rapire*) kidnap; (*legge*) impound; (*segregare*) segregate. **seque'stro** *n.m.* (*per debiti*) distress; (*di persona*) kidnapping.

se'r|a *n.f.* evening. **di** ∼**a** in the evening. ∼**a'le** *a.* evening. ∼**alme'nte** *adv.* every evening. ∼**a'ta** *n.f.* evening; (*ricevimento*) party.

serba're *v.t.* keep; (*odio*) harbour; (*speranza*) cherish.

serbato'io *n.m.* tank. ∼ **d'acqua** reservoir.

se'rbo *n.m.* **mettere in** ∼ put aside.

serena'ta *n.f.* serenade.

sere'n|o *a.* serene; (*cielo*) clear. ∼**ità** *n.f.* serenity.

serge'nte *n.m.* sergeant.

se'rie *n.f. invar.* series; (*complesso*) set. **fuori** ∼ custom-built. **produzione in** ∼ mass production.

se'ri|o *a.* serious; (*degno di fiducia*) reliable. **sul** ∼**o** seriously; (*davvero*) really. ∼**età** *n.f.* seriousness.

sermo'ne *n.m.* sermon.

serpeggia're *v.i.* meander; (*diffondersi*) spread.

serpe'nte *n.m.* snake. ∼ **a sonagli** rattlesnake.

se'rra *n.f.* greenhouse.

serra'nda *n.f.* shutter.

serra're *v.t.* shut; (*stringere*) tighten; (*incalzare*) press on.

serratu'ra *n.f.* lock.

servi'r|e *v.t.* serve; (*al ristorante*) wait on. −*v.i.* serve; (*essere utile*) be of use. ∼**si** *v.r.* (*di cibo*) help oneself. ∼**si da** buy from. ∼**si di** use. **non serve** it is no good.

servi'zi|o *n.m.* service; (*da caffè ecc.*) set. ∼ *n.m. pl.* bathroom and kitchen. **donna di** ∼**o** maid. **essere di** ∼**o** be on duty. **fare** ∼**o** (*di autobus ecc.*) run. ∼**e'vole** *a.* obliging.

se'rv|o, a *n.m., f.* servant. ∼**itù** *n.f.* servitude; (*personale di servizio*) servants *pl.*

sessa'nt|a *a. & n.m.* sixty. ∼**i'na** *n.f.* **una** ∼**ina** about sixty.

sessio'ne *n.f.* session.

se'ss|o *n.m.* sex. ∼**ua'le** *a.* sexual. ∼**ualità** *n.f.* sexuality.

se'sto[1] *a. & n.m.* sixth.

se'sto[2] *n.m.* (*ordine*) order.

se'ta *n.f.* silk.

seta'cci|o *n.m.* sieve. ∼**a're** *v.t.* sieve.

se'te *n.f.* thirst. **avere** ∼ be thirsty.

se'tola *n.f.* bristle.

se'tta *n.f.* sect.

setta'nt|a *a. & n.m.* seventy. ∼**i'na** *n.f.* **una** ∼**ina** about seventy.

se'tte *a. & n.m.* seven.

settece'nto *a. & n.m.* seven hundred. **il S**∼ the eighteenth century.

sette'mbre *n.m.* September.

settentrio'n|e *n.m.* north. ∼**a'le** *a.* northern; *n.m./f.* northerner.

se'ttico *a.* septic.

settima'n|a *n.f.* week. ∼**a'le** *a. & n.m.* weekly.

se'ttimo *a. & n.m.* seventh.

setto're *n.m.* sector.

seve'r|o *a.* severe; (*rigoroso*) strict. ∼**ità** *n.f.* severity.

sevi'zi|e *n.f. pl.* torture *s.* ∼**a're** *v.t.* torture.

sezio'n|e *n.f.* section; (*reparto*) department; (*med.*) dissection. ∼**a're** *v.t.* divide; dissect.

sfaccenda're *v.i.* bustle about.

sfaccenda'to *a.* idle.

sfacchina'|re *v.i.* toil. ∼**ta** *n.f.* drudgery.

sfaccia't|o *a.* cheeky. ∼**a'ggine** *n.f.* cheek.

sface'lo *n.m.* ruin.

sfalda'rsi *v.r.* flake off.

sfama're *v.t.* feed.

sfa'rz|o *n.m.* pomp. ∼**o'so** *a.* sumptuous.

sfasa'to *a.* (*fam.*) confused.

sfascia'r|e *v.t.* unbandage; (*fracassare*) smash. ∼**si** *v.r.* fall to pieces.

sfavilla'|re *v.i.* sparkle. ∼**nte** *a.* sparkling.

sfavore'vole *a.* unfavourable.

sfe'r|a *n.f.* sphere. ∼**ico** *a.* spherical.

sferra're *v.t.* (*cavallo*) unshoe; (*scagliare*) land.

sfe'rz|a *n.f.* whip. ∼**a're** *v.t.* whip.

sfibra'|re *v.t.* exhaust. ∼**to** *a.* exhausted.

sfi'd|a *n.f.* challenge. ∼**a're** *v.t.* challenge.

sfidu'ci|a *n.f.* mistrust. ∼**a'to** *a.* discouraged.

sfigura're *v.t.* disfigure. −*v.i.* (*far cattiva figura*) cut a poor figure.

sfilaccia'r|e *v.t.*, ∼**si** *v.r.* fray.

sfila'r|e *v.t.* unthread; (*togliere di dosso*) take off. −*v.i.* (*truppe*) march past; (*in parata*) parade. ∼**si** *v.r.* come unthreaded; take off.

sfila'ta *n.f.* parade; (*sfilza*) series. ∼ **di moda** fashion show.

sfi'nge *n.f.* sphinx.

sfini'to *a.* worn out.

sfiora're *v.t.* skim; (*argomento*) touch on.

sfiori're *v.i.* wither.

sfi'tto *a.* vacant.

sfoca'to *a.* out of focus.

sfocia're *v.i.* ∼ **in** flow into.

sfodera'to *a.* unlined.

sfoga'r|e *v.t.* vent. ∼**si** *v.r.* give vent to one's feelings.

sfoggia're *v.t./i.* show off.

sfo'glia *n.f.* sheet of pastry. **pasta** ∼ puff pastry.

sfoglia're *v.t.* leaf through.

sfo'go *n.m.* outlet; (*fig.*) outburst; (*med.*) rash.

sfolgora're *v.i.* blaze. ~**nte** *a.* blazing.

sfolla're *v.t.* clear. —*v.i.* (*mil.*) evacuate.

sfolti're *v.t.* thin (out).

sfonda're *v.t.* break down. —*v.i.* (*aver successo*) make one's name.

sfo'ndo *n.m.* background.

sforma'|rsi *v.i.* lose one's shape. ~**to** *n.m.* (*culin.*) flan.

sforni'to *a.* ~ **di** (*negozio*) out of.

sfortu'n|a *n.f.* bad luck; misfortune. ~**a'to** *a.* unlucky.

sforza'r|e *v.t.* force. ~**si** *v.r.* try hard. **sfo'rzo** *n.m.* effort; (*tensione*) strain.

sfratta're *v.t.* evict. **sfra'tto** *n.m.* eviction.

sfrega're *v.t.* rub.

sfregia're *v.t.* slash. **sfre'gio** *n.m.* slash.

sfrena'|rsi *v.r.* run wild. ~**to** *a.* wild.

sfronta'to *a.* shameless.

sfrutta're *v.t.* exploit.

sfugge'nte *a.* receding.

sfuggi'|re *v.i.* escape. ~**ta** *adv.* **di** ~**ta** in passing.

sfuma'|re *v.i.* (*svanire*) vanish; (*colore*) shade off. —*v.t.* (*colore*) soften. ~**tu'ra** *n.f.* shade.

sfuria'ta *n.f.* outburst (of anger).

sgabe'llo *n.m.* stool.

sgabuzzi'no *n.m.* closet.

sgamb|etta're *v.i.* kick one's legs. ~**e'tto** *n.m.* **fare lo** ~**etto a qcno.** trip s.o. up.

sganascia'rsi *v.r.* ~ **dalle risa** roar with laughter.

sgancia'r|e *v.t.* unhook; (*ferrovia*) uncouple; (*bombe*) drop. ~**si** *v.r.* (*fig.*) get away.

sganghera'to *a.* ramshackle.

sgarba'to *a.* rude. **sga'rbo** *n.m.* discourtesy.

sgargia'nte *a.* garish.

sgattaiola're *v.i.* slip away.

sgela're *v.t./i.* thaw.

sghe'mbo *a.* slanting. **a** ~ obliquely.

sghignazza're *v.i.* laugh scornfully.

sgobb|a're *v.i.* slog; (*sl.*, *di studente*) swot. ~**o'ne, a** *n.m.*, *f.* slogger; swot.

sgocciola're *v.i.* drip.

sgola'rsi *v.r.* shout oneself hoarse.

sgomb(e)ra're *v.t.* clear (out). **sgo'mbro** *a.* clear; *n.m.* (*trasloco*) removal; (*pesce*) mackerel.

sgomenta'r|e *v.t.* dismay. ~**si** *v.r.* be dismayed. **sgome'nto** *n.m.* dismay.

sgonfia'r|e *v.t.* deflate. ~**si** *v.r.* go down.

sgo'rbio *n.m.* scrawl; (*fig.*, *vista sgradevole*) sight.

sgorga're *v.i.* gush (out).

sgozza're *v.t.* cut someone's throat.

sgrad|e'vole *a.* disagreeable. ~**i'to** *a.* unwelcome.

sgrana're *v.t.* (*piselli*) shell; (*occhi*) open wide.

sgranchi'r|e *v.t.*, ~**si** *v.r.* stretch.

sgranocchia're *v.t.* munch.

sgrazia'to *a.* ungainly.

sgretola'r|e *v.t.*, ~**si** *v.r.* crumble.

sgrida'|re *v.t.* scold. ~**ta** *n.f.* scolding.

sguaia'to *a.* coarse.

sgualci're *v.t.* crumple.

sgualdri'na *n.f.* slut.

sgua'rdo *n.m.* look; (*breve*) glance.

sgua'ttera *n.f.* scullery maid.

sguazza're *v.i.* splash; (*nel fango*) wallow.

sguinzaglia're *v.t.* unleash.

sguscia're *v.t.* shell. —*v.i.* (*sfuggire*) slip (away).

si *pron. r.* oneself; *m.* himself; *f.* herself; *neutro* itself; *pl.* themselves; (*reciproco*) each other; (*tra più di due*) one another; (*indef.*) one; you; we; they. **non** ~ **sa mai** one never can tell; you never know. —*n.m.* (*mus.*) te.

sì *adv.* yes.

si'a *conj.* ~ ... ~ (*o ... o*) whether ... or; either ... or; (*entrambi*) both. ~ **che venga** ~ **che non venga** whether he comes or not. ~ **questo** ~ **quello** either this or that. **verranno** ~ **Giuseppe** ~ **Giacomo** both Joseph and James are coming.

siame'se *a.* Siamese.

sibila're *v.i.* hiss. **si'bilo** *n.m.* hiss.

sica'rio *n.m.* (*hired*) killer.

sicché *conj.* (*perciò*) so (that); (*allora*) then.

siccità *n.f.* drought.

sicco'me *conj.* as.

Sici'li|a *n.f.* Sicily. **s**~**a'no, a** *a.* & *n.m.*, *f.* Sicilian.

sicu'ra *n.f.* safety-catch.

sicu'r|o *a.* (*non pericoloso*) safe; (*certo*) sure; (*saldo*) steady; (*comm.*) sound. —*adv.* certainly. —*n.m.* safety. ~**e'zza** *n.f.* (*certezza*) certainty; (*salvezza*) safety.

siderurgi'a *n.f.* iron and steel industry.

si'dro *n.m.* cider.

sie'pe *n.f.* hedge.

sie'ro *n.m.* serum.

sie'sta *n.f.* (afternoon) nap.

sifo'ne *n.m.* siphon.

Sig. *abbr.* (*di signore*) Mr.

sigare'tta *n.f.* cigarette.

si'garo *n.m.* cigar.

Sigg. *abbr.* (*di signori*) Messrs.

sigi'll|o *n.m.* seal. ~a're *v.t.* seal.

si'gl|a *n.f.* initials *pl.* ~a musicale signature tune. ~a're *v.t.* initial.

Sig.na *abbr.* (*di signorina*) Miss.

significa'|re *v.t.* mean. ~nte, ~ti'vo *adjs.* significant. ~to *n.m.* meaning.

signo'r|e, a *n.m.,f.* man, woman; (*gentiluomo, donna distinta*) gentleman, lady; (*padrone, padrona*) master, mistress; (*davanti a nome proprio*) Mr (*abbr. di* Mister), Mrs *o* Ms (*abbr. di* Mistress); (*in lettere ufficiali*) Sir, Madam.

signori'le *a.* gentlemanly; (*di lusso*) luxury.

signori'na *n.f.* young lady; (*seguito da nome proprio*) Miss.

Sig.ra *abbr.* (*di signora*) Mrs, Ms.

silenziato're *n.m.* silencer.

sile'nzi|o *n.m.* silence. ~o'so *a.* silent.

sili'cio *n.m.* piastrina di ~ silicon chip.

si'llaba *n.f.* syllable.

sillaba'rio *n.m.* primer.

silu'r|o *n.m.* torpedo. ~a're *v.t.* torpedo.

si'mb|olo *n.m.* symbol. ~oleggia're *v.t.* symbolize. ~o'lico *a.* symbolic(al). ~oli'smo *n.m.* symbolism.

si'mil|e *a.* similar; (*tale*) such. ~e a like. —*n.m.* (*il prossimo*) fellow creature. ~arità *n.f.* similarity. ~me'nte *adv.* similarly.

simm|etri'a *n.f.* symmetry. ~e'trico *a.* symmetric(al).

simp|ati'a *n.f.* liking; (*compenetrazione*) sympathy. ~a'tico *a.* nice; (*piacente*) likeable. ~atizza're *v.t.* ~atizzare con take a liking to.

simpo'sio *n.m.* symposium.

simula'|re *v.t.* feign. ~zio'ne *n.f.* simulation.

simulta'neo *a.* simultaneous.

sinago'ga *n.f.* synagogue.

since'r|o *a.* sincere. ~ità *n.f.* sincerity.

si'ncope *n.f.* syncopation; (*med.*) fainting fit.

sincronizza're *v.t.* synchronize.

sindaca'|to *n.m.* (trade) union; (*industriale*) syndicate. ~le *a.* (trade-) union. ~li'sta *n.m.|f.* trade-unionist.

si'ndaco *n.m.* mayor.

sinfoni'a *n.f.* symphony.

singhio'zz|o *n.m.* hiccup; (*di pianto*) sob. ~a're *v.i.* hiccup; sob.

singola're *a.* singular. —*n.m.* singular; (*tennis*) single.

si'ngolo *a.* single. —*n.m.* individual; (*tennis*) single.

sini'str|o, a *a.* left(-hand); (*avverso*) sinister. —*n.m.* accident. —*n.f.* left (hand); (*pol.*) left (wing). a ~a on the left. girare a ~a a turn to the left.

si'no *prep.* = fino.

sino'nimo *a.* synonymous. —*n.m.* synonym.

sinta'ssi *n.f.* syntax.

si'ntesi *n.f.* synthesis; (*riassunto*) summary.

sinte'ti|co *a.* synthetic. ~zza're *v.t.* synthesize.

si'ntom|o *n.m.* symptom. ~a'tico *a.* symptomatic.

sinuo'so *a.* (*strada*) winding.

sipa'rio *n.m.* curtain.

sire'na *n.f.* siren.

Si'ri|a *n.f.* Syria. s~a'no, a *a.* & *n.m.,f.* Syrian.

siri'nga *n.f.* syringe.

si'smico *a.* seismic.

siste'm|a *n.m.* system. ~a'tico *a.* systematic. ~a'r|e *v.t.* (*mettere*) place; (*definire*) settle; (*procurare lavoro, collocare*) fix up. ~a'rsi *v.r.* settle (down); (*trovare un lavoro*) find a job. ~azio'ne *n.f.* arrangement; (*accomodamento*) settlement; (*lavoro*) job.

situa're *v.t.* place.

situazio'ne *n.f.* situation.

slaccia're *v.t.* unfasten.

slancia'rsi *v.r.* hurl oneself. **sla'ncio** *n.m.* impetus; (*impulso*) impulse.

slancia'to *a.* slender.

slava'to *a.* faded; (*viso*) washed out.

sla'vo *a.* Slav(onic).

slea'l|e *a.* disloyal. ~tà *n.f.* disloyalty.

slega're *v.t.* untie.

sli'tt|a *n.f.* sledge, sleigh. ~i'no *n.m.* toboggan.

slitta'|re *v.i.* (*auto*) skid. ~ta *n.f.* skid.

sloga'|re *v.t.* dislocate. ~tu'ra *n.f.* dislocation.

sloggia're *v.t.* dislodge. —*v.i.* move out.

smacchia're *v.t.* clean.

sma'cco *n.m.* humiliating defeat.

smaglia'nte *a.* dazzling.

smaglia'|rsi *v.r.* (*calza*) ladder. ∼**tu'ra** *n.f.* ladder.

smalta're *v.t.* enamel; (*ceramica*) glaze; (*unghie*) varnish. **sma'lto** *n.m.* enamel; glaze; (*per le unghie*) nail varnish.

smalti're *v.t.* (*merce*) sell off; (*fig.*) get through.

sma'ni|a *n.f.* fidgets *pl.*; (*desiderio*) longing. ∼**a're** *v.i.* have the fidgets; long. ∼**o'so** *a.* restless.

smantella're *v.t.* dismantle.

smarri'|re *v.t.* lose; (*temporaneamente*) mislay. ∼**rsi** *v.r.* get lost; (*turbarsi*) be bewildered. ∼**me'nto** *n.m.* loss; bewilderment.

smaschera're *v.t.* unmask.

smemora'to, a *a.* forgetful. —*n.m., f.* scatterbrain.

smenti'|re *v.t.* deny. ∼**ta** *n.f.* denial.

smera'ldo *n.m.* emerald.

smercia're *v.t.* sell off.

smeri'gli|o *n.m.* emery. ∼**a'to** *a.* emery. **vetro** ∼**ato** frosted glass.

sme'sso *p.p. di* **smettere.** —*a.* (*di abiti*) cast-off.

sme'tt|ere *v.t.* stop; (*abiti*) stop wearing. ∼**ila!** stop it!

smidolla'to *a.* spineless.

smi'lzo *a.* thin.

sminuir|e *v.t.* diminish. ∼**si** *v.r.* (*fig.*) belittle oneself.

sminuzza're *v.t.* crumble.

smista'|re *v.t.* sort out; (*mil.*) post. ∼**me'nto** *n.m.* clearing; (*postale*) sorting.

smisura'to *a.* boundless; (*esorbitante*) excessive.

smobilita'|re *v.t.* demobilize. ∼**zio'ne** *n.f.* demobilization.

smoda'to *a.* immoderate.

smoking *n.m. invar.* dinner-jacket.

smonta'r|e *v.t.* take to pieces; (*scoraggiare*) dishearten. —*v.i.* (*da veicolo*) get off; (*da cavallo*) dismount; (*dal servizio*) go off duty. ∼**si** *v.r.* lose heart.

smo'rfi|a *n.f.* grimace; (*moina*) simper. **fare** ∼**e** make faces. ∼**o'so** *a.* affected.

smo'rto *a.* pale; (*colore*) dull.

smorza're *v.t.* (*luce*) dim; (*colori*) tone down; (*suoni*) deaden; (*sete*) quench.

smo'sso *p.p. di* **smuovere.**

smottame'nto *n.m.* landslide.

smu'nto *a.* emaciated.

smuo'ver|e *v.t.* shift; (*commuovere*) move. ∼**si** *v.r.* move; be moved.

smussa'r|e *v.t.* round (off). ∼**si** *v.r.* get blunt.

snatura'to *a.* unnatural.

sne'll|o *a.* slender. ∼**i'rsi** *v.r.* slim down.

snerva'|re *v.t.* enervate. ∼**rsi** *v.r.* get exhausted. ∼**nte** *a.* enervating.

snida're *v.t.* drive out.

snob|ba're *v.t.* snub. ∼**i'smo** *n.m.* snobbery.

snocciola're *v.t.* stone; (*fig.*) blurt out.

snoda'r|e *v.t.* untie; (*sciogliere*) loosen. ∼**si** *v.r.* come untied; (*di strada*) wind.

soa've *a.* gentle.

sobbalza're *v.i.* jerk; (*trasalire*) start. **sobba'lzo** *n.m.* jerk; start.

sobbarca'rsi *v.r.* ∼ **a** undertake.

sobbo'rgo *n.m.* suburb.

sobilla're *v.t.* stir up.

so'brio *a.* sober.

socchiu'|dere *v.t.* half-close. ∼**so** *p.p. di* ∼**dere;** *a.* (*porta*) ajar.

socco'mbere *v.i.* succumb.

socco'r|rere *v.t.* assist. ∼**so** *p.p. di* ∼**rere;** *n.m.* assistance. ∼**si** *n.m. pl.* (*rifornimenti*) supplies. **pronto** ∼**so** first aid.

socialdemocra'|tico, a *a.* Social Democratic. —*n.m., f.* Social Democrat. ∼**zi'a** *n.f.* Social Democracy.

soci|a'le *a.* social. ∼**alizza're** *v.t.* socialize. ∼**e'vole** *a.* sociable.

sociali's|mo *n.m.* Socialism. ∼**ta** *a. & n.m./f.* Socialist.

società *n.f.* society; (*comm.*) company.

so'cio, a *n.m., f.* member; (*comm.*) partner.

sociol|ogi'a *n.f.* sociology. ∼**o'gico** *a.* sociological.

so'da *n.f.* soda.

soddisfa'|re *v.t./i.* satisfy; (*richiesta*) meet; (*offesa*) make amends for. ∼**tto** *p.p. di* ∼**re;** *a.* satisfied. ∼**zio'ne** *n.f.* satisfaction.

so'do *a.* hard; (*fig.*) firm. **uovo** ∼ hard-boiled egg. —*adv.* hard. **dormire** ∼ sleep soundly.

sofà *n.f.* sofa.

soffere'n|te *a.* (*malato*) ill. ∼**za** *n.f.* suffering.

sofferma'rsi *v.r.* pause. ∼ **su** dwell on.

soffe'rto *p.p. di* **soffrire.**

soffia're *v.t.* blow; (*segreto*) reveal; (*rubare*) pinch (*fam.*). —*v.i.* blow.

so'ffice *a.* soft.

soffie'tto *n.m.* bellows *pl.* ∼ **editoriale** blurb.

so'ffio *n.m.* puff; (*med.*) murmur. **in un** ∼ (*sottovoce*) in a whisper.

soffi'tta *n.f.* attic.

soffi'tto *n.m.* ceiling.

soffoca'|re *v.t./i.* choke; (*fig.*) stifle. ∼**zio'ne** *n.f.* suffocation.

soffri'ggere *v.t.* fry lightly.

soffri're *v.t./i.* suffer; (*sopportare*) bear. ∼ **di** suffer from.

soffri'tto *p.p. di* **soffriggere.**

sofistica'|re *v.t.* (*adulterare*) adulterate. —*v.i.* (*sottilizzare*) quibble. ∼**to** *a.* sophisticated.

sogge'tt|o *a. & n.m.* subject. ∼**i'vo** *a.* subjective.

soggezio'ne *n.f.* (*rispetto*) awe; (*imbarazzo*) uneasiness.

soggh|igna're *v.i.* sneer. ∼**i'gno** *n.m.* sneer.

soggioga're *v.t.* subdue.

soggiorna're *v.i.* stay. **soggio'rno** *n.m.* stay; (*stanza*) living-room.

soggiu'ngere *v.t.* add.

so'glia *n.f.* threshold.

so'gliola *n.f.* sole.

sogna'|re *v.t./i.* dream. ∼**re a occhi aperti** day-dream. ∼**to're,** ∼**tri'ce** *n.m., f.* dreamer. **so'gno** *n.m.* dream. **neanche per sogno!** not at all!

so'ia *n.f.* soya.

sol *n.m.* (*mus.*) soh.

sola'io *n.m.* attic.

solame'nte *adv.* only.

so'lco *n.m.* furrow; (*di ruota*) track; (*di nave*) wake; (*di disco*) groove.

solda'to *n.m.* soldier. ∼ **semplice** private.

so'ld|o *n.m.* copper. ∼**i** *n.m. pl.* (*denaro*) money *s.* **senza un** ∼**o** penniless.

so'l|e *n.m.* sun; (*luce del sole*) sunlight. **prendere il** ∼**e** sunbathe. ∼**a're** *a.* solar, sun. ∼**eggia'to** *a.* sunny.

sole'nn|e *a.* solemn. ∼**ità** *n.f.* solemnity.

sole're *v.i.* be in the habit of; (*al passato*) used to. **come si suol dire** as they say.

solfa'to *n.m.* sulphate.

so'lfuro *n.m.* sulphur.

solida'le *a.* in agreement.

solidarietà *n.f.* solidarity.

solidifica'r|e *v.t./i.,* ∼**si** *v.r.* solidify.

so'lid|o *a.* solid; (*robusto*) sturdy; (*di colore*) fast. ∼**ità** *n.f.* solidity; fastness.

solilo'quio *n.m.* soliloquy.

soli'sta *a.* solo. —*n.m./f.* soloist.

solita'rio *a.* solitary; (*isolato*) lonely. —*n.m.* (*brillante*) solitaire; (*gioco di carte*) patience.

so'lit|o *a.* usual. **essere** ∼**o fare** be in the habit of doing. —*n.m.* the usual. **di** ∼**o,** ∼**ame'nte** usually.

solitu'dine *n.f.* solitude.

sollecita'|re *v.t.* speed up; (*persona*) urge. ∼**zio'ne** *n.f.* (*richiesta*) request; (*preghiera*) entreaty.

solle'cit|o *a.* prompt. —*n.m.* reminder. ∼**u'dine** *n.f.* promptness; (*interessamento*) concern.

soll|etica're *v.t.* tickle. ∼**e'tico** *n.m.* tickling. **fare il** ∼**etico a qcno.** tickle s.o. **soffrire il** ∼**etico** be ticklish.

solleva'r|e *v.t.* lift; (*elevare*) raise; (*confortare*) comfort. ∼**si** *v.r.* rise; (*riaversi*) recover.

sollie'vo *n.m.* relief.

so'lo *a.* alone; (*isolato*) lonely; (*unico*) only. —*adv.* only. **da** ∼ by oneself. —*n.m.* **il** ∼ the only one.

solsti'zio *n.m.* solstice.

solta'nto *adv.* only.

solu'bile *a.* soluble.

soluzio'ne *n.f.* solution.

solve'nte *a. & n.m.* solvent.

so'ma *n.f.* load. **bestia da** ∼ beast of burden.

soma'ro *n.m.* ass, donkey.

somiglia'|re *v.i.* ∼**re a** resemble. ∼**rsi** *v.r.* be alike. ∼**nza** *n.f.* resemblance.

so'mm|a *n.f.* sum; (*math.*) addition. ∼**a're** *v.t.* add; (*totalizzare*) sum up. **tutto** ∼**a'to** everything considered.

somma'rio *a. & n.m.* summary.

somme'r|gere *v.t.* submerge. ∼**so** *p.p. di* ∼**gere.**

sommergi'bile *n.m.* submarine.

somme'sso *a.* soft; (*sottomesso*) submissive.

somministra're *v.t.* administer.

sommità *n.f.* summit.

so'mmo *a.* highest; (*fig.*) supreme. —*n.m.* summit.

sommo'ssa *n.f.* rising.

sona'glio *n.m.* bell.

so'nd|a *n.f.* (*mech.*) drill; (*spaziale, med.*) probe. ∼**a'ggio** *n.m.* drilling; probing; (*indagine*) survey. ∼**aggio**

d'opinioni opinion poll. ∼**a're** *v.t.* sound; (*investigare*) probe.

sone'tto *n.m.* sonnet.

sonna'mbulo, a *n.m.,f.* sleep-walker.

sonnecchia're *v.i.* doze.

sonni'fero *n.m.* sleeping-pill.

so'nno *n.m.* sleep. **aver** ∼ be sleepy. ∼**le'nza** *n.f.* sleepiness.

sono'ro *a.* resonant; (*rumoroso*) loud; (*onde*) sound.

sontuo'so *a.* sumptuous.

sopori'fero *a.* soporific.

soppesa're *v.t.* weigh (up).

soppia'tto *adv.* **di** ∼ furtively.

sopporta're *v.t.* support; (*tollerare*) stand; (*dolore*) bear.

soppressio'ne *n.f.* suppression.

soppre'sso *p.p. di* **sopprimere.**

soppri'mere *v.t.* suppress.

so'pra *prep.* on; (*in alto*) above; (*senza contatto*) over; (*al piano superiore*) upstairs. —*adv.* on top; upstairs. **al di** ∼ **di** over; (*oltre*) above. **dormirci** ∼ sleep on it. **pensarci** ∼ think about it.

sopra'bito *n.m.* overcoat.

sopracci'glio *n.m.* (*pl. f.* **sopracci-glia**) eyebrow.

sopraccope'rta *n.f.* (*di letto*) bed-spread; (*di libro*) (dust-)jacket.

sopradde'tto *a.* above-mentioned.

sopraffa'|re *v.t.* overwhelm. ∼**tto** *p.p. di* ∼**re.**

sopraffi'no *a.* excellent; (*fig.*) highly refined.

sopraggiu'ngere *v.i.* come unexpectedly; (*accadere*) happen.

soprammo'bile *n.m.* ornament.

soprannatura'le *a.* & *n.m.* supernatural.

sopranno'me *n.m.* nickname.

sopra'no *n.m./f.* soprano.

soprappensie'ro *adv.* lost in thought.

soprassa'lto *n.m.* **di** ∼ with a start.

soprassede're *v.i.* ∼ **a** postpone.

soprattu'tto *adv.* above all.

sopravveni're *v.i.* turn up; (*accadere*) happen.

sopravve'nto *n.m.* (*fig.*) upper hand.

sopravvissu'to *p.p. di* **sopravvivere.**

sopravvi'vere *v.i.* survive. ∼ **a** (*persona*) outlive.

soprintende'n|te *n.m./f.* supervisor; (*di museo ecc.*) keeper. ∼**za** *n.f.* supervision; (*ente*) board.

sopru'so *n.m.* abuse of power.

soqqua'dro *n.m.* **mettere a** ∼ turn upside-down.

sorbe'tto *n.m.* sorbet.

sorbi're *v.t.* sip; (*fig.*) put up with.

so'rdido *a.* sordid; (*avaro*) stingy.

sordi'na *n.f.* **in** ∼ on the quiet.

so'rd|o, a *a.* deaf; (*di rumore, dolore*) dull. —*n.m.,f.* deaf person. ∼**ità** *n.f.* deafness. ∼**omu'to, a** *a.* deaf-and-dumb; *n.m.,f.* deaf mute.

sore'll|a *n.f.* sister. ∼**a'stra** *n.f.* step-sister.

sorge'nte *n.f.* spring; (*fonte*) source.

sorgere *v.i.* rise; (*fig.*) arise.

sormonta're *v.t.* surmount.

sornio'ne *a.* sly.

sorpassa're *v.t.* surpass; (*eccedere*) exceed; (*veicolo*) overtake. **sorpa'sso** *n.m.* overtaking.

sorpassa'to *a.* old-fashioned.

sorpre'nd|ere *v.t.* surprise; (*cogliere in flagrante*) catch. ∼**e'nte** *a.* surprising; (*straordinario*) remarkable.

sorpre's|a *n.f.* surprise. ∼**o** *p.p. di* **sorprendere.**

sorre'|ggere *v.t.* support; (*tenere*) hold up. ∼**tto** *p.p. di* ∼**ggere.**

sorri'|dere *v.i.* smile. ∼**de'nte** *a.* smiling. ∼**so** *p.p. di* ∼**dere;** *n.m.* smile.

so'rs|o *n.m.* sip; (*piccola quantità*) drop. ∼**eggia're** *v.t.* sip.

so'rta *n.f.* sort. **di** ∼ whatever. **ogni** ∼ **di** all kinds of.

so'rte *n.f.* fate; (*caso imprevisto*) chance. **tirare a** ∼ draw lots.

sorte'ggi|o *n.m.* draw. ∼**a're** *v.t.* draw lots.

sortile'gio *n.m.* witchcraft.

sorti're *v.i.* come out.

sorti'ta *n.f.* (*mil.*) sortie.

so'rto *p.p. di* **sorgere.**

sorveglia'|re *v.t.* watch over; (*controllare*) oversee. ∼**nte** *n.m./f.* keeper; overseer. ∼**nza** *n.f.* watch; (*mil.*) surveillance.

sorvola're *v.t.* fly over; (*fig.*) skip.

so'sia *n.m. invar.* double.

sospe'|ndere *v.t.* hang (up); (*interrompere*) stop; (*privare di una carica*) suspend. ∼**nsio'ne** *n.f.* suspension. ∼**so** *p.p. di* ∼**ndere;** *a.* (*ansioso*) anxious. **in** ∼**so** pending. ∼**so a** hanging from.

sosp|etta're *v.t./i.* suspect. ∼**e'tto** *a.* suspicious; *n.m.* suspicion. ∼**etto'so** *a.* suspicious.

sospi'n|gere *v.t.* drive. ∼**to** *p.p. di* ∼**gere.**

sosp|ira're *v.i.* sigh. —*v.t.* long for. ∼**i'ro** *n.m.* sigh.

so'st|a *n.f.* stop; (*pausa*) pause. **senza ∼a** incessantly. **∼a're** *v.i.* stop; pause.

sostanti'vo *n.m.* noun.

sosta'nz|a *n.f.* substance. **∼e** *n.f. pl.* (*patrimonio*) property *s.* **in ∼a** to sum up. **∼io'so** *a.* substantial; (*cibo*) nourishing.

soste'gno *n.m.* support.

sostene'r|e *v.t.* support; (*prendere su di sé*) bear; (*resistere*) withstand; (*affermare*) maintain; (*nutrire*) sustain. **∼si** *v.r.* support oneself; (*mantenersi*) sustain oneself.

sosteni|to're, ∼tri'ce *n.m., f.* supporter.

sostentame'nto *n.m.* maintenance.

sostenu'to *a.* stiff; (*di stile*) distinguished.

sostit|ui're *v.t.* substitute. **∼u'to, a** *n.m., f.* substitute. **∼uzio'ne** *n.f.* substitution.

sottace't|o *a.* pickled. **∼i** *n.m. pl.* pickles.

sotta'na *n.f.* petticoat; (*gonna*) skirt.

sotterfu'gio *n.m.* subterfuge. **di ∼** secretly.

sotterra'neo, a *a.* underground. **—***n.m.* (*cantina*) cellar. **—***n.f.* (*ferrovia*) underground.

sotterra're *v.t.* bury.

sottiglie'zza *n.f.* slimness; (*fig.*) subtlety.

sotti'l|e *a.* thin; (*fine*) fine; (*penetrante*) subtle. **∼izza're** *v.i.* split hairs.

sottinte'|ndere *v.t.* imply. **∼so** *p.p. di* **∼ndere**; *n.m.* allusion. **senza ∼si** openly.

so'tto *prep.* under; (*più in basso*) below; (*disotto*) underneath. **—***adv.* below; underneath; (*al piano di sotto*) downstairs. **mettersi ∼** (*fig.*) get down to it. **∼ la pioggia** in the rain. **∼ ∼** deep down; (*di nascosto*) on the quiet.

sottobicchie're *n.m.* coaster.

sottobo'sco *n.m.* undergrowth.

sottobra'ccio *adv.* arm in arm.

sottolinea're *v.t.* underline; (*fig.*) stress.

sottoma'no *adv.* (*di nascosto*) underhand.

sottomari'no *a. & n.m.* submarine.

sottome'tter|e *v.t.* subdue. **∼si** *v.r.* submit (oneself).

sottome'sso *p.p. di* **sottomettere**. **—***a.* (*remissivo*) submissive.

sottopassa'ggio *n.m.* underpass; (*pedonale*) subway.

sottopo'r|re *v.t.* submit; (*costringere*) subject. **∼si** *v.r.* submit oneself. **∼si a** undergo.

sottopo'sto *p.p. di* **sottoporre**.

sottoscri'tto *p.p. di* **sottoscrivere**. **—***n.m.* undersigned.

sottoscri'|vere *v.t.* subscribe. **—***v.i.* **∼vere a** subscribe to. **∼zio'ne** *n.f.* subscription.

sottosegreta'rio *n.m.* under-secretary.

sottoso'pra *adv.* upside-down.

sottosta'nte *a.* below.

sottosuo'lo *n.m.* subsoil.

sottotene'nte *n.m.* second lieutenant; (*naut.*) sub-lieutenant.

sottote'rra *adv.* underground.

sottoti'tolo *n.m.* subtitle.

sottovaluta're *v.t.* underestimate.

sottove'ste *n.f.* petticoat.

sottovo'ce *adv.* in a low voice.

sottra'|rre *v.t.* take away; (*math.*) subtract. **∼rsi** *v.r.* **∼rsi a** escape from. **∼tto** *p.p. di* **∼rre**. **∼zio'ne** *n.f.* subtraction; (*asportazione*) removal.

sottufficia'le *n.m.* non-commissioned officer; (*naut.*) petty officer.

sove'nte *adv.* (*lit.*) often.

soverchieri'|a *n.f.* bullying. **fare ∼e** bully.

sovie'tico, a *a. & n.m., f.* Soviet.

sovracca'ric|o, a *a.* **∼o (di)** overloaded (with). **—***n.m.* overload. **∼a're** *v.t.* overload.

sovra'no, a *a.* sovereign; (*fig.*) supreme. **—***n.m., f.* sovereign.

sovrappo'r|re *v.t.* superimpose. **∼si** *v.r.* overlap.

sovrasta're *v.i.* dominate. **—***v.t.* overhang.

sovrintende'n|te, ∼za = **soprintenden|te, ∼za**.

sovruma'no *a.* superhuman.

sovvenzio'ne *n.f.* subsidy.

sovversi'vo *a.* subversive.

so'zzo *a.* filthy.

spacca'|re *v.t.* split; (*legna*) chop. **∼rsi** *v.r.* split. **∼tu'ra** *n.f.* split.

spaccia'|re *v.t.* sell (off); (*mettere in circolazione*) spread; (*fam., dichiarare inguaribile*) give s.o. up. **∼rsi** *v.r.* **∼rsi per** pass oneself off as. **∼to're, ∼tri'ce** *n.m., f.* peddler; (*di droga*) pusher. **spa'ccio** *n.m.* sale; (*negozio*) shop.

spa'cco *n.m.* split; (*di vestito*) slit; (*di giacca*) vent.

spacco'ne, a *n.m., f.* boaster.

spa'da *n.f.* sword. **~cci'no** *n.m.* swordsman.

spadroneggia're *v.i.* play the master.

spaesa'to *a.* out of one's element.

spaghe'tti *n.m. pl.* spaghetti *s.*

Spa'gn|a *n.f.* Spain. **s~o'lo, a** *a.* Spanish; *n.m., f.* Spaniard; *n.m.* (*lingua*) Spanish.

spagnole'tta *n.f.* spool.

spa'go *n.m.* string.

spaia'to *a.* odd.

spalanca'r|e *v.t.*, **~si** *v.r.* open wide.

spala're *v.t.* shovel.

spa'll|a *n.f.* shoulder. **~e** *n.f. pl.* (*schiena*) back. **~eggia're** *v.t.* back up.

spalle'tta *n.f.* parapet.

spallie'ra *n.f.* back; (*di letto*) headboard; (*ginnastica*) wall bars *pl.*

spalma're *v.t.* spread.

spa'nder|e *v.t.* spread; (*versare*) spill. **~si** *v.r.* spread.

spara'|re *v.t./i.* shoot. **~rle grosse** talk big. **~to're** *n.m.* shooter. **~to'ria** *n.f.* shooting. **spa'ro** *n.m.* shot.

sparecchia're *v.t.* clear.

spare'ggio *n.m.* (*comm.*) deficit; (*sport*) play-off.

spa'rg|ere *v.t.* scatter; (*diffondere*) spread; (*lacrime, sangue*) shed. **~ersi** *v.r.* spread. **~ime'nto** *n.m.* scattering; shedding. **~imento di sangue** bloodshed.

spari'|re *v.i.* disappear. **~zio'ne** *n.f.* disappearance.

sparla're *v.i.* **~ di** speak ill of.

sparpaglia'r|e *v.t.*, **~si** *v.r.* scatter.

spa'rso *p.p. di* **spargere**. **~a.** scattered; (*sciolto*) loose.

sparti're *v.t.* share out; (*separare*) separate.

spartitra'ffico *n.m. invar.* traffic island.

sparu'to *a.* gaunt.

sparvie'ro *n.m.* sparrow-hawk.

spasima'|re *v.i.* suffer agonies; (*fig.*) yearn. **~re per** be madly in love with. **~nte** *n.m.* (*hum.*) admirer.

spa'simo *n.m.* spasm.

spasmo'dico *a.* spasmodic.

spass|a'rsi *v.r.* amuse oneself. **spa'sso** *n.m.* fun. **andare a spasso** go for a stroll. **essere a spasso** be out of work. **~o'so** *a.* funny.

spa'tola *n.f.* spatula.

spaura'cchio *n.m.* scarecrow; (*fig.*) bugbear.

spauri're *v.t.* frighten.

spava'ldo *a.* defiant.

spaventapa'sseri *n.m. invar.* scarecrow.

spave'nt|o *n.m.* fright. **~a're** *v.t.* frighten. **~a'rsi** *v.r.* be scared. **~o'so** *a.* frightening.

spazienti'rsi *v.r.* lose one's patience.

spa'zi|o *n.m.* space. **~a'le** *a.* (*cosmico*) space. **~o'so** *a.* spacious.

spazzacami'no *n.m.* chimney-sweep.

spazz|a're *v.t.* sweep. **~atu'ra** *n.f.* (*immondizia*) rubbish. **~i'no** *n.m.* road sweeper; (*netturbino*) dustman.

spa'zzol|a *n.f.* brush. **~a're** *v.t.* brush. **~i'no** *n.m.* (small) brush. **~ino da denti** toothbrush.

specchia'rsi *v.r.* look at oneself in a mirror; (*riflettersi*) be mirrored. **~ in qcno.** model oneself on s.o. **spe'cchio** *n.m.* mirror.

specia'l|e *a.* special. **~ità** *n.f.* speciality. **~me'nte** *adv.* especially.

speciali'|sta *n.m./f.* specialist. **~zza're** *v.t.*, **~zza'rsi** *v.r.* specialize. **~zza'to** *a.* (*di operaio*) skilled.

spe'cie *n.f.* (*scientifico*) species *pl. invar.*; (*tipo*) kind. **fare ~ a** surprise. **in ~** especially.

spec|ifica're *v.t.* specify. **~i'fico** *a.* specific.

specula'|re *v.i.* speculate. **—*v.t.* ~re su** (*indagare*) speculate on; (*comm.*) speculate in. **~zio'ne** *n.f.* speculation.

spedi'|re *v.t.* send. **~zio'ne** *n.f.* (*di lettere ecc.*) dispatch; (*comm.*) consignment; (*scientifica*) expedition.

spedi'to *a.* quick; (*di parlata*) fluent.

spe'gner|e *v.t.* put out; (*gas, luce*) turn off; (*motore*) switch off; (*fig.*) stifle. **~si** *v.r.* go out; (*morire*) pass away.

spella'r|e *v.t.* skin; (*fig.*) fleece. **~si** *v.r.* peel off.

spe'nd|ere *v.t.* spend. **~accio'ne, a** *n.m., f.* spendthrift.

spenna're *v.t.* pluck.

spensiera't|o *a.* carefree. **~e'zza** *n.f.* lightheartedness.

spe'nto *p.p. di* **spegnere**. **—*a.* out; (*smorto*) dull.

spera'nza *n.f.* hope. **pieno di ~** hopeful. **senza ~** hopeless.

spera're *v.t.* hope for; (*aspettarsi*) expect. **—*v.i.* ~ in** trust in. **spero di sì** I hope so.

spe'rd|ersi *v.r.* lose oneself. ∼**u'to** *a.* lost; (*isolato*) secluded.

spergiu'ro, a *n.m., f.* perjurer. −*n.m.* perjury.

sperimenta'|re *v.t.* experiment. ∼**le** *a.* experimental.

spe'rma *n.m.* sperm.

spero'ne *n.m.* spur.

sperpera're *v.t.* squander. **spe'rpero** *n.m.* waste.

spe's|a *n.f.* expense; (*acquisto*) purchase. **andare a far** ∼**e** go shopping. **fare la** ∼**a** do the shopping.

spe'so *p.p. di* **spendere.**

spe'ss|o¹ *a.* thick. ∼**o're** *n.m.* thickness.

spe'sso² *adv.* often.

spetta'bile *a.* respectable (*comm. abbr.* **Spett.**). **S**∼ **ditta Rossi** Messrs Rossi.

spetta'col|o *n.m.* spectacle; (*rappresentazione*) show. ∼**o'so** *a.* spectacular.

spetta'nza *n.f.* concern.

spetta're *v.i.* ∼ **a** be up to; (*di diritto*) be due to.

spetta|to're, ∼**tri'ce** *n.m., f.* spectator. ∼**tori** *n.m. pl.* (*di cinema ecc.*) audience *s.*

spettina'r|e *v.t.* ∼**e qcno.** ruffle s.o.'s hair. ∼**si** *v.r.* ruffle one's hair.

spe'ttr|o *n.m.* ghost; (*fisica*) spectrum. ∼**a'le** *a.* ghostly.

spe'zie *n.f. pl.* spices.

spezza'r|e *v.t.,* ∼**si** *v.r.* break.

spezzati'no *n.m.* stew.

spezzetta're *v.t.* break into small pieces.

spi'|a *n.f.* spy; (*della polizia*) informer; (*di porta*) peep-hole. ∼**a luminosa** warning light. ∼**a're** *v.t.* spy on; (*occasione ecc.*) wait for.

spiace'nte *a.* sorry.

spiace'vole *a.* unpleasant.

spia'ggia *n.f.* beach.

spiana're *v.t.* level; (*rendere liscio*) smooth; (*pasta*) roll out; (*edificio*) raze to the ground.

spia'no *n.m.* open space. **a tutto** ∼ without a break.

spianta'to *a.* (*fig.*) penniless.

spiattella're *v.t.* blurt out.

spia'zzo *n.m.* (*radura*) clearing.

spicca'|re *v.t.* (*parole*) pronounce distinctly. ∼**re il volo** take flight. −*v.i.* stand out. ∼**to** *a.* marked.

spi'cchio *n.m.* (*di agrumi*) segment; (*di aglio*) clove.

spiccia'|rsi *v.r.* hurry up. ∼**ti'vo** *a.* speedy.

spi'cciol|o *a.* **moneta** ∼**a,** ∼**i** *n.m. pl.* (small) change *s.*

spi'cco *n.m.* relief. **fare** ∼ stand out.

spie'd|o *n.m.* spit. ∼**i'no** *n.m.* kebab.

spiega'|re *v.t.* explain; (*stendere*) spread out; (*vele*) unfurl. ∼**rsi** *v.r.* explain oneself; (*dispiegarsi*) unfold. ∼**zio'ne** *n.f.* explanation.

spieta'to *a.* ruthless.

spiffera're *v.t.* blurt out. −*v.i.* (*di vento*) whistle. **spi'ffero** *n.m.* (*corrente d'aria*) draught.

spi'ga *n.f.* spike; (*bot.*) ear.

spiglia'to *a.* self-possessed.

spigola're *v.t.* glean.

spi'golo *n.m.* edge; (*angolo*) corner.

spi'lla *n.f.* pin; (*gioiello*) brooch.

spilla're *v.t.* tap.

spi'llo *n.m.* pin. ∼ **di sicurezza** safety-pin.

spilo'rcio *a.* stingy.

spi'n|a *n.f.* thorn; (*di pesce*) bone; (*electr.*) plug. ∼**a dorsale** spine. ∼**a'le** *a.* spinal. ∼**o'so** *a.* thorny.

spina'ci *n.m. pl.* spinach *s.*

spi'nger|e *v.t.* push; (*fig.*) drive. ∼**si** *v.r.* push on; (*gettarsi*) throw oneself.

spi'nta *n.f.* push; (*violenta*) thrust; (*fig.*) spur.

spi'nto *p.p. di* **spingere.**

spiona'ggio *n.m.* espionage.

spio'vere *v.i.* stop raining; (*ricadere*) fall; (*scorrere*) flow down.

spi'ra *n.f.* coil.

spira'glio *n.m.* small opening; (*soffio d'aria*) breath of air; (*raggio di luce*) gleam of light.

spira'le *a.* spiral.

spira're *v.i.* (*soffiare*) blow; (*morire*) pass away.

spirit|i'smo *n.m.* spiritualism. ∼**a'to** *a.* possessed; (*espressione*) wild. ∼**ua'le** *a.* spiritual.

spi'rit|o *n.m.* spirit; (*arguzia*) wit; (*intelletto*) mind. ∼**osa'ggine** *n.f.* witticism. ∼**o'so** *a.* witty.

sple'nd|ere *v.i.* shine. ∼**e'nte** *a.* shining.

sple'ndido *a.* splendid; (*di persona*) generous.

splendo're *n.m.* splendour.

spodesta're *v.t.* dispossess; (*re*) depose.

spoetizza're *v.t.* disenchant.

spo'gli|a *n.f.* (*di animale*) skin. ∼**e** *n.f.*

pl. (*salma*) mortal remains; (*bottino*) spoils.

spoglia're *v.t.* strip; (*svestire*) undress; (*fare lo spoglio*) go through. ~re'llo *n.m.* strip-tease. ~to'io *n.m.* dressing-room. **spo'glio** *a.* undressed; (*nudo*) bare; *n.m.* (*scrutinio*) perusal. **spoglio di** (*privo*) lacking in.

spo'la *n.f.* shuttle. **fare la** ~ go to and fro.

spole'tta *n.f.* spool.

spolpa're *v.t.* take the flesh off; (*fig.*) fleece.

spolvera're *v.t.* dust; (*spazzolare*) brush.

spo'nda *n.f.* (*di mare, lago*) shore; (*di fiume*) bank; (*bordo*) edge.

sponsorizza're *v.t.* sponsor.

sponta'neo *a.* spontaneous.

spopola're *v.t.* depopulate. —*v.i.* (*avere successo*) draw the crowds.

spora'dico *a.* sporadic.

sporc|a're *v.t.* dirty; (*macchiare*) soil. ~a'rsi *v.r.* get dirty. ~accio'ne, a *n.m., f.* dirty person. ~i'zia *n.f.* dirt.

spo'rco *a.* dirty. **avere la coscienza** ~a have a bad conscience.

sporge'n|te *a.* jutting (out). ~za *n.f.* projection.

spo'rger|e *v.t.* stretch out. —*v.i.* jut out. ~si *v.r.* lean out. ~e querela contro take legal action against.

sport *n.m. invar.* sport. ~i'vo, a *a.* sports; (*persona*) sporty; *n.m., f.* sportsman, sportswoman.

spo'rta *n.f.* shopping basket.

sporte'llo *n.m.* door; (*di banca ecc.*) window.

spo'rto *p.p. di* **sporgere**.

spo's|o, a *n.m., f.* bridegroom, bride. ~ali'zio *n.m.* wedding. ~a're *v.t.* marry. ~a'rsi *v.r.* get married. ~a'to *a.* married.

spossa't|o *a.* worn out. ~e'zza *n.f.* exhaustion.

sposta'|re *v.t.* move; (*differire*) postpone; (*cambiare*) change. ~rsi *v.r.* move.

sposta'to, a *a.* ill-adjusted. —*n.m., f.* (*disadattato*) misfit.

spra'ng|a *n.f.* bar. ~a're *v.t.* bar.

spra'zzo *n.m.* flash; (*fig.*) gleam.

spreca're *v.t.* waste. **spre'co** *n.m.* waste.

sprege'vole *a.* despicable.

spregiudica'to *a.* unprejudiced; (*pej.*) unscrupulous.

spre'mere *v.t.* squeeze.

spremu'ta *n.f.* juice.

sprezza'nte *a.* contemptuous.

sprigiona'r|e *v.t.* emit. ~si *v.r.* burst out.

sprizza're *v.t./i.* spurt; (*salute, gioia*) be bursting with.

sprofonda'r|e *v.i.* sink; (*crollare*) collapse. ~si *v.r.* ~si in sink into; (*fig.*) be engrossed in.

sprona're *v.t.* spur (on). **spro'ne** *n.m.* spur; (*sartoria*) yoke.

sproporzio'n|e *n.f.* disproportion. ~a-'to *a.* disproportionate.

spropo'sit|o *n.m.* blunder; (*eccesso*) excessive amount. **a** ~o inopportunely. ~a'to *a.* full of blunders; (*enorme*) huge.

sprovvedu'to *a.* unprepared. ~ di lacking in.

sprovvi'st|o *a.* ~o di out of. **alla** ~a unexpectedly.

spruzza'|re *v.t.* sprinkle; (*vaporizzare*) spray; (*inzaccherare*) spatter. ~to're *n.m.* spray; **spru'zzo** *n.m.* spray; (*di fango*) splash.

spudora't|o *a.* impudent. ~e'zza *n.f.* impudence.

spu'gn|a *n.f.* sponge; (*tessuto*) towelling. ~o'so *a.* spongy.

spu'm|a *n.f.* foam; (*schiuma*) froth. ~eggia're *v.i.* foam.

spuma'nte *n.m.* sparkling wine.

spunta'r|e *v.t.* (*rompere la punta*) break the point of; (*capelli*) trim. ~la (*fig.*) win through. —*v.i.* (*di pianta*) sprout; (*di capelli*) begin to grow; (*sorgere*) rise; (*apparire*) appear. ~si *v.r.* get blunt.

spunti'no *n.m.* snack.

spu'nto *n.m.* cue; (*fig.*) starting point.

spurga'r|e *v.t.* purge. ~si *v.r.* (*med.*) expectorate.

sputa're *v.t./i.* spit. **spu'to** *n.m.* spit.

squa'dr|a *n.f.* (*gruppo*) team; (*di polizia ecc.*) squad; (*da disegno*) square. ~a're *v.t.* square; (*guardare*) look up and down.

squadr|i'glia *n.f.* ~o'ne *n.m.* squadron.

squaglia'r|e *v.t.*, ~si *v.r.* melt. ~sela (*fam., svignarsela*) steal out.

squali'fic|a *n.f.* disqualification. ~a're *v.t.* disqualify.

squa'll|ido *a.* squalid. ~o're *n.m.* squalor.

squa'lo *n.m.* shark.

squa'm|a *n.f.* scale. ~a're *v.t.* scale.

~a'rsi *v.r.* (*di pelle*) flake off. ~o'so *a.* scaly.

squarciago'la *adv.* a ~ at the top of one's voice.

squarta're *v.t.* quarter.

squattrina'to *a.* penniless.

squilibra'|re *v.t.* unbalance. ~to, a *a.* unbalanced; *n.m.*, *f.* lunatic. **squi-li'brio** *n.m.* unbalance.

squilla'|re *v.i.* (*di campana*) peal; (*di tromba*) blare; (*di telefono*) ring. **squi'llo** *n.m.* blare; ring. **ragazza squillo** call-girl.

squisi'to *a.* exquisite.

sradica're *v.t.* eradicate.

sragiona're *v.i.* rave.

sregola'to *a.* inordinate; (*dissoluto*) dissolute.

sta'bil|e *a.* stable; (*permanente*) lasting; (*saldo*) steady. **compagnia** ~e (*theatr.*) repertory company. —*n.m.* (*edificio*) building. ~ità *n.f.* stability.

stabilime'nto *n.m.* factory; (*industriale*) plant; (*edificio*) establishment.

stabili'r|e *v.t.* establish; (*decidere*) decide. ~si *v.r.* settle.

stabilizza'|re *v.t.* stabilize. ~to're *n.m.* stabilizer.

stacca'r|e *v.t.* detach; (*parole*) pronounce clearly; (*separare*) separate. ~si *v.r.* come off. ~si da move away from; (*abbandonare*) give up.

sta'dio *n.m.* stadium.

sta'ffa *n.f.* stirrup.

staffe'tta *n.f.* dispatch-rider.

stagio'n|e *n.f.* season. ~a'le a. seasonal. ~a're *v.t.* season.

taglia'rsi *v.r.* stand out.

stagna'|re *v.t.* (*saldare*) solder. —*v.i.* (*di acqua ecc.*) stagnate. ~nte a. stagnant. **sta'gno** *a.* (*a tenuta d'acqua*) watertight; *n.m.* (*acqua ferma*) pond; (*metallo*) tin.

stagno'la *n.f.* tin foil.

stalagmi'te *n.f.* stalagmite.

stalatti'te *n.f.* stalactite.

sta'll|a *n.f.* stable; (*per buoi*) cowshed. ~ie're *n.m.* groom.

stallo'ne *n.m.* stallion.

stama'ni, stamatti'na *advs.* this morning.

stambe'rga *n.f.* hovel.

sta'mp|a *n.f.* (*typ.*) printing; (*giornali, giornalisti*) press; (*riproduzione*) print. ~a're *v.t.* print; (*imprimere*) imprint.

stampate'llo *n.m.* block letters *pl.*

stampe'lla *n.f.* crutch.

sta'mpo *n.m.* mould.

stana're *v.t.* drive out.

stanc|a're *v.t.* tire; (*annoiare*) bore. ~a'rsi *v.r.* get tired. ~he'zza *n.f.* tiredness. **sta'nco** *a.* tired. ~o (**di**) (*stufo*) fed up (with).

standardizza're *v.t.* standardize.

sta'ng|a *n.f.* bar. ~he'tta *n.f.* (*di occhiali*) bar.

stanga'ta *n.f.* (*fig.*) blow.

stano'tte *n.f.* tonight; (*la notte scorsa*) last night.

sta'nte *prep.* on account of. **a sé** ~ separate.

stanti'o *a.* stale.

stantu'ffo *n.m.* piston.

sta'nza *n.f.* room; (*metrica*) stanza.

stanzia're *v.t.* allocate.

stappa're *v.t.* uncork.

sta'r|e *v.i.* (*rimanere*) stay; (*essere*) be; (*abitare*) live. ~e a (*attenersi*) keep to; (*spettare*) be up to. ~e bene (*economicamente*) be well off; (*di salute*) be well; (*addirsi*) suit. ~e dietro a (*seguire*) follow; (*sorvegliare*) keep an eye on; (*corteggiare*) run after. ~e in piedi stand. ~e per be about to. **ben ti sta!** it serves you right! **come stai?** how are you? **lasciar** ~e leave alone. ~ci (*essere contenuto*) go into; (*essere d'accordo*) agree. ~sene *v.r.* (*rimanere*) stay.

starn|uti're *v.i.* sneeze. ~u'to *n.m.* sneeze.

stase'ra *adv.* this evening, tonight.

stata'le *a.* state. —*n.m.|f.* state employee.

Sta'ti Uni'ti (d'America) *n.m. pl.* **gli** ~ ~ the United States (of America).

sta'tico *a.* static.

stati'sta *n.m.* statesman.

stati'stic|a *n.f.* statistics *s.* ~o *a.* statistical.

sta'to *p.p. di* **essere, stare.** —*n.m.* state; (*posizione sociale*) position; (*legge*) status. ~ **d'animo** frame of mind. **S**~ **Maggiore** (*mil.*) General Staff.

sta'tua *n.f.* statue.

statu'ra *n.f.* height. **di alta** ~ tall. **di bassa** ~ short.

statu'to *n.m.* statute.

staziona'rio *a.* stationary.

stazio'ne *n.f.* station. ~ **balneare** seaside resort.

ste'cca *n.f.* stick; (*di ombrello*) rib; (*da biliardo*) cue; (*med.*) splint; (*di* *sigarette*) carton; (*di busto*) whalebone. **fare una ~** (*mus.*) fluff a note.

stecca'to *n.m.* fence.

stecchi'to *a.* skinny; (*rigido*) stiff.

ste'll|a *n.f.* star. **~a alpina** edelweiss. **~a di mare** starfish. **~a filante** streamer. **~a'to** *a.* starry.

ste'lo *n.m.* stem. **lampada a ~** standard lamp.

ste'mma *n.m.* coat of arms.

stempera're *v.t.* dilute.

stempia'to *a.* bald at the temples.

stenda'rdo *n.m.* standard.

ste'nder|e *v.t.* spread (out); (*appendere*) hang out; (*distendere*) stretch (out). **~si** *v.r.* stretch out.

stenodattilo'graf|o, a *n.m., f.* shorthand typist. **~i'a** *n.f.* shorthand typing.

stenograf|a're *v.t.* take down in shorthand. **~i'a** *n.f.* shorthand.

stenta're *v.i.* **~ a** find it hard to. **ste'nto** *n.m.* effort. **a stento** with difficulty.

ste'rco *n.m.* dung.

ste'reo(fo'nico) *a.* stereo(phonic).

stereotipa'to *a.* stereotyped.

ste'ril|e *a.* sterile; (*terreno*) barren. **~ità** *n.f.* sterility.

sterilizza're *v.t.* sterilize. **~zio'ne** *n.f.* sterilization.

sterli'na *n.f.* pound (sterling).

sterm|ina're *v.t.* exterminate. **~i'nio** *n.m.* extermination.

stermina'to *a.* immense.

ste'rno *n.m.* breastbone.

stern|uti're, ~u'to = **starnutire, starnuto**.

ste'rpo *n.m.* dry twig.

ste'rz|o *n.m.* steering. **~a're** *v.t./i.* steer.

ste'so *p.p. di* **stendere.**

ste'sso *a.* same; (*rafforzativo, personale*) **io ~** I myself, **tu ~** you yourself; (*rafforzativo, preciso*) **in quel momento ~** at that very moment; (*riflessivo*) **me ~** myself, **se ~** himself. **lo ~** *n.m.* the same; *adv.* (*in ogni modo*) all the same.

stesu'ra *n.f.* drawing up; (*documento*) draft.

stetosco'pio *n.m.* stethoscope.

sti'gma *n.m.* stigma.

stigma'te *n.f. pl.* stigmata.

stila're *v.t.* draw up.

sti'l|e *n.m.* style. **~i'sta** *n.m./f.* stylist. **~izza'to** *a.* stylized.

stilla'r|e *v.i.* ooze. **~si** *v.r.* **~si il cervello** rack one's brains.

stilogra'fic|o *a.* **penna ~a** fountainpen.

sti'm|a *n.f.* esteem; (*valutazione*) estimate. **~a're** *v.t.* esteem; estimate; (*ritenere*) consider.

stimola're *v.t.* stimulate; (*incitare*) incite. **~nte** *a.* stimulating; *n.m.* stimulant.

sti'molo *n.m.* stimulus; (*fitta*) pang.

sti'nco *n.m.* shin.

sti'n|gere *v.t./i.* fade. **~to** *p.p. di* **~gere**.

stipa'r|e *v.t.* cram. **~si** *v.r.* crowd together.

stipe'ndio *n.m.* salary.

sti'pite *n.m.* doorpost.

stipula're *v.t.* stipulate. **~zio'ne** *n.f.* (*accordo*) agreement.

stira're *v.t.* iron; (*distendere*) stretch. **~tu'ra** *n.f.* ironing. **sti'ro** *n.m.* **ferro da stiro** iron.

sti'rpe *n.f.* stock.

sti'tic|o *a.* constipated. **~he'zza** *n.f.* constipation.

sti'va *n.f.* (*naut.*) hold.

stiva'le *n.m.* boot.

sti'zz|a *n.f.* anger. **~o'so** *a.* peevish.

stizzi'r|e *v.t.* irritate. **~si** *v.r.* get cross.

stoccafi'sso *n.m.* stockfish.

stocca'ta *n.f.* stab; (*battuta pungente*) gibe.

sto'ffa *n.f.* material; (*fig.*) stuff.

sto'ic|o *a.* stoic. **~i'smo** *n.m.* stoicism.

sto'la *n.f.* stole.

sto'lto *a.* foolish.

sto'maco *n.m.* stomach. **mal di ~** stomach-ache.

stona're *v.t./i.* sing/play out of tune. **—v.i.** (*non intonarsi*) clash. **~to** *a.* out of tune; clashing; (*confuso*) bewildered. **~tu'ra** *n.f.* false note.

sto'ppa *n.f.* tow.

sto'ppia *n.f.* stubble.

stoppi'no *n.m.* wick.

sto'rcer|e *v.t.*, **~si** *v.r.* twist. **~si dal dolore** writhe in pain.

stordi'r|e *v.t.* stun; (*intontire*) daze. **~rsi** *v.r.* dull one's senses. **~to** *a.* stunned; dazed; (*sventato*) heedless.

sto'ri|a *n.f.* history; (*racconto, bugia*) story; (*pretesto*) excuse. **senza ~e!** no fuss! **~co** *a.* historic(al); *n.m.* historian.

storio'ne *n.m.* sturgeon.

stormi're *v.i.* rustle.

sto'rmo *n.m.* flock.

storna're *v.t.* avert; (*somma*) transfer.

sto'rno *n.m.* starling.

storpia're *v.t.* cripple; (*parole*) mangle. **sto'rpio, a** *a.* crippled; *n.m., f.* cripple.

sto'rto, a *p.p. di* storcere. —*a.* crooked; (*ritorto*) twisted; (*di gambe*) bandy; (*fig.*) wrong. —*n.f.* (*distorsione*) sprain.

stovi'glie *n.f. pl.* crockery *s.*

stra'b|ico *a.* cross-eyed. **essere ~ico** have a squint. **~i'smo** *n.m.* squint.

straca'rico *a.* overloaded.

stracci|a're *v.t.* tear. **~a'to** *a.* torn; (*di persona*) in rags. **stra'ccio** *a.* torn; (*di carta*) waste; *n.m.* rag; (*strofinaccio*) cloth; (*per la polvere*) duster. **~o'ne** *n.m.* ragamuffin.

straco'tto *a.* overdone. —*n.m.* stew.

stra'd|a *n.f.* road; (*di città*) street; (*fig., cammino*) way. **essere fuori ~a** be on the wrong track. **fare ~a** lead the way. **farsi ~a** make one's way. **~a a senso unico** one-way street. **~a maestra** main road. **~a senza uscita** blind alley. **~a'le** *a.* road.

strafalcio'ne *n.m.* blunder.

strafa're *v.i.* overdo.

strafo'ro *adv.* **di ~** on the sly.

strafotte'nte *a.* insolent.

stra'ge *n.f.* slaughter.

straluna'|re *v.t.* **~re gli occhi** open one's eyes wide. **~to** *a.* (*di occhi*) staring; (*di persona*) distraught.

stramazza're *v.i.* fall heavily.

stra'mb|o *a.* strange. **~eri'a** *n.f.* oddity.

strampala'to *a.* odd.

strangola're *v.t.* strangle.

stranie'ro, a *a.* foreign. —*n.m., f.* foreigner.

stra'n|o *a.* strange. **~e'zza** *n.f.* strangeness.

straordina'rio *a.* extraordinary; (*notevole*) remarkable. **lavoro ~** overtime. **treno ~** special train.

strapazza'r|e *v.t.* ill-treat; (*uovo*) scramble. **~si** *v.r.* tire oneself out. **strapa'zzo** *n.m.* strain. **da strapazzo** (*fig.*) worthless.

strapio'mbo *n.m.* projection. **a ~** sheer.

strappa'r|e *v.t.* tear (up); (*tirar via*) pull away; (*sradicare*) pull up; (*estorcere*) wring. **~si** *v.r.* get torn; (*allontanarsi*) tear oneself away. **stra'ppo** *n.m.* tear; (*muscolare*) sprain; (*strat-*

tone) jerk. **fare uno strappo alla regola** make an exception to the rule.

strapunti'no *n.m.* folding seat.

straripa're *v.i.* flood.

strascica're *v.t.* trail; (*piedi*) shuffle.

stra'scico *n.m.* train; (*fig.*) after-effect.

strass *n.m.* rhinestone.

stratage'mma *n.m.* stratagem.

strat|egi'a *n.f.* strategy. **~e'gico** *a.* strategic.

stra'to *n.m.* layer; (*di vernice ecc.*) coat; (*roccioso*) stratum.

stratosfe'ra *n.f.* stratosphere.

stravaga'n|te *a.* extravagant; (*eccentrico*) eccentric. **~za** *n.f.* extravagance; eccentricity.

stravede're *v.t.* see wrongly. **~ per** worship.

stravi'zio *n.m.* excess.

stravo'lgere *v.t.* twist; (*turbare*) upset.

strazia'|re *v.t.* tear apart. **~nte** *a.* heart-rending; (*dolore*) agonizing. **stra'zio** *n.m.* agony.

stre'g|a *n.f.* witch. **~a're** *v.t.* bewitch. **~o'ne** *n.m.* wizard.

stre'gua *n.f.* **alla ~ di** like.

strema'|re *v.t.* exhaust. **~to** *a.* exhausted.

stre'nna *n.f.* present.

stre'nuo *a.* strenuous.

strepit|a're *v.i.* make a din. **~o'so** *a.* noisy; (*fig.*) striking.

stre'tt|o, a *p.p. di* stringere. —*a.* narrow; (*serrato*) tight; (*vicino*) close; (*di dialetto*) broad; (*rigoroso*) strict. —*n.m.* (*geog.*) strait. —*n.f.* grasp. **essere alle ~e** be in dire straits. **lo ~o necessario** the bare minimum. **~a di mano** handshake. **~e'zza** *n.f.* narrowness. **~ezze** *n.f. pl.* (*difficoltà finanziarie*) financial difficulties.

stretto'ia *n.f.* bottleneck; (*fam., difficoltà*) tight spot.

stria'to *a.* striped.

stride'nte *a.* strident.

stri'd|ere *v.i.* squeak; (*fig.*) clash. **~o're** *n.m.* screech(ing).

stri'dulo *a.* shrill.

strill|a're *v.i.* scream. **stri'llo** *n.m.* scream. **~o'ne** *n.m.* newspaper seller.

striminzi'to *a.* skimpy; (*magro*) skinny.

strimpella're *v.t.* strum.

stri'nga *n.f.* lace.

stringa'to *a.* (*fig.*) terse.

stri'nger|e *v.t.* press; (*serrare*)

squeeze; (*tenere stretto*) hold tight; (*abito*) take in; (*comprimere*) be tight; (*restringere*) tighten. —*v.i.* (*premere*) press. ∾**si** *v.r.* ∾**si (a)** (*accostarsi*) draw close (to); (*avvicinarsi*) squeeze up. ∾**e la mano (a)** shake hands (with).

stri'sc|ia *n.f.* strip; (*riga*) stripe. ∾**e (pedonali)** *n.f. pl.* zebra crossing *s.*

striscia'r|e *v.i.* crawl; (*sfiorare*) graze. —*v.t.* (*piedi*) drag; graze. ∾**si** *v.r.* ∾**si a** rub against. **stri'scio** *n.m.* graze; (*med.*) smear. **colpire di striscio** graze.

stritola're *v.t.* grind.

strizza're *v.t.* squeeze; (*torcere*) wring (out). ∾ **l'occhio** wink.

stro'fa *n.f.* strophe.

strofina'ccio *n.m.* cloth; (*per spolverare*) duster.

strofina're *v.t.* rub.

stronca're *v.t.* cut off; (*reprimere*) crush.

stropiccia'r|e *v.t.* rub; (*vestito*) crumple.

strozza'|re *v.t.* strangle. ∾**tu'ra** *n.f.* strangling; (*di strada*) narrowing.

strozzi'no *n.m.* (*pej.*) usurer; (*truffatore*) shark.

stru'gg|ere *v.t.* melt; (*fig.*) consume. ∾**ersi** *v.r.* pine (away). ∾**e'nte** *a.* all-consuming.

strume'nt|o *n.m.* instrument; (*arnese*) tool. ∾**o a corda/fiato** string/wind instrument. ∾**a'le** *a.* instrumental. ∾**azio'ne** *n.f.* instrumentation.

struscia're *v.t.* rub.

stru'tto *n.m.* lard.

struttu'r|a *n.f.* structure. ∾**a'le** *a.* structural.

stru'zzo *n.m.* ostrich.

stucca'|re *v.t.* stucco. ∾**to're** *n.m.* plasterer. **stu'cco** *n.m.* stucco.

stucche'vole *a.* nauseating.

stude'nt|e *n.m.*, ∾**e'ssa** *n.f.* student; (*di scuola*) schoolboy, schoolgirl. ∾**e'sco** *a.* student; school.

stu'di|o *n.m.* studying; (*stanza, ricerca*) study; (*di artista, TV, ecc.*) studio; (*di professionista*) office. ∾**a're** *v.t.* study. ∾**a'rsi** *v.r.* ∾**arsi di** try to. ∾**o'so, a** *a.* studious; *n.m.*, *f.* scholar.

stu'fa *n.f.* stove. ∾ **elettrica** electric fire.

stufa'r|e *v.t.* (*culin.*) stew; (*dare fastidio*) bore. ∾**si** *v.r.* get bored. **stu'fo** *a.* bored. **essere stufo di** be fed up with.

stufa'to *n.m.* stew.

stuo'ia *n.f.* mat.

stupeface'nte *a.* amazing. —*n.m.* drug.

stupe'ndo *a.* stupendous.

stu'pid|o *a.* stupid. ∾**a'ggine** *n.f.* (*azione*) stupid thing; (*cosa da poco*) nothing. ∾**ità** *n.f.* stupidity.

stupi'r|e *v.t.* astonish. —*v.i.*, ∾**si** *v.r.* be astonished.

stupo're *n.m.* amazement.

stu'pro *n.m.* rape.

stu'r|a *n.f.* uncorking. ∾**a're** *v.t.* uncork; (*lavandino*) clear.

stuzzicade'nti *n.m. invar.* toothpick.

stuzzica're *v.t.* prod (at); (*denti*) pick; (*fuoco*) poke; (*molestare*) tease; (*l'appetito*) whet.

su *prep.* on, upon; (*senza contatto*) over; (*al di sopra di*) above; (*circa, intorno a*) about. ∾ **due piedi** on the spot. ∾ **misura** made to measure. **uno** ∾ **dieci** one out of ten. —*adv.* (*sopra*) up (above); (*al piano di sopra*) upstairs; (*indosso*) on. ∾**!** come on!

suba'cqueo *a.* underwater.

subalte'rno *a.* & *n.m.* subordinate.

subbu'glio *n.m.* turmoil.

subcoscie'nte *a.* & *n.m.* subconscious.

su'bdolo *a.* underhand; (*fam.*) sneaky.

subentra're *v.i.* take the place (of).

subi're *v.t.* undergo; (*patire*) suffer.

subi'ss|o *n.m.* ruin. ∾**a're** *v.t.* (*fig.*) ∾ **are di** overwhelm with.

subita'neo *a.* sudden.

su'bito *adv.* at once. ∾ **dopo** soon afterwards.

subli'me *a.* sublime.

subodora're *v.t.* suspect.

subordina'to, a *a.* & *n.m.*, *f.* subordinate.

suburba'no *a.* suburban.

succe'der|e *v.i.* (*accadere*) happen. ∾**e a** succeed; (*venire dopo*) follow. ∾**e al trono** succeed to the throne. ∾**si** *v.r.* follow each other.

successi|o'ne *n.f.* succession. ∾**i'vo** *a.* successive. ∾**o're** *n.m.* successor.

succe'sso *p.p. di* **succedere**. —*n.m.* success; (*esito*) outcome; (*di disco ecc.*) hit.

succhia're *v.t.* suck (up).

succi'nto *a.* (*conciso*) concise; (*di abito*) scanty.

su'cc|o *n.m.* juice; (*fig.*) essence. ∾**o'so** *a.* juicy. ∾**ule'nto** *a.* succulent.

succursa'le *n.f.* branch (office).

sud *n.m.* south. **del** ∾ southern.

~-e'st *n.m.* south-east. ~-o'vest *n.m.* south-west.

sud|a're *v.i.* perspire, sweat. ~are freddo be in a cold sweat. ~a'ta *n.f.* sweat. ~a'to *a.* perspiring. ~o're *n.m.* perspiration, sweat.

sudde'tto *a.* above-mentioned.

su'ddito, a *n.m.,f.* subject.

suddivi'|dere *v.t.* subdivide. ~sio'ne *n.f.* subdivision.

su'dici|o *a.* dirty; (*più forte*) filthy. ~u'me *n.m.* dirt; filth.

sufficie'n|te *a.* sufficient; (*presuntuoso*) conceited. —*n.m.* bare essentials *pl.*; (*schol.*) pass-mark. ~za *n.f.* sufficiency; conceit; pass. a ~za enough.

suffi'sso *n.m.* suffix.

suffra'gio *n.m.* (*voto*) vote.

suffumica're *v.t.* fumigate.

suggeri'|re *v.t.* suggest; (*theatr.*) prompt. ~me'nto *n.m.* suggestion. ~to're, ~tri'ce *n.m.,f.* prompter.

suggestio'n|e *n.f.* suggestion. ~a'bile *a.* easily influenced. ~a're *v.t.* influence.

suggesti'vo *a.* suggestive; (*di musica ecc.*) evocative.

su'ghero *n.m.* cork.

su'gna *n.f.* suet.

su'go *n.m.* (*di frutta*) juice; (*di carne*) gravy; (*salsa*) sauce.

suici'd|io *n.m.* suicide. ~a *a.* suicidal; *n.m./f.* suicide. ~a'rsi *v.r.* commit suicide.

sui'n|o *a.* carne ~a pork. —*n.m.* swine.

sul = su + il. su'llo = su + lo. su'lla = su + la. su'i = su+ i. su'gli = su + gli. su'lle = su + le.

sultani'na *a.* uva ~ sultana.

sulta'n|o *n.m.* sultan. ~a *n.f.* sultana.

su'nto *n.m.* summary.

su'o, a *a.* (*pl.* suoi, sue) (*di lui*) his; (*di lei*) her; (*di esso*) its; (*forma di cortesia*) your. —*pron.* his, hers, its; (*nella chiusa delle lettere*) S~ Yours.

suo'cer|o *n.m.* father-in-law. ~a *n.f.* mother-in-law.

suo'la *n.f.* sole.

suo'lo *n.m.* ground; (*terreno*) soil.

suona'|re *v.t./i.* (*mus.*) play; (*campanello*) ring; (*allarme, clacson*) sound; (*orologio*) strike. ~to're, ~tri'ce *n.m.,f.* player.

suo'no *n.m.* sound.

suo'ra *n.f.* nun. **Suor Maria** Sister Mary.

supera're *v.t.* surpass; (*eccedere*) exceed; (*vincere*) overcome; (*veicolo*) overtake; (*esame*) get through.

supe'rb|ia *n.f.* haughtiness. ~o *a.* haughty; (*magnifico*) superb.

superfi'ci|e *n.f.* surface; (*area*) area. ~a'le *a.* superficial.

supe'rfluo *a.* superfluous.

superio'r|e *a.* superior; (*di grado*) senior; (*più elevato*) higher; (*sovrastante*) upper; (*al di sopra*) above. ~e, a *n.m., f.* superior. ~ità *n.f.* superiority.

superlati'vo *a.* & *n.m.* superlative.

supermerca'to *n.m.* supermarket.

superso'nico *a.* supersonic.

supe'rstite *a.* surviving. —*n.m./f.* survivor.

superstizio'|ne *n.f.* superstition. ~so *a.* superstitious.

superuo'mo *n.m.* superman.

supi'no *a.* supine.

suppelle'ttili *n.f. pl.* furnishings.

suppergiù *adv.* about.

suppleme'nt|o *n.m.* supplement. ~a're *a.* supplementary.

supple'nte *a.* temporary. —*n.m./f.* (*schol.*) supply teacher.

su'pplic|a *n.f.* plea; (*domanda*) petition. ~a're *v.t.* beg.

suppli're *v.t.* replace. —*v.i.* ~ a (*compensare*) make up for.

suppli'zio *n.m.* torture.

suppo'rre *v.t.* suppose.

suppo'rto *n.m.* support.

supposizio'ne *n.f.* supposition.

suppo'sta *n.f.* suppository.

suppo'sto *p.p.* di supporre.

suppura're *v.i.* fester.

supremazi'a *n.f.* supremacy.

supre'mo *a.* supreme.

surgela'|re *v.t.* deep-freeze. ~ti *n.m. pl.* frozen foods.

surreali's|mo *n.m.* surrealism. ~ta *n.m./f.* surrealist.

surroga'to *n.m.* substitute.

suscetti'bil|e *a.* susceptible. ~ità *n.f.* susceptibility.

suscita're *v.t.* stir up; (*ammirazione ecc.*) arouse.

susi'n|a *n.f.* plum. ~o *n.m.* plum-tree.

sussegue'nte *a.* subsequent.

sussegui'r|e *v.t.* follow. ~si *v.r.* follow one another.

sussidia'rio *a.* subsidiary.

sussi'di|o *n.m.* subsidy; (*aiuto*) aid. ~a're *v.t.* subsidize.

sussie'go *n.m.* haughtiness.

suss|iste'nza *n.f.* subsistence. ~i'-
stere *v.i.* subsist; (*essere valido*) hold
good.
suss|ulta're *v.i.* start. ~u'lto *n.m.*
start.
suss|urra're *v.t.* whisper. ~u'rro
n.m. whisper.
sutu'r|a *n.f.* suture. ~a're *v.t.* suture.
svaga'r|e *v.t.* amuse. ~si *v.r.* amuse
oneself. **sva'go** *n.m.* diversion.
svaligia're *v.t.* rob; (*casa*) burgle.
svaluta'|re *v.t.* devalue; (*fig.*) under-
estimate. ~zio'ne *n.f.* devaluation.
svani're *v.i.* vanish.
svanta'ggio *n.m.* disadvantage.
svapora're *v.i.* evaporate.
svaria'to *a.* varied.
svasa't|o *a.* flared. ~u'ra *n.f.* flare.
sva'stica *n.f.* swastika.
svede'se *a. & n.m.* (*lingua*) Swedish.
—*n.m.|f.* Swede.
sve'glia *n.f.* (*segnale*) call; (*orologio*)
alarm (clock).
sveglia'r|e *v.t.* wake up; (*fig.*) awaken.
~si *v.r.* wake up. **sve'glio** *a.* awake;
(*di mente*) quick-witted.
svela're *v.t.* reveal.
svelti'r|e *v.t.* quicken. ~si *v.r.* (*di
persona*) liven up. **sve'lto** *a.* quick;
(*slanciato*) svelte. **alla svelta** quickly.
sve'nd|ere *v.t.* undersell. ~ita *n.f.*
(clearance) sale.
sveni'|re *v.i.* faint. ~me'nto fainting
fit.
sventa're *v.t.* foil.
sventa'to *a.* careless.
sventola're *v.t./i.* wave.
sventra're *v.t.* disembowel.

sventu'r|a *n.f.* misfortune. ~a'to *a.*
unfortunate.
svenu'to *p.p. di* **svenire.**
svergogna'to *a.* shameless.
sverna're *v.i.* winter.
svesti'r|e *v.t.*, ~si *v.r.* undress.
Sve'zia *n.f.* Sweden.
svezza're *v.t.* wean.
svia'r|e *v.t.* divert; (*corrompere*) lead
astray. ~si *v.r.* go astray.
svigna'rsela *v.r.* slip away.
sviluppa'r|e *v.t.*, ~si *v.r.* develop. **svi-
lu'ppo** *n.m.* development.
svincola'r|e *v.t.* release; (*merce*) clear.
~si *v.r.* free oneself. **svi'ncolo** *n.m.*
clearance; (*di autostrada*) exit.
svisa're *v.t.* distort.
sviscera'|re *v.t.* gut; (*fig.*) dissect. ~to
a. (*amore*) passionate; (*ossequioso*)
obsequious.
svi'sta *n.f.* oversight.
svita're *v.t.* unscrew.
Svi'zzer|a *n.f.* Switzerland. **s~o, a**
a. & n.m., f. Swiss.
svoglia'to *a.* lazy.
svolazza'|re *v.i.* flutter. ~nte *a.* (*di
capelli*) wind-swept.
svo'lger|e *v.t.* unwind; (*pacco*) un-
wrap; (*risolvere*) solve; (*portare a termine*) carry out; (*sviluppare*) develop.
~si *v.r.* (*accadere*) take place.
svolgime'nto *n.m.* course; (*sviluppo*)
development.
svo'lt|a *n.f.* turning; (*fig.*) turning-
point. ~a're *v.i.* turn.
svo'lto *p.p. di* **svolgere.**
svuota're *v.t.* empty (out).

T

taba'cc|o *n.m.* tobacco. ∼a'io, a *n.m.*, *f.* tobacconist. ∼heri'a *n.f.* tobacconist's (shop).

tabe'lla *n.f.* table; (*lista*) list.

taberna'colo *n.m.* tabernacle.

tabù *a.* & *n.m.* taboo.

ta'cca *n.f.* notch; (*fig.*) quality.

tacca'gno *a.* (*fam.*) stingy.

tacche'ggio *n.m.* shop-lifting.

tacchi'no *n.m.* turkey.

ta'ccia *n.f.* (*cattiva fama*) bad reputation.

ta'cco *n.m.* heel.

taccui'no *n.m.* notebook.

tace're *v.i.* be silent. —*v.t.* say nothing (about).

tachi'metro *n.m.* speedometer.

ta'cito *a.* silent; (*inespresso*) tacit.

tacitu'rno *a.* taciturn.

tafa'no *n.m.* horse-fly.

tafferu'glio *n.m.* scuffle.

ta'glia *n.f.* (*riscatto*) ransom; (*ricompensa*) reward; (*statura*) height; (*misura*) size.

tagliaca'rte *n.m. invar.* paper-knife.

taglia'ndo *n.m.* coupon.

taglia're *v.t.* cut; (*attraversare*) cut across; (*interrompere*) cut off; (*togliere*) cut out; (*carne*) carve; (*erba*) mow. —*v.i.* cut. ta'glio *n.m.* cut; (*il tagliare*) cutting; (*di stoffa*) length; (*parte tagliente*) edge.

taglie'nte *a.* sharp.

taglio'la *n.f.* trap.

tagliuzza're *v.t.* cut into small pieces.

ta'lco *n.m.* talcum powder.

ta'le *a.* such; (*così grande*) such a. il ∼ giorno on such and such a day. quel tal signore that gentleman. ∼ padre ∼ figlio like father like son. ∼ quale just like. —*pron.* un ∼ someone.

tale'nto *n.m.* talent.

talisma'no *n.m.* talisman.

tallonci'no *n.m.* coupon.

tallo'ne *n.m.* heel.

talme'nte *adv.* so.

talo'ra *adv.* = talvolta.

ta'lpa *n.f.* mole.

talvo'lta *adv.* sometimes.

tambure'llo *n.m.* tambourine.

tambu'r|o *n.m.* drum. ∼i'no *n.m.* drummer.

Tami'gi *n.m.* Thames.

tampona're *v.t.* (*urtare*) crash into; (*otturare*) plug.

tampo'ne *n.m.* plug; (*med.*) tampon; (*ferrovia*) buffer.

ta'na *n.f.* den.

ta'nfo *n.m.* stench.

tange'nte *a.* & *n.f.* tangent.

tangi'bile *a.* tangible.

ta'ngo *n.m.* tango.

tanti'no *adv.* un ∼ a little (bit).

ta'nto *a. indef.* (so) much (*pl.* (so) many); (*così lungo*) so long; (*in correlazione con quanto*) as much (*pl.* as many). —*pron.* so much (*pl.* so many); (*molto*) a lot. —*conj.* (*comunque*) in any case. —*adv.* (*così*) so; (*così a lungo*) so long. di ∼ in ∼ every now and then. ∼ l'uno come l'altro both. ∼ quanto as much as. tre volte ∼ three times as much. una volta ∼ once in a while.

ta'ppa *n.f.* stop; (*parte di viaggio*) stage.

tappa're *v.t.* plug; (*bottiglia*) cork. ∼ la bocca a qcno. (*fam.*) shut s.o. up.

tappare'lla *n.f.* (*fam.*) (roller) blind.

tappe'to *n.m.* carpet; (*piccolo*) rug.

tappezza're *v.t.* (*pareti*) paper; (*rivestire*) cover.

tappezz|eri'a *n.f.* tapestry; (*di carta*) wallpaper; (*arte*) upholstery. ∼ie're *n.m.* upholsterer.

ta'ppo *n.m.* plug; (*di sughero*) cork; (*fam., persona piccola*) short person.

tara'ntola *n.f.* tarantula.

tarchia'to *a.* stocky.

tarda're *v.i.* be late. —*v.t.* delay.

ta'rd|i *adv.* late. al più ∼i at the latest. più ∼i later (on). sul ∼i late in the day. ∼i'vo *a.* late; (*di persona*) retarded. ∼o *a.* slow; (*di tempo*) late.

ta'rg|a *n.f.* plate; (*auto*) number-plate. ∼he'tta *n.f.* (*di porta*) door-plate.

tari'ffa *n.f.* rate, tariff.

ta'rl|o *n.m.* woodworm. ∼a'rsi *v.r.* get wormeaten.

ta'rm|a *n.f.* moth. ∼a'rsi *v.r.* get moth-eaten.

taro'cco *n.m.* tarot.

tarpa're *v.t.* clip.

tartaglia're *v.i.* stutter.

ta'rtaro *a.* & *n.m.* tartar.

tartaru'ga *n.f.* tortoise; (*di mare*) turtle; (*per pettine ecc.*) tortoiseshell.

tarti'na *n.f.* canapé.

tartu'fo *n.m.* truffle.

ta'sc|a *n.f.* pocket. ~**a'bile** *a.* pocket. ~**hi'no** *n.m.* breast pocket.

tascapa'ne *n.m.* haversack.

ta'ss|a *n.f.* tax; (*d'iscrizione ecc.*) fee; (*doganale*) duty. ~**a're** *v.t.* tax. ~**azio'ne** *n.f.* taxation.

tassa'metro *n.m.* taximeter.

tassati'vo *a.* peremptory.

tasse'llo *n.m.* wedge; (*di stoffa*) gusset.

tass|ì *n.m. invar.* taxi. ~**i'sta** *n.m./f.* taxi-driver.

ta'sso *n.m.* (*bot.*) yew; (*animale*) badger; (*comm.*) rate.

tasta're *v.t.* feel; (*sondare*) sound. ~ **il terreno** (*fig.*) feel one's way.

ta'st|o *n.m.* key; (*tatto*) touch. ~**ie'ra** *n.f.* keyboard.

tasto'ni *adv.* **a** ~ gropingly.

ta'ttic|o *a.* tactical. ~**a** *n.f.* tactics *pl.*

ta'tto *n.m.* (*senso*) touch; (*accortezza*) tact. **aver** ~ be tactful.

tatua'|ggio *n.m.* tattoo. ~**re** *v.t.* tattoo.

tave'rna *n.f.* tavern; (*trattoria*) inn.

ta'vol|a *n.f.* table; (*asse*) plank; (*di marmo*) slab. ~**a calda** snack-bar. ~**i'no** *n.m.* small table. ~**o** *n.m.* table. ~**o da stiro** ironing-board.

tavola'to *n.m.* boarding; (*di pavimento*) wood floor.

tavole'tta *n.f.* bar; (*medicinale*) tablet.

tavolo'zza *n.f.* palette.

ta'zza *n.f.* cup. ~ **da caffè/tè** coffee-cup/teacup.

te *pron.* you; (*termine*) (to) you; (*te stesso*) yourself.

tè *n.m. invar.* tea.

tea'tr|o *n.m.* theatre. ~**o d'avanguardia** fringe theatre. ~**a'le** *a.* theatrical.

te'cnic|o, a *a.* technical. —*n.m.*, *f.* technician. —*n.f.* technique.

tecnologi'a *n.f.* technology.

tede'sco, a *a. & n.m.*, *f.* German.

te'di|o *n.m.* tedium. ~**o'so** *a.* tedious.

tega'me *n.m.* saucepan.

te'glia *n.f.* baking tin.

te'gola *n.f.* tile; (*fig.*) blow.

teie'ra *n.f.* teapot.

te'la *n.f.* cloth; (*per quadri, vele*) canvas; (*theatr.*) curtain. ~ **cerata** oilcloth. ~ **di lino** linen.

tela'io *n.m.* loom; (*cornice*) frame.

teleca'mera *n.f.* television camera.

telecoma'ndo *n.m.* remote control.

telecomunicazio'ni *n.f.* *pl.* telecommunications.

telecro'n|aca *n.f.* newsreel. ~**i'sta** *n.m./f.* television commentator.

telefe'rica *n.f.* cableway.

tele'f|ono *n.m.* telephone. ~**ono a gettoni** coin-box. ~**ona're** *v.t./i.* (tele)phone, ring. ~**ona'ta** *n.f.* (telephone) call. ~**onata interurbana** trunk call. ~**o'nico** *a.* (tele)phone. ~**oni'sta** *n.m./f.* (telephone) operator.

telegiorna'le *n.m.* television news.

tele'gr|afo *n.m.* telegraph (office). ~**afa're** *v.t.* telegraph. ~**afi'a** *n.f.* telegraphy. ~**a'fico** *a.* telegraphic.

telegra'mma *n.m.* telegram.

telep|ati'a *n.f.* telepathy. ~**a'tico** *a.* telepathic.

teleroma'nzo *n.m.* television serial.

telesco'pio *n.m.* telescope.

teleselezio'ne *n.f.* subscriber trunk dialling (*abbr.* STD).

telespetta|to're, ~tri'ce *n.m.,f.* (tele)viewer.

televis|io'ne *n.f.* television. ~**o're** *n.m.* television set.

te'ma *n.m.* theme; (*schol.*) essay.

temera'rio *a.* reckless.

teme're *v.t.* fear, be afraid of.

temperamati'te *n.m. invar.* pencil-sharpener.

temperame'nto *n.m.* temperament.

tempera'|re *v.t.* temper; (*matita*) sharpen. ~**to** *a.* temperate.

temperatu'ra *n.f.* temperature.

temperi'no *n.m.* penknife.

tempe'st|a *n.f.* storm. ~**o'so** *a.* stormy.

tempesti'vo *a.* timely.

te'mpia *n.f.* temple.

te'mpio *n.m.* temple.

te'mpo *n.m.* time; (*atmosferico*) weather; (*mus.*) tempo; (*gram.*) tense; (*di film, gioco*) part. **a suo** ~ in due course. ~ **fa** some time ago. **un** ~ once.

tempora'le *a.* temporal. —*n.m.* (thunder)storm.

tempora'neo *a.* temporary.

temporeggia're *v.i.* temporize.

tempra're *v.t.* temper.

tena'c|e *a.* tenacious. ~**ia** *n.f.* tenacity.

tena'glia *n.f.* pincers *pl.*

te'nda *n.f.* curtain; (*per campeggio*) tent; (*tendone*) awning.

tende'nza *n.f.* tendency.

te'ndere *v.t.* (*allargare*) stretch (out); (*tirare*) tighten; (*porgere*) hold out; (*fig., trappola*) lay. —*v.i.* ~ a aim at; (*essere inclinato*) tend.

te'ndine *n.m.* tendon.

tendo'ne *n.m.* awning; (*di circo*) tent.

te'nebr|e *n.f. pl.* darkness *s.* ~o'so *a.* gloomy.

tene'nte *n.m.* lieutenant.

tene'r|e *v.t.* hold; (*mantenere*) keep; (*gestire*) run; (*prendere*) take; (*seguire*) follow; (*considerare*) consider. —*v.i.* hold. ~ci, ~e a be keen on. ~e per (*essere a favore di*) be for. ~si *v.r.* keep oneself. ~si a hold on to; (*seguire*) stick to. ~si indietro stand back.

te'ner|o *a.* tender. ~e'zza *n.f.* tenderness.

te'nia *n.f.* tapeworm.

te'nnis *n.m.* tennis.

teno're *n.m.* standard; (*mus.*) tenor. a ~ di legge by law. ~ di vita standard of living.

tensio'ne *n.f.* tension.

tenta'colo *n.m.* tentacle.

tenta'|re *v.t.* attempt; (*sperimentare*) try; (*indurre in tentazione*) tempt. ~ti'vo *n.m.* attempt. ~zio'ne *n.f.* temptation.

tentenna're *v.i.* waver; (*esitare*) hesitate. —*v.t.* shake.

tento'ni *adv.* a ~ gropingly.

te'nue *a.* fine; (*debole*) weak; (*esiguo*) small; (*leggero*) slight.

tenu'ta *n.f.* (*capacità*) capacity; (*possedimento*) estate; (*divisa*) uniform; (*abbigliamento*) clothes *pl.* a ~ d'aria airtight.

teol|ogi'a *n.f.* theology. ~o'gico *a.* theological. **teo'logo** *n.m.* theologian.

teore'ma *n.m.* theorem.

teori'a *n.f.* theory. **teo'rico** *a.* theoretic(al).

tepo're *n.m.* warmth.

te'pp|a *n.f.* mob. ~i'smo *n.m.* hooliganism. ~i'sta *n.m.* hooligan.

terap|i'a *n.f.* therapy. ~e'utico *a.* therapeutic(al).

tergicrista'llo *n.m.* windscreen wiper.

tergiversa're *v.i.* hesitate.

te'rgo *n.m.* a ~ behind. **segue a** ~ please turn over (*abbr.* PTO).

te'rm|e *n.f. pl.* thermal baths. ~a'le *a.* thermal. **stazione** ~ale spa.

te'rmico *a.* thermic.

termina'le *a.* & *n.m.* terminal.

termina're *v.t./i.* finish, end.

te'rmine *n.m.* (*limite*) limit; (*fine*) end; (*condizione, espressione*) term.

terminologi'a *n.f.* terminology.

te'rmite *n.f.* termite.

termocope'rta *n.f.* electric blanket.

termo'metro *n.m.* thermometer.

te'rmos *n.m. invar.* thermos.

termosifo'ne *n.m.* radiator; (*sistema*) central heating.

termo'stato *n.m.* thermostat.

te'rra *n.f.* earth; (*regione*) land; (*terreno*) ground; (*argilla*) clay. **per** ~ on the ground. **sotto** ~ underground.

terraco'tta *n.f.* terracotta. **vasellame di** ~ earthenware.

terrafe'rma *n.f.* dry land.

terrapie'no *n.m.* embankment.

terra'zz|a *n.f.*, ~o *n.m.* terrace.

terremo'to *n.m.* earthquake.

terre'no *a.* earthly. —*n.m.* ground; (*suolo*) soil; (*proprietà terriera*) land.

terre'stre *a.* earthly. **esercito** ~ land forces *pl.*

terri'bile *a.* terrible.

terrifica'nte *a.* terrifying.

terri'na *n.f.* tureen.

territo'ri|o *n.m.* territory. ~a'le *a.* territorial.

terro'r|e *n.m.* terror. ~i'smo *n.m.* terrorism. ~i'sta *n.m./f.* terrorist. ~izza're *v.t.* terrorize.

te'rso *a.* clear.

te'rz|o *a.* third. —*n.m.* third. ~i *n.m. pl.* (*legge*) third party *s.*

te'sa *n.f.* brim.

te'schio *n.m.* skull.

te'si *n.f.* thesis.

te'so *p.p. di* **tendere**. —*a.* taut; (*fig.*) tense.

teso'r|o *n.m.* treasure; (*tesoreria*) treasury. ~eri'a *n.f.* treasury. ~ie're *n.m.* treasurer.

te'ssera *n.f.* card.

te'ss|ere *v.t.* weave. ~ito're, ~tri'ce *n.m., f.* weaver. ~itu'ra *n.f.* weaving.

te'ssil|e *a.* textile. ~i *n.m. pl.* textiles; (*operai*) textile workers.

tessu'to *n.m.* fabric; (*anat.*) tissue.

te'sta *n.f.* head; (*cervello*) brain. **essere in** ~ a be ahead of. **in** ~ (*sport*) in the lead.

testame'nto *n.m.* will. T~ (*relig.*) Testament.

testa'rd|o *a.* stubborn. **~a'ggine** *n.f.* stubbornness.

testa'ta *n.f.* head; (*intestazione*) heading; (*colpo*) butt.

te'ste *n.m.|f.* witness.

testi'colo *n.m.* testicle.

testimo'n|e *n.m.|f.* witness. **~ia'nza** *n.f.* testimony. **~ia're** *v.t.* witness; *v.i.* give evidence.

te'st|o *n.m.* text. **far ~o** be an authority. **~ua'le** *a.* textual.

testo'ne, a *n.m., f.* blockhead.

te'tano *n.m.* tetanus.

te'tro *a.* gloomy.

te'tt|o *n.m.* roof. **~o'ia** *n.f.* roofing.

Te'vere *n.m.* Tiber.

ti *pron.* you; (*termine*) (to) you; (*riflessivo*) yourself. **eccoti!** here you are! **sbrigati!** hurry up!

tia'ra *n.f.* tiara.

tic *n.m. invar.* tic.

ticchett|a're *v.i.* tick. **~i'o** *n.m.* ticking.

ti'cchio *n.m.* tic; (*ghiribizzo*) whim.

tie'pido *a.* lukewarm.

ti'f|o *n.m.* (*med.*) typhus. **far il ~o per** (*fig.*) be a fan of. **~a're** *v.i.* **~are per** shout for. **~o'so, a** *n.m., f.* fan.

tifoide'a *n.f.* typhoid.

tifo'ne *n.m.* typhoon.

ti'glio *n.m.* lime.

ti'gre *n.f.* tiger.

timba'llo *n.m.* (*culin.*) pie.

ti'mbr|o *n.m.* stamp; (*di voce*) tone. **~a're** *v.t.* stamp.

ti'mid|o *a.* shy. **~e'zza** *n.f.* shyness.

ti'mo *n.m.* thyme.

timo'n|e *n.m.* rudder. **~ie're** *n.m.* helmsman.

timo'r|e *n.m.* fear; (*soggezione*) awe. **~o'so** *a.* timorous.

ti'mpano *n.m.* eardrum; (*mus.*) kettledrum.

tine'llo *n.m.* morning-room.

ti'n|o *n.m.*, **~o'zza** *n.f.* tub.

ti'nt|a *n.f.* dye; (*colore*) colour. **~ori'a** *n.f.* (*negozio*) cleaner's. **~u'ra** *n.f.* dyeing; (*colorante*) dye.

tintare'lla *n.f.* (*fam.*) sun-tan.

tintinna're *v.i.* tinkle.

ti'nto *p.p. di* **tingere.**

ti'pico *a.* typical.

ti'po *n.m.* type; (*fam., individuo*) chap.

tip|ografi'a *n.f.* typography. **~ogra'fico** *a.* typographic(al). **~o'grafo** *n.m.* printer.

tira'ggio *n.m.* draught.

tira'nn|o, a *a.* tyrannical. —*n.m., f.* tyrant. **~eggia're** *v.t.* tyrannize. **~i'a** *n.f.* tyranny.

tirapie'di *n.m.* (*pej.*) hanger-on.

tira'r|e *v.t.* pull; (*gettare*) throw; (*tracciare*) draw; (*stampare*) print. —*v.i.* draw; (*vento*) blow; (*abito*) be tight; (*sparare*) shoot. **~e avanti** struggle on. **~e su** (*bambino*) bring up. **~si** *v.r.* draw (oneself). **~si indietro** move back.

tirasse'gno *n.m.* darts *pl.*

tirato're *n.m.* shot. **~ scelto** marksman.

tiratu'ra *n.f.* printing; (*di giornali*) circulation; (*di libri*) run.

ti'rchi|o *a.* mean. **~eri'a** *n.f.* meanness.

ti'ro *n.m.* (*traino*) draught; (*lancio*) throw; (*sparo*) shot; (*scherzo*) trick. **~ a segno** rifle-range.

tiroci'nio *n.m.* apprenticeship.

tiro'ide *n.f.* thyroid.

Tirre'no *n.m.* **il (mar) ~** the Tyrrhenian Sea.

tisa'na *n.f.* herb tea.

titilla're *v.t.* titillate.

titola're *a.* regular. —*n.m.|f.* principal; (*proprietario*) owner; (*calcio*) regular player.

ti'tolo *n.m.* title; (*accademico*) qualification; (*comm.*) security. **a ~ di** as.

tituba'|re *v.i.* hesitate. **~nte** *a.* hesitant.

ti'zio *n.m.* fellow.

tizzo'ne *n.m.* brand.

tocca'|re *v.t.* touch; (*tastare*) feel; (*riguardare*) concern; (*fare scalo*) call at. —*v.i.* **~re a** (*capitare*) happen; (*spettare*) be up to; (*essere obbligato*) have to. **tocca a te** it is your turn. **~nte** *a.* touching. **to'cco** *n.m.* touch; (*di pennello, campana*) stroke.

to'glier|e *v.t.* take away/off; (*strappar via*) remove. **~si** *v.r.* get away/out; (*abito*) take off.

tole'tta *n.f.* toilet; (*mobile*) dressing-table.

tollera'|re *v.t.* tolerate. **~nte** *a.* tolerant. **~nza** *n.f.* tolerance.

to'lto *p.p. di* **togliere.**

toma'ia *n.f.* upper.

to'mba *n.f.* grave, tomb.

tombi'no *n.m.* manhole cover.

to'mbola *n.f.* bingo; (*caduta*) tumble.

to'mo *n.m.* tome.

to'naca *n.f.* habit.

to'ndo *a.* round.

to'nfo *n.m.* thud; (*in acqua*) splash.

to'nico *a.* & *n.m.* tonic.
tonifica're *v.t.* brace.
tonnella'|ta *n.f.* ton. **~ggio** *n.m.* tonnage.
to'nno *n.m.* tunny (fish).
to'no *n.m.* tone; (*mus.*, *armonia*) tune.
tonsi'll|a *n.f.* tonsil. **~i'te** *n.f.* tonsillitis.
tonsu'ra *n.f.* tonsure.
to'nto *a.* (*fam.*) thick.
topa'zio *n.m.* topaz.
to'po *n.m.* mouse.
topogr|afi'a *n.f.* topography. **~a'fico** *a.* topographic(al).
to'ppa *n.f.* (*rattoppo*) patch; (*serratura*) keyhole.
tora'ce *n.m.* chest.
to'rba *n.f.* peat.
to'rbido *a.* muddy; (*fig.*) troubled.
to'rcer|e *v.t.* twist; (*biancheria*) wring (out). **~si** *v.r.* twist.
to'rchio *n.m.* press.
to'rcia *n.f.* torch.
torcico'llo *n.m.* stiff neck.
to'rdo *n.m.* thrush.
Tori'no *n.f.* Turin.
torme'nta *n.f.* snowstorm.
torm|enta're *v.t.* torment. **~e'nto** *n.m.* torment.
tornaco'nto *n.m.* profit.
torna'nte *n.m.* hairpin bend.
torna're *v.i.* return, go/come back; (*risultare*) be; (*ridiventare*) become again.
torne'o *n.m.* tournament.
to'rnio *n.m.* lathe.
to'ro *n.m.* bull; (*astr.*) Taurus.
torpe'din|e *n.f.* torpedo. **~ie'ra** *n.f.* torpedo-boat.
torpedo'ne *n.m.* coach.
torpo're *n.m.* torpor.
to'rre *n.f.* tower; (*scacchi*) castle.
torrefazio'ne *n.f.* roasting.
torre'n|te *n.m.* torrent. **~zia'le** *a.* torrential.
torre'tta *n.f.* turret.
to'rrido *a.* torrid.
torrio'ne *n.m.* keep.
torro'ne *n.m.* nougat.
torsio'ne *n.f.* twisting.
to'rso *n.m.* torso.
to'rsolo *n.m.* core.
to'rta *n.f.* cake; (*crostata*) tart.
tortie'ra *n.f.* baking tin.
to'rto *p.p. di* **torcere**. —*a.* twisted. —*n.m.* wrong; (*colpa*) fault. **aver ~** be wrong.
to'rtora *n.f.* turtle-dove.

tortuo'so *a.* winding; (*ambiguo*) tortuous.
tortu'r|a *n.f.* torture. **~a're** *v.t.* torture.
to'rvo *a.* grim.
tosa're *v.t.* shear. **~tu'ra** *n.f.* shearing.
Tosca'na *n.f.* Tuscany.
to'ss|e *n.f.* cough. **~i're** *v.i.* cough.
to'ssico *a.* toxic. —*n.m.* poison.
tossico'mane *n.m.|f.* drug addict.
tostapa'ne *n.m.* toaster.
tosta're *v.t.* (*pane*) toast; (*caffè*) roast.
to'st|o *adv.* (*subito*) soon. —*a.* **faccia ~a** cheek.
tota'l|e *a.* total. **~ità** *n.f.* totality. **~izza're** *v.t.* total. **~me'nte** *adv.* totally.
totalita'rio *a.* totalitarian.
totoca'lcio *n.m.* (football) pools *pl.*
tova'gli|a *n.f.* tablecloth. **~o'lo** *n.m.* napkin.
to'zzo *a.* squat. —*n.m.* **~ di pane** crust of bread.
tra *prep.* = **fra**.
traballa'|re *v.i.* stagger; (*di veicolo*) jolt. **~nte** *a.* staggering; (*di sedia*) rickety.
trabocca're *v.i.* overflow.
trabocche'tto *n.m.* trap.
tracanna're *v.t.* gulp down.
tra'cci|a *n.f.* track; (*orma*) footstep; (*striscia*) trail; (*residuo*) trace; (*fig.*) sign. **~a're** *v.t.* trace; (*schema*) sketch out; (*linea*) draw. **~a'to** *n.m.* (*schema*) layout.
trache'a *n.f.* windpipe.
traco'lla *n.f.* shoulder-strap. **borsa a ~** shoulder-bag.
traco'll|o *n.m.* collapse. **~a're** *v.i.* lose one's balance.
tradi'|re *v.t.* betray; (*moglie*, *marito*) be unfaithful to. **~me'nto** *n.m.* betrayal; (*pol.*) treason. **~to're**, **~tri'ce** *n.m.*, *f.* traitor.
tradizio'n|e *n.f.* tradition. **~a'le** *a.* traditional. **~ali'sta** *n.m.|f.* traditionalist.
trado'tto *p.p. di* **tradurre**.
tradu'|rre *v.t.* translate. **~tto're**, **~ttri'ce** *n.m.*, *f.* translator. **~zio'ne** *n.f.* translation.
trae'nte *n.m.|f.* (*comm.*) drawer.
trafela'to *a.* breathless.
traffica'|re *v.i.* **~re (in)** trade (in); (*affaccendarsi*) busy oneself. **~nte** *n.m.|f.* dealer. **~nte di droga** (drug) pusher.
tra'ffico *n.m.* traffic; (*comm.*) trade.

trafi'ggere *v.t.* stab; (*straziare*) pierce.

trafo'r|o *n.m.* boring; (*galleria*) tunnel. **~a're** *v.t.* bore; (*terreno*) drill.

trage'dia *n.f.* tragedy.

traghe'tt|o *n.m.* ferrying; (*nave*) ferry-(boat). **~a're** *v.t.* ferry.

tra'gico *a.* tragic. —*n.m.* (*autore*) tragedian.

tragi'tto *n.m.* journey; (*per mare*) crossing.

tragua'rdo *n.m.* finishing-post; (*meta*) goal.

traietto'ria *n.f.* trajectory.

traina're *v.t.* drag; (*rimorchiare*) tow.

tralascia're *v.t.* interrupt; (*omettere*) leave out.

tra'lcio *n.m.* shoot.

trali'ccio *n.m.* (*tela*) ticking; (*struttura*) trellis.

traluce'nte *a.* shining.

tram *n.m. invar.* tram.

tra'm|a *n.f.* weft; (*di film ecc.*) plot. **~a're** *v.t.* weave; (*macchinare*) plot.

tramanda're *v.t.* hand down.

trambu'sto *n.m.* turmoil.

tramesti'o *n.m.* bustle.

tramezzi'no *n.m.* sandwich.

trame'zzo *n.m.* partition.

tra'mite *prep.* through.

tramonta'na *n.f.* north wind.

tram|onta're *v.i.* set. **~o'nto** *n.m.* sunset.

tramorti're *v.t.* stun. —*v.i.* faint.

trampoli'no *n.m.* springboard; (*per lo sci*) ski-jump.

tra'mpolo *n.m.* stilt.

tramuta're *v.t.* transform.

tra'ncia *n.f.* shearing machine.

trane'llo *n.m.* trap.

trangugia're *v.t.* gulp down.

tranne *prep.* except.

tranqui'll|o *a.* quiet; (*pacifico*) peaceful; (*coscienza*) easy. **~a'nte** *n.m.* tranquillizer. **~ità** *n.f.* calm; (*di spirito*) tranquillity. **~izza're** *v.t.* reassure.

transatla'ntico *a.* transatlantic. —*n.m.* (ocean) liner.

transa'tto *p.p. di* **transigere.**

transazio'ne *n.f.* compromise; (*comm.*) transaction.

transi'gere *v.i.* reach an agreement; (*cedere*) yield.

transiti'vo *a.* transitive.

tra'nsi|to *n.m.* transit. **diritto di ~to** right of way. **divieto di ~to** no thoroughfare. **~ta'bile** *a.* passable.

~ta're *v.i.* pass. **~zio'ne** *n.f.* transition.

transito'rio *a.* transitory.

trantra'n *n.m.* (*fam.*) routine.

tranvi'a *n.f.* tramway.

tra'pano *n.m.* drill.

trapassa're *v.t.* pierce. —*v.i.* (*morire*) pass away.

trapa'sso *n.m.* passage.

trapela're *v.i.* (*di liquido, fig.*) leak out.

trape'zio *n.m.* trapeze; (*math.*) trapezium.

trapi|anta're *v.t.* transplant. **~a'nto** *n.m.* transplant.

tra'ppola *n.f.* trap.

trapu'nta *n.f.* quilt.

tra'rre *v.t.* draw; (*ricavare*) obtain. **~ in inganno** deceive.

trasali're *v.i.* start.

trasanda'to *a.* shabby.

trasborda're *v.t.* transfer; (*naut.*) trans-ship. —*v.i.* change.

trascendenta'le *a.* transcendental.

trasce'ndere *v.t.* transcend. —*v.i.* (*eccedere*) go too far.

trascina'r|e *v.t.* drag. **~si** *v.r.* drag oneself.

trasco'rrere *v.t.* spend. —*v.i.* pass.

trascri'|vere *v.t.* transcribe. **~tto** *p.p. di* **~vere.** **~zio'ne** *n.f.* transcription.

trascura'|re *v.t.* neglect; (*non tenere conto di*) disregard. **~bile** *a.* negligible. **~te'zza** *n.f.* negligence. **~to** *a.* negligent; (*curato male*) neglected; (*nel vestire*) slovenly.

trasecola'to *a.* amazed.

trasferi'|re *v.t.* transfer. **~rsi** *v.r.* move. **~me'nto** *n.m.* transfer; move.

trasfe'rta *n.f.* transfer; (*indennità*) subsistence allowance; (*sport*) away match.

trasfigura're *v.t.* transfigure.

trasforma'|re *v.t.* transform. **~to're** *n.m.* transformer. **~zio'ne** *n.f.* transformation.

trasfusio'ne *n.f.* transfusion.

trasgre|di're *v.t.* disobey; (*legge*) infringe. **~ssio'ne** *n.f.* infringement.

trasla'to *a.* metaphoric.

trasloca'r|e *v.t.* move. **~si** *v.r.* move house. **traslo'co** *n.m.* removal.

trasme'sso *p.p. di* **trasmettere.**

trasme'tt|ere *v.t.* pass on; (*TV, radio*) broadcast; (*techn., med.*) transmit. **~ito're** *n.m.* transmitter.

trasmi|ssio'ne *n.f.* transmission; (*TV,*

radio) broadcast. ∼**tte'nte** *n.m.* transmitter; *n.f.* broadcasting station.

trasogna'|re *v.i.* day-dream. ∼**to** *a.* dreamy.

traspare'n|te *a.* transparent. ∼**za** *n.f.* transparency. **in** ∼**za** against the light.

traspari're *v.i.* show (through).

traspira'|re *v.i.* perspire; (*fig.*) transpire. ∼**zio'ne** *n.f.* perspiration.

traspo'rre *v.t.* transpose.

trasp|orta're *v.t.* transport. **lasciarsi** ∼**ortare da** let oneself get carried away by. ∼**o'rto** *n.m.* transport.

trastulla'r|e *v.t.* amuse. ∼**si** *v.r.* amuse oneself.

trasuda're *v.t.* ooze with. —*v.i.* sweat.

trasversa'le *a.* transverse.

trasvola're *v.t.* fly (across). —*v.i.* skim over.

tra'tta *n.f.* (*traffico illegale*) trade; (*comm.*) draft.

trattame'nto *n.m.* treatment.

tratta'|re *v.t.* treat; (*commerciare*) deal; (*negoziare*) negotiate. —*v.i.* deal (with). **di che si tratta?** what is it about? **si tratta di** it is a question of. ∼**ti've** *n.f. pl.* negotiations. ∼**to** *n.m.* treaty; (*opera scritta*) treatise.

tratteggia're *v.t.* outline; (*ombreggiare*) hatch.

trattene'r|e *v.t.* hold; (*reprimere*) repress; (*frenare*) restrain; (*far restare*) keep; (*non consegnare*) withhold. ∼**si** *v.r.* restrain oneself; (*fermarsi*) stop. ∼**si su** (*indugiare*) dwell on.

trattenime'nto *n.m.* entertainment; (*ricevimento*) party.

tratti'no *n.m.* dash; (*in parole composte*) hyphen.

tra'tt|o *p.p. di* **trarre.** —*n.m.* (*di spazio, tempo*) stretch; (*di penna*) stroke; (*linea*) line; (*modo di fare*) manners *pl.*; (*brano*) passage. ∼**i** *n.m. pl.* (*lineamenti*) features. **a** ∼**i** at intervals. **ad un** ∼**o** suddenly.

tratto're *n.m.* tractor.

trattori'a *n.f.* restaurant.

tra'um|a *n.m.* trauma. ∼**a'tico** *a.* traumatic.

trava'glio *n.m.* labour; (*angoscia*) anguish.

travasa're *v.t.* decant.

tra'v|e *n.f.* beam. ∼**atu'ra** *n.f.* beams *pl.*

travede're *v.i.* be mistaken. ∼ **per** be crazy about.

trave'rsa *n.f.* crossbar; (*via*) sideroad.

traversa'|re *v.t.* cross. ∼**ta** *n.f.* crossing.

traversi'e *n.f. pl.* misfortunes.

traversi'na *n.f.* (*ferrovia*) sleeper.

trave'rs|o *a.* crosswise. **di** ∼**o** *adv.* askew. **andare di** ∼**o** (*cibo*) go down the wrong way. **guardare qcno. di** ∼**o** look askance at s.o. **per vie** ∼**e** (*fam.*) by underhand methods.

travesti'|re *v.t.* disguise. ∼**rsi** *v.r.* disguise oneself. ∼**me'nto** *n.m.* disguise. ∼**to** *a.* disguised; *n.m.* transvestite.

travia're *v.t.* lead astray.

travisa're *v.t.* distort.

travo'lg|ere *v.t.* sweep away; (*sopraffare*) overwhelm. ∼**e'nte** *a.* overwhelming.

travo'lto *p.p. di* **travolgere.**

trazio'ne *n.f.* traction.

tre *a. & n.m.* three.

trebbia'|re *v.t.* thresh. ∼**tri'ce** *n.f.* threshing-machine.

tre'ccia *n.f.* plait, braid.

trece'nto *a. & n.m.* three hundred. **il T**∼ the fourteenth century.

tre'dici *a. & n.m.* thirteen.

tre'gua *n.f.* truce; (*fig.*) respite.

trema'r|e *v.i.* tremble; (*di freddo*) shiver. ∼**e'lla** *n.f.* (*fam.*) shivers *pl.*

treme'ndo *a.* terrible.

trementi'na *n.f.* turpentine.

tremi'la *a. & n.m.* three thousand.

tre'm|ito *n.m.* tremble. ∼**o're** *n.m.* trembling.

tremola're *v.i.* shake; (*di luce*) flicker.

tre'no *n.m.* train.

tre'nt|a *a. & n.m.* thirty. ∼**e'simo** *a. & n.m.* thirtieth. ∼**i'na** *n.f.* **una** ∼**ina** about thirty.

tre'pid|o *a.* anxious. ∼**a're** *v.i.* be anxious.

treppie'de *n.m.* tripod.

tre'sca *n.f.* intrigue; (*amorosa*) affair.

tre'spolo *n.m.* trestle.

tria'ngol|o *n.m.* triangle. ∼**a're** *a.* triangular.

tribolazio'ne *n.f.* tribulation.

trib|ù *n.f.* tribe. ∼**a'le** *a.* tribal.

tribu'na *n.f.* tribune; (*per uditori*) gallery; (*sport*) stand.

tribuna'le *n.m.* court.

tributa're *v.t.* bestow.

tribu't|o *n.m.* tribute; (*tassa*) tax. ∼**a'rio** *a.* tributary.

triche'co *n.m.* walrus.

trici'clo *n.m.* tricycle.

tricolo're *a.* three-coloured. —*n.m.* (*bandiera*) tricolour.

tride'nte *n.m.* trident.

trifo'glio *n.m.* clover.

tri'glia *n.f.* mullet.

trigonometri'a *n.f.* trigonometry.

trilla're *v.i.* trill.

trilogi'a *n.f.* trilogy.

trime'stre *n.m.* quarter; (*schol.*) term.

tri'na *n.f.* lace.

trince'|a *n.f.* trench. **~ra're** *v.t.* entrench.

trincia're *v.t.* cut up.

Trinità *n.f.* Trinity.

tri'o *n.m.* trio.

trio'nf|o *n.m.* triumph. **~a'le** *a.* triumphal. **~a'nte** *a.* triumphant. **~a're** *v.i.* triumph. **~are su** triumph over.

tri'plic|e *a.* triple. **in ~e** in triplicate. **~a're** *v.t.* triple.

tri'plo *a.* treble. —*n.m.* **il ~ (di)** three times as much (as).

tri'pode *n.m.* tripod.

tri'ppa *n.f.* tripe.

tripu'di|o *n.m.* jubilation; (*baldoria*) riot. **~a're** *v.i.* rejoice.

tri'st|e *a.* sad; (*luogo*) gloomy. **~e'zza** *n.f.* sadness.

tri'sto *a.* wicked; (*meschino*) miserable.

trita'|re *v.t.* mince. **~ca'rne** *n.m. invar.* mincer.

tri'ttico *n.m.* triptych.

triumvira'to *n.m.* triumvirate.

trive'll|a *n.f.* drill. **~a're** *v.t.* drill.

trivia'le *a.* vulgar.

trofe'o *n.m.* trophy.

tro'golo *n.m.* trough.

tro'ia *n.f.* sow.

tro'mba *n.f.* trumpet; (*auto*) horn; (*delle scale*) well. **~ d'aria** whirlwind.

trombo'ne *n.m.* trombone.

trombo'si *n.f.* thrombosis.

tronca're *v.t.* cut off; (*fig.*) break off.

tro'nc|o *a.* cut off; (*gram.*) truncated. —*n.m.* trunk; (*di strada*) section. **~o'ne** *n.m.* stump.

troneggia're *v.i.* **~ (su)** tower (over).

tro'no *n.m.* throne.

tro'pic|o *n.m.* tropic. **~a'le** *a.* tropical.

tro'ppo *a. & pron.* too much (*pl.* too many). —*adv.* (*con a. e adv.*) too; (*con v.*) too much. **sentirsi di ~** feel unwanted.

tro'ta *n.f.* trout.

tro'tt|o *n.m.* trot. **andare al ~o** trot.

~a're *v.i.* trot. **~erella're** *v.i.* trot along; (*di bimbo*) toddle.

tro'ttola *n.f.* (spinning) top.

trova'r|e *v.t.* find; (*scoprire*) find out; (*incontrare*) meet; (*ritenere*) think. **andare a ~e** go and see. **~si** *v.r.* find oneself; (*di luogo*) be; (*sentirsi*) feel.

trova'ta *n.f.* bright idea.

trovate'llo, a *n.m., f.* foundling.

tru'cc|o *n.m.* (*cosmetico*) make-up; (*imbroglio*) trick. **~a're** *v.t.* make up; (*falsificare*) fix (*sl.*). **~a'rsi** *v.r.* make up. **~ato're, ~atri'ce** *n.m., f.* make-up artist.

tru'ce *a.* grim.

trucida're *v.t.* slay.

tru'ciolo *n.m.* shaving.

trucule'nto *a.* truculent.

tru'ff|a *n.f.* fraud. **~a're** *v.t.* swindle.

tru'ppa *n.f.* troops *pl.*

tu *pron.* you. **a ~ per ~** face to face. **darsi del ~** be on familiar terms (with someone).

tu'ba *n.f.* (*mus.*) tuba; (*cappello*) top hat.

tuba're *v.i.* coo.

tubercolo'si *n.f.* tuberculosis.

tu'b|o *n.m.* pipe; (*anat.*) canal. **~atu'ra, ~azio'ne** *ns.f.* piping. **~e'tto** *n.m.* tube. **~ola're** *a.* tubular.

tu'ff|o *n.m.* dive. **~a're** *v.t.* plunge. **~a'rsi** *v.r.* dive. **~ato're, ~atri'ce** *n.m., f.* diver.

tugu'rio *n.m.* hovel.

tulipa'no *n.m.* tulip.

tu'lle *n.m.* tulle.

tumefazio'ne *n.f.* swelling.

tu'mido *a.* swollen.

tumo're *n.m.* tumour.

tumulazio'ne *n.f.* burial.

tumu'lt|o *n.m.* turmoil; (*sommossa*) riot. **~uo'so** *a.* uproarious.

tu'nica *n.f.* tunic.

Tunisi'a *n.f.* Tunisia.

tu'nnel *n.m.* tunnel.

tu'o, a *a.* (*pl.* **tuo'i, tu'e**) your. —*pron.* yours. **i tuoi** your family. **un ~ amico** a friend of yours.

tuo'n|o *n.m.* thunder. **~a're** *v.i.* thunder.

tuo'rlo *n.m.* yolk.

tura'cciolo *n.m.* stopper; (*di sughero*) cork.

tura'r|e *v.t.* stop; (*bottiglia*) cork. **~si** *v.r.* become blocked. **~si il naso** hold one's nose.

turba'nte *n.m.* turban.

turba'|re *v.t.* upset. **~rsi** *v.r.* get

upset. **∼me'nto** *n.m.* disturbance; (*sconvolgimento*) upsetting.

turbi'na *n.f.* turbine.

tu'rbin|e *n.m.* whirl. **∼e di vento** whirlwind. **∼a're** *v.i.* whirl.

turbole'n|to *a.* turbulent. **∼za** *n.f.* turbulence.

turboreatto're *n.m.* turbo-jet (engine).

turche'se *a.* & *n.m./f.* turquoise.

Turchi'a *n.f.* Turkey. **tu'rco, a** *a.* Turkish; *n.m.*, *f.* Turk, Turkish woman; *n.m.* (*lingua*) Turkish.

turchi'no *a.* & *n.m.* deep blue.

tu'rgido *a.* turgid.

turi's|mo *n.m.* tourism. **∼ta** *n.m./f.* tourist. **∼tico** *a.* tourist.

tu'rno *n.m.* turn. **a ∼** in turn. **di ∼** on duty. **fare a ∼** take turns. **∼ di notte** night-shift.

tu'rp|e *a.* base. **∼ilo'quio** *n.m.* foul language.

tu'ta *n.f.* overalls *pl.*; (*sport*) track suit. **∼ spaziale** spacesuit.

tute'l|a *n.f.* (*legge*) guardianship; (*protezione*) protection. **∼a're** *v.t.* protect.

tu|to're, ∼tri'ce *n.m., f.* guardian.

tuttavi'a *conj.* nevertheless, still.

tu'tt|o *a.* all (*pl.* all); (*intero*) a/the whole; (*ogni*) every. —*adv.* all. —*n.m.* whole. **a ∼a velocità** at full speed. **del ∼o** completely. **di ∼o punto** entirely. **in ∼o il mondo** all over the world. **noi ∼i** all of us. **∼'a un tratto** all at once. **∼'altro** not at all. **∼'altro che** anything but. **∼i e due** both. **∼i e tre** all three. **∼o il giorno** all day (long).

tuttofa're *a.* general. —*n.m./f.* general servant.

tutto'ra *adv.* still.

U

ubbidie'n|te *a.* obedient. ∼**za** *n.f.* obedience.

ubbidi're *v.i.* ∼ (a) obey.

ubiquità *n.f.* ubiquity.

ubria'c|o, a *a.* drunk; tight (*fam.*). −*n.m.*, *f.* drunk. ∼**a're** *v.t.* get s.o. drunk. ∼**a'rsi** *v.r.* get drunk. ∼**arsi di** (*fig.*) become inebriated with. ∼**he'zza** *n.f.* drunkenness. ∼**o'ne** *n.m.* drunkard.

ucce'll|o *n.m.* bird. ∼**ie'ra** *n.f.* aviary.

ucci'der|e *v.t.* kill. ∼**si** *v.r.* kill oneself.

uccis|io'ne *n.f.* killing. ∼**o're** *n.m.* killer.

udi'bile *a.* audible.

udie'nza *n.f.* audience; (*colloquio*) interview; (*legge*) hearing.

udi'|re *v.t.* hear. ∼**ti'vo** *a.* auditory. ∼**to** *n.m.* hearing. ∼**to're**, ∼**tri'ce** *n.m.|f.* listener; (*schol.*) unregistered student.

udito'rio *n.m.* audience.

ufficia'le *a.* official. −*n.m.* officer; (*funzionario*) official. ∼ **dello Stato civile** registrar.

uffi'cio *n.m.* office; (*dovere*) duty. ∼ **di collocamento** employment office.

ufficio'so *a.* unofficial.

u'fo *adv.* **a** ∼ free.

uggio'so *a.* boring.

uguaglia'|nza *n.f.* equality. ∼**re** *v.t.* make equal; (*essere uguale*) equal; (*livellare*) level. ∼**rsi** *v.r.* ∼**rsi a** compare oneself to.

ugua'l|e *a.* equal; (*lo stesso*) the same; (*simile*) like. ∼**me'nte** *adv.* equally; (*malgrado tutto*) all the same.

u'lcera *n.f.* ulcer.

ulterio're *a.* ulterior; (*nuovo*) further.

ultima're *v.t.* complete.

ultima'tum *n.m.* ultimatum.

u'ltimo *a.* last; (*notizie ecc.*) latest; (*più lontano*) farthest; (*fig.*) ultimate. −*n.m.* (the) last. **fino all'**∼ to the last. **in** ∼ at the end. **l'** ∼ **piano** the top floor.

ultraviole'tto *a.* ultraviolet.

ulula'|re *v.i.* howl. ∼**to** *n.m.* howling.

uman|e'simo *n.m.* humanism. ∼**i'sta** *n.m.|f.* humanist.

uma'n|o *a.* human; (*benevolo*) humane. ∼**ità** *n.f.* humanity. ∼**ita'rio** *a.* humanitarian.

umidificato're *n.m.* humidifier.

u'mid|o *a.* damp; (*di clima*) humid; (*mani, occhi*) moist. −*n.m.* dampness. **in** ∼**o** (*culin.*) stewed. ∼**ità** *n.f.* dampness; humidity.

u'mil|e *a.* humble. ∼**ia're** *v.t.* humiliate. ∼**iazio'ne** *n.f.* humiliation. ∼**tà** *n.f.* humility.

umo're *n.m.* humour; (*stato d'animo*) mood. **essere di buon** ∼ be in a good temper.

umori's|mo *n.m.* humour. ∼**ta** *n.m.|f.* humorist. ∼**tico** *a.* humorous.

un, una *vedi* **uno**.

una'nim|e *a.* unanimous. ∼**ità** *n.f.* unanimity. **all'**∼**ità** unanimously.

uncine'tto *n.m.* crochet hook.

unci'no *n.m.* hook.

u'ndici *a. & n.m.* eleven.

u'nger|e *v.t.* grease; (*relig.*) anoint; (*blandire*) flatter. ∼**si** *v.r.* grease oneself.

Ungher|i'a *n.f.* Hungary. **u**∼**e'se** *a. & n.m.|f.* Hungarian.

u'nghi|a *n.f.* nail; (*di animale*) claw. ∼**a'ta** *n.f.* (*graffio*) scratch.

ungue'nto *n.m.* ointment.

u'nic|o *a.* only; (*singolo*) single; (*incomparabile*) unique. ∼**ame'nte** *adv.* only.

unico'rno *n.m.* unicorn.

unifica'|re *v.t.* unify. ∼**zio'ne** *n.f.* unification.

unifo'rm|e *a. & n.f.* uniform. ∼**ità** *n.f.* uniformity.

unilatera'le *a.* unilateral.

unio'ne *n.f.* union; (*armonia*) unity.

uni'|re *v.t.* unite; (*collegare*) join; (*colori ecc.*) blend. ∼**rsi** *v.r.* unite; join. ∼**to** *a.* united; (*tinta*) plain.

uni'sono *n.m.* **all'**∼ in unison.

unità *n.f.* unity; (*math., mil.*) unit. ∼**rio** *a.* unitary.

università *n.f.* university. ∼**rio, a** *a.* university; *n.m.*, *f.* (*insegnante*) university lecturer; (*studente*) undergraduate.

unive'rs|o *n.m.* universe. ∼**a'le** *a.* universal.

u'no, un, u'na *indef. art.* a; (*davanti a vocale o h*) an. **uno** *a. & n.m.* one;

pron. one; (*un tale*) somebody. **a ~ a ~** one by one. **~ alla volta** one at a time. **~ di noi** one of us. **~ su dieci** one out of ten.

u'nt|o *p.p. di* **ungere.** —*a.* greasy. —*n.m.* grease. **~uo'so** *a.* greasy.

uo'mo *n.m.* (*pl.* **uomini**) man. **~ d'affari** business man.

uo'vo *n.m.* (*pl. f.* **uova**) egg. **~ in camicia** poached egg. **~ sodo** hard-boiled egg. **~ strapazzato** scrambled egg.

uraga'no *n.m.* hurricane.

ura'nio *n.m.* uranium.

urba'no *a.* urban; (*cortese*) urbane.

urban|e'simo *n.m.* urbanization. **~i'-stica** *n.f.* town planning.

urge'n|te *a.* urgent. **~za** *n.f.* urgency. **in caso d'~za** in an emergency.

u'rgere *v.i.* be urgent.

uri'na *n.f.* = **orina.**

urla're *v.i.* shout; (*di cane, vento*) howl. **u'rlo** *n.m.* (*pl. m.* **urli**, *f.* **urla**) shout; howling.

u'rna *n.f.* urn; (*elettorale*) ballot-box.

urrà *int.* hurrah.

URSS *abbr. f.* (*di* **Unione delle Repubbliche Socialiste Sovietiche**). **l'~** the USSR.

urta'r|e *v.t.* knock (against); (*scontrarsi*) bump into; (*fig.*) irritate. **~si** *v.r.* collide; (*fig.*) clash.

u'rto *n.m.* knock; (*scontro*) crash; (*contrasto*) conflict; (*fig.*) clash.

usa'nza *n.f.* custom; (*moda*) fashion.

usa'|re *v.t.* use; (*impiegare*) employ; (*esercitare*) exercise. —*v.i.* use; (*essere di moda*) be fashionable. **non si usa**

più it is out of fashion. **~to** *a.* used; (*non nuovo*) second-hand.

uscie're *n.m.* usher.

u'scio *n.m.* door.

usci're *v.i.* go out; (*venir fuori*) come out, get out; (*lasciare un luogo*) leave; (*sfuggire*) slip; (*di strada*) lead into; (*essere sorteggiato*) be drawn; (*sporgere*) jut out; (*di giornale*) be published.

usci'ta *n.f.* exit, way out; (*mil.*) sortie; (*spesa*) outlay; (*sbocco*) outlet; (*battuta*) witty remark. **giorno di libera ~** day off. **~ di sicurezza** emergency exit.

usigno'lo *n.m.* nightingale.

u'so *n.m.* use; (*abitudine*) custom; (*usanza*) usage. **fuori ~** out of use.

ustio'ne *n.f.* burn.

usua'le *a.* usual.

usufrui're *v.i.* **~ di** take advantage of.

usu'r|a *n.f.* usury. **~a'io** *n.m.* usurer.

usurpa're *v.t.* usurp.

utensi'l|e *n.m.* utensil. **cassetta degli ~i** tool-box.

ute'nte *n.m.|f.* user.

u'tero *n.m.* womb.

u'til|e *a.* useful. —*n.m.* (*vantaggio*) advantage; (*profitto*) profit. **~ità** *n.f.* usefulness. **~ita'rio, a** *a.* utilitarian; *n.f.* (*auto*) small car.

utilizza'|re *v.t.* utilize. **~zio'ne** *n.f.* utilization.

u'va *n.f.* grapes *pl.* **chicco d'~** grape. **~ passa** raisins *pl.* **~ sultanina** currants *pl.*

V

vaca′nte *a*. vacant.

vaca′nza *n.f.* holiday; (*posto vacante*) vacancy. **essere in ∼** be on holiday.

va′cca *n.f.* cow.

vacc|ina′re *v.t.* vaccinate. **∼ina-zio′ne** *n.f.* vaccination. **∼i′no** *n.m.* vaccine.

vacilla′|re *v.i.* totter; (*di cosa*) wobble; (*di luce*) flicker; (*fig.*) waver. **∼nte** *a*. tottering; wobbly; flickering; wavering.

va′cuo *a*. (*vano*) vain; (*fig.*) empty. —*n.m.* vacuum.

vagabo′nd|o, a *n.m.*, *f.* vagabond; (*fannullone*) idler. **∼a′re** *v.i.* wander.

vaga′re *v.i.* wander.

vagheggia′re *v.t.* long for.

vagi′na *n.f.* vagina.

vagi′|re *v.i.* whimper. **∼to** *n.m.* whimper.

va′glia *n.m. invar.* money order. **∼ bancario** bank draft. **∼ postale** postal order.

vaglia′re *v.t.* sift; (*fig.*) weigh. **va′glio** *n.m.* sieve.

va′go *a*. vague.

vago′ne *n.m.* (*per passeggeri*) carriage; (*per merci*) wagon. **∼ letto** sleeping-car.

vaio′lo *n.m.* smallpox.

vala′nga *n.f.* avalanche.

vale′nte *a*. skilful.

vale′r|e *v.i.* be worth; (*contare*) count; (*aver vigore*) be in force; (*giovare*) be of use; (*essere valido*) be valid. —*v.t.* (*procurare*) earn. **∼si di** avail oneself of. **far ∼e i propri diritti** assert one's rights. **farsi ∼e** make oneself appreciated. **ne vale la pena?** is it worthwhile? **non vale!** it is not fair! **tanto vale che** we may as well.

vale′vole *a*. valid.

valica′re *v.t.* cross.

va′lico *n.m.* pass.

va′lid|o *a*. valid; (*efficace*) efficient. **∼o a** fit for. **∼ità** *n.f.* validity.

valigeri′a *n.f.* (*fabbrica*) leather factory; (*negozio*) leather goods shop.

vali′gi|a *n.f.* suitcase. **fare le ∼e** pack. **∼a diplomatica** diplomatic bag.

va′ll|e *n.f.* valley. **a ∼e** downstream. **∼a′ta** *n.f.* valley.

valle′tto *n.m.* valet.

valo′r|e *n.m.* value, worth; (*merito*) merit; (*coraggio*) valour. **∼i** *n.m. pl.* (*comm.*) securities. **campione senza ∼e** free sample. **oggetti di ∼e** valuables. **senza ∼e** worthless.

valorizza′re *v.t.* use to advantage; (*aumentare di valore*) increase the value of.

valoro′so *a*. valiant.

va′lso *p.p. di valere*.

valu′ta *n.f.* currency.

valuta′|re *v.t.* value. **∼zio′ne** *n.f.* valuation.

va′lva *n.f.* valve.

va′lvola *n.f.* valve; (*electr.*) fuse.

va′lzer *n.m. invar.* waltz.

vampa′ta *n.f.* blaze; (*al viso*) (hot) flush.

vampi′ro *n.m.* vampire.

va′ndal|o *n.m.* vandal. **∼i′smo** *n.m.* vandalism.

vaneggia′re *v.i.* rave.

va′ng|a *n.f.* spade. **∼a′re** *v.t.* dig.

Vange′lo *n.m.* Gospel.

vani′glia *n.f.* vanilla.

vanit|à *n.f.* vanity. **∼o′so** *a*. vain.

va′no *a*. vain. —*n.m.* (*stanza*) room; (*spazio vuoto*) hollow.

vanta′ggi|o *n.m.* advantage; (*sport*) lead; (*tennis*) advantage. **∼o′so** *a*. advantageous.

vant|a′re *v.t.* praise. **∼a′rsi** *v.r.* boast. **∼eri′a** *n.f.* boasting. **va′nto** *n.m.* boast.

va′nvera *n.f.* **a ∼** at random. **parlare a ∼** talk nonsense.

vapo′r|e *n.m.* vapour; (*acqueo*) steam; (*piroscafo*) steamer. **a ∼e** steam. **al ∼e** (*culin.*) steamed. **∼e′tto** *n.m.* steamboat. **∼ie′ra** *n.f.* steam-engine.

vaporizza′|re *v.t.* vaporize. **∼to′re** *n.m.* vaporizer.

vaporo′so *a*. (*di vestito*) flimsy.

vara′re *v.t.* launch. **va′ro** *n.m.* launch.

varca′re *v.t.* cross.

va′rco *n.m.* passage. **aspettare al ∼** lie in wait.

varia′|re *v.t./i.* vary. **∼re di umore** change one's mood. **∼bile** *a*. variable; *n.f.* (*math.*) variable. **∼nte** *n.f.* variant. **∼zio′ne** *n.f.* variation.

varice′lla *n.f.* chicken-pox.

varico′so *a*. varicose.

variega'to *a.* variegated.

varietà *n.f.* variety. —*n.m.* variety show.

va'ri|o *a.* varied; (*al pl.*, *parecchi*) various. ∼ *pl.* (*molti*) several.

variopi'nto *a.* multicoloured.

va'sca *n.f.* tub. ∼ **da bagno** bath.

vasce'llo *n.m.* vessel. **capitano di** ∼ captain.

vaseli'na *n.f.* vaseline.

vasella'me *n.m.* china. ∼ **d'oro/ d'argento** gold/silver plate.

va's|o *n.m.* pot; (*da fiori*) vase; (*anat.*) vessel; (*per cibi*) jar. ∼**a'io** *n.m.* potter.

vasso'io *n.m.* tray.

va'st|o *a.* vast. **di** ∼**e vedute** broadminded. ∼**ità** *n.f.* vastness.

Vatica'no *n.m.* Vatican.

ve *pron.* & *adv.* **vedi vi.**

ve'cchi|o, a *a.* old. —*n.m.*, *f.* old man/ woman. **i** ∼ *pl.* old people. ∼**a'ia** *n.f.* old age.

ve'c|e *n.f.* **in** ∼**e di** in place of. **fare le** ∼**i di qcno.** take s.o.'s place.

vede'r|e *v.t./i.* see. **far** ∼**e** show. **farsi** ∼**e** show one's face. ∼**si** *v.r.* see oneself; (*reciproco*) meet each other.

vede'tta *n.f.* (*luogo*) look-out; (*naut.*) patrol vessel.

ve'dovo, a *n.m.*, *f.* widower, widow.

vedu'ta *n.f.* view.

veeme'nte *a.* vehement.

vegeta'le *a.* & *n.m.* vegetable.

vegeta're *v.i.* vegetate.

vegetaria'no, a *a.* & *n.m.*, *f.* vegetarian.

vegetazio'ne *n.f.* vegetation.

ve'geto *a.* thriving; (*persona*) vigorous.

ve'glia *n.f.* watch. **fare la** ∼ keep watch. ∼ **funebre** vigil.

veglia're *v.i.* be awake. ∼ **su** watch over.

vei'colo *n.m.* vehicle.

ve'l|a *n.f.* sail; (*sport*) sailing. **a gonfie** ∼**e** (*fig.*) at a fine pace. **far** ∼**a** set sail.

vela'|re *v.t.* veil; (*nascondere*) hide. ∼**rsi** *v.r.* (*annebbiarsi*) mist; (*di voce*) grow husky. ∼**to** *a.* veiled.

veleggia're *v.i.* sail.

vele'n|o *n.m.* poison. ∼**o'so** *a.* poisonous.

vele'tta *n.f.* (*di cappello*) veil.

velie'ro *n.m.* sailing-ship.

veli'na *n.f.* (**carta**) ∼ tissue-paper; (*copia*) carbon copy.

veli'volo *n.m.* aircraft.

velleità *n.f.* foolish ambition.

ve'llo *n.m.* fleece.

vellu't|o *n.m.* velvet. ∼**o a coste** corduroy. ∼**a'to** *a.* velvety.

ve'lo *n.m.* veil; (*tessuto*) voile.

velo'c|e *a.* fast. ∼**i'sta** *n.m./f.* (*sport*) sprinter. ∼**ità** *n.f.* speed; (*auto.*, *marcia*) gear.

velo'dromo *n.m.* cycle-track.

ve'na *n.f.* vein. **essere in** ∼ **di** be in the mood for.

vena'le *a.* venal.

vende'mmi|a *n.f.* (grape) harvest. ∼**a're** *v.t.* harvest.

ve'nder|e *v.t.* sell. ∼**si** *v.r.* sell oneself.

vende'tta *n.f.* revenge.

vendica'|re *v.t.* revenge. ∼**rsi** *v.r.* revenge oneself. ∼**ti'vo** *a.* vindictive.

ve'ndit|a *n.f.* sale. **in** ∼**a** on sale. ∼**a all'asta** auction sale. ∼**o're** *n.m.* seller.

venera'|bile, ∼**ndo** *adjs.* venerable.

venera're *v.t.* revere. ∼**zio'ne** *n.f.* reverence.

venerdì *n.m.* Friday. **di** ∼ on Fridays. **V**∼ **Santo** Good Friday.

Ve'nere *n.f.* Venus.

vene'reo *a.* venereal.

Vene'zi|a *n.f.* Venice. **v**∼**a'no, a** *a.* & *n.m.*, *f.* Venetian; *n.f.* (*persiana*) Venetian blind.

venia'le *a.* venial.

veni'r|e *v.i.* come; (*riuscire*) turn out; (*costare*) cost. ∼**e a sapere** learn. ∼**e in mente** occur. ∼ **meno** (*svenire*) faint. ∼ **meno a qcno.** fail s.o. ∼ **via** come away; (*staccarsi*) come off. **mi viene da piangere** I feel like crying. **vieni a prendermi** call for me. **vieni a trovarmi** come and see me.

venta'glio *n.m.* fan.

ve'nt|i *a.* & *n.m.* twenty. ∼**e'nne** *a.* & *n.m./f.* twenty-year-old. ∼**e'simo** *a.* & *n.m.* twentieth. ∼**i'na** *n.f.* **una** ∼**ina** (*circa venti*) about twenty.

ventila'|re *v.t.* air. ∼**to're** *n.m.* fan. ∼**zio'ne** *n.f.* ventilation.

ve'nt|o *n.m.* wind. ∼**a'ta** *n.f.* gust (of wind). ∼**o'so** *a.* windy.

vento'sa *n.f.* sucker.

ve'ntre *n.m.* stomach.

ventri'loquo *n.m.* ventriloquist.

ventu'ra *n.f.* fortune. **andare alla** ∼ trust to luck.

ventu'ro *a.* next.

venu'ta *n.f.* coming.

verame'nte *adv.* really.

vera'nda *n.f.* veranda.

verba'le *a.* verbal. —*n.m.* (*di riunione*) minutes *pl.*

ve'rbo *n.m.* verb. **il V~** (*relig.*) the Word.

verbo'so *a.*verbose.

ve'rde *a.* & *n.m.* green. **essere al ~** be hard up.

verdera'me *n.m.* verdigris.

verde'tto *n.m.* verdict.

verdu'ra *n.f.* vegetables *pl.*

vereco'ndo *a.* bashful.

ve'rga *n.f.* rod.

verga'to *a.* lined.

ve'rgin|e *n.f.* virgin; (*astr.*) Virgo. —*a.* virgin. **~a'le** *a.* virginal. **~ità** *n.f.* virginity.

vergo'gn|a *n.f.* shame; (*timidezza*) shyness. **~a'rsi** *v.r.* feel ashamed; feel shy. **~o'so** *a.* ashamed; shy; (*disonorevole*) shameful.

veri'fic|a *n.f.* check. **~a're** *v.t.* check. **~a'rsi** *v.r.* come true.

verit|à *n.f.* truth. **~ie'ro** *a.* truthful.

ve'rme *n.m.* worm.

vermi'glio *a.* & *n.m.* vermilion.

ve'rmut *n.m.* vermouth.

verna'colo *n.m.* vernacular.

verni'c|e *n.f.* paint; (*trasparente*) varnish; (*pelle*) patent leather; (*fig.*) veneer. **~ia're** *v.t.* paint; varnish. **~iatu'ra** *n.f.* painting; (*fig.*) gloss.

ve'r|o *a.* true; (*autentico*) real; (*perfetto*) perfect. **è ~o?** is that so? —*n.m.* truth; (*realtà*) life. **~i'smo** *n.m.* realism.

verosi'mile *a.* likely.

verru'ca *n.f.* verruca.

versa'nte *n.m.* slope.

versa'|re *v.t.* pour; (*spargere*) shed; (*rovesciare*) spill; (*denaro*) pay. **~rsi** *v.r.* spill; (*sfociare*) flow. **~me'nto** *n.m.* shedding; (*pagamento*) payment; (*in banca*) deposit.

versa'tile *a.* versatile.

versa'to *a.* (*pratico*) versed.

verse'tto *n.m.* verse.

versio'ne *n.f.* version; (*traduzione*) translation.

ve'rso[1] *n.m.* verse; (*grido*) cry; (*gesto*) gesture; (*senso*) direction; (*modo*) manner. **fare il ~ a qcno.** ape s.o. **non c'è ~ di** there is no way of.

ve'rso[2] *prep.* towards; (*contro*) against; (*nei pressi di*) near. **~ dove?** which way?

ve'rtebra *n.f.* vertebra.

vertica'le *a.* & *n.f.* vertical.

ve'rtice *n.m.* summit; (*math.*) vertex. **conferenza al ~** summit conference.

verti'gin|e *n.f.* dizziness; (*med.*) vertigo. **aver le ~i** feel dizzy. **~o'so** *a.* dizzy; (*di velocità*) breakneck.

vesci'ca *n.f.* bladder; (*sulla pelle*) blister.

ve'scovo *n.m.* bishop.

ve'spa *n.f.* wasp.

ve'spro *n.m.* vespers *pl.*

vessi'llo *n.m.* standard.

vesta'glia *n.f.* dressing-gown.

ve'st|e *n.f.* dress; (*rivestimento*) covering; (*capacità*) capacity. **~i** *n.m. pl.*, **~ia'rio** *n.m.* clothes *pl.*

vesti'bolo *n.m.* hall.

vesti'gio *n.m.* (*pl. m.* vestigi, *f.* vestigia) trace.

vesti'|re *v.t.* dress; (*indossare*) wear. **~rsi** *v.r.* get dressed. **~to** *a.* dressed; *n.m.* (*da uomo*) suit; (*da donna*) dress. **~ti** *n.m. pl.* clothes.

vetera'no, a *a.* & *n.m., f.* veteran.

veterina'rio, a *a.* veterinary. —*n.m.* veterinary surgeon. —*n.f.* veterinary science.

ve'to *n.m. invar.* veto.

vetri'n|a *n.f.* (shop-) window; (*armadio*) display cabinet. **~i'sta** *n.m./f.* window-dresser.

vetrio'lo *n.m.* vitriol.

ve'tr|o *n.m.* glass; (*di finestra, porta*) pane. **~a'io** *n.m.* glazier. **~a'to, a** *a.* glazed; *n.f.* glass door/window. **~eri'a** *n.f.* glass works. **~o'so** *a.* vitreous.

ve'tta *n.f.* peak.

vetto're *n.m.* vector.

vettova'glie *n.f. pl.* provisions.

vettu'r|a *n.f.* coach; (*ferroviaria*) carriage; (*auto*) car. **~i'no** *n.m.* coachman.

vezzeggia'|re *v.t.* fondle. **~ti'vo** *n.m.* pet name.

ve'zz|o *n.m.* habit. **~i** *n.m. pl.* (*moine*) affectation *s.* **~o'so** *a.* charming.

vi (*davanti a lo, la, li, le, ne* ve) *pron.* you; (*con v.r.*) yourselves; (*reciproco*) each other; (*dimostrativo*) it. —*adv.* (*lì*) there; (*qui*) here. **ve ne sono due** there are two. **~ vidi** I saw you.

vi'a[1] *n.f.* street, road; (*fig.*) way; (*anat.*) tract. **in ~ di** in the course of. **per ~ di** on account of. **~ ~ che** as.

vi'a[2] *adv.* away; (*fuori*) out. **e così ~** and so on. —*int.* **~!** go away!; (*sport*) go!; (*andiamo*) come on! —*n.m.* starting signal.

viabilità *n.f.* road conditions *pl.*

viado'tto *n.m.* viaduct.

viaggia'|re *v.i.* travel. ~to're, ~tri'ce *a.* travelling; *n.m., f.* traveller.

via'ggio *n.m.* journey; (*breve*) trip.

via'le *n.m.* avenue; (*privato*) drive.

viava'i *n.m.* coming and going.

vibra'|re *v.i.* vibrate; (*fremere*) quiver. ~nte *a.* vibrant. ~zio'ne *n.f.* vibration.

vica'rio *n.m.* vicar.

vi'ce *n.m.|f.* deputy. —*pref.* ~- vice-. ~direttore assistant manager. ~rè viceroy.

vice'nda *n.f.* event. a ~ (*fra due*) each other; (*a turno*) in turn(s).

viceve'rsa *adv.* vice versa.

vicina'nz|a *n.f.* nearness. ~e *n.f. pl.* (*paraggi*) neighbourhood.

vicina'to *n.m.* neighbourhood; (*vicini*) neighbours *pl.*

vici'no, a *a.* near; (*accanto*) next. —*adv.* near, close. —*n.m., f.* neighbour. ~ a *prep.* near (to).

vicissitu'dine *n.f.* vicissitude.

vi'colo *n.m.* alley.

vi'deo *n.m.* video. ~registrato're *n.m.* video-recorder.

vieta'|re *v.t.* forbid. **sosta** ~ta no parking.

vige'nte *a.* in force.

vigila'|re *v.t.* keep an eye on. —*v.i.* keep watch. ~nte *a.* vigilant. ~nza *n.f.* vigilance.

vi'gile *a.* watchful. —*n.m.* ~ (**urbano**) policeman. ~ **del fuoco** fireman.

vigi'lia *n.f.* eve; (*relig.*) fasting.

viglia'cc|o, a *a.* cowardly. —*n.m., f.* coward. ~heri'a *n.f.* cowardice.

vi'gn|a *n.f.*, ~e'to *n.m.* vineyard.

vigne'tta *n.f.* cartoon.

vigo'r|e *n.m.* vigour. **entrare in** ~e come into force. ~o'so *a.* vigorous.

vi'l|e *a.* cowardly; (*abietto*) vile. ~tà *n.f.* cowardice.

vi'll|a *n.f.* (country) house. ~i'no *n.m.* cottage.

villa'ggio *n.m.* village.

villa'n|o *a.* rude. —*n.m.* boor; (*contadino*) peasant. ~i'a *n.f.* rudeness.

villeggia'|re *v.i.* spend one's holidays. ~nte *n.m.|f.* holiday-maker. ~tu'ra *n.f.* holiday(s) (*pl.*).

vi'min|e *n.m.* wicker. **sedia di** ~i wicker chair.

vi'nc|ere *v.t.* win; (*sconfiggere*) beat; (*superare*) overcome. ~ita *n.f.* win;

(*somma vinta*) winnings. ~ito're, ~itri'ce *n.m., f.* winner.

vincola're *v.t.* bind; (*comm.*) tie up.

vi'ncolo *n.m.* bond.

vi'n|o *n.m.* wine. ~i'colo *a.* wine.

vi'nto *p.p. di* vincere.

vio'la *n.f.* (*bot.*) violet; (*mus.*) viola.

violaccio'cca *n.f.* stock.

viola'|re *v.t.* violate. ~zio'ne *n.f.* violation.

violenta're *v.t.* rape.

viole'n|to *a.* violent. ~za *n.f.* violence.

viole'tto, a *a.* & *n.m.* (*colore*) violet. —*n.f.* violet.

violi'n|o *n.m.* violin. ~i'sta *n.m.|f.* violinist.

violonce'llo *n.m.* cello.

vio'ttolo *n.m.* path.

vi'pera *n.f.* viper.

vira'|ggio *n.m.* (*fotografia*) toning; (*naut., aeron.*) turn. ~re *v.i.* turn. ~re di bordo veer.

vi'rgol|a *n.f.* comma. **punto e** ~a semicolon. ~e'tte *n.f. pl.* inverted commas.

viri'l|e *a.* virile; (*da uomo*) manly. ~ità *n.f.* virility; manliness.

virt|ù *n.f.* virtue. ~uo'so *a.* virtuous; *n.m.* (*mus.*) virtuoso.

virule'nto *a.* virulent.

vi'rus *n.m.* virus.

vi'scer|e *n.m.* internal organ. ~e *n.f. pl.* (*fig., intestini*) bowels; (*di animale*) entrails.

vi'schio *n.m.* mistletoe.

vi'scido *a.* slimy.

visco'nt|e *n.m.* viscount. ~e'ssa *n.f.* viscountess.

visco'so *a.* viscous.

visi'bil|e *a.* visible. ~ità *n.f.* visibility.

visibi'lio *n.m.* profusion. **andare in** ~ go into ecstasies.

visie'ra *n.f.* (*di elmo*) visor; (*di berretto*) peak.

visio'ne *n.f.* vision. **prima** ~ (*cinema*) first showing.

vi'sit|a *n.f.* visit; (*breve*) call; (*med.*) examination. ~a're *v.t.* visit; call on; examine; ~ato're, ~atri'ce *n.m., f.* visitor.

visi'vo *a.* visual.

vi'so *n.m.* face.

viso'ne *n.m.* mink.

vi'spo *a.* lively.

vissu'to *p.p. di* vivere. —*a.* experienced.

vi'sta *n.f.* sight; (*veduta*) view. a ~

d'occhio as far as the eye can see. **crescere a ~ d'occhio** grow very fast. **in ~ di** considering. **perdere di ~ qcno.** lose sight of s.o.

vi'sto *p.p. di* vedere. —*n.m.* visa.

visto'so *a.* showy; (*notevole*) considerable.

visua'le *a.* visual.

vi'ta *n.f.* life; (*durata della vita*) lifetime; (*anat.*) waist. **a ~ for** life. **essere in fin di ~** be at death's door. **essere in ~** be alive.

vita'l|e *a.* vital. **~ità** *n.f.* vitality.

vitali'zio *a.* life. —*n.m.* (life) annuity.

vitami'na *n.f.* vitamin.

vi'te *n.f.* (*mech.*) screw; (*bot.*) vine.

vite'llo *n.m.* calf; (*culin.*) veal.

viti'ccio *n.m.* tendril.

viticolt|o're *n.m.* wine-grower. **~u'ra** *n.f.* wine-growing.

vi'treo *a.* vitreous; (*sguardo*) glassy.

vi'ttima *n.f.* victim.

vi'tto *n.m.* food; (*pasti*) board. **~ e alloggio** board and lodging.

vitto'ri|a *n.f.* victory. **~o'so** *a.* victorious.

vittoria'no *a.* Victorian.

vitup|era're *v.t.* vituperate. **~e'rio** *n.m.* insult.

viu'zza *n.f.* narrow lane.

vi'va *int.* hurrah. **~ la Regina!** long live the Queen!

viva'c|e *a.* vivacious; (*mente*) lively; (*colore*) bright. **~ità** *n.f.* vivacity; liveliness; brightness.

viva'io *n.m.* nursery; (*per pesci*) pond.

viva'nda *n.f.* food; (*piatto*) dish.

vive'nte *a.* living.

vi'vere *v.i.* live. —*v.t.* (*passare*) go through. —*n.m.* life. **~ di** live on.

vi'veri *n.m. pl.* provisions.

vi'vido *a.* vivid.

vivifica're *v.t.* enliven.

vivisezio'ne *n.f.* vivisection.

vi'vo *a.* alive; (*vivente*) living; (*vivace*) lively; (*colore*) bright. —*n.m.* living person; (*parte sensibile*) quick. **farsi ~** give news of oneself. **trasmissione dal ~** live transmission.

vizia'|re *v.t.* (*bambino ecc.*) spoil; (*guastare*) vitiate. **~to** *a.* spoilt; (*di aria*) stale.

vi'zi|o *n.m.* vice; (*cattiva abitudine*) bad habit; (*difetto*) flaw. **~o'so** *a.* dissolute; (*difettoso*) faulty. **circolo ~oso** vicious circle.

vocabola'rio *n.m.* dictionary; (*lessico*) vocabulary.

voca'bolo *n.m.* word.

voca'le *a.* vocal. —*n.f.* vowel.

vocazio'ne *n.f.* vocation.

vo'ce *n.f.* voice; (*diceria*) rumour.

vocia're *v.i.* shout.

vocifera're *v.i.* shout. **si vocifera che** it is rumoured that.

vo'g|a *n.f.* rowing; (*lena*) enthusiasm; (*moda*) vogue. **essere in ~a** be in fashion. **~a're** *v.i.* row. **~ato're** *n.m.* oarsman.

vo'glia *n.f.* desire; (*volontà*) will; (*della pelle*) birthmark. **non ho ~ di mangiare** I don't feel like eating.

vo'i *pron.* you. **~a'ltri** *pron.* you (people).

vola'no *n.m.* shuttlecock; (*mech.*) flywheel.

vola'nte *a.* flying. **disco ~** flying saucer. —*n.m.* steering-wheel.

volanti'no *n.m.* leaflet.

vola'|re *v.i.* fly. **~ta** *n.f.* flight; (*corsa*) rush; (*di uccelli*) flock; (*sport*) final sprint.

vola'tile *a.* (*di liquido*) volatile. —*n.m.* bird.

volentie'ri *adv.* willingly. **~!** with pleasure!

vole'r|e *v.t.* want; (*desiderare*) wish; (*gradire*) like. **senza ~e** without meaning to. **~ bene** love. **~ dire** mean. **~ci** (*essere necessario, riferito a cose*) need; (*di tempo, quantità*) take. **~ne a** have a grudge against. —*n.m.* will. **~i** *n.m. pl.* wishes.

volga'r|e *a.* vulgar; (*popolare*) common. **~ità** *n.f.* vulgarity. **~izza're** *v.t.* popularize.

vo'lger|e *v.t./i.* turn. **~si** *v.r.* turn (round). **~si a** (*dedicarsi*) take up.

vo'lgo *n.m.* common people.

volie'ra *n.f.* aviary.

voliti'vo *a.* strong-minded.

vo'lo *n.m.* flight. **al ~** quickly. **alzarsi in ~** (*di aereo*) take off. **in ~** airborne. **~ a vela** gliding.

volontà *n.f.* will; (*forza di volontà*) will-power. **a ~** at pleasure.

volonta'rio *a.* voluntary. —*n.m.* volunteer.

volontero'so *a.* willing.

vo'lpe *n.f.* fox.

vo'lt|a *n.f.* time; (*turno*) turn; (*curva*) bend; (*archit.*) vault. **a ~e** sometimes. **c'era una ~a** once upon a time. **due ~e** twice. **una ~a** once. **una ~a per tutte** once and for all. **uno per ~a** one at a time.

voltafa'ccia *n.m. invar.* volte-face.
volta'ggio *n.m.* voltage.
volta'|re *v.t./i.* turn; (*rigirare*) turn round; (*rivoltare*) turn over. ∼**rsi** *v.r.* turn (round). ∼**ta** *n.f.* turning.
volteggia're *v.i.* circle; (*ginnastica*) vault.
vo'lto *p.p. di* volgere. −*n.m.* face.
volu'bile *a.* fickle.
volu'm|e *n.m.* volume. ∼**ino'so** *a.* voluminous.
volutt|à *n.f.* voluptuousness. ∼**uo'so** *a.* voluptuous.
vomita're *v.t.* vomit, be sick. **vo'mito** *n.m.* vomit.
vo'ngola *n.f.* clam.
vora'ce *a.* voracious.
vora'gine *n.f.* abyss.
vo'rtice *n.m.* whirl; (*gorgo*) whirlpool; (*di vento*) whirlwind.

vo'stro *a. & pron.* your; (*vostro proprio*) your own. **il** ∼ yours. **un** ∼ **amico** a friend of yours.
vota'|re *v.i.* vote. ∼**nte** *n.m./f.* voter. ∼**zio'ne** *n.f.* voting; (*schol.*) marks *pl.*
vo'to *n.m.* vote; mark; (*relig.*) vow.
vs. *abbr.* (*di* vostro, *comm.*) yours.
vulca'n|o *n.m.* volcano. ∼**ico** *a.* volcanic.
vulnera'bil|e *a.* vulnerable. ∼**ità** *n.f.* vulnerability.
vuo't|o *a.* empty; (*non occupato*) vacant. ∼**o di** (*sprovvisto*) devoid of. −*n.m.* empty space; (*fisica*) vacuum; (*fig.*) void. **assegno a** ∼**o** dud cheque. ∼**o d'aria** air pocket. ∼**a're** *v.t.*, ∼**a'rsi** *v.r.* empty.

W

W *abbr.* (*di* viva) long live.
water *n.m.* toilet; (*fam.*) loo.

watt *n.m. invar.* watt.

X

X, x *a.* **raggi X** X-rays. **il giorno X** D-day.
xe'res *n.m. invar.* sherry.

xeroco'pia *n.f.* xerox.
xilo'fono *n.m.* xylophone.

Y

yacht *n.m. invar.* yacht.
yo'ga *n.m.* yoga; (*praticante*) yogi.

yo'ghurt *n.m.* yoghurt.

Z

zabaglio'ne *n.m.* zabaglione.

za'cchera *n.f.* splash of mud.

zaffa'ta *n.f.* stench.

zaffera'no *n.m.* saffron.

za'ffiro *n.m.* sapphire.

za'gara *n.f.* orange-blossom.

za'ino *n.m.* knapsack.

za'mpa *n.f.* paw; (*di uccello*) claw; (*di maiale, culin.*) trotter.

zampi'll|o *n.m.* spurt. ~a're *v.i.* spurt.

zampo'gn|a *n.f.* bagpipe. ~a'ro *n.m.* piper.

za'nna *n.f.* fang; (*di elefante*) tusk.

zanza'ra *n.f.* mosquito.

za'pp|a *n.f.* hoe. ~a're *v.t.* hoe.

za'ttera *n.f.* raft.

zavo'rra *n.f.* ballast.

za'zzera *n.f.* mop of hair.

ze'br|a *n.f.* zebra. ~e *n.f. pl.* (*passaggio pedonale*) zebra crossing.

ze'cca¹ *n.f.* mint. **nuovo di ~** brand-new.

ze'cca² *n.f.* (*parassita*) tick.

zecchi'no *n.m.* sequin. **oro ~** pure gold.

ze'l|o *n.m.* zeal. ~a'nte *a.* zealous.

ze'nit *n.m.* zenith.

ze'nzero *n.m.* ginger.

ze'ppa *n.f.* wedge.

ze'ppo *a.* (packed) full. **pieno ~ di** crammed with.

zerbi'no *n.m.* doormat.

ze'ro *n.m.* nought, zero; (*calcio*) nil; (*tennis*) love.

ze'ta *n.f.* zed.

zibelli'no *n.m.* sable.

zi'gomo *n.m.* cheek-bone.

zigza'g *n.m. invar.* zigzag. **andare a ~** zigzag.

zimbe'llo *n.m.* (*oggetto di scherno*) laughing-stock.

zi'nco *n.m.* zinc.

zi'ngaro, a *n.m., f.* gypsy.

zi'|o *n.m.* uncle. ~a *n.f.* aunt.

zite'lla *n.f.* spinster; (*pej.*) old maid.

zi'tto *a.* silent. **sta' ~!** keep quiet!

zizza'nia *n.f.* (*fig.*) discord.

zo'ccolo *n.m.* clog; (*di cavallo*) hoof; (*di parete*) wainscot; (*di colonna*) base.

zodi'aco *n.m.* zodiac.

zo'lfo *n.m.* sulphur.

zo'lla *n.f.* clod; (*di zucchero*) lump.

zo'na *n.f.* zone; (*area*) area. ~ **verde** green belt.

zo'nzo *adv.* **andare a ~** stroll about.

zoo *n.m. invar.* zoo.

zo|ologi'a *n.f.* zoology. ~olo'gico *a.* zoological. ~o'logo, a *n.m., f.* zoologist.

zoppica're *v.i.* limp; (*essere debole*) be shaky.

zo'ppo, a *a.* lame. —*n.m., f.* cripple.

zo'tic|o *a.* uncouth. ~o'ne *n.m.* boor.

zua'va *n.f.* **calzoni alla ~** plus-fours.

zu'cca *n.f.* marrow.

zu'ccher|o *n.m.* sugar. ~a're *v.t.* sugar. ~ie'ra *n.f.* sugar-bowl. ~ifi'cio *n.m.* sugar-refinery. ~i'no *a.* sugary. ~o'so *a.* (*fig.*) honeyed.

zucchi'n|a *n.f.*, ~o *n.m.* courgette.

zucco'ne *n.m.* blockhead.

zu'ffa *n.f.* scuffle.

zufola're *v.t./i.* whistle.

zuma're *v.i.* zoom.

zu'pp|a *n.f.* soup. ~a **inglese** trifle. ~ie'ra *n.f.* (soup) tureen.

zu'ppo *a.* soaked.

A

a /ə, eɪ/ *indef. art.* (*before vowel* **an**) un, uno *m.*; un', una *f.*

aback /ə'bæk/ *adv.* **taken** ~ preso alla sprovvista.

abacus /'æbəkəs/ *n.* abaco *m.*

abandon /ə'bændən/ *v.t.* abbandonare. ~**ed** *a.* abbandonato; (*behaviour*) dissoluto. ~**ment** *n.* abbandono *m.*

abase /ə'beɪs/ *v.t.* degradare. ~**ment** *n.* degradazione *f.*

abashed /ə'bæʃt/ *a.* confuso.

abate /ə'beɪt/ *v.t.* diminuire. —*v.i.* calmarsi. ~**ment** *n.* diminuzione *f.*

abattoir /'æbətwɑ:(r)/ *n.* mattatoio *m.*

abbey /'æbɪ/ *n.* abbazia *f.*

abb|ot /'æbət/ *n.* abate *m.* ~**ess** /'æbis/ badessa *f.*

abbreviat|e /ə'bri:vɪeɪt/ *v.t.* abbreviare. ~**ion** /-'eɪʃn/ *n.* abbreviazione *f.*

ABC /'eɪbi:'si:/ *n.* abbicì *m.*

abdicat|e /'æbdɪkeɪt/ *v.t./i.* abdicare (a). ~**ion** /-'eɪʃn/ *n.* abdicazione *f.*

abdom|en /'æbdəmən/ *n.* addome *m.* ~**inal** /-'dɒmɪnl/ *a.* addominale.

abduct /æb'dʌkt/ *v.t.* rapire. ~**ion** /-ʃn/ *n.* rapimento *m.* ~**or** *n.* rapitore, -trice *m.*, *f.*

aberration /æbə'reɪʃn/ *n.* aberrazione *f.*

abet /ə'bet/ *v.t.* (*p.t.* **abetted**) (*jurid.*) farsi complice di.

abeyance /ə'beɪəns/ *n.* **in** ~ in sospeso.

abhor /əb'hɔ:(r)/ *v.t.* (*p.t.* **abhorred**) aborrire. ~**rence** /-'hɒrəns/ *n.* aborrimento *m.* ~**rent** /-'hɒrənt/ *a.* ripugnante.

abide /ə'baɪd/ *v.t.* (*p.t.* **abided**) sopportare. —*v.i.* (*old use*, *p.t.* **abode**) abitare. ~ **by** conformarsi a.

abiding /ə'baɪdɪŋ/ *a.* perpetuo; (*steady*) costante.

ability /ə'bɪlətɪ/ *n.* capacità *f.*; (*cleverness*) abilità *f.*

abject /'æbdʒekt/ *a.* (*depressed*) abbattuto; (*vile*) abietto.

ablaze /ə'bleɪz/ *a.* in fiamme; (*fig.*) splendente.

abl|e /'eɪbl/ *a.* (**-er, -est**) capace, abile.

be ~**e** potere; (*know how to*) riuscire. ~**y** *adv.* abilmente.

ablutions /ə'blu:ʃnz/ *n.pl.* abluzioni *f.pl.*

abnormal /æb'nɔ:ml/ *a.* anormale. ~**ity** /-'mælətɪ/ *n.* anormalità *f.*

aboard /ə'bɔ:d/ *adv. & prep.* a bordo.

abode /ə'bəʊd/ *see* **abide**. —*n.* (*old use*) dimora *f.*

aboli|sh /ə'bɒlɪʃ/ *v.t.* abolire. ~**tion** /æbə'lɪʃn/ *n.* abolizione *f.*

abominable /ə'bɒmɪnəbl/ *a.* abominevole.

abominat|e /ə'bɒmɪneɪt/ *v.t.* abominare. ~**ion** /-'neɪʃn/ *n.* abominazione *f.*

aborigin|al /æbə'rɪdʒənl/ *a. & n.* aborigeno *m.* ~**es** /-i:z/ *n.pl.* aborigeni *m.pl.*

abort /ə'bɔ:t/ *v.t.* fare abortire. —*v.i.* abortire. ~**ion** /-ʃn/ *n.* aborto *m.* ~**ionist** *n.* procura|tore, -trice di aborti *m.*, *f.* ~**ive** *a.* abortivo.

abound /ə'baʊnd/ *v.i.* abbondare (**in**, **di**).

about /ə'baʊt/ *adv.* (*approximately*) circa; (*here and there*) qua e là; (*in existence*) in giro. —*prep.* intorno a; (*somewhere in*) verso. ~**-face**, ~**turn** *ns.* dietrofront *m. invar.* **be** ~ **to** stare per. **be up and** ~ essere alzato. **man** ~ **town** *n.* uomo di mondo *m.* **talk** ~ parlare di.

above /ə'bʌv/ *adv.* sopra. —*prep.* al disopra di. ~ **all** soprattutto. ~**board** *a.* onesto. ~**-mentioned** *a.* suddetto.

abrasion /ə'breɪʒn/ *n.* abrasione *f.*; (*injury*) scalfittura *f.*

abrasive /ə'breɪsɪv/ *a. & n.* abrasivo *m.*

abreast /ə'brest/ *adv.* di fianco. **keep** ~ **of** andare di pari passo con.

abridge /ə'brɪdʒ/ *v.t.* abbreviare. ~**ment** *n.* abbreviazione *f.* ~**d edition** *n.* edizione ridotta *f.*

abroad /ə'brɔ:d/ *adv.* all'estero; (*far and wide*) dappertutto.

abrupt /ə'brʌpt/ *a.* (*sudden*) inaspettato; (*of manners*) brusco; (*steep*) scosceso. **~ness** n. subitaneità f.; (of manners) rudezza f.; (steepness) ripidezza f.

abscess /'æbsɪs/ n. ascesso m.

abscond /əb'skɒnd/ v.i. nascondersi.

absence /'æbsəns/ assenza f.; (lack) mancanza f.

absent[1] /'æbsənt/ a. assente. **~ly** adv. distrattamente. **~-minded** a. distratto. **~-mindedness** n. distrazione f.

absent[2] /æb'sent/ v.r. **~ o.s.** assentarsi.

absentee /æbsən'ti:/ n. assente m./f. **~ism** n. assenteismo m.

absinthe /'æbsɪnθ/ n. assenzio m.

absolute /'æbsəlu:t/ a. assoluto. **~ly** adv. assolutamente.

absolution /æbsə'lu:ʃn/ n. assoluzione f.

absolve /əb'zɒlv/ v.t. (from sin) assolvere; (from vow) sciogliere.

absor|b /əb'zɔːb/ v.t. assorbire. **~bent** a. assorbente. **~ption** n. assorbimento m.

abst|ain /əb'steɪn/ v.i. astenersi (da). **~ention** /-'stenʃn/ n. astensione f.

abstemious /əb'sti:mɪəs/ a. astemio.

abstinen|ce /'æbstɪnəns/ n. astinenza f. **~t** a. astinente.

abstract[1] /'æbstrækt/ a. astratto. —n. (quality) astratto m.; (summary) riassunto m.

abstract[2] /əb'strækt/ v.t. astrarre; (take away) sottrarre. **~ion** /-ʃn/ n. astrazione f.

abstruse /əb'stru:s/ a. astruso.

absurd /əb'sɜːd/ a. assurdo. **~ity** n. assurdità f.

abundan|t /ə'bʌndənt/ a. abbondante. **~ce** n. abbondanza f.

abuse[1] /ə'bju:z/ v.t. (misuse) abusare di; (ill-treat) maltrattare; (insult) insultare.

abus|e[2] /ə'bju:s/ n. abuso m.; (insult) insulto m. **~ive** a. ingiurioso.

abut /ə'bʌt/ v.i. (p.t. **abutted**) confinare (con).

abysmal /ə'bɪzməl/ a. abissale; (fam., bad) pessimo.

abyss /ə'bɪs/ n. abisso m.

acacia /ə'keɪʃə/ n. acacia f.

academic /ækə'demɪk/ a. accademico; (scholarly) dotto; (pej.) teorico. —n. accademico m. **~ally** adv. accademicamente.

academ|y /ə'kædəmɪ/ n. accademia f.

~y of music conservatorio m. **~ician** /-'mɪʃn/ n. accademico, a m.,f.

accede /ək'si:d/ v.i. **~ to** (request) acconsentire a; (office) assumere. **~ to the throne** salire al trono.

accelerat|e /ək'seləreɪt/ v.t. accelerare. **~ion** /-'reɪʃn/ n. accelerazione f.

accelerator /ək'seləreɪtə(r)/ n. acceleratore m.

accent[1] /'æksənt/ n. accento m.

accent[2] /æk'sent/ v.t. accentare; (emphasize) accentuare.

accentuate /ək'sentʃueɪt/ v.t. accentuare.

accept /ək'sept/ v.t. accettare. **~able** a. accettabile. **~ance** n. accettazione f.; (approval) approvazione f.

access /'ækses/ accesso m. **~ible** /ək'sesəbl/ a. accessibile. **~ibility** /-ɪ'bɪlətɪ/ n. accessibilità f.

accession /æk'seʃn/ n. accessione f.; (thing added) aggiunta f.

accessory /ək'sesərɪ/ a. accessorio. —n. accessorio m.; (jurid.) complice m./f.

accident /'æksɪdənt/ accidente m.; (chance) caso m. **~al** /-'dentl/ a. accidentale. **~ally** /-'dentəlɪ/ adv. accidentalmente.

acclaim /ə'kleɪm/ v.t. acclamare. —n. acclamazione f.

acclimatiz|e /ə'klaɪmətaɪz/ v.t. acclimatare. —v.i. acclimatarsi. **~ation** /-'zeɪʃn/ n. acclimatazione f.

accolade /'ækəleɪd/ (of knight) accollata f.; (praise) encomio m.

accommodat|e /ə'kɒmədeɪt/ v.t. (supply) fornire; (give hospitality to) ospitare; (adapt) adattare. **~ing** a. accomodante. **~ion** /-'deɪʃn/ n. accomodamento m.; (rooms) alloggio m.

accompan|y /ə'kʌmpənɪ/ v.t. accompagnare. **~iment** n. accompagnamento m. **~ist** n. accompagna|tore, -trice m.,f.

accomplice /ə'kʌmplɪs/ n. complice m./f.

accomplish /ə'kʌmplɪʃ/ v.t. compiere; (achieve) portare a termine. **~ed** a. compiuto. **~ment** n. realizzazione f.; (ability) talento m.

accord /ə'kɔːd/ v.i. accordarsi. —v.t. accordare. —n. accordo m. **of one's own ~** spontaneamente. **~ance** n. **in ~ance with** in conformità con.

according /ə'kɔːdɪŋ/ adv. **~ to** secondo. **~ly** adv. di conseguenza.

accordion /ə'kɔːdɪən/ n. fisarmonica f.

accost /ə'kɒst/ *v.t.* accostare.

account /ə'kaʊnt/ *n.* conto *m.*; (*description*) resoconto *m.*; (*importance*) importanza *f.* —*v.t.* considerare. ~ **for** render conto di. **on** ~ **of** a causa di. **on no** ~ per nulla. **on this** ~ per questo. **take into** ~ tenere in considerazione. **statement of** ~ estratto conto. ~**able** *a.* responsabile (di). ~**ability** /-ə'bɪlətɪ/ *n.* responsabilità *f.*

accountan|t /ə'kaʊntənt/ *n.* contabile *m./f.* ~**cy** *n.* contabilità *f.*

accoutrements /ə'ku:trəmənts/ *n.pl.* equipaggiamento *m.s.*

accredited /ə'kredɪtɪd/ *a.* accreditato.

accru|e /ə'kru:/ *v.i.* accumularsi. ~**al** *n.* accumulazione *f.*

accumulat|e /ə'kju:mjʊleɪt/ *v.t./i.* accumulare, accumularsi. ~**ion** /-'leɪʃn/ *n.* accumulazione *f.*

accumulator /ə'kju:mjʊleɪtə(r)/ *n.* (*electr.*) accumulatore *m.*

accura|te /'ækjərət/ *a.* preciso. ~**cy** *n.* precisione *f.*

accus|e /ə'kju:z/ *v.t.* accusare. ~**ation** /-'zeɪʃn/ *n.* accusa *f.*

accustom /ə'kʌstəm/ *v.t.* abituare. ~**ed** *a.* abituato. **get** ~**ed (to)** abituarsi (a).

ace /eɪs/ *n.* asso *m.*

acetate /'æsɪteɪt/ *n.* acetato *m.*

ache /eɪk/ *n.* dolore, male *m.* —*v.i.* dolere, far male. ~ **all over** essere tutto indolenzito. ~ **for** desiderare ardentemente.

achieve /ə'tʃi:v/ *v.t.* realizzare; (*success*) ottenere. ~**ment** *n.* realizzazione *f.*; (*feat*) successo *m.*

acid /'æsɪd/ *a. & n.* acido *m.* ~**ity** /ə'sɪdətɪ/ *n.* acidità *f.*

acknowledge /ək'nɒlɪdʒ/ *v.t.* riconoscere. ~ **receipt of** accusare ricevuta di. ~**ment** *n.* riconoscimento *m.*; (*letter etc.*) ricevuta *f.*

acme /'ækmɪ/ *n.* acme *m.*

acne /'æknɪ/ *n.* acne *f.*

acorn /'eɪkɔ:n/ *n.* ghianda *f.*

acoustic /ə'ku:stɪk/ *a.* acustico. ~**s** *n.pl.* acustica *f.s.*

acquaint /ə'kweɪnt/ *v.t.* ~ **s.o. with** mettere qcno. al corrente di. **be** ~**ed with** (*person*) conoscere; (*fact*) sapere. ~**ance** *n.* conoscenza *f.*; (*person*) conoscente *m./f.*

acquiesce /ækwɪ'es/ *v.i.* acconsentire. ~**nce** *n.* acquiescenza *f.*

acqui|re /ə'kwaɪə(r)/ *v.t.* acquisire. ~**sition** /ækwɪ'zɪʃn/ *n.* acqui-

sizione; (*fig.*) acquisto *m.* ~**sitive** /-'kwɪzətɪv/ *a.* avido.

acquit /ə'kwɪt/ *v.t.* (*p.t.* **acquitted**) assolvere. ~ **o.s. well** comportarsi bene. ~**tal** *n.* assoluzione *f.*

acre /'eɪkə(r)/ *n.* acro *m.* ~**age** *n.* numero di acri *m.*

acrid /'ækrɪd/ *a.* acre.

acrimon|ious /ækrɪ'məʊnɪəs/ *a.* acrimonioso. ~**y** /'ækrɪmənɪ/ *n.* acrimonia *f.*

acrobat /'ækrəbæt/ *n.* acrobata *m./f.* ~**ic** /-'bætɪk/ *a.* acrobatico. ~**ics** /-'bætɪks/ *n.pl.* acrobazie *f. pl.*

acronym /'ækrənɪm/ *n.* acronimo *m.*

across /ə'krɒs/ *adv. & prep.* (*side to side*) da un lato all'altro; (*on other side*) dall'altra parte (di); (*crosswise*) attraverso. **go** *or* **walk** ~ attraversare.

act /ækt/ *n.* atto *m.*; (*action*) azione *f.*; (*decree*) legge *f.* —*v.i.* agire. —*v.t./i.* recitare; (*pretend*) fingere. ~ **as** fingere da. ~ **for** agire per conto di. ~**ing** *a.* facente funzione di; *n.* (*theatr.*) recitazione *f.* **do some** ~**ing** fare del teatro.

action /'ækʃn/ *n.* azione *f.*; (*mil.*) combattimento *m.*; (*jurid.*) processo *m.* **out of** ~ fuori servizio. **take** ~ agire.

activate /'æktɪveɪt/ *v.t.* attivare.

activ|e /'æktɪv/ *a.* attivo; (*energetic*) agile. ~**ity** /-'tɪvətɪ/ *n.* attività *f.*

ac|tor /'æktə(r)/ *n.* attore *m.* ~**tress** *n.* attrice *f.*

actual /'æktʃʊəl/ *a.* attuale. ~**ity** /-'ælətɪ/ *n.* attualità *f.* ~**ly** *adv.* effettivamente.

actuary /'æktʃʊərɪ/ *n.* attuario, a *m.*, *f.*

actuat|e /'æktjʊeɪt/ *v.t.* mettere in azione. ~**ion** /-'eɪʃn/ *n.* azionamento *m.*

acumen /ə'kju:men/ *n.* acume *m.*

acupunctur|e /'ækjʊpʌŋktʃə(r)/ *n.* agopuntura *f.* ~**ist** *n.* agopunturista *m./f.*

acute /ə'kju:t/ *a.* acuto; (*mind*) perspicace. ~**ly** *adv.* acutamente. ~**ness** *n.* acutezza *f.*

ad /æd/ *n.* (*fam.*) avviso *m.*; (*newspaper*) inserzione *f.*

AD /eɪ'di:/ *abbr.* (*of* **Anno Domini**) d.C.

adamant /'ædəmənt/ *a.* inflessibile.

Adam's apple /'ædəmz'æpl/ *n.* pomo d'Adamo *m.*

adapt /ə'dæpt/ *v.t.* adattare. —*v.i.* adattarsi. ~**ation** /ædæp'teɪʃn/ *n.* adattamento *m.* ∿or (*electr.*) spina differenziale *f.*

adaptab|le /ə'dæptəbl/ *a.* adattabile. ∿ility /-'bɪlətɪ/ *n.* adattabilità *f.*

add /æd/ *v.t./i.* aggiungere. ∿ up addizionare. ∿ up to ammontare *a.* ∿ing machine (macchina) addizionatrice *f.*

adder /'ædə(r)/ *n.* vipera *f.*

addict /'ædɪkt/ *n.* tossicomane *m.|f.*; (*fig.*) fanatico, a *m., f.*

addict|ed /ə'dɪktɪd/ *a.* ∿ed to dedito *a.* ∿ion /-ʃn/ *n.* (*med.*) tossicomania *f.* ∿ive *a.* che dà assuefazione.

addition /ə'dɪʃn/ *n.* addizione *f.* in ∿ per aggiunta. ∿al /-ʃənl/ *a.* addizionale.

additive /'ædɪtɪv/ *a.* & *n.* additivo *m.*

address /ə'dres/ *n.* indirizzo *m.*; (*speech*) discorso *m.* —*v.t.* indirizzare; (*speak to*) rivolgersi *a.* ∿ee /ædre'si:/ *n.* destinatario, a *m., f.*

adenoids /'ædɪnɔɪdz/ *n.pl.* adenoidi *f.pl.*

adept /'ædept/ *a.* & *n.* esperto, a *m., f.*

adequa|te /'ædɪkwət/ *a.* adeguato. ∿cy *n.* adeguatezza *f.* ∿tely *adv.* adeguatamente.

adhere /əd'hɪə(r)/ *v.i.* aderire (a). ∿nce /-rəns/ *n.* aderenza *f.*

adhesion /əd'hi:ʒn/ *n.* adesione *f.*

adhesive /əd'hi:sɪv/ *a.* & *n.* adesivo *m.* *ad infinitum* /ædmfɪ'naɪtəm/ *adv.* in infinità.

adjacent /ə'dʒeɪsnt/ *a.* adiacente.

adjective /'ædʒɪktɪv/ *n.* aggettivo *m.*

adjoin /ə'dʒɔɪn/ *v.t.* confinare con. ∿ing *a.* adiacente.

adjourn /ə'dʒɜ:n/ *v.t.* aggiornare. —*v.i.* trasferirsi.

adjudicate /ə'dʒu:dɪkeɪt/ *v.t./i.* aggiudicare.

adjust /ə'dʒʌst/ *v.t.* aggiustare. —*v.i.* ∿ (to) adattarsi (a). ∿able *a.* regolabile. ∿ment *n.* adattamento *m.*; (*techn.*) regolamento *m.*

ad lib /æd'lɪb/ *a.* improvvisato. —*v.i.* (*p.t.* -libbed) (*fam.*) improvvisare.

administer /əd'mɪnɪstə(r)/ *v.t.* amministrare; (*medicine etc.*) somministrare.

administrat|e /əd'mɪnɪstreɪt/ *v.t./i.* amministrare. ∿ion /-'streɪʃn/ *n.* amministrazione *f.* ∿or *n.* amministra|tore, -trice *m., f.*

admirable /'ædmərəbl/ *a.* ammirevole.

admiral /'ædmərəl/ *n.* ammiraglio *m.*

admir|e /əd'maɪə(r)/ *v.t.* ammirare. ∿ation /ædmə'reɪʃn/ *n.* ammirazione *f.* ∿er /-'maɪərə(r)/ *n.* ammira|tore, -trice *m., f.*

admissible /əd'mɪsəbl/ *a.* ammissibile.

admission /əd'mɪʃn/ *n.* ammissione *f.*; (*entry*) ingresso *m.*

admit /əd'mɪt/ *v.t.* (*p.t.* **admitted**) far entrare; (*acknowledge*) riconoscere. ∿ to confessare. ∿tance *n.* ammissione *f.* ∿tedly *adv.* indubbiamente.

admoni|sh /əd'mɒnɪʃ/ *v.t.* ammonire. ∿tion /-'nɪʃn/ *n.* ammonimento *m.*

ado /ə'du:/ *n.* chiasso *m.* without more ∿ senza altre difficoltà.

adolescen|t /ædə'lesnt/ *a.* & *n.* adolescente *m.|f.* ∿ce *n.* adolescenza *f.*

adopt /ə'dɒpt/ *v.t.* adottare. ∿ion /-ʃn/ *n.* adozione *f.* ∿ive *a.* adottivo.

ador|e /ə'dɔ:(r)/ *v.t.* adorare. ∿able *a.* adorabile. ∿ation /ædə'reɪʃn/ *n.* adorazione *f.*

adorn /ə'dɔ:n/ *v.t.* adornare. ∿ment *n.* ornamento *m.*

adrenalin /ə'drenəlɪn/ *n.* adrenalina *f.*

Adriatic (Sea) /eɪdrɪ'ætɪk(si:)/ *n.* Adriatico *m.*

adrift /ə'drɪft/ *a.* & *adv.* alla deriva.

adroit /ə'drɔɪt/ *a.* abile.

adulation /ædju'leɪʃn/ *n.* adulazione *f.*

adult /'ædʌlt/ *a.* & *n.* adulto, a *m., f.* ∿hood *n.* maturità *f.*

adulterat|e /ə'dʌltəreɪt/ *v.t.* adulterare. ∿ion /-'reɪʃn/ *n.* adulterazione *f.*

adulter|y /ə'dʌltərɪ/ *n.* adulterio *m.* ∿er *n.* adultero *m.* ∿ess *n.* adultera *f.* ∿ous *a.* adultero.

advance /əd'vɑːns/ *v.t./i.* avanzare; (*money*) anticipare. —*n.* avanzamento *m.*; (*payment*) anticipo *m.* in ∿ anticipatamente. ∿d *a.* avanzato; (*studies*) superiore. ∿ment *n.* avanzamento *m.*

advantage /əd'vɑːntɪdʒ/ *n.* vantaggio *m.* take ∿ of trarre vantaggio da; (*person*) approfittare di. ∿ous /ædvən'teɪdʒəs/ *a.* vantaggioso.

advent /'ædvənt/ *n.* avvento *m.* A∿ *n.* Avvento *m.*

adventur|e /əd'ventʃə(r)/ *n.* avventura *f.* ∿er *n.* avventuriero, a *m., f.* ∿ous *a.* avventuroso.

adverb /'ædvɜːb/ *n.* avverbio *m.*

adversary /'ædvəsərɪ/ *n.* avversario, a *m., f.*

advers|e /'ædvɜːs/ *a.* avverso. ∿ity /əd'vɜːsətɪ/ *n.* avversità *f.*

advert /'ædvɜːt/ *n.* (*fam.*) annunzio *m.*

~isement /əd'vɜːtɪsmənt/ n. annunzio pubblicitario m.; (in paper etc.) inserzione f.

advertise /'ædvətaɪz/ v.t./i. fare pubblicità; (seek, sell) fare un'inserzione. ~r /-ə(r)/ n. inserzionista m.|f.

advice /əd'vaɪs/ n. consigli m. pl.; (comm.) avviso m.

advis|e /əd'vaɪz/ v.t. consigliare; (inform) avvertire. ~e against sconsigliare. ~able a. consigliabile. ~er n. consulente m.|f. ~ory a. consultivo.

advocate[1] /'ædvəkət/ n. sostenitore; (Amer., mil.) avvocato m.

advocate[2] /'ædvəkeɪt/ v.t. raccomandare.

aegis /'iːdʒɪs/ n. under the ~ of sotto la protezione di.

aeon /'iːən/ n. eternità f.

aerial /'eərɪəl/ a. aereo. —n. antenna f.

aerobatics /eərə'bætɪks/ n.pl. acrobazie aeree f.pl.

aerobics /eə'rɒbɪks/ n.pl. aerobica f.s.

aerodrome /'eərədrəʊm/ n. aerodromo m.

aerodynamic /eərəʊdaɪ'næmɪk/ a. aerodinamico.

aeroplane /'eərəpleɪn/ n. aeroplano m.

aerosol /'eərəsɒl/ n. aerosol m.

aesthetic /iːs'θetɪk/ a. estetico.

afar /ə'faː(r)/ adv. lontano.

affable /'æfəbl/ a. affabile.

affair /ə'feə(r)/ n. faccenda f. (love)~ relazione (amorosa) f.

affect /ə'fekt/ v.t. agire su; (concern) concernere; (pretend) simulare. ~ation /æfek'teɪʃn/ n. affettazione f. ~ed a. affettato.

affection /ə'fekʃn/ n. affetto m.; (disease) affezione f. ~ate /-ʃənət/ a. affettuoso.

affiliat|e /ə'fɪlɪeɪt/ v.t. affiliare. ~ion /-'eɪʃn/ n. affiliazione f.

affinity /ə'fɪnətɪ/ n. affinità f.

affirm /ə'fɜːm/ v.t. affermare. ~ation /æfə'meɪʃn/ n. affermazione f.

affirmative /ə'fɜːmətɪv/ a. affermativo. —n. affermativa f.

affix /ə'fɪks/ v.t. attaccare; (signature) apporre.

afflict /ə'flɪkt/ v.t. affliggere. ~ion /-ʃn/ n. afflizione f.

affluen|t /'æfluənt/ a. ricco. ~ce n. ricchezza f.

afford /ə'fɔːd/ v.t. permettersi; (provide) fornire.

affray /ə'freɪ/ n. rissa f.

affront /ə'frʌnt/ n. affronto m. —v.t. insultare.

afield /ə'fiːld/ adv. far ~ lontano.

aflame /ə'fleɪm/ adv. & a. in fiamme.

afloat /ə'fləʊt/ adv. a galla.

afoot /ə'fʊt/ adv. in corso.

aforesaid /ə'fɔːsed/ a. (jurid.) suddetto.

afraid /ə'freɪd/ a. timoroso. be ~ aver paura; (be sorry) essere spiacente.

afresh /ə'freʃ/ adv. di nuovo.

African /'æfrɪkən/ a. & n. africano, a m., f.

after /'aːftə(r)/ adv. & prep. dopo. —conj. dopo che. —a. seguente. ~-effect n. effetto ritardato m. be ~ (seek) cercare. look ~ aver cura di.

afterbirth /'aːftəbɜːθ/ n. placenta f.

aftermath /'aːftəmæθ/ n. conseguenze f.pl.

afternoon /aːftə'nuːn/ n. pomeriggio m.

aftershave /'aːftəʃeɪv/ n. lozione (dopo barba) f.

afterthought /'aːftəθɔːt/ n. ripensamento m.

afterwards /'aːftəwədʒ/ adv. dopo.

again /ə'gen/ adv. di nuovo; (besides) inoltre. never ~ mai più. now and ~ ogni tanto.

against /ə'genst/ prep. contro.

age /eɪdʒ/ n. età f. —v.t./i. (pres. p. ageing) invecchiare. ~s (fam.) secoli. of ~ maggiorenne. under ~ minorenne. ~less a. sempre giovane.

aged[1] /'eɪdʒd/ a. dell'età di.

aged[2] /'eɪdʒɪd/ a. vecchio.

agen|cy /'eɪdʒənsɪ/ n. agenzia f.; (means) intervento m. ~t n. agente m.|f.

agenda /ə'dʒendə/ n.pl. ordine del giorno m.s.

agglomeration /əglɒmə'reɪʃn/ n. agglomerazione f.

aggravat|e /'ægrəveɪt/ v.t. aggravare; (fam., irritate) esasperare. ~ion /-'veɪʃn/ n. aggravamento m.; esasperazione f.

aggregate[1] /'ægrɪgət/ a. & n. totale m.

aggregate[2] /'ægrɪgeɪt/ v.t./i. aggregare.

aggress|ive /ə'gresɪv/ a. aggressivo. ~ion /-ʃn/ n. aggressione f. ~iveness n. aggressività f. ~or n. aggressore m.

aggrieved /ə'griːvd/ a. addolorato.

aggro /'ægrəʊ/ n. (fam.) irritazione f.

aghast /ə'gaːst/ a. inorridito.

agil|e /'ædʒaɪl/ *a.* agile. **~ity** /ə'dʒɪlətɪ/ *n.* agilità *f.*

agitat|e /'ædʒɪteɪt/ *v.t.* agitare. **~ion** /-'teɪʃn/ *n.* agitazione *f.* **~or** *n.* agita|tore, -trice *m., f.*

agnostic /æg'nɒstɪk/ *a.* & *n.* agnostico, a *m., f.* **~ism** /-sɪzəm/ *n.* agnosticismo *m.*

ago /ə'gəʊ/ *adv.* fa. **a long time ~** molto tempo fa.

agog /ə'gɒg/ *a.* impaziente.

agon|y /'ægənɪ/ *n.* agonia *f.*; (*mental*) angoscia *f.* **~ize** *v.i.* tormentarsi. **~izing** *a.* angoscioso.

agree /ə'griː/ *v.t./i.* convenire; (*of figures*) concordare; (*get on*) andare d'accordo. **~ with** (*of food etc.*) confarsi a. **~d** *a.* (*time, place*) convenuto.

agreeable /ə'griːəbl/ *a.* gradevole; (*in favour of*) favorevole.

agreement /ə'griːmənt/ *n.* accordo *m.* **in ~** d'accordo.

agricultur|e /'ægrɪkʌltʃə(r)/ *n.* agricoltura *f.* **~al** /-'kʌltʃərəl/ *a.* agricolo.

aground /ə'graʊnd/ *adv.* **run ~** (*of ship*) arenarsi.

ahead /ə'hed/ *adv.* avanti, in avanti. **be ~ of** essere più avanti di. **go ~!** (*fam.*) fa' pure!

aid /eɪd/ *v.t.* aiutare. **—***n.* aiuto *m.* **in ~ of** a favore di.

aide /eɪd/ *n.* (*Amer.*) assistente *m./f.*

ail /eɪl/ *v.t.* affliggere. **~ing** *a.* sofferente. **~ment** *n.* indisposizione *f.*

aim /eɪm/ *v.t.* puntare. **—***v.i.* mirare. **—***n.* mira *f.*; (*fig.*) scopo *m.* **~less** *a.*, **~lessly** *adv.* senza scopo.

air /eə(r)/ *n.* aria *f.* **—***v.t.* arieggiare; (*views*) rendere manifesto. **—***a.* (*base etc.*) aereo. **~-conditioned** *a.* ad aria condizionata. **~-borne** *a.* in volo. **A~ Force** aviazione *f.* **~ mail** posta aerea *f.* **be on the ~** essere in onda. **put on ~s** darsi arie.

aircraft /'eəkrɑːft/ *n.* (*pl. invar.*) aereo *m.*

airfield /'eəfiːld/ *n.* campo d'aviazione *m.*

airgun /'eəgʌn/ *n.* fucile pneumatico *m.*

airlift /'eəlɪft/ *n.* ponte aereo *m.*

airline /'eəlaɪn/ *n.* linea aerea *f.*

airlock /'eəlɒk/ *n.* bolla d'aria *f.*

airman /'eəmən/ (*pl.* -men) *n.* aviatore *m.*

airport /'eəpɔːt/ *n.* aeroporto *m.*

airtight /'eətaɪt/ *a.* ermetico.

airworthy /'eəwɜːðɪ/ *a.* abilitato al volo.

airy /'eərɪ/ *a.* (**-ier, -iest**) arieggiato; (*manner*) spensierato.

aisle /aɪl/ *n.* navata *f.*; (*gangway*) passaggio *m.*

ajar /ə'dʒɑː(r)/ *adv.* & *a.* socchiuso.

akin /ə'kɪn/ *a.* affine.

alabaster /'æləbɑːstə(r)/ *n.* alabastro *m.*

alacrity /ə'lækrətɪ/ *n.* alacrità *f.*

alarm /ə'lɑːm/ *n.* allarme *m.*; (*clock*) sveglia *f.* **—***v.t.* allarmare. **~ist** *n.* allarmista *m./f.*

alas /ə'læs/ *int.* ahimè.

albatross /'ælbətrɒs/ *n.* albatro *m.*

albino /æl'biːnəʊ/ *n.* albino *m./f.*

album /'ælbəm/ *n.* album *m. invar.*

alchem|y /'ælkɪmɪ/ *n.* alchimia *f.* **~ist** *n.* alchimista *m./f.*

alcohol /'ælkəhɒl/ *n.* alcool *m.* **~ic** /-'hɒlɪk/ *a.* (*drink*) alcolico; (*person*) alcolizzato; *n.* alcolizzato, a *m., f.* **~ism** *n.* alcolismo *m.*

alcove /'ælkəʊv/ *n.* alcova *f.*

ale /eɪl/ *n.* birra *f.*

alert /ə'lɜːt/ *a.* svelto; (*watchful*) vigile. **—***n.* segnale d'allarme *m.* **—***v.t.* avvertire. **on the ~** all'erta. **~ness** *n.* vigilanza *f.*

algebra /'ældʒɪbrə/ *n.* algebra *f.*

Algeria /æl'dʒɪərɪə/ *n.* Algeria *f.* **~n** *a.* & *n.* algerino, a *m., f.*

alias /'eɪlɪəs/ *n.* (*pl.* -ases) falso nome *m.* **—***adv.* altrimenti detto.

alibi /'ælɪbaɪ/ *m.* (*pl.* -is) alibi *m.*

alien /'eɪlɪən/ *n.* & *a.* straniero, a *m., f.*

alienat|e /'eɪlɪəneɪt/ *v.t.* alienare. **~ion** /-'neɪʃn/ *n.* alienazione *f.*

alight[1] /ə'laɪt/ *v.i.* discendere; (*of bird*) posarsi.

alight[2] /ə'laɪt/ *a.* in fiamme; (*light*) acceso.

align /ə'laɪn/ *v.t.* allineare. **~ment** *n.* allineamento *m.*

alike /ə'laɪk/ *a.* simile. **—***adv.* similmente. **look** *or* **be ~** rassomigliarsi.

alimony /'ælɪmənɪ/ *n.* alimenti *m.pl.*

alive /ə'laɪv/ *a.* vivo. **~ to** sensibile a. **~ with** brulicante di.

alkali /'ælkəlaɪ/ *n.* (*pl.* -is) alcali *m.* **~ne** *a.* alcalino.

all /ɔːl/ *a.* tutto. **—***pron.* tutto. **—***adv.* completamente. **~ but one** tutti tranne uno. **~-clear** *n.* cessato allarme *m.* **~ in** *a.* (*fam.*) esausto. **~ of a sudden** all'improvviso. **~ of it** tutto. **~-out** *a.* massimo. **~ over**

(*finished*) finito; (*everywhere*) dapper-tutto. ~ **right!** va bene! ~ **round** *a.* completo. **be** ~ **for** essere a favore di. **not at** ~ niente affatto.

allay /ə'leɪ/ *v.t.* placare.

allegation /ælɪ'geɪʃn/ *n.* allegazione *f.*

allege /ə'ledʒ/ *v.t.* allegare. ~**dly** /-ɪdlɪ/ *adv.* secondo quanto si dice.

allegiance /ə'li:dʒəns/ *n.* fedeltà *f.*

allegor|y /'ælɪgərɪ/ *n.* allegoria *f.* ~**ical** /-'gɒrɪkl/ *a.* allegorico.

allerg|y /'ælədʒɪ/ *n.* allergia *f.* ~**ic** /ə'lɜ:dʒɪk/ *a.* allergico.

alleviat|e /ə'li:vɪeɪt/ *v.t.* alleviare. ~**ion** /-'eɪʃn/ *n.* alleviamento *m.*

alley /'ælɪ/ (*pl.* **-eys**) *n.* vicolo *m.*; (*for bowling etc.*) corsia *f.*

alliance /ə'laɪəns/ *n.* alleanza *f.*

allied /'ælaɪd/ *a.* alleato.

alligator /'ælɪgeɪtə(r)/ *n.* alligatore *m.*

allocat|e /'æləkeɪt/ *v.t.* assegnare; (*share out*) distribuire. ~**ion** /-'keɪʃn/ *n.* assegnazione *f.*; distribuzione *f.*

allot /ə'lɒt/ *v.t.* (*p.t.* **allotted**) distribuire. ~**ment** *n.* distribuzione *f.*; (*share*) porzione *f.*; (*land*) lotto di terra *m.*

allow /ə'laʊ/ *v.t.* permettere; (*grant*) accordare; (*reckon on*) calcolare; (*agree*) ammettere. ~ **for** tener conto di.

allowance /ə'laʊəns/ *n.* indennità *f.*; (*pension*) pensione *f.*; (*comm.*) riduzione *f.* **make** ~**s for** essere indulgente verso; (*take into account*) tener conto di.

alloy[1] /'ælɔɪ/ *n.* lega *f.*

alloy[2] /ə'lɔɪ/ *v.t.* legare.

allude /ə'lu:d/ *v.i.* alludere.

allure /ə'lʊə(r)/ *v.t.* attrarre. —*n.* attrattiva *f.*

allusion /ə'lu:ʒn/ *n.* allusione *f.*

ally[1] /'ælaɪ/ *n.* alleato, a *m.,f.*

ally[2] /ə'laɪ/ *v.t.* alleare.

almanac /'ɔ:lmənæk/ *n.* almanacco *m.*

almighty /ɔ:l'maɪtɪ/ *a.* onnipotente; (*fam.*, *big*) grande. —*n.* **the A**~ Dio *m.*

almond /'ɑ:mənd/ *n.* mandorla *f.*; (*tree*) mandorlo *m.*

almost /'ɔ:lməʊst/ *adv.* quasi.

alms /ɑ:mz/ *n.* elemosina *f.*

almshouse /'ɑ:mzhaʊs/ *n.* ospizio di carità *m.*

alone /ə'ləʊn/ *a.* solo. —*adv.* da solo.

along /ə'lɒŋ/ *prep.* lungo. —*adv.* ~ **with** assieme a. **all** ~ tutto il tempo. **come** ~ vieni.

alongside /əlɒŋ'saɪd/ *adv.* (*naut.*) lungo bordo. —*prep.* a fianco di.

aloof /ə'lu:f/ *adv.* in disparte. —*a.* distante. ~**ness** *n.* riserbo *m.*

aloud /ə'laʊd/ *adv.* ad alta voce.

alphabet /'ælfəbet/ *n.* alfabeto *m.* ~**ical** /-'betɪkl/ *a.* alfabetico.

alpine /'ælpaɪn/ *a.* alpestre.

Alpine /'ælpaɪn/ *a.* alpino.

Alps /ælps/ *n.pl.* **the** ~ le Alpi *f.pl.*

already /ɔ:l'redɪ/ *adv.* (di) già.

Alsatian /æl'seɪʃn/ *n.* (*geog.*) alsaziano, a *m.*,*f.*; (*dog*) cane-lupo *m.*

also /'ɔ:lsəʊ/ *adv.* anche, pure.

altar /'ɔ:ltə(r)/ *n.* altare *m.*

alter /'ɔ:ltə(r)/ *v.t./i.* alterare, alterarsi. ~**ation** /-'reɪʃn/ *n.* modifica *f.*

alternate[1] /ɔ:l'tɜ:nət/ *a.* alterno; (*by turns*) alternato. ~**ly** *adv.* alternatamente.

alternate[2] /'ɔ:ltəneɪt/ *v.i.* alternarsi. —*v.t.* alternare.

alternative /ɔ:l'tɜ:nətɪv/ *a.* alternativo. —*n.* alternativa *f.* ~**ly** *adv.* alternativamente.

although /ɔ:l'ðəʊ/ *conj.* sebbene, benché.

altitude /'æltɪtju:d/ *n.* altitudine *f.*

altogether /ɔ:ltə'geðə(r)/ *adv.* completamente; (*on the whole*) nell'insieme.

altruism /'æltru:ɪzəm/ *n.* altruismo *m.*

altruist /'æltru:ɪst/ *n.* altruista *m.*|*f.* ~**ic** /-'ɪstɪk/ *a.* altruistico.

aluminium /æljʊ'mɪnɪəm/ *n.* alluminio *m.*

always /'ɔ:lweɪz/ *adv.* sempre.

am /æm/ *see* be.

a.m. /'eɪem/ *a. abbr.* (*of* ante meridiem) antimeridiano.

amalgamate /ə'mælgəmeɪt/ *v.t./i.* amalgamare, amalgamarsi.

amass /ə'mæs/ *v.t.* ammassare.

amateur /'æmətə(r)/ *n.* amatore *m.* —*a.* dilettante. ~**ish** *a.* (*pej.*) da dilettante.

amaz|e /ə'meɪz/ *v.t.* stupire. ~**ed** *a.* stupito. ~**ingly** *adv.* sorprendentemente. ~**ement** *n.* stupore *m.*

ambassador /æm'bæsədə(r)/ *n.* ambascia|tore, -trice *m.*,*f.*

amber /'æmbə(r)/ *n.* ambra *f.*

ambidextrous /æmbɪ'dekstrəs/ *a.* ambidestro.

ambience /'æmbɪəns/ *n.* ambiente *m.*

ambigu|ous /æm'bɪgjʊəs/ *a.* ambiguo. ~**ity** /-'gju:ətɪ/ *n.* ambiguità *f.*

ambit /'æmbɪt/ *n.* ambito *m.*; (*bounds*) limite *m.*

ambiti|on /æm'bɪʃn/ *n.* ambizione *f.*
~**ous** *a.* ambizioso.
ambivalen|t /æm'bɪvələnt/ *a.* ambiva-
lente. ~**ce** *n.* ambivalenza *f.*
amble /'æmbl/ *v.i.* camminare lentamente.
ambulance /'æmbjʊləns/ *n.* ambu-
lanza *f.*
ambush /'æmbʊʃ/ *n.* imboscata *f.*
—*v.t.* tendere un'imboscata a.
amen /ɑː'men/ *int.* così sia.
amenable /ə'miːnəbl/ *a.* ~ to (*responsive*) ben disposto a.
amend /ə'mend/ *v.t.* modificare. **make**
~**s** fare ammenda. ~**ment** *n.* modifica *f.*
amenities /ə'miːnətɪz/ *n.pl.* attrattive
f.pl.
America /ə'merɪkə/ *n.* America *f.* ~**n**
a. & *n.* americano, a *m.*, *f.* ~**nism** *n.*
americanismo *m.* ~**nize** *v.t.* ame-
ricanizzare.
amethyst /'æmɪθɪst/ *n.* ametista *f.*
amiable /'eɪmɪəbl/ *a.* amabile.
amicabl|e /'æmɪkəbl/ *a.* amichevole.
~**y** *adv.* amichevolmente.
amid(st) /ə'mɪd(st)/ *prep.* in mezzo a.
amiss /ə'mɪs/ *a.* & *adv.* sbagliato. **take
it** ~ prendersela.
ammonia /ə'məʊnɪə/ *n.* ammoniaca *f.*
ammunition /æmjʊ'nɪʃn/ *n.* munizioni *f.pl.*
amnesia /æm'niːzɪə/ *n.* amnesia *f.*
amnesty /'æmnəstɪ/ *n.* amnistia *f.*
amok /ə'mɒk/ *adv.* **run** ~ essere in
preda a furore.
among(st) /ə'mʌŋ(st)/ *prep.* tra, fra.
amoral /eɪ'mɒrəl/ *a.* amorale.
amorous /'æmərəs/ *a.* amoroso.
amorphous /ə'mɔːfəs/ *a.* amorfo.
amount /ə'maʊnt/ *n.* ammontare *m.*;
(*total*) totale *m.*; (*sum of money*)
somma *f.* —*v.i.* ~ to ammontare a;
(*fig.*) equivalere a.
amp(ere) /'æmp(eə(r))/ *n.* ampère *m.*
amphibi|an /æm'fɪbɪən/ *n.* anfibio *m.*
~**ous** *a.* anfibio.
amphitheatre /'æmfɪθɪətə(r)/ *n.*
anfiteatro *m.*
ampl|e /'æmpl/ *a.* (-er, -est) ampio;
(*enough*) abbondante. ~**y** *adv.* ampiamente.
amplif|y /'æmplɪfaɪ/ *v.t.* amplificare.
~**ier** *n.* amplificatore *m.*
amputat|e /'æmpjʊteɪt/ *v.t.* amputare.
~**ion** /-'teɪʃn/ *n.* amputazione *f.*
amus|e /ə'mjuːz/ *v.t.* divertire. ~**e-**

ment *n.* divertimento *m.* ~**ing** *a.*
divertente.
an /ən, æn/ *see* **a.**
anachronism /ə'nækrənɪzəm/ *n.* ana-
cronismo *m.*
anaemi|a /ə'niːmɪə/ *n.* anemia *f.* ~**c** *a.*
anemico.
anaesthesia /ænɪs'θiːzɪə/ *n.* anestesia
f.
anaesthet|ic /ænɪs'θetɪk/ *n.* anestetico
m. ~**ist** /ə'niːsθɪtɪst/ *n.* anestetista
m.|*f.*
anagram /'ænəgræm/ *n.* anagramma
m.
analogy /ə'nælədʒɪ/ *n.* analogia *f.*
analys|e /'ænəlaɪz/ *v.t.* analizzare. ~**t**
/-ɪst/ *n.* analista *m.*|*f.*
analysis /ə'næləsɪs/ *n.* (*pl.* -**yses** /-siːz/)
n. analisi *f.*
analytic(al) /ænə'lɪtɪk(əl)/ *a.* anali-
tico.
anarch|y /'ænəkɪ/ *n.* anarchia *f.* ~**ist**
n. anarchico, a *m.*, *f.*
anathema /ə'næθəmə/ *n.* anatema *m.*
anatom|y /ə'nætəmɪ/ *n.* anatomia *f.*
~**ical** /ænə'tɒmɪkl/ *a.* anatomico.
ancest|or /'ænsestə(r)/ *n.* antenato, a
m., *f.* ~**ral** /-'sestrəl/ *a.* ancestrale.
ancestry /'ænsestrɪ/ *n.* antenati *m.pl.*
anchor /'æŋkə(r)/ *n.* ancora *f.* —*v.t.*
ancorare. —*v.i.* gettar l'ancora.
anchovy /'æntʃəvɪ/ *n.* acciuga *f.*
ancient /'eɪnʃənt/ *a.* antico.
ancillary /æn'sɪlərɪ/ *a.* ausiliario.
and /ənd, ænd/ *conj.* e, ed. **more** ~
more sempre più. **try** ~ **come** cerca
di venire.
anecdote /'ænɪkdəʊt/ *n.* aneddoto *m.*
anew /ə'njuː/ *adv.* di nuovo.
angel /'eɪndʒl/ *n.* angelo *m.* ~**ic**
/æn'dʒelɪk/ *a.* angelico.
anger /'æŋgə(r)/ *n.* collera *f.* —*v.t.* far
andare in collera.
angle[1] /'æŋgl/ *n.* angolo *m.*; (*fig.*) punto
di vista *m.*
angle[2] /'æŋgl/ *v.i.* pescare (con la
lenza). ~ **for** (*fig.*) cercare. ~**r** /-ə(r)/
n. pesca|tore, -trice *m.*, *f.*
Anglican /'æŋglɪkən/ *a.* & *n.* angli-
cano, a *m.*, *f.*
Anglo- /'æŋgləʊ/ *pref.* anglo-.
Anglo-Saxon /'æŋgləʊ'sæksn/ *a.* & *n.*
anglo-sassone *m.*|*f.*
angr|y /'æŋgrɪ/ *a.* (-ier, -iest) arrab-
biato. **get** ~**y** arrabbiarsi. ~**ily** *adv.*
rabbiosamente.
anguish /'æŋgwɪʃ/ *n.* angoscia *f.*
angular /'æŋgjʊlə(r)/ *a.* angolare.

animal 212 any

animal /'ænɪməl/ a. & n. animale m.

animate[1] /'ænɪmət/ a. animato.

animat|e[2] /'ænɪmeɪt/ v.t. animare. **~ion** /-'meɪʃn/ n. animazione f.

animosity /ænɪ'mɒsətɪ/ n. animosità f.

aniseed /'ænɪsiːd/ n. seme d'anice m.

ankle /'æŋkl/ n. caviglia f. **~ sock** calzino m.

annals /'ænlz/ n.pl. annali m.pl.

annex /ə'neks/ v.t. annettere. **~ation** /ænek'seɪʃn/ n. annessione f.

annexe /'æneks/ n. annesso m.

annihilat|e /ə'naɪəleɪt/ v.t. annientare. **~ion** /-'leɪʃn/ n. annientamento m.

anniversary /ænɪ'vɜːsərɪ/ n. anniversario m.

annotat|e /'ænəteɪt/ v.t. annotare. **~ation** /-'teɪʃn/ n. annotazione f.

announce /ə'naʊns/ v.t. annunciare. **~ment** n. annuncio m. **~r** /-e(r)/ n. (radio, TV) annuncia|tore, -trice m., f.

annoy /ə'nɔɪ/ v.t. seccare, importunare. **~ance** n. seccatura f. **~ed** a. seccato. **~ing** a. seccante.

annual /'ænjʊəl/ a. annuale. —n. annuario m. **~ly** adv. annualmente.

annuity /ə'njuːətɪ/ n. annualità f. **life ~** vitalizio m.

annul /ə'nʌl/ v.t. (p.t. **annulled**) annullare. **~ment** n. annullamento m.

anoint /ə'nɔɪnt/ v.t. ungere.

anomal|y /ə'nɒməlɪ/ n. anomalia f. **~ous** a. anomalo.

anon /ə'nɒn/ adv. (old use) fra poco.

anonymous /ə'nɒnɪməs/ a. anonimo.

anorak /'ænəræk/ n. giacca a vento f.

another /ə'nʌðə(r)/ a. & pron. un altro, un'altra. **in ~ way** diversamente. **one ~** l'un l'altro.

answer /'ɑːnsə(r)/ n. risposta f.; (solution) soluzione f. —v.t./i. rispondere (a); (prayer) esaudire. **~ back** ribattere. **~ for** essere responsabile di. **~ the door** aprire la porta. **~able** a. responsabile. **~ing-machine** n. segreteria telefonica f.

ant /ænt/ n. formica f.

antagonis|m /æn'tægənɪzəm/ n. antagonismo m. **~tic** /-'nɪstɪk/ a. antagonistico.

antagonize /æn'tægənaɪz/ v.t. provocare l'ostilità di.

Antarctic /æn'tɑːktɪk/ a. antartico. —n. Antartico m.

ante- /'æntɪ/ pref. anti-.

antecedent /æntɪ'siːdnt/ n. antecedente m.

antelope /'æntɪləʊp/ n. antilope m.

antenatal /'æntmeɪtl/ a. prenatale.

antenna /æn'tenə/ n. antenna f.

anthem /'ænθəm/ n. inno m.

anthill /'ænthɪl/ n. formicaio m.

anthology /æn'θɒlədʒɪ/ n. antologia f.

anthropolog|y /ænθrə'pɒlədʒɪ/ n. antropologia f. **~ist** n. antropologo, a m., f.

anti- /'æntɪ/ pref. anti-, contro. **~aircraft** a. antiaereo.

antibiotic /æntɪbaɪ'ɒtɪk/ a. & n. antibiotico m.

antibody /'æntɪbɒdɪ/ n. anticorpo m.

antic /'æntɪk/ n. buffonata f.

anticipat|e /æn'tɪsɪpeɪt/ v.t. anticipare; (foresee) prevedere; (forestall) prevenire. **~ion** /-'peɪʃn/ n. anticipazione f.

anticlimax /æntɪ'klaɪmæks/ n. smontatura f.

anticlockwise /æntɪ'klɒkwaɪz/ adv. & a. in senso antiorario.

anticyclone /æntɪ'saɪkləʊn/ n. anticiclone m.

antidote /'æntɪdəʊt/ m. antidoto m.

antifreeze /'æntɪfriːz/ n. antigelo m.

antipathy /æn'tɪpəθɪ/ n. antipatia f.

antiquarian /æntɪ'kweərɪən/ a. & n. antiquario, a m., f.

antiquated /'æntɪkweɪtɪd/ a. antiquato.

antique /æn'tiːk/ a. antico. —n. antichità f. **~ dealer** antiquario, a m., f. **~ trade** antiquariato m.

antiquity /æn'tɪkwətɪ/ n. antichità f.

anti-Semitic /æntɪsɪ'mɪtɪk/ a. antisemita.

antiseptic /æntɪ'septɪk/ a. & n. antisettico m.

antisocial /æntɪ'səʊʃl/ a. antisociale.

antithesis /æn'tɪθəsɪs/ n. (pl. **-eses** /-siːz/) antitesi f.

antler /'æntlər/ n. corno (di cervo) m.

anus /'eɪnəs/ n. ano m.

anvil /'ænvɪl/ n. incudine f.

anxiety /æŋ'zaɪətɪ/ n. ansietà f.; (eagerness) (forte) desiderio m.

anxious /'æŋkʃəs/ a. ansioso; (eager) impaziente. **~ly** adv. ansiosamente; impazientemente.

any /'enɪ/ a. qualche, qualunque, qualsiasi, del; (every) ogni. **not ~** non alcuno, nessuno. **have you ~ wine?** avete del vino? —pron. alcuno, nessuno; (anybody) chiunque; (not fol-

lowed by noun) ne. **have we** ∼? ne abbiamo? *—adv.* nulla; (*a little*) un po'. **is it** ∼ **better?** è un po' meglio? **it isn't** ∼ **good** non serve a nulla.
anybody /'enɪbɒdɪ/ *pron.* qualcuno; (*after negative*) nessuno. ∼ **can do that** chiunque sa farlo.
anyhow /'enɪhaʊ/ *adv.* comunque; (*badly*) alla buona.
anyone /'enɪwʌn/ *pron.* = anybody.
anything /'enɪθɪŋ/ *pron.* qualche cosa, qualcosa; (*after negative*) niente. ∼ **but** tutt'altro che.
anyway /'enɪweɪ/ *adv.* ad ogni modo.
anywhere /'enɪweə(r)/ *adv.* dovunque; (*after negative*) in nessun luogo.
apace /ə'peɪs/ *adv.* velocemente.
apart /ə'pɑːt/ *adv.* a parte; (*separated*) distante; (*into pieces*) a pezzi. ∼ **from** a parte, oltre.
apartheid /ə'pɑːtheɪt/ *n.* discriminazione razziale *f.*
apartment /ə'pɑːtmənt/ *n.* (*Amer.*) appartamento *m.*
apath|y /'æpəθɪ/ *n.* apatia *f.* ∼**etic** /-'θetɪk/ *a.* apatico.
ape /eɪp/ *n.* scimmia. *f.* *—v.t.* scimmiottare.
aperient /ə'pɪərɪənt/ *a.* & *n.* lassativo *m.*
aperitif /ə'perətɪf/ *n.* aperitivo *m.*
aperture /'æpətʃʊə(r)/ *n.* apertura *f.*
apex /'eɪpeks/ *n.* apice *m.*
aphorism /'æfərɪzəm/ *n.* aforisma *m.*
aphrodisiac /æfrə'dɪzɪæk/ *a.* & *n.* afrodisiaco *m.*
apiece /ə'piːs/ *adv.* a testa.
aplomb /ə'plɒm/ *n.* disinvoltura *f.*
apologetic /əpɒlə'dʒetɪk/ *a.* contrito. **be** ∼ essere spiacente.
apologize /ə'pɒlədʒaɪz/ *v.i.* chiedere scusa.
apology /ə'pɒlədʒɪ/ *n.* scusa *f.*; (*poor specimen*) esemplare meschino *m.*
apople|xy /'æpəpleksɪ/ *n.* apoplessia *f.* ∼**ctic** /-'plektɪk/ *a.* apoplettico.
apostle /ə'pɒsl/ *n.* apostolo *m.*
apostrophe /ə'pɒstrəfɪ/ *n.* apostrofo *m.*
appal /ə'pɔːl/ *v.t.* (*p.t.* **appalled**) atterrire. ∼**ling** *a.* spaventoso.
apparatus /æpə'reɪtəs/ *n.* apparato *m.*
apparel /ə'pærəl/ *n.* abbigliamento *m.*
apparent /ə'pærənt/ *a.* evidente. ∼**ly** *adv.* evidentemente.
apparition /æpə'rɪʃn/ *n.* apparizione *f.*
appeal /ə'piːl/ *v.i.* fare appello; (*attract*)

attrarre. *—n.* appello *m.* ∼**ing** *a.* attraente.
appear /ə'pɪə(r)/ *v.i.* apparire; (*arrive*) presentarsi; (*seem*) sembrare; (*publication*) essere pubblicato; (*theatr.*) esibirsi. ∼**ance** *n.* apparenza *f.*; (*aspect*) sembianza *f.*
appease /ə'piːz/ *v.t.* placare.
append /ə'pend/ *v.t.* appendere.
appendage /ə'pendɪdʒ/ *n.* aggiunta *f.*
appendicitis /əpendɪ'saɪtɪs/ *n.* appendicite *f.*
appendix /ə'pendɪks/ *n.* (*pl.* **-ices** /-siːz/) (*of book*) appendice *f.*; (*pl.* **-ixes**) (*anat.*) appendice *f.*
appertain /æpə'teɪn/ *v.i.* essere pertinente.
appetite /'æpɪtaɪt/ *n.* appetito *m.*
appetiz|er /'æpɪtaɪzə(r)/ *n.* stuzzichino *m.* ∼**ing** *a.* appetitoso.
applau|d /ə'plɔːd/ *v.t./i.* applaudire. ∼**se** *n.* applauso *m.*
apple /'æpl/ *n.* mela *f.* ∼**-tree** *n.* melo *m.*
appliance /ə'plaɪəns/ *n.* apparecchio *m.*
applicable /'æplɪkəbl/ *a.* applicabile.
applicant /'æplɪkənt/ *n.* candidato, a *m.,f.*
application /æplɪ'keɪʃn/ *n.* applicazione *f.*; (*request*) domanda *f.* ∼ **form** modulo *m.* **on** ∼ su richiesta.
appl|y /ə'plaɪ/ *v.t./i.* applicare, applicarsi; (*refer*) riferirsi; (*ask*) rivolgersi. ∼**y for** (*job etc.*) fare domanda per. ∼**ied** *a.* applicato.
appoint /ə'pɔɪnt/ *v.t.* nominare; (*fix*) designare. **well-**∼**ed** *a.* ben equipaggiato. ∼**ment** *n.* appuntamento *m.*; (*job*) posto *m.*
apportion /ə'pɔːʃn/ *v.t.* distribuire.
apposite /'æpəzɪt/ *a.* appropriato.
apprais|e /ə'preɪz/ *v.t.* valutare. ∼**al** *n.* valutazione *f.*
appreciable /ə'priːʃəbl/ *a.* apprezzabile.
appreciat|e /ə'priːʃɪeɪt/ *v.t.* (*like*) apprezzare; (*understand*) comprendere. *—v.i.* (*increase value*) aumentare di valore. ∼**ion** /-'eɪʃn/ *n.* apprezzamento *m.*; aumento *m.* ∼**ive** /ə'priːʃɪətɪv/ *a.* sensibile.
apprehen|d /æprɪ'hend/ *v.t.* arrestare; (*understand*) comprendere. ∼**sion** /-ʃn/ *n.* arresto *m.*; (*fear*) apprensione *f.*
apprehensive /æprɪ'hensɪv/ *a.* apprensivo.

apprentice /ə'prentıs/ n. apprendista m./f. −v.t. mettere in tirocinio. ∼**ship** n. tirocinio m.

approach /ə'prəʊtʃ/ v.t./i. accostare, accostarsi. −n. avvicinamento m. **make** ∼**es to** fare degli approcci con. ∼**able** a. accessibile.

approbation /æprə'beıʃn/ n. approvazione f.

appropriate[1] /ə'prəʊprıət/ a. appropriato. ∼**ly** adv. in modo appropriato.

appropriate[2] /ə'prəʊprıeıt/ v.t. appropriarsi.

approval /ə'pru:vl/ n. approvazione f. **on** ∼ in prova.

approv|e /ə'pru:v/ v.t./i. approvare. ∼**ingly** adv. con approvazione.

approximate[1] /ə'prɒksımət/ a. approssimativo. ∼**ly** adv. approssimativamente.

approximat|e[2] /ə'prɒksımeıt/ v.t. avvicinarsi a. ∼**ion** /-'meıʃn/ n. approssimazione f.

apricot /'eıprıkɒt/ n. albicocca f. ∼ **tree** n. albicocco m.

April /'eıprəl/ n. aprile m. ∼ **fool!** pesce d'aprile!

apron /'eıprən/ n. grembiule m.

apropos /'æprəpəʊ/ adv. a proposito.

apse /æps/ n. abside f.

apt /æpt/ a. atto; (pupil) sveglio; (tendency) propenso. ∼**ly** adv. giustamente.

aptitude /'æptıtju:d/ n. attitudine f.

aqualung /'ækwəlʌŋ/ n. autorespiratore m.

aquarium /ə'kweərıəm/ n. (pl. -ums) acquario m.

Aquarius /ə'kweərıəs/ n. Acquario m.

aquatic /ə'kwætık/ a. acquatico.

aqueduct /'ækwıdʌkt/ n. acquedotto m.

aquiline /'ækwılaın/ a. aquilino.

Arab /'ærəb/ a. & n. arabo, a m.,f. ∼**ic** a. & n. (lang.) arabo m. ∼**ic numerals** numeri arabici m.pl.

Arabian /ə'reıbıən/ a. arabo.

arable /'ærəbl/ a. arabile.

arbiter /'ɑ:bıtə(r)/ arbitro m.

arbitrary /'ɑ:bıtrərı/ a. arbitrario.

arbitrat|e /'ɑ:bıtreıt/ v.i. arbitrare. ∼**ion** /-'treıʃn/ n. arbitraggio m., ∼**or** n. arbitro m.

arc /ɑ:k/ n. arco m.

arcade /ɑ:'keıd/ n. (covered area) portico m.; (shops) galleria f. **amusement** ∼ galleria dei divertimenti f.

arcane /ɑ:'keın/ a. misterioso.

arch[1] /ɑ:tʃ/ n. arco m.; (in church etc.) volta f.; (anat.) arcata f. − v.t./i. inarcare.

arch[2] /ɑ:tʃ/ a. birichino.

archaeolg|y /ɑ:kı'ɒlədʒı/ n. archeologia f. ∼**ical** /-ə'lɒdʒıkl/ a. archeologico. ∼**ist** n. archeologo, a m.,f.

archaic /ɑ:'keıık/ a. arcaico.

archbishop /ɑ:tʃ'bıʃəp/ n. arcivescovo m.

arch-enemy /ɑ:tʃ'enəmı/ n. arcinemico m.

archer /'ɑ:tʃə(r)/ n. arciere m. ∼**y** n. tiro all'arco m.

archetype /'ɑ:kıtaıp/ n. prototipo m.

archipelago /ɑ:kı'peləgəʊ/ n. (pl. -os) arcipelago m.

architect /'ɑ:kıtekt/ n. architetto m.

architectur|e /'ɑ:kıtektʃə(r)/ n. architettura f. ∼**al** /-'tektʃərəl/ a. architetturale.

archiv|es /'ɑ:kaıvz/ n.pl. archivio m.s. ∼**ist** /-ıvıst/ n. archivista m./f.

archway /'ɑ:tʃweı/ n. arco m.

Arctic /'ɑ:ktık/ a. & n. artico m. **arctic** a. glaciale.

ardent /'ɑ:dənt/ a. ardente. ∼**ly** adv. ardentemente.

ardour /'ɑ:də(r)/ n. ardore m.; (enthusiasm) zelo m.

arduous /'ɑ:djʊəs/ a. arduo.

are /ɑ:(r)/ see **be**.

area /'eərıə/ n. (surface) superficie f.; (region) zona f.; (fig.) campo m.

arena /ə'ri:nə/ n. arena f.

aren't /ɑ:nt/ = **are not**.

Argentin|a /ɑ:dʒən'ti:nə/ n. Argentina f. ∼**ian** /-'tınıən/ a. & n. argentino, a m.,f.

argu|e /'ɑ:gju:/ v.i. litigare; (reason) ragionare; (debate) dibattere. ∼**able** a. discutibile.

argument /'ɑ:gjʊmənt/ n. argomento m.; (reasoning) ragionamento m. ∼**ative** /-'mentətıv/ a. polemico.

arid /'ærıd/ a. arido.

Aries /'eəri:z/ n. Ariete m.

arise /ə'raız/ v.i. (p.t. **arose**, p.p. **arisen**) levarsi, alzarsi; (fig.) nascere. ∼ **from** risultare da.

aristocracy /ærı'stɒkrəsı/ n. aristocrazia f.

aristocrat /'ærıstəkræt/ n. aristocratico, a m.,f. ∼**ic** /-'krætık/ a. aristocratico.

arithmetic /ə'rıθmətık/ n. aritmetica f.

ark /ɑ:k/ n. (relig.) arca f.

arm /ɑ:m/ *n.* braccio *m.*; (*mil.*) arma *f.*; (*pl., weapons*) armi *f.pl.* ~ **in arm** a braccetto. —*v.t.* armare. ~**ed robbery** rapina a mano armata *f.*

armada /ɑ:ˈmɑːdə/ *n.* armata *f.*

armament /ˈɑːməmənt/ *n.* armamento *m.*

armchair /ˈɑːmtʃeə(r)/ *n.* poltrona *f.*

armful /ˈɑːmfʊl/ *n.* bracciata *f.*

armistice /ˈɑːmɪstɪs/ *n.* armistizio *m.*

armlet /ˈɑːmlɪt/ *n.* bracciale *m.*

armour /ˈɑːmə(r)/ *n.* armatura *f.* ~**ed** *a.* blindato.

armoury /ˈɑːmərɪ/ *n.* arsenale *m.*

armpit /ˈɑːmpɪt/ *n.* ascella *f.*

army /ˈɑːmɪ/ *n.* esercito *m.*

aroma /əˈrəʊmə/ *n.* aroma *f.* ~**tic** /ærəˈmætɪk/ *a.* aromatico.

arose /əˈrəʊz/ *see* **arise**.

around /əˈraʊnd/ *adv.* intorno. —*prep.* attorno a; (*Amer.*) circa. **all** ~ da tutte le parti.

arouse /əˈraʊz/ *v.t.* destare; (*excite*) stimolare.

arrange /əˈreɪndʒ/ *v.t.* sistemare; (*fix*) combinare. ~**ment** *n.* (*order*) disposizione *f.*; (*pl., plans*) piani *m.pl.*

array /əˈreɪ/ *v.t.* (*dress*) abbigliare; (*mil.*) schierare. —*n.* abbigliamento *m.*; schiera *f.*

arrears /əˈrɪəz/ *n.pl.* arretrati *m.pl.*

arrest /əˈrest/ *v.t.* arrestare; (*attention*) attirare. —*n.* arresto *m.* **under** ~ in stato d'arresto.

arrival /əˈraɪvl/ *n.* arrivo *m.* **new** ~**s** nuovi arrivati *m.pl.*

arrive /əˈraɪv/ *v.i.* arrivare.

arrogan|t /ˈærəgənt/ *a.* arrogante. ~**ce** *n.* arroganza *f.* ~**tly** *adv.* con arroganza.

arrow /ˈærəʊ/ *n.* freccia *f.*

arsenal /ˈɑːsənl/ *n.* arsenale *m.*

arsenic /ˈɑːsnɪk/ *n.* arsenico *m.*

arson /ˈɑːsn/ *n.* incendio doloso *m.* ~**ist** *n.* incendiario *m.*

art[1] /ɑːt/ *n.* arte *f.* **A**~**s** *n.pl.* (*Univ.*) facoltà di lettere *f.s.* ~ **gallery** galleria d'arte *f.* **fine** ~**s** belle arti *f.pl.*

art[2] /ɑːt/ (*old use, with* **thou**) = **are**.

artefact /ˈɑːtɪfækt/ *n.* manufatto *m.*

arter|y /ˈɑːtərɪ/ *n.* arteria *f.* ~**ial** /-ˈtɪərɪəl/ *a.* arteriale. ~**ial road** *n.* strada nazionale *f.*

artesian /ɑːˈtiːzjən/ *a.* ~ **well** pozzo artesiano *m.*

artful /ˈɑːtfʊl/ *a.* furbo. ~**ness** *n.* furberia *f.*

arthriti|s /ɑːˈθraɪtɪs/ *n.* artrite *f.* ~**c** /-ɪtɪk/ *a.* artritico.

artichoke /ˈɑːtɪtʃəʊk/ *n.* carciofo *m.* **Jerusalem** ~ topinamburo *m.*

article /ˈɑːtɪkl/ *n.* articolo *m.* **leading** ~ articolo di fondo *m.*

articulate[1] /ɑːˈtɪkjʊlət/ *a.* articolato.

articulat|e[2] /ɑːˈtɪkjʊleɪt/ *v.t./i.* articolare. ~**ed lorry** *n.* autotreno *m.* ~**ion** /-ˈleɪʃn/ *n.* articolazione *f.*

artific|e /ˈɑːtɪfɪs/ *n.* artificio *m.* ~**ial** /-ˈfɪʃl/ *a.* artificiale.

artillery /ɑːˈtɪlərɪ/ *n.* artiglieria *f.*

artisan /ɑːtɪˈzæn/ *n.* artigiano *m.*

artist /ˈɑːtɪst/ *n.* artista *m./f.* ~**ic** /-ˈtɪstɪk/ *a.* artistico. ~**ry** *n.* arte *f.*

artiste /ɑːˈtiːst/ *n.* (*theatr.*) artista *m./f.*

artless /ˈɑːtlɪs/ *a.* senz'arte; (*simple*) naturale.

arty /ˈɑːtɪ/ *a.* (*fam.*) che si atteggia ad artista.

as /æz, əz/ *adv. & conj.* come; (*since*) poiché; (*while*) mentre. ~ **far as** (*distance*) fino a; (*qualitative*) in quanto a. ~ **long as** finché, purché. ~ **much as** tanto quanto. ~ **as soon as** appena. ~ **well** anche.

ascend /əˈsend/ *v.t./i.* salire. ~**ant** *n.* ascendente *m.*

ascent /əˈsent/ *n.* ascesa *f.*

ascertain /æsəˈteɪn/ *v.t.* accertare.

ascetic /əˈsetɪk/ *a.* ascetico. —*n.* asceta *m./f.*

ascribe /əˈskraɪb/ *v.t.* attribuire.

ash[1] /æʃ/ *n.* ~(-**tree**) frassino *m.*

ash[2] /æʃ/ *n.* cenere *f.* **A**~ **Wednesday** Mercoledì delle Ceneri. ~**en** *a.* cinereo.

ashamed /əˈʃeɪmd/ *a.* vergognoso. **be** ~ aver vergogna.

ashore /əˈʃɔː(r)/ *adv.* a terra. **go** ~ sbarcare.

ashtray /ˈæʃtreɪ/ *n.* portacenere *m.*

Asia /ˈeɪʃə/ *n.* Asia *f.* ~**n** *a. & n.* asiatico, a *m., f.* ~**tic** /-ˈætɪk/ *a.* asiatico.

aside /əˈsaɪd/ *adv.* da parte —*n.* (*theatr.*) a parte *m.*

asinine /ˈæsɪnaɪn/ *a.* asinino.

ask /ɑːsk/ *v.t.* chiedere; (*question*) domandare; (*invite*) invitare. ~ **about** informarsi di. ~ **after** chiedere notizie di. ~ **for help** chiedere aiuto. ~ **for trouble** andare in cerca di guai. ~ **s.o. in** invitare qcno. ad entrare.

askance /əˈskæns/ *adv.* **look** ~ **at** guardare qcno. di traverso.

askew /əˈskjuː/ *adv. & a.* di traverso.

asleep /ə'sli:p/ *adv.* & *a.* addormentato. **fall ~** addormentarsi.

asparagus /ə'spærəgəs/ *n.* asparagi *m.pl.*

aspect /'æspekt/ *n.* aspetto *m.*; (*of house etc.*) esposizione *f.*

aspersions /ə'spɜːʃnz/ *n.pl.* **cast ~ on** diffamare.

asphalt /'æsfælt/ *n.* asfalto *m.* —*v.t.* asfaltare.

asphyxia /æs'fɪksɪə/ *n.* asfissia *f.*

asphyxiat|e /əs'fɪksɪeɪt/ *v.t.* asfissiare. **~ion** /-'eɪʃn/ *n.* asfissia *f.*

aspic /'æspɪk/ *n.* gelatina *f.*

aspir|e /əs'paɪə(r)/ *v.i.* aspirare. **~ation** /æspə'reɪʃn/ *n.* aspirazione *f.*

aspirin /'æsprɪn/ *n.* aspirina *f.*

ass /æs/ *n.* asino *m.*; (*fam.*,*fig.*) stupido, a *m.*, *f.*

assail /ə'seɪl/ *v.t.* assalire. **~ant** *n.* aggressore *m.*

assassin /ə'sæsɪn/ *n.* assassino, a *m.*, *f.*

assassinat|e /ə'sæsɪneɪt/ *v.t.* assassinare. **~ion** /-'eɪʃn/ *n.* assassinio *m.*

assault /ə'sɔːlt/ *n.* (*mil.*) assalto *m.*; (*jurid.*) aggressione *f.* —*v.t.* aggredire.

assembl|e /ə'sembl/ *v.t.* riunire; (*mech.*) montare. —*v.i.* riunirsi. **~age** *n.* assembramento *m.*; (*mech.*) montaggio *m.*

assembly /ə'semblɪ/ *n.* assemblea *f.* **~ line** catena di montaggio *f.*

assent /ə'sent/ *n.* assentimento *m.* —*v.i.* acconsentire.

assert /ə'sɜːt/ *v.t.* asserire; (*one's rights*) far valere. **~ion** /-ʃn/ *n.* asserzione *f.* **~ive** *a.* assertivo.

assess /ə'ses/ *v.t.* valutare; (*tax*) tassare. **~ment** *n.* valutazione *f.*

asset /'æset/ *n.* (*advantage*) vantaggio *m.*; (*pl.*, *comm.*) beni *m.pl.*

assiduous /ə'sɪdjʊəs/ *a.* assiduo.

assign /ə'saɪn/ *v.t.* assegnare; (*jurid.*) delegare. **~ment** *n.* assegnazione *f.*; (*task*) compito *m.*

assignation /æsɪg'neɪʃn/ *n.* assegnazione *f.*; (*jurid.*) cessione *f.*; (*meeting*) appuntamento *m.*

assimilat|e /ə'sɪmɪleɪt/ *v.t.*/*i.* assimilare. **~ion** /-'eɪʃn/ *n.* assimilazione *f.*

assist /ə'sɪst/ *v.t.*/*i.* assistere. **~ance** *n.* assistenza *f.*

assistant /ə'sɪstənt/ *n.* assistente *m.*/*f.*; (*shop*) commesso, a *m.*, *f.* —*a.* assistente.

associat|e[1] /ə'səʊʃɪeɪt/ *v.t.*/*i.* associare, associarsi. **~e with** frequentare.

~ion /-'eɪʃn/ *n.* associazione *f.* **Association football** (gioco del) calcio *m.*

associate[2] /ə'səʊʃɪət/ *a.* associato. —*n.* collega *m.*/*f.*

assort|ed /ə'sɔːtɪd/ *a.* assortito. **~ment** *n.* assortimento *m.*

assume /ə'sjuːm/ *v.t.* supporre; (*power*, *attitude*) prendere; (*role*, *burden*) assumere.

assumption /ə'sʌmpʃn/ *n.* supposizione *f.* **the A~** l'Assunzione *f.*

assurance /ə'ʃʊərəns/ *n.* assicurazione *f.*

assure /ə'ʃʊə(r)/ *v.t.* assicurare. **~d** *a.* sicuro. **~dly** /-rɪdlɪ/ *adv.* sicuramente.

asterisk /'æstərɪsk/ *n.* asterisco *m.*

astern /ə'stɜːn/ *adv.* a poppa.

asthma /'æsmə/ *n.* asma *f.* **~tic** /-'mætɪk/ *a.* & *n.* asmatico, a *m.*, *f.*

astonish /ə'stɒnɪʃ/ *v.t.* sorprendere. **~ing** *a.* sorprendente. **~ment** *n.* stupore *m.*

astound /ə'staʊnd/ *v.t.* stupire.

astray /ə'streɪ/ *adv.* & *a.* fuori strada. **go ~** smarrirsi. **lead ~** traviare.

astride /ə'straɪd/ *adv.* & *prep.* a cavalcioni.

astringent /ə'strɪndʒənt/ *a.* astringente; (*fig.*) austero. —*n.* astringente *m.*

astrolog|y /ə'strɒlədʒɪ/ *n.* astrologia *f.* **~er** astrologo, a *m.*, *f.*

astronaut /'æstrənɔːt/ *n.* astronauta *m.*/*f.*

astronom|y /ə'strɒnəmɪ/ *n.* astronomia *f.* **~er** *n.* astronomo, a *m.*, *f.* **~ical** /æstrə'nɒmɪkl/ *a.* astronomico.

astute /ə'stjuːt/ *a.* astuto. **~ness** *n.* astuzia *f.*

asunder /ə'sʌndə(r)/ *adv.* separatamente.

asylum /ə'saɪləm/ *n.* asilo *m.* **lunatic ~** manicomio *m.*

at /ət, æt/ *prep.* a, in, da. **~ home** a casa. **~ Robert's** da Roberto. **~ the station** alla stazione. **~ once** subito; (*simultaneously*) nello stesso tempo. **~ times** talvolta. **not ~ all** per niente.

ate /eɪt/ *see* **eat**.

atheis|t /'eɪθɪɪst/ *n.* ateo, a *m.*, *f.* **~m** /-zəm/ *n.* ateismo *m.*

athlet|e /'æθliːt/ *n.* atleta *m.*/*f.* **~ic** /-'letɪk/ *a.* atletico. **~ics** /-'letɪks/ *n.pl.* atletica *f.s.*

Atlantic /ət'læntɪk/ *a.* & *n.* atlantico

m. —n. ~ **(Ocean)** Oceano Atlantico *m.*

atlas /'ætləs/ *n.* atlante *m.*

atmospher|e /'ætməsfiə(r)/ *n.* atmosfera *f.* ~**ic** /-'ferɪk/ *a.* atmosferico. ~**ics** /-'ferɪks/ *n.pl.* scariche *f.pl.*

atom /'ætəm/ *n.* atomo *m.* ~**ic** /ə'tɒmɪk/ *a.* atomico.

atomize /'ætəmaɪz/ *v.t.* atomizzare. ~**r** /-ə(r)/ *n.* spruzzatore *m.*

atone /ə'təʊn/ *v.i.* ~ **for** espiare. ~**ment** *n.* espiazione *f.*

atrocious /ə'trəʊʃəs/ *a.* atroce.

atrocity /ə'trɒsəti/ *n.* atrocità *f.*

atrophy /'ætrəfi/ *n.* atrofia *f.*

attach /ə'tætʃ/ *v.t./i.* attaccare, attaccarsi. ~**ed** *a.* (*bound by affection*) legato. ~**ment** *n.* (*affection*) attaccamento *m.*; (*tool*) accessorio *m.*

attaché /ə'tæʃeɪ/ *n.* addetto *m.* ~ **case** borsa (per documenti) *f.*

attack /ə'tæk/ *n.* attacco *m.* —*v.t./i.* attaccare. ~**er** *n.* assali|tore, -trice *m., f.*

attain /ə'teɪn/ *v.t.* raggiungere. ~**able** *a.* raggiungibile. ~**ment** *n.* raggiungimento *m.* ~**ments** *n.pl.* cognizioni *f.pl.*

attempt /ə'tempt/ *v.t.* tentare. —*n.* tentativo *m.*

attend /ə'tend/ *v.t.* assistere; (*school*) frequentare; (*escort*) accompagnare. —*v.i.* prestare attenzione. ~ **to** badare a. ~**ance** *n.* presenza *f.*; (*service*) servizio *m.*

attendant /ə'tendənt/ *a.* che accompagna. —*n.* guardiano, a *m., f.*; (*servant*) inserviente *m.|f.*

attention /ə'tenʃn/ *n.* attenzione *f.* ~! (*mil.*) attenti! **pay** ~ stare attento.

attentive /ə'tentɪv/ *a.* attento; (*considerate*) sollecito. ~**ness** *n.* attenzione *f.*

attenuate /ə'tenjʊeɪt/ *v.t.* attenuare.

attest /ə'test/ *v.t./i.* attestare. ~**ation** /æte'steɪʃn/ *n.* attestazione *f.*

attic /'ætɪk/ *n.* attico *m.*

attire /ə'taɪə(r)/ *n.* abbigliamento *m.* —*v.t.* vestire.

attitude /'ætɪtjuːd/ *n.* attitudine *f.*

attorney /ə'tɜːni/ *n.* (*pl.* **-eys**) procuratore *m.*; (*Amer.*) avvocato *m.*

attract /ə'trækt/ *v.t.* attirare. ~**ion** /-ʃn/ *n.* attrazione *f.*; (*charm*) fascino *m.*

attractive /ə'træktɪv/ *a.* (*of magnet*) attrattivo; (*of person*) attraente. ~**ness** *n.* attrattiva *f.*

attribute[1] /ə'trɪbjuːt/ *v.t.* attribuire.

attribute[2] /'ætrɪbjuːt/ *n.* attributo *m.*

attrition /ə'trɪʃn/ *n.* attrito *m.*

aubergine /'əʊbəʒiːn/ *n.* melanzana *f.*

auburn /'ɔːbən/ *a.* castano ramato.

auction /'ɔːkʃn/ *n.* asta *f.* ~ **sale** vendita all'asta. —*v.t.* vendere all'asta. ~**eer** /-ə'nɪə(r)/ *n.* venditore all'asta *m.*

audaci|ous /ɔː'deɪʃəs/ *a.* audace. ~**ty** /-æsəti/ *n.* audacità *f.*

audible /'ɔːdəbl/ *a.* udibile.

audience /'ɔːdɪəns/ *n.* udienza *f.*; (*theatr.*, *radio*) pubblico *m.*

audio-visual /ɔːdɪəʊ'vɪʒʊəl/ *a.* audiovisivo.

audit /'ɔːdɪt/ *n.* verifica dei conti *f.* —*v.t.* verificare.

audition /ɔː'dɪʃn/ *n.* audizione *f.* —*v.t./i.* fare il provino.

auditor /'ɔːdɪtə(r)/ *n.* revisore di conti *m.*

auditorium /ɔːdɪ'tɔːrɪəm/ *n.* sala *f.*

augment /ɔːg'ment/ *v.t.* aumentare.

augur /'ɔːgə(r)/ *v.i.* predire. **it** ~**s well** promette bene.

august /ɔː'gʌst/ *a.* augusto.

August /'ɔːgəst/ *n.* agosto *m.*

aunt /ɑːnt/ *n.* zia *f.*

au pair /əʊ'peə(r)/ *n.* ragazza alla pari *f.*

aura /'ɔːrə/ *n.* aura *f.*

auspices /'ɔːspɪsɪz/ *n.pl.* auspici *m.pl.*; (*protection*) patronato *m.s.*

auspicious /ɔː'spɪʃəs/ *a.* propizio.

auster|e /ɔː'stɪə(r)/ *a.* austero. ~**ity** /-erəti/ *n.* austerità *f.*

Australia /ɒ'streɪlɪə/ *n.* Australia *f.* ~**n** *a.* & *n.* australiano, a *m., f.*

Austria /'ɒstrɪə/ *n.* Austria *f.* ~**n** *a.* & *n.* austriaco, a *m., f.*

authentic /ɔː'θentɪk/ *a.* autentico. ~**ity** /-ən'tɪsəti/ *n.* autenticità *f.*

authenticate /ɔː'θentɪkeɪt/ *v.t.* autenticare.

author /'ɔːθə(r)/ *n.* autore *m.* ~**ess** autrice *f.* ~**ship** *n.* professione di scrittore *f.*; (*origin*) paternità (di un'opera ecc.) *f.*

authoritarian /ɔːθɒrɪ'teərɪən/ *a.* autoritario.

authorit|y /ɔː'θɒrəti/ *n.* autorità *f.*; (*permission*) autorizzazione *f.* ~**ative** /-ɪtətɪv/ *a.* autorevole; (*manner*) imperativo.

authoriz|e /'ɔːθəraɪz/ *v.t.* autorizzare. ~**ation** /-'zeɪʃn/ *n.* autorizzazione *f.*

autistic /ɔː'tɪstɪk/ *a.* autistico.

autobiography /ɔːtəbaɪˈɒɡrəfɪ/ n. autobiografia f.

autocracy /ɔːˈtɒkrəsɪ/ n. autocrazia f.

autocrat /ˈɔːtəkræt/ n. autocrate m. ~**ic** /-ˈkrætɪk/ a. autocratico.

autograph /ˈɔːtəɡrɑːf/ n. autografo m. —v.t. autografare.

automat|e /ˈɔːtəmeɪt/ v.t. automatizzare. ~**ion** /-ˈmeɪʃn/ n. automazione f.

automatic /ɔːtəˈmætɪk/ a. automatico.

automaton /ɔːˈtɒmətən/ n. automa m.

automobile /ˈɔːtəməbiːl/ n. (Amer.) automobile f.

autonom|y /ɔːˈtɒnəmɪ/ n. autonomia f. ~**ous** a. autonomo.

autopsy /ˈɔːtɒpsɪ/ n. autopsia f.

autumn /ˈɔːtəm/ n. autunno m. ~**al** /-ˈtʌmnəl/ a. autunnale.

auxiliary /ɔːɡˈzɪlɪərɪ/ a. ausiliario. —n. ausiliare m./f.

avail /əˈveɪl/ v.t./i. servire (a). ~ **oneself of** approfittarsi di. —n. vantaggio m. **to no** ~ inutile.

availab|le /əˈveɪləbl/ a. disponibile. ~**ility** /-ˈbɪlətɪ/ n. disponibilità f.

avalanche /ˈævəlɑːnʃ/ n. valanga f.

avaric|e /ˈævərɪs/ n. avarizia f. ~**ious** /-ˈrɪʃəs/ a. avaro.

avenge /əˈvendʒ/ v.t. vendicare.

avenue /ˈævənjuː/ n. viale m.; (fig.) via f.

average /ˈævərɪdʒ/ n. media f. —a. medio. —v.t./i. raggiungere una media di. **on** ~ in media.

avers|e /əˈvɜːs/ a. avverso. ~**ion** /-ʃn/ n. avversione f.

avert /əˈvɜːt/ v.t. (turn away) distogliere; (ward off) sviare.

aviary /ˈeɪvɪərɪ/ n. uccelliera f.

aviation /eɪvɪˈeɪʃn/ n. aviazione f.

aviator /ˈeɪvɪeɪtə(r)/ n. (old use) avia|tore, -trice m., f.

avid /ˈævɪd/ a. avido. ~**ity** /-ˈvɪdətɪ/ n. avidità f.

avocado /ævəˈkɑːdəʊ/ n. (pl. -os) pera avocado f.

avoid /əˈvɔɪd/ v.t. evitare. ~**able** a. evitabile. ~**ance** n. l'evitare m.

avuncular /əˈvʌŋkjʊlə(r)/ a. da zio.

await /əˈweɪt/ v.t. attendere.

awake /əˈweɪk/ v.t./i. (p.t. **awoke**, p.p. **awoken**) svegliare, svegliarsi. —a. sveglio. **wide** ~ ben sveglio.

awaken /əˈweɪkən/ v.t./i. risvegliare. ~**ing** n. risveglio m.

award /əˈwɔːd/ v.t. assegnare. —n. ricompensa f.; (scholarship) borsa di studio f.

aware /əˈweə(r)/ a. conscio. ~**ness** n. consapevolezza f.

awash /əˈwɒʃ/ a. inondato.

away /əˈweɪ/ adv. via; (absent) fuori; (far) lontano; (persistently) di continuo. —a. & n. ~ (**match**) partita fuori casa f.

awe /ɔː/ n. timore m. ~**some** a. imponente. ~**struck** a. atterrito.

awful /ˈɔːfʊl/ a. terribile. ~**ly** adv. terribilmente; (fam.) molto.

awhile /əˈwaɪl/ adv. un po'.

awkward /ˈɔːkwəd/ a. goffo; (clumsy) maldestro; (embarrassing) imbarazzante. ~**ly** adv. goffamente; in modo imbarazzante. ~**ness** n. goffaggine f.; (discomfort) imbarazzo m.

awning /ˈɔːnɪŋ/ n. tendone m.

awoke, awoken /əˈwəʊk, əˈwəʊkən/ see **awake**.

awry /əˈraɪ/ adv. & a. di traverso.

axe /æks/ n. scure f. —v.t. (pres. p. **axing**) tagliare con la scure; (fig.) cancellare.

axiom /ˈæksɪəm/ n. assioma m.

axis /ˈæksɪs/ n. (pl. **axes** /-iːz/) asse m.

axle /ˈæksl/ n. asse m.

ay(e) /aɪ/ adv. & n. sì m. invar.

B

BA *abbr. see* **bachelor.**

babble /'bæbl/ *v.i.* balbettare; (*of stream*) gorgogliare. —*n.* mormorio *m.*

baboon /bə'bu:n/ *n.* babbuino *m.*

baby /'beɪbɪ/ *n.* bebè *m.*; (*Amer. sl.*) ragazza *f.* ~**-sit** *v.i.* fare da babysitter. ~**-sitter** *n.* babysitter *m./f.*

babyish /'beɪbɪʃ/ *a.* bambinesco.

bachelor /'bætʃələ(r)/ *n.* scapolo *m.* **B~ of Arts (BA)** laureato, a in lettere *m., f.* **B~ of Science (B.Sc.)** laureato, a in scienze *m., f.*

back /bæk/ *n.* dorso *m.*, schiena *f.*; (*of car*) retro *m.*; (*of chair*) schienale *m.*; (*of cloth*) rovescio *m.*; (*of house*) retro *m.* —*a.* posteriore; (*taxes*) arretrato. —*adv.* indietro; (*returned*) di ritorno. —*v.t.* appoggiare; (*betting*) scommettere su; (*car*) far marcia indietro. —*v.i.* rinculare. ~**-bencher** *n.* (*pol.*) parlamentare senza potere amministrativo *m.* ~ **down** *v.i.* andare in ritirata. ~ **of beyond** posto fuori mano *m.* ~ **out** *v.i.* ritirarsi (da un'impresa). ~ **up** *v.i.* (*auto.*) fare marcia indietro. ~**-up** *n.* sostegno *m.*

backache /'bækeɪk/ *n.* mal di schiena *m.*

backbiting /'bækbaɪtɪŋ/ *n.* maldicenza *f.*

backbone /'bækbəʊn/ *n.* spina dorsale *f.*

backchat /'bæktʃæt/ *n.* risposta (impertinente) *f.*

backdate /bæk'deɪt/ *v.t.* retrodatare.

backer /'bækə(r)/ *n.* sostenitore *m.*; (*comm.*) finanziatore *m.*

backfire /bæk'faɪə(r)/ *v.i.* (*auto.*) far ritorno di fiamma; (*fig.*) fallire.

backgammon /bæk'gæmən/ *n.* trictrac *m.*

background /'bækgraʊnd/ *n.* sfondo *m.*; (*environment*) ambiente *m.*

backhand /'bækhænd/ *n.* (*sport*) rovescio *m.* ~**ed** *a.* di rovescio. ~**ed blow** manrovescio *m.* ~**er** *n.* (*sport*) rovescio *m.*; (*fig.*) attacco indiretto *m.*

backing /'bækɪŋ/ *n.* appoggio *m.*

backlash /'bæklæʃ/ *n.* contraccolpo *m.*; (*fig.*) ripercussione *f.*

backlog /'bæklɒg/ *n.* ~ **of work** lavoro arretrato *m.*

backside /bæk'saɪd/ *n.* (*fam.*) sedere *m.*

backstage /bæk'steɪdʒ/ *a.* & *adv.* dietro la scena.

backstroke /'bækstrəʊk/ *n.* (*sport*) rovescio *m.*; (*swimming*) nuoto sul dorso *m.*

backward /'bækwəd/ *a.* tardivo.

backwards /'bækwədz/ *adv.* indietro; (*fall*) all'indietro; (*walk*) in senso inverso. **go ~ and forwards** andare avanti e indietro.

backwater /'bækwɔ:tə(r)/ *n.* acqua stagnante *f.*; (*fig.*) luogo isolato *m.*

bacon /'beɪkən/ *n.* pancetta *f.*

bacteria /bæk'tɪərɪə/ *n.pl.* batteri *m.pl.* ~**l** *a.* batterico.

bad /bæd/ *a.* (**worse, worst**) cattivo; brutto; (*wicked*) malvagio; (*harmful*) nocivo; (*accident*) grave; (*food*) guasto. ~ **language** linguaggio osceno *m.* ~**-mannered** *a.* maleducato. ~**-tempered** *a.* irascibile. **feel ~** sentirsi male. ~**ly** *adv.* male. ~**ly off** povero. **want ~ly** aver urgente bisogno di.

bade /beɪd/ *see* **bid.**

badge /bædʒ/ *n.* distintivo *m.*

badger /'bædʒə(r)/ *n.* tasso *m.* —*v.t.* tormentare.

badminton /'bædmɪntən/ *n.* gioco del volano *m.*

baffle /'bæfl/ *v.t.* confondere.

bag /bæg/ *n.* sacco *m.*; (*handbag*) borsa *f.* ~**s** *n.pl.* (*luggage*) bagagli *m.pl.*; (*under eyes*) borse *f.pl.* —*v.t.* (*p.t.* **bagged**) insaccare; (*take*) impadronirsi di. ~**s of** (*fam.*) un sacco di.

baggage /'bægɪdʒ/ *n.* bagaglio *m.*

baggy /'bægɪ/ *a.* (*clothes*) sformato.

bagpipes /'bægpaɪps/ *n.pl.* cornamusa *f.s.*

Bahamas /bə'hɑ:məz/ *n.pl.* **the ~** le isole Bahama *f.pl.*

bail[1] /beɪl/ *n.* cauzione *f.* —*v.t.* mettere in libertà provvisoria. ~ **s.o. out** ottenere per qcno. la libertà provvisoria.

bail[2] /beɪl/ *n.* (*cricket*) sbarretta *f.*

bail[3] /beɪl/ *v.t.* (*naut.*) aggottare.

bailiff /'beɪlɪf/ *n.* usciere *m.*; (*estate*) fattore *m.*

bait /beɪt/ *n.* esca *f.* —*v.t.* inescare; (*torment*) esasperare.

bak|e /beɪk/ *v.t.* cuocere al forno. —*v.i.* cuocersi al forno. ~**er** *n.* fornaio, a, panettiere, a *m.*, *f.* ~**ing** *n.* cottura al forno *f.*; (*of bread*) infornata *f.* ~**ing-powder** *n.* lievito *m.* ~**ing tin** *n.* teglia *f.*

bakery /'beɪkərɪ/ *n.* panificio, forno *m.*

balance /'bæləns/ *n.* equilibrio *m.*; (*comm.*) bilancio *m.*; (*sum*) saldo *m.*; (*scales*) bilancia *f.*; (*clock*) bilanciere *m.* —*v.t.* bilanciare; (*comm.*) fare il bilancio. —*v.i.* bilanciarsi. ~**d** *a.* equilibrato.

balcony /'bælkənɪ/ *n.* balcone *m.*

bald /bɔ:ld/ *a.* (-er, -est) calvo; (*tyre*) liscio. ~**ly** *adv.* schiettamente. ~**ness** *n.* calvizie *f.*

balderdash /'bɔ:ldədæʃ/ *n.* sciocchezze *f.pl.*

bale[1] /beɪl/ *n.* balla (di merce) *f.*

bale[2] /beɪl/ *v.i.* ~ **out** lanciarsi col paracadute.

baleful /'beɪlfʊl/ *a.* funesto.

balk /bɔ:k/ *v.t.* ostacolare. —*v.i.* ~ **(at)** impennarsi (davanti a).

ball[1] /bɔ:l/ *n.* palla *f.*; (*football*) pallone *m.*; (*of yarn*) gomitolo *m.* ~-**bearing** *n.* cuscinetto a sfera *m.* ~**boy** *n.* raccattapalle *m.* ~-**cock** *n.* rubinetto a galleggiante *m.*; ~-**pen** *n.* biro *f.* ~-**shaped** *a.* sferico.

ball[2] /bɔ:l/ *n.* (*dance*) ballo *m.*

ballad /'bæləd/ *n.* ballata *f.*

ballast /'bæləst/ *n.* zavorra *f.*

ballet /'bæleɪ/ *n.* balletto *m.*

ballistic /bə'lɪstɪk/ *a.* balistico. ~**s** *n.* balistica *f.s.*

balloon /bə'lu:n/ *n.* pallone *m.*

balloonist /bə'lu:nɪst/ *n.* aeronauta *m.|f.*

ballot /'bælət/ *n.* scrutinio *m.* ~ (-**paper**) scheda di votazione *f.* ~-**box** urna *f.*

ballroom /'bɔ:lru:m/ *n.* sala da ballo *f.*

ballyhoo /bælɪ'hu:/ *n.* (*publicity*) pubblicità chiassosa *f.*; (*uproar*) baccano *m.*

balm /bɑ:m/ *n.* balsamo *m.* ~**y** *a.* (*of air*) dolce, mite; (*sl.*) matto.

baloney /bə'ləʊnɪ/ *n.* (*sl.*) idiozie *f.pl.*

balsam /'bɔ:lsəm/ *n.* balsamo *m.*

balustrade /bælə'streɪd/ *n.* balaustrata *f.*

bamboo /bæm'bu:/ *n.* bambù *m.*

bamboozle /bæm'bu:zl/ *v.t.* imbrogliare.

ban /bæn/ *v.t.* (*p.t.* **banned**) proibire. ~ **from** escludere da. —*n.* bando *m.*

banal /bə'nɑ:l/ *a.* banale. ~**ity** /-ælətɪ/ *n.* banalità *f.*

banana /bə'nɑ:nə/ *n.* banana *f.* ~-**tree** banano *m.*

band /bænd/ *n.* banda *f.*; (*mus.*) orchestrina *f.*; (*mil.*) fanfara *f.* —*v.i.* ~ **together** riunirsi.

bandage /'bændɪdʒ/ *n.* benda *f.* —*v.t.* bendare.

bandit /'bændɪt/ *n.* bandito *m.*

bandstand /'bændstænd/ *n.* palco dell'orchestra *m.*

bandwagon /'bændwægən/ *n.* **jump on the** ~ (*fig.*) seguire la corrente.

bandy[1] /'bændɪ/ *v.t.* ~ **about** far circolare.

bandy[2] /'bændɪ/ *a.* (-ier, -iest) ~-**legged** dalle gambe storte.

bane /beɪn/ *n.* (*fig.*) veleno *m.* ~**ful** *a.* malefico.

bang /bæŋ/ *n.* (*noise*) rumore *m.*; (*blow*) colpo *m.*; (*of gun*) detonazione *f.*; (*of door*) sbattuta *f.* —*v.t./i.* battere; sbattere. —*adv.* esattamente. ~! *int.* bum!

banger /'bæŋə(r)/ *n.* petardo *m.*; (*sl.*, *culin.*) salsiccia *f.*

bangle /'bæŋgl/ *n.* braccialetto *m.*

banish /'bænɪʃ/ *v.t.* bandire.

banisters /'bænɪstəz/ *n.pl.* ringhiera *f.s.*

banjo /'bændʒəʊ/ *n.* (*pl.* -os) banjo *m.*

bank[1] /bæŋk/ *n.* riva *f.*; (*of river*) sponda *f.*; (*of sand*) banco *m.* —*v.t.* arginare; (*fire*) ammassare. —*v.i.* (*aeron.*) inclinarsi in virata.

bank[2] /bæŋk/ *n.* banca *f.* ~ **holiday** *n.* giorno di vacanza nazionale *m.* —*v.t.* depositare in banca. —*v.i.* ~ **with** avere un conto in banca da. ~ **on** *v.t.* contare su. ~**er** *n.* banchiere *m.* ~**ing** *n.* attività bancaria *f.*

banknote /'bæŋknəʊt/ *n.* banconota *f.*

bankrupt /'bæŋkrʌpt/ *a.* fallito. **go** ~ fallire. —*n.* fallito, a *m.*, *f.* —*v.t.* far fallire. ~**cy** *n.* bancarotta *f.*

banner /'bænə(r)/ *n.* stendardo *m.*

banns /bænz/ *n.pl.* pubblicazioni matrimoniali *f.pl.*

banquet /'bæŋkwɪt/ *n.* banchetto *m.*

bantamweight /'bæntəmweɪt/ *n.* peso gallo *m.*

banter /'bæntə(r)/ *n.* motteggio *m.* —*v.i.* motteggiare.

bap /bæp/ *n.* panino soffice *m.*

baptism /'bæptɪzəm/ *n.* battesimo *m.*

Baptist /'bæptɪst/ *n.* battista *m./f.*

baptize /bæp'taɪz/ *v.t.* battezzare.

bar /bɑː(r)/ *n.* sbarra *f.*; (*on window* & *jurid.*) barra *f.*; (*of chocolate*) tavoletta *f.*; (*café*) bar *m.*; (*counter*) banco *m.*; (*mus.*) battuta *f.*; (*fig.*) ostacolo *m.* —*v.t.* (*p.t.* **barred**) sbarrare; (*exclude*) escludere; (*prohibit*) proibire. —*prep.* tranne.

barbarian /bɑː'beərɪən/ *a.* & *n.* barbaro, a *m.*, *f.*

barbar|ic /bɑː'bærɪk/ *a.* barbarico. ~**ity** /-ətɪ/ *n.* barbarie *f.* ~**ous** *a.* /'bɑːbərəs/ *a.* barbaro.

barbecue /'bɑːbɪkjuː/ *n.* barbecue *m.* —*v.t.* arrostire all'aperto.

barbed /bɑːbd/ *a.* ~ **wire** filo spinato.

barber /'bɑːbə(r)/ *n.* barbiere *m.*

barbiturate /bɑː'bɪtjʊrət/ *n.* barbiturico *m.*

bare /beə(r)/ *a.* (-er, est) nudo; (*room*) spoglio; (*mere*) semplice. —*v.t.* mettere a nudo. ~ **one's teeth** digrignare i denti. ~**ly** *adv.* appena. ~**ness** *n.* nudità *f.*; (*di stanza*) squallore *m.*

bareback /'beəbæk/ *adv.* senza sella.

barefaced /'beəfeɪst/ *a.* sfacciato.

bareheaded /'beəhedɪd/ *a.* a capo scoperto.

bargain /'bɑːgɪn/ *n.* (*agreement*) patto *m.*; (*good buy*) occasione *f.* —*v.i.* contrattare; (*haggle*) mercanteggiare. ~ **for** aspettarsi.

barge /bɑːdʒ/ *n.* barcone *m.* —*v.i.* ~ **in** intervenire a sproposito.

baritone /'bærɪtəʊn/ *n.* baritono *m.*

barium /'beərɪəm/ *n.* bario *m.*

bark[1] /bɑːk/ *n.* (*of tree*) corteccia *f.*

bark[2] /bɑːk/ *n.* (*of dog*) latrato *m.* —*v.i.* abbaiare.

barley /'bɑːlɪ/ *n.* orzo *m.* ~**-water** *n.* orzata *f.*

barmaid /'bɑːmeɪd/ *n.* cameriera al banco *f.*

barman /'bɑːmən/ *n.* (*pl.* -**men**) barista *m.*

barmy /'bɑːmɪ/ *a.* (*sl.*) matto.

barn /bɑːn/ *n.* granaio *m.*

barometer /bə'rɒmɪtə(r)/ *n.* barometro *m.*

baron /'bærən/ *n.* barone *m.* ~**ess** *n.* baronessa *f.*

baroque /bə'rɒk/ *a.* & *n.* barocco *m.*

barracks /'bærəks/ *n.pl.* caserma *f.s.*

barrage /'bærɑːʒ/ *n.* sbarramento *m.*

barrel /'bærəl/ *m.* barile *m.*, botte *f.*; (*of gun*) canna *f.* ~**-organ** *n.* organetto a cilindro *m.*

barren /'bærən/ *a.* sterile. ~**ness** *n.* sterilità *f.*

barricade /bærɪ'keɪd/ *n.* barricata *f.* —*v.t.* barricare.

barrier /'bærɪə(r)/ *n.* barriera *f.*

barring /'bɑːrɪŋ/ *prep.* salvo.

barrister /'bærɪstə(r)/ *n.* avvocato *m.*, avvocatessa *f.*

barrow /'bærəʊ/ *n.* carretto *m.*; (*wheelbarrow*) carriola *f.*

barter /'bɑːtə(r)/ *n.* baratto *m.* —*v.t.* barattare.

base /beɪs/ *n.* base *f.* —*v.t.* basare. —*a.* vile. ~**less** *a.* infondato.

baseball /'beɪsbɔːl/ *n.* baseball *m.*

basement /'beɪsmənt/ *n.* seminterrato *m.*

bash /bæʃ/ *v.t.* colpire (violentemente). —*n.* colpo (violento) *m.* **have a** ~ (*sl.*) provare.

bashful /'bæʃfl/ *a.* timido.

basic /'beɪsɪk/ *a.* fondamentale. ~**ally** *adv.* fondamentalmente.

basil /'bæzl/ *n.* basilico *m.*

basilica /bə'zɪlɪkə/ *n.* basilica *f.*

basin /'beɪsn/ *n.* bacile *m.*; (*for washing*) lavabo *m.*; (*for food*) scodella *f.*; (*geog.*) bacino *m.*

basis /'beɪsɪs/ *n.* (*pl.* **bases** /-siːz/) base *f.*

bask /bɑːsk/ *v.i.* crogiolarsi.

basket /'bɑːskɪt/ *n.* cestino *m.*

basketball /'bɑːskɪtbɔːl/ *n.* pallacanestro *f.*

Basque /bɑːsk/ *a.* & *n.* basco, a *m.*, *f.*

baste /beɪst/ *v.t.* (*sew*) imbastire; (*culin.*) ungere con grasso.

bastion /'bæstɪən/ *n.* bastione *m.*

bat[1] /bæt/ *n.* mazza *f.*; (*for table tennis*) racchetta *f.* —*v.t./i.* (*p.t.* **batted**) battere. ~ **an eyelid** batter ciglio. **off one's own** ~ da solo.

bat[2] /bæt/ *n.* (*mammal*) pipistrello *m.*

batch /bætʃ/ *n.* (*of people*) gruppo *m.*; (*of papers*) mucchio *m.*; (*of goods*) lotto *m.*; (*of bread*) infornata *f.*

bated /'beɪtɪd/ *a.* **with** ~ **breath** col fiato sospeso.

bath /bɑːθ/ *n.* (*pl.* -**s** /bɑːðz/) bagno *m.*; (*tub*) vasca da bagno *f.* ~**s** bagni pubblici *m.pl.* —*v.t./i.* fare il bagno.

bathe /beɪð/ *v.t.* bagnare. —*v.i.* farsi il bagno. —*n.* bagno (di mare) *m.* ~**r** /-ə(r)/ *n.* bagnante *m./f.*

bathing /'beɪðɪŋ/ *n.* bagni *m.pl.* ~**-costume** *n.* costume da bagno *m.*

bathroom /'bɑːθrʊm/ *n.* stanza da bagno *f.*

baton /'bætən/ *n.* manganello *m.*; (*mus.*) bacchetta *f.*

batman /'bætmən/ *n.* (*pl.* -men) (*mil.*) ordinanza *f.*

batsman /'bætsmən/ *n.* (*pl.* -men) battitore *m.*

battalion /bə'tælɪən/ *n.* battaglione *m.*

batter /'bætə(r)/ *v.t.* battere. —*n.* pastella *f.* ~ed *a.* (*car etc.*) malandato; (*wife etc.*) maltrattato. ~ing *n.* (*fam.*) bastonatura *f.*

battery /'bætərɪ/ *n.* batteria *f.*; (*of car*) accumulatore *m.*; (*of torch, radio*) pila *f.*

battle /'bætl/ *n.* battaglia *f.*; (*fig.*) lotta *f.* —*v.i.* lottare.

battleaxe /'bætlæks/ *n.* (*fam.*) donna battagliera *f.*

battlefield /'bætlfi:ld/ *n.* campo di battaglia *m.*

battlements /'bætlmənts/ *n.pl.* merli *m.pl.*; (*wall*) bastioni *m.pl.*

battleship /'bætlʃɪp/ *n.* corazzata *f.*

batty /'bætɪ/ *a.* (*sl.*) toccato.

baulk /bɔ:lk/ *v.t./i.* = **balk**.

bawd|y /'bɔ:dɪ/ *a.* (-ier, -iest) osceno. ~iness *n.* oscenità *f.*

bawl /bɔ:l/ *v.t./i.* urlare.

bay[1] /beɪ/ *n.* (*bot.*) lauro *m.*

bay[2] /beɪ/ *n.* (*geog.*) baia *f.*; ~ **window** finestra sporgente *f.* **keep at** ~ tenere a bada.

bay[3] /beɪ/ *n.* (*of dog*) latrato *m.* —*v.i.* latrare.

bayonet /'beɪənɪt/ *n.* baionetta *f.*

bazaar /bə'zɑ:(r)/ *n.* bazar *m.*

b. & b. *abbr. see* **bed.**

BC *abbr.* (*of* **before Christ**) a.C.

be /bi:/ *v.i.* (*pres.* **am, are, is**; *p.t.* **was, were**; *p.p.* **been**) essere. ~ **cold/hot**, etc. aver freddo/ caldo, ecc. **it is cold/hot**, etc. (*weather*) fa freddo/caldo, ecc. **how are you?** come stai? **how much is it?** quanto costa? ~ **reading/ walking**, etc. (*aux.*) leggere/camminare, ecc. **have been to** essere stato a.

beach /bi:tʃ/ *n.* spiaggia *f.* ~**head** *n.* testa di sbarco *f.*

beachcomber /'bi:tʃkəʊmə(r)/ *n.* accattone *m.*

beacon /'bi:kən/ *n.* faro *m.*; (*light*) fanale *m.*

bead /bi:d/ *n.* perlina *f.*

beak /bi:k/ *n.* becco *m.*

beaker /'bi:kə(r)/ *n.* coppa *f.*

beam /bi:m/ *n.* trave *f.*; (*of light*) raggio *m.*; (*naut.*) baglio *m.* **be on**

one's ~**-ends** (*fig.*) essere agli estremi. —*v.i.* irradiare. ~**ing** *a.* raggiante.

bean /bi:n/ *n.* fagiolo *m.*; (*of coffee*) chicco *m.*

beano /'bi:nəʊ/ *n.* (*pl.* -os) (*fam.*) baldoria *f.*

bear[1] /beə(r)/ *n.* orso *m.*

bear[2] /beə(r)/ *v.t./i.* (*p.t.* **bore**, *p.p.* **borne**) portare; (*endure*) sopportare; (*child*) metter al mondo. ~ **in mind** tenere a mente. ~ **right** svoltare a destra. ~ **with** aver pazienza con. ~**able** *a.* sopportabile. ~**er** *n.* porta|tore, -trice *m.*, *f.*

beard /bɪəd/ *n.* barba *f.* ~**ed** *a.* barbuto.

bearing /'beərɪŋ/ *n.* portamento *m.*; (*relevance*) rapporto *m.*; (*mech.*) cuscinetto *m.* ~**s** *n.pl.* (*fig.*) senso di direzione *m.s.*

beast /bi:st/ *n.* bestia *f.*; (*person*) bruto *m.*

beastly /'bi:stlɪ/ *a.* (-ier, -iest) (*fam.*) bestiale.

beat /bi:t/ *v.t./i.* (*p.t.* **beat**, *p.p.* **beaten**) battere; (*culin.*) sbattere. —*n.* battito *m.*; (*mus.*) battuta *f.*; (*of policeman*) ronda *f.* ~ **a retreat** (*mil.*) battere in ritirata; ~ **it** (*sl.*) darsela a gambe. ~ **up** picchiare. ~**er** *n.* battitore *m.* ~**ing** *n.* bastonata *f.*

beautician /bju:'tɪʃn/ *n.* estetista *m.*/*f.*

beautiful /'bju:tɪfl/ *a.* bello, bellissimo. ~**ly** *adv.* splendidamente.

beautify /'bju:tɪfaɪ/ *v.t.* abbellire.

beauty /'bju:tɪ/ *n.* bellezza *f.* ~**parlour** *n.* istituto di bellezza *m.* ~ **spot** (*on face*) neo *m.*; (*site*) luogo pittoresco *m.*

beaver /'bi:və(r)/ *n.* castoro *m.*

became /bɪ'keɪm/ *see* **become.**

because /bɪ'kɒz/ *conj.* perché; poiché. —*adv.* ~ **of** a causa di.

beck /bek/ *n.* **at the** ~ **and call of** agli ordini di.

beckon /'bekən/ *v.t./i.* ~ **(to)** chiamare con un cenno.

become /bɪ'kʌm/ *v.t./i.* (*p.t.* **became**, *p.p.* **become**) diventare; (*of clothes*) star bene. **what has** ~ **of her?** che ne è di lei?

becoming /bɪ'kʌmɪŋ/ *a.* adatto; (*of clothes*) grazioso.

bed /bed/ *n.* letto *m.*; (*layer*) strato *m.*; (*of sea, river*) fondo *m.*; (*of flowers*) aiuola *f.*; ~ **and breakfast** (**b. & b.**) camera con colazione *f.* —*v.i.* (*p.t.*

bedded) ~ **down** coricarsi. ~**ding** n. biancheria da letto f.

bedbug /'bedbʌg/ n. cimice f.

bedclothes /'bedkləʊðz/ n.pl. coperte da letto f.pl.

bedevil /bɪ'devl/ v.t. (p.t. **bedevilled**) tormentare ferocemente.

bedlam /'bedləm/ n. baraonda f.

bedpan /'bedpæn/ n. padella (per malati) f.

bedpost /'bedpəʊst/ n. colonna del letto f.

bedraggled /bɪ'drægld/ a. inzaccherato.

bedridden /'bedrɪdn/ a. costretto a letto.

bedroom /'bedrʊm/ n. camera da letto f.

bedside /'bedsaɪd/ n. capezzale m. ~ **manner** (of doctor) modi rassicuranti m.pl.

bed-sitting-room /bed'sɪtɪŋruːm/ n. monolocale m.

bedspread /'bedspred/ n. copriletto m.

bedtime /'bedtaɪm/ n. l'ora di coricarsi f.

bee /biː/ n. ape f. **make a ~-line for** precipitarsi verso.

beech /biːtʃ/ n. faggio m.

beef /biːf/ n. manzo m. —v.i. (sl.) brontolare. ~**steak** n. bistecca f.

beefburger /'biːfbɜːgə(r)/ n. hamburger m.

beefeater /'biːfiːtə(r)/ n. guardia della Torre di Londra f.

beefy /'biːfɪ/ a. (-ier, -iest) muscoloso.

beehive /'biːhaɪv/ n. alveare m.

been /biːn/ see **be**.

beer /bɪə(r)/ n. birra f.

beet /biːt/ n. bietola f.

beetle /'biːtl/ n. scarafaggio m.

beetroot /'biːtruːt/ n. invar. barbabietola f.

befall /bɪ'fɔːl/ v.t./i. (p.t. **befell**, p.p. **befallen**) accadere (a).

befit /bɪ'fɪt/ v.t. (p.t. **befitted**) convenire a.

before /bɪ'fɔː(r)/ prep. (time) prima di; (place) davanti a. —adv. (place) avanti; (time) prima. —conj. (time) prima che.

beforehand /bɪ'fɔːhænd/ adv. in anticipo.

befriend /bɪ'frend/ v.t. trattare da amico.

beg /beg/ v.t./i. (p.t. **begged**) mendicare; (entreat) supplicare; (ask)

chiedere. ~ **s.o.'s pardon** chiedere scusa a qcno.

began /bɪ'gæn/ see **begin**.

beget /bɪ'get/ v.t. (p.t. **begot**, p.p. **begotten**, pres. p. **begetting**) procreare.

beggar /'begə(r)/ n. mendicante m./f. **lucky ~**! (fam.) beato te!

begin /bɪ'gɪn/ v.t./i. (p.t. **began**, p.p. **begun**, pres. p. **beginning**) cominciare. ~**ner** n. principiante m./f. ~**ning** n. principio m.

begot, begotten /bɪ'gɒt, bɪ'gɒtn/ see **beget**.

begrudge /bɪ'grʌdʒ/ v.t. invidiare; (give) dare malvolentieri.

beguile /bɪ'gaɪl/ v.t. ingannare; (entertain) intrattenere.

begun /bɪ'gʌn/ see **begin**.

behalf /bɪ'hɑːf/ n. **on ~ of** a nome di.

behave /bɪ'heɪv/ v.i. comportarsi. ~ **(o.s.)** comportarsi bene.

behaviour /bɪ'heɪvjə(r)/ n. comportamento m., condotta f.

behead /bɪ'hed/ v.t. decapitare.

beheld /bɪ'held/ see **behold**.

behind /bɪ'haɪnd/ prep. dietro (di). —adv. dietro, indietro; (late) in ritardo. —n. (fam.) sedere m.

behold /bɪ'həʊld/ v.t. (p.t. **beheld**) (old use) guardare.

beholden /bɪ'həʊldən/ a. obbligato.

being /'biːɪŋ/ n. essere m. **come into ~** nascere.

belated /bɪ'leɪtɪd/ a. tardivo.

belch /beltʃ/ v.i. ruttare. —v.t. ~ **out** (smoke) eruttare.

belfry /'belfrɪ/ n. campanile m.

Belgi|um /'beldʒəm/ n. Belgio m. ~**an** a. & n. belga m./f.

belie /bɪ'laɪ/ v.t. smentire.

belief /bɪ'liːf/ n. (trust) fede f.; (opinion) convinzione f.

believe /bɪ'liːv/ v.t./i. credere. **make ~** fingere. ~**r** /-ə(r)/ n. credente m./f.

belittle /bɪ'lɪtl/ v.t. rimpicciolire; (fig.) denigrare.

bell /bel/ n. campana f.; (on door) campanello m.

belligerent /bɪ'lɪdʒərənt/ a. & n. belligerante m./f.

bellow /'beləʊ/ v.t./i. muggire.

bellows /'beləʊz/ n.pl. soffietto m.s.

belly /'belɪ/ n. ventre m., pancia f.

bellyful /'belɪfʊl/ n. scorpacciata f. **have a ~ of** (sl.) essere stufo di.

belong /bɪ'lɒŋ/ v.i. appartenere; (club) essere socio di.

belongings /br'lɒŋɪŋz/ *n.pl.* roba *f.s.* **personal ~** effetti personali *m.pl.*

beloved /br'lʌvɪd/ *a. & n.* amato, a *m., f.*

below /br'ləu/ *prep.* sotto, al disotto di; (*rank*) inferiore a. —*adv.* sotto, di sotto.

belt /belt/ *n.* cintura *f.*; (*area*) zona *f.* —*v.t.* (*fig.*) circondare; (*sl.*) picchiare.

bemused /br'mju:zd/ *a.* stupefatto.

bench /bentʃ/ *n.* panca *f.*; (*workingtable*) banco *m.* **the B~** (*jurid.*) la magistratura *f.*

bend /bend/ *v.t./i.* (*p.t. & p.p.* **bent**) piegare, piegarsi. —*n.* curva *f.*; (*of river*) gomito *m.* **~ down/over** chinarsi.

beneath /br'ni:θ/ *prep.* sotto, al di sotto di. —*adv.* giù, abbasso. **~ contempt** indegno.

benediction /benr'dɪkʃn/ *n.* benedizione *f.*

benefactor /'benɪfæktə(r)/ *n.* benefat|tore, -trice *m., f.*

beneficial /benɪ'fɪʃl/ *a.* benefico.

beneficiary /benɪ'fɪʃərɪ/ *a. & n.* beneficiario, a *m., f.*

benefit /'benɪfɪt/ *n.* vantaggio *m.*; (*allowance*) indennità *f.* —*v.t./i.* (*p.t.* **benefited**, *pres. p.* **benefiting**) giovare a.

benevolen|t /br'nevələnt/ *a.* benevolo. **~ce** *n.* benevolenza *f.*

benign /br'naɪn/ *a.* benevolo; (*med.*) benigno.

bent /bent/ *see* **bend.** —*n.* disposizione *f.* —*a.* curvato; (*sl.*) corrotto.

bequeath /br'kwi:ð/ *v.t.* lasciare per testamento.

bequest /br'kwest/ *n.* lascito *m.*

bereave|d /br'ri:vd/ *n.* **the ~d** i familiari del defunto *m.pl.* **~ment** *n.* lutto *m.*

bereft /br'reft/ *a.* **~ of** privato di.

beret /'bereɪ/ *n.* berretto *m.*

Bermuda /bə'mju:də/ *n.* le Bermude *f.pl.*

berry /'berɪ/ *n.* bacca *f.*

berserk /bə'sɜ:k/ *a.* **go ~** diventare una furia.

berth /bɜ:θ/ *n.* cuccetta *f.*; (*anchorage*) posto d'ormeggio *m.* —*v.i.* attraccare. **give a wide ~ to** evitare.

beseech /br'si:tʃ/ *v.t.* (*p.t.* **besought**) supplicare.

beset /br'set/ *v.t.* (*p.t.* **beset**, *pres. p.* **besetting**) assalire.

beside /br'saɪd/ *prep.* accanto a. **~ o.s.** fuori di sé.

besides /br'saɪdz/ *prep.* oltre a. (*except*) tranne. —*adv.* inoltre, per di più.

besiege /br'si:dʒ/ *v.t.* assediare; (*fig.*) assalire.

besought /br'sɔ:t/ *see* **beseech.**

bespoke /br'spəuk/ *a.* (*tailor*) che lavora su ordinazione.

best /best/ *a.* migliore. —*adv.* meglio, nel modo migliore. —*n.* (il) meglio *m.* **at ~** tutt'al più. **~ man** testimone *m.* **do one's ~** fare il proprio meglio. **like ~** preferire.

bestow /br'stəu/ *v.t.* accordare.

bestseller /best'selə(r)/ *n.* libro di grande successo *m.*

bet /bet/ *n.* scommessa *f.* —*v.t./i.* (*p.t.* **bet** *or* **betted**) scommettere.

betray /br'treɪ/ *v.t.* tradire. **~al** *n.* tradimento *m.*

betroth|ed /br'trəuðd/ *n.* fidanzato, a *m., f.* **~al** *n.* fidanzamento *m.*

better /'betə(r)/ *a.* migliore, meglio. —*adv.* meglio. —*v.t.* migliorare. —*n.* **one's ~s** i propri superiori *m.pl.* **all the ~** tanto meglio. **~ off** più ricco. **get ~** migliorare; (*recover*) rimettersi. **the sooner the ~** prima è, meglio è.

between /br'twi:n/ *prep.* fra, tra. —*adv.* in mezzo.

beverage /'bevərɪdʒ/ *n.* bevanda *f.*

bevy /'bevɪ/ *n.* frotta *f.*

beware /br'weə(r)/ *v.i.* guardarsi (da).

bewilder /br'wɪldə(r)/ *v.t.* disorientare. **~ment** *n.* smarrimento *m.*

bewitch /br'wɪtʃ/ *v.t.* stregare.

beyond /br'jɒnd/ *prep.* oltre, di là di. —*adv.* più in là. **~ doubt** oltre ogni dubbio. **~ reason** irragionevole.

bias /'baɪəs/ *n.* preconcetto *m.*; (*pej.*) pregiudizio *m.*; (*preference*) preferenza *f.*; (*sewing*) cucitura diagonale *f.* —*v.t.* (*p.t.* **biased**) influenzare. **~ed** *a.* prevenuto.

bib /bɪb/ *n.* bavaglino *m.*

Bible /'baɪbl/ *n.* Bibbia *f.*

biblical /'bɪblɪkl/ *a.* biblico.

bibliography /bɪblɪ'ɒgrəfɪ/ *n.* bibliografia *f.*

biceps /'baɪseps/ *n.* bicipite *m.*

bicker /'bɪkə(r)/ *v.i.* altercare.

bicycle /'baɪsɪkl/ *n.* bicicletta *f.* —*v.i.* andare in bicicletta.

bid[1] /bɪd/ *n.* (*offer*) offerta *f.*; (*attempt*) tentativo *m.* —*v.t./i.* (*p.t.* **bid**, *pres. p.*

bidding) offrire. ~**der** *n.* offerente *m.|f.* ~**ding** *n.* offerta *f.*

bid² /bɪd/ *v.t.* (*p.t.* **bid**, *p.p.* **bidden**, *pres. p.* **bidding**) (*command*) comandare; (*say*) dire. ~**ding** *n.* comando *m.*

bide /baɪd/ *v.t.* ~ **one's time** aspettare il momento buono.

biennial /baɪ'enɪəl/ *a. & n.* biennale *f.*

bifocals /baɪ'fəʊklz/ *n.pl.* occhiali bifocali *m.pl.*

big /bɪg/ *a.* (**bigger**, **biggest**) grande, grosso; (*sl.*) generoso. —*adv.* **talk** ~ esagerare. ~-**headed** *a.* presuntuoso.

bigam|y /'bɪgəmɪ/ *n.* bigamia *f.* ~**ist** *n.* bigamo, a *m., f.* ~**ous** *a.* bigamo.

bigot /'bɪgət/ *n.* bigotto, a *m., f.* ~**ed** *a.* bigotto. ~**ry** *n.* bigotteria *f.*

bigwig /'bɪgwɪg/ *n.* (*fam.*) pezzo grosso *m.*

bike /baɪk/ *n.* (*fam.*) bici *f. invar.*

bikini /bɪ'kiːnɪ/ *n.* (*pl.* -**is**) bikini *m. invar.*

bilberry /'bɪlbərɪ/ *n.* mirtillo *m.*

bile /baɪl/ *n.* bile *f.*

bilingual /baɪ'lɪŋgwəl/ *a.* bilingue.

bilious /'bɪlɪəs/ *a.* (*med.*) biliare; (*of temperament*) collerico.

bill¹ /bɪl/ *n.* fattura *f.*; (*in restaurant etc.*) conto *m.*; (*theatr.*) cartellone *m.*; (*comm.*) cambiale *f.*; (*Amer.*) biglietto di banca *m.*; (*pol.*) progetto di legge *m.* —*v.t.* fatturare; (*theatr.*) mettere in programma.

bill² /bɪl/ *n.* (*of bird*) becco *m.*

billet /'bɪlɪt/ *n.* (*mil.*) alloggio *m.* —*v.t.* alloggiare.

billiards /'bɪlɪədz/ *n.* biliardo *m.*

billion /'bɪlɪən/ *n.* bilione *m.*; (*Amer.*) miliardo *m.*

billy-goat /'bɪlɪgəʊt/ *n.* capro *m.*

bin /bɪn/ *n.* recipiente *m.*; (*for rubbish*) bidone *m.*

bind /baɪnd/ *v.t.* (*p.t.* **bound**) legare; (*book*) rilegare; (*jurid.*) obbligare; (*sl.*) brontolare. —*n.* (*sl.*) scocciatura *f.*

binding /'baɪndɪŋ/ *n.* (*of books*) rilegatura *f.*; (*braid*) bordura *f.*; (*sl.*) brontolamento *m.*

binge /bɪndʒ/ *n.* (*sl.*) **go on a** ~ **far** baldoria.

bingo /'bɪŋgəʊ/ *n.* gioco simile alla tombola *m.*

binoculars /bɪ'nɒkjʊləz/ *n.pl.* binocolo *m.s.*

biochemistry /baɪəʊ'kemɪstrɪ/ *n.* biochimica *f.*

biograph|y /baɪ'ɒgrəfɪ/ *n.* biografia *f.* ~**er** *n.* biografo, a *m., f.*

biolog|y /baɪ'ɒlədʒɪ/ *n.* biologia *f.* ~**ical** /-ə'lɒdʒɪkl/ *a.* biologico. ~**ist** *n.* biologo, a *m., f.*

biped /'baɪped/ *n.* bipede *m.*

birch /bɜːtʃ/ *n.* (*tree*) betulla *f.*; (*whip*) verga *f.*

bird /bɜːd/ *n.* uccello *m.*; (*fam.*) tipo *m.*; (*girl, sl.*) ragazza *f.*

Biro /'baɪərəʊ/ *n.* (*pl.* -**os**) (*P.*) biro *f.*

birth /bɜːθ/ *n.* nascita *f.* ~-**control** *n.* controllo delle nascite *m.*

birthday /'bɜːθdeɪ/ *n.* compleanno *m.*

birthmark /'bɜːθmɑːk/ *n.* voglia *f.*

birthright /'bɜːθraɪt/ *n.* diritto di nascita *m.*

biscuit /'bɪskɪt/ *n.* biscotto *m.*

bisect /baɪ'sekt/ *v.t.* dividere in due (parti).

bishop /'bɪʃəp/ *n.* vescovo *m.*

bit¹ /bɪt/ *n.* pezzettino *m.*; (*quantity*) pochino *m.*; (*of horse*) morso *m.*; (*mech.*) punta *f.*

bit² /bɪt/ *see* **bite**.

bitch /bɪtʃ/ *n.* cagna *f.*; (*fam.*) (*donna*) maligna *f.* —*v.i.* (*fam.*) sparlare. ~**y** *a.* malevolo.

bite /baɪt/ *v.t./i.* (*p.t.* **bit**, *p.p.* **bitten**) mordere; (*one's nails*) mangiarsi. —*n.* morso *m.*; (*mouthful*) boccone *m.*

biting /'baɪtɪŋ/ *a.* mordente.

bitter /'bɪtə(r)/ *a.* amaro; (*of weather*) rigido. —*n.* birra amara *f.* **to the** ~ **end** *a* oltranza. ~**ly** *adv.* amaramente. ~**ness** *n.* amarezza *f.*; (*resentment*) rancore *m.*

bizarre /bɪ'zɑː(r)/ *a.* bizzarro.

blab /blæb/ *v.i.* (*p.t.* **blabbed**) cianciare.

black /blæk/ *a.* (-**er**, -**est**) nero. —*n.* nero *m.* —*v.t.* annerire; (*shoes*) lucidare (con crema nera). ~ **out** cancellare; (*make dark*) oscurare. **be** ~ **and blue** essere pieno di lividi.

blackball /'blækbɔːl/ *v.t.* votare contro.

blackberry /'blækbərɪ/ *n.* mora *f.* ~ **bush** *n.* rovo *m.*

blackbird /'blækbɜːd/ *n.* merlo *m.*

blackboard /'blækbɔːd/ *n.* lavagna *f.*

blackcurrant /blæk'kʌrənt/ *n.* ribes *m.*

blacken /'blækən/ *v.t./i.* annerire.

blackguard /'blægɑːd/ *n.* mascalzone *m.*

blackleg /'blækleg/ *n.* crumiro *m.*

blacklist /'blæklɪst/ v.t. mettere sulla lista nera.

blackmail /'blækmeɪl/ n. ricatto m. —v.t. ricattare. ~er n. ricatta|tore, -trice m., f.

black-out /'blækaʊt/ n. oscuramento m.; (med.) svenimento m.

blacksmith /'blæksmɪθ/ n. fabbro m.

bladder /'blædə(r)/ n. vescica f.

blade /bleɪd/ n. lama f. ~ of grass filo d'erba.

blame /bleɪm/ v.t. biasimare. —n. colpa f. free from ~ irreprensibile. ~less a. innocente.

blanch /blɑːntʃ/ v.t./i. immergere (in acqua bollente); (almonds) mondare.

bland /blænd/ a. (-er, -est) mite; (taste) blando.

blandishments /'blændɪʃmənts/ n.pl. lusinghe f.pl.

blank /blæŋk/ a. bianco; (fig.) vuoto; (comm.) in bianco. —n. spazio vuoto m. ~ verse versi sciolti m.pl. ~ wall parete nuda f.

blanket /'blæŋkɪt/ n. coperta f.; (fig.) coltre f. —v.t. (p.t. blanketed) (fig.) ammantare.

blare /bleə(r)/ v.t./i. squillare. —n. squillo m.

blarney /'blɑːnɪ/ n. lusinga f.

blasé /'blɑːzeɪ/ a. blasé.

blaspheme /blæs'fiːm/ v.t./i. bestemmiare. ~r n. blasfemo, a m., f.

blasphem|y /'blæsfəmɪ/ n. bestemmia f. ~ous a. blasfemo.

blast /blɑːst/ n. esplosione f.; (gust) raffica f.; (sound) scoppio m. —v.t. far saltare; (fam., curse) maledire. ~ furnace m. altoforno m. ~-off n. (of missile) lancio m.

blatant /'bleɪtnt/ a. assordante; (shameless) sfacciato.

blaze /'bleɪz/ n. fiammata f.; (fig.) splendore m. —v.i. ardere. ~ a trail tracciare una via.

blazer /'bleɪzə(r)/ n. blazer m. invar.

bleach /bliːtʃ/ n. decolorante m.; (household) candeggina f. —v.t./i. sbiancare. ~ed hair capelli ossigenati m.pl.

bleak /bliːk/ a. (-er, -est) squallido.

bleary /'blɪərɪ/ a. velato.

bleat /bliːt/ n. belato m. —v.i. belare.

bleed /bliːd/ v.t./i. (p.t. bled) sanguinare.

bleep /bliːp/ n. bip m. —v.i. chiamare (all'interfono). ~er n. interfono m.

blemish /'blemɪʃ/ n. macchia f.

blend /blend/ v.t./i. mescolare, mescolarsi. —n. miscela f.

bless /bles/ v.t. benedire. ~ed a. benedetto. be ~ed with essere dotato di. ~ing n. benedizione f.

blew /bluː/ see blow¹.

blight /blaɪt/ n. ruggine f.; (fig.) influsso malefico m. —v.t. far avvizzire; (fig.) rovinare.

blighter /'blaɪtə(r)/ n. (sl.) tizio m.

blind /blaɪnd/ a. cieco. —v.t. accecare. —n. cortina f.; (fig.) pretesto m. ~ alley vicolo cieco m. ~ly adv. ciecamente. ~ness n. cecità f.

blindfold /'blaɪndfəʊld/ a. & adv. con gli occhi bendati. —n. benda f. —v.t. bendare gli occhi a.

blink /blɪŋk/ v.i. battere gli occhi; (of light) tremolare.

blinkers /'blɪŋkəz/ n.pl. paraocchi m.pl.

bliss /blɪs/ n. beatitudine f. ~ful a. beato. ~fully adv. beatamente.

blister /'blɪstə(r)/ n. vescica f. —v.i. coprirsi di vesciche.

blithe /blaɪð/ a. gioioso.

blitz /blɪts/ n. bombardamento aereo m. —v.t. danneggiare (con attacco aereo).

blizzard /'blɪzəd/ n. tormenta f.

bloated /'bləʊtɪd/ a. gonfio.

bloater /'bləʊtə(r)/ n. aringa affumicata f.

blob /blɒb/ n. goccia f.; (stain) macchia f.

bloc /blɒk/ n. (pol.) blocco m.

block /blɒk/ n. blocco m.; (of flats) isolato m.; (in pipe) ostruzione f. —v.t. bloccare. in ~ letters a stampatello m. traffic ~ ingorgo stradale m. ~age n. ostruzione f.

blockade /blɒ'keɪd/ n. blocco m. —v.t. bloccare.

blockhead /'blɒkhed/ n. (fam.) testone, a m., f.

bloke /bləʊk/ n. (fam.) tizio m.

blond /blɒnd/ a. & n. biondo m. ~e a. & n. bionda f.

blood /blʌd/ n. sangue m. ~ count conteggio dei globuli m. ~-curdling a. raccapricciante. ~-pressure pressione del sangue f. ~ sport sport sanguinario.

bloodhound /'blʌdhaʊnd/ n. segugio m.

bloodshed /'blʌdʃed/ n. spargimento di sangue m.

bloodshot /'blʌdʃɒt/ a. iniettato di sangue.

bloodstream /'blʌdstri:m/ n. flusso del sangue m.

bloodthirsty /'blʌdθɜːstɪ/ a. assetato di sangue.

bloody /'blʌdɪ/ a. (-ier, -iest) insanguinato; (sl.) maledetto. ~-minded a. (fam.) perverso; (stubborn) ostinato.

bloom /blu:m/ n. fiore m. —v.i. fiorire; (fig.) rifiorire. ~ing a. fiorente; (fam.) dannato.

bloomer /'blu:mə(r)/ n. (sl.) papera f. ~s n.pl. (fam.) mutandoni m.pl.

blossom /'blɒsəm/ n. fiore (d'albero) m. —v.i. sbocciare. ~ out (into) (fig.) divenire.

blot /blɒt/ n. macchia f. —v.t. (p.t. blotted) macchiare; (dry) asciugare. ~ out oscurare. ~ter, ~ting-paper ns. carta assorbente f.

blotch /blɒtʃ/ n. macchia f. ~y a. chiazzato.

blouse /blaʊz/ n. blusa f.

blow[1] /bləʊ/ v.t./i. (p.t. blew, p.p. blown) soffiare; (fuse) saltare; (trumpet) suonare; (whistle) fischiare. ~ down v.t. abbattere. ~-dry v.t. asciugare. ~ out (candle) soffiare. ~-out n. (of tyre) scoppio m. ~ over passare. ~ up gonfiare; (far) saltare. ~-up n. (photo) ingrandimento m.

blow[2] /bləʊ/ n. colpo m.; (puff) soffio m.

blowlamp /'bləʊlæmp/ n. fiamma ossidrica f.

blown /bləʊn/ see blow[1].

blowzy /'blaʊzɪ/ a. trasandato.

blubber /'blʌbə(r)/ n. grasso di balena m.

bludgeon /'blʌdʒən/ n. randello m. —v.t. colpire con un randello.

blue /blu:/ a. (-er, -est) blu. —n. blu m. have the ~s essere depresso. out of the ~ inaspettatamente.

bluebell /'blu:bel/ n. giacinto di bosco m.

bluebottle /'blu:bɒtl/ n. moscone m.

blueprint /'blu:prɪnt/ n. progetto m.

bluff[1] /blʌf/ v.i. (poker) bluffare. —n. (poker) bluff m. invar.

bluff[2] /blʌf/ a. (person) brusco.

blunder /'blʌndə(r)/ v.i. commettere un errore grossolano. —n. errore grossolano m.

blunt /blʌnt/ a. spuntato; (person) reciso. —v.t. smussare. ~ly adv. schiettamente. ~ness n. schiettezza f.

blur /blɜː(r)/ n. offuscamento m. —v.t. (p.t. blurred) rendere confuso.

blurb /blɜːb/ n. soffietto editoriale m.

blurt /blɜːt/ v.t. ~ out spifferare.

blush /blʌʃ/ v.i. arrossire. —n. rossore m.

bluster /'blʌstə(r)/ v.i. (weather) infuriare; (person) strepitare. ~y a. furioso.

boar /bɔː(r)/ n. cinghiale m.

board /bɔːd/ n. tavola f.; (for notices) tabellone m.; (food) vitto m.; (admin.) consiglio m. above ~ corretto. ~ and lodging vitto e alloggio. full ~ pensione completa f. go by the ~ essere abbandonato. —v.t./i. (naut.) montare a bordo; (live as a boarder) far pensione. ~er n. pensionante m./f.; (schol.) convit|tore, -trice m., f. ~ing-house n. pensione f. ~ing-school n. collegio m.

boast /bəʊst/ v.i. vantarsi. —v.t. vantare. —n. vanto m. ~er n. spaccone, a m., f. ~ful a. vanaglorioso.

boat /bəʊt/ n. barca f.; (large) battello m. ~er n. (hat) paglietta f.

boatswain /'bəʊsn/ n. nostromo m.

bob[1] /bɒb/ v.i. (p.t. bobbed) sobbalzare; (curtsy) inchinarsi; (hair) tagliare i capelli corti. ~ up venire improvvisamente a galla.

bob[2] /bɒb/ n. invar. (sl.) scellino m.

bobbin /'bɒbɪn/ n. bobina f.

bobby /'bɒbɪ/ n. (fam.) poliziotto m.

bobsleigh /'bɒbsleɪ/ n. bob m.

bode /bəʊd/ v.i. presagire. ~ well/ill essere di buono/cattivo augurio.

bodice /'bɒdɪs/ n. corpetto m.

bodily /'bɒdɪlɪ/ a. fisico. —adv. di persona, fisicamente.

body /'bɒdɪ/ n. corpo m. ~work n. carrozzeria f.

bodyguard /'bɒdɪgɑːd/ n. guardia del corpo f.

boffin /'bɒfɪn/ n. (sl.) scienziato m.

bog /bɒg/ n. palude f. —v.t. impantanarsi.

boggle /'bɒgl/ v.i. trasalire.

bogus /'bəʊgəs/ a. falso.

bogy /'bəʊgɪ/ n. spauracchio m.

boil[1] /bɔɪl/ n. foruncolo m.

boil[2] /bɔɪl/ v.t./i. (far) bollire. ~ away evaporare. ~ down condensare. ~ up (fig.) eccitarsi. ~ing hot a. bollente.

boiler /'bɔɪlə(r)/ n. caldaia f. ~ suit n. tuta f.

boisterous /'bɔɪstərəs/ a. chiassoso; (of wind) tempestoso.

bold /bəʊld/ a. (-er, -est) audace. ~**ness** n. audacia f.

Bolivia /bə'lɪvɪə/ n. Bolivia f. ~**n** a. & n. boliviano, a m., f.

bollard /'bɒləd/ n. colonnina f.

bolster /'bəʊlstə(r)/ n. cuscino m. —v.t. ~ **up** sostenere.

bolt /bəʊlt/ n. catenaccio m.; (for nut) bullone m.; (lightning) saetta f.; (leap) balzo m. —v.t. lanciare; (food) trangugiare. —v.i. svignarsela. ~ **upright** adv. diritto come un fuso.

bomb /bɒm/ n. bomba f. —v.t. bombardare. ~**er** n. bombardiere m. ~**ing** n. bombardamento m. ~**shell** n. granata f.; (fig.) notizia sconvolgente f.

bombard /bɒm'bɑːd/ v.t. bombardare.

bombastic /bɒm'bæstɪk/ a. ampolloso.

bonanza /bə'nænzə/ n. (fig.) miniera d'oro f.

bond /bɒnd/ n. legame m.; (comm.) obbligazione f.

bondage /'bɒndɪdʒ/ n. schiavitù f.

bone /bəʊn/ n. osso m. (pl. ossa f.); (of fish) spina f. —v.t. disossare. ~**-dry** a. secco. ~ **idle** a. fannullone.

bonfire /'bɒnfaɪə(r)/ n. falò m. invar.

bonnet /'bɒnɪt/ n. cuffia f.; (auto.) cofano m.

bonny /'bɒnɪ/ a. (-ier, -iest) grazioso.

bonus /'bəʊnəs/ n. premio m.

bony /'bəʊnɪ/ a. (-ier, -iest) ossuto; (of fish) pieno di spine.

boo /buː/ int. puh! —v.t./i. fischiare.

boob /buːb/ n. (sl.) gaffe f. —v.i. (sl.) fare una gaffe.

booby /'buːbɪ/ n. sciocco, a m., f. ~ **trap** trappola f.; (mil.) ordigno esplosivo m.

book /bʊk/ n. libro m.; (comm.) registro m.; (of tickets etc.) blocchetto m. —v.t./i. (enter) registrare; (reserve) prenotare; (motorist) multare. ~**able** a. che si può prenotare. ~**ing-office** biglietteria f.

bookcase /'bʊkkeɪs/ n. libreria f.

bookkeeping /'bʊkkiːpɪŋ/ n. contabilità f.

booklet /'bʊklɪt/ n. opuscolo m.

bookmaker /'bʊkmeɪkə(r)/ n. allibratore m.

bookmark /'bʊkmɑː(r)k/ n. segnalibro m.

bookseller /'bʊkselə(r)/ n. libraio, a m., f.

bookshop /'bʊkʃɒp/ n. libreria f.

bookstall /'bʊkstɔːl/ n. edicola f.

bookworm /'bʊkwɜːm/ n. (fig.) topo di biblioteca m.

boom /buːm/ v.i. rimbombare; (fig.) prosperare. —n. rimbombo m.; (comm.) boom m.

boon /buːn/ n. vantaggio m.

boor /bʊə(r)/ n. zoticone m. ~**ish** a. maleducato.

boost /buːst/ v.t. spingere (in su); (product) lanciare. —n. spinta (in su) f. ~**er** n. (med.) dose supplementare f.

boot /buːt/ n. stivale m.; (auto) portabagagli m. invar. **get the** ~ (sl.) essere licenziato.

booth /buːð/ n. cabina f.

booty /'buːtɪ/ n. bottino m.

booze /buːz/ v.i. (fam.) sbronzarsi. —n. (fam.) bevanda alcolica f.; (spree) sbornia f.

border /'bɔːdə(r)/ n. bordo m.; (frontier) frontiera f.; (in garden) bordura f. —v.i. ~ **on** confinare con.

borderline /'bɔːdəlaɪn/ n. linea di demarcazione f.

bore[1] /bɔː(r)/ see **bear**[2].

bore[2] /bɔː(r)/ v.t./i. (techn.) forare.

bore[3] /bɔː(r)/ v.t. annoiare. —n. (person) secca|tore, -trice m., f.; (thing) seccatura f. ~**dom** n. noia f. **boring** a. noioso.

born /bɔːn/ a. nato. **be** ~ nascere.

borne /bɔːn/ see **bear**[2].

borough /'bʌrə/ n. municipalità f.

borrow /'bɒrəʊ/ v.t. prendere a prestito.

Borstal /'bɔːstl/ n. riformatorio m.

bosh /bɒʃ/ int. & n. (sl.) sciocchezze f.pl.

bosom /'bʊzəm/ n. seno m. ~ **friend** amico, a del cuore m., f.

boss /bɒs/ n. (fam.) capo m., dirigente m./f. —v.t. (fam.) spadroneggiare.

bossy /'bɒsɪ/ a. autoritario.

botan|y /'bɒtənɪ/ n. botanica f. ~**ical** /bə'tænɪkl/ a. botanico. ~**ist** n. botanico, a m., f.

botch /bɒtʃ/ v.t. rattoppare malamente.

both /bəʊθ/ a. ambedue. —pron. tutti e due, entrambi. —adv. nello stesso tempo.

bother /'bɒðə(r)/ v.t./i. seccare; (disturb) dar disturbo. —n. (worry) preoccupazione f.; (minor trouble) fastidio m. ~ **it!** int. che seccatura! ~ **about** preoccuparsi di.

bottle /'bɒtl/ n. bottiglia f. —v.t. imbottigliare. ~-**opener** n. apribottiglie m. invar. ~ **up** (fig.) reprimere.

bottleneck /'bɒtlnek/ n. (traffic jam) ingorgo m.

bottom /'bɒtəm/ n. fondo m.; (of hill) bassopiano m.; (buttocks) sedere m. —a. ultimo. ~**less** a. senza fondo.

bough /baʊ/ n. ramoscello m.

bought /bɔːt/ see buy.

boulder /'bəʊldə(r)/ n. masso m.

boulevard /'buːləvɑːd/ n. viale m.

bounce /baʊns/ v.i. rimbalzare; (person) saltellare; (cheque, sl.) essere respinto. —v.t. far rimbalzare. —n. rimbalzo m. ~**r** n. buttafuori m. invar.

bouncing /'baʊnsɪŋ/ a. robusto.

bound¹ /baʊnd/ v.i. balzare. —n. balzo m.

bound² /baʊnd/ see bind. —a. be ~ **for** essere diretto a. ~ **to** obbligato a; (certain) sicuro di.

boundary /'baʊndərɪ/ n. limite m.

bound|s /'baʊndz/ n.pl. limiti m.pl. **out of** ~**s** fuori dai limiti. ~**less** a. illimitato.

bountiful /'baʊntɪfl/ a. abbondante.

bouquet /bʊ'keɪ/ n. mazzo di fiori m.; (perfume) aroma f.

bout /baʊt/ n. periodo m.; (med.) attacco m.; (sport) incontro m.

bow¹ /bəʊ/ n. arco m.; (mus.) archetto m.; (knot) nodo m. ~-**legged** a. dalle gambe storte. ~-**tie** n. cravatta a farfalla f.

bow² /baʊ/ n. inchino m. —v.i. inchinarsi. —v.t. piegare.

bow³ /baʊ/ n. (naut.) prua f.

bowels /'baʊəlz/ n.pl. intestini m.pl.; (fig.) viscere f.pl.

bowl¹ /bəʊl/ n. scodella f.; (of pipe) fornello m.; (of spoon) cavità f.

bowl² /bəʊl/ n. (ball) boccia f. —v.t./i. (cricket) servire. ~ **over** buttar giù. ~**ing** n. gioco delle bocce m.

bowler¹ /'bəʊlə(r)/ n. (cricket) giocatore che serve la palla m.

bowler² /'bəʊlə(r)/ n. ~ **hat** bombetta f.

box¹ /bɒks/ n. scatola f.; (theatr.) palco m. ~-**office** n. botteghino m. ~-**room** n. ripostiglio m.

box² /bɒks/ v.t./i. fare a pugni. ~ **s.o.'s ears** schiaffeggiare qcno. ~**er** n. pugile m. ~**ing** n. pugilato m. **Boxing Day** n. (giorno di) Santo Stefano m.

boy /bɔɪ/ n. ragazzo m. ~-**friend** n.

ragazzo m. ~**hood** n. fanciullezza f. ~**ish** a. fanciullesco.

boycott /'bɔɪkɒt/ v.t. boicottare. —n. boicottaggio m.

bra /brɑː/ n. reggipetto m.

brace /breɪs/ n. sostegno m.; (dental) apparecchio m. ~**s** n.pl. bretelle f.pl. —v.t. sostenere. ~ **o.s.** farsi forza.

bracelet /'breɪslɪt/ n. braccialetto m.

bracing /'breɪsɪŋ/ a. tonificante.

bracken /'brækən/ n. felce f.

bracket /'brækɪt/ n. mensola f.; (group) categoria f.; (typ.) parentesi f. invar. —v.t. mettere fra parentesi.

brag /bræg/ v.i. (p.t. **bragged**) vantarsi.

braid /breɪd/ n. passamano m.; (of hair) treccia f.

brain /breɪn/ n. cervello m. ~**s** n.pl. (fig.) testa f.s. —v.t. fracassare la testa. ~-**child** n. invenzione personale f. ~**less** a. senza cervello. ~**storm** n. attacco di pazzia m. ~**wave** n. lampo di genio m.

brainwash /'breɪnwɒʃ/ v.t. fare il lavaggio del cervello.

brainy /'breɪnɪ/ a. (-ier, -iest) intelligente.

braise /breɪz/ v.t. brasare.

brake /breɪk/ n. freno m. —v.t./i. frenare.

bramble /'bræmbl/ n. rovo m.

bran /bræn/ n. crusca f.

branch /brɑːntʃ/ n. ramo m.; (of road) diramazione f.; (comm.) succursale f. —v.i. ~ **off** biforcarsi. ~ **out** estendersi.

brand /brænd/ n. marca f. —v.t. marcare; (reputation) tacciare. ~-**new** a. nuovo fiammante.

brandish /'brændɪʃ/ v.t. brandire.

brandy /'brændɪ/ n. cognac m.

brash /bræʃ/ a. sfacciato.

brass /brɑːs/ n. ottone m. **get down to** ~ **tacks** (fig.) venire al sodo. **top** ~ (sl.) pezzi grossi m.pl. ~**y** a. (-ier, -iest) volgare.

brassière /'bræsjeə(r)/ n. reggipetto m.

brat /bræt/ n. (pej.) marmocchio, a m., f.

bravado /brə'vɑːdəʊ/ n. bravata f.

brave /breɪv/ a. (-er, -est) coraggioso. —n. prode m. —v.t. affrontare. ~**ry** /-ərɪ/ n. coraggio m.

brawl /brɔːl/ n. rissa f. —v.i. rissare.

brawn /brɔːn/ n. muscolo m. ~**y** a. muscoloso.

bray /breɪ/ *n.* raglio *m.* —*v.i.* ragliare.

brazen /'breɪzn/ *a.* sfrontato.

brazier /'breɪzɪə(r)/ *n.* braciere *m.*

Brazil /brə'zɪl/ *n.* Brasile *m.* ∼**ian** *a.* & *n.* brasiliano, a *m.*, *f.*

breach /briːtʃ/ *n.* violazione *f.*; (*of contract*) rottura *f.*; (*gap*) breccia *f.* —*v.t.* aprire una breccia.

bread /bred/ *n.* pane *m.* ∼**-winner** *n.* sostegno della famiglia *m.* **loaf of** ∼ pagnotta *f.*

breadcrumbs /'bredkrʌmz/ *n.pl.* briciole *f.pl.*; (*culin.*) pangrattato *m.*

breadline /'bredlaɪn/ *n.* **on the** ∼ in povertà.

breadth /bredθ/ *n.* larghezza *f.*

break /breɪk/ *v.t.* (*p.t.* **broke**, *p.p.* **broken**) rompere, spezzare; (*law*) violare; (*a record*) battere; (*news*) rivelare; (*journey*) interrompere. —*v.i.* spezzarsi; (*news*) diffondersi. —*n.* rottura *f.*; (*interval*) intervallo *m.*; (*fam.*, *chance*) opportunità *f.* ∼ **away** scappare. ∼ **down** crollare; (*figures*) analizzare. ∼ **faith** venir meno (alla parola). ∼ **into** irrompere in. ∼ **off** interrompersi. ∼ **out** scoppiare; (*run away*) fuggire. ∼ **up** disperdersi; (*friendship*) rompere; (*schools*) iniziare le vacanze. ∼**able** *a.* fragile. ∼**age** *n.* rottura *f.*

breakdown /'breɪkdaʊn/ *n.* (*techn.*) guasto *m.*; (*med.*) esaurimento nervoso; (*of figures*) analisi *f. invar.*

breaker /'breɪkə(r)/ *n.* (*wave*) frangente *m.*

breakfast /'brekfəst/ *n.* (prima) colazione *f.*

breakthrough /'breɪkθruː/ *n.* scoperta *f.*

breakwater /'breɪkwɔːtə(r)/ *n.* frangiflutti *m. invar.*

breast /brest/ *n.* seno *m.*; (*chest*) petto *m.* ∼**-stroke** *n.* nuoto a rana *m.*

breath /breθ/ *n.* respiro, fiato *m.* **out of** ∼ senza fiato. **under one's** ∼ sottovoce.

breathalyser /'breθəlaɪzə(r)/ *n.* palloncino (per la prova dell'alcool) *m.*

breath|e /briːð/ *v.t./i.* respirare. ∼**ing** *n.* respirazione *f.*

breather /'briːðə(r)/ *n.* pausa *f.*

breathtaking /'breθteɪkɪŋ/ *a.* strabiliante.

bred /bred/ *see* **breed.**

breeches /'brɪtʃɪz/ *n.pl.* calzoni *m.pl.*

breed /briːd/ *v.t./i.* (*p.t.* **bred**) allevare; (*fig.*) generare. —*n.* razza *f.* ∼**er** *n.*

alleva|tore, **-trice** *m.*, *f.* ∼**ing** *n.* allevamento *m.*; (*manners*) educazione *f.*

breez|e /briːz/ *n.* brezza *f.* ∼**y** *a.* ventoso; (*person*) spigliato.

Breton /'bretən/ *a.* & *n.* bretone *m.*/*f.*

brew /bruː/ *v.t.* (*beer*) fabbricare; (*tea*) mettere in infusione. —*v.i.* essere in fermentazione. —*n.* infuso *m.* ∼**er** *n.* birraio *m.* ∼**ery** *n.* fabbrica di birra *f.*

bribe /braɪb/ *n.* bustarella *f.* —*v.t.* corrompere. ∼**ry** /-ərɪ/ *n.* corruzione *f.*

brick /brɪk/ *n.* mattone *m.* —*v.t.* ∼ **up** murare.

bricklayer /'brɪkleɪə(r)/ *n.* muratore *m.*

brid|e /braɪd/ *n.* sposa *f.* ∼**al** *a.* nuziale.

bridegroom /'braɪdgrʊm/ *n.* sposo *m.*

bridesmaid /'braɪdzmeɪd/ *n.* damigella d'onore *f.*

bridge[1] /brɪdʒ/ *n.* ponte *m.*; (*of nose*) dorso *m.* —*v.t.* ∼ **a gap** colmare una lacuna.

bridge[2] /brɪdʒ/ *n.* (*cards*) bridge *m.*

bridle /'braɪdl/ *n.* briglia *f.* —*v.t.* imbrigliare. ∼**-path** *n.* mulattiera *f.*

brief[1] /briːf/ *a.* (**-er**, **-est**) breve. ∼**s** *n.pl.* slip *m.s.* ∼**ly** *adv.* brevemente.

brief[2] /briːf/ *n.* (*jurid.*) fascicolo *m.* —*v.t.* dare istruzioni a.

briefcase /'briːfkeɪs/ *n.* valigetta *f.*

brigad|e /brɪ'geɪd/ *n.* brigata *f.* ∼**ier** /-ə'dɪə(r)/ *n.* generale di brigata *m.*

bright /braɪt/ *a.* (**-er**, **-est**) brillante, luminoso; (*day*, *room*) chiaro; (*clever*) intelligente. ∼**ly** *adv.* brillantemente. ∼**ness** *n.* luminosità *f.*

brighten /'braɪtn/ *v.t.* illuminare. —*v.i.* (*of weather*) rischiararsi; (*of face*) ravvivarsi.

brillian|t /'brɪljənt/ *a.* brillante; (*light*) lucente. ∼**ce** *n.* lucentezza *f.*; (*of brains*) vivezza d'ingegno *f.*

brim /brɪm/ *n.* bordo *m.* —*v.i.* (*p.t.* **brimmed**) ∼ **over** traboccare.

brine /braɪn/ *n.* salamoia *f.*

bring /brɪŋ/ *v.t.* (*p.t.* **brought**) portare. ∼ **about** causare. ∼ **back** restituire. ∼ **down** abbattere. ∼ **off** portare a compimento. ∼ **on** cagionare. ∼ **out** mettere in evidenza; (*book*) pubblicare. ∼ **round/to** (*unconscious person*) far rinvenire; ∼ **up** (*med.*) vomitare; (*children*) allevare; (*question*) introdurre l'argomento.

brink /brɪŋk/ *n.* orlo *m.*

brisk /brɪsk/ a. (-er, -est) svelto. ∼**ness** n. sveltezza f.

bristl|e /'brɪsl/ n. setola f. —v.i. rizzarsi. ∼**ing with** pieno di.

Britain /'brɪtən/ n. Gran Bretagna f.

British /'brɪtɪʃ/ a. britannico. **the** ∼ il popolo britannico m.

Briton /'brɪtən/ n. britanno, a m.,f.

Brittany /'brɪtənɪ/ n. Bretagna f.

brittle /'brɪtl/ a. fragile.

broach /brəʊtʃ/ v.t. intavolare.

broad /brɔːd/ a. (-er, -est) largo, ampio. **in** ∼ **daylight** in pieno giorno. ∼ **bean** n. fava f. ∼**-minded** a. di larghe vedute. ∼**ly** adv. largamente.

broadcast /'brɔːdkɑːst/ n. trasmissione f. —v.t. (p.t. **broadcast**) trasmettere. —v.i. fare una trasmissione. ∼**ing** a. & n. radio-diffusione f.

broaden /'brɔːdn/ v.t./i. allargare, allargarsi.

brocade /brə'keɪd/ n. broccato m.

broccoli /'brɒkəlɪ/ n. invar. broccoletti m.pl.

brochure /'brəʊʃə(r)/ n. opuscolo m.

brogue /brəʊg/ n. scarpa da campagna f.; (accent) cadenza dialettale f.

broke /brəʊk/ see **break**. —a. (sl.) al verde.

broken /'brəʊkən/ see **break**. —a. ∼ **English** inglese scorretto. ∼-**hearted** a. dal cuore spezzato.

broker /'brəʊkə(r)/ n. sensale m.

brolly /'brɒlɪ/ n. (fam.) ombrello m.

bronchitis /brɒŋ'kaɪtɪs/ n. bronchite f.

bronze /brɒnz/ n. bronzo m. —v.t./i. abbronzare, abbronzarsi.

brooch /brəʊtʃ/ n. fermaglio m.

brood /bruːd/ n. covata f.; (joc.) prole f. —v.i. covare; (fig.) meditare. ∼**y** a. meditabondo.

brook[1] /brʊk/ n. ruscello m.

brook[2] /brʊk/ v.t. sopportare.

broom /bruːm/ n. ginestra f.; (brush) scopa f.

broomstick /'bruːmstɪk/ n. manico di scopa m.

broth /brɒθ/ n. brodo m.

brothel /'brɒθl/ n. bordello m.

brother /'brʌðə(r)/ n. fratello m. ∼-**in-law** n. cognato m. ∼**ly** a. fraterno. ∼**hood** n. fratellanza f.

brought /brɔːt/ see **bring**.

brow /braʊ/ n. fronte f.; (of hill) cima f.

browbeat /'braʊbiːt/ v.t. (p.t. -**beat**, p.p. -**beaten**) intimidire.

brown /braʊn/ a. (-er, -est) marrone. —n. marrone m. —v.t./i. brunire; (culin.) rosolare. **be** ∼**ed off** (sl.) essere stufo.

Brownie /'braʊnɪ/ n. giovane esploratrice f.

browse /braʊz/ v.i. (in a shop) curiosare; (of animal) brucare.

bruise /bruːz/ n. contusione f. —v.t. ammaccare. —v.i. farsi un livido. ∼**d** a. contuso.

brunch /brʌntʃ/ n. (fam.) pasto unico (di prima e seconda colazione) m.

brunette /bruː'net/ n. brunetta f.

brunt /brʌnt/ n. **the** ∼ **of** il peso maggiore di.

brush /brʌʃ/ n. spazzola f.; (skirmish) rissa f. —v.t. spazzolare. ∼ **against** sfiorare. ∼ **aside** mettere da parte. ∼ **off** (reject) liberarsi di. ∼ **up (on)** ripassare.

brusque /bruːsk/ a. brusco. ∼**ly** adv. bruscamente.

Brussels /'brʌslz/ n. Bruxelles f.

brutal /'bruːtl/ a. brutale. ∼**ity** /-'tælətɪ/ n. brutalità f.

brute /bruːt/ n. bruto m. ∼ **force** forza bruta f.

B.Sc. abbr. see **bachelor**.

bubble /'bʌbl/ n. bolla f. —v.i. far bolle. ∼ **over** traboccare.

bubbly /'bʌblɪ/ a. pieno di bolle. —n. (fam.) spumante m.

buck[1] /bʌk/ n. cervo. —v.i. (of horse) impennarsi. ∼ **up** (sl.) rincorarsi; (rush) sbrigarsi.

buck[2] /bʌk/ n. (Amer., sl.) dollaro m.

buck[3] /bʌk/ n. **pass the** ∼ scaricare la responsabilità.

bucket /'bʌkɪt/ n. secchio m.

buckle /'bʌkl/ n. fibbia f. —v.t. affibbiare. —v.i. (di metallo) piegarsi. ∼ **down to** mettersi con impegno a.

bud /bʌd/ n. bocciolo m. —v.i. (p.t. **budded**) sbocciare. ∼**ding** a. in boccio; (fig.) in erba.

Buddhis|t /'bʊdɪst/ a. & n. buddista m.|f. ∼**m** /-zəm/ n. buddismo m.

buddy /'bʌdɪ/ n. (fam.) compagno m.

budge /bʌdʒ/ v.t./i. spostare, spostarsi.

budgerigar /'bʌdʒərɪgɑː(r)/ n. cocorita f.

budget /'bʌdʒɪt/ n. bilancio m. —v.i. (p.t. **budgeted**) fare il bilancio.

buff /bʌf/ n. (colour) (color) camoscio

m.; (*Amer., fam.*) fanatico, a *m., f.*
—*v.t.* lucidare.
buffalo / 'bʌfələʊ/ *n.* (*pl.* -oes *or* -o)
bufalo *m.*
buffer /'bʌfə(r)/ *n.* (*auto*) paraurti *m.*
old ∼ (*person, sl.*) incompetente *m.*
buffet[1] /'bʊfeɪ/ *n.* (*meal, counter*) buffet
m. invar.
buffet[2] /'bʌfɪt/ *n.* buffetto *m.* —*v.t.* (*p.t.*
buffeted) schiaffeggiare.
buffoon /bə'fuːn/ *n.* buffone, a *m., f.*
bug /bʌg/ *n.* cimice *f.*; (*germ, sl.*) germe
m.; (*device, sl.*) microfono segreto
m. —*v.t.* (*p.t.* **bugged**) mettere micro-
foni segreti; (*Amer., sl.*) irritare.
bugbear /'bʌgbeə(r)/ *n.* spauracchio
m.
buggy /'bʌgɪ/ *n.* **baby** ∼ carrozzino *m.*
bugle /'bjuːgl/ *n.* tromba *f.*
build /bɪld/ *v.t./i.* (*p.t.* **built**) costruire. —*n.* (*of person*) corporatura
f. ∼ **up** *v.t.* costruire; (*door, window,
etc.*) murare. ∼-**up** *n.* (*of gas etc.*)
accumulo *m.*; (*fig.*) battage pubblicitario *m.* ∼**er** *n.* costruttore *m.*
built /bɪlt/ *see* **build**. ∼-**in** *a.* a muro.
∼-**up area** *n.* abitato *m.*
bulb /bʌlb/ *n.* bulbo *m.*; (*electr.*) lampadina *f.* ∼**ous** *a.* bulboso.
Bulgaria /bʌl'geərɪə/ *n.* Bulgaria *f.* ∼**n**
a. & n. bulgaro, a *m., f.*
bulg|e /bʌldʒ/ *n.* rigonfiamento *m.*
—*v.i.* esser gonfio; (*jut out*) sporgere. ∼**ing** *a.* gonfio.
bulk /bʌlk/ *n.* volume *m.* **in** ∼ all'in-
grosso; (*loose*) alla rinfusa. **the** ∼ **of**
il grosso di. ∼**y** *a.*, voluminoso.
bull /bʊl/ *n.* toro *m.* ∼**s-eye** *n.* centro
del bersaglio *m.*
bulldog /'bʊldɒg/ *n.* mastino *m.*
bulldozer /'bʊldəʊzə(r)/ *n.* livellatrice
f.
bullet /'bʊlɪt/ *n.* pallottola *f.* ∼-**proof**
a., a prova di pallottole; (*vehicle*) blindato.
bulletin /'bʊlətɪn/ *n.* bollettino *m.*
bullfight /'bʊlfaɪt/ *n.* corrida *f.* ∼**er** *n.*
torero *m.*
bullion /'bʊljən/ *n.* oro/argento in
verghe *m.*
bullring /'bʊlrɪŋ/ *n.* arena *f.*
bully /'bʊlɪ/ *n.* bullo *m.* —*v.t.* tiranneg-
giare. ∼**ing** *n.* prepotenze *f.pl.*
bum[1] /bʌm/ *n.* (*sl.*) sedere *m.*
bum[2] /bʌm/ *n.* (*Amer., sl.*) vagabondo,
a *m., f.*
bumble-bee /'bʌmblbiː/ *n.* calabrone
m.

bump /bʌmp/ *v.t./i.* urtare. ∼ **into**
cozzare con; (*meet*) incontrare. —*n.*
botta *f.*; (*swelling*) bernoccolo *m.*
bumper /'bʌmpə(r)/ *n.* paraurti *m.*
invar. —*a.* abbondante.
bumpkin /'bʌmpkɪn/ *n.* zoticone, a *m.*,
f.
bumptious /'bʌmpʃəs/ *a.* presuntuoso.
bun /bʌn/ *n.* panino *m.*; (*hair*) chignon
m.
bunch /bʌntʃ/ *n.* mazzo *m.*; (*of people*)
gruppo *m.*; (*of grapes*) grappolo *m.*
bundle /'bʌndl/ *n.* fascio *m.* —*v.t.* affa-
stellare.
bung /bʌŋ/ *n.* tappo *m.* —*v.t.* tappare;
(*sl.*) scagliare.
bungalow /'bʌŋgələʊ/ *n.* casetta a un
piano *f.*
bungle /'bʌŋgl/ *v.t.* abborracciare.
bunion /'bʌnjən/ *n.* callo *m.*
bunk /bʌŋk/ *n.* cuccetta *f.* ∼-**bed** letto
a castello *m.*
bunker /'bʌŋkə(r)/ *n.* carbonile *m.*;
(*golf*) ostacolo *m.*; (*mil.*) bunker *m.*
invar.
bunkum /'bʌŋkəm/ *n.* fandonie *f.pl.*
bunny /'bʌnɪ/ *n.* coniglietto *m.*
buoy /bɔɪ/ *n.* boa *f.* —*v.t.* ∼ **up** sostenere.
buoyan|t /'bɔɪənt/ *a.* galleggiante; (*fig.*)
allegro. ∼**cy** *n.* galleggiabilità *f.*; (*fig.*)
esuberanza *f.*
burden /'bɜːdn/ *n.* carico *m.* —*v.t.* caricare. ∼**some** *a.* pesante.
bureau /'bjʊərəʊ/ *n.* (*pl.* -**eaux** /-əʊz/)
scrivania *f.*; (*office*) ufficio *m.*
bureaucracy /bjʊə'rɒkrəsɪ/ *n.* burocrazia *f.*
bureaucrat /'bjʊərəkræt/ *n.* burocrate
m./*f.* ∼**ic** /-'krætɪk/ *a.* burocratico.
burgeon /'bɜːdʒən/ *v.i.* germogliare.
burglar /'bɜːglə(r)/ *n.* ladro *m.* ∼**y** *n.*
furto *m.*
burgle /'bɜːgl/ *v.t.* svaligiare.
Burgundy /'bɜːgəndɪ/ *n.* Borgogna *f.*;
(*wine*) vino di Borgogna *m.*
burial /'berɪəl/ *n.* sepoltura *f.*
burlesque /bɜː'lesk/ *n.* parodia *f.*
burly /'bɜːlɪ/ *a.* (-**ier, -iest**) corpulento.
Burm|a /'bɜːmə/ Birmania *f.* ∼**ese**
/-'miːz/ *a. & n.* birmano, a *m., f.*
burn /bɜːn/ *v.t./i.* (*p.t.* **burned** *or*
burnt) bruciare. —*n.* bruciatura *f.* ∼ *v.t.* ∼**er**
down *v.t.* distruggere col fuoco. ∼**er**
n. bruciatore *m.*; (*gas*) becco *m.* ∼**ing**
a. (*fig.*) cocente.
burnish /'bɜːnɪʃ/ *v.t.* lustrare.

burnt /bɜːnt/ *see* **burn.**
burp /bɜːp/ *n.* (*fam.*) rutto *m.* —*v.i.*
(*fam.*) ruttare.
burr /bɜː(r)/ *n.* ronzio *m.*
burrow /'bʌrəʊ/ *n.* tana *f.* —*v.t.* scavare (una tana).
bursar /'bɜːsə(r)/ *n.* tesoriere, a *m.*,*f.*
bursary /'bɜːsərɪ/ *n.* borsa di studio *f.*
burst /bɜːst/ *v.t./i.* (*p.t.* **burst**) scoppiare. —*n.* scoppio *m.*; (*surge*) slancio
m.; (*mil.*) raffica *f.*
bury /'berɪ/ *v.t.* seppellire; (*hide*) nascondere.
bus /bʌs/ *n.* (*pl.* **buses**) autobus *m.*
invar. —*v.i.* (*p.t.* **bussed**) prendere
l'autobus. **~-stop** *n.* fermata dell'autobus *f.*
bush /bʊʃ/ *n.* cespuglio *m.*; (*land*) boscaglia *f.* **~y** *a.* folto.
bushel /'bʊʃl/ *n.* staio *m.*
business /'bɪznɪs/ *n.* affare *m.*; (*comm.*)
affari *m.pl.*; (*fig.*) compito *m.* **~-like**
a. efficiente. **~ man** uomo d'affari *m.*
mind one's own ~ farsi i fatti propri.
busker /'bʌskə(r)/ *n.* suona|tore, -trice
ambulante *m.*,*f.*
bust[1] /bʌst/ *n.* busto *m.*; (*chest*) petto
m.
bust[2] /bʌst/ *v.t./i.* (*p.t.* **busted** *or* **bust**)
(*sl.*) spezzare, scoppiare. —*a.* rotto.
~-up *n.* (*sl.*) lite *f.* **go ~** (*sl.*) fallire.
bustle /'bʌsl/ *v.i.* agitarsi. —*n.* trambusto *m.*; (*of dress*) puf *m. invar.*
bus|y /'bɪzɪ/ *a.* (*-ier*, *-iest*) occupato;
(*street*) pieno di traffico; (*day*) intenso. —*v.t.* **~ o.s. with** occuparsi di.
~ily *adv.* alacremente.
busybody /'bɪzɪbɒdɪ/ *n.* ficcanaso *m.*|*f.
invar.*
but /bʌt/ *conj.* ma. —*prep.* eccetto,
tranne. —*adv.* soltanto. **~ for** senza.
last ~ one penultimo.
butane /'bjuːteɪn/ *n.* butano *m.*
butcher /'bʊtʃə(r)/ *n.* macellaio *m.*
—*v.t.* massacrare. **~y** *n.* macello *m.*;
(*shop*) macelleria *f.*; (*fig.*) strage *f.*

butler /'bʌtlə(r)/ *n.* maggiordomo *m.*
butt /bʌt/ *n.* (*of gun*) calcio *m.*; (*of
cigarette*) mozzicone *m.*; (*target*) bersaglio *m.* —*v.i.* cozzare. **~ in** immischiarsi.
butter /'bʌtə(r)/ *n.* burro *m.* —*v.t.* im-
burrare. **~-bean** *n.* fagiolo di Lima
m. **~-fingers** *n.* mani di ricotta *f.pl.*
~ up *v.t.* (*fam.*) adulare.
buttercup /'bʌtəkʌp/ *n.* ranuncolo *m.*
butterfly /'bʌtəflaɪ/ *n.* farfalla *f.*
buttock /'bʌtək/ *n.* natica *f.*
button /'bʌtn/ *n.* bottone *m.* —*v.t./i.*
abbottonare, abbottonarsi.
buttonhole /'bʌtnhəʊl/ *n.* occhiello
m. —*v.t.* (*fig.*) attaccare un bottone.
buttress /'bʌtrɪs/ *n.* contrafforte *m.*
—*v.t.* sostenere.
buxom /'bʌksəm/ *a.* (*of woman*) formo-
sa.
buy /baɪ/ *v.t.* (*p.t.* **bought**) comprare.
—*n.* compera *f.* **~er** *n.* compra|tore,
-trice *m.*,*f.*
buzz /bʌz/ *n.* ronzio *m.* —*v.i.* ronzare;
(*news*) circolare; (*techn.*) chiamare
qcno. col vibratore a cicala. **~ off** (*sl.*)
svignarsela. **~er** *n.* cicalino *m.*
by /baɪ/ *prep.* per, di, da; (*near*) vicino
a; (*time*) entro; (*measure*, *weight*) per.
~ and large in complesso. **~ car**
in macchina. **~-election** *n.* elezione
straordinaria *f.* **~-law** *n.* legge locale
f. **~ oneself** da solo. **~-product** *n.*
sottoprodotto *m.* **put ~** mettere da
parte.
bye-bye /'baɪbaɪ/ *int.* (*fam.*) arrivederci.
bygone /'baɪgɒn/ *a.* passato.
bypass /'baɪpɑːs/ *n.* circonvallazione
f. —*v.t.* girare intorno a.
bystander /'baɪstændə(r)/ *n.* spetta|
tore, -trice *m.*,*f.*
byword /'baɪwɜːd/ *n.* sinonimo *m.*

C

cab /kæb/ n. tassì m. invar.; (of lorry, train) cabina f.

cabaret /'kæbəreɪ/ n. spettacolo di varietà m.

cabbage /'kæbɪdʒ/ n. cavolo m.

cabin /'kæbɪn/ n. capanna f.; (in ship, plane) cabina f.

cabinet /'kæbɪnɪt/ n. armadietto m. C~ (pol.) gabinetto m. ~-maker n. ebanista m.

cable /'keɪbl/ n. cavo m. —v.t. telegrafare. ~ railway n. funicolare f.

cache /kæʃ/ n. nascondiglio m. —v.t. nascondere.

cackle /'kækl/ n. schiamazzo m. —v.i. schiamazzare.

cacophon|ous /kæ'kɔfənəs/ a. cacofonico. ~y n. cacofonia f.

cactus /'kæktəs/ n. (pl. -ti /-taɪ/) cacto m.

cad /kæd/ n. canaglia f. ~dish a. ignobile.

caddie /'kædɪ/ n. (golf) portabastoni m. invar.

caddy /'kædɪ/ n. scatola da tè f.

cadence /'keɪdəns/ n. cadenza f.

cadet /kə'det/ n. cadetto m.

cadge /kædʒ/ v.t./i. scroccare. ~r /-ə(r)/ n. scroccone, a m., f.

Caesarean /sɪ'zeərɪən/ a. cesareo. ~ section parto cesareo m.

café /'kæfeɪ/ n. caffè m.

cafeteria /kæfɪ'tɪərɪə/ n. tavola calda f.

caffeine /'kæfiːn/ n. caffeina f.

cage /keɪdʒ/ n. gabbia f. —v.t. mettere in gabbia.

cagey /'keɪdʒɪ/ a. (fam.) diffidente.

Cairo /'kaɪərəʊ/ n. il Cairo m.

cajole /kə'dʒəʊl/ v.t. allettare. ~ry n. raggiro m.

cake /keɪk/ n. torta f. ~ of soap saponetta f. ~d a. incrostato.

calamit|y /kə'læmətɪ/ n. calamità f. ~ous a. disastroso.

calcium /'kælsɪəm/ n. calcio m.

calculat|e /'kælkjʊleɪt/ v.t./i. calcolare; (Amer.) supporre. ~ing a. calcolatore. ~ion /-'leɪʃn/ n. calcolo m. ~or n. calcolatrice f.

calculus /'kælkjʊləs/ n. (pl. -li) calcolo m.

calendar /'kælɪndə(r)/ n. calendario m.

calf[1] /kɑːf/ n. (pl. calves) vitello m.

calf[2] /kɑːf/ n. (pl. calves) (of leg) polpaccio m.

calibre /'kælɪbə(r)/ n. calibro m.

calico /'kælɪkəʊ/ n. calico m.

call /kɔːl/ v.t./i. chiamare. —n. appello m.; (phone) telefonata f.; (shout) grido m.; (visit) visita f. be on ~ essere di guardia. ~ back richiamare. ~-box n. cabina telefonica f. ~ for chiedere; (fetch) passare a prendere. ~ off disdire. ~ on visitare. ~ out gridare. ~ together riunire. ~ up (mil.) richiamare; (phone) chiamare. long distance ~ n. chiamata interurbana f. ~er n. visita|tore, -trice m.,f.; (phone) chi telefona. ~ing n. vocazione f.

callous /'kæləs/ a. senza cuore. ~ness n. durezza di cuore f.

callow /'kæləʊ/ a. (-er, -est) imberbe.

calm /kɑːm/ a. (-er, -est) calmo. —n. calma f. —v.t./i. calmare, calmarsi. ~ness n. calma f.

calorie /'kælərɪ/ n. caloria f.

camber /'kæmbə(r)/ n. curvatura f.

Cambodia /kæm'bəʊdɪə/ n. Cambogia f. ~n a. & n. cambogiano, a m., f.

came /keɪm/ see come.

camel /'kæml/ n. cammello m.

camellia /kə'miːljə/ n. camelia f.

cameo /'kæmɪəʊ/ n. (pl. -os) cammeo m.

camera /'kæmərə/ n. macchina fotografica f.; (TV) telecamera f. ~man n. (pl. -men) operatore m.

camouflage /'kæməflɑːʒ/ n. mimetizzazione f. —v.t. mimetizzare.

camp[1] /kæmp/ n. campeggio m.; (mil.) campo m. —v.i. campeggiare; accamparsi. ~-bed n. letto da campo m. ~er n. campeggia|tore, -trice m., f. ~ing n. campeggio m.

camp[2] /kæmp/ a. (affected) affettato.

campaign /kæm'peɪn/ n. campagna f. —v.i. fare una campagna.

campsite /'kæmpsaɪt/ n. campeggio m.

campus /'kæmpəs/ n. (pl. -puses) città universitaria f.

can[1] /kæn/ n. scatola, latta f. —v.t. (p.t. canned) mettere in scatola. ~ned music musica riprodotta f.

can[2] /kæn/ *v. aux.* (*p.t.* **could**) (*be able to*) potere; (*know how to*) sapere. **~not** (*neg.*), **~'t** (*neg., fam.*) I **~not/~'t** go non posso andare.

Canad|a /'kænədə/ *n.* Canada *m.* **~ian** /kə'neɪdɪən/ *a.* & *n.* canadese *m./f.*

canal /kə'næl/ *n.* canale *m.*

canary /kə'neərɪ/ *n.* canarino *m.*

cancel /'kænsl/ *v.t./i.* (*p.t.* **cancelled**) cancellare; (*annul*) disdire. **~lation** /-'leɪʃn/ *n.* cancellazione *f.*; disdetta *f.*

cancer /'kænsə(r)/ *n.* cancro *m.* **C~** *n.* (*Astr.*) Cancro *m.* **~ous** *a.* canceroso.

candid /'kændɪd/ *a.* candido, franco.

candida|te /'kændɪdeɪt/ *n.* candidato *m.* **~cy** /-əsɪ/ *n.* candidatura *f.*

candle /'kændl/ *n.* candela *f.*

candlestick /'kændlstɪk/ *n.* candelabro *m.*

candour /'kændə(r)/ *n.* franchezza *f.*

candy /'kændɪ/ *n.* (*Amer.*) caramella *f.* **~-floss** *n.* zucchero filato *m.*

cane /keɪn/ *n.* canna *f.*; (*for baskets*) vimini *m. invar.*; (*stick*) bastoncino *m.* —*v.t.* (*chair*) impagliare; (*strike*) bastonare.

canine /'keɪnaɪn/ *a.* canino.

canister /'kænɪstə(r)/ *n.* scatola *f.*

cannabis /'kænəbɪs/ *n.* hascisc *m.*

cannibal /'kænɪbl/ *n.* cannibale *m./f.* **~ism** *n.* cannibalismo *m.*

cannon /'kænən/ *n. invar.* cannone *m.* **~ shot** cannonata *f.*

cannot /'kænət/ *see* **can**[2].

canny /'kænɪ/ *a.* astuto, accorto.

canoe /kə'nu:/ *n.* canotto *m.* —*v.i.* andare in canotto. **~ist** *n.* canottiere, a *m., f.*

canon /'kænən/ *n.* canone *m.*; (*rule*) regola *f.*; (*person*) canonico *m.*

canonize /'kænənaɪz/ *v.t.* canonizzare.

canopy /'kænəpɪ/ *n.* baldacchino *m.*; (*of parachute*) calotta *f.*

cant /kænt/ *n.* gergo *m.*

can't /kɑ:nt/ *see* **can**[2].

cantankerous /kæn'tæŋkərəs/ *a.* stizzoso.

canteen /kæn'ti:n/ *n.* mensa *f.*; (*for cutlery*) portaposate *m. invar.*

canter /'kæntə(r)/ *n.* piccolo galoppo *m.* —*v.i.* andare a piccolo galoppo.

canvas /'kænvəs/ *n.* tela *f.*

canvass /'kænvəs/ *v.i.* far campagna elettorale. **~ing** *n.* sollecitazione (di voti) *f.*

canyon /'kænjən/ *n.* canyon *m. invar.*

cap /kæp/ *n.* berretto *m.*; (*academic*) tocco *m.*; (*of cartridge*) capsula *f.*;

(*mech.*) tappo *m.* —*v.t.* (*p.t.* **capped**) tappare; (*outdo*) superare.

capab|le /'keɪpəbl/ *a.* capace, abile. **~ility** /-'bɪlətɪ/ *n.* capacità *f.* **~ly** *adv.* con abilità.

capacity /kə'pæsətɪ/ *n.* capacità *f.*; (*function*) qualità *f.*

cape[1] /keɪp/ *n.* (*cloak*) cappa *f.*

cape[2] /keɪp/ *n.* (*geog.*) capo *m.*

caper[1] /'keɪpə(r)/ *v.i.* saltellare. —*n.* capriola *f.*; (*fig.*) stramberia *f.*

caper[2] /'keɪpə(r)/ *n.* (*culin.*) cappero *m.*

capital /'kæpɪtl/ *a.* capitale. —*n.* (*town*) capitale *f.*; (*money*) capitale *m.* **~ letter** lettera maiuscola *f.*

capitalis|t /'kæpɪtəlɪst/ *a.* & *n.* capitalista *m./f.* **~m** /-zəm/ *n.* capitalismo *m.*

capitalize /'kæpɪtəlaɪz/ *v.t.* capitalizzare; (*provide capital*) finanziare; (*typ.*) scrivere con maiuscola.

capitulat|e /kə'pɪtʃʊleɪt/ *v.i.* arrendersi. **~ion** /-'leɪʃn/ *n.* capitolazione *f.*

capon /'keɪpən/ *n.* cappone *m.*

capricious /kə'prɪʃəs/ *a.* capriccioso.

Capricorn /'kæprɪkɔ:n/ *n.* Capricorno *m.*

capsicum /'kæpsɪkəm/ *n.* peperone *m.*

capsize /kæp'saɪz/ *v.t./i.* capovolgere, capovolgersi.

capsule /'kæpsju:l/ *n.* capsula *f.*

captain /'kæptɪn/ *n.* capitano *m.* —*v.t.* comandare.

caption /'kæpʃn/ *n.* (*heading*) intestazione *f.*; (*jurid.*) arresto *m.*

captivate /'kæptɪveɪt/ *v.t.* cattivare.

captiv|e /'kæptɪv/ *a.* & *n.* prigioniero, a *m., f.* **~ity** /-'tɪvətɪ/ *n.* prigionia *f.*

capture /'kæptʃə(r)/ *v.t.* catturare; (*attention*) attirare. —*n.* cattura *f.*

car /kɑ:(r)/ *n.* macchina *f.* **~-ferry** traghetto per le automobili *m.* **~-park** parcheggio *m.*

carafe /kə'ræf/ *n.* caraffa *f.*

caramel /'kærəmel/ *n.* caramello *m.*

carat /'kærət/ *n.* carato *m.*

caravan /'kærəvæn/ *n.* carovana *f.*

carbohydrate /kɑ:bəʊ'haɪdreɪt/ *n.* carboidrato *m.*

carbon /'kɑ:bən/ *n.* carbonio *m.*; (*paper*) carta carbone *f.* **~ copy** copia carbone *f.*

carburettor /kɑ:bjʊ'retə(r)/ *n.* carburatore *m.*

carcass /'kɑ:kəs/ *n.* carcassa *f.*

card[1] /kɑ:d/ *n.* biglietto *m.*; (*invitation, greeting*) cartolina *f.*; (*game*) carta

(da gioco); (*membership*) tessera *f*. ~-
index *n*. schedario *m*.
cardboard /'kɑːdbɔːd/ *n*. cartone *m*.
cardiac /'kɑːdɪæk/ *a*. cardiaco.
cardigan /'kɑːdɪgən/ *n*. cardigan *m*.
invar.
cardinal /'kɑːdɪnəl/ *a*. cardinale. —*n*.
cardinale *m*.
care /keə(r)/ *n*. cura, attenzione *f*.;
(*worry*) preoccupazione *f*.; (*protection*) responsabilità *f*. —*v.i.* ~
about interessarsi di. ~ **for** aver
cura di; (*like*) voler bene. ~ **of** presso.
I don't ~ non mi importa. **in** ~ **in**
custodia. **take** ~ **of** occuparsi di.
career /kə'rɪə(r)/ *n*. carriera *f*. —*v.i.*
andare a gran velocità.
carefree /'keəfriː/ *a*. spensierato.
careful /'keəfʊl/ *a*. attento; (*cautious*)
prudente. ~**ly** *adv*. con cura.
careless /'keəlɪs/ *a*. negligente; (*not
careful*) incauto; (*not worried*)
spensierato. ~**ly** *adv*. negligen-
temente. ~**ness** *n*. noncuranza *f*.;
spensieratezza *f*.
caress /kə'res/ *n*. carezza *f*. —*v.t.* carez-
zare.
caretaker /'keəteɪkə(r)/ *n*. custode
m.|f.
cargo /'kɑːgəʊ/ *n*. (*pl*. **-oes**) carico *m*.
Caribbean /kærɪ'biːən/ *a*. caraibico.
~ **Sea** Mar dei Caraibi *m*.
caricature /'kærɪkətʃʊə(r)/ *n*. caricatura *f*. —*v.t.* mettere in caricatura.
carnage /'kɑːnɪdʒ/ *n*. carneficina *f*.
carnal /'kɑːnl/ *a*. carnale.
carnation /kɑː'neɪʃn/ *n*. garofano *m*.
carnival /'kɑːnɪvl/ *n*. carnevale *m*.
carol /'kærəl/ *n*. cantico *m*. **Christmas**
~ cantico di Natale.
carouse /kə'raʊz/ *v.i.* gozzovigliare.
~**l** /-'zel/ *n*. carosello *m*.
carp[1] /kɑːp/ *n*. *invar*. carpa *f*.
carp[2] /kɑːp/ *v.i.* ~ **at** trovare a ridire
su.
carpent|er /'kɑːpɪntə(r)/ *n*. falegname
m. ~**ry** *n*. falegnameria *f*.
carpet /'kɑːpɪt/ *n*. tappeto *m*. —*v.t.*
coprire con tappeto. **be on the** ~
essere ammonito. ~**-sweeper** *n*. spazzola per tappeti *f*.
carriage /'kærɪdʒ/ *n*. carrozza *f*.;
(*mech*.) carrello *m*.; (*of goods*) trasporto *m*.; (*cost*) porto *m*.; (*bearing*)
portamento *m*.
carriageway /'kærɪdʒweɪ/ *n*. strada
carrozzabile *f*.
carrier /'kærɪə(r)/ *n*. corriere *m*.;

(*comm*.) spedizioniere *m*.; (*mech*.) trasportatore *m*; (*med*.) portatore (di
germi) *m*. ~**-bag** sacchetto (per la
spesa) *m*.
carrot /'kærət/ *n*. carota *f*.
carry /'kærɪ/ *v.t./i.* portare; (*goods*) trasportare; (*sounds*) trasmettere;
(*math*.) riportare; (*involve*) implicare.
~**-cot** *n*. culla portabile *f*. ~ **off** portar
via; (*prize*) vincere. ~ **on** continuare;
(*fam., flirt*) filare. ~ **out** eseguire;
(*duty*) compiere; (*investigation*) svolgere.
cart /kɑːt/ *n*. carretto *m*. —*v.t.* trasportare; (*fam., carry*) portare.
cartilage /'kɑːtɪlɪdʒ/ *n*. cartilagine *f*.
carton /'kɑːtən/ *n*. scatola di cartone
f.; (*for drinks*) cartoccio *m*.; (*of ciga-
rettes*) stecca *f*.
cartoon /kɑː'tuːn/ *n*. vignetta *f*.; (*cinema*) cartone animato *m*. ~**ist** *n*.
caricaturista *m.|f*.
cartridge /'kɑːtrɪdʒ/ *n*. cartuccia *f*.
carve /kɑːv/ *v.t.* scolpire; (*meat*) tagliare.
cascade /kæs'keɪd/ *n*. cascata *f*. —*v.i.*
cascare.
case /keɪs/ *n*. caso *m*.; (*jurid*.) processo
m.; (*crate*) cassa *f*.; (*box*) scatola *f*.;
(*suitcase*) valigia *f*. **glass** ~ vetrina *f*.
show~ bacheca *f*. **upper/lower** ~
lettere maiuscole/minuscole *f.pl*.
cash /kæʃ/ *n*. denaro contante *m*.
—*v.t.* incassare. **pay (in)** ~ pagare in
contanti. ~ **desk** *n*. cassa *f*. ~ **in (on)**
approfittarsi di; (*comm*.) realizzare
da.
cashew /kæ'ʃuː/ *n*. anacardio *m*.
cashier /kæ'ʃɪə(r)/ *n*. cassiere, a *m.*, *f*.
cashmere /kæʃ'mɪə(r)/ *n*. cachemire
m. invar.
casino /kə'siːnəʊ/ *n*. (*pl*. **-os**) casinò *m*.
invar.
cask /kɑːsk/ *n*. barile *m*.
casket /'kɑːskɪt/ *n*. scrigno *m*.
casserole /'kæsərəʊl/ *n*. casseruola *f*.;
(*stew*) stufato *m*.
cassette /kə'set/ *n*. cassetta *f*.
cast /kɑːst/ *v.t.* (*p.t.* **cast**) gettare;
(*shed*) buttare; (*metal*) fondere; (*vote*)
dare; (*theatr*.) assegnare (le parti).
—*n*. getto *m*.; (*theatr*.) complesso
m.; (*mould*) forma *f*. ~ **iron** *n*. ghisa
f. ~**-iron** *a*. di ghisa; (*fig*.) solido.
~**-offs** *n.pl*. abiti smessi *m.pl*.
castanets /kæstə'nets/ *n.pl*. nacchere
f.pl.

castaway /ˈkɑːstəweɪ/ *n.* naufrago, a *m., f.*

caste /kɑːst/ *n.* casta *f.*

castle /ˈkɑːsl/ *n.* castello *m.*; (*chess*) torre *f.*

castor /ˈkɑːstə(r)/ *n.* rotella *f.* ~ **oil** olio di ricino *m.* ~ **sugar** zucchero raffinato *m.*

castrat|e /kæˈstreɪt/ *v.t.* castrare. ~**ion** /-ʃn/ *n.* castrazione *f.*

casual /ˈkæʒʊəl/ *a.* casuale; (*work*) saltuario; (*attitude*) semplice; (*clothes*) pratico. ~**ly** *adv.* casualmente; semplicemente.

casualt|y /ˈkæʒʊəltɪ/ *n.* incidente *m.*; (*wounded person*) vittima *f.* ~**ies** *n.pl.* (*mil.*) perdite *f.pl.*

cat /kæt/ *n.* gatto *m.*; (*pej.*) donna maldicente *f.* ~**'s eyes** *n.pl.* catarifrangente *m.s.*

cataclysm /ˈkætəklɪzəm/ *n.* cataclisma *m.*

catacomb /ˈkætəkəʊm/ *n.* catacomba *f.*

catalogue /ˈkætəlɒg/ *n.* catalogo *m.* —*v.t.* catalogare.

catalyst /ˈkætəlɪst/ *n.* catalizzatore *m.*

catamaran /kætəməˈræn/ *n.* catamarano *m.*

catapult /ˈkætəpʌlt/ *n.* catapulta *f.*; (*child's*) fionda *f.*

cataract /ˈkætərækt/ *n.* cataratta *f.*

catarrh /kəˈtɑː(r)/ *n.* catarro *m.*

catastroph|e /kəˈtæstrəfɪ/ *n.* catastrofe *f.* ~**ic** /kætəˈstrɒfɪk/ *a.* catastrofico.

catch /kætʃ/ *v.t.* (*p.t.* **caught**) afferrare; (*grab*) acchiappare; (*train, bus*) prendere. —*v.i.* (*get stuck*) impigliarsi; (*fire*) prendere. —*n.* presa *f.*; (*of fish*) pesca *f.*; (*on door*) fermo *m.*; (*on window*) gancio *m.* ~ **a cold** prendersi un raffreddore. ~ **on** (*fam.*) diventare popolare. ~**-phrase** *n.* frase fatta *f.* ~ **sight of** avvistare. ~ **up** riguadagnare il tempo perduto. ~ **up with** raggiungere.

catching /ˈkætʃɪŋ/ *a.* contagioso.

catchment /ˈkætʃmənt/ *n.* ~ **area** circoscrizione scolare *f.*; (*of rain*) bacino pluviale *m.*

catchword /ˈkætʃwɜːd/ *n.* slogan *m.* invar.

catchy /ˈkætʃɪ/ *a.* orecchiabile.

catechism /ˈkætɪkɪzəm/ *n.* catechismo *m.*

categorical /kætɪˈgɒrɪkl/ *a.* categorico.

category /ˈkætɪgərɪ/ *n.* categoria *f.*

cater /ˈkeɪtə(r)/ *v.i.* provvedere cibo. ~ **for** (*needs*) provvedere a. ~**er** *n.* fornitore (di cibo) *m.*

caterpillar /ˈkætəpɪlə(r)/ *n.* bruco *m.*

cathedral /kəˈθiːdrəl/ *n.* cattedrale *f.*

catholic /ˈkæθəlɪk/ *a.* universale. **C~** *a. & n.* cattolico, a *m., f.* **C~ism** /kəˈθɒlɪsɪzəm/ *n.* cattolicesimo *m.*

catnap /ˈkætnæp/ *n.* pisolino *m.*

cattle /ˈkætl/ *n.pl.* bestiame *m.s.*

catty /ˈkætɪ/ *a.* dispettoso.

catwalk /ˈkætwɔːk/ *n.* passerella *f.*

caucus /ˈkɔːkəs/ *n.* comitato elettorale *m.*

caught /kɔːt/ *see* **catch.**

cauldron /ˈkɔːldrən/ *n.* calderone *m.*

cauliflower /ˈkɒlɪflaʊə(r)/ *n.* cavolfiore *m.*

cause /kɔːz/ *n.* causa *f.* —*v.t.* causare.

causeway /ˈkɔːzweɪ/ *n.* strada sopraelevata *f.*

caustic /ˈkɔːstɪk/ *a. & n.* caustico *m.*

cauterize /ˈkɔːtəraɪz/ *v.t.* cauterizzare.

cauti|on /ˈkɔːʃn/ *n.* cautela, prudenza *f.*; (*warning*) avviso *m.* —*v.t.* mettere in guardia; (*jurid.*) ammonire. ~**ous** *a.* cauto. ~**ously** *adv.* cautamente.

cavalcade /kævəlˈkeɪd/ *n.* cavalcata *f.*

cavalier /kævəˈlɪə(r)/ *a.* altezzoso.

cavalry /ˈkævəlrɪ/ *n.* cavalleria *f.*

cave /keɪv/ *n.* caverna *f.* —*v.i.* ~ **in** franare. ~**-man** *n.* (*pl.* **-men**) uomo delle caverne *m.*

cavern /ˈkævən/ *n.* caverna *f.*

caviare /ˈkævɪɑː(r)/ *n.* caviale *m.*

caving /ˈkeɪvɪŋ/ *n.* speleologia *f.*

cavity /ˈkævətɪ/ *n.* cavità *f.*

cavort /kəˈvɔːt/ *v.i.* saltellare.

cease /siːs/ *v.t./i.* cessare. ~**-fire** *n.* tregua *f.* **without** ~ incessantemente. ~**less** *a.* incessante.

cedar /ˈsiːdə(r)/ *n.* cedro *m.*

cede /siːd/ *v.t.* cedere; (*rights etc.*) rinunciare *a.*

cedilla /sɪˈdɪlə/ *n.* cediglia *f.*

ceiling /ˈsiːlɪŋ/ *n.* soffitto *m.*

celebrat|e /ˈselɪbreɪt/ *v.t.* celebrare. —*v.i.* far festa. ~**ion** /-ˈbreɪʃn/ *n.* celebrazione *f.*

celebrated /ˈselɪbreɪtɪd/ *a.* celebre.

celebrity /sɪˈlebrətɪ/ *n.* celebrità *f.*

celery /ˈselərɪ/ *n.* sedano *m.*

celestial /sɪˈlestjəl/ *a.* celestiale.

celiba|te /ˈselɪbət/ *a. & n.* celibe *m.* ~**cy** *n.* celibato *m.*

cell /sel/ *n.* cella *f.*; (*biol.*) cellula *f.*; (*electr.*) elemento *m.*

cellar /'selə(r)/ *n.* scantinato *m.*; (*for wine*) cantina *f.*

cell|o /'tʃeləʊ/ *n.* (*pl.* **-os**) violoncello *m.* **~ist** *n.* violoncellista *m.*/*f.*

Cellophane /'seləfeɪn/ *n.* (*P.*) cellofane *m.*

cellular /'seljʊlə(r)/ *a.* cellulare.

celluloid /'seljʊlɔɪd/ *n.* celluloide *f.*

cellulose /'seljʊləʊs/ *n.* cellulosa *f.*

Celt /kelt/ *n.* celta *m.*/*f.* **~ic** *a.* celtico.

cement /sɪ'ment/ *n.* cemento *m.* —*v.t.* cementare; (*fig.*) consolidare.

cemetery /'semətrɪ/ *n.* cimitero *m.*

cenotaph /'senəta:f/ *n.* cenotafio *m.*

censor /'sensə(r)/ *n.* censore *m.* —*v.t.* censurare. **~ship** *n.* censura *f.*

censorious /sen'sɔːrɪəs/ *a.* ipercritico.

censure /'senʃə(r)/ *n.* biasimo *m.* —*v.t.* biasimare.

census /'sensəs/ *n.* censimento *m.*

cent /sent/ *n.* centesimo *m.*

centenary /sen'tiːnərɪ/ *n.* centenario *m.*

centigrade /'sentɪgreɪd/ *a.* centigrado.

centilitre /'sentɪliːtə(r)/ *n.* centilitro *m.*

centimetre /'sentɪmiːtə(r)/ *n.* centimetro *m.*

centipede /'sentɪpiːd/ *n.* millepiedi *m. invar.*

central /'sentrəl/ *a.* centrale. **~ize** *v.t.* centralizzare. **~ly** *adv.* al centro.

centre /'sentə(r)/ *n.* centro *m.* —*v.t.* (*p.t.* **centred**) centrare. —*v.i.* concentrarsi.

centrifugal /sen'trɪfjʊgəl/ *a.* centrifugo.

century /'sentʃərɪ/ *n.* secolo *m.*

ceramic /sɪ'ræmɪk/ *a.* ceramico. **~s** *n.pl.* (*art*) ceramica *f.s.*; (*objects*) ceramiche *f.pl.*

cereal /'sɪərɪəl/ *n.* cereale *m.*

cerebral /'serɪbrəl/ *a.* cerebrale.

ceremonial /serɪ'məʊnɪəl/ *a.* da cerimonia. —*n.* cerimoniale *m.*

ceremon|y /'serɪmənɪ/ *n.* cerimonia *f.* **~ious** /-'məʊnɪəs/ *a.* cerimonioso.

certain /'sɜːtn/ *a.* certo. **for ~** di sicuro. **make ~ of** assicurarsi di. **~ly** *adv.* certamente. **~ty** *n.* certezza *f.*

certificate /sə'tɪfɪkət/ *n.* certificato *m.*

certify /'sɜːtɪfaɪ/ *v.t.* certificare.

cessation /se'seɪʃən/ *n.* cessazione *f.*

cesspit, cesspool /'sespɪt, 'sespuːl/ *ns.* pozzo nero *m.*; (*fam.*) fogna *f.*

chafe /tʃeɪf/ *v.t.*/*i.* strofinare; (*fig.*) irritare, irritarsi.

chaffinch /'tʃæfɪntʃ/ *n.* fringuello *m.*

chagrin /'ʃægrɪn/ *n.* dispiacere *m.* **~ed** *a.* contrariato.

chain /tʃeɪn/ *n.* catena *f.* —*v.t.* incatenare. **~ reaction** reazione a catena *f.* **~-smoker** *n.* fumatore accanito *m.* **~ store** negozio a catena *m.*

chair /tʃeə(r)/ *n.* sedia *f.*; (*univ.*) cattedra *f.* —*v.t.* presiedere. **~-lift** *n.* seggiovia *f.*

chairman /'tʃeəmən/ *n.* (*pl.* **-men**) presidente *m.*

chalet /'ʃæleɪ/ *n.* villino *m.*

chalice /'tʃælɪs/ *n.* calice *m.*

chalk /tʃɔːk/ *n.* gesso *m.* **~y** *a.* gessoso.

challeng|e /'tʃælɪndʒ/ *n.* sfida *f.*; (*mil.*) intimazione *f.* —*v.t.* sfidare; (*question the truth*) mettere in dubbio. **~ing** *a.* impegnativo.

chamber /'tʃeɪmbə(r)/ *n.* (*old use*) camera *f.* **~-pot** *n.* vaso da notte *m.* **~s** *n.pl.* ufficio (d'avvocato) *m.s.*

chambermaid /'tʃeɪmbəmeɪd/ *n.* cameriera (d'albergo) *f.*

chameleon /kə'miːljən/ *n.* camaleonte *m.*

chamois /'ʃæmɪ/ *n.* pelle di camoscio *f.*

champagne /ʃæm'peɪn/ *n.* sciampagna *f.*

champion /'tʃæmpɪən/ *n.* campione *m.* —*v.t.* difendere. **~ship** *n.* campionato *m.*

chance /tʃɑːns/ *n.* caso *m.*; (*likelihood*) possibilità *f.*; (*opportunity*) occasione *f.*; (*risk*) rischio *m.* —*a.* fortuito. —*v.t.*/*i.* accadere; (*risk*) rischiare. **by ~** per caso.

chancellor /'tʃɑːnsələ(r)/ *n.* cancelliere *m.*

chancy /'tʃɑːnsɪ/ *a.* rischioso, incerto.

chandelier /ʃændə'lɪə(r)/ *n.* lampadario *m.*

change /tʃeɪndʒ/ *v.t.* cambiare; (*substitute*) scambiare. —*v.i.* cambiarsi. —*n.* cambiamento *m.*; (*money*) resto *m.*; (*small coins*) spiccioli *m.pl.* **~ of life** *n.* menopausa *f.* **~ one's mind** cambiare idea. **~-over** *n.* cambiamento totale *m.* **~able** *a.* mutevole; (*weather*) variabile.

channel /'tʃænl/ *n.* canale *m.*; (*fig.*) via *f.*, mezzo *m.* —*v.t.* (*p.t.* **channelled**) scavare un canale; (*fig.*) incanalare. **the C~ Islands** le Isole Normanne. **the (English) C~** la Manica.

chant /tʃɑːnt/ *n.* cantilena *f.* —*v.t.*/*i.* cantare.

chao|s /ˈkeɪɒs/ *n.* caos *m.* **~tic** /-ˈɒtɪk/ *a.* caotico.

chap¹ /tʃæp/ *n.* (*fam.*) tipo *m.*

chap² /tʃæp/ *n.* screpolatura *f.* —*v.t./i.* (*p.t.* **chapped**) screpolare, screpolarsi.

chapel /ˈtʃæpl/ *n.* cappella *f.*

chaperon /ˈʃæpərəʊn/ *n.* chaperon *f. invar.* —*v.t.* fare da chaperon.

chaplain /ˈtʃæplɪn/ *n.* cappellano *m.*

chapter /ˈtʃæptə(r)/ *n.* capitolo *m.*

char¹ /tʃɑː(r)/ *n.* donna ad ore *f.*

char² /tʃɑː(r)/ *v.t.* (*p.t.* **charred**) carbonizzare.

character /ˈkærəktə(r)/ *n.* carattere *m.*; (*theatr.*) personaggio *m.* **in ~** caratteristico. **~ize** *v.t.* caratterizzare.

characteristic /kærəktəˈrɪstɪk/ *a.* caratteristico. **~ally** *adv.* tipicamente.

charade /ʃəˈrɑːd/ *n.* sciarada *f.*

charcoal /ˈtʃɑːkəʊl/ *n.* carbonella *f.*

charge /tʃɑːdʒ/ *n.* prezzo *m.*; (*electr., mil.*) carica *f.*; (*jurid.*) accusa *f.*; (*task, custody*) cura *f.* —*v.t./i.* far pagare; (*electr., mil.*) caricare; (*jurid.*) accusare; (*entrust*) affidare. **~ to** addebitare. **in ~ of** responsabile di. **take ~ of** incaricarsi di. **~able** *a.* a carico (di).

chariot /ˈtʃærɪət/ *n.* cocchio *m.*

charis|ma /kəˈrɪzmə/ *n.* carisma *m.* **~matic** /-ˈmætɪk/ *a.* carismatico.

charit|y /ˈtʃærətɪ/ *n.* carità *f.*; (*society*) istituto di carità *m.* **~able** *a.* caritatevole.

charlatan /ˈʃɑːlətən/ *n.* ciarlatano *m.*

charm /tʃɑːm/ *n.* fascino *m.*; (*on bracelet*) ciondolo *m.* —*v.t.* affascinare. **~ing** *a.* affascinante. **~er** *n.* incantatore *m.*; (*woman*) ammaliatrice *f.*

chart /tʃɑːt/ *n.* carta nautica *f.*; (*table*) tabella *f.* —*v.t.* fare la carta nautica.

charter /ˈtʃɑːtə(r)/ *n.* carta *f.* **~** (**flight**) (volo) charter *m.* —*v.t.* noleggiare. **~ed accountant** commercialista *m./f.*

charwoman /ˈtʃɑːwʊmən/ *n.* (*pl.* -women) donna ad ore *f.*

chary /ˈtʃeərɪ/ *a.* cauto, circospetto.

chase /tʃeɪs/ *v.t.* inseguire. —*v.i.* correre. —*n.* caccia *f.*, inseguimento *m.*

chasm /ˈkæzəm/ *n.* abisso *m.*

chassis /ˈʃæsɪ/ *n.* telaio *m.*

chaste /tʃeɪst/ *a.* casto.

chastise /tʃæsˈtaɪz/ *v.t.* castigare.

chastity /ˈtʃæstətɪ/ *n.* castità *f.*

chat /tʃæt/ *n.* chiacchierata *f.* —*v.i.*

chatted) chiacchierare. **have a ~** fare due chiacchiere. **~ty** *a.* chiacchierone; (*style*) familiare.

chattel /ˈtʃætl/ *n.* beni mobili *m.pl.*

chatter /ˈtʃætə(r)/ *n.* ciarle *f.pl.* —*v.i.* ciarlare. **his teeth are ~ing** batte i denti.

chatterbox /ˈtʃætəbɒks/ *n.* chiacchierone, a *m., f.*

chauffeur /ˈʃəʊfə(r)/ *n.* autista *m.*

chauvinis|t /ˈʃəʊvɪnɪst/ *n.* sciovinista *m./f.* **~m** /-zəm/ *n.* sciovinismo *m.*

cheap /tʃiːp/ *a.* (**-er, -est**) a buon mercato; (*poor quality*) scadente; (*rate*) economico. **~(ly)** *adv.* a buon mercato. **~ness** *n.* prezzo basso *m.*; (*fig.*) meschinità *f.*

cheapen /ˈtʃiːpən/ *v.t.* deprezzare; (*fig.*) screditare.

cheat /tʃiːt/ *v.t./i.* truffare; (*at cards*) barare. —*n.* truffa *f.*; (*person*) truffa| tore, -trice *m., f.*

check¹ /tʃek/ *v.t./i.* verificare; (*tickets*) controllare; (*curb*) moderare; (*chess*) dare scacco a. —*n.* verifica *f.*; (*tickets*) controllo *m.*; (*curb*) freno *m.*; (*chess*) scacco *m.*; (*bill, Amer.*) conto *m.* **~ in** registrare all'arrivo. **~ out** saldare il conto. **~ up** accertare. **check-up** *n.* visita di controllo *f.* **~ up on** prendere informazioni su.

check² /tʃek/ *n.* stoffa a quadri *f.* —*a.* a quadri.

checkmate /ˈtʃekmeɪt/ *n.* scacco matto *m.* —*v.t.* dare scacco matto a.

cheek /tʃiːk/ *n.* guancia *f.*; (*fig.*) sfacciataggine *f.* **~-bone** *n.* zigomo *m.* **~y** *a.* sfacciato.

cheep /tʃiːp/ *v.i.* pigolare.

cheer /tʃɪə(r)/ *n.* allegria *f.*; (*applause*) applauso *m.* —*v.t./i.* rallegrare; (*applaud*) applaudire. **~s!** salute! **~ up!** su, allegro! **~ful** *a.* allegro. **~fulness** *n.* allegria *f.*

cheerio /tʃɪərɪˈəʊ/ *int.* (*fam.*) arrivederci.

cheerless /ˈtʃɪəlɪs/ *a.* triste, tetro.

cheese /tʃiːz/ *n.* formaggio *m.*

cheetah /ˈtʃiːtə/ *n.* ghepardo *m.*

chef /ʃef/ *n.* capocuoco *m.*

chemical /ˈkemɪkl/ *a.* chimico. —*n.* prodotto chimico *m.*

chemist /ˈkemɪst/ *n.* farmacista *m./f.*; (*scientist*) chimico, a *m., f.* **~ry** *n.* chimica *f.*

cheque /tʃek/ *n.* assegno *m.* **~-book** *n.* libretto d'assegni *m.*

chequered /'tʃekəd/ *a.* a scacchi. ∼ **career** carriera con alti e bassi *f.*

cherish /'tʃerɪʃ/ *v.t.* curare teneramente; (*love*) amare; (*hope*) nutrire.

cherry /'tʃerɪ/ *n.* ciliegia *f.* ∼- **tree** *n.* ciliegio *m.*

cherub /'tʃerəb/ *n.* (*pl.* **-im**) (*angel*) cherubino *m.*; (*pl.* ∼**s**) (*art*) putto *m.*; (*fam.*, *child*) angioletto *m.*

chess /tʃes/ *n.* scacchi *m.pl.* ∼- **board** *n.* scacchiera *f.*

chest /tʃest/ *n.* petto *m.*; (*box*) cassapanca *f.* ∼ **of drawers** *n.* cassettone *m.*

chestnut /'tʃesnʌt/ *n.* castagna *f.* ∼- **tree** *n.* castagno *m.*

chew /tʃuː/ *v.t.* masticare; (*fig.*) rimuginare.

chic /ʃiːk/ *a.* & *n.* chic *m. invar.*

chick /tʃɪk/ *n.* pulcino *m.*

chicken /'tʃɪkɪn/ *n.* pollo *m.* —*a.* (*sl.*) timido. —*v.i.* ∼ **out** (*sl.*) ritirarsi. ∼- **pox** *n.* varicella *f.*

chicory /'tʃɪkərɪ/ *n.* cicoria *f.*

chide /tʃaɪd/ *v.t.* (*p.t.* **chided**) rimproverare.

chief /tʃiːf/ *n.* capo *m.* —*a.* principale. ∼**ly** *adv.* principalmente.

chilblain /'tʃɪlbleɪn/ *n.* gelone *m.*

child /tʃaɪld/ *n.* (*pl.* **children** /'tʃɪldrən/) bambino, a *m.*, *f.* ∼**hood** *n.* fanciullezza *f.* ∼**ish** *a.* bambinesco. ∼**less** *a.* senza figli. ∼**like** *a.* infantile.

childbirth /'tʃaɪldbɜːθ/ *n.* parto *m.*

Chile /'tʃɪlɪ/ *n.* Cile *m.* ∼**an** *a.* & *n.* cileno, a *m.*, *f.*

chill /tʃɪl/ *n.* freddo *m.*; (*illness*) infreddatura *f.* —*a.* freddo. —*v.t./i.* raffreddare, raffreddarsi. ∼**y** *a.* freddo, gelido.

chilli /'tʃɪlɪ/ *n.* (*pl.* **-ies**) peperoncino *m.*

chime /tʃaɪm/ *n.* scampanio *m.* —*v.t./i.* scampanare.

chimney /'tʃɪmnɪ/ *n.* (*pl.* **-eys**) camino *m.* ∼**-pot** *n.* comignolo *m.* ∼**-sweep** *n.* spazzacamino *m.*

chimpanzee /tʃɪmpæn'ziː/ *n.* scimpanzè *m.*

chin /tʃɪn/ *n.* mento *m.*

china /'tʃaɪnə/ *n.* porcellana *f.*

Chin|a /'tʃaɪnə/ *n.* Cina *f.* ∼**ese** /-'niːz/ *a.* & *n.* cinese *m.*/*f.*

chink[1] /tʃɪŋk/ *n.* fessura *f.*

chink[2] /tʃɪŋk/ *n.* tintinnio *m.* —*v.t./i.* (far) tintinnare.

chip /tʃɪp/ *n.* scheggia *f.*; (*culin.*) pata-

tina fritta *f.*; (*gambling*) gettone *m.* —*v.t./i.* (*pt.* **chipped**) scheggiare. ∼ **in** (*fam.*) intervenire; (*with money*) contribuire. **have a** ∼ **on one's shoulder** covare risentimenti. ∼**pings** *n.pl.* schegge *f.pl.*

chiropodist /kɪ'rɒpədɪst/ *n.* pedicure *m.*/*f.*

chirp /tʃɜːp/ *n.* cinguettio *m.* —*v.i.* cinguettare.

chirpy /'tʃɜːpɪ/ *a.* vivace, allegro.

chisel /'tʃɪzl/ *n.* scalpello *m.* —*v.t.* (*p.t.* **chiselled**) scalpellare.

chit /tʃɪt/ *n.* bigliettino *m.*; (*child*) marmocchio, a *m.*, *f.*

chit-chat /'tʃɪttʃæt/ *n.* chiacchiera *f.*

chivalr|y /'ʃɪvəlrɪ/ *n.* cavalleria *f.* ∼**ous** *a.* cavalleresco.

chive /tʃaɪv/ *n.* erba cipollina *f.*

chivvy /'tʃɪvɪ/ *v.t.* (*fam.*) far premura.

chlorine /'klɔːriːn/ *n.* cloro *m.*

chock /tʃɒk/ *n.* cuneo *m.* ∼**-a-block**, ∼**-full** *adjs.* pieno zeppo.

chocolate /'tʃɒklɪt/ *n.* cioccolato *m.*; (*drink*) cioccolata *f.*; (*sweet*) cioccolatino *m.*

choice /tʃɔɪs/ *n.* scelta *f.* —*a.* scelto.

choir /'kwaɪə(r)/ *n.* coro *m.*

choirboy /'kwaɪəbɔɪ/ *n.* corista *m.*

choke /tʃəʊk/ *v.t./i.* soffocare, soffocarsi. —*n.* (*auto*) valvola dell'aria *f.*

cholera /'kɒlərə/ *n.* colera *m.*

cholesterol /kə'lestərɒl/ *n.* colesterolo *m.*

choose /tʃuːz/ *v.t./i.* (*p.t.* **chose**, *p.p.* **chosen**) scegliere; (*prefer*) preferire.

choosey /'tʃuːzɪ/ *a.* (*fam.*) difficile (da accontentare).

chop /tʃɒp/ *v.t./i.* (*p.t.* **chopped**) tagliare. —*n.* colpo (d'ascia) *m.*; (*culin.*) costata *f.* ∼ **down** abbattere. ∼ **off** spaccare. ∼**per** *n.* accetta *f.*; (*sl.*) elicottero *m.*

choppy /'tʃɒpɪ/ *a.* increspato.

chopstick /'tʃɒpstɪk/ *n.* bastoncino *m.*

choral /'kɔːrəl/ *a.* corale.

chord /kɔːd/ *n.* corda *f.*

chore /tʃɔː(r)/ *n.* lavoro *m.* **household** ∼**s** *n.pl.* faccende domestiche *f.pl.*

choreographer /kɒrɪ'ɒgrəfə(r)/ *n.* coreografo, a *m.*, *f.*

chorister /'kɒrɪstə(r)/ *n.* corista *m.*/*f.*

chortle /'tʃɔːtl/ *n.* risata sonora *f.* —*v.i.* ridacchiare.

chorus /'kɔːrəs/ *n.* coro *m.*; (*of song*) ritornello *m.*

chose, chosen /tʃəuz, 'tʃəuzn/ *see* **choose.**

Christ /kraɪst/ *n.* Cristo *m.*

christen /'krɪsn/ *v.t.* battezzare. ~**ing** *n.* battesimo *m.*

Christian /'krɪstjən/ *a. & n.* cristiano, a *m., f.* ~ **name** nome di battesimo *m.*

Christmas /'krɪsməs/ *n.* Natale *m.* —*a.* di Natale. ~**-box** *n.* mancia natalizia *f.* ~ **Eve** la vigilia di Natale *f.*

chrome /krəum/ *n.* cromo *m.*

chromium /'krəumɪəm/ *n.* cromo *m.* ~ **plating** cromatura *f.*

chromosome /'krəuməsəum/ *n.* cromosoma *m.*

chronic /'krɒnɪk/ *a.* cronico.

chronicle /'krɒnɪkl/ *n.* cronaca *f.* —*v.t.* fare la cronaca di.

chronolog|y /krə'nɒlədʒɪ/ *n.* cronologia *f.* ~**ical** /krɒnə'lɒdʒɪkl/ *a.* cronologico.

chrysanthemum /krɪ'sænθəməm/ *n.* crisantemo *m.*

chubby /'tʃʌbɪ/ *a.* (-**ier**, -**iest**) paffuto.

chuck /tʃʌk/ *v.t.* (*fam.*) buttare. ~ **out** buttar fuori.

chuckle /'tʃʌkl/ *n.* riso represso *m.* —*v.i.* ridere sotto i baffi.

chuffed /tʃʌft/ *a.* (*sl.*) contento.

chug /tʃʌg/ *v.i.* (*p.t.* **chugged**) (*of motor*) sbuffare.

chum /tʃʌm/ *n.* amico, compagno *m.* ~**my** *a.* amichevole.

chump /tʃʌmp/ *n.* (*sl.*) testone, a *m., f.* ~ **chop** *n.* costata di montone *f.*

chunk /tʃʌŋk/ *n.* grosso pezzo *m.*

chunky /'tʃʌŋkɪ/ *a.* tozzo.

church /'tʃɜːtʃ/ *n.* chiesa *f.*

churchyard /'tʃɜːtʃjɑːd/ *n.* cimitero *m.*

churlish /'tʃɜːlɪʃ/ *a.* sgarbato.

churn /'tʃɜːn/ *n.* zangola *f.* —*v.t.* agitare. ~ **out** produrre. **milk** ~ bidone *m.*

chute /ʃuːt/ *n.* scivolo *m.*; (*for rubbish*) canale di scarico *m.*

chutney /'tʃʌtnɪ/ *n.* (*pl.* -**eys**) salsa piccante *f.*

cider /'saɪdə(r)/ *n.* sidro *m.*

cigar /sɪ'gɑː(r)/ *n.* sigaro *m.*

cigarette /sɪgə'ret/ *n.* sigaretta *f.* ~**holder** *n.* bocchino *m.*

cine-camera /'sɪnɪkæmərə/ *n.* macchina da presa *f.*

cinema /'sɪnəmə/ *n.* cinema *m. invar.*

cinnamon /'sɪnəmən/ *n.* cannella *f.*

cipher /'saɪfə(r)/ *n.* (*math.*) zero *m.*; (*fig.*) nullità *f.*; (*secret system*) cifrario *m.*

circle /'sɜːkl/ *n.* circolo *m.*; (*theatr.*) galleria *f.* —*v.t.* accerchiare. —*v.i.* girare, muoversi in cerchio.

circuit /'sɜːkɪt/ *n.* circuito *m.*

circuitous /sɜː'kjuːɪtəs/ *a.* indiretto.

circular /'sɜːkjulə(r)/ *a. & n.* circolare *f.*

circularize /'sɜːkjuləraɪz/ *v.t.* inviare circolari (a).

circulat|e /'sɜːkjuleɪt/ *v.t./i.* (far) circolare. ~**ion** /-'leɪʃn/ *n.* circolazione *f.*; (*of journals*) tiratura *f.*

circumcis|e /'sɜːkəmsaɪz/ *v.t.* circoncidere. ~**ion** /-'sɪʒn/ *n.* circoncisione *f.*

circumference /sə'kʌmfərəns/ *n.* circonferenza *f.*

circumflex /'sɜːkəmfleks/ *a. & n.* circonflesso *m.*

circumspect /'sɜːkəmspekt/ *a.* circospetto.

circumstance /'sɜːkəmstəns/ *n.* circostanza *f.* ~**s** (*means*) *n.pl.* condizioni finanziarie *f.pl.*

circus /'sɜːkəs/ *n.* circo *m.*

cistern /'sɪstən/ *n.* cisterna *f.*

citadel /'sɪtədl/ *n.* cittadella *f.*

cit|e /saɪt/ *v.t.* citare. ~**ation** /-'teɪʃn/ *n.* citazione *f.*

citizen /'sɪtɪzn/ *n.* cittadino, a *m., f.*; (*of town*) abitante *m./f.* ~**ship** *n.* cittadinanza *f.*

citrus /'sɪtrəs/ *n.* agrume *m.*

city /'sɪtɪ/ *n.* città *f.* **the C**~ la City (di Londra).

civic /'sɪvɪk/ *a.* civico. ~**s** *n.pl.* educazione civica *f.s.*

civil /'sɪvl/ *a.* civile. **C**~ **Servant** impiegat|o, -a statale *m., f.* **C**~ **Service** amministrazione pubblica *f.* ~**ity** /-'vɪlətɪ/ *n.* cortesia *f.*

civilian /sɪ'vɪlɪən/ *a. & n.* civile *m./f.* **in** ~ **clothes** in borghese.

civiliz|e /'sɪvəlaɪz/ *v.t.* civilizzare. ~**ation** /-'zeɪʃn/ *n.* civiltà *f.*

civvies /'sɪvɪz/ *n.pl.* **in** ~ (*sl.*) in borghese.

clad /klæd/ *see* **clothe.**

claim /kleɪm/ *v.t.* reclamare; (*assert*) pretendere. —*n.* rivendicazione *f.*; (*comm.*) reclamo *m.*; (*right*) diritto *m.* ~**ant** *n.* reclamante *m./f.*

clairvoyant /kleə'vɔɪənt/ *n.* chiaroveggente *m./f.*

clam /klæm/ *n.* mollusco *m.*

clamber /'klæmbə(r)/ v.i. arrampicarsi.

clammy /'klæmɪ/ a. (-ier, -iest) viscido.

clamour /'klæmə(r)/ n. (noise) clamore m.; (protest) rimostranza f. —v.i. ~ for chiedere a gran voce.

clamp /klæmp/ n. morsa f. —v.t. ammorsare. ~ down on reprimere.

clan /klæn/ n. clan m. invar.

clandestine /klæn'destɪn/ a. clandestino.

clang /klæŋ/ n. clangore m.

clanger /'klæŋə(r)/ n. (sl.) gaffe f.

clap /klæp/ v.t./i. (p.t. clapped) applaudire; (hands) battere. —n. applauso m.; (of thunder) scoppio m.

claptrap /'klæptræp/ n. imbonimento m.

claret /'klærət/ n. (vino) chiaretto m.

clarif|y /'klærɪfaɪ/ v.t./i. chiarificare. ~ication /-ɪ'keɪʃn/ n. chiarimento m.

clarinet /klærɪ'net/ n. clarinetto m.

clarity /'klærətɪ/ n. chiarezza f.

clash /klæʃ/ n. scontro m.; (fig.) contrasto m. —v.t. cozzare. —v.i. (fig.) essere in contrasto.

clasp /klɑːsp/ n. fermaglio m. —v.t. agganciare.

class /klɑːs/ n. classe f.; (lessons) corso m. —v.t. classificare. **evening** ~ corso serale.

classic /'klæsɪk/ a. & n. classico m. ~s n.pl. classici m.pl. ~al a. classico.

classif|y /'klæsɪfaɪ/ v.t. classificare. ~ication /-ɪ'keɪʃn/ n. classificazione f.

classroom /'klɑːsruːm/ n. aula f.

classy /'klɑːsɪ/ a. (sl.) di classe.

clatter /'klætə(r)/ n. fracasso m. —v.i. far fracasso.

clause /klɔːz/ n. clausola f.; (gram.) proposizione f.

claustrophob|ia /klɔːstrə'fəubɪə/ n. claustrofobia f. ~ic a. & n. claustrofobico, a m., f.

claw /klɔː/ n. artiglio m.; (device) tenaglia f. —v.t. afferrare.

clay /kleɪ/ n. argilla f.

clean /kliːn/ a. (-er, -est) pulito, lindo; (stroke) netto. —adv. completamente. —v.t. pulire. —v.i. ~ up far pulizia. ~-cut a. ben delineato. ~er n. donna ad ore f.

cleanliness /'klenlɪnɪs/ n. pulizia f.

cleans|e /klenz/ v.t. pulire; (fig.) purificare. ~ing cream n. crema detergente f.

clear /klɪə(r)/ a. (-er, -est) chiaro; (glass) trasparente; (without obstacles) libero; (profit) netto; (sky) sereno. —adv. chiaramente. —v.t. sgombrare; (goods) liquidare; (jurid.) discolpare; (obstacle) superare; (table) sparecchiare. —v.i. (weather) rasserenarsi. ~ off or out v.i. (sl.) andarsene. ~ up v.t. (tidy) riordinare; (mystery) chiarire; v.i. (weather) schiarirsi. **keep** ~ **of** tenersi lontano da. ~ly adv. chiaramente.

clearance /'klɪərəns/ n. spazio libero m.; (authorization) autorizzazione f.; (customs) sdoganamento m. ~ **sale** liquidazione f.

clearing /'klɪərɪŋ/ n. radura f.

clearway /'klɪəweɪ/ n. strada con divieto di sosta f.

cleavage /'kliːvɪdʒ/ n. spaccatura f.; (fig.) scollatura f.

cleave /kliːv/ v.t./i. (p.t. cleaved, clove or cleft; p.p. cloven or cleft) fendere, fendersi.

clef /klef/ n. (mus.) chiave f.

cleft /kleft/ see **cleave**. —n. fenditura f.

clemen|t /'klemənt/ a. clemente. ~cy n. clemenza f.

clench /klentʃ/ v.t. serrare.

clergy /'klɜːdʒɪ/ n. clero m. ~man n. (pl. -men) prete m.

cleric /'klerɪk/ n. chierico m. ~al a. clericale; (of clerks) di impiegato.

clerk /klɑːk/ n. impiegato, a m., f.

clever /'klevə(r)/ a. (-er, -est) intelligente; (skilful) abile. ~ly adv. intelligentemente; abilmente. ~ness n. intelligenza f.

cliché /'kliːʃeɪ/ n. cliché m. invar.

click /klɪk/ n. scatto m. —v.i. scattare; (sl.) andar d'accordo.

client /'klaɪənt/ n. cliente m./f.

clientele /kliːən'tel/ n. clientela f.

cliff /klɪf/ n. rupe f.

climat|e /'klaɪmɪt/ n. clima f. ~ic /-'mætɪk/ a. climatico.

climax /'klaɪmæks/ n. punto culminante m.

climb /klaɪm/ v.t./i. (stairs) salire; (hill) scalare; (tree) arrampicarsi su; (plants) arrampicarsi. —n. salita f. ~ **down** scendere; (fig.) tirarsi indietro. ~ **over** scavalcare. ~er n. (sport) alpinista m./f.; (plant) rampicante m.

clinch /klɪntʃ/ v.t. (deal) concludere.

cling /klɪŋ/ v.i. (p.t. clung) aggrapparsi; (*stick*) aderire. ~ **film** pellicola trasparente *f.*

clinic /'klɪnɪk/ *n.* ambulatorio *m.*; (*private*) clinica *f.*

clinical /'klɪnɪkl/ *a.* clinico.

clink /klɪŋk/ *n.* tintinnio *m.* —*v.t./i.* (far) tintinnare.

clinker /'klɪŋkə(r)/ *n.* scoria *f.*

clip[1] /klɪp/ *n.* (*for paper*) graffa *f.*; (*for hair*) molletta *f.* —*v.t.* (*p.t.* **clipped**) attaccare insieme.

clip[2] /klɪp/ *v.t.* tagliare; (*with shears*) tosare; (*fam.*) picchiare. —*n.* taglio *m.*; (*fam., blow*) scappellotto *m.* ~**ping** *n.* ritaglio *m.*

clippers /'klɪpəz/ *n.pl.* macchinetta per tosare *f.s.*; (*for nails*) forbicine (per le unghie) *f.pl.*

clique /kliːk/ *n.* cricca *f.*

cloak /kləʊk/ *n.* mantello *m.*

cloakroom /'kləʊkruːm/ *n.* guardaroba *m. invar.*; (*toilet*) toletta *f.*

clobber /'klɒbə(r)/ *n.* (*sl.*) indumenti *m.pl.* —*v.t.* (*sl.*) picchiare.

clock /klɒk/ *n.* orologio *m.* —*v.i.* cronometrare. ~ **in** timbrare il cartellino. **grandfather** ~ orologio a pendolo *m.*

clockwise /'klɒkwaɪz/ *a. & adv.* in senso orario.

clockwork /'klɒkwɜːk/ *n.* meccanismo a orologeria *m.* **like** ~ a perfezione.

clod /klɒd/ *n.* zolla *f.*

clog /klɒg/ *n.* zoccolo *m.* —*v.t./i.* (*p.t.* **clogged**) intasare, intasarsi.

cloister /'klɔɪstə(r)/ *n.* chiostro *m.*

close[1] /kləʊs/ *a.* (**-er, -est**) vicino; (*together*) accanto; (*friend*) intimo; (*weather*) afoso. —*adv.* (da) vicino. —*n.* recinto chiuso *m.* ~**-up** *n.* (*cinema etc.*) primo piano *m.* **have a** ~ **shave** (*fig.*) scamparla bella. ~**ly** *adv.* da vicino; (*with attention*) attentamente. ~**ness** *n.* prossimità *f.*; (*togetherness*) intimità *f.*

close[2] /kləʊz/ *v.t.* chiudere. —*v.i.* chiudersi; (*end*) terminare. —*n.* fine *f.* ~**d shop** azienda che assume solamente aderenti ai sindacati.

closet /'klɒzɪt/ *n.* (*Amer.*) armadio *m.*

closure /'kləʊʒə(r)/ *n.* chiusura *f.*

clot /klɒt/ *n.* grumo *m.*; (*sl.*) testone, a *m., f.* —*v.i.* (*p.t.* **clotted**) coagularsi. ~**ted cream** *n.* panna rappresa *f.*

cloth /klɒθ/ *n.* tessuto *m.*; (*duster*) straccio *m.*; (*table-cloth*) tovaglia *f.*

cloth|e /kləʊð/ *v.t.* (*p.t.* **clothed** *or* **clad**) vestire. ~**ing** *n.* vestiario *m.*

clothes /kləʊðz/ *n.pl.* vestiti, abiti *m.pl.*

cloud /klaʊd/ *n.* nuvola *f.* —*v.i.* annuvolarsi. ~**y** *a.* (**-ier, -iest**) nuvoloso; (*liquid*) torbido.

cloudburst /'klaʊdbɜːst/ *n.* acquazzone *m.*

clout /klaʊt/ *n.* colpo *m.* —*v.t.* colpire.

clove /kləʊv/ *see* **cleave.** —*n.* chiodo di garofano *m.* ~ **of garlic** spicchio d'aglio.

clover /'kləʊvə(r)/ *n.* trifoglio *m.*

clown /klaʊn/ *n.* pagliaccio *m.* —*v.i.* fare il pagliaccio.

cloy /klɔɪ/ *v.t.* saziare.

club /klʌb/ *n.* club, circolo *m.*; (*weapon*) mazza *f.*; (*sport*) bastone *m.*; (*at cards*) fiori *m.pl.* —*v.t./i.* (*p.t.* **clubbed**) bastonare. ~ **together** unirsi.

cluck /klʌk/ *v.i.* chiocciare.

clue /kluː/ *n.* indizio *m.*; (*in crosswords*) definizione *f.* **not to have a** ~ non aver la minima idea.

clump /klʌmp/ *n.* blocco *m.*; (*of trees*) gruppo *m.* —*v.t./i.* camminare pesantemente; (*group together*) ammucchiare.

clums|y /'klʌmzɪ/ *a.* (**-ier, -iest**) maldestro, goffo. ~**iness** *n.* goffaggine *f.*

clung /klʌŋ/ *see* **cling.**

cluster /'klʌstə(r)/ *n.* gruppo *m.* —*v.i.* raggrupparsi.

clutch /klʌtʃ/ *v.t.* afferrare. —*n.* stretta *f.*; (*auto.*) frizione *f.*

clutter /'klʌtə(r)/ *n.* disordine *m.* —*v.t.* ingombrare.

coach /kəʊtʃ/ *n.* pullman *m.*; (*of train*) vagone *m.*; (*horse-drawn*) carrozza *f.*; (*sport*) allena|tore, -trice *m., f.* —*v.t.* insegnare (privatamente); (*sport*) allenare.

coagulate /kəʊ'ægjʊleɪt/ *v.t./i.* coagulare, coagularsi.

coal /kəʊl/ *n.* carbone *m.*

coalfield /'kəʊlfiːld/ *n.* bacino carbonifero *m.*

coalition /kəʊə'lɪʃn/ *n.* coalizione *f.*

coarse /kɔːs/ *a.* (**-er, -est**) grossolano; (*of material*) ruvido. ~**ness** *n.* grossolanità *f.*; ruvidezza *f.*

coast /kəʊst/ *n.* costa *f.* —*v.i.* (*with cycle*) scendere a ruota libera; (*with car*) discendere in folle. ~**al** *a.* costiero.

coaster /'kəʊstə(r)/ *n.* (*for glass*) sottobicchiere *m. invar.*; (*for bottle*) sottobottiglia *m. invar.*

coastguard /'kəʊstgɑ:d/ n. guardia costiera f.

coastline /'kəʊstlaɪn/ n. litorale m.

coat /kəʊt/ n. cappotto m.; (of animal) manto m.; (of paint) mano f. —v.t. coprire. ∼ of arms stemma m. ∼ing n. rivestimento m.

coax /kəʊks/ v.t. persuadere con moine.

cob /kɒb/ n. (of corn) pannocchia f.

cobble[1] /'kɒbl/ n. ciottolo m.

cobble[2] /'kɒbl/ v.t. rappezzare.

cobbler /'kɒblə(r)/ n. (old use) ciabattino m.

cobweb /'kɒbweb/ n. ragnatela f.

cocaine /kəʊ'keɪn/ n. cocaina f.

cock /kɒk/ n. gallo m.; (mech.) valvola f.; (of gun) cane m. —v.t. drizzare; (gun) caricare. ∼-and-bull story panzana f. ∼-eyed a. (sl.) storto. ∼-up n. (sl.) pasticcio m.

cockerel /'kɒkərəl/ n. galletto m.

cockle /'kɒkl/ n. vongola f.

cockney /'kɒknɪ/ a. & n. (pl. -eys) londinese m./f.

cockpit /'kɒkpɪt/ n. (in aircraft) cabina f.

cockroach /'kɒkrəʊtʃ/ n. scarafaggio m.

cocksure /kɒk'ʃʊə(r)/ a. presuntuoso.

cocktail /'kɒkteɪl/ n. cocktail m. invar.

cocky /'kɒkɪ/ a. (-ier, -iest) impertinente.

cocoa /'kəʊkəʊ/ n. cacao m.

coconut /'kəʊkənʌt/ n. noce di cocco f.

cocoon /kə'ku:n/ n. bozzolo m.

cod /kɒd/ n. (pl. cod) merluzzo m. ∼-liver oil olio di fegato di merluzzo m.

coddle /'kɒdl/ v.t. coccolare; (culin.) far bollire (un uovo) lentamente.

code /kəʊd/ n. codice m.

codify /'kəʊdɪfaɪ/ v.t. codificare.

coeducational /kəʊedʒʊ'keɪʃənl/ a. misto.

coerc|e /kəʊ'ɜ:s/ v.t. costringere. ∼ion /-ʃn/ n. forza f.

coexist /kəʊɪg'zɪst/ v.i. coesistere. ∼ence n. coesistenza f.

coffee /'kɒfɪ/ n. caffè m. ∼-mill macinino del caffè m. ∼-pot caffettiera f.

coffer /'kɒfə(r)/ n. forziere m.

coffin /'kɒfɪn/ n. bara f.

cog /kɒg/ n. dente (di ruota) m.

cogent /'kəʊdʒənt/ a. persuasivo.

cohabit /kəʊ'hæbɪt/ v.i. convivere.

coherent /kəʊ'hɪərənt/ a. coerente.

coil /kɔɪl/ v.t. avvolgere. —n. rotolo m.; (one ring) spira f.

coin /kɔɪn/ n. moneta f. —v.t. (word, phrase) coniare. ∼age n. sistema monetario m.

coincide /kəʊɪn'saɪd/ v.i. coincidere.

coinciden|ce /kəʊ'ɪnsɪdəns/ n. coincidenza f. ∼tal /-'dentl/ a. coincidente.

coke /kəʊk/ n. (carbone) coke m.

colander /'kʌləndə(r)/ n. colabrodo m. invar.

cold /kəʊld/ a. (-er, -est) freddo. be ∼ aver freddo. it is ∼ fa freddo. —n. freddo m.; (med.) raffreddore m. ∼-blooded a. insensibile. ∼ cream crema emolliente f. ∼ feet (fig.) fifa f. ∼-shoulder v.t. snobbare. in ∼ storage in frigorifero. ∼ness n. freddezza f.

coleslaw /'kəʊlslɔ:/ n. insalata di cavolo crudo f.

colic /'kɒlɪk/ n. colica f.

collaborat|e /kə'læbəreɪt/ v.i. collaborare. ∼ion /-'reɪʃn/ n. collaborazione f. ∼or n. collabora|tore, -trice m., f.

collage /'kɒlɑ:ʒ/ n. collage m. invar.

collapse /kə'læps/ v.i. crollare; (med.) avere un collasso. —n. crollo m.; (med.) collasso m.

collapsible /kə'læpsəbl/ a. pieghevole.

collar /'kɒlə(r)/ n. colletto m. —v.t. (fam.) afferrare. ∼-bone n. clavicola f.

colleague /'kɒli:g/ n. collega m./f.

collect /kə'lekt/ v.t. raccogliere; (hobby) collezionare; (pick up) andare a prendere; (rent) riscuotere. —v.i. riunirsi; (of dust) raccogliersi. ∼ion /-ʃn/ n. collezione f.; (in church) colletta f.; (of post) levata f. ∼or n. collezionista m./f.; (of taxes) esattore m.

collected /kə'lektɪd/ a. padrone di sé.

collective /kə'lektɪv/ a. collettivo.

college /'kɒlɪdʒ/ n. collegio m.

collide /kə'laɪd/ v.i. scontrarsi.

colliery /'kɒlɪərɪ/ n. miniera di carbone f.

collision /kə'lɪʒn/ n. investimento m.; (fig.) conflitto m.

colloquial /kə'ləʊkwɪəl/ a. familiare. ∼ism n. expressione familiare f.

collusion /kə'lu:ʒn/ n. collusione f.

colon /'kəʊlən/ n. (gram.) due punti m. invar.; (med.) colon m. invar.

colonel /'kɜ:nl/ n. colonnello m.

colonize /'kɒlənaɪz/ v.t. colonizzare.

colon|y /'kɒlənɪ/ n. colonia f. ∼ial /kə'ləʊnɪəl/ a. coloniale.

colossal /kə'lɒsl/ a. colossale.

colour /'kʌlə(r)/ *n.* colore *m.*; (*complexion*) colorito *m.* ~s *n.pl.* (*flag*) bandiera *f.s.* —*a.* a colori. —*v.t.* colorare; (*dye*) tingere. —*v.i.* (*blush*) arrossire. ~ **bar** *n.* discriminazione razziale *f.* ~-**blind** *a.* daltonico. **off** ~ (*fig.*) giù di corda. ~**ful** *a.* pieno di colore; (*fig.*) pittoresco. ~**less** *a.* incolore.

coloured /'kʌləd/ *a.* (*person*) di colore; (*pencil*) a colori.

colt /kəʊlt/ *n.* puledro *m.*

column /'kɒləm/ *n.* colonna *f.*

columnist /'kɒləmnɪst/ *n.* cronista *m.|f.*

coma /'kəʊmə/ *n.* coma *m.*

comb /kəʊm/ *n.* pettine *m.* —*v.t.* pettinare; (*search*) rastrellare.

combat /'kɒmbæt/ *n.* combattimento *m.* —*v.t.* (*p.t.* **combated**) combattere. ~**ant** /-ətənt/ *n.* combattente *m.|f.*

combination /kɒmbɪ'neɪʃn/ *n.* combinazione *f.*

combine[1] /kəm'baɪn/ *v.t.* combinare. —*v.i.* unirsi.

combine[2] /'kɒmbaɪn/ *n.* associazione *f.* ~ **harvester** *n.* mietitrebbia *f.*

combustion /kəm'bʌstʃən/ *n.* combustione *f.*

come /kʌm/ *v.i.* (*p.t.* **came**, *p.p.* **come**) venire; (*occur*) accadere. ~ **about** succedere. ~ **across** (*person*) imbattersi in; (*object*) trovare. ~ **apart** staccarsi. ~ **away** venir via. ~ **back** ritornare. ~-**back** *n.* ritorno *m.*; (*retort*) replica *f.* ~ **by** ottenere; (*pass*) passare. ~ **down** scendere; (*price*) calare. ~-**down** *n.* rovescio di fortuna *m.* ~ **in** entrare. ~ **in for** ricevere. ~ **into** (*money*) ereditare. ~ **off** cadere da; (*succeed*) riuscire. ~ **off it!** (*fam.*) basta! ~ **out** venir fuori; (*result*) risultare. ~ **round** (*after fainting*) riaversi; (*be converted*) cambiare opinione. ~ **to** (*decision etc.*) raggiungere. ~ **up** salire; (*fig.*) saltar fuori. ~-**uppance** *n.* (*Amer.*) giusta punizione *f.* ~ **up with** (*idea*) proporre.

comedian /kə'miːdɪən/ *n.* comico *m.*

comedy /'kɒmədɪ/ *n.* commedia *f.*

comely /'kʌmlɪ/ *a.* (-**ier**, -**iest**) (*old use*) avvenente.

comet /'kɒmɪt/ *n.* cometa *f.*

comfort /'kʌmfət/ *n.* conforto *m.* —*v.t.* confortare. ~**able** *a.* comodo; (*wealthy*) agiato.

comfy /'kʌmfɪ/ *a.* (*fam.*) comodo.

comic /'kɒmɪk/ *a.* comico. —*n.* comico *m.*; (*periodical*) fumetto *m.* ~ **strip** racconto a fumetti *m.* ~**al** *a.* comico.

coming /'kʌmɪŋ/ *n.* venuta *f.* —*a.* prossimo. ~ **and going** andirivieni *m. invar.*

comma /'kɒmə/ *n.* virgola *f.*

command /kə'mɑːnd/ *n.* comando *m.*; (*mastery*) padronanza *f.* —*v.t.* comandare; (*deserve*) meritare. ~**er** *n.* capo *m.*; (*mil.*) comandante *m.* ~**ing** *a.* imponente.

commandment /kə'mɑːndmənt/ *n.* comandamento *m.*

commando /kə'mɑːndəʊ/ *n.* (*pl.* -**os**) commando *m. invar.*

commemorat|e /kə'meməreɪt/ *v.t.* commemorare. ~**ion** /-'reɪʃn/ *n.* commemorazione *f.* ~**ive** /-ətɪv/ *a.* commemorativo.

commence /kə'mens/ *v.t.|i.* cominciare. ~**ment** *n.* inizio *m.*

commend /kə'mend/ *v.t.* lodare; (*entrust*) affidare. ~**able** *a.* lodevole. ~**ation** /kɒmen'deɪʃn/ *n.* elogio *m.*

commensurate /kə'menʃərət/ *a.* proporzionato.

comment /'kɒment/ *n.* commento *m.* —*v.i.* commentare.

commentary /'kɒməntrɪ/ *n.* commentario *m.*; (*radio*, *TV*) cronaca *f.*

commentat|e /'kɒmənteɪt/ *v.i.* fare la radiocronaca. ~**or** *n.* (*radio*) radiocronista *m.|f.*; (*TV*) telecronista *m.|f.*

commerce /'kɒmɜːs/ *n.* commercio *m.*

commercial /kə'mɜːʃl/ *a.* commerciale. —*n.* pubblicità commerciale *f.* ~**ize** *v.t.* commercializzare.

commiserat|e /kə'mɪzəreɪt/ *v.t.|i.* commiserare. ~**ion** /-'reɪʃn/ *n.* commiserazione *f.*

commission /kə'mɪʃn/ *n.* commissione *f.* —*v.t.* commissionare; (*mil.*) nominare (al comando). **out of** ~ fuori servizio. ~**er** *n.* commissario *m.*; (*of police*) questore *m.*

commissionaire /kəmɪʃə'neə(r)/ *n.* portiere *m.*

commit /kə'mɪt/ *v.t.* (*p.t.* **committed**) commettere; (*entrust*) affidare. ~ **o.s.** impegnarsi. ~ **to memory** imparare a memoria. ~**ment** *n.* impegno *m.*

committee /kə'mɪtɪ/ *n.* comitato *m.*

commodity /kə'mɒdətɪ/ *n.* prodotto *m.*

common /'kɒmən/ *a.* (-**er**, -**est**) comune; (*usual*) solito. —*n.* prato pubblico *m.* ~ **law** diritto consuetudinario *m.* **C**~ **Market** Mercato Comune *m.* ~-**room** sala dei professori/degli studenti *f.* ~ **sense** buon senso *m.* **House of C~s** Camera dei Comuni *f.* ~**ly** *adv.* comunemente.

commoner /'kɒmənə(r)/ *n.* cittadino, a comune *m., f.*

commonplace /'kɒmənpleɪs/ *a.* banale. —*n.* banalità *f.*

Commonwealth /'kɒmənwelθ/ *n.* **the** ~ il Commonwealth *m.*

commotion /kə'məʊʃn/ *n.* confusione *f.*

communal /'kɒmjʊnl/ *a.* comune.

commune[1] /kə'mju:n/ *v.i.* confidarsi.

commune[2] /'kɒmju:n/ *n.* comune *m.*; (*of students*) comune *f.*

communicat|e /kə'mju:nɪkeɪt/ *v.t./i.* comunicare. ~**ion** /-'keɪʃn/ *n.* comunicazione *f.* ~**ive** /-ətɪv/ *a.* comunicativo.

communion /kə'mju:nɪən/ *n.* comunione *f.*

communiqué /kə'mju:nɪkeɪ/ *n.* comunicato *m.*

communis|t /'kɒmjʊnɪst/ *n.* comunista *m./f.* ~**m** /-zəm/ *n.* comunismo *m.*

community /kə'mju:nətɪ/ *n.* comunità *f.* ~ **centre** centro sociale *m.*

commute /kə'mju:t/ *v.i.* viaggiare giornalmente. —*v.t.* (*jurid.*) commutare. ~**r** /-ə(r)/ *n.* (viaggia|tore, -trice) pendolare *m., f.*

compact[1] /kəm'pækt/ *a.* compatto.

compact[2] /'kɒmpækt/ *n.* portacipria *m. invar.*

companion /kəm'pænɪən/ *n.* compagno, a *m., f.* ~**ship** *n.* compagnia *f.*

company /'kʌmpənɪ/ *n.* compagnia *f.*; (*fam., guests*) ospiti *m.pl.*

comparable /'kɒmpərəbl/ *a.* paragonabile.

compar|e /kəm'peə(r)/ *v.t./i.* paragonare, paragonarsi. ~**ative** /-'pærətɪv/ *a.* comparativo; (*fig.*) relativo; *n.* (*gram.*) comparativo *m.*

comparison /kəm'pærɪsn/ *n.* paragone *m.*

compartment /kəm'pɑːtmənt/ *n.* compartimento *m.*; (*on train*) scompartimento *m.*

compass /'kʌmpəs/ *n.* bussola *f.* ~**es** *n.pl.* compasso *m.s.*

compassion /kəm'pæʃn/ *n.* compassione *f.* ~**ate** *a.* compassionevole.

compatib|le /kəm'pætəbl/ *a.* compatibile. ~**ility** /-'bɪlətɪ/ *n.* compatibilità *f.*

compatriot /kəm'pætrɪət/ *n.* compatriota *m./f.*

compel /kəm'pel/ *v.t.* (*p.t.* **compelled**) costringere. ~**ling** *a.* irresistibile.

compendium /kəm'pendɪəm/ *n.* compendio *m.*

compensat|e /'kɒmpənseɪt/ *v.t./i.* compensare; (*for loss*) risarcire. ~**ion** /-'seɪʃn/ *n.* compenso *m.*; (*financial*) risarcimento *m.*

compère /'kɒmpeə(r)/ *n.* presenta|tore, -trice *m., f.* —*v.t.* presentare.

compete /kəm'piːt/ *v.i.* competere.

competen|t /'kɒmpɪtənt/ *a.* competente. ~**ce** *n.* competenza *f.*

competition /kɒmpə'tɪʃn/ *n.* (*contest*) competizione *f.*; (*comm.*) concorrenza *f.*

competitive /kəm'petətɪv/ *a.* competitivo. ~ **prices** prezzi di concorrenza *m.pl.*

competitor /kəm'petɪtə(r)/ *n.* concorrente *m./f.*

compile /kəm'paɪl/ *v.t.* compilare. ~**r** /-ə(r)/ *n.* compila|tore, -trice *m., f.*

complacen|t /kəm'pleɪsnt/ *a.* compiaciuto. ~**cy** *n.* compiacimento *m.*

complain /kəm'pleɪn/ *v.i.* ~ (**about**) lagnarsi (di). ~ **of** (*med.*) accusare.

complaint /kəm'pleɪnt/ *n.* lagnanza *f.*; (*med.*) malattia *f.*

complement /'kɒmplɪmənt/ *n.* complemento *m.* —*v.t.* completare. ~**ary** /-'mentrɪ/ *a.* complementare.

complet|e /kəm'pliːt/ *a.* completo; (*finished*) finito; (*downright*) perfetto. —*v.t.* completare; (*a form*) riempire. ~**ely** *adv.* completamente. ~**ion** /-ʃn/ *n.* completamento *m.*

complex /'kɒmpleks/ *a.* complesso. —*n.* complesso *m.* ~**ity** /kəm'pleksətɪ/ *n.* complessità *f.*

complexion /kəm'plekʃn/ *n.* carnagione *f.*; (*fig.*) carattere *m.*

complian|ce /kəm'plaɪəns/ *n.* acquiescenza *f.*; (*agreement*) osservanza *f.* ~**t** *a.* acquiescente.

complicat|e /'kɒmplɪkeɪt/ *v.t.* complicare. ~**ed** *a.* complicato. ~**ion** /-'keɪʃn/ *n.* complicazione *f.*

complicity /kəm'plɪsətɪ/ *n.* complicità *f.*

compliment /'kɒmplɪmənt/ *n.* complimento *m.* ~**s** *n.pl.* omaggi *m.pl.* —*v.t.* complimentare. ~**ary** /-'mentrɪ/ *a.* complimentoso; (*given free*) in omaggio.

comply /kəm'plaɪ/ *v.i.* ~ **with** conformarsi a.

component /kəm'pəunənt/ *a.* & *n.* componente *m.*

compose /kəm'pəuz/ *v.t.* comporre. ~ **o.s.** calmarsi. ~**d** *a.* composto, calmo. ~**r** /-ə(r)/ *n.* compositore *m.*

composition /kɒmpə'zɪʃn/ *n.* composizione *f.*

compost /'kɒmpɒst/ *n.* composta *f.*

composure /kəm'pəuʒə(r)/ *n.* calma *f.*

compound[1] /'kɒmpaund/ *n.* composto *m.*; (*enclosure*) recinto *m.* —*a.* composto.

compound[2] /kəm'paund/ *v.t.* comporre. —*v.i.* (*settle*) accordarsi.

comprehen|d /kɒmprɪ'hend/ *v.t.* comprendere; (*include*) includere. ~**sion** *n.* comprensione *f.*

comprehensive /kɒmprɪ'hensɪv/ *a.* comprensivo. ~ **school** scuola media unica *f.*

compress[1] /kəm'pres/ *v.t.* comprimere. ~**ion** /-ʃn/ *n.* compressione *f.*

compress[2] /'kɒmpres/ *n.* (*med.*) compressa *f.*

comprise /kəm'praɪz/ *v.t.* comprendere.

compromise /'kɒmprəmaɪz/ *n.* compromesso *m.* —*v.t.* compromettere. —*v.i.* giungere a un compromesso.

compulsion /kəm'pʌlʃn/ *n.* desiderio irresistibile *m.*

compulsive /kəm'pʌlsɪv/ *a.* coercitivo; (*psych.*) incorreggibile.

compulsory /kəm'pʌlsərɪ/ *a.* obbligatorio.

compunction /kəm'pʌŋkʃn/ *n.* scrupolo *m.*

computer /kəm'pju:tə(r)/ *n.* computer *m.* ~**ize** *v.t.* computerizzare.

comrade /'kɒmreɪd/ *n.* camerata *m.*/*f.* ~**ship** *n.* cameratismo *m.*

con[1] /kɒn/ *v.t.* (*p.t.* **conned**) (*fam.*) imbrogliare. —*n.* (*fam.*) truffa *f.* ~**man** *n.* (*fam.*) truffatore *m.*

con[2] /kɒn/ *see* **pro and con.**

concave /'kɒŋkeɪv/ *a.* concavo.

conceal /kən'si:l/ *v.t.* celare. ~**ment** *n.* celamento *m.*

concede /kən'si:d/ *v.t.* concedere.

conceit /kən'si:t/ *n.* vanità *f.* ~**ed** *a.* vanitoso.

conceivabl|e /kən'si:vəbl/ *a.* concepibile. ~**y** *adv.* in modo concepibile.

conceive /kən'si:v/ *v.t.*/*i.* concepire.

concentrat|e /'kɒnsəntreɪt/ *v.t.*/*i.* concentrare, concentrarsi. ~**ion** /-'treɪʃn/ *n.* concentrazione *f.* ~**ion camp** campo di concentramento *m.*

concept /'kɒnsept/ *n.* concetto *m.* ~**ual** /kən'septʃuəl/ *a.* concettuale.

conception /kən'sepʃn/ *n.* concezione *f.*

concern /kən'sɜ:n/ *n.* affare *m.*; (*worry*) ansietà *f.*; (*comm.*) azienda *f.* —*v.t.* riguardare. **be** ~**ed about** essere preoccupato per. ~**ing** *prep.* riguardo a.

concert /'kɒnsət/ *n.* concerto *m.* **in** ~ di comune accordo. ~**ed** /-'sɜ:tɪd/ *a.* concertato.

concertina /kɒnsə'ti:nə/ *n.* piccola fisarmonica *f.*

concerto /kən'tʃɜ:təu/ *n.* (*pl.* **-os**) concerto *m.*

concession /kən'seʃn/ *n.* concessione *f.*

conciliat|e /kən'sɪlɪeɪt/ *v.t.* conciliare. ~**ion** /-'eɪʃn/ *n.* conciliazione *f.*

concise /kən'saɪs/ *a.* conciso. ~**ly** *adv.* concisamente. ~**ness** *n.* concisione *f.*

conclu|de /kən'klu:d/ *v.t.*/*i.* concludere. ~**ding** *a.* finale. ~**sion** *n.* conclusione *f.*

conclusive /kən'klu:sɪv/ *a.* conclusivo. ~**ly** *adv.* in modo conclusivo.

concoct /kən'kɒkt/ *v.t.* confezionare; (*fig.*) inventare. ~**ion** /-ʃn/ *n.* mistura *f.*

concourse /'kɒŋkɔ:s/ *n.* (*rail.*) atrio *m.*

concrete /'kɒŋkri:t/ *n.* calcestruzzo *m.* —*a.* concreto. —*v.t.* ricoprire di calcestruzzo. —*v.i.* solidificarsi.

concur /kən'kɜ:(r)/ *v.i.* (*p.t.* **concurred**) essere d'accordo.

concussion /kən'kʌʃn/ *n.* commozione cerebrale *f.*

condemn /kən'dem/ *v.t.* condannare. ~**ation** /kɒndem'neɪʃn/ *n.* condanna *f.*

condens|e /kən'dens/ *v.t.*/*i.* condensare, condensarsi. ~**ation** /kɒnden'seɪʃn/ *n.* condensazione *f.*

condescend /kɒndɪ'send/ *v.i.* condiscendere. ~**ing** *a.* condiscendente.

condiment /'kɒndɪmənt/ *n.* condimento *m.*

condition /kən'dɪʃn/ *n.* condizione *f.* —*v.t.* condizionare. **on** ~ **that** a condizione che. ~**al** *a.* condizionale. ~**er** *n.* balsamo (per capelli) *m.*

condolences /kən'dəulənsɪz/ *n.pl.* condoglianze *f.pl.*

condone /kən'dəun/ *v.t.* condonare.

conducive /kən'dju:sɪv/ *a.* **be** ~ **to** contribuire a.

conduct[1] /kən'dʌkt/ *v.t.* condurre; (*orchestra*) dirigere.

conduct[2] /'kɒndʌkt/ *n.* condotta *f.*

conduct|or /kən'dʌktə(r)/ *n.* direttore d'orchestra *m.*; (*of bus*) bigliettaio *m.* ~ress *n.* bigliettaia *f.*

cone /kəʊn/ *n.* cono *m.*

confectioner /kən'fekʃnə(r)/ *n.* pasticciere, a *m.*, *f.* ~y *n.* pasticceria *f.*

confederation /kənfedə'reɪʃn/ *n.* confederazione *f.*

confer /kən'fɜː(r)/ *v.t./i.* (*p.t.* **conferred**) conferire.

conference /'kɒnfərəns/ *n.* conferenza *f.*

confess /kən'fes/ *v.t./i.* confessare, confessarsi. ~ion /-ʃn/ *n.* confessione *f.* ~ional *n.* confessionale *m.* ~or *n.* confessore *m.*

confetti /kən'fetɪ/ *n.* coriandoli *m.pl.*

confide /kən'faɪd/ *v.t./i.* confidare, confidarsi.

confiden|t /'kɒnfɪdənt/ *a.* sicuro. ~ce *n.* (*trust*) fiducia *f.*; (*self-assurance*) sicurezza di sé *f.*; (*secret*) confidenza *f.* ~ce trick truffa *f.*

confidential /kɒnfɪ'denʃl/ *a.* confidenziale.

confine /kən'faɪn/ *v.t.* relegare; (*limit*) limitare. ~ment *n.* detenzione *f.*; (*med.*) parto *m.*

confines /'kɒnfaɪnz/ *n.pl.* confini *m.pl.*

confirm /kən'fɜːm/ *v.t.* confermare. ~ation /kɒnfə'meɪʃn/ *n.* conferma *f.* ~ed *a.* inveterato.

confiscat|e /'kɒnfɪskeɪt/ *v.t.* confiscare. ~ion /-'keɪʃn/ *n.* confisca *f.*

conflagration /kɒnflə'greɪʃn/ *n.* conflagrazione *f.*

conflict[1] /'kɒnflɪkt/ *n.* conflitto *m.*

conflict[2] /kən'flɪkt/ *v.i.* essere in conflitto. ~ing *a.* contrastante.

conform /kən'fɔːm/ *v.t./i.* conformare, conformarsi. ~ist *n.* conformista *m./f.*

confound /kən'faʊnd/ *v.t.* confondere. ~ed *a.* (*fam.*) maledetto.

confront /kən'frʌnt/ *v.t.* confrontare; (*face*) affrontare. ~ation /kɒnfrʌn'teɪʃn/ *n.* confronto *m.*

confus|e /kən'fjuːz/ *v.t.* confondere. ~ing *a.* che confonde. ~ion /-ʒn/ *n.* confusione *f.*

congeal /kən'dʒiːl/ *v.t./i.* congelare, congelarsi.

congenial /kən'dʒiːnɪəl/ *a.* simpatico.

congenital /kən'dʒenɪtl/ *a.* congenito.

congest|ed /kən'dʒestɪd/ *a.* congestionato. ~ion /-tʃən/ *n.* congestione *f.*

congratulat|e /kən'grætjʊleɪt/ *v.t.* congratularsi con. ~ions /-'leɪʃnz/ *n.pl.* congratulazioni *f.pl.*

congregat|e /'kɒŋgrɪgeɪt/ *v.i.* congregarsi. ~ion /-'geɪʃn/ *n.* assemblea *f.*

congress /'kɒŋgres/ *n.* congresso *m.* C~ (*Amer.*) il Congresso *m.*

conic(al) /'kɒnɪk(l)/ *a.* conico.

conifer /'kɒnɪfə(r)/ *n.* conifero *m.*

conjecture /kən'dʒektʃə(r)/ *n.* congettura *f.* —*v.t./i.* congetturare.

conjugal /'kɒndʒʊgl/ *a.* coniugale.

conjugate /'kɒndʒʊgeɪt/ *v.t.* coniugare. ~ion /-'geɪʃn/ *n.* coniugazione *f.*

conjunction /kən'dʒʌŋkʃn/ *n.* congiunzione *f.*

conjur|e /'kʌndʒə(r)/ *v.i.* fare giochi di prestigio. —*v.t.* ~e up evocare. ~or *n.* prestigia|tore, -trice *m.*, *f.*

conk /kɒŋk/ *n.* (*sl.*) naso *m.* —*v.t.* (*sl.*) colpire. —*v.i.* ~ out (*sl.*) guastarsi; (*person*) svenire.

conker /'kɒŋkə(r)/ *n.* (*fam.*) castagna *f.*

connect /kə'nekt/ *v.t./i.* collegare, collegarsi; (*of train*) far coincidenza. ~ed *a.* connesso. be ~ed with far parte di. be well ~ed aver conoscenze influenti.

connection /kə'nekʃn/ *n.* connessione *f.*; (*rail.*) coincidenza *f.*; (*mech.*) attacco *m.* ~s *n.pl.* conoscenze *f.pl.* in ~ with con riferimento a.

conniv|e /kə'naɪv/ *v.i.* ~e at essere connivente a. ~ance *n.* connivenza *f.*

connoisseur /kɒnə'sɜː(r)/ *n.* intendi|tore, -trice *m.*, *f.*

connot|e /kə'nəʊt/ *v.t.* implicare. ~ation /kɒnə'teɪʃn/ *n.* connotazione *f.*

conquer /'kɒŋkə(r)/ *v.t.* conquistare; (*fig.*) superare. ~or *n.* conquistatore *m.*

conquest /'kɒŋkwest/ *n.* conquista *f.*

conscience /'kɒnʃəns/ *n.* coscienza *f.*

conscientious /kɒnʃɪ'enʃəs/ *a.* coscienzioso.

conscious /'kɒnʃəs/ *a.* conscio. ~ly *adv.* consapevolmente. ~ness *n.* consapevolezza *f.*; (*med.*) conoscenza *f.*

conscript[1] /kən'skrɪpt/ *v.t.* chiamare alle armi. ~ion /-ʃn/ *n.* coscrizione, leva *f.*

conscript[2] /'kɒnskrɪpt/ *n.* coscritto *m.*

consecrat|e /'kɒnsɪkreɪt/ *v.t.* consacrare. ~ion /-'kreɪʃn/ *n.* consacrazione *f.*

consecutive /kən'sekjʊtɪv/ *a.* consecutivo.

consensus /kən'sensəs/ *n.* consenso *m.*

consent /kən'sent/ *v.i.* consentire. —*n.* consenso *m.*

consequence /'kɒnsɪkwəns/ *n.* conseguenza *f.*

consequent /'kɒnsɪkwənt/ *a.* conseguente. ~ly *adv.* di conseguenza.

conservation /kɒnsə'veɪʃn/ *n.* conservazione *f.*

conservationist /kɒnsə'veɪʃənɪst/ *n.* sosteni|tore, -trice della preservazione di risorse naturali *m.*, *f.*

conservative /kən'sɜːvətɪv/ *a.* conservativo; (*modest*) cauto. C~ *a.* & *n.* conserva|tore, -trice *m.*, *f.*

conservatory /kən'sɜːvətrɪ/ *n.* serra *f.*

conserve /kən'sɜːv/ *v.t.* conservare.

consider /kən'sɪdə(r)/ *v.t.* considerare; (*take into account*) tener conto di. ~ation /-'reɪʃn/ *n.* considerazione *f.*; (*respect*) deferenza *f.* ~ing *prep.* in considerazione di.

considerabl|e /kən'sɪdərəbl/ *a.* considerevole. ~y *adv.* notevolmente.

considerate /kən'sɪdərət/ *a.* sollecito.

consign /kən'saɪn/ *v.t.* consegnare; (*send*) spedire. ~ment *n.* consegna *f.*

consist /kən'sɪst/ *v.i.* ~ of essere composto di.

consisten|t /kən'sɪstənt/ *a.* coerente; (*unchanging*) costante. ~t with compatibile con. ~cy *n.* consistenza *f.*; ~tly *adv.* costantemente.

consol|e /kən'səʊl/ *v.t.* consolare. ~ation /kɒnsə'leɪʃn/ *n.* consolazione *f.*

consolidat|e /kən'splɪdeɪt/ *v.t./i.* consolidare, consolidarsi. ~ion /-'deɪʃn/ *n.* consolidazione *f.*

consonant /'kɒnsənənt/ *n.* consonante *f.*

consort¹ /'kɒnsɔːt/ *n.* consorte *m.*/*f.*

consort² /kən'sɔːt/ *v.i.* ~ with frequentare.

consortium /kən'sɔːtɪəm/ *n.* (*pl.* -tia) consorzio *m.*

conspicuous /kən'spɪkjʊəs/ *a.* cospicuo.

conspiracy /kən'spɪrəsɪ/ *n.* cospirazione *f.*

conspire /kən'spaɪə(r)/ *v.i.* cospirare.

constable /'kʌnstəbl/ *n.* poliziotto *m.*

constabulary /kən'stæbjʊlərɪ/ *n.* corpo di polizia *m.*

constant /'kɒnstənt/ *a.* costante; (*un-*

ceasing) continuo. ~ly *adv.* costantemente.

constellation /kɒnstə'leɪʃn/ *n.* costellazione *f.*

consternation /kɒnstə'neɪʃn/ *n.* costernazione *f.*

constipat|ed /'kɒnstɪpeɪtɪd/ *a.* stitico. ~ion /-'peɪʃn/ *n.* stitichezza *f.*

constituency /kən'stɪtjʊənsɪ/ *n.* collegio elettorale *m.*

constituent /kən'stɪtjʊənt/ —*n.* elemento costituente *m.*; (*pol.*) elet|tore, -trice *m.*, *f.*

constitut|e /'kɒnstɪtjuːt/ *v.t.* costituire. ~ion /-'tjuːʃn/ *n.* costituzione *f.* ~ional /-'tjuːʃnl/ *a.* costituzionale; *n.* passeggiata igienica *f.*

constrain /kən'streɪn/ *v.t.* costringere.

constraint /kən'streɪnt/ *n.* costrizione *f.*

constrict /kən'strɪkt/ *v.t.* restringere. ~ion /-ʃn/ *n.* restringimento *m.*

construct /kən'strʌkt/ *v.t.* costruire. ~ion /-ʃn/ *n.* costruzione *f.*

constructive /kən'strʌktɪv/ *a.* costruttivo.

construe /kən'struː/ *v.t.* interpretare; (*gram.*) costruire.

consul /'kɒnsl/ *n.* console *m.* ~ar /-jʊlə(r)/ *a.* consolare. ~ate /-ət/ *n.* consolato *m.*

consult /kən'sʌlt/ *v.t./i.* consultare, consultarsi. ~ation /kɒnsl'teɪʃn/ *n.* consultazione *f.*; (*med.*) consulto *m.*

consultant /kən'sʌltənt/ *n.* consulente *m.*/*f.*

consume /kən'sjuːm/ *v.t.* consumare. ~r /-ə(r)/ *n.* consuma|tore, -trice *m.*, *f.*; *a.* di consumo.

consumerism /kən'sjuːmərɪzəm/ *n.* protezione dei consumatori *f.*

consummat|e /'kɒnsəmeɪt/ *v.t.* consumare. ~ion /-'meɪʃn/ *n.* consumazione *f.*

consumption /kən'sʌmpʃn/ *n.* consumo *m.*; (*med.*) tisi *f.*

contact /'kɒntækt/ *n.* contatto *m.* —*v.t.* mettersi in contatto con.

contagious /kən'teɪdʒəs/ *a.* contagioso.

contain /kən'teɪn/ *v.t.* contenere. ~ o.s. controllarsi. ~er *n.* recipiente *m.*; (*comm.*) container *m.*

contaminat|e /kən'tæmɪneɪt/ *v.t.* contaminare. ~ion /-'neɪʃn/ *n.* contaminazione *f.*

contemplat|e /'kɒntempleɪt/ *v.t.*

contemplare; (*consider*) intendere. ~ion /-'pleɪʃn/ *n.* contemplazione *f.*

contemporary /kən'tempərərɪ/ *a. & n.* contemporaneo, a *m., f.*

contempt /kən'tempt/ *n.* disprezzo *m.* ~ible *a.* spregevole. ~uous /-tʃʊəs/ *a.* sprezzante.

contend /kən'tend/ *v.t./i.* contendere; (*assert*) sostenere. ~er *n.* contendente *m./f.*

content[1] /kən'tent/ *a.* soddisfatto. —*v.t.* contentare. ~ed *a.* soddisfatto. ~ment *n.* contentezza *f.*

content[2] /'kɒntent/ *n.* contenuto *m.*

contention /kən'tenʃn/ *n.* contesa *f.*; (*opinion*) opinione *f.*

contest[1] /'kɒntest/ *n.* (*fight*) contesa *f.*; (*sport*) gara *f.*

contest[2] /kən'test/ *v.t.* contestare; (*dispute*) disputare. ~ant *n.* concorrente *m./f.*

context /'kɒntekst/ *n.* contesto *m.*

continent /'kɒntɪnənt/ *n.* continente *m.* the C~ l'Europa (continentale) *f.* ~al /-'nentl/ *a.* continentale.

contingen|t /kən'tɪndʒənt/ *a.* contingente. —*n.* contingenza *f.* ~cy *n.* contingenza *f.*

continual /kən'tɪnjʊəl/ *a.* continuo.

continu|e /kən'tɪnjuː/ *v.t./i.* continuare; (*resume*) riprendere. ~ance *n.* continuità *f.* ~ation /-ʊ'eɪʃn/ *n.* continuazione *f.* ~ed *a.* continuo.

continuous /kən'tɪnjʊəs/ *a.* continuo. ~ly *adv.* continuamente.

continuity /kɒntɪ'njuːətɪ/ *n.* continuità *f.* ~ girl (*cinema, TV*) segretaria di produzione *f.*

contort /kən'tɔːt/ *v.t.* contorcere. ~ion /-ʃn/ *n.* contorcimento *m.* ~ionist /-ʃənɪst/ *n.* contorsionista *m./f.*

contour /'kɒntʊə(r)/ *n.* contorno, profilo *m.*

contraband /'kɒntrəbænd/ *n.* contrabbando *m.*

contraception /kɒntrə'sepʃn/ *n.* controllo delle nascite *m.*

contraceptive /kɒntrə'septɪv/ *a. & n.* contraccettivo *m.*

contract[1] /'kɒntrækt/ *n.* contratto *m.*

contract[2] /kən'trækt/ *v.t./i.* contrarre. ~ion /-ʃn/ *n.* contrazione *f.*

contractor /kən'træktə(r)/ *n.* imprenditore *m.*

contradict /kɒntrə'dɪkt/ *v.t.* contraddire. ~ion /-ʃn/ *n.* contraddizione *f.* ~ory *a.* contraddittorio.

contraption /kən'træpʃn/ *n.* (*fam.*) aggeggio *m.*

contrary[1] /'kɒntrərɪ/ *a.* contrario. —*n.* contrario *m.* —*adv.* ~ to contrariamente a. **on the** ~ al contrario.

contrary[2] /kən'treərɪ/ *a.* avverso.

contrast[1] /'kɒntrɑːst/ *n.* contrasto *m.*

contrast[2] /kən'trɑːst/ *v.t./i.* contrastare. ~ing *a.* contrastante.

contraven|e /kɒntrə'viːn/ *v.t.* trasgredire. ~tion /-'venʃn/ *n.* trasgressione *f.*

contribut|e /kən'trɪbjuːt/ *v.t./i.* contribuire. ~e to (*newspaper*) scrivere per. ~ion /kɒntrɪ'bjuːʃn/ *n.* contribuzione *f.* ~or *n.* contribu|tore, -trice *m., f.*; (*to newspaper*) collabora|tore, -trice *m., f.*

contrite /'kɒntraɪt/ *a.* pentito.

contriv|e /kən'traɪv/ *v.t.* escogitare. ~ance *n.* escogitazione *f.*

control /kən'trəʊl/ *v.t.* (*p.t.* **controlled**) (*a firm etc.*) dirigere; (*check*) controllare; (*restrain*) trattenere. —*n.* controllo *m.*; (*mastery*) padronanza *f.* ~s *n.pl.* (*mech.*) comandi *m.pl.*

controversial /kɒntrə'vɜːʃl/ *a.* controverso.

controversy /'kɒntrəvɜːsɪ/ *n.* controversia *f.*

conundrum /kə'nʌndrəm/ *n.* enigma *m.*

conurbation /kɒnɜː'beɪʃn/ *n.* conurbazione *f.*

convalesce /kɒnvə'les/ *v.i.* essere in convalescenza. ~nce *n.* convalescenza *f.* ~nt *a. & n.* convalescente *m./f.* ~nt home convalescenziario *m.*

convector /kən'vektə(r)/ *n.* convettore *m.*

convene /kən'viːn/ *v.t.* convocare. —*v.i.* radunarsi.

convenience /kən'viːnɪəns/ *n.* convenienza *f.* ~s *n.pl.* gabinetti pubblici *m.pl.*

convenient /kən'viːnɪənt/ *a.* conveniente, comodo; (*accessible*) vicino. ~ly *adv.* convenientemente.

convent /'kɒnvənt/ *n.* convento *m.*

convention /kən'venʃn/ *n.* convenzione *f.*; (*custom*) consuetudine *f.* ~al *a.* convenzionale.

converge /kən'vɜːdʒ/ *v.i.* convergere.

conversant /kən'vɜːsənt/ *a.* ~ with pratico di.

conversation /kɒnvə'seɪʃn/ *n.* conversazione *f.* ~al *a.* di conversazione.

~alist *n.* abile conversa|tore, -trice *m.*, *f.*

converse[1] /kən'vɜːs/ *v.i.* conversare.

converse[2] /'kɒnvɜːs/ *a.* & *n.* inverso *m.* ~ly *adv.* viceversa.

conver|t[1] /kən'vɜːt/ *v.t.* convertire. ~sion /-ʃn/ *n.* conversione *f.* ~tible *a.* convertibile. —*n.* (*auto*) macchina decappottabile *f.*

convert[2] /'kɒnvɜːt/ *n.* convertito, a *m.*, *f.*

convex /'kɒnveks/ *a.* convesso.

convey /kən'veɪ/ *v.t.* portare; (*goods*) trasportare; (*idea*) rendere. ~ance *n.* trasporto *m.* ~or belt *n.* nastro trasportatore *m.*

convict[1] /kən'vɪkt/ *v.t.* giudicare colpevole. ~ion /-ʃn/ *n.* condanna *f.*; (*belief*) convinzione *f.*

convict[2] /'kɒnvɪkt/ *n.* condannato *m.*

convinc|e /kən'vɪns/ *v.t.* convincere. ~ing *a.* convincente.

convivial /kən'vɪvɪəl/ *a.* conviviale.

convoke /kən'vəʊk/ *v.t.* convocare.

convoluted /'kɒnvəluːtɪd/ *a.* attorcigliato.

convoy /'kɒnvɔɪ/ *n.* convoglio *m.*

convuls|e /kən'vʌls/ *v.t.* sconvolgere. be ~ed with laughter contorcersi dalle risa. ~ion /-ʃn/ *n.* convulsione *f.*

coo /kuː/ *v.i.* tubare.

cook /kʊk/ *v.t.*/*i.* cucinare, cucinarsi; (*fam.*, *alter*) falsificare. —*n.* cuoco, a *m.*, *f.* ~ up (*fam.*) architettare.

cooker /'kʊkə(r)/ *n.* fornello *m.*, cucina *f.*

cookery /'kʊkərɪ/ *n.* cucina *f.*

cookie /'kʊkɪ/ *n.* (*Amer.*) biscotto *m.*

cool /kuːl/ *a.* (-er, -est) fresco; (*calm*) calmo; (*unfriendly*) freddo. —*n.* fresco *m.*; (*sl.*) calma *f.* —*v.t.*/*i.* rinfrescare, rinfrescarsi. ~ down calmare. ~ly *adv.* freddamente. ~ness *n.* freddezza *f.*

coop /kuːp/ *n.* pollaio *m.* —*v.t.* ~ up rinchiudere.

co-operat|e /kəʊ'ɒpəreɪt/ *v.i.* cooperare. ~ion /-'reɪʃn/ *n.* cooperazione *f.*

co-operative /kəʊ'ɒpərətɪv/ *a.* cooperativo. —*n.* cooperativa *f.*

co-opt /kəʊ'ɒpt/ *v.t.* eleggere.

co-ordinat|e /kəʊ'ɔːdɪneɪt/ *v.t.* coordinare. ~ion /-'neɪʃn/ *n.* coordinazione *f.*

cop /kɒp/ *v.t.* (*p.t.* copped) (*sl.*) prendere. —*n.* (*sl.*) poliziotto *m.*

cope /kəʊp/ *v.i.* (*fam.*) farcela. ~ with affrontare.

copious /'kəʊpɪəs/ *a.* copioso.

copper[1] /'kɒpə(r)/ *n.* rame *m.*; (*coin*) moneta *f.* —*a.* di rame.

copper[2] /'kɒpə(r)/ *n.* (*sl.*) poliziotto *m.*

coppice, copse /'kɒpɪs, kɒps/ *ns.* boschetto *m.*

Coptic /'kɒptɪk/ *a.* copto.

copulat|e /'kɒpjʊleɪt/ *v.i.* accoppiarsi. ~ion /-'leɪʃn/ *n.* copulazione *f.*

copy /'kɒpɪ/ *n.* copia *f.*; (*typ.*) materiale *m.* —*v.t.* copiare. ~-writer *n.* redattore pubblicitario *m.*

copyright /'kɒpɪraɪt/ *n.* diritto d'autore *m.*

coral /'kɒrəl/ *n.* corallo *m.*

cord /kɔːd/ *n.* corda *f.*; (*fabric*) velluto a coste *m.* ~s *n.pl.* pantaloni di velluto a coste *m.pl.*

cordial /'kɔːdɪəl/ *a.* cordiale. —*n.* cordiale *m.*

cordon /'kɔːdn/ *n.* cordone *m.* —*v.t.* ~ off mettere un cordone intorno a.

corduroy /'kɔːdərɔɪ/ *n.* velluto a coste *m.*

core /kɔː(r)/ *n.* (*of apple*) torsolo *m.*; (*fig.*) cuore *m.*

cork /kɔːk/ *n.* sughero *m.*; (*for bottle*) turacciolo *m.* —*v.t.* tappare.

corkscrew /'kɔːkskruː/ *n.* cavatappi *m.*

corn[1] /kɔːn/ *n.* grano *m.*; (*Amer.*) granturco *m.*

corn[2] /kɔːn/ *n.* (*hard skin*) callo *m.*

corned /kɔːnd/ *a.* ~ beef manzo salato *m.*

corner /'kɔːnə(r)/ *n.* angolo *m.*; (*football*) calcio d'angolo *m.* —*v.t.* mettere in un angolo; (*comm.*) accaparrare. ~-stone *n.* pietra angolare *f.*

cornet /'kɔːnɪt/ *n.* (*mus.*) cornetta *f.*; (*for ice-cream*) cono *m.*

cornflakes /'kɔːnfleɪks/ *n.pl.* fiocchi di granturco *m.pl.*

cornflour /'kɔːnflaʊə(r)/ *n.* farina di granturco *f.*

cornice /'kɔːnɪs/ *n.* cornicione *m.*

cornucopia /kɔːnjʊ'kəʊpɪə/ *n.* cornucopia *f.*

Corn|wall /'kɔːnwəl/ *n.* Cornovaglia *f.* ~ish *a.* della Cornovaglia.

corny /'kɔːnɪ/ *a.* (*fam.*) banale.

corollary /kə'rɒlərɪ/ *n.* corollario *m.*

coronary /'kɒrənərɪ/ *n.* infarto *m.*

coronation /kɒrə'neɪʃn/ *n.* incoronazione *f.*

coroner /'kɒrənə(r)/ *n.* coroner *m.* *invar.*

corporal[1] /'kɔːpərəl/ *n.* caporale *m.*
corporal[2] /'kɔːpərəl/ *a.* corporale.
corporate /'kɔːpərət/ *a.* corporativo.
corporation /kɔːpə'reɪʃn/ *n.* ente *m.*; (*of town*) consiglio municipale *m.*
corps /kɔː(r)/ *n.* (*pl.* **corps** /kɔːz/) corpo *m.*
corpse /kɔːps/ *n.* cadavere *m.*
corpulent /'kɔːpjʊlənt/ *a.* corpulento.
corpuscle /'kɔːpʌsl/ *n.* globulo *m.*
corral /kə'rɑːl/ *n.* (*Amer.*) recinto *m.*
correct /kə'rekt/ *a.* corretto; (*time*) giusto; (*dress*) adatto. —*v.t.* correggere. **~ion** /-ʃn/ *n.* correzione *f.*
correlat|e /'kɒrəleɪt/ *v.t.* mettere in correlazione. **~ion** /-'leɪʃn/ *n.* correlazione *f.*
correspond /kɒrɪ'spɒnd/ *v.i.* corrispondere. **~ence** *n.* corrispondenza *f.* **~ent** *n.* corrispondente *m.*/*f.*
corridor /'kɒrɪdɔː(r)/ *n.* corridoio *m.*
corroborate /kə'rɒbəreɪt/ *v.t.* corroborare.
corro|de /kə'rəʊd/ *v.t.*/*i.* corrodere, corrodersi. **~sion** *n.* corrosione *f.*
corrugated /'kɒrəgeɪtɪd/ *a.* ondulato. **~ iron** lamiera ondulata *f.*
corrupt /kə'rʌpt/ *a.* corrotto. —*v.t.* corrompere. **~ion** /-ʃn/ *n.* corruzione *f.*
corset /'kɔːsɪt/ *n.* busto *m.*
Corsica /'kɔːsɪkə/ *n.* Corsica. *f.* **~n** *a.* & *n.* corso, a *m.*, *f.*
cortège /'kɔːteɪʒ/ *n.* corteo *m.*
cos /kɒs/ *n.* lattuga romana *f.*
cosh /kɒʃ/ *n.* randello *m.* —*v.t.* bastonare.
cosmetic /kɒz'metɪk/ *a.* & *n.* cosmetico *m.* **~ surgery** chirurgia estetica *f.*
cosmic /'kɒzmɪk/ *a.* cosmico.
cosmonaut /'kɒzmənɔːt/ *n.* cosmonauta *m.*/*f.*
cosmopolitan /kɒzmə'pɒlɪtən/ *a.* & *n.* cosmopolita *m.*/*f.*
cosmos /'kɒzmɒs/ *n.* cosmo *m.*
Cossack /'kɒsæk/ *n.* cosacco *m.*
cosset /'kɒsɪt/ *v.t.* (*p.t.* **cosseted**) coccolare.
cost /kɒst/ *v.i.* (*p.t.* **cost**) costare. —*v.t.* (*p.t.* **costed**) stabilire il prezzo di. —*n.* costo *m.* **~s** *n.pl.* (*jurid.*) spese processuali. **at all ~s** a tutti i costi. **to one's ~** a proprie spese.
costly /'kɒstlɪ/ *a.* (**-ier, -iest**) costoso.
costume /'kɒstjuːm/ *n.* costume *m.*
cos|y /'kəʊzɪ/ *a.* (**-ier, -iest**) intimo, accogliente. —*n.* copriteiera *f.* **~iness** *n.* intimità *f.*
cot /kɒt/ *n.* lettino *m.*

cottage /'kɒtɪdʒ/ *n.* villino *m.* **~ loaf** pagnotta *f.* **~ pie** pasticcio di carne e patate *m.*
cotton /'kɒtn/ *n.* cotone *m.* —*v.i.* **~ on** (*sl.*) comprendere. **~ wool** cotone idrofilo *m.*
couch /kaʊtʃ/ *n.* divano *m.* —*v.t.* esprimere.
couchette /kuː'ʃet/ *n.* cuccetta *f.*
cough /kɒf/ *v.i.* tossire. —*n.* tosse *f.* **~ up** (*sl.*) sborsare.
could /kʊd, kəd/ *p.t. of* **can**[2].
couldn't /'kʊdnt/ = **could not**.
council /'kaʊnsl/ *n.* consiglio *m.* **~ house** casa popolare *f.*
councillor /'kaʊnsələ(r)/ *n.* consigliere, a *m.*, *f.*
counsel /'kaʊnsl/ *n.* parere *m.*; (*pl. invar.*) (*jurid.*) avvocato *m.* **~lor** *n.* consigliere, a *m.*, *f.*
count[1] /kaʊnt/ *n.* (*nobleman*) conte *m.*
count[2] /kaʊnt/ *v.t.*/*i.* contare. —*n.* conto *m.*
countdown /'kaʊntdaʊn/ *m.* conteggio alla rovescia *m.*
countenance /'kaʊntɪnəns/ *n.* espressione *f.* —*v.t.* approvare.
counter[1] /'kaʊntə(r)/ *n.* (*in shop etc.*) banco *m.*; (*token*) gettone *m.*
counter[2] /'kaʊntə(r)/ *adv.* **~ to** contro, in contrasto a. —*a.* opposto. —*v.t.* opporre; (*blow*) parare. —*v.i.* contrattaccare.
counter- /'kaʊntə(r)/ *pref.* contro-.
counteract /kaʊntər'ækt/ *v.t.* neutralizzare.
counter-attack /'kaʊntərətæk/ *n.* contrattacco *m.* —*v.t.*/*i.* contrattaccare.
counterbalance /'kaʊntəbæləns/ *n.* contrappeso *m.* —*v.t.*/*i.* controbilanciare.
counterfeit /'kaʊntəfɪt/ *a.* contraffatto. —*n.* falsificazione *f.* —*v.t.* falsificare.
counterfoil /'kaʊntəfɔɪl/ *n.* matrice *f.*
counterpart /'kaʊntəpɑːt/ *n.* equivalente *m.*; (*of document*) copia *f.*
counter-productive /'kaʊntəprə'dʌktɪv/ *a.* inefficace.
countersign /'kaʊntəsaɪn/ *v.t.* controfirmare.
countess /'kaʊntɪs/ *n.* contessa *f.*
countless /'kaʊntlɪs/ *a.* innumerevole.
countrified /'kʌntrɪfaɪd/ *a.* campagnolo.
country /'kʌntrɪ/ *n.* paese *m.*; (*native land*) patria *f.* (*countryside*) campagna *f.* **~ folk** gente di campagna *f.* **go to**

the ~ andare in campagna; (*pol.*) indire le elezioni.

countryman /'kʌntrɪmən/ *n.* (*pl.* -men) contadino *m.*; (*of one's own country*) compatriota *m.*

countryside /'kʌntrɪsaɪd/ *n.* campagna *f.*

county /'kaʊntɪ/ *n.* contea *f.*

coup /kuː/ *n.* colpo *m.*

coupé /'kuːpeɪ/ *n.* coupé *m.*

couple /'kʌpl/ *n.* coppia *f.* —*v.t./i.* accoppiare, accoppiarsi. **a ~ of** un paio di.

coupon /'kuːpɒn/ *n.* scontrino *m.*; (*comm.*) buono *m.*

courage /'kʌrɪdʒ/ *n.* coraggio *m.* ~**ous** /kə'reɪdʒəs/ *a.* coraggioso. ~**ously** *adv.* coraggiosamente.

courgette /kʊə'ʒet/ *n.* zucchino *m.*

courier /'kʊrɪə(r)/ *n.* messaggero, a *m.,f.*; (*for tourists*) guida *f.*

course /kɔːs/ *n.* corso *m.*; (*behaviour*) condotta *f.*; (*aeron., naut.*) rotta *f.*; (*culin.*) portata *f.*; (*for golf*) campo *m.* **in due ~** a tempo debito. **in the ~ of** durante. **of ~** naturalmente.

court /kɔːt/ *n.* corte *f.*; (*tennis*) campo *m.* —*v.t.* fare la corte (a); (*danger*) cercare. ~ **martial** *m.* (*pl.* **courts martial**) corte marziale *f.* ~**-martial** *v.t.* (*p.t.* ~**-martialled**) portare davanti alla corte marziale.

courteous /'kɜːtɪəs/ *a.* cortese.

courtesan /kɔːtɪ'zæn/ *n.* (*old use*) cortigiana *f.*

courtesy /'kɜːtəsɪ/ *n.* cortesia *f.*

courtier /'kɔːtɪə(r)/ *n.* (*old use*) cortigiano *m.*

courtship /'kɔːtʃɪp/ *n.* corteggiamento *m.*

courtyard /'kɔːtjaːd/ *n.* cortile *m.*

cousin /'kʌzn/ *n.* cugino, a *m.,f.* **first/second ~** cugino, a di primo/secondo grado *m.,f.*

cove /kəʊv/ *n.* insenatura *f.*

covenant /'kʌvənənt/ *n.* accordo *m.*

Coventry /'kɒvntrɪ/ *n.* **send to ~** mandare al diavolo.

cover /'kʌvə(r)/ *v.t.* coprire; (*journalism*) fare la cronaca di. —*n.* copertura *f.*; (*shelter*) riparo *m.*; (*lid*) coperchio *m.*; (*of book*) copertina *f.* ~ **charge** coperto *m.* ~ **up** coprire; (*fig.*) nascondere. ~**ing** *n.* copertura *f.*; (*fig.*) protezione *f.*

coverage /'kʌvərɪdʒ/ *n.* servizio di cronaca *m.*

covet /'kʌvɪt/ *v.t.* bramare.

cow /kaʊ/ *n.* vacca *f.*

coward /'kaʊəd/ *n.* vigliacco, a *m.,f.* ~**ly** *a.* vile.

cowardice /'kaʊədɪs/ *n.* viltà *f.*

cowboy /'kaʊbɔɪ/ *n.* cowboy *m. invar.*

cower /'kaʊə(r)/ *v.i.* acquattarsi.

cowl /kaʊl/ *n.* cappuccio *m.*; (*of chimney*) cappa *f.*

cowshed /'kaʊʃed/ *n.* stalla *f.*

coxswain /'kɒksn/ *n.* timoniere, a *m.,f.*

coy /kɔɪ/ *a.* (-er, -est) ritroso.

crab /kræb/ *n.* granchio *m.* —*v.i.* (*p.t.* **crabbed**) denigrare. ~**-apple** *n.* mela selvatica *f.* ~**by** *a.* sgarbato.

crack /kræk/ *n.* scoppio *m.*; (*in ceiling*) crepa *f.*; (*sl.*) battuta spiritosa *f.* —*a.* (*fam.*) di prim'ordine. —*v.t.* spaccare; (*whip*) schioccare; (*nut*) schiacciare; (*joke*) raccontare; (*problem*) risolvere. ~ **down on** (*fam.*) trattare più severamente. ~ **up** *v.i.* crollare. **get** ~**ing** (*fam.*) sbrigarsi.

cracked /krækt/ *a.* (*sl.*) matto.

cracker /'krækə(r)/ *n.* petardo *m.*; (*culin.*) biscotto cracker *m.*

crackers /'krækəz/ *a.* (*sl.*) matto.

crackle /'krækl/ *v.i.* crepitare. —*n.* crepitio *m.*

crackling /'kræklɪŋ/ *n.* crepitio *m.*; (*of pork*) cotenna croccante *f.*

crackpot /'krækpɒt/ *n.* (*sl.*) picchiatello, a *m.,f.*

cradle /'kreɪdl/ *n.* culla *f.* —*v.t.* cullare.

craft[1] /krɑːft/ *n.* mestiere *m.*; (*technique*) arte *f.*; (*cunning*) astuzia *f.*

craft[2] /krɑːft/ *n. invar.* (*boat*) imbarcazione *f.*

craftsman /'krɑːftsmən/ *n.* (*pl.* -men) artigiano *m.* ~**ship** *n.* artigianato *m.*

crafty /'krɑːftɪ/ *a.* (-ier, -iest) astuto.

crag /kræg/ *n.* rupe *f.* ~**gy** *a.* scosceso.

cram /kræm/ *v.t./i.* (*p.t.* **crammed**) calcare, calcarsi; (*for exams*) sgobbare. ~**-full** *a.* pieno zeppo.

cramp /kræmp/ *n.* crampo *m.*

cramped /kræmpt/ *a.* ristretto.

cranberry /'krænbərɪ/ *n.* mirtillo rosso *m.*

crane /kreɪn/ *n.* gru *f.*

crank[1] /kræŋk/ *n.* manovella *f.*

crank[2] /kræŋk/ *n.* eccentrico, a *m.,f.* ~**y** *a.* eccentrico.

cranny /'krænɪ/ *n.* fessura *f.*

crash /kræʃ/ *n.* (*noise*) fragore *m.*; (*collision*) scontro *m.*; (*comm.*) crollo *m.* —*v.t./i.* fracassare, fracassarsi; scontrarsi; crollare; (*of plane*) precipitare. ~ **course** n. corso intensivo m. ~**-helmet** n. casco m. ~**-land** v.i. fare un atterraggio forzato.

crass /kræs/ a. crasso.

crate /kreɪt/ n. cassa da imballaggio f. —v.t. imballare.

crater /'kreɪtə(r)/ n. cratere m.

cravat /krə'væt/ n. cravatta, sciarpa f.

crav|e /kreɪv/ v.i. ~**e for** desiderare ardentemente. ~**ing** n. voglia f.

crawl /krɔːl/ v.i. andare carponi; (move slowly) avanzare lentamente. ~ **to** cercare d'ingraziarsi. ~ **with** brulicare di. —n. (swimming) crawl m. invar. **at a** ~ molto lentamente.

crayon /'kreɪən/ n. matita colorata f.

craze /kreɪz/ n. voga f.

craz|y /'kreɪzɪ/ a. (-**ier**, -**iest**) matto. **be** ~**y about** andar matto per. ~**y paving** n. lastricato rustico m. ~**i-ness** n. follia f.

creak /kriːk/ n. scricchiolio m. —v.i. scricchiolare.

cream /kriːm/ n. crema f.; (fresh) panna f.; (fig.) fior fiore m. —a. (colour) colour crema. —v.t. (remove) scremare; (beat) sbattere. ~ **cheese** formaggio cremoso m. ~**y** a. cremoso.

crease /kriːs/ n. piega f.; (crumple) grinza f. —v.t./i. sgualcire, sgualcirsi.

creat|e /kriː'eɪt/ v.t. creare. ~**ion** /-ʃn/ n. creazione f. ~**ive** a. creativo. ~**or** n. crea|tore, -trice m., f.

creature /'kriːtʃə(r)/ n. creatura f.

crèche /kreɪʃ/ n. asilo m.

credence /'kriːdns/ n. fede f.

credentials /krɪ'denʃlz/ n.pl. credenziali f.pl.

credib|le /'kredəbl/ a. verosimile. ~**ility** /-'bɪlətɪ/ n. credibilità f.

credit /'kredɪt/ n. credito m.; (honour) onore m. —v.t. (p.t. **credited**) accreditare. ~ **card** n. carta di credito f. ~ **s.o. with** attribuire a qcno. **take the** ~ **for** farsi il merito di. ~**able** a. lodevole. ~**or** n. credi|tore, -trice m., f.

credulous /'krɛdjʊləs/ a. credulo.

creed /kriːd/ n. credo m.

creek /kriːk/ n. insenatura f. **up the** ~ (sl.) nei guai.

creep /kriːp/ v.i. (p.t. **crept**) strisciare; (plant) arrampicarsi. —n. (sl.) persona sgradevole f. ~**er** n. pianta rampicante f.

creeps /kriːps/ n.pl. **give s.o. the** ~ far venire a qcno. la pelle d'oca.

cremat|e /krɪ'meɪt/ v.t. cremare. ~**ion** /-ʃn/ n. cremazione f.

crematorium /kremə'tɔːrɪəm/ n. (pl. -**ia**) n. crematorio m.

Creole /'kriːəʊl/ a. & n. creolo, a m., f.

crêpe /kreɪp/ n. crespo m. ~ **paper** carta crespata f.

crept /krept/ see **creep**.

crescendo /krɪ'ʃendəʊ/ n. (pl. -**os**) crescendo m.

crescent /'kresnt/ n. mezzaluna f.; (street) strada a semicerchio f.

cress /kres/ n. crescione m.

crest /krest/ n. cresta f.; (coat of arms) cimiero m.

Crete /kriːt/ n. Creta f.

cretin /'kretɪn/ n. cretino, a m., f.

crevasse /krɪ'væs/ n. crepaccio m.

crevice /'krevɪs/ n. crepa f.

crew /kruː/ see **crow**. —n. equipaggio m.; (gang) gruppo m. ~ **cut** taglio a spazzola m. ~ **neck** girocollo m.

crib[1] /krɪb/ n. culla f.; (relig.) presepio m.

crib[2] /krɪb/ v.t./i. (p.t. **cribbed**) plagiare. —n. plagio m.

crick /krɪk/ n. crampo m.

cricket[1] /'krɪkɪt/ n. cricket m. ~**er** n. giocatore di cricket m.

cricket[2] /'krɪkɪt/ n. (insect) grillo m.

crime /kraɪm/ n. delitto m.; (acts) delinquenza f.

criminal /'krɪmɪnl/ a. & n. criminale m./f.

crimp /krɪmp/ v.t. arricciare.

crimson /'krɪmzn/ a. & n. cremisi m.

cringe /krɪndʒ/ v.i. acquattarsi; (fig.) umiliarsi.

crinkle /'krɪŋkl/ v.t./i. spiegazzare, spiegazzarsi. —n. crespa f.

crinoline /'krɪnəliːn/ n. crinolina f.

cripple /'krɪpl/ n. & n. storpio, a m., f. —v.t. storpiare; (fig.) danneggiare.

crisis /'kraɪsɪs/ n. (pl. **crises** /'kraɪsiːz/) crisi f. invar.

crisp /krɪsp/ a. (-**er**, -**est**) (culin.) croccante; (air) frizzante; (style) incisivo. ~**s** n.pl. patatine fritte f.pl.

criss-cross /'krɪskrɒs/ a. a linee incrociate. —v.t./i. incrociare, incrociarsi.

criterion /kraɪ'tɪərɪən/ n. (pl. -**ia**) criterio m.

critic /'krɪtɪk/ n. critico, a m., f. ~**al** a. critico. ~**ally** adv. in modo critico; (ill) gravemente.

criticism /'krɪtɪsɪzəm/ n. critica f.

criticize /'krɪtɪsaɪz/ v.t./i. criticare.

croak /krəʊk/ *n.* gracidio *m.* —*v.i.* gracidare.

crochet /ˈkrəʊʃeɪ/ *n.* lavoro all'uncinetto *m.* —*v.t.* lavorare all'uncinetto.

crock /krɒk/ *n.* vaso (di terracotta) *m.*; (*fam.*) rudere *m.*; (*old car*) macinino *m.*

crockery /ˈkrɒkərɪ/ *n.* stoviglie *f.pl.*

crocodile /ˈkrɒkədaɪl/ *n.* coccodrillo *m.* ~ **tears** lacrime di coccodrillo *f.pl.*

crocus /ˈkrəʊkəs/ *n.* (*pl.* -es) croco *m.*

crony /ˈkrəʊnɪ/ *n.* amico intimo *m.*

crook /krʊk/ *n.* (*fam.*) delinquente *m.*; (*stick*) bastone (da pastore) *m.*; (*of arm*) piegatura *f.*

crooked /ˈkrʊkɪd/ *a.* storto; (*winding*) tortuoso; (*dishonest*) disonesto.

croon /kruːn/ *v.t./i.* cantare sottovoce.

crop /krɒp/ *n.* raccolto *m.*; (*fig.*) quantità *f.*; taglio corto di capelli *m.* —*v.t.* (*p.t.* **cropped**) raccogliere. —*v.i.* ~ **up** presentarsi.

cropper /ˈkrɒpər/ *n.* **come a** ~ (*fam.*) far fiasco.

croquet /ˈkrəʊkeɪ/ *n.* pallamaglio *m.*

croquette /krəʊˈket/ *n.* crocchetta *f.*

cross /krɒs/ *n.* croce *f.*; (*of animals*) incrocio *m.* —*v.t./i.* traversare; (*legs, animals*) incrociare; (*cheque*) sbarrare; (*oppose*) intralciare. —*a.* arrabbiato. ~ **off** *or* **out** cancellare. ~ **oneself** farsi la croce. ~ **s.o.'s mind** venire in mente a qcno. **talk at** ~ **purposes** fraintendersi. ~**ly** *adv.* di malumore.

crossbar /ˈkrɒsbɑː(r)/ *n.* traversa *f.*

cross-examine /krɒsɪgˈzæmɪn/ *v.t.* sottoporre a controinterrogatorio.

cross-eyed /ˈkrɒsaɪd/ *a.* strabico.

crossfire /ˈkrɒsfaɪə(r)/ *n.* fuoco incrociato *m.*

crossing /ˈkrɒsɪŋ/ *n.* (*by boat*) traversata *f.*; (*on road*) passaggio pedonale *m.*

cross-reference /krɒsˈrefrəns/ *n.* rimando *m.*

crossroads /ˈkrɒsrəʊdz/ *n.* bivio *m.*

cross-section /krɒsˈsekʃn/ *n.* sezione trasversale *f.*; (*fig.*) rappresentanza *f.*

crosswise /ˈkrɒswaɪz/ *adv.* di traverso.

crossword /ˈkrɒswɜːd/ *n.* parole incrociate *f.pl.*

crotch /krɒtʃ/ *n.* inforcatura *f.*; (*of trousers*) cavallo *m.*

crotchety /ˈkrɒtʃɪtɪ/ *a.* stizzoso.

crouch /kraʊtʃ/ *v.i.* rannicchiarsi.

crow /krəʊ/ *n.* corvo *m.* —*v.i.* (*p.t.* **crew**) cantare. **as the** ~ **flies** in linea d'aria.

crowbar /ˈkrəʊbɑː(r)/ *n.* palanchino *m.*

crowd /kraʊd/ *n.* folla *f.* —*v.t./i.* affollare, affollarsi. ~**ed** *a.* affollato.

crown /kraʊn/ *n.* corona *f.*; (*top part*) sommità *f.* —*v.t.* incoronare; (*tooth*) incapsulare. **C**~ **Court** Corte d'Assise *f.* **C**~ **prince** principe ereditario *m.*

crucial /ˈkruːʃl/ *a.* cruciale.

crucifix /ˈkruːsɪfɪks/ *n.* crocifisso *m.*

crucif|**y** /ˈkruːsɪfaɪ/ *v.t.* crocifiggere. ~**ixion** /-ˈfɪkʃn/ *n.* crocifissione *f.*

crude /kruːd/ *a.* (-**er**, -**est**) (*raw*) crudo; (*rough*) rozzo.

cruel /krʊəl/ *a.* (**crueller, cruellest**) crudele. ~**ty** *n.* crudeltà *f.*

cruet /ˈkruːɪt/ *n.* oliera *f.*

cruis|**e** /kruːz/ *n.* crociera *f.* —*v.i.* fare una crociera; (*of car*) andare a piccola velocità *f.* ~**er** *n.* (*warship*) incrociatore *m.*; (*motorboat*) motoscafo *m.*

crumb /krʌm/ *n.* briciola *f.*

crumble /ˈkrʌmbl/ *v.t./i.* sbriciolare, sbriciolarsi; (*collapse*) crollare.

crummy /ˈkrʌmɪ/ *a.* (-**ier**, -**iest**) (*sl.*) squallido, sudicio.

crumpet /ˈkrʌmpɪt/ *n.* pasticcino *m.*

crumple /ˈkrʌmpl/ *v.t./i.* spiegazzare, spiegazzarsi.

crunch /krʌntʃ/ *v.t.* sgranocchiare. —*n.* (*fig.*) momento decisivo *m.*

crusade /kruːˈseɪd/ *n.* crociata *f.* ~**r** /-ə(r)/ *n.* crociato *m.*

crush /krʌʃ/ *v.t.* schiacciare; (*clothes*) sgualcire. —*n.* (*mass of people*) calca *f.*; (*of fruit*) spremuta *f.* **have a** ~ **on** (*sl.*) prendersi una cotta per.

crust /krʌst/ *n.* crosta *f.* ~**y** crostoso.

crutch /krʌtʃ/ *n.* gruccia *f.*; (*anat.*) inforcatura *f.*

crux /krʌks/ *n.* (*pl.* **cruxes**) culmine *m.*

cry /kraɪ/ *n.* grido *m.* —*v.i.* piangere; (*call out*) gridare. ~**-baby** *n.* piagnucolone, a *m.*, *f.* ~ **off** tirarsi indietro. **a far** ~ **from** (*fig.*) molto diverso da.

crypt /krɪpt/ *n.* cripta *f.*

cryptic /ˈkrɪptɪk/ *a.* criptico.

crystal /ˈkrɪstl/ *n.* cristallo *m.* ~**lize** *v.t./i.* cristallizzare, cristallizzarsi.

cub /kʌb/ *n.* cucciolo *m.*

Cuba /ˈkjuːbə/ *n.* Cuba *m.* ~**n** *a.* & *n.* cubano, a *m.*, *f.*

cubby-hole /ˈkʌbɪhəʊl/ *n.* cantuccio *m.*

cub|**e** /kjuːb/ *n.* cubo *m.* ~**ic** *a.* cubico.

cubicle /ˈkjuːbɪkl/ *n.* cubicolo *m.*

cubis|m /'kju:bɪzm/ *n.* cubismo. **~t** *a.* & *n.* cubista *m./f.*

cuckold /'kʌkəld/ *n.* cornuto *m.*

cuckoo /'kuku:/ *n.* cuculo *m.*

cucumber /'kju:kʌmbə(r)/ *n.* cetriolo *m.*

cuddl|e /'kʌdl/ *v.t./i.* stringersi al petto. —*n.* abbraccio *m.* **~y** *a.* coccolone.

cudgel /'kʌdʒl/ *n.* randello *m.* —*v.t.* (*p.t.* **cudgelled**) randellare. **~ one's brains** (*fig.*) lambiccarsi il cervello.

cue[1] /kju:/ *n.* spunto *m.*; (*theatr.*) battuta d'entrata *f.*

cue[2] /kju:/ *n.* (*billiards*) stecca *f.*

cuff /kʌf/ *n.* polsino *m.*; (*blow*) scapaccione *m.* —*v.t.* schiaffeggiare. **~-link** *n.* gemello *m.* **speak off the ~** parlare improvvisando.

cul-de-sac /'kʌldəsæk/ *n.* vicolo cieco *m.*

culinary /'kʌlɪnərɪ/ *a.* culinario.

cull /kʌl/ *v.t.* (*flowers*) cogliere; (*animals*) selezionare e uccidere.

culminat|e /'kʌlmɪneɪt/ *v.i.* culminare. **~ion** /-'neɪʃn/ *n.* culminazione *f.*

culottes /ku'lɒts/ *n.pl.* gonna pantalone *f.s.*

culprit /'kʌlprɪt/ *n.* colpevole *m./f.*

cult /kʌlt/ *n.* culto *m.*

cultivat|e /'kʌltɪveɪt/ *v.t.* coltivare. **~ion** /-'veɪʃn/ *n.* coltivazione *f.*

cultural /'kʌltʃərəl/ *a.* culturale.

culture /'kʌltʃə(r)/ *n.* cultura *f.* **~d** *a.* colto.

cumbersome /'kʌmbəsəm/ *a.* ingombrante.

cumulative /'kju:mjʊlətɪv/ *a.* cumulativo.

cunning /'kʌnɪŋ/ *a.* furbo. —*n.* astuzia *f.*

cup /kʌp/ *n.* tazza *f.*; (*prize*) coppa *f.* **C~ Final** finale di campionato *m.*

cupboard /'kʌbəd/ *n.* armadio *m.*

cupful /'kʌpfʊl/ *n.* tazza piena *f.*

cupidity /kju:'pɪdɪtɪ/ *n.* cupidigia *f.*

curable /'kjʊərəbl/ *a.* curabile.

curate /'kjʊərət/ *n.* curato *m.*

curator /kjʊə'reɪtə(r)/ *n.* curatore *m.*

curb /kɜːb/ *n.* freno *m.* —*v.t.* tenere a freno.

curdle /'kɜːdl/ *v.t.* cagliare. —*v.i.* coagularsi.

curds /kɜːdz/ *n.pl.* latte cagliato *m.s.*

cure /kjʊə(r)/ *v.t.* curare; (*culin.*) affumicare. —*n.* cura *f.*

curfew /'kɜːfju:/ *n.* coprifuoco *m.*

curio /'kjʊərɪəʊ/ *n.* (*pl.* **-os**) curiosità *f.*

curi|ous /'kjʊərɪəs/ *a.* curioso; (*strange*) strano. **~osity** /-'ɒsətɪ/ *n.* curiosità *f.*

curl /kɜːl/ *v.t./i.* arricciare, arricciarsi. —*n.* ricciolo *m.* **~ o.s. up** raggomitolarsi.

curler /'kɜːlə(r)/ *n.* bigodino *m.*

curly /'kɜːlɪ/ *a.* (**-ier, -iest**) riccio.

currant /'kʌrənt/ *n.* uva passa *f.*

currency /'kʌrənsɪ/ *n.* valuta *f.*; (*acceptance*) uso corrente *m.*

current /'kʌrənt/ *a.* corrente. —*n.* corrente *f.* **~ events** attualità *f.pl.* **~ly** *adv.* attualmente.

curriculum /kə'rɪkjʊləm/ *n.* (*pl.* **-la**) programma di studi *m.* **~ vitae** curriculum vitae *m. invar.*

curry /'kʌrɪ/ *n.* curry *m. invar.* —*v.t.* **~ favour with** cercare d'ingraziarsi con.

curse /kɜːs/ *n.* maledizione *f.*; (*oath*) bestemmia *f.* —*v.t.* maledire. —*v.i.* bestemmiare.

cursory /'kɜːsərɪ/ *a.* rapido.

curt /kɜːt/ *a.* brusco.

curtail /kɜː'teɪl/ *v.t.* abbreviare; (*expenses*) ridurre.

curtain /'kɜːtn/ *n.* tenda *f.*; (*theatr.*) sipario *m.*

curtsy /'kɜːtsɪ/ *n.* inchino *m.* —*v.i.* inchinarsi.

curve /kɜːv/ *n.* curva *f.* —*v.t./i.* curvare, curvarsi; (*of road*) svoltare.

cushion /'kʊʃn/ *n.* cuscino *m.* —*v.t.* (*a blow*) attutire; (*fig.*) proteggere.

cushy /'kʊʃɪ/ *a.* (**-ier, -iest**) (*fam.*) comodo.

custard /'kʌstəd/ *n.* crema pasticciera *f.*

custodian /kʌ'stəʊdɪən/ *n.* custode *m./f.*

custody /'kʌstədɪ/ *n.* custodia *f.*; (*jurid.*) detenzione *f.*

custom /'kʌstəm/ *n.* usanza *f.*; (*comm.*) clientela *f.* **~ary** *a.* abituale.

customer /'kʌstəmə(r)/ *n.* cliente *m./f.*

customs /'kʌstəmz/ *n.pl.* dogana *f.* **~ officer** *n.* doganiere *m.*

cut /kʌt/ *v.t./i.* (*p.t.* **cut**, *pres.p.* **cutting**) tagliare; (*prices*) ridurre. —*n.* taglio *m.*; (*of clothes*) linea *f.*; (*reduction*) riduzione *f.* **~ across** *or* **through** attraversare. **~ back** *or* **down** ridurre. **~ in** intromettersi. **~ off** tagliar via; (*phone*) interrompere; (*fig.*) isolare. **~ out** ritagliare; (*omit*) eliminare. **~-price** *a.* a prezzo ri-

dotto. ~ up tagliare a pezzi. be ~
up about (*fig.*) essere addolorato
per.

cute /kjuːt/ *a.* (-er, -est) (*fam.*) abile;
(*Amer.*) grazioso.

cuticle /'kjuːtɪkl/ *n.* cuticola *f.*

cutlery /'kʌtlərɪ/ *n.* posateria *f.*

cutlet /'kʌtlɪt/ *n.* cotoletta *f.*

cut-throat /'kʌtθrəʊt/ *a.* spietato.

cutting /'kʌtɪŋ/ *a.* caustico. —*n.* (*from
newspaper*) ritaglio *m.*; (*of plant*) talea
f.

cyanide /'saɪənaɪd/ *n.* cianuro *m.*

cybernetics /saɪbə'netɪks/ *n.* ciberne-
tica *f.*

cyclamen /'sɪkləmən/ *n.* ciclamino *m.*

cycl|e /'saɪkl/ *n.* ciclo *m.*; (*bicycle*) bici-
cletta *f.* —*v.i.* andare in bicicletta.

~ing *n.* ciclismo *m.* ~ist *n.* ciclista
m./*f.*

cyclic(al) /'saɪklɪk(l)/ *a.* ciclico.

cyclone /'saɪkləʊn/ *n.* ciclone *m.*

cylind|er /'sɪlɪndə(r)/ *n.* cilindro
m. ~rical /-'lɪndrɪkl/ *a.* cilindrico.

cymbal /'sɪmbl/ *n.* cembalo *m.*

cynic /'sɪnɪk/ *n.* cinico, a *m.*, *f.* ~al *a.*
cinico. ~ism /-sɪzəm/ *n.* cinismo *m.*

cypress /'saɪprəs/ *n.* cipresso *m.*

Cypr|us /'saɪprəs/ *n.* Cipro *m.* ~iot
/'sɪprɪət/ *a.* & *n.* cipriota *m.*/*f.*

cyst /sɪst/ *n.* ciste *f.*

czar /zɑː(r)/ *n.* zar *m.*

Czech /tʃek/ *a.* & *n.* ceco, a *m.*, *f.*

Czechoslovak /tʃekəʊ'sləʊvæk/ *a.* &
n. cecoslovacco, a *m.*, *f.* ~ia /-ə'vækɪə/
n. Cecoslovacchia *f.*

D

dab /dæb/ v.t. (p.t. **dabbed**) toccare leggermente. —n. colpetto m. **a ~ of** un pochino di.

dabble /'dæbl/ v.i. **~ in** dilettarsi in. **~r** /ə(r)/ n. dilettante m./f.

dad /dæd/ n. (fam.) papà m. **~dy** n. (children's use) papà m. **~dy-long-legs** n. tipula f.

daffodil /'dæfədɪl/ n. trombone m.

daft /dɑːft/ a. (-er, -est) sciocco.

dagger /'dægə(r)/ n. stiletto m.

dahlia /'deɪlɪə/ n. dalia f.

daily /'deɪlɪ/ a. giornaliero. —adv. giornalmente. —n. quotidiano m.; (fam., cleaner) donna a ore f.

dainty /'deɪntɪ/ a. (-ier, -iest) grazioso.

dairy /'deərɪ/ n. caseificio m.; (shop) latteria f.

dais /deɪs/ n. predella f.

daisy /'deɪzɪ/ n. margheritina f.

dale /deɪl/ n. valle f.

dally /'dælɪ/ v.i. gingillarsi.

dam /dæm/ n. diga f. —v.t. (p.t. **dammed**) arginare.

damag|e /'dæmɪdʒ/ n. danno m.; (pl., jurid.) risarcimento m.s. —v.t. danneggiare; (fig.) nuocere. **~ing** a. dannoso.

damask /'dæməsk/ n. damasco m.

dame /deɪm/ n. (old use) dama f. **D~** Donna f.

damn /dæm/ v.t. dannare; (curse) maledire. —int. accidenti! —n. **not care a ~** non importarsene. —a. dannato. **~ation** /-'neɪʃn/ n. dannazione f.

damp /dæmp/ n. umidità f. —a. (-er, -est) umido. —v.t. inumidire; (fig.) deprimere. **~ness** n. umidità f.

damper /'dæmpə(r)/ n. (fig.) guastafeste m./f.

damsel /'dæmzl/ n. (old use) donzella f.

dance /dɑːns/ v.t./i. ballare. —n. danza f.; (gathering) festa da ballo f. **~-hall** sala da ballo f. **~r** /-ə(r)/ n. ballerino, a m., f.

dandelion /'dændɪlaɪən/ n. dente di leone m.

dandruff /'dændrəf/ n. forfora f.

dandy /'dændɪ/ n. bellimbusto m.

Dane /deɪn/ n. danese m./f.

danger /'deɪndʒə(r)/ n. pericolo m.; (risk) rischio m. **~ous** a. pericoloso.

dangle /'dæŋgl/ v.t./i. penzolare, far penzolare.

Danish /'deɪnɪʃ/ a. danese. —n. (lang.) danese m.

dank /dæŋk/ a. (-er, -est) umido, malsano.

dare /deə(r)/ v.t. osare; (challenge) sfidare. —n. sfida f. **I ~ say** molto probabilmente.

daredevil /'deədevɪl/ n. rompicollo m.

daring /'deərɪŋ/ a. audace.

dark /dɑːk/ a. (-er, -est) buio; (colour) scuro; (gloomy) tetro. —n. buio m.; (nightfall) tenebre f.pl. **~ horse** n. vincitore imprevisto m. **~-room** n. camera oscura f. **in the ~** all'oscuro. **~ness** n. oscurità f.

darken /'dɑːkən/ v.t./i. oscurare, oscurarsi.

darling /'dɑːlɪŋ/ a. diletto. —n. tesoro m.

darn /dɑːn/ v.t. rammendare.

dart /dɑːt/ n. dardo m. **~s** n.pl. (gioco delle) freccette (m.) f.pl. —v.i. lanciarsi; (run) precipitarsi.

dartboard /'dɑːtbɔːd/ n. bersaglio (per freccette) m.

dash /dæʃ/ v.i. scagliarsi. —v.t. gettare; (hopes) infrangere; (write hastily) buttar giù. —n. slancio m.; (small amount) pochino m.; (stroke) lineetta f. **cut a ~** far colpo. **~ off** scappar via. **~ out** precipitarsi fuori.

dashboard /'dæʃbɔːd/ n. cruscotto m.

dashing /'dæʃɪŋ/ a. ardito.

data /'deɪtə/ n.pl. dati m.pl. **~ processing** elaborazione di dati f.

date¹ /deɪt/ n. data f.; (fam.) appuntamento m. —v.t./i. datare; (Amer., fam.) dare appuntamento a. **to ~** fino ad oggi. **~d** a. fuori moda.

date² /deɪt/ n. (fruit) dattero m.

daub /dɔːb/ v.t. spalmare.

daughter /'dɔːtə(r)/ n. figlia f. **~-in-law** n. nuora f.

daunt /dɔːnt/ v.t. intimorire.

dauntless /'dɔːntlɪs/ a. intrepido.

dawdle /'dɔːdl/ v.i. bighellonare. **~r** /-ə(r)/ n. bighellone, a m., f.

dawn /dɔːn/ n. alba f. —v.i. albeggiare; (fig.) venire in mente.

day /deɪ/ n. giorno m.; (whole day) giornata f.; (period) epoca f. **~-break**

n. alba *f.* ~**-dream** *n.* sogno ad occhi aperti *m.*; *v.i.* sognare ad occhi aperti.
daylight /'deɪlaɪt/ *n.* luce del giorno *f.*
daytime /'deɪtaɪm/ *n.* giorno *m.*
daze /deɪz/ *v.t.* stordire —*n.* stordimento *m.* **in a** ~ stordito.
dazzle /'dæzl/ *v.t.* abbagliare.
deacon /'diːkən/ *n.* diacono *m.*
dead /ded/ *a.* morto; (*numb*) esanime. —*adv.* completamente. —*n.* **the** ~ **i** morti *m.pl.* ~ **beat** stanco morto. ~ **end** *n.* vicolo cieco *m.* ~ **on time** in perfetto orario. ~**-pan** *a.* impassibile. ~ **slow** lentissimo. **stop** ~ fermarsi di colpo.
deaden /'dedn/ *v.t.* (*sound, blow*) ammortire; (*pain*) calmare.
deadline /'dedlaɪn/ *n.* termine definitivo *m.*
deadlock /'dedlɒk/ *n.* punto morto *m.*
deadly /'dedlɪ/ *a.* (-ier, -iest) mortale; (*harmful*) micidiale; (*dreary*) insopportabile.
deaf /def/ *a.* (-er, -est) sordo. ~**-aid** *n.* apparecchio acustico *m.* ~ **mute** sordomuto. ~**ness** *n.* sordità *f.*
deafen /'defn/ *v.t.* assordare. ~**ing** *a.* assordante.
deal /diːl/ *v.t.* (*p.t.* **dealt**) distribuire; (*a blow*) assestare; (*cards*) dare. —*v.i.* ~ **in** trattare in. —*v.t.* ~ **with** (*handle*) occuparsi di. —*n.* affare *m.*; (*cards*) mano *f.*; (*treatment*) trattamento *m.* **a great** ~ moltissimo. ~**er** *n.* commerciante *m.*/*f.*
dealings /'diːlɪŋz/ *n.pl.* rapporti *m.pl.*
dean /diːn/ *n.* decano *m.*; (*univ.*) preside di facoltà *m.*
dear /dɪə(r)/ *a.* (-er, -est) caro. —*n.* caro, a *m.*, *f.* —*adv.* a caro prezzo. —*int.* ~ **me!** Dio mio! ~**ly** *adv.* caramente.
dearth /dɜːθ/ *n.* penuria *f.*
death /deθ/ *n.* morte *f.* ~ **duty** tassa di successione *f.* ~**'s head** *n.* teschio *m.* ~**-trap** *n.* tranello *m.* ~**ly** *a.* mortale.
débâcle /deɪ'bɑːkl/ *n.* sfacelo *m.*
debar /dɪ'bɑː(r)/ *v.t.* (*p.t.* **debarred**) escludere.
debase /dɪ'beɪs/ *v.t.* degradare.
debat|e /dɪ'beɪt/ *n.* dibattito *m.* —*v.t.* dibattere. —*v.i.* (*consider*) considerare. ~**able** *a.* discutibile.
debauch /dɪ'bɔːtʃ/ *v.t.* corrompere. ~**ery** *n.* dissolutezza *f.*
debilitate /dɪ'bɪlɪteɪt/ *v.t.* debilitare.
debility /dɪ'bɪlətɪ/ *n.* debolezza *f.*

debit /'debɪt/ *n.* debito *m.* —*v.t.* addebitare.
debonair /debə'neə(r)/ *a.* disinvolto.
debris /'debriː/ *n.* macerie *f.pl.*
debt /det/ *n.* debito *m.* **in** ~ nei debiti. ~**or** *n.* debi|tore, -trice *m.*, *f.*
debutante /'debjuːtɑːnt/ *n.* (*old use*) debuttante *f.*
decade /'dekeɪd/ *n.* decennio *m.*
decaden|t /'dekədənt/ *a.* decadente. ~**ce** *n.* decadenza *f.*
decant /dɪ'kænt/ *v.t.* travasare. ~**er** /ə(r)/ *n.* caraffa *f.*
decapitate /dɪ'kæpɪteɪt/ *v.t.* decapitare.
decay /dɪ'keɪ/ *v.i.* imputridire; (*of tooth*) cariarsi. —*n.* decadenza *f.*; carie *f.*
deceased /dɪ'siːst/ *a.* defunto.
deceit /dɪ'siːt/ *n.* inganno *m.* ~**ful** *a.* falso. ~**fully** *adv.* falsamente.
deceive /dɪ'siːv/ *v.t.* ingannare.
December /dɪ'sembə(r)/ *n.* dicembre *m.*
decen|t /'diːsnt/ *a.* decente; (*good, fam.*) buono; (*kind, fam.*) bravo. ~**cy** *n.* decenza *f.* ~**tly** *adv.* decentemente.
decentralize /diː'sentrəlaɪz/ *v.t.* decentrare.
decept|ive /dɪ'septɪv/ *a.* ingannevole. ~**ion** /-ʃn/ *n.* inganno *m.*
decibel /'desɪbel/ *n.* decibel *m.*
decide /dɪ'saɪd/ *v.t.*/*i.* decidere, decidersi. ~**d** /-ɪd/ *a.* risoluto; (*clear*) netto. ~**dly** /-ɪdlɪ/ *adv.* risolutamente; senza dubbio.
decimal /'desɪml/ *a.* decimale. —*n.* numero decimale *m.* ~ **point** punto *m.*
decimate /'desɪmeɪt/ *v.t.* decimare.
decipher /dɪ'saɪfə(r)/ *v.t.* decifrare.
decision /dɪ'sɪʒn/ *n.* decisione *f.*
decisive /dɪ'saɪsɪv/ *a.* decisivo; (*manner*) deciso. ~**ly** *adv.* decisamente.
deck[1] /dek/ *n.* ponte *m.* ~**-chair** *n.* sedia a sdraio *f.* **top** ~ (*of bus*) imperiale *m.*
deck[2] /dek/ *v.t.* abbigliare.
declaim /dɪ'kleɪm/ *v.t.* declamare.
declar|e /dɪ'kleə(r)/ *v.t.* dichiarare. ~**a-tion** /deklə'reɪʃn/ *n.* dichiarazione *f.*
decline /dɪ'klaɪn/ *v.t.* rifiutare; (*gram.*) declinare. —*v.i.* diminuire; (*health*) deperire. —*n.* declino *m.*
decode /diː'kəʊd/ *v.t.* decifrare.
decompos|e /diːkəm'pəʊz/ *v.t.*/*i.* decomporre, decomporsi. ~**ition** /-ɒmpə'zɪʃn/ *n.* decomposizione *f.*
décor /'deɪkɔː(r)/ *n.* decorazione *f.*; (*furnishing*) disposizione dei mobili *f.*

decorat|e /'dekəreɪt/ v.t. decorare; (*room*) tappezzare. ∼**ion** /-'reɪʃn/ n. decorazione f. ∼**ive** /-ətɪv/ a. decorativo.

decorator /'dekəreɪtə(r)/ n. decora|tore, -trice m., f. **interior** ∼ arreda|tore, -trice m., f.

decorum /dɪ'kɔːrəm/ n. decoro m.

decoy[1] /'diːkɔɪ/ n. esca f.

decoy[2] /dɪ'kɔɪ/ v.t. adescare.

decrease[1] /dɪ'kriːs/ v.t./i. diminuire.

decrease[2] /'diːkriːs/ n. diminuzione f.

decree /dɪ'kriː/ n. decreto m.; (*jurid.*) sentenza f. −v.t. (*p.t.* **decreed**) decretare.

decrepit /dɪ'krepɪt/ a. decrepito.

decry /dɪ'kraɪ/ v.t. denigrare; (*censure*) biasimare.

dedicat|e /'dedɪkeɪt/ v.t. dedicare. ∼**ion** /-'keɪʃn/ n. dedicazione f.; (*in book*) dedica f.

deduce /dɪ'djuːs/ v.t. dedurre.

deduct /dɪ'dʌkt/ v.t. dedurre. ∼**ion** /-ʃn/ n. deduzione f.

deed /diːd/ n. atto m.

deem /diːm/ v.t. ritenere.

deep /diːp/ a. (-er, est) profondo. −adv. profondamente. ∼**-freeze** n. congelatore m. **go off the** ∼ **end** arrabbiarsi. **in** ∼ **waters** in cattive acque. ∼**ly** adv. profondamente.

deepen /'diːpən/ v.t./i. approfondire, approfondirsi.

deer /dɪə(r)/ n. invar. cervo m.

deface /dɪ'feɪs/ v.t. sfigurare.

defamation /defə'meɪʃn/ n. diffamazione f.

default /dɪ'fɔːlt/ v.i. venir meno a un impegno. −n. inadempienza f. **in** ∼ **of** per mancanza di.

defeat /dɪ'fiːt/ v.t. sconfiggere; (*frustrate*) frustrare. −n. sconfitta f.; (*of plan etc.*) fallimento m.

defeatis|t /dɪ'fiːtɪst/ n. disfattista m./f. ∼**m** n. disfattismo m.

defect[1] /'diːfekt/ n. difetto m. ∼**ive** /dɪ'fektɪv/ a. difettoso.

defect[2] /dɪ'fekt/ v.i. fare defezione. ∼**ion** n. defezione f.

defence /dɪ'fens/ n. difesa f. ∼**less** a. indifeso.

defend /dɪ'fend/ v.t. difendere. ∼**ant** n. (*jurid.*) imputato, a m., f.

defensive /dɪ'fensɪv/ a. difensivo. −n. difensiva f.

defer /dɪ'fɜː(r)/ v.t. (*p.t.* **deferred**) rinviare.

deferen|ce /'defərəns/ n. deferenza f. ∼**tial** /-'renʃl/ a. deferente.

defian|ce /dɪ'faɪəns/ n. sfida f. ∼**t** a. spavaldo. ∼**tly** adv. spavaldamente.

deficien|t /dɪ'fɪʃnt/ a. deficiente. **be** ∼**t in** mancare di. ∼**cy** n. insufficienza f.

deficit /'defɪsɪt/ n. deficit m.

defile /dɪ'faɪl/ v.t. contaminare.

define /dɪ'faɪn/ v.t. definire.

definite /'defɪnɪt/ a. definito; (*clear*) preciso; (*firm*) categorico. ∼**ly** adv. definitivamente.

definition /defɪ'nɪʃn/ n. definizione f.

definitive /dɪ'fɪnətɪv/ a. definitivo.

deflat|e /dɪ'fleɪt/ v.t./i. sgonfiare, sgonfiarsi. ∼**ion** /-ʃn/ n. (*comm.*) deflazione f.

deflect /dɪ'flekt/ v.t./i. deflettere.

deform /dɪ'fɔːm/ v.t. deformare. ∼**ed** a. deforme. ∼**ity** n. deformità f.

defraud /dɪ'frɔːd/ v.t. defraudare.

defray /dɪ'freɪ/ v.t. pagare il costo.

defrost /diː'frɒst/ v.t. disgelare.

deft /deft/ a. (-er, -est) destro. ∼**ness** n. destrezza f.

defunct /dɪ'fʌŋkt/ a. defunto.

defuse /diː'fjuːz/ v.t. disinnescare.

defy /dɪ'faɪ/ v.t. sfidare; (*attempts*) resistere a.

degenerate[1] /dɪ'dʒenəreɪt/ v.i. degenerare.

degenerate[2] /dɪ'dʒenərət/ a. & n. degenerato, a m., f.

degrad|e /dɪ'greɪd/ v.t. degradare. ∼**ation** /degrə'deɪʃn/ n. degradazione f.

degree /dɪ'griː/ n. grado m.; (*univ.*) laurea f.; (*rank*) rango m. **to a** ∼ (*fam.*) estremamente.

dehydrate /diː'haɪdreɪt/ v.t./i. disidratare, disidratarsi.

de-ice /diː'aɪs/ v.t. togliere il ghiaccio.

deign /deɪn/ v.i. accondiscendere.

deity /'diːɪtɪ/ n. deità f.

deject|ed /dɪ'dʒektɪd/ a. demoralizzato. ∼**ion** /-ʃn/ n. abbattimento m.

delay /dɪ'leɪ/ v.t. ritardare. −v.i. indugiare. −n. ritardo m.

delectable /dɪ'lektəbl/ a. dilettevole.

delegat|e[1] /'delɪgət/ n. delegato, a m., f. ∼**ion** /-'geɪʃn/ n. delegazione f.

delegate[2] /'delɪgeɪt/ v.t. delegare.

delet|e /dɪ'liːt/ v.t. cancellare. ∼**ion** /-ʃn/ n. cancellatura f.

deliberate[1] /dɪ'lɪbərət/ a. intenzionale; (*steps etc.*) misurato. ∼**ly** adv. deliberatamente.

deliberat|e² /dɪ'lɪbəreɪt/ v.t./i. delibe-rare. ~**ion** /-'reɪʃn/ n. deliberazione f.

delica|te /'delɪkət/ a. delicato. ~**cy** n. delicatezza f.; (food) piatto prelibato m.

delicatessen /delɪkə'tesn/ n. negozio di specialità gastronomiche m.

delicious /dɪ'lɪʃəs/ a. delizioso.

delight /dɪ'laɪt/ n. piacere m. —v.t. deliziare. —v.i. dilettarsi. ~**ed** a. lieto. ~**ful** a. delizioso.

delineat|e /dɪ'lɪnɪeɪt/ v.t. delineare. ~**ion** /-'eɪʃn/ n. delineazione f.

delinquen|t /dɪ'lɪŋkwənt/ a. & n. delin-quente m./f. ~**cy** n. delinquenza f.

deliri|ous /dɪ'lɪrɪəs/ a. delirante. ~**um** n. delirio m.

deliver /dɪ'lɪvə(r)/ v.t. consegnare; (ut-ter) pronunciare; (aim) lanciare; (set free) liberare; (med.) far partorire. ~**ance** n. liberazione f. ~**y** n. con-segna f.; (of post) distribuzione f.; (med.) parto m.

delta /'deltə/ n. delta m.

delu|de /dɪ'lu:d/ v.t. ingannare. ~**de o.s.** illudersi. ~**sion** /-ʒn/ n. illusione f.

deluge /'delju:dʒ/ n. diluvio m.

de luxe /dɪ'lʌks/ a. di lusso.

delve /delv/ v.i. far ricerche.

demagogue /'deməgɒg/ n. demagogo, a m., f.

demand /dɪ'mɑ:nd/ v.t. esigere. —n. richiesta f. ~**s** n.pl. esigenze f.pl. **in** ~ ricercato. **on** ~ a richiesta. ~**ing** a. esigente.

demarcation /di:mɑ:'keɪʃn/ n. demar-cazione f.

demean /dɪ'mi:n/ v.t. ~ **o.s.** abbas-sarsi.

demeanour /dɪ'mi:nə(r)/ n. com-portamento m.

demented /dɪ'mentɪd/ a. demente.

demerara /demə'reərə/ n. ~ **sugar** zucchero non raffinato m.

demise /dɪ'maɪz/ n. decesso m.

demo /'deməʊ/ n. (pl. -os) (fam.) dimo-strazione f.

demobilize /di:'məʊbəlaɪz/ v.t. smobi-litare.

democracy /dɪ'mɒkrəsɪ/ n. demo-crazia f.

democrat /'deməkræt/ n. democratico, a m., f. ~**ic** /-'krætɪk/ a. democratico.

demoli|sh /dɪ'mɒlɪʃ/ v.t. demolire. ~**tion** /demə'lɪʃn/ n. demolizione f.

demon /'di:mən/ n. demonio m.

demonstrat|e /'demənstreɪt/ v.t.

dimostrare. —v.i. fare una dimostra-zione. ~**ion** /-'streɪʃn/ n. dimostra-zione f. ~**or** n. dimostra|tore, -trice m., f.

demonstrative /dɪ'mɒnstrətɪv/ a. dimostrativo.

demoralize /dɪ'mɒrəlaɪz/ v.t. demora-lizzare.

demote /dɪ'məʊt/ v.t. retrocedere di grado.

demure /dɪ'mjʊə(r)/ a. contegnoso.

den /den/ n. tana f.

denial /dɪ'naɪəl/ n. rinnegamento m.; (statement) diniego m.

denigrate /'denɪgreɪt/ v.t. denigrare.

denim /'denɪm/ n. tessuto di cotone ritorto m. ~**s** n.pl. blue-jeans m.pl.

Denmark /'denmɑ:k/ n. Danimarca f.

denomination /dɪnɒmɪ'neɪʃn/ n. deno-minazione f.; (relig.) setta f.

denote /dɪ'nəʊt/ v.t. denotare.

denounce /dɪ'naʊns/ v.t. denunciare.

dens|e /dens/ a. (-er, -est) denso; (per-son) ottuso. ~**ely** adv. densamente. ~**ity** n. densità f.

dent /dent/ n. ammaccatura f. —v.t. ammaccare.

dental /'dentl/ a. dei denti. ~ **surgeon** n. dentista m./f.

dentist /'dentɪst/ n. dentista m./f. ~**ry** n. odontoiatria f.

denture /'dentʃə(r)/ n. dentiera f.

denude /dɪ'nju:d/ v.t. denudare.

denunciation /dɪnʌnsɪ'eɪʃn/ n. denun-cia f.

deny /dɪ'naɪ/ v.t. negare; (rumour) smentire; (disown) rinnegare.

deodorant /di:'əʊdərənt/ a. & n. deodorante m.

depart /dɪ'pɑ:t/ v.i. andarsene. ~ **from** abbandonare.

department /dɪ'pɑ:tment/ n. reparto m.; (geog., univ.) dipartimento m. ~ **store** n. grande magazzino m.

departure /dɪ'pɑ:tʃə(r)/ n. partenza f. ~ **from** (fig.) allontanamento da.

depend /dɪ'pend/ v.i. ~ **on** dipendere (da); (rely) contare su. ~**able** a. fidato. ~**ence** n. dipendenza f. ~**ent** a. dipendente. **be** ~**ent on** essere a carico di.

dependant /dɪ'pendənt/ n. dipendente m./f.

depict /dɪ'pɪkt/ v.t. dipingere; (in words) descrivere.

deplete /dɪ'pli:t/ v.t. esaurire.

deplor|e /dɪ'plɔ:(r)/ v.t. deplorare. ~**able** a. deplorevole.

deploy /dɪ'plɔɪ/ *v.t./i.* (*mil.*) spiegare, spiegarsi.

depopulate /di:'pɒpjʊleɪt/ *v.t.* spopolare.

deport /dɪ'pɔːt/ *v.t.* deportare. **~ation** /di:pɔ'teɪʃn/ *n.* deportazione *f.*

depose /dɪ'pəʊz/ *v.t.* deporre.

deposit /dɪ'pɒzɪt/ *v.t.* (*p.t.* **deposited**) depositare. —*n.* deposito *m.*; (*first instalment*) caparra *f.* **~or** *n.* depositante *m./f.*

depot /'depəʊ/ *n.* deposito *m.*; (*Amer.*) stazione ferroviaria *f.*

deprav|e /dɪ'preɪv/ *v.t.* depravare. **~ity** /-'prævəti/ *n.* depravazione *f.*

deprecate /'deprɪkeɪt/ *v.t.* disapprovare.

depreciat|e /dɪ'priːʃɪeɪt/ *v.t./i.* deprezzare, deprezzarsi. **~ion** /-'eɪʃn/ *n.* deprezzamento *m.*

depress /dɪ'pres/ *v.t.* deprimere; (*press down*) premere. **~ion** /-ʃn/ *n.* depressione *f.*

deprivation /deprɪ'veɪʃn/ *n.* privazione *f.*

deprive /dɪ'praɪv/ *v.t.* privare.

depth /depθ/ *n.* profondità *f.* **be out of one's ~** non toccare il fondo; (*fig.*) sentirsi in alto mare. **in the ~s of** nel più profondo di.

deputation /depjʊ'teɪʃn/ *n.* deputazione *f.*

deputize /'depjʊtaɪz/ *v.i.* **~ for** fare le veci di.

deputy /'depjʊti/ *n.* sostituto, a *m.*, *f.* **~ chairman** vicepresidente *m.*

derail /dɪ'reɪl/ *v.t.* deragliare. **~ment** *n.* deragliamento *m.*

deranged /dɪ'reɪndʒd/ *a.* (*mind*) squilibrato.

Derby /'dɑːbɪ/ *n.* **the D~** il Derby *m.*

derelict /'derəlɪkt/ *a.* abbandonato.

deri|de /dɪ'raɪd/ *v.t.* deridere. **~sion** /-'rɪʒn/ *n.* derisione *f.* **~sive** *a.* derisorio.

derisory /dɪ'raɪsərɪ/ *a.* derisorio; (*offer etc.*) irrisorio.

derivative /dɪ'rɪvətɪv/ *a.* & *n.* derivato *m.*

deriv|e /dɪ'raɪv/ *v.t./i.* derivare. **~ation** /derɪ'veɪʃn/ *n.* derivazione *f.*

derogatory /dɪ'rɒɡətrɪ/ *a.* degradante; (*remark*) spregiativo.

derv /dɜːv/ *n.* gasolio *m.*

descend /dɪ'send/ *v.t./i.* discendere. **~ant** *n.* discendente *m./f.*

descent /dɪ'sent/ *n.* discesa *f.*; (*lineage*) origine *f.*

descri|be /dɪs'kraɪb/ *v.t.* descrivere. **~ption** /-'krɪpʃn/ *n.* descrizione *f.* **~ptive** /-'krɪptɪv/ *a.* descrittivo.

desecrat|e /'desɪkreɪt/ *v.t.* profanare. **~ion** /-'kreɪʃn/ *n.* profanazione *f.*

desert[1] /'dezət/ *a.* & *n.* deserto *m.*

desert[2] /dɪ'zɜːt/ *v.t./i.* abbandonare; (*mil.*) disertare. **~er** *n.* disertore *m.*

deserts /dɪ'zɜːts/ *n.pl.* meriti *m.pl.* **get one's ~** ottenere ciò che ci si merita.

deserv|e /dɪ'zɜːv/ *v.t.* meritare. **~edly** *adv.* meritatamente. **~ing** *a.* (*person*) meritevole; (*action*) meritorio.

design /dɪ'zaɪn/ *n.* disegno *m.*; (*comm.*) progetto *m.*; (*pattern*) modello *m.*; (*aim*) proposito *m.* —*v.t.* disegnare; (*plan*) progettare. **have ~s on** aver mire su. **~er** *n.* disegna|tore, -trice *m.*, *f.*; (*theatr.*) costumista *m./f.*

designat|e /'dezɪɡneɪt/ *v.t.* designare. **~ion** /-'neɪʃn/ *n.* designazione *f.*

desir|e /dɪ'zaɪə(r)/ *n.* desiderio *m.* —*v.t.* desiderare. **~able** *a.* desiderabile. **~ability** /-ə'bɪləti/ *n.* desiderabilità *f.*

desist /dɪ'zɪst/ *v.i.* desistere.

desk /desk/ *n.* scrivania *f.*; (*at school*) banco *m.*; (*comm.*) cassa *f.*

desolat|e /'desələt/ *a.* desolato; (*uninhabited*) disabitato. **~ion** /-'leɪʃn/ *n.* desolazione *f.*

despair /dɪ'speə(r)/ *n.* disperazione *f.* —*v.i.* **~ of** disperare di.

desperat|e /'despərət/ *a.* disperato. **~ely** *adv.* disperatamente. **~ion** /-'reɪʃn/ *n.* disperazione *f.*

despicable /dɪ'spɪkəbl/ *a.* disprezzevole.

despise /dɪ'spaɪz/ *v.t.* disprezzare.

despite /dɪ'spaɪt/ *prep.* malgrado.

desponden|t /dɪ'spɒndənt/ *a.* scoraggiato. **~cy** *n.* abbattimento *m.*

despot /'despɒt/ *n.* despota *m.*

dessert /dɪ'zɜːt/ *n.* dolce *m.* **~-spoon** *n.* cucchiaio da dolce *m.*

destination /destɪ'neɪʃn/ *n.* destinazione *f.*

destine /'destɪn/ *v.t.* destinare.

destiny /'destɪnɪ/ *n.* destino *m.*

destitute /'destɪtjuːt/ *a.* bisognoso. **~ of** privo di.

destr|oy /dɪ'strɔɪ/ *v.t.* distruggere. **~uction** /-'trʌkʃn/ *n.* distruzione *f.* **~uctive** *a.* distruttivo.

destroyer /dɪ'strɔɪə(r)/ *n.* (*naut.*) cacciatorpediniere *m.*

desultory /'desəltrɪ/ *a.* irregolare.

detach /dɪ'tætʃ/ *v.t.* staccare. **~able** *a.*

separabile. ~ed *a*. distaccato. ~ed house villa *f*.

detachment /dɪ'tætʃmənt/ *n*. distacco *m*.; (*mil*.) distaccamento *m*.; (*fig*.) indifferenza *f*.

detail /'di:teɪl/ *n*. dettaglio *m*. —*v.t.* esporre dettagliatamente; (*mil*.) assegnare. ~ed *a*. dettagliato.

detain /dɪ'teɪn/ *v.t.* trattenere; (*prisoner*) detenere. ~ee /di:teɪ'ni:/ *n*. detenuto, a *m*., *f*.

detect /dɪ'tekt/ *v.t.* percepire; (*discover*) scoprire. ~ion /-ʃn/ *n*. scoperta *f*. ~or *n*. rivelatore *m*.

detective /dɪ'tektɪv/ *n*. investigatore *m*. ~ story racconto poliziesco *m*.

detention /dɪ'tenʃn/ *n*. detenzione *f*.; (*schol*.) punizione *f*.

deter /dɪ'tɜ:(r)/ *v.t.* (*p.t.* deterred) impedire.

detergent /dɪ'tɜ:dʒənt/ *a*. & *n*. detersivo *m*.

deteriorat|e /dɪ'tɪərɪəreɪt/ *v.t./i.* deteriorare, deteriorarsi. ~ion /-'reɪʃn/ *n*. deterioramento *m*.

determin|e /dɪ'tɜ:mɪn/ *v.t.* determinare; (*decide*) decidere. ~ation /-'neɪʃn/ *n*. determinazione *f*. ~ed *a*. determinato; (*resolute*) deciso.

deterrent /dɪ'terənt/ *n*. deterrente *m*.

detest /dɪ'test/ *v.t.* detestare. ~-able *a*. detestabile.

detonat|e /'detəneɪt/ *v.t./i.* (far) detonare. ~ion /-'neɪʃn/ *n*. detonazione *f*. ~or *n*. detonatore *m*.

detour /'di:tʊə(r)/ *n*. deviazione *f*.

detract /dɪ'trækt/ *v.i.* ~ from detrarre da.

detriment /'detrɪmənt/ *n*. detrimento *m*. ~al /-'mentl/ *a*. dannoso.

devalu|e /di:'vælju:/ *v.t.* svalutare. ~ation /-'eɪʃn/ *n*. svalutazione *f*.

devastat|e /'devəsteɪt/ *v.t.* devastare. ~ing *a*. devastante.

develop /dɪ'veləp/ *v.t./i.* sviluppare, svilupparsi; (*an illness*) contrarre; (*land*) valorizzare; (*show*) manifestarsi. ~ into divenire. ~er *n*. sviluppatore *m*.; (*of land*) imprendi|tore, -trice *m*., *f*. ~ment *n*. sviluppo *m*.

deviant /'di:vɪənt/ *a*. deviato.

deviat|e /'di:vɪeɪt/ *v.i.* deviare. ~ion /-'eɪʃn/ *n*. deviazione *f*.

device /dɪ'vaɪs/ *n*. arnese *m*.; (*scheme*) progetto *m*.

devil /'devl/ *n*. diavolo *m*. ~ish *a*. diabolico.

devious /'di:vɪəs/ *a*. tortuoso.

devise /dɪ'vaɪz/ *v.t.* escogitare.

devoid /dɪ'vɔɪd/ *a*. ~ of privo di.

devolution /di:və'lu:ʃn/ *n*. (*of power*) decentramento *m*.

devot|e /dɪ'vəʊt/ *v.t.* dedicare. ~ed *a*. devoto. ~edly *adv*. con devozione. ~ion /-ʃn/ *n*. devozione *f*. ~ions *n.pl.* (*relig*.) preghiere *f.pl.*

devotee /devə'ti:/ *n*. appassionato, a *m*., *f*.

devour /dɪ'vaʊə(r)/ *v.t.* divorare.

devout /dɪ'vaʊt/ *a*. devoto.

dew /dju:/ *n*. rugiada *f*.

dext|erity /dek'sterətɪ/ *n*. destrezza *f*. ~rous /'dekstrəs/ *a*. destro.

diabet|es /daɪə'bi:tɪz/ *n*. diabete *m*. ~ic /-'betɪk/ *a*. & *n*. diabetico, a *m*., *f*.

diabolical /daɪə'bɒlɪkl/ *a*. diabolico.

diadem /'daɪədem/ *n*. diadema *m*.

diagnose /'daɪəgnəʊz/ *v.t.* diagnosticare.

diagnosis /daɪəg'nəʊsɪs/ *n*. (*pl.* -oses /-si:z/) diagnosi *f*.

diagonal /daɪ'ægənl/ *a*. & *n*. diagonale *f*.

diagram /'daɪəgræm/ *n*. diagramma *m*.

dial /'daɪəl/ *n*. quadrante *m*.; (*on phone*) disco combinatore *m*. —*v.t.* (*p.t.* dialled) fare il numero. ~ling tone segnale di linea libera *m*.

dialect /'daɪəlekt/ *n*. dialetto *m*.

dialogue /'daɪəlɒg/ *n*. dialogo *m*.

diameter /daɪ'æmɪtə(r)/ *n*. diametro *m*.

diamond /'daɪəmənd/ *n*. diamante, brillante *m*.; (*shape*) losanga *f*. ~s *n.pl.* (*cards*) quadri *m.pl.*

diaper /'daɪəpə(r)/ *n*. (*Amer*.) pannolino *m*.

diaphanous /daɪ'æfənəs/ *a*. diafano.

diaphragm /'daɪəfræm/ *n*. diaframma *m*.

diarrhoea /daɪə'rɪə/ *n*. diarrea *f*.

diary /'daɪərɪ/ *n*. diario *m*.; (*for desk*) agenda *f*.

diatribe /'daɪətraɪb/ *n*. diatriba *f*.

dice /daɪs/ *n. invar.* dadi *m.pl.* —*v.t.* (*culin*.) tagliare a dadini.

dicey /'daɪsɪ/ *a*. (*sl*.) rischioso.

dicker /'dɪkə(r)/ *v.i.* (*fam*.) mercanteggiare.

dictat|e /dɪk'teɪt/ *v.t./i.* dettare. ~ion /-ʃn/ *n*. dettato *m*.

dictates /'dɪkteɪts/ *n.pl.* dettami *m.pl.*.

dictator /dɪk'teɪtə(r)/ *n*. dittatore *m*. ~ship *n*. dittatura *f*.

diction /'dɪkʃn/ *n*. dizione *f*.

dictionary /'dɪkʃənərɪ/ *n.* dizionario *m.*

did /dɪd/ *see* do.

didactic /dɪ'dæktɪk/ *a.* didattico.

diddle /'dɪdl/ *v.t.* (*sl.*) gabbare.

didn't /'dɪdnt/ = **did not.**

die[1] /daɪ/ *v.i.* (*pres. p.* **dying**) morire. ~ **down** calmarsi. ~ **out** estinguersi. **be dying to** morire dal desiderio di.

die[2] /daɪ/ *n.* (*techn.*) stampo *m.*

die-hard /'daɪhɑːd/ *n.* ostinato, a *m.,f.*

diesel /'diːzl/ *n.* (motore) diesel *m.*

diet /'daɪət/ *n.* regime alimentare *m.*; (*restricted*) dieta *f.* —*v.i.* essere a dieta.

diet|etic /daɪə'tetɪk/ *a.* dietetico. ~**i-tian** *n.* dietologo, a *m.,f.*

differ /'dɪfə(r)/ *v.i.* differire; (*disagree*) non essere d'accordo.

differen|t /'dɪfrənt/ *a.* differente. ~**ce** *n.* differenza *f.*; (*disagreement*) divergenza *f.* ~**tly** *adv.* diversamente.

differential /dɪfə'renʃl/ *a.* & *n.* differenziale *m.*

differentiate /dɪfə'renʃɪeɪt/ *v.t./i.* differenziare, differenziarsi.

difficult /'dɪfɪkəlt/ *a.* difficile. ~**ty** *n.* difficoltà *f.*

diffiden|t /'dɪfɪdənt/ *a.* timido, incerto. ~**ce** *n.* timidezza *f.*

diffuse[1] /dɪ'fjuːs/ *a.* diffuso.

diffus|e[2] /dɪ'fjuːz/ *v.t./i.* diffondere, diffondersi. ~**ion** /-ʒn/ *n.* diffusione *f.*

dig /dɪg/ *v.t./i.* (*p.t.* **dug**, *pres. p.* **digging**) scavare; (*thrust*) conficcare. —*n.* (*poke*) spinta *f.*; (*remark*) frecciata *f.*; (*archaeol.*) scavo *m.* ~**s** *n.pl.* (*fam.*) camera ammobiliata *f.s.* ~ **out** tirar fuori. ~ **up** (*find*) scovare; (*tree*) sradicare.

digest[1] /dɪ'dʒest/ *v.t.* digerire. ~**ible** *a.* digeribile. ~**ion** /-ʃn/ *n.* digestione *f.* ~**ive** *a.* digestivo.

digest[2] /'daɪdʒest/ *n.* compendio *m.*

digger /'dɪgə(r)/ *n.* (*mech.*) scavatrice *f.*

digit /'dɪdʒɪt/ *n.* cifra *f.*; (*finger*) dito *m.*

digital /'dɪdʒɪtl/ *a.* digitale.

dignif|y /'dɪgnɪfaɪ/ *v.t.* nobilitare. ~**ied** *a.* dignitoso.

dignitary /'dɪgnɪtərɪ/ *n.* dignitario *m.*

dignity /'dɪgnətɪ/ *n.* dignità *f.*

digress /daɪ'gres/ *v.i.* divagare. ~ **from** allontanarsi da. ~**ion** /-ʃn/ *n.* digressione *f.*

dike /daɪk/ *n.* diga *f.*

dilapidat|ed /dɪ'læpɪdeɪtɪd/ *a.* cadente. ~**ion** /-'deɪʃn/ *n.* dilapidazione *f.*

dilat|e /daɪ'leɪt/ *v.t./i.* dilatare, dilatarsi. ~**ion** /-ʃn/ *n.* dilatazione *f.*

dilatory /'dɪlətərɪ/ *a.* dilatorio.

dilemma /dɪ'lemə/ *n.* dilemma *m.*

diligen|t /'dɪlɪdʒənt/ *a.* diligente. ~**ce** *n.* diligenza *f.*

dilly-dally /'dɪlɪdælɪ/ *v.i.* (*fam.*) tentennare.

dilute /daɪ'ljuːt/ *v.t.* diluire.

dim /dɪm/ *a.* (**dimmer, dimmest**) (*weak*) debole; (*dark*) offuscato; (*fam.*, *stupid*) ottuso. —*v.t./i.* (*p.t.* **dimmed**) (*light*) affievolire. ~ **the headlights** spegnere gli abbaglianti. ~**ness** *n.* debolezza *f.*; oscurità *f.*

dime /daɪm/ *n.* (*Amer.*) moneta da dieci centesimi *f.*

dimension /daɪ'menʃn/ *n.* dimensione *f.*

diminish /dɪ'mɪnɪʃ/ *v.t./i.* diminuire.

diminutive /dɪ'mɪnjʊtɪv/ *a.* minuscolo. —*n.* diminutivo *m.*

dimple /'dɪmpl/ *n.* fossetta *f.* ~**d** *a.* a fossette.

din /dɪn/ *n.* baccano *m.*

dine /daɪn/ *v.i.* pranzare. ~**r** /-ə(r)/ *n.* commensale *m./f.*; (*rail.*) vagone ristorante *m.*

dinghy /'dɪŋgɪ/ *n.* dinghy *m.*; (*naut.*) canotto pneumatico *m.*

ding|y /'dɪndʒɪ/ *a.* (**-ier, -iest**) squallido. ~**iness** *n.* squallore *m.*

dining-room /'daɪnɪŋruːm/ *n.* sala da pranzo *f.*

dinner /'dɪnə(r)/ *n.* pranzo *m.* ~-**jacket** *n.* smoking *m.* ~ **party** cena *f.*

dinosaur /'daɪnəsɔː(r)/ *n.* dinosauro *m.*

dint /dɪnt/ *n.* **by** ~ **of** a forza di.

diocese /'daɪəsɪs/ *n.* diocesi *f. invar.*

dip /dɪp/ *v.t./i.* (*p.t.* **dipped**) immergere; (*pen*) intingere; (*lower*) abbassare. —*n.* (*slope*) inclinazione *f.*; (*in sea*) breve bagno *m.* ~ **into** (*book*) scorrere.

diphtheria /dɪf'θɪərɪə/ *n.* difterite *f.*

diphthong /'dɪfθɒŋ/ *n.* dittongo *m.*

diploma /dɪ'pləʊmə/ *n.* diploma *m.*

diplomacy /dɪ'pləʊməsɪ/ *n.* diplomazia *f.*

diplomat /'dɪpləmæt/ *n.* diplomatico, a *m.,f.* ~**ic** /-'mætɪk/ *a.* diplomatico.

dire /daɪə(r)/ *a.* (**-er, -est**) terribile; (*med.*) estremo.

direct /dɪ'rekt/ *a.* diretto. —*adv.* direttamente. —*v.t.* dirigere; (*show the* *way*) indicare (la via); (*attention*) rivolgere.

direction /dɪ'rekʃn/ *n.* direzione *f.*; (*theatr.*) regia *f.* ∼s *n.pl.* indicazioni *m.pl.*

directly /dɪ'rektlɪ/ *adv.* direttamente; (*at once*) subito. —*conj.* (*fam.*) appena.

director /dɪ'rektə(r)/ *n.* diret|tore, -trice *m.*, *f.*; (*theatr.*) regista *m.|f.*

directory /dɪ'rektərɪ/ *n.* annuario *m.*

dirge /dɜːdʒ/ *n.* canto funebre *m.*

dirt /dɜːt/ *n.* sporcizia *f.* ∼-**track** *n.* (*sport*) pista battuta di cenere *f.*

dirty /'dɜːtɪ/ *a.* (-**ier**, -**iest**) sporco. ∼ **trick** brutto scherzo *m.* ∼ **word** parolaccia *f.* —*v.t.|i.* sporcare, sporcarsi.

disability /dɪsə'bɪlətɪ/ *n.* infermità *f.*

disable /dɪs'eɪbl/ *v.t.* rendere incapace. ∼**d** *a.* invalido.

disabuse /dɪsə'bjuːz/ *v.t.* disingannare.

disadvantage /dɪsəd'vɑːntɪdʒ/ *n.* svantaggio *m.* ∼**d** *a.* svantaggiato.

disagree /dɪsə'griː/ *v.i.* non andare d'accordo; (*of food*, *climate*) far male. ∼**ment** *n.* disaccordo *m.*; (*quarrel*) dissidio *m.*

disagreeable /dɪsə'griːəbl/ *a.* sgradevole.

disappear /dɪsə'pɪə(r)/ *v.i.* scomparire. ∼**ance** *n.* scomparsa *f.*

disappoint /dɪsə'pɔɪnt/ *v.t.* deludere. ∼**ment** *n.* delusione *f.*

disapprov|**e** /dɪsə'pruːv/ *v.i.* disapprovare. ∼**al** *n.* disapprovazione *f.*

disarm /dɪs'ɑːm/ *v.t.|i.* disarmare, disarmarsi. ∼**ament** *n.* disarmo *m.*

disarray /dɪsə'reɪ/ *n.* disordine *m.*

disast|**er** /dɪ'zɑːstə(r)/ *n.* disastro *m.* ∼**rous** *a.* disastroso.

disband /dɪs'bænd/ *v.t.|i.* disperdere, disperdersi.

disbelief /dɪsbɪ'liːf/ *n.* incredulità *f.*

disc /dɪsk/ *n.* disco *m.* ∼ **jockey** presentatore di programma *m.* **slipped** ∼ ernia del disco *f.*

discard /dɪs'kɑːd/ *v.t.* scartare; (*beliefs etc.*) abbandonare.

discern /dɪ'sɜːn/ *v.t.* discernere. ∼**ible** *a.* discernibile. ∼**ing** *a.* perspicace.

discharge /dɪs'tʃɑːdʒ/ *v.t.* scaricare; (*mil.*) congedare; (*dismiss*) licenziare; (*jurid.*) assolvere. —*n.* scarico *m.*; (*electr.*) scarica *f.*; (*med.*) emissione *f.*; (*mil.*) congedo *m.*; (*dismissal*) licenziamento *m.*

disciple /dɪ'saɪpl/ *n.* discepolo *m.*

disciplinarian /dɪsəplɪ'neərɪən/ *n.* disciplina|tore, -trice *m.*, *f.*

disciplin|**e** /'dɪsɪplɪn/ *n.* disciplina *f.* —*v.t.* disciplinare; (*punish*) punire. ∼**ary** *a.* disciplinare.

disclaim /dɪs'kleɪm/ *v.t.* disconoscere. ∼**er** *n.* rifiuto *m.*

disclos|**e** /dɪs'kləʊz/ *v.t.* scoprire. ∼**ure** /-ʒə(r)/ *n.* rivelazione *f.*

disco /'dɪskəʊ/ *n.* (*pl.* -**os**) (*fam.*) discoteca *f.*

discolo|**ur** /dɪs'kʌlə(r)/ *v.t.|i.* scolorire, scolorirsi. ∼**ration** /-'reɪʃn/ *n.* scoloramento *m.*

discomfort /dɪs'kʌmfət/ *n.* disagio *m.*; (*lack of comfort*) scomodità *f.*

disconcert /dɪskən'sɜːt/ *v.t.* sconcertare.

disconnect /dɪskə'nekt/ *v.t.* sconnettere; (*electr.*) staccare.

disconsolate /dɪs'kɒnsələt/ *a.* sconsolato.

discontent /dɪskən'tent/ *n.* scontentezza *f.* ∼**ed** *a.* scontento.

discontinue /dɪskən'tɪnjuː/ *v.t.* cessare, smettere.

discord /'dɪskɔːd/ *n.* discordia *f.* ∼**ant** /-'skɔːdənt/ *a.* discorde.

discothèque /'dɪskətek/ *n.* discoteca *f.*

discount[1] /'dɪskaʊnt/ *n.* sconto *m.*

discount[2] /dɪs'kaʊnt/ *v.t.* non credere a; (*comm.*) scontare.

discourage /dɪs'kʌrɪdʒ/ *v.t.* scoraggiare.

discourse /'dɪskɔːs/ *n.* discorso *m.*

discourteous /dɪs'kɜːtɪəs/ *a.* scortese.

discover /dɪs'kʌvə(r)/ *v.t.* scoprire. ∼**y** *n.* scoperta *f.*

discredit /dɪs'kredɪt/ *v.t.* (*p.t.* **discredited**) screditare. —*n.* discredito *m.*

discreet /dɪs'kriːt/ *a.* discreto. ∼**ly** *adv.* discretamente.

discrepancy /dɪ'skrepənsɪ/ *n.* discrepanza *f.*

discretion /dɪ'skreʃn/ *n.* discrezione *f.*

discriminat|**e** /dɪs'krɪmɪneɪt/ *v.t.|i.* discriminare. ∼**e between** distinguere tra. ∼**ing** *a.* discriminante. ∼**ion** /-'neɪʃn/ *n.* discriminazione *f.*

discus /'dɪskəs/ *n.* disco *m.*

discuss /dɪs'kʌs/ *v.t.* discutere; (*argue about*) dibattere. ∼**ion** /-ʃn/ *n.* discussione *f.*

disdain /dɪs'deɪn/ *n.* sdegno *m.* —*v.t.* sdegnare. ∼**ful** *a.* sdegnoso.

disease /dɪ'ziːz/ *n.* malattia *f.* ∼**d** *a.* malato.

disembark /dɪsɪm'baːk/ v.t./i. sbarcare.

disembodied /dɪsɪm'bɒdɪd/ a. disincarnato.

disenchant /dɪsɪn'tʃɑːnt/ v.t. disincantare. ~ment n. disincanto m.

disengage /dɪsɪn'geɪdʒ/ v.t. disimpegnare. ~ment n. disimpegno m.

disentangle /dɪsɪn'tæŋgl/ v.t. districare.

disfavour /dɪs'feɪvə(r)/ n. sfavore m.

disfigure /dɪs'fɪgə(r)/ v.t. deformare.

disgorge /dɪs'gɔːdʒ/ v.t. rigettare; (of river) scaricare; (fig.) restituire.

disgrace /dɪs'greɪs/ n. vergogna f.; (disfavour) disgrazia f. —v.t. disonorare. ~ful a. vergognoso.

disgruntled /dɪs'grʌntld/ a. malcontento.

disguise /dɪs'gaɪz/ v.t. travestire. —n. travestimento m. in ~ travestito.

disgust /dɪs'gʌst/ n. disgusto m. —v.t. disgustare. ~ing a. disgustoso.

dish /dɪʃ/ n. piatto m. —v.t. ~ out (fam.) distribuire. ~ up servire.

dishcloth /'dɪʃklɒθ/ n. strofinaccio m.

dishearten /dɪs'hɑːtn/ v.t. scoraggiare.

dishevelled /dɪ'ʃevld/ a. scompigliato.

dishonest /dɪs'ɒnɪst/ a. disonesto. ~y n. disonestà f.

dishonour /dɪs'ɒnə(r)/ n. disonore m. —v.t. disonorare. ~able a. disonorevole. ~ably adv. in modo disonorevole.

dishwasher /'dɪʃwɒʃə(r)/ n. lavapiatti f.

disillusion /dɪsɪ'luːʒn/ v.t. disilludere. ~ment n. disillusione f.

disincentive /dɪsɪn'sentɪv/ n. freno m.

disinclined /dɪsɪn'klaɪnd/ a. riluttante.

disinfect /dɪsɪn'fekt/ v.t. disinfettare. ~ant n. disinfettante m.

disinherit /dɪsɪn'herɪt/ v.t./i. diseredare.

disintegrate /dɪs'ɪntɪgreɪt/ v.t./i. disintegrare, disintegrarsi.

disinterested /dɪs'ɪntrəstɪd/ a. disinteressato.

disjointed /dɪs'dʒɔɪntɪd/ a. sconnesso.

disk /dɪsk/ = disc.

dislike /dɪs'laɪk/ n. avversione f. —v.t. provare avversione per.

dislocat|e /'dɪsləkeɪt/ v.t. (limb) slogare. ~ion /-'keɪʃn/ n. slogatura f.

dislodge /dɪs'lɒdʒ/ v.t. sloggiare.

disloyal /dɪs'lɔɪəl/ a. sleale. ~ty n. slealtà f.

dismal /'dɪzməl/ a. tetro.

dismantle /dɪs'mæntl/ v.t. smantellare.

dismay /dɪs'meɪ/ n. costernazione f. —v.t. costernare.

dismiss /dɪs'mɪs/ v.t. congedare; (reject) scacciare. ~al n. congedo m.; (of idea) abbandono m.

dismount /dɪs'maʊnt/ v.i. smontare.

disobedien|t /dɪsə'biːdɪənt/ a. disubbidiente. ~ce n. disubbidienza f.

disobey /dɪsə'beɪ/ v.t./i. disubbidire.

disorder /dɪs'ɔːdə(r)/ n. disordine m.; (ailment) disturbo m. ~ly a. disordinato.

disorganize /dɪs'ɔːgənaɪz/ v.t. disorganizzare.

disorientate /dɪs'ɔːrɪənteɪt/ v.t. disorientare.

disown /dɪs'əʊn/ v.t. ripudiare.

disparaging /dɪs'pærɪdʒɪŋ/ a. sprezzante. ~ly adv. sprezzantemente.

disparity /dɪs'pærətɪ/ n. disparità f.

dispassionate /dɪs'pæʃənət/ a. spassionato.

dispatch /dɪs'pætʃ/ v.t. spedire. —n. spedizione f.; (report) dispaccio m. ~-box n. cassetta dei dispacci f. ~-rider n. staffetta f. with ~ con prontezza.

dispel /dɪs'pel/ v.t. (p.t. dispelled) dissipare.

dispensable /dɪs'pensəbl/ a. dispensabile.

dispensary /dɪs'pensərɪ/ n. farmacia f.

dispensation /dɪspen'seɪʃn/ n. distribuzione f.; (relig.) dispensa f.

dispense /dɪs'pens/ v.t. distribuire; (med.) preparare; (relig.) dispensare; (justice) amministrare. ~ with fare a meno di. ~r /-ə(r)/ n. (mech.) distributore m.; (med.) farmacista m./f.

dispers|e /dɪ'spɜːs/ v.t./i. disperdere, disperdersi. ~al n. dispersione f.

dispirited /dɪs'pɪrɪtɪd/ a. scoraggiato.

displace /dɪs'pleɪs/ v.t. spostare.

display /dɪs'pleɪ/ v.t. mostrare; (goods) esporre; (feelings) manifestare. —n. mostra f.; (of goods) esposizione f.; (of feelings) manifestazione f.; (pej.) ostentazione f.

displeas|e /dɪs'pliːz/ v.t. non piacere a. be ~ed with essere scontento di. ~ure /-'pleʒə(r)/ n. malcontento m.

disposable /dɪs'pəʊzəbl/ a. disponibile.

dispos|e /dɪs'pəʊz/ v.t. disporre. —v.i. ~e of disfarsi di. be well ~ed essere ben disposto. ~al n. (of waste) eliminazione *f*. **at s.o.'s ~al** a disposizione di qcno.

disposition /dɪspə'zɪʃn/ *n*. disposizione *f*.; (*character*) indole *m*.

disproportionate /dɪsprə'pɔːʃənət/ *a*. sproporzionato.

disprove /dɪs'pruːv/ *v.t.* confutare.

dispute /dɪs'pjuːt/ *v.t.* contestare. —*n*. disputa *f*. **in ~** in discussione.

disqualif|y /dɪs'kwɒlɪfaɪ/ *v.t.* rendere incapace; (*sport*) squalificare. **~ica-tion** /-ɪ'keɪʃn/ *n*. squalifica *f*.

disquiet /dɪs'kwaɪət/ *n*. inquietudine *f*.

disregard /dɪsrɪ'gɑːd/ *v.t.* ignorare. —*n*. mancanza di riguardo *f*.

disrepair /dɪsrɪ'peə(r)/ *n*. cattivo stato *m*.

disreputable /dɪs'repjʊtəbl/ *a*. malfamato.

disrepute /dɪsrɪ'pjuːt/ *n*. discredito *m*.

disrespect /dɪsrɪs'pekt/ *n*. mancanza di rispetto *f*.

disrobe /dɪs'rəʊb/ *v.t./i.* svestire, svestirsi.

disrupt /dɪs'rʌpt/ *v.t.* spezzare; (*plans*) sconvolgere. **~ion** /-ʃn/ *n*. scompiglio *m*. **~ive** *a*. disgregante.

dissatisf|ied /dɪ'sætɪsfaɪd/ *a*. scontento. **~action** /dɪsætɪs'fækʃn/ *n*. malcontento *m*.

dissect /dɪ'sekt/ *v.t.* sezionare. **~ion** /-ʃn/ *n*. dissezione *f*.

disseminat|e /dɪ'semɪneɪt/ *v.t.* disseminare. **~ion** /-'neɪʃn/ *n*. disseminazione *f*.

dissent /dɪ'sent/ *v.i.* dissentire. —*n*. dissenso *m*. **~er** /-ə(r)/ *n*. dissidente *m./f*.

dissertation /dɪsə'teɪʃn/ *n*. dissertazione *f*.

disservice /dɪs'sɜːvɪs/ *n*. cattivo servizio *m*.

dissident /'dɪsɪdənt/ *a*. & *n*. dissidente *m./f*.

dissimilar /dɪ'sɪmɪlə(r)/ *a*. dissimile.

dissipate /'dɪsɪpeɪt/ *v.t.* dissipare; (*fig.*) sprecare. **~d** *a*. dissipato.

dissociate /dɪ'səʊʃɪeɪt/ *v.t.* dissociare.

dissolute /'dɪsəljuːt/ *a*. dissoluto.

dissolution /dɪsə'luːʃn/ *n*. dissoluzione *f*.

dissolve /dɪ'zɒlv/ *v.t./i.* dissolvere, dissolversi.

dissuade /dɪ'sweɪd/ *v.t.* dissuadere.

distance /'dɪstəns/ *n*. distanza *f*. **from a ~** da lontano. **in the ~** in lontananza.

distant /'dɪstənt/ *a*. distante.

distaste /dɪs'teɪst/ *n*. avversione *f*. **~ful** *a*. sgradevole.

distemper /dɪ'stempə(r)/ *n*. (*of dogs*) cimurro *m*.; (*paint*) intonaco *m*. —*v.t.* intonacare.

distend /dɪs'tend/ *v.t./i.* dilatare, dilatarsi.

distil /dɪs'tɪl/ *v.t.* (*p.t.* **distilled**) distillare. **~lation** /-'leɪʃn/ *n*. distillazione *f*.

distillery /dɪs'tɪlərɪ/ *n*. distilleria *f*.

distinct /dɪs'tɪŋkt/ *a*. chiaro; (*marked*) netto. **~ion** /-ʃn/ *n*. distinzione *f*.; (*honour*) onorificenza *f*. **~ive** *a*. caratteristico. **~ly** *adv*. chiaramente.

distinguish /dɪs'tɪŋgwɪʃ/ *v.t./i.* distinguere. **~ed** *a*. distinto.

distort /dɪs'tɔːt/ *v.t.* distorcere. **~ion** /-ʃn/ *n*. distorsione *f*.; (*fig.*) alterazione *f*.

distract /dɪs'trækt/ *v.t.* distrarre. **~ed** *a*. sconvolto. **~ing** *a*. sconvolgente. **~ion** /-ʃn/ *n*. distrazione *f*.; (*frenzy*) follia *f*.

distraught /dɪs'trɔːt/ *a*. sconvolto.

distress /dɪs'tres/ *n*. angoscia *f*.; (*poverty*) miseria *f*.; (*danger*) pericolo *m*. —*v.t.* affliggere. **~ing** *a*. penoso.

distribut|e /dɪs'trɪbjuːt/ *v.t.* distribuire. **~ion** /-'bjuːʃn/ *n*. distribuzione *f*. **~or** *n*. distributore *m*.

district /'dɪstrɪkt/ *n*. distretto *m*.; (*of town*) quartiere *m*.

distrust /dɪs'trʌst/ *n*. sfiducia *f*. —*v.t.* sospettare.

disturb /dɪs'tɜːb/ *v.t.* disturbare; (*perturb*) turbare; (*move*) spostare. **~ance** *n*. disturbo *m*.; (*tumult*) tumulto *m*. **~ed** *a*. turbato. **~ing** *a*. sconvolgente.

disused /dɪs'juːzd/ *a*. fuori uso.

ditch /dɪtʃ/ *n*. fosso *m*. —*v.t.* (*sl.*) abbandonare.

dither /'dɪðə(r)/ *v.i.* vacillare. —*n*. (*fam.*) stato di eccitazione *m*.

ditto /'dɪtəʊ/ *n*. idem *m. invar*.

divan /dɪ'væn/ *n*. divano *m*.

div|e /daɪv/ *v.i.* tuffarsi; (*rush*) precipitarsi. —*n*. tuffo *m*.; (*of plane*) picchiata *f*.; (*fam., place*) bettola *f*. **~er** *n*. tuffa|tore, -trice *m.,f*.; (*underwater*) palombaro *m*. **~ing-board** *n*. trampolino *m*. **~ing-suit** *n*. scafandro *m*.

diverge /daɪ'vɜːdʒ/ *v.i.* divergere.

divergent /daɪ'vɜːdʒənt/ *a*. divergente.

diverse /daɪ'vɜːs/ *a*. diverso.

diversify /daɪ'vɜːsɪfaɪ/ *v.t.* diversificare.

diversity /dar'vɜːsətɪ/ *n*. diversità *f*.

diver|t /daɪ'vɜːt/ *v.t.* deviare; (*entertain*) distrarre. **~sion** /-ʃn/ *n.* deviazione *f.*; (*distraction*) diversivo *m.*

divest /daɪ'vest/ *v.t.* **~ of** privare di.

divide /dɪ'vaɪd/ *v.t./i.* dividere, dividersi.

dividend /'dɪvɪdend/ *n.* dividendo *m.*

divine /dɪ'vaɪn/ *a.* divino.

divinity /dɪ'vɪnɪtɪ/ *n.* divinità *f.*

division /dɪ'vɪʒn/ *n.* divisione *f.*

divorce /dɪ'vɔːs/ *n.* divorzio *m.* —*v.t./i.* divorziare, divorziarsi.

divorcee /dɪvɔː'siː/ *n.* divorziato, a *m.*, *f.*

divulge /daɪ'vʌldʒ/ *v.t.* divulgare.

DIY *abbr. see* **do-it-yourself.**

dizz|y /'dɪzɪ/ *a.* (-ier, -iest) vertiginoso. **be** *or* **feel ~y** avere le vertigini. **~iness** *n.* vertigine *f.*

do /duː/ *v.t./i.* (*3 sing. pres.* **does,** *p.t.* **did,** *p.p.* **done**) fare; (*fare, be suitable*) andare; (*be enough*) bastare; (*sl., swindle*) ingannare. **done for** (*fam.*) rovinato. **done in** (*fam.*) esausto. **well done!** bravo! —*v. aux.* **~ you speak Italian? Yes I ~** parla italiano? Sì. **don't you?, doesn't he?** vero? (*emphatic*) **~ come in!** entrate! —*n.* (*pl.* **dos** *or* **do's**) (*fam.*) festa *f.* **~ away with** abolire. **~ in** (*fam., deceive*) ingannare; (*sl., kill*) uccidere. **~ out** pulire. **~ up** (*coat etc.*) abbottonare; (*house*) rimettere a nuovo. **~ with** fare di; (*need*) aver bisogno di. **~ without** fare a meno di.

docile /'dəʊsaɪl/ *a.* docile.

dock[1] /dɒk/ *n.* bacino *m.* —*v.t./i.* entrare in bacino. **~er** *n.* scaricatore di porto *m.*

dock[2] /dɒk/ *n.* (*jurid.*) banco degli imputati *m.*

docket /'dɒkɪt/ *n.* bolletta *f.*; (*voucher*) scontrino *m.*

dockyard /'dɒkjɑːd/ *n.* cantiere navale *m.*

doctor /'dɒktə(r)/ *n.* dottore *m.*, dottoressa *f.* —*v.t.* (*cat*) castrare; (*fig.*) adulterare.

doctorate /'dɒktərət/ *n.* dottorato *m.*

doctrine /'dɒktrɪn/ *n.* dottrina *f.*

document /'dɒkjʊmənt/ *n.* documento *m.* **~ary** /-'mentrɪ/ *a.* & *n.* documentario *m.*

doddering /'dɒdərɪŋ/ *a.* barcollante.

dodge /dɒdʒ/ *v.t./i.* scansare, scansarsi. —*n.* balzo *m.*; (*fam.*) trucco *m.* **~r** *n.* (*fam.*) furbacchione, a *m.*, *f.*

dodgems /'dɒdʒəmz/ *n.pl.* autoscontro *m.s.*

dodgy /'dɒdʒɪ/ *a.* (-ier, -iest) (*awkward*) difficile.

does /dʌz/ *see* **do.**

doesn't /'dʌznt/ = **does not.**

dog /dɒg/ *n.* cane *m.* —*v.t.* (*p.t.* **dogged**) pedinare. **~-collar** *n.* (*fam., relig.*) collare *m.* **~-eared** *a.* (*book*) con orecchie. **~-house** *n.* (*Amer.*) canile *m.* **in the ~house** (*sl.*) in disgrazia.

dogged /'dɒgɪd/ *a.* ostinato.

dogma /'dɒgmə/ *n.* dogma *m.* **~tic** /-'mætɪk/ *a.* dogmatico.

dogsbody /'dɒgzbɒdɪ/ *n.* (*fam.*) facchino *m.*

doh /dəʊ/ *n.* (*mus.*) do *m.*

doily /'dɔɪlɪ/ *n.* centrino *m.*

doings /'duːɪŋz/ *n.pl.* (*fam.*) attività *f.pl.*

do-it-yourself /duːɪtjɔː'self/ (*abbr.* **DIY**) *n.* il far da sé *m.*

doldrums /'dɒldrəmz/ *n.pl.* **be in the ~** essere giù.

dole /dəʊl/ *v.t.* **~ out** distribuire. —*n.* (*fam.*) sussidio di disoccupazione *m.* **on the ~** (*fam.*) disoccupato.

doleful /'dəʊlfl/ *a.* triste.

doll /dɒl/ *n.* bambola *f.* —*v.t.* **~ up** (*fam.*) agghindare.

dollar /'dɒlə(r)/ *n.* dollaro *m.*

dollop /'dɒləp/ *n.* (*fam.*) cucchiaiata *f.*; (*of cream*) palla *f.*

dolphin /'dɒlfɪn/ *n.* delfino *m.*

domain /dəʊ'meɪn/ *n.* dominio *m.*

dome /dəʊm/ *n.* cupola *f.* **~d** *a.* a cupola.

domestic /də'mestɪk/ *a.* domestico; (*trade, flights, etc.*) interno. **~ science** *n.* economia domestica *f.* **~ servant** *n.* domestico, a *m.*, *f.* **~ated** *a.* (*animal*) addomesticato.

domesticity /dɒme'stɪsətɪ/ *n.* vita familiare *f.*

dominant /'dɒmɪnənt/ *a.* dominante.

dominat|e /'dɒmɪneɪt/ *v.t./i.* dominare. **~ion** /-'neɪʃn/ *n.* dominazione *f.*

domineer /dɒmɪ'nɪə(r)/ *v.i.* spadroneggiare.

dominion /də'mɪnjən/ *n.* dominio *m.*

domino /'dɒmɪnəʊ/ *n.* (*pl.* **~oes**) domino *m.*

don[1] /dɒn/ *v.t.* (*p.t.* **donned**) indossare.

don[2] /dɒn/ *n.* docente universitario, a *m.*, *f.*

donat|e /dəʊ'neɪt/ *v.t.* donare. **~ion** /-ʃn/ *n.* donazione *f.*

done /dʌn/ *see* **do.**

donkey /'dɒŋkɪ/ *n.* asino *m.* ~ **jacket** giaccone *m.* ~ **-work** *n.* sgobbata *f.*

donor /'dəʊnə(r)/ *n.* (*of blood*) dona|tore, -trice *m.*, *f.*

don't /dəʊnt/ = **do not**.

doodle /'duːdl/ *v.i.* scarabocchiare.

doom /duːm/ *n.* fato (crudele) *m.* —*v.t.* **be** ~**ed to** essere condannato a.

doomsday /'duːmzdeɪ/ *n.* giudizio universale *m.*

door /dɔː(r)/ *n.* porta *f.*

doorman /'dɔːmən/ *n.* (*pl.* **-men**) portiere *m.*

doormat /'dɔːmæt/ *n.* stuoia *f.*

doorstep /'dɔːstep/ *n.* gradino di entrata *m.*

doorway /'dɔːweɪ/ *n.* vano della porta *f.*

dope /dəʊp/ *n.* (*fam.*) stupefacente *m.*; (*sl.*, *information*) informazione segreta *f.*; (*sl.*, *idiot*) idiota *m.*|*f.* —*v.t.* (*fam.*) drogare. ~**y** *a.* (*sl.*) inebetito.

dormant /'dɔːmənt/ *a.* inattivo.

dormer /'dɔːmə(r)/ *n.* ~ **(window)** abbaino *m.*

dormitory /'dɔːmɪtrɪ/ *n.* dormitorio *m.*

dormouse /'dɔːmaʊs/ *n.* (*pl.* **-mice**) ghiro *m.*

dos|e /dəʊs/ *n.* dose *f.* ~**age** *n.* dosatura *f.*; (*on label*) dosaggio *m.*

doss /dɒs/ *v.i.* (*sl.*) coricarsi. ~ **house** *n.* dormitorio pubblico *m.*

dot /dɒt/ *n.* punto *m.* —*v.t.* (*p.t.* **dotted**) punteggiare. **be** ~**ted with** essere punteggiato di. ~**ted line** linea tratteggiata *f.* **on the** ~ puntuale.

dote /dəʊt/ *v.i.* ~ **on** stravedere per.

dotty /'dɒtɪ/ *a.* (**-ier**, **-iest**) (*fam.*) picchiatello.

double /'dʌbl/ *a.* doppio. —*adv.* in due, due volte. —*n.* doppio *m.*; (*person*) sosia *m.* ~**s** (*tennis*) doppio *m.* —*v.t.*/*i.* raddoppiare; (*fold*) piegare in due; (*turn back*) ripiegare. **at the** ~ a passo di corsa. ~**-bass** *n.* contrabbasso *m.* ~ **bed** letto matrimoniale *m.* ~**-breasted** *a.* a doppio petto. ~ **chin** doppio mento *m.* ~**-cross** *v.t.* ingannare. ~**-dealing** *n.* duplicità *f.* ~**-decker** *n.* autobus a due piani *m.* ~ **Dutch** ostrogoto *m.* ~**-jointed** *a.* snodato. **doubly** *adv.* doppiamente.

doubt /daʊt/ *n.* dubbio *m.* —*v.t.* dubitare. ~**ful** *a.* dubbio; (*person*) titubante. ~**less** *adv.* indubbiamente.

dough /dəʊ/ *n.* pasta *f.*; (*for bread*) impasto *m.*; (*sl.*) quattrini *m.pl.*

doughnut /'dəʊnʌt/ *n.* frittella dolce *f.*

dove /dʌv/ *n.* colomba *f.*

dowager /'daʊədʒə(r)/ *n.* vedova nobile *f.*

dowdy /'daʊdɪ/ *a.* (**-ier**, **-iest**) trasandato.

down[1] /daʊn/ *n.* (*feathers*) piumino *m.*

down[2] /daʊn/ *n.* (*open land*) duna *f.* ~**s** *n.pl.* colline *f.pl.*

down[3] /daʊn/ *adv.* giù, abbasso, sotto. —*prep.* giù per. —*a.* discendente. —*v.t.* (*fam.*) buttar giù. **come** *or* **go** ~ discendere. ~**-and-out** *n.* squattrinato *m.* ~**-hearted** *a.* scoraggiato. ~ **payment** deposito *m.* ~**-to-earth** *a.* pratico. ~ **under** agli antipodi. ~ **with** abbasso.

downcast /'daʊnkɑːst/ *a.* scoraggiato.

downfall /'daʊnfɔːl/ *n.* caduta *f.*

downgrade /daʊn'greɪd/ *v.t.* degradare.

downhill /daʊn'hɪl/ *adv.* **go** ~ andare in discesa.

downpour /'daʊnpɔː(r)/ *n.* acquazzone *m.*

downright /'daʊnraɪt/ *a.* vero; (*honest*) franco. —*adv.* veramente.

downstairs /daʊn'steəz/ *adv.* dabbasso. — /'daʊnsteəz/ *a.* di sotto.

downstream /'daʊnstriːm/ *adv.* a valle.

downtrodden /'daʊntrɒdn/ *a.* calpestato.

downward /'daʊnwəd/ *a.* & *adv.*, ~**s** *adv.* verso il basso.

dowry /'daʊərɪ/ *n.* dote *f.*

doze /dəʊz/ *v.i.* sonnecchiare. ~ **off** assopirsi. —*n.* sonnellino *m.*

dozen /'dʌzn/ *n.* dozzina *f.* ~**s of** (*fam.*) decine di.

Dr *abbr.* (*of* **Doctor**) Dott. *m.*

drab /dræb/ *a.* tetro.

draft[1] /drɑːft/ *n.* abbozzo *m.*; (*comm.*) cambiale *f.*; (*mil.*) distaccamento *m.*; (*Amer.*) leva *f.* —*v.t.* abbozzare; (*mil.*) distaccare; (*Amer.*) arruolare.

draft[2] /drɑːft/ *n.* (*Amer.*) = **draught**.

drag /dræg/ *v.t.*/*i.* (*p.t.* **dragged**) trascinare, trascinarsi; (*river*) dragare. —*n.* (*fam.*) noia *f.* **in** ~ (*sl.*, *man*) travestito da donna.

dragon /'drægən/ *n.* drago *m.*

dragon-fly /'drægənflaɪ/ *n.* libellula *f.*

drain /dreɪn/ *v.t.* (*land*) prosciugare; (*vegetables*) scolare; (*med.*) drenare; (*tank*, *glass*) vuotare; (*fig.*) esaurire. —*n.* canale di scolo *m.* **be a** ~ **on** essere un peso per. ~**ing-board** *n.* scolapiatti *m.*

drama /'drɑːmə/ *n.* arte drammatica *f.*; (*event*) dramma *m.* ~**tic** /drə'mætɪk/ *a.* drammatico. ~**tist** /'dræmətɪst/ *n.* drammaturgo *m.* ~**tize** /'dræmətaɪz/ *v.t.* adattare per il teatro; (*fig.*) drammatizzare.

drank /dræŋk/ *see* **drink.**

drape /dreɪp/ *v.t.* drappeggiare.

drastic /'dræstɪk/ *a.* drastico.

draught /drɑːft/ *n.* corrente (d'aria) *f.*; (*pulling*) tiro *m.* ~**s** *n. pl.* (*game*) (giuoco della) dama (*m.*) *f. s.* ~ **beer** birra alla spina *f.* ~**y** *a.* pieno di correnti d'aria.

draughtsman /'drɑːftsmən/ *n.* (*pl.* -**men**) disegna|tore, -trice *m.*, *f.*

draw /drɔː/ *v.t.* (*p.t.* **drew,** *p.p.* **drawn**) tirare; (*attract*) attirare; (*picture*) disegnare; (*line*) tracciare; (*money*) ritirare. —*v.i.* (*sport*) pareggiare; (*in lottery*) sorteggiare. —*n.* (*sport*) pareggio *m.*; (*in lottery*) sorteggio *m.* ~ **in** (*days*) accorciarsi. ~ **out** (*days*) diventare lunghi. ~ **the line at** porre un limite a. ~ **up** fermarsi; (*document*) redigere; (*chair*) accostare.

drawback /'drɔːbæk/ *n.* inconveniente *m.*

drawbridge /'drɔːbrɪdʒ/ *n.* ponte levatoio *m.*

drawer /drɔː(r)/ *n.* cassetto *m.*

drawers /drɔːz/ *n.pl.* mutandoni *f.pl.*

drawing /'drɔːɪŋ/ *n.* disegno *m.* ~**-pin** *n.* puntina *f.* ~**-room** *n.* salotto *m.*

drawl /drɔːl/ *n.* pronuncia strascicata *f.*

drawn /drɔːn/ *see* **draw.** —*a.* (*features*) tirato.

dread /dred/ *n.* timore *m.* —*v.t.* temere.

dreadful /'dredfl/ *a.* terribile. ~**ly** *adv.* terribilmente.

dream /driːm/ *n.* sogno *m.* —*v.t./i.* (*p.t.* **dreamed** *or* **dreamt**) sognare —*a.* di sogno. ~ **up** inventare. ~**er** *n.* sogna|tore, -trice *m.*, *f.* ~**y** *a.* sognante.

drear|y /'drɪərɪ/ *a.* (-**ier**, -**iest**) tetro; (*boring*) monotono. ~**iness** *n.* desolazione *f.*; monotonia *f.*

dredge /dredʒ/ *n.* draga *f.* —*v.t./i.* dragare. ~**r** *n.* draga *f.*; (*for sugar*) spargizucchero *m. invar.*

dregs /dregz/ *n.pl.* feccia *f.s.*

drench /drentʃ/ *v.t.* inzuppare.

dress /dres/ *n.* vestito *m.*; (*clothing*) abbigliamento *m.* —*v.t./i.* vestire, vestirsi; (*decorate*) adornare; (*med.*) fasciare; (*culin.*) condire. ~ **circle** *n.* prima galleria *f.* ~ **rehearsal** *n.* prova generale *f.*

dresser /'dresə(r)/ *n.* (*theatr.*) costumista *f.*; (*furniture*) credenza *f.*

dressing /'dresɪŋ/ *n.* (*sauce*) condimento *m.*; (*bandage*) benda *f.*; (*stiffener*) conciatura *f.* ~**-case** *n.* borsa da toletta *f.* ~ **down** *n.* sgridata *f.* ~**-gown** *n.* vestaglia *f.* ~**-room** *n.* spogliatoio *m.*; (*theatr.*) camerino *m.* ~**-table** *n.* toletta *f.*

dressmak|er /'dresmeɪkə(r)/ *n.* sarta *f.* ~**ing** *n.* confezioni (per donna) *f.pl.*

dressy /'dresɪ/ *a.* (-**ier**, -**iest**) elegante.

drew /druː/ *see* **draw.**

dribble /'drɪbl/ *v.i.* gocciolare; (*baby*) sbavare; (*in football*) filtrare.

dribs and drabs /drɪbzn'dræbz/ *n.pl.* **in** ~ alla spicciolata *f.*

dried /draɪd/ *a.* (*of food*) secco.

drier /'draɪə(r)/ *n.* asciugatoio *m.*

drift /drɪft/ *v.i.* essere trasportato; (*of snow*) ammucchiarsi. —*n.* (*movement*) direzione *f.*; (*of snow*) cumulo *m.*; (*meaning*) senso *m.* ~ **apart** (*of persons*) perdersi di vista. ~**er** *n.* persona senza meta *f.*

driftwood /'drɪftwʊd/ *n.* pezzi di legno galleggianti *m.pl.*

drill /drɪl/ *n.* (*tool*) trapano *m.*; (*training*) esercitazione *f.*; (*fig.*) procedura *f.* —*v.t.* trapanare; (*train*) esercitare. —*v.i.* esercitarsi.

drily /'draɪlɪ/ *adv.* seccamente.

drink /drɪŋk/ *v.t./i.* (*p.t.* **drank,** *p.p.* **drunk**) bere. —*n.* bibita *f.* ~**able** *a.* potabile. ~**er** *n.* bevi|tore, -trice *m.*, *f.* ~**ing-water** *n.* acqua potabile *f.*

drip /drɪp/ *v.i.* (*p.t.* **dripped**) gocciolare; (*of sweat*) grondare. —*n.* gocciolamento *m.*; (*med.*) fleboclisi *f.*; (*sl.*, *person*) persona insipida *f.* ~**-dry** *a.* che non si stira.

dripping /'drɪpɪŋ/ *n.* grasso d'arrosto *m.*

drive /draɪv/ *v.t./i.* (*p.t.* **drove,** *p.p.* **driven**) condurre; (*car etc.*) guidare; (*fig.*) spingere. —*n.* gita *f.*; (*road*) viale *m.*; (*fig.*) energia *f.*; (*pol.*) campagna *f.* ~ **at** mirare a. ~ **in** conficcare; (*car*) entrare (con un veicolo). ~ **s.o. mad** far impazzire qcno.

driver /'draɪvə(r)/ *n.* guida|tore, -trice *m.*, *f.*

drivel /'drɪvl/ *n.* sciocchezze *f.pl.*

driving /'draɪvɪŋ/ *n.* guida *f.* ~**-li-**

cence *n.* patente *f.* ~ **school** *n.* scuola guida *f.*

drizzl|e /'drɪzl/ *n.* pioggerella *f.* —*v.i.* piovigginare. ~**y** *a.* piovigginoso.

dromedary /'drɒmədərɪ/ *n.* dromedario *m.*

drone /drəʊn/ *n.* fuco *m.*; (*fam.*, *lay-about*) fannullone, a *m.*, *f.* —*v.i.* ronzare; (*fig.*) parlare con voce monotona; (*fam.*, *idle*) oziare.

drool /druːl/ *v.i.* sbavare.

droop /druːp/ *v.t./i.* abbassare, abbassarsi; (*of flowers*) appassirsi.

drop /drɒp/ *n.* goccia *f.*; (*fall*) caduta *f.*; (*of cliff*) discesa *f.* —*v.t./i.* (*p.t.* dropped) (far) cadere; (*fall*, *lower*) abbassare. ~ **in on** passare da. ~ **off** assopirsi. ~ **out** ritirarsi; (*of student*) abbandonare gli studi. ~**-out** *n.* persona emarginata dalla società *f.*

droppings /'drɒpɪŋz/ *n.pl.* sterco *m.*

dross /drɒs/ *n.* scoria *f.*

drought /draʊt/ *n.* siccità *f.*

drove /drəʊv/ *see* **drive.** —*n.* branco *m.*

drown /draʊn/ *v.t./i.* annegare.

drowsy /'draʊzɪ/ *a.* sonnolento.

drudge /drʌdʒ/ *n.* sgobbone, a *m.*, *f.* ~**ry** /-ərɪ/ *n.* lavoro monotono *m.*

drug /drʌg/ *n.* droga *f.*; (*med.*) farmaco *m.* —*v.t.* (*p.t.* drugged) drogare. ~ **addict** *n.* tossicomane, a *m.*, *f.*

drugstore /'drʌgstɔ:(r)/ *n.* (*Amer.*) drugstore *m. invar.*

drum /drʌm/ *n.* tamburo *m.*; (*for oil*) bidone *m.*; (*mech.*) cilindro *m.* —*v.i.* (*p.t.* drummed) suonare il tamburo. —*v.t.* ~ **into s.o.** inculcare nella mente di qcno. ~**mer** *n.* batterista *m./f.*

drumstick /'drʌmstɪk/ *n.* bacchetta (di tamburo) *f.*; (*culin.*) zampa di pollo *f.*

drunk /drʌŋk/ *see* **drink.** —*a.* ubriaco. **get** ~ ubriacarsi. ~**ard** *n.* ubriacone, a *m.*, *f.* ~**en** *a.* ubriaco. ~**enness** *n.* ubriachezza *f.*

dry /draɪ/ *a.* (**drier, driest**) asciutto. —*v.t./i.* asciugare. ~**-clean** *v.t.* pulire a secco. ~**-cleaner** *n.* smacchiatore a secco *m.*; (*shop*) tintoria *f.* ~ **up** asciugare le stoviglie; (*fam.*) smettere di parlare. ~**ness** *n.* siccità *f.*

dual /'djuːəl/ *a.* doppio. ~ **carriageway** *n.* strada a doppia carreggiata *f.* ~**-purpose** *a.* a doppio uso.

dub /dʌb/ *v.t.* (*p.t.* dubbed) (*film*) doppiare; (*nickname*) soprannominare.

dubious /'djuːbɪəs/ *a.* dubbio; (*person*) dubbioso.

duchess /'dʌtʃɪs/ *n.* duchessa *f.*

duck /dʌk/ *n.* anitra *f.* —*v.t./i.* immergere, immergersi; (*head*) abbassare. ~**ling** *n.* anatroccolo *m.*

duct /dʌkt/ *n.* condotto *m.*

dud /dʌd/ *a.* inutile; (*cheque*) a vuoto; (*coin*) falso.

due /djuː/ *a.* dovuto; (*expected*) atteso. —*adv.* ~ **north** direttamente a nord. —*n.* il dovuto *m.* ~**s** *n.pl.* diritti *m.pl.* ~ **to** a causa di.

duel /'djuːəl/ *n.* duello *m.*

duet /djuː'et/ *n.* duetto *m.*

duffle /'dʌfl/ *a.* ~ **bag** sacco *m.* ~**-coat** *n.* montgomery *m. invar.*

dug /dʌg/ *see* **dig.**

duke /djuːk/ *n.* duca *m.*

dull /dʌl/ *a.* (**-er, -est**) ottuso; (*of sky*) cupo; (*colour*) smorto; (*person, play, etc.*) monotono; (*sound*) soffocato; (*knife*) spuntato. —*v.t.* (*pain*) ammortire; (*mind*) intorpidire.

duly /'djuːlɪ/ *adv.* debitamente.

dumb /dʌm/ *a.* (**-er, -est**) muto; (*fam.*) ottuso.

dumbfound /dʌm'faʊnd/ *v.t.* sbalordire.

dummy /'dʌmɪ/ *n.* fantoccio *m.*; (*of tailor*) manichino *m.*; (*of baby*) succhiotto *m.* —*a.* finto. ~ **run** *n.* prova *f.*

dump /dʌmp/ *v.t./i.* scaricare; (*fam.*) sbarazzarsi di. —*n.* luogo di scarico *m.*; (*mil.*) deposito *m.*; (*fam.*) posto squallido *m.* **be down in the** ~**s** essere depresso.

dumpling /'dʌmplɪŋ/ *n.* gnocco *m.*

dumpy /'dʌmpɪ/ *a.* (**-ier, -iest**) tarchiato.

dunce /dʌns/ *n.* zuccone, a *m.*, *f.*

dung /dʌŋ/ *n.* letame *m.*

dungarees /dʌŋgə'riːz/ *n.pl.* tuta *f.s.*

dungeon /'dʌndʒən/ *n.* prigione sotterranea *f.*

dunk /dʌŋk/ *v.t.* intingere.

duo /'djuːəʊ/ *n.* duetto *m.*

dupe /djuːp/ *v.t.* gabbare. —*n.* credulone, a *m.*, *f.*

duplicate[1] /'djuːplɪkət/ *n.* copia *f.* —*a.* doppio.

duplicat|e[2] /'djuːplɪkeɪt/ *v.t.* raddoppiare; (*on machine*) ciclostilare. ~**or** *n.* ciclostile *m.*

duplicity /djuː'plɪsətɪ/ *n.* duplicità *f.*

durable /'djʊərəbl/ *a.* resistente; (*enduring*) durevole.

duration /djʊ'reɪʃn/ *n.* durata *f.*

duress /djʊ'res/ *n.* costrizione *f.* **under** ~ sotto minaccia.

during /'djʊərɪŋ/ *prep.* durante.

dusk /dʌsk/ *n.* crepuscolo *m.*

dusky /'dʌskɪ/ *a.* (**-ier, -iest**) oscuro.

dust /dʌst/ *n.* polvere *f.* —*v.t.* spolverare; (*sprinkle*) cospargere. ~-**cover, ~-jacket** *ns.* sopraccoperta *f.*

dustbin /'dʌstbɪn/ *n.* pattumiera *f.*

duster /'dʌstə(r)/ *n.* strofinaccio *m.*

dustman /'dʌstmən/ *n.* (*pl.* -**men**) spazzino *m.*

dustpan /'dʌstpən/ *n.* paletta per la spazzatura *f.*

dusty /'dʌstɪ/ *a.* (**-ier, -iest**) polveroso.

Dutch /dʌtʃ/ *a.* & *n.* olandese *m./f.* ~**man,** ~**woman** *n.* olandese *m./f.* **go** ~ fare alla romana.

dutiful /'dju:tɪfl/ *a.* rispettoso.

duty /'dju:tɪ/ *n.* dovere *m.*; (*tax*) dogana *f.* **on** ~ di servizio. ~-**free** *a.* esente da dogana.

duvet /'dju:veɪ/ *n.* piumone *m.*

dwarf /dwɔːf/ *n.* (*pl.* -**s**) nano, a *m., f.* —*v.t.* rimpicciolire.

dwell /dwel/ *v.i.* (*p.t.* **dwelt**) dimorare. ~ **on** soffermarsi su. ~**er** *n.* abitante *m./f.* ~**ing** *n.* abitazione *f.*

dwindle /'dwɪndl/ *v.i.* diminuire.

dye /daɪ/ *v.t.* (*pres. p.* **dyeing**) tingere. —*n.* tintura *f.*

dying /'daɪɪŋ/ *see* **die**[1].

dynamic /daɪ'næmɪk/ *a.* dinamico. ~**s** *n.pl.* dinamica *f.s.*

dynamite /'daɪnəmaɪt/ *n.* dinamite *f.* —*v.t.* far saltare con la dinamite.

dynamo /'daɪnəməʊ/ *n.* dinamo *f. invar.*

dynasty /'dɪnəstɪ/ *n.* dinastia *f.*

dysentery /'dɪsəntrɪ/ *n.* dissenteria *f.*

dyslexia /dɪs'leksɪə/ *n.* dislessia *f.*

E

each /iːtʃ/ *a.* ogni. —*pron.* ognuno. ~ **one** ciascuno. ~ **other** l'un l'altro. **they love** ~ **other** si amano.

eager /'iːgə(r)/ *a.* desideroso; (*enthusiastic*) avido. ~**ly** *adv.* ansiosamente. ~**ness** *n.* zelo *m.*, premura *f.*

eagle /'iːgl/ *n.* aquila *f.*

ear[1] /ɪə(r)/ *n.* orecchio *m.* ~**-drum** *n.* timpano *m.* ~**-ring** *n.* orecchino *m.*

ear[2] /ɪə(r)/ *n.* (*of corn*) spiga *f.*

earache /'ɪəreɪk/ *n.* mal d'orecchi *m.*

earl /ɜːl/ *n.* conte *m.*

early /'ɜːlɪ/ *a.* (-**ier, -iest**) primo; (*morning*) mattutino; (*before expected time*) prematuro. —*adv.* presto. **arrive** ~ arrivare in anticipo. **in the** ~ **spring** al principio della primavera.

earmark /'ɪəmɑːk/ *v.t.* ~ **for** destinare a.

earn /ɜːn/ *v.t.* guadagnare; (*deserve*) meritare.

earnest /'ɜːnɪst/ *a.* serio. **in** ~ sul serio.

earnings /'ɜːnɪŋz/ *n.pl.* guadagni *m.pl.*; (*salary*) stipendio *m.s.*

earphones /'ɪəfəʊnz/ *n.pl.* cuffia *f.s.*

earshot /'ɪəʃɒt/ *n.* **within** ~ a portata d'orecchio.

earth /ɜːθ/ *n.* terra *f.* —*v.t.* (*electr.*) mettere a terra. ~**ly** *a.* terrestre.

earthenware /'ɜːθnweə(r)/ *n.* terraglia *f.*

earthquake /'ɜːθkweɪk/ *n.* terremoto *m.*

earthy /'ɜːθɪ/ *a.* terroso; (*coarse*) grossolano.

earwig /'ɪəwɪg/ *n.* forfecchia *f.*

ease /iːz/ *n.* agio *m.*; (*comfort*) benessere *m.* —*v.t./i.* calmare, calmarsi; (*relax*) rilassarsi; (*slow down*) rallentare; (*loosen*) allentare. **at** ~ a proprio agio; (*mil.*) a riposo. **ill at** ~ a disagio. **with** ~ con facilità.

easel /'iːzl/ *n.* cavalletto *m.*

east /iːst/ *n.* est *m.* —*a.* dell'est. —*adv.* verso est. ~**erly** *a.* da levante. ~**ern** *a.* orientale. ~**ward, ~wards** *advs.* verso est.

Easter /'iːstə(r)/ *n.* Pasqua *f.* ~ **egg** uovo di Pasqua *m.*

easy /'iːzɪ/ *a.* (-**ier, -iest**) facile; (*relaxed*) agevole. ~ **chair** *n.* poltrona *f.* ~**!** piano! ~**-going** *a.* accomodante.

go ~ **on** (*fam.*) andare piano con. **take it** ~ prendersela con calma.

eat /iːt/ *v.t./i.* (*p.t.* **ate**, *p.p.* **eaten**) mangiare. ~ **into** corrodere. ~**able** *a.* mangiabile. ~**er** *n.* mangia|tore, -trice *m.*, *f.*

eau-de-Cologne /əʊdəkə'ləʊn/ *n.* acqua di Colonia *f.*

eaves /iːvz/ *n.pl.* cornicione *m.s.*

eavesdrop /'iːvzdrɒp/ *v.i.* (*p.t.* -**dropped**) origliare.

ebb /eb/ *n.* riflusso *m.* —*v.i.* rifluire; (*fig.*) declinare.

ebony /'ebənɪ/ *n.* ebano *m.*

ebullient /ɪ'bʌlɪənt/ *a.* esuberante.

eccentric /ɪk'sentrɪk/ *a.* & *n.* eccentrico, a *m.*, *f.* ~**ity** /eksen'trɪsətɪ/ *n.* eccentricità *f.*

ecclesiastical /ɪkliːzɪ'æstɪkl/ *a.* ecclesiastico.

echelon /'eʃəlɒn/ *n.* scaglione *m.*

echo /'ekəʊ/ *n.* (*pl.* -**oes**) eco *m.* —*v.t./i.* (*p.t.* **echoed**, *pres. p.* **echoing**) echeggiare; (*imitate*) ripetere.

eclectic /ɪk'lektɪk/ *a.* & *n.* eclettico *m.*

eclipse /ɪ'klɪps/ *n.* eclissi *f.* —*v.t.* eclissare.

ecology /iː'kɒlədʒɪ/ *n.* ecologia *f.*

economic /iːkə'nɒmɪk/ *a.* economico. ~**al** *a.* economico. ~**s** *n.* economia *f.*

economist /ɪ'kɒnəmɪst/ *n.* economista *m.|f.*

econom|y /ɪ'kɒnəmɪ/ *n.* economia *f.* ~**ize** *v.i.* economizzare.

ecstasy /'ekstəsɪ/ *n.* estasi *f. invar.*

ecstatic /ɪk'stætɪk/ *a.* estatico. ~**ally** *adv.* estaticamente.

ecumenical /iːkjuː'menɪkl/ *a.* ecumenico.

eddy /'edɪ/ *n.* vortice *m.*

edge /edʒ/ *n.* bordo *m.*; (*of knife*) filo *m.*; (*of road*) ciglio *m.* —*v.t.* bordare; (*move*) muovere. **have the** ~ **on** (*fam.*) essere in vantaggio su. **on** ~ con i nervi tesi. ~**ways** *adv.* di fianco.

edging /'edʒɪŋ/ *n.* bordo *m.*

edgy /'edʒɪ/ *a.* nervoso.

edible /'edɪbl/ *a.* mangiabile.

edict /'iːdɪkt/ *n.* editto *m.*

edifice /'edɪfɪs/ *n.* edificio *m.*

edify /'edɪfaɪ/ *v.t.* edificare.

edit /'edɪt/ *v.t.* (*newspaper*) dirigere;

(*text*) curare l'edizione di; (*film*) montare. ~ed by a cura di.

edition /ɪ'dɪʃn/ *n*. edizione *f*.

editor /'edɪtə(r)/ *n*. redat|tore, -trice *m*., *f*.; (*of text*) cura|tore, -trice *m*., *f*. ~ in chief redattore capo *m*.

editorial /edɪ'tɔ:rɪəl/ *a*. redazionale. —*n*. articolo di fondo *m*.

educat|e /'edʒʊkeɪt/ *v.t.* istruire; (*mind, public*) educare. ~ed *a*. istruito. ~ion /-'keɪʃn/ *n*. istruzione *f*.; (*culture*) cultura, educazione *f*. ~ional /-'keɪʃənl/ *a*. istruttivo.

EEC /i:i:'si:/ *abbr*. (*of* **European Economic Community**) MCE (Mercato Comune Europeo) *m*.

eel /i:l/ *n*. anguilla *f*.

eerie /'ɪərɪ/ *a*. (**-ier, -iest**) misterioso, inquietante.

efface /ɪ'feɪs/ *v.t.* cancellare.

effect /ɪ'fekt/ *n*. effetto *m*. —*v.t.* effettuare. in ~ in effetti. take ~ entrare in vigore.

effective /ɪ'fektɪv/ *a*. efficace; (*striking*) che colpisce; (*mil*.) effettivo. ~ly *adv*. efficacemente. ~ness *n*. efficacia *f*.

effeminate /ɪ'femɪnət/ *a*. effeminato.

effervescent /efə'vesnt/ *a*. effervescente.

effete /e'fi:t/ *a*. esausto.

efficien|t /ɪ'fɪʃnt/ *a*. efficiente. ~cy *n*. efficienza *f*. ~tly *adv*. efficientemente.

effigy /'efɪdʒɪ/ *n*. effigie *f*.

effort /'efət/ *n*. sforzo *m*. ~less *a*. facile.

effrontery /ɪ'frʌntərɪ/ *n*. sfrontatezza *f*.

effusive /ɪ'fju:sɪv/ *a*. espansivo.

e.g. *abbr*. (*of* **exempli gratia**) p. es. (per esempio).

egalitarian /ɪgælɪ'teərɪən/ *a*. & *n*. egalitario, a *m*., *f*.

egg[1] /eg/ *n*. uovo *m*. ~-**cup** *n*. portauovo *m*. ~-**plant** *n*. melanzana *f*. ~**shell** *n*. guscio d'uovo *m*.

egg[2] /eg/ *v.t.* ~ on (*fam*.) incitare.

ego /'egəʊ/ *n*. (*pl*. **-os**) ego *m*. ~(t)ism *n*. egoismo *m*. ~(t)ist *n*. egoista *m*./*f*.

egocentric /egəʊ'sentrɪk/ *a*. egocentrico.

Egypt /'i:dʒɪpt/ *n*. Egitto *m*. ~ian /ɪ'dʒɪpʃn/ *a*. & *n*. egiziano, a *m*., *f*.

eh /eɪ/ *int*. (*fam*.) eh?

eiderdown /'aɪdədaʊn/ *n*. piumino *m*.

eight /eɪt/ *a*. & *n*. otto *m*. **eighth** /eɪtθ/ *a*. & *n*. ottavo, a *m*., *f*.

eighteen /eɪ'ti:n/ *a*. & *n*. diciotto *m*. ~th *a*. & *n*. diciottesimo, a *m*., *f*.

eight|y /'eɪtɪ/ *a*. & *n*. ottanta *m*. ~ieth *a*. & *n*. ottantesimo, a *m*., *f*.

either /'aɪðə(r)/ *a*. & *pron*. o l'uno o l'altro; (*with negative*) né l'uno né l'altro; (*each*) ciascuno. —*adv*. (*negative*) neanche. —*conj*. ~ he or o lui o; (*with negative*) né lui né.

ejaculate /ɪ'dʒækjʊleɪt/ *v.t.*/*i*. eiaculare; (*exclaim*) esclamare.

eject /ɪ'dʒekt/ *v.t.* emettere; (*throw out*) espellere.

eke /i:k/ *v.t.* ~ out far bastare; (*increase*) arrotondare.

elaborate[1] /ɪ'læbərət/ *a*. elaborato.

elaborate[2] /ɪ'læbəreɪt/ *v.t.*/*i*. elaborare.

elapse /ɪ'læps/ *v.i.* (*of time*) trascorrere.

elastic /ɪ'læstɪk/ *a*. & *n*. elastico *m*. ~ **band** elastico *m*. ~ity /elæ'stɪsətɪ/ *n*. elasticità *f*.

elat|ed /ɪ'leɪtɪd/ *a*. esultante. ~ion /-ʃn/ *n*. esultanza *f*.

elbow /'elbəʊ/ *n*. gomito *m*.

elder[1] /'eldə(r)/ *a*. & *n*. maggiore *m*./*f*.

elder[2] /'eldə(r)/ *n*. (*tree*) sambuco *m*.

elderly /'eldəlɪ/ *a*. anziano.

eldest /'eldɪst/ *a*. & *n*. maggiore *m*./*f*.

elect /ɪ'lekt/ *v.t.* eleggere. —*a*. scelto. ~ to do decidere di fare. ~ion /-ʃn/ *n*. elezione *f*.

elector /ɪ'lektə(r)/ *n*. elet|tore, -trice *m*., *f*. ~al *a*. elettorale. ~ate *n*. elettorato *m*.

electric /ɪ'lektrɪk/ *a*. elettrico. ~ **blanket** *n*. termocoperta *f*. ~al *a*. elettrico.

electrician /ɪlek'trɪʃn/ *n*. elettricista *m*.

electricity /ɪlek'trɪsətɪ/ *n*. elettricità *f*.

electrify /ɪ'lektrɪfaɪ/ *v.t.* elettrificare; (*fig*.) elettrizzare.

electrocute /ɪ'lektrəkju:t/ *v.t.* fulminare.

electrolysis /ɪlek'trɒlɪsɪs/ *n*. elettrolisi *f*.

electron /ɪ'lektrɒn/ *n*. elettrone *m*.

electronic /ɪlek'trɒnɪk/ *a*. elettronico. ~s *n*. elettronica *f*.

elegan|t /'elɪgənt/ *a*. elegante. ~ce *n*. eleganza *f*. ~tly *adv*. elegantemente.

element /'elɪmənt/ *n*. elemento *m*. ~ary /-'mentrɪ/ *a*. elementare.

elephant /'elɪfənt/ *n*. elefante *m*.

elevat|e /'elɪveɪt/ *v.t.* elevare. ~ion /-'veɪʃn/ *n*. elevazione *f*.

elevator /'elɪveɪtə(r)/ n. (*Amer.*) ascensore m.

eleven /ɪ'levn/ a. & n. undici m. ~th a. & n. undicesimo, a m.,f.

elf /elf/ n. (*pl.* **elves**) elfo m.

elicit /ɪ'lɪsɪt/ v.t. trarre fuori.

eligible /'elɪdʒəbl/ a. eleggibile. **be ~ for** aver diritto a. **~ young man** buon partito.

eliminat|e /ɪ'lɪmɪneɪt/ v.t. eliminare. ~**ion** /-'neɪʃn/ n. eliminazione f.

élite /eɪ'li:t/ n. il fior fiore m.

elixir /ɪ'lɪksə(r)/ n. elisir m. *invar.*

ellip|se /ɪ'lɪps/ n. ellisse f. ~**tical** a. ellittico.

elm /elm/ n. olmo m.

elocution /elə'kju:ʃn/ n. elocuzione f.

elongate /'i:lɒŋgeɪt/ v.t. allungare.

elope /ɪ'ləʊp/ v.i. fuggire con l'amante. ~**ment** n. fuga f.

eloquen|t /'eləkwənt/ a. eloquente. ~**ce** n. eloquenza f. ~**tly** adv. con eloquenza.

else /els/ adv. altro. **nothing ~** nient'altro. **or ~** altrimenti. ~**where** adv. altrove.

elucidate /ɪ'lu:sɪdeɪt/ v.t. delucidare.

elude /ɪ'lu:d/ v.t. eludere.

elusive /ɪ'lu:sɪv/ a. elusivo.

emaciated /ɪ'meɪʃɪeɪtɪd/ a. emaciato.

emanate /'eməneɪt/ v.i. emanare.

emancipat|e /ɪ'mænsɪpeɪt/ v.t. emancipare. ~**ion** /-'peɪʃn/ n. emancipazione f.

embalm /ɪm'bɑ:m/ v.t. imbalsamare.

embankment /ɪm'bæŋkmənt/ n. (*of river*) argine m.; (*of railway*) terrapieno m.

embargo /ɪm'bɑ:gəʊ/ n. (*pl.* **-oes**) embargo m.

embark /ɪm'bɑ:k/ v.t./i. imbarcare, imbarcarsi. **~ on** intraprendere. ~**ation** /embɑ:'keɪʃn/ n. imbarco m.

embarrass /ɪm'bærəs/ v.t. imbarazzare. ~**ment** n. imbarazzo m.

embassy /'embəsɪ/ n. ambasciata f.

embed /ɪm'bed/ v.t. (*p.t.* **embedded**) incastrare; (*fig.*) incidere.

embellish /ɪm'belɪʃ/ v.t. abbellire. ~**ment** n. abbellimento m.

embers /'embəz/ n.pl. braci f.pl.

embezzle /ɪm'bezl/ v.t. appropriarsi indebitamente. ~**ment** n. appropriazione indebita f.

embitter /ɪm'bɪtə(r)/ v.t. amareggiare.

emblem /'embləm/ n. emblema m.

embod|y /ɪm'bɒdɪ/ v.t. incorporare; (*in-*

clude) racchiudere. ~**iment** n. incarnazione f.

emboss /ɪm'bɒs/ v.t. (*metal*) sbalzare; (*paper*) stampare in rilievo. ~**ed** a. in rilievo.

embrace /ɪm'breɪs/ v.t./i. abbracciare, abbracciarsi. —n. abbraccio m.

embroider /ɪm'brɔɪdə(r)/ v.t. ricamare. ~**y** n. ricamo m.

embroil /ɪm'brɔɪl/ v.t. ingarbugliare.

embryo /'embrɪəʊ/ n. (*pl.* **-os**) embrione m. ~**nic** /-'ɒnɪk/ a. embrionale.

emend /ɪ'mend/ v.t. emendare.

emerald /'emərəld/ n. smeraldo m.

emerge /ɪ'mɜ:dʒ/ v.i. emergere. ~**nce** /-əns/ n. apparizione f.

emergency /ɪ'mɜ:dʒənsɪ/ n. emergenza f. **~ exit** uscita di sicurezza f. **in an ~** in caso di emergenza.

emery /'eməri/ n. smeriglio m. **~-board** n. limetta (per le unghie) f.

emigrant /'emɪgrənt/ n. emigrante m./f.

emigrat|e /'emɪgreɪt/ v.i. emigrare. ~**ion** /-'greɪʃn/ n. emigrazione f.

eminen|t /'emɪnənt/ a. eminente. ~**ce** n. eminenza f. ~**tly** adv. eminentemente.

emissary /'emɪsərɪ/ n. emissario m.

emi|t /ɪ'mɪt/ v.t. (*p.t.* **emitted**) emettere. ~**ssion** n. emissione f.

emollient /ɪ'mɒlɪənt/ a. & n. emolliente m.

emotion /ɪ'məʊʃn/ n. emozione f. ~**al** a. commovente; (*person*) emotivo.

emotive /ɪ'məʊtɪv/ a. emotivo.

empathy /'empəθɪ/ n. comprensione reciproca f.

emperor /'empərə(r)/ n. imperatore m.

empha|sis /'emfəsɪs/ n. (*pl.* ~**ses** /-si:z/) enfasi f.

emphatic /ɪm'fætɪk/ a. enfatico; (*manner*) risoluto.

emphasize /'emfəsaɪz/ v.t. accentuare, mettere in evidenza.

empire /'empaɪə(r)/ n. impero m.

empirical /ɪm'pɪrɪkl/ a. empirico.

employ /ɪm'plɔɪ/ v.t. impiegare. ~**ee** /emplɔɪ'i:/ n. impiegato, a m.,f. ~**er** n. datore di lavoro m. ~**ment** n. impiego m. ~**ment agency** ufficio di collocamento m.

empower /ɪm'paʊə(r)/ v.t. autorizzare; (*enable*) mettere in grado.

empress /'emprɪs/ n. imperatrice f.

empt|y /'emptɪ/ a. vuoto; (*promise*) vano. —v.t./i. vuotare, vuotarsi. **on**

an ~y stomach a digiuno. ~ies n.pl.
vuoti m.pl. ~iness n. vuoto m.
emulate /'emjʊleɪt/ v.t. emulare.
emulsion /ɪ'mʌlʃn/ n. emulsione f.
enable /ɪ'neɪbl/ v.t. ~ s.o. to mettere
qcno. in grado di.
enact /ɪ'nækt/ v.t. (jurid.) decretare;
(theatr.) rappresentare.
enamel /ɪ'næml/ n. smalto. —v.t. (p.t.
enamelled) smaltare.
enamoured /ɪ'næməd/ a. be ~ of essere innamorato di.
encampment /ɪn'kæmpmənt/ n. accampamento m.
encase /ɪn'keɪs/ v.t. rinchiudere.
enchant /ɪn'tʃɑːnt/ v.t. incantare.
~ing a. incantevole. ~ment n. in-
canto m.
encircle /ɪn'sɜːkl/ v.t. circondare.
enclave /'enkleɪv/ n. territorio circondato da paesi stranieri m.
enclose /ɪn'kləʊz/ v.t. (land) circondare; (with letter) allegare; (in receptacle) racchiudere. ~d a. (space)
chiuso; (comm.) allegato.
enclosure /ɪn'kləʊʒə(r)/ n. chiusura f.;
(area) recinto m.; (comm.) allegato m.
encompass /ɪn'kʌmpəs/ v.t. circondare.
encore /'ɒŋkɔː(r)/ int. & n. bis m. invar.
encounter /ɪn'kaʊntə(r)/ v.t. incontrare. —n. incontro m.; (battle) scontro m.
encourage /ɪn'kʌrɪdʒ/ v.t. incoraggiare. ~ment n. incoraggiamento
m.
encroach /ɪn'krəʊtʃ/ v.i. ~ on (land)
invadere; (time) abusare di. ~ment
n. usurpazione f.
encumb|er /ɪn'kʌmbə(r)/ v.t. ingom-
brare. be ~ered with essere carico
di. ~rance n. ingombro m.
encyclical /ɪn'sɪklɪkl/ n. enciclica f.
encyclopaed|ia /ɪnsaɪklə'piːdɪə/ n. en-
ciclopedia f. ~ic a. enciclopedico.
end /end/ n. fine f.; (furthest point)
termine m. —v.t./i. finire. in the ~
infine. make ~s meet sbarcare il
lunario. no ~ (fam.) molto. on ~ in
piedi; (consecutive) di fila.
endanger /ɪn'deɪndʒə(r)/ v.t. rischiare.
endear|ing /ɪn'dɪərɪŋ/ a. accattivante.
~ment n. tenerezza f.
endeavour /ɪn'devə(r)/ n. tentativo
m. —v.i. ~ to sforzarsi di.
ending /'endɪŋ/ n. fine f.
endive /'endɪv/ n. indivia f.

endless /'endlɪs/ a. interminabile; (patience) infinita.
endorse /ɪn'dɔːs/ v.t. (comm.) girare;
(fig.) approvare; (jurid.) registrare.
~ment n. (comm.) girata f.; (fig.) conferma f.; (jurid.) registrazione su patente di un reato f.
endow /ɪn'daʊ/ v.t. dotare.
endur|e /ɪn'djʊə(r)/ v.t. sopportare.
—v.i. durare. ~able a. sopportabile.
~ance n. resistenza f. ~ing a.
duraturo.
enemy /'enəmɪ/ n. & a. nemico, a
m., f.
energetic /enə'dʒetɪk/ a. energico.
energy /'enədʒɪ/ n. energia f.
enervat|e /'enəːveɪt/ v.t. infiacchire.
~ing a. debilitante.
enfold /ɪn'fəʊld/ v.t. avviluppare.
enforce /ɪn'fɔːs/ v.t. imporre. ~d a.
imposto.
engage /ɪn'geɪdʒ/ v.t./i. (staff) assumere; (reserve) prenotare; (attention) occupare; (activity) impegnare;
(mech.) ingranare. ~d a. fidanzato;
(busy) impegnato. get ~d fidanzarsi.
~ment n. fidanzamento m.; (meeting)
appuntamento m.; (undertaking) impegno m.
engaging /ɪn'geɪdʒɪŋ/ a. attraente.
engender /ɪn'dʒendə(r)/ v.t. generare.
engine /'endʒɪn/ n. motore m.; (of
train) locomotrice f. ~-driver n.
macchinista m.
engineer /endʒɪ'nɪə(r)/ n. ingegnere
m. —v.t. costruire; (fig.) macchinare.
~ing n. ingegneria f.
England /'ɪŋglənd/ n. Inghilterra f.
English /'ɪŋglɪʃ/ a. inglese. —n. (lang.)
inglese m. the ~ Channel la Manica
f. ~man, ~woman ns. inglese m., f.
engrave /ɪn'greɪv/ v.t. incidere. ~ing
n. stampa f.
engrossed /ɪn'grəʊst/ a. assorbito.
engulf /ɪn'gʌlf/ v.t. ingolfare.
enhance /ɪn'hɑːns/ v.t. accrescere.
enigma /ɪ'nɪgmə/ n. enigma m. ~tic
/enɪg'mætɪk/ a. enigmatico.
enjoy /ɪn'dʒɔɪ/ v.t. godere. ~ o.s. divertirsi. ~able a. piacevole. ~ment n.
godimento m.
enlarge /ɪn'lɑːdʒ/ v.t./i. ingrandire, in-
grandirsi. ~ upon dilungarsi su.
~ment n. ingrandimento m.
enlighten /ɪn'laɪtn/ v.t. illuminare.
~ment n. progresso culturale m. the
E~ment l'illuminismo m.

enlist /ɪn'lɪst/ *v.t.* reclutare; (*fig.*) ottenere. —*v.i.* arruolarsi.

enliven /ɪn'laɪvn/ *v.t.* rianimare.

enmity /'enmətɪ/ *n.* inimicizia *f.*

ennoble /ɪ'nəʊbl/ *v.t.* nobilitare.

enormity /ɪ'nɔːmətɪ/ *n.* enormità *f.*

enormous /ɪ'nɔːməs/ *a.* enorme.

enough /ɪ'nʌf/ *a.* & *adv.* abbastanza, sufficiente. —*n.* il necessario *m.* —*int.* basta!

enquir|e /ɪn'kwaɪə(r)/ *v.t./i.* domandare. ∼**e about** chiedere informazioni su. ∼**y** *n.* domanda *f.*

enrage /ɪn'reɪdʒ/ *v.t.* fare arrabbiare.

enrapture /ɪn'ræptʃə(r)/ *v.t.* estasiare.

enrich /ɪn'rɪtʃ/ *v.t.* arricchire.

enrol /ɪn'rəʊl/ *v.t./i.* (*p.t.* **enrolled**) arruolare, arruolarsi. ∼**ment** *n.* arruolamento *m.*

ensconce /ɪn'skɒns/ *v.t.* ∼ **o.s.** sistemarsi.

ensemble /ɒn'sɒmbl/ *n.* complesso *m.*

enshrine /ɪn'ʃraɪn/ *v.t.* racchiudere.

ensign /'ensən/ *n.* insegna *f.*

enslave /ɪn'sleɪv/ *v.t.* render schiavo.

ensue /ɪn'ʃjuː/ *v.i.* risultare.

ensure /ɪn'ʃʊə(r)/ *v.t.* assicurare. ∼ **that** assicurarsi che.

entail /ɪn'teɪl/ *v.t.* comportare.

entangle /ɪn'tæŋgl/ *v.t.* impigliare. ∼**ment** *n.* groviglio *m.*; (*mil.*) reticolato *m.*

enter /'entə(r)/ *v.t./i.* entrare; (*list, school, etc.*) iscriversi; (*competition*) partecipare a.

enterprise /'entəpraɪz/ *n.* impresa *f.*; (*fig.*) iniziativa *f.*

enterprising /'entəpraɪzɪŋ/ *a.* intraprendente.

entertain /entə'teɪn/ *v.t.* intrattenere; (*guests*) ricevere; (*ideas, hopes*) nutrire; (*consider*) prendere in considerazione. ∼**ment** *n.* (*amusement*) intrattenimento *m.*; (*performance*) spettacolo *m.*; (*reception*) trattenimento *m.*

enthral /ɪn'θrɔːl/ *v.t.* (*p.t.* **enthralled**) incantare.

enthuse /ɪn'θjuːz/ *v.i.* ∼ **over** entusiasmarsi per.

enthusias|m /ɪn'θjuːzɪæzəm/ *n.* entusiasmo *m.* ∼**tic** /-'æstɪk/ *a.* entusiastico. ∼**tically** /-'æstɪklɪ/ *adv.* entusiasticamente.

enthusiast /ɪn'θjuːzɪæst/ *n.* entusiasta *m.|f.*

entice /ɪn'taɪs/ *v.t.* attirare.

entire /ɪn'taɪə(r)/ *a.* intero. ∼**ly** *adv.* interamente.

entirety /ɪn'taɪərətɪ/ *n.* **in its** ∼ nell'insieme.

entitle /ɪn'taɪtl/ *v.t.* intitolare; (*give a right*) qualificare. **be** ∼**d to** aver diritto a. ∼**ment** *n.* diritto *m.*

entity /'entətɪ/ *n.* entità *f.*

entomb /ɪn'tuːm/ *v.t.* seppellire.

entrails /'entreɪlz/ *n.pl.* intestini *m.pl.*

entrance[1] /'entrəns/ *n.* entrata *f.*; (*right to enter*) ammissione *f.*

entrance[2] /ɪn'trɑːns/ *v.t.* estasiare.

entrant /'entrənt/ *n.* concorrente *m.|f.*

entreat /ɪn'triːt/ *v.t.* supplicare. ∼**y** *n.* supplica *f.*

entrench /ɪn'trentʃ/ *v.t.* fortificare.

entrust /ɪn'trʌst/ *v.t.* affidare.

entry /'entrɪ/ *n.* entrata *f.*; (*on list*) ammissione *f.*

entwine /ɪn'twaɪn/ *v.t.* intrecciare.

enumerate /ɪ'njuːməreɪt/ *v.t.* enumerare.

enunciate /ɪ'nʌnsɪeɪt/ *v.t.* enunciare; (*state*) affermare.

envelop /ɪn'veləp/ *v.t.* (*p.t.* **enveloped**) avviluppare.

envelope /'envələʊp/ *n.* busta *f.*

enviable /'envɪəbl/ *a.* invidiabile.

envious /'envɪəs/ *a.* invidioso. ∼**ly** *adv.* con invidia.

environment /ɪn'vaɪərənmənt/ *n.* ambiente *m.* ∼**al** /-'mentl/ *a.* ambientale.

envisage /ɪn'vɪzɪdʒ/ *v.t.* prevedere.

envoy /'envɔɪ/ *n.* inviato, a *m., f.*

envy /'envɪ/ *n.* invidia *f.* —*v.t.* invidiare.

enzyme /'enzaɪm/ *n.* enzima *f.*

epaulette /'epəʊlet/ *n.* spallina *f.*

ephemeral /ɪ'femərəl/ *a.* effimero.

epic /'epɪk/ *n.* epopea *f.* —*a.* epico.

epicentre /'epɪsentə(r)/ *n.* epicentro *m.*

epicure /'epɪkjʊə(r)/ *n.* buongustaio, a *m., f.*

epidemic /epɪ'demɪk/ *n.* epidemia *f.*

epilep|sy /'epɪlepsɪ/ *n.* epilessia *f.* ∼**tic** /-'leptɪk/ *a.* & *n.* epilettico, a *m., f.*

epilogue /'epɪlɒg/ *n.* epilogo *m.*

episode /'epɪsəʊd/ *n.* episodio *m.*

epistle /ɪ'pɪsl/ *n.* epistola *f.*

epitaph /'epɪtɑːf/ *n.* epitaffio *m.*

epithet /'epɪθet/ *n.* epiteto *m.*

epitom|e /ɪ'pɪtəmɪ/ *n.* epitome *m.* ∼**ize** *v.t.* compendiare.

epoch /'iːpɒk/ *n.* epoca *f.* ∼- **making** *a.* che fa epoca.

equal /'iːkwəl/ *a.* uguale. —*n.* pari *m. invar.* —*v.t.* (*p.t.* **equalled**) uguaglia-

re. ~ **to** (*task*) all'altezza di. ~**ity**
/ɪ'kwɒlətɪ/ *n.* uguaglianza *f.* ~**ly** *adv.*
ugualmente.

equalize /'iːkwəlaɪz/ *v.t./i.* uguagliare,
uguagliarsi; (*wages*) livellare; (*sport*)
pareggiare. ~**r** /-ə(r)/ *n.* (*sport*) pareggio *m.*

equanimity /ekwə'nɪmətɪ/ *n.* equani-
mità *f.*

equate /ɪ'kweɪt/ *v.t.* uguagliare.

equation /ɪ'kweɪʒn/ *n.* equazione *f.*

equator /ɪ'kweɪtə(r)/ *n.* equatore *m.*
~**ial** /ekwə'tɔːrɪəl/ *a.* equatoriale.

equerry /'ekwərɪ/ *n.* scudiero *m.*

equestrian /ɪ'kwestrɪən/ *a.* equestre.

equilateral /iːkwɪ'lætərl/ *a.* equi-
latero.

equilibrium /iːkwɪ'lɪbrɪəm/ *n.* equilibrio *m.*

equinox /'iːkwɪnɒks/ *n.* equinozio *m.*

equip /ɪ'kwɪp/ *v.t.* (*p.t.* **equipped**) equipaggiare. ~**ment** *n.* equipaggiamento
m.

equitable /'ekwɪtəbl/ *a.* giusto.

equit|y /'ekwətɪ/ *n.* equità *f.* ~**ies** *n.pl.*
(*comm.*) azioni ordinarie *f.pl.*

equivalen|t /ɪ'kwɪvələnt/ *a.* & *n.* equi-
valente *m.|f.* ~**ce** *n.* equivalenza *f.*

equivocal /ɪ'kwɪvəkl/ *a.* equivoco.

era /'ɪərə/ *n.* era *f.*

eradicate /ɪ'rædɪkeɪt/ *v.t.* sradicare.

erase /ɪ'reɪz/ *v.t.* cancellare. ~**r** /-ə(r)/
n. gomma *f.*

erect /ɪ'rekt/ *a.* eretto. —*v.t.* erigere.
~**ion** /-ʃn/ *n.* erezione *f.*

ermine /'ɜːmɪn/ *n.* ermellino *m.*

ero|de /ɪ'rəʊd/ *v.t.* erodere. ~**sion** /-ʒn/
n. erosione *f.*

erotic /ɪ'rɒtɪk/ *a.* erotico. ~**ism**
/-sɪzəm/ *n.* erotismo *m.*

err /ɜː(r)/ *v.i.* errare; (*sin*) peccare.

errand /'erənd/ *n.* commissione *f.*

erratic /ɪ'rætɪk/ *a.* irregolare; (*person*)
imprevedibile.

erroneous /ɪ'rəʊnɪəs/ *a.* erroneo.

error /'erə(r)/ *n.* errore *m.*

erudit|e /'eruːdaɪt/ *a.* erudito. ~**ion**
/-'dɪʃn/ *n.* erudizione *f.*

erupt /ɪ'rʌpt/ *v.i.* eruttare; (*fig.*) scoppiare. ~**ion** /-ʃn/ *n.* eruzione *f.*;
scoppio *m.*

escalat|e /'eskəleɪt/ *v.t./i.* crescere ra-
pidamente. ~**ion** /-'leɪʃn/ *n.* aumento
m.

escalator /'eskəleɪtə(r)/ *n.* scala
mobile *f.*

escapade /eskə'peɪd/ *n.* scappatella *f.*

escape /ɪ'skeɪp/ *v.i.* evadere. —*v.t.* sfug-

gire; (*gas*) uscire. —*n.* fuga *f.*; (*of
prisoner*) evasione *f.*; (*fig.*) modo d'e-
vadere *m.*; (*mech.*) scappamento *m.*

have a narrow ~ cavarsela per mi-
racolo.

escapism /ɪ'skeɪpɪzəm/ *n.* evasione
(dalla realtà) *f.*

escarpment /ɪs'kaːpmənt/ *n.* scarpata
f.

escort[1] /'eskɔːt/ *n.* sco ·ta *f.*; (*of person*)
accompagnatore *m.*

escort[2] /ɪ'skɔːt/ *v.t.* scortare.

Eskimo /'eskɪməʊ/ *n.* (*pl.* -**os**, -**o**) esqui-
mese *m.|f.*

especial /ɪ'speʃl/ *a.* speciale. ~**ly** *adv.*
particolarmente.

espionage /'espɪɑːnɑːʒ/ *n.* spionaggio
m.

esplanade /esplə'neɪd/ *n.* spianata *f.*

Esq. /ɪ'skwaɪə(r)/ *n.* (*abbr. of* **Esquire**)
(*in address*) **R. Andrews,** ~ Egregio
Signor R. Andrews.

essay /'eseɪ/ *n.* saggio *m.*; (*at school*)
tema *m.*

essence /'esns/ *n.* essenza *f.* **in** ~ in
sostanza.

essential /ɪ'senʃl/ *a.* & *n.* essenziale *m.*
~**ly** *adv.* essenzialmente.

establish /ɪ'stæblɪʃ/ *v.t.* stabilire; (*a
business*) impiantare; (*prove*) confermare. ~**ment** *n.* stabilimento *m.* **the
E**~**ment** il potere tradizionalista *m.*

estate /ɪ'steɪt/ *n.* tenuta *f.*; (*possessions*)
patrimonio *m.* ~ **agent** agente immobiliare *m,* ~ **car** giardiniera *f.*

esteem /ɪ'stiːm/ *v.t.* stimare. —*n.* stima
f.

estimate[1] /'estɪmət/ *n.* valutazione *f.*;
(*comm.*) preventivo *m.*

estimat|e[2] /'estɪmeɪt/ *v.t.* stimare.
~**ion** /-'meɪʃn/ *n.* stima *f.*; (*opinion*)
punto di vista *m.*

estranged /ɪs'treɪndʒt/ *a.* alienato.

estuary /'estʃʊərɪ/ *n.* estuario *m.*

etc. /ɪt'setrə/ (*abbr. of* **et cetera**) ecc.
(eccetera).

etching /'etʃɪŋ/ *n.* acquaforte *f.*

eternal /ɪ'tɜːnl/ *a.* eterno.

eternity /ɪ'tɜːnətɪ/ *n.* eternità *f.*

ether /'iːθə(r)/ *n.* etere *m.*

ethereal /ɪ'θɪərɪəl/ *a.* etereo.

ethic /'eθɪk/ *n.* etica *f.* ~**s** *n.pl.* morale
f. ~**al** *a.* etico.

ethnic /'eθnɪk/ *a.* etnico.

ethos /'iːθɒs/ *n.* carattere particolare
(di un popolo) *m.*

etiquette /'etɪket/ *n.* etichetta *f.*

etymology /etɪ'mɒlədʒɪ/ *n.* etimologia *f.*

eucalyptus /juːkə'lɪptəs/ *n.* (*pl.* **-tuses**) eucalipto *m.*

eulogy /'juːlədʒɪ/ *n.* elogio *m.*

euphemism /'juːfəmɪzəm/ *n.* eufemismo *m.*

euphoria /juːˈfɔːrɪə/ *n.* euforia *f.*

Europe /'jʊərəp/ *n.* Europa *f.* ~**an** /-ˈpɪən/ *a. & n.* europeo, a *m., f.*

euthanasia /juːθəˈneɪzɪə/ *n.* eutanasia *f.*

evacuat|e /ɪ'vækjʊeɪt/ *v.t.* evacuare. ~**ion** /-ˈeɪʃn/ *n.* evacuazione *f.*

evade /ɪ'veɪd/ *v.t.* evadere.

evaluate /ɪ'væljʊeɪt/ *v.t.* valutare.

evangelical /iːvænˈdʒelɪkl/ *a.* evangelico.

evangelist /ɪ'vændʒəlɪst/ *n.* evangelista *m.*

evaporat|e /ɪ'væpəreɪt/ *v.i.* evaporare; (*fig.*) svanire. ~**ion** /-ˈreɪʃn/ *n.* evaporazione *f.*

evasion /ɪ'veɪʒn/ *n.* evasione *f.*; (*excuse*) pretesto *m.*

evasive /ɪ'veɪsɪv/ *a.* evasivo.

eve /iːv/ *n.* vigilia *f.*

even /'iːvn/ *a.* regolare; (*surface*) piatto; (*amount*) uguale; (*number*) pari. —*v.t.* appianare. ~ **up** *v.i.* pareggiare. —*adv.* anche, ancora. ~ **if** persino se. ~ **so** con tutto ciò. **get** ~ **with** vendicarsi di.

evening /'iːvnɪŋ/ *n.* sera *f.*; (*whole evening, event*) serata *f.*

evensong /'iːvənsɒŋ/ *n.* vespro *m.*

event /ɪ'vent/ *n.* evento *m.*; (*sport*) gara *f.* **in the** ~ **of** nell'eventualità di. ~**ful** *a.* movimentato.

eventual /ɪ'ventʃʊəl/ *a.* finale, definitivo. ~**ity** /-ˈælətɪ/ *n.* eventualità *f.* ~**ly** *adv.* alla fine.

ever /'evə(r)/ *adv.* mai.; (*at all times*) sempre. ~ **after** da allora in poi. ~ **since** da quando; da allora. ~ **so** (*fam.*) veramente. **for** ~ per sempre. **hardly** ~ quasi mai.

evergreen /'evəgriːn/ *a. & n.* sempreverde *m.*

everlasting /'evəlɑːstɪŋ/ *a.* eterno.

every /'evrɪ/ *a.* ogni. ~ **one** ciascuno. ~ **other day** un giorno sì un giorno no.

everybody /'evrɪbɒdɪ/ *pron.* tutti.

everyday /'evrɪdeɪ/ *a.* quotidiano, di ogni giorno.

everyone /'evrɪwʌn/ *pron.* ognuno. ~ **else** tutti gli altri.

everything /'evrɪθɪŋ/ *pron.* ogni cosa.

everywhere /'evrɪweə(r)/ *adv.* dovunque.

evict /ɪ'vɪkt/ *v.t.* sfrattare. ~**ion** /-ʃn/ *n.* sfratto *m.*

evidence /'evɪdəns/ *n.* evidenza *f.*; (*jurid.*) testimonianza *f.* ~ **of** segni di. **in** ~ in vista.

evident /'evɪdənt/ *a.* evidente. ~**ly** *adv.* evidentemente.

evil /'iːvl/ *a.* cattivo. —*n.* male *m.*

evo|ke /ɪ'vəʊk/ *v.t.* evocare. ~**cative** /ɪ'vɒkətɪv/ *a.* evocativo.

evolution /iːvə'luːʃn/ *n.* evoluzione *f.*

evolve /ɪ'vɒlv/ *v.t./i.* evolvere, evolversi.

ewe /juː/ *n.* pecora *f.*

ex /eks/ *pref.* ex.

exacerbate /ɪg'zæsəbeɪt/ *v.t.* esacerbare.

exact[1] /ɪg'zækt/ *a.* esatto. ~**ly** *adv.* esattamente. ~**itude** *n.* esattezza *f.*

exact[2] /ɪg'zækt/ *v.t.* esigere. ~**ing** *a.* esigente.

exaggerat|e /ɪg'zædʒəreɪt/ *v.t./i.* esagerare. ~**ion** /-ˈreɪʃn/ *n.* esagerazione *f.*

exalt /ɪg'zɔːlt/ *v.t.* elevare; (*praise*) vantare.

exam /ɪg'zæm/ *n.* (*fam.*) esame *m.*

examination /ɪgzæmɪ'neɪʃn/ *n.* esame *m.*

examine /ɪg'zæmɪn/ *v.t.* esaminare; (*med.*) visitare; (*jurid.*) interrogare. ~**r** /-ə(r)/ *n.* esamina|tore, -trice *m., f.*

example /ɪg'zɑːmpl/ *n.* esempio *m.* **make an** ~ **of** dare una punizione esemplare a.

exasperat|e /ɪg'zæspəreɪt/ *v.t.* esasperare. ~**ion** /-ˈreɪʃn/ *n.* esasperazione *f.*

excavat|e /'ekskəveɪt/ *v.t.* scavare. ~**ion** /-ˈveɪʃn/ *n.* scavo *m.*

exceed /ɪk'siːd/ *v.t.* eccedere. ~**ingly** *adv.* estremamente.

excel /ɪk'sel/ *v.i.* (*p.t.* **excelled**) eccellere. —*v.t.* superare.

excellen|t /'eksələnt/ *a.* eccellente. ~**ce** *n.* eccellenza *f.* ~**tly** *adv.* eccellentemente.

except /ɪk'sept/ *prep.* eccetto. —*v.t.* eccettuare. ~ **for** tranne per. ~**ing** *prep.* tranne.

exception /ɪk'sepʃən/ *n.* eccezione *f.* **take** ~ **to** fare obiezioni a.

exceptional /ɪk'sepʃənl/ *a.* eccezionale. ~**ly** *adv.* eccezionalmente.

excerpt /'eksɜːpt/ *n.* estratto *m.*

excess[1] /ık'ses/ *n.* eccesso *m.*
excess[2] /'ekses/ *a.* in eccedenza. ~
fare *n.* supplemento *m.* ~ **luggage**
n. bagaglio in eccedenza *m.*
excessive /ık'sesıv/ *a.* eccessivo. ~**ly**
adv. eccessivamente.
exchange /ık'stʃeındʒ/ *v.t.* scambiare. —*n.* scambio *m.*; (*comm.*) cambio *m.* (**telephone**) ~ centrale
(telefonica) *f.*
exchequer /ıks'tʃekə(r)/ *n.* (*pol.*) tesoro *m.*
excise /'eksaız/ *n.* dazio *m.* —*v.t.* /-'saız/
recidere.
excit|e /ık'saıt/ *v.t.* eccitare; (*cause*)
suscitare. ~**able** *a.* eccitabile. ~**ed**
a. eccitato. ~**ement** *n.* eccitazione *f.*
~**ing** *a.* eccitante.
exclaim /ık'skleım/ *v.i.* esclamare.
exclamation /eksklə'meıʃn/ *n.* escla-
mazione *f.* ~ **mark** *n.* punto esclamativo *m.*
exclu|de /ık'sklu:d/ *v.t.* escludere.
~**sion** /-ʒən/ *n.* esclusione *f.*
exclusive /ık'sklu:sıv/ *a.* (*rights etc.*)
esclusivo; (*club*) signorile; (*person*)
altezzoso. ~ **of** all'infuori di. ~**ly**
adv. esclusivamente.
excommunicate /ekskə'mju:nıkeıt/
v.t. scomunicare.
excrement /'ekskrımənt/ *n.* escre-
mento *m.*
excruciating /ık'skru:ʃıeıtıŋ/ *a.*
straziante.
excursion /ık'skɜ:ʃn/ *n.* escursione *f.*
excus|e[1] /ık'skju:z/ *v.t.* scusare. ~
from esonerare da. ~**able** *a.* perdo-
nabile.
excuse[2] /ık'skju:s/ *n.* scusa *f.*
ex-directory /eksdı'rektərı/ *a.* con numero privato.
execrable /'eksıkrəbl/ *a.* esecrabile.
execute /'eksıkju:t/ *v.t.* eseguire.
execution /eksı'kju:ʃn/ *n.* esecuzione
f. ~**er** *n.* boia *m. invar.*
executive /ıg'zekjʊtıv/ *n.* dirigente
m./f. —*a.* esecutivo.
executor /ıg'zekjʊtə(r)/ *n.* (*jurid.*) ese-
cu|tore, -trice testamentario, a *m., f.*
exemplary /ıg'zemplərı/ *a.* esemplare.
exemplify /ıg'zemplıfaı/ *v.t.* esempli-
ficare.
exempt /ıg'zempt/ *a.* esente. —*v.t.*
esentare. ~**ion** /-ʃn/ *n.* esenzione *f.*
exercise /'eksəsaız/ *n.* esercizio *m.*;
(*mil.*) esercitazione *f.* —*v.t./i.* esercitare, esercitarsi. ~ **book** *n.* quaderno
m.

exert /ıg'zɜ:t/ *v.t.* esercitare. ~ **o.s.**
sforzarsi. ~**ion** /-ʃn/ *n.* sforzo *m.*
exhal|e /eks'heıl/ *v.t./i.* esalare. ~**a-
tion** /-ə'leıʃn/ *n.* esalazione *f.*
exhaust /ıg'zɔ:st/ *v.t.* esaurire. —*n.*
(*auto*) scappamento *m.* ~**ed** *a.* esausto. ~**ion** /-stʃən/ *n.* esaurimento *m.*
exhaustive /ıg'zɔ:stıv/ *a.* esauriente.
exhibit /ıg'zıbıt/ *v.t.* esporre; (*jurid.*)
esibire; (*fig.*) dimostrare. —*n.* oggetto
esposto *m.*; (*jurid.*) documento *m.*
~**or** *n.* esposi|tore, -trice *m., f.*
exhibition /eksı'bıʃn/ *n.* esposizione
f.; (*act of showing*) dimostrazione *f.*;
(*schol.*) borsa di studio *f.* ~**ist** *n.* esi-
bizionista *m./f.*
exhilarat|e /ıg'zıləreıt/ *v.t.* esilarare.
~**ion** /-'reıʃn/ *n.* ilarità *f.*
exhort /ıg'zɔ:t/ *v.t.* esortare.
exile /'eksaıl/ *n.* esilio *m.*; (*person*)
esule *m./f.* —*v.t.* esiliare.
exist /ıg'zıst/ *v.i.* esistere. ~**ence** *n.*
esistenza *f.* **in** ~**ence** esistente.
existentialism /egzıs'tenʃəlızəm/ *n.*
esistenzialismo *m.*
exit /'eksıt/ *n.* uscita *f.*
exodus /'eksədəs/ *n.* esodo *m.*
exonerate /ıg'zɒnəreıt/ *v.t.* esonerare.
exorbitant /ıg'zɔ:bıtənt/ *a.* esorbitante.
exorcis|e /'eksɔ:saız/ *v.t.* esorcizzare.
~**m** /-sızəm/ *n.* esorcismo *m.*
exotic /ıg'zɒtık/ *a.* esotico.
expan|d /ık'spænd/ *v.t./i.* espandere,
espandersi; (*metal*) dilatare, dilatarsi;
(*explain better*) spiegare. ~**sion** *n.*
espansione; dilatazione *f.*
expanse /ık'spæns/ *n.* estensione *f.*
expansive /ık'spænsıv/ *a.* espansivo.
expatriate /eks'pætrıət/ *a. & n.* espa-
triato, a *m., f.*
expect /ık'spekt/ *v.t.* aspettare; (*suppose*) pensare; (*demand*) esigere. **I** ~
so credo di sì. ~**ation** /ekspek'teıʃn/
n. attesa, aspettativa *f.* ~**ation of life**
probabilità di vita *f.*
expectan|t /ık'spektənt/ *a.* in attesa.
~**t mother** donna incinta *f.* ~**cy** *n.*
aspettativa *f.*
expedien|t /ık'spi:dıənt/ *a.* con-
veniente. ~**cy** *n.* convenienza *f.*
expedite /'ekspıdaıt/ *v.t.* accelerare.
expedition /ekspı'dıʃn/ *n.* spedizione
f.; (*promptness*) sollecitudine *f.* ~**ary**
a. (*mil.*) di spedizione.
expel /ık'spel/ *v.t.* (*p.t.* **expelled**) espellere.

expend /ɪk'spend/ *v.t.* spendere. ~**able** *a.* spendibile.

expenditure /ɪk'spendɪtʃə(r)/ *n.* spesa *f.*

expense /ɪk'spens/ *n.* spesa *f.*; (*fig.*) costo *m.* **at s.o.'s** ~ alle spalle di qcno.

expensive /ɪk'spensɪv/ *a.* caro, costoso. ~**ly** *adv.* costosamente.

experience /ɪk'spɪərɪəns/ *n.* esperienza *f.* —*v.t.* provare. ~**d** *a.* esperto.

experiment /ɪk'sperɪmənt/ *n.* esperimento *m.* —*v.i.* sperimentare. ~**al** /-'mentl/ *a.* sperimentale.

expert /'ekspɜːt/ *a.* & *n.* esperto, a *m.*, *f.* ~**ly** *adv.* abilmente.

expertise /ekspɜː'tiːz/ *n.* competenza *f.*

expir|e /ɪk'spaɪə(r)/ *v.i.* scadere; (*die*) spirare. ~**y** *n.* scadenza *f.*

expla|in /ɪk'spleɪn/ *v.t.* spiegare. ~**nation** /eksplə'neɪʃn/ *n.* spiegazione *f.* ~**natory** /ɪks'plænətərɪ/ *a.* esplicativo.

expletive /ɪk'spliːtɪv/ *n.* imprecazione *f.*

explicit /ɪk'splɪsɪt/ *a.* esplicito.

explo|de /ɪk'spləʊd/ *v.t./i.* (fare) esplodere. ~**sion** /-ʒn/ *n.* esplosione *f.* ~**sive** *a.* & *n.* esplosivo *m.*

exploit[1] /'eksplɔɪt/ *n.* impresa *f.*

exploit[2] /ɪk'splɔɪt/ *v.t.* sfruttare. ~**ation** /eksplɔɪ'teɪʃn/ *n.* sfruttamento *m.*

exploratory /ɪk'splɒrətrɪ/ *a.* esplorativo.

explor|e /ɪk'splɔː(r)/ *v.t.* esplorare; (*fig.*) studiare. ~**ation** /eksplə'reɪʃn/ *n.* esplorazione *f.* ~**er** *n.* explora|tore, -trice *m.*, *f.*

exponent /ɪk'spəʊnənt/ *n.* esponente *m.*/*f.*

export[1] /ɪk'spɔːt/ *v.t.* esportare.

export[2] /'ekspɔːt/ *n.* esportazione *f.* ~**er** /ɪks'pɔːtə(r)/ esporta|tore, -trice *m.*, *f.*

expos|e /ɪk'spəʊz/ *v.t.* esporre; (*reveal*) svelare. ~**ure** /-ʒə(r)/ *n.* esposizione *f.*; (*photo*) posa *f.*; (*med.*) assideramento *m.*

expound /ɪk'spaʊnd/ *v.t.* spiegare.

express[1] /ɪk'spres/ *a.* & *n.* espresso *m.* —*adv.* per espresso. ~**ly** *adv.* espressamente.

express[2] /ɪk'spres/ *v.t.* esprimere. ~**ion** /-ʃn/ *n.* espressione *f.* ~**ive** *a.* espressivo.

expulsion /ɪk'spʌlʃn/ *n.* espulsione *f.*

expurgate /'ekspəgeɪt/ *v.t.* espurgare.

exquisite /'ekskwɪzɪt/ *a.* squisito. ~**ly** *adv.* squisitamente.

ex-serviceman /eks'sɜːvɪsmən/ *n.* (*pl.* -**men**) ex-combattente *m.*

extant /ek'stænt/ *a.* ancora esistente.

extempore /ek'stempərɪ/ *a.* & *adv.* senza preparazione.

exten|d /ɪk'stend/ *v.t.* estendere; (*offer*) porgere; (*a visit*) prolungare. —*v.i.* estendersi. ~**sion** *n.* estensione *f.*; (*comm.*) proroga *f.*; (*telephone*) (numero) interno *m.*

extensive /ɪk'stensɪv/ *a.* ampio, vasto. ~**ly** ampiamente.

extent /ɪk'stent/ *n.* estensione *f.* **to a certain** ~ fino a un certo punto.

extenuate /ɪk'stenjʊeɪt/ *v.t.* attenuare.

exterior /ɪk'stɪərɪə(r)/ *a.* & *n.* esterno *m.*

exterminat|e /ɪk'stɜːmɪneɪt/ *v.t.* sterminare. ~**ion** /-'neɪʃn/ *n.* sterminio *m.*

external /ɪk'stɜːnl/ *a.* esterno. ~**ly** *adv.* esternamente.

extinct /ɪk'stɪŋkt/ *a.* estinto. ~**ion** /-ʃn/ *n.* estinzione *f.*

extinguish /ɪk'stɪŋgwɪʃ/ *v.t.* estinguere. ~**er** *n.* estintore *m.*

extol /ɪk'stəʊl/ *v.t.* (*p.t.* **extolled**) lodare.

extort /ɪk'stɔːt/ *v.t.* estorcere. ~**ion** /-ʃn/ *n.* estorsione *f.*

extortionate /ɪk'stɔːʃənət/ *a.* esorbitante.

extra /'ekstrə/ *a.* straordinario, extra. —*adv.* in più. —*n.* supplemento *m.*; (*cinema*) comparso, a *m.*, *f.*

extract[1] /ɪk'strækt/ *v.t.* estrarre; (*fig.*) strappare. ~**ion** /-ʃn/ *n.* estrazione *f.*; (*lineage*) origine *f.*

extract[2] /'ekstrækt/ *n.* estratto *m.*

extradit|e /'ekstrədaɪt/ *v.t.* estradare. ~**ion** /-'dɪʃn/ *n.* estradizione *f.*

extramarital /ekstrə'mærɪtl/ *a.* extraconiugale.

extramural /ekstrə'mjʊərəl/ *a.* extrauniversitario.

extraordinary /ɪk'strɔːdnrɪ/ *a.* straordinario.

extra-sensory /ekstrə'sensərɪ/ *a.* extrasensoriale.

extravagan|t /ɪk'strævəgənt/ *a.* stravagante; (*wasteful*) prodigo. ~**ce** *n.* stravaganza *f.*; prodigalità *f.*

extrem|e /ɪk'striːm/ *a.* & *n.* estremo *m.* ~**ely** *adv.* estremamente. ~**ist** *n.* estremista *m.*/*f.*

extremity /ɪk'stremətɪ/ *n.* estremità *f.*

extricate /'ekstrɪkeɪt/ *v.t.* districare.

extrovert /'ekstrəvɜːt/ *n.* estroverso, a *m., f.*

exuberan|t /ɪg'zjuːbərənt/ *a.* esuberante. ~**ce** *n.* esuberanza *f.*

exude /ɪg'zjuːd/ *v.t.* stillare; (*charm etc.*) manifestare un'abbondanza di.

exult /ɪg'zʌlt/ *v.i.* esultare.

eye /aɪ/ *n.* occhio *m.* —*v.t.* (*p.t.* **eyed,** *pres. p.* **eyeing**) guardare. ~**-opener** *n.* (*fam.*) rivelazione *f.* ~**-shadow** *n.* ombretto *m.* **keep an** ~ **on** tener d'occhio. **see** ~ **to** ~ aver le stesse idee.

eyeball /'aɪbɔːl/ *n.* bulbo oculare *m.*

eyebrow /'aɪbraʊ/ *n.* sopracciglio *m.* (*pl.* sopracciglia *f.*).

eyeful /'aɪfʊl/ *n.* (*fam.*) spettacolo sorprendente *m.*

eyelash /'aɪlæʃ/ *n.* ciglio *m.* (*pl.* ciglia *f.*).

eyelet /'aɪlɪt/ *n.* occhiello *m.*

eyelid /'aɪlɪd/ *n.* palpebra *f.*

eyesight /'aɪsaɪt/ *n.* vista *f.*

eyesore /'aɪsɔː(r)/ *n.* (*fam., fig.*) pugno nell'occhio *m.*

eyewitness /'aɪwɪtnɪs/ *n.* testimone oculare *m./f.*

F

fable /'feɪbl/ n. fiaba f.

fabric /'fæbrɪk/ n. tessuto m.

fabrication /fæbrɪ'keɪʃn/ n. invenzione f.

fabulous /'fæbjʊləs/ a. favoloso.

façade /fə'sɑːd/ n. facciata f.; (fig.) apparenza f.

face /feɪs/ n. faccia f., viso m.; (grimace) smorfia f.; (of clock) quadrante m. —v.t. essere di fronte a; (confront) affrontare. —v.i. voltarsi; (of house) essere esposto (a). ∼-**lift** n. plastica facciale f. ∼ **up to** accettare. **in the** ∼ **of** di fronte a. **pull** ∼s far boccacce.

faceless /'feɪslɪs/ a. anonimo.

facet /'fæsɪt/ n. sfaccettatura f.; (fig.) aspetto m.

facetious /fə'siːʃəs/ a. faceto.

facial /'feɪʃl/ a. facciale. —n. trattamento di bellezza al viso m.

facile /'fæsaɪl/ a. facile.

facilitate /fə'sɪlɪteɪt/ v.t. facilitare.

facilit|y /fə'sɪlətɪ/ n. facilità f. ∼ies facilitazioni f.pl.

facing /'feɪsɪŋ/ n. rivestimento m. ∼s n.pl., (on clothes) risvolti m.pl.

fact /fækt/ n. fatto m. **as a matter of** ∼ in realtà. **in** ∼ infatti.

faction /'fækʃn/ n. fazione f.

factor /'fæktə(r)/ n. fattore m.

factory /'fæktərɪ/ n. fabbrica f.

factual /'fæktʃʊəl/ a. effettivo.

faculty /'fækltɪ/ n. facoltà f.

fad /'fæd/ n. capriccio m.

fade /feɪd/ v.i. sbiadire; (flower) appassire; (light) affievolirsi.

fag /fæg/ n. (chore) fatica f.; (cigarette, sl.) sigaretta f.

fagged /fægd/ a. ∼ **out** stanco morto.

fah /fɑː/ n. (mus.) fa m.

fail /feɪl/ v.t. (exam) non superare; (candidate) bocciare; (memory etc.) mancare. —v.i. fallire; (health etc.) venire a mancare. **without** ∼ senz'altro.

failing /'feɪlɪŋ/ n. difetto m. —prep. in mancanza di.

failure /'feɪljə(r)/ n. fallimento m.; (person) incapace m./f.; (mech.) guasto m.; (med.) collasso m.; (fig.) disastro m.

faint /feɪnt/ a. (-er, -est) debole, leggero. —v.i. svenire. —n. svenimento m. **feel** ∼ sentirsi venir meno. **the**

∼**est idea** la più pallida idea. ∼-**hearted** a. timido. ∼**ly** adv. debolmente; (slightly) leggermente. ∼**ness** n. debolezza f.

fair[1] /feə(r)/ n. fiera.

fair[2] /feə(r)/ a. (-er, -est) (hair, person) biondo; (skin etc.) chiaro; (just) giusto; (weather) bello; (amount) sufficiente. —adv. giustamente. ∼ **copy** n. bella copia f. ∼ **play** n. correttezza f. ∼**ly** adv. con giustizia; (rather) discretamente. ∼**ness** n. giustizia f.

fairy /'feərɪ/ n. fata f. ∼**land** n. paese delle fate m. ∼ **story**, ∼-**tale** ns. fiaba f.

faith /feɪθ/ n. fede f. ∼-**healer** n. guari-|tore, -trice m., f.

faithful /'feɪθfl/ a. fedele. ∼**ly** adv. fedelmente. ∼**ness** n. fedeltà f.

fake /feɪk/ n. falsificazione f.; (person) impostore m. —a. falso. —v.t. falsificare; (pretend) fingere.

fakir /'feɪkɪə(r)/ n. fachiro m.

falcon /'fɔːlkən/ n. falcone m.

fall /fɔːl/ v.i. (p.t. **fell**, p.p. **fallen**) cadere. —n. caduta f.; (Amer., autumn) autunno m.; (in price) ribasso m. ∼ **back on** ritornare su. ∼ **down** or **off** cadere. ∼ **for** (fam., person) innamorarsi di; (a trick) cascarci dentro. ∼ **in** crollare; (mil.) mettersi in riga. ∼ **in with** (meet) imbattersi in; (agree) concordare con. ∼ **off** (diminish) diminuire. ∼ **out** (friends) litigare. ∼-**out** n. pioggia radioattiva f. ∼ **short** mancare. ∼ **through** (plan) andare a monte.

fallacy /'fæləsɪ/ n. errore m.

fallible /'fæləbl/ a. fallibile.

fallow /'fæləʊ/ a. incolto.

false /fɔːls/ a. falso. ∼**hood** n. menzogna f. ∼**ly** adv. falsamente. ∼**ness** n. falsità f.

falsify /'fɔːlsɪfaɪ/ v.t. falsificare.

falter /'fɔːltə(r)/ v.i. vacillare.

fame /feɪm/ n. fama f.

famed /feɪmd/ a. rinomato.

familiar /fə'mɪlɪə(r)/ a. familiare. **be** ∼ **with** conoscere. ∼**ity** /-'ærətɪ/ n. familiarità f. ∼**ize** v.t. familiarizzare.

family /'fæməlɪ/ n. famiglia f. —a. di famiglia, familiare.

famine /'fæmɪn/ n. carestia f.

famished /'fæmɪʃt/ *a.* be ~ (*fam.*)
avere una fame da lupo.

famous /'feɪməs/ *a.* famoso. ~ly *adv.*
(*fam.*) a meraviglia.

fan¹ /fæn/ *n.* ventaglio *m.*; (*mech.*) ventilatore *m.* —*v.t.* (*p.t.* **fanned**) far
vento a. —*v.i.* ~ **out** spiegarsi a ventaglio. ~ **belt** *n.* cinghia per ventilatore
f.

fan² /fæn/ *n.* ammira|tore, -trice *m.*,
f.; (*sport*) tifoso, a *m.*, *f.*; (*devotee*)
appassionato, a *m.*, *f.*

fanatic /fə'nætɪk/ *n.* fanatico, a *m.*, *f.*
~**al** *a.* fanatico. ~**ism** /-sɪzəm/ *n.*
fanatismo *m.*

fancier /'fænsɪə(r)/ *n.* (**dog etc.**) ~
amatore (di cani ecc.) *m.*

fanciful /'fænsɪfl/ *a.* fantasioso.

fancy /'fænsɪ/ *n.* fantasia *f.*; (*desire*)
desiderio *m.* —*a.* (a) fantasia; (*of
price*) eccessivo. —*v.t.* (*want, fam.*)
aver desiderio di; (*suppose*) pensare,
supporre. ~ **dress** *n.* costume (per
maschera) *m.* **take a** ~ **to** incapric-
ciarsi di.

fanfare /'fænfeə(r)/ *n.* fanfara *f.*

fang /fæŋ/ *n.* zanna *f.*; (*of snake*) dente
m.

fanlight /'fænlaɪt/ *n.* lunetta *f.*

fantastic /fæn'tæstɪk/ *a.* fantastico.

fantas|y /'fæntəsɪ/ *n.* fantasia *f.*; (*day-
dream*) fantasticheria *f.* ~**ize** *v.i.* fan-
tasticare.

far /fɑ:(r)/ *adv.* lontano; (*much*) molto;
(*very*) di gran lunga. —*a.* (**further,
furthest** *or* **farther, farthest**) lontano; (*end, side*) altro. **as** ~ **as** (*up to*)
fino a. **as** ~ **as I know** per quanto io
sappia. **by** ~ di gran lunga. ~ **away**
a. lontano. **the F**~ **East** *n.* l'Estremo
Oriente *m.* ~-**fetched** *a.* improbabile.
~-**off** *a.* remoto. ~-**reaching** *a.* di
larga portata. ~-**seeing** *a.* lungimi-
rante. ~-**sighted** *a.* presbite; (*fig.*)
prudente.

farc|e /fɑ:s/ *n.* farsa *f.* ~**ical** *a.* ridico-
lo.

fare /feə(r)/ *n.* tariffa *f.*; (*food*) vitto
m. —*v.i.* passarsela.

farewell /feə'wel/ *int.* & *n.* addio *m.*

farm /fɑ:m/ *n.* fattoria *f.* —*v.t.* coltivare. —*v.i.* fare l'agricoltore. ~ **out**
delegare (lavoro). ~**er** *n.* agricoltore
m. ~**ing** *n.* agricoltura *f.*

farmhouse /'fɑ:mhaʊs/ *n.* casa co-
lonica *f.*

farmyard /'fɑ:mjɑ:d/ *n.* aia *f.*

farther, farthest /'fɑ:ðə(r), 'fɑ:ðɪst/ *see*
far.

fascinat|e /'fæsmeɪt/ *v.t.* affascinare.
~**ion** /-'neɪʃn/ *n.* fascino *m.*

fascis|t /'fæʃɪst/ *a.* & *n.* fascista *m.*/*f.*
~**m** /-zəm/ *n.* fascismo *m.*

fashion /'fæʃn/ *n.* moda *f.*; (*manner*)
maniera *f.* ~**able** *a.* di moda.

fast¹ /fɑ:st/ *a.* (**-er, -est**) veloce; (*of
watch*) in anticipo; (*immoral*) dissoluto; (*of colour*) indelebile; (*fig.*)
saldo. —*adv.* velocemente; (*firmly*)
fermamente. ~ **asleep** profondamente addormentato.

fast² /fɑ:st/ *v.i.* digiunare. —*n.* digiuno
m.

fasten /'fɑ:sn/ *v.t.*/*i.* allacciare, allac-
ciarsi; (*window, bolt, etc.*) fermare.
~**er**, ~**ing** *ns.* gancio *m.*, chiusura *f.*

fastidious /fə'stɪdɪəs/ *a.* fastidioso.

fat /fæt/ *n.* grasso *m.* —*a.* (**fatter,
fattest**) grasso. ~**head** *n.* (*sl.*) zuccone, a *m.*, *f.* **a** ~ **lot** (*sl.*) un bel
niente. ~**ness** *n.* grassezza *f.*

fatal /'feɪtl/ *a.* mortale. ~**ity** /fə'tælətɪ/
n. morte *f.* ~**ly** *adv.* mortalmente.

fatalis|t /'feɪtəlɪst/ *n.* fatalista *m.*/*f.* ~**m**
n. fatalismo *m.*

fate /feɪt/ *n.* destino *m.*; (*one's lot*) sorte
f. ~**d** *a.* destinato. ~**ful** *a.* fatidico.

father /'fɑ:ðə(r)/ *n.* padre *m.* ~-**in-law**
n. (*pl.* ~**s-in-law**) suocero *m.* ~**hood**
n. paternità *f.* ~**ly** *a.* paterno.

fathom /'fæðəm/ *n.* braccio *m.* —*v.t.* ~
(**out**) comprendere.

fatigue /fə'ti:g/ *n.* fatica *f.* —*v.t.* affati-
care.

fatten /'fætn/ *v.t.*/*i.* ingrassare, ingrassarsi. ~**ing** *a.* ingrassante.

fatty /'fætɪ/ *a.* grasso, untuoso. —*n.*
(*fam.*) ciccione, a *m.*, *f.*

fatuous /'fætʃʊəs/ *a.* fatuo.

fault /fɔ:lt/ *n.* difetto *m.*; (*blame*) colpa
f.; (*geol.*) faglia *f.*; (*tennis*) fallo *m.*
—*v.t.* criticare. ~**less** *a.* impeccabile.
~**y** *a.* difettoso.

fauna /'fɔ:nə/ *n.* fauna *f.*

favour /'feɪvə(r)/ *n.* favore *m.* —*v.t.*
favorire; (*prefer*) preferire; (*support*)
favoreggiare. ~**able** *a.* favorevole.
~**ably** *adv.* favorevolmente.

favourit|e /'feɪvərɪt/ *a.* & *n.* prediletto,
a *m.*, *f.* ~**ism** *n.* favoritismo *m.*

fawn¹ /fɔ:n/ *n.* cerbiatto *m.* —*a.* fulvo.

fawn² /fɔ:n/ *v.i.* ~ **on** adulare.

fear /fɪə(r)/ *n.* timore *m.* —*v.t.* temere.
~**ful** *a.* timoroso; (*awful*) terribile.

~less *a.* impavido. ~lessness *n.* impavidità *f.*

fearsome /'fɪəsəm/ *a.* spaventoso.

feasib|le /'fiːzəbl/ *a.* fattibile; (*likely*) probabile. ~ility /-'bɪlətɪ/ *n.* praticabilità *f.*

feast /fiːst/ *n.* festa *f.*; (*banquet*) banchetto *m.* —*v.i.* banchettare. ~ on godersi.

feat /fiːt/ *n.* impresa *f.*

feather /'feðə(r)/ *n.* piuma *f.* —*v.t.* ~ one's nest arricchirsi. ~-brained *a.* sciocco.

featherweight /'feðəweɪt/ *n.* peso piuma *m. invar.*

feature /'fiːtʃə(r)/ *n.* lineamento *m.*; (*quality*) specialità *f.*; (*in newspaper*) articolo *m.* ~ film *n.* lungometraggio *m.* —*v.t.* (*film*) avere come protagonista; (*represent*) rappresentare. —*v.i.* figurare.

February /'februərɪ/ *n.* febbraio *m.*

feckless /'feklɪs/ *a.* inetto.

fed /fed/ *see* feed. —*a.* ~ up (*sl.*) stufo (with, di).

federa|l /'fedərəl/ *a.* federale. ~tion /-'reɪʃn/ *n.* federazione *f.*

fee /fiː/ *n.* onorario *m.*; (*price*) quota *f.* school ~(s) retta *f.*

feeble /'fiːbl/ *a.* (-er, -est) fiacco. ~-minded *a.* debole di mente.

feed /fiːd/ *v.t.* (*p.t.* fed) nutrire; (*animals*) dar da mangiare a; (*supply*) alimentare. —*v.i.* nutrirsi. —*n.* pasto *m.* ~er *n.* (*bottle*) poppatoio *m.*; (*bib*) bavaglino *m.*

feedback /'fiːdbæk/ *n.* controreazione *f.*

feel /fiːl/ *v.t.* (*p.t.* felt) sentire; (*experience*) provare; (*think*) pensare; (*touch*) tastare. ~ hot/hungry aver caldo/fame. ~ like sentirsi di. ~ up to sentirsi in grado di.

feeler /'fiːlə(r)/ *n.* (*in animals*) antenna *f.* put out a ~ tastare il terreno.

feeling /'fiːlɪŋ/ *n.* sentimento *m.*; (*awareness*) sensazione *f.*

feet /fiːt/ *see* foot.

feign /feɪn/ *v.t.* simulare.

feint /feɪnt/ *n.* finta *f.*

felicitous /fə'lɪsɪtəs/ *a.* ben appropriato.

feline /'fiːlaɪn/ *a.* felino.

fell¹ /fel/ *v.t.* abbattere.

fell² /fel/ *see* fall.

fellow /'feləʊ/ *n.* compagno *m.*; (*of society*) socio *m.*; (*fam.*) tipo *m.* ~-countryman *n.* compatriota *m.*

~ship *n.* cameratismo *m.*; (*group*) associazione *f.*

felony /'felənɪ/ *n.* (*old use*) delitto *m.*

felt¹ /felt/ *n.* feltro *m.* ~-tipped pen *n.* pennarello *m.*

felt² /felt/ *see* feel.

female /'fiːmeɪl/ *a.* femminile. —*n.* femmina *f.*

feminin|e /'femənɪn/ *a.* & *n.* femminile *m.* ~ity /-'nɪnətɪ/ *n.* femminilità *f.*

feminist /'femɪnɪst/ *n.* femminista *m.*/*f.*

fenc|e /fens/ *n.* recinto *m.*; (*person*) ricettatore *m.* —*v.t.* ~ in chiudere in un recinto. —*v.i.* tirar di scherma. ~er *n.* (*sport*) schermidore *m.* ~ing *n.* steccato *m.*; (*sport*) scherma *f.*

fend /fend/ *v.i.* ~ for o.s. badare a se stesso. —*v.t.* ~ off parare.

fender /'fendə(r)/ *n.* parafuoco *m. invar.*; (*naut.*) parabordo *m.*

fennel /'fenl/ *n.* finocchio *m.*

ferment¹ /fə'ment/ *v.t.*/*i.* (far) fermentare. ~ation /fɜːmen'teɪʃn/ *n.* fermentazione *f.*

ferment² /'fɜːment/ *n.* fermento *m.*

fern /fɜːn/ *n.* felce *f.*

feroc|ious /fə'rəʊʃəs/ *a.* feroce. ~ity /-'rɒsətɪ/ *n.* ferocia *f.*

ferret /'ferɪt/ *n.* furetto *m.* —*v.i.* (*p.t.* ferreted) cacciare. —*v.t.* ~ out scovare.

ferry /'ferɪ/ *n.* traghetto *m.* —*v.t.*/*i.* traghettare.

fertil|e /'fɜːtaɪl/ *a.* fertile. ~ity /fə'tɪlətɪ/ *n.* fertilità *f.* ~ize /-əlaɪz/ *v.t.* fertilizzare.

fertilizer /'fɜːtəlaɪzə(r)/ *n.* fertilizzante *m.*

fervent /'fɜːvənt/ *a.* fervente.

fervour /'fɜːvə(r)/ *n.* fervore *m.*

fester /'festə(r)/ *v.t.*/*i.* (far) suppurare; (*fig.*) amareggiare.

festival /'festɪvl/ *n.* festival *m.*; (*relig.*) festa *f.*

festiv|e /'festɪv/ *a.* festivo. ~ity /fe'stɪvətɪ/ *n.* festività *f.*

festoon /fe'stuːn/ *v.i.* ~ with ornare di festoni.

fetch /fetʃ/ *v.t.* andare a prendere; (*bring*) portare; (*be sold for*) raggiungere (il prezzo di).

fetching /'fetʃɪŋ/ *a.* attraente.

fête /feɪt/ *n.* festa *f.* —*v.t.* festeggiare.

fetid /'fetɪd/ *a.* fetido.

fetish /'fetɪʃ/ *n.* idolo *m.*

fetter /'fetə(r)/ *v.t.* incatenare. ~s *n.pl.* catene *f.pl.*

fettle /'fetl/ *n.* condizione *f.* **be in good** ~ essere in buona forma.

feud /fju:d/ *n.* ostilità *f.*

feudal /'fju:dl/ *a.* feudale. ~**ism** *n.* feudalismo *m.*

fever /'fi:və(r)/ *n.* febbre *f.* ~**ish** *a.* febbricitante; (*fig.*) febbrile.

few /fju:/ *a. & n.* pochi. **a** ~ *a.* qualche; *pron.* alcuni. **a good** ~, **quite a** ~ (*fam.*) parecchi. ~**er** *a. & n.* meno (di). ~**est** *a. & n.* il minor numero di.

fiancé /fɪ'ɒnseɪ/ *n.* fidanzato *m.* **fiancée** *n.* fidanzata *f.*

fiasco /fɪ'æskəʊ/ *n.* (*pl.* -os) fiasco *m.*

fib /fɪb/ *n.* bugia *f.* ~**ber** *n.* bugiardo, a *m., f.*

fibre /'faɪbə(r)/ *n.* fibra *f.*

fibreglass /'faɪbəglɑːs/ *n.* lana di vetro *f.*

fickle /'fɪkl/ *a.* incostante.

fiction /'fɪkʃn/ *n.* finzione *f.*; (*lit.*) (prosa) narrativa *f.* ~ **writer** romanziere, a *m., f.* ~**al** *a.* immaginario.

fictitious /fɪk'tɪʃəs/ *a.* fittizio.

fiddle /'fɪdl/ *n.* (*fam., mus.*) violino *m.*; (*sl., cheating*) imbroglio *m.* —*v.i.* gingillarsi; (*sl., cheat*) imbrogliare. ~**r** /-ə(r)/ *n.* (*fam.*) violinista *m.*/*f.*; (*sl., cheat*) truffa/tore, trice *m., f.*

fidelity /fɪ'delətɪ/ *n.* fedeltà *f.*

fidget /'fɪdʒɪt/ *v.i.* agitarsi. —*n.* irrequieto, a *m., f.* ~**y** *a.* agitato.

field /fi:ld/ *n.* campo *m.*; (*fig.*) settore *m.* ~**-day** *n.* giornata campale *f.* ~ **events** *n.pl.* atletica leggera *f.s.* ~**glasses** *n.pl.* binocolo *m.s.* **F**~ **Marshal** *n.* feldmaresciallo *m.*

fieldwork /'fi:ldwɜːk/ *n.* ricerche *f.pl.*

fiend /fi:nd/ *n.* demonio *m.* ~**ish** *a.* diabolico.

fierce /fɪəs/ *a.* (-**er**, -**est**) feroce; (*attack*) violento. ~**ness** *n.* ferocia *f.*

fiery /'faɪərɪ/ *a.* (-**ier**, -**iest**) focoso.

fifteen /fɪf'ti:n/ *a. & n.* quindici *m.* ~**th** *a. & n.* quindicesimo, a *m., f.*

fifth /fɪfθ/ *a. & n.* quinto, a *m., f.*

fift|y /'fɪftɪ/ *a. & n.* cinquanta *m.* ~**ieth** *a. & n.* cinquantesimo, a *m., f.*

fig /fɪg/ *n.* fico *m.*

fight /faɪt/ *v.t./i.* (*p.t.* **fought**) combattere; (*struggle*) lottare; (*physical*) azzuffarsi. —*n.* lotta *f.*; (*brawl*) zuffa *f.*; (*mil.*) battaglia *f.* ~ **off** respingere. ~ **shy of** evitare. ~**er** *n.* combattente *m.*/*f.*; (*plane*) caccia *m. invar.* ~**ing** *n.* combattimento *m.*

figment /'fɪgmənt/ *n.* invenzione *f.*

figurative /'fɪgjərətɪv/ *a.* figurativo.

figure /'fɪgə(r)/ *n.* cifra *f.*; (*diagram*) figura *f.*; (*shape*) forma *f.*; (*of woman*) linea *f.* ~**s** *n.pl.* aritmetica *f.* —*v.t.* immaginare. —*v.i.* figurare. ~ **out** calcolare. ~**head** *n.* figura simbolica *f.* ~ **of speech** modo di dire *m.*

filament /'fɪləmənt/ *n.* filamento *m.*

filch /fɪltʃ/ *v.t.* rubacchiare.

fil|e[1] /faɪl/ *n.* (*tool*) lima *f.* —*v.t.* limare. ~**ings** *n.pl.* limatura *f.s.*

file[2] /faɪl/ *n.* schedario *m.*; (*row*) fila *f.* —*v.t.* (*papers*) schedare. —*v.i.* sfilare.

fill /fɪl/ *v.t./i.* riempire, riempirsi; (*tooth*) otturare. —*n.* pieno *m.* ~ **in** compilare. ~ **out** riempire; (*get fat*) ingrassarsi. ~ **up** (*auto*) fare il pieno.

fillet /'fɪlɪt/ *n.* filetto *m.* —*v.t.* (*p.t.* **filleted**) disossare.

filling /'fɪlɪŋ/ *n.* (*culin.*) ripieno *m.*; (*of tooth*) piombatura *f.* ~ **station** stazione di rifornimento *f.*

filly /'fɪlɪ/ *n.* puledra *f.*

film /fɪlm/ *n.* strato sottile *m.*; (*photo*) pellicola *f.*; (*cinema*) film *m. invar.* —*v.t.* (*cinema*) girare un film. ~ **industry** industria cinematografica *f.* ~ **star** divo, a *m., f.*

filter /'fɪltə(r)/ *n.* filtro *m.* —*v.t.* filtrare. —*v.i.* infiltrarsi. ~ **out** diffondersi; (*facts*) venir fuori. ~**-tip** *n.* filtro *m.*

filth /fɪlθ/ *n.* sudiciume *m.* ~**iness** *n.* sporcizia *f.* ~**y** *a.* sudicio.

fin /fɪn/ *n.* pinna *f.*; (*aeron.*) aletta *f.*

final /'faɪnl/ *a.* finale; (*conclusive*) decisivo. —*n.* (*sport*) finale *f.* ~**s** *n.pl.* (*schol.*) esami finali *m.pl.* ~**ist** *n.* finalista *m.*/*f.* ~**ity** /-'nælətɪ/ *n.* finalità *f.* ~**ly** *adv.* infine, finalmente.

finale /fɪ'nɑːlɪ/ *n.* finale *m.*

finalize /'faɪnəlaɪz/ *v.t.* portare a termine.

financ|e /faɪ'næns/ *n.* finanza *f.* —*v.t.* finanziare. ~**ier** *n.* finanziere *m.*

financial /faɪ'nænʃl/. *a.* finanziario. ~**ly** *adv.* finanziariamente.

finch /fɪntʃ/ *n.* fringuello *m.*

find /faɪnd/ *v.t.* (*p.t.* **found**) trovare; (*jurid.*) dichiarare. —*n.* scoperta *f.* ~ **out** scoprire. ~**ings** *n.pl.* conclusioni *f.pl.*

fine[1] /faɪn/ *n.* multa *f.* —*v.t.* multare.

fine[2] /faɪn/ *a.* (-**er**, -**est**) bello; (*slender*) fine. —*adv.* bene. ~ **arts** *n.pl.* belle arti *f.pl.* ~**ly** *adv.* (*cut*) finemente.

finery /'faɪnərɪ/ *n.* splendore *m.*

finesse /fɪ'nes/ *n.* finezza *f.*

finger /'fɪŋgə(r)/ *n.* dito *m.* (*pl.* dita *f.*). —*v.t.* tastare. ~-**mark** *n.* ditata *f.* ~-**nail** *n.* unghia *f.* ~-**stall** *n.* copridito *m.*

fingerprint /'fɪŋgəprɪnt/ *n.* impronta digitale *f.*

fingertip /'fɪŋgətɪp/ *n.* punta del dito *f.*

finicking, finicky /'fɪnɪkɪŋ, 'fɪnɪkɪ/ *adjs.* meticoloso.

finish /'fɪnɪʃ/ *v.t./i.* finire. —*n.* fine *f.*; (*appearance*) finitura *f.*

finite /'faɪnaɪt/ *a.* limitato.

Fin|land /'fɪnlənd/ *n.* Finlandia *f.* ~**n** *n.* finlandese *m.|f.* ~**nish** *a.* finlandese; *n.* (*lang.*) finlandese *m.*

fiord /fjɔːd/ *n.* fiordo *m.*

fir /fɜː(r)/ *n.* abete *m.*

fire /'faɪə(r)/ *n.* fuoco *m.*; (*destructive burning*) incendio *m.* —*v.t.* dar fuoco a; (*bullet etc.*) sparare; (*dismiss*) licenziare; (*fig.*) infiammare. ~ **brigade** *n.* vigili del fuoco *m.pl.* ~-**engine** *n.* autopompa *f.* ~-**escape** *n.* uscita di sicurezza *f.*

firearm /'faɪərɑːm/ *n.* arma da fuoco *f.*

firelight /'faɪəlaɪt/ *n.* luce del fuoco *f.*

fireman /'faɪəmən/ *n.* (*pl.* -men) pompiere *m.*

firep ace /'faɪəpleɪs/ *n.* caminetto *m.*

fireside /'faɪəsaɪd/ *n.* focolare *m.*

firewood /'faɪəwʊd/ *n.* legna (da ardere) *f.*

firework /'faɪəwɜːk/ *n.* fuoco d'artificio *m.*

firing-squad /'faɪərɪŋskwɒd/ *n.* plotone d'esecuzione *m.*

firm[1] /fɜːm/ *n.* ditta, azienda *f.*

firm[2] /fɜːm/ *a.* (-**er**, -**est**) fermo; (*steady*) stabile; (*resolute*) risoluto. ~**ly** *adv.* decisamente. ~**ness** *n.* fermezza *f.*

first /fɜːst/ *a.* primo. —*n.* primo, a *m.*, *f.* —*adv.* per primo, innanzitutto. **at** ~ all'inizio. ~ **aid** *n.* pronto soccorso *m.* ~-**born** *a.* & *n.* primogenito *m.* ~-**class** *a.* & *adv.* di prim'ordine. ~-**name** *n.* nome di battesimo *m.* ~-**rate** *a.* ottimo. ~**ly** *adv.* in primo luogo.

fiscal /'fɪskl/ *a.* fiscale.

fish /fɪʃ/ *n.* (*usually invar.*) pesce *m.* —*v.t./i.* pescare. ~ **for** sollecitare. ~ **out** tirar fuori. ~**ing** *n.* pesca *f.* ~ **finger** *n.* bastoncino di pesce *m.* ~**monger** *n.* pescivendolo *m.* ~**y** *a.* (*fam.*) sospetto.

fisherman /'fɪʃəmən/ *n.* (*pl.* -men) pescatore *m.*

fission /'fɪʃn/ *n.* fissione *f.*

fist /fɪst/ *n.* pugno *m.*

fit[1] /fɪt/ *n.* attacco *m.*; (*of rage*) accesso *m.*; (*of generosity*) slancio *m.*

fit[2] /fɪt/ *a.* (**fitter, fittest**) adatto; (*good enough*) giusto; (*healthy*) in buona salute. —*v.t./i.* (*p.t.* **fitted**) (*clothes*) provare; (*adapt*) adattare; (*prepare*) mettere in grado di; (*install*) installare. —*n.* (*of clothes*) taglio *m.* ~ **out**, ~**up** equipaggiare. ~**ness** *n.* buona salute *f.*; (*of remark*) appropriatezza *f.* ~**ted carpet** *n.* moquette *f. invar.*

fitful /'fɪtfl/ *a.* irregolare.

fitment /'fɪtmənt/ *n.* mobile a muro *m.*

fitting /'fɪtɪŋ/ *a.* appropriato. —*n.* (*of clothes*) prova *f.*; (*mech.*) montaggio *m.*

fittings /'fɪtɪŋz/ *n.pl.* accessori *m.pl.*

five /faɪv/ *a.* & *n.* cinque *m.*

fiver /'faɪvə(r)/ *n.* (*fam.*) biglietto da cinque sterline *m.*

fix /fɪks/ *v.t./i.* fissare, fissarsi; (*repair*) aggiustare; (*deal with, sl.*) sistemare. —*n.* difficoltà *f.* ~**ed** *a.* fisso.

fixation /fɪk'seɪʃn/ *n.* fissazione *f.*

fixative /'fɪksətɪv/ *n.* fissativo *m.*

fixture /'fɪkstʃə(r)/ *n.* installazione *f.*; (*sport*) gara *f.*

fizz /fɪz/ *v.i.* frizzare. —*n.* effervescenza *f.* ~**y** *a.* gassoso.

fizzle /'fɪzl/ *v.i.* spumeggiare. ~ **out** finire in nulla.

flab /flæb/ *n.* (*fam.*) flaccidità *f.* ~**by** *a.* floscio.

flabbergast /'flæbəgɑːst/ *v.t.* sbalordire.

flag[1] /flæg/ *n.* bandiera *f.* —*v.t.* (*p.t.* **flagged**)) ~ **down** far segno di fermarsi. ~-**pole** *n.* asta della bandiera *f.* ~**ship** *n.* nave ammiraglia *f.*

flag[2] /flæg/ *v.i.* (*p.t.* **flagged**) affievolirsi; (*droop*) venir meno.

flagon /'flægən/ *n.* bottiglione *m.*

flagrant /'fleɪgrənt/ *a.* flagrante.

flagstone /'flægstəʊn/ *n.* pietra da lastricare *f.*

flair /fleə(r)/ *n.* attitudine *f.*

flak|e /fleɪk/ *n.* fiocco *m.*; (*of paint, soap*) scaglia *f.* —*v.i.* cadere in fiocchi. ~**e out** (*fam.*) crollare. ~**y** *a.* a scaglie.

flamboyant /flæm'bɔɪənt/ *a.* fastoso.

flame /fleɪm/ *n.* fiamma *f.* —*v.i.* fiammeggiare.

flamingo /flə'mɪŋgəʊ/ *n.* (*pl.* -os) fenicottero *m.*

flammable /'flæməbl/ *a.* infiammabile.

flan /flæn/ *n.* sformato *m.*

flank /flæŋk/ *n.* fianco *m.* —*v.t.* fian-cheggiare.

flannel /'flænl/ *n.* flanella *f.* **face-~** *n.* guanto di spugna *m.* **~s** *n.pl.* pantaloni di flanella *m.pl.*

flannellette /flænə'let/ *n.* flanella di cotone *f.*

flap /flæp/ *v.i.* (*p.t.* **flapped**) sbattere; (*sl.*) agitarsi. —*v.t.* **~ its wings** battere le ali. —*n.* (*of pocket*) patta *f.*; (*of table*) ribalta *f.*; (*sl.*) agitazione *f.*

flare /fleə(r)/ *v.i.* **~ up** infiammarsi. —*n.* fiammata *f.*; (*device*) razzo *m.*; (*in skirt*) svasatura *f.* **~d** *a.* svasato.

flash /flæʃ/ *v.t./i.* scintillare; (*move rapidly*) saettare; (*signal*) trasmettere; (*flaunt*) ostentare; (*on and off*) lampeggiare. —*n.* lampo *m.*; (*of news*) notizia lampo *f.* **~ past** passare come un bolide. **in a ~** in un attimo. **~er** *n.* (*auto*) lampeggiatore *m.*

flashback /'flæʃbæk/ *n.* scena retrospettiva *f.*

flashlight /'flæʃlaɪt/ *n.* torcia elettrica *f.*; (*photo*) flash *m. invar.*

flashy /'flæʃɪ/ *a.* vistoso.

flask /flɑːsk/ *n.* fiasco *m.*; (*vacuum flask*) termos *m. invar.*

flat /flæt/ *a.* (**flatter, flattest**) piatto; (*tyre*) a terra; (*refusal*) reciso; (*fare, rate*) fisso; (*depressed*) giù di morale; (*mus.*) stonato. —*adv.* in posizione piatta. —*n.* appartamento *m.*; (*mus.*) bemolle *m.* **~ out** (*tired*) esausto. **~ rate** tariffa unica *f.* **~ly** *adv.* categoricamente.

flatten /'flætn/ *v.t./i.* appiattire, appiattirsi.

flatter /'flætə(r)/ *v.t.* adulare. **~er** *n.* adula|tore, -trice *m., f.* **~ing** *a.* lusinghiero. **~y** *n.* adulazione *f.*

flatulence /'flætjʊləns/ *n.* flatulenza *f.*

flaunt /flɔːnt/ *v.t.* ostentare.

flautist /'flɔːtɪst/ *n.* flautista *m.*/*f.*

flavour /'fleɪvə(r)/ *n.* sapore *m.* —*v.t.* condire. **~ing** *n.* condimento *m.*

flaw /flɔː/ *n.* difetto *m.* **~less** *a.* perfetto.

flax /flæks/ *n.* lino *m.* **~en** *a.* di lino.

flea /fliː/ *n.* pulce *f.* **~ market** *n.* (*hum.*) mercato delle pulci *m.*

fleck /flek/ *n.* macchiolina *f.*

fled /fled/ *see* **flee.**

fledged /fledʒd/ *a.* **fully-~** totalmente maturo.

fledgeling /'fledʒlɪŋ/ *n.* uccellino *m.*

flee /fliː/ *v.t./i.* (*p.t.* **fled**) fuggire.

fleece /fliːs/ *n.* vello *m.* —*v.t.* tosare.

fleet /fliːt/ *n.* flotta *f.*; (*of cars*) colonna *f.*

fleeting /'fliːtɪŋ/ *a.* fugace.

Flemish /'flemɪʃ/ *a.* & *n.* fiammingo *m.*

flesh /fleʃ/ *n.* carne *f.* **in the ~** in persona. **one's own ~ and blood** il proprio sangue. **~y** *a.* carnoso.

flew /fluː/ *see* **fly²**.

flex /fleks/ *n.* filo *m.*

flexib|le /'fleksəbl/ *a.* flessibile. **~ility** /-'bɪlətɪ/ *n.* flessibilità *f.*

flexitime /'fleksɪtaɪm/ *n.* orario flessibile *m.*

flick /flɪk/ *n.* buffetto *m.* **~s** *n.pl.* (*fam.*) cinema *f.s.* —*v.t.* dare un buffetto. **~ through** sfogliare. **~-knife** *n.* coltello a serramanico *m.*

flicker /'flɪkə(r)/ *v.i.* tremolare. —*n.* tremolio *m.*; (*light*) guizzo *m.*

flier /'flaɪə(r)/ *n.* = **flyer.**

flight¹ /flaɪt/ *n.* volo *m.* **~-deck** *n.* ponte di volo *m.* **~ of stairs** *n.* rampa *f.*

flight² /flaɪt/ *n.* fuga *f.* **take (to) ~** darsi alla fuga.

flighty /'flaɪtɪ/ *a.* (**-ier, -iest**) frivolo.

flimsy /'flɪmzɪ/ *a.* (**-ier, -iest**) leggero.

flinch /flɪntʃ/ *v.i.* (*wince*) sussultare; (*draw back*) ritirarsi.

fling /flɪŋ/ *v.t.* (*p.t.* **flung**) gettare. —*n.* getto *m.* **have a ~** godersela. **in full ~** in piena attività.

flint /flɪnt/ *n.* pietra focaia *f.*; (*for lighter*) pietrina *f.*

flip /flɪp/ *v.t./i.* (*p.t.* **flipped**) dare un colpetto. —*n.* colpetto *m.* **the ~ side** l'altro lato. **~ through** sfogliare.

flippant /'flɪpənt/ *a.* irriverente.

flipper /'flɪpə(r)/ *n.* pinna *f.*

flirt /flɜːt/ *v.t.* flirtare. —*n.* civetta *f.* **~ation** /-'teɪʃn/ *n.* flirt *m. invar.* **~atious** /-'teɪʃəs/ *a.* civettuolo.

flit /flɪt/ *v.i.* (*p.t.* **flitted**) volteggiare; (*leave stealthily*) andarsene.

float /fləʊt/ *v.t./i.* galleggiare. —*n.* galleggiante *m.*; (*low cart*) carro *m.*; (*money*) riserva di cassa *f.*

flock /flɒk/ *n.* gregge *m.*; (*of people*) frotta *f.* —*v.i.* affollarsi.

floe /fləʊ/ *n.* banchisa *f.*

flog /flɒg/ *v.t.* (*p.t.* **flogged**) bastonare; (*sl.*) vendere.

flood /flʌd/ *n.* allagamento *m.*; (*of tears, rain*) diluvio *m.*; (*of river*) straripamento *m.* —*v.t.* allagare. —*v.i.* straripare.

floodlight /'flʌdlaɪt/ *n.* riflettore *m.*

—*v.t.* (*p.t.* **floodlit**) illuminare con riflettori.

floor /flɔː(r)/ *n.* pavimento *m.*; (*storey*) piano *m.*; (*for dancing*) pista *f.* —*v.t.* pavimentare; (*baffle*) confondere. ∼ **show** *n.* spettacolo di varietà *m.*

flop /flɒp/ *v.i.* (*p.t.* **flopped**) muoversi goffamente; (*drop*) piombare; (*sl.*) far fiasco. —*n.* tonfo *m.*; (*sl.*) fiasco *m.* ∼**py** *a.* floscio.

flora /'flɔːrə/ *n.* flora *f.*

floral /'flɔːrəl/ *a.* floreale.

Floren|ce /'flɒrəns/ *n.* Firenze *f.* ∼**tine** *a.* & *n.* fiorentino, a *m.*, *f.*

florid /'flɒrɪd/ *a.* florido.

florist /'flɒrɪst/ *n.* fioraio, a *m.*, *f.*

flounce /flaʊns/ *n.* balza *f.*

flounder /'flaʊndə(r)/ *v.i.* dibattersi.

flour /'flaʊə(r)/ *n.* farina *f.* ∼**y** *a.* farinoso.

flourish /'flʌrɪʃ/ *v.i.* prosperare. —*v.t.* brandire. —*n.* gesto drammatico *m.*; (*scroll*) ghirigoro *m.* ∼**ing** *a.* prosperoso.

flout /flaʊt/ *v.t.* schernire.

flow /fləʊ/ *v.i.* scorrere; (*hang loosely*) ricadere. —*n.* flusso *m.* ∼ **out** sgorgare.

flower /'flaʊə(r)/ *n.* fiore. —*v.i.* fiorire. ∼**-bed** *n.* aiuola *f.* ∼**ed** *a.* a fiori. ∼**y** *a.* fiorito.

flown /fləʊn/ *see* **fly²**.

flu /fluː/ *n.* (*fam.*) influenza *f.*

fluctuat|e /'flʌktʃʊeɪt/ *v.i.* fluttuare. ∼**ion** /-'eɪʃn/ *n.* fluttuazione *f.*

flue /fluː/ *n.* gola del camino *f.*

fluen|t /'fluːənt/ *a.* spedito. **speak** ∼**t Italian** parlare correntemente l'italiano. ∼**cy** *n.* scioltezza *f.* ∼**tly** *adv.* speditamente.

fluff /flʌf/ *n.* peluria *f.* —*v.t.*/*i.* arruffare, arruffarsi; (*sl.*) sbagliare. ∼**y** *a.* (**-ier**, **-iest**) vaporoso.

fluid /'fluːɪd/ *a.* & *n.* fluido *m.*

fluke /fluːk/ *n.* colpo di fortuna *m.*

flung /flʌŋ/ *see* **fling**.

flunk /flʌŋk/ *v.t.* (*Amer.*, *fam.*) essere bocciato.

fluorescent /flʊə'resnt/ *a.* fluorescente.

fluoride /'flʊəraɪd/ *n.* fluoruro *m.*

flurry /'flʌrɪ/ *n.* raffica *f.*; (*fig.*) agitazione *f.*

flush¹ /flʌʃ/ *v.i.* arrossire. —*v.t.* lavare con un getto d'acqua. —*n.* vampa *f.*; (*of water*) getto d'acqua *m.*; (*fig.*) impeto *m.* —*a.* a livello; (*fam.*,

affluent) ben fornito. ∼ **the toilet** tirare l'acqua.

flush² /flʌʃ/ *v.t.*/*i.* (far) volar via.

fluster /'flʌstə(r)/ *v.t.* confondere.

flute /fluːt/ *n.* flauto *m.*

flutter /'flʌtə(r)/ *v.i.* svolazzare; (*of wings*) battere. —*n.* battito *m.*; (*fig.*) confusione *f.*

flux /flʌks/ *n.* flusso *m.*

fly¹ /flaɪ/ *n.* mosca *f.*

fly² /flaɪ/ *v.i.* (*p.t.* **flew**, *p.p.* **flown**) volare; (*of flag*) sventolare; (*rush*) precipitarsi. —*v.t.* pilotare; (*passengers*) trasportare (in aereo). ∼ **open** *v.i.* spalancarsi. —*n.* (*of trousers*) patta *f.*

flyer /'flaɪə(r)/ *n.* aviatore *m.*

flying /'flaɪɪŋ/ *a.* volante; (*visit*) breve. —*n.* volo *m.* ∼ **saucer** *n.* disco volante *m.* **get off to a** ∼ **start** partire come un razzo. **with** ∼ **colours** splendidamente.

flyleaf /'flaɪliːf/ *n.* (*pl.* **-leaves** /'flaɪliːvz/) risguardo *m.*

flyover /'flaɪəʊvə(r)/ *n.* cavalcavia *m. invar.*

flyweight /'flaɪweɪt/ *n.* peso mosca *m.*

foal /fəʊl/ *n.* puledro *m.*

foam /fəʊm/ *n.* schiuma *f.* —*v.i.* spumare. ∼ **at the mouth** far la bava alla bocca. ∼ **rubber** *n.* gommapiuma *f.*

fob /fɒb/ *v.t.* (*p.t.* **fobbed**) ∼ **off on** affibbiare a.

focal /'fəʊkl/ *a.* focale.

focus /'fəʊkəs/ *n.* (*pl.* **-cuses** *or* **-ci** /-saɪ/) (*optical*) fuoco *m.*; (*fig.*) centro *m.* —*v.t.*/*i.* (*p.t.* **focused**) mettere a fuoco; (*fig.*) concentrare. **in** ∼ a fuoco. **out of** ∼ sfocato.

fodder /'fɒdə(r)/ *n.* foraggio *m.*

foe /fəʊ/ *n.* nemico, a *m.*, *f.*

foetus /'fiːtəs/ *n.* (*pl.* **-tuses**) feto *m.*

fog /fɒg/ *n.* nebbia *f.* —*v.t.*/*i.* (*p.t.* **fogged**) annebbiare, annebbiarsi. ∼**-horn** *n.* sirena da nebbia *f.* ∼**gy** *a.* nebbioso.

fogey /'fəʊgɪ/ *n.* (*pl.* **-gies**) persona antiquata *f.*

foible /'fɔɪbl/ *n.* punto debole *m.*

foil¹ /fɔɪl/ *n.* lamina di metallo *f.*; (*fig.*) contrasto *m.*

foil² /fɔɪl/ *v.t.* frustrare.

foist /fɔɪst/ *v.t.* appioppare (**on**, a).

fold¹ /fəʊld/ *v.t.*/*i.* piegare, piegarsi; (*arms*) incrociare; (*fail*) crollare. —*n.* piega *f.* ∼**er** *n.* cartella *f.*; (*leaflet*) volantino *m.* ∼**ing** *a.* pieghevole.

fold² /fəʊld/ *n.* ovile *m.*

foliage /'fəʊlɪdʒ/ *n.* fogliame *m.*

folk /fəʊk/ *n.* gente *m.* **my** ~**s** *n.pl.* i miei *m.pl.* ~**-dance** *n.* danza popolare *f.* ~**-song** *n.* canto popolare *m.*

folklore /'fəʊklɔː(r)/ *n.* folclore *m.*

follow /'fɒləʊ/ *v.t./i.* seguire. **it** ~**s that** consegue che. ~ **suit** fare lo stesso. ~**-up** *n.* seguito *m.* ~**er** *n.* seguace *m./f.*

following /'fɒləʊɪŋ/ *n.* seguito *m.* −*a.* seguente. −*prep.* in seguito a.

folly /'fɒlɪ/ *n.* follia *f.*

foment /fəʊ'ment/ *v.t.* fomentare.

fond /fɒnd/ *a.* (**-er, -est**) affezionato; (*hope*) vivo. **be** ~ **of** (*person*) voler bene a; (*music etc.*) essere appassionato di. ~**ness** *n.* affetto *m.*; (*for things*) passione *f.*

fondle /'fɒndl/ *v.t.* coccolare.

font /fɒnt/ *n.* fonte battesimale *f.*

food /fuːd/ *n.* cibo *m.*

fool /fuːl/ *n.* sciocco, a *m., f.*; (*culin.*) crema *f.* −*v.t.* prendere in giro. −*v.i.* scherzare.

foolhardy /'fuːlhɑːdɪ/ *a.* temerario.

foolish /'fuːlɪʃ/ *a.* stolto. ~**ly** *adv.* scioccamente. ~**ness** *n.* sciocchezza *f.*

foolproof /'fuːlpruːf/ *a.* facilissimo.

foolscap /'fuːlskæp/ *n.* carta protocollo *f.*

foot /fʊt/ *n.* (*pl.* **feet**) piede *m.*; (*measure*) piede (= *30.48 cm.*). −*v.t.* ~ **it** camminare. ~**-bridge** *n.* passerella *f.* ~ **the bill** saldare il conto. **on** ~ a piedi. **on one's feet** in piedi. **put one's** ~ **in it** fare una gaffe.

footage /'fʊtɪdʒ/ *n.* (*cinema*) metraggio *m.*

football /'fʊtbɔːl/ *n.* pallone *m.*; (*game*) calcio *m.* ~ **pools** totocalcio *m.* ~**er** *n.* giocatore di calcio *m.*

foothills /'fʊthɪlz/ *n.pl.* colline pedemontane *f.pl.*

foothold /'fʊthəʊld/ *n.* punto d'appoggio *m.*

footing /'fʊtɪŋ/ *n.* posizione del piede *f.* **on an equal** ~ in condizioni di parità.

footlights /'fʊtlaɪts/ *n.pl.* luci della ribalta *f.pl.*

footloose /'fʊtluːs/ *a.* libero.

footman /'fʊtmən/ *n.* (*pl.* **-men**) valletto *m.*

footnote /'fʊtnəʊt/ *n.* nota a piè pagina *f.*

footpath /'fʊtpɑːθ/ *n.* (*in country*) sentiero *m.*; (*in town*) marciapiede *m.*

footprint /'fʊtprɪnt/ *n.* orma *f.*

footsore /'fʊtsɔː(r)/ *a.* con i piedi doloranti.

footstep /'fʊtstep/ *n.* passo *m.*

footstool /'fʊtstuːl/ *n.* sgabellino *m.*

footwear /'fʊtweə(r)/ *n.* calzature *f.pl.*

for /fə(r), fɔː(r)/ *prep.* per; (*in favour of*) a favore di; (*direction*) verso; (*time*) da; (*attitude, tendency*) adatto a; (*in spite of*) malgrado. −*conj.* poiché, perché.

forage /'fɒrɪdʒ/ *v.i.* foraggiare. −*n.* foraggio *m.*

foray /'fɒreɪ/ *n.* incursione *f.*

forbade /fə'beɪd/ *see* **forbid.**

forbear /fɔː'beə(r)/ *v.t./i.* (*p.t.* **forbore**, *p.p.* **forborne**) astenersi. ~**ance** *n.* pazienza *f.*

forbid /fə'bɪd/ *v.t.* (*p.t.* **forbade**, *p.p.* **forbidden**) proibire.

forbidding /fə'bɪdɪŋ/ *a.* severo; (*of prices*) proibitivo.

force /fɔːs/ *n.* forza *f.* −*v.t.* forzare. ~ **on** imporre a. **come into** ~ entrare in vigore. ~**d** *a.* forzato. ~**ful** *a.* energico.

force-feed /'fɔːsfiːd/ *v.t.* (*p.t.* **-fed**) nutrire per forza.

forceps /'fɔːseps/ *n. invar.* forcipe *m.*

forcibl|e /'fɔːsəbl/ *a.* forzato. ~**y** *adv.* forzatamente.

ford /fɔːd/ *n.* guado *m.*

fore /fɔː(r)/ *a.* anteriore. −*n.* **to the** ~ in vista.

forearm /'fɔːrɑːm/ *n.* avambraccio *m.*

foreboding /fɔː'bəʊdɪŋ/ *n.* presentimento *m.*

forecast /'fɔːkɑːst/ *v.t.* (*p.t.* **forecast**) prevedere. −*n.* previsione *f.*

forecourt /'fɔːkɔːt/ *n.* cortile anteriore *m.*

forefathers /'fɔːfɑːðəz/ *n.pl.* antenati *m.pl.*

forefinger /'fɔːfɪŋgə(r)/ *n.* (dito) indice *m.*

forefront /'fɔːfrʌnt/ *n.* parte anteriore *f.*

foregone /'fɔːgɒn/ *a.* ~ **conclusion** risultato previsto.

foreground /'fɔːgraʊnd/ *n.* primo piano *m.*

forehead /'fɒrɪd/ *n.* fronte *f.*

foreign /'fɒrən/ *a.* straniero; (*trade*) estero; (*not belonging*) estraneo. **F~ Secretary** Ministro degli Esteri *m.* ~**er** *n.* straniero, a *m., f.*

foreman /'fɔːmən/ *n.* (*pl.* **-men**) capoparto *m.*

foremost /'fɔːməʊst/ *a.* principale. —*adv.* in primo luogo.

forensic /fə'rensɪk/ *a.* ~ **medicine** medicina legale.

forerunner /'fɔːrʌnə(r)/ *n.* precursore *m.*

foresee /fɔː'siː/ *v.t.* (*p.t.* **-saw**, *p.p.* **-seen**) prevedere. ~**able** *a.* prevedibile.

foreshadow /fɔː'ʃædəʊ/ *v.t.* presagire.

foresight /'fɔːsaɪt/ *n.* previdenza *f.*

forest /'fɒrɪst/ *n.* foresta *f.*

forestall /fɔː'stɔːl/ *v.t.* prevenire.

forestry /'fɒrɪstrɪ/ *n.* silvicoltura *f.*

foretaste /'fɔːteɪst/ *n.* pregustazione *f.*

foretell /fɔː'tel/ *v.t.* (*p.t.* **foretold**) predire.

forever /fə'revə(r)/ *adv.* per sempre.

forewarn /fɔː'wɔːn/ *v.t.* avvertire.

foreword /'fɔːwɜːd/ *n.* prefazione *f.*

forfeit /'fɔːfɪt/ *n.* pegno *m.*; (*jurid.*) penalità *f.* —*v.t.* perdere.

forgave /fə'geɪv/ *see* **forgive**.

forge[1] /fɔːdʒ/ *v.i.* avanzare. ~ **ahead** farsi strada.

forge[2] /fɔːdʒ/ *n.* fucina *f.* —*v.t.* fucinare; (*copy*) contraffare. ~**r** /-ə(r)/ *n.* contraffattore *m.* ~**ry** /-ərɪ/ *n.* contraffazione *f.*; (*crime*) falso *m.*

forget /fə'get/ *v.t./i.* (*p.t.* **forgot**, *p.p.* **forgotten**) dimenticare, dimenticarsi. ~**-me-not** *n.* non-ti-scordar-di-me *m.* ~ **o.s.** perdere la padronanza di sé. ~**ful** *a.* smemorato. ~**ful of** dimentico di.

forgive /fə'gɪv/ *v.t.* (*p.t.* **forgave**, *p.p.* **forgiven**) perdonare. ~**ness** *n.* perdonó *m.*

forgo /fɔː'gəʊ/ *v.t.* (*p.t.* **forwent**, *p.p.* **forgone**) rinunciare a.

fork /fɔːk/ *n.* forchetta *f.*; (*for digging*) forca *f.*; (*in road*) bivio *m.* —*v.t./i.* inforcare; (*road*) biforcarsi. ~**-lift truck** *n.* carrello automotore *m.* ~ **out** (*sl.*) sborsare. ~**ed** *a.* biforcato.

forlorn /fə'lɔːn/ *a.* derelitto. ~ **hope** speranza vana *f.*

form /fɔːm/ *n.* forma *f.*; (*in school*) classe *f.*; (*document*) modulo *m.* —*v.t./i.* formare, formarsi.

formal /'fɔːml/ *a.* formale; (*person*) formalista. ~ **dress** abito da cerimonia *m.* ~**ity** /-'mælətɪ/ *n.* formalità *f.* ~**ly** *adv.* ufficialmente.

format /'fɔːmæt/ *n.* formato *m.*

formation /fɔː'meɪʃn/ *n.* formazione *f.*

formative /'fɔːmətɪv/ *a.* formativo.

former /'fɔːmə(r)/ *a.* precedente; (*first*

of two) primo (di due). ~**ly** *adv.* in altri tempi.

formidable /'fɔːmɪdəbl/ *a.* formidabile.

formless /'fɔːmlɪs/ *a.* informe.

formula /'fɔːmjʊlə/ *n.* (*pl.* **-ae** *or* **-as** /-iː, -əz/) formula *f.*

formulate /'fɔːmjʊleɪt/ *v.t.* formulare.

fornicat|e /'fɔːnɪkeɪt/ *v.i.* fornicare. ~**ion** /-'keɪʃn/ *n.* fornicazione *f.*

forsake /fə'seɪk/ *v.t.* (*p.t.* **forsook**, *p.p.* **forsaken**) abbandonare.

forsythia /fɔː'saɪθɪə/ *n.* forsizia *f.*

fort /fɔːt/ *n.* forte *m.*

forth /fɔːθ/ *adv.* avanti. **and so** ~ e così via.

forthcoming /fɔːθ'kʌmɪŋ/ *a.* prossimo; (*fam.*, *person*) socievole.

forthright /'fɔːθraɪt/ *a.* schietto.

forthwith /fɔːθ'wɪθ/ *adv.* immediatamente.

fortif|y /'fɔːtɪfaɪ/ *v.t.* fortificare. ~**ication** /-ɪ'keɪʃn/ *n.* fortificazione *f.*

fortitude /'fɔːtɪtjuːd/ *n.* coraggio *m.*

fortnight /'fɔːtnaɪt/ *n.* quindicina *f.* ~**ly** *a.* bimensile; *adv.* ogni due settimane.

fortress /'fɔːtrɪs/ *n.* fortezza *f.*

fortuitous /fɔː'tjuːɪtəs/ *a.* fortuito.

fortunate /'fɔːtʃənət/ *a.* fortunato. ~**ly** *adv.* fortunatamente.

fortune /'fɔːtʃuːn/ *n.* fortuna *f.* ~**-teller** *n.* indovino, a *m.*, *f.*

fort|y /'fɔːtɪ/ *a.* & *n.* quaranta *m.* ~**y winks** sonnellino *m.* ~**ieth** *a.* & *n.* quarantesimo, a *m.*, *f.*

forum /'fɔːrəm/ *n.* foro *m.*

forward /'fɔːwəd/ *a.* in avanti; (*advanced*) precoce; (*pert*) sfacciato. —*n.* (*sport*) attaccante *m.* —*adv.* avanti. —*v.t.* (*letter*) inoltrare; (*goods*) spedire; (*help*) promuovere. ~**ness** *n.* precocità *f.* ~**s** *adv.* avanti.

fossil /'fɒsl/ *a.* & *n.* fossile *m.* ~**ize** /-sɪlaɪz/ *v.t./i.* fossilizzare, fossilizzarsi.

foster /'fɒstə(r)/ *v.t.* (*promote*) incoraggiare; (*child*) allevare. ~**child** *n.* figlio, a adottivo, a *m.*, *f.* ~**-mother** *n.* madre adottiva *f.*

fought /fɔːt/ *see* **fight**.

foul /faʊl/ *a.* (-**er**, -**est**) sporco; (*of air*) viziato; (*of smell, taste, etc.*) cattivo; (*of language*) osceno. —*n.* (*sport*) fallo *m.* —*v.t.* sporcare, contaminare. ~**-mouthed** *a.* osceno. ~ **play** (*jurid.*) delitto *m.*; (*sport*) gioco sleale *m.*

found[1] /faʊnd/ *see* **find**.

found[2] /faʊnd/ v.t. fondare. ~ation
/-'deɪʃn/ n. fondazione f.; (basis)
fondamento m.

founder[1] /'faʊndə(r)/ n. fonda|tore,
-trice m., f.

founder[2] /'faʊndə(r)/ v.i. (of ship)
affondare.

foundling /'faʊndlɪŋ/ n. trovatello,
a m., f.

foundry /'faʊndrɪ/ n. fonderia. f.

fountain /'faʊntɪn/ n. fontana f. ~-pen
n. penna stilografica f.

four /fɔ:(r)/ a. & n. quattro m. ~fold
a. quadruplo; adv. quattro volte. ~-
poster n. letto a baldacchino m. ~th
a. & n. quarto, a m., f.

foursome /'fɔ:səm/ n. quartetto m.

fourteen /fɔ:'ti:n/ a. & n. quattordici
m. ~th a. & n. quattordicesimo, a m.,
f.

fowl /faʊl/ n. pollame m.

fox /fɒks/ n. volpe f. —v.t. ingannare.
be ~ed essere perplesso.

foyer /'fɔɪeɪ/ n. ridotto m.

fraction /'frækʃn/ n. frazione f.

fractious /'frækʃəs/ a. stizzoso.

fracture /'fræktʃə(r)/ n. frattura f.
—v.t./i. fratturare, fratturarsi.

fragile /'frædʒaɪl/ a. fragile.

fragment /'frægmənt/ n. frammento
m. ~ary a. frammentario.

fragran|t /'freɪɡrənt/ a. fragrante. ~ce
n. fragranza f.

frail /freɪl/ a. (-er, -est) delicato.

frame /freɪm/ n. telaio m.; (for picture)
cornice f.; (anat.) ossatura f.; (of spectacles) montatura f.; (in garden) cassa
di vetri f. —v.t. incorniciare; (fig.)
formulare; (sl.) montare un'accusa.
~ of mind n. stato d'animo m. ~-up
n. (sl.) complotto m.

framework /'freɪmwɜːk/ n. struttura
f.

France /frɑ:ns/ n. Francia f.

franchise /'fræntʃaɪz/ n. (pol.) diritto
di voto m.; (comm.) franchigia f.

frank[1] /fræŋk/ a. franco. ~ly adv.
francamente. ~ness n. franchezza f.

frank[2] /fræŋk/ v.t. affrancare.

frantic /'fræntɪk/ a. frenetico.

fratern|al /frə'tɜːnəl/ a. fraterno. ~ity
n. fraternità f.; (club) associazione f.

fraternize /'frætənaɪz/ v.i. frater-
nizzare.

fraud /frɔ:d/ n. frode f.; (person) impostore m. ~ulent a. fraudolento.

fraught /frɔ:t/ a. ~ with carico di.

fray[1] /freɪ/ n. mischia f.

fray[2] /freɪ/ v.t./i. sfilacciare, sfilac-
ciarsi.

freak /fri:k/ n. fenomeno m. —a. anormale. ~ish a. strambo.

freckle /'frekl/ n. lentiggine f. ~d a.
lentigginoso.

free /fri:/ a. (freer, freest) libero; (gratis) gratuito; (comm.) franco; (lavish)
generoso. —v.t. (p.t. freed) liberare;
(clear) sgombrare; (disentangle) svin-
colare. ~-lance a. indipendente. ~-
range a. (eggs) di fattoria. ~ speech
n. libertà di parola f. ~ly adv. liberamente.

freedom /'fri:dəm/ n. libertà f.

freehold /'fri:həʊld/ n. proprietà (fon-
diaria) assoluta f.

Freemason /'fri:meɪsn/ n. massone m.
~ry n. massoneria f.

freesia /'fri:zjə/ n. fresia f.

freez|e /fri:z/ v.t./i. (p.t. froze, p.p.
frozen) gelare; (food) congelare; (fig.)
agghiacciare; (econ.) bloccare. —n.
gelo m.; blocco m. ~er n. congelatore
m. ~ing a. gelido; n. congelamento
m.

freight /freɪt/ n. carico m. ~er n.
(ship) nave da carico f.

French /frentʃ/ a. & n. francese m./f.
f~ window n. porta-finestra f.
~man, ~woman ns. francese m./f.

frenz|y /'frenzɪ/ n. frenesia f. ~ied a.
frenetico.

frequen|t[1] /'fri:kwənt/ a. frequente.
~cy n. frequenza f. ~tly adv. fre-
quentemente.

frequent[2] /frɪ'kwent/ v.t. frequentare.

fresco /'freskəʊ/ n. (pl. -os) affresco m.

fresh /freʃ/ a. (-er, -est) fresco; (ad-
ditional) nuovo; (Amer.) sfacciato. ~
water acqua dolce f. ~ly adv. di
recente. ~man n. matricola f. ~ness
n. freschezza f.

freshen /'freʃn/ v.i. rinfrescarsi. —v.t.
(fig.) rinnovare.

fret /fret/ v.i. (p.t. fretted) inquietarsi.
~ful a. irritabile.

Freudian /'frɔɪdjən/ a. freudiano.

friar /'fraɪə(r)/ n. frate m.

friction /'frɪkʃn/ n. frizione f.

Friday /'fraɪdɪ/ n. venerdì m. Good ~
Venerdì Santo m.

fridge /frɪdʒ/ n. (fam.) frigo m.

fried /fraɪd/ see fry. —a. fritto.

friend /frend/ n. amico, a m., f. ~ship
n. amicizia f.

friendl|y /'frendlɪ/ a. (-ier, -iest)
amichevole. F~y Society n. società

di mutuo soccorso *f*. **~iness** *n*. amiche-
volezza *f*.

frieze /friːz/ *n*. fregio *m*.

frigate /'frɪgət/ *n*. fregata *f*.

fright /fraɪt/ *n*. paura *f*.; (*person, thing*)
orrore *m*. **~ful** *a*. terribile. **~fully**
adv. terribilmente.

frighten /'fraɪtn/ *v.t*. impaurire. **~ off**
far scappare. **~ed** *a*. spaventato. **be
~ed** aver paura.

frigid /'frɪdʒɪd/ *a*. frigido. **~ity**
/-'dʒɪdətɪ/ *n*. freddezza *f*.

frill /frɪl/ *n*. trina *f*. **~s** *n.pl*. (*fig*.)
fronzoli *m.pl*.

fringe /frɪndʒ/ *n*. frangia *f*.; (*of hair*)
frangetta *f*.; (*of area, society*) margine
m. **~ benefits** *n.pl*. proventi vari
m.pl. **~ theatre** *n*. teatro d'avanguardia *m*.

frisk /frɪsk/ *v.t./i*. saltellare; (*search*)
perquisire.

frisky /'frɪskɪ/ *a*. (-ier, -iest) vispo.

fritter[1] /'frɪtə(r)/ *n*. frittella *f*.

fritter[2] /'frɪtə(r)/ *v.t*. **~ away** sprecare.

frivol|ous /'frɪvələs/ *a*. frivolo. **~ity**
/-'vɒlətɪ/ *n*. frivolezza *f*.

frizzy /'frɪzɪ/ *a*. crespo.

fro /frəʊ/ *see* **to and fro.**

frock /frɒk/ *n*. abito *m*.

frog /frɒg/ *n*. rana *f*. **~ in the throat**
raucedine *f*.

frogman /'frɒgmən/ *n*. (*pl*. -men)
uomo rana *m*.

frolic /'frɒlɪk/ *v.i*. (*pl*. **frolicked**) fol-
leggiare. *—n*. scherzo *m*.

from /frəm, frɒm/ *prep*. da; (*time*) fin
da; (*cause*) per.

front /frʌnt/ *n*. parte anteriore *f*.;
(*archit*.) facciata *f*.; (*in war*) fronte
m.; (*of clothes*) davanti *m*.; (*seafront*)
lungomare *m*. *—a*. davanti; (*in front*)
anteriore. **~ door** *m*. porta d'entrata
f. **~ page** *n*. prima pagina *f*. **in ~ of**
davanti *a*. **put a bold ~ on**
affrontare. **~age** *n*. facciata *f*. **~al** *a*.
frontale.

frontier /'frʌntɪə(r)/ *n*. frontiera *f*.

frost /frɒst/ *n*. gelo *m*. **~-bite** *n*. congelamento *m*. **~-bitten** *a*. congelato.
~ed *a*. (*glass*) smerigliato. **~y** *a*.
gelido.

froth /frɒθ/ *n*. schiuma *f*. *—v.i*. far
schiuma.

frown /fraʊn/ *v.i*. aggrottare le ciglia. *—n*. cipiglio *m*. **~ on** disapprovare.

froze, frozen /frəʊz, 'frəʊzn/ *see*
freeze.

frugal /'fruːgl/ *a*. frugale. **~ly** *adv*.
frugalmente.

fruit /fruːt/ *n*. frutto *m*.; (*at table*)
frutta *f*. **~ machine** *n*. (*fam*.) macchina mangiasoldi *f*. **~ salad** *n*. mace-
donia di frutta *f*. **~erer** *n*.
fruttivendolo, a *m*., *f*. **~y** *a*. che sa di
frutta.

fruit|ful /'fruːtfl/ *a*. fecondo; (*fig*.) frut-
tuoso. **~less** *a*. inutile.

fruition /fruː'ɪʃn/ *n*. realizzazione *f*.

frump /frʌmp/ *n*. sciattona *f*.

frustrat|e /frʌ'streɪt/ *v.t*. frustrare.
~ion /-ʃn/ *n*. frustrazione *f*.

fry[1] /fraɪ/ *v.t./i*. (*p.t*. **fried**) (far) frig-
gere. **~ing-pan** *n*. padella *f*.

fry[2] /fraɪ/ *n*. (*pl*. **fry**) **small ~** nonnulla
m. invar.

fuchsia /'fjuːʃə/ *n*. fucsia *f*.

fuddy-duddy /'fʌdɪdʌdɪ/ *n*. (*fam*.) ma-
tusa *m*.

fudge /fʌdʒ/ *n*. dolce caramellato *m*.

fuel /'fjuːəl/ *n*. combustibile *m*.; (*fig*.)
alimento *m*. **~ oil** nafta *f*. *—v.t*. (*p.t*.
fuelled) alimentare.

fugitive /'fjuːdʒətɪv/ *n. & a*. fuggiasco,
a *m*., *f*.

fugue /fjuːg/ *n*. fuga *f*.

fulfil /fʊl'fɪl/ *v.t*. (*p.t*. **fulfilled**) compiere; (*task*) eseguire. **~ o.s.** realizzarsi.
~ling *a*. soddisfacente. **~ment** *n*.
appagamento *m*.

full /fʊl/ *a*. (-er, -est) pieno; (*bus, hotel*)
completo; (*dress*) ampio. *—adv*. pro-
prio. **at ~ speed** a tutta velocità. **~-
blooded** *a*. vigoroso. **~ face** *a*. di
faccia. **~-scale** *a*. in grande. **~ stop**
n. punto *m*. **~-time** *a*. (*work*) a tempo
pieno. **in ~** per intero. **in ~ swing**
in piena attività. **~y** *adv*. completamente.

fulsome /'fʊlsəm/ *a*. esagerato.

fumble /'fʌmbl/ *v.i*. annaspare.

fume /fjuːm/ *v.i*. essere furioso. **~s**
n.pl. fumi *m.pl*.

fumigate /'fjuːmɪgeɪt/ *v.t*. suffumigare.

fun /fʌn/ *n*. divertimento *m*. **~-fair** *n*.
luna park *m*. **have ~** divertirsi.
make ~ of canzonare.

function /'fʌŋkʃn/ *n*. funzione *f*.; (*ceremony*) cerimonia *f*. *—v.i*. funzionare. **~al** *a*. funzionale.

fund /fʌnd/ *n*. fondo *m*. *—v.t*. procurare fondi (per).

fundamental /fʌndə'mentl/ *a*. fondamentale.

funeral /'fjuːnərəl/ *n*. funerale *m*. *—a*.
funebre.

fungus /'fʌŋgəs/ n. (pl. -gi /-gaɪ/) fungo m.

funicular /fjuːˈnɪkjʊlə(r)/ n. funicolare f.

funk /fʌŋk/ n. (sl.) tremarella f. —v.i. (sl.) tirarsi indietro.

funnel /'fʌnl/ n. imbuto m.; (of ship) ciminiera f.

funn|y /'fʌnɪ/ a. (-ier, -iest) buffo; (odd) strano. ~y-bone n. punta del gomito f. ~y business inganno m. ~ily adv. comicamente; stranamente.

fur /fɜː(r)/ n. pelo m.; (skin) pelliccia f.; (in kettle) deposito m. ~ry a. peloso.

furbish /'fɜːbɪʃ/ v.t. lustrare; (renovate) mettere a nuovo.

furious /'fjʊərɪəs/ a. furioso. ~ly adv. furiosamente.

furnace /'fɜːnɪs/ n. fornace f.

furnish /'fɜːnɪʃ/ v.t. ammobiliare; (supply) fornire. ~ings n.pl. mobili m.pl.

furniture /'fɜːnɪtʃə(r)/ n. mobili m.pl.

furrier /'fʌrɪə(r)/ n. pellicciaio, a m.,f.

furrow /'fʌrəʊ/ n. solco m.

furthe|r /'fɜːðə(r)/ see far. —a. (additional) ulteriore. —adv. più lontano; (more) in più. —v.t. pro-

muovere. ~st see far; adv. (il) più lontano.

furthermore /'fɜːðəmɔː(r)/ adv. per di più.

furthermost /'fɜːðəməʊst/ a. il più remoto.

furtive /'fɜːtɪv/ a. furtivo.

fury /'fjʊərɪ/ n. furia f.

fuse[1] /fjuːz/ v.t./i. fondere, fondersi; (electr.) saltare. —n. (electr.) valvola f. ~-box n. scatola dei fusibili f.

fuse[2] /fjuːz/ n. (of bomb) detonatore m.

fuselage /'fjuːzəlɑːʒ/ n. fusoliera f.

fusion /'fjuːʒn/ n. fusione f.

fuss /fʌs/ n. storie f.pl.; (confusion) confusione f. —v.t./i. agitarsi. **make a ~ of** colmare di attenzioni. ~y a. (-ier, -iest) esigente, fastidioso; (of clothes etc.) carico.

fusty /'fʌstɪ/ a. (-ier, -iest) stantio.

futile /'fjuːtaɪl/ a. futile.

future /'fjuːtʃə(r)/ a. futuro. —n. avvenire m.; (gram.) futuro m. **in ~** d'ora innanzi.

futuristic /fjuːtʃəˈrɪstɪk/ a. futuristico.

fuzz /fʌz/ n. peluria f.

fuzzy /'fʌzɪ/ a. (hair) increspato; (photo) sfocato.

G

gab /gæb/ *n.* (*fam.*) parlantina *f.*

gabardine /gæbə'di:n/ *n.* gabardine *f.*

gabble /'gæbl/ *v.i.* borbottare. —*n.* borbottio *m.*

gable /'geɪbl/ *n.* frontone *m.*

gad /gæd/ *v.i.* (*p.t.* **gadded**) ~ **about** gironzolare.

gadget /'gædʒɪt/ *n.* aggeggio *m.*

Gaelic /'geɪlɪk/ *a.* & *n.* gaelico *m.*

gaffe /gæf/ *n.* gaffe *f.*

gag /gæg/ *n.* bavaglio *m.*; (*joke*) battuta comica *f.* —*v.t.* (*p.t.* **gagged**) imbavagliare. —*v.i.* dire battute comiche.

gaga /'gɑːgɑː/ *a.* (*sl.*) rimbambito.

gaiety /'geɪətɪ/ *n.* gaiezza *f.*

gaily /'geɪlɪ/ *adv.* gaiamente.

gain /geɪn/ *v.t.* guadagnare; (*acquire*) acquistare. —*v.i.* (*of clock*) andare avanti. —*n.* guadagno *m.*; (*increase*) aumento *m.* ~**ful** *a.* profittevole.

gainsay /geɪn'seɪ/ *v.t.* (*p.t.* **gainsaid**) (*formal*) negare.

gait /geɪt/ *n.* andatura *f.*

gala /'gɑːlə/ *n.* gala *f.*

galaxy /'gæləksɪ/ *n.* galassia *f.*

gale /geɪl/ *n.* bufera di vento *f.*

gall /gɔːl/ *n.* bile *f.*; (*impudence*) sfacciataggine *f.* ~-**bladder** *n.* cistifellea *f.*

gallant /'gælənt/ *a.* coraggioso; (*chivalrous*) galante. ~**ry** *n.* coraggio *m.*

galleon /'gælɪən/ *n.* galeone *m.*

gallery /'gælərɪ/ *n.* galleria *f.*

galley /'gælɪ/ *n.* (*pl.* -**eys**) galera *f.*; (*ship's kitchen*) cambusa *f.*; ~(-**proof**) *n.* (*typ.*) bozza in colonna *f.*

Gallic /'gælɪk/ *a.* gallico. ~**ism** /-sɪzəm/ *n.* gallicismo *m.*

gallivant /gælɪ'vænt/ *v.i.* (*fam.*) gironzolare.

gallon /'gælən/ *n.* gallone *m.* (= 4.556 litri).

gallop /'gæləp/ *n.* galoppo *m.* —*v.i.* (*p.t.* **galloped**) galoppare.

gallows /'gæləʊz/ *n.* forca *f.*

galore /gə'lɔː(r)/ *adv.* a bizzeffe.

galosh /gə'lɒʃ/ *n.* caloscia *f.*

galvanize /'gælvənaɪz/ *v.t.* galvanizzare.

gambit /'gæmbɪt/ *n.* prima mossa *f.*

gamble /'gæmbl/ *v.t./i.* giocare; (*fig.*) speculare. —*n.* gioco d'azzardo *m.* ~**e**

on contare su. ~**er** *n.* giocatore, -trice *m.*, *f.* ~**ing** *n.* gioco *m.*

game[1] /geɪm/ *n.* gioco *m.*; (*match*) partita *f.*; (*animals*) selvaggina *f.* —*a.* coraggioso. ~ **for** disposto a.

game[2] /geɪm/ *a.* (*lame*) zoppo.

gamekeeper /'geɪmki:pə(r)/ *n.* guardacaccia *m. invar.*

gammon /'gæmən/ *n.* prosciutto affumicato *m.*

gamut /'gæmət/ *n.* (*mus.*) estensione *f.*; (*fig.*) gamma *f.*

gander /'gændə(r)/ *n.* oca maschio *f.*

gang /gæŋ/ *n.* banda *f.*; (*of workmen*) squadra *f.* —*v.i.* ~ **up** formare una combriccola.

gangling /'gæŋglɪŋ/ *a.* spilungone.

gangrene /'gæŋgri:n/ *n.* cancrena *f.*

gangster /'gæŋstə(r)/ *n.* gangster *m. invar.*

gangway /'gæŋweɪ/ *n.* passaggio *m.*; (*of ship*) passerella *f.*

gaol /dʒeɪl/ *n.* carcere *m.* —*v.t.* incarcerare. ~**er** *n.* carceriere *m.*

gaolbird /'dʒeɪlbɜːd/ *n.* avanzo di galera *m.*

gap /gæp/ *n.* breccia *f.*; (*deficiency*) lacuna *f.*; (*interval*) pausa *f.*

gape /geɪp/ *v.i.* restare a bocca aperta; (*be wide open*) aprirsi. ~**ing** *a.* aperto.

garage /'gærɑːʒ/ *n.* garage *m.* —*v.t.* mettere in garage.

garb /gɑːb/ *n.* abito *m.*

garbage /'gɑːbɪdʒ/ *n.* immondizie *f.pl.*

garble /'gɑːbl/ *v.t.* ingarbugliare.

garden /'gɑːdn/ *n.* giardino *m.* —*v.i.* fare il giardinaggio. ~**er** *n.* giardiniere, a *m.*, *f.* ~**ing** *n.* giardinaggio *m.*

gargantuan /gɑː'gæntjʊən/ *a.* gigantesco.

gargle /'gɑːgl/ *v.i.* far gargarismi. —*n.* gargarismo *m.*

gargoyle /'gɑːgɔɪl/ *n.* grondone *m.*

garish /'geərɪʃ/ *a.* sgargiante.

garland /'gɑːlənd/ *n.* ghirlanda *f.*

garlic /'gɑːlɪk/ *n.* aglio *m.*

garment /'gɑːmənt/ *n.* indumento *m.*

garnet /'gɑːnɪt/ *n.* granato *m.*

garnish /'gɑːnɪʃ/ *v.t.* guarnire. —*n.* guarnizione *f.*

garret /'gærət/ *n.* soffitta *f.*

garrison /'gærɪsn/ *n.* guarnigione *f.*

garrulous /'gærələs/ a. garrulo.

garter /'gɑːtə(r)/ n. giarrettiera f.

gas /gæs/ n. (pl. **gases**, p.t. **gassed**) gas m.; (med.) anestetico m.; (Amer., fam.) benzina f. —v.t. asfissiare. —v.i. (fam.) ciarlare. ~ **mask** n. maschera antigas f. ~ **meter** n. contatore (del gas) m. ~ **ring** n. fornello (a gas) m. ~**sy** a. gassoso; (fam., talkative) verboso.

gash /gæʃ/ n. sfregio m. —v.t. sfregiare.

gasket /'gæskɪt/ n. guarnizione f.

gasoline /'gæsəliːn/ n. (Amer.) benzina f.

gasometer /gə'sɒmɪtə(r)/ n. gassometro m.

gasp /gɑːsp/ v.i. ansimare; (fig.) rimanere senza fiato. —n. ansimo m.

gastric /'gæstrɪk/ a. gastrico.

gastronomy /gæ'strɒnəmɪ/ n. gastronomia f.

gate /geɪt/ n. cancello m.; (of metal) chiusa f. —v.t. (at college) vietare la libera uscita.

gâteau /'gætəʊ/ n. torta f.

gatecrash /'geɪtkræʃ/ v.t./i. entrare senza invito.

gateway /'geɪtweɪ/ n. ingresso m.

gather /'gæðə(r)/ v.t./i. raccogliere; (obtain gradually) acquistare; (understand) dedurre; (cloth) increspare. ~**ing** n. riunione f.

gauche /gəʊʃ/ a. goffo.

gaudy /'gɔːdɪ/ a. (-ier, -iest) fastoso.

gauge /geɪdʒ/ n. misura f. —v.t. misurare; (fig.) stimare.

gaunt /gɔːnt/ a. sparuto; (grim) desolato.

gauntlet /'gɔːntlɪt/ n. **run the** ~ essere oggetto di critica.

gauze /gɔːz/ n. garza f.

gave /geɪv/ see **give**.

gawky /'gɔːkɪ/ a. (-ier, -iest) sgraziato.

gawp /gɔːp/ v.i. (fam.) guardare come uno stupido.

gay /geɪ/ a. (-er, -est) gaio; (fam., homosexual) omosessuale.

gaze /geɪz/ v.i. ~ **at** fissare. —n. sguardo fisso m.

gazebo /gə'ziːbəʊ/ n. belvedere m.

gazelle /gə'zel/ n. gazzella f.

gazette /gə'zet/ n. gazzetta f.

gazump /gə'zʌmp/ v.t. (sl., comm.) accettare un prezzo più alto da un altro compratore.

GB abbr. of **Great Britain.**

gear /gɪə(r)/ n. equipaggiamento m.;

(techn.) ingranaggio m.; (auto.) marcia f. **in** ~ in marcia. **out of** ~ in folle.

gearbox /'gɪəbɒks/ n. scatola del cambio f.

geese /giːs/ see **goose.**

geezer /'giːzə(r)/ n. (sl.) tipo m.

gel /dʒel/ n. gel m. invar.

gelatine /dʒelə'tiːn/ n. gelatina f.

gelignite /'dʒelɪgnaɪt/ n. nitroglicerina f.

gem /dʒem/ n. gemma f.

Gemini /'dʒemɪnaɪ/ n. (astr.) Gemelli m.pl.

gen /dʒen/ n. (sl.) informazione f.

gender /'dʒendə(r)/ n. genere m.

gene /dʒiːn/ n. gene m.

genealogy /dʒiːnɪ'ælədʒɪ/ n. genealogia f.

general /'dʒenrəl/ a. generale. —n. generale m. ~ **election** n. elezioni f.pl. ~ **practitioner** n. medico generico m. ~**ly** adv.; **in** ~ generalmente.

generaliz|e /'dʒenrəlaɪz/ v.t./i. generalizzare. ~**ation** /-'zeɪʃn/ n. generalizzazione f.

generate /'dʒenəreɪt/ v.t. generare.

generation /dʒenə'reɪʃn/ n. generazione f.

generator /'dʒenəreɪtə(r)/ n. generatore m.

gener|ous /'dʒenərəs/ a. generoso; (plentiful) abbondante. ~**osity** /-'rɒsətɪ/ n. generosità f.

genetic /dʒɪ'netɪk/ a. genetico. ~**s** n. genetica f.

Geneva /dʒɪ'niːvə/ n. Ginevra f.

genial /'dʒiːnɪəl/ a. gioviale.

genital /'dʒenɪtl/ a. genitale. ~**s** n.pl. genitali m.pl.

genitive /'dʒenɪtɪv/ a. & n. genitivo m.

genius /'dʒiːnɪəs/ n. (pl. -uses) genio m.

genocide /'dʒenəsaɪd/ n. genocidio m.

genre /ʒɑːŋr/ n. genere (letterario) m.

gent /dʒent/ n. (sl.) signore m.

genteel /dʒen'tiːl/ a. raffinato.

gentl|e /'dʒentl/ a. (-er, -est) dolce; (slight) leggero. ~**eness** n. dolcezza f. ~**y** adv. delicatamente.

gentlefolk /'dʒentlfəʊk/ n.pl. persone per bene f.pl.

gentleman /'dʒentlmən/ n. (pl. -men) signore m.; (well bred) gentiluomo m. ~**ly** a. da gentiluomo.

gentlewoman /'dʒentlwʊmən/ n. (pl. -women) gentildonna f.

gentry /'dʒentrɪ/ n.pl. piccola nobiltà f.s.

genuflect /'dʒenjuːflekt/ *v.i.* genuflettersi.

genuine /'dʒenjʊɪn/ *a.* genuino.

geograph|y /dʒɪˈɒɡrəfɪ/ *n.* geografia *f.* ~**er** *n.* geografo, a *m.*, *f.* ~**ical** /dʒɪəˈɡræfɪkl/ *a.* geografico.

geolog|y /dʒɪˈɒlədʒɪ/ *n.* geologia *f.* ~**ical** /dʒɪəˈlɒdʒɪkl/ *a.* geologico. ~**ist** *n.* geologo, a *m.*, *f.*

geomet|ry /dʒɪˈɒmɪtrɪ/ *n.* geometria *f.* ~**er** /-ˈɒmɪtə(r)/ *n.* geometra *m.|f.* ~**rical** /dʒɪəˈmetrɪkl/ *a.* geometrico.

geranium /dʒəˈreɪnɪəm/ *n.* geranio *m.*

geriatrics /dʒerɪˈætrɪks/ *n.* geriatria. *f.*

germ /dʒɜːm/ *n.* germe *m.*

German /'dʒɜːmən/ *a.* & *n.* tedesco, a *m.*, *f.* ~ **measles** *n.* rosolia *f.* ~**ic** /dʒəˈmænɪk/ *a.* germanico. ~**y** *n.* Germania *f.*

germicide /'dʒəːmɪsaɪd/ *n.* germicida *m.*

germinate /'dʒɜːmɪneɪt/ *v.i.* germinare.

gerrymander /'dʒerɪmændə(r)/ *n.* broglio elettorale *m.*

gestation /dʒeˈsteɪʃn/ *n.* gestazione *f.*

gesticulate /dʒesˈtɪkjʊleɪt/ *v.i.* gesticolare.

gesture /'dʒestʃə(r)/ *n.* gesto *m.*

get /get/ *v.t./i.* (*p.t.* **got**, *pres. p.* **getting**) avere, ottenere, guadagnare; (*catch, buy*) prendere; (*fetch*) andare a prendere; (*fam., understand*) comprendere. ~ **s.o. to do** far fare. —*v.i.* andare, arrivare; (*become*) diventare. ~ **at** arrivare; (*fam., understand*) capire; (*imply*) insinuare. ~ **away** scappare. ~ **by** (*manage*) cavarsela. ~ **done with** farla finita. ~ **in** entrare. ~ **nowhere** non concludere nulla. ~ **off** scendere; (*leave*) andarsene; (*jurid.*) essere assolto. ~ **on** (*succeed*) riuscire; (*be on good terms*) andare d'accordo. ~ **out** uscire. ~ **out of** (*fig.*) tirarsi fuori da. ~ **over** (*illness*) riprendersi da; (*fence etc.*) scavalcare. ~ **round** (*rule*) aggirare; (*person*) rigirare. ~ **through** (*phone*) avere la linea. ~ **up** alzarsi; (*climb*) salire. ~-**up** *n.* tenuta *f.*

get-away /'getəweɪ/ *n.* fuga *f.*

geyser /'giːzə(r)/ *n.* scaldabagno *m.*; (*geol.*) geyser *m. invar.*

ghastly /'ɡɑːstlɪ/ *a.* (-**ier**, -**iest**) orrendo; (*pale*) spettrale.

gherkin /'ɡɜːkɪn/ *n.* cetriolino *m.*

ghetto /'ɡetəʊ/ *n.* (*pl.* -**os**) ghetto *m.*

ghost /ɡəʊst/ *n.* fantasma *m.* ~ **writer** *n.* collaboratore anonimo *m.*

ghoulish /'ɡuːlɪʃ/ *a.* mostruoso.

giant /'dʒaɪənt/ *n.* & *a.* gigante *m.*

gibberish /'dʒɪbərɪʃ/ *n.* borbottio *m.*; (*fig.*) discorso incomprensibile *m.*

gibe /dʒaɪb/ *n.* scherno *m.* —*v.i.* ~ **at** beffarsi di.

giblets /'dʒɪblɪts/ *n.pl.* frattaglie *f.pl.*

giddy /'ɡɪdɪ/ *a.* (-**ier**, -**iest**) vertiginoso. **be** *or* **feel** ~ aver le vertigini.

gift /ɡɪft/ *n.* dono *m.* ~-**wrap** *v.t.* (*p.t.* ~-**wrapped**) fare un pacco-regalo.

gifted /'ɡɪftɪd/ *a.* dotato (di talento).

gig /ɡɪɡ/ *n.* (*fam.*) sessione di jazz ecc.

gigantic /dʒaɪˈɡæntɪk/ *a.* gigantesco.

giggle /'ɡɪɡl/ *v.i.* ridacchiare. —*n.* risolino *m.*

gild /ɡɪld/ *v.t.* dorare.

gills /ɡɪlz/ *n.pl.* branchia *f.s.*

gilt /ɡɪlt/ *a.* dorato. —*n.* doratura *f.* ~-**edged stocks** *n.pl.* titoli di stato *m.pl.*

gimmick /'ɡɪmɪk/ *n.* trucco *m.*

gin /dʒɪn/ *n.* gin *m. invar.*

ginger /'dʒɪndʒə(r)/ *n.* zenzero *m.* —*a.* color zenzero. —*v.t.* ~ **up** ravvivare. ~ **ale**, ~ **beer** *ns.* bibita allo zenzero *f.* ~**bread** *n.* pan di zenzero *m.*

gingerly /'dʒɪndʒəlɪ/ *adv.* con precauzione.

gingham /'ɡɪŋəm/ *n.* percalle (a quadretti) *m.*

gipsy /'dʒɪpsɪ/ = **gypsy.**

giraffe /dʒɪˈrɑːf/ *n.* giraffa *f.*

girder /'ɡɜːdə(r)/ *n.* trave *f.*

girdle /'ɡɜːdl/ *n.* cintura *f.*; (*elastic corset*) fascetta *f.*

girl /ɡɜːl/ *n.* ragazza *f.*; (*female child*) (figlia) femmina *f.* ~-**friend** *n.* amica *f.*; (*of boy*) ragazza *f.* ~**hood** *n.* fanciullezza *f.* ~**ish** *a.* da ragazza.

giro /'dʒaɪərəʊ/ *n.* trasferimento bancario *m.*

girth /ɡɜːθ/ *n.* circonferenza *f.*

gist /dʒɪst/ *n.* sostanza *f.*

give /ɡɪv/ *v.t./i.* (*p.t.* **gave**, *p.p.* **given**) dare; (*supply, offer*) offrire, porgere; (*utter*) emettere; (*yield*) cedere. —*n.* elasticità *f.* ~ **away** dar via; (*secret*) tradire. ~ **back** restituire. ~ **birth** dare alla luce. ~ **in** arrendersi. ~ **off** emanare. ~ **o.s. to** darsi a. ~ **out** (*announce*) annunciare. ~ **over** (*fam.*) smetterla. ~ **o.s. up** arrendersi. ~ **up** rinunziare. ~ **way** cedere; (*collapse*) crollare.

given /'ɡɪvn/ *see* **give.** —*a.* dato. ~ **name** nome di battesimo *m.*

glacier /'glæsɪə(r)/ n. ghiacciaio m.

glad /glæd/ a. contento. ~ly adv. con piacere.

gladden /'glædn/ v.t. rallegrare.

glade /gleɪd/ n. radura. f.

gladiator /'glædɪeɪtə(r)/ n. gladiatore m.

gladiolus /glædɪ'əʊləs/ n. (pl. -li /-laɪ/) gladiolo m.

glam|our /'glæmə(r)/ n. fascino m. ~orize v.t. rendere affascinante. ~orous a. affascinante.

glance /glɑːns/ n. sguardo m. —v.i. ~ at dare uno sguardo a.

gland /glænd/ n. glandola f.

glar|e /gleə(r)/ v.i. abbagliare; (stare angrily) guardare in cagnesco. —n. bagliore m.; (look) sguardo minaccioso m. ~ing a. sfolgorante; (mistake) madornale.

glass /glɑːs/ n. vetro m.; (mirror) specchio m.; (for drinking) bicchiere m. ~es n.pl. occhiali m.pl. ~y a. vitreo.

glaze /gleɪz/ v.t. (door, window) mettere vetri a; (pottery) smaltare. —n. vernice f. ~d a. (eye) vitreo.

gleam /gliːm/ n. barlume m. —v.i. luccicare.

glean /gliːn/ v.t. racimolare.

glee /gliː/ n. gioia. f. ~ club gruppo corale m. ~ful a. gioioso.

glen /glen/ n. gola f.

glib /glɪb/ a. loquace. ~ly adv. con prontezza.

glid|e /glaɪd/ v.i. scorrere; (of plane) planare. ~er /-ə(r)/ n. aliante m. ~ing n. volo a vela m.

glimmer /'glɪmə(r)/ n. barlume m. —v.i. luccicare.

glimpse /glɪmps/ n. occhiata f. —v.t. intravvedere.

glint /glɪnt/ n. scintillio m. —v.i. scintillare.

glisten /'glɪsn/ v.i. luccicare.

glitter /'glɪtə(r)/ v.i. brillare. —n. lucchicio m.

gloat /gləʊt/ v.i. ~ over guardare avidamente.

global /'gləʊbl/ a. mondiale.

globe /gləʊb/ n. globo m.

globule /'glɒbjuːl/ n. globulo m.

gloom /gluːm/ n. oscurità f.; (sadness) tristezza f. ~y a. (-ier, -iest) cupo.

glorify /'glɔːrɪfaɪ/ v.t. glorificare.

glorious /'glɔːrɪəs/ a. splendido; (deed, hero, etc.) glorioso.

glory /'glɔːrɪ/ n. gloria f.; (beauty) splendore m. —v.i. ~ in vantarsi di. ~-hole n. (sl.) ripostiglio m.

gloss /glɒs/ n. lucentezza f. —v.t. ~ over minimizzare. ~y a. lucente.

glossary /'glɒsərɪ/ n. glossario m.

glove /glʌv/ n. guanto m. ~ compartment cassetto (del cruscotto) m. ~d a. inguantato.

glow /gləʊ/ v.i. risplendere; (of person) avvampare. —n. splendore m.; rossore m.

glower /'glaʊə(r)/ v.i. ~ (at) guardare in cagnesco.

glowing /'gləʊɪŋ/ a. ardente; (fig.) entusiastico.

glucose /'gluːkəʊs/ n. glucosio m.

glue /gluː/ n. colla f. —v.t. (pres. p. gluing) incollare.

glum /glʌm/ a. (glummer, glummest) tetro.

glut /glʌt/ n. eccesso m.

glutton /'glʌtn/ n. ghiottone, a m., f. ~ous a. ghiotto. ~y n. ingordigia f.

glycerine /'glɪsəriːn/ n. glicerina f.

gnarled /nɑːld/ a. nodoso.

gnash /næʃ/ v.t. ~ one's teeth digrignare i denti.

gnat /næt/ n. moscerino m.

gnaw /nɔː/ v.t./i. rosicchiare.

gnome /nəʊm/ n. gnomo m.

go /gəʊ/ v.i. (p.t. went, p.p. gone) andare; (leave) andar via; (work) funzionare; (become) diventare; (be sold) vendersi; (vanish) sparire. —n. (pl. goes) energia f.; (try) tentativo m.; (turn) turno m. be going to stare per. ~ about girare. ~-ahead n. via m.; a. intraprendente. ~ and see andare a vedere. ~ away andarsene. ~ back ritornare. ~-between n. intermediario, a m., f. ~ by passare. ~ down scendere; (of sun) tramontare. ~ for andare a prendere; (sl.) attaccare. ~-getter n. persona ambiziosa f. ~ in entrare. ~ out uscire; (of light, fire) spegnersi. ~ over or through (examine) ispezionare. ~ round (be enough) bastare. ~ shopping andare a far la spesa. ~-slow n. sciopero a singhiozzo m. ~ under soccombere; (fail) fallire. ~ up salire. ~ with accompagnare. ~ without fare a meno di. on the ~ in movimento.

goad /gəʊd/ v.t. incitare.

goal /gəʊl/ n. gol m. invar.; (fig.) fine m. ~-post n. palo m. ~ie n. (fam.) portiere m.

goalkeeper /'gəʊkiːpə(r)/ *n.* portiere *m.*

goat /gəʊt/ *n.* capra *f.*

goatee /gəʊ'tiː/ *n.* pizzo *m.*

gobble /'gɒbl/ *v.t.* ~ **down**, ~ **up** trangugiare (in fretta).

goblet /'gɒblɪt/ *n.* calice *m.*

goblin /'gɒblɪn/ *n.* folletto *m.*

God /gɒd/ *n.* Dio *m.* ~-**forsaken** *a.* sperduto.

god /gɒd/ *n.* dio *m.* ~**dess** *n.* dea *f.* ~**ly** *a.* devoto.

god|child /'gɒdtʃaɪld/ *n.* (*pl.* ~**children**) figlioccio, a *m.*, *f.* ~**daughter** *n.* figlioccia *f.* ~**father** *n.* padrino *m.* ~**mother** *n.* madrina *f.* ~**son** *n.* figlioccio *m.*

godsend /'gɒdsend/ *n.* manna *f.*

goggle /'gɒgl/ *v.i.* strabuzzare gli occhi.

goggles /'gɒglz/ *n.pl.* occhialoni a visiera *m.pl.*

going /'gəʊɪŋ/ *n.* l'andare *m.* —*a.* che va. ~**s-on** *n.pl.* avvenimenti *m.pl.*

gold /gəʊld/ *n.* oro *m.* —*a.* d'oro. ~ **mine** *n.* miniera d'oro *f.*

golden /'gəʊldən/ *a.* dorato. ~ **handshake** liquidazione generosa *f.* ~ **wedding** nozze d'oro *f.pl.*

goldfish /'gəʊldfɪʃ/ *n.* invar. pesce rosso *m.*

goldsmith /'gəʊldsmɪθ/ *n.* orefice *m.*

golf /gɒlf/ *n.* golf *m.* ~-**course** *n.* campo di golf *m.* ~**er** *n.* gioca|tore, -trice di golf *m.*, *f.*

golliwog /'gɒlɪwɒg/ *n.* bambolotto negro *m.*

gone /gɒn/ *see* **go**. —*a.* andato. **be far** ~ essere gravemente ammalato.

gong /gɒŋ/ *n.* gong *m.* invar.

good /gʊd/ *a.* (**better**, **best**) buono; (*capable, well behaved*) bravo. —*n.* bene *m.* **a** ~ **deal** molto. **as** ~ **as** quasi. **for** ~ per sempre. ~**afternoon**, ~-**morning** *ints.* & *ns.* buon giorno *m.* ~-**evening** *int.* & *n.* buona sera *f.* ~-**for-nothing** *a.* & *n.* buono a nulla *m.* **G**~ **Friday** Venerdì Santo *m.* ~-**looking** *a.* bello. **have a** ~ **time** divertirsi. **it's no** ~ è inutile. ~**ness** *n.* bontà *f.*

goodbye /gʊd'baɪ/ *int.* & *n.* arrivederci *m.*

goods /gʊdz/ *n.pl.* merce *f.s.*

goodwill /gʊd'wɪl/ *n.* buona volontà *f.*

goody /'gʊdɪ/ *n.* (*fam.*) leccornia *f.* ~**goody** *a.* & *n.* santarello, a *m.*, *f.*

gooey /'guːɪ/ *a.* (*sl.*) appiccicoso; (*fig.*) sdolcinato.

goofy /'guːfɪ/ *a.* (*sl.*) sciocco.

goose /guːs/ *n.* (*pl.* **geese**) oca *f.* ~-**flesh**, ~-**pimples** *ns.* pelle d'oca *f.s.*

gooseberry /'gʊzbərɪ/ *n.* uva spina *f.*

gore[1] /gɔː(r)/ *n.* sangue (coagulato) *m.*

gore[2] /gɔː(r)/ *v.t.* incornare.

gorge /gɔːdʒ/ *n.* gola *f.* —*v.t./i.* rimpinzare, rimpinzarsi.

gorgeous /'gɔːdʒəs/ *a.* magnifico.

gorilla /gə'rɪlə/ *n.* gorilla *m.*

gormless /'gɔːmlɪs/ *a.* (*fam.*) stupido.

gorse /gɔːs/ *n.* ginestra spinosa *f.*

gory /'gɔːrɪ/ *a.* (-**ier**, -**iest**) cruento.

gosh /gɒʃ/ *int.* (*sl.*) caspita.

gospel /'gɒspl/ *n.* vangelo *m.* ~ **truth** verità sacrosanta *f.*

gossip /'gɒsɪp/ *n.* pettegolezzo *m.*; (*person*) pettegolo, a *m.*, *f.* —*v.i.* (*p.t.* **gossiped**) pettegolare. ~**y** *a.* pettegolo.

got /gɒt/ *see* **get**. **have** ~ avere. **have** ~ **to do it** dover fare.

Gothic /'gɒθɪk/ *a.* gotico.

gouge /gaʊdʒ/ *v.t.* ~ **out** cavare.

gourmet /'gʊəmeɪ/ *n.* buongustaio, a *m.*, *f.*

gout /gaʊt/ *n.* gotta *f.*

govern /'gʌvn/ *v.t./i.* governare. ~**or** *n.* governatore *m.*; (*fam.*) principale *m.*

governess /'gʌvənɪs/ *n.* istitutrice *f.*

government /'gʌvənmənt/ *n.* governo *m.* ~**al** /-'mentl/ *a.* governativo.

gown /gaʊn/ *n.* abito *m.*; (*of judge, teacher*) toga *f.*

GP *abbr. see* **general practitioner.**

grab /græb/ *v.t.* (*p.t.* **grabbed**) afferrare.

grace /greɪs/ *n.* grazia *f.* —*v.t.* aggraziare. ~**ful** *a.* aggraziato.

gracious /'greɪʃəs/ *a.* benevolo; (*elegant*) leggiadro.

gradation /grə'deɪʃn/ *n.* gradazione *f.*

grade /greɪd/ *n.* rango *m.*; (*of goods*) qualità *f.*; (*schol.*) voto *m.* —*v.t.* graduare; (*schol.*) classificare.

gradient /'greɪdɪənt/ *n.* pendenza *f.*

gradual /'grædʒʊəl/ *a.* graduale. ~**ly** *adv.* gradatamente.

graduate[1] /'grædʒʊət/ *n.* laureato, a *m.*, *f.*

graduat|e[2] /'grædʒʊeɪt/ *v.i.* laurearsi. —*v.t.* graduare. ~**ion** /-'eɪʃn/ *n.* laurea *f.*

graffiti /grə'fiːtɪ/ *n.pl.* graffiti *m.pl.*

graft[1] /grɑːft/ *n.* innesto *m.* —*v.t.* innestare.

graft[2] /grɑːft/ *n.* corruzione *f.*

grain /greɪn/ *n.* grano *m.*; (*of sand*)

granello *m.*; (*of coffee, rice*) chicco *m.*; (*in leather*) grana *f.*; (*in wood*) venatura *f.*

gram /græm/ *n.* grammo *m.*

gramma|r /'græmə(r)/ *n.* grammatica *f.* **~atical** /grə'mætɪkl/ *a.* grammaticale.

gramophone /'græməfəʊn/ *n.* grammofono *m.*

grand /grænd/ *a.* (**-er, -est**) grandioso; (*fam.*) eccellente. **~ piano** *n.* pianoforte a coda *m.*

grand|child /'grændtʃaɪld/ *n.* (*pl.* -children) nipote *m./f.* **~daughter** *n.* nipote *f.* **~father** *n.* nonno *m.* **~mother** *n.* nonna *f.* **~parents** *n.pl.* nonni *m.pl.* **~son** *n.* nipote *m.*

grandeur /'grændʒə(r)/ *n.* grandiosità *f.*

grandiose /'grændɪəʊs/ *a.* grandioso.

grandstand /'grændstænd/ *n.* tribuna *f.*

granite /'grænɪt/ *n.* granito *m.*

granny /'grænɪ/ *n.* (*fam.*) nonna *f.*

grant /grɑːnt/ *v.t.* accordare; (*concede*) ammettere. *—n.* concessione *f.*; (*for study*) borsa di studio *f.* **take for granted** dare per scontato.

granulated /'grænjʊleɪtɪd/ *a.* **~ sugar** zucchero cristallizzato *m.*

granule /'grænjuːl/ *n.* granulo *m.*

grape /greɪp/ *n.* acino *m.*

grapefruit /'greɪpfruːt/ *n.* pompelmo *m.*

graph /grɑːf/ *n.* grafico *m.* **~ic** *a.* grafico.

grapple /græpl/ *v.i.* **~ with** essere alle prese con.

grasp /grɑːsp/ *v.t.* afferrare. *—n.* stretta *f.*; (*understanding*) comprensione *f.*; (*reach*) capacità *f.*

grasping /'grɑːspɪŋ/ *a.* avido.

grass /grɑːs/ *n.* erba *f.* **~ roots** *n.pl.* fondamenta *f.pl.* **~y** *a.* erboso.

grasshopper /'grɑːshɒpə(r)/ *n.* cavalletta *f.*

grassland /'grɑːslænd/ *n.* prateria *f.*

grate[1] /greɪt/ *n.* grata *f.*; (*hearth*) focolare *m.*

grate[2] /greɪt/ *v.t.* grattugiare. *—v.i.* stridere. **~r** /-ə(r)/ *n.* grattugia *f.*

grateful /'greɪtfl/ *a.* grato. **~ly** *adv.* con gratitudine.

gratif|y /'grætɪfaɪ/ *v.t.* appagare. **~ied** *a.* compiaciuto. **~ying** *a.* piacevole.

grating /'greɪtɪŋ/ *n.* grata *f.*

gratis /'greɪtɪs/ *adv.* gratis.

gratitude /'grætɪtjuːd/ *n.* gratitudine *f.*

gratuitous /grə'tjuːɪtəs/ *a.* gratuito.

gratuity /grə'tjuːətɪ/ *n.* gratifica *f.*

grave[1] /greɪv/ *n.* tomba *f.* **~-digger** *n.* becchino *m.*

grave[2] /greɪv/ *a.* (**-er, -est**) grave. **~ly** *adv.* gravemente.

grave[3] /grɑːv/ *a.* **~ accent** accento grave.

gravel /'grævl/ *n.* ghiaia *f.*

gravestone /'greɪvstəʊn/ *n.* lapide *f.*

graveyard /'greɪvjɑːd/ *n.* cimitero *m.*

gravitat|e /'grævɪteɪt/ *v.i.* gravitare. **~ion** /-'teɪʃn/ *n.* gravitazione *f.*

gravity /'grævətɪ/ *n.* gravità *f.*

gravy /'greɪvɪ/ *n.* sugo (di carne) *m.*

graze[1] /greɪz/ *v.t./i.* pascolare.

graze[2] /greɪz/ *v.t.* sfiorare; (*scrape*) scalfire. *—n.* scalfittura *f.*

greas|e /griːs/ *n.* grasso *m.* *—v.t.* ungere. **~e-paint** *n.* cerone *m.* **~e-proof paper** *n.* carta oleata *f.* **~y** *a.* unto.

great /greɪt/ *a.* (**-er, -est**) grande; (*fam.*) splendido. **~-grandfather** *n.* bisnonno *m.* **~-grandmother** *n.* bisnonna *f.* **~ly** *adv.* molto. **~ness** *n.* grandezza *f.*

Great Britain /greɪt'brɪtən/ *n.* Gran Bretagna *f.*

Greece /griːs/ *n.* Grecia *f.*

greed /griːd/ *n.* avidità *f.*; (*for food*) ingordigia *f.* **~y** *a.* avido; ingordo.

Greek /griːk/ *a. & n.* greco, a *m., f.*

green /griːn/ *a.* (**-er, -est**) verde. *—n.* verde *m.*; (*grass*) prato *m.* **~s** *n.pl.* verdura *f.* **~ belt** zona verde *f.* **~ fingers** il pollice verde *m.* **~ light** (*fam.*) permesso di procedere *m.* **~ery** *n.* vegetazione *f.*

greengage /'griːngeɪdʒ/ *n.* susina verde *f.*

greengrocer /'griːngrəʊsə(r)/ *n.* fruttivendolo, a *m., f.*

greenhouse /'griːnhaʊs/ *n.* serra *f.*

greet /griːt/ *v.t.* salutare. **~ing** *n.* saluto *m.*

gregarious /grɪ'geərɪəs/ *a.* gregario; (*person*) socievole.

grenade /grɪ'neɪd/ *n.* granata *f.*

grew /gruː/ *see* grow.

grey /greɪ/ *a.* (**-er, -est**) grigio; (*fig.*) triste. *—n.* grigio *m.* *—v.i.* diventare grigio.

greyhound /'greɪhaʊnd/ *n.* levriero *m.*

grid /grɪd/ *n.* griglia *f.*; (*electr.*) rete *f.*; (*on map*) reticolato *m.*

grief /griːf/ *n.* dolore *m.* **come to ~** andare in rovina.

grievance /'griːvns/ *n.* lagnanza *f.*

grieve /griːv/ *v.t./i.* affliggere, affliggersi.

grievous /'griːvəs/ doloroso; (*serious*) grave.

grill /gril/ *n.* graticola *f.*; (*for grilling*) griglia *f.* —*v.t./i.* arrostire; (*question*) sottoporre a severo interrogatorio.

grille /gril/ *n.* grata *f.*

grim /grim/ *a.* (**grimmer, grimmest**) arcigno.

grimace /grɪ'meɪs/ *n.* smorfia *f.* —*v.i.* fare una smorfia.

grim|e /graɪm/ *n.* sudiciume *m.* **~y** *a.* sudicio.

grin /grin/ *v.i.* (*p.t.* **grinned**) fare un (largo) sorriso. —*n.* (largo) sorriso *m.*

grind /graɪnd/ *v.t.* (*p.t.* **ground**) macinare; (*crush*) schiacciare; (*sharpen*) affilare. —*n.* fatica *f.*

grip /grip/ *v.t.* (*p.t.* **gripped**) afferrare; (*attention*) tenere avvinto. —*n.* stretta *f.*; (*control*) controllo *m.* **be in the ~ of** essere in preda a.

gripes /graɪps/ *n.pl.* colica *f.s.*

grisly /'grɪzlɪ/ *a.* (**-ier, -iest**) orribile.

gristle /'grɪsl/ *n.* cartilagine *f.*

grit /grit/ *n.* graniglia *f.*; (*fig.*) coraggio *m.* —*v.t.* (*p.t.* **gritted**) stridere; (*clench*) serrare.

grizzl|e /'grɪzl/ *v.i.* piagnucolare. **~y** *a.* grigio.

groan /grəʊn/ *v.i.* gemere. —*n.* gemito *m.*

grocer /'grəʊsə(r)/ *n.* droghiere, a *m.*, *f.* **~ies** *n.pl.* generi alimentari *m.pl.* **~y** *n.* drogheria *f.*

grog /grɒg/ *n.* grog *m. invar.*

groggy /'grɒgɪ/ *a.* barcollante.

groin /grɔɪn/ *n.* inguine *m.*

groom /gruːm/ *n.* stalliere *m.*; (*palace official*) gentiluomo di corte *m.*; (*bridegroom*) sposo *m.* —*v.t.* strigliare; (*fig.*) preparare. **well ~ed** ben curato.

groove /gruːv/ *n.* scanalatura *f.*

grope /grəʊp/ *v.i.* brancolare. **~ for** cercare a tastoni.

gross /grəʊs/ *a.* (**-er, -est**) grossolano; (*comm.*) lordo. —*n.* (*pl.* **gross**) (*twelve dozen*) grossa *f.* **~ly** *adv.* grossolanamente; (*very*) enormemente.

grotesque /grəʊ'tesk/ *a.* grottesco.

grotto /'grɒtəʊ/ *n.* (*pl.* **-oes**) grotta *f.*

grotty /'grɒtɪ/ *a.* (*sl.*) squallido.

grouch /graʊtʃ/ *v.i.* (*fam.*) brontolare.

ground[1] /graʊnd/ *n.* terra *f.*; (*area*) terreno *m.*; (*reason*) ragione *f.* **~s** *n.pl.* (*of coffee*) sedimenti *m.pl.* —*v.t./i.* fare arenare, arenarsi; (*plane*) costringere ad atterrare. **~ floor** *n.* pianterreno *m.* **~rent** *n.* affitto del terreno *m.* **~ swell** *n.* mare lungo *m.* **~less** *a.* infondato.

ground[2] /graʊnd/ *see* **grind**.

grounding /'graʊndɪŋ/ *n.* base *f.*

groundsheet /'graʊndʃiːt/ *n.* telone impermeabile *m.*

groundwork /'graʊndwɜːk/ *n.* preparativi *m.pl.*

group /gruːp/ *n.* gruppo *m.* —*v.t./i.* aggruppare, aggrupparsi.

grouse[1] /graʊs/ *n.* (*pl.* **grouse**) gallo cedrone *m.*

grouse[2] /graʊs/ *v.i.* (*fam.*) borbottare.

grove /grəʊv/ *n.* boschetto *m.*

grovel /'grɒvl/ *v.i.* (*p.t.* **grovelled**) prosternarsi.

grow /grəʊ/ *v.t./i.* (*p.t.* **grew**, *p.p.* **grown**) crescere; (*become*) diventare; (*of plant*) coltivare. **~ up** diventare adulto. **~er** *n.* coltiva|tore, -trice *m.*, *f.*

growl /graʊl/ *v.i.* ringhiare. —*n.* grugnito *m.*

grown /grəʊn/ *see* **grow**. —*a.* adulto. **~-up** *a.* & *n.* adulto, a *m.*, *f.*

growth /grəʊθ/ *n.* crescita *f.*; (*increase*) aumento *m.*; (*med.*) tumore *m.*

grub /grʌb/ *n.* larva *f.*; (*sl.*) mangiare *m.*

grubby /'grʌbɪ/ *a.* (**-ier, -iest**) sporco.

grudg|e /grʌdʒ/ *v.t.* dare a malincuore. —*n.* rancore *m.* **bear a ~e against** aver rancore verso. **~ingly** *adv.* a malincuore.

gruelling /'gruːəlɪŋ/ *a.* estenuante.

gruesome /'gruːsəm/ *a.* macabro.

gruff /grʌf/ *a.* (**-er, -est**) burbero.

grumble /'grʌmbl/ *v.i.* brontolare.

grumpy /'grʌmpɪ/ *a.* (**-ier, -iest**) irritabile.

grunt /grʌnt/ *v.i.* grugnire. —*n.* grugnito *m.*

guarant|ee /gærən'tiː/ *n.* garanzia *f.* —*v.t.* garantire. **~or** *n.* garante *m.*/*f.*

guard /gɑːd/ *v.t.* proteggere; (*watch*) sorvegliare. —*v.i.* **~ against** guardarsi da. —*n.* guardia *f.*; (*on train*) capotreno *m.* **~ian** *n.* guardiano, a *m.*, *f.*; (*of minor*) tu|tore, -trice *m.*, *f.*

guarded /'gɑːdɪd/ *a.* guardingo.

guerrilla /gə'rɪlə/ *n.* guerrigliero *m.* **~ warfare** guerriglia *f.*

guess /ges/ v.t./i. indovinare; (*Amer.*) ritenere. —n. congettura f.

guesswork /'gesw₃:k/ n. supposizione f.

guest /gest/ n. ospite m.|f.; (*in hotel*) cliente m.|f. ∼-house n. pensione f.

guffaw /gə'fɔ:/ n. sghignazzata f. —v.i. sghignazzare.

guidance /'gaɪdəns/ n. direzione, guida f.

guide /gaɪd/ n. guida f. —v.t. guidare. ∼d missile n. missile teleguidato m.

guidebook /'gaɪdbʊk/ n. guida turistica f.

guild /gɪld/ n. corporazione f. G∼ Hall Palazzo delle Corporazioni m.

guile /gaɪl/ n. astuzia f.

guillotine /'gɪləti:n/ n. ghigliottina f.; (*for paper*) taglierina f.

guilt /gɪlt/ n. colpa f. ∼y a. colpevole.

guinea-pig /'gɪnɪpɪg/ n. porcellino d'India m.

guise /gaɪz/ n. foggia f.

guitar /gɪ'tɑː(r)/ n. chitarra f. ∼ist n. chitarrista m.|f.

gulf /gʌlf/ n. golfo m.; (*hollow*) abisso m.

gull /gʌl/ n. gabbiano m.

gullet /'gʌlɪt/ n. esofago m.

gullible /'gʌləbl/ a. credulo.

gully /'gʌlɪ/ n. burrone m.; (*drain*) cunetta f.

gulp /gʌlp/ v.t. trangugiare. —v.i. (*a sob*) soffocare. —n. boccone m.; (*of liquid*) sorso m.

gum¹ /gʌm/ n. (*anat.*) gengiva f.

gum² /gʌm/ n. gomma f.; (*chewing-gum*) chewing-gum m. —v.t. (*p.t.* gummed) ingommare.

gumboot /'gʌmbuːt/ n. stivale di gomma m.

gumption /'gʌmpʃn/ n. (*fam.*) buon senso m.

gun /gʌn/ n. cannone m.; (*rifle*) fucile m.; (*pistol*) rivoltella f. —v.t. (*p.t.* gun-ned) ∼ down freddare. ∼ner n. artigliere m.

gunfire /'gʌnfaɪə(r)/ n. cannoneggiamento m.

gunman /'gʌnmən/ n. (*pl.* -men) bandito armato m.

gunpowder /'gʌnpaʊdə(r)/ n. polvere da sparo f.

gunshot /'gʌnʃɒt/ n. colpo (d'arma da fuoco) m.

gurgle /'gɜːgl/ n. gorgoglio m. —v.i. gorgogliare.

guru /'gʊruː/ n. (*pl.* -us) guru m. invar.

gush /gʌʃ/ v.i. sgorgare; (*fig.*) ciarlare. —n. fiotto m.; (*fig.*) effusione f. ∼ing a. effusivo.

gusset /'gʌsɪt/ n. gherone m.; (*of pants*) tassello m.

gust /gʌst/ n. raffica f.; (*of rain*) scroscio m. ∼y a. ventoso.

gusto /'gʌstəʊ/ n. fervore m.

gut /gʌt/ n. budello m. (*pl.* budella f.) ∼s n.pl. pancia f.; (*fam., courage*) coraggio m. —v.t. (*p.t.* gutted) sventrare.

gutter /'gʌtə(r)/ n. grondaia f.; (*in street*) cunetta f.; (*slum*) bassifondi m.pl. ∼snipe n. scugnizzo m.

guttural /'gʌtərəl/ a. gutturale.

guy /gaɪ/ n. (*sl.*) tipo, tizio m.

guzzle /'gʌzl/ v.t./i. ingozzare.

gym /dʒɪm/ n. (*fam., gymnasium*) palestra f.; (*gymnastics*) ginnastica f. ∼slip n. tunica f.

gymkhana /dʒɪm'kɑːnə/ n. gimkhana f.

gymnast /'dʒɪmnæst/ n. ginnasta m.|f. ∼ics /-'næstɪks/ n.pl. ginnastica f.

gynaecolog|y /gaɪnɪ'kɒlədʒɪ/ ginecologia f. ∼ist n. ginecologo, a m., f.

gypsy /'dʒɪpsɪ/ n. zingaro, a m., f.

gyrate /dʒaɪ'reɪt/ v.i. roteare.

gyroscope /'dʒaɪərəskəʊp/ n. giroscopio m.

H

haberdashery /ˈhæbəˈdæʃərɪ/ n. merceria f.

habit /ˈhæbɪt/ n. abitudine f.; (costume) abito m.

habit|able /ˈhæbɪtəbl/ a. abitabile. ~ation /-ˈteɪʃn/ n. abitazione f.

habitat /ˈhæbɪtæt/ n. habitat m. invar.

habitual /həˈbɪtʃʊəl/ a. abituale; (smoker, liar) inveterato. ~ly adv. abitualmente.

hack[1] /hæk/ n. cavallo da nolo m.; (writer) scribacchino, a m., f.

hack[2] /hæk/ v.t. tagliare. ~ to pieces tagliare a pezzi.

hackney /ˈhæknɪ/ a. ~ carriage vettura pubblica f.

hackneyed /ˈhæknɪd/ a. trito, banale.

had /hæd/ see have.

haddock /ˈhædək/ n. invar. aglefino m.

haemorrhage /ˈhemərɪdʒ/ n. emorragia f.

haemorrhoids /ˈhemərɔɪdz/ n.pl. emorroidi f.pl.

hag /hæg/ n. megera f.

haggard /ˈhægəd/ a. disfatto.

haggle /ˈhægl/ v.i. mercanteggiare.

hail[1] /heɪl/ v.t. salutare; (taxi) chiamare. —v.i. ~ from provenire da.

hail[2] /heɪl/ n. grandine f. —v.i. grandinare. ~stone n. chicco di grandine m. ~storm n. grandinata f.

hair /heə(r)/ n. (on head) capelli m.pl.; (on body, of animals) pelo m. ~-do n. (fam.) acconciatura f. ~-dryer n. asciugacapelli m. invar. ~-raising a. terrificante. ~-style n. pettinatura f.

hairbrush /ˈheəbrʌʃ/ n. spazzola per capelli f.

haircut /ˈheəkʌt/ n. taglio dei capelli m.

hairdresser /ˈheədresə(r)/ n. parrucchiere, a m., f.

hairpin /ˈheəpɪn/ n. forcina f. ~ bend n. curva a gomito f.

hairy /ˈheərɪ/ a. (-ier, -iest) peloso; (sl.) raccapricciante.

hake /heɪk/ n. invar. nasello m.

halcyon /ˈhælsɪən/ a. sereno.

hale /heɪl/ a. vigoroso.

half /hɑːf/ n. (pl. halves) metà f., mezzo m. —a. mezzo. —adv. a metà. ~ a dozen mezza dozzina. ~ an hour mezz'ora. ~-caste n. meticcio, a m.,

f. ~-hearted a. esitante. ~-term n. vacanza di metà trimestre f. ~-time n. intervallo m. ~-way a. & adv. a metà strada. ~-wit n. idiota m./f.

halibut /ˈhælɪbət/ n. invar. ippoglosso m.

hall /hɔːl/ n. sala f.; (entrance) ingresso m.; (mansion) palazzo m. ~ of residence n. casa dello studente f.

hallelujah /hælɪˈluːjə/ int. & n. alleluia f.

hallmark /ˈhɔːlmɑːk/ n. marchio di garanzia m.; (fig.) (qualità) caratteristica f.

hallo /həˈləʊ/ int. & n. ciao m.; (telephone) pronto m. say ~ to salutare.

hallow /ˈhæləʊ/ v.t. santificare.

hallucination /həluːsɪˈneɪʃn/ n. allucinazione f.

halo /ˈheɪləʊ/ n. (pl. -oes) alone m.

halt /hɔːlt/ n. alt m. invar. —v.t./i. fermare, fermarsi.

halting /ˈhɔːltɪŋ/ a. esitante.

halve /hɑːv/ v.t. dividere a metà.

ham /hæm/ n. prosciutto m.; (sl., theatr.) at|tore, -trice da strapazzo m., f.

hamburger /ˈhæmbɜːgə(r)/ n. amburger m. invar.

hamlet /ˈhæmlɪt/ n. paesino m.

hammer /ˈhæmə(r)/ n. martello m. —v.t. martellare.

hammock /ˈhæmək/ n. amaca f.

hamper[1] /ˈhæmpə(r)/ n. paniere m.

hamper[2] /ˈhæmpə(r)/ v.t. intralciare.

hamster /ˈhæmstə(r)/ n. criceto m.

hand /hænd/ n. mano f.; (of clock) lancetta f.; (writing) scrittura f. —v.t. porgere. at ~, to ~ a portata di mano. by ~ a mano. ~ down tramandare. ~ in or over consegnare. ~ out distribuire. ~ over passare. on the one ~ da un lato. on the other ~ d'altra parte. out of ~ incontrollabile.

handbag /ˈhændbæg/ n. borsa (da signora) f.

handbook /ˈhændbʊk/ n. manuale m.

handcuff /ˈhændkʌf/ n. manetta f. —v.t. ammanettare.

handful /ˈhændfʊl/ n. manciata f.; (fig.) persona incontrollabile f.

handicap /ˈhændɪkæp/ n. handicap m.

invar. —*v.t.* (*p.t.* **handicapped**) handicappare.

handicraft /'hændɪkrɑːft/ *n.* artigianato *m.*

handiwork /'hændɪwɜːk/ *n.* opera *f.*

handkerchief /'hæŋkətʃɪf/ *n.* (*pl.* -fs) fazzoletto *m.*

handle /'hændl/ *n.* manico *m.*; (*of door*) maniglia *f.* —*v.t.* maneggiare; (*deal with*) occuparsi di; (*control*) dirigere.

handlebar /'hændlbɑː(r)/ *n.* manubrio *m.*

handshake /'hændʃeɪk/ *n.* stretta di mano *f.*

handsome /'hænsəm/ *a.* bello; (*fig.*) generoso.

handstand /'hændstænd/ *n.* verticale *f.*

handwriting /'hændraɪtɪŋ/ *n.* calligrafia *f.*

handy /'hændɪ/ *a.* (-ier, -iest) utile; (*of person*) abile.

handyman /'hændɪmæn/ *n.* (*pl.* -men) tuttofare *m. invar.*

hang /hæŋ/ *v.t.* (*p.t.* **hung**) sospendere, appendere; (*p.t.* **hanged**) (*criminal*) impiccare. —*v.i.* pendere; (*hair*) scendere. —*n.* **get the ~ of** (*fam.*) afferrare il senso di. **~ about** gironzolare. **~ fire** (*of events*) tardare. **~-glider** *n.* deltaplano *m.* **~-gliding** *n.* volo col deltaplano *m.* **~ on** tenersi stretto; (*sl.*) aspettare. **~ out** (*sl.*) abitare. **~ over** sovrastare. **~-up** *n.* (*sl.*) inibizione *f.* **~ up** (*telephone*) riattaccare.

hangar /'hæŋə(r)/ *n.* hangar *m. invar.*

hanger /'hæŋə(r)/ *n.* gruccia *f.* **~-on** *n.* tirapiedi *m.*/*f.*

hangman /'hæŋmən/ *n.* (*pl.* -men) boia *m.*

hangover /'hæŋəʊvə(r)/ *n.* malessere (dopo una sbornia) *m.*

hanker /'hæŋkə(r)/ *v.i.* **~ after** agognare.

hanky-panky /'hæŋkɪpæŋkɪ/ *n.* (*sl.*) imbroglio *m.*

haphazard /hæp'hæzəd/ *a.*, **~ly** *adv.* a casaccio.

hapless /'hæplɪs/ *a.* sfortunato.

happen /'hæpən/ *v.i.* accadere. **as it ~s** si dà il caso. **I ~ed to meet him** mi capitò di incontrarlo. **~ing** *n.* avvenimento *m.*

happ|y /'hæpɪ/ *a.* (-ier, -iest) felice. **~y-go-lucky** *a.* spensierato. **~ily** *adv.* felicemente. **~iness** *n.* felicità *f.*

harangue /hə'ræŋ/ *n.* arringa *f.* —*v.t.* arringare.

harass /'hærəs/ *v.t.* angustiare. **~ment** *n.* tormento *m.*

harbour /'hɑːbə(r)/ *n.* porto *m.* —*v.t.* dare asilo a; (*fig.*) covare.

hard /hɑːd/ *a.* (-er, -est) duro. —*adv.* molto, duro; (*think*) intensamente; (*pull*) forte. **~back** *n.* libro rilegato *m.* **~-boiled egg** uovo sodo *m.* **~ by** vicino. **~ done by** trattato male. **~-headed** *a.* ostinato. **~ up** (*fam.*) al verde. **~-working** *a.* diligente. **~ness** *n.* durezza *f.*

hardboard /'hɑːdbɔːd/ *n.* legno precompresso *m.*

harden /'hɑːdn/ *v.t.*/*i.* indurire, indurirsi.

hardly /'hɑːdlɪ/ *adv.* appena. **~ ever** quasi mai.

hardship /'hɑːdʃɪp/ *n.* avversità *f.*

hardware /'hɑːdweə(r)/ *n.* ferramenta *f.pl.*

hardy /'hɑːdɪ/ *a.* (-ier, -iest) forte, resistente.

hare /heə(r)/ *n.* lepre *f.* **~-brained** *a.* sventato.

harem /'hɑːriːm/ *n.* harem *m. invar.*

haricot /'hærɪkəʊ/ *n.* **~ bean** fagiolo (secco) *m.*

hark /hɑːk/ *v.i.* **~ back to** ritornare su.

harlot /'hɑːlət/ *n.* (*old use*) prostituta *f.*

harm /hɑːm/ *n.* male *m.*; (*wrong*) torto *m.* —*v.t.* danneggiare; far male (a). **~ful** *a.* dannoso. **~less** *a.* innocuo.

harmonica /hɑː'mɒnɪkə/ *n.* armonica *f.*

harmon|y /'hɑːmənɪ/ *n.* armonia *f.* **~ious** /-'məʊnɪəs/ *a.* armonioso. **~ize** *v.t.*/*i.* armonizzare.

harness /'hɑːnɪs/ *n. invar.* finimenti *m.pl.* —*v.t.* bardare.

harp /hɑːp/ *n.* arpa *f.* —*v.i.* **~ on about** insistere su. **~ist** *n.* arpista *m.*/*f.*

harpoon /hɑː'puːn/ *n.* fiocina *f.*

harpsichord /'hɑːpsɪkɔːd/ *n.* clavicembalo *m.*

harrow /'hærəʊ/ *n.* erpice *m.*

harrowing /'hærəʊɪŋ/ *a.* straziante.

harsh /hɑːʃ/ *a.* (-er, -est) severo; (*disagreeable*) sgradevole; (*light*) abbagliante. **~ly** *adv.* duramente. **~ness** *n.* durezza *f.*

harvest /'hɑːvɪst/ *n.* mietitura *f.* —*v.t.* mietere. **~er** *n.* mietitrice *f.*

has /hæz/ *see* have.

hash /hæʃ/ *n.* carne cotta tritata *f.*; (*fig.*) pasticcio *m.* **make a** ∼ **of** (*sl.*) impasticciare.`

hashish /'hæʃiːʃ/ *n.* hascisc *m.*

hassle /'hæsl/ *n.* (*fam.*) trambusto *m.* —*v.t.* (*fam.*) opprimere.

haste /heɪst/ *n.* fretta *f.* **make** ∼ affrettarsi.

hasten /'heɪsn/ *v.t./i.* affrettare, affrettarsi.

hast|y /'heɪstɪ/ *a.* (-ier, -iest) frettoloso. ∼ily *adv.* frettolosamente.

hat /hæt/ *n.* cappello *m.*

hatch[1] /hætʃ/ *n.* (*for food*) portello di servizio *m.*

hatch[2] /hætʃ/ *v.t./i.* covare; (*a plot*) tramare.

hatchback /'hætʃbæk/ *n.* (*auto.*) tre *or* cinque porte *f. invar.*

hatchet /'hætʃɪt/ *n.* ascia *f.*

hate /heɪt/ *n.* odio *m.* —*v.t.* odiare. ∼ful *a.* odioso.

hatred /'heɪtrɪd/ *n.* odio *m.*

haughty /'hɔːtɪ/ *a.* (-ier, -iest) altezzoso.

haul /hɔːl/ *v.t.* trascinare; (*goods*) trasportare. —*n.* tirata *f.*; (*profit*) guadagno *m.*; (*loot*) bottino *m.* ∼age *n.* trasporto *m.* ∼ier *n.* imprenditore di trasporti *m.*

haunch /hɔːntʃ/ *n.* anca *f.*

haunt /hɔːnt/ *v.t.* frequentare; (*linger in the mind*) perseguitare. —*n.* ritrovo *m.* ∼ed house casa stregata *f.*

have /hæv/ *v.t.* (*3 s. pres.* has; *p.t.* had) avere; (*meal, bath, walk*) fare. —*v. aux.* (*used with p.p.*) avere. ∼ done aver fatto. ∼ sthg. done far fare. ∼ to do dover fare. the haves and have-nots i ricchi e i poveri *m.pl.*

haven /'heɪvn/ *n.* rifugio *m.*

haversack /'hævəsæk/ *n.* bisaccia *f.*

havoc /'hævək/ *n.* strage *f.*

haw /hɔː/ *see* hum.

hawk[1] /hɔːk/ *n.* falco *m.*

hawk[2] /hɔːk/ *v.t.* portare in giro per vendere. ∼er *n.* vendi|tore, -trice ambulante *m.,f.*

hawthorn /'hɔːθɔːn/ *n.* biancospino *m.*

hay /heɪ/ *n.* fieno *m.* ∼ fever febbre del fieno *f.* ∼loft fienile *m.* ∼stack *n.* mucchio di fieno *m.*

haywire /'heɪwaɪə(r)/ *a.* go ∼ (*fam.*) confondersi.

hazard /'hæzəd/ *n.* rischio *m.* —*v.t.* rischiare. ∼ous *a.* azzardato.

haze /heɪz/ *n.* foschia *f.*

hazel /'heɪzl/ *n.* nocciolo *m.*; (*colour*) (color) nocciola *m.* ∼nut *n.* nocciola *f.*

hazy /'heɪzɪ/ *a.* (-ier, -iest) nebbioso; (*fig.*) confuso.

he /hiː/ *pron.* egli, lui. —*n.* maschio *m.*

head /hed/ *n.* testa *f.*; (*chief*) capo *m.* —*v.t.* essere in testa a; (*letter*) intestare. —*v.i.* ∼ for dirigersi verso. ∼-dress, ∼gear *ns.* acconciatura *f.* ∼ first a capofitto. ∼-on *a.* frontale; *adv.* frontalmente. heads or tails? testa o croce? ∼ waiter *n.* capocameriere *m.* ∼er *n.* (*football*) rinvio di testa *m.* ∼y *a.* (-ier, -iest) che dà alla testa.

headache /'hedeɪk/ *n.* mal di testa *m.*

heading /'hedɪŋ/ *n.* intestazione *f.*

headlamp, headlight /'hedlæmp, 'hedlaɪt/ *ns.* fanale *m.*

headline /'hedlaɪn/ *n.* titolo *m.*

headlong /'hedlɒŋ/ *a. & adv.* a capofitto.

headmaster, headmistress /hed'mɑːstə(r), hed'mɪstrɪs/ *ns.* preside *m.|f.*; diret|tore, -trice *m., f.*

headphone /'hedfəʊn/ *n.* cuffia (ricevente) *f.*

headquarters /'hedkwɔːtəz/ *n.pl.* sede *f.s.*; (*mil.*) quartiere generale *m.s.*

headstrong /'hedstrɒŋ/ *a.* testardo.

headway /'hedweɪ/ *n.* progresso *m.*

heal /hiːl/ *v.t./i.* guarire.

health /helθ/ *n.* salute *f.* ∼y *a.* (-ier, -iest) sano; (*beneficial*) salubre.

heap /hiːp/ *n.* mucchio *m.* —*v.t.* ammucchiare. ∼s of (*fam.*) moltissimi.

hear /hɪə(r)/ *v.t./i.* (*p.t.* heard) sentire. hear, hear! bravo! ∼ from aver notizie di. ∼ of sentir parlare di. ∼ing *n.* udito *m.*; (*jurid.*) udienza *f.* ∼ing-aid *n.* apparecchio acustico *m.*

hearsay /'hɪəseɪ/ *n.* diceria *f.*

hearse /hɜːs/ *n.* carro funebre *m.*

heart /hɑːt/ *n.* cuore *m.* by ∼ a memoria. ∼ attack attacco cardiaco *m.* ∼break *n.* crepacuore *m.* ∼broken *a.* straziato. ∼-searching *n.* esame di coscienza *m.* ∼-to-∼ *a.* a cuore aperto. lose ∼ perdersi di coraggio.

heartache /'hɑːteɪk/ *n.* angoscia *f.*

heartburn /'hɑːtbɜːn/ *n.* bruciore di stomaco *m.*

hearten /'hɑːtn/ *v.t.* incoraggiare.

heartfelt /'hɑːtfelt/ *a.* sentito.

hearth /hɑːθ/ *n.* focolare *m.*

heartless /'hɑːtlɪs/ *a.* spietato.

heart|y /'hɑːtɪ/ *a.* (-ier, -iest) caloroso;

(*meal*) copioso. ~**ily** *adv*. di cuore; (*eat*) con appetito.

heat /hi:t/ *n*. calore *m*.; (*contest*) prova *f*. —*v.t./i*. scaldare, scaldarsi. ~ **stroke** *n*. insolazione *f*. ~ **wave** *n*. ondata di calore *f*. ~**er** *n*. stufa *f*. ~**ing** *n*. riscaldamento *m*.

heated /'hi:tɪd/ *a*. (*discussion*) animato.

heath /hi:θ/ *n*. brughiera *f*.

heathen /'hi:ðn/ *n*. pagano, a *m*., *f*.

heather /'heðə(r)/ *n*. erica *f*.

heave /hi:v/ *v.t./i*. sollevare, sollevarsi; (*a sigh*) emettere; (*fam*.) gettare.

heaven /'hevn/ *n*. cielo *m*.; (*bliss*) paradiso *m*. ~**ly** *a*. celeste; (*fam*.) delizioso.

heav|y /'hevɪ/ *a*. (-ier, -iest) pesante; (*cold, sea, etc*.) forte; (*traffic*) denso. ~**ily** *adv*. pesantemente; (*smoke, drink, etc*.) molto.

heavyweight /'hevɪweɪt/ *n*. peso massimo *m*.

Hebrew /'hi:bru:/ *a*. ebreo. —*n*. ebreo, a *m*., *f*.; (*lang*.) ebraico *m*.

heckle /'hekl/ *v.t*. tempestare di domande.

hectic /'hektɪk/ *a*. febbrile.

hedge /hedʒ/ *n*. siepe *f*. —*v.t*. circondare con siepe. —*v.i*. evadere (a una domanda).

hedgehog /'hedʒhɒg/ *n*. riccio *m*.

heed /hi:d/ *v.t*. fare attenzione a. —*n*. **pay** ~ **to** fare attenzione a. ~**less** *a*. disattento.

heel /hi:l/ *n*. tallone *m*.; (*of shoe*) tacco *m*. **down at** ~ trasandato. **take to one's** ~**s** darsela a gambe.

hefty /'heftɪ/ *a*. (-ier, -iest) massiccio.

heifer /'hefə(r)/ *n*. giovenca *f*.

height /haɪt/ *n*. altezza *f*.; (*of plane*) altitudine *f*.; (*of season*) culmine *m*.; (*fig*.) colmo *m*.

heighten /'haɪtn/ *v.t*. innalzare; (*fig*.) accrescere.

heinous /'heɪnəs/ *a*. nefando.

heir, heiress /eə(r), 'eərɪs/ *ns*. erede *m*./*f*.

heirloom /'eəlu:m/ *n*. cimelio di famiglia *m*.

held /held/ *see* **hold**[1].

helicopter /'helɪkɒptə(r)/ *n*. elicottero *m*.

heliport /'helɪpɔ:t/ *n*. eliporto *m*.

hell /hel/ *n*. inferno *m*. ~**-bent** *a*. accanito. ~**ish** *a*. infernale.

hello /hə'ləʊ/ *int*. & *n*. = **hallo**.

helm /helm/ *n*. timone *m*.

helmet /'helmɪt/ *n*. casco *m*.

help /help/ *v.t./i*. aiutare. —*n*. aiuto *m*.; (*charwoman*) donna di servizio *f*. ~ **o.s. to** servirsi di. **it cannot be** ~**ed** è inevitabile. ~**er** *n*. aiutante *m*./*f*. ~**ful** *a*. utile; (*person*) di aiuto. ~**less** *a*. (*unable to manage*) incapace; (*powerless*) indifeso.

helping /'helpɪŋ/ *n*. porzione *f*.

helter-skelter /heltə'skeltə(r)/ *adv*. alla rinfusa. —*n*. otto volante *m*.

hem /hem/ *n*. orlo *m*. —*v.t*. (*p.t.* hemmed) orlare. ~ **in** rinchiudere.

hemisphere /'hemɪsfɪə(r)/ *n*. emisfero *m*.

hemp /hemp/ *n*. canapa *f*.; (*drug*) hascisc *m*.

hen /hen/ *n*. gallina *f*. ~**-party** *n*. (*fam*.) riunione di donne *f*.

hence /hens/ *adv*. da qui; (*for this reason*) quindi; (*from now on*) da questo momento. ~**forth** *adv*. d'ora in poi.

henchman /'hentʃmən/ *n*. (*pl.* -men) seguace *m*.

henna /'henə/ *n*. enné *m*.

henpecked /'henpekt/ *a*. tiranneggiato dalla moglie.

her /hɜ:(r)/ *a*. suo, sua, suoi, sue. —*pron*. lei, la, le; (*after prep*.) lei.

herald /'herəld/ *v.t*. annunciare.

heraldry /'herəldrɪ/ *n*. araldica *f*.

herb /hɜ:b/ *n*. erba *f*. ~**s** *n.pl*. erbette *f.pl*.

herbaceous /hɜ:'beɪʃəs/ *a*. erbaceo.

herbalist /'hɜ:bəlɪst/ *n*. erborista *m*./*f*.

herculean /hɜ:kjʊ'li:ən/ *a*. erculeo.

herd /hɜ:d/ *n*. gregge *m*. —*v.i*. ~ **together** raggrupparsi.

here /hɪə(r)/ *adv*. qui, qua. ~ **is,** ~ **are** ecco.

hereafter /hɪər'ɑ:ftə(r)/ *adv*. in futuro.

hereby /hɪə'baɪ/ *adv*. qui vicino; (*comm*.) con la presente.

hereditary /hɪ'redɪtrɪ/ *a*. ereditario.

heredity /hɪ'redətɪ/ *n*. eredità *f*.

here|sy /'herəsɪ/ *n*. eresia *f*. ~**tic** *n*. eretico, a *m*., *f*.

herewith /hɪə'wɪð/ *adv*. con la presente.

heritage /'herɪtɪdʒ/ *n*. eredità *f*.

hermetic /hɜ:'metɪk/ *a*. ermetico.

hermit /'hɜ:mɪt/ *n*. eremita *m*./*f*.

hernia /'hɜ:nɪə/ *n*. ernia *f*.

hero /'hɪərəʊ/ *n*. (*pl.* -oes) eroe *m*. ~**ine** /'herəʊɪn/ *n*. eroina *f*. ~**ism** /'herəʊɪzəm/ *n*. eroismo *m*.

heroic /hɪ'rəʊɪk/ *a*. eroico.

heroin /'herəʊɪn/ n. eroina f.

heron /'herən/ n. airone m.

herring /'herɪŋ/ n. aringa f.

hers /hɜːz/ poss. pron. suo, sua, suoi, sue. **a friend of ~** un suo amico.

herself /hɜː'self/ pron. sé; se stessa; (r.) si; (emphatic) (proprio) lei. **by ~** da sola.

hesitant /'hezɪtənt/ a. esitante.

hesitat|e /'hezɪteɪt/ v.i. esitare. **~ion** /-'teɪʃn/ n. esitazione f.

hessian /'hesɪən/ n. tela di canapa f.

het /het/ a. **~ up** (sl.) eccitato.

heterogeneous /hetərə'dʒiːnɪəs/ a. eterogeneo.

heterosexual /hetərə'seksjʊəl/ a. eterosessuale.

hew /hjuː/ v.t. (p.p. hewn) spaccare.

hexagon /'heksəgən/ n. esagono m. **~al** /-'ægənl/ a. esagonale.

hey /heɪ/ int. ehi.

heyday /'heɪdeɪ/ n. fiore m.

hi /haɪ/ int. salve.

hiatus /haɪ'eɪtəs/ n. (pl. -tuses) iato m.

hibernat|e /'haɪbəneɪt/ v.i. svernare. **~ion** /-'neɪʃn/ n. ibernazione f.

hibiscus /hɪ'bɪskəs/ n. ibisco m.

hiccup /'hɪkʌp/ n. singulto m. —v.i. avere il singhiozzo.

hide[1] /haɪd/ v.t./i. (p.t. hid, p.p. hidden) nascondere, nascondersi. **~-out** n. (fam.) nascondiglio m.

hide[2] /haɪd/ n. pelle di animale f.

hideous /'hɪdɪəs/ a. atroce.

hiding /'haɪdɪŋ/ n. (fam.) bastonatura f. **go into ~** nascondersi.

hierarchy /'haɪərɑːkɪ/ n. gerarchia f.

hieroglyph /'haɪərəglɪf/ n. geroglifico m.

hi-fi /haɪ'faɪ/ a. (fam.) ad alta fedeltà.

higgledy-piggledy /'hɪgldɪ'pɪgldɪ/ adv. alla rinfusa.

high /haɪ/ a. (-er, -est) alto; (wind) forte; (intoxicated) brillo; (of food) passato. —n. livello alto m. —adv. alto. **~-falutin** a. pomposo. **~-handed** a. prepotente. **~ Mass** n. Messa solenne f. **~-rise** a. (of building) molto alto. **~ road** n. strada maestra f. **~ school** n. scuola media f. **~ street** n. strada principale f. **~ tea** n. pasto serale con tè e cibo m. **~-up** a. altolocato. **~er education** n. insegnamento superiore m. **~ness** n. altezza f.

highbrow /'haɪbraʊ/ a. & n. intellettuale m./f.

highlight /'haɪlaɪt/ n. punto cul-

minante m. **~s** n.pl. (in hair) mèche f.pl. —v.t. dar rilievo a.; (hair) fare le mèche.

highly /'haɪlɪ/ adv. altamente, molto; (paid) bene. **~-strung** a. con i nervi tesi. **think ~ of** stimare molto.

highway /'haɪweɪ/ n. strada maestra f.

highwayman /'haɪweɪmən/ n. (pl. -men) bandito di strada m.

hijack /'haɪdʒæk/ v.t. dirottare. —n. dirottamento m. **~er** n. dirottatore m.

hike /haɪk/ n. camminata f. —v.i. fare un'escursione a piedi. **~r** /-ə(r)/ n. escursionista m./f.

hilarious /hɪ'leərɪəs/ a. ilare.

hill /hɪl/ n. collina f.; (in road) altura f.; **~-billy** n. (Amer.) montanaro m. **~y** a. collinoso.

hillside /'hɪlsaɪd/ n. pendio m.

hilt /hɪlt/ n. impugnatura f. **to the ~** completamente.

him /hɪm/ pron. lui, lo, gli. **I spoke to ~** gli parlai. **it is ~** è lui. **she loves ~** lo ama.

himself /hɪm'self/ pron. sé, se stesso; (r.) si; (emphatic) (proprio) lui. **by ~** da solo.

hind /haɪnd/ a. posteriore.

hind|er /'hɪndə(r)/ v.t. intralciare. **~rance** n. intralcio m.

hindsight /'haɪndsaɪt/ n. **with ~** retrospettivamente.

Hindu /hɪn'duː/ n. & a. indù m./f. **~ism** /'hɪnduːɪzəm/ n. induismo m.

hinge /hɪndʒ/ n. cardine m. —v.i. (fig.) **~ on** dipendere da.

hint /hɪnt/ n. accenno m.; (indirect suggestion) allusione f.; (advice) suggerimento m. —v.i. accennare. **~ at** alludere a.

hinterland /'hɪntəlænd/ n. retroterra m.

hip /hɪp/ n. fianco m.

hippie /'hɪpɪ/ n. hippie m./f. invar.

hippopotamus /hɪpə'pɒtəməs/ n. (pl. -muses or -mi /-məsaɪz, -maɪ/) ippopotamo m.

hire /'haɪə(r)/ v.t. noleggiare; (person) assumere. —n. noleggio m. **~-purchase** n. vendita a rate f.

hirsute /'hɜːsjuːt/ a. irsuto.

his /hɪz/ a. suo, sua, suoi, sue. —poss. pron. il suo, la sua, i suoi, le sue.

hiss /hɪs/ n. sibilo m. —v.t./i. sibilare.

historian /hɪ'stɔːrɪən/ n. storico, a m., f.

histor|y /'hɪstərɪ/ n. storia f. **make ~y**

passare alla storia. ∼**ic(al)** /hɪ's-tɒrɪk(l)/ *a.* storico.

histrionic /hɪstrɪ'ɒnɪk/ *a.* istrionico. ∼**s** *n.pl.* commedia *f.s.*

hit /hɪt/ *v.t./i.* (*p.t.* **hit**, *pres. p.* **hitting**) colpire; (*against*) urtare; (*find*) trovare. —*n.* colpo *m.*; (*fig.*) successo *m.* ∼ **it off** andare d'accordo. ∼ **on** scoprire. ∼**-or-miss** *a.* alla buona. ∼ **upon** (*answer*) trovare. ∼ **the roof** infuriarsi.

hitch /hɪtʃ/ *v.t.* attaccare. —*n.* (*snag*) intoppo *m.* ∼ **a lift**, ∼**-hike** *v.i.* fare l'autostop. ∼**-hiker** *n.* autostoppista *m.*/*f.*

hither /'hɪðə/ *adv.* di qua. ∼ **and thither** di qua e di là.

hitherto /hɪðə'tu:/ *adv.* finora.

hive /haɪv/ *n.* alveare *m.* —*v.t.* ∼ **off** separarsi dal gruppo. ∼ **of industry** *n.* fucina di lavoro *f.*

hoard /hɔːd/ *v.t.* accumulare. —*n.* provvista *f.*; (*of money*) gruzzolo *m.*

hoarding /'hɔːdɪŋ/ *n.* palizzata *f.*

hoar-frost /'hɔːfrɒst/ *n.* brina *f.*

hoarse /hɔːs/ *a.* (**-er**, **-est**) rauco. ∼**ness** *n.* raucedine *f.*

hoax /həʊks/ *n.* burla *f.* —*v.t.* burlare. ∼**er** /'həʊksə(r)/ burlone, a *m.*, *f.*

hob /hɒb/ *n.* piastra (con fornelli) *f.*

hobble /'hɒbl/ *v.i.* zoppicare.

hobby /'hɒbɪ/ *n.* hobby *m. invar.*; passatempo *m.* ∼**-horse** *n.* cavalluccio di legno *m.*; (*fixation*) pallino *m.*

hobnail /'hɒbneɪl/ *n.* chiodo per scarponi *m.*

hob-nob /'hɒbnɒb/ *v.i.* (*p.t.*- **nobbed**) ∼ **with the great** frequentare persone influenti.

hock /hɒk/ *n.* vino del Reno *m.*

hockey /'hɒkɪ/ *n.* hockey *m.*

hoe /həʊ/ *n.* zappa *f.* —*v.t.* (*pres. p.* **hoeing**) zappare.

hog /hɒg/ *n.* maiale *m.*; (*fam.*, *greedy*) ingordo, a *m.*, *f.* —*v.t.* (*p.p.* **hogged**) (*fam.*) accaparrarsi.

hoist /hɔɪst/ *v.t.* innalzare; (*anchor*) levare. —*n.* (*mech.*) montacarichi *m. invar.*; (*fam.*, *push*) spinta (in alto) *f.*

hold[1] /həʊld/ *v.t./i.* (*p.t.* **held**) tenere; (*contain*) contenere; (*interest*) tenere alto; (*breath*) trattenere; (*believe*) mantenere; (*weather*) durare. —*n.* presa *f.*; (*influence*) ascendente *m.* **get** ∼ **of** afferrare; (*fig.*) trovare. ∼ **back** *v.t.* trattenere; *v.i.* esitare. ∼ **on** (*fam.*) attendere. ∼ **on to** aggrapparsi a. ∼ **one's tongue** tacere. ∼ **out** (*give*)

dare; (*resist*) resistere. ∼ **over** rimandare. ∼ **up** (*hinder*) ostruire; (*attack*) assalire. ∼**-up** *n.* (*delay*) ritardo *m.*; (*attack*) rapina a mano armata *f.* ∼ **with** (*sl.*) approvare. ∼**er** *n.* possessore *m.*; (*of post*) titolare *m.*/*f.*; (*container*) astuccio *m.*

hold[2] /həʊld/ *n.* (*of ship*) stiva *f.*

holdall /'həʊldɔːl/ *n.* sacca *f.*

holding /'həʊldɪŋ/ *n.* (*land*) podere *m.*; (*comm.*) azioni *m.pl.*

hole /həʊl/ *n.* buco *m.* —*v.t.* bucare.

holiday /'hɒlədeɪ/ *n.* vacanza *f.*, ferie *f.pl.* —*v.i.* andare in vacanza. ∼ **maker** *n.* villeggiante *m.*/*f.*

holiness /'həʊlɪnɪs/ *n.* santità *f.*

Holland /'hɒlənd/ *n.* Olanda *f.*

hollow /'hɒləʊ/ *a.* vuoto, cavo. —*n.* cavità *f.* —*v.t.* ∼ **out** scavare.

holly /'hɒlɪ/ *n.* agrifoglio *m.* ∼**hock** *n.* malvone *m.*

holocaust /'hɒləkɔːst/ *n.* olocausto *m.*

holster /'həʊlstə(r)/ *n.* fondina *f.*

holy /'həʊlɪ/ *a.* (**-ier**, **-iest**) santo, sacro; (*water*) benedetto. **H**∼ **Ghost** *n.* Spirito Santo *m.*

homage /'hɒmɪdʒ/ *n.* omaggio *m.*

home /həʊm/ *n.* casa *f.*; (*institution*) ospizio *m.*; (*native land*) terra natia *f.* —*a.* familiare; (*pol.*) nazionale. —*adv.* a casa. **H**∼ **Counties** *n.pl.* regioni intorno a Londra *m.pl.* **H**∼ **Office** *n.* Ministero degli Interni *m.* **H**∼ **Secretary** *n.* Ministro degli Interni *m.* ∼ **town** *n.* città natia *f.* ∼ **truth** *n.* verità amara *f.* ∼**less** *a.* senza tetto.

homeland /'həʊmlænd/ *n.* patria *f.*

homely /'həʊmlɪ/ *a.* (**-ier**, **-iest**) semplice; (*Amer.*) bruttino.

homesick /'həʊmsɪk/ *a.* **be** ∼ **(for)** avere nostalgia (di).

homeward /'həʊmwəd/ *a.* di ritorno. —*adv.* verso casa.

homework /'həʊmwɜːk/ *n.* compiti *m.pl.*

homicide /'hɒmɪsaɪd/ *n.* omicidio *m.*; (*person*) omicida *m.*/*f.*

homoeopath|ic /həʊmɪə'pæθɪk/ *a.* omeopatico. ∼**y** /-'ɒpəθɪ/ *n.* omeopatia *f.*

homogeneous /hɒmə'dʒiːnɪəs/ *a.* omogeneo.

homosexual /hɒmə'sekʃʊəl/ *a.* & *n.* omosessuale *m.*/*f.*

hone /həʊn/ *v.t.* affilare.

honest /'ɒnɪst/ *a.* onesto; (*frank*)

aperto. **~ly** adv. onestamente. **~y** n.
onestà f.

honey /'hʌnɪ/ n. (pl. **-eys**) miele m.;
(darling, fam.) tesoro m.

honeycomb /'hʌnɪkəʊm/ n. favo m.

honeymoon /'hʌnɪmuːn/ n. luna di
miele f.

honeysuckle /'hʌnɪsʌkl/ n. caprifoglio
m.

honk /hɒŋk/ v.i. suonare il clacson.

honorary /'ɒnərərɪ/ a. onorario.

honour /'ɒnə(r)/ n. onore m. —v.t. ono-
rare. **~able** a. onorevole. **~s degree**
n. laurea con lode f.

hood /hʊd/ n. cappuccio m.; (of car)
cofano m.; (of chimney) cappa f.

hoodlum /'huːdləm/ n. giovinastro m.

hoodwink /'hʊdwɪŋk/ v.t. infinoc-
chiare.

hoof /huːf/ n. (pl. **hooves**) zoccolo m.

hook /hʊk/ n. gancio m.; (for crochet)
uncinetto m.; (for fishing) amo m.
—v.t./i. agganciare, agganciarsi. **by
~ or by crook** a qualunque costo. **~
it** (sl.) squagliarsela. **off the ~** libe-
rato dall'angoscia; (telephone) stac-
cato.

hooked /hʊkt/ a. adunco. **~ on** (sl.)
dedito a.

hookey /'hʊkɪ/ n. **play ~** (Amer. sl.)
marinare la scuola.

hooligan /'huːlɪgən/ n. teppista m.
~ism /-ɪzəm/ n. teppismo m.

hoop /huːp/ n. cerchio m.

hooray /'huːreɪ/ int. & n. = **hurrah**.

hoot /huːt/ n. colpo di clacson m.
—v.t./i. suonare il clacson; (jeer) fischiare. **~er** n. clacson m. invar.; (of
factory) sirena f.

Hoover /'huːvə(r)/ n. (P.) aspirapolvere m. invar. —v.t. passare l'aspirapolvere.

hop[1] /hɒp/ (p.t. **hopped**) saltellare.
—n. saltello m.; (flight) tappa f.
caught on the ~ preso alla sprovvista. **~ in** (fam.) saltar dentro. **~ it!**
(sl.) vattene! **~ out** (fam.) uscire.

hop[2] /hɒp/ n. (plant) luppolo m.

hope /həʊp/ n. speranza f. —v.t./i. spe-
rare. **~ful** a. pieno di speranza;
(promising) promettente. **~fully** adv.
se tutto va bene. **~less** a. senza
speranza; (incompetent) incapace.
~lessness n. disperazione f.

hopscotch /'hɒpskɒtʃ/ n. gioco della
campana m.

horde /hɔːd/ n. orda f.

horizon /hə'raɪzn/ n. orizzonte m.

horizontal /hɒrɪ'zɒntl/ a. orizzontale.
~ly adv. orizzontalmente.

hormone /'hɔːməʊn/ n. ormone m.

horn /hɔːn/ n. corno m.; (of car) clacson m. invar. **~ed** a. cornuto. **~y** a.
calloso.

hornet /'hɔːnɪt/ n. calabrone m.

horoscope /'hɒrəskəʊp/ n. oroscopo
m.

horrible /'hɒrəbl/ a. orribile.

horrid /'hɒrɪd/ a. orrendo.

horrific /hə'rɪfɪk/ a. raccapricciante.

horr|or /'hɒrə(r)/ n. orrore m. **~or
film** film dell'orrore m. **~ify** v.t. far
inorridire.

hors-d'œuvre /ɔː'dɜːvr/ n. antipasto
m.

horse /hɔːs/ n. cavallo m. **~-chestnut**
n. ippocastano m. **~-racing** n. ippica
f. **~-radish** n. rafano m. **~ sense**
(fam.) buon senso m.

horseback /'hɔːsbæk/ n. **on ~** a cavallo.

horseplay /'hɔːspleɪ/ n. scherzo grossolano m.

horsepower /'hɔːspaʊə(r)/ n. cavallo
(vapore) m.

horseshoe /'hɔːsʃuː/ n. ferro di cavallo
m.

horsy /'hɔːsɪ/ a. appassionato di
cavalli.

horticultur|e /'hɔːtɪkʌltʃə(r)/ n. orti-
coltura f. **~al** /-'kʌltʃərəl/ a. di orticol-
tura.

hose /həʊz/ n. (pipe) tubo (flessibile)
m. —v.t. innaffiare.

hosiery /'həʊzɪərɪ/ n. calze f./pl.

hospice /'hɒspɪs/ n. ospizio m.

hospit|able /hɒ'spɪtəbl/ a. ospitale.
~ably adv. con ospitalità. **~ality**
/-'tælətɪ/ n. ospitalità f.

hospital /'hɒspɪtl/ n. ospedale m.

host[1] /həʊst/ n. **a ~ of** una moltitudine
di.

host[2] /həʊst/ n. ospite m. **~ess** n.
padrona di casa f.; (aeron.) hostess f.
invar.

host[3] /həʊst/ n. (relig.) ostia f.

hostage /'hɒstɪdʒ/ n. ostaggio m.

hostel /'hɒstl/ n. ostello m.

hostil|e /'hɒstaɪl/ a. ostile. **~ity**
/hɒ'stɪlətɪ/ n. ostilità f.

hot /hɒt/ a. (**hotter, hottest**) caldo,
ardente; (culin.) piccante. **be or feel
~** aver caldo. **it is ~** fa caldo. —v.t.
(p.t. **hotted**) **~ up** riscaldare. **~ dog**
n. panino imbottito con salsiccia m.

~-water bottle *n.* borsa dell'acqua calda *f.* in ~ water (*fam.*) nei guai.

hotbed /'hɒtbed/ *n.* focolaio *m.*

hotchpotch /'hɒtʃpɒtʃ/ *n.* miscuglio *m.*

hotel /həʊ'tel/ *n.* albergo *m.* ~ier /həʊ'telɪə(r)/ *n.* alberga|tore, -trice *m., f.*

hothead /'hɒthed/ *n.* persona impetuosa *f.* ~ed *a.* impetuoso.

hothouse /'hɒthaʊs/ *n.* serra *f.*

hotplate /'hɒtpleɪt/ *n.* piastra riscaldante *f.*

hound /haʊnd/ *n.* cane da caccia *m.* —*v.t.* cacciare; (*fig.*) perseguitare.

hour /'aʊə(r)/ *n.* ora *f.* ~ly *a.* ad ogni ora; *adv.* ogni ora.

house¹ /haʊs/ *n.* casa *f.*; (*pol.*) Camera *f.*; (*theatr.*) sala *f.* ~-proud *a.* orglioso della propria casa. ~-warming *n.* inaugurazione della casa *f.*

house² /haʊz/ *v.t.* alloggiare; (*store*) riporre; (*mech.*) incastrare.

houseboat /'haʊsbəʊt/ *n.* casa galleggiante *f.*

housebreaking /'haʊsbreɪkɪŋ/ *n.* furto con scasso *m.*

household /'haʊshəʊld/ *n.* casa, famiglia *f.* ~er *n.* capo di famiglia *m.*

housekeep|er /'haʊski:pə(r)/ *n.* governante di casa *f.* ~ing *n.* governo della casa *m.*

housemaid /'haʊsmeɪd/ *n.* donna di servizio *f.*

housewife /'haʊswaɪf/ *n.* (*pl.* -wives) casalinga *f.*

housework /'haʊswɜ:k/ *n.* lavoro domestico *m.*

housing /'haʊzɪŋ/ *n.* alloggio *m.* ~ estate zona residenziale *f.*

hovel /'hɒvl/ *n.* tugurio *m.*

hover /'hɒvə(r)/ *v.i.* librarsi; (*linger*) indugiare.

hovercraft /'hɒvəkrɑːft/ *n.* aeronave *f.*

how /haʊ/ *adv.* come. ~ about che ne diresti. ~ do you do? (*in introduction*) molto lieto. ~ long quanto tempo. ~ many quanti. ~ much quanto. ~ often ogni quanto. and ~! eccome!

however /haʊ'evə(r)/ *adv.* per quanto; (*nevertheless*) comunque.

howl /haʊl/ *n.* ululato *m.* —*v.i.* ululare.

howler /'haʊlə(r)/ *n.* (*fam.*) strafalcione *m.*

HP *abbr. see* hire-purchase.

hub /hʌb/ *n.* mozzo *m.*; (*fig.*) centro *m.*

hubbub /'hʌbʌb/ *n.* baccano *m.*

huddle /'hʌdl/ *v.i.* rannicchiarsi.

hue¹ /hju:/ *n.* colore *m.*

hue² /hju:/ *n.* ~ and cry clamore *m.*

huff /hʌf/ *n.* in a ~ imbronciato.

hug /hʌg/ *v.t.* (*p.t.* hugged) abbracciare; (*keep close to*) tenersi vicino a. —*n.* abbraccio *m.*

huge /hju:dʒ/ *a.* enorme.

hulk /hʌlk/ *n.* carcassa *f.*; (*person*) omaccione *m.* ~ing *a.* (*fam.*) grosso.

hull /hʌl/ *n.* (*of ship*) scafo *m.*

hullabaloo /hʌləbə'lu:/ *n.* baccano *m.*

hullo /hə'ləʊ/ *int.* & *n.* = hallo.

hum /hʌm/ *v.t./i.* (*p.t.* hummed) canticchiare; (*of insect, engine*) ronzare; (*fig.*) fervere (di attività). —*n.* ronzio *m.* ~ and haw esitare.

human /'hju:mən/ *a.* umano. —*n.* essere umano *m.* ~ism /-nɪzəm/ *n.* umanesimo *m.* ~itarian /-mænɪ'teərɪən/ *a.* & *n.* umanitario, a *m., f.*

humane /hju:'meɪn/ *a.* benevolo.

humanit|y /hju:'mænətɪ/ *n.* umanità *f.* ~ies *n.pl.* (*univ.*) dottrine umanistiche *f.pl.*

humbl|e /hʌmbl/ *a.* (-er, -est) umile. —*v.t.* umiliare. ~y *adv.* umilmente.

humbug /'hʌmbʌg/ *n.* inganno *m.*; (*person*) imbroglione, a *m., f.*

humdrum /'hʌmdrʌm/ *a.* noioso.

humid /'hju:mɪd/ *a.* umido. ~ity /-'mɪdətɪ/ *n.* umidità *f.*

humidifier /hju:'mɪdɪfaɪə(r)/ *n.* umidificatore *m.*

humiliat|e /hju:'mɪlɪeɪt/ *v.t.* umiliare. ~ion /-'eɪʃn/ *n.* umiliazione *f.*

humility /hju:'mɪlətɪ/ *n.* umiltà *f.*

humorist /'hju:mərɪst/ *n.* umorista *m./f.*

hum|our /'hju:mə(r)/ *n.* umorismo *m.*; (*state of mind*) umore *m.* —*v.t.* compiacere. ~orous *a.* umoristico. ~orously *adv.* con spirito.

hump /hʌmp/ *n.* protuberanza *f.*; (*of the spine*) gobba *f.* the ~ (*sl.*) malumore *m.* —*v.t.* inarcare; (*hoist up*) portare sulle spalle.

hunch /hʌntʃ/ *v.t.* curvare. —*n.* gobba *f.*; (*intuition*) intuizione *f.* ~ed up incurvato.

hunchback /'hʌntʃbæk/ *n.* gobbo, a *m., f.*

hundred /'hʌndrəd/ *a.* & *n.* cento *m.* ~s of centinaia di. ~fold *a.* & *n.* centuplo *m.*; *adv.* cento volte. ~th *a.* & *n.* centesimo *m.*

hundredweight /'hʌndrədweɪt/ n. cinquanta chili m.

hung /hʌŋ/ see **hang.**

Hungar|y /'hʌŋgərɪ/ n. Ungheria f. ~**ian** /-'geərɪən/ a. & n. ungherese m.|f.

hunger /'hʌŋgə(r)/ n. fame f. —v.i. ~ **for** aver fame di. ~-**strike** n. sciopero della fame m.

hungr|y /'hʌŋgrɪ/ a. (-ier, -iest) affamato. **be** ~**y** aver fame. ~**ily** adv. con appetito.

hunk /hʌŋk/ n. (grosso) pezzo m.

hunt /hʌnt/ v.t./i. andare a caccia. —n. caccia f. ~ **for** cercare. ~**er** n. cacciatore m. ~**ing** n. caccia f.

hurdle /'hɜːdl/ n. ostacolo m.

hurdy-gurdy /'hɜːdɪgɜːdɪ/ n. organetto m.

hurl /hɜːl/ v.t. scagliare.

hurly-burly /'hɜːlɪbɜːlɪ/ n. subbuglio m.

hurrah, hurray /hʊ'rɑː, hʊ'reɪ/ int. & n. urrà m.

hurricane /'hʌrɪkən/ n. uragano m.

hurried /'hʌrɪd/ a. affrettato. ~**ly** adv. in fretta.

hurry /'hʌrɪ/ v.t./i. affrettare, affrettarsi. —n. fretta f. **be in a** ~ aver fretta.

hurt /hɜːt/ v.t./i. (p.t. hurt) far male (a); (injure, offend) ferire. —n. male m.; (fig.) ferita f. ~**ful** a. doloroso; (fig.) offensivo.

hurtle /'hɜːtl/ v.t./i. lanciare, lanciarsi.

husband /'hʌzbənd/ n. marito m.

hush /hʌʃ/ v.t. far tacere. —n. silenzio m. ~-**hush** a. (fam.) segretissimo. ~ **up** mettere a tacere.

husk /hʌsk/ n. guscio m.

husky /'hʌskɪ/ a. (-ier, -iest) rauco.

hussy /'hʌsɪ/ n. sfacciatella f.

hustle /'hʌsl/ v.t./i. affrettare, affrettarsi. —n. attività incessante f. ~ **and bustle** n. trambusto m.

hut /hʌt/ n. capanna f.

hutch /hʌtʃ/ n. conigliera f.

hyacinth /'haɪəsɪnθ/ n. giacinto m.

hybrid /'haɪbrɪd/ a. & n. ibrido m.

hydrangea /haɪ'dreɪndʒə/ n. ortensia f.

hydrant /'haɪdrənt/ n. idrante m.

hydraulic /haɪ'drɔːlɪk/ a. idraulico.

hydroelectric /haɪdrəʊɪ'lektrɪk/ a. idroelettrico.

hydrofoil /'haɪdrəfɔɪl/ n. aliscafo m.

hydrogen /'haɪdrədʒən/ n. idrogeno m. ~ **bomb** n. bomba all'idrogeno f. ~ **peroxide** n. acqua ossigenata f.

hyena /haɪ'iːnə/ n. iena f.

hygien|e /'haɪdʒiːn/ n. igiene m. ~**ist** /-'dʒiːnɪst/ n. igienista m.|f.

hygienic /haɪ'dʒiːnɪk/ a. igienico.

hymn /hɪm/ n. inno m.

hyper- /'haɪpə(r)/ pref. iper-.

hypermarket /'haɪpəmɑːkɪt/ n. complesso di supermercati m.

hyphen /'haɪfn/ n. lineetta f. ~**ate** v.t. unire con lineetta.

hypno|sis /hɪp'nəʊsɪs/ n. ipnosi f. ~**tic** /-'nɒtɪk/ a. ipnotico.

hypnot|ize /'hɪpnətaɪz/ v.t. ipnotizzare. ~**ism** n. ipnotismo m. ~**ist** n. ipnotizzatore m.

hypochondriac /haɪpə'kɒndrɪæk/ n. ipocondriaco, a m., f.

hypocri|sy /hɪ'pɒkrəsɪ/ n. ipocrisia f. ~**te** /'hɪpəkrɪt/ n. ipocrita m.|f. ~**tical** /-'krɪtɪkl/ a. ipocrita.

hypodermic /haɪpə'dɜːmɪk/ a. ipodermico. —n. siringa ipodermica f.

hypothe|sis /haɪ'pɒθəsɪs/ n. (pl. -theses /-siːz/) ipotesi f. ~**tical** /-ə'θetɪkl/ a. ipotetico.

hysteri|a /hɪs'tɪərɪə/ n. isterismo m. ~**cal** /-'terɪkl/ a. isterico. ~**cs** /-'terɪks/ n.pl. attacco isterico m.

I

I /aɪ/ *pron.* io.

ice /aɪs/ *n.* ghiaccio *m.* —*v.t.* ghiacciare; (*culin.*) candire. ~**-cream** *n.* gelato *m.* ~ **hockey** *n.* hockey su ghiaccio *m.* ~ **lolly** *n.* ghiacciolo *m.* ~ **rink** *n.* pista di pattinaggio *f.*

iceberg /'aɪsbɜːg/ *n.* iceberg *m. invar.*; (*fig.*) pezzo di ghiaccio *m.*

Iceland /'aɪslənd/ *n.* Islanda *f.* ~**er** *n.* islandese *m./f.* ~**ic** /-'lændɪk/ *a.* & *n.* (*lang.*) islandese *m.*

icicle /'aɪsɪkl/ *n.* ghiacciolo *m.*

icing /'aɪsɪŋ/ *n.* glassa *f.*

icon /'aɪkɒn/ *n.* icona *f.*

ic|y /'aɪsɪ/ *a.* (**-ier, -iest**) gelido. ~**ily** *adv.* gelidamente.

idea /aɪ'dɪə/ *n.* idea *f.*; (*impression*) impressione *f.*

ideal /aɪ'dɪəl/ *a.* & *n.* ideale *m.* ~**ize** *v.t.* idealizzare. ~**ly** *adv.* idealmente.

idealis|t /aɪ'dɪəlɪst/ *n.* idealista *m./f.* ~**m** /-zəm/ *n.* idealismo *m.* ~**tic** /-'lɪstɪk/ *a.* idealistico.

identical /aɪ'dentɪkl/ *a.* identico.

identif|y /aɪ'dentɪfaɪ/ *v.t.* identificare. —*v.i.* ~ **with** identificarsi con. ~**ication** /-ɪ'keɪʃn/ *n.* identificazione *f.*

identikit /aɪ'dentɪkɪt/ *n.* identikit *m. invar.*

identity /aɪ'dentɪtɪ/ *n.* identità *f.*

ideolog|y /aɪdɪ'ɒlədʒɪ/ *n.* ideologia *f.* ~**ical** /-'lɒdʒɪkl/ *a.* ideologico. ~**ist** *n.* ideologo, a *m., f.*

idiocy /'ɪdɪəsɪ/ *n.* idiozia *f.*

idiom /'ɪdɪəm/ *n.* idioma *m.* ~**atic** /-'mætɪk/ *a.* idiomatico.

idiosyncrasy /ɪdɪə'sɪŋkrəsɪ/ *n.* idiosincrasia *f.*

idiot /'ɪdɪət/ *n.* idiota *m./f.* ~**ic** /-'ɒtɪk/ *a.* idiota.

idl|e /'aɪdl/ *a.* (**-er, -est**) ozioso; (*lazy*) pigro; (*vain*) inutile; (*mech.*) fermo. —*v.t./i.* oziare; (*mech.*) girare a vuoto. ~**eness** *n.* ozio *m.* ~**er** /-ə(r)/ *n.* ozioso, a *m., f.* ~**y** *adv.* oziosamente.

idol /'aɪdl/ *n.* idolo *m.* ~**atry** /-'ɒlətrɪ/ *n.* idolatria *f.* ~**ize** /-əlaɪz/ *v.t.* idolatrare.

idyllic /ɪ'dɪlɪk/ *a.* idillico.

i.e. *abbr.* (*of* id est) cioè.

if /ɪf/ *conj.* se.

igloo /'ɪgluː/ *n.* igloo *m. invar.*

ignite /ɪg'naɪt/ *v.t./i.* dar fuoco a, prender fuoco.

ignition /ɪg'nɪʃn/ *n.* ignizione *f.*

ignoble /ɪg'nəʊbl/ *a.* ignobile.

ignomin|y /'ɪgnəmɪnɪ/ *n.* ignominia *f.* ~**ious** /-'mɪnɪəs/ *a.* infamante.

ignoramus /ɪgnə'reɪməs/ *n.* (*pl.* **-muses**) ignorante *m./f.*

ignoran|t /'ɪgnərənt/ *a.* ignorante; (*lacking knowledge*) ignaro. ~**ce** *n.* ignoranza *f.* ~**tly** *adv.* con ignoranza.

ignore /ɪg'nɔː(r)/ *v.t.* ignorare.

ilk /ɪlk/ *n.* (*fam.*) **of that** ~ dello stesso genere.

ill /ɪl/ *a.* ammalato; (*bad*) cattivo. —*adv.* male. —*n.* male *m.* ~**-advised** *a.* malaccorto. ~ **at ease** *a.* a disagio. ~**-bred** *a.* maleducato. ~**gotten** *a.* illecito. ~**-natured** *a.* di cattivo carattere. ~**-starred** *a.* sfortunato. ~**-treat** *v.t.* maltrattare. ~ **will** *n.* malanimo *m.*

illegal /ɪ'liːgl/ *a.* illegale. ~**ly** *adv.* illegalmente.

illegibl|e /ɪ'ledʒəbl/ *a.* illeggibile. ~**y** *adv.* in modo illeggibile.

illegitima|te /ɪlɪ'dʒɪtɪmət/ *a.* illegittimo. ~**cy** *n.* illegittimità *f.*

illicit /ɪ'lɪsɪt/ *a.* illecito. ~**ly** *adv.* illecitamente.

illitera|te /ɪ'lɪtərət/ *a.* & *n.* analfabeta *m./f.* ~**cy** *n.* analfabetismo *m.*

illness /'ɪlnɪs/ *n.* malattia *f.*

illogical /ɪ'lɒdʒɪkl/ *a.* illogico.

illuminat|e /ɪ'ljuːmɪneɪt/ *v.t.* illuminare. ~**ion** /-'neɪʃn/ *n.* illuminazione *f.*

illusion /ɪ'luːʒn/ *n.* illusione *f.* ~**ist** *n.* illusionista *m./f.*

illusory /ɪ'luːsərɪ/ *a.* illusorio.

illustrat|e /'ɪləstreɪt/ *v.t.* illustrare. ~**ion** /-'streɪʃn/ *n.* illustrazione *f.* ~**ive** /-ətɪv/ *a.* illustrativo.

illustrious /ɪ'lʌstrɪəs/ *a.* illustre.

image /'ɪmɪdʒ/ *n.* immagine *f.* ~**ry** /-ərɪ/ *n.* immagini *f.pl.*

imaginati|on /ɪmædʒɪ'neɪʃn/ *n.* immaginazione *f.* ~**ve** /ɪ'mædʒɪnətɪv/ *a.* pieno di fantasia.

imagin|e /ɪ'mædʒɪn/ *v.t.* immaginare. ~**able** *a.* immaginabile. ~**ary** *a.* immaginario.

imbalance /ɪmˈbæləns/ n. squilibrio m.

imbecile /ˈɪmbəsiːl/ a. & n. imbecille m./f.

imbibe /ɪmˈbaɪb/ v.t. assorbire.

imbroglio /ɪmˈbrəʊlɪəʊ/ n. (pl. -os) pasticcio m.

imbue /ɪmˈbjuː/ v.t. impregnare.

imitat|e /ˈɪmɪteɪt/ v.t. imitare. ~ion /-ˈteɪʃn/ n. imitazione f. ~ive a. imitativo. ~or n. imita|tore, -trice m., f.

immaculate /ɪˈmækjʊlət/ a. immacolato. ~ly adv. immacolatamente.

immaterial /ɪməˈtɪərɪəl/ a. immateriale; (fig.) irrilevante.

immatur|e /ɪməˈtjʊə(r)/ a. immaturo. ~ity n. immaturità f.

immeasurabl|e /ɪˈmeʒərəbl/ a. incommensurabile. ~y adv. incommensurabilmente.

immediate /ɪˈmiːdɪət/ a. immediato. ~ly adv. immediatamente; conj. (non) appena.

immemorial /ɪmɪˈmɔːrɪəl/ a. immemorabile.

immens|e /ɪˈmens/ a. immenso. ~ely adv. immensamente. ~ity n. immensità f.

immers|e /ɪˈmɜːs/ v.t. immergere. ~ion /-ʃn/ n. immersione f. ~ion heater n. riscaldatore ad immersione m.

immigra|te /ˈɪmɪgreɪt/ v.i. immigrare. ~nt a. & n. immigrante m./f. ~tion /-ˈgreɪʃn/ n. immigrazione f.

imminen|t /ˈɪmɪnənt/ a. imminente. ~ce n. imminenza f.

immobile /ɪˈməʊbaɪl/ a. immobile.

immobiliz|e /ɪˈməʊbɪlaɪz/ v.t. immobilizzare. ~ation /-ˈzeɪʃn/ n. immobilizzazione f.

immoderate /ɪˈmɒdərət/ a. smodato. ~ly adv. smoderatamente.

immodest /ɪˈmɒdɪst/ a. immodesto.

immoral /ɪˈmɒrəl/ a. immorale. ~ly adv. immoralmente. ~ity /ɪməˈrælətɪ/ n. immoralità f.

immortal /ɪˈmɔːtl/ a. immortale. ~ity /-ˈtælətɪ/ n. immortalità f. ~ize v.t. immortalare.

immovabl|e /ɪˈmuːvəbl/ a. irremovibile. ~y adv. irremovibilmente.

immun|e /ɪˈmjuːn/ a. immune. ~ity n. immunità f.

immuniz|e /ˈɪmjʊnaɪz/ v.t. immunizzare. ~ation /-ˈzeɪʃn/ n. immunizzazione f.

imp /ɪmp/ n. diavoletto m.; (child) monello, a m., f.

impact /ˈɪmpækt/ n. urto m.; (fig.) forte effetto m.

impair /ɪmˈpeə(r)/ v.t. danneggiare. ~ment n. menomazione f.

impale /ɪmˈpeɪl/ v.t. impalare. ~ment n. impalamento m.

impalpable /ɪmˈpælpəbl/ a. impalpabile.

impart /ɪmˈpɑːt/ v.t. impartire.

impartial /ɪmˈpɑːʃl/ a. imparziale. ~ity /-ˈrælətɪ/ n. imparzialità f.

impassable /ɪmˈpɑːsəbl/ a. impraticabile.

impasse /æmˈpɑːs/ n. vicolo cieco m.

impassioned /ɪmˈpæʃnd/ a. appassionato.

impassive /ɪmˈpæsɪv/ a. impassibile.

impatien|t /ɪmˈpeɪʃənt/ a. impaziente. ~ce n. impazienza f. ~tly adv. impazientemente.

impeach /ɪmˈpiːtʃ/ v.t. accusare; (pol.) incriminare. ~ment n. accusa f.; incriminazione f.

impeccable /ɪmˈpekəbl/ a. impeccabile.

impecunious /ɪmprˈkjuːnjəs/ a. indigente.

impede /ɪmˈpiːd/ v.t. impedire.

impediment /ɪmˈpedɪmənt/ n. impedimento m.

impel /ɪmˈpel/ v.t. (p.t. impelled) costringere.

impending /ɪmˈpendɪŋ/ a. imminente.

impenetrable /ɪmˈpenɪtrəbl/ a. impenetrabile.

impenitent /ɪmˈpenɪtənt/ a. impenitente.

imperative /ɪmˈperətɪv/ a. & n. imperativo m.

imperceptibl|e /ɪmpəˈseptəbl/ a. impercettibile.

imperfect /ɪmˈpɜːfɪkt/ a. imperfetto; (faulty) difettoso. ~ion /-əˈfekʃn/ n. imperfezione f.

imperial /ɪmˈpɪərɪəl/ a. imperiale; (measure) legale. ~ism n. imperialismo m. ~ist n. imperialista m./f.

imperil /ɪmˈperəl/ v.t. (p.t. imperilled) mettere in pericolo.

imperious /ɪmˈpɪərɪəs/ a. imperioso.

impermanent /ɪmˈpɜːmənənt/ a. temporaneo.

impersonal /ɪmˈpɜːsənl/ a. impersonale. ~ly adv. impersonalmente.

impersonat|e /ɪmˈpɜːsəneɪt/ v.t.

impersonare; (*theatr.*) interpretare. **~or** /-ə(r)/ *n.* impersona|tore, -trice *m.*, *f.*

impertinen|t /ɪm'pɜ:tɪmənt/ *a.* impertinente. **~ce** *n.* impertinenza *f.*

imperturbable /ɪmpə'tɜ:bəbl/ *a.* imperturbabile.

impervious /ɪm'pɜ:vjəs/ *a.* impervio.

impetuous /ɪm'petjʊəs/ *a.* impetuoso.

impetus /'ɪmpɪtəs/ *n.* impeto *m.*

impinge /ɪm'pɪndʒ/ *v.i.* **~ on** (*person*) colpire; (*rights*) nuocere.

impish /'ɪmpɪʃ/ *a.* birichino.

implacable /ɪm'plækəbl/ *a.* implacabile.

implant[1] /ɪm'plɑ:nt/ *v.t.* piantare; (*fig.*) inculcare.

implant[2] /'ɪmplɑ:nt/ *n.* trapianto *m.*

implausible /ɪm'plɔ:zɪbl/ *a.* improbabile.

implement[1] /'ɪmplɪmənt/ *n.* attrezzo *m.*

implement[2] /'ɪmplɪmənt/ *v.t.* effettuare.

implicat|e /'ɪmplɪkeɪt/ *v.t.* implicare. **~ion** /-'keɪʃn/ *n.* implicazione *f.*

implicit /ɪm'plɪsɪt/ *a.* implicito; (*absolute*) assoluto. **~ly** *adv.* implicitamente.

implore /ɪm'plɔ:(r)/ *v.t.* implorare.

imply /ɪm'plaɪ/ *v.t.* implicare; (*insinuate*) insinuare.

impolite /ɪmpə'laɪt/ *a.* sgarbato.

impolitic /ɪm'pɒlɪtɪk/ *a.* inopportuno.

imponderable /ɪm'pɒndərəbl/ *a.* imponderabile.

import[1] /ɪm'pɔ:t/ *v.t.* importare. **~ation** /-'teɪʃn/ *n.* importazione *f.* **~er** *n.* importa|tore, -trice *m.*, *f.*

import[2] /'ɪmpɔ:t/ *n.* importazione *f.*; (*value*) importanza *f.*

importan|t /ɪm'pɔ:tnt/ *a.* importante. **~ce** *n.* importanza *f.*

importunate /ɪm'pɔ:tjʊnət/ *a.* importuno.

impos|e /ɪm'pəʊz/ *v.t.*/*i.* imporre, imporsi. **~e on** abusare di. **~ition** /-ə'zɪʃn/ *n.* imposizione *f.*

imposing /ɪm'pəʊzɪŋ/ *a.* imponente.

impossib|le /ɪm'pɒsəbl/ *a.* impossibile. **~ility** /-'bɪlətɪ/ *n.* impossibilità *f.* **~ly** *adv.* impossibilmente.

impost|or /ɪm'pɒstə(r)/ *n.* impostore *m.*

impoten|t /'ɪmpətənt/ *a.* impotente. **~ce** *n.* impotenza *f.*

impound /ɪm'paʊnd/ *v.t.* confiscare.

impoverish /ɪm'pɒvərɪʃ/ *v.t.* impoverire. **~ment** *n.* impoverimento *m.*

impracticab|le /ɪm'præktɪkəbl/ *a.* impraticabile.

impractical /ɪm'præktɪkl/ *a.* non pratico.

imprecis|e /ɪmprɪ'saɪs/ *a.* impreciso. **~ion** /-'sɪʒn/ *n.* imprecisione *f.*

impregnab|le /ɪm'pregnəbl/ *a.* imprendibile.

impregnate /'ɪmpregneɪt/ *v.t.* impregnare (**with,** di).

impresario /ɪmpre'sɑ:rɪəʊ/ *n.* (*pl.* -os) impresario *m.*

impress /ɪm'pres/ *v.t.* imprimere; (*fig.*) colpire.

impressi|on /ɪm'preʃn/ *n.* impressione *f.* **~onable** *a.* impressionabile. **~ve** *a.* imponente.

impressionis|m /ɪm'preʃnɪzəm/ *n.* impressionismo *m.* **~t** *n.* impressionista *m.*/*f.*

imprint[1] /'ɪmprɪnt/ *n.* impressione *f.*

imprint[2] /ɪm'prɪnt/ *v.t.* imprimere.

imprison /ɪm'prɪzn/ *v.t.* imprigionare. **~ment** *n.* imprigionamento *m.*

improbab|le /ɪm'prɒbəbl/ *a.* improbabile; (*incredible*) inverosimile. **~ility** /-'bɪlətɪ/ *n.* improbabilità *f.*; inverosimiglianza *f.*

impromptu /ɪm'prɒmptju:/ *a.* estemporaneo. *—adv.* in modo improvvisato. *—n.* improvvisazione *f.*

improp|er /ɪm'prɒpə(r)/ *a.* disadatto; (*indecent, incorrect*) scorretto. **~erly** *adv.* scorrettamente. **~riety** /-ə'praɪətɪ/ *n.* scorrettezza *f.*

improve /ɪm'pru:v/ *v.t.*/*i.* migliorare. **~ (up)on** perfezionare. **~ment** *n.* miglioramento *m.*

improviden|t /ɪm'prɒvɪdənt/ *a.* imprevidente. **~ce** *n.* imprevidenza *f.*

improvis|e /'ɪmprəvaɪz/ *v.t.* improvvisare. **~ation** /-'zeɪʃn/ *n.* improvvisazione *f.*

impruden|t /ɪm'pru:dənt/ *a.* imprudente. **~ce** *n.* imprudenza *f.*

impuden|t /'ɪmpjʊdənt/ *a.* sfrontato. **~ce** *n.* sfrontatezza *f.*

impugn /ɪm'pju:n/ *v.t.* contestare.

impuls|e /'ɪmpʌls/ *n.* impulso *m.* **~ive** *a.* impulsivo. **~ively** *adv.* impulsivamente.

impunity /ɪm'pju:nətɪ/ *n.* impunità *f.*

impur|e /ɪm'pjʊə(r)/ *a.* impuro. **~ity** *n.* impurità *f.*

imput|e /ɪm'pju:t/ *v.t.* imputare. **~ation** /-'teɪʃn/ *n.* imputazione *f.*

in /ɪn/ *prep.* in, a, fra. —*adv.* dentro; (*at home*) a casa; (*in fashion*) di moda. —*a.* interno. ~ **itself** in se stesso. ~-**patient** *n.* degente *m.*/*f.* ~ **so far as** in quanto a. ~ **that** in quanto che. ~ **the main** per la maggior parte. ~ **the rain** sotto la pioggia. ~ **the sun** al sole. **the** ~**s and outs** i dettagli.

inability /məˈbɪlətɪ/ *n.* incapacità *f.*

inaccessible /ɪnækˈsesəbl/ *a.* inaccessibile.

inaccura|te /ɪnˈækjərət/ *a.* inesatto. ~**cy** *n.* inesattezza *f.*

inactiv|e /ɪnˈæktɪv/ *a.* inattivo. ~**ity** /-ˈtɪvətɪ/ *n.* inattività *f.*

inadequa|te /ɪnˈædɪkwət/ *a.* inadeguato. ~**cy** *n.* inadeguatezza *f.* ~**tely** *adv.* inadeguatamente.

inadmissible /ɪnədˈmɪsəbl/ *a.* inammissibile.

inadvertent /ɪnədˈvɜːtənt/ *a.* involontario.

inadvisable /ɪnədˈvaɪzəbl/ *a.* sconsigliabile.

inane /ɪˈneɪn/ *a.* inane.

inanimate /ɪnˈænɪmət/ *a.* esanime.

inapplicable /ɪnˈæplɪkəbl/ *a.* inapplicabile.

inappropriate /ɪnəˈprəʊprɪət/ *a.* inadatto.

inarticulate /ɪnɑːˈtɪkjʊlət/ *a.* inarticolato; (*of person*) incapace di esprimersi chiaramente.

inattenti|ve /ɪnəˈtentɪv/ *a.* disattento. ~**on** /-ʃn/ *n.* disattenzione *f.*

inaudible /ɪnˈɔːdəbl/ *a.* impercettibile.

inaugura|te /ɪˈnɔːgjʊreɪt/ *v.t.* inaugurare. ~**l** *a.* inaugurale. ~**tion** /-ˈreɪʃn/ *n.* inaugurazione *f.*

inauspicious /ɪnɔːˈspɪʃəs/ *a.* infausto.

inborn /ˈɪnbɔːn/ *a.* innato.

inbred /ɪnˈbred/ *a.* congenito.

incalculable /ɪnˈkælkjʊləbl/ *a.* incalcolabile.

incandescen|t /ɪnkænˈdesnt/ *a.* incandescente. ~**ce** *n.* incandescenza *f.*

incantation /ɪnkænˈteɪʃn/ *n.* incantesimo *m.*

incapab|le /ɪnˈkeɪpəbl/ *a.* incapace. ~**ility** /-ˈbɪlətɪ/ *n.* incapacità *f.*

incapacit|ate /ɪnkəˈpæsɪteɪt/ *v.t.* rendere incapace. ~**y** *n.* incapacità *f.*

incarcerat|e /ɪnˈkɑːsəret/ *v.t.* incarcerare. ~**ion** /-ˈreɪʃn/ *n.* incarcerazione *f.*

incarnat|e /ɪnˈkɑːnɪt/ *a.* incarnato. ~**ion** /-ˈneɪʃn/ *n.* incarnazione *f.*

incautious /ɪnˈkɔːʃəs/ *a.* incauto. ~**ly** *adv.* incautamente.

incendiary /ɪnˈsendɪərɪ/ *a.* & *n.* incendiario *m.*

incense[1] /ˈɪnsens/ *n.* incenso *m.*

incense[2] /ɪnˈsens/ *v.t.* esasperare.

incentive /ɪnˈsentɪv/ *n.* incentivo *m.*

inception /ɪnˈsepʃn/ *n.* inizio *m.*

incertitude /ɪnˈsɜːtɪtjuːd/ *n.* incertezza *f.*

incessant /ɪnˈsesnt/ *a.* incessante.

incest /ˈɪnsest/ *n.* incesto *m.*

inch /ɪntʃ/ *n.* pollice *m.* (=2.54 *cm*). —*v.t.*/*i.* muovere, muoversi gradatamente.

incidence /ˈɪnsɪdəns/ *n.* incidenza *f.*

incident /ˈɪnsɪdənt/ *n.* incidente *m.*

incidental /ɪnsɪˈdentl/ *a.* incidentale; (*expenses*) casuale. ~**ly** *adv.* incidentalmente; (*by the way*) a proposito.

incinerat|e /ɪnˈsɪnəreɪt/ *v.t.* incenerire. ~**or** /-ə(r)/ *n.* inceneritore *m.*

incipient /ɪnˈsɪpɪənt/ *a.* incipiente.

incis|e /ɪnˈsaɪz/ *v.t.* incidere. ~**ion** /-ˈsɪʒn/ *n.* incisione *f.*

incisive /ɪnˈsaɪsɪv/ *a.* incisivo.

incite /ɪnˈsaɪt/ *v.t.* incitare. ~**ment** *n.* incitamento *m.*

incivility /ɪnsɪˈvɪlətɪ/ *n.* scortesia *f.*

inclement /ɪnˈklemənt/ *a.* inclemente.

inclination /ɪnklɪˈneɪʃn/ *n.* inclinazione *f.*

incline[1] /ɪnˈklaɪn/ *v.t.*/*i.* inclinare, inclinarsi.

incline[2] /ˈɪnklaɪn/ *n.* pendio *m.*

inclu|de /ɪnˈkluːd/ *v.t.* includere. ~**ding** *a.* incluso. ~**sion** /-ʒn/ *n.* inclusione *f.*

inclusive /ɪnˈkluːsɪv/ *a.* inclusivo. **be** ~ **of** comprendere.

incognito /ɪnkɒgˈniːtəʊ/ *adv.* in incognito.

incoherent /ɪnkəʊˈhɪərənt/ *a.* incoerente. ~**ly** *adv.* incoerentemente.

income /ˈɪnkʌm/ *n.* reddito *m.* ~ **tax** *n.* imposta sul reddito *f.*

incoming /ˈɪnkʌmɪŋ/ *a.* in arrivo. ~ **tide** marea montante *f.*

incommunicado /ɪnkəmjuːnɪˈkɑːdəʊ/ *a.* in segregazione.

incomparable /ɪnˈkɒmprəbl/ *a.* incomparabile.

incompatib|le /ɪnkəmˈpætəbl/ *a.* incompatibile. ~**ility** /-ˈbɪlətɪ/ *n.* incompatibilità *f.*

incompeten|t /ɪnˈkɒmpɪtənt/ *a.* incompetente. ~**ce** *n.* incompetenza *f.*

incomplete /ɪnkəm'pliːt/ *a.* incompleto.

incomprehensi|ble /ɪnkɒmprɪ'hensəbl/ *a.* incomprensibile. ~**on** /-ʃn/ *n.* incomprensione *f.*

inconceivabl|e /ɪnkən'siːvəbl/ *a.* inconcepibile. ~**y** *adv.* inconcepibilmente.

inconclusive /ɪnkən'kluːsɪv/ *a.* inconcludente.

incongruous /ɪn'kɒŋgrʊəs/ *a.* incongruo.

inconsequential /ɪnkɒnsɪ'kwənʃl/ *a.* senza importanza.

inconsiderable /ɪnkən'sɪdərəbl/ *a.* trascurabile.

inconsiderate /ɪnkən'sɪdərət/ *a.* sconsiderato.

inconsisten|t /ɪnkən'sɪstənt/ *a.* inconsistente. **be** ~**t with** essere contrario a. ~**cy** *n.* inconsistenza *f.*

inconsolable /ɪnkən'səʊləbl/ *a.* inconsolabile.

inconspicuous /ɪnkən'spɪkjʊəs/ *a.* non apparisce. ~**ly** *adv.* modestamente.

incontestable /ɪnkən'testəbl/ *a.* incontestabile.

incontinen|t /ɪn'kɒntɪnənt/ *a.* incontinente. ~**ce** *n.* incontinenza *f.*

incontrovertible /ɪnkɒntrə'vɜːtəbl/ *a.* incontestabile.

inconvenien|t /ɪnkən'viːnɪənt/ *a.* scomodo; (*time, place*) inopportuno. ~**ce** *n.* scomodità *f.*; (*drawback*) inconveniente *m.* **put s.o. to** ~**ce** dare disturbo a qcno.

incorporat|e /ɪn'kɔːpəreɪt/ *v.t.* incorporare. ~**ion** /-'reɪʃn/ *n.* incorporazione *f.*

incorrect /ɪnkə'rekt/ *a.* incorretto. ~**ly** *adv.* scorrettamente.

incorrigible /ɪn'kɒrɪdʒəbl/ *a.* incorreggibile.

incorruptible /ɪnkə'rʌptəbl/ *a.* incorruttibile.

increas|e[1] /ɪn'kriːs/ *v.t./i.* aumentare. ~**ingly** *adv.* sempre più.

increase[2] /'ɪnkriːs/ *n.* aumento *m.*

incredibl|e /ɪn'kredəbl/ *a.* incredibile. ~**y** *adv.* incredibilmente.

incredulous /ɪn'kredjʊləs/ *a.* incredulo.

increment /'ɪŋkrəmənt/ *n.* incremento *m.*

incriminat|e /ɪn'krɪmɪneɪt/ *v.t.* incriminare. ~**ion** /-'neɪʃn/ *n.* incriminazione *f.*

incubat|e /'ɪŋkjʊbeɪt/ *v.t.* incubare. ~**ion** /-'beɪʃn/ *n.* incubazione *f.* ~**or** /-ə(r)/ *n.* incubatrice *f.*

incubus /'ɪŋkjʊbəs/ *n.* (*pl.* -**uses**) incubo *m.*

inculcate /'ɪnkʌlkeɪt/ *v.t.* inculcare.

incumbent /ɪn'kʌmbənt/ *a.* **be** ~ **on** incombere a.

incur /ɪn'kɜː(r)/ *v.t.* (*p.t.* **incurred**) incorrere; (*debts*) contrarre.

incurabl|e /ɪn'kjʊərəbl/ *a.* incurabile. ~**y** *adv.* incurabilmente.

incursion /ɪn'kɜːʃn/ *n.* incursione *f.*

indebted /ɪn'detɪd/ *a.* ~ **to** obbligato verso.

indecen|t /ɪn'diːsnt/ *a.* indecente. ~**cy** *n.* indecenza *f.*

indecision /ɪndɪ'sɪʒn/ *n.* indecisione *f.*

indecisi|ve /ɪndɪ'saɪsɪv/ *a.* indeciso.

indecorous /ɪn'dekərəs/ *a.* indecoroso.

indeed /ɪn'diːd/ *adv.* difatti, davvero. **very much** ~ moltissimo.

indefatigable /ɪndɪ'fætɪgəbl/ *a.* instancabile.

indefinable /ɪndɪ'faɪnəbl/ *a.* indefinibile.

indefinite /ɪn'defɪnət/ *a.* indefinito. ~**ly** *adv.* indefinitamente.

indelibl|e /ɪn'delɪbl/ *a.* indelebile.

indelicate /ɪn'delɪkət/ *a.* indelicato.

indemni|fy /ɪn'demnɪfaɪ/ *v.t.* indennizzare. ~**ty** /-əti/ *n.* indennità *f.*; (*compensation*) risarcimento *m.*

indent /ɪn'dent/ *v.t.* intaccare. ~**ation** /-'teɪʃn/ *n.* intaccatura *f.*; (*typewriter*) rientranza dal margine *f.*

independen|t /ɪndɪ'pendənt/ *a.* indipendente. ~**ce** *n.* indipendenza *f.* ~**tly** *adv.* indipendentemente.

indescribabl|e /ɪndɪ'skraɪbəbl/ *a.* indescrivibile. ~**y** *adv.* indescrivibilmente.

indestructible /ɪndɪ'strʌktəbl/ *a.* indistruttibile.

indeterminate /ɪndɪ'tɜːmɪnət/ *a.* indeterminato.

index /'ɪndeks/ *n.* (*pl.* **indexes**) indice *m.*; (*in library*) catalogo *m.* —*v.t.* preparare l'indice di. **card** ~ *n.* schedario *m.* ~ (**finger**) *n.* (dito) indice *m.* ~-**linked** *a.* legato al costo della vita.

India /'ɪndjə/ *n.* India *f.* ~**n** *a.* & *n.* indiano, a *m.,f.* ~**n ink** inchiostro di China *m.* ~**n summer** estate di San Martino *f.* **Red** ~**n** pellerossa *m./f.*

indicat|e /'ɪndɪkeɪt/ *v.t.* indicare; (*state briefly*) accennare. ~**ion** /-'keɪʃn/ *n.*

indicazione *f.* ~or *n.* indicatore *m.*; (*auto.*) freccia *f.*

indicative /ɪn'dɪkətɪv/ *a.* & *n.* indicativo *m.*

indict /ɪn'daɪt/ *v.t.* accusare. ~ment *n.* accusa *f.*

indifferen|t /ɪn'dɪfrənt/ *a.* indifferente; (*not good*) mediocre. ~ce *n.* indifferenza *f.*

indigenous /ɪn'dɪdʒɪnəs/ *a.* indigeno.

indigent /'ɪndɪdʒənt/ *a.* bisognoso.

indigesti|ble /ɪndɪ'dʒestəbl/ *a.* indigesto. ~on /-tʃən/ *n.* indigestione *f.*

indigna|nt /ɪn'dɪgnənt/ *a.* indignato. ~tion /-'neɪʃn/ *n.* indignazione *f.* ~ntly *adv.* con indignazione.

indignity /ɪn'dɪgnətɪ/ *n.* affronto *m.*

indigo /'ɪndɪgəʊ/ *n.* indaco *m.*

indirect /ɪndɪ'rekt/ *a.* indiretto. ~ly *adv.* indirettamente.

indiscre|et /ɪndɪ'skriːt/ *a.* indiscreto. ~tion /-'kreʃn/ *n.* indiscrezione *f.*

indiscriminate /ɪndɪ'skrɪmɪnət/ *a.* indiscriminato. ~ly *adv.* senza distinzione.

indispensable /ɪndɪ'spensəbl/ *a.* indispensabile.

indispos|ed /ɪndɪ'spəʊzd/ *a.* indisposto. ~ition /-ə'zɪʃn/ *n.* indisposizione *f.*

indisputabl|e /ɪndɪ'spjuːtəbl/ *a.* indisputabile. ~y *adv.* indisputabilmente.

indissoluble /ɪndɪ'sɒljʊbl/ *a.* indissolubile.

indistinct /ɪndɪ'stɪŋkt/ *a.* indistinto. ~ly *adv.* indistintamente.

indistinguishable /ɪndɪ'stɪŋgwɪʃəbl/ *a.* indistinguibile.

individual /ɪndɪ'vɪdʒʊəl/ *a.* individuale. —*n.* individuo *m.* ~ist *n.* individualista *m./f.* ~ity /-'ælətɪ/ *n.* individualità *f.* ~ly *adv.* individualmente.

indivisible /ɪndɪ'vɪzəbl/ *a.* indivisibile.

indoctrinat|e /ɪn'dɒktrɪneɪt/ *v.t.* indottrinare. ~ion /-'neɪʃn/ *n.* indottrinamento *m.*

indolen|t /'ɪndələnt/ *a.* indolente. ~ce *n.* indolenza *f.*

indomitable /ɪn'dɒmɪtəbl/ *a.* indomito.

Indonesia /ɪndəʊ'niːzɪə/ *n.* Indonesia *f.* ~n *a.* & *n.* indonesiano, a *m.*, *f.*

indoor /'ɪndɔː(r)/ *a.* interno; (*undercover*) coperto. ~s /-'dɔːz/ *adv.* in casa.

indubitabl|e /ɪn'djuːbɪtəbl/ *a.* indubitabile. ~y *adv.* indubitabilmente.

induce /ɪn'djuːs/ *v.t.* indurre; (*produce*) causare. ~ment *n.* incentivo *m.*

induct /ɪn'dʌkt/ *v.t.* investire; (*electr.*) indurre. ~ion /-ʃn/ *n.* investitura *f.*; induzione *f.*

indulge /ɪn'dʌldʒ/ *v.t.* soddisfare; (*child*) viziare. —*v.i.* ~ in concedersi. ~nce *n.* lusso *m.*; (*leniency*) indulgenza *f.* ~nt *a.* indulgente.

industrial /ɪn'dʌstrɪəl/ *a.* industriale. ~ist *n.* industriale *m.* ~ized /-aɪzd/ *a.* industrializzato.

industrious /ɪn'dʌstrɪəs/ *a.* industrioso.

industry /'ɪndəstrɪ/ *n.* industria *f.*; (*zeal*) zelo *m.*

inebriated /ɪ'niːbrɪeɪtɪd/ *a.* ubriaco.

inedible /ɪn'edɪbl/ *a.* immangiabile.

ineffable /ɪn'efəbl/ *a.* ineffabile.

ineffective /ɪnɪ'fektɪv/ *a.* inefficace.

ineffectual /ɪnɪ'fektʃʊəl/ *a.* inutile; (*person*) incapace.

inefficien|t /ɪnɪ'fɪʃnt/ *a.* inefficiente. ~cy *n.* inefficienza *f.*

ineligible /ɪn'elɪdʒəbl/ *a.* inadatto.

inept /ɪ'nept/ *a.* inetto. ~itude /-tɪtjuːd/ *n.* inettitudine *f.*

inequality /ɪnɪ'kwɒlətɪ/ *n.* ineguaglianza *f.*

inequitable /ɪn'ekwɪtəbl/ *a.* ingiusto.

ineradicable /ɪnɪ'rædɪkəbl/ *a.* inestirpabile.

inert /ɪ'nɜːt/ *a.* inerte. ~ia /-ʃə/ *n.* inerzia *f.*

inescapable /ɪnɪs'keɪpəbl/ *a.* inevitabile.

inestimable /ɪn'estɪməbl/ *a.* inestimabile.

inevitabl|e /ɪn'evɪtəbl/ *a.* inevitabile. ~y *adv.* inevitabilmente.

inexact /ɪnɪg'zækt/ *a.* inesatto.

inexcusabl|e /ɪnɪk'skjuːzəbl/ *a.* imperdonabile.

inexhaustible /ɪnɪg'zɔːstəbl/ *a.* inesauribile.

inexorabl|e /ɪn'eksərəbl/ *a.* inesorabile.

inexpedient /ɪnɪk'spiːdɪənt/ *a.* inopportuno.

inexpensive /ɪnɪk'spensɪv/ *a.* poco costoso.

inexperience /ɪnɪk'spɪərɪəns/ *n.* inesperienza *f.* ~d *a.* inesperto.

inexplicabl|e /ɪnɪk'splɪkəbl/ *a.* inesplicabile.

inextricabl|e /ɪnɪk'strɪkəbl/ *a.* inestricabile.

infallib|le /ɪnˈfæləbl/ *a.* infallibile. **~ility** /-ˈbɪlətɪ/ *n.* infallibilità *f.*

infam|ous /ˈɪnfəməs/ *a.* infame. **~y** *n.* infamia *f.*

infan|cy /ˈɪnfənsɪ/ *n.* infanzia *f.* **~t** *n.* neonato, a *m.*, *f.* **~tile** /-taɪl/ *a.* infantile.

infantry /ˈɪnfəntrɪ/ *n.* fanteria *f.* **~man** (*pl.* -men) *n.* fante *m.*

infatuat|ed /ɪnˈfætʃʊeɪtɪd/ *a.* infatuato. **~ion** /-ˈeɪʃn/ *n.* infatuazione *f.*

infect /ɪnˈfekt/ *v.t.* infettare. **~ed with** (*illness*) affetto da. **~ion** /-ʃn/ *n.* infezione *f.* **~ious** *a.* infettivo.

infer /ɪnˈfɜː(r)/ *v.t.* (*p.t.* **inferred**) dedurre. **~ence** /ˈɪnfərəns/ *n.* deduzione *f.*

inferior /ɪnˈfɪərɪə(r)/ *a.* inferiore; (*goods*) scadente. *—n.* inferiore *m.*|*f.*; (*in rank*) subalterno, a *m.*, *f.* **~ity** /-ˈɒrətɪ/ *n.* inferiorità *f.*

infernal /ɪnˈfɜːnl/ *a.* infernale. **~ly** *adv.* infernalmente.

inferno /ɪnˈfɜːnəʊ/ *n.* (*pl.* -os) inferno *m.*

infertil|e /ɪnˈfɜːtaɪl/ *a.* sterile. **~ity** /-ˈtɪlətɪ/ *n.* sterilità *f.*

infest /ɪnˈfest/ *v.t.* infestare. **~-ation** /-ˈteɪʃn/ *n.* infestazione *f.*

infidelity /ɪnfɪˈdelətɪ/ *n.* infedeltà *f.*

infighting /ˈɪnfaɪtɪŋ/ *n.* lotta per il potere *f.*

infiltrat|e /ˈɪnfɪltreɪt/ *v.t.* infiltrare. **~ion** /-ˈtreɪʃn/ *n.* infiltrazione *f.*

infinite /ˈɪnfɪnət/ *a.* infinito. **~ly** *adv.* infinitamente.

infinitesimal /ɪnfɪnɪˈtesɪml/ *a.* infinitesimo.

infinitive /ɪnˈfɪnətɪv/ *n.* infinito *m.*

infinity /ɪnˈfɪnətɪ/ *n.* infinità *f.*

infirm /ɪnˈfɜːm/ *a.* debole. **~ity** *n.* debolezza *f.*

infirmary /ɪnˈfɜːmərɪ/ *n.* infermeria *f.*

inflam|e /ɪnˈfleɪm/ *v.t.* infiammare. **~mable** /-ˈæməbl/ *a.* infiammabile. **~mation** /-əˈmeɪʃn/ *n.* infiammazione *f.*

inflammatory /ɪnˈflæmətrɪ/ *a.* incendiario.

inflat|e /ɪnˈfleɪt/ *v.t.* gonfiare.

inflation /ɪnˈfleɪʃn/ *n.* inflazione *f.* **~ary** *a.* inflazionario.

inflexible /ɪnˈfleksəbl/ *a.* inflessibile.

inflexion /ɪnˈflekʃn/ *n.* inflessione *f.*

inflict /ɪnˈflɪkt/ *v.t.* infliggere (**on**, a). **~ion** /-ʃn/ *n.* inflizione *f.*

inflow /ˈɪnfləʊ/ *n.* afflusso *m.*

influen|ce /ˈɪnflʊəns/ *n.* influenza *f.*; (*power*) ascendente *m.* *—v.t.* influenzare. **~tial** /-ˈenʃl/ *a.* autorevole. **~tial relatives** parenti altolocati *m.pl.*

influenza /ɪnflʊˈenzə/ *n.* influenza *f.*

influx /ˈɪnflʌks/ *n.* affluenza *f.*

inform /ɪnˈfɔːm/ *v.t.*/*i.* informare. **~ant** *n.* informa|tore, -trice *m.*, *f.* **~er** /ə(r)/ *n.* dela|tore, -trice *m.*, *f.* **~ against** denunziare. **keep s.o. ~ed** tenere qcno. al corrente.

informal /ɪnˈfɔːml/ *a.* semplice, senza cerimonia. **~ity** /-ˈmælətɪ/ *n.* assenza di formalità *f.* **~ly** *adv.* senza formalità *f.*

informati|on /ɪnfəˈmeɪʃn/ *n.* informazione *f.* **~ve** /-ˈfɔːmətɪv/ *a.* informativo.

infra-red /ɪnfrəˈred/ *a.* infrarosso.

infrastructure /ˈɪnfrəstrʌktʃə(r)/ *n.* infrastruttura *f.*

infrequent /ɪnˈfriːkwənt/ *a.* infrequente. **~ly** *adv.* raramente.

infringe /ɪnˈfrɪndʒ/ *v.t.* contravvenire *a.* *—v.i.* **~ on** usurpare. **~ment** *n.* infrazione *f.*

infuriat|e /ɪnˈfjʊərɪeɪt/ *v.t.* infuriare. **~ing** *a.* esasperante.

infus|e /ɪnˈfjuːz/ *v.t.* infondere; (*steep in liquid*) fare un'infusione di. **~ion** /-ʒn/ *n.* infusione *f.*

ingenious /ɪnˈdʒiːnɪəs/ *a.* ingegnoso.

ingenuous /ɪnˈdʒenjʊəs/ *a.* ingenuo.

ingest /ɪnˈdʒest/ *v.t.* ingerire.

ingle-nook /ˈɪŋglnʊk/ *n.* cantuccio del focolare *m.*

ingot /ˈɪŋgət/ *n.* lingotto *m.*

ingrained /ɪnˈgreɪnd/ *a.* radicato.

ingratiate /ɪnˈgreɪʃɪeɪt/ *v.t.* **~ o.s. with** ingraziarsi.

ingratitude /ɪnˈgrætɪtjuːd/ *n.* ingratitudine *f.*

ingredient /ɪnˈgriːdjənt/ *n.* ingrediente *m.*

ingrowing /ˈɪngrəʊɪŋ/ *a.* (*of nail*) incarnito.

inhabit /ɪnˈhæbɪt/ *v.t.* abitare. **~ant** *n.* abitante *m.*|*f*

inhal|e /ɪnˈheɪl/ *v.t.* inalare. *—v.i.* (*cigarette*) aspirare. **~ation** /-əˈleɪʃn/ *n.* inalazione *f.* **~er** /-ə(r)/ *n.* inalatore *m.*

inherent /ɪnˈhɪərənt/ *a.* inerente.

inherit /ɪnˈherɪt/ *v.t.* ereditare. **~ance** *n.* eredità *f.*

inhibit /ɪnˈhɪbɪt/ *v.t.* inibire; (*prevent*) impedire. **~ion** /-ˈbɪʃn/ *n.* inibizione *f.*

inhospitable /ɪn'hɒspɪtəbl/ a. inospitale.

inhuman /ɪn'hju:mən/ a. disumano. ∼ity /-'mænətɪ/ n. inumanità f.

inimical /ɪ'nɪmɪkl/ a. ostile.

inimitable /ɪ'nɪmɪtəbl/ a. inimitabile.

iniquit|ous /ɪ'nɪkwɪtəs/ a. ingiusto. ∼y /-ətɪ/ n. ingiustizia f.

initial /ɪ'nɪʃl/ a. & n. iniziale f. —v.t. (p.t. **initialled**) siglare. ∼ly adv. all'inizio.

initiat|e /ɪ'nɪʃɪeɪt/ v.t. iniziare. ∼ion /-'eɪʃn/ n. iniziazione f.

initiative /ɪ'nɪʃətɪv/ n. iniziativa f.

inject /ɪn'dʒekt/ v.t. iniettare. ∼ion /-ʃn/ n. iniezione f.

injudicious /ɪndʒʊ'dɪʃəs/ a. avventato.

injure /'ɪndʒə(r)/ v.t. ferire; (harm) nuocere.

injury /'ɪndʒərɪ/ n. ferita f.; (wrong) torto m.

injustice /ɪn'dʒʌstɪs/ n. ingiustizia f.

ink /ɪŋk/ n. inchiostro m. ∼-well n. calamaio m. ∼y a. sporco d'inchiostro.

inkling /'ɪŋklɪŋ/ n. sentore m.

inlaid /ɪn'leɪd/ see inlay¹.

inland /'ɪnlənd/ a. interno. —adv. all'interno. **I∼ Revenue** n. fisco m.

in-laws /'ɪnlɔ:z/ n.pl. (fam.) parenti acquisiti m.pl.

inlay¹ /ɪn'leɪ/ v.t. (p.t. **inlaid**) intarsiare.

inlay² /'ɪnleɪ/ n. intarsio m.

inlet /'ɪnlet/ n. insenatura f.; (mech.) entrata f.

inmate /'ɪnmeɪt/ n. (of hospital) degente m./f.; (of prison) carcerato, a m., f.

inn /ɪn/ n. locanda f.

innards /'ɪnədz/ n.pl. (fam.) frattaglie f.pl.

innate /ɪ'neɪt/ a. innato.

inner /'ɪnə(r)/ a. interno. ∼most a. il più profondo. ∼ tube n. camera d'aria f.

innings /'ɪnɪŋz/ n. invar. (sport) turno m.; (fig.) periodo di predominio m.

innkeeper /'ɪnki:pə(r)/ n. locandiere, a m., f.

innocen|t /'ɪnəsnt/ a. & n. innocente m./f. ∼ce n. innocenza f. ∼tly adv. innocentemente.

innocuous /ɪ'nɒkjʊəs/ a. innocuo.

innovat|e /'ɪnəveɪt/ v.i. innovare. ∼ion /-'veɪʃn/ n. innovazione f. ∼or n. innova|tore, -trice m., f.

innuendo /ɪnju:'endəʊ/ n. (pl. -os) insinuazione f.

innumerable /ɪ'nju:mərəbl/ a. innumerevole.

inoculat|e /ɪ'nɒkjʊleɪt/ v.t. inoculare. ∼ion /-'leɪʃn/ n. inoculazione f.

inoffensive /ɪnə'fensɪv/ a. inoffensivo.

inoperable /ɪn'ɒpərəbl/ a. inoperabile.

inoperative /ɪn'ɒpərətɪv/ a. inefficace.

inopportune /ɪn'ɒpətju:n/ a. inopportuno.

inordinate /ɪ'nɔ:dɪnət/ a. smodato. ∼ly adv. smoderatamente.

input /'ɪnpʊt/ n. input m. invar.; (electr.) energia f.

inquest /'ɪnkwest/ n. inchiesta f.

inquir|e /ɪn'kwaɪə(r)/ v.i. informarsi. —v.t. domandare. ∼e into v.t. fare indagini su. ∼y n. domanda f.; (jurid.) inchiesta f.

inquisition /ɪnkwɪ'zɪʃn/ n. investigazione f.

inquisitive /ɪn'kwɪzətɪv/ a. curioso.

inroad /'ɪnrəʊd/ n. incursione f.

inrush /'ɪnrʌʃ/ n. irruzione f.

insan|e /ɪn'seɪn/ a. pazzo; (fig.) insensato. ∼ity /ɪn'sænətɪ/ n. pazzia f.

insanitary /ɪn'sænɪtrɪ/ a. malsano.

insatiable /ɪn'seɪʃəbl/ a. insaziabile.

inscri|be /ɪn'skraɪb/ v.t. iscrivere. ∼ption /-ɪpʃn/ n. iscrizione f.

inscrutable /ɪn'skru:təbl/ a. impenetrabile.

insect /'ɪnsekt/ n. insetto m. ∼icide /ɪn'sektɪsaɪd/ n. insetticida m.

insecur|e /ɪnsɪ'kjʊə(r)/ a. malsicuro; (person) insicuro. ∼ity n. mancanza di sicurezza f.

insemination /ɪnsemɪ'neɪʃn/ n. inseminazione f.

insensible /ɪn'sensəbl/ a. insensibile; (unconscious) privo di sensi.

insensitive /ɪn'sensətɪv/ a. insensibile.

inseparable /ɪn'seprəbl/ a. inseparabile.

insert¹ /ɪn'sɜ:t/ v.t. inserire. ∼ion /-ʃn/ n. inserzione f.

insert² /'ɪnsɜ:t/ n. inserto m.

inside /ɪn'saɪd/ n. interno m. ∼s n.pl. (fam.) stomaco m.s. —adv. dentro. —prep. all'interno di; (of time) in meno di. ∼ out adv. a rovescio; (thoroughly) a fondo.

insidious /ɪn'sɪdɪəs/ a. insidioso.

insight /'ɪnsaɪt/ n. intuito m.

insignia /ɪn'sɪgnɪə/ n.pl. insegne f.pl.

insignificant /ɪnsɪg'nɪfɪkənt/ *a.* insignificante.

insincer|e /ɪnsɪn'sɪə(r)/ *a.* poco sincero. ~**ity** /-'serətɪ/ *n.* mancanza di sincerità *f.*

insinuat|e /ɪn'sɪnjʊeɪt/ *v.t.* insinuare. ~**ion** /-'eɪʃn/ *n.* insinuazione *f.*

insipid /ɪn'sɪpɪd/ *a.* insipido.

insist /ɪn'sɪst/ *v.t./i.* insistere.

insisten|t /ɪn'sɪstənt/ *a.* insistente. ~**ce** *n.* insistenza *f.* ~**tly** *adv.* insistentemente.

insolen|t /'ɪnsələnt/ *a.* insolente. ~**ce** *n.* insolenza *f.*

insoluble /ɪn'sɒljʊbl/ *a.* insolubile.

insolvent /ɪn'sɒlvənt/ *a.* insolvente.

insomnia /ɪn'sɒmnɪə/ *n.* insonnia *f.* ~**c** /-ˈæk/ *n.* insonne *m./f.*

inspect /ɪn'spekt/ *v.t.* ispezionare; (*tickets*) controllare. ~**ion** /-ʃn/ *n.* ispezione *f.*; controllo *m.* ~**or** *n.* ispet|tore, -trice *m., f.*; controllore *m.*

inspir|e /ɪn'spaɪə(r)/ *v.t.* ispirare. ~**ation** /-ə'reɪʃn/ *n.* ispirazione *f.*

instability /ɪnstə'bɪlətɪ/ *n.* instabilità *f.*

install /ɪn'stɔːl/ *v.t.* installare. ~**ation** /-ə'leɪʃn/ *n.* installazione *f.*

instalment /ɪn'stɔːlmənt/ *n.* (*comm.*) rata *f.*; (*of serial*) puntata *f.*

instance /'ɪnstəns/ *n.* esempio *m.* **in the first** ~ in primo luogo.

instant /'ɪnstənt/ *a.* immediato; (*food*) espresso; (*comm., abbr.* **inst.**) corrente. —*n.* istante *m.* ~**ly** *adv.* immediatamente.

instantaneous /ɪnstən'teɪnɪəs/ *a.* istantaneo.

instead /ɪn'sted/ *adv.* invece. ~ **of** anziché; (*person*) al posto di.

instep /'ɪnstep/ *n.* collo del piede *m.*

instigat|e /'ɪnstɪgeɪt/ *v.t.* istigare. ~**ion** /-'geɪʃn/ *n.* istigazione *f.* ~**or** *n.* istiga|tore, -trice *m., f.*

instil /ɪn'stɪl/ *v.t.* (*p.t.* **instilled**) inculcare.

instinct /'ɪnstɪŋkt/ *n.* istinto *m.* ~**ive** /ɪn'stɪŋktɪv/ *a.* istintivo.

institut|e /'ɪnstɪtjuːt/ *n.* istituto *m.* —*v.t.* istituire; (*rule*) stabilire; (*legal action*) intentare. ~**ion** /-'tjuːʃn/ *n.* istituzione *f.*

instruct /ɪn'strʌkt/ *v.t.* istruire; (*order*) ordinare. ~**ion** /-ʃn/ *n.* istruzione *f.* ~**ions** /-ʃnz/ *n.pl.* (*orders*) ordini *m.pl.* ~**ive** *a.* istruttivo. ~**or** *n.* istruttore *m.*

instrument /'ɪnstrʊmənt/ *n.* strumento *m.*

instrumental /ɪnstrʊ'mentl/ *a.* strumentale. **be** ~ **in** contribuire a. ~**ist** *n.* strumentista *m./f.*

insubordinat|e /ɪnsə'bɔːdɪnət/ *a.* insubordinato. ~**ion** /-'neɪʃn/ *n.* insubordinazione *f.*

insubstantial /ɪnsəb'stænʃl/ *a.* inconsistente.

insufferable /ɪn'sʌfrəbl/ *a.* insopportabile.

insufficient /ɪnsə'fɪʃnt/ *a.* insufficiente. ~**ly** *adv.* insufficientemente.

insular /'ɪnsjʊlə(r)/ *a.* insulare; (*narrow-minded*) gretto.

insulat|e /'ɪnsjʊleɪt/ *v.t.* isolare. ~**ion** /-'leɪʃn/ *n.* isolamento *m.*

insulin /'ɪnsjʊlɪn/ *n.* insulina *f.*

insult¹ /ɪn'sʌlt/ *v.t.* insultare.

insult² /'ɪnsʌlt/ *n.* insulto *m.*

insuperable /ɪn'sjuːprəbl/ *a.* insuperabile.

insur|e /ɪn'ʃʊə(r)/ *v.t.* assicurare. ~**ance** *n.* assicurazione *f.*

insurgent /ɪn'sɜːdʒənt/ *a.* & *n.* ribelle *m./f.*

insurrection /ɪnsə'rekʃn/ *n.* insurrezione *f.*

intact /ɪn'tækt/ *a.* intatto.

intake /'ɪnteɪk/ *n.* immissione *f.*; (*mech.*) presa *f.*; (*of food*) consumo *m.*

intangible /ɪn'tændʒbl/ *a.* intangibile.

integral /'ɪntɪgrəl/ *a.* integrale.

integrat|e /'ɪntɪgreɪt/ *v.t./i.* integrare, integrarsi. ~**ion** /-'greɪʃn/ *n.* integrazione *f.*

integrity /ɪn'tegrətɪ/ *n.* integrità *f.*

intellect /'ɪntəlekt/ *n.* intelletto *m.* ~**ual** /-'lektʃʊəl/ *a.* & *n.* intellettuale *m./f.*

intelligen|t /ɪn'telɪdʒənt/ *a.* intelligente. ~**ce** *n.* intelligenza *f.*; (*mil.*) informazioni *f.pl.* ~**tly** *adv.* intelligentemente.

intelligentsia /ɪntelɪ'dʒentsɪə/ *n.* intellettuali *m.pl.*

intelligible /ɪn'telɪdʒəbl/ *a.* intelligibile.

intemperance /ɪn'tempərəns/ *n.* intemperanza *f.*

intend /ɪn'tend/ *v.t.* destinare; (*have in mind*) aver intenzione di. ~**ed** *a.* intenzionale; (*future*) futuro.

intens|e /ɪn'tens/ *a.* intenso; (*person*) emotivo. ~**ely** *adv.* intensamente;

(*very*) estremamente. ∼**ity** *n*. intensità *f*.

intensif|y /ɪn'tensɪfaɪ/ *v.t.* intensificare. ∼**ication** /-ɪ'keɪʃn/ *n*. intensificazione *f*.

intensive /ɪn'tensɪv/ *a*. intensivo. ∼ **course** *n*. corso accelerato *m*.

intent /ɪn'tent/ *n*. intenzione *f*. —*a*. intento. ∼ **on** deciso a; (*absorbed*) preso da. ∼**ly** *adv*. attentamente.

intention /ɪn'tenʃn/ *n*. intenzione *f*. ∼**al** *a*. intenzionale. ∼**ally** *adv*. apposta.

inter /ɪn'tɜ:(r)/ *v.t.* (*p.t.* **interred**) interrare.

inter- /'ɪntə(r)/ *pref.* inter-.

interact /ɪntə'rækt/ *v.i.* reagire reciprocamente. ∼**ion** /-ʃn/ *n*. azione reciproca *f*.

intercede /ɪntə'si:d/ *v.i.* intercedere.

intercept /ɪntə'sept/ *v.t.* intercettare. ∼**ion** /-ʃn/ *n*. intercettamento *m*.

interchange[1] /ɪntə'tʃeɪndʒ/ *v.t.* scambiare. ∼**able** *a*. scambievole.

interchange[2] /'ɪntətʃeɪndʒ/ *n.* scambio *m*.; (*road junction*) incrocio (autostradale) *m*.

intercom /'ɪntəkɒm/ *n*. citofono *m*.

interconnected /ɪntəkə'nektɪd/ *a*. collegato.

intercourse /'ɪntəkɔ:s/ *n*. rapporto *m*.; (*sexual*) rapporti sessuali *m.pl*.

interest /'ɪntrəst/ *n*. interesse *m*.; (*advantage*) tornaconto *m*. —*v.t.* interessare. ∼**ed** *a*. interessato. ∼**ing** *a*. interessante.

interfer|e /ɪntə'fɪə(r)/ *v.i.* intromettersi. ∼**e with** interferire con. ∼**ance** *n*. interferenza *f*.

interim /'ɪntərɪm/ *n*. **in the** ∼ nel frattempo. —*a*. temporaneo.

interior /ɪn'tɪərɪə(r)/ *n*. interno *m*. —*a*. interiore.

interjection /ɪntə'dʒekʃn/ *n*. interiezione *f*.

interlock /ɪntə'lɒk/ *v.t./i.* congiungere, congiungersi.

interloper /'ɪntələʊpə(r)/ *n*. intruso, a *m., f*.

interlude /'ɪntəlu:d/ *n*. intervallo *m*.; (*theatr*.) intermezzo *m*.

intermarr|iage /ɪntə'mærɪdʒ/ *n*. matrimonio fra parenti *m*. ∼**y** *v.i.* sposarsi tra parenti; (*of tribes etc.*) sposarsi con membri di razza diversa.

intermediary /ɪntə'mi:dɪərɪ/ *a*. & *n*. intermediario, a *m., f*.

intermediate /ɪntə'mi:dɪət/ *a*. intermedio.

interminable /ɪn'tɜ:mɪnəbl/ *a*. interminabile.

intermission /ɪntə'mɪʃn/ *n*. intervallo *m*.

intermittent /ɪntə'mɪtnt/ *a*. intermittente. ∼**ly** *adv*. intermittentemente.

intern /ɪn'tɜ:n/ *v.t.* internare. ∼**ee** /-'ni:/ *n*. internato, a *m., f*. ∼**ment** *n*. internamento *m*.

internal /ɪn'tɜ:nl/ *a*. interno. ∼**ly** *adv*. internamente.

international /ɪntə'næʃnəl/ *a*. internazionale. —*n*. competi|tore, -trice in gare internazionali *m., f*.

interplay /'ɪntəpleɪ/ *n*. azione reciproca *f*.

interpolate /ɪn'tɜ:pəleɪt/ *v.t.* interpolare.

interpose /ɪntə'pəʊz/ *v.t.* frapporre.

interpret /ɪn'tɜ:prɪt/ *v.t.* interpretare. —*v.i.* fare l'interprete. ∼**ation** /-'teɪʃn/ *n*. interpretazione *f*. ∼**er** *n*. interprete *m./f*.

interrelated /ɪntərɪ'leɪtɪd/ *a*. in correlazione.

interrogat|e /ɪn'terəgeɪt/ *v.t.* interrogare. ∼**ion** /-'geɪʃn/ *n*. interrogazione *f*.; (*of police*) interrogatorio *m*.

interrogative /ɪntə'rɒgətɪv/ *a*. & *n*. interrogativo *m*.

interrupt /ɪntə'rʌpt/ *v.t.* interrompere. ∼**ion** /-ʃn/ *n*. interruzione *f*.

intersect /ɪntə'sekt/ *v.t./i.* intersecare, intersecarsi. ∼**ion** /-ʃn/ *n*. intersezione *f*.; (*of roads*) incrocio *m*.

intersperse /ɪntə'spɜ:s/ *v.t.* inframezzare.

intertwine /ɪntə'twaɪn/ *v.t./i.* attorcigliare, attorcigliarsi.

interval /'ɪntəvl/ *n*. intervallo *m*.

interven|e /ɪntə'vi:n/ *v.i.* intervenire. ∼**tion** /-'venʃn/ *n*. intervento *m*.

interview /'ɪntəvju:/ *n*. intervista *f*.; (*for job*) colloquio *m*. —*v.t.* intervistare. ∼**er** *n*. intervista|tore, -trice *m., f*.

interweave /ɪntə'wi:v/ *v.t.* (*p.t.* **interwove**, *p.p.* **interwoven**) intessere.

intestin|e /ɪn'testɪn/ *n*. intestino *m*. ∼**al** *a*. intestinale.

intima|te[1] /'ɪntɪmət/ *a*. intimo. ∼**cy** *n*. intimità *f*. ∼**tely** *adv*. intimamente.

intimate[2] /'ɪntɪmeɪt/ *v.t.* notificare; (*imply*) suggerire.

intimidat|e /ɪn'tɪmɪdeɪt/ v.t. intimidire. ~ion /-'deɪʃn/ n. intimidazione f.

into /'ɪntu:/ prep. dentro, in. **get ~ trouble** mettersi nei guai. **run ~ s.o.** imbattersi in qcno.

intolerable /ɪn'tɒlərəbl/ a. intollerabile.

intoleran|t /ɪn'tɒlərənt/ a. intollerante. ~ce n. intolleranza f.

intonation /ɪntə'neɪʃn/ n. intonazione f.

intoxicat|ed /ɪn'tɒksɪkeɪtɪd/ a. inebriato. ~ion /-'keɪʃn/ n. ebbrezza f.

intractable /ɪn'træktəbl/ a. intrattabile.

intransigent /ɪn'trænsɪdʒənt/ a. intransigente.

intransitive /ɪn'trænsətɪv/ a. intransitivo.

intravenous /ɪntrə'vi:nəs/ a. endovenoso.

intrepid /ɪn'trepɪd/ a. intrepido.

intrica|te /'ɪntrɪkət/ a. complesso. ~cy n. complessità f.

intrigu|e /ɪn'tri:g/ v.t./i. intrigare; (interest) interessare. —n. intrigo m. ~ing a. affascinante.

intrinsic /ɪn'trɪnsɪk/ a. intrinseco.

introduce /ɪntrə'dju:s/ v.t. presentare; (bring in, insert) introdurre; (initiate) iniziare.

introduct|ion /ɪntrə'dʌkʃn/ n. introduzione f.; (of person) presentazione f. ~ory a. introduttivo.

introspective /ɪntrə'spektɪv/ a. introspettivo.

introvert /'ɪntrəvɜ:t/ n. introverso, a m., f.

intru|de /ɪn'tru:d/ v.i. intrudere. ~der n. intruso, a m., f. ~sion n. intrusione f.

intuit|ion /ɪntju:'ɪʃn/ n. intuito m. ~ive /ɪn'tju:ɪtɪv/ a. intuitivo.

inundat|e /'ɪnʌndeɪt/ v.t. inondare. ~ion /-'deɪʃn/ n. inondazione f.

invade /ɪn'veɪd/ v.t. invadere. ~r /-ə(r)/ n. invasore m.

invalid[1] /'ɪnvəlɪd/ n. invalido, a m., f.

invalid[2] /ɪn'vælɪd/ a. non valido. ~ate v.t. invalidare.

invaluable /ɪn'væljʊəbl/ a. inestimabile.

invariabl|e /ɪn'veərɪəbl/ a. invariabile. ~y adv. invariabilmente.

invasion /ɪn'veɪʒn/ n. invasione f.

invective /ɪn'vektɪv/ n. invettiva f.

inveigh /ɪn'veɪ/ v.i. inveire.

inveigle /ɪn'vi:gl/ v.t. indurre con inganno.

invent /ɪn'vent/ v.t. inventare. ~ive a. inventivo. ~or n. inven|tore, -trice m., f.

inventory /'ɪnventrɪ/ n. inventario m.

inverse /ɪn'vɜ:s/ a. & n. inverso m. ~ly adv. inversamente.

inver|t /ɪn'vɜ:t/ v.t. invertire. ~sion n. inversione f. ~ted commas n.pl. virgolette f.pl.

invest /ɪn'vest/ v.t. investire. —v.i. fare investimenti. ~ in (fam.) comprare. ~ment n. investimento m. ~or n. investitore m.

investigat|e /ɪn'vestɪgeɪt/ v.t. investigare. ~ion /-'geɪʃn/ n. investigazione f.

investiture /ɪn'vestɪtʃə(r)/ n. investitura f.

inveterate /ɪn'vetərət/ a. inveterato.

invidious /ɪn'vɪdɪəs/ a. odioso.

invigilat|e /ɪn'vɪdʒɪleɪt/ v.i. sorvegliare. ~or n. sorvegliante m./f.

invigorate /ɪn'vɪgəreɪt/ v.t. rinvigorire.

invincible /ɪn'vɪnsɪbl/ a. invincibile.

inviolable /ɪn'vaɪələbl/ a. inviolabile.

invisible /ɪn'vɪzəbl/ a. invisibile.

invit|e /ɪn'vaɪt/ v.t. invitare; (attract) provocare. ~ation /ɪnvɪ'teɪʃn/ n. invito m. ~ing a. invitante.

invoice /'ɪnvɔɪs/ n. fattura f. —v.t. fatturare.

invoke /ɪn'vəʊk/ v.t. invocare.

involuntary /ɪn'vɒləntrɪ/ a. involontario.

involve /ɪn'vɒlv/ v.t. comportare; (include, affect) coinvolgere. ~d a. complesso. ~d in coinvolto in. ~ment n. coinvolgimento m.

invulnerable /ɪn'vʌlnərəbl/ a. invulnerabile.

inward /'ɪnwəd/ a. interiore. ~ly adv. interiormente. ~s adv. verso l'interno.

iodine /'aɪədi:n/ n. iodio m.

iota /aɪ'əʊtə/ n. (amount) briciolo m.

IOU n. (abbr. of I owe you) pagherò m. invar.

IQ n. (abbr. of intelligence quotient) quoziente d'intelligenza m.

Iran /ɪ'rɑːn/ n. Iran m. ~ian /ɪ'reɪnɪən/ a. & n. iraniano, a m., f.

Iraq /ɪ'rɑːk/ n. Irak m. ~i a. & n. iracheno, a m., f.

irascible /ɪ'ræsəbl/ a. irascibile.

irate /aɪ'reɪt/ a. adirato.

ire /'aɪə(r)/ *n.* ira *f.*

Ireland /'aɪələnd/ *n.* Irlanda *f.*

iridescent /ɪrɪ'desnt/ *a.* iridescente.

iris /'aɪərɪs/ *n.* iride *f.*

Irish /'aɪərɪʃ/ *a.* & *n.* irlandese *m.* ~**man**, ~**woman** *ns.* irlandese *m., f.*

irk /ɜːk/ *v.t.* infastidire. ~**some** *a.* fastidioso.

iron /'aɪən/ *n.* ferro *m.*; (*appliance*) ferro (da stiro) *m.* —*a.* di ferro. —*v.t.* stirare. **I~ Curtain** *n.* cortina di ferro *f.* ~ **out** *v.t.* appianare. ~**ing-board** *n.* tavolo da stiro *m.*

ironic(al) /aɪ'rɒnɪk(l)/ *a.* ironico.

ironmonger /'aɪənmʌŋgə(r)/ *n.* negoziante in ferramenta *m.*

ironworks /'aɪənwɜːks/ *n.pl.* ferriera *f.s.*

irony /'aɪərənɪ/ *n.* ironia *f.*

irradiate /ɪ'reɪdɪeɪt/ *v.t.* irradiare.

irrational /ɪ'ræʃənl/ *a.* irrazionale.

irreconcilable /ɪrekən'saɪləbl/ *a.* irreconciliabile.

irrefutable /ɪrɪ'fjuːtəbl/ *a.* irrefutabile.

irregular /ɪ'regjʊlə(r)/ *a.* irregolare. ~**ity** /-'lærətɪ/ *n.* irregolarità *f.*

irrelevan|t /ɪ'reləvənt/ *a.* non pertinente. ~**ce** *n.* non pertinenza *f.*

irreparabl|e /ɪ'repərəbl/ *a.* irreparabile. ~**y** *adv.* irreparabilmente.

irreplaceable /ɪrɪ'pleɪsəbl/ *a.* insostituibile.

irrepressible /ɪrɪ'presəbl/ *a.* irrefrenabile.

irreproachable /ɪrɪ'prəʊtʃəbl/ *a.* irreprensibile.

irresistible /ɪrɪ'zɪstəbl/ *a.* irresistibile.

irresolute /ɪ'rezəluːt/ *a.* irresoluto.

irrespective /ɪrɪs'pektɪv/ *a.* ~ **of** senza riguardo a.

irresponsible /ɪrɪ'spɒnsəbl/ *a.* irresponsabile.

irretrievable /ɪrɪ'triːvəbl/ *a.* irrecuperabile.

irreverent /ɪ'revərənt/ *a.* irriverente.

irreversible /ɪrɪ'vɜːsəbl/ *a.* irreversibile.

irrevocable /ɪ'revəkəbl/ *a.* irrevocabile.

irrigat|e /'ɪrɪgeɪt/ *v.t.* irrigare. ~**ion** /-'geɪʃn/ *n.* irrigazione *f.*

irritable /'ɪrɪtəbl/ *a.* irritabile.

irritat|e /'ɪrɪteɪt/ *v.t.* irritare. ~**ion** /-'teɪʃn/ *n.* irritazione *f.*

is /ɪz/ *see* **be**.

Islam /'ɪzlɑːm/ *n.* Islam *m.* ~**ic** /ɪz'læmɪk/ *a.* islamico.

island /'aɪlənd/ *n.* isola *f.* **traffic** ~ isola pedonale *f.* ~**er** *n.* isolano, a *m., f.*

isle /aɪl/ *n.* isola *f.*

isolat|e /'aɪsəleɪt/ *v.t.* isolare. ~**ion** /-'leɪʃn/ *n.* isolamento *m.*

Israel /'ɪzreɪl/ *n.* Israele *m.* ~**i** /ɪz'reɪlɪ/ *a.* & *n.* israeliano, a *m., f.*

issue /'ɪʃuː/ *n.* uscita *f.*, sbocco *m.*; (*outcome*) risultato *m.*; (*of magazine etc.*) numero *m.*; (*of stamps etc.*) emissione *f.*; (*offspring*) figli *m.pl.* —*v.t.* distribuire; (*orders etc.*) emettere; (*book*) pubblicare. —*v.i.* ~ **from** uscire da. **at ~** in questione. **take ~** entrare in discussione.

isthmus /'ɪsməs/ *n.* (*pl.* **-muses**) istmo *m.*

it /ɪt/ *pron.* (*subject*) esso, essa; (*object*) lo, la, ciò; (*usually omitted before verb*) ~ **is hot** fa caldo. **it's me** sono io.

Ital|y /'ɪtəlɪ/ *n.* Italia *f.* ~**ian** /ɪ'taljən/ *a.* & *n.* italiano, a *m., f.*; (*lang.*) italiano *m.*

italic /ɪ'tælɪk/ *a.* italico. ~**s** *n.pl.* corsivo *m.s.*

itch /ɪtʃ/ *n.* prurito *m.* —*v.i.* avere prurito, prudere. **be ~ing to** aver voglia matta di. ~**y** *a.* che prude.

item /'aɪtəm/ *n.* articolo *m.*; (*on agenda*) punto *m.* ~**ize** *v.t.* dettagliare.

itinerant /aɪ'tɪnərənt/ *a.* girovago; (*musician*) ambulante.

itinerary /aɪ'tɪnərərɪ/ *n.* itinerario *m.*

its /ɪts/ *poss. pron.* suo, sua, suoi, sue.

it's /ɪts/ = **it is**, **it has**.

itself /ɪt'self/ *pron.* si; (*emphatic*) esso stesso, essa stessa.

ITV *n.* (*abbr. of* **Independent Television**) canale televisivo commerciale *m.*

ivory /'aɪvərɪ/ *n.* avorio *m.* —*a.* d'avorio.

ivy /'aɪvɪ/ *n.* edera *f.*

J

jab /dʒæb/ v.t. (p.t. jabbed) punzecchiare. —n. colpo secco m.; (fam.,
med.) puntura f.

jabber /'dʒæbə(r)/ v.i. borbottare. —n.
borbottio m.

jack /dʒæk/ n. (techn.) cricco m.; (flag)
bandiera (di nave) f.; (cards) fante
m. —v.t. ~ up sollevare (con cricco).

jackal /'dʒækɔːl/ n. sciacallo m.

jackass /'dʒækæs/ n. asino m.

jackdaw /'dʒækdɔː/ n. taccola f.

jacket /'dʒækɪt/ n. giacca f.; (of book)
sopraccoperta f.

jack-knife /'dʒæknaɪf/ n. coltello a serramanico m.

jackpot /'dʒækpɒt/ n. premio (di una
lotteria) m. hit the ~ vincere tutto.

jade /dʒeɪd/ n. giada f.

jaded /'dʒeɪdɪd/ a. spossato.

jagged /'dʒægɪd/ a. dentellato.

jaguar /'dʒægjʊə(r)/ n. giaguaro m.

jail /dʒeɪl/ = gaol.

jalopy /dʒə'lɒpɪ/ n. vecchia carcassa
(d'auto) f.

jam¹ /dʒæm/ n. marmellata f.

jam² /dʒæm/ v.t. (p.t. jammed) ingombrare; (mech.) bloccare; (radio)
disturbare. —v.i. incepparsi. —n.
pigiamento m.; (mech.) blocco m.; (of
traffic) ingorgo m.; (fam., difficulty)
guaio m. ~-packed a. (fam.) pieno
zeppo.

jamboree /dʒæmbə'riː/ n. baldoria f.;
(rally) raduno m.

Jamaica /dʒə'meɪkə/ n. Giamaica f.

jangle /dʒæŋgl/ n. suono stridente
m. —v.t./i. stridere.

janitor /'dʒænɪtə(r)/ n. portiere m.

January /'dʒænjʊərɪ/ n. gennaio m.

Japan /dʒə'pæn/ n. Giappone m. ~ese
/dʒæpə'niːz/ a. & n. giapponese m./f.

jar¹ /dʒɑː(r)/ n. vaso m., brocca f.

jar² /dʒɑː(r)/ v.i. (p.t. jarred) disso-
nare; (of colours etc.) discordare. —n.
dissonanza f. ~ring a. dissonante.

jargon /'dʒɑːgən/ n. gergo m.

jasmine /'dʒæsmɪn/ n. gelsomino m.

jaundice /'dʒɔːndɪs/ n. itterizia f.

jaundiced /'dʒɔːndɪst/ a. itterico; (fig.)
distorto.

jaunt /dʒɔːnt/ n. gita f.

jaunty /'dʒɔːntɪ/ a. (-ier, -iest) allegro.

javelin /'dʒævlɪn/ n. giavellotto m.

jaw /dʒɔː/ n. mascella f. —v.i. (fam.)
ciarlare.

jay /dʒeɪ/ n. ghiandaia f. ~-walker n.
pedone distratto m.

jazz /dʒæz/ n. jazz m. —v.t. ~ up
ravvivare. ~y a. vistoso.

jealous /'dʒeləs/ a. geloso. ~y n. gelo-
sia f.

jeans /dʒiːnz/ n.pl. blue jeans m.pl.

jeep /dʒiːp/ n. jeep f. invar., camionetta
f.

jeer /dʒɪə(r)/ v.t./i. ~ at prendersi
gioco di; (boo) fischiare. —n. scherno
m.

jell /dʒel/ v.i. concretarsi.

jell|y /'dʒelɪ/ n. gelatina. ~ied a. in
gelatina.

jellyfish /'dʒelɪfɪʃ/ n. medusa f.

jeopard|y /'dʒepədɪ/ n. pericolo m.
~ize v.t. mettere in pericolo.

jerk /dʒɜːk/ n. scatto m., scossa f.
—v.t./i. scattare. ~ily adv. a scatti.
~y a. traballante.

jersey /'dʒɜːzɪ/ n. (pl. -eys) jersey m.;
(pullover) maglia f.

jest /dʒest/ n. scherzo m. —v.i. scherzare. ~er n. buffone m.

Jesus /'dʒiːzəs/ n. Gesù m.

jet¹ /dʒet/ n. ambra nera f. ~-black a.
nero ebano.

jet² /dʒet/ n. getto m.; (plane) aviogetto
m., jet m. invar.; ~ lag n. stanchezza
(causata da volo attraverso il fuso
orario) f. ~-propelled a. a reazione.

jettison /'dʒetɪsn/ v.t. gettare a mare.

jetty /'dʒetɪ/ n. molo m.

Jew /dʒuː/ n. ebreo m. ~ess n. ebrea
f.

jewel /'dʒuːəl/ n. gioiello m. ~ler n.
gioielliere, a m., f. ~lery n. gioielli
m.pl.

Jewish /'dʒuːɪʃ/ a. ebreo.

jib /dʒɪb/ v.i. (p.t. jibbed) recalcitrare.
~ at mostrare ripugnanza per.

jiffy /'dʒɪfɪ/ n. (fam.) in a ~ in un batter
d'occhio.

jig /dʒɪg/ n. giga f.

jiggle /'dʒɪgl/ v.t. (far) oscillare.

jigsaw /'dʒɪgsɔː/ ~ (puzzle) n. puzzle
m. invar.

jilt /dʒɪlt/ v.t. piantare in asso.

jingle /'dʒɪŋgl/ v.t./i. (far) tintinnare.
—n. tintinnio m.

jinx /dʒɪŋks/ *n.* (*fam.*) malocchio *m.*

jitter|s /'dʒɪtəz/ *n.pl.* (*fam.*) fifa *f.s.* **~y** /-ərɪ/ *a.* (*fam.*) nervoso.

job /dʒɒb/ *n.* lavoro *m.*; (*post*) posto *m.*; (*fam., thing*) faccenda *f.* **it's a good ~ that** meno male che. **~less** *a.* senza lavoro.

job centre /'dʒɒbsentə(r)/ *n.* ufficio statale di collocamento *m.*

jockey /'dʒɒkɪ/ *n.* (*pl.* **-eys**) fantino *m.* **disc ~** *n.* presentatore di programma di dischi *m.*

jocular /'dʒɒkjʊlə(r)/ *a.* scherzoso.

jog /dʒɒg/ *v.t.* (*p.t.* **jogged**) sballottare; (*memory*) rinfrescare. —*v.i.* fare il footing. —*n.* colpetto *m.*; (*pace*) andatura lenta *f.* **~ging** *n.* jogging *m. invar.*

join /dʒɔɪn/ *v.t.* raggiungere, riunire; (*become member of*) iscriversi a. —*v.i.* (*of roads etc.*) congiungersi. —*n.* giuntura *f.* **~ in** *v.i.* partecipare a. **~ up** *v.i.* (*mil.*) arruolarsi.

joiner /'dʒɔɪnə(r)/ *n.* falegname *m.*

joint /dʒɔɪnt/ *a.* comune. —*n.* giuntura *f.*; (*anat.*) articolazione *f.*; (*culin.*) arrosto *m.*; (*sl., tavern*) bettola *f.*; (*sl., drug*) sigaretta alla marijuana *f.* **~ly** *adv.* unitamente.

joist /dʒɔɪst/ *n.* travetto *m.*

jok|e /dʒəʊk/ *n.* scherzo *m.*; (*funny story*) barzelletta *f.* —*v.i.* scherzare. **~er** *n.* burlone, a *m., f.*; (*cards*) jolly *m. invar.* **~ingly** *adv.* per scherzo.

joll|y /'dʒɒlɪ/ *a.* (**-ier, -iest**) allegro. —*adv.* (*fam.*) molto. **~ification** /-fɪ'keɪʃn/, **~ity** *ns.* allegria *f.*

jolt /dʒəʊlt/ *v.t./i.* (far) sobbalzare. —*n.* scossa *f.*, sobbalzo *m.*

Jordan /'dʒɔːdən/ *n.* Giordania *f.*

jostle /'dʒɒsl/ *v.t./i.* spingere, spingersi.

jot /dʒɒt/ *n.* nulla *m.* —*v.t.* (*p.t.* **jotted**) annotare. **~ter** *n.* taccuino *m.*

journal /'dʒɜːnl/ *n.* giornale *m.* **~ism** *n.* giornalismo *m.* **~ist** *n.* giornalista *m./f.*

journalese /dʒɜːnə'liːz/ *n.* gergo giornalistico *m.*

journey /'dʒɜːnɪ/ *n.* (*pl.* **-eys**) viaggio *m.*; (*distance*) tragitto *m.* —*v.i.* viaggiare.

jovial /'dʒəʊvɪəl/ *a.* gioviale.

jowl /'dʒaʊl/ *n.* mascella *f.*

joy /dʒɔɪ/ *n.* gioia *f.* **~-ride** *n.* (*fam.*) gita in macchina (specialmente rubata) *f.* **~ful, ~ous** *adjs.* gioioso.

jubil|ant /'dʒuːbɪlənt/ *a.* giubilante. **~ation** /-'leɪʃn/ *n.* giubilo *m.*

jubilee /'dʒuːbɪliː/ *n.* giubileo *m.*

Judaism /'dʒuːdeɪɪzəm/ *n.* giudaismo *m.*

judge /dʒʌdʒ/ *n.* giudice *m.* —*v.t.* giudicare. **~ment** *n.* giudizio *m.*

judic|iary /dʒuː'dɪʃərɪ/ *n.* magistratura *f.* **~ial** *a.* giudiziario.

judicious /dʒuː'dɪʃəs/ *a.* giudizioso.

judo /'dʒuːdəʊ/ *n.* judo *m.*

jug /dʒʌg/ *n.* boccale *m.*

juggernaut /'dʒʌgənɔːt/ *n.* (*fam.*) grosso autotreno *m.*

juggle /'dʒʌgl/ *v.i.* fare giochi di destrezza. **~r** /-ə(r)/ *n.* giocoliere, a *m.*, *f.*

juic|e /dʒuːs/ *n.* succo *m.* **~y** *a.* succoso; (*fam., story*) piccante.

juke-box /'dʒuːkbɒks/ *n.* juke-box *m. invar.*

July /dʒuː'laɪ/ *n.* luglio *m.*

jumble /'dʒʌmbl/ *v.t.* mischiare. —*n.* miscuglio *m.* **~ sale** *n.* vendita di beneficenza *f.*

jumbo /'dʒʌmbəʊ/ *n.* (*pl.* **-os**) **~ jet** jumbo jet *m. invar.*

jump /dʒʌmp/ *v.t./i.* saltare; (*start*) sussultare; (*of prices*) salire rapidamente; (*abscond*) fuggire da. —*n.* salto *m.*; (*of prices*) sbalzo *m.* **~ at** accettare con entusiasmo. **~ the gun** agire prematuramente. **~ the queue** non rispettare la fila. **~ed-up** *a.* arrivato.

jumper /'dʒʌmpə(r)/ *n.* maglione *m.*

jumpy /'dʒʌmpɪ/ *a.* nervoso.

junction /'dʒʌŋkʃn/ *n.* congiunzione *f.*; (*of roads*) bivio *m.*

juncture /'dʒʌŋktʃə(r)/ *n.* **at this ~** a questo punto.

June /dʒuːn/ *n.* giugno *m.*

jungle /'dʒʌŋgl/ *n.* giungla *f.*

junior /'dʒuːnɪə(r)/ *a.* più giovane (**to,** di); (*in rank*) subalterno. **~ school** *n.* scuola elementare *f.*

junk /dʒʌŋk/ *n.* cianfrusaglie *f.pl.* **~shop** *n.* negozio di rigattiere *m.*

junkie /'dʒʌŋkɪ/ *n.* (*sl.*) tossicomane *m./f.*

junta /'dʒʌntə/ *n.* giunta *f.*

jurisdiction /dʒʊərɪs'dɪkʃn/ *n.* giurisdizione *f.*

jurisprudence /dʒʊərɪs'pruːdns/ *n.* giurisprudenza *f.*

juror /'dʒʊərə(r)/ *n.* giurato *m.*

jury /'dʒʊərɪ/ *n.* giuria *f.*

just /dʒʌst/ *a.* giusto. —*adv.* esattamente; (*merely*) appena; (*really*) veramente. **~ly** *adv.* giustamente.

justice /'dʒʌstɪs/ *n.* giustizia *f.* **court of ~** *n.* tribunale *m.* **J~ of the Peace** *n.* giudice conciliatore *m.*

justifiabl|e /dʒʌstɪ'faɪəbl/ *a.* giustificabile. **~y** *adv.* giustificabilmente.

justif|y /'dʒʌstɪfaɪ/ *v.t.* giustificare. **~ication** /-ɪ'keɪʃn/ *n.* giustificazione *f.*

jut /dʒʌt/ *v.i.* (*p.t.* **jutted**) **~ out** sporgere.

juvenile /'dʒuːvənaɪl/ *a.* giovanile; (*for the young*) per i giovani. —*n.* giovane *m./f.*

juxtapose /dʒʌkstə'pəʊz/ *v.t.* giustapporre.

K

kaleidoscope /kə'laɪdəskəʊp/ *n.* caleidoscopio *m.*

kangaroo /kæŋgə'ruː/ *n.* canguro *m.*

kapok /'keɪpɒk/ *n.* capoc *m.*

karate /kə'rɑːtɪ/ *n.* karatè *m.*

kebab /kə'bæb/ *n.* spiedino di carne *m.*

keel /kiːl/ *n.* chiglia *f.* —*v.i.* ~ **over** capovolgersi.

keen /kiːn/ *a.* (-**er**, -**est**) (*interest*) vivo; (*sharp*) tagliente; (*intense*) acuto; (*eager*) entusiastico. ~ **on** entusiasta di. ~**ly** *adv.* intensamente. ~**ness** *n.* intensità *f.*; entusiasmo *m.*

keep /kiːp/ *v.t.* (*p.t.* **kept**) tenere; (*promise, family*) mantenere; (*detain*) trattenere; (*rules etc.*) rispettare. —*v.i.* tenersi; (*remain*) rimanere. —*n.* mantenimento *m.*; (*of castle*) maschio *m.* **for** ~**s** (*fam.*) per sempre. ~ **back** *v.t.* trattenere; *v.i.* tenersi indietro. ~ **in with** *v.i.* mantenersi in buoni rapporti con. ~ (**on**) continuare (a). ~ **up with** *v.i.* seguire da vicino; stare al passo con. ~**er** *n.* custode *m./f.*

keeping /'kiːpɪŋ/ *n.* custodia *f.* **in** ~ **with** in armonia con.

keepsake /'kiːpseɪk/ *n.* ricordo *m.*

keg /keg/ *n.* barilotto *m.*

kennel /'kenl/ *n.* canile *m.*

Kenya /'kenjə/ *n.* Kenia *m.*

kept /kept/ *see* keep.

kerb /kɜːb/ *n.* bordo del marciapiede *m.*

kerfuffle /kə'fʌfl/ *n.* (*fam.*) trambusto *m.*

kernel /'kɜːnl/ *n.* nocciolo *m.*

kerosene /'kerəsiːn/ *n.* cherosene *m.*

ketchup /'ketʃəp/ *n.* salsa piccante *f.*

kettle /'ketl/ *n.* bollitore *m.*

key /kiː/ *n.* chiave *f.*; (*of piano, typewriter*) tasto *m.* ~**-ring** *n.* anello portachiavi *m.* —*v.t.* ~ **up** (*fig.*) stimolare.

keyboard /'kiːbɔːd/ *n.* tastiera *f.*

keyhole /'kiːhəʊl/ *n.* buco della serratura *m.*

keynote /'kiːnəʊt/ *n.* nota dominante *f.*

keystone /'kiːstəʊn/ *n.* chiave di volta *f.*

khaki /'kɑːkɪ/ *a.* & *n.* cachi *m.*

kick /kɪk/ *v.t./i.* dar calci; (*of gun*) rinculare. —*n.* calcio *m.*; (*fam., thrill*) piacere *m.* ~**-off** *n.* calcio d'inizio *m.* ~ **up a row** fare una scenata.

kickback /'kɪkbæk/ *n.* contraccolpo *m.*; (*sl., percentage*) tangente *f.*

kid /kɪd/ *n.* capretto *m.*; (*child*) ragazzino, a *m.,f.* —*v.i.* (*p.t.* **kidded**) (*fam.*) scherzare. —*v.t.* (*fam.*) prendere in giro.

kidnap /'kɪdnæp/ *v.t.* (*p.t.* **kidnapped**) rapire. ~**ping** *n.* rapimento *m.*

kidney /'kɪdnɪ/ *n.* (*pl.* -**eys**) rene *m.*; (*culin.*) rognone *m.*

kill /kɪl/ *v.t.* uccidere; (*fig.*) metter fine a. —*n.* uccisione *f.*; (*in hunt*) cacciagione *f.* ~**er** *n.* uccisore *m.* ~**ing** *n.* uccisione *f.*; *a.* (*unbearable*) micidiale; (*funny, fam.*) molto divertente.

killjoy /'kɪldʒɔɪ/ *n.* guastafeste *m./f. invar.*

kiln /kɪln/ *n.* forno *m.*

kilo /'kiːləʊ/ *n.* (*pl.* -**os**) chilo *m.*

kilogram /'kɪləgræm/ *n.* chilogrammo *m.*

kilometre /'kɪləmiːtə(r)/ *n.* chilometro *m.*

kilowatt /'kɪləwɒt/ *n.* chilowatt *m. invar.*

kilt /kɪlt/ *n.* gonnellino degli scozzesi *m.*

kin /kɪn/ *n.* congiunti *m.pl.* **next of** ~ parenti più stretti *m.pl.*

kind[1] /kaɪnd/ *n.* genere *m.*, specie *f.* **in** ~ in natura. ~ **of** (*fam.*) alquanto. **two of a** ~ due della stessa specie.

kind[2] /kaɪnd/ *a.* (-**er**, -**est**) gentile, buono. ~ **regards** cordiali saluti *m.pl.* ~**ness** *n.* gentilezza *f.*

kindergarten /'kɪndəgɑːtn/ *n.* asilo infantile *m.*

kindle /'kɪndl/ *v.t./i.* accendere, accendersi.

kindly /'kaɪndlɪ/ *a.* (-**ier**, -**iest**) benevolo. —*adv.* gentilmente; (*please*) per favore.

kindred /'kɪndrɪd/ *n.* parentela *f.* —*a.* imparentato.

kinetic /kɪ'netɪk/ *a.* cinetico.

king /kɪŋ/ *n.* re *m. invar.* ~**-size(d)** *a.* extra-lungo, grande.

kingdom /'kɪŋdəm/ *n.* regno *m.*

kingpin /'kɪŋpɪn/ *n.* perno *m.*

kink /kɪŋk/ n. nodo m.; (fig.) bizzarria f. ~y a. bizzarro; (perverted) pervertito.

kiosk /'kiːɒsk/ n. chiosco m. **telephone** ~ cabina telefonica f.

kip /kɪp/ n. (sl.) pisolino m. —v.i. (p.t. **kipped**) (sl.) dormire.

kipper /'kɪpə(r)/ n. aringa affumicata f.

kiss /kɪs/ n. bacio m. —v.t./i. baciare, baciarsi.

kit /kɪt/ n. equipaggiamento m.; (tools) attrezzi m.pl. —v.t. (p.t. **kitted**) ~ **out** equipaggiare.

kitbag /'kɪtbæg/ n. sacco a spalla m.

kitchen /'kɪtʃɪn/ n. cucina f. ~ **garden** n. orto m.

kitchenette /kɪtʃɪ'net/ n. cucinino m.

kite /kaɪt/ n. (toy) aquilone m.

kith /kɪθ/ n. ~ **and kin** amici e parenti m.pl.

kitten /'kɪtn/ n. gattino m.

kitty /'kɪtɪ/ n. fondo comune m.

kleptomaniac /kleptəʊ'meɪnɪæk/ n. cleptomane m./f.

knack /næk/ n. destrezza f.

knapsack /'næpsæk/ n. sacco da montagna m.

knead /niːd/ v.t. impastare.

knee /niː/ n. ginocchio m. ~**s-up** n. (fam.) festa f.

kneecap /'niːkæp/ n. rotella f.

kneel /niːl/ v.i. (p.t. **knelt**) inginocchiarsi.

knell /nel/ n. campana a morto f.

knelt /nelt/ see **kneel**.

knew /njuː/ see **know**.

knickerbockers /'nɪkəbɒkəz/ n.pl. pantaloni alla zuava m.pl.

knickers /'nɪkəz/ n.pl. mutandine f.pl.

knick-knack /'nɪknæk/ n. gingillo m.

knife /naɪf/ n. (pl. **knives**) coltello m. —v.t. accoltellare.

knight /naɪt/ n. cavaliere m.; (chess) cavallo m. —v.t. creare cavaliere. ~**hood** n. rango di cavaliere m.

knit /nɪt/ v.t./i. (p.t. **knitted** or **knit**) lavorare a maglia; (fig.) unire. ~ **one's brow** corrugare la fronte. ~**ting** n. lavoro a maglia m.

knitwear /'nɪtweə(r)/ n. maglieria f.

knob /nɒb/ n. pomo m. ~**bly** a. nodoso.

knock /nɒk/ v.t./i. battere; (at door) bussare; (sl.) denigrare. —n. colpo m. ~ **about** v.t. malmenare. ~ **down** v.t. (demolish) abbattere; (reduce) ribassare. ~**-down** a. molto basso. ~**kneed** a. dalle gambe storte. ~ **off** v.t. (fam.) sottrarre; v.i. (cease work) smettere. ~ **out** v.t. mettere fuori combattimento. ~**-out** n. (boxing) knock-out m. ~ **over** v.t. rovesciare. ~ **up** v.t. (meal etc.) preparare. ~**er** n. battente m.

knot /nɒt/ n. nodo m. —v.t. (p.t. **knotted**) annodare.

knotty /'nɒtɪ/ a. (-ier, -iest) nodoso.

know /nəʊ/ v.t./i. (p.t. **knew**, p.p. **known**) sapere; (person, place) conoscere. —n. **in the** ~ (fam.) al corrente. ~**-all** n. (fam.) sapientone, a m.,f. ~**-how** n. abilità f. ~**ingly** adv. consapevolmente.

knowledge /'nɒlɪdʒ/ n. conoscenza f. ~**able** a. ben informato.

known /nəʊn/ see **know** —a. noto.

knuckle /'nʌkl/ n. nocca f. —v.i. ~ **under** sottomettersi.

Koran /kə'rɑːn/ n. Corano m.

Korea /kə'rɪə/ n. Corea f.

kosher /'kəʊʃə(r)/ a. kasher.

kowtow /kaʊ'taʊ/ v.i. prostrarsi.

kudos /'kjuːdɒs/ n. (fam.) onore m.

L

lab /læb/ *n.* (*fam.*) laboratorio *m.*
label /'leɪbl/ *n.* etichetta *f.* —*v.t.* (*p.t.* **labelled**) mettere un'etichetta (a).
laboratory /lə'bɒrətrɪ/ *n.* laboratorio *m.*
laborious /lə'bɔːrɪəs/ *a.* laborioso.
labour /'leɪbə(r)/ *n.* lavoro *m.*; (*workers*) manodopera *f.* **be in** ~ (*med.*) avere le doglie. —*v.t./i.* lavorare; (*hard*) sgobbare. ~ **at** affaticarsi. ~**ed** *a.* difficile.
Labour /'leɪbə(r)/ *n.* ~ **Party** partito laburista *m.*
labourer /'leɪbərə(r)/ *n.* manovale *m.*
labyrinth /'læbərɪnθ/ *n.* labirinto *m.*
lace /leɪs/ *n.* merletto *m.*; (*of shoe*) laccio *m.* —*v.t.* allacciare; (*drink*) correggere.
lacerate /'læsəreɪt/ *v.t.* lacerare.
lack /læk/ *n.* mancanza *f.* —*v.t.* mancare di.
lackadaisical /lækə'deɪzɪkl/ *a.* apatico.
lackey /'lækɪ/ *n.* lacchè *m.*
laconic /lə'kɒnɪk/ *a.* laconico.
lacquer /'lækə(r)/ *n.* lacca *f.*
lad /læd/ *n.* ragazzo *m.*
ladder /'lædə(r)/ *n.* scala *f.*; (*in tights*) smagliatura *f.* —*v.i.* smagliarsi.
laden /'leɪdn/ *a.* carico (*with*, di).
ladle /'leɪdl/ *n.* mestolo *m.*
lady /'leɪdɪ/ *n.* signora *f.* ~**-in- waiting** *n.* dama di corte *f.* ~**like** *a.* signorile.
ladybird /'leɪdɪbɜːd/ *n.* coccinella *f.*
ladyship /'leɪdɪʃɪp/ *n.* Signoria *f.*
lag /læg/ *v.i.* (*p.t.* **lagged**) (*go slow*) attardarsi. ~ **behind** restare indietro. ~**gard** *n.* infingardo, a *m.*, *f.*
lager /'lɑːgə(r)/ *n.* birra chiara *f.*
lagging /'lægɪŋ/ *n.* materiale isolante *m.*
lagoon /lə'guːn/ *n.* laguna *f.*
lah /lɑː/ *n.* (*mus.*) la *m.*
laid /leɪd/ *see* **lay²**.
lain /leɪn/ *see* **lie²**.
lair /leə(r)/ *n.* tana *f.*
laity /'leɪətɪ/ *n.* laicato *m.*
lake /leɪk/ *n.* lago *m.*
lamb /læm/ *n.* agnello *m.* ~**'s-wool** *n.* lana d'agnello *f.*
lame /leɪm/ *a.* (**-er, -est**) zoppo; (*argument*) debole.
lament /lə'ment/ *n.* lamento *m.* —*v.t./i.* lamentare, lamentarsi. ~**able** *a.* lamentevole.
laminated /'læmɪneɪtɪd/ *a.* laminato.
lamp /læmp/ *n.* lampada *f.*
lamp-post /'læmppəʊst/ *n.* lampione *m.*
lampshade /'læmpʃeɪd/ *n.* paralume *m.*
lance /lɑːns/ *n.* lancia *f.* —*v.t.* (*med.*) incidere. ~**-corporal** *n.* appuntato *m.*
lancet /'lɑːnsɪt/ *n.* (*med.*) bisturi *m.*
land /lænd/ *n.* terra *f.*, terreno *m.*; (*country*) paese *m.* —*v.t./i.* sbarcare; (*aeron.*) atterrare; (*fall*) cadere; (*a blow, fam.*) assestare; (*reach*) trovarsi; (*obtain*) assicurarsi. ~**-locked** *a.* circondato da terra. ~**ed** *a.* terriero.
landing /'lændɪŋ/ *n.* sbarco *m.*; (*aeron.*) atterraggio *m.*; (*top of stairs*) pianerottolo *m.* ~**-stage** *n.* pontile da sbarco *m.*
land\|lady /'lændleɪdɪ/ *n.* proprietaria *f.*; (*of inn etc.*) affittacamere *f.* *invar.* ~**lord** *n.* proprietario *m.*; padrone *m.*; (*of pub etc.*) oste *m.*
landmark /'lændmɑːk/ *n.* punto di riferimento *m.*; (*fig.*) pietra miliare *f.*
landscape /'lændskeɪp/ *n.* paesaggio *m.*
landslide /'lændslaɪd/ *n.* frana *f.*; (*pol.*) valanga di voti *f.*
lane /leɪn/ *n.* sentiero *m.*; (*of traffic*) corsia *f.*; (*aeron.*) rotta *f.*
language /'læŋgwɪdʒ/ *n.* lingua *f.*; (*speech, style*) linguaggio *m.*
languid /'læŋgwɪd/ *a.* languido.
lang\|uish /'læŋgwɪʃ/ *v.i.* languire. ~**uor** /-ə(r)/ *n.* languore *m.*
lank /læŋk/ *a.* allampanato; (*of hair*) liscio.
lanky /'læŋkɪ/ *a.* (**-ier, -iest**) dinoccolato.
lantern /'læntən/ *n.* lanterna *f.*
lap¹ /læp/ *n.* grembo *m.*; (*of dress*) lembo *m.*; (*sport, journey*) tappa *f.* —*v.t./i.* (*p.t.* **lapped**) ~ **over** sovrapporre, sovrapporsi.
lap² /læp/ *v.t.* (*p.t.* **lapped**) ~ **up** bere avidamente.
lapel /lə'pel/ *n.* risvolto *m.*
lapse /læps/ *v.i.* scivolare; (*expire*)

scadere. —*n.* sbaglio *m.*; (*of time*) intervallo *m.* ~ **into** cadere in.

larceny /'lɑːsənɪ/ *n.* ladrocinio *m.*

lard /lɑːd/ *n.* strutto *m.*

larder /'lɑːdə(r)/ *n.* dispensa *f.*

large /lɑːdʒ/ *a.* (**-er, -est**) grande, grosso. **at** ~ in libertà; (*as a whole*) in generale. **by and** ~ in complesso. ~**ly** *adv.* ampiamente. ~**ness** *n.* grandezza *f.* ~**sse** /-'dʒes/ *n.* generosità *f.*

lark[1] /lɑːk/ *n.* (*bird*) allodola *f.*

lark[2] /lɑːk/ *n.* (*joke*) burla *f.* —*v.i.* ~ **about** giocherellare.

larva /'lɑːvə/ *n.* (*pl.* **-vae** /-viː/) larva *f.*

laryngitis /lærɪn'dʒaɪtɪs/ *n.* laringite *f.*

larynx /'lærɪŋks/ *n.* laringe *f.*

lascivious /lə'sɪvɪəs/ *a.* lascivo.

laser /'leɪzə(r)/ *n.* laser *m.*

lash /læʃ/ *v.t.* frustare. —*n.* frustata *f.*; (*eyelash*) ciglio *m.* ~ **out** attaccare; (*spend*) sperperare.

lashings /'læʃɪŋz/ *n.pl.* ~ **of** (*sl.*) abbondanza di *f.s.*

lass /læs/ *n.* ragazzina *f.*

lassitude /'læsɪtjuːd/ *n.* stanchezza *f.*

lasso /læ'suː/ *n.* (*pl.* **-os**) laccio *m.*

last[1] /lɑːst/ *a.* ultimo; (*recent*) scorso. —*adv.* per ultimo; (*most recently*) l'ultima volta. —*n.* ultimo, a *m.*, *f.* **at** ~! finalmente! **at** (**long**) ~ alla fine. ~ **but one** penultimo. ~ **night** ieri sera. **the** ~ **straw** il colmo. ~**ly** *adv.* infine.

last[2] /lɑːst/ *v.i.* durare. ~ **out** sopravvivere. ~**ing** *a.* durevole.

last[3] /lɑːst/ *n.* (*block*) forma (da scarpa) *f.*

latch /lætʃ/ *n.* chiavistello *m.*; (*on gate*) saliscendi *m.*

late /leɪt/ *a.* (**-er, -est**) in ritardo; (*at a late hour*) tardo; (*recent*) recente; (*former*) ex; (*deceased*) defunto. —*adv.* tardi. **of** ~ recentemente. ~**ness** *n.* ora tarda *f.*

lately /'leɪtlɪ/ *adv.* recentemente.

latent /'leɪtnt/ *a.* latente.

lateral /'lætərəl/ *a.* laterale.

lathe /leɪð/ *n.* tornio *m.*

lather /'lɑːðə(r)/ *n.* schiuma *f.* —*v.t.* insaponare. —*v.i.* far schiuma.

Latin /'lætɪn/ *a.* & *n.* latino *m.*

latitude /'lætɪtjuːd/ *n.* latitudine *f.*

latrine /lə'triːn/ *n.* latrina *f.*

latter /'lætə(r)/ *a.* più recente, ultimo. ~**-day** *a.* moderno. ~**ly** *adv.* ultimamente.

lattice /'lætɪs/ *n.* traliccio *m.*

laudable /'lɔːdəbl/ *a.* lodevole.

laugh /lɑːf/ *v.i.* ridere (**at**, di). —*n.* risata *f.* ~**able** *a.* ridicolo. ~**ing-stock** *n.* zimbello *m.*

laughter /'lɑːftə(r)/ *n.* risata *f.*

launch[1] /lɔːntʃ/ *v.t.* lanciare; (*ship*) varare; (*attack*) sferrare. —*n.* lancio *m.*; varo *m.* ~ (**out**) **into** intraprendere. ~**ing pad** *n.* piattaforma di lancio *f.*

launch[2] /lɔːntʃ/ *n.* lancia *f.*

laund|er /'lɔːndə(r)/ *v.t.* lavare e stirare. ~**ress** *n.* lavandaia *f.*

launderette /lɔːn'dret/ *n.* lavanderia automatica *f.*

laundry /'lɔːndrɪ/ *n.* lavanderia *f.*; (*clothes*) bucato *m.*

laurel /'lɒrəl/ *n.* lauro *m.*

lava /'lɑːvə/ *n.* lava *f.*

lavatory /'lævətrɪ/ *n.* gabinetto *m.*

lavender /'lævəndə(r)/ *n.* lavanda *f.*

lavish /'lævɪʃ/ *a.* prodigo; (*plentiful*) copioso. —*v.t.* profondere. ~**ly** *adv.* copiosamente.

law /lɔː/ *n.* legge *f.* ~**-abiding** *a.* disciplinato. ~ **and order** *n.* ordine pubblico *m.* ~**ful** *a.* legittimo. ~**fully** *adv.* legalmente. ~**less** *a.* senza legge. **L**~ **Courts** *n.pl.* tribunale *m.*

lawn /lɔːn/ *n.* prato *m.* ~**-mower** *n.* falciatrice *f.*

lawsuit /'lɔːsjuːt/ *n.* causa *f.*

lawyer /'lɔːjə(r)/ *n.* avvocato *m.*

lax /læks/ *a.* negligente; (*morals etc.*) rilassato. ~**ity** *n.* negligenza *f.*

laxative /'læksətɪv/ *n.* lassativo *m.*

lay[1] /leɪ/ *a.* laico; (*opinion etc.*) profano.

lay[2] /leɪ/ *v.t.* (*p.t.* **laid**) porre, mettere; (*eggs*) fare (le uova); (*table*) apparecchiare; (*trap*) tendere; (*siege*) porre. ~ **aside** *v.t.* mettere da parte. ~ **down** *v.t.* posare; (*conditions, rules*) stabilire. ~ **hands on** *v.i.* impadronirsi di. ~ **hold of** *v.t.* afferrare. ~ **into** *v.i.* (*sl.*) picchiare. ~ **off** *v.t.* licenziare. ~ **on** *v.t.* (*organize*) organizzare. ~ **out** *v.t.* stendere; (*spend*) sborsare. ~ **up** *v.t.* (*store*) accumulare.

layabout /'leɪəbaʊt/ *n.* fannullone, a *m.*, *f.*

lay-by /'leɪbaɪ/ *n.* corsia di sosta *f.*

layer /'leɪə(r)/ *n.* strato *m.*

layette /leɪ'et/ *n.* corredino (da neonato) *m.*

layman /'leɪmən/ *n.* (*pl.* -**men**) profano *m.*

layout /'leɪaʊt/ *n.* disposizione *f.*

laze /leɪz/ *v.i.* oziare.

laz|y /'leɪzɪ/ *a.* (-**ier**, -**iest**) pigro. ~**iness** *n.* pigrizia *f.* ~**y-bones** *n.* poltrone, a *m.*, *f.*

lead[1] /liːd/ *v.t.*/*i.* (*p.t.* **led**) condurre; (*team etc.*) dirigere; (*induce*) indurre; (*at cards*) giocare (per primo). —*n.* guida *f.*; (*leash*) guinzaglio *m.*; (*theatr.*) parte principale *f.*; (*wire*) filo *m.* **in the** ~ in testa. ~ **away** *v.t.* portar via. ~ **up to** *v.t.* preludere.

lead[2] /led/ *n.* piombo *m.*; (*of pencil*) mina *f.* ~**en** *a.* di piombo.

leader /'liːdə(r)/ *n.* capo *m.*; (*in newspaper*) articolo di fondo *m.* ~**ship** *n.* direzione *f.*

leading /'liːdɪŋ/ *a.* principale. ~ **question** *n.* domanda tendenziosa *f.*

leaf /liːf/ *n.* (*pl.* **leaves**) foglia *f.*; (*of book*) foglio *m.*; (*of metal*) lamina *f.*; (*of table*) asse *f.* —*v.i.* ~ **through** sfogliare. ~**y** *a.* frondoso.

leaflet /'liːflɪt/ *n.* dépliant *m.*; manifestino *m.*

league /liːg/ *n.* lega *f.* **be in** ~ **with** essere in combutta con.

leak /liːk/ *n.* fessura *f.*; (*of gas*) fuga *f.* —*v.i.* colare. —*v.t.* perdere; (*fig.*) far trapelare. ~**age** *n.* perdita *f.*; fuga *f.* ~**y** *a.* che perde.

lean[1] /liːn/ *a.* (-**er**, -**est**) magro; (*fig.*) povero. ~**ness** *n.* magrezza *f.*

lean[2] /liːn/ *v.t.*/*i.* (*p.t.* **leaned**, *p.p.* **leant** /lent/) (far) pendere. ~ **against** appoggiare, appoggiarsi a. ~ **back** sdraiarsi. ~ **forward** *or* **over** piegarsi. ~ (**up**)**on** dipendere da. ~ **towards** tendere verso. ~-**to** *n.* baracca *f.*

leaning /'liːnɪŋ/ *a.* pendente. —*n.* tendenza *f.*

leap /liːp/ *v.i.* (*p.t.* **leaped**, *p.p.* **leapt** /lept/) saltare. —*n.* salto *m.* ~-**frog** *n.* saltamontone *m.*; *v.i.* (*p.t.* -**frogged**) giocare alla cavallina. ~ **year** *n.* anno bisestile *m.*

learn /lɜːn/ *v.t.*/*i.* (*p.t.* **learned**, *p.p.* **learnt**) imparare. ~**er** *n.* principiante *m.*/*f.*; (*apprentice*) apprendista *m.*/*f.*

learn|ed /'lɜːnɪd/ *a.* colto. ~**ing** *n.* cultura *f.*

lease /liːs/ *n.* contratto d'affitto *m.* —*v.t.* affittare. ~**hold** *n.* proprietà in affitto *f.*

leash /liːʃ/ *n.* guinzaglio *m.*

least /liːst/ *a.* il più piccolo; (*slightest*) il minimo; (*smallest amount*) il meno. —*n.* il meno *m.* —*adv.* meno, minimamente. **at** ~ almeno. **not in the** ~ niente affatto.

leather /'leðə(r)/ *n.* cuoio *m.*

leave /liːv/ *v.t.* (*p.t.* **left**) lasciare; (*go away*) partire. —*n.* permesso *m.* ~ **out** omettere. **on** ~ in licenza. **take one's** ~ accomiatarsi.

leavings /'liːvɪŋz/ *n.pl.* resti *m.pl.*

Leban|on /'lebənən/ *n.* Libano *m.* ~**ese** /-'niːz/ *a.* & *n.* libanese *m.*/*f.*

lecher /'letʃə(r)/ *n.* libertino *m.* ~**ous** *a.* lascivo. ~**y** *n.* lascivia *f.*

lectern /'lektən/ *n.* leggio *m.*

lecture /'lektʃə(r)/ *n.* conferenza *f.*; (*univ.*) lezione *f.*; (*reproof*) ramanzina *f.* —*v.i.* fare una conferenza; fare lezioni. —*v.t.* fare una ramanzina. ~**r** *n.* conferenziere, a *m.*, *f.*; (*univ.*) docente universitario, a *m.*, *f.*

led /led/ *see* **lead**[1].

ledge /ledʒ/ *n.* sporgenza *f.*; (*of window*) davanzale *m.*

ledger /'ledʒə(r)/ *n.* libro mastro *m.*

lee /liː/ *n.* riparo *m.*

leech /liːtʃ/ *n.* sanguisuga *f.*

leek /liːk/ *n.* porro *m.*

leer /lɪə(r)/ *v.i.* ~ (**at**) sbirciare. —*n.* sbirciata *f.*

leeway /'liːweɪ/ *n.* deriva *f.*; (*fig.*) libertà di azione *f.*

left[1] /left/ *see* **leave**. ~ **luggage** (**office**) *n.* deposito bagagli *m.* ~-**overs** *n.pl.* rimasugli *m.pl.*

left[2] /left/ *a.* sinistro. —*adv.* a sinistra. —*n.* sinistra *f.* ~-**handed** *a.* mancino. ~ **wing** *a.* (*pol.*) di sinistra.

leftist /'leftɪst/ *n.* sinistroide *m.*/*f.*

leg /leg/ *n.* gamba *f.*; (*of animal*) zampa *f.*; (*of furniture*) piede *m.*; (*of journey*) tappa *f.* ~-**warmer** *n.* scaldamuscoli *m. invar.*

legacy /'legəsɪ/ *n.* lascito *m.*

legal /'liːgl/ *a.* legale. ~ **aid** *n.* patrocinio gratuito *m.* ~**ity** /-'gæləti/ *n.* legalità *f.* ~**ly** *adv.* legalmente.

legalize /'liːgəlaɪz/ *v.t.* legalizzare.

legation /lɪ'geɪʃn/ *n.* legazione *f.*

legend /'ledʒənd/ *n.* leggenda *f.* ~**ary** *a.* leggendario.

legib|le /'ledʒəbl/ *a.* leggibile. ~**ility** /-'bɪlətɪ/ *n.* leggibilità *f.* ~**ly** *adv.* in modo leggibile.

legion /'liːdʒən/ *n.* legione *f.*

legislat|e /'ledʒɪsleɪt/ v.i. legiferare. **~ion** /-'leɪʃn/ n. legislazione f.

legislat|ive /'ledʒɪslətɪv/ a. legislativo. **~ure** /-eɪtʃə(r)/ n. legislatura f.

legitima|te /lɪ'dʒɪtɪmət/ a. legittimo. **~cy** n. legittimità f.

leisure /'leʒə(r)/ n. tempo libero m. **at ~ con comodo. ~ly** a. & adv. senza fretta.

lemon /'lemən/ n. limone m.

lemonade /lemə'neɪd/ n. limonata f.

lend /lend/ v.t. (p.t. **lent**) prestare; (contribute) dare. **~er** n. presta|tore, -trice m.,f. **~ing library** n. biblioteca per il prestito f.

length /leŋθ/ n. lunghezza f.; (of cloth) taglio m.; (of time) durata f. **at ~ a** lungo. **~y** a. (-ier, -iest) lungo.

lengthen /'leŋθən/ v.t./i. allungare, allungarsi.

lengthways /'leŋθweɪz/ adv. per il lungo.

lenien|t /'liːnɪənt/ a. indulgente. **~ce** n. indulgenza f. **~tly** adv. con indulgenza.

lens /lenz/ n. lente f.; (of camera) obiettivo m.

lent /lent/ see **lend.**

Lent /lent/ n. Quaresima f.

lentil /'lentl/ n. lenticchia f.

Leo /'liːəʊ/ n. (astr.) Leone m.

leopard /'lepəd/ n. leopardo m.

leotard /'liːəʊtɑːd/ n. calzamaglia f.

leper /'lepə(r)/ n. lebbroso, a m.,f.

leprosy /'leprəsɪ/ n. lebbra f.

lesbian /'lezbɪən/ a. lesbico. —n. lesbica f.

lesion /'liːʒn/ n. lesione f.

less /les/ a. meno di, minore. —adv., n. & prep. meno. **any the ~** per niente meno. **~ and ~** sempre meno. **none the ~** non di meno. **~er** a. minore.

lessen /'lesn/ v.t./i. diminuire.

lesson /'lesn/ n. lezione f.

lest /lest/ conj. per paura che.

let /let/ v.t./i. (p.t. **let**, pres. p. **letting**) lasciare, permettere; (lease) affittare. —v. aux. **~ us go** andiamo. **~ him do it** che lo faccia. —n. affitto m. **~ down** v.t. abbassare; (dress) allungare; (fig.) deludere. **~-down** n. delusione f. **~ in/out** v.t. far entrare /uscire. **~ o.s. in for** coinvolgersi (in). **~ off** v.t. far partire; (excuse) perdonare. **~ off steam** (fig.) scaricarsi. **~ on** v.t. (sl.) rivelare. **~ through** v.t. far passare. **~ up** v.t.

(fam.) diminuire. **~-up** n. (fam.) pausa f.

lethal /'liːθl/ a. letale.

letharg|y /'leθədʒɪ/ n. letargo m. **~ic** /lɪ'θɑːdʒɪk/ a. letargico.

letter /'letə(r)/ n. lettera f. **~- bomb** n. lettera esplosiva f. **~-box** n. buca per le lettere f. **~-head** n. carta intestata f. **~ing** n. caratteri m.pl.

lettuce /'letɪs/ n. lattuga f.

leukaemia /luː'kiːmɪə/ n. leucemia f.

level /'levl/ a. piano; (on surface) orizzontale; (in height) allo stesso livello; (spoonful etc.) raso. —n. livello m. —v.t. (p.t. **levelled**) livellare; (aim) puntare. **~ crossing** n. passaggio a livello m. **~-headed** a. equilibrato.

lever /'liːvə(r)/ n. leva f. —v.t. far leva.

leverage /'liːvərɪdʒ/ n. azione di una leva f.

levity /'levətɪ/ n. leggerezza f.

levy /'levɪ/ v.t. imporre. —n. imposta f.

lewd /luːd/ a. (-er, -est) lascivo.

lexicography /leksɪ'kɒɡrəfɪ/ n. lessicografia f.

lexicon /'leksɪkn/ n. lessico m.

liable /'laɪəbl/ a. responsabile (**to,** di, per); (likely to) soggetto a.

liabilit|y /laɪə'bɪlətɪ/ n. responsabilità f.; (of person, fam.) peso m. **~ies** debiti m.pl.

liaise /lɪ'eɪz/ v.i. (fam.) fare da intermediario.

liaison /lɪ'eɪzn/ n. legame m.; (mil.) collegamento m.

liar /'laɪə(r)/ n. bugiardo, a m.,f.

libel /'laɪbl/ n. diffamazione f. —v.t. (p.t. **libelled**) diffamare.

liberal /'lɪbərəl/ a. generoso; (tolerant) di larghe vedute. **~ly** adv. liberalmente.

Liberal /'lɪbərəl/ a. & n. liberale m./f.

liberat|e /'lɪbəreɪt/ v.t. liberare. **~ed** /-reɪtɪd/ a. (of woman) emancipata. **~ion** /-'reɪʃn/ n. liberazione f.

libertine /'lɪbətiːn/ n. libertino m.

liberty /'lɪbətɪ/ n. libertà f. **take the ~ of** permettersi di. **take liberties** prendersi libertà.

libido /lɪ'biːdəʊ/ n. (pl. -os) libido m.

Libra /'liːbrə/ n. (astr.) Bilancia f.

librar|y /'laɪbrərɪ/ n. biblioteca f. **~ian** /-'breərɪən/ n. bibliotecario, a m.,f.

Libya /'lɪbɪə/ n. Libia f. **~n** a. & n. libico, a m.,f.

lice /laɪs/ n. see **louse.**

licence /'laɪsns/ n. licenza f.; (for television) canone televisivo m.; (for driv-

ing) patente *f*.; (*disregard of rules*) sregolatezza *f*.

license /'laɪsns/ *v.t.* autorizzare.

licentious /laɪ'senʃəs/ *a*. licenzioso.

lichen /'laɪkən/ *n*. lichene *m*.

lick /lɪk/ *v.t.* leccare; (*sl*.) battere. —*n*. leccata *f*.

lid /lɪd/ *n*. coperchio *m*.

lido /'liːdəʊ/ *n*. stabilimento balneare *m*.

lie[1] /laɪ/ *n*. bugia *f*. —*v.i.* (*p.t.* **lied**, *pres. p.* **lying**) mentire. **give the ~ to** smentire.

lie[2] /laɪ/ *v.i.* (*p.t.* **lay**, *p.p.* **lain**, *pres. p.* **lying**) giacere; (*remain*) rimanere; (*be*) restare. —*n*. posizione *f*. **~ down** sdraiarsi. **~ in**, **~ up** restare a letto. **~ low** tenersi nascosto.

lieu /luː/ *n*. **in ~ of** in luogo di.

lieutenant /lef'tenənt/ *n*. tenente *m*.

life /laɪf/ *n*. (*pl*. **lives**) vita *f*. **~ cycle** *n*. ciclo vitale *m*. **~-guard** *n*. bagnino *m*. **~-jacket** *n*. giubbotto di salvataggio *m*. **~-size(d)** *a*. in grandezza naturale.

lifebelt /'laɪfbelt/ *n*. cintura di salvataggio *f*.

lifeboat /'laɪfbəʊt/ *n*. lancia di salvataggio *f*.

lifebuoy /'laɪfbɔɪ/ *n*. salvagente *m*.

lifeless /'laɪflɪs/ *a*. inanimato; (*lacking liveliness*) scialbo.

lifelike /'laɪflaɪk/ *a*. realistico.

lifeline /'laɪflaɪn/ *n*. sagola di salvataggio *f*.; (*fig*.) linea di comunicazione vitale *f*.

lifelong /'laɪflɔŋ/ *a*. di tutta la vita.

lifetime /'laɪftaɪm/ *n*. vita *f*. **the chance of a ~** un'occasione unica.

lift /lɪft/ *v.t.* sollevare; (*fam*., *steal*) rubare. —*v.i.* (*of fog*) alzarsi. —*n*. ascensore *m*. **give a ~ to** dare un passaggio a. **~-off** *n*. decollo *m*.

ligament /'lɪgəmənt/ *n*. legamento *m*.

light[1] /laɪt/ *n*. luce *f*.; (*lamp*) lampada *f*.; (*flame*) fuoco *m*. —*a*. luminoso; (*pale*) chiaro. —*v.t.* (*p.t.* **lit** *or* **lighted**) accendere; (*brighten*) illuminare. **bring to ~** rivelare. **come to ~** essere rivelato. **~-year** *n*. anno luce *m*.

light[2] /laɪt/ *a*. (**-er**, **-est**) leggero. **~-fingered** *a*. (*thief*) svelto di mano. **~-headed** *a*. sventato; (*delirious*) vaneggiante. **~-hearted** *a*. gaio. **~ly** *adv*. leggermente. **~ness** *n*. leggerezza *f*.

lighten[1] /'laɪtn/ *v.t./i.* illuminare, illuminarsi.

lighten[2] /'laɪtn/ *v.t.* alleggerire; (*fig*.) alleviare.

lighter /'laɪtə(r)/ *n*. accendino *m*.

lighthouse /'laɪthaʊs/ *n*. faro *m*.

lighting /'laɪtɪŋ/ *n*. illuminazione *f*.

lightning /'laɪtnɪŋ/ *n*. lampo, fulmine *m*. —*a*. lampo.

lightweight /'laɪtweɪt/ *a*. leggero. —*n*. peso leggero *m*.

like[1] /laɪk/ *a*. simile. —*prep*. come. —*conj*. (*fam*., *as*) come. —*n*. simile *m*. **~-minded** *a*. degli stessi gusti.

like[2] /laɪk/ *v.t.* piacere, gradire. **~s** *n.pl*. cose che piacciono *f.pl*. **I ~ him** mi piace. **I should ~** vorrei, gradirei. **~able** *a*. simpatico.

likel|y /'laɪklɪ/ *a*. (**-ier**, **-iest**) probabile. —*adv*. probabilmente. **not ~y!** (*fam*.) neanche per sogno! **~ihood** *n*. probabilità *f*.

liken /'laɪkən/ *v.t.* paragonare.

likeness /'laɪknɪs/ *n*. somiglianza *f*.

likewise /'laɪkwaɪz/ *adv*. parimenti.

liking /'laɪkɪŋ/ *n*. gusto *m*.; (*for person*) simpatia *f*.

lilac /'laɪlək/ *n*. lillà *m*. —*a*. color lillà.

lilt /lɪlt/ *n*. cadenza *f*.

lily /'lɪlɪ/ *n*. giglio *m*. **~ of the valley** *n*. mughetto *m*.

limb /lɪm/ *n*. arto *m*. **out on a ~** isolato.

limber /'lɪmbə(r)/ *v.i.* **~ up** sciogliersi i muscoli.

limbo /'lɪmbəʊ/ *n*. (*pl*. **-os**) limbo *m*.

lime[1] /laɪm/ *n*. calce *f*.

lime[2] /laɪm/ *n*. (*fruit*) cedro *m*.; (*tree*) tiglio *m*.

limelight /'laɪmlaɪt/ *n*. luce della ribalta *f*. **be in the ~** essere molto in vista.

limerick /'lɪmərɪk/ *n*. limerick *m*. *invar*.

limestone /'laɪmstəʊn/ *n*. calcare *m*.

limit /'lɪmɪt/ *n*. limite *m*. —*v.t.* limitare. **~ation** /-'teɪʃn/ *n*. limite *m*. **~ed** *a*. ristretto. **~ed company** *n*. società anonima *f*.

limousine /'lɪməziːn/ *n*. limousine *f*. *invar*.

limp[1] /lɪmp/ *v.i.* zoppicare. —*n*. andatura zoppicante *f*.

limp[2] /lɪmp/ *a*. (**-er**, **-est**) floscio.

limpid /'lɪmpɪd/ *a*. limpido.

linctus /'lɪŋktəs/ *n*. sciroppo per la tosse *m*.

line /laɪn/ *n*. linea *f*.; (*piece of cord, wire, etc*.) filo *m*.; (*wrinkle*) ruga *f*.; (*row*) fila *f*.; (*of poem*) verso *m*.; (*of* *goods*) articolo *m.*; (*of railway*) binario *m.*; (*on page*) riga *f.* —*v.t.*/*i.* segnare; (*paper*) rigare; (*streets etc.*) fiancheggiare; (*garment*) foderare. **be on the** ~ (*fig.*) avere un futuro incerto. **in** ~ **with** in conformità con. ~ **up** *v.i.* allinearsi.

lineage /'lɪnɪɪdʒ/ *n.* lignaggio *m.*

linear /'lɪnɪə(r)/ *a.* lineare.

linen /'lɪnɪn/ *n.* lino *m.*; (*articles*) biancheria *f.*

liner /'laɪnə(r)/ *n.* nave di linea *f.*

linesman /'laɪnzmən/ *n.* (*pl.* -men) (*football*) segnalinee *m. invar.*

linger /'lɪŋɡə(r)/ *v.i.* indugiare.

lingerie /'lænʒərɪ/ *n.* biancheria (da donna) *f.*

lingo /'lɪŋɡəʊ/ *n.* (*pl.* -os) (*fam.*) gergo *m.*

linguist /'lɪŋɡwɪst/ *n.* linguista *m.*/*f.*

linguistic /lɪŋ'ɡwɪstɪk/ *a.* linguistico. ~**s** *n.pl.* linguistica *f.s.*

lining /'laɪnɪŋ/ *n.* fodera *f.*

link /lɪŋk/ *n.* anello *m.*; (*fig.*) legame *m.* —*v.t.* collegare. ~ **up with** unirsi a.

links /lɪŋks/ *n.pl.* campo da golf *m.s.*

linoleum /lɪ'nəʊlɪəm/ *n.* linoleum *m. invar.*

lint /lɪnt/ *n.* garza *f.*

lion /'laɪən/ *n.* leone *m.* ~**ess** *n.* leonessa *f.*

lionize /'laɪənaɪz/ *v.t.* trattare da celebrità.

lip /lɪp/ *n.* labbro *m.* (*pl.* labbra *f.*); (*edge*) bordo *m.* ~**-read** *v.t.*/*i.* leggere dal movimento delle labbra. **pay** ~**service** approvare soltanto a parole. **stiff upper** ~ imperturbabilità *f.*

lipsalve /'lɪpsɑːv/ *n.* burro di cacao *m.*

lipstick /'lɪpstɪk/ *n.* rossetto (per le labbra) *m.*

liquefy /'lɪkwɪfaɪ/ *v.t.*/*i.* liquefare, liquefarsi.

liqueur /lɪ'kjʊə(r)/ *n.* liquore *m.*

liquid /'lɪkwɪd/ *n.* & *a.* liquido *m.* ~**ize** *v.t.* rendere liquido. ~**izer** *n.* frullatore *m.*

liquidat|e /'lɪkwɪdeɪt/ *v.t.* liquidare. ~**ion** /-'deɪʃn/ *n.* liquidazione *f.*

liquor /'lɪkə(r)/ *n.* bevanda alcoolica *f.*; (*juice*) brodo *m.*

liquorice /'lɪkərɪs/ *n.* liquirizia *f.*

lisle /laɪl/ *n.* filo di Scozia *m.*

lisp /lɪsp/ *n.* pronuncia blesa *f.* —*v.t.*/*i.* parlare bleso.

lissom /'lɪsəm/ *a.* flessibile.

list[1] /lɪst/ *n.* lista *f.* —*v.t.* elencare.

list[2] /lɪst/ *v.i.* (*of ship*) inclinarsi.

listen /'lɪsn/ *v.i.* ascoltare. ~ **to s.o.** ascoltare qcno. ~ **in** (*broadcast*) ascoltare un programma. ~**er** *n.* ascolta|tore, -trice *m.*, *f.*

listless /'lɪstlɪs/ *a.* svogliato.

lit /lɪt/ *see* **light**[1].

litany /'lɪtənɪ/ *n.* litania *f.*

literal /'lɪtərəl/ *a.* testuale; (*fig.*) prosaico. ~**ly** *adv.* letteralmente.

literary /'lɪtərərɪ/ *a.* letterario.

litera|te /'lɪtərət/ *a.* che sa leggere e scrivere. ~**cy** *n.* il saper leggere e scrivere *m.*

literature /'lɪtərətʃə(r)/ *n.* letteratura *f.*; (*fig.*) documentazione *f.*

lithe /laɪð/ *a.* snello.

lithograph /'lɪθəɡrɑːf/ *n.* litografia *f.*

litigation /lɪtɪ'ɡeɪʃn/ *n.* causa *f.*

litre /'liːtə(r)/ *n.* litro *m.*

litter /'lɪtə(r)/ *n.* (*rubbish*) immondizie *f.pl.*; (*animals*) figliata *f.* —*v.t.* (*make untidy*) ingombrare. ~**-bin** *n.* bidone per le immondizie *m.* ~**ed with** ingombrato di.

little /'lɪtl/ *a.* piccolo; (*not much*) (un) poco. —*n.* poco *m.* —*adv.* poco. **a** ~ **water** un po' d'acqua. ~ **by** ~ a poco a poco.

liturgy /'lɪtədʒɪ/ *n.* liturgia *f.*

live[1] /laɪv/ *a.* vivo; (*wire*) carico; (*broadcast*) in diretta. ~ **wire** (*fig.*) dinamico.

live[2] /lɪv/ *v.t.*/*i.* vivere. ~ **down** far dimenticare. ~ **it up** far bella vita. ~ **on** vivere di; (*continue*) sopravvivere. ~ **up to** vivere all'altezza di. ~ **with** convivere con.

livelihood /'laɪvlɪhʊd/ *n.* sostentamento *m.*

livel|y /'laɪvlɪ/ *a.* (-ier, -iest) vivace. ~**iness** *n.* vivacità *f.*

liven /'laɪvn/ *v.t.*/*i.* ~ **up** animare, animarsi; (*room etc.*) ravvivare.

liver /'lɪvə(r)/ *n.* fegato *m.*

livery /'lɪvərɪ/ *n.* livrea *f.*

livestock /'laɪvstɒk/ *n.* bestiame *m.*

livid /'lɪvɪd/ *a.* livido; (*fam.*) furioso.

living /'lɪvɪŋ/ *a.* vivo. —*n.* vita *f.*, vivere *m.* ~**-room** *n.* soggiorno *m.*

lizard /'lɪzəd/ *n.* lucertola *f.*

llama /'lɑːmə/ *n.* lama *m.*

load /ləʊd/ *n.* carico *m.*; (*fig.*) peso *m.* ~**s of** (*fam.*) un sacco di. —*v.t.* caricare. ~**ed** *a.* carico; (*fam.*, *rich*) ricchissimo. ~**ed question** *n.* domanda esplosiva *f.*

loaf[1] /ləʊf/ *n.* (*pl.* **loaves**) pane *m.*

loaf[2] /ləʊf/ *v.i.* oziare. ~**er** *n.* ozioso, a *m., f.*

loam /ləʊm/ *n.* terriccio *m.*

loan /ləʊn/ *n.* prestito *m.* —*v.t.* (*fam.*) prestare. **on** ~ in prestito.

loath /ləʊθ/ *a.* riluttante.

loath|e /ləʊð/ *v.t.* detestare. ~**ing** *n.* disgusto *m.* ~**some** *a.* disgustoso.

lobby /lɒbɪ/ *n.* atrio *m.*; (*pol.*) gruppo di manovratori *m.* —*v.i.* far manovre di anticamera.

lobe /ləʊb/ *n.* lobo *m.*

lobster /lɒbstə(r)/ *n.* aragosta *f.*

local /ləʊkl/ *a.* locale. —*n.* abitante del luogo *m./f.*; (*fam.*) pub del rione *m.* ~**ly** *adv.* localmente; (*nearby*) nelle vicinanze.

locale /ləʊˈkɑːl/ *n.* luogo dell'azione *m.*

locality /ləʊˈkælətɪ/ *n.* località *f.*

localized /ləʊkəlaɪzd/ *a.* localizzato.

locat|e /ləʊˈkeɪt/ *v.t.* individuare; (*situate*) collocare. ~**ion** /-ʃn/ *n.* posizione *f.* **on** ~**ion** (*cinema*) all'esterno.

lock[1] /lɒk/ *n.* (*hair*) ciocca *f.*; ~**s** *n.pl.* capelli *m.pl.*

lock[2] /lɒk/ *n.* (*on door etc.*) serratura *f.*; (*on canal*) chiusa *f.*; (*mech.*) blocco *m.* —*v.t./i.* chiudere a chiave; bloccare. ~ **out** chiudere fuori. ~**-out** *n.* serrata *f.* ~**-up** *n.* (*prison*) guardina *f.*

locker /lɒkə(r)/ *n.* armadietto *m.*

locket /lɒkɪt/ *n.* medaglione *m.*

locksmith /lɒksmɪθ/ *n.* fabbro *m.*

locomotion /ləʊkəˈməʊʃn/ *n.* locomozione *f.*

locomotive /ləʊkəməʊtɪv/ *n.* locomotiva *f.*

locum /ləʊkəm/ *n.* interino, a *m., f.*

locust /ləʊkəst/ *n.* locusta *f.*

lodge /lɒdʒ/ *n.* casetta *f.*; (*of porter*) portineria *f.*; (*masonic*) loggia *f.* —*v.t./i.* alloggiare; (*deposit*) depositare; (*become fixed*) conficcarsi. ~**r** /-ə(r)/ *n.* inquilino, a *m., f.*

lodgings /lɒdʒɪŋz/ *n.pl.* camere in affitto *f.pl.*; (*flat*) alloggio *m.*

loft /lɒft/ *n.* attico *m.*; (*for hay*) fienile *m.*

lofty /lɒftɪ/ *a.* (**-ier, -iest**) alto; (*haughty*) altezzoso.

log /lɒg/ *n.* ceppo *m.*; (*log-book, naut.*) giornale di bordo *m.* ~**-book** (*auto.*) *n.* libretto di circolazione *m.* **sleep like a** ~ dormire come un ghiro. —*v.t.* (*p.t.* **logged**) registrare.

logarithm /lɒgərɪðəm/ *n.* logaritmo *m.*

loggerheads /lɒgəhedz/ *n.pl.* **at** ~ in disaccordo.

logic /lɒdʒɪk/ *n.* logica *f.* ~**al** *a.* logico. ~**ally** *adv.* logicamente.

logistics /ləˈdʒɪstɪks/ *n.* logistica *f.*

logo /ləʊgəʊ/ *n.* (*pl.* **-os**) (*fam.*) emblema *m.*

loin /lɔɪn/ *n.* (*culin.*) lombata *f.* ~**s** *n.pl.* reni *f.pl.*

loiter /lɔɪtə(r)/ *v.i.* gironzolare.

loll /lɒl/ *v.i.* stare sdraiato.

loll|ipop /lɒlɪpɒp/ *n.* lecca-lecca *m.* ~**y** *n.* (*fam.*) lecca-lecca *m.*; (*sl.*) soldi *m.pl.*

London /lʌndən/ *n.* Londra *f.* ~**er** londinese *m./f.*

lone /ləʊn/ *a.* solitario. ~**r** /-ə(r)/ *n.* persona solitaria *f.* ~**some** *a.* solitario.

lonely /ləʊnlɪ/ *a.* (**-ier, -iest**) solitario. **feel** ~ sentirsi solo.

long[1] /lɒŋ/ *a.* (**-er, -est**) lungo. —*adv.* a lungo, lungamente. **how** ~ **is?** quanto è lungo?; (*in time*) quanto dura? **a** ~ **time** molto tempo. **a** ~ **way** distante. **as** *or* **so** ~ **as** purché. **before** ~ fra breve. ~**-distance** *a.* a grande distanza; (*call*) interurbano. ~ **johns** *n.pl.* (*fam.*) mutandoni *m.pl.* ~ **jump** *n.* salto in lungo *m.* ~**-playing record** *n.* (*disco*) microsolco *m.* ~**-range** *a.* a lunga portata; (*forecast*) a lungo termine. ~**-sighted** *a.* presbite. ~**-standing** *a.* di vecchia durata. ~**-term** *a.* a lunga scadenza. ~**-winded** *a.* prolisso. **in the** ~ **run** a lungo andare. **so** ~**!** (*fam.*) ciao!

long[2] /lɒŋ/ *v.i.* ~ **for** desiderare ardentemente. ~**ing** *n.* brama *f.*; *a.* desideroso.

longevity /lɒnˈdʒevətɪ/ *n.* longevità *f.*

longhand /lɒŋhænd/ *n.* scrittura ordinaria *f.*

longitude /lɒndʒɪtjuːd/ *n.* longitudine *f.*

loo /luː/ *n.* (*fam.*) gabinetto *m.*

loofah /luːfə/ *n.* luffa *f.*

look /lʊk/ *v.t./i.* guardare; (*seem*) sembrare. —*n.* occhiata *f.*; (*appearance*) aspetto *m.* (**good**) ~**s** bellezza *f.* ~ **after** badare a. ~ **at** guardare. ~ **down on** guardare dall'alto in basso. ~ **for** cercare. ~ **forward to** attendere con ansia. ~ **in** on passare da. ~ **into** esaminare. ~ **like** (*resemble*) assomigliare a; (*seem*) sembrare. ~ **on to** (*of room, window*) dare su. ~ **out** fare attenzione. ~ **out for**

cercare. ∼-**out** *n.* guardia *f.*; (*prospect*) prospettiva *f.* ∼ **through** ripassare. ∼ **up** (*word*) cercare; (*visit*) andare a trovare. ∼ **up to** rispettare. ∼**er-on** *n.* (*pl.* **lookers-on**) spetta| tore, -trice *m.*, *f.* ∼**ing glass** *n.* specchio *m.*

loom[1] /luːm/ *n.* telaio *m.*

loom[2] /luːm/ *v.i.* apparire; (*fig.*) profilarsi.

loony /'luːnɪ/ *n.* & *a.* (*sl.*) matto, a *m.*, *f.* ∼-**bin** *n.* (*sl.*) manicomio *m.*

loop /luːp/ *n.* cappio *m.* —*v.t.* fare un cappio.

loophole /'luːphəʊl/ *n.* (*in rule*) scappatoia *f.*

loose /luːs/ *a.* (**-er, -est**) libero; (*of knot etc.*) allentato; (*page etc.*) sciolto; (*clothes*) largo; (*morals*) dissoluto; (*inexact*) vago. **at a** ∼ **end** sfaccendato. ∼**ly** *adv.* scioltamente; vagamente.

loosen /'luːsn/ *v.t.* sciogliere.

loot /luːt/ *n.* bottino *m.* —*v.t.* depredare. ∼**er** *n.* preda|tore, -trice *m.*, *f.* ∼**ing** *n.* saccheggio *m.*

lop /lɒp/ *v.t.* (*p.t.* **lopped**) ∼ **off** potare.

lop-sided /lɒp'saɪdɪd/ *a.* sbilenco.

loquacious /ləʊ'kweɪʃəs/ *a.* loquace.

lord /lɔːd/ *n.* signore *m.*; (*British title*) Lord *m.* **the L**∼ il Signore *m.* **good L**∼! Dio mio! ∼**ly** *a.* altezzoso. ∼**ship** *n.* signoria *f.*

lore /lɔː(r)/ *n.* tradizioni *f.pl.*

lorgnette /lɔː'njet/ *n.* occhialino *m.*

lorry /'lɒrɪ/ *n.* camion *m. invar.*

lose /luːz/ *v.t./i.* (*p.t.* **lost**) perdere. **get lost** perdersi. ∼**r** *n.* perdente *m./f.*

loss /lɒs/ *n.* perdita *f.* **be at a** ∼ essere perplesso. **be at a** ∼ **for words** non trovare le parole.

lost /lɒst/ *see* **lose.** —*a.* perduto.

lot[1] /lɒt/ *n.* sorte *f.*; (*comm.*) partita (di merce) *f.* (*piece of land*) appezzamento *m.*; (*at auction*) lotto *m.*

lot[2] /lɒt/ *n.* **the** ∼ (il) tutto *m.*; (*people*) tutti, e *m.*, *f.pl.* **a** ∼ **of,** ∼**s of** (*fam.*) un sacco di.

lotion /'ləʊʃn/ *n.* lozione *f.*

lottery /'lɒtərɪ/ *n.* lotteria *f.*

lotto /'lɒtəʊ/ *n.* tombola *f.*

lotus /'ləʊtəs/ *n.* (*pl.* **-uses**) loto *m.*

loud /laʊd/ *a.* (**-er, -est**) sonoro, alto. —*adv.* forte. ∼ **hailer** *n.* megafono *m.* **out** ∼ ad alta voce. ∼**ly** *adv.* forte.

loudspeaker /laʊd'spiːkə(r)/ *n.* altoparlante *m.*

lounge /laʊndʒ/ *v.i.* poltrire. —*n.* salotto *m.* ∼ **suit** abito da passeggio *m.*

louse /laʊs/ *n.* (*pl.* **lice**) pidocchio *m.*

lousy /'laʊzɪ/ *a.* (**-ier, -iest**) pidocchioso; (*sl.*) schifoso, pessimo.

lout /laʊt/ *n.* zoticone *m.*

lovable /'lʌvəbl/ *a.* amabile.

love /lʌv/ *n.* amore *m.*; (*in tennis*) zero *m.* —*v.t.* amare; (*like greatly*) provare piacere (per). **be** *or* **fall in** ∼ innamorarsi (**with,** di). ∼-**affair** *n.* relazione amorosa *f.*

lovely /'lʌvlɪ/ *a.* (**-ier, -iest**) bello, attraente; (*fam.*, *excellent*) eccellente. **have a** ∼ **time** divertirsi.

lover /'lʌvə(r)/ *n.* amante *m./f.*; (*devotee*) appassionato, a *m.*, *f.*

loving /'lʌvɪŋ/ *a.* affettuoso.

low[1] /ləʊ/ *v.i.* muggire.

low[2] /ləʊ/ *a.* (**-er, -est**) basso; (*depressed*) depresso. —*adv.* in basso. —*n.* minimo *m.*; (*low pressure*) depressione *f.* ∼-**cut** *a.* (*clothes*) scollato. ∼-**down** *a.* meschino; *n.* (*fam.*) verità *f.* ∼-**grade** *a.* di qualità inferiore. ∼-**key** *a.* contenuto.

lowbrow /'ləʊbraʊ/ *a.* di scarsa cultura.

lower /'ləʊə(r)/ *a.* & *adv. see* **low**[2] —*v.t./i.* abbassare. ∼ **o.s.** abbassarsi.

lowlands /'ləʊləndz/ *n.pl.* pianure *f.pl.*

lowly /'ləʊlɪ/ *a.* (**-ier, -iest**) umile.

loyal /'lɔɪəl/ *a.* leale. ∼**ly** *adv.* lealmente. ∼**ty** *n.* lealtà *f.*

lozenge /'lɒzɪndʒ/ *n.* losanga *f.*; (*tablet*) pastiglia *f.*

LP *abbr. see* **long-playing record.**

Ltd. *abbr. of* **limited.**

lubric|ate /'luːbrɪkeɪt/ *v.t.* lubrificare. ∼**ant** *n.* lubrificante *m.* ∼**ation** /-'keɪʃn/ *n.* lubrificazione *f.*

lucid /'luːsɪd/ *a.* chiaro; (*sane*) lucido. ∼**ity** /-'sɪdətɪ/ *n.* lucidità *f.*

luck /lʌk/ *n.* fortuna *f.* **bad** ∼ sfortuna *f.*

luck|y /'lʌkɪ/ *a.* (**-ier, -iest**) fortunato; (*number etc.*) che porta fortuna; (*event etc.*) felice. ∼**y charm** *n.* portafortuna *m.* ∼**ily** *adv.* fortunatamente.

lucrative /'luːkrətɪv/ *a.* lucrativo.

lucre /'luːkə(r)/ *n.* (*pej.*) soldi *m.pl.*

ludicrous /'luːdɪkrəs/ *a.* ridicolo.

lug /lʌg/ *v.t.* (*p.t.* **lugged**) trascinare.

luggage /'lʌgɪdʒ/ *n.* bagaglio *m.* ∼-**rack** *n.* portabagagli *m.* ∼-**van** *n.* bagagliaio *m.*

lugubrious /luˈgjuːbrɪəs/ *a.* lugubre.

lukewarm /'luːkwɔːm/ *a.* tiepido.

lull /lʌl/ *v.t.* cullare. —*n.* pausa *f.*

lullaby /'lʌləbaɪ/ *n.* ninna nanna *f.*

lumbago /lʌmˈbeɪɡəʊ/ *n.* lombaggine *f.*

lumber /ˈlʌmbə(r)/ *n.* cianfrusaglie *f.pl.*; (*timber*) legname *m.* —*v.t.* ingombrare.

lumberjack /ˈlʌmbədʒæk/ *n.* tagliaboschi *m.invar.*

luminous /ˈluːmɪnəs/ *a.* luminoso.

lump[1] /lʌmp/ *n.* protuberanza *f.*; (*swelling*) gonfiore *m.*; (*in liquid*) grumo *m.*; (*of sugar*) zolletta *f.*; (*in throat*) nodo *m.*; (*dull person*) persona goffa *f.* —*v.t.* ~ **together** ammucchiare. ~ **sum** *n.* somma globale *f.* ~**y** *a.* grumoso.

lump[2] /lʌmp/ *v.t.* ~ **it** (*fam.*) sopportare controvoglia.

lunacy /ˈluːnəsɪ/ *n.* follia *f.*

lunar /ˈluːnə(r)/ *a.* lunare.

lunatic /ˈluːnətɪk/ *n.* pazzo, a *m.*, *f.*

lunch /lʌntʃ/ *n.* pranzo *m.* —*v.i.* pranzare. ~**eon** /ˈlʌntʃən/ *n.* (*formal*) pranzo *m.* ~**eon voucher** *n.* buono pasto *m.*

lung /lʌŋ/ *n.* polmone *m.*

lunge /lʌndʒ/ *n.* balzo *m.* —*v.i.* lanciarsi.

lurch[1] /lɜːtʃ/ *n.* **leave in the** ~ lasciare nei guai.

lurch[2] /lɜːtʃ/ *v.i.* barcollare.

lure /lʊə(r)/ *v.t.* adescare. —*n.* esca *f.*; (*fig.*) lusinga *f.*

lurid /ˈlʊərɪd/ *a.* sensazionale; (*gaudy*) sgargiante.

lurk /lɜːk/ *v.i.* nascondersi.

luscious /ˈlʌʃəs/ *a.* succulento; (*fig.*) stucchevole.

lush /lʌʃ/ *a.* lussureggiante.

lust /lʌst/ *n.* lussuria *f.*; (*fig.*) brama *f.* —*v.i.* ~ **after** desiderare (fortemente). ~**ful** *a.* lussurioso.

lustre /ˈlʌstə(r)/ *n.* lustro *m.*

lusty /ˈlʌstɪ/ *a.* (**-ier, -iest**) vigoroso.

lute /luːt/ *n.* liuto *m.*

Luxemburg /ˈlʌksəmbɜːɡ/ *n.* Lussemburgo *m.*

luxuriant /lʌɡˈʒʊərɪənt/ *a.* lussureggiante.

luxurious /lʌɡˈʒʊərɪəs/ *a.* lussuoso.

luxury /ˈlʌkʃərɪ/ *n.* lusso *m.* —*a.* di lusso.

lying /ˈlaɪɪŋ/ *see* **lie**[1], **lie**[2]. —*n.* mentire *m.*

lynch /lɪntʃ/ *v.t.* linciare.

lynx /lɪŋks/ *n.* lince *f.*

lyre /ˈlaɪə(r)/ *n.* lira *f.*

lyric /ˈlɪrɪk/ *a.* lirico. ~**s** *n.pl.* parole *f.pl.* ~**al** lirico. ~**ism** /-sɪzəm/ *n.* lirismo *m.*

M

MA *abbr. of* **Master of Arts.**

mac /mæk/ *m.* (*fam.*) impermeabile *m.*

macabre /mə'kɑ:brə/ *a.* macabro.

macaroni /mækə'rəʊnɪ/ *n.* maccheroni *m.pl.*

macaroon /mækə'ru:n/ *n.* amaretto *m.*

mace[1] /meɪs/ *n.* (*staff*) mazza *f.*

mace[2] /meɪs/ *n.* (*spice*) macis *m.*

mach /mɑːk/ *n.* ~ (**number**) (numero di) mach *m.*

machiavellian /mækɪə'velɪən/ *a.* machiavellico.

machinations /mækɪ'neɪʃnz/ *n.pl.* macchinazione *f.s.*

machine /mə'ʃi:n/ *n.* macchina *f.* —*v.t.* (*sew*) cucire a macchina; (*techn.*) eseguire a macchina. ~-**gun** *n.* mitragliatrice *f.*; *v.t.* mitragliare. ~ **tool** *n.* macchina utensile *f.*

machinery /mə'ʃi:nərɪ/ *n.* macchinario *m.*; (*working parts, fig.*) meccanismo *m.*

machinist /mə'ʃi:nɪst/ *n.* macchinista *m.|f.*; (*on sewing machine*) lavorante *m.|f.*

machismo /mæ'tʃɪzməʊ/ *n.* gallismo *m.*

macho /'mætʃəʊ/ *a.* maschilista.

mackerel /'mækrəl/ *n. invar.* sgombro *m.*

mackintosh /'mækɪntɒʃ/ *n.* impermeabile *m.*

macrobiotic /mækrəʊbaɪ'ɒtɪk/ *a.* macrobiotico.

mad /mæd/ *a.* (**madder, maddest**) pazzo, matto; (*foolish*) insensato; (*angry, fam.*) furente. **like** ~ come un pazzo. ~**ly** *adv.* follemente. ~**ness** *n.* pazzia *f.*

madam /'mædəm/ *n.* signora *f.*

madcap /'mædkæp/ *a.* & *n.* scervellato, a *m., f.*

madden /'mædn/ *v.t.* esasperare.

made /meɪd/ *see* **make.** ~ **to measure** *a.* fatto su misura.

madhouse /'mædhaʊs/ *n.* (*fam.*) manicomio *m.*

madman /'mædmən/ *n.* (*pl.* **-men**) pazzo *m.*

madonna /mə'dɒnə/ *n.* madonna *f.*

madrigal /'mædrɪgl/ *n.* madrigale *m.*

maelstrom /'meɪlstrəm/ *n.* vortice *m.*

magazine /mægə'zi:n/ *n.* rivista *f.*; (*arms store*) deposito *m.*; (*of camera*) magazzino *m.*

magenta /mə'dʒentə/ *a.* & *n.* magenta *f.*

maggot /'mægət/ *n.* verme *m.* ~**y** *a.* bacato.

Magi /'meɪdʒaɪ/ *n.pl.* **the** ~ i Re Magi *m.pl.*

magic /'mædʒɪk/ *n.* magia *f.* —*a.* magico. ~**al** *a.* magico.

magician /mə'dʒɪʃn/ *n.* mago *m.*

magisterial /mædʒɪ'stɪərɪəl/ *a.* di magistrato; (*imperious*) autoritario.

magistrate /'mædʒɪstreɪt/ *n.* magistrato, a *m., f.*

magnanim|ous /mæg'nænɪməs/ *a.* magnanimo. ~**ity** /-ə'nɪmətɪ/ *n.* magnanimità *f.*

magnate /'mægneɪt/ *n.* magnate *m.*

magnesia /mæg'ni:ʃə/ *n.* magnesia *f.*

magnet /'mægnɪt/ *n.* magnete *m.*, calamita *f.* ~**ic** /-'netɪk/ *a.* magnetico. ~**ism** *n.* magnetismo *m.* ~**ize** *v.t.* magnetizzare.

magnificen|t /mæg'nɪfɪsnt/ *a.* magnifico. ~**ce** *n.* magnificenza *f.*

magnif|y /'mægnɪfaɪ/ *v.t.* ingrandire; (*fig.*) esagerare. ~**ication** /-ɪ'keɪʃn/ *n.* ingrandimento *m.* ~**ier,** ~**ying glass** *ns.* lente d'ingrandimento *f.*

magnitude /'mægnɪtjuːd/ *n.* grandezza *f.*

magnolia /mæg'nəʊlɪə/ *n.* magnolia *f.*

magnum /'mægnəm/ *n.* bottiglione *m.*

magpie /'mægpaɪ/ *n.* gazza *f.*

mahogany /mə'hɒgənɪ/ *n.* mogano *m.*

maid /meɪd/ *n.* cameriera *f.* ~ **of all work** donna tutto fare *f.* ~ **of honour** damigella d'onore *f.* **old** ~ (*pej.*) zitellona *f.*

maiden /'meɪdn/ *n.* (*old use*) fanciulla *f.* —*a.* verginale; (*speech, voyage*) inaugurale. ~ **aunt** zia nubile *f.* ~ **name** nome da ragazza *m.* ~**ly** *a.* verginale.

maidenhood /'meɪdnhʊd/ *n.* verginità *f.*

mail[1] /meɪl/ *n.* posta *f.* —*a.* (*bag, van*) postale. —*v.t.* impostare. ~**ing list** *n.* elenco d'indirizzi *m.* ~ **order** *n.* ordinazione per posta *f.*

mail[2] /meɪl/ *n.* (*armour*) cotta *f.*

maim /meɪm/ *v.t.* mutilare.

main[1] /meɪn/ *a.* principale. —*n.* **in the** ~ in complesso. ~ **street** *n.* corso *m.* ~**ly** *adv.* principalmente.

main[2] /meɪn/ *n.* (*water*, *gas*) conduttura principale *f.*

mainland /'meɪnlənd/ *n.* continente *m.*

mainspring /'meɪnsprɪŋ/ *n.* (*techn.*) molla principale *f.*; (*motive*) stimolo *m.*

mainstay /'meɪnsteɪ/ *n.* (*naut.*) straglio di maestra *m.*; (*support*) sostegno *m.*

mainstream /'meɪnstriːm/ *n.* tendenza generale *f.*

maintain /meɪn'teɪn/ *v.t.* mantenere; (*keep in repair*) curare la manutenzione (di).

maintenance /'meɪntənəns/ *n.* mantenimento *m.*; (*care*) manutenzione *f.*; (*alimony*) alimenti *m.pl.*

maisonette /meɪzə'net/ *n.* appartamento a due piani *m.*

maize /meɪz/ *n.* granoturco *m.*

majestic /mə'dʒestɪk/ *a.* maestoso.

majesty /'mædʒəstɪ/ *n.* maestà *f.*

major /'meɪdʒə(r)/ *a.* maggiore. —*n.* maggiore *m.* —*v.i.* ~ **in** (*Amer.*) specializzarsi in.

Majorca /mə'dʒɔːkə/ *n.* Maiorca *f.*

majority /mə'dʒɒrətɪ/ *n.* maggioranza *f.*; (*age*) maggiore età *f.*

make /meɪk/ *v.t./i.* (*p.t.* **made**) fare, farsi; (*decision*) prendere; (*destination*) arrivare a. —*n.* fattura *f.*; (*brand*) marca *f.* ~ **as if to** fare per. ~ **believe** fingere. ~-**believe** *a.* finto; *n.* finzione *f.* ~ **do** arrangiarsi. ~ **for** dirigersi verso. ~ **good** *v.i.* riuscire; *v.t.* (*loss*) compensare; (*damage*) riparare. ~ **it up** riconciliarsi. ~ **little-/much of** dare poca/molta importanza a. ~ **off** fuggire. ~ **out** distinguere; (*cheque*) rilasciare. ~ **over** cedere. ~ **up** completare; (*story*) inventare; (*apply cosmetics*) truccare. ~-**up** *n.* trucco *m.*; (*character*) natura *f.*; (*object*) costituzione *f.* ~ **up for** compensare. ~ **up one's mind** decidersi. ~ **up to** cercare d'ingraziarsi con.

maker /'meɪkə(r)/ *n.* fabbricante *m.* **M**~ Creatore *m.*

makeshift /'meɪkʃɪft/ *n.* espediente *m.* —*a.* improvvisato.

makeweight /'meɪkweɪt/ *n.* aggiunta *f.*

making /'meɪkɪŋ/ *n.* formazione *f.* **be the** ~ **of** essere la causa del successo

di. **have the** ~**s of** aver la stoffa di. **in the** ~ in formazione.

maladjust|ed /mælə'dʒʌstɪd/ *a.* disadattato. ~**ment** *n.* disadattamento *m.*; (*mech.*) regolazione difettosa *f.*

maladministration /mælədmɪnɪ'streɪʃn/ *n.* cattiva amministrazione *f.*

malady /'mælədɪ/ *n.* malattia *f.*

malaise /mæ'leɪz/ *n.* malessere *m.*

malaria /mə'leərɪə/ *n.* malaria *f.*

Malay /mə'leɪ/ *a.* & *n.* malese *m./f.* ~**sia** *n.* Malesia *f.*

male /meɪl/ *a.* maschile. —*n.* maschio *m.* **on the** ~ **side** da parte del padre.

malefactor /'mælɪfæktə(r)/ *n.* malfattore *m.*

malevolen|t /mə'levəlnt/ *a.* malevolo. ~**ce** *n.* malevolenza *f.*

malform|ation /mælfɔː'meɪʃn/ *n.* malformazione *f.* ~**ed** /-'fɔːmd/ *a.* malformato.

malfunction /mæl'fʌŋkʃn/ *n.* funzionamento imperfetto *m.*

malice /'mælɪs/ *n.* malignità *f.* **bear s.o.** ~ covare rancore verso qcno.

malicious /mə'lɪʃəs/ *a.* maligno. ~**ly** *adv.* con malignità.

malign /mə'laɪn/ *a.* malefico. —*v.t.* malignare (su).

malignan|t /mə'lɪgnənt/ *a.* maligno. ~**cy** *n.* malignità *f.*

malinger /mə'lɪŋgə(r)/ *v.i.* fingersi malato. ~**er** *n.* scansafatiche *m./f. invar.*

malleable /'mælɪəbl/ *a.* malleabile.

mallet /'mælɪt/ *n.* martello di legno *m.*

malnutrition /mælnjuː'trɪʃn/ *n.* malnutrizione *f.*

malpractice /mæl'præktɪs/ *n.* negligenza *f.*

malt /mɔːlt/ *n.* malto *m.*

Malt|a /'mɔːltə/ *n.* Malta *f.* ~**ese** /-'tiːz/ *a.* & *n.* maltese *m./f.*

maltreat /mæl'triːt/ *v.t.* maltrattare. ~**ment** *n.* maltrattamento *m.*

mammal /'mæml/ *n.* mammifero *m.*

mammoth /'mæməθ/ *n.* mammut *m.* —*a.* mastodontico.

man /mæn/ *n.* (*pl.* **men**) uomo *m.*; (*in sports*) giocatore *m.*; (*chess*) pedina *f.* —*v.t.* (*p.t.* **manned**) fornire di uomini; (*be on duty*) essere di servizio. ~ **about town** uomo di mondo. ~-**hour** *n.* ora lavorativa *f.* ~-**hunt** *n.* caccia all'uomo *f.* ~ **in the street** uomo qualunque. ~-**made** *a.* artificiale. ~ **of letters** letterato *m.*

∼-of-war *n.* nave da guerra *f.* **∼ to man** *a.* & *adv.* da uomo a uomo.

manacle /'mænəkl/ *n.* manetta *f.* —*v.t.* ammanettare.

manage /'mænɪdʒ/ *v.t.* dirigere; (*shop*, *affairs*) gestire; (*take charge of*) occuparsi (di). —*v.i.* riuscire; (*make do*) arrangiarsi. **∼able** *a.* maneggevole. **∼ment** *n.* direzione *f.*; (*of shop*) gestione *f.* **managing director** *n.* direttore generale *m.*

manager /'mænɪdʒə(r)/ *n.* direttore *m.*; (*theatr.*, *cinema*) impresario *m.* **∼ess** /-'res/ *n.* direttrice *f.* **∼ial** /-'dʒɪərɪəl/ *a.* direttivo.

mandarin /'mændərɪn/ *n.* mandarino *m.*

mandate /'mændeɪt/ *n.* mandato *m.*

mandatory /'mændətrɪ/ *a.* obbligatorio.

mane /meɪn/ *n.* criniera *f.*

manful /'mænfl/ *a.* coraggioso.

manganese /mæŋgə'niːz/ *n.* manganese *m.*

manger /'meɪndʒə(r)/ *n.* mangiatoia *f.*

mangle[1] /'mæŋgl/ *n.* mangano *m.* —*v.t.* manganare.

mangle[2] /'mæŋgl/ *v.t.* (*damage*) maciullare.

mango /'mæŋgəʊ/ *n.* (*pl.* -oes) mango *m.*

mangy /'meɪndʒɪ/ *a.* rognoso.

manhandle /'mænhændl/ *v.t.* malmenare.

manhole /'mænhəʊl/ *n.* botola *f.* **∼ cover** tombino *m.*

manhood /'mænhʊd/ *n.* età virile *f.*; (*quality*) virilità *f.*

mania /'meɪnɪə/ *n.* mania *f.* **∼c** /-ɪæk/ *n.* maniaco, a *m.*, *f.*

manicur|e /'mænɪkjʊə(r)/ *n.* manicure *f.* —*v.t.* fare la manicure. **∼ist** *n.* manicure *f.*

manifest /'mænɪfest/ *a.* & *n.* manifesto *m.* —*v.t.* manifestare. **∼ation** /-'steɪʃn/ *n.* manifestazione *f.*

manifold /'mænɪfəʊld/ *a.* molteplice.

manipulat|e /mə'nɪpjʊleɪt/ *v.t.* manipolare. **∼ion** /-'leɪʃn/ *n.* manipolazione *f.*

mankind /mæn'kaɪnd/ *n.* genere umano *m.*

manly /'mænlɪ/ *a.* virile.

mannequin /'mænɪkɪn/ *n.* indossatrice *f.*

manner /'mænə(r)/ *n.* maniera *f.*; (*attitude*) atteggiamento *m.*; (*kind*) sorta *f.* **∼s** *n.pl.* usanze *f.pl.*; (*behaviour*)

maniere *f.pl.* **have no ∼s** essere senza educazione. **∼ed** *a.* manierato. **bad ∼ed** *a.* maleducato.

mannerism /'mænərɪzəm/ *n.* manierismo *m.*

mannish /'mænɪʃ/ *a.* (*of woman*) mascolina.

manœuvre /mə'nuːvə(r)/ *n.* manovra *f.* —*v.i.* far manovre. —*v.t.* manovrare.

manor /'mænə(r)/ *n.* maniero *m.*

manpower /'mænpaʊə(r)/ *n.* mano d'opera *f.*

manservant /'mænsɜːvənt/ *n.* (*pl.* **menservants**) domestico *m.*

mansion /'mænʃn/ *n.* palazzo *m.*

manslaughter /'mænslɔːtə(r)/ *n.* omicidio colposo *m.*

mantelpiece /'mæntlpiːs/ *n.* mensola di caminetto *f.*

mantilla /mæn'tɪlə/ *n.* mantiglia *f.*

mantle /'mæntl/ *n.* mantello *m.*

manual /'mænjʊəl/ *a.* & *n.* manuale *m.*

manufacture /mænjʊ'fæktʃə(r)/ *v.t.* fabbricare. —*n.* fabbricazione *f.* **∼r** /-ə(r)/ *n.* fabbricante *m.*

manure /mə'njʊə(r)/ *n.* concime *m.*

manuscript /'mænjʊskrɪpt/ *n.* manoscritto *m.*

many /'menɪ/ *a.* & *pron.* molti, molte. **a great ∼** moltissimi. **as ∼** altrettanti. **∼ a time** molte volte. **too ∼** troppi.

map /mæp/ *n.* carta geografica *f.*; (*of streets etc.*) mappa *f.* —*v.t.* (*p.t.* **mapped**) tracciare una mappa. **∼ out** abbozzare un piano.

maple /'meɪpl/ *n.* acero *m.*

mar /mɑː(r)/ *v.t.* (*p.t.* **marred**) guastare.

marathon /'mærəθən/ *n.* maratona *f.*

marauder /mə'rɔːdə(r)/ *n.* predone *m.*

marble /'mɑːbl/ *n.* marmo *m.*; (*for game*) pallina *f.*

March /mɑːtʃ/ *n.* marzo *m.*

march /mɑːtʃ/ *v.i.* marciare. —*v.t.* far marciare. —*n.* marcia *f.* **∼ past** *n.* sfilata *f.*

marchioness /mɑːʃənɪs/ *n.* marchesa *f.*

mare /'meə(r)/ *n.* giumenta *f.*

margarine /mɑːdʒə'riːn/ *n.* margarina *f.*

margin /'mɑːdʒɪn/ *n.* margine *m.* **∼al** *a.* marginale. **∼ally** *adv.* marginalmente.

marguerite /mɑːgə'riːt/ *n.* margherita *f.*

marigold /'mærɪgəʊld/ *n.* calendula *f.*
marijuana /mærɪ'wɑːnə/ *n.* marijuana
f.
marina /mə'riːnə/ *n.* porticciolo *m.*
marinade /mærɪ'neɪd/ *n.* salamoia
f. —*v.t.* marinare.
marine /mə'riːn/ *a.* marino. —*n.* marina mercantile *f.*; (*sailor*) soldato di
fanteria marina *m.*
marionette /mærɪə'net/ *n.* marionetta
f.
marital /'mærɪtl/ *a.* coniugale.
maritime /'mærɪtaɪm/ *a.* marittimo.
marjoram /'mɑːdʒərəm/ *n.* mag-
giorana *f.*
mark[1] /mɑːk/ *n.* (*currency*) marco *m.*
mark[2] /mɑːk/ *n.* segno *m.*; (*trace*) traccia *f.*; (*schol.*) voto *m.*; (*target*) bersaglio *m.* —*v.t.* segnare; (*characterize*)
caratterizzare; (*schol.*) correggere;
(*notice*) notare. ~ **out** delimitare;
(*fig.*) designare. ~ **time** segnare il
passo. ~**er** *n.* (*sport*) segnatore *m.*;
(*for book*) segnalibro *m.* ~**ing** *n.* mar-
catura *f.*
marked /mɑːkt/ *a.* marcato. ~**ly** /-ɪdlɪ/
adv. notevolmente.
market /'mɑːkɪt/ *n.* mercato *m.* —*v.t./i.*
comprare *or* vendere al mercato;
(*launch*) commercializzare. ~
garden *n.* orto *m.* **on the** ~ in vendita. ~**ing** *n.* marketing *m.*
marksman /'mɑːksmən/ *n.* (*pl.* -**men**)
tiratore scelto *m.* ~**ship** *n.* abilità nel
tiro *f.*
marmalade /'mɑːməleɪd/ *n.* marmellata d'arance *f.*
marmot /'mɑːmət/ *n.* marmotta *f.*
maroon[1] /mə'ruːn/ *a.* & *n.* marrone
rossastro *m.*
maroon[2] /mə'ruːn/ *v.t.* **be** ~**ed in**
essere abbandonato in.
marquee /mɑː'kiː/ *n.* padiglione *m.*
marquetry /'mɑːkɪtrɪ/ *n.* intarsio *m.*
marquis /'mɑːkwɪs/ *n.* marchese *m.*
marriage /'mærɪdʒ/ *n.* matrimonio *m.*
~**able** *a.* da marito.
marrow /'mærəʊ/ *n.* midollo *m.*; (*vegetable*) zucca *f.*
marr|y /'mærɪ/ *v.t./i.* sposare, sposarsi;
(*give in marriage*) maritare. ~**ied** *a.*
sposato; (*life*) coniugale.
marsh /mɑːʃ/ *n.* palude *f.* ~**y** *a.* paludoso.
marshal /'mɑːʃl/ *n.* maresciallo *m.*;
(*at event*) cerimoniere *m.* —*v.t.* (*p.t.*
marshalled) schierare; (*fig.*) scortare.

marsh mallow /mɑːʃ'mæləʊ/ *n.* caramella gommosa e pastosa *f.*
martial /'mɑːʃl/ *a.* marziale.
Martian /'mɑːʃn/ *a.* & *n.* marziano, a
m., *f.*
martinet /mɑːtɪ'net/ *n.* fanatico della
disciplina *m.*
martyr /'mɑːtə(r)/ *n.* martire *m.*|*f.*
—*v.t.* martoriare. ~**dom** *n.* martirio
m.
marvel /'mɑːvəl/ *n.* meraviglia *f.*
—*v.i.* (*p.t.* **marvelled**) meravigliarsi
(**at**, di).
marvellous /'mɑːvələs/ *a.* meraviglioso.
Marxis|t /'mɑːksɪst/ *a.* & *n.* marxista
m.|*f.* ~**m** /-zəm/ *n.* marxismo *m.*
marzipan /'mɑːzɪpæn/ *n.* marzapane
m.
mascara /mæ'skɑːrə/ *n.* mascara *m.*
mascot /'mæskət/ *n.* mascotte *f. invar.*
masculin|e /'mæskjʊlɪm/ *a.* ma-
schile. —*n.* genere maschile *m.* ~**ity**
/-'lɪnətɪ/ *n.* mascolinità *f.*
mash /mæʃ/ *n.* pastone *m.*; (*culin.*)
purè *m.* —*v.t.* impastare. ~**ed potatoes** purè di patate *m.*
mask /mɑːsk/ *n.* maschera *f.* —*v.t.*
mascherare.
masochis|t /'mæsəkɪst/ *n.* masochista
m.|*f.* ~**m** /-zəm/ *n.* masochismo *m.*
mason /'meɪsn/ *n.* muratore *m.* ~**ry** *n.*
massoneria *f.*
Mason /'meɪsn/ *n.* (**Free**)~ massone
m. ~**ic** /mə'sɒnɪk/ *a.* massonico.
masquerade /mɑːskə'reɪd/ *n.* masche-
rata *f.* —*v.i.* mascherarsi. ~ **as** farsi
passare per.
mass[1] /mæs/ *n.* (*relig.*) messa *f.*
mass[2] /mæs/ *n.* massa *f.* —*v.t.*|*i.* am-
massare, ammassarsi. ~-**media** *n.*
comunicazioni di massa *f.pl.* ~-
produce *v.t.* produrre in serie.
massacre /'mæsəkə(r)/ *n.* massacro
m. —*v.t.* massacrare.
massage /'mæsɑːʒ/ *n.* massaggio *m.*
—*v.t.* massaggiare.
masseu|r /mæ'sɜː(r)/ *n.* massaggiatore
m. ~**se** *n.* massaggiatrice *f.*
massive /'mæsɪv/ *a.* enorme; (*fig.*) imponente.
mast /mɑːst/ *n.* (*naut.*) albero *m.*; (*for
flag*) asta *f.*; (*for radio*) antenna *f.*
master /'mɑːstə(r)/ *n.* (*in school*) professore *m.*; (*in control*) maestro, padrone *m.*; (*employer*) principale *m.*;
(*of merchant ship*) capitano *m.*
M~ (*boy*) Signorino *m.* —*v.t.* essere

padrone (di), dominare. **~-mind** *n.* mente superiore *f.*; *v.t.* ideare e dirigere. **M~ of Arts** laureato in Lettere *m.* **~-stroke** *n.* colpo magistrale *m.* **~y** *n.* padronanza *f.*

masterly /'mɑːstəlɪ/ *a.* magistrale.

masterpiece /'mɑːstəpiːs/ *n.* capolavoro *m.*

masturbat|e /'mæstəbeɪt/ *v.i.* masturbarsi. **~ion** /-'beɪʃn/ *n.* masturbazione *f.*

mat /mæt/ *n.* (*at door*) stuoia *f.*; (*on table*) sottopiatto *m.*

match[1] /mætʃ/ *n.* fiammifero *m.*

match[2] /mætʃ/ *n.* (*sport*) partita *f.*; (*equal*) uguale *m.*/*f.*; (*marriage*) matrimonio *m.*; (*s.o. to marry*) partito *m.* —*v.t.*/*i.* contrapporre; (*be like*) andare con; (*curtains etc.*) intonarsi; (*put together*) accoppiare. **~ing** *a.* intonato.

matchbox /'mætʃbɒks/ *n.* scatola di fiammiferi *f.*

mate[1] /meɪt/ *n.* compagno, a *m.*, *f.* —*v.t.*/*i.* accoppiare, accoppiarsi.

mate[2] /meɪt/ *n.* (*chess*) scacco matto *m.*

material /mə'tɪərɪəl/ *n.* materiale *m.*; (*cloth*) stoffa *f.* —*a.* materiale. **raw ~s** *n.pl.* materie prime *f.pl.* **~istic** /-'lɪstɪk/ *a.* materialistico.

materialize /mə'tɪərɪəlaɪz/ *v.i.* materializzarsi.

maternal /mə'tɜːnl/ *a.* materno.

maternity /mə'tɜːnɪtɪ/ *n.* maternità *f.* **~ clothes** *n.pl.* abiti premaman *m.pl.*

matey /'meɪtɪ/ *a.* (*fam.*) amichevole.

mathematic|s /mæθə'mætɪks/ *n.* & *n.pl.* matematica *f.s.* **~ian** /-ə'tɪʃn/ *n.* matematico, a *m.*, *f.* **~al** *a.* matematico. **maths** *n.pl.* (*fam.*) matematica *f.*

matinée /'mætɪneɪ/ *n.* matinée *m.*

matriculat|e /mə'trɪkjʊleɪt/ *v.t.*/*i.* immatricolare, immatricolarsi. **~ion** /-'leɪʃn/ *n.* immatricolazione *f.*

matrimon|y /'mætrɪmənɪ/ *n.* matrimonio *m.* **~ial** /-'məʊnɪəl/ *a.* matrimoniale.

matrix /'meɪtrɪks/ *n.* (*pl.* **matrices** /-siːz/) matrice *f.*

matron /'meɪtrən/ *n.* matrona *f.*; (*of school etc.*) governante *f.* **~ly** *a.* matronale.

matt /mæt/ *a.* opaco.

matted /'mætɪd/ *a.* **~ hair** capelli arruffati.

matter /'mætə(r)/ *n.* materia *f.*; (*affair*) faccenda *f.*; (*pus*) pus *m.* —*v.i.* importare. **as a ~ of fact** in verità. **it**

does not ~ non importa. **~-of-fact** *a.* pratico. **what is the ~?** che cosa c'è (che non va)?

matting /'mætɪŋ/ *n.* materiale per stuoie *m.*

mattress /'mætrɪs/ *n.* materasso *m.*

matur|e /mə'tjʊə(r)/ *a.* maturo. —*v.t.*/*i.* maturare, far maturare. **~ity** *n.* maturità *f.*

maul /mɔːl/ *v.t.* malmᵊnare.

Mauritius /mə'rɪʃəs/ *n.* l'isola Maurizio *f.*

mausoleum /mɔːsə'liːəm/ *n.* mausoleo *m.*

mauve /məʊv/ *a.* & *n.* malva *f.*

mawkish /'mɔːkɪʃ/ *a.* sdolcinato.

maxim /'mæksɪm/ *n.* massima *f.*

maxim|um /'mæksɪməm/ *a.* & *n.* (*pl.* **maxima**) massimo *m.* **~ize** *v.t.* massimizzare.

may /meɪ/ *v. aux.* (*p.t.* **might**) potere. **it ~/might be true** può/potrebbe esser vero. **~ I come in?** posso entrare?

May /meɪ/ *n.* maggio *m.* **~ Day** *n.* il primo maggio *m.*

maybe /'meɪbɪ/ *adv.* forse, può darsi.

mayhem /'meɪhem/ *n.* azione brutale *f.*

mayonnaise /meɪə'neɪz/ *n.* maionese *f.*

mayor /'meə(r)/ *n.* sindaco *m.* **~ess** *n.* sindaca *f.*; moglie del sindaco *f.*

maze /meɪz/ *n.* labirinto *m.*

me[1] /miː/ *pron.* me, mi, a me. **it is ~** sono io.

me[2] /miː/ *n.* (*mus.*) mi *m.*

meadow /'medəʊ/ *n.* prato *m.*

meagre /'miːɡə(r)/ *a.* scarso.

meal[1] /miːl/ *n.* pasto *m.*

meal[2] /miːl/ *n.* (*grain*) farina *f.*

mealy-mouthed /miːlɪ'maʊðd/ *a.* ipocrita.

mean[1] /miːn/ *a.* (**-er, -est**) avaro; (*low in rank*) basso; (*unkind*) indegno. **~ness** *n.* meschinità *f.*; avarizia *f.*

mean[2] /miːn/ *a.* medio. —*n.* media *f.* **Greenwich ~ time** ora media di Greenwich.

mean[3] /miːn/ *v.t.* (*p.t.* **meant**) voler dire, significare; (*intend*) intendere. **~ well** aver buone intenzioni. **be meant for** essere destinato a.

meander /mɪ'ændə(r)/ *v.i.* vagare.

meaning /'miːnɪŋ/ *n.* significato *m.* **~ful** *a.* significativo. **~less** *a.* senza senso.

means /miːnz/ *n.* mezzo *m.* —*n.pl.*

(*resources*) mezzi *m.pl.* **by all** ~ certamente. **by no** ~ niente affatto. ~ **test** *n.* accertamento patrimoniale *m.*

meant /ment/ *see* **mean**³.

meantime, meanwhile /'mi:ntaɪm, 'mi:nwaɪl/ *advs.* intanto. **in the mean time** nel frattempo.

measles /'mi:zlz/ *n.* morbillo *m.*

measly /'mi:zlɪ/ *a.* (*sl.*) meschino.

measurable /'meʒərəbl/ *a.* misurabile.

measure /'meʒə(r)/ *n.* misura *f.* —*v.t./i.* misurare. ~ **up to** essere all'altezza di. ~**d** *a.* misurato. ~**ment** *n.* misura *f.*

meat /mi:t/ *n.* carne *f.* ~**y** *a.* (**-ier, -iest**) carnoso; (*fig.*) sostanzioso.

mechanic /mɪ'kænɪk/ *n.* meccanico *m.*

mechanic|al /mɪ'kænɪkl/ *a.* meccanico. ~**s** *n.* meccanica *f.*; *n.pl.* meccanismo *m.s.*

mechan|ism /'mekənɪzəm/ *n.* meccanismo *m.* ~**ize** *v.t.* meccanizzare.

medal /'medl/ *n.* medaglia *f.* ~**list** *n.* vinci|tore, -trice di una medaglia *m.*, *f.*

medallion /mɪ'dælɪən/ *n.* medaglione *m.*

meddle /'medl/ *v.i.* immischiarsi (**in,** di). ~ **with** (*tinker*) toccare. ~**some** *a.* ficcanaso.

media /'mi:dɪə/ *see* **medium.** —*n.pl.* mezzi pubblicitari *m.pl.*

mediat|e /'mi:dɪeɪt/ *v.i.* fare da mediatore. ~**ion** /-'eɪʃn/ *n.* mediazione *f.* ~**or** media|tore, -trice *m.*, *f.*

medical /'medɪkl/ *a.* medico; (*student*) in medicina. —*n.* (*fam.*) visita medica *f.*

medicat|e /'medɪkeɪt/ *v.t.* medicare. ~**ion** /-'keɪʃn/ *n.* medicazione *f.*

medicinal /mɪ'dɪsɪnl/ *a.* medicinale.

medicine /'medsn/ *n.* medicina *f.*

medieval /medɪ'i:vl/ *a.* medievale.

mediocr|e /mi:dɪ'əʊkə(r)/ *a.* mediocre. ~**ity** /-'ɒkrətɪ/ *n.* mediocrità *f.*

meditat|e /'medɪteɪt/ *v.t./i.* meditare. ~**ion** /-'teɪʃn/ *n.* meditazione *f.*

Mediterranean /medɪtə'reɪnɪən/ *a.* mediterraneo. —*n.* **the** ~ (**Sea**) il (mare) Mediterraneo *m.*

medium /'mi:dɪəm/ *n.* (*pl.* **media**) mezzo *m.*; (*pl.* **mediums**) (*person*) medium *m./f.* —*a.* medio.

medley /'medlɪ/ *n.* (*pl.* **-eys**) miscuglio *m.*

meek /mi:k/ *a.* (**-er, -est**) mite, mansueto.

meet /mi:t/ *v.t./i.* (*p.t.* **met**) incontrare;

(*at station etc.*) andare incontro (a); (*be introduced to*) fare la conoscenza di; (*face*) far fronte (a). ~ **the bill** pagare il conto. ~ **with** (*obstacles*) imbattersi in. —*n.* raduno *m.*

meeting /'mi:tɪŋ/ *n.* riunione *f.*; (*of two people*) incontro *m.*

megalomania /megələʊ'meɪnɪə/ *n.* megalomania *f.*

megaphone /'megəfəʊn/ *n.* megafono *m.*

melanchol|y /'melənkɒlɪ/ *n.* malinconia *f.* —*a.* malinconico. ~**ic** /-'kɒlɪk/ *a.* melanconico.

mêlée /'meleɪ/ *n.* mischia *f.*

mellow /'meləʊ/ *a.* (**-er, -est**) (*fruit*) maturo; (*wine*) generoso; (*person*) dolce; (*sound, colour*) caldo. —*v.i.* (*person*) addolcirsi.

melodious /mɪ'ləʊdɪəs/ *a.* melodioso.

melodrama /'melədrɑ:mə/ *n.* melodramma *m.* ~**tic** /-ə'mætɪk/ *a.* melodrammatico.

melod|y /'melədɪ/ *n.* melodia *f.* ~**ic** /mɪ'lɒdɪk/ *a.* melodico.

melon /'melən/ *n.* melone *m.*

melt /melt/ *v.t./i.* sciogliere, sciogliersi. ~**ing-pot** *n.* crogiuolo *m.*

member /'membə(r)/ *n.* membro *m.* **M~ of Parliament** deputato *m.* ~**ship** *n.* associazione *f.*; (*members*) soci *m.pl.*

membrane /'membreɪn/ *n.* membrana *f.*

memento /mɪ'mentəʊ/ *n.* (*pl.* **-oes**) ricordo *m.*

memo /'meməʊ/ *n.* (*pl.* **-os**) (*fam.*) nota *f.*

memoir /'memwɑ:(r)/ *n.* nota biografica *f.* ~**s** *n.pl.* ricordi *m.pl.*

memorable /'memərəbl/ *a.* memorabile.

memorandum /memə'rændəm/ *n.* (*pl.* **-ums**) appunto *m.*

memorial /mɪ'mɔ:rɪəl/ *n.* monumento *m.* —*a.* commemorativo.

memorize /'meməraɪz/ *v.t.* imparare a memoria.

memory /'memərɪ/ *n.* memoria *f.*; (*thing remembered*) ricordo *m.* **in** ~ **of** a ricordo di.

men /men/ *see* **man.**

menac|e /'menəs/ *n.* minaccia *f.*; (*nuisance*) peste *f.* —*v.t.* minacciare. ~**ingly** *adv.* minacciosamente.

menagerie /mɪ'nædʒərɪ/ *n.* serraglio *m.*

mend /mend/ *v.t.* riparare; (*darn*)

rammendare. —*n.* rattoppo *m.* **on the** ~ in via di guarigione.

menfolk /'menfəʊk/ *n.pl.* uomini *m.pl.*

menial /'mi:nɪəl/ *a.* umile.

meningitis /menɪn'dʒaɪtɪs/ *n.* meningite *f.*

menopause /'menəpɔ:z/ *n.* menopausa *f.*

menstruat|e /'menstrʊeɪt/ *v.i.* mestruare. ~**ion** /-'eɪʃn/ *n.* mestruazione *f.*

mental /'mentl/ *a.* mentale.

mentality /men'tælətɪ/ *n.* mentalità *f.*

mention /'menʃn/ *v.t.* menzionare. —*n.* menzione *f.* **don't** ~ **it!** prego!

mentor /'mentɔ:(r)/ *n.* mentore *m.*

menu /'menju:/ *n.* (*pl.* **-us**) menu *m. invar.*

mercantile /'mɜ:kəntaɪl/ *a.* mercantile.

mercenary /'mɜ:sɪnərɪ/ *a.* & *n.* mercenario *m.*

merchandise /'mɜ:tʃəndaɪz/ *n.* merce *f.*

merchant /'mɜ:tʃənt/ *n.* mercante *m.* —*a.* mercantile.

merciful /'mɜ:sɪfl/ *a.* misericordioso. ~**ly** *adv.* (*fam.*) grazie a Dio.

merciless /'mɜ:sɪlɪs/ *a.* spietato.

mercur|y /'mɜ:kjʊrɪ/ *n.* mercurio *m.* ~**ial** /mɜ:'kjʊərɪəl/ *a.* di mercurio; (*fig.*) attivo.

mercy /'mɜ:sɪ/ *n.* misericordia *f.* **at the** ~ **of** alla mercè di.

mere /mɪə(r)/ *a.* solo; (*lit.*) mero. ~**ly** *adv.* solamente. ~**st** *a.* minimo.

merge /mɜ:dʒ/ *v.t./i.* fondere, fondersi; (*comm.*) amalgamare. ~**r** /-ə(r)/ *n.* fusione *f.*

meridian /mə'rɪdɪən/ *n.* meridiano *m.*

meringue /mə'ræŋ/ *n.* meringa *f.*

merit /'merɪt/ *n.* merito *m.* —*v.t.* meritare. ~**orious** /-'tɔ:rɪəs/ *a.* benemerito.

mermaid /'mɜ:meɪd/ *n.* sirena *f.*

merry /'merɪ/ *a.* (**-ier, -est**) allegro. **make** ~ far festa. ~**-go-round** *n.* giostra *f.* ~**-making** *n.* festa *f.* **merrily** *adv.* allegramente. **merriment** *n.* baldoria *f.*

mesh /meʃ/ *n.* maglia *f.*

mesmerize /'mezməraɪz/ *v.t.* ipnotizzare; (*fig.*) affascinare.

mess /mes/ *n.* disordine *m.*; (*something spilt*) sporco *m.*; (*trouble*) guaio *m.*; (*mil.*) mensa *f.* —*v.t.* ~ **up** mettere in disordine. —*v.i.* ~ **about** perder tempo. **make a** ~ **of** fare un pasticcio di.

message /'mesɪdʒ/ *n.* messaggio *m.*

messenger /'mesɪndʒə(r)/ *n.* messaggero *m.*

Messiah /mɪ'saɪə/ *n.* Messia *m.*

Messrs /'mesəz/ *n.pl. see* **Mr.**

messy /'mesɪ/ *a.* (**-ier, -iest**) disordinato; (*slovenly*) sciatto.

met /met/ *see* **meet.**

metabolism /mɪ'tæbəlɪzəm/ *n.* metabolismo *m.*

metal /'metl/ *n.* metallo *m.* —*a.* di metallo. ~**lic** /mɪ'tælɪk/ *a.* metallico.

metallurgy /mɪ'tælədʒɪ/ *n.* metallurgia *f.*

metamorphosis /metə'mɔ:fəsɪs/ *n.* (*pl.* **-phoses** /-si:z/) metamorfosi *f. invar.*

metaphor /'metəfə(r)/ *n.* metafora *f.* ~**ical** /-'fɒrɪkl/ *a.* metaforico.

mete /mi:t/ *v.t.* ~ **out** distribuire.

meteor /'mi:tɪə(r)/ *n.* meteora *f.*

meteorolog|y /mi:tɪə'rɒlədʒɪ/ *n.* meteorologia *f.* ~**ical** /-ə'lɒdʒɪkl/ *a.* meteorologico.

meter[1] /'mi:tə(r)/ *n.* contatore *m.*

meter[2] /'mi:tə(r)/ *n.* (*Amer.*) = **metre.**

method /'meθəd/ *n.* metodo *m.*

methodical /mɪ'θɒdɪkl/ *a.* metodico.

Methodist /'meθədɪst/ *n.* metodista *m./f.*

methylated /'meθɪleɪtɪd/ *a.* ~ **spirit** alcool denaturato *m.*

meticulous /mɪ'tɪkjʊləs/ *a.* meticoloso.

metre /'mi:tə(r)/ *n.* metro *m.*

metric /'metrɪk/ *a.* metrico. ~**ation** /-'keɪʃn/ *n.* conversione al sistema metrico *f.*

metropol|is /mə'trɒpəlɪs/ *n.* metropoli *f. invar.* ~**itan** /metrə'pɒlɪtən/ *a.* metropolitano.

mettle /'metl/ *n.* tempra *f.*

mew /mju:/ *n.* miao *m.* —*v.i.* miagolare.

mews /mju:z/ *n.* casetta (ricavata da un'ex scuderia) *f.*

mezzanine /'mezəni:n/ *n.* mezzanino *m.*

Mexic|o /'meksɪkəʊ/ *n.* Messico *m.* ~**an** *a.* & *n.* messicano, a *m., f.*

miaow /mi:'aʊ/ *n.* & *v.i.* = **mew.**

mice /maɪs/ *see* **mouse.**

mickey /'mɪkɪ/ *n.* **take the** ~ **out of** prendere in giro.

micro- /'maɪkrəʊ/ *pref.* micro-.

microbe /'maɪkrəʊb/ *n.* microbo *m.*

microchip /'maɪkrəʊtʃɪp/ *n.* microchip *m.*

microfilm /'maɪkrəʊfɪlm/ *n.* microfilm
m.

microphone /'maɪkrəfəʊn/ *n.* microfono *m.*

microprocessor /maɪkrəʊ'prəʊse-
sə(r)/ *n.* micro-processore *m.*

microscop|e /'maɪkrəskəʊp/ *n.* micro-
scopio *m.* **~ic** /-'skɒpɪk/ *a.* micro-
scopico.

microwave /'maɪkrəʊweɪv/ *n.* mi-
croonda *f.*

mid /mɪd/ *a.* in mezzo. **in ~ air** a
mezz'aria.

midday /mɪd'deɪ/ *n.* mezzogiorno *m.*

middle /'mɪdl/ *a.* di centro; (*quality*)
medio. *—n.* mezzo *m.* **in the ~ of** in
mezzo a. **~-aged** *a.* di mezza età. **the
M~ Ages** *n.pl.* il Medio Evo *m.s.* **~-
class** *a.* borghese. **the ~ classes** *n.pl.*
la classe media *f.s.* **M~ East** *n.* Medio
Oriente *m.*

middleman /'mɪdlmæn/ *n.* (*pl.* **-men**)
intermediario *m.*

middling /'mɪdlɪŋ/ *a.* discreto.

midge /mɪdʒ/ *n.* moscerino *m.*

midget /'mɪdʒɪt/ *n.* nano, a *m.*, *f.*

Midlands /'mɪdləndz/ *n.pl.* the ~
l'Inghilterra centrale *f.s.*

midnight /'mɪdnaɪt/ *n.* mezzanotte *f.*

midriff /'mɪdrɪf/ *n.* diaframma *m.*;
(*fam.*) pancia *f.*

midst /mɪdst/ *n.* **in the ~ of** in mezzo
a.

midsummer /mɪd'sʌmə(r)/ *n.* mezza
estate *f.*

midway /mɪd'weɪ/ *adv.* a metà strada.

midwife /'mɪdwaɪf/ *n.*(*pl.*-**wives**) leva-
trice *f.*

midwinter /mɪd'wɪntə(r)/ *n.* cuore
dell'inverno *m.*

might[1] /maɪt/ *n.* potere *m.* **~y** *a.*
(**-ier, -iest**) potente; (*fig.*) grande; *adv.*
(*fam.*) molto.

might[2] /maɪt/ *see* **may.**

migraine /'miːɡreɪn/ *n.* emicrania *f.*

migrant /'maɪɡrənt/ *a.* & *n.* migratore
m.; (*person*) emigrante *m.|f.*

migrat|e /maɪ'ɡreɪt/ *v.i.* migrare. **~ion**
/-ʃn/ *n.* migrazione *f.*

mike /maɪk/ *n.* (*fam.*) microfono *m.*

Milan /mɪ'læn/ *n.* Milano *f.*

mild /maɪld/ *a.* (**-er, -est**) mite; (*illness*)
lieve. **~ly** *adv.* moderatamente.
~ness *n.* dolcezza *f.*

mildew /'mɪldjuː/ *n.* muffa *f.*

mile /maɪl/ *n.* miglio *m.* **~s nicer**
(*fam.*) molto più bello. **~s too big**

(*fam.*) eccessivamente grande. **~age**
n. chilometraggio *m.*

milestone /'maɪlstəʊn/ *n.* pietra miliare *f.*

milieu /'miːljɜː/ *n.* ambiente *m.*

militant /'mɪlɪtənt/ *a.* & *n.* militante
m.|f.

military /'mɪlɪtrɪ/ *a.* militare.

militate /'mɪlɪteɪt/ *v.i.* militare. **~
against** opporsi a.

militia /mɪ'lɪʃə/ *n.* milizia *f.*

milk /mɪlk/ *n.* latte *m.* *—v.t.* mungere;
(*fig.*) sfruttare. **~ shake** *n.* frullato
di latte *m.* **~y** *a.* latteo; (*tea etc.*)
biancastro.

milkman /'mɪlkmən/ *n.* (*pl.* **-men**) lat-
taio *m.*

mill /mɪl/ *n.* mulino *m.*; (*for coffee
etc.*) macinino *m.* *—v.t./i.* macinare;
(*metals*) laminare. **~ about** *v.i.* assie-
parsi. **~er** *n.* mugnaio *m.*

millennium /mɪ'leniəm/ *n.* (*pl.* **-ums**)
millennio *m.*

millet /'mɪlɪt/ *n.* miglio *m.*

milligram /'mɪlɪɡræm/ *n.* milli-
grammo *m.*

millimetre /'mɪlɪmiːtə(r)/ *n.* milli-
metro *m.*

milliner /'mɪlɪnə(r)/ *n.* modista *f.* **~y**
n. modisteria *f.*

million /'mɪliən/ *n.* milione *m.* **a ~
pounds** un milione di sterline. **~aire**
/-'neə(r)/ *n.* milionario *m.*

millstone /'mɪlstəʊn/ *n.* macina *f.*;
(*fig.*) peso *m.*

mime /maɪm/ *n.* mimo *m.* *—v.t./i.* mi-
mare.

mimic /'mɪmɪk/ *v.t.* (*p.t.* **mimicked**)
imitare. *—n.* imita|tore, -trice *m.*,
f. **~ry** *n.* mimica *f.*

mimosa /mɪ'məʊzə/ *n.* mimosa *f.*

minaret /mɪnə'ret/ *n.* minareto *m.*

mince /mɪns/ *v.t.* tritare. *—n.* carne
tritata *f.* **~ pie** *n.* pasticcino (a base
di frutta secca) *m.* **not to ~ words**
non misurare le parole. **~r** /-ə(r)/ *n.*
tritacarne *m.*

mincemeat /'mɪnsmiːt/ *n.* composto
di frutta secca *m.* **make ~ of** (*fig.*)
demolire.

mind /maɪnd/ *n.* mente *f.*; (*intention*)
proposito *m.*; (*sanity*) ragione *f.*
—v.t. (*look after*) badare (a); (*object
to*) essere dispiaciuto; (*be careful*) fare
attenzione. **never ~** non importa.
~ful *a.* **~ful of** conscio di. **~less** *a.*
noncurante.

minder /'maɪndə(r)/ *n.* sorvegliante *m.*/*f.*

mine[1] /maɪn/ *poss. pron.* mio, mia, miei, mie.

min|**e**[2] /maɪn/ *n.* miniera *f.*; (*explosive*) mina *f.* —*v.t.* estrarre (minerali); (*mil.*) minare. ~**er** *n.* minatore *m.* ~**ing** *n.* industria mineraria *f.*; *a.* minerario.

minefield /'maɪnfiːld/ *n.* campo minato *m.*

mineral /'mɪnərəl/ *n.* & *a.* minerale *m.*

minesweeper /'maɪnswiːpə(r)/ *n.* dragamine *m. invar.*

mingle /'mɪŋgl/ *v.t.* mescolare. —*v.i.* ~ **with** mescolarsi a.

mingy /'mɪndʒɪ/ *a.* (*fam.*) gretto.

mini- /'mɪnɪ/ *pref.* mini-.

miniature /'mɪnɪətʃə(r)/ *a.* & *n.* miniatura *f.*

minibus /'mɪnɪbʌs/ *n.* minibus *m.*

minim /'mɪnɪm/ *n.* (*mus.*) minima *f.*

minim|**um** /'mɪnɪməm/ *a.* & *n.* (*pl.* -**ima**) minimo *m.* ~**al** *a.* minimo. ~**ize** *v.t.* minimizzare.

miniskirt /'mɪnɪskɜːt/ *n.* minigonna *f.*

minist|**er** /'mɪnɪstə(r)/ *n.* ministro *m.*; (*relig.*) pastore *m.* ~**erial** /-'stɪərɪəl/ *a.* ministeriale. ~**ry** *n.* ministero *m.*

mink /mɪŋk/ *n.* visone *m.*

minor /'maɪnə(r)/ *a.* minore. —*n.* minorenne *m.*/*f.*

minority /maɪ'nɒrətɪ/ *n.* minoranza *f.*; (*age*) età minore *f.*

minstrel /'mɪnstrəl/ *n.* menestrello *m.*

mint[1] /mɪnt/ *n.* zecca *f.*; (*fig.*) gran quantità *f.* —*v.t.* coniare. **in** ~ **condition** in condizione perfetta.

mint[2] /mɪnt/ *n.* menta *f.*

minuet /mɪnjʊ'et/ *n.* minuetto *m.*

minus /'maɪnəs/ *prep.* meno; (*fam.*) senza. —*n.* meno *m.*

minuscule /'mɪnəskjuːl/ *a.* minuscolo.

minute[1] /'mɪnɪt/ *n.* minuto *m.* ~**s** *n.pl.* (*of meeting*) verbale *m.s.*

minute[2] /maɪ'njuːt/ *a.* minuto; (*precise*) minuzioso.

minx /mɪŋks/ *n.* sfacciatella *f.*

mirac|**le** /'mɪrəkl/ *n.* miracolo *m.* ~**ulous** /mɪ'rækjʊləs/ *a.* miracoloso.

mirage /'mɪrɑːʒ/ *n.* miraggio *m.*

mire /'maɪə(r)/ *n.* pantano *m.*

mirror /'mɪrə(r)/ *n.* specchio *m.* —*v.t.* rispecchiare.

mirth /mɜːθ/ *n.* allegria *f.*

misadventure /mɪsəd'ventʃə(r)/ *n.* disavventura *f.*

misanthrope /'mɪsənθrəʊp/ *n.* misantropo, a *m.*, *f.*

misapprehension /mɪsæprɪ'henʃn/ *n.* malinteso *m.*

misbehav|**e** /mɪsbɪ'heɪv/ *v.i.* comportarsi male. ~**iour** *n.* comportamento scorretto *m.*

miscalculat|**e** /mɪs'kælkjʊleɪt/ *v.t.*/*i.* calcolare male. ~**ion** /-'leɪʃn/ *n.* calcolo sbagliato *m.*

miscarr|**y** /mɪs'kærɪ/ *v.i.* abortire. ~**iage** /-ɪdʒ/ *n.* aborto *m.* ~**iage of justice** errore giudiziario *m.*

miscellaneous /mɪsə'leɪnɪəs/ *a.* assortito.

mischief /'mɪstʃɪf/ *n.* birichinata *f.*; (*harm*) danno *m.* **make** ~ seminare zizzania.

mischievous /'mɪstʃɪvəs/ *a.* birichino; (*malicious*) dannoso.

misconception /mɪskən'sepʃən/ *n.* concetto erroneo *m.*

misconduct /mɪs'kɒndʌkt/ *n.* cattiva condotta *f.*

misconstrue /mɪskən'struː/ *v.t.* fraintendere.

misdeed /mɪs'diːd/ *n.* misfatto *m.*

misdemeanour /mɪsdɪ'miːnə(r)/ *n.* reato *m.*

miser /'maɪzə(r)/ *n.* avaro *m.* ~**ly** *a.* avaro.

miserable /'mɪzrəbl/ *a.* infelice; (*fig.*) deprimente.

misery /'mɪzərɪ/ *n.* miseria *f.*; (*pain*) sofferenze *f.pl.*; (*person, fam.*) piagnone, a *m.*, *f.*

misfire /mɪs'faɪə(r)/ *v.i.* (*of gun*) far cilecca; (*go wrong*) non riuscire.

misfit /'mɪsfɪt/ *n.* disadattato, a *m.*, *f.*

misfortune /mɪs'fɔːtʃuːn/ *n.* sfortuna *f.*

misgiving(s) /mɪs'gɪvɪŋ(z)/ *n.* (*pl.*) dubbi *m.pl.*; (*anxiety*) apprensione *f.*

misguided /mɪs'gaɪdɪd/ *a.* fuorviato.

mishap /'mɪshæp/ *n.* infortunio *m.*

misinform /mɪsɪn'fɔːm/ *v.t.* informar male.

misinterpret /mɪsɪn'tɜːprɪt/ *v.t.* fraintendere.

misjudge /mɪs'dʒʌdʒ/ *v.t.* giudicar male.

mislay /mɪs'leɪ/ *v.t.* (*p.t.* **mislaid**) smarrire.

mislead /mɪs'liːd/ *v.t.* (*p.t.* **misled**) sviare. ~**ing** *a.* ingannevole.

mismanage /mɪs'mænɪdʒ/ *v.t.* amministrare male. ~**ment** *n.* cattiva amministrazione *f.*

misnomer /mɪs'nəʊmə(r)/ *n.* termine improprio *m.*

misplace /mɪs'pleɪs/ *v.t.* mettere in posto sbagliato. ～ **one's trust** riporre male la propria fiducia.

misprint /'mɪsprɪnt/ *n.* errore di stampa *m.*

misquote /mɪs'kwəʊt/ *v.t.* citare erroneamente.

misrepresent /mɪsreprɪ'zent/ *v.t.* rappresentare male.

miss /mɪs/ *v.t./i.* fallire; (*lack*) mancare; (*feel loss*) sentire la mancanza (di); (*train etc.*) perdere. —*n.* colpo mancato *m.* ～ **out** *v.t.* saltare, omettere. ～ **the point** non capire.

Miss /mɪs/ *n.* (*pl.* **Misses**) signorina *f.*

misshapen /mɪs'ʃeɪpən/ *a.* malformato.

missile /'mɪsaɪl/ *n.* missile *m.*

missing /'mɪsɪŋ/ *a.* mancante; (*lost*) smarrito; (*mil.*) disperso.

mission /'mɪʃn/ *n.* missione *f.*

missionary /'mɪʃənrɪ/ *n.* missionario, a *m., f.*

missive /'mɪsɪv/ *n.* missiva *f.*

misspell /mɪs'spel/ *v.t.* (*p.t.* **misspelt**) sbagliare l'ortografia.

mist /mɪst/ *n.* foschia *f.*; (*fig.*) velo *m.* —*v.t./i.* appannare, appannarsi.

mistake /mɪ'steɪk/ *n.* sbaglio *m.* —*v.t.* (*p.t.* **mistook**, *p.p.* **mistaken**) sbagliare; (*choose wrongly*) scambiare; (*understand wrongly*) fraintendere. ～**n** *a.* sbagliato. ～**nly** *adv.* erroneamente.

mistletoe /'mɪsltəʊ/ *n.* vischio *m.*

mistreat /mɪs'triːt/ *v.t.* maltrattare.

mistress /'mɪstrɪs/ *n.* padrona *f.*; (*teacher*) maestra *f.*; (*man's lover*) amante *f.*

mistrust /mɪs'trʌst/ *v.t.* non aver fiducia. —*n.* sfiducia *f.*

misty /'mɪstɪ/ *a.* (-ier, -iest) nebbioso; (*indistinct*) indistinto.

misunderstand /mɪsʌndə'stænd/ *v.t.* (*p.t.* -stood) fraintendere. ～**ing** *n.* malinteso *m.*

misuse[1] /mɪs'juːz/ *v.t.* usare male.

misuse[2] /mɪs'juːs/ *n.* cattivo uso *m.*

mite /maɪt/ *n.* (*child*) piccino, a *m., f.*

mitigate /'mɪtɪɡeɪt/ *v.t.* attenuare.

mitre /'maɪtə(r)/ *n.* mitra *f.*

mitten /'mɪtn/ *n.* manopola *f.*

mix /mɪks/ *v.t./i.* mischiare, mischiarsi. —*n.* miscuglio *m.* ～ **up** mescolare; (*fig.*) confondere. ～**up** *n.* confusione *f.* ～ **with** frequentare.

～**er** *n.* (*culin.*) frullatore *m.* **be a good** ～**er** essere socievole.

mixed /mɪkst/ *a.* misto. ～**up** *a.* (*fam.*) disadattato.

mixture /'mɪkstʃə(r)/ *n.* mescolanza *f.*; (*blend*) miscela *f.*; (*for cough*) sciroppo *m.*

moan /məʊn/ *n.* lamento *m.* —*v.i.* lamentarsi. ～**er** *n.* brontolone, a *m., f.*

moat /məʊt/ *n.* fossato *m.*

mob /mɒb/ *n.* folla *f.*; (*sl., gang*) banda *f.* —*v.t.* (*p.t.* **mobbed**) assalire.

mobil|e /'məʊbaɪl/ *a.* mobile. —*n.* composizione mobile *f.* ～**ity** /-'bɪlətɪ/ *n.* mobilità *f.*

mobiliz|e /'məʊbɪlaɪz/ *v.t./i.* mobilitare. ～**ation** /-'zeɪʃn/ *n.* mobilitazione *f.*

moccasin /'mɒkəsɪn/ *n.* mocassino *m.*

mock /mɒk/ *v.t./i.* canzonare. —*a.* finto. ～**-up** *n.* modello in scala *m.*

mockery /'mɒkərɪ/ *n.* derisione *f.* **a** ～ **of** una parodia di.

mode /məʊd/ *n.* modo *m.*

model /'mɒdl/ *n.* modello *m.*; (*for fashion*) indossa|tore, -trice *m., f.* —*a.* esemplare. —*v.t.* (*p.t.* **modelled**) modellare. —*v.i.* fare l'indossa|tore, -trice; (*for artist*) posare.

moderate[1] /'mɒdərət/ *a.* & *n.* moderato, a *m., f.* ～**ly** *adv.* moderatamente.

moderat|e[2] /'mɒdəreɪt/ *v.t./i.* moderare, moderarsi. ～**ion** /-'reɪʃn/ *n.* moderazione *f.*

modern /'mɒdn/ *a.* moderno. ～ **times** tempi presenti *m.pl.* ～**ize** *v.t.* modernizzare

modest /'mɒdɪst/ *a.* modesto. ～**y** *n.* modestia *f.*

modicum /'mɒdɪkəm/ *n.* **a** ～ **of** un po' di.

modif|y /'mɒdɪfaɪ/ *v.t.* modificare. ～**ication** /-ɪ'keɪʃn/ *n.* modificazione *f.*

modulat|e /'mɒdjʊleɪt/ *v.t./i.* modulare. ～**ion** /-'leɪʃn/ *n.* modulazione *f.*

module /'mɒdjuːl/ *n.* modulo *m.*

mogul /'məʊɡʊl/ *n.* (*fam.*) pezzo grosso *m.*

mohair /'məʊheə(r)/ *n.* mohair *m.*

moist /mɔɪst/ *a.* (-er, -est) umido. ～**ure** /'mɔɪstʃə(r)/ *n.* umidità *f.*

moisten /'mɔɪsn/ *v.t.* inumidire.

moisturize /'mɔɪstʃəraɪz/ *v.t.* (*cosmetic*) idratare. ～**r** /-ə(r)/ *n.* (crema) idratante *f.*

molar /'məʊlə(r)/ *n.* molare *m.*

molasses /mə'læsɪz/ *n.* melassa *f.*

mole[1] /məʊl/ *n.* (*on skin*) neo *m.*
mole[2] /məʊl/ *n.* (*animal*) talpa *f.* ~**hill** *n.* monticello *m.*
mole[3] /məʊl/ *n.* (*breakwater*) molo *m.*
molecule /'mɒlɪkjuːl/ *n.* molecola *f.*
molest /mə'lest/ *v.t.* molestare.
mollify /'mɒlɪfaɪ/ *v.t.* placare.
mollusc /'mɒləsk/ *n.* mollusco *m.*
mollycoddle /'mɒlɪkɒdl/ *v.t.* coccolare.
molten /'məʊltən/ *a.* fuso.
moment /'məʊmənt/ *n.* momento *m.*
momentar|y /'məʊməntrɪ/ *a.* momentaneo. ~**ily** *adv.* momentaneamente.
momentous /mə'mentəs/ *a.* importante.
momentum /mə'mentəm/ *n.* impeto *m.*
monarch /'mɒnək/ *n.* monarca *m.* ~**ist** *n.* monarchico, a *m.*, *f.* ~**y** *n.* monarchia *f.*
monast|ery /'mɒnəstrɪ/ *n.* monastero *m.* ~**ic** /mə'næstɪk/ *a.* monastico.
Monday /'mʌndɪ/ *n.* lunedí *m.*
monetarist /'mʌnɪtərɪst/ *n.* monetarista *m.*/*f.*
monetary /'mʌnɪtrɪ/ *a.* monetario.
money /'mʌnɪ/ *n.* denaro *m.* ~**s** *n.pl.* somme *f.pl.* ~**-box** *n.* salvadanaio *m.* ~**-lender** *n.* usuraio *m.* ~ **order** *n.* vaglia *m. invar.* ~**-spinner** *n.* (*fam.*) miniera d'oro *f.* ~**ed** *a.* danaroso.
mongol /'mɒŋgl/ *n.* & *a.* (*med.*) mongoloide *m.*/*f.*
mongrel /'mʌŋgrəl/ *n.* (cane) bastardo *m.*
monitor /'mɒnɪtə(r)/ *n.* (*schol.*) capoclasse *m.*/*f.*; (*techn.*) dispositivo di controllo *m.* —*v.t.* controllare; (*a broadcast*) ascoltare.
monk /mʌŋk/ *n.* monaco *m.*'
monkey /'mʌŋkɪ/ *n.* (*pl.* -**eys**) scimmia *f.* ~**-jacket** *n.* giubbotto *m.* ~**-nut** *n.* nocciolina americana *f.* ~**-wrench** *n.* chiave inglese a rullino *f.*
mono /'mɒnəʊ/ *a.* & *n.* (*pl.* -**os**) mono *m. invar.*
monocle /'mɒnəkl/ *n.* monocolo *m.*
monogram /'mɒnəgræm/ *n.* monogramma *m.*
monologue /'mɒnəlɒg/ *n.* monologo *m.*
monopol|y /mə'nɒpəlɪ/ *n.* monopolio *m.* ~**ize** *v.t.* monopolizzare.
monosyllab|le /'mɒnəsɪləbl/ *n.* monosillabo *m.* ~**ic** /-'læbɪk/ *a.* monosillabico.

monotone /'mɒnətəʊn/ *n.* tono uniforme *m.*
monoton|ous /mə'nɒtənəs/ *a.* monotono. ~**y** *n.* monotonia *f.*
monsoon /mɒn'suːn/ *n.* monsone *m.*
monst|er /'mɒnstə(r)/ *n.* mostro *m.* ~**rous** *a.* mostruoso.
monstrosity /mɒn'strɒsətɪ/ *n.* mostruosità *f.*
montage /mɒn'tɑːʒ/ *n.* montaggio *m.*
month /mʌnθ/ *n.* mese *m.*
monthly /'mʌnθlɪ/ *a.* mensile. —*adv.* mensilmente. —*n.* (*periodical*) rivista mensile *f.*
monument /'mɒnjʊmənt/ *n.* monumento *m.* ~**al** /-'mentl/ *a.* monumentale.
moo /muː/ *n.* muggito *m.* —*v.i.* muggire.
mooch /muːtʃ/ *v.i.* (*sl.*) bighellonare.
mood /muːd/ *n.* umore *m.* **be in the ~ for** aver voglia di. ~**y** *a.* (-**ier**, -**est**) di malumore; (*variable*) capriccioso.
moon /muːn/ *n.* luna *f.*
moon|light /'muːnlaɪt/ *n.* chiaro di luna *m.* ~**lit** *a.* illuminato dalla luna.
moonlighting /'muːnlaɪtɪŋ/ *n.* (*fam.*) lavoro nero *m.*
moor[1] /mʊə(r)/ *n.* brughiera *f.*
moor[2] /mʊə(r)/ *v.t.* ormeggiare. ~**ings** *n.pl.* ormeggi *m.pl.*
moose /muːs/ *n.* (*pl.* **moose**) alce *m.*
moot /muːt/ *a.* discutibile. —*v.t.* sollevare (una domanda).
mop /mɒp/ *n.* strofinaccio *m.*; (*of hair*) zazzera *f.* —*v.t.* (*p.t.* **mopped**) ~ **up** pulire (con uno strofinaccio).
mope /məʊp/ *v.i.* essere depresso.
moped /'məʊped/ *n.* ciclomotore *m.*
moral /'mɒrəl/ *a.* morale. —*n.* morale *f.* ~**s** *n.pl.* moralità *f.* ~**ize** *v.i.* moraleggiare. ~**ly** *adv.* moralmente.
morale /mə'rɑːl/ *n.* morale *m.*
moralist /'mɒrəlɪst/ *n.* moralista *m.*/*f.*
morality /mə'rælətɪ/ *n.* moralità *f.*
morass /mə'ræs/ *n.* palude *f.*
morbid /'mɔːbɪd/ *a.* morboso.
more /mɔː(r)/ *a.* & *pron.* più, di più. —*adv.* (di) più; (*again*) ancora. ~ **and more** sempre più. ~ **or less** più o meno. **once** ~ ancora una volta. **some** ~ ancora un po'.
moreover /mɔː'rəʊvə(r)/ *adv.* inoltre.
morgue /mɔːg/ *n.* obitorio *m.*
moribund /'mɒrɪbʌnd/ *a.* moribondo.
morning /'mɔːnɪŋ/ *n.* mattino, a *m.*, *f.*; (*whole morning*) mattinata *f.* ~**-room** *n.* soggiorno *m.*

Morocc|o /mə'rɒkəʊ/ *n.* Marocco *m.*
~an *a.* & *n.* marocchino, a *m.*, *f.*
moron /'mɔːrɒn/ *n.* deficiente *m.*/*f.*
morose /mə'rəʊs/ *a.* scontroso.
morphine /'mɔːfiːn/ *n.* morfina *f.*
Morse /mɔːs/ *n.* ~ **(code)** Morse *m.*
morsel /'mɔːsl/ *n.* boccone *m.*
mortal /'mɔːtl/ *a.* & *n.* mortale *m.*/*f.*
~ity /mɔː'tælətɪ/ *n.* mortalità *f.*
mortar /'mɔːtə(r)/ *n.* mortaio *m.*
mortgage /'mɔːgɪdʒ/ *n.* ipoteca *f.*;
(*loan*) prestito ipotecario *m.* —*v.t.* ipotecare.
mortify /'mɔːtɪfaɪ/ *v.t.* mortificare.
mortuary /'mɔːtʃərɪ/ *n.* camera mortuaria *f.*
mosaic /məʊ'zeɪk/ *n.* mosaico *m.*
mosque /mɒsk/ *n.* moschea *f.*
mosquito /məs'kiːtəʊ/ *n.* (*pl.* **-oes**) zanzara *f.* **~-net** *n.* zanzariera *f.*
moss /mɒs/ *n.* muschio *m.* **~y** *a.* muschioso.
most /məʊst/ *a.* il più; (*majority*) la maggior parte di. —*n.* massimo *m.* —*adv.* di più, maggiormente. **at ~** al massimo. **for the ~ part** per lo più. **make the ~ of** sfruttare al massimo. **~ly** *adv.* per lo più.
MOT *n.* (*abbr. of* **Ministry of Transport**) **~ (test)** revisione obbligatoria di autoveicoli *f.*
motel /məʊ'tel/ *n.* motel *m.*
moth /mɒθ/ *n.* farfalla (notturna) *f.*
(**clothes-**) **~** tarma *f.* **~-ball** *n.* pallina antitarme *f.* **~-eaten** *a.* tarmato.
mother /'mʌðə(r)/ *n.* madre *f.*; (*mummy, fam.*) mamma *f.* —*v.t.* fare da madre (a). **~hood** *n.* maternità *f.* **~-in-law** *n.* (*pl.* **~s-in-law**) suocera *f.* **~land** *n.* patria *f.* **~-of-pearl** *n.* madreperla *f.* **~ tongue** *n.* madrelingua *f.*
motherly /'mʌðəlɪ/ *a.* materno.
motif /məʊ'tiːf/ *n.* motivo *m.*
motion /'məʊʃn/ *n.* moto *m.*; (*proposal*) mozione *f.*; (*gesture*) gesto *m.* —*v.t.*/*i.* **~ (to)** fare cenno a. **~less** *a.* immoto.
motivat|e /'məʊtɪveɪt/ *v.t.* motivare. **~ion** /-'veɪʃn/ *n.* motivazione *f.*
motive /'məʊtɪv/ *n.* motivo *m.*
motley /'mɒtlɪ/ *a.* screziato.
motor /'məʊtə(r)/ *n.* motore *m.* —*a.* a motore. —*v.i.* andare in automobile. **~ bike** *n.* (*fam.*) moto *f.* **~ boat** *n.* motoscafo *m.* **~ car** *n.* automobile *f.* **~ cycle** *n.* motocicletta *f.* **~-cyclist** *n.* motociclista *m.*/*f.* **~ing** *n.* auto-

mobilismo *m.* **~ist** *n.* automobilista *m.*/*f.*
motorcade /'məʊtəkeɪd/ *n.* (*Amer.*) corteo di automobili *m.*
motorize /'məʊtəraɪz/ *v.t.* motorizzare.
motorway /'məʊtəweɪ/ *n.* autostrada *f.*
mottled /'mɒtld/ *a.* chiazzato.
motto /'mɒtəʊ/ *n.* (*pl.* **-oes**) motto *m.*
mould[1] /məʊld/ *n.* stampo *m.* —*v.t.* foggiare; (*fig.*) formare. **~ing** *n.* (*archit.*) cornicione *m.*
mould[2] /məʊld/ *n.* (*rot*) muffa *f.* **~y** *a.* ammuffito.
moult /məʊlt/ *v.i.* perdere il pelo.
mound /maʊnd/ *n.* mucchio *m.*
mount[1] /maʊnt/ *n.* monte *m.*
mount[2] /maʊnt/ *v.t.*/*i.* montare; (*photo*) incorniciare. —*v.i.* **~ up** aumentare —*n.* montatura *f.*
mountain /'maʊntɪn/ *n.* montagna *f.* **~ous** *a.* montagnoso.
mountaineer /maʊntɪ'nɪə(r)/ *n.* alpinista *m.*/*f.* **~ing** *n.* alpinismo *m.*
mourn /mɔːn/ *v.t.* lamentare. —*v.i.* **~ for** piangere la morte di. **~er** *n.* persona che segue un funerale *f.* **~ing** *n.* lutto *m.*
mournful /'mɔːnfl/ *a.* triste.
mouse /maʊs/ *n.* (*pl.* **mice**) topo *m.* **~trap** *n.* trappola (per topi) *f.*
moustache /mə'stɑːʃ/ *n.* baffi *m.pl.*
mousy /'maʊsɪ/ *a.* (*colour*) grigio topo; (*person*) timido, ritroso.
mouth[1] /maʊθ/ *n.* bocca *f.* **~-organ** *n.* armonica (a bocca) *f.* **~wash** *n.* acqua dentifricia *f.*
mouth[2] /maʊð/ *v.t.* declamare.
mouthful /'maʊθfʊl/ *n.* boccone *m.*
mouthpiece /'maʊθpiːs/ *n.* imboccatura *f.*; (*fig.*) portavoce *m. invar.*
movable /'muːvəbl/ *a.* movibile.
move /muːv/ *v.t.*/*i.* muovere, muoversi; (*furniture etc.*) spostare; (*progress*) procedere; (*induce*) indurre; (*provoke emotion*) commuovere; (*propose*) proporre. —*n.* mossa *f.*; (*action*) movimento *m.*; (*removal*) trasloco *m.* **~ along** andare avanti. **~ away** allontanarsi. **~ forward** avanzare. **~ in** (*to a house*) entrare (in casa nuova). **~ out** (*of house*) sgombrare. **~ over!** spostati! **on the ~** in movimento.
movement /'muːvmənt/ *n.* movimento *m.*
movie /'muːvɪ/ *n.* (*Amer.*) film *m. invar.*

moving /'mu:vɪŋ/ a. mobile; (touching) commovente.

mow /məʊ/ v.t. (p.p. **mown**) falciare; (lawn) tagliare. ~ **down** sterminare. ~**er** n. falciatrice f.

MP ʻ(abbr.) see **Member of Parliament.**

Mr /'mɪstə(r)/ n. (pl. **Messrs**) Signor m.

Mrs /'mɪsɪz/ n. (pl. **Mrs**) Signora f.

Ms /mɪz/ n. Signora f., Signorina f.

much /mʌtʃ/ a., pron. & adv. molto. **how** ~ quanto. ~ **as** per quanto. ~ **the same** quasi uguale. **so** ~ tanto. **too** ~ troppo.

muck /mʌk/ n. letame m.; (fig.) sudiciume m.; (fam., filth) porcheria f. —v.i. ~ **about** (fam.) perder tempo. ~ **in** (fam.) adattarsi. —v.t. ~ **up** (sl.) sporcare; (make a mess of sthg.) impasticciare. ~**y** a. (-ier, -iest) sudicio.

mucus /'mju:kəs/ n. muco m.

mud /mʌd/ n. fango m. ~**dy** a. (-ier, -iest) fangoso.

muddle /'mʌdl/ v.t. confondere. —v.i. ~ **through** arrabattarsi. —n. disordine m.; (mix-up) confusione f.

mudguard /'mʌdgɑ:d/ n. parafango m.

muff /mʌf/ n. manicotto m.

muffin /'mʌfɪn/ n. focaccina da tè f.

muffle /'mʌfl/ v.t. imbacuccare; (sound) smorzare. ~**r** n. sciarpa f.

mug[1] /mʌg/ n. bicchierone m.; (face, sl.) muso m.; (simpleton, sl.) sempliciotto m.

mug[2] /mʌg/ v.t. (p.t. **mugged**) aggredire e derubare. ~**ger** n. rapinatore m. ~**ging** n. aggressione f.

muggy /'mʌgɪ/ a. (-ier, -iest) afoso.

mule[1] /mju:l/ n. mulo m.

mule[2] /mju:l/ n. (slipper) ciabatta f.

mull[1] /mʌl/ v.t. riscaldare con aromi. ~**ed wine** n. vino caldo m.

mull[2] /mʌl/ v.t. ~ **over** rimuginare su.

multi- /'mʌltɪ/ pref. multi-.

multifarious /mʌltɪ'feərɪəs/ a. svariato.

multinational /mʌltɪ'næʃənl/ a. & n. multinazionale m.|f.

multiple /'mʌltɪpl/ a. & n. multiplo m.

multipl|y /'mʌltɪplaɪ/ v.t. moltiplicare. ~**ication** /-ɪ'keɪʃn/ n. moltiplicazione f.

multitude /'mʌltɪtju:d/ n. moltitudine f.

mum[1] /mʌm/ a. **keep** ~ (fam.) star zitto.

mum[2] /mʌm/ n. (fam.) mamma f.

mumble /'mʌmbl/ v.t./i. borbottare.

mumm|y[1] /'mʌmɪ/ n. (body) mummia f. ~**ify** v.t. mummificare.

mummy[2] /'mʌmɪ/ n. (fam.) mamma f.

mumps /mʌmps/ n. orecchioni m.pl.

munch /mʌntʃ/ v.t./i. sgranocchiare.

mundane /mʌn'deɪn/ a. monotono; (wordly) mondano.

municipal /mju:'nɪsɪpl/ a. municipale. ~**ity** /-'pælətɪ/ n. municipalità f.

munificent /mju:'nɪfɪsnt/ a. munifico.

munitions /mju:'nɪʃnz/ n.pl. munizioni f.pl.

mural /'mjʊərəl/ a. murale. —n. affresco m.

murder /'mɜ:də(r)/ n. assassinio m. —v.t. assassinare; (fig.) massacrare. ~**er** n. assassino m. ~**ess** n. assassina f. ~**ous** a. omicida.

murky /'mɜ:kɪ/ a. (-ier, -iest) oscuro.

murmur /'mɜ:mə(r)/ n. mormorio m. —v.t./i. mormorare.

muscle /'mʌsl/ n. muscolo m. —v.i. ~ **in** (sl.) entrare di prepotenza.

muscular /'mʌskjʊlə(r)/ a. muscolare.

muse /mju:z/ v.i. meditare.

museum /mju:'zɪəm/ n. museo m.

mush /mʌʃ/ n. poltiglia f. ~**y** a. poltiglioso.

mushroom /'mʌʃrʊm/ n. fungo m. —v.i. svilupparsi rapidamente.

music /'mju:zɪk/ n. musica f. ~**al** a. musicale; (talented) dotato di senso musicale; n. commedia musicale f. ~**centre** n. impianto stereo m. ~**-hall** n. teatro di varietà m.

musician /mju:'zɪʃn/ n. musicista m.|f.

musk /mʌsk/ n. muschio m.

Muslim /'mʊzlɪm/ a. & n. mussulmano, a m., f.

muslin /'mʌzlɪn/ n. mussolina f.

musquash /'mʌskwɒʃ/ n. topo muschiato m.

mussel /'mʌsl/ n. cozza f.

must /mʌst/ v. aux. dovere. ~ **you go?** devi andartene? **you** ~ **come** devi venire. —n. **a** ~ (fam.) cosa da vedere/fare f.

mustard /'mʌstəd/ n. senape f.

muster /'mʌstə(r)/ v.t./i. radunare, radunarsi.

musty /'mʌstɪ/ a. (-ier, -iest) stantio.

mutation /mju:'teɪʃn/ n. mutamento m.

mute /mju:t/ a. & n. muto, a m., f.

muted /'mju:tɪd/ a. smorzato.

mutilat|e /'mju:tɪleɪt/ v.t. mutilare.
∼ion /-'leɪʃn/ n. mutilazione f.
mutin|y /'mju:tɪnɪ/ n. ammutinamento
m. —v.i. ammutinarsi. **∼ous** a. am-
mutinato.
mutter /'mʌtə(r)/ v.t./i. borbottare.
—n. borbottio m.
mutton /'mʌtn/ n. carne di montone f.
mutual /'mju:tʃʊəl/ a. mutuo; (common, fam.) comune. **∼ly** adv. mu-
tuamente.
muzzle /'mʌzl/ n. (of animal) muso m.;
(for dogs) museruola f.; (of firearm)
bocca f. —v.t. far tacere.

my /maɪ/ a. mio, mia, miei, mie.
myriad /'mɪrɪəd/ n. miriade f.
myself /maɪ'self/ pron. me stesso; (reflexive) mi; (after prep.) me.
mysterious /mɪ'stɪərɪəs/ a. misterioso.
mystery /'mɪstərɪ/ n. mistero m.
mystic /'mɪstɪk/ a. & n. mistico, a m.,
f. **∼al** a. mistico. **∼ism** /-sɪzəm/ n.
misticismo m.
mystif|y /'mɪstɪfaɪ/ v.t. mistificare.
∼ication /-ɪ'keɪʃn/ n. mistificazione f.
mystique /mɪ'sti:k/ n. mistica f.
myth /mɪθ/ n. mito m. **∼ical** a. mitico.
mythology /mɪ'θɒlədʒɪ/ n. mitologia f.

N

nab /næb/ *v.t.* (*p.t.* **nabbed**) (*sl.*) afferrare.

nag /næg/ *v.t.*/*i.* (*p.t.* **nagged**) criticare; (*pester*) tormentare. **~ging** *a.* (*pain etc.*) persistente.

nail /neɪl/ *n.* chiodo *m.*; (*of finger, toe*) unghia *f.* —*v.t.* inchiodare. **~ polish** smalto (per unghie) *m.* **on the ~** subito.

naive /naɪ'iːv/ *a.* ingenuo, candido.

naked /'neɪkɪd/ *a.* nudo. **~ truth** verità nuda e cruda *f.* **~ness** *n.* nudità *f.*

namby-pamby /næmbɪ'pæmbɪ/ *a.* & *n.* effeminato *m.*

name /neɪm/ *n.* nome *m.*; (*fig.*) reputazione *f.* —*v.t.* nominare; (*give as name*) chiamare. **be ~d after** portare il nome di. **~less** *a.* senza nome.

namely /'neɪmlɪ/ *adv.* cioè.

namesake /'neɪmseɪk/ *n.* omonimo *m.*

nanny /'nænɪ/ *n.* bambinaia *f.* **~-goat** *n.* capra *f.*

nap[1] /næp/ *n.* pisolino *m.* —*v.i.* (*p.t.* **napped**) fare un pisolino.

nap[2] /næp/ *n.* (*fibres*) pelo *m.*

nape /neɪp/ *n.* nuca *f.*

napkin /'næpkɪn/ *n.* tovagliolo *m.*; (*for baby*) pannolino *m.*

Naples /'neɪpəlz/ *n.* Napoli *f.*

nappy /'næpɪ/ *n.* pannolino *m.*

narcotic /nɑː'kɒtɪk/ *a.* & *n.* narcotico *m.*

narrat|e /nə'reɪt/ *v.t.* narrare. **~ion** /-ʃn/ *n.* narrazione *f.* **~or** *n.* narra|tore, -trice *m.*, *f.*

narrative /'nærətɪv/ *a.* narrativo. —*n.* narrazione *f.*

narrow /'nærəʊ/ *a.* (-er, -est) stretto; (*fig.*) ristretto. —*v.t.*/*i.* restringere, restringersi. **have a ~ escape** scamparla per un pelo. **~-minded** *a.* di idee ristrette. **~ly** *adv.* per poco.

nasal /'neɪzl/ *a.* nasale.

nast|y /'nɑːstɪ/ *a.* (-ier, -iest) sgradevole; (*of weather*) brutto. **turn ~y** diventare cattivo. **~ily** *adv.* sgradevolmente. **~iness** *n.* cattiveria *f.*

natal /'neɪtl/ *a.* natale.

nation /'neɪʃn/ *n.* nazione *f.* **~-wide** *a.* nazionale.

national /'næʃnəl/ *a.* nazionale. —*n.* cittadino a *m.*, *f.* **~ anthem** inno nazionale *m.* **N~ Health Service** Servizio sanitario *m.* **~ism** *n.* nazionalismo *m.* **~ize** *v.t.* nazionalizzare. **~ly** *adv.* a livello nazionale.

nationality /næʃə'nælətɪ/ *n.* nazionalità *f.*

native /'neɪtɪv/ *a.* nativo; (*of quality*) innato. —*n.* nativo, a *m.*, *f.*; (*outside Europe*) indigeno, a *m.*, *f.* **go ~** vivere da indigeno. **~ land** terra natia *f.* **~ language** lingua madre *f.*

nativity /nə'tɪvɪtɪ/ *n.* nascita *f.* **the N~** la Natività *f.*

natter /'nætə(r)/ *v.i.* (*fam.*) chiacchierare. —*n.* (*fam.*) chiacchierata *f.*

natural /'nætʃrəl/ *a.* naturale. **~ist** *n.* naturalista *m.*/*f.* **~ly** *adv.* naturalmente.

naturaliz|e /'nætʃrəlaɪz/ *v.t.* naturalizzare. **~ation** /-'zeɪʃn/ *n.* naturalizzazione *f.*

nature /'neɪtʃə(r)/ *n.* natura *f.*; (*kind*) genere *m.*; (*of person*) indole *f.*

naught /nɔːt/ *n.* (*old use*) niente *m.*; (*math.*) zero *m.*

naught|y /'nɔːtɪ/ *a.* (-ier, -iest) cattivo; (*indecent*) piccante. **~ily** *adv.* male.

nause|a /'nɔːsɪə/ *n.* nausea *f.* **~ous**, **~ating** *adjs.* nauseante.

nauseate /'nɔːsɪeɪt/ *v.t.* nauseare.

nautical /'nɔːtɪkl/ *a.* nautico.

naval /'neɪvl/ *a.* navale. **~ officer** *n.* ufficiale di marina *m.*

nave /neɪv/ *n.* navata *f.*

navel /'neɪvl/ *n.* ombelico *m.*

navigable /'nævɪgəbl/ *a.* navigabile.

navigat|e /'nævɪgeɪt/ *v.t.* navigare. —*v.i.* dirigere. **~ion** /-'geɪʃn/ *n.* navigazione *f.* **~or** *n.* navigatore *m.*

navvy /'nævɪ/ *n.* manovale *m.*

navy /'neɪvɪ/ *n.* marina *f.* **~ (blue)** blu (marino) *m. invar.*

Neapolitan /nɪə'pɒlɪtən/ *a.* & *n.* napoletano, a *m.*, *f.*

near /nɪə(r)/ *a.* (-er, -est) vicino. —*adv.* vicino, presso. —*prep.* vicino (a); (*nearly*) quasi. —*v.t.*/*i.* avvicinarsi. **~ at hand** *adv.* a portata di mano. **~ by** *adv.* vicino. **N~ East** *n.* Vicino Oriente *m.* **~ness** *n.* vicinanza *f.*

nearby /'nɪəbaɪ/ *a.* vicino.

nearly /'nɪəlɪ/ *adv.* quasi; (*closely*) strettamente. **not ~** affatto.

neat /niːt/ *a.* (-er, -est) nitido; (*room etc.*) pulito; (*undiluted*) liscio; (*plan etc.*) ben indovinato. ∿ly *adv.* ordinatamente; abilmente. ∿-ness *n.* pulizia *f.*

nebulous /ˈnebjʊləs/ *a.* nebuloso.

necessar|y /ˈnesəsərɪ/ *a.* necessario. ∿ies *n.pl.* necessità *f.pl.* ∿ily *adv.* necessariamente.

necessitate /nɪˈsesɪteɪt/ *v.t.* necessitare.

necessity /nɪˈsesətɪ/ *n.* necessità *f.*

neck /nek/ *n.* collo *m.*; (*of dress*) colletto *m.* ∿ **and** ∿ testa a testa.

necklace /ˈneklɪs/ *n.* collana *f.*

neckline /ˈneklaɪn/ *n.* scollatura *f.*

necktie /ˈnektaɪ/ *n.* cravatta *f.*

nectar /ˈnektə(r)/ *n.* nettare *m.*

nectarine /ˈnektərɪn/ *n.* noce pesca *f.*

née /neɪ/ *a.* nata.

need /niːd/ *n.* bisogno *m.* —*v.t.* aver bisogno di. —*v. aux.* occorrere. **he** ∿ **not go** non occorre che vada. ∿ **I come?** devo venire? ∿less *a.* inutile. ∿lessly *adv.* inutilmente.

needle /ˈniːdl/ *n.* ago *m.*; (*of record-player*) puntina *f.*; (*for knitting*) ferro *m.* —*v.t.* punzecchiare.

needlework /ˈniːdlwɜːk/ *n.* cucito *m.*

needy /ˈniːdɪ/ *a.* (-ier, -iest) bisognoso.

negation /nɪˈgeɪʃn/ *n.* negazione *f.*

negative /ˈnegətɪv/ *a.* negativo. —*n.* negazione *f.*; (*photo*) negativa *f.* ∿ly *adv.* negativamente.

neglect /nɪˈglekt/ *v.t.* trascurare. —*n.* trascuratezza *f.* ∿ **to do** tralasciare di fare. **state of** ∿ stato di abbandono *m.* ∿ful *a.* negligente.

négligé /ˈneglɪʒeɪ/ *n.* négligé *m.*

negligen|t /ˈneglɪdʒənt/ *a.* negligente. ∿ce *n.* negligenza *f.*

negligible /ˈneglɪdʒəbl/ *a.* trascurabile.

negotiable /nɪˈgəʊʃɪəbl/ *a.* negoziabile.

negotiat|e /nɪˈgəʊʃɪeɪt/ *v.t./i.* negoziare. ∿ion /-ˈeɪʃn/ *n.* trattativa *f.* ∿or *n.* negozia|tore, -trice *m.*, *f.*

Negr|o /ˈniːgrəʊ/ *a.* & *n.* (*pl.* -oes) negro *m.* ∿ess *n.* negra *f.*

neigh /neɪ/ *n.* nitrito *m.* —*v.i.* nitrire.

neighbour /ˈneɪbə(r)/ *n.* vicino, a *m.*, *f.* ∿hood *n.* vicinato *m.* **in the** ∿hood **of** nei dintorni di; (*fig.*) circa. ∿ing *a.* adiacente.

neighbourly /ˈneɪbəlɪ/ *a.* amichevole.

neither /ˈnaɪðə(r)/ *a.* & *pron.* né l'uno

né l'altro. —*adv.* né. —*conj.* nemmeno, neanche.

neon /ˈniːɒn/ *n.* neon *m.* —*a.* al neon.

nephew /ˈnevjuː/ *n.* nipote *m.*

nepotism /ˈnepətɪzəm/ *n.* nepotismo *m.*

nerve /nɜːv/ *n.* nervo *m.*; (*courage, cheek, fam.*) coraggio *m.* ∿racking *a.* esasperante.

nervous /ˈnɜːvəs/ *a.* nervoso; (*agitated*) irrequieto. **be** ∿ essere apprensivo. ∿ly *adv.* nervosamente. ∿ness *n.* nervosismo *m.*; (*fear*) apprensione *f.*

nervy /ˈnɜːvɪ/ *a.* = **nervous**.

nest /nest/ *n.* nido *m.* —*v.i.* fare il nido. ∿-egg *n.* gruzzolo *m.*

nestle /ˈnesl/ *v.i.* rannicchiarsi.

net[1] /net/ *n.* rete *f.* —*v.t.* (*p.t.* **netted**) (*catch*) catturare. ∿ting *n.* reticolato *m.*

net[2] /net/ *a.* netto. —*v.t.* (*p.t.* **netted**) incassare.

netball /ˈnetbɔːl/ *n.* palla-rete *f.*

Netherlands /ˈneðələndz/ *n.pl.* **the** ∿ i Paesi Bassi *m.pl.*

nettle /ˈnetl/ *n.* ortica *f.*

network /ˈnetwɜːk/ *n.* rete *f.*

neuralgia /njʊəˈrældʒə/ *n.* nevralgia *f.*

neuro|sis /njʊəˈrəʊsɪs/ *n.* (*pl.* -oses /-siːz/) nevrosi *f.* ∿tic /-ˈrɒtɪk/ *a.* & *n.* neurotico, a *m.*, *f.*

neuter /ˈnjuːtə(r)/ *a.* & *n.* neutro *m.* —*v.t.* castrare.

neutral /ˈnjuːtrəl/ *a.* neutrale. —*n.* **in** ∿ (*auto*) in folle. ∿ity /-ˈtrælətɪ/ *n.* neutralità *f.*

neutron /ˈnjuːtrɒn/ *n.* neutrone *m.*

never /ˈnevə(r)/ *adv.* mai; (*not, fam.*) impossibile. ∿ **again** mai più. ∿-ending *a.* interminabile. ∿ **mind** non importa.

nevertheless /nevəðəˈles/ *adv.* comunque.

new /njuː/ *a.* (-er, -est) nuovo, novello. ∿-born *a.* neonato. ∿ **year** anno nuovo *m.* N∿ **Year's Day** *n.* Capodanno *m.* N∿ **Year's Eve** *n.* (notte di) San Silvestro *f.* N∿ **Zealand** *n.* Nuova Zelanda *f.* ∿ness *n.* novità *f.*

newcomer /ˈnjuːkʌmə(r)/ *n.* nuovo, a arrivato, a *m.*, *f.*

newfangled /njuːˈfæŋgld/ *a.* (*pej.*) nuovo e strano.

newly /ˈnjuːlɪ/ *adv.* nuovamente. ∿weds *n.pl.* sposini *m.pl.*

news /njuːz/ *n.* notizie *f.pl.*; (*radio*) giornale radio *m.*; (*TV*) telegiornale *m.* ∼y *a.* (*fam., letter*) pieno di notizie. ∼ **flash** *n.* notizia lampo *f.*

newsagent /'nju:zeɪdʒənt/ *n.* giornalaio, a *m., f.*

newsletter /'nju:zletə(r)/ *n.* bollettino d'informazione *m.*

newspaper /'nju:zpeɪpə(r)/ *n.* giornale *m.*

newsreel /'nju:zri:l/ *n.* telecronaca *f.*

newt /nju:t/ *n.* tritone *m.*

next /nekst/ *a.* prossimo; (*adjoining*) vicino. —*adv.* dopo. —*n.* seguente *m./f.* ∼ **best** migliore alternativa *f.* ∼ **door** accanto. ∼ **of kin** *n.* parente più prossimo *m.* ∼ **to nothing** quasi niente.

nib /nɪb/ *n.* pennino *m.*

nibble /'nɪbl/ *v.t./i.* rosicchiare. —*n.* bocconcino *m.*

nice /naɪs/ *a.* (-er, -est) bello; (*kind*) gentile; (*agreeable*) simpatico; (*pleasant*) piacevole. ∼ly *adv.* gentilmente; piacevolmente; (*well*) bene.

niceties /'naɪsətɪz/ *n.pl.* finezze *f.pl.*

niche /nɪtʃ/ *n.* nicchia *f.*

nick /nɪk/ *n.* tacca *f.*; (*sl.*) prigione *f.* —*v.t.* intaccare; (*sl.*) rubare. **in the** ∼ **of time** appena in tempo.

nickel /'nɪkl/ *n.* nichel *m.*; (*Amer.*) moneta da cinque centesimi *f.*

nickname /'nɪkneɪm/ *n.* soprannome *m.* —*v.t.* soprannominare.

nicotine /'nɪkəti:n/ *n.* nicotina *f.*

niece /ni:s/ *n.* nipote *f.*

Nigeria /naɪ'dʒɪərɪə/ *n.* Nigeria *f.* ∼n *a. & n.* nigeriano, a *m., f.*

niggardly /'nɪgədlɪ/ *a.* avaro.

niggl|e /'nɪgl/ *v.i.* ∼ **over sthg.** perdersi nei dettagli. ∼**ing** *a.* insignificante; (*of pain*) fastidioso.

night /naɪt/ *n.* notte *f.*; (*evening*) sera *f.* —*a.* di notte. ∼**-club** night *m.* ∼**-dress**, ∼**-gown** *ns.* camicia da notte *f.* ∼**-life** *n.* vita notturna *f.* ∼**-school** *n.* scuola serale *f.* ∼**-watchman** *n.* guardiano notturno *m.*

nightfall /'naɪtfɔ:l/ *n.* crepuscolo *m.*

nightingale /'naɪtɪŋgeɪl/ *n.* usignolo *m.*

nightly /'naɪtlɪ/ *a.* di notte, di sera; (*by night*) notturno. —*adv.* ogni notte.

nightmare /'naɪtmeə(r)/ *n.* incubo *m.*

nil /nɪl/ *n.* nulla *m.*; (*sport*) zero *m.*

nimble /'nɪmbl/ *a.* (-er, -est) agile.

nin|e /naɪn/ *a. & n.* nove *m.* ∼th *a. & n.* nono, a *m., f.*

nineteen /naɪn'ti:n/ *a. & n.* diciannove

m. ∼th *a. & n.* diciannovesimo, a *m., f.*

ninet|y /'naɪntɪ/ *a. & n.* novanta *m.* ∼ieth *a. & n.* novantesimo, a *m., f.*

nip /nɪp/ *v.t.* (*p.t.* **nipped**) pizzicare. —*v.i.* (*fam.*) affrettarsi. —*n.* pizzico *m.*; (*cold*) freddo pungente *m.*

nipper /'nɪpə(r)/ *n.* (*sl.*) ragazzino, a *m., f.*

nipple /'nɪpl/ *n.* capezzolo *m.*

nippy /'nɪpɪ/ *a.* (-ier, -iest) (*fam., cold*) pungente; (*fam., quick*) svelto.

nitrogen /'naɪtrədʒən/ *n.* azoto *m.*

nitwit /'nɪtwɪt/ *n.* (*fam.*) imbecille *m./f.*

no /nəʊ/ *a.* nessuno. —*adv.* no, non. —*n.* (*pl.* **noes**) no *m. invar.* ∼ **go** (*fam.*) è inutile. ∼ **man's land** *n.* terra di nessuno *f.* ∼ **one** = **nobody.** ∼ **parking** sosta vietata. ∼ **smoking** è proibito fumare.

nob|le /'nəʊbl/ *a.* (-er, -est) nobile. ∼**ility** /-'bɪlətɪ/ *n.* nobiltà *f.*

nobleman /'nəʊblmən/ *n.* (*pl.* -men) nobiluomo *m.*

nobody /'nəʊbʊdɪ/ *pron.* nessuno. —*n.* nullità *f.*

nocturnal /nɒk'tɜ:nl/ *a.* notturno.

nod /nɒd/ *v.t./i.* (*p.t.* **nodded**) accennare (col capo). —*n.* cenno del capo *m.* ∼ **off** *v.i.* addormentarsi.

nodule /'nɒdju:l/ *n.* nodulo *m.*

noise /nɔɪz/ *n.* rumore *m.* ∼**less** *a.* silenzioso.

nois|y /'nɔɪzɪ/ *a.* (-ier, -iest) rumoroso. ∼**ily** *adv.* rumorosamente.

nomad /'nəʊmæd/ *n.* nomade *m./f.* ∼**ic** /-'mædɪk/ *a.* nomade.

nominal /'nɒmɪnl/ *a.* nominale; (*of fee*) simbolico.

nominat|e /'nɒmɪneɪt/ *v.t.* nominare; (*appoint*) designare. ∼**ion** /-'neɪʃn/ *n.* nomina *f.*

non- /nɒn/ *pref.* non-.

nonagenarian /nɒnədʒɪ'neərɪən/ *a.* nonagenario.

nonchalant /'nɒnʃələnt/ *a.* noncurante.

non-commissioned /nɒnkə'mɪʃnd/ *a.* ∼ **officer** sottufficiale *m.*

non-committal /nɒnkə'mɪtl/ *a.* evasivo.

nondescript /'nɒndɪskrɪpt/ *a.* indefinito.

none /nʌn/ *pron.* (*person*) nessuno; (*thing*) niente. ∼ **of them** nessuno di loro. ∼ **of this** niente di tutto ciò. —*adv.* niente affatto. ∼ **too soon** non certo troppo presto.

nonentity /nɒˈnentətɪ/ n. nullità f.

non-event /nɒnɪˈvent/ n. fiasco m.

non-existent /nɒnɪgˈzɪstənt/ a. inesistente.

nonplussed /nɒnˈplʌst/ a. perplesso.

nonsens|e /ˈnɒnsns/ n. sciocchezza f. ~ical /-ˈsensɪkl/ a. assurdo.

non-starter /nɒnˈstɑːtə(r)/ n. (fam.) progetto impossibile m.

non-stop /nɒnˈstɒp/ a. diretto. —adv. senza pausa.

noodles /ˈnuːdlz/ n.pl. tagliatelle f.pl.

nook /nʊk/ n. cantuccio m.

noon /nuːn/ n. mezzogiorno m.

noose /nuːs/ n. nodo scorsoio m.

nor /nɔː(r)/ conj. né, e neppure.

Nordic /ˈnɔːdɪk/ a. nordico.

norm /nɔːm/ n. norma f.

normal /ˈnɔːməl/ a. normale. ~ity /-ˈmælətɪ/ n. normalità f. ~ly adv. normalmente.

Normandy /ˈnɔːməndɪ/ n. Normandia f.

north /nɔːθ/ n. nord, settentrione m. —a. del nord, settentrionale. —adv. a nord. N~ America n. America del Nord f. ~-east, ~-west ns. nord-est, nord-ovest m. N~ Sea n. Mare del Nord m. ~erly /ˈnɔːðəlɪ/ a. del nord. ~ward a. a nord. ~wards adv. verso nord.

northern /ˈnɔːðən/ a. del nord, settentrionale. ~er n. settentrionale m./f.

Norw|ay /ˈnɔːweɪ/ n. Norvegia f. ~egian /-ˈwiːdʒən/ a. & n. norvegese m./f.

nose /nəʊz/ n. naso m. —v.i. ~ about curiosare.

nosebleed /ˈnəʊzbliːd/ n. emorragia dal naso f.

nosedive /ˈnəʊzdaɪv/ n. picchiata f.

nostalg|ia /nɒˈstældʒə/ n. nostalgia f. ~ic a. nostalgico.

nostril /ˈnɒstrɪl/ n. narice f.

nosy /ˈnəʊzɪ/ a. (-ier, -iest) (fam.) ficcanaso.

not /nɒt/ adv. non, no. if ~ se no. ~ at all niente affatto. ~ even neanche. ~ yet non ancora.

notable /ˈnəʊtəbl/ a. notevole. —n. notabile m.

notably /ˈnəʊtəblɪ/ adv. notevolmente.

notary /ˈnəʊtərɪ/ n. notaio m.

notation /nəʊˈteɪʃn/ n. notazione f.

notch /nɒtʃ/ n. tacca f. —v.t. intaccare. ~ up segnare (punti).

note /nəʊt/ n. nota f.; (short letter, banknote) biglietto m.; (written com-

ment) appunto m. —v.t. notare. ~ down annotare.

notebook /ˈnəʊtbʊk/ n. taccuino m.

noted /ˈnəʊtɪd/ a. noto.

notepaper /ˈnəʊtpeɪpə(r)/ n. carta da lettere f.

noteworthy /ˈnəʊtwɜːðɪ/ a. degno di nota.

nothing /ˈnʌθɪŋ/ pron. niente. —n. niente m.; (person) nullità f. —adv. niente affatto. ~ but nient'altro che. ~ much poco o nulla. ~ to do with nulla a che fare con.

notice /ˈnəʊtɪs/ n. avviso m.; (termination of employment) licenziamento m.; (announcement) annuncio m. —v.t. notare. (advance) ~ n. preavviso m. ~-board n. tabellone per annunci m. take ~ of fare attenzione a.

noticeabl|e /ˈnəʊtɪsəbl/ a. notevole. ~y adv. notevolmente.

notif|y /ˈnəʊtɪfaɪ/ v.t. notificare. ~ication /-ɪˈkeɪʃn/ n. notifica f.

notion /ˈnəʊʃn/ n. nozione f.

notori|ous /nəʊˈtɔːrɪəs/ a. famigerato. ~ety /-əˈraɪətɪ/ n. notorietà f.

notwithstanding /nɒtwɪθˈstændɪŋ/ prep. malgrado. —adv. nondimeno.

nougat /ˈnuːgɑː/ n. torrone m.

nought /nɔːt/ n. zero m.

noun /naʊn/ n. nome m.

nourish /ˈnʌrɪʃ/ v.t. nutrire. ~ment n. nutrimento m.

novel /ˈnɒvl/ n. romanzo m. —a. nuovo, novello. ~ist n. romanziere, a m., f. ~ty n. novità f.

November /nəʊˈvembə(r)/ n. novembre m.

novice /ˈnɒvɪs/ n. novizio, a m., f.

now /naʊ/ adv. ora, adesso. —conj. ~ (that) ora che. ~ and again, ~ and then ogni tanto.

nowadays /ˈnaʊədeɪz/ adv. oggigiorno.

nowhere /ˈnəʊweə(r)/ adv. in nessun posto.

noxious /ˈnɒkʃəs/ a. nocivo.

nozzle /ˈnɒzl/ n. beccuccio m.

nuance /ˈnjuːɑːns/ n. sfumatura f.

nuclear /ˈnjuːklɪə(r)/ a. nucleare.

nucleus /ˈnjuːklɪəs/ n. (pl. -lei /-lɪaɪ/) nucleo m.

nud|e /njuːd/ a. & n. nudo m. ~ity n. nudità f.

nudge /nʌdʒ/ v.t. dare di gomito a —n. gomitata f.

nudis|t /ˈnjuːdɪst/ n. nudista m./f. ~m /-zəm/ n. nudismo m.

nugget /'nʌgɪt/ n. pepita f.
nuisance /'nju:sns/ n. seccatura f.
null /nʌl/ a. nullo. ∼ity n. nullità f.
nullify /'nʌlɪfaɪ/ v.t. annullare.
numb /nʌm/ a. intirizzito. —v.t. intirizzire.
number /'nʌmbə(r)/ n. numero m. —v.t. numerare; (include) contare. ∼-plate n. targa f.
numera|cy /'nju:mərəsɪ/ n. cultura matematica f. ∼te a. dotato di cultura matematica.
numeral /'nju:mərəl/ n. cifra f.
numerical /nju:'merɪkl/ a. numerico.
numerous /'nju:mərəs/ a. numeroso.
nun /nʌn/ n. suora f.
nuptial /'nʌpʃəl/ a. nuziale.
nurs|e /nɜ:s/ n. infermiere, a m., f.; (nanny) bambinaia f. —v.t. curare; (fig.) nutrire. ∼ing n. professione d'infermiere, a f. ∼ing home n. clinica f.

nursery /'nɜ:sərɪ/ n. stanza dei bambini f.; (for plants) vivaio m. (day) ∼, ∼ school ns. asilo m. ∼ rhyme n. filastrocca f.
nurture /'nɜ:tʃə(r)/ v.t. nutrire.
nut /nʌt/ n. noce f.; (mech.) dado m.; (sl.) testa f. be ∼s (fam.) essere matto.
nutcrackers /'nʌtkrækəz/ n.pl. schiaccianoci m. invar.
nutmeg /'nʌtmeg/ n. noce moscata f.
nutrient /'nju:trɪənt/ a. nutriente. —n. sostanza nutritiva f.
nutritio|n /nju:'trɪʃn/ n. nutrizione f. ∼us a. nutriente.
nutshell /'nʌtʃel/ n. guscio di noce m. in a ∼ in poche parole.
nuzzle /'nʌzl/ v.t. frugare col muso.
nylon /'naɪlɒn/ n. nailon m. ∼s n.pl. calze di nailon f.pl.
nymph /nɪmf/ n. ninfa f.

O

oaf /əʊf/ n. (pl. **oafs**) zoticone, a m., f.
oak /əʊk/ n. quercia f.
OAP abbr. of **old-age pensioner** n. pensionato, a m., f.
oar /ɔ:(r)/ n. remo m.
oarsman /'ɔ:zmən/ n. (pl. -men) rematore m.
oasis /əʊ'eɪsɪs/ n. (pl. **oases** /-si:z/) oasi f. invar.
oath /əʊθ/ n. giuramento m.; (swearword) bestemmia f.
oatmeal /'əʊtmi:l/ n. farina d'avena f.
oats /əʊts/ n.pl. avena f.s.
obedien|t /ə'bi:dɪənt/ a. ubbidiente. ~ce n. ubbidienza f. ~tly adv. ubbidientemente.
obelisk /'ɒbɪlɪsk/ n. obelisco m.
obes|e /əʊ'bi:s/ a. obeso. ~ity n. obesità f.
obey /ə'beɪ/ v.t./i. ubbidire (a); (instructions) osservare.
obituary /ə'bɪtʃʊərɪ/ n. necrologio m.
object[1] /'ɒbdʒɪkt/ n. oggetto m.; (intention) obiettivo m. ~-lesson n. esempio pratico m.
object[2] /əb'dʒekt/ v.i. obiettare; (protest) opporsi. ~ion /-ʃn/ n. obiezione f. ~or n. opposi|tore, trice m., f.
objectionable /əb'dʒekʃnəbl/ a. discutibile; (unpleasant) sgradevole.
objective /əb'dʒektɪv/ a. oggettivo. —n. obiettivo m. ~ly adv. obiettivamente.
obligation /ɒblɪ'geɪʃn/ n. obbligo m. **be under an ~ to** avere un obbligo verso.
obligatory /ə'blɪɡətrɪ/ a. obbligatorio.
oblig|e /ə'blaɪdʒ/ v.t. obbligare; (do a small service) fare una cortesia a. ~ed a. obbligato. ~ing a. cortese.
oblique /ə'bli:k/ a. obliquo.
obliterat|e /ə'blɪtəreɪt/ v.t. obliterare. ~ion /-'reɪʃn/ n. obliterazione f.
oblivion /ə'blɪvɪən/ n. oblio m.
oblivious /ə'blɪvɪəs/ a. immemore.
oblong /'ɒblɒŋ/ a. oblungo. —n. rettangolo m.
obnoxious /əb'nɒkʃəs/ a. detestabile.
oboe /'əʊbəʊ/ n. oboe m.
obscen|e /əb'si:n/ a. osceno. ~ity /-enətɪ/ n. oscenità f.
obscur|e /əb'skjʊə(r)/ a. oscuro. —v.t.

oscurare; (conceal) celare. ~ity n. oscurità f.
obsequious /əb'si:kwɪəs/ a. ossequioso.
observan|t /əb'zɜ:vənt/ a. attento. ~ce n. osservanza f.
observatory /əb'zɜ:vətrɪ/ n. osservatorio m.
observ|e /əb'zɜ:v/ v.t. osservare. ~ation /ɒbzə'veɪʃn/ n. osservazione f. ~er n. osserva|tore, -trice m., f.
obsess /əb'ses/ v.t. ossessionare. ~ion /-ʃn/ n. ossessione f. ~ive a. ossessivo.
obsolete /'ɒbsəli:t/ a. disusato.
obstacle /'ɒbstəkl/ n. ostacolo m.
obstetrics /əb'stetrɪks/ n. ostetricia f.
obstina|te /'ɒbstɪnət/ a. ostinato. ~cy n. ostinazione f. ~tely adv. ostinatamente.
obstreperous /ɒb'strepərəs/ a. turbolento.
obstruct /əb'strʌkt/ v.t. ostruire. ~ion /-ʃn/ n. ostruzione f.
obtain /əb'teɪn/ v.t. ottenere. —v.i. prevalere. ~able a. ottenibile.
obtrusive /əb'tru:sɪv/ a. importuno.
obtuse /əb'tju:s/ a. ottuso.
obviate /'ɒbvɪeɪt/ v.t. ovviare (a); evitare.
obvious /'ɒbvɪəs/ a. ovvio. ~ly ovviamente.
occasion /ə'keɪʒn/ n. occasione f. —v.t. cagionare. **on ~** talvolta.
occasional /ə'keɪʒənl/ a. saltuario. ~ly adv. ogni tanto.
occult /ɒ'kʌlt/ a. occulto.
occupation /ɒkjʊ'peɪʃn/ n. occupazione f.; (job) mestiere m. ~al a. professionale. ~al therapy n. ergoterapia f.
occup|y /'ɒkjʊpaɪ/ v.t. occupare. ~ant, ~ier ns. occupante m./f.
occur /ə'kɜ:(r)/ v.i. (p.t. **occurred**) accadere; (exist) trovarsi. **it ~red to me that** mi venne in mente che.
occurrence /ə'kʌrəns/ n. evenienza f.
ocean /'əʊʃn/ n. oceano m.
o'clock /ə'klɒk/ adv. **it is 7 ~** sono le sette.
octagon /'ɒktəɡən/ n. ottagono m.
octane /'ɒkteɪn/ n. ottano m.
octave /'ɒktɪv/ n. ottava f.

October /ɒk'təʊbə(r)/ *n.* ottobre *m.*

octopus /'ɒktəpəs/ *n.* (*pl.* **-puses**) polipo *m.*

oculist /'ɒkjʊlɪst/ *n.* oculista *m./f.*

odd /ɒd/ *a.* (**-er**, **-est**) dispari; (*not of set*) scompagnato; (*occasional*) saltuario; (*strange*) strano. **fifty-~** cinquanta e rotti. **the ~ one out** l'eccezione *f.* **~ity** *n.* stranezza *f.*; (*person*) eccentrico, a *m.*, *f.* **~ly** *adv.* stranamente. **~ly enough** strano a dirsi.

oddment /'ɒdmənt/ *n.* avanzo *m.*

odds /ɒdz/ *n.pl.* probabilità *f.pl.*; (*in betting*) posta *f.* **at ~** in disaccordo. **~ and ends** cianfrusaglie *f.pl.*

ode /əʊd/ *n.* ode *f.*

odious /'əʊdɪəs/ *a.* odioso.

odour /'əʊdə(r)/ *n.* odore *m.* **~less** *a.* inodoro.

of /əv, ɒv/ *prep.* di. **a friend ~ mine** un mio amico. **how kind ~ you** com'è gentile da parte tua.

off /ɒf/ *adv.* lontano, via; (*light etc.*) spento; (*tap*) chiuso; (*of food*) passato. **—***prep.* da; (*distant from*) lontano da. **be better ~ than** essere più ricco di. **be ~** andar via. **day ~** *n.* giorno libero *m.* **~-beat** *a.* insolito. **~ chance** possibilità remota *f.* **~ colour** *a.* giù di forma. **~-licence** *n.* spaccio di bevande alcooliche *m.* **~-load** *v.t.* scaricare. **~-putting** *a.* (*fam.*) ributtante. **~-stage** *a.* fra le quinte. **~-white** *a.* bianco avorio.

offal /'ɒfl/ *n.* frattaglie *f.pl.*

offence /ə'fens/ *n.* offesa *f.*; (*illegal act*) delitto *m.* **take ~** offendersi.

offend /ə'fend/ *v.t.* offendere. **~er** *n.* delinquente *m./f.*

offensive /ə'fensɪv/ *a.* offensivo; (*disgusting*) disgustoso. **—***n.* offensiva *f.*

offer /'ɒfə(r)/ *v.t.* offrire. **—***n.* offerta *f.* **on ~** in vendita.

offhand /ɒf'hænd/ *a.* improvvisato; (*brusque*) spicciativo; (*casual*) disinvolto. **—***adv.* lì per lì.

office /'ɒfɪs/ *n.* ufficio *m.*; (*post*) carica *f.*

officer /'ɒfɪsə(r)/ *n.* ufficiale *m.*; (*policeman*) agente *m.*; (*of organization*) funzionario *m.*

official /ə'fɪʃl/ *a.* ufficiale. **—***n.* funzionario *m.* **~ly** *adv.* ufficialmente.

officiate /ə'fɪʃɪeɪt/ *v.i.* officiare. **~ as** fungere da.

officious /ə'fɪʃəs/ *a.* invadente.

offing /'ɒfɪŋ/ *n.* **in the ~** in vista.

offset /'ɒfset/ *v.t.* (*p.t.* **-set**, *pres. p.* **-setting**) controbilanciare.

offshoot /'ɒfʃuːt/ *n.* ramo *m.*

offside /ɒf'saɪd/ *a.* (*sport*) fuori gioco.

offspring /'ɒfsprɪŋ/ *n. invar.* prole *f.*

often /'ɒfn/ *adv.* spesso. **how ~** ogni quanto tempo.

ogle /'əʊgl/ *v.t.* occhieggiare.

ogre /'əʊgə(r)/ *n.* orco *m.*

oh /əʊ/ *int.* oh!

oil /ɔɪl/ *n.* olio *m.*; (*petroleum*) petrolio *m.*; (*for heating*) nafta *f.* **—***v.t.* oliare. **~-painting** *n.* quadro a olio *m.* **~y** *a.* untuoso.

oilfield /'ɔɪlfiːld/ *n.* giacimento di petrolio *m.*

oil-rig /'ɔɪlrɪg/ *n.* piattaforma per trivellazioni subacquee *f.*

oilskins /'ɔɪlskɪnz/ *n.pl.* vestiti di tela cerata *m.pl.*

ointment /'ɔɪntmənt/ *n.* pomata *f.*

OK /əʊ'keɪ/ *a.* esatto. **—***adv.* bene, d'accordo.

old /əʊld/ *a.* (**-er**, **-est**) vecchio; (*not modern*) antico. **how ~ is she?** quanti anni ha? **she is ten years ~** ha dieci anni. **of ~** nei tempi antichi. **~ age** *n.* vecchiaia *f.* **~-fashioned** *a.* antiquato. **~ maid** *n.* zitella *f.* **~-world** *a.* all'antica.

oleander /əʊlɪ'ændə(r)/ *n.* oleandro *m.*

olive /'ɒlɪv/ *n.* (*fruit*) oliva *f.*; (*tree*) ulivo *m.* **—***a.* d'oliva; (*colour*) olivastro.

Olympic /ə'lɪmpɪk/ *a.* olimpico. **~s**, **~ Games** *ns.* Olimpiadi *f.pl.*

omelette /'ɒmlɪt/ *n.* omelette *f.*

omen /'əʊmen/ *n.* presagio *m.*

ominous /'ɒmɪnəs/ *a.* sinistro.

omi|t /ə'mɪt/ *v.t.* (*p.t.* **omitted**) omettere. **~ssion** /-ʃn/ *n.* omissione *f.*

omnipotent /ɒm'nɪpətənt/ *a.* onnipotente.

on /ɒn/ *prep.* su, sopra. **—***adv.* (*light etc.*) acceso; (*put on*) addosso; (*machine*) in funzione; (*happening*) in programma. **and so ~** e così via. **be ~ at** (*fam.*) criticare. **go ~** continuare. **later ~** più tardi. **~ and off** a intervalli. **~ and ~** senza fermarsi. **~ foot** a piedi. **~ Monday** lunedì. **~ Mondays** tutti i lunedì. **~ the way** in viaggio.

once /wʌns/ *adv.* una volta; (*formerly*) un tempo. **—***conj.* non appena. **at ~** subito. **~-over** *n.* (*fam.*) scorsa *f.*

oncoming /'ɒnkʌmɪŋ/ *a.* che si avvicina.

one /wʌn/ *a.* uno, una. —*n.* uno, a *m.,f.* —*pron.* uno; (*impersonal*) si. ~ **another** l'un l'altro. ~ **by** ~ a uno a uno. ~ **never knows** non si sa mai. ~**-sided** *a.* unilaterale. ~**-way** *a.* (*street*) a senso unico; (*ticket*) semplice.

onerous /'ɒnərəs/ *a.* oneroso.

oneself /wʌn'self/ *pron.* si, se stesso. **by** ~ da solo.

onion /'ʌnɪən/ *n.* cipolla *f.*

onlooker /'ɒnlʊkə(r)/ *n.* spetta|tore, -trice *m.,f.*

only /'əʊnlɪ/ *a.* solo. —*adv.* solamente, soltanto. —*conj.* solo che. **an** ~ **son** un figlio unico. ~ **just** appena. ~ **too** veramente.

onset /'ɒnset/ *n.* inizio *m.*; (*attack*) attacco *m.*

onslaught /'ɒnslɔːt/ *n.* assalto *m.*

onus /'əʊnəs/ *n.* onere *m.*

onward(s) /'ɒnwəd(z)/ *a.* & *adv.* in avanti.

onyx /'ɒnɪks/ *n.* onice *f.*

ooze /uːz/ *v.i.* fluire. —*v.t.* colare.

opal /'əʊpl/ *n.* opale *f.*

opaque /əʊ'peɪk/ *a.* opaco.

open /'əʊpən/ *a.* aperto; (*free to all*) pubblico; (*uncertain*) incerto; (*available*) disponibile; (*cheque*) non sbarrato. —*v.t./i.* aprire, aprirsi. **half~** *a.* socchiuso. ~**-ended** *a.* senza limite di tempo. ~**-minded** *a.* di larghe vedute. ~ **sea** alto mare *m.* ~ **secret** segreto di Pulcinella *m.* **O~** University *n.* università dell'aria *f.* **the** ~ *n.* l'aria aperta *f.*

opener /'əʊpənə(r)/ *n.* (*for tins*) apriscatole *m. invar.*; (*for bottles*) apribottiglie *m. invar.* **eye-~** *n.* (*fam.*) rivelazione *f.*

opening /'əʊpənɪŋ/ *n.* apertura *f.*; (*beginning*) inizio *m.*; (*job*) posto libero *m.*

openly /'əʊpənlɪ/ *adv.* apertamente.

opera /'ɒprə/ *n.* opera *f.* ~**-glasses** *n.pl.* binocolo da teatro *m.s.* ~**tic** /ɒpə'rætɪk/ *a.* di opera.

operat|e /'ɒpəreɪt/ *v.t./i.* operare; (*techn.*) (far) funzionare; (*control*) gestire. ~**e on** operare. ~**ion** /-'reɪʃn/ *n.* operazione *f.*; (*mech.*) funzionamento *m.* **in** ~**ion** in vigore. ~**or** *n.* opera|tore, -trice *m.,f.*; (*telephonist*) centralinista *m.|f.*

operational /ɒpə'reɪʃnl/ *a.* operativo.

operative /'ɒpərətɪv/ *a.* operante; (*law etc.*) in vigore.

operetta /ɒpə'retə/ *n.* operetta *f.*

opinion /ə'pɪnɪən/ *n.* opinione *f.* **in my** ~ secondo me. ~**ated** *a.* dogmatico.

opium /'əʊpɪəm/ *n.* oppio *m.*

opponent /ə'pəʊnənt/ *n.* avversario, a *m.,f.*

opportune /'ɒpətjuːn/ *a.* opportuno.

opportunist /ɒpə'tjuːnɪst/ *n.* opportunista *m.|f.*

opportunity /ɒpə'tjuːnətɪ/ *n.* opportunità *f.*

oppos|e /ə'pəʊz/ *v.t.* opporsi. ~**ed to** contrario a.

opposite /'ɒpəzɪt/ *a.* opposto. —*n.* contrario *m.* —*adv.* dirimpetto. —*prep.* di fronte (a). ~ **number** equivalente *m.|f.*

opposition /ɒpə'zɪʃn/ *n.* opposizione *f.*

oppress /ə'pres/ *v.t.* opprimere. ~**ion** /-ʃn/ *n.* oppressione *f.* ~**ive** *a.* oppressivo. ~**or** *n.* oppressore *m.*

opt /ɒpt/ *v.i.* ~ **for** scegliere. ~ **out** dissociarsi.

optical /'ɒptɪkl/ *a.* ottico.

optician /ɒp'tɪʃn/ *n.* ottico, a *m.,f.*

optimis|t /'ɒptɪmɪst/ *n.* ottimista *m.|f.* ~**m** /-zəm/ *n.* ottimismo *m.* ~**tic** /-'mɪstɪk/ *a.* ottimistico.

optimum /'ɒptɪməm/ *n.* posizione ideale *f.*

option /'ɒpʃn/ *n.* scelta *f.*; (*comm.*) opzione *f.*

optional /'ɒpʃənl/ *a.* facoltativo.

opulen|t /'ɒpjʊlənt/ *a.* opulento. ~**ce** *n.* opulenza *f.*

or /ɔː(r)/ *conj.* o, oppure; (*after negative*) né. ~ **else** se no.

oracle /'ɒrəkl/ *n.* oracolo *m.*

oral /'ɔːrəl/ *a.* orale. —*n.* (*fam.*) esame orale *m.*

orange /'ɒrɪndʒ/ *n.* arancia *f.*; (*tree*) arancio *m.* —*a.* & *n.* (*colour*) arancione *m.* ~**ade** *n.* aranciata *f.*

orator /'ɒrətə(r)/ *n.* ora|tore, -trice *m., f.*

oratorio /ɒrə'tɔːrɪəʊ/ *n.* (*pl.* **-os**) oratorio *m.*

oratory /'ɒrətrɪ/ *n.* oratorio *m.*

orb /ɔːb/ *n.* orbe *m.*

orbit /'ɔːbɪt/ *n.* orbita *f.* —*v.t.* orbitare.

orchard /'ɔːtʃəd/ *n.* frutteto *m.*

orchestra /'ɔːkɪstrə/ *n.* orchestra *f.* ~**l** /-'kestrəl/ *a.* orchestrale.

orchestrate /'ɔːkɪstreɪt/ *v.t.* orchestrare.

orchid /'ɔːkɪd/ *n.* orchidea *f.*

ordain /ɔː'deɪn/ *v.t.* decretare; (*relig.*) ordinare.

ordeal /ɔːˈdiːl/ *n*. (dura) prova *f*.

order /ˈɔːdə(r)/ *n*. ordine *m*.; (*comm*.) ordinazione *f*. —*v.t*. ordinare. **in ~ to** *or* **that** al fine di.

orderly /ˈɔːdəlɪ/ *a*. ordinato. —*n*. (*mil*.) ordinanza *f*., attendente *m*.; (*med*.) inserviente *m*.

ordinary /ˈɔːdɪnrɪ/ *a*. ordinario; (*average*) comune.

ordination /ɔːdɪˈneɪʃn/ *n*. ordinazione *f*.

ore /ɔː(r)/ *n*. minerale *m*.

organ /ˈɔːgən/ *n*. organo *m*. **~ist** *n*. organista *m*./*f*.

organic /ɔːˈgænɪk/ *a*. organico.

organism /ˈɔːgənɪzəm/ *n*. organismo *m*.

organiz|e /ˈɔːgənaɪz/ *v.t*. organizzare. **~ation** /-ˈzeɪʃn/ *n*. organizzazione *f*. **~er** *n*. organizza|tore, -trice *m*., *f*.

orgasm /ˈɔːgæzəm/ *n*. orgasmo *m*.

orgy /ˈɔːdʒɪ/ *n*. orgia *f*.

Orient /ˈɔːrɪənt/ *n*. **the ~** l'Oriente *m*. **~al** /-ˈentl/ *a*. & *n*. orientale *m*./*f*.

orientat|e /ˈɔːrɪənteɪt/ *v.t*. orientare. **~ation** /-ˈteɪʃn/ *n*. orientamento *m*.

orifice /ˈɒrɪfɪs/ *n*. apertura *f*.

origin /ˈɒrɪdʒɪn/ *n*. origine *f*.

original /əˈrɪdʒənl/ *a*. originario; (*not copied*) autentico; (*new*) originale. **~ity** /-ˈnælətɪ/ *n*. originalità *f*. **~ly** *adv*. originariamente.

originat|e /əˈrɪdʒɪneɪt/ *v.i*. **~e from** provenire da. **~or** *n*. inizia|tore, -trice *m*., *f*.

ormolu /ˈɔːməluː/ *n*. similoro *m*.

ornament /ˈɔːnəmənt/ *n*. ornamento *m*. **~al** /-ˈmentl/ *a*. ornamentale. **~ation** /-enˈteɪʃn/ *n*. decorazione *f*.

ornate /ɔːˈneɪt/ *a*. adorno.

ornithology /ɔːnɪˈθɒlədʒɪ/ *n*. ornitologia *f*.

orphan /ˈɔːfn/ *n*. orfano, a *m*., *f*. —*v.t*. rendere orfano. **~age** *n*. orfanotrofio *m*.

orthodox /ˈɔːθədɒks/ *a*. ortodosso. **~y** *n*. ortodossia *f*.

orthopaedic /ɔːθəˈpiːdɪk/ *a*. ortopedico.

oscillate /ˈɒsɪleɪt/ *v.i*. oscillare.

ossify /ˈɒsɪfaɪ/ *v.t*./*i*. ossificare, ossificarsi.

ostensibl|e /ɒsˈtensəbl/ *a*. apparente. **~y** *adv*. apparentemente.

ostentat|ion /ɒstenˈteɪʃn/ *n*. ostentazione *f*. **~ious** *a*. ostentato.

osteopath /ˈɒstɪəpæθ/ *n*. osteopata *m*./*f*. **~y** /-ˈɒpəθɪ/ *n*. osteopatia *f*.

ostracize /ˈɒstrəsaɪz/ *v.t*. bandire.

ostrich /ˈɒstrɪtʃ/ *n*. struzzo *m*.

other /ˈʌðə(r)/ *a*. altro. —*n*. & *pron*. altro, a *m*., *f*. **~ than** altro che. **the ~ one** l'altro, a *m*., *f*.

otherwise /ˈʌðəwaɪz/ *adv*. altrimenti.

otter /ˈɒtə(r)/ *n*. lontra *f*.

ouch /aʊtʃ/ *int*. ahi!

ought /ɔːt/ *v. aux*. dovere. **I ~ to see it.** dovrei vederlo. **he ~ to have done it** avrebbe dovuto farlo.

ounce /aʊns/ *n*. oncia *f*. (=28.35 *grams*.)

our /ˈaʊə(r)/ *a*. (il) nostro, (la) nostra.

ours /ˈaʊəz/ *poss. pron*. (il) nostro, (la) nostra.

ourselves /aʊəˈselvz/ *pron*. noi stessi; (*reflexive*) ci; (*after prep*.) noi (stessi).

oust /aʊst/ *v.t*. estromettere.

out /aʊt/ *adv*. fuori; (*light*) spento; (*in blossom*) sbocciato; (*in error*) sbagliato. **be ~ of** essere senza. **be ~ to** essere deciso di. **~-and-~** *a*. perfetto. **~ of date** antiquato. **~ of order** guasto. **~ of place** spostato; (*fig*.) inopportuno. **~ of print/stock** esaurito. **~ of sorts** indisposto. **~ of tune** (*singer*) stonato; (*instrument*) scordato. **~ of work** disoccupato. **~-patient** *n*. paziente non ricoverato, a *m*., *f*. **~-patient's department** ambulatorio *m*.

outbid /aʊtˈbɪd/ *v.t*. (*p.t*. -**bid**, *pres. p*. -**bidding**) fare un'offerta superiore a.

outboard /ˈaʊtbɔːd/ *a*. fuoribordo.

outbreak /ˈaʊtbreɪk/ *n*. (*of anger*) esplosione *f*.; (*of war*) scoppio *m*.; (*of disease*) epidemia *f*.

outbuilding /ˈaʊtbɪldɪŋ/ *n*. annesso *m*.

outburst /ˈaʊtbɜːst/ *n*. esplosione *f*.

outcast /ˈaʊtkɑːst/ *n*. esule *m*./*f*.; (*social*) paria *m. invar*.

outcome /ˈaʊtkʌm/ *n*. risultato *m*.

outcry /ˈaʊtkraɪ/ *n*. scalpore *m*.

outdated /aʊtˈdeɪtɪd/ *a*. sorpassato.

outdo /aʊtˈduː/ *v.t*. (*p.t*. -**did**, *p.p*. **~done**) superare.

outdoor /ˈaʊtdɔː(r)/ *a*. all'aperto. **~s** /-ˈdɔːz/ *adv*. all'aria aperta.

outer /ˈaʊtə(r)/ *a*. esteriore.

outfit /ˈaʊtfɪt/ *n*. equipaggiamento *m*.; (*clothes*) completo *m*. **~ter** *n*. fornitore *m*.

outgoing /ˈaʊtgəʊɪŋ/ *a*. uscente; (*of mail etc*.) in partenza; (*sociable*) estroverso. **~s** *n.pl*. uscite *f.pl*.

outgrow /æʊtˈgrəʊ/ *v.t*. (*p.t*. -**grew**,

p.p. **-grown)** diventare troppo grande per; (*height, quantity*) sorpassare.

outhouse /'aʊthaʊs/ *n.* costruzione annessa *f.*

outing /'aʊtɪŋ/ *n.* gita *f.*

outlandish /aʊt'lændɪʃ/ *a.* bizzarro.

outlaw /'aʊtlɔː/ *n.* fuorilegge *m./f. invar.* —*v.t.* bandire.

outlay /'aʊtleɪ/ *n.* spesa *f.*

outlet /'aʊtlet/ *n.* sbocco *m.*; (*for feelings*) sfogo *m.*; (*comm.*) punto di vendita *m.*

outline /'aʊtlaɪn/ *n.* contorno *m.*; (*summary*) sommario *m.* —*v.t.* tracciare il contorno; (*describe*) descrivere.

outlive /aʊt'lɪv/ *v.t.* sopravvivere a.

outlook /'aʊtlʊk/ *n.* vista *f.*; (*future prospect*) prospettiva *f.*

outlying /'aʊtlaɪŋ/ *a.* remoto.

outmoded /aʊt'məʊdɪd/ *a.* fuori moda.

outnumber /aʊt'nʌmbə(r)/ *v.t.* superare in numero.

outpost /'aʊtpəʊst/ *n.* avamposto *m.*

output /'aʊtpʊt/ *n.* produzione *f.*

outrage /'aʊtreɪdʒ/ *n.* oltraggio *m.* —*v.t.* oltraggiare.

outrageous /aʊt'reɪdʒəs/ *a.* oltraggioso.

outright /'aʊtraɪt/ *adv.* completamente; (*at once*) immediatamente; (*frankly*) francamente. —*a.* completo; (*refusal*) netto.

outset /'aʊtset/ *n.* inizio *m.*

outside[1] /'aʊtsaɪd/ *a. & n.* esterno *m.*

outside[2] /aʊt'saɪd/ *adv.* all'esterno, fuori. —*prep.* fuori di.

outsider /aʊt'saɪdə(r)/ *n.* estraneo, a *m., f.*; (*in race*) outsider *m.*

outsize /'aʊtsaɪz/ *a.* fuori misura.

outskirts /'aʊtskɜːts/ *n.pl.* sobborghi *m.pl.*

outspoken /aʊt'spəʊkn/ *a.* schietto.

outstanding /aʊt'stændɪŋ/ *a.* eccezionale; (*not settled*) in sospeso; (*conspicuous*) prominente.

outstretched /aʊt'stretʃt/ *a.* allungato.

outstrip /aʊt'strɪp/ *v.t.* (*p.t.* **-stripped**) superare.

outward /'aʊtwəd/ *a.* esterno; (*journey*) di andata. — **~(s)** *adv.* verso l'esterno. **~ly** *adv.* al di fuori.

outweigh /aʊt'weɪ/ *v.t.* aver maggior peso di; (*fig.*) superare in importanza.

outwit /aʊt'wɪt/ *v.t.* (*p.t.* **-witted**) battere in astuzia.

oval /'əʊvl/ *n. & a.* ovale *m.*

ovary /'əʊvərɪ/ *n.* ovaia *f.*

ovation /əʊ'veɪʃn/ *n.* ovazione *f.*

oven /'ʌvn/ *n.* forno *m.*

over /'əʊvə(r)/ *prep.* sopra; (*across*) dall'altra parte; (*during*) durante; (*more than*) più di. —*adv.* di sopra; (*ended*) finito; (*more*) più. **all ~** dappertutto. **~ again** un'altra volta. **~ and above** oltre a. **~ and ~** più e più volte. **~ here** qui. **~ there** là.

over- /'əʊvə(r)/ *pref.* troppo.

overall[1] /'əʊvərɔːl/ *n.* camice *m.* **~s** *n.pl.* tuta *f.s.*

overall[2] /əʊvər'ɔːl/ *a.* totale. —*adv.* complessivamente.

overawe /əʊvər'ɔː/ *v.t.* intimidire.

overbalance /əʊvə'bæləns/ *v.t./i.* (*far*) perdere l'equilibrio.

overbearing /əʊvə'beərɪŋ/ *a.* dominante.

overboard /'əʊvəbɔːd/ *adv.* in mare.

overbook /əʊvə'bʊk/ *v.t.* sopraprenotare.

overcast /əʊvə'kɑːst/ *a.* coperto.

overcharge /əʊvə'tʃɑːdʒ/ *v.t.* (*fill too much*) sovraccaricare; (*charge too much*) far pagare troppo caro.

overcoat /'əʊvəkəʊt/ *n.* cappotto *m.*

overcome /əʊvə'kʌm/ *v.t.* (*p.t.* **-came,** *p.p.* **-come**) superare. **be ~ by** essere sopraffatto da.

overcrowded /əʊvə'kraʊdɪd/ *a.* sovraffollato.

overdo /əʊvə'duː/ *v.t.* (*p.t.* **-did,** *p.p.* **-done**) esagerare; (*culin.*) cuocere troppo.

overdose /'əʊvədəʊs/ *n.* dose eccessiva *f.*

overdraft /'əʊvədrɑːft/ *n.* scoperto *m.*

overdraw /əʊvə'drɔː/ *v.t.* (*p.t.* **-drew,** *p.p.* **-drawn**) prelevare in scoperto.

overdue /əʊvə'djuː/ *a.* in ritardo; (*belated*) tardivo.

overestimate /əʊvər'estɪmeɪt/ *v.t.* sopravvalutare.

overflow[1] /əʊvə'fləʊ/ *v.i.* straripare.

overflow[2] /'əʊvəfləʊ/ *n.* (*excess*) eccesso *m.*; (*outlet*) scarico *m.*

overgrown /əʊvə'grəʊn/ *a.* cresciuto troppo; (*garden*) coperto di erbacce.

overhang /əʊvə'hæŋ/ *v.t./i.* (*p.t.* **-hung**) sovrastare; (*fig.*) incombere. —*n.* sporgenza *f.*

overhaul[1] /əʊvə'hɔːl/ *v.t.* revisionare.

overhaul[2] /'əʊvəhɔːl/ *n.* revisione *f.*

overhead[1] /əʊvə'hed/ *adv.* al di sopra.

overhead[2] /'əʊvəhed/ *a.* sopra la testa. **~s** *n.pl.* spese generali *f.pl.*

overhear /əʊvə'hɪə(r)/ v.t. (p.t. -heard) udire per caso.

overjoyed /əʊvə'dʒɔɪd/ a. felicissimo.

overland /'əʊvəlænd/ a. & adv. via terra.

overlap /əʊvə'læp/ v.t./i. (p.t. -lapped) sovrapporre, sovrapporsi.

overleaf /əʊvə'liːf/ adv. sul retro.

overload /əʊvə'ləʊd/ v.t. sovraccaricare.

overlook /əʊvə'lʊk/ v.t. dominare; (fail to see) lasciarsi sfuggire; (oversee) ispezionare; (forgive) condonare.

overnight /əʊvə'naɪt/ adv. per la notte. —a. notturno.

overpass /'əʊvəpɑːs/ n. cavalcavia m. invar.

overpay /əʊvə'peɪ/ v.t. (p.t. -paid) strapagare.

overpower /əʊvə'paʊə(r)/ v.t. sopraffare. ~ing a. insostenibile.

overpriced /əʊvə'praɪst/ a. troppo caro.

overrate /əʊvə'reɪt/ v.t. sopravvalutare.

overreact /əʊvərɪ'ækt/ v.i. reagire eccessivamente.

overreach /əʊvə'riːtʃ/ v.r. ~ o.s. fallire per aver tentato troppo.

overrid|e /əʊvə'raɪd/ v.t. (p.t. -rode, p.p. -ridden) passare sopra a. ~ing a. dominante.

overripe /'əʊvəraɪp/ a. troppo maturo.

overrule /əʊvə'ruːl/ v.t. annullare; (a claim) respingere.

overrun /əʊvə'rʌn/ v.t. (p.t. -ran, p.p. -run, pres. p. -running) invadere; (a limit) oltrepassare.

overseas /əʊvə'siːz/ a. d'oltremare. —adv. oltremare.

oversee /əʊvə'siː/ v.t. (p.t. -saw, p.p. -seen) sorvegliare. ~r /'əʊvəsɪə(r)/ n. sorvegliante m.

overshadow /əʊvə'ʃædəʊ/ v.t. adombrare.

overshoot /əʊvə'ʃuːt/ v.t. (p.t. -shot) passare il segno.

oversight /'əʊvəsaɪt/ n. svista f.

oversleep /əʊvə'sliːp/ v.i. (p.t. -slept) svegliarsi tardi.

overstep /əʊvə'step/ v.t. (p.t. -stepped) oltrepassare.

overt /'əʊvɜːt/ a. chiaro, palese.

overtak|e /əʊvə'teɪk/ v.t./i. (p.t. -took, p.p. -taken) sorpassare. ~ing n. sorpasso m.

overtax /əʊvə'tæks/ v.t. abusare (di).

overthrow[1] /əʊvə'θrəʊ/ v.t. (p.t. -threw, p.p. -thrown) rovesciare.

overthrow[2] /'əʊvəθrəʊ/ n. crollo m.

overtime /'əʊvətaɪm/ n. lavoro straordinario m. —adv. oltre l'ora fissata.

overtone /'əʊvətəʊn/ n. (fig.) implicazione f.

overture /'əʊvətjʊə(r)/ n. preludio m. ~s n.pl. (fig.) approccio m.s.

overturn /əʊvə'tɜːn/ v.t./i. capovolgere, capovolgersi.

overweight /'əʊvəweɪt/ a. troppo pesante. be ~ pesare troppo.

overwhelm /əʊvə'welm/ v.t. sommergere; (with emotion) confondere. ~ing a. travolgente.

overwork /əʊvə'wɜːk/ v.t./i. (far) lavorare eccessivamente. —n. lavoro eccessivo m.

overwrought /əʊvə'rɔːt/ a. esausto.

ovulation /əʊvjʊ'leɪʃn/ n. ovulazione f.

ow|e /əʊ/ v.t. dovere. ~ing a. dovuto. ~ing to a causa di.

owl /aʊl/ n. gufo m.

own[1] /əʊn/ a. proprio. get one's ~ back (fam.) vendicarsi. hold one's ~ tener duro. on one's ~ da solo.

own[2] /əʊn/ v.t. possedere. —v.i. ~ up (to) (fam.) confessare. ~er n. proprietario, a m., f. ~ership n. proprietà f.

ox /ɒks/ n. (pl. oxen) bue m. (pl. buoi).

oxide /'ɒksaɪd/ n. ossido m.

oxygen /'ɒksɪdʒən/ n. ossigeno m.

oyster /'ɔɪstə(r)/ n. ostrica f.

P

pace /peɪs/ n. passo m. —v.i. ~ **up and
down** camminare avanti e indietro.
keep ~ with camminare di pari
passo con. **~-maker** n. (runner) battistrada m.; (med.) pacemaker m.

Pacific /pə'sɪfɪk/ a. pacifico. —n. ~
(Ocean) (Oceano) Pacifico m.

pacifist /'pæsɪfɪst/ n. pacifista m./f.

pacify /'pæsɪfaɪ/ v.t. pacificare.

pack /pæk/ n. pacco m.; (of cards)
mazzo m.; (of hounds) muta f.; (of
wolves) branco m.; (large amount)
mucchio m. —v.t. impaccare; (suitcase) fare; (press down) pigiare. —v.i.
fare i bagagli. **~ed lunch** pranzo al
sacco m. **~ed out** (fam.) pieno zeppo.
send ~ing mandar via.

package /'pækɪdʒ/ n. pacco m. —v.t.
impacchettare. **~ deal** n. accordo globale m. **~ tour** n. viaggio organizzato
m.

packet /'pækɪt/ n. pacchetto m.

pact /pækt/ n. patto m.

pad[1] /pæd/ n. imbottitura f.; (for writing) blocco m.; (fam., flat) (piccolo)
appartamento m. —v.t. (p.t. **padded**)
imbottire. **~ding** n. imbottitura f.

pad[2] /pæd/ v.i. (p.t. **padded**) camminare con passo felpato.

paddle[1] /'pædl/ n. pagaia f. **~-steamer**
n. piroscafo a ruota m.

paddle[2] /'pædl/ v.i. sguazzare in acqua.

paddock /'pædək/ n. recinto m.

paddy /'pædɪ/ n. riso vestito m. **~-field**
n. risaia f.

padlock /'pædlɒk/ n. lucchetto
m. —v.t. chiudere col lucchetto.

paediatrician /piːdɪə'trɪʃn/ n. pedia-
tra m./f.

pagan /'peɪgən/ a. & n. pagano, a m., f.

page[1] /peɪdʒ/ n. pagina f.

page[2] /peɪdʒ/ n. paggio m.; (in hotel)
fattorino m. —v.t. (in hotel) (far) chiamare.

pageant /'pædʒənt/ n. parata f. **~ry** n.
cerimoniale m.

pagoda /pə'gəʊdə/ n. pagoda f.

paid /peɪd/ see **pay**. —a. **put ~ to**
(fam.) finire definitivamente.

pail /peɪl/ n. secchio m.

pain /peɪn/ n. dolore m. **~s** n.pl. (effort)
sforzo m.s. —v.t. addolorare. **be at
~s** darsi da fare. **be in ~** soffrire. **~**
in the neck (fam.) scocciatura f. **~-
killer** n. calmante m.

pain|ful /'peɪnfl/ a. doloroso; (labori-
ous) penoso. **~less** a. indolore.

painstaking /'peɪnzteɪkɪŋ/ a. minuzioso.

paint /peɪnt/ n. pittura f. **~s** n.pl.
colori m.pl. —v.t./i. pitturare. **~er** n.
(artist) pit|tore, -trice m., f.; (decor-
ator) imbianchino m. **~ing** n. pittura
f.; (picture) dipinto m.

pair /peə(r)/ n. paio m. (pl.f. paia);
(of people) coppia f. **~ of trousers**
pantaloni m.pl. —v.t./i. appaiare, ap-
paiarsi. **~ off** mettere, mettersi in
due.

Pakistan /pɑːkɪ'stɑːn/ n. Pakistan m.
~i a. & n. pakistano, a m., f.

pal /pæl/ n. (fam.) amico m.

palace /'pælɪs/ n. palazzo m.

palat|e /'pælət/ n. palato m. **~able** a.
gustoso.

palatial /pə'leɪʃl/ a. sontuoso.

palaver /pə'lɑːvə(r)/ n. (fam.) trambusto m.

pale[1] /peɪl/ a. (-er, -est) pallido; (of
colour, light) chiaro. —v.i. impallidire. **~ness** n. pallore m.

pale[2] /peɪl/ n. palo m.

Palestin|e /'pælɪstaɪn/ n. Palestina f.
~ian /-'stɪnɪən/ a. & n. palestinese
m./f.

palette /'pælɪt/ n. tavolozza f. **~-knife**
n. spatola f.

pall /pɔːl/ n. drappo funebre m.; (fig.)
cappa f. —v.i. **~ (on)** stancare.

pallid /'pælɪd/ a. pallido.

palm /pɑːm/ n. (of hand) palmo m.;
(tree) palma f.; (symbol) vittoria f.
—v.t. **~ off** appioppare (**on, a**).
P~ Sunday n. Domenica delle Palme
f.

palmist /'pɑːmɪst/ n. chiromante
m./f.

palpable /'pælpəbl/ a. palpabile.

palpitat|e /'pælpɪteɪt/ v.i. palpitare.
~ion /-'teɪʃn/ n. palpitazione f.

paltry /'pɔːltrɪ/ a. (-ier, -iest) insignificante.

pamper /'pæmpə(r)/ v.t. viziare.

pamphlet /'pæmflɪt/ n. opuscolo m.

pan /pæn/ n. tegame m.; (for frying)
padella f.; (of scales) piatto m. —v.t.

(*p.t.* **panned**) (*fam.*) criticare severamente.

panacea /pænə'sɪə/ *n.* panacea *f.*

panache /pæ'næʃ/ *n.* stile *m.*

pancake /'pænkeɪk/ *n.* frittella *f.*

panda /'pændə/ *n.* panda *m.* ~ **car** *n.* macchina della polizia *f.*

pandemonium /pændɪ'məʊnɪəm/ *n.* pandemonio *m.*

pander /'pændə(r)/ *v.i.* ~ **to** concedere tutto a.

pane /peɪn/ *n.* (*of glass*) vetro *m.*; (*on door*) pannello *m.*

panel /'pænl/ *n.* pannello *m.*; (*group of people*) giuria *f.* ~**ling** *n.* pannelli *m.pl.*

pang /pæŋ/ *n.* fitta *f.*; (*of hunger*) spasimo *m.*

panic /'pænɪk/ *n.* panico *m.* —*v.i.* (*p.t.* **panicked**) lasciarsi prendere dal panico. ~-**stricken** *a.* in preda al panico.

panoram|a /pænə'rɑ:mə/ *n.* panorama *m.* ~**ic** *a.* panoramico.

pansy /'pænzɪ/ *n.* viola del pensiero *f.*; (*fam.*, *effeminate man*) finocchio *m.*

pant /pænt/ *v.i.* ansimare.

pantechnicon /pæn'teknɪkən/ *n.* furgone per traslochi *m.*

panther /'pænθə(r)/ *n.* pantera *f.*

panties /'pæntɪz/ *n.pl.* mutandine *f.pl.*

pantomime /'pæntəmaɪm/ *n.* pantomima *f.*

pantry /'pæntrɪ/ *n.* dispensa *f.*

pants /pænts/ *n.pl.* (*underwear*, *fam.*) mutande *f.pl.*; (*trousers*, *fam.*) pantaloni *m.pl.*

papa|cy /'peɪpəsɪ/ *n.* papato *m.* ~**l** *a.* papale.

papaw /'pəpɔ:/ *n.* papaia *f.*

paper /'peɪpə(r)/ *n.* carta *f.*; (*newspaper*) giornale *m.*; (*exam*) esame *m.*; (*document*) relazione *f.* —*v.t.* tappezzare. **on** ~ in teoria. ~-**clip** *n.* graffetta *f.* ~**work** *n.* lavoro d'ufficio *m.*

paperback /'peɪpəbæk/ *a.* & *n.* edizione economica *f.*

paperweight /'peɪpəweɪt/ *n.* fermacarte *m.* *invar.*

papier mâché /pæpɪeɪ'mæʃeɪ/ *n.* cartapesta *f.*

par /pɑ:(r)/ *n.* pari *f.* **feel below** ~ sentirsi un po' giù. **on a** ~ **with** alla pari con.

parable /'pærəbl/ *n.* parabola *f.*

parachut|e /'pærəʃu:t/ *n.* paracadute *m.* —*v.i.* lanciarsi col paracadute. ~**ist** *n.* paracadutista *m./f.*

parade /pə'reɪd/ *n.* parata militare *f.*; (*street*) lungomare *m.*; (*display*) sfoggio *m.* —*v.i.* sfilare. —*v.t.* far sfoggio.

paradise /'pærədaɪs/ *n.* paradiso *m.*

paradox /'pærədɒks/ *n.* paradosso *m.* ~**ical** /-'dɒksɪkl/ *a.* paradossale.

paraffin /'pærəfɪn/ *n.* paraffina *f.*

paragon /'pærəgən/ *n.* modello di perfezione *m.*

paragraph /'pærəgrɑ:f/ *n.* paragrafo *m.*

parallel /'pærəlel/ *a.* parallelo. —*n.* parallelo *m.*; (*line*) parallela *f.* —*v.t.* essere paragonabile a.

paralyse /'pærəlaɪz/ *v.t.* paralizzare.

paraly|sis /pə'ræləsɪs/ *n.* (*pl.* -**ses** /-si:z/) paralisi *f. invar.* ~**tic** /pærə'lɪtɪk/ *a.* & *n.* paralitico, a *m.*,*f.*

parameter /pə'ræmɪtə(r)/ *n.* parametro *m.*

paramount /'pærəmaʊnt/ *a.* supremo.

paranoia /pærə'nɔɪə/ *n.* paranoia *f.*

parapet /'pærəpɪt/ *n.* parapetto *m.*

paraphernalia /pærəfə'neɪlɪə/ *n.* oggetti vari *m.pl.*

paraphrase /'pærəfreɪz/ *n.* parafrasi *f.* —*v.t.* parafrasare.

paraplegic /pærə'pli:dʒɪk/ *n.* paraplegico, a *m.*,*f.*

parasite /'pærəsaɪt/ *n.* parassita *m./f.*

parasol /'pærəsɒl/ *n.* parasole *m.*

paratrooper /'pærətru:pə(r)/ *n.* paracadutista *m.*

parcel /'pɑ:sl/ *n.* pacco *m.*

parch /pɑ:tʃ/ *v.t.* disseccare. **be** ~**ed** aver molta sete.

parchment /'pɑ:tʃmənt/ *n.* pergamena *f.*

pardon /'pɑ:dn/ *n.* perdono *m.*; (*jurid.*) grazia *f.* —*v.t.* perdonare; graziare. **I beg your** ~! (mi) scusi! **I beg your** ~? prego?

pare /peə(r)/ *v.t.* pareggiare; (*peel*) pelare.

parent /'peərənt/ *n.* geni|tore, -trice *m.*, *f.*; (*source*) fonte *f.* ~**s** *n.pl.* genitori *m.pl.* ~ **al** /pə'rentl/ *a.* paterno, materno. ~**hood** *n.* paternità *f.*, maternità *f.*

parenthesis /pə'renθəsɪs/ *n.* (*pl.* -**theses** /-si:z/) parentesi *f. invar.*

Paris /'pærɪs/ *n.* Parigi *f.* ~**ian** /pə'rɪzɪən/ *a.* & *n.* parigino, a *m.*,*f.*

parish /'pærɪʃ/ *n.* parrocchia *f.*; (*municipal*) comune *m.* ~**ioner** /pə'rɪʃənə(r)/ *n.* parrocchiano, a *m.*,*f.*

parity /'pærɪtɪ/ *n.* parità *f.*

park /pɑ:k/ *n.* parco *m.* —*v.t./i.* posteg

giare. ~ **oneself** *v.r.* (*fam.*) installarsi. ~**ing-meter** *n.* parchimetro *m.*

parka /'pɑːkə/ *n.* parka *m.*

parliament /'pɑːləmənt/ *n.* parlamento *m.* ~**ary** /-'mentrɪ/ *a.* parlamentare.

parlour /'pɑːlə(r)/ *n.* salone *m.*; (*of house*) salotto *m.*

parochial /pə'rəʊkɪəl/ *a.* parrocchiale; (*fig.*) ristretto.

parody /'pærədɪ/ *n.* paródia *f.* —*v.t.* parodiare.

parole /pə'rəʊl/ *n.* **on** ~ sulla parola. —*v.t.* mettere in libertà sulla parola.

paroxysm /'pærəksɪzəm/ *n.* parossismo *m.*

parquet /'pɑːkeɪ/ *n.* ~ **floor** parquet *m.*

parrot /'pærət/ *n.* pappagallo *m.*

parry /'pærɪ/ *v.t.* scansare. —*n.* parata *f.*

parsimonious /pɑːsɪ'məʊnɪəs/ *a.* parsimonioso.

parsley /'pɑːslɪ/ *n.* prezzemolo *m.*

parsnip /'pɑːsnɪp/ *n.* pastinaca *f.*

parson /'pɑːsn/ *n.* parroco *m.*

part /pɑːt/ *n.* parte *f.*; (*of machine*) pezzo *m.* —*adv.* in parte. —*v.t./i.* separare, separarsi. **on the** ~ **of** da parte di. ~-**time** *a.* & *adv.* a mezzo tempo. ~ **with** *v.t.* separarsi da.

partake /pɑː'teɪk/ *v.t.* (*p.t.* -**took**, *p.p.* -**taken**) partecipare.

partial /'pɑːʃl/ *a.* parziale. **be** ~ **to** aver un debole per. ~**ity** /-ɪ'ælətɪ/ *n.* parzialità *f.*; predilezione *f.* ~**ly** *adv.* parzialmente.

particip|ate /pɑː'tɪsɪpeɪt/ *v.i.* partecipare (**in,** a) ~**ant** *n.* partecipante *m./f.* ~**ation** /-'peɪʃn/ *n.* partecipazione *f.*

participle /'pɑːtɪsɪpl/ *n.* participio *m.*

particle /'pɑːtɪkl/ *n.* particella *f.*

particular /pə'tɪkjʊlə(r)/ *a.* particolare; (*precise*) meticoloso. ~**s** *n.pl.* dettagli *m.pl.* **in** ~ specialmente. ~**ly** *adv.* particolarmente.

parting /'pɑːtɪŋ/ *n.* separazione *f.*; (*in hair*) scriminatura *f.* —*a.* d'addio.

partisan /pɑːtɪ'zæn/ *n.* partigiano, a *m., f.*

partition /pɑː'tɪʃn/ *n.* (*pol.*) partizione *f.*; (*wall*) parete divisoria *f.* —*v.t.* dividere in parti.

partly /'pɑːtlɪ/ *adv.* in parte.

partner /'pɑːtnə(r)/ *n.* socio, a *m., f.*; (*sport*) compagno, a *m., f.* ~**ship** *n.* società *f.*

partridge /'pɑːtrɪdʒ/ *n.* pernice *f.*

party /'pɑːtɪ/ *n.* ricevimento *m.*; (*group*) gruppo *m.*; (*pol.*) partito *m.*; (*jurid.*) parte (in causa) *f.* ~ **line** *n.* (*telephone*) duplex *m.* *invar.*

pass /pɑːs/ *v.t./i.* passare; (*overtake*) sorpassare; (*in exam*) essere promosso; (*utter*) proferire. —*n.* lasciapassare *m.* *invar.*; (*in mountains*) passo *m.*; (*sport*) passaggio *m.* **make a** ~ **at** (*fam.*) far proposte (indiscrete) a. ~ **away** morire. ~ **down** trasmettere. ~ (-**mark**) *n.* (*schol.*) (voto) sufficiente *m.* ~ **out** (*fam.*) svenire. ~ **over** sorvolare. ~ **round** distribuire. ~ **through** attraversare. ~ **up** (*fam.*) lasciar perdere.

passable /'pɑːsəbl/ *a.* passabile; (*of road*) praticabile.

passage /'pæsɪdʒ/ *n.* passaggio *m.*; (*voyage*) traversata *f.*; (*corridor*) corridoio *m.*; (*in book*) brano *m.*

passenger /'pæsɪndʒə(r)/ *n.* passeggero, a *m., f.*

passer-by /pɑːsə'baɪ/ *n.* (*pl.* **passers-by**) passante *m./f.*

passion /'pæʃn/ *n.* passione *f.* ~**ate** *a.* appassionato. ~**ately** *adv.* appassionatamente.

passive /'pæsɪv/ *a.* passivo. ~**ness** *n.* passività *f.*

Passover /'pɑːsəʊvə(r)/ *n.* Pasqua ebraica *f.*

passport /'pɑːspɔːt/ *n.* passaporto *m.*

password /'pɑːswɜːd/ *n.* parola d'ordine *f.*

past /pɑːst/ *a.* & *n.* passato *m.* —*prep.* & *adv.* oltre. **in times** ~ nei tempi andati. **the** ~ **week** la settimana scorsa.

paste /peɪst/ *n.* pasta *f.*; (*adhesive*) colla *f.* —*v.t.* incollare. ~ **jewellery** gioielli d'imitazione *m.pl.*

pasteboard /'peɪstbɔːd/ *n.* cartone *m.*

pastel /'pæstl/ *a.* & *n.* pastello *m.*

pasteurize /'pæstʃəraɪz/ *v.t.* pastorizzare.

pastiche /pæ'stiːʃ/ *n.* pastiche *m.*

pastille /'pæstɪl/ *n.* pastiglia *f.*

pastime /'pɑːstaɪm/ *n.* passatempo *m.*

pastoral /'pɑːstərəl/ *a.* pastorale.

pastry /'peɪstrɪ/ *n.* pasta *f.*

pasture /'pɑːstʃə(r)/ *n.* pascolo *m.*

pasty[1] /'pæstɪ/ *n.* pasticcio *m.*

pasty[2] /'peɪstɪ/ *a.* smorto.

pat /pæt/ *v.t.* (*p.t.* **patted**) dare un buffetto. —*n.* buffetto *m.*; (*of butter*) pezzetto *m.* —*adv.* al momento giusto.

patch /pætʃ/ n. pezza f.; (period) periodo m.; (piece of ground) appezzamento m. —v.t. ~ up rappezzare; (fig.) appianare. not a ~ on (fam.) molto inferiore a. ~y a. irregolare.

pâté /'pæteɪ/ n. pâté m.

patent /'peɪtnt/ a. evidente. —n. brevetto m. —v.t. brevettare. ~ **leather** n. vernice f. ~**ly** adv. evidentemente.

paternal /pə'tɜːnl/ a. paterno.

paternity /pə'tɜːnətɪ/ n. paternità f.

path /pɑːθ/ n. (pl. -s /pɑːðz/) sentiero m.; (sport) pista f.; (of rocket) traiettoria f.; (fig.) via f.

pathetic /pə'θetɪk/ a. pietoso.

pathology /pə'θɒlədʒɪ/ n. patologia f.

pathos /'peɪθɒs/ n. pathos m.

patience /'peɪʃns/ n. pazienza f.

patient /'peɪʃnt/ a. & n. paziente m./f. ~**ly** adv. pazientemente.

patio /'pætɪəʊ/ n. (pl. -os) patio m.

patriarch /'peɪtrɪɑːk/ n. patriarca m.

patrician /pə'trɪʃn/ a. & n. patrizio, a m., f.

patriot /'pætrɪət/ n. patriota m./f. ~**ic** /-'ɒtɪk/ a. patriottico. ~**ism** n. patriottismo m.

patrol /pə'trəʊl/ n. pattuglia f. —v.t./i. pattugliare.

patron /'peɪtrən/ n. patrono m.; (of charity) benefat|tore, -trice m.,f.; (customer) cliente (abituale) m./f.

patron|age /'pætrənɪdʒ/ n. patronato m.; (of shop etc.) clientela f. ~**ize** v.t. essere cliente abituale di; (fig.) trattare con condiscendenza.

patter[1] /'pætə(r)/ n. picchiettio m. —v.i. picchiettare.

patter[2] /'pætə(r)/ n. (speech) gergo m.; (chatter) cicaleccio m.

pattern /'pætn/ n. disegno (stampato) m.; (model) modello m.; (sample) campione m.; (manner) modo m.

paunch /pɔːntʃ/ n. pancia f.

pauper /'pɔːpə(r)/ n. povero, a m., f.

pause /pɔːz/ n. pausa f. —v.i. fare una pausa.

pav|e /peɪv/ v.t. pavimentare. ~**e the way for** aprire la strada a. ~**ing-stone** n. lastra f.

pavement /'peɪvmənt/ n. marciapiede m.

pavilion /pə'vɪlɪən/ n. padiglione m.

paw /pɔː/ n. zampa f. —v.i. dar zampate.

pawn[1] /pɔːn/ n. (chess, fig.) pedina f.

pawn[2] /pɔːn/ v.t. impegnare. —n. in

~ in pegno. ~**shop** n. monte di pietà m.

pawnbroker /'pɔːnbrəʊkə(r)/ n. prestatore su pegno m.

pay /peɪ/ v.t./i. (p.t. **paid**) pagare; (attention) prestare; (compliment) fare; (be profitable) rendere. —n. paga f. **in the ~ of** al servizio di. ~ **back** ripagare. ~ **cash** pagare in contanti. ~ **in** versare. ~ **off** or **out** or **up** pagare (completamente). ~**off** n. (sl.) liquidazione f.; (fig.) resa dei conti f.

payable /'peɪəbl/ a. pagabile.

payment /'peɪmənt/ n. pagamento m.

payroll /'peɪrəʊl/ n. libro-paga m.

pea /piː/ n. pisello m.

peace /piːs/ n. pace f. ~ **of mind** tranquillità (d'animo) f. ~**able** a. pacifico.

peaceful /'piːsfl/ a. calmo, sereno.

peacemaker /'piːsmeɪkə(r)/ n. pacifica|tore, -trice m., f.

peach /piːtʃ/ n. pesca f.; (tree) pesco m.

peacock /'piːkɒk/ n. pavone m.

peak /piːk/ n. picco m.; (maximum) massimo m. ~ **hours** n.pl. ore di punta f.pl. ~**ed cap** n. berretto a punta m.

peaky /'piːkɪ/ a. malaticcio.

peal /piːl/ n. scampanio m.; (of laughter) scoppio m.

peanut /'piːnʌt/ n. nocciolina americana f. ~**s** (sl.) quattro soldi m.pl.

pear /peə(r)/ n. pera f.; (tree) pero m.

pearl /pɜːl/ n. perla f. ~**y** a. perlaceo.

peasant /'peznt/ n. contadino, a m., f.

peat /piːt/ n. torba f.

pebble /'pebl/ n. sassolino m.

peck /pek/ v.t./i. beccare; (fam., kiss) dare un bacetto. —n. beccata f.; bacetto m.

peckish /'pekɪʃ/ a. be ~ (fam.) aver un po' di fame.

peculiar /pɪ'kjuːlɪə(r)/ a. originale; (special) particolare. ~**ity** /-'ærətɪ/ n. stranezza f.; (feature) particolarità f.

pedal /'pedl/ n. pedale m. —v.i. pedalare.

pedantic /pɪ'dæntɪk/ a. pedante.

peddle /'pedl/ v.t. vendere al minuto.

pedestal /'pedɪstl/ n. piedistallo m.

pedestrian /pɪ'destrɪən/ n. pedone m. —a. pedonale; (dull) prosaico. ~ **crossing** n. passaggio pedonale m.

pedicure /'pedɪkjʊə(r)/ n. pedicure f.

pedigree /'pedɪgriː/ n. lignaggio m.; (of animal) pedigree m. —a. (of animal) di razza.

pedlar /'pedlə(r)/ *n.* venditore ambulante *m.*

peek /piːk/ *v.i.* guardare furtivamente.

peel /piːl/ *n.* buccia *f.* —*v.t.* sbucciare. —*v.i.* (*of skin*) spellarsi; (*of paint*) staccarsi. ~**ings** *n.pl.* bucce *f.pl.*

peep[1] /piːp/ *v.i.* guardare furtivamente. —*n.* occhiata furtiva *f.* ~**-hole** *n.* spiraglio *m.*

peep[2] /piːp/ *v.i.* (*cheep*) pigolare. —*n.* pigolio *m.*

peer[1] /pɪə(r)/ *v.i.* ~ **at** scrutare.

peer[2] /pɪə(r)/ *n.* pari *m.* ~**age** *n.* pari *m.pl.*

peeved /piːvd/ *a.* (*sl.*) irritato.

peevish /'piːvɪʃ/ *a.* stizzoso.

peg /peg/ *n.* piolo *m.*; (*for clothes*) molletta *f.* —*v.t.* (*p.t.* **pegged**) stabilizzare. **off the** ~ confezionato. ~ **away** sgobbare.

pejorative /pɪ'dʒɒrətɪv/ *a.* peggiorativo.

pelican /'pelɪkən/ *n.* pellicano *m.* ~ **crossing** *n.* passaggio pedonale controllato *m.*

pellet /'pelɪt/ *n.* pallottolina *f.*; (*for gun*) pallottola *f.*

pelt[1] /pelt/ *n.* pelle (di animale da pelliccia) *f.*

pelt[2] /pelt/ *v.t.* colpire. —*v.i.* (*of rain etc.*) cadere violentemente.

pelvis /'pelvɪs/ *n.* bacino *m.*

pen[1] /pen/ *n.* (*enclosure*) recinto *m.*

pen[2] /pen/ *n.* penna *f.* ~**-name** *n.* pseudonimo *m.*

penal /'piːnl/ *a.* penale. ~**ize** *v.t.* penalizzare.

penalty /'penltɪ/ *n.* penalità *f.*; (*fine*) multa *f.* ~ **kick** *n.* (*football*) calcio di rigore *m.*

penance /'penəns/ *n.* penitenza *f.*

pence /pens/ *see* **penny.**

pencil /'pensl/ *n.* matita *f.* —*v.t.* (*p.t.* **pencilled**) segnare a matita. ~**-sharpener** *n.* temperamatite *m. invar.*

pendant /'pendənt/ *n.* ciondolo *m.*

pending /'pendɪŋ/ *a.* in sospeso. —*prep.* in attesa di.

pendulum /'pendjʊləm/ *n.* pendolo *m.*

penetrat|e /'penɪtreɪt/ *v.t.*/*i.* penetrare. ~**ing** *a.* perspicace; (*of sound*) penetrante. ~**ion** /-'treɪʃn/ *n.* penetrazione *f.*

penguin /'peŋgwɪn/ *n.* pinguino *m.*

penicillin /penɪ'sɪlɪn/ *n.* penicillina *f.*

peninsula /pə'nɪnsjʊlə/ *n.* penisola *f.*

penis /'piːnɪs/ *n.* pene *m.*

peniten|t /'penɪtənt/ *a.* & *n.* penitente *m.*/*f.* ~**ce** *n.* penitenza *f.*

penitentiary /penɪ'tenʃərɪ/ *n.* (*Amer.*) penitenziario *m.*

penknife /'pennaɪf/ *n.* (*pl.* **penknives**) temperino *m.*

pennant /'penənt/ *n.* banderuola *f.*

penniless /'penɪlɪs/ *a.* senza un soldo.

penny /'penɪ/ *n.* (*pl.* **pennies** *or* **pence**) penny *m.* (*pl.* pence).

pension /'penʃn/ *n.* pensione *f.* —*v.t.* ~ **off** mettere in pensione. ~**able** *a.* pensionabile. ~**er** *n.* pensionato, a *m.*, *f.*

pensive /'pensɪv/ *a.* pensoso.

pent-up /pent'ʌp/ *a.* contenuto.

pentagon /'pentəgən/ *n.* pentagono *m.*

Pentecost /'pentɪkɒst/ *n.* Pentecoste *f.*

penthouse /'penthaʊs/ *n.* attico *m.*

penultimate /pen'ʌltɪmət/ *a.* penultimo.

penury /'penjʊərɪ/ *n.* penuria *f.*

peony /'pɪənɪ/ *n.* peonia *f.*

people /'piːpl/ *n.pl.* persone *f.pl.*, gente *f.s.*; (*citizens*) popolo *m.s.* —*v.t.* popolare. **my** ~ (*fam.*) i miei *m.pl.* ~ **say** si dice.

pep /pep/ *n.* vigore *m.* ~ **talk** discorso d'incoraggiamento *m.* —*v.t.* ~ **up** ravvivare.

pepper /'pepə(r)/ *n.* pepe *m.*; (*vegetable*) peperone *m.* —*v.t.* pepare. ~**y** *a.* pepato.

peppercorn /'pepəkɔːn/ *n.* grano di pepe *m.* ~ **rent** affitto nominale *m.*

peppermint /'pepəmɪnt/ *n.* menta piperita *f.*; (*sweet*) caramella di menta *f.*

per /pɜː(r)/ *prep.* per. ~ **annum** all'anno. ~ **head** a testa.

perceive /pə'siːv/ *v.t.* percepire; (*notice*) accorgersi di.

percentage /pə'sentɪdʒ/ *n.* percentuale *f.*

perceptible /pə'septəbl/ *a.* percettibile.

percept|ion /pə'sepʃn/ *n.* percezione *f.* ~**ive** *a.* perspicace.

perch /pɜːtʃ/ *n.* posatoio *m.* —*v.i.* appollaiarsi.

percolat|e /'pɜːkəleɪt/ *v.t.* filtrare. —*v.i.* infiltrarsi. ~**or** *n.* macchinetta per il caffè *f.*

percussion /pə'kʌʃn/ *n.* percussione *f.*

peremptory /pə'remptərɪ/ *a.* perentorio.

perennial /pə'renɪəl/ *a.* perenne. —*n.* pianta perenne *f.*

perfect[1] /'pɜːfɪkt/ *a.* perfetto. ~**ly** *adv.* perfettamente.

perfect[2] /pə'fekt/ *v.t.* perfezionare. ~**ion** /-ʃn/ *n.* perfezione *f.* **to** ~**ion** alla perfezione. ~**ionist** *n.* perfezionista *m./f.*

perforat|e /'pɜːfəreɪt/ *v.t.* perforare. ~**ion** /-'reɪʃn/ *n.* perforazione *f.*

perform /pə'fɔːm/ *v.t.* compiere, fare; (*theatr.*) recitare; (*operation*) eseguire. ~**ance** *n.* esecuzione *f.*; (*theatr.*) rappresentazione *f.*; (*of car*) rendimento *m.*; (*fam.*, *behaviour*) traffico *m.* ~**er** *n.* artista *m./f.*

perfume /'pɜːfjuːm/ *n.* profumo *m.* ~**ry** /-'fjuːmərɪ/ *n.* profumeria *f.*

perfunctory /pə'fʌŋktərɪ/ *a.* superficiale.

perhaps /pə'hæps/ *adv.* forse.

peril /'perəl/ *n.* pericolo *m.* ~**ous** *a.* rischioso.

perimeter /pə'rɪmɪtə(r)/ *n.* perimetro *m.*

period /'pɪərɪəd/ *n.* periodo *m.*; (*schol.*) lezione *f.*; (*gram.*) punto fermo *m.* —*a.* d'epoca. ~**ic** /-'ɒdɪk/ *a.* periodico. ~**ically** /-'ɒdɪklɪ/ *adv.* periodicamente.

periodical /pɪərɪ'ɒdɪkl/ *n.* rivista *f.*

peripher|y /pə'rɪfərɪ/ *n.* periferia *f.* ~**al** *a.* periferico.

periscope /'perɪskəʊp/ *n.* periscopio *m.*

perish /'perɪʃ/ *v.i.* perire; (*rot*) deteriorare. ~**able** *a.* deteriorabile. ~**ing** *a.* (*fam.*) da morire.

perjur|e /'pɜːdʒə(r)/ *v.r.* ~**e o.s.** spergiurare. ~**y** *n.* spergiuro *m.*

perk[1] /pɜːk/ *v.t./i.* ~ **up** rianimare, rianimarsi. ~**y** *a.* baldanzoso.

perk[2] /pɜːk/ *n.* (*fam.*) gratifica *f.*

perm /pɜːm/ *n.* permanente *f.* —*v.t.* fare la permanente a.

permanen|t /'pɜːmənənt/ *a.* permanente. ~**ce** *n.* permanenza *f.* ~**tly** *adv.* permanentemente.

permeable /'pɜːmɪəbl/ *a.* permeabile.

permeate /'pɜːmɪeɪt/ *v.t.* impregnare.

permissible /pə'mɪsəbl/ *a.* tollerabile.

permission /pə'mɪʃn/ *n.* permesso *m.*

permissive /pə'mɪsɪv/ *a.* indulgente. ~ **society** società permissiva *f.* ~**ness** *n.* rilassatezza *f.*

permit[1] /pə'mɪt/ *v.t.* (*p.t.* **permitted**) permettere.

permit[2] /'pɜːmɪt/ *n.* permesso *m.*

permutation /pɜːmjuː'teɪʃn/ *n.* permutazione *f.*

pernicious /pə'nɪʃəs/ *a.* pernicioso.

peroxide /pə'rɒksaɪd/ *n.* acqua ossigenata *f.*

perpendicular /pɜːpən'dɪkjʊlə(r)/ *a.* & *n.* perpendicolare *f.*

perpetrat|e /'pɜːpɪtreɪt/ *v.t.* perpetrare. ~**or** *n.* autore *m.*

perpetual /pə'petʃʊəl/ *a.* perpetuo.

perpetuat|e /pə'petʃʊeɪt/ *v.t.* perpetuare. ~**ion** /-'eɪʃn/ *n.* perpetuazione *f.*

perplex /pə'pleks/ *v.t.* rendere perplesso. ~**ed** *a.* perplesso. ~**ing** *a.* che confonde. ~**ity** *n.* perplessità *f.*

persecut|e /'pɜːsɪkjuːt/ *v.t.* perseguitare. ~**ion** /-'kjuːʃn/ *n.* persecuzione *f.*

persever|e /pɜːsɪ'vɪə(r)/ *v.i.* perseverare. ~**ance** *n.* perseveranza *f.*

Persian /'pɜːʃn/ *a.* & *n.* (*lang.*) persiano *m.* **the** ~ **Gulf** *n.* il Golfo Persico *m.*

persist /pə'sɪst/ *v.i.* persistere (**in**, a). ~**ence** *n.* persistenza *f.* ~**ent** *a.* persistente; (*persevering*) insistente. ~**ently** *adv.* persistentemente.

person /'pɜːsn/ *n.* persona *f.*

personal /'pɜːsənl/ *a.* personale. ~**ly** *adv.* personalmente.

personality /pɜːsə'nælətɪ/ *n.* personalità *f.*; (*on TV*) personaggio *m.*

personify /pə'sɒnɪfaɪ/ *v.t.* personificare.

personnel /pɜːsə'nel/ *n.* personale *m.*

perspective /pə'spektɪv/ *n.* prospettiva *f.*

perspicacious /pɜːspɪ'keɪʃəs/ *a.* perspicace.

perspir|e /pəs'paɪə(r)/ *v.i.* sudare. ~**ation** /-ə'reɪʃn/ *n.* sudore *m.*

persua|de /pə'sweɪd/ *v.t.* persuadere. ~**sion** *n.* persuasione *f.*

persuasive /pə'sweɪsɪv/ *a.* persuasivo. ~**ly** *adv.* persuasivamente.

pert /pɜːt/ *a.* sfacciato; (*Amer.*) sveglio. ~**ly** *adv.* sfacciatamente.

pertain /pə'teɪn/ *v.i.* ~ **to** appartenere a.

pertinent /'pɜːtɪnənt/ *a.* pertinente. ~**ly** *adv.* pertinentemente.

perturb /pə'tɜːb/ *v.t.* perturbare.

Peru /pə'ruː/ *n.* Perù *m.* ~**vian** *a.* & *n.* peruviano, a *m.*, *f.*

perus|e /pə'ruːz/ *v.t.* leggere attentamente. ~**al** *n.* lettura attenta *f.*

perva|de /pə'veɪd/ *v.t.* pervadere. ~**sive** *a.* pervasivo.

perverse 369 **pick**

perverse /pə'vɜːs/ *a.* perverso; (*of behaviour*) irrazionale. ~**ity** *n.* perversità *f.*

perver|t¹ /pə'vɜːt/ *v.t.* pervertire. ~**sion** *n.* perversione *f.*

pervert² /'pɜːvɜːt/ *n.* pervertito, a *m., f.*

pessimis|t /'pesɪmɪst/ *n.* pessimista *m./f.* ~**m** /-zəm/ *n.* pessimismo *m.* ~**tic** /-'mɪstɪk/ *a.* pessimistico.

pest /pest/ *n.* insetto nocivo *m.*; (*person*) peste *f.*

pester /'pestə(r)/ *v.t.* importunare.

pesticide /'pestɪsaɪd/ *n.* insetticida *m.*

pet /pet/ *n.* animale domestico *m.*; (*favourite*) prediletto, a *m., f. —a.* preferito. —*v.t.* (*p.t.* **petted**) coccolare. ~ **name** vezzeggiativo *m.*

petal /'petl/ *n.* petalo *m.*

peter /'piːtə(r)/ *v.i.* ~ **out** esaurirsi.

petite /pə'tiːt/ *a.* (*of woman*) minuta.

petition /pɪ'tɪʃn/ *n.* petizione *f. —v.t.* fare una petizione.

petrify /'petrɪfaɪ/ *v.t./i.* pietrificare, pietrificarsi.

petrol /'petrəl/ *n.* benzina *f.* ~ **station** *n.* stazione di rifornimento *f.*

petroleum /pɪ'trəʊliəm/ *n.* petrolio *m.*

petticoat /'petɪkəʊt/ *n.* sottoveste *f.*

pett|y /'petɪ/ *a.* (**-ier, -iest**) insignificante; (*mean*) meschino. ~**y cash** *n.* piccola cassa *f.* ~**y officer** *n.* sottufficiale di marina *m.* ~**iness** *n.* meschinità *f.*

petulan|t /'petjʊlənt/ *a.* petulante. ~**ce** *n.* petulanza *f.*

pew /pjuː/ *n.* banco (di chiesa) *m.*

pewter /'pjuːtə(r)/ *n.* peltro *m.*

phallic /'fælɪk/ *a.* fallico.

phantom /'fæntəm/ *n.* fantasma *m.*

pharmaceutical /fɑːmə'sjuːtɪkl/ *a.* farmaceutico.

pharmac|y /'fɑːməsɪ/ *n.* farmacia *f.* ~**ist** *n.* farmacista *m./f.*

pharyngitis /færɪn'dʒaɪtɪs/ *n.* faringite *f.*

phase /feɪz/ *n.* fase *f. —v.t.* ~ **in**/ **out** introdurre/eliminare gradualmente.

Ph.D. *abbr. of* **Doctor of Philosophy** *n.* dottorato di ricerca *m.*

pheasant /'feznt/ *n.* fagiano *m.*

phenomen|on /fɪ'nɒmɪnən/ *n.* (*pl.* **-a**) fenomeno *m.* ~**al** *a.* fenomenale.

phew /fjuː/ *int.* perbacco!

phial /'faɪəl/ *n.* fiala *f.*

philanderer /fɪ'lændərə(r)/ *n.* donnaiolo *m.*

philanthrop|ist /fɪ'lænθrəpɪst/ *n.*

filantropo, a *m., f.* ~**ic** /-ən'θrɒpɪk/ *a.* filantropico.

philatel|y /fɪ'lætəlɪ/ *n.* filatelia *f.* ~**ist** *n.* filatelico, a *m., f.*

philharmonic /fɪlɑː'mɒnɪk/ *a.* filarmonico.

Philippines /'fɪlɪpiːnz/ *n.pl.* (isole) Filippine *f.pl.*

philistine /'fɪlɪstaɪn/ *a.* & *n.* filisteo, a *m., f.*

philosoph|y /fɪ'lɒsəfɪ/ *n.* filosofia *f.* ~**er** *n.* filosofo, a *m., f.* ~**ical** /-ə'sɒfɪkl/ *a.* filosofico.

phlegm /flem/ *n.* flemma *f.*

phlegmatic /fleg'mætɪk/ *a.* flemmatico.

phobia /'fəʊbɪə/ *n.* fobia *f.*

phone /fəʊn/ *n.* (*fam.*) telefono *m.* —*v.t./i.* telefonare. ~ **back** richiamare. ~ **box** *n.* cabina telefonica *f.*

phonetic /fə'netɪk/ *a.* fonetico. ~**s** *n.* fonetica *f.*

phoney /'fəʊnɪ/ *a.* (**-ier, -iest**) (*sl.*) falso. —*n.* (*sl.*) impostore *m.*

phosphate /'fɒsfeɪt/ *n.* fosfato *m.*

phosphorous /'fɒsfərəs/ *n.* fosforo *m.*

photo /'fəʊtəʊ/ *n.* (*pl.* **-os**) (*fam.*) foto *f.*

photocopy /'fəʊtəʊkɒpɪ/ *n.* fotocopia *f.* —*v.t.* fotocopiare.

photogenic /fəʊtəʊ'dʒenɪk/ *a.* fotogenico.

photograph /'fəʊtəgrɑːf/ *n.* fotografia *f.* —*v.t.* fotografare. ~**er** /fə'tɒgrəfə(r)/ *n.* fotografo, a *m., f.* ~**ic** /-'græfɪk/ *a.* fotografico. ~**y** /fə'tɒgrəfɪ/ *n.* fotografia *f.*

phrase /freɪz/ *n.* espressione *f. —v.t.* esprimere. ~**-book** *n.* libro di fraseologia *m.*

physical /'fɪzɪkl/ *a.* fisico.

physician /fɪ'zɪʃn/ *n.* medico *m.*

physicist /'fɪzɪsɪst/ *n.* fisico, a *m., f.*

physics /'fɪzɪks/ *n.* fisica *f.*

physiology /fɪzɪ'ɒlədʒɪ/ *n.* fisiologia *f.*

physiotherap|y /fɪzɪəʊ'θerəpɪ/ *n.* fisioterapia *f.* ~**ist** *n.* fisioterapista *m./f.*

physique /fɪ'ziːk/ *n.* fisico *m.*

pian|o /pɪ'ænəʊ/ *n.* (*pl.* **-os**) piano *m.* ~**ist** /'pɪənɪst/ *n.* pianista *m./f.*

pick¹ /pɪk/ *n.* piccone *m.*

pick² /pɪk/ *v.t.* scegliere; (*flowers etc.*) cogliere; (*a lock*) forzare; (*dig*) scavare; (*pockets*) borseggiare. —*n.* scelta *f.* ~ **a quarrel** attaccar lite. ~ **holes in** trovar da ridire su. ~ **on** *v.t.* (*nag*) punzecchiare. ~ **out** *v.t.* (*identify*) individuare; (*colour*) mettere in risalto. ~ **up** *v.t.* sollevare;

(*learn*) imparare; (*information*) raccogliere; (*passenger, habit, etc.*) prendere; (*illness*) contrarre; ~ o.s. up *v.i.* riprendersi. ~-up *n.* conoscenza casuale *f.*; (*truck*) furgone *m.*; (*stylusholder*) pick-up *m.*

pickaxe /ˈpɪkæks/ *n.* picco *m.*

picket /ˈpɪkɪt/ *n.* picchetto *m.* −*v.t./i.* picchettare. ~ **line** *n.* controllo del picchetto *m.*

pickle /ˈpɪkl/ *n.* salamoia *f.* ~s *n.pl.* sottaceti *m.pl.* −*v.t.* mettere sottaceto. **in a** ~ (*fam.*) nei guai.

pickpocket /ˈpɪkpɒkɪt/ *n.* borsaiolo *m.*

picnic /ˈpɪknɪk/ *n.* picnic *m.* −*v.i.* (*p.t.* **picnicked**) fare un picnic.

pictorial /pɪkˈtɔːrɪəl/ *a.* illustrato.

picture /ˈpɪktʃə(r)/ *n.* (*painting*) quadro *m.*; (*photo*) fotografia *f.*; (*drawing*) disegno *m.*; (*beautiful thing*) cosa meravigliosa *f.*; (*fig.*) descrizione *f.*; (*film*) film *m.* **the** ~**s** il cinema. −*v.t.* ritrarre; (*imagine*) immaginare.

picturesque /pɪktʃəˈresk/ *a.* pittoresco.

piddling /ˈpɪdlɪŋ/ *a.* (*fam.*) insignificante.

pidgin /ˈpɪdʒɪn/ *a.* ~ **English** inglese corrotto.

pie /paɪ/ *n.* crostata *f.*

piebald /ˈpaɪbɔːld/ *a.* pezzato.

piece /piːs/ *n.* pezzo *m.*; (*coin*) moneta *f.*; (*in game*) pedina *f.* −*v.t.* mettere assieme. **a** ~ **of news/advice** una notizia/un consiglio. ~-**work** *n.* lavoro a cottimo *m.* **take to** ~**s** smontare.

piecemeal /ˈpiːsmiːl/ *a. & adv.* pezzo a pezzo.

pier /pɪə(r)/ *n.* molo *m.*

pierc|e /pɪəs/ *v.t.* perforare. ~**ing** *a.* penetrante.

piety /ˈpaɪətɪ/ *n.* pietà *f.*

piffl|e /ˈpɪfl/ *n.* (*sl.*) sciocchezza *f.* ~**ing** *a.* (*sl.*) futile.

pig /pɪg/ *n.* maiale *m.* ~-**headed** *a.* ostinato.

pigeon /ˈpɪdʒɪn/ *n.* piccione *m.* ~-**hole** *n.* casella *f.*

piggy /ˈpɪgɪ/ *a.* (*fam.*) ingordo. ~-**back** *adv.* sulle spalle. ~ **bank** *n.* salvadanaio *m.*

pigment /ˈpɪgmənt/ *n.* pigmento *m.* ~**ation** /-ˈteɪʃn/ *n.* pigmentazione *f.*

pigskin /ˈpɪgskɪn/ *n.* pelle di cinghiale *f.*

pigsty /ˈpɪgstaɪ/ *n.* porcile *m.*

pigtail /ˈpɪgteɪl/ *n.* codino *m.*; (*plait*) treccia *f.*

pike /paɪk/ *n. invar.* (*fish*) luccio *m.*; (*shaft*) picca *f.*

pilchard /ˈpɪltʃəd/ *n.* sardella *f.*

pile¹ /paɪl/ *n.* mucchio *m.* −*v.t.* ~ **up** accatastare; *v.i.* ammucchiarsi. ~ **it on** esagerare. ~-**up** *n.* tamponamento a catena *m.*

pile² /paɪl/ *n.* (*of fabric*) pelo *m.*

piles /paɪlz/ *n.pl.* emorroidi *f.pl.*

pilfer /ˈpɪlfə(r)/ *v.t./i.* rubacchiare. ~**age** *n.* furto *m.* ~**ing** *n.* rubacchiare *m.*

pilgrim /ˈpɪlgrɪm/ *n.* pellegrino *m.* ~**age** *n.* pellegrinaggio *m.*

pill /pɪl/ *n.* pillola *f.*

pillage /ˈpɪlɪdʒ/ *n.* saccheggio *m.* −*v.t.* saccheggiare.

pillar /ˈpɪlə(r)/ *n.* pilastro *m.* ~-**box** *n.* buca delle lettere *f.*

pillion /ˈpɪlɪən/ *n.* sellino posteriore *m.* **ride** ~ viaggiare sul sellino posteriore.

pillory /ˈpɪlərɪ/ *n.* berlina *f.*

pillow /ˈpɪləʊ/ *n.* cuscino *m.*

pillowcase /ˈpɪləʊkeɪs/ *n.* federa *f.*

pilot /ˈpaɪlət/ *n.* pilota *m./f.* −*v.t.* pilotare. ~-**light** *n.* lampada spia *f.*

pimp /pɪmp/ *n.* sfruttatore *m.*

pimple /ˈpɪmpl/ *n.* foruncolo *m.*

pin /pɪn/ *n.* spillo *m.*; (*mech.*) perno *m.* −*v.t.* (*p.t.* **pinned**) appuntare; (*hold down*) immobilizzare; (*fix*) fermare. ~ **s.o. down to** costringere qcno. a. ~-**point** *v.t.* definire con precisione. ~**s and needles** formicolio *m.* ~-**stripe** *a.* righettato. ~ **up** puntare; (*on wall*) affiggere. ~-**up** *n.* (*fam.*) ragazza da copertina *f.*

pinafore /ˈpɪnəfɔː(r)/ *n.* grembiulino *m.* ~ **dress** *n.* scamiciato *m.*

pincers /ˈpɪnsəz/ *n.pl.* tenaglie *f.pl.*

pinch /pɪntʃ/ *v.t.* pizzicare; (*steal, sl.*) rubare; (*arrest, sl.*) arrestare. −*v.i.* (*shoe*) stringere. −*n.* pizzicotto *m.*; (*small amount*) presa *f.* **at a** ~ in caso di bisogno.

pincushion /ˈpɪnkʊʃn/ *n.* puntaspilli *m. invar.*

pine¹ /paɪn/ *n.* pino *m.*

pine² /paɪn/ *v.i.* ~ **away** struggersi. ~ **for** desiderare ardentemente.

pineapple /ˈpaɪnæpl/ *n.* ananas *m. invar.*

ping /pɪŋ/ *n.* colpo secco *m.*

ping-pong /ˈpɪŋpɒŋ/ *n.* pingpong *m.*

pinion /ˈpɪnjən/ *v.t.* immobilizzare.

pink /pɪŋk/ *a. & n.* rosa *m.*

pinnacle /'pɪnəkl/ *n.* pinnacolo *m.*

pint /paɪnt/ *n.* pinta *f.* (= *0.57 litre*).

pioneer /paɪə'nɪə(r)/ *n.* pioniere, a *m.*, *f.* −*v.t.* fare da pioniere.

pious /'paɪəs/ *a.* pio.

pip[1] /pɪp/ *n.* (*seed*) seme *m.*

pip[2] /pɪp/ *n.* (*sound*) pip *m.*

pip[3] /pɪp/ *n.* (*on uniform*) stelletta *f.*

pipe /paɪp/ *n.* tubo *m.*; (*mus.*) piffero *m.*; (*for smoking*) pipa *f.* −*v.t.* far arrivare con tubature; (*naut.*) chiamare col fischio; (*music etc.*) trasmettere per filo. **~-cleaner** *n.* nettapipe *m. invar.* **~ down** (*fam.*) abbassare il tono della voce. **~-dream** *n.* illusione *f.* **~r** *n.* suonatore di piffero *m.*

pipeline /'paɪplaɪn/ *n.* conduttura *f.* **in the ~** in preparazione.

piping /'paɪpɪŋ/ *n.* tubatura *f.* **~ hot** caldo bollente.

piquant /'piːkənt/ *a.* piccante.

pique /piːk/ *n.* picca *f.*

piqué /'piːkeɪ/ *n.* picché *m.*

pira|te /'paɪərət/ *n.* pirata *m.* **~cy** *n.* pirateria *f.*

pirouette /pɪru'et/ *n.* piroetta *f.* −*v.i.* piroettare.

Pisces /'paɪsiːz/ *n.* (*astr.*) Pesci *m.pl.*

pistol /'pɪstl/ *n.* pistola *f.*

piston /'pɪstən/ *n.* pistone *m.*

pit /pɪt/ *n.* fossa *f.*; (*mine*) miniera *f.*; (*theatr.*) platea *f.*; (*of stomach*) bocca *f.* −*v.t.* (*p.t.* **pitted**) butterare; (*fig.*) opporre. **~ o.s. against** opporsi a.

pitch[1] /pɪtʃ/ *n.* pece *f.* **~-black** *a.* nero come la pece.

pitch[2] /pɪtʃ/ *v.t.* erigere. −*v.i.* precipitare. −*n.* posteggio *m.*; (*of voice*) tono *m.*; (*of sound*) altezza *f.*; (*sport*) campo *m.*; (*fig.*) grado *m.* **~ed battle** *n.* battaglia campale *f.* **~ in** (*fam.*) contribuire. **~ into** (*fam.*) dar addosso.

pitcher /'pɪtʃə(r)/ *n.* brocca *f.*

pitchfork /'pɪtʃfɔːk/ *n.* forca *f.*

piteous /'pɪtɪəs/ *a.* pietoso.

pitfall /'pɪtfɔːl/ *n.* trappola *f.*

pith /pɪθ/ *n.* (*of orange, lemon*) interno della buccia *m.*; (*fig.*) essenza *f.*

pithy /'pɪθɪ/ *a.* (**-ier, -iest**) conciso.

piti|ful /'pɪtɪfl/ *a.* pietoso. **~less** *a.* spietato.

pittance /'pɪtns/ *n.* compenso esiguo *m.*

pity /'pɪtɪ/ *n.* pietà *f.*; (*regret*) peccato *m.* −*v.t.* aver pietà (di).

pivot /'pɪvət/ *n.* perno. −*v.t./i.* imperniare, imperniarsi.

pixie /'pɪksɪ/ *n.* folletto *m.*

placard /'plækɑːd/ *n.* cartellone *m.*

placate /plə'keɪt/ *v.t.* placare.

place /pleɪs/ *n.* posto *m.*; (*duty*) compito *m.*; (*in book*) segno *m.*; (*house, fam.*) casa *f.* −*v.t.* collocare; (*in competition*) classificare; (*remember*) identificare; (*an order*) dare. **be ~d** (*in race*) essere classificato ai primi posti. **~-mat** *n.* sottopiatto *m.* **take ~** aver luogo.

placement /'pleɪsmənt/ *n.* collocamento *m.*

placid /'plæsɪd/ *a.* placido.

plagiar|ize /'pleɪdʒəraɪz/ *v.t.* plagiare. **~ism** *n.* plagio *m.*

plague /pleɪɡ/ *n.* peste *f.* −*v.t.* tormentare.

plaice /pleɪs/ *n. invar.* pianuzza *f.*

plaid /plæd/ *n.* plaid *m. invar.*

plain /pleɪn/ *a.* (**-er, -est**) chiaro; (*simple*) semplice; (*not pretty*) scialbo. −*adv.* chiaramente. −*n.* pianura *f.* **in ~ clothes** in borghese. **~ly** *adv.* francamente. **~ness** *n.* chiarezza *f.*

plaintiff /'pleɪntɪf/ *n.* parte lesa *f.*

plait /plæt/ *v.t.* intrecciare. −*n.* treccia *f.*

plan /plæn/ *n.* progetto *m.*, piano *m.* −*v.t.* (*p.t.* **planned**) progettare.

plane[1] /pleɪn/ *n.* (*tree*) platano *m.*

plane[2] /pleɪn/ *n.* (*level*) piano *m.*; (*aeron.*) aeroplano *m.*

plane[3] /pleɪn/ *n.* (*tool*) pialla *f.* −*v.t.* piallare.

planet /'plænɪt/ *n.* pianeta *m.* **~ary** *a.* planetario.

plank /plæŋk/ *n.* asse *f.*

planning /'plænɪŋ/ *n.* pianificazione *f.* **family ~** *n.* controllo delle nascite *m.* **town ~** *n.* urbanistica *f.*

plant /plɑːnt/ *n.* pianta *f.*; (*mech.*) impianto *m.*; (*factory*) stabilimento *m.* −*v.t.* piantare; (*place in position*) mettere.

plantation /plæn'teɪʃn/ *n.* piantagione *f.*

plaque /plɑːk/ *n.* placca *f.*

plasma /'plæzmə/ *n.* plasma *m.*

plaster /'plɑːstə(r)/ *n.* intonaco *m.*; (*adhesive*) impiastro *m.* **~ of Paris** *n.* gesso *m.* −*v.t.* intonacare; (*med.*) ingessare; (*cover*) ricoprire. **~ed** *a.* (*fam.*) ubriaco.

plastic /'plæstɪk/ *a.* plastico. −*n.*

plastica *f.* ~ **surgery** chirurgia plastica *f.*

Plasticine /'plæstɪsiːn/ *n.* (*P.*) Plastilina *f.*

plate /pleɪt/ *n.* piatto *m.*; (*of metal*) placca *f.*; (*gold and silverware*) argenteria *f.*; (*in book*) tavola fuori testo *f.* —*v.t.* (*cover with metal*) placcare. ~**ful** *n.* (*pl.* **-fuls**) piatto *m.*

plateau /'plætəʊ/ *n.* (*pl.* **plateaux**) *n.* altopiano *m.*

platform /'plætfɔːm/ *n.* piattaforma *f.*; (*rail.*) marciapiede *m.*

platinum /'plætɪnəm/ *n.* platino *m.*

platitude /'plætɪtjuːd/ *n.* luogo comune *m.*

platonic /plə'tɒnɪk/ *a.* platonico.

platoon /plə'tuːn/ *n.* plotone *m.*

platter /'plætə(r)/ *n.* piatto (grande) *m.*

plausible /'plɔːzəbl/ *a.* plausibile.

play /pleɪ/ *v.t./i.* giocare (a); (*act*) recitare (una parte); (*instrument*) suonare. —*n.* gioco *m.*; (*theatr.*) lavoro teatrale *m.*, commedia *f.*; (*free movement*) libertà di movimento *f.* ~**-act** *v.i.* fingere. ~ **down** *v.t.* minimizzare. ~**-group** *n.* asilo-nido *m.* ~ **on** *v.t.* approfittare di. ~ **on words** *n.* gioco di parole *m.* ~**ed out** sfinito. ~**-pen** *n.* recinto *m.* ~ **safe** non prendere rischi. ~**thing** *n.* giocattolo *m.* ~ **up** *v.i.* (*fam.*) comportarsi male. ~**er** *n.* gioca|tore, -trice *m.*, *f.*

playboy /'pleɪbɔɪ/ *n.* playboy *m.*

playful /'pleɪfl/ *a.* scherzoso. ~**ly** *adv.* scherzosamente.

playground /'pleɪgraʊnd/ *n.* cortile (per la ricreazione) *m.*

playing /'pleɪɪŋ/ *n.* gioco *m.* ~**-card** *n.* carta da gioco *f.* ~**-field** *n.* campo da gioco *m.*

playmate /'pleɪmeɪt/ *n.* compagno, a di gioco *m.*, *f.*

playwright /'pleɪraɪt/ *n.* drammaturgo, a *m.*, *f.*

plc (*abbr. of* **public limited company**) *n.* società anonima *f.*

plea /pliː/ *n.* richiesta *f.*; (*excuse*) scusa *f.*; (*jurid.*) difesa *f.*

plead /pliːd/ *v.t./i.* dichiararsi; (*jurid.*) perorare; (*as excuse*) scusarsi. ~ **with** implorare.

pleasant /'pleznt/ *a.* piacevole.

pleas|e /pliːz/ *v.t.* far piacere (a). —*v.i.* **do as you** ~**e** fa come vuoi. —*adv.* per favore, prego. ~**e oneself** fare il proprio comodo. ~**ed** *a.* lieto. ~**ed with** contento di. ~**ing** *a.* piacevole.

pleasur|e /'pleʒə(r)/ *n.* piacere *m.* ~**able** *a.* gradevole.

pleat /pliːt/ *n.* piega *f.* —*v.t.* pieghettare.

plebiscite /'plebɪsɪt/ *n.* plebiscito *m.*

plectrum /'plektrəm/ *n.* plettro *m.*

pledge /pledʒ/ *n.* pegno *m.*; (*promise*) promessa *f.* —*v.t.* impegnare; promettere.

plentiful /'plentɪfl/ *a.* abbondante.

plenty /'plentɪ/ *n.* abbondanza *f.* ~ (**of**) molto, un sacco di.

pleurisy /'plʊərəsɪ/ *n.* pleurite *f.*

pliable /'plaɪəbl/ *a.* flessibile.

pliers /'plaɪəz/ *n.pl.* pinze *f.pl.*

plight /plaɪt/ *n.* situazione difficile *f.*

plimsolls /'plɪmsəlz/ *n.pl.* scarpe di tela *f.pl.*

plinth /plɪnθ/ *n.* plinto *m.*

plod /plɒd/ *v.i.* (*p.t.* **plodded**) camminare faticosamente; (*work hard*) sgobbare. ~**der** *n.* sgobbone, a *m.*, *f.*

plonk /plɒŋk/ *n.* (*sl.*) vino ordinario *m.*

plop /plɒp/ *n.* tonfo *m.* —*v.i.* (*p.t.* **plopped**) cadere con un tonfo.

plot /plɒt/ *n.* complotto *m.*; (*of novel etc.*) intreccio *m.*; (*piece of land*) appezzamento *m.* —*v.t./i.* (*p.t.* **plotted**) complottare; (*mark out*) tracciare.

plough /plaʊ/ *n.* aratro *m.* —*v.t./i.* arare. ~ **through** procedere a fatica.

ploy /plɔɪ/ *n.* (*fam.*) manovra *f.*

pluck /plʌk/ *v.t.* strappare; (*eyebrows*) depilare; (*bird*) spennare; (*flowers*) cogliere. —*n.* coraggio *m.* ~ **up courage** farsi coraggio. ~**y** *a.* (**-ier**, **-iest**) coraggioso.

plug /plʌg/ *n.* tappo *m.*; (*electr.*) spina *f.* —*v.t./i.* (*p.t.* **plugged**) tappare; (*fam.*, *advertise*) pubblicizzare con insistenza. ~ **in** (*electr.*) inserire la spina.

plum /plʌm/ *n.* prugna *f.*; (*tree*) prugno *m.* ~ **job** *n.* (*fam.*) posto eccellente *m.* ~ **pudding** *n.* budino natalizio *m.*

plumage /'pluːmɪdʒ/ *n.* piume *f.pl.*

plumb /plʌm/ *a.* verticale. —*n.* piombino *m.* —*adv.* esattamente. —*v.t.* misurare la profondità di.

plumb|er /'plʌmə(r)/ *n.* idraulico *m.* ~**ing** *n.* impianto idraulico *m.*

plume /pluːm/ *n.* piuma *f.*

plummet /'plʌmɪt/ *n.* piombino *m.* —*v.i.* cadere a piombo.

plummy /'plʌmɪ/ *a.* (**-ier**, **-iest**) (*of voice*) affettata.

plump /plʌmp/ *a.* (**-er**, **-est**) paffuto.

—v.t. ~ **for** scegliere. ~**ness** n.
paffutezza f.
plunder /'plʌndə(r)/ n. preda f. —v.t.
saccheggiare.
plung|e /plʌndʒ/ v.t./i. tuffare, tuf-
farsi. —n. tuffo m. ~**er** n. (mech.)
stantuffo m. ~**ing** a. (neckline) profondo.
plural /'plʊərəl/ a. & n. plurale m.
plus /plʌs/ prep. più. —a. & adv. in
più. —n. più m. **five** ~ più di cinque.
~**-fours** n.pl. pantaloni alla zuava
m.pl.
plush /plʌʃ/ n. felpa f. —a. lussuoso.
~**y** a. elegante.
plutocrat /'plu:təkræt/ n. plutocrate
m.
plutonium /plu:'təʊnjəm/ n. plutonio
m.
ply[1] /plaɪ/ n. (of thread) capo m.; (layer)
spessore m. ~**wood** n. (legno) com-
pensato m.
ply[2] /plaɪ/ v.t. maneggiare; (trade)
esercitare. ~ **s.o. with drink** dare
da bere a qcno. continuamente.
p.m. adv. (abbr. of **post meridiem**)
del pomeriggio.
pneumatic /nju:'mætɪk/ a. pneumatico.
pneumonia /nju:'məʊnjə/ n. pol-
monite f.
P.O. abbr. see **Post Office**.
poach /pəʊtʃ/ v.t. (culin.) cuocere in
camicia; (steal) cacciare/ pescare di
frodo. ~**er** n. bracconiere m.
pocket /'pɒkɪt/ n. tasca f.; (of air) vuoto
m.; (of resistance) sacca f. —v.t. inta-
scare. **be in/out of** ~ guada-
gnarci/rimetterci. ~**-book** n.
taccuino m. ~**-money** n. denaro per
le piccole spese m.
pock-marked /'pɒkmɑ:kt/ a. butte-
rato.
pod /pɒd/ n. guscio m.
podgy /'pɒdʒɪ/ a. (-ier, -iest) grassoccio.
poem /'pəʊɪm/ n. poesia f.
poet /'pəʊɪt/ n. poeta m. ~**ess** n. poe-
tessa f. **P~ Laureate** n. poeta laureato m. ~**ic**, ~**ical** /-'etɪk, -'etɪkl/ adjs.
poetico.
poetry /'pəʊɪtrɪ/ n. poesia f.
poignant /'pɔɪnjənt/ a. vivo, doloroso.
point /pɔɪnt/ n. punto m.; (sharp end)
punta f.; (meaning) senso m.; (electr.)
presa di corrente f. —v.t./i. puntare;
(sharpen) appuntire. **good** ~**s** qualità
f.pl. ~**-blank** a. & adv. a bruciapelo.

~**-duty** n. (of policeman) servizio m.
~ **out** indicare. **to the** ~ pertinente.
up to a ~ fino a un certo punto. **what
is the** ~? a che scopo?
pointed /'pɔɪntɪd/ a. appuntito; (fig.)
evidente.
pointer /'pɔɪntə(r)/ n. indicatore m.;
(dog) pointer m.
pointless /'pɔɪntlɪs/ a. inutile.
poise /pɔɪz/ v.t./i. bilanciare, bilanciarsi. —n. equilibrio m.; (fig.) padronanza di sé f.
poison /'pɔɪzn/ n. veleno m. —v.t. av-
velenare. ~**ous** a. velenoso.
poke /pəʊk/ v.t./i. spingere; (pry)
frugare; (fire) attizzare; (put) ficcare. —n. (piccola) spinta f. ~ **fun at**
farsi beffe di.
poker[1] /'pəʊkə(r)/ n. attizzatoio m.
poker[2] /'pəʊkə(r)/ n. (cards) poker m.
~**-face** n. persona impassibile f.
poky /'pəʊkɪ/ a. (-ier, -iest) angusto.
Pol|and /'pəʊlənd/ n. Polonia f. ~**e** n.
polacco, a m., f.
polar /'pəʊlə(r)/ a. polare. ~ **bear** n.
orso bianco m.
polarize /'pəʊləraɪz/ v.t./i. polarizzare.
pole[1] /pəʊl/ n. palo m.
pole[2] /pəʊl/ n. (geog.) polo m. ~**-star**
n. stella polare f.
polemic /pə'lemɪk/ a. polemico. —n.
polemica f.
police /pə'li:s/ n. polizia f. —v.t. proteggere (con la polizia). ~ **record** n.
fedina penale f. ~ **state** n. stato di
polizia m. ~ **station** n. commis-
sariato m.
police|man /pə'li:smən/ n. (pl. -men)
poliziotto m. ~**woman** /-wʊmən/ n.
(pl. -women) donna poliziotto f.
policy[1] /'pɒlɪsɪ/ n. linea di condotta f.,
politica f.
policy[2] /'pɒlɪsɪ/ n. **insurance** ~
polizza d'assicurazione f.
polio(myelitis) /'pəʊlɪəʊ(maɪə'laɪtɪs)/
n. polio(mielite) f.
polish /'pɒlɪʃ/ n. lucentezza f.; (substance) lucido m.; (fig.) raffinatezza
f. —v.t./i. lucidare. **nail** ~ smalto (per
le unghie) m. ~ **off** finire (in fretta).
~**ed** a. lucido; (of manner) raffinato.
~**er** n. lucidatore m.; (machine) luci-
datrice f.
Polish /'pəʊlɪʃ/ a. polacco. —n. (lang.)
polacco m.
polite /pə'laɪt/ a. cortese. ~**ly** adv.
cortesemente. ~**ness** n. cortesia f.

politic|ian /pɒlɪ'tɪʃn/ *n.* politico *m.*
~**al** /-'lɪtɪkl/ *a.* politico.

politics /'pɒlətɪks/ *n.* politica *f.*

polka /'pɒlkə/ *n.* polca *f.* ~ **dots** pois
m.pl.

poll /pəʊl/ *n.* votazione *f.* —*v.t./i.*
(*votes*) ottenere. **opinion** ~ sondag-
gio d'opinione *m.* ~**ing-booth** *n.*
cabina elettorale *f.*

pollen /'pɒlən/ *n.* polline *m.*

pollut|e /pə'luːt/ *v.t.* inquinare. ~**ion**
/-ʃn/ *n.* inquinamento *m.*

polo /'pəʊləʊ/ *n.* polo *m.* ~-**neck** *n.*
collo alla ciclista *m.*

poltergeist /'pɒltəgaɪst/ *n.* spirito (fra-
cassone) *m.*

polychrome /'pɒlɪkrəʊm/ *a.* poli-
cromo.

polyester /pɒlɪ'estə(r)/ *n.* poliestere *m.*

polygam|y /pə'lɪgəmɪ/ *n.* poligamia *f.*
~**ist** *n.* poligamo *m.* ~**ous** *a.* poligamo.

polyglot /'pɒlɪglɒt/ *a.* & *n.* poliglotta
m./f.

polygon /'pɒlɪgən/ *n.* poligono *m.*

polyp /'pɒlɪp/ *n.* polipo *m.*

polystyrene /pɒlɪ'staɪriːn/ *n.* poli-
stirene *m.*

polytechnic /pɒlɪ'teknɪk/ *n.* poli-
tecnico *m.*

polythene /'pɒlɪθiːn/ *n.* politene *m.* ~
bag *n.* sacchetto di plastica *m.*

pomander /pəʊ'mændə(r)/ *n.* sfera
profumata *f.*

pomegranate /'pɒmɪgrænɪt/ *n.* mela-
grana *f.*

pommel /'pʌml/ *n.* pomo *m.*

pomp /pɒmp/ *n.* pompa *f.*

pompon /'pɒmpɒn/ *n.* pompon *m.*

pomp|ous /'pɒmpəs/ *a.* pomposo.
~**osity** /-'pɒsətɪ/ *n.* pomposità *f.*

poncho /'pɒntʃəʊ/ *n.* (*pl.* -os) poncio
m.

pond /pɒnd/ *n.* laghetto *m.*

ponder /'pɒndə(r)/ *v.t./i.* ponderare.

ponderous /'pɒndərəs/ *a.* ponderoso.

pong /pɒŋ/ *n.* (*sl.*) puzzo *m.* —*v.i.* (*sl.*)
puzzare.

pontif|f /'pɒntɪf/ *n.* pontefice *m.* ~**ical**
/-'tɪfɪkl/ *a.* pontificio; (*fig.*) ampolloso.

pontificate /pɒn'tɪfɪkeɪt/ *v.i.* pon-
tificare.

pontoon /pɒn'tuːn/ *n.* pontone *m.* ~
bridge ponte di barche *m.*

pony /'pəʊnɪ/ *n.* pony *m.* ~-**tail** *n.* coda
di cavallo *f.* ~-**trekking** *n.* escursio-
nismo col pony *m.*

poodle /'puːdl/ *n.* barboncino *m.*

pool[1] /puːl/ *n.* pozzanghera *f.* (**swim-
ming-**)~ *n.* piscina *f.*

pool[2] /puːl/ *n.* (*common fund*) banco
m. ~**s** *n.pl.* totocalcio *m.s.* —*v.t.* mettere in un fondo comune.

poor /pʊə(r)/ *a.* (**-er, -est**) povero;
(*quantity*) scarso; (*not good*) scadente.
be in ~ **health** essere in cattiva
salute. ~**ly** *a.* (*fam.*) indisposto; *adv.*
male.

pop[1] /pɒp/ *n.* scoppio *m.* —*v.t./i.* (*p.t.*
popped) (far) scoppiare; (*put*) mettere. ~ **in** *v.i.* fare una visitina. ~
out *v.i.* fare un salto fuori. ~ **up** *v.i.*
saltar su.

pop[2] /pɒp/ *a.* popolare, pop. —*n.* (*fam.*)
musica pop *f.* ~ **art** arte pop *f.*

popcorn /'pɒpkɔːn/ *n.* granoturco
soffiato *m.*

pope /pəʊp/ *n.* papa *m.*

popgun /'pɒpgʌn/ *n.* pistola ad aria
compressa *f.*

poplar /'pɒplə(r)/ *n.* pioppo *m.*

poplin /'pɒplɪn/ *n.* popeline *f.*

poppet /'pɒpɪt/ *n.* (*fam.*) tesoro *m.*

poppy /'pɒpɪ/ *n.* papavero *m.*

popular /'pɒpjʊlə(r)/ *a.* popolare. ~**ity**
/-'lærətɪ/ *n.* popolarità *f.* ~**ize** *v.t.* popo-
larizzare.

populat|e /'pɒpjʊleɪt/ *v.t.* popolare.
~**ion** /-'leɪʃn/ *n.* popolazione *f.*

porcelain /'pɔːsəlɪn/ *n.* porcellana *f.*

porch /pɔːtʃ/ *n.* portico *m.*

porcupine /'pɔːkjʊpaɪn/ *n.* porcospino
m.

pore[1] /pɔː(r)/ *n.* poro *m.*

pore[2] /pɔː(r)/ *v.i.* ~ **over** studiare attentamente.

pork /pɔːk/ *n.* carne di maiale *f.*

porn /pɔːn/ *n.* (*fam.*) pornografia *f.* ~**o**
a. (*fam.*) porno.

pornograph|y /pɔː'nɒgrəfɪ/ *n.* porno-
grafia *f.* ~**ic** /-ə'græfɪk/ *a.* pornografi-
co.

porous /'pɔːrəs/ *a.* poroso.

porpoise /'pɔːpəs/ *n.* focena *f.*

porridge /'pɒrɪdʒ/ *n.* farinata di fiocchi
d'avena *f.*

port[1] /pɔːt/ *n.* porto *m.*; (*porthole*) oblò
m.

port[2] /pɔːt/ *a.* & *n.* (*naut.*) babordo *m.*

port[3] /pɔːt/ *n.* (*wine*) porto *m.*

portable /'pɔːtəbl/ *a.* portabile.

portal /'pɔːtl/ *n.* portale *m.*

portent /'pɔːtent/ *n.* presagio *m.*

porter /'pɔːtə(r)/ *n.* portiere *m.*; (*for
luggage*) facchino *m.* ~**age** *n.* facchi-
naggio *m.*

portfolio /pɔːtˈfəʊljəʊ/ n. (pl. -os) cartella f.

porthole /ˈpɔːthəʊl/ n. oblò m.

portico /ˈpɔːtɪkəʊ/ n. (pl. -oes) portico m.

portion /ˈpɔːʃn/ n. porzione f. —v.t. dividere (in porzioni).

portly /ˈpɔːtlɪ/ a. (-ier, -iest) corpulento.

portrait /ˈpɔːtrɪt/ n. ritratto m.

portray /pɔːˈtreɪ/ v.t. ritrarre; (represent) rappresentare. ~al n. ritratto m.

Portug|al /ˈpɔːtjʊgl/ n. Portogallo m. ~uese /-ˈgiːz/ a. & n. portoghese m.|f.

pose /pəʊz/ n. posa f. —v.t. mettere in posa; (present) proporre. —v.i. posare. ~ as atteggiarsi a.

poser /ˈpəʊzə(r)/ n. domanda imbarazzante f.

posh /pɒʃ/ a. (sl.) lussuoso.

position /pəˈzɪʃn/ n. posizione f.; (job) impiego m.; (status) rango m. —v.t. mettere in posizione.

positive /ˈpɒzətɪv/ a. positivo; (real) concreto; (certain) sicuro. —n. positivo m.; (photo) positiva f. ~ly adv. positivamente.

possess /pəˈzes/ v.t. possedere. ~or n. possessore m.

possession /pəˈzeʃn/ n. possesso m. ~s n.pl. beni m.pl.

possessive /pəˈzesɪv/ a. possessivo. ~ness n. carattere possessivo m.

possib|le /ˈpɒsəbl/ a. possibile. ~ility /-ˈbɪlətɪ/ n. possibilità f. ~ly adv. possibilmente.

post[1] /pəʊst/ n. (pole) palo m. —v.t. (notice) affiggere.

post[2] /pəʊst/ n. (place) posto m. —v.t. appostare.

post[3] /pəʊst/ n. (mail) posta f. —v.t. impostare. **keep s.o. ~ed** tenere qcno. informato. **~-box** n. cassetta postale f.; (P.O. box) casella postale f. **~-code** n. codice postale m. **P~ Office** n. ufficio postale m. **~age** n. affrancatura f.

post- /pəʊst/ pref. dopo.

postal /ˈpəʊstl/ a. postale. ~ **order** n. vaglia postale m.

postcard /ˈpəʊstkɑːd/ n. cartolina f.

post-date /pəʊstˈdeɪt/ v.t. postdatare.

poster /ˈpəʊstə(r)/ n. cartellone m.

poste restante /pəʊstˈrestɑːnt/ n. fermo posta m.

posterior /pɒˈstɪərɪə(r)/ a. posteriore. —n. deretano m.

posterity /pɒsˈterətɪ/ n. posterità f.

posthumous /ˈpɒstjʊməs/ a. postumo. ~ly adv. dopo la morte.

postman /ˈpəʊstmən/ n. (pl. -men) postino m.

postmark /ˈpəʊstmɑːk/ n. timbro postale m.

postmaster, postmistress /ˈpəʊstmɑːstə(r), ˈpəʊstmɪstrɪs/ ns. direttore, direttrice di ufficio postale m., f.

post-mortem /ˈpəʊstmɔːtəm/ n. autopsia f.

postpone /pəʊstˈpəʊn/ v.t. posporre. ~ment n. rinvio m.

postscript /ˈpəʊsskrɪpt/ n. poscritto m.

postulant /ˈpɒstjʊlənt/ n. postulante m.|f.

postulate /ˈpɒstjʊleɪt/ v.t. postulare.

posture /ˈpɒstʃə(r)/ n. posizione f. —v.i. mettersi in posa.

posy /ˈpəʊzɪ/ n. mazzolino di fiori m.

pot /pɒt/ n. vaso m.; (for cooking) pentola f.; (sl.) sacco m.; (marijuana, sl.) erba f. —v.t. (p.t. potted) piantare (in vaso). **go to ~** (sl.) andare in malora. **~-belly** n. pancione m. **~-boiler** n. lavoro letterario scritto solo per guadagno m. **~ luck** n. pasto alla buona m. **~-shot** n. colpo sparato a casaccio m.

potassium /pəˈtæsjəm/ n. potassio m.

potato /pəˈteɪtəʊ/ n. (pl. -oes) patata f.

poten|t /ˈpəʊtnt/ a. potente. ~cy n. potenza f.

potentate /ˈpəʊtənteɪt/ n. potentato m.

potential /pəʊˈtenʃl/ a. & n. potenziale m. ~ity /-ʃɪˈælətɪ/ n. potenzialità f. ~ly adv. potenzialmente.

pot-hole /ˈpɒthəʊl/ n. marmitta f.; (in road) buca f. ~r n. speleologo, a m., f.

potion /ˈpəʊʃn/ n. pozione f.

potted /ˈpɒtɪd/ see **pot**. —a. conservato.

potter[1] /ˈpɒtə(r)/ n. vasaio, a m., f.

potter[2] /ˈpɒtə(r)/ v.i. gingillarsi.

pottery /ˈpɒtərɪ/ n. ceramiche f.pl.

potty /ˈpɒtɪ/ a. (-ier, -iest) (sl.) matto.

pouch /paʊtʃ/ n. borsa f.

pouffe /puːf/ n. (stool) pouf m. invar.

poult|erer /ˈpəʊltərə(r)/ n. pollivendolo, a m., f. ~ry n. pollame m.

poultice /ˈpəʊltɪs/ n. cataplasma m.

pounce /paʊns/ v.i. balzare. —n. balzo m.

pound[1] /paʊnd/ n. libbra f. (= 0.454 kg.); (money) sterlina f.

pound[2] /paʊnd/ n. recinto m.; (for cars) deposito auto m.

pound[3] /paʊnd/ v.t./i. battere; (run/ walk heavily) correre/ camminare pesantemente.

pour /pɔː(r)/ v.t. versare. —v.i. riversarsi; (rain) piovere a dirotto. ~ **in** entrare a fiotti. ~ **out** riversarsi fuori; (a drink) mescere. ~**ing rain** pioggia torrenziale f.

pout /paʊt/ v.i. fare il broncio. —n. broncio m.

poverty /'pɒvətɪ/ n. povertà f.

powder /'paʊdə(r)/ n. polvere f.; (cosmetic) cipria f. —v.t. polverizzare; (face) incipriare. ~**y** a. polveroso.

power /'paʊə(r)/ n. potere m.; (electr.) corrente f. ~**-station** n. centrale elettrica f. ~**ed** a. a motore. ~**ful** a. potente. ~**less** a. impotente.

powwow /'paʊwaʊ/ n. riunione f.

practicable /'præktɪkəbl/ a. praticabile.

practical /'præktɪkl/ a. pratico; (virtual) effettivo. ~ **joke** burla f. ~**ly** adv. praticamente; (almost) quasi.

practice /'præktɪs/ n. pratica f.; (custom) usanza f.; (exercise) esercizio m.; (sport) allenamento m.; (of doctor) clientela f. **out of** ~ fuori esercizio.

practise /'præktɪs/ v.t./i. esercitarsi; (carry out) mettere in pratica; (sport) allenarsi; (a profession) esercitare. ~**d** a. esperto.

practitioner /præk'tɪʃənə(r)/ n. professionista m. **general** ~ n. medico generico m.

pragmatic /præg'mætɪk/ a. pragmatico.

prairie /'preərɪ/ n. prateria f.

praise /preɪz/ v.t. lodare. —n. lode f. ~**worthy** a. lodevole.

pram /præm/ n. carrozzella f.

prance /prɑːns/ v.i. saltellare.

prank /præŋk/ n. tiro m.

prattle /'prætl/ v.i. cinguettare. —n. cinguettio m.

prawn /prɔːn/ n. gambero m.

pray /preɪ/ v.t./i. pregare.

prayer /preə(r)/ n. preghiera f.

pre- /priː/ pref. pre-.

preach /priːtʃ/ v.t./i. predicare. ~**er** n. predicatore m.

preamble /priː'æmbl/ n. preambolo m.

pre-arrange /priːə'reɪndʒ/ v.t. predisporre. ~**ment** n. predisposizione f.

precarious /prɪ'keərɪəs/ a. precario. ~**ly** adv. precariamente.

precaution /prɪ'kɔːʃn/ n. precauzione f. ~**ary** a. preventivo.

preced|e /prɪ'siːd/ v.t. precedere. ~**ing** a. precedente.

preceden|ce /'presɪdəns/ n. precedenza f. ~**t** n. precedente m.

precept /'priːsept/ n. precetto m.

precinct /'priːsɪŋkt/ n. recinto m. **pedestrian** ~ n. zona pedonale f. ~**s** n.pl. dintorni m.pl.

precious /'preʃəs/ a. prezioso. —adv. (fam.) molto.

precipice /'presɪpɪs/ n. precipizio m.

precipitat|e[1] /prɪ'sɪpɪteɪt/ v.t. precipitare. ~**ion** /-'teɪʃn/ n. precipitazione f.

precipitate[2] /prɪ'sɪpɪtɪt/ n. precipitato m. —a. precipitoso.

precipitous /prɪ'sɪpɪtəs/ a. scosceso.

précis /'preɪsiː/ n. (pl. précis /-siːz/) riassunto m.

precis|e /prɪ'saɪs/ a. preciso. ~**ely** adv. precisamente. ~**ion** /-'sɪʒn/ n. precisione f.

preclude /prɪ'kluːd/ v.t. precludere.

precocious /prɪ'kəʊʃəs/ a. precoce. ~**ly** adv. precocemente.

preconce|ived /priːkən'siːvd/ a. preconcetto. ~**ption** /-'sepʃn/ n. preconcetto m.

precursor /priː'kɜːsə(r)/ n. precursore m.

predator /'predətə(r)/ n. predatore m. ~**y** a. rapace.

predecease /priːdɪ'siːs/ v.t. morire prima (di).

predecessor /'priːdɪsesə(r)/ n. predecessore m.

predestin|e /priː'destɪn/ v.t. predestinare. ~**ation** /-'neɪʃn/ n. predestinazione f.

predicament /prɪ'dɪkəmənt/ n. situazione difficile f.

predicat|e /'predɪkɪt/ n. predicato m. ~**ive** /prɪ'dɪkətɪv/ a. predicativo.

predict /prɪ'dɪkt/ v.t. predire. ~**ion** /-ʃn/ n. predizione f.

predilection /priːdɪ'lekʃn/ n. predilezione f.

predispose /priːdɪ'spəʊz/ v.t. predisporre.

predomin|ate /prɪ'dɒmɪneɪt/ v.i. predominare. ~**ant** a. predominante.

pre-eminent /priː'emɪnənt/ a. preminente.

pre-empt /priː'empt/ v.t. assicurarsi.

preen /priːn/ v.t. lisciarsi. ~ **o.s.** agghindarsi.

prefab /'priːfæb/ n. (fam.) casa pre-

fabbricata *f.* ~**ricated** /-'fæbrɪkeɪtɪd/ *a.* prefabbricato.
preface /'prefɪs/ *n.* prefazione *f.*
prefect /'priːfekt/ *n.* capoclasse *m./f.*; (*official*) prefetto *m.*
prefer /prɪ'fɜː(r)/ *v.t.* (*p.t.* **preferred**) preferire. ~**able** /'prefrəbl/ *a.* preferibile.
preferen|ce /'prefrəns/ *n.* preferenza *f.* ~**tial** /-ə'renʃl/ *a.* preferenziale.
prefix /'priːfɪks/ *n.* (*pl.* -**ixes**) prefisso *m.*
pregnan|t /'pregnənt/ *a.* incinta. ~**cy** *n.* gravidanza *f.*
prehistoric /priːhɪ'stɒrɪk/ *a.* preistorico.
prejudge /priː'dʒʌdʒ/ *v.t.* giudicare prematuramente.
prejudice /'predʒʊdɪs/ *n.* pregiudizio *m.*; (*harm*) danno *m.* —*v.t.* pregiudicare; danneggiare. ~**d** *a.* prevenuto.
prelate /'prelət/ *n.* prelato *m.*
preliminar|y /prɪ'lɪmɪnərɪ/ *a.* preliminare. ~**ies** *n.pl.* preliminari *m.pl.*
prelude /'preljuːd/ *n.* preludio *m.*
pre-marital /priː'mærɪtl/ *a.* prematrimoniale.
premature /'premətjʊə(r)/ *a.* prematuro.
premeditated /priː'medɪteɪtɪd/ *a.* premeditato.
premier /'premɪə(r)/ *a.* primario. —*n.* (*pol.*) primo ministro *m.*
première /'premɪə(r)/ *n.* prima *f.*
premises /'premɪsɪz/ *n.pl.* locali *m.pl.* **on the** ~ sul posto.
premiss /'premɪs/ *n.* premessa *f.*
premium /'priːmɪəm/ *n.* premio *m.* **at a** ~ molto ricercato.
premonition /priːmə'nɪʃn/ *n.* presentimento *m.*
preoccup|ation /priːɒkjʊ'peɪʃn/ *n.* preoccupazione *f.* ~**ied** /-'ɒkjʊpaɪd/ *a.* preoccupato.
prep /prep/ *n.* compiti *m.pl.* ~ **school** scuola (elementare) privata *f.*
preparation /prepə'reɪʃn/ *n.* preparazione *f.* ~**s** *n.pl.* preparativi *m.pl.*
preparatory /prɪ'pærətrɪ/ *a.* preparatorio. ~ **school** *n.* scuola (elementare) privata *f.*
prepare /prɪ'peə(r)/ *v.t./i.* preparare, prepararsi. ~**d to** disposto a.
prepay /priː'peɪ/ *v.t.* (*p.t.* -**paid**) pagare in anticipo.
preponderance /prɪ'pɒndərəns/ *n.* preponderanza *f.*

preposition /prepə'zɪʃn/ *n.* preposizione *f.*
prepossessing /priːpə'zesɪŋ/ *a.* attraente.
preposterous /prɪ'pɒstərəs/ *a.* assurdo.
prerequisite /priː'rekwɪzɪt/ *n.* requisito essenziale *m.*
prerogative /prɪ'rɒgətɪv/ *n.* prerogativa *f.*
Presbyterian /prezbɪ'tɪərɪən/ *a. & n.* presbiteriano, a *m., f.*
prescri|be /prɪ'skraɪb/ *v.t.* prescrivere. ~**ption** /-'ɪpʃn/ *n.* prescrizione *f.*; (*med.*) ricetta *f.*
presence /'prezns/ *n.* presenza *f.* ~ **of mind** presenza di spirito *f.*
present[1] /'preznt/ *a. & n.* presente *m.* **at** ~ attualmente. **for the** ~ per il momento.
present[2] /'preznt/ *n.* (*gift*) regalo *m.*
present[3] /prɪ'zent/ *v.t.* regalare; (*film etc.*) presentare. ~ **s.o. with** offrire a qcno. ~**able** *a.* presentabile. ~**ation** /prezn'teɪʃn/ *n.* presentazione *f.*
presently /'prezntlɪ/ *adv.* fra poco.
preservative /prɪ'zɜːvətɪv/ *n.* conservante *m.*
preserv|e /prɪ'zɜːv/ *v.t.* preservare; (*maintain, culin.*) conservare. —*n.* riserva *f.*; (*jam*) marmellata *f.* ~**ation** /prezə'veɪʃn/ *n.* conservazione *f.*
preside /prɪ'zaɪd/ *v.i.* presiedere. ~ **over** presiedere a.
presiden|t /'prezɪdənt/ *n.* presidente *m.* ~**cy** *n.* presidenza *f.* ~**tial** /-'denʃl/ *a.* presidenziale.
press /pres/ *v.t./i.* premere; (*squeeze*) stringere; (*urge*) pressare; (*iron*) stirare. —*n.* pressione *f.*; (*mech.*) pressa *f.*; (*printing*) stamperia *f.*; (*newspapers*) stampa *f.* **be** ~**ed for** essere a corto di. **in the** ~ nei giornali. ~ **cutting** ritaglio di giornale *m.* ~ **on** procedere. ~-**stud** *n.* (bottone) automatico *m.*
pressing /'presɪŋ/ *a.* urgente.
pressure /'preʃə(r)/ *n.* pressione *f.* —*v.t.* far pressione su. ~-**cooker** *n.* pentola a pressione *f.* ~ **group** *n.* gruppo di pressione *m.*
pressurize /'preʃəraɪz/ *v.t.* far pressione su.
prestige /pre'stiːʒ/ *n.* prestigio *m.*
prestigious /pre'stɪdʒəs/ *a.* prestigioso.
presumably /prɪ'zjuːməblɪ/ *adv.* presumibilmente.

presum|e /prɪ'zjuːm/ v.t. presumere. ~**e (up)on** v.i. approfittare (di). ~**ption** /-'zʌmpʃn/ n. presunzione f.

presumptuous /prɪ'zʌmptʃʊəs/ a. presuntuoso.

presuppose /priːsə'pəʊz/ v.t. presupporre.

pretence /prɪ'tens/ n. finzione f.; (claim) pretesa f.; (pretext) pretesto m.

pretend /prɪ'tend/ v.t./i. fingere, fingersi. ~ **to** (lay claim) pretendere (a).

pretentious /prɪ'tenʃəs/ a. pretenzioso.

pretext /'priːtekst/ n. pretesto m.

pretty /'prɪtɪ/ a. (-ier, -iest) grazioso. —adv. abbastanza.

prevail /prɪ'veɪl/ v.i. predominare; (win) prevalere. ~ **on** persuadere.

prevalen|t /'prevələnt/ a. prevalente. ~**ce** n. prevalenza f.

prevaricate /prɪ'værɪkeɪt/ v.i. tergiversare.

prevent /prɪ'vent/ v.t. impedire. ~**able** a. evitabile. ~**ion** /-ʃn/ n. prevenzione f. ~**ive** a. preventivo.

preview /'priːvjuː/ n. anteprima f.

previous /'priːvɪəs/ a. precedente. ~ **to** prima di. ~**ly** adv. precedentemente.

pre-war /priː'wɔː(r)/ a. anteguerra.

prey /preɪ/ n. preda f. —v.i. ~ **on** far preda di; (worry) tormentare. **bird of** ~ n. uccello rapace m.

price /praɪs/ n. prezzo m. —v.t. fissare il prezzo. ~**less** a. inestimabile; (fam., amusing) straordinario. ~**y** a. (fam.) caro.

prick /prɪk/ v.t./i. pungere, pungersi. —n. puntura f. ~ **up one's ears** rizzare le orecchie.

prickl|e /'prɪkl/ n. spina f.; (sensation) formicolio m. ~**y** a. pungente; (person) permaloso.

pride /praɪd/ n. orgoglio m. —v.r. ~ **o.s. on** vantarsi di. ~ **of place** n. posizione alta f.

priest /priːst/ n. prete m. ~**hood** n. sacerdozio m. ~**ly** a. sacerdotale.

prig /prɪg/ n. presuntuoso m. ~**gish** a. pedante.

prim /prɪm/ a. (**primmer, primmest**) compassato.

primar|y /'praɪmərɪ/ a. primario; (chief) principale. ~**ily** adv. in primo luogo. ~**y school** n. scuola elementare f.

prime[1] /praɪm/ a. principale, primo; (first rate) eccellente. **be in one's** ~ essere nel fiore degli anni. **P~ Minister** Primo Ministro m.

prime[2] /praɪm/ v.t. (gun) caricare; (prepare) preparare; (surface) mesticare.

primer[1] /'praɪmə(r)/ n. (of paint) prima mano f.

primer[2] /'praɪmə(r)/ n. (schol.) sillabario m.

primeval /praɪ'miːvl/ a. primitivo.

primitive /'prɪmɪtɪv/ a. primitivo.

primrose /'prɪmrəʊz/ n. primula f.

prince /prɪns/ n. principe m. ~**ly** a. principesco.

princess /prɪn'ses/ n. principessa f.

principal /'prɪnsəpl/ a. principale. —n. (schol.) preside m. ~**ly** adv. principalmente.

principality /prɪnsɪ'pælətɪ/ n. principato m.

principle /'prɪnsəpl/ n. principio m. **in** ~ in teoria. **on** ~ per principio.

print /prɪnt/ v.t. imprimere; (typ.) stampare; (write in capitals) scrivere in stampatello. —n. impronta f.; (letters) stampatello m.; (of design) stampato m.; (picture) stampa f.; (photo) copia f. **in** ~ (of book) in vendita. **out of** ~ esaurito. ~**ed matter** n. stampe f.pl. ~**out** n. tabulato m.

print|er /'prɪntə(r)/ n. tipografo m. ~**ing** n. tipografia f.

prior[1] /'praɪə(r)/ a. precedente. ~ **to** prima di.

prior[2] /'praɪə(r)/ n. priore m. ~**y** n. prioria f.

priority /praɪ'ɒrətɪ/ n. precedenza f.

prise /praɪz/ v.t. forzare.

prism /'prɪzəm/ n. prisma m.

prison /'prɪzn/ n. prigione f. ~**er** n. prigioniero, a m., f.

pristine /'prɪstiːn/ a. originario; (unspoilt) intatto.

privacy /'prɪvəsɪ/ n. vita privata f. **in** ~ in intimità.

private /'praɪvɪt/ a. privato; (confidential) personale. —n. soldato semplice m. **in** ~ in privato. ~ **eye** n. (fam.) investigatore privato m. ~**ly** adv. privatamente.

privation /praɪ'veɪʃn/ n. privazione f. ~**s** n.pl. stenti m.pl.

privet /'prɪvɪt/ n. ligustro m.

privilege /'prɪvəlɪdʒ/ n. privilegio m. ~**d** a. privilegiato.

privy /'prɪvɪ/ a. ~ **to** al corrente di.

prize /praɪz/ n. premio m. —a. (idiot

etc.) perfetto. —*v.t.* apprezzare. **~-fighter** *n.* pugile professionista *m.* **~-giving** *n.* premiazione *f.*

pro /prəʊ/ *n.* **~s and cons** il pro e il contro *m.*

pro- /prəʊ/ *pref.* pro-.

probab|le /'prɒbəbl/ *a.* probabile. **~ility** /-'bɪlətɪ/ *n.* probabilità *f.* **~ly** *adv.* probabilmente.

probation /prə'beɪʃn/ *n.* prova *f.*; (*jurid.*) libertà vigilata *f.* **~ary** *a.* in prova.

probe /prəʊb/ *n.* sonda *f.*; (*fig.*) indagine *f.* —*v.t.* sondare. —*v.i.* **~ into** esaminare a fondo.

problem /'prɒbləm/ *n.* problema *m.* —*a.* difficile. **~atic** /-'mætɪk/ *a.* problematico.

procedure /prə'si:dʒə(r)/ *n.* procedimento *m.*

proceed /prə'si:d/ *v.i.* procedere; (*originate*) provenire. **~ing** *n.* procedimento *m.*

proceedings /prə'si:dɪŋz/ *n.pl.* (*report*) atti *m.pl.*; (*jurid.*) azione legale *f.s.*

proceeds /'prəʊsi:dz/ *n.pl.* ricavo *m.s.*

process /'prəʊses/ *n.* processo *m.*; (*jurid.*) azione legale *f.* —*v.t.* trattare; (*photo*) sviluppare. **in ~ of** in corso di. **in the ~** nel mentre.

procession /prə'seʃn/ *n.* processione *f.*

procl|aim /prə'kleɪm/ *v.t.* proclamare. **~amation** /prɒklə'meɪʃn/ *n.* proclamazione *f.*

procrastinate /prəʊ'kræstɪneɪt/ *v.i.* procrastinare.

procreation /prəʊkrɪ'eɪʃn/ *n.* procreazione *f.*

proctor /'prɒktə(r)/ *n.* (*univ.*) prefetto *m.*

procure /prə'kjʊə(r)/ *v.t.* ottenere.

prod /prɒd/ *v.t./i.* (*p.t.* **prodded**) punzecchiare; (*fig.*) incitare. —*n.* colpetto *m.*

prodigal /'prɒdɪgl/ *a.* prodigo.

prodigious /prə'dɪdʒəs/ *a.* prodigioso.

prodigy /'prɒdɪdʒɪ/ *n.* prodigio *m.*

produc|e[1] /prə'dju:s/ *v.t./i.* (*show*) presentare; (*theatr.*) mettere in scena; (*cause*) causare; (*manufacture*) produrre. **~er** *n.* produttore *m.*; (*theatr.*, *TV*) regista *m.* **~tion** /-'dʌkʃn/ *n.* produzione *f.*; regia *f.*

produce[2] /'prɒdju:s/ *n.* prodotti *m.pl.*

product /'prɒdʌkt/ *n.* prodotto *m.*

productiv|e /prə'dʌktɪv/ *a.* produttivo. **~ity** /prɒdʌk'tɪvətɪ/ *n.* produttività *f.*

profan|e /prə'feɪn/ *a.* profano; (*blasphemous*) blasfemo. **~ity** /-'fænətɪ/ *n.* profanità *f.*

profess /prə'fes/ *v.t.* professare; (*pretend*) pretendere.

profession /prə'feʃn/ *n.* professione *f.* **~al** *a.* professionale; (*man*) di professione; *n.* professionista *m.|f.*

professor /prə'fesə(r)/ *n.* professore (universitario) *m.*

proffer /'prɒfə(r)/ *v.t.* offrire.

proficien|t /prə'fɪʃnt/ *a.* competente. **~cy** *n.* competenza *f.*

profile /'prəʊfaɪl/ *n.* profilo *m.*; (*character study*) breve biografia *f.*

profit /'prɒfɪt/ *n.* profitto *m.* —*v.i.* **~ from** trarre profitto da. **~able** *a.* vantaggioso.

profiteer /prɒfɪ'tɪə(r)/ *n.* profitta|tore, -trice *m.*, *f.*

profound /prə'faʊnd/ *a.* profondo. **~ly** *adv.* profondamente.

profus|e /prə'fju:s/ *a.* profuso. **~ely** *adv.* profusamente. **~ion** /-ʒn/ *n.* profusione *f.*

progeny /'prɒdʒənɪ/ *n.* progenie *f.*

prognosis /prɒg'nəʊsɪs/ *n.* (*pl.* **-oses**) prognosi *f.*

program /'prəʊgræm/ *n.* (**computer**) **~** programma *m.* —*v.t.* (*p.t.* **programmed**) programmare. **~mer** *n.* programma|tore, -trice *m.*, *f.*

programme /'prəʊgræm/ *n.* programma *m.*

progress[1] /'prəʊgres/ *n.* progresso *m.* **in ~** in corso.

progress[2] /prə'gres/ *v.i.* progredire. **~ion** *n.* progresso *m.*

progressive /prə'gresɪv/ *a.* progressivo; (*reforming*) progressista. **~ly** *adv.* progressivamente.

prohibit /prə'hɪbɪt/ *v.t.* proibire. **~ive** /-bətɪv/ *a.* proibitivo.

project[1] /prə'dʒekt/ *v.t.* progettare. —*v.i.* (*stick out*) sporgere.

project[2] /'prɒdʒekt/ *n.* progetto *m.*

projectile /prə'dʒektaɪl/ *n.* proiettile *m.*

projector /prə'dʒektə(r)/ *n.* proiettore *m.*

proletari|at /prəʊlɪ'teərɪət/ *n.* proletariato *m.* **~an** *a.* & *n.* proletario, a *m.*, *f.*

proliferat|e /prə'lɪfəreɪt/ *v.i.* proliferare. **~ion** /-'reɪʃn/ *n.* proliferazione *f.*

prolific /prə'lɪfɪk/ *a.* prolifico.

prologue /'prəʊlɒg/ *n.* prologo *m.*

prolong /prə'lɒŋ/ *v.t.* prolungare.
promenade /prɒmə'nɑ:d/ *n.* passeggiata *f.* —*v.t./i.* passeggiare. ~ **concert** *n.* concerto (popolare) di musica classica *f.*
prominen|t /'prɒmɪnənt/ *a.* prominente; (*important*) importante; (*conspicuous*) cospicuo. ~**ce** *n.* prominenza *f.*
promiscu|ous /prə'mɪskjʊəs/ *a.* promiscuo. ~**ity** /prɒmɪ'skju:ətɪ/ *n.* promiscuità *f.*
promis|e /'prɒmɪs/ *n.* promessa *f.* —*v.t./i.* promettere. ~**ing** *a.* promettente.
promontory /'prɒməntrɪ/ *n.* promontorio *m.*
promot|e /prə'məʊt/ *v.t.* promuovere. ~**ion** /-'məʊʃn/ *n.* promozione *f.*
prompt /prɒmpt/ *a.* pronto; (*punctual*) puntuale. —*adv.* preciso. —*v.t.* incitare; (*theatr.*) suggerire. ~**er** *n.* suggeri|tore, -trice *m.*, *f.* ~**ly** *adv.* puntualmente. ~**ness** *n.* prontezza *f.*
promulgate /'prɒməlgeɪt/ *v.t.* promulgare.
prone /prəʊn/ *a.* prono. ~ **to incline** a.
prong /prɒŋ/ *n.* dente (di forchetta) *m.*
pronoun /'prəʊnaʊn/ *n.* pronome *m.*
pronounce /prə'naʊns/ *v.t.* pronunciare; (*declare*) dichiarare. ~**ment** *n.* dichiarazione *f.*
pronunciation /prənʌnsɪ'eɪʃn/ *n.* pronuncia *f.*
pronounced /prə'naʊnst/ *a.* pronunciato; (*noticeable*) marcato.
proof /pru:f/ *n.* prova *f.*; (*typ.*) bozza *f.*; (*of alcohol*) grado *m.* —*a.* ~ **against** a prova di. ~-**reading** *n.* correzione delle bozze *f.*
prop¹ /prɒp/ *n.* puntello *m.*; (*fig.*) sostegno *m.* —*v.t.* (*p.t.* **propped**) puntellare; sostenere. ~ **against** (*lean*) appoggiare a.
prop² /prɒp/ *n.* (*theatr.*, *fam.*) materiale di scena *m.*
propaganda /prɒpə'gændə/ *n.* propaganda *f.*
propagat|e /'prɒpəgeɪt/ *v.t./i.* propagare, propagarsi. ~**ion** /-'geɪʃn/ *n.* propagazione *f.*
propel /prə'pel/ *v.t.* (*p.t.* **propelled**) spingere (avanti).
propeller /prə'pelə(r)/ *n.* elica *f.*
propensity /prə'pensətɪ/ *n.* tendenza *f.*
proper /'prɒpə(r)/ *a.* corretto; (*suit-*

able) adatto; (*gram.*) proprio; (*fam.*, *real*) vero e proprio. ~**ly** *adv.* correttamente.
property /'prɒpətɪ/ *n.* proprietà *f.* **real** ~ beni immobili *m.pl.*
prophecy /'prɒfəsɪ/ *n.* profezia *f.*
prophesy /'prɒfɪsaɪ/ *v.t./i.* profetizzare.
prophet /'prɒfɪt/ *n.* profeta *m.* ~**ic** /prə'fetɪk/ *a.* profetico.
propitious /prə'pɪʃəs/ *a.* propizio.
proportion /prə'pɔ:ʃn/ *n.* proporzione *f.* ~**al**, ~**ate** *adjs.* proporzionale.
proposal /prə'pəʊzl/ *n.* proposta *f.*; (*of marriage*) offerta di matrimonio *f.*
propos|e /prə'pəʊz/ *v.t.* proporre. —*v.i.* fare un' offerta di matrimonio. ~**ition** /prɒpə'zɪʃn/ *n.* proposta *f.*; (*gram.*) proposizione *f.*; (*fam.*, *project*) affare *m.*
propound /prə'paʊnd/ *v.t.* proporre.
proprietor /prə'praɪətə(r)/ *n.* proprietario, a *m.*, *f.*
propriety /prə'praɪətɪ/ *n.* correttezza *f.*
propulsion /prə'pʌlʃn/ *n.* propulsione *f.*
prosaic /prə'zeɪk/ *a.* prosaico.
proscribe /prə'skraɪb/ *v.t.* proscrivere.
prose /prəʊz/ *n.* prosa *f.*
prosecut|e /'prɒsɪkju:t/ *v.t.* processare; (*carry on*) proseguire. ~**ion** /-'kju:ʃn/ *n.* processo *m.*; esecuzione *f.* ~**or** *n.* accusatore *m.* **Public P~or** Ministero Pubblico *m.*
prospect¹ /'prɒspekt/ *n.* vista *f.*; (*expectation*) prospettiva *f.*
prospect² /prə'spekt/ *v.i.* esplorare. ~**or** *n.* cercatore *m.*
prospective /prə'spektɪv/ *a.* probabile; (*future*) futuro.
prospectus /prə'spektəs/ *n.* prospetto *m.*
prosper /'prɒspə(r)/ *v.i.* prosperare.
prosper|ous /'prɒspərəs/ *a.* prospero. ~**ity** /-'sperətɪ/ *n.* prosperità *f.*
prostitut|e /'prɒstɪtju:t/ *n.* prostituta *f.* ~**ion** /-'tju:ʃn/ *n.* prostituzione *f.*
prostrate /'prɒstreɪt/ *a.* prostrato; (*fig.*) affranto.
protagonist /prə'tægənɪst/ *n.* protagonista *m.|f.*
protect /prə'tekt/ *v.t.* proteggere. ~**ion** /-ʃn/ *n.* protezione *f.* ~**or** *n.* protet|tore, -trice *m.*, *f.*
protective /prə'tektɪv/ *a.* protettivo.
protégé /'prɒtɪʒeɪ/ *n.* protetto *m.* ~**e** *n.* protetta *f.*

protein /'prəuti:n/ *n.* proteina *f.*

protest[1] /'prəutest/ *n.* protesta *f.*

protest[2] /prə'test/ *v.t./i.* protestare. ~**er** *n.* contesta|tore, -trice *m., f.*

Protestant /'prɒtɪstənt/ *a. & n.* protestante *m.|f.*

protocol /'prəutəkɒl/ *n.* protocollo *m.*

prototype /'prəutətaɪp/ *n.* prototipo *m.*

protract /prə'trækt/ *v.t.* protrarre.

protractor /prə'træktə(r)/ *n.* goniometro *m.*

protrude /prə'tru:d/ *v.i.* sporgere.

protuberance /prə'tju:bərəns/ *n.* protuberanza *f.*

proud /praud/ *a.* fiero. ~**ly** *adv.* fieramente.

prove /pru:v/ *v.t.* provare. —*v.i.* rivelarsi. ~**n** *a.* provato.

provenance /'prɒvənəns/ *n.* provenienza *f.*

proverb /'prɒvɜ:b/ *n.* proverbio *m.* ~**ial** /prə'vɜ:bɪəl/ *a.* proverbiale.

provide /prə'vaɪd/ *v.t./i.* provvedere. ~ **against** premunirsi (contro). ~ **for** badare a.

provided /prə'vaɪdɪd/ *conj.* ~ **(that)** purché.

providen|ce /'prɒvɪdəns/ *n.* providenza *f.* ~**t** *a.* previdente.

providential /prɒvɪ'denʃl/ *a.* provvidenziale.

providing /prə'vaɪdɪŋ/ *conj.* = **provided.**

province /'prɒvɪns/ *n.* provincia *f.*; (*fig.*) competenza *f.*

provincial /prə'vɪnʃl/ *a.* provinciale.

provision /prə'vɪʒn/ *n.* provvedimento *m.* ~**s** *n.pl.* provviste *f.pl.*

provisional /prə'vɪʒənl/ *a.* provvisorio. ~**ly** *adv.* provvisoriamente.

proviso /prə'vaɪzəu/ *n.* (*pl.* **-os**) condizione *f.*

provo|ke /prə'vəuk/ *v.t.* provocare. ~**cation** /prɒvə'keɪʃn/ *n.* provocazione *f.* ~**cative** /-'vɒkətɪv/ *a.* provocante.

prow /prau/ *n.* prua *f.*

prowess /'prauɪs/ *n.* prodezza *f.*

prowl /praul/ *v.i.* girovagare. —*n.* **on the** ~ in cerca di preda. ~**er** *n.* predone *m.*

proximity /prɒk'sɪmətɪ/ *n.* prossimità *f.*

proxy /'prɒksɪ/ *n.* procura *f.*

prud|e /pru:d/ *n.* persona eccessivamente pudica *f.* ~**ish** *a.* pudico.

pruden|t /'pru:dnt/ *a.* prudente. ~**ce** *n.* prudenza *f.* ~**tly** *adv.* prudentemente.

prune[1] /pru:n/ *n.* prugna secca *f.*

prune[2] /pru:n/ *v.t.* potare.

prurient /'pruərɪənt/ *a.* lascivo.

pry /praɪ/ *v.i.* ficcare il naso.

psalm /sɑ:m/ *n.* salmo *m.*

pseudo- /'sju:dəu/ *pref.* pseudo-.

pseudonym /'sju:dənɪm/ *n.* pseudonimo *m.*

psychedelic /'saɪkədelɪk/ *a.* psichedelico.

psychiatr|y /saɪ'kaɪətrɪ/ *n.* psichiatria *f.* ~**ic** /-ɪ'ætrɪk/ *a.* psichiatrico. ~**ist** *n.* psichiatra *m.|f.*

psychic /'saɪkɪk/ *a.* psichico.

psycho-analysis /saɪkəuə'næləsɪs/ *n.* psicanalisi *f.*

psycho-analys|e /saɪkəu'ænəlaɪz/ *v.t.* psicanalizzare. ~**t** /-ɪst/ *n.* psicanalista *m.|f.*

psycholog|y /saɪ'kɒlədʒɪ/ *n.* psicologia *f.* ~**ical** /-ə'lɒdʒɪkl/ *a.* psicologico. ~**ist** *n.* psicologo, a *m., f.*

psychopath /'saɪkəupæθ/ *n.* psicopatico, a *m., f.*

pub /pʌb/ *n.* pub *m.*

puberty /'pju:bətɪ/ *n.* pubertà *f.*

pubic /'pju:bɪk/ *a.* pubico.

public /'pʌblɪk/ *a.* pubblico. ~ **house** *n.* pub *m.* ~ **library** *n.* biblioteca comunale *f.* ~ **school** *n.* scuola privata *f.* ~**-spirited** *a.* dotato di senso civico. ~**ly** *adv.* pubblicamente.

publican /'pʌblɪkən/ *n.* gestore di un pub *m.*

publication /pʌblɪ'keɪʃn/ *n.* pubblicazione *f.*

publicity /pʌb'lɪsətɪ/ *n.* pubblicità *f.*

publicize /'pʌblɪsaɪz/ *v.t.* pubblicizzare.

publish /'pʌblɪʃ/ *v.t.* pubblicare. ~**er** *n.* editore *m.* ~**ing** *n.* editoria *f.*; (*of book*) pubblicazione *f.*

puck /pʌk/ *n.* (*ice hockey*) disco di gomma *m.*

pucker /'pʌkə(r)/ *v.t./i.* raggrinzare, raggrinzarsi.

pudding /'pudɪŋ/ *n.* budino *m.*

puddle /'pʌdl/ *n.* pozzanghera *f.*

pudgy /'pʌdʒɪ/ *a.* (**-ier, -iest**) grassoccio.

puerile /'pjuəraɪl/ *a.* puerile.

puff /pʌf/ *n.* sbuffo *m.*; (*of wind*) soffio *m.*; (*for powder*) piumino *m.*; (*in advertising*) montatura *f.* — *v.t./i.* sbuffare; (*become inflated*) gonfiarsi. ~ **at** (*pipe*) tirare (boccate). ~ **out** (*candle*) soffiare (per spegnere). ~ **pastry** n. pasta sfoglia f. ~**ed** a. (out of breath) senza fiato.

puffy /'pʌfɪ/ a. gonfio.

pug-nosed /'pʌgnəʊzd/ a. dal naso schiacciato.

pugnacious /pʌg'neɪʃəs/ a. pugnace.

pull /pʊl/ v.t./i. tirare; (tooth) estrarre; (muscle) stirarsi. —n. tirata f.; (fig.) influenza f. ~ **a fast one** giocare un brutto tiro. ~ **down** (building) demolire. ~ **faces** far boccacce. ~ **in** (auto) avvicinarsi. ~ **off** togliere; (fig.) portare a buon fine. ~ **o.s. to-gether** farsi coraggio. ~ **one's weight** mettercela tutta. ~ **s.o.'s leg** prendere in giro qcno. ~ **through** farcela. ~ **up** fermarsi; (reprimand) rimproverare.

pulley /'pʊlɪ/ n. puleggia f.

pullover /'pʊləʊvə(r)/ n. pullover m.

pulp /pʌlp/ n. polpa f.; (for paper) pasta f.; (fam.) letteratura scadente f.

pulpit /'pʊlpɪt/ n. pulpito m.

pulsate /'pʌlseɪt/ v.i. battere.

pulse /pʌls/ n. polso m.

pulverize /'pʌlvəraɪz/ v.t. polverizzare.

pumice /'pʌmɪs/ n. pomice f.

pummel /'pʌml/ v.t. (p.t. **pummelled**) picchiare.

pump[1] /pʌmp/ n. pompa f. —v.t./i. pompare; (fig.) strappare informazioni da. ~ **up** gonfiare.

pump[2] /pʌmp/ n. (shoe) scarpa scollata f.

pumpkin /'pʌmpkɪn/ n. zucca f.

pun /pʌn/ n. gioco di parole m.

punch[1] /pʌntʃ/ v.t. dare un pugno; (perforate) perforare. —n. pugno m.; (sl.) energia f.; (device) stampo m. ~**drunk** a. stordito. ~ **line** n. battuta culminante f. ~**up** n. rissa f.

punch[2] /pʌntʃ/ n. (drink) ponce m.

punctilious /pʌŋk'tɪlɪəs/ a. meticoloso.

punctual /'pʌŋktʃʊəl/ a. puntuale. ~**ity** /-'ælətɪ/ n. puntualità f. ~**ly** adv. puntualmente.

punctuat|e /'pʌŋkʃʊeɪt/ v.t. punteggiare. ~**ion** /-'eɪʃn/ n. punteggiatura f.

puncture /'pʌŋktʃə(r)/ n. puntura f.; (tyre) foratura f. —v.t./i. pungere; perforare.

pundit /'pʌndɪt/ n. esperto m.

pungen|t /'pʌndʒənt/ a. acre; (remark) mordace. ~**cy** n. asprezza f.

punish /'pʌnɪʃ/ v.t. punire. ~**able** a. punibile. ~**ment** n. punizione f.

punitive /'pju:nɪtɪv/ a. punitivo.

punk /pʌŋk/ n. (music, person) punk m.

punnet /'pʌnɪt/ n. cestello (per frutta) m.

punt[1] /pʌnt/ n. (boat) barchino m.

punt[2] /pʌnt/ v.i. puntare, scommettere. ~**er** n. puntatore m.

puny /'pju:nɪ/ a. (-ier, -iest) piccino.

pup, puppy /pʌp, 'pʌpɪ/ ns. cucciolo m.

pupil /'pju:pl/ n. alunno, a m., f.; (of eye) pupilla f.

puppet /'pʌpɪt/ n. marionetta f.

purchase /'pɜ:tʃəs/ v.t. acquistare. —n. acquisto m. ~**r** n. acquirente m./f.

pur|e /'pjʊə(r)/ a. (-er, -est) puro. ~**ely** adv. puramente. ~**ity** n. purità f.

purée /'pjʊəreɪ/ n. puré m.

purgatory /'pɜ:gətrɪ/ n. purgatorio m.

purge /pɜ:dʒ/ v.t. purgare; (pol.) epurare. —n. purga f.; epurazione f.

purif|y /'pjʊərɪfaɪ/ v.t. purificare. ~**ication** /-ɪ'keɪʃn/ n. purificazione f.

purist /'pjʊərɪst/ n. purista m./f.

puritan /'pjʊərɪtən/ n. puritano, a m., f. ~**ical** /-'tænɪkl/ a. puritano.

purl /pɜ:l/ n. (knitting) punto rovescio m.

purple /'pɜ:pl/ a. porporino. —n. porpora f.

purport /pə'pɔ:t/ v.t. ~ **to be** pretendere di essere.

purpose /'pɜ:pəs/ n. scopo m.; (determination) fermezza f. **on** ~ apposta. ~**-built** a. costruito con un preciso scopo. **to no** ~ con nessun risultato. ~**ful** a. deciso. ~**ly** adv. di proposito.

purr /pɜ:(r)/ v.i. fare le fusa.

purse /pɜ:s/ n. borsellino m.; (Amer.) borsa f. —v.t. aggrottare.

pursue /pə'sju:/ v.t. inseguire. ~**r** n. insegui|tore, -trice m., f.

pursuit /pə'sju:t/ n. inseguimento m.; (fig.) attività f.

purveyor /pə'veɪə(r)/ n. fornitore m.

pus /pʌs/ n. pus m.

push /pʊʃ/ v.t./i. spingere, spingersi; (button) premere; (make demands) far pressione (su). —n. spinta f.; (effort) sforzo m.; (drive) iniziativa f. **at a** ~ in caso di bisogno. **get the** ~ (sl.) essere licenziato. ~ **aside** v.t. scostare. ~ **back** v.t. respingere. ~**button telephone** n. telefono a pulsante m. ~**-chair** n. passeggino m.

~ **off** *v.i.* (*sl.*) andarsene. ~ **on** *v.i.* continuare. ~**-over** *n.* (*fam.*) cosa da niente *f.* ~ **up** *v.t.* alzare. ~**y** *a.* (*pej.*) carrierista.

pushing /'puʃɪŋ/ *a.* ambizioso.

puss /pus/ *n.* micio *m.*

put /put/ *v.t.* (*p.t.* **put**, *pres. p.* **putting**) mettere, posare; (*express*) esprimere; (*say*) dire; (*estimate*) valutare. ~ **across** comunicare; (*deceive*) ingannare. ~ **aside** mettere da parte. ~ **away** riporre. ~ **back** rimettere; (*clock*) mettere indietro. ~ **by** risparmiare. ~ **down** mettere giù; (*suppress*) reprimere; (*write*) annotare; (*kill*) sopprimere. ~ **forward** avanzare. ~ **in** introdurre; (*submit*) presentare. ~ **in for** far domanda. ~ **off** posporre; (*repel*) ripugnare. ~ **on** (*wear*) indossare; (*speed*) aumentare; (*light*) accendere. ~ **one's foot down** rimanere fermo. ~ **out** (*extinguish*) spegnere; (*inconvenience*) scomodare; (*hand*) stendere; (*disconcert*) mettere in difficoltà. ~ **to sea** salpare. ~ **through** portare a termine; (*phone*) mettere in comunicazione. ~ **up** alzare; (*price*) aumentare; (*guest*) ospitare. ~**-up job** *n.* affare losco *m.* ~ **up with** sopportare. —*a.* **stay** ~ (*fam.*) stare fermo.

putrefy /'pju:trɪfaɪ/ *v.i.* putrefarsi.

putt /pʌt/ *n.* (*golf*) colpo *m.*

putty /'pʌtɪ/ *n.* mastice *m.*

puzzl|e /'pʌzl/ *n.* enigma *m.*; (*jigsaw*) puzzle *m.* —*v.t.* rendere perplesso. —*v.i.* scervellarsi. ~**ing** *a.* inspiegabile.

pygmy /'pɪgmɪ/ *n.* pigmeo *m.*

pyjamas /pə'dʒɑ:məz/ *n.pl.* pigiama *m.s.*

pylon /'paɪlɒn/ *n.* pilone *m.*

pyramid /'pɪrəmɪd/ *n.* piramide *f.*

python /'paɪθn/ *n.* pitone *m.*

Q

quack[1] /kwæk/ *n.* (*of duck*) qua qua *m.*

quack[2] /kwæk/ *n.* ciarlatano *m.* ~ **doctor** *n.* medicastro *m.*

quadrangle /'kwɒdræŋgl/ *n.* quadrangolo *m.*; (*court*) cortile quadrangolare *m.*

quadruped /'kwɒdruped/ *n.* quadrupede *m.*

quadruple /'kwɒdru:pl/ *a. & n.* quadruplo *m.* —*v.t./i.* quadruplicare. ~**t** /-plət/ *n.* uno, a di quattro gemelli *m.*, *f.*

quagmire /'kwægmaɪə(r)/ *n.* pantano *m.*

quail /kweɪl/ *n.* quaglia *f.*

quaint /kweɪnt/ *a.* (**-er, -est**) pittoresco; (*odd*) bizzarro.

quake /kweɪk/ *v.i.* tremare. —*n.* (*fam.*) terremoto *m.*

Quaker /'kweɪkə(r)/ *n.* quacchero, a *m.*, *f.*

qualification /kwɒlɪfɪ'keɪʃn/ *n.* qualifica *f.*; (*ability*) requisito *m.*; (*fig.*) riserva *f.*

qualif|y /'kwɒlɪfaɪ/ *v.t./i.* qualificare, qualificarsi; (*limit*) precisare. ~**ied** *a.* qualificato; (*limited*) limitato.

qualit|y /'kwɒləti/ *n.* qualità *f.* ~**ative** *a.* /-ɪtətɪv/ qualitativo.

qualm /kwɑ:m/ *n.* scrupolo *m.*

quandary /'kwɒndrɪ/ *n.* **in a** ~ in un dilemma.

quantit|y /'kwɒntəti/ *n.* quantità *f.* **in** ~**y** in abbondanza. ~**ative** /-ɪtətɪv/ *a.* quantitativo.

quarantine /'kwɒrənti:n/ *n.* quarantena *f.*

quarrel /'kwɒrəl/ *n.* lite *f.* —*v.i.* (*p.t.* **quarrelled**) litigare. ~**some** *a.* litigioso.

quarry[1] /'kwɒrɪ/ *n.* (*animal*) preda *f.*

quarry[2] /'kwɒrɪ/ *n.* (*excavation*) cava *f.*

quart /kwɔ:t/ *n.* litro *m.*

quarter /'kwɔ:tə(r)/ *n.* quarto *m.*; (*of year*) trimestre *m.*; (*district*) quartiere *m.* ~**s** *n.pl.* alloggio *m.s.*; (*mil.*) alloggi *m.pl.* —*v.t.* dividere in quattro; (*mil.*) acquartierare. **from all** ~**s** da tutte le parti. ~**-final** *n.* quarto di finale *m.* ~**ly** *a.* trimestrale; *adv.* trimestralmente.

quartermaster /'kwɔ:təmɑ:stə(r)/ *n.* (*mil.*) furiere *m.*

quartet /kwɔ:'tet/ *n.* quartetto *m.*

quartz /kwɔ:ts/ *n.* quarzo *m.* —*a.* (*watch etc.*) al quarzo.

quash /kwɒʃ/ *v.t.* annullare.

quasi- /'kweɪsaɪ/ *pref.* quasi.

quaver /'kweɪvə(r)/ *v.i.* tremolare. —*n.* (*mus.*) croma *f.*

quay /ki:/ *n.* banchina *f.*

queasy /'kwi:zɪ/ *a.* delicato (di stomaco).

queen /kwi:n/ *n.* regina *f.* ~ **mother** *n.* regina madre *f.*

queer /kwɪə(r)/ *a.* (**-er, -est**) strano; (*dubious*) sospetto; (*ill*) indisposto. —*n.* (*sl.*) finocchio *m.*

quell /kwel/ *v.t.* reprimere.

quench /kwentʃ/ *v.t.* estinguere. ~ **one's thirst** dissetarsi.

querulous /'kwerʊləs/ *a.* querulo.

query /'kwɪərɪ/ *n.* domanda *f.* —*v.t.* indagare; (*doubt*) dubitare.

quest /kwest/ *n.* ricerca *f.*

question /'kwestʃən/ *n.* domanda *f.*; (*for discussion*) questione *f.* —*v.t.* interrogare; (*doubt*) mettere in dubbio. **in** ~ in questione. **out of the** ~ fuori discussione. ~ **mark** punto interrogativo *m.* **without** ~ senza dubbio.

questionable /'kwestʃənəbl/ *a.* discutibile.

questionnaire /kwestʃə'neə(r)/ *n.* questionario *m.*

queue /kju:/ *n.* fila *f.* —*v.i.* (*pres. p.* **queuing**) mettersi in fila.

quibble /'kwɪbl/ *v.i.* cavillare.

quick /kwɪk/ *a.* (**-er, -est**) veloce. —*adv.* in fretta. —*n.* **to the** ~ sul vivo *m.* **be** ~! sbrigati! ~**-tempered** *a.* collerico. ~**ly** *adv.* presto.

quicken /'kwɪkən/ *v.t./i.* affrettare, affrettarsi.

quicksand /'kwɪksænd/ *n.* sabbia mobile *f.*

quid /kwɪd/ *n. invar.* (*sl.*) sterlina *f.*

quiet /'kwaɪət/ *a.* (**-er, -est**) quieto; (*calm*) tranquillo; (*silent*) silenzioso. —*n.* quiete *f.* **on the** ~ di nascosto. ~**ly** *adv.* silenziosamente. ~**ness** *n.* tranquillità *f.*

quieten /'kwaɪətn/ *v.t./i.* calmare, calmarsi.

quill /kwɪl/ *n.* penna (d'oca) *f.*

quilt /kwɪlt/ *n.* trapunta *f.* **continental** ∼ piumone *m.* —*v.t.* trapuntare.

quince /kwɪns/ *n.* cotogna *f.* ∼ tree *n.* melo cotogno *m.*

quinine /kwɪˈniːn/ *n.* chinino *m.*

quintessence /kwɪnˈtesns/ *n.* quintessenza *f.*

quintet /kwɪnˈtet/ *n.* quintetto *m.*

quintuplet /ˈkwɪntjuːplət/ *n.* uno, a di cinque gemelli *m.*, *f.*

quip /kwɪp/ *n.* battuta spiritosa *f.* —*v.t.* (*p.t.* **quipped**) fare dello spirito.

quirk /kwɜːk/ *n.* stranezza *f.*

quit /kwɪt/ *v.t./i.* (*p.t.* **quitted**) andar via; (*cease*, *fam.*) smettere.

quite /kwaɪt/ *adv.* abbastanza; (*completely*) completamente; (*really*) ve-ramente. ∼ (**so**)! davvero! ∼ **a few** parecchi.

quits /kwɪts/ *a.* pari.

quiver /ˈkwɪvə(r)/ *v.i.* tremare.

quixotic /kwɪkˈsɒtɪk/ *a.* cavalleresco.

quiz /kwɪz/ *n.* (*pl.* **quizzes**) quesito *m.*; (*game*) quiz *m.* —*v.t.* (*pt.* **quizzed**) interrogare.

quizzical /ˈkwɪzɪkl/ *a.* canzonatorio.

quorum /ˈkwɔːrəm/ *n.* quorum *m.*

quota /ˈkwəʊtə/ *n.* quota *f.*

quotation /kwəʊˈteɪʃn/ *n.* citazione *f.*; (*price*) preventivo *m.* ∼ **marks** *n.pl.* virgolette *f.pl.*

quote /kwəʊt/ *v.t.* citare; (*price*) quotare. —*n.* (*fam.*) citazione *f.*; (*price*) preventivo *m.* ∼s *n.pl.* virgolette *f.pl.*

quotient /ˈkwəʊʃnt/ *n.* quoziente *m.*

R

rabbi /'ræbaɪ/ *n.* rabbino *m.*
rabbit /'ræbɪt/ *n.* coniglio *m.*
rabble /'ræbl/ *n.* calca *f.* the ∼ (*pej.*) la plebaglia *f.*
rabid /'ræbɪd/ *a.* rabbioso; (*dog*) idrofobo.
rabies /'reɪbi:z/ *n.* rabbia *f.*
race[1] /reɪs/ *n.* corsa *f.* −*v.t.* gareggiare con; (*horse*) fare correre. −*v.i.* (*run*) correre. ∼-track *n.* pista *f.* racing *n.* corse *f.pl.* racing car *n.* macchina da corsa *f.*
race[2] /reɪs/ *n.* razza *f.* ∼ riots *n.pl.* disordini di carattere razziale *m.pl.*
racecourse /'reɪskɔ:s/ *n.* ippodromo *m.*
racehorse /'reɪshɔ:s/ *n.* cavallo da corsa *m.*
racial /'reɪʃl/ *a.* razziale. ∼ism /-ɪzəm/ *n.* razzismo *m.*
racis|t /'reɪsɪst/ *a.* & *n.* razzista *m.*|*f.* ∼m /-zəm/ *n.* razzismo *m.*
rack[1] /ræk/ *n.* rastrelliera *f.*; (*for luggage*) portabagagli *m. invar.*; (*for plates*) scolapiatti *m. invar.* −*v.t.* ∼ one's brains scervellarsi.
rack[2] /ræk/ *n.* go to ∼ and ruin andare in rovina.
racket[1] /'rækɪt/ *n.* racchetta *f.*
racket[2] /'rækɪt/ *n.* (*din*) fracasso *m.*; (*swindle*) truffa *f.*: (*crime*) racket *m. invar.* ∼eer /-ə'tɪə(r)/ *n.* truffatore *m.*
raconteur /rækɒn'tɜ:/ *n.* narratore *m.*
racy /'reɪsɪ/ *a.* (-ier, -iest) arguto, vivace.
radar /'reɪdɑ:(r)/ *n.* radar *m.*
radian|t /'reɪdɪənt/ *a.* raggiante. ∼ce *n.* fulgore *m.* ∼tly *adv.* con fulgore.
radiat|e /'reɪdɪeɪt/ *v.t.*/*i.* irradiare, irradiarsi. ∼ion /-'eɪʃn/ *n.* radiazione *f.*
radiator /'reɪdɪeɪtə(r)/ *n.* radiatore *m.*
radical /'rædɪkl/ *a.* & *n.* radicale *m.*|*f.*
radio /'reɪdɪəʊ/ *n.* (*pl.* -os) radio *f.* −*v.t.* radiotelegrafare.
radioactiv|e /reɪdɪəʊ'æktɪv/ *a.* radioattivo. ∼ity /-'tɪvətɪ/ *n.* radioattività *f.*
radiograph|er /reɪdɪ'ɒgrəfə(r)/ *n.* radiologo, a *m.*, *f.* ∼y *n.* radiografia *f.*
radish /'rædɪʃ/ *n.* ravanello *m.*
radius /'reɪdɪəs/ *n.* (*pl.* -dii /-dɪaɪ/) raggio *m.*
raffish /'ræfɪʃ/ *a.* dissoluto.
raffle /ræfl/ *n.* lotteria *f.*

raft /rɑ:ft/ *n.* zattera *f.*
rafter /'rɑ:ftə(r)/ *n.* trave *f.*
rag[1] /ræg/ *n.* straccio *m.*; (*pej.*, *newspaper*) giornalaccio *m.* ∼s *n.pl.* abiti a brandelli *m.pl.*
rag[2] /ræg/ *v.t.* (*p.t.* ragged) (*sl.*) stuzzicare. −*n.* burla *f.*; (*univ.*) festa studentesca *f.*
ragamuffin /'rægəmʌfɪn/ *n.* straccione *m.*
rage /reɪdʒ/ *n.* rabbia *f.*; (*fashion*) gran moda *f.* −*v.i.* infuriarsi; (*of storm*) infuriare.
ragged /'rægɪd/ *a.* logoro; (*coastline*) frastagliato.
raid /reɪd/ *n.* (*mil.*, *police, etc.*) irruzione *f.*; (*by thieves*) rapina *f.* −*v.t.* fare un'incursione; rapinare. ∼er *n.* predone *m.*
rail[1] /reɪl/ *n.* ringhiera *f.*; (*for train*) binario *m.*; (*rod*) asta *f.* by ∼ per ferrovia.
rail[2] /reɪl/ *v.i.* ∼ against/at inveire contro.
railing /'reɪlɪŋ/ *n.* inferriata *f.*
railroad /'reɪlrəʊd/ *n.* (*Amer.*) = railway.
railway /'reɪlweɪ/ *n.* ferrovia *f.* ∼man *n.* (*pl.* -men) ferroviere *m.* ∼ station *n.* stazione ferroviaria *f.*
rain /reɪn/ *n.* pioggia *f.* −*v.i.* piovere. ∼-water *n.* acqua piovana *f.*
rainbow /'reɪnbəʊ/ *n.* arcobaleno *m.*
raincoat /'reɪnkəʊt/ *n.* impermeabile *m.*
rainfall /'reɪnfɔ:l/ *n.* precipitazione (atmosferica) *f.*
rainy /'reɪnɪ/ *a.* (-ier, -iest) piovoso.
raise /reɪz/ *v.t.* alzare; (*breed*) allevare; (*money etc.*) ottenere; (*question*) sollevare; (*hat, glass*) levare. −*n.* (*Amer.*) aumento *m.*
raisin /'reɪzn/ *n.* uva passa *f.*
rake[1] /reɪk/ *n.* rastrello *m.* −*v.t.* rastrellare; (*search*) frugare. ∼-off *n.* (*fam.*) percentuale *f.* ∼ up rivangare.
rake[2] /reɪk/ *n.* (*man*) scapestrato *m.*
rally /'rælɪ/ *v.t.*/*i.* radunare, radunarsi; (*in sickness*) riaversi. −*n.* raduno *m.*; (*recovery*) recupero *m.*; (*auto.*) rally *m. invar.*
ram /ræm/ *n.* montone *m.* −*v.t.* (*p.t.* rammed) cozzare (contro).

ramble 387 raven

rambl|e /'ræmbl/ *n.* escursione *f.* —*v.i.* gironzolare; (*in speech*) divagare. **~e on** parlare sconnessamente. **~er** *n.* escursionista *m./f.* **~ing** *a.* sconnesso.

ramification /ræmɪfɪ'keɪʃn/ *n.* ramificazione *f.*

ramp /ræmp/ *n.* rampa *f.*

rampage[1] /ræm'peɪdʒ/ *v.i.* andare su tutte le furie.

rampage[2] /'ræmpeɪdʒ/ *n.* **go on the ~** = **rampage**[1].

rampant /'ræmpənt/ *a.* (*disease etc.*) dilagante.

rampart /'ræmpɑːt/ *n.* bastione *m.*

ramshackle /'ræmʃækl/ *a.* sgangherato; (*house*) cadente.

ran /ræn/ *see* **run.**

ranch /rɑːntʃ/ *n.* ranch *m.*

rancid /'rænsɪd/ *a.* rancido.

rancour /'ræŋkə(r)/ *n.* rancore *m.*

random /'rændəm/ *a.* a caso. —*n.* **at ~** a casaccio.

randy /'rændɪ/ *a.* (-**ier,** -**iest**) lascivo.

rang /ræŋ/ *see* **ring**[2].

range /reɪndʒ/ *n.* (*series*) serie *f.*; (*of mountains*) catena *f.*; (*distance*) portata *f.*; (*comm., mus.*) gamma *f.*; (*open area*) pascolo *m.*; (*kitchen*) fornello *m.* —*v.i.* estendersi; (*vary*) variare.

ranger /'reɪndʒə(r)/ *n.* guardaboschi *m. invar.*

rank[1] /ræŋk/ *n.* riga *f.*; (*social position*) rango *m.* **~s** *n.pl.* soldati semplici *m.pl.* —*v.t./i.* schierare; (*place*) collocare. **the ~ and file** la bassa forza.

rank[2] /ræŋk/ *a.* (-**er,** -**est**) rigoglioso; (*smell*) puzzolente; (*fig.*) vero e proprio.

rankle /'ræŋkl/ *v.i.* (*fig.*) bruciare.

ransack /'rænsæk/ *v.t.* rovistare; (*pillage*) saccheggiare.

ransom /'rænsəm/ *n.* riscatto *m.* —*v.t.* riscattare; (*redeem*) redimere. **hold s.o. to ~** tenere qcno. in ostaggio.

rant /rænt/ *v.i.* declamare.

rap /ræp/ *n.* colpo (secco) *m.* —*v.t./i.* (*p.t.* **rapped**) picchiare.

rapacious /rə'peɪʃs/ *a.* rapace.

rap|e /reɪp/ *v.t.* violentare. —*n.* stupro *m.* **~ist** *n.* violentatore *m.*

rapid /'ræpɪd/ *a.* rapido. **~ity** /rə'pɪdətɪ/ *n.* rapidità *f.*

rapids /'ræpɪdz/ *n.pl.* rapida *f.s.*

rapport /ræ'pɔː(r)/ *n.* rapporto *m.*

rapt /ræpt/ *a.* rapito. **~ in** assorto in.

raptur|e /'ræptʃə(r)/ *n.* estasi *f.* **~ous** *a.* estatico.

rar|e[1] /reə(r)/ *a.* (-**er,** -**est**) raro. **~ely** *adv.* raramente. **~ity** *n.* rarità *f.*

rare[2] /reə(r)/ *a.* (*culin.*) al sangue.

rarefied /'reərɪfaɪd/ *a.* rarefatto.

raring /'reərɪŋ/ *a.* (*fam.*) **~ to** impaziente di.

rascal /'rɑːskl/ *n.* mascalzone *m.*

rash[1] /ræʃ/ *n.* eruzione *f.*

rash[2] /ræʃ/ *a.* (-**er,** -**est**) avventato. **~ly** *adv.* avventatamente. **~ness** *n.* avventatezza *f.*

rasher /'ræʃə(r)/ *n.* fetta (di pancetta) *f.*

rasp /rɑːsp/ *n.* stridio *m.* **~ing** *a.* stridente.

raspberry /'rɑːzbrɪ/ *n.* lampone *m.*

rat /ræt/ *n.* topo *m.* —*v.i.* (*p.t.* **ratted**) **~ on** far la spia a. **~ race** arrivismo *m.*

rate /reɪt/ *n.* andamento *m.*; (*speed*) velocità *f.*; (*price*) prezzo *m.*; (*comm.*) tasso *m.* **~s** *n.pl.* (*taxes*) imposte comunali *f.pl.* —*v.t.* valutare. —*v.i.* essere considerato. **at any ~** in ogni caso. **at this ~** di questo passo. **~able value** *n.* valore imponibile *m.*

ratepayer /'reɪtpeɪə(r)/ *n.* contribuente *m./f.*

rather /'rɑːðə(r)/ *adv.* piuttosto; (*fairly*) alquanto; (*int.*) eccome! **I would ~ not** preferirei di no.

ratif|y /'rætɪfaɪ/ *v.t.* ratificare. **~ication** /-ɪ'keɪʃn/ *n.* ratifica *f.*

rating /'reɪtɪŋ/ *n.* valutazione *f.*; (*sailor*) marinaio semplice *m.*

ratio /'reɪʃɪəʊ/ *n.* (*pl.* -**os**) proporzione *f.*

ration /'ræʃn/ *n.* razione *f.* —*v.t.* razionare.

rational /'ræʃnəl/ *a.* razionale.

rationalize /'ræʃnəlaɪz/ *v.t.* razionalizzare.

rattle /rætl/ *v.i.* tintinnare. —*v.t.* (*shake*) agitare; (*sl.*) innervosire. —*n.* tintinnio *m.*; (*toy*) sonaglio *m.* **~ off** *v.t.* (*fig.*) snocciolare.

rattlesnake /'rætlsneɪk/ *n.* serpente a sonagli *m.*

ratty /'rætɪ/ *a.* (-**ier,** -**iest**) (*sl.*) irritabile.

raucous /'rɔːkəs/ *a.* rauco.

ravage /'rævɪdʒ/ *v.t.* devastare.

ravages /'rævɪdʒɪz/ *n.pl.* danni *m.pl.*

rav|e /reɪv/ *v.i.* vaneggiare; (*in anger*) infuriarsi. **~e about** andare in estasi per. **~ings** *n.pl.* vaneggiamenti *m.pl.*

raven /'reɪvn/ *n.* cornacchia *f.* —*a.* (*of hair*) corvino.

ravenous /'rævənəs/ *a.* vorace; (*person*) affamato.

ravine /rə'vi:n/ *n.* burrone *m.*

raving /'reɪvɪŋ/ *a.* ~ **mad** matto da legare.

ravish /'rævɪʃ/ *v.t.* (*delight*) estasiare. ~**ing** *a.* affascinante.

raw /rɔ:/ *a.* (-**er**, -**est**) crudo; (*not processed*) grezzo; (*wound*) vivo; (*inexperienced*) inesperto; (*weather*) gelido. ~ **deal** *n.* trattamento ingiusto *m.* ~ **materials** *n.pl.* materie prime *f.pl.*

ray[1] /reɪ/ *n.* raggio *m.*

ray[2] /reɪ/ *n.* (*mus.*) re *m.*

raze /reɪz/ *v.t.* radere al suolo.

razor /'reɪzə(r)/ *n.* rasoio *m.*

re /ri:/ *prep.* riguardo a.

re- /ri:/ *pref.* ri-, di nuovo.

reach /ri:tʃ/ *v.t.* (*extend*) allungare; (*arrive at*) arrivare a; (*achieve*, *contact*) raggiungere; (*hand over*) prendere. —*v.i.* estendersi. —*n.* portata *f.*; (*of river*) tratto *m.* **within** ~ **of** alla portata di; (*close to*) a breve distanza da.

react /rɪ'ækt/ *v.i.* reagire.

reaction /rɪ'ækʃn/ *n.* reazione *f.* ~**ary** *a.* & *n.* reazionario, a *m.*, *f.*

reactor /rɪ'æktə(r)/ *n.* reattore *m.*

read /ri:d/ *v.t./i.* (*p.t.* **read** /red/) leggere; (*study*) studiare; (*interpret*) interpretare; (*of instrument*) indicare. —*n.* (*fam.*) lettura *f.* ~ **out** *v.t.* leggere ad alta voce. ~**able** *a.* piacevole a leggersi; (*clear*) leggibile. ~**ing** *n.* lettura *f.*

reader /'ri:də(r)/ *n.* let|tore, -trice *m.*, *f.* ~**ship** *n.* numero di lettori *m.*; (*univ.*) incarico universitario *m.*

readily /'redɪlɪ/ *adv.* volentieri; (*easily*) facilmente.

readiness /'redɪnɪs/ *n.* prontezza *f.* **in** ~ pronto.

readjust /ri:ə'dʒʌst/ *v.t.* riaggiustare. —*v.r.* adattarsi (**to**, a).

ready /'redɪ/ *a.* (-**ier**, -**iest**) pronto; (*quick*) veloce. **get** ~ prepararsi. ~-**made** *a.* confezionato. ~ **money** *n.* denaro in contanti *m.* ~ **reckoner** *n.* prontuario *m.*

real /rɪəl/ *a.* reale, vero. —*adv.* (*Amer. fam.*) veramente. ~ **estate** *n.* beni immobili *m.pl.*

realis|t /'rɪəlɪst/ *n.* realista *m.*/*f.* ~**m** /-zəm/ *n.* realismo *m.* ~**tic** /-'lɪstɪk/ *a.* realistico. ~**tically** /-'lɪstɪklɪ/ *adv.* realisticamente.

reality /rɪ'ælətɪ/ *n.* realtà *f.*

realiz|e /'rɪəlaɪz/ *v.t.* rendersi conto; (*fulfil*, *comm.*) realizzare. ~**ation** /-'zeɪʃn/ *n.* realizzazione *f.*; (*comm.*) realizzo *m.*

really /'rɪəlɪ/ *adv.* veramente.

realm /relm/ *n.* reame *m.*

ream /ri:m/ *n.* risma *f.*

reap /ri:p/ *v.t.* mietere; (*fig.*) raccogliere.

reappear /ri:ə'pɪə(r)/ *v.i.* riapparire.

reappraisal /ri:ə'preɪzl/ *n.* rivalutazione *f.*

rear[1] /rɪə(r)/ *n.* parte posteriore *f.* —*a.* posteriore. ~-**admiral** *n.* contrammiraglio *m.*

rear[2] /rɪə(r)/ *v.t.* allevare. —*v.i.* ~ (**up**) (*of horse*) impennarsi.

rearguard /'rɪəgɑ:d/ *n.* retroguardia *f.*

rearm /ri:'ɑ:m/ *v.t./i.* riarmare, riarmarsi.

rearrange /ri:ə'reɪndʒ/ *v.t.* riordinare.

reason /'ri:zn/ *n.* ragione *f.* —*v.i.* ragionare. **within** ~ nei limiti del ragionevole. ~**ing** *n.* ragionamento *m.*

reasonable /'ri:znəbl/ *a.* ragionevole.

reassur|e /ri:ə'ʃʊə(r)/ *v.t.* rassicurare. ~**ance** *n.* rassicurazione *f.*

rebate /'ri:beɪt/ *n.* rimborso *m.*; (*discount*) sconto *m.*

rebel[1] /'rebl/ *n.* ribelle *m.*/*f.*

rebel[2] /rɪ'bel/ *v.i.* (*p.t.* **rebelled**) ribellarsi. ~**lion** *n.* ribellione *f.* ~**lious** *a.* ribelle.

rebound[1] /rɪ'baʊnd/ *v.i.* rimbalzare; (*fig.*) ricadere.

rebound[2] /'ri:baʊnd/ *n.* rimbalzo *m.* **on the** ~ (*fig.*) per reazione.

rebuff /rɪ'bʌf/ *v.t.* respingere. —*n.* diniego *m.*

rebuild /ri:'bɪld/ *v.t.* (*p.t.* **rebuilt**) ricostruire.

rebuke /rɪ'bju:k/ *v.t.* rimproverare. —*n.* rimprovero *m.*

rebuttal /rɪ'bʌtl/ *n.* rifiuto *m.*

recall /rɪ'kɔ:l/ *v.t.* richiamare; (*remember*) rievocare. —*n.* richiamo *m.*

recant /rɪ'kænt/ *v.i.* ripudiare.

recap /'ri:kæp/ *v.t./i.* (*p.t.* **recapped**) (*fam.*) ricapitolare. —*n.* (*fam.*) ricapitolazione *f.*

recapitulat|e /ri:kə'pɪtʃʊleɪt/ *v.t./i.* ricapitolare. ~**ion** /-'leɪʃn/ *n.* ricapitolazione *f.*

recapture /ri:'kæptʃə(r)/ *v.t.* riconquistare; (*fig.*) ritrovare.

reced|e /rɪ'si:d/ *v.i.* recedere. ~**ing** *a.* (*forehead*) sfuggente.

receipt /rɪ'siːt/ *n.* ricevuta *f.* ∼s *n.pl.* (*comm.*) introiti *m.pl.*

receive /rɪ'siːv/ *v.t.* ricevere. ∼r /-ə(r)/ *n.* (*of stolen goods*) ricetta|tore, -trice *m.*, *f.*; (*of phone*) ricevitore *m.*

recent /'riːsnt/ *a.* recente. ∼ly *adv.* recentemente.

receptacle /rɪ'septəkl/ *n.* recipiente *m.*

reception /rɪ'sepʃn/ *n.* ricevimento *m.*; (*welcome*) accoglienza *f.*; (*radio etc.*) ricezione *f.* ∼ist *n.* segretaria *f.*

receptive /rɪ'septɪv/ *a.* ricettivo.

recess /rɪ'ses/ *n.* rientranza *f.*; (*fig.*) recesso *m.*; (*holiday*) vacanza *f.*

recession /rɪ'seʃn/ *n.* recessione *f.*

recharge /riː'tʃɑːdʒ/ *v.t.* ricaricare.

recipe /'resəpɪ/ *n.* ricetta *f.*

recipient /rɪ'sɪpɪənt/ *n.* ricevente *m.*/*f.*; (*of letter*) destinatario, a *m.*, *f.*

reciprocal /rɪ'sɪprəkl/ *a.* reciproco.

reciprocate /rɪ'sɪprəkeɪt/ *v.t.* contraccambiare.

recital /rɪ'saɪtl/ *n.* racconto *m.*; (*theatr.*) recital *m.*

recite /rɪ'saɪt/ *v.t.* recitare; (*list*) elencare.

reckless /'reklɪs/ *a.* incauto. ∼ly *adv.* incautamente. ∼ness *n.* imprudenza *f.*

reckon /'rekən/ *v.t.*/*i.* calcolare; (*consider*) considerare. ∼ on (*rely*) contare su. ∼ing *n.* conto *m.*

reclaim /rɪ'kleɪm/ *v.t.* reclamare; (*land*) bonificare.

reclin|e /rɪ'klaɪn/ *v.i.* sdraiarsi. ∼ing *a.* sdraiato; (*seat*) ribaltabile.

recluse /rɪ'kluːs/ *n.* recluso, a *m.*, *f.*

recognition /rekəg'nɪʃn/ *n.* riconoscimento *m.* **beyond** ∼ irriconoscibile.

recognize /'rekəgnaɪz/ *v.t.* riconoscere.

recoil /rɪ'kɔɪl/ *v.i.* rimbalzare; (*in fear*) indietreggiare. −*n.* rimbalzo *m.*

recollect /rekə'lekt/ *v.t.* ricordare. ∼ion /-ʃn/ *n.* ricordo *m.*

recommend /rekə'mend/ *v.t.* raccomandare. ∼ation /-'deɪʃn/ *n.* raccomandazione *f.*

recompense /'rekəmpens/ *v.t.* ricompensare. −*n.* ricompensa *f.*

reconcil|e /'rekənsaɪl/ *v.t.* (*people*) riconciliare; (*facts*) conciliare. ∼e o.s. rassegnarsi. ∼iation /-sɪlɪ'eɪʃn/ *n.* riconciliazione *f.*

recondition /riːkən'dɪʃn/ *v.t.* ripristinare.

reconn|oitre /rekə'nɔɪtə(r)/ *v.t.*/*i.* (*pres. p.* -**tring**) (*mil.*) fare una ricognizione di. ∼aissance /rɪ'kɒnɪsns/ *n.* ricognizione *f.*

reconsider /riːkən'sɪdə(r)/ *v.t.* riconsiderare.

reconstruct /riːkən'strʌkt/ *v.t.* ricostruire. ∼ion /-ʃn/ *n.* ricostruzione *f.*

record[1] /rɪ'kɔːd/ *v.t.*/*i.* registrare. ∼ing *n.* registrazione *f.*

record[2] /'rekɔːd/ *n.* (*file*) documentazione *f.*; (*mus.*) disco *m.*; (*sport*) record *m.* **off the** ∼ in confidenza. ∼-player *n.* giradischi *m. invar.*

record|er /rɪ'kɔːdə(r)/ *n.* registratore *m.*; (*mus.*) flauto dolce *m.* ∼ing *n.* registrazione *f.*

recount /rɪ'kaʊnt/ *v.t.* raccontare.

re-count[1] /riː'kaʊnt/ *v.t.* ricontare.

re-count[2] /'riːkaʊnt/ *n.* (*pol.*) nuovo computo *m.*

recoup /rɪ'kuːp/ *v.t.* ricuperare.

recourse /rɪ'kɔːs/ *n.* ricorso *m.* **have** ∼ **to** rivolgersi a.

recover /rɪ'kʌvə(r)/ *v.t.* ricuperare. −*v.i.* riprendersi. ∼y *n.* ricupero *m.*; (*of health*) guarigione *f.*

recreation /rekrɪ'eɪʃn/ *n.* ricreazione *f.* ∼al *a.* ricreativo.

recrimination /rɪkrɪmɪ'neɪʃn/ *n.* recriminazione *f.*

recruit /rɪ'kruːt/ *n.* recluta *f.* −*v.t.* reclutare. ∼ment *n.* reclutamento *n.*

rectang|le /'rektæŋgl/ *n.* rettangolo *m.* ∼ular /-'tæŋgjʊlə(r)/ *a.* rettangolare.

rectif|y /'rektɪfaɪ/ *v.t.* rettificare. ∼ication /-ɪ'keɪʃn/ *n.* rettificazione *f.*

rector /'rektə(r)/ *n.* parroco *m.*; (*of college*) rettore *m.* ∼y *n.* presbiterio *m.*

recumbent /rɪ'kʌmbənt/ *a.* supino.

recuperat|e /rɪ'kjuːpəreɪt/ *v.i.* ristabilirsi. ∼ion /-'reɪʃn/ *n.* ricupero *m.*

recur /rɪ'kɜː(r)/ *v.i.* (*p.t.* **recurred**) ricorrere.

recurren|t /rɪ'kʌrənt/ *a.* ricorrente. ∼ce *n.* ricorrenza *f.*

recycle /riː'saɪkl/ *v.t.* riciclare.

red /red/ *a.* (**redder, reddest**) rosso. −*n.* rosso *m.* **in the** ∼ (*account*) scoperto. ∼-**handed** *a.* in flagrante. ∼ **herring** *n.* (*fig.*) falsa pista *f.* ∼-**hot** *a.* rovente. **R**∼ **Indian** pellerossa *m.*/*f.* ∼-**letter day** *n.* giorno memorabile *m.* ∼ **light** *n.* segnale di pericolo *m.* ∼ **tape** *n.* (*fig.*) burocrazia *f.* ∼ness *n.* rossore *m.*

redbreast /'redbrest/ *n.* pettirosso *m.*

redbrick /'redbrɪk/ a. (*univ.*) di recente fondazione.
redd|en /'redn/ v.t. arrossare. —v.i.
arrossire. **~ish** a. rossastro.
redecorate /ri:'dekəreɪt/ v.t. ridipin-
gere.
red|eem /rɪ'di:m/ v.t. riscattare.
~eeming quality caratteristica che
salva f. **~emption** /-'dempʃn/ n.
riscatto m.
redeploy /ri:dɪ'plɔɪ/ v.t. ridistribuire.
rediffusion /ri:dɪ'fju:ʒn/ n. filo-
diffusione f.
redirect /ri:daɪə'rekt/ v.t. riindi-
rizzare.
redo /ri:'du:/ v.t. (*p.t.* **redid,** *p.p.*
redone) rifare.
redouble /rɪ'dʌbl/ v.t. raddoppiare.
redress /rɪ'dres/ v.t. riparare. —n. riparazione f.
reduc|e /rɪ'dju:s/ v.t. ridurre. —v.i.
(*slim*) dimagrire. **~tion** /-'dʌkʃn/ n.
riduzione f.
redundan|t /rɪ'dʌndənt/ a. superfluo.
be made ~t venir licenziato (per
eccesso di personale). **~cy** n. licenziamento (per eccesso di personale) m.;
cassa integrazione f.
reed /ri:d/ n. canna f.; (*mus.*) ancia f.
reef /ri:f/ n. scogliera f.
reefer /'ri:fə(r)/ n. giubbotto a doppio
petto m.; (*sl.*) sigaretta alla marijuana
f.
reek /ri:k/ n. puzzo m. —v.i. **~ (of)**
puzzare (di).
reel /ri:l/ n. bobina f. —v.i. girare;
(*stagger*) vacillare. —v.t. **~ off** (*fig.*)
snocciolare.
refectory /rɪ'fektərɪ/ n. refettorio m.
refer /rɪ'fɜ:(r)/ v.t./i. (*p.t.* **referred**) **~
to** fare allusione a; (*concern*) riguardare; (*for information*) indirizzare a;
(*consult*) rivolgersi a.
referee /refə'ri:/ n. arbitro m.; (*comm.*)
garante m./f. —v.i. (*p.t.* **refereed**) fare
da arbitro.
reference /'refrəns/ n. riferimento m.;
(*mention*) allusione f.; (*comm.*) refe-
renza f. **in** *or* **with ~ to** con riferimento a. **~ book** libro di
consultazione m.
referendum /refə'rendəm/ n. (*pl.*
-ums) referendum m.
refill[1] /ri:'fɪl/ v.t. riempire (di nuovo);
(*pen etc.*) ricaricare.
refill[2] /'ri:fɪl/ n. ricambio m.
refine /rɪ'faɪn/ v.t. raffinare. **~d** a.
raffinato. **~ment** n. raffinatezza f.;

(*techn.*) raffinazione f. **~ry** /-ərɪ/ n.
raffineria f.
reflation /ri:'fleɪʃn/ n. nuova inflazione f.
reflect /rɪ'flekt/ v.t./i. riflettere, riflettersi; (*of mirror*) rispecchiare. **~
upon** ripercuotersi su. **~ion** /-ʃn/ n.
riflessione f.; (*image*) riflesso m. **~or**
n. riflettore m.
reflective /rɪ'flektɪv/ a. riflessivo.
reflex /'ri:fleks/ a. & n. riflesso m.
reflexive /rɪ'fleksɪv/ a. (*gram.*) riflessivo.
reform /rɪ'fɔ:m/ v.t. riformare. —v.i.
correggersi. —n. riforma f. **~er** n.
riforma|tore, -trice m., f.
refract /rɪ'frækt/ v.t. rifrangere.
refrain[1] /rɪ'freɪn/ n. ritornello m.
refrain[2] /rɪ'freɪn/ v.i. astenersi (**from,**
da).
refresh /rɪ'freʃ/ v.t. rinfrescare. **~ing**
a. rinfrescante. **~ments** n.pl. rinfre-
sco m.s.
refresher /rɪ'freʃə(r)/ **~ course** n.
corso d'aggiornamento m.
refrigerat|e /rɪ'frɪdʒəreɪt/ v.t. refrige-
rare. **~or** n. frigorifero m.
refuel /ri:'fju:əl/ v.t./i. (*p.t.* **refuelled**)
rifornire, rifornirsi (di carburante).
refuge /'refju:dʒ/ n. rifugio m. **take ~**
rifugiarsi.
refugee /refju'dʒi:/ n. rifugiato, a m., f.
refund[1] /rɪ'fʌnd/ v.t. rimborsare.
refund[2] /'ri:fʌnd/ n. rimborso m.
refurbish /ri:'fɜ:bɪʃ/ v.t. rimettere a
nuovo.
refus|e[1] /rɪ'fju:z/ v.t./i. rifiutare, rifiu-
tarsi. **~al** n. rifiuto m.
refuse[2] /'refju:s/ n. immondizie f.pl.
refute /rɪ'fju:t/ v.t. confutare.
regain /rɪ'geɪn/ v.t. riguadagnare.
regal /'ri:gl/ a. regale.
regale /rɪ'geɪl/ v.t. deliziare.
regalia /rɪ'geɪlɪə/ n.pl. insegne f.pl.
regard /rɪ'gɑ:d/ v.t. guardare; (*consider*) considerare. —n. riguardo m.
~s n.pl. saluti m.pl. **as ~s, ~ing**
preps. per quanto riguarda.
regardless /rɪ'gɑ:dlɪs/ adv. lo stesso.
~ of senza badare a.
regatta /rɪ'gætə/ n. regata f.
regenerate /rɪ'dʒenəreɪt/ v.t. rigene-
rare.
regen|t /'ri:dʒənt/ n. reggente m./f.
~cy n. reggenza f.
regime /reɪ'ʒi:m/ n. regime m.
regiment /'redʒɪmənt/ n. reggimento
m. **~al** /-'mentl/ a. reggimentale.

~**ation** /-en'teɪʃn/ *n.* irreggimentazione *f.*

region /'riːdʒən/ *n.* regione *f.* **in the** ~ **of** approssimativamente. ~**al** *a.* regionale.

regist|er /'redʒɪstə(r)/ *n.* registro *m.* —*v.t./i.* registrare; (*vehicle*) immatricolare; (*letter*) raccomandare; (*luggage*) assicurare. ~**ration** /-'streɪʃn/ *n.* registrazione *f.*; immatricolazione *f.*; raccomandazione *f.*; assicurazione *f.* ~**ry** *or* ~**er office** *n.* anagrafe *f.*

registrar /redʒɪ'strɑː(r)/ *n.* ufficiale di stato civile *m.*; (*univ.*) segretario *m.*

regression /rɪ'greʃn/ *n.* regressione *f.*

regret /rɪ'gret/ *n.* rammarico *m.* —*v.t.* (*p.t.* **regretted**) rimpiangere. **I** ~ **that** mi rincresce che. ~**fully** *adv.* con rammarico. ~**table** *a.* spiacevole. ~**tably** *adv.* spiacevolmente. (*before adjective*) deplorevolmente.

regular /'regjʊlə(r)/ *a.* regolare. (*usual*) abituale. —*n.* (*fam.*) cliente abituale *m./f.* ~**ity** /-'lærəti/ *n.* regolarità *f.* ~**ly** *adv.* regolarmente.

regulat|e /'regjʊleɪt/ *v.t.* regolare. ~**ion** /-'leɪʃn/ *n.* regolamento *m.*

rehabilitat|e /riːə'bɪlɪteɪt/ *v.t.* riabilitare. ~**ion** /-'teɪʃn/ *n.* riabilitazione *f.*

rehash[1] /riː'hæʃ/ *v.t.* rimaneggiare.

rehash[2] /'riːhæʃ/ *n.* rimaneggiamento *m.*

rehears|e /rɪ'hɜːs/ *v.t.* fare le prove. ~**al** *n.* prova *f.*

reign /reɪn/ *n.* regno *m.* —*v.i.* regnare.

reimburse /riːɪm'bɜːs/ *v.t.* rimborsare.

reins /reɪnz/ *n.pl.* redini *f.pl.*

reindeer /'reɪndɪə(r)/ *n. invar.* renna *f.*

reinforce /riːɪn'fɔːs/ *v.t.* rinforzare. ~**ment** *n.* rinforzo *m.*

reinstate /riːɪn'steɪt/ *v.t.* reintegrare.

reiterate /riː'ɪtəreɪt/ *v.t.* reiterare.

reject[1] /rɪ'dʒekt/ *v.t.* scartare; (*refuse to accept*) respingere. ~**ion** /-ʃn/ *n.* scarto *m.*; ripulsa *f.*

reject[2] /'riːdʒekt/ *n.* rifiuto, scarto *m.*

rejoic|e /rɪ'dʒɔɪs/ *v.i.* gioire. ~**ing** *n.* gioia *f.*

rejoin /rɪ'dʒɔɪn/ *v.t.* raggiungere; (*answer*) replicare.

rejoinder /rɪ'dʒɔɪndə(r)/ *n.* replica *f.*

rejuvenate /riː'dʒuːvəneɪt/ *v.t.* ringiovanire.

rekindle /riː'kɪndl/ *v.t.* riaccendere.

relapse /rɪ'læps/ *n.* ricaduta *f.* —*v.i.* ricadere.

relate /rɪ'leɪt/ *v.t.* riportare; (*connect*) collegare. —*v.i.* ~ **to** riferirsi a; (*identify with*) aver rapporto con. ~**d** *a.* imparentato; (*ideas etc.*) affine.

relation /rɪ'leɪʃn/ *n.* rapporto *m.*; (*person*) parente *m./f.* ~**ship** *n.* rapporto *m.*; (*blood tie*) parentela *f.*; (*affair*) relazione *f.*

relative /'relətɪv/ *n.* parente *m./f.* —*a.* relativo. ~**ly** *adv.* relativamente.

relax /rɪ'læks/ *v.t./i.* rilassare, rilassarsi; (*pace, grip, etc.*) allentare. ~**ation** /riːlæk'seɪʃn/ *n.* rilassamento *m.*; (*recreation*) svago *m.* ~**ing** *a.* distensivo.

relay[1] /'riːleɪ/ *n.* turno *m.* ~ (**race**) *n.* corsa a staffetta *f.*

relay[2] /rɪ'leɪ/ *v.t.* ritrasmettere.

release /rɪ'liːs/ *v.t.* liberare; (*film*) distribuire; (*mech.*) sganciare; (*brake*) allentare; (*information etc.*) rilasciare. —*n.* liberazione *f.*; distribuzione *f.*; rilascio *m.*

relegate /'relɪgeɪt/ *v.t.* relegare.

relent /rɪ'lent/ *v.i.* cedere. ~**less** *a.* inflessibile.

relevan|t /'reləvənt/ *a.* pertinente. ~**ce** *n.* pertinenza *f.*

reliab|le /rɪ'laɪəbl/ *a.* fidato. ~**ility** /-'bɪləti/ *n.* affidabilità *f.*

relian|ce /rɪ'laɪəns/ *n.* affidamento *m.*; (*trust*) fiducia *f.* ~**t** *a.* fiducioso.

relic /'relɪk/ *n.* reliquia *f.* ~**s** *n.pl.* resti *m.pl.*

relief /rɪ'liːf/ *n.* sollievo *m.*; (*assistance*) soccorso *m.*; (*distraction*) diversivo *m.*; (*replacement*) sostituto *m.*; (*outline*) rilievo *m.* ~ **road** *n.* strada sussidiaria *f.*

relieve /rɪ'liːv/ *v.t.* alleviare; (*take over from*) dare il cambio a.

religion /rɪ'lɪdʒən/ *n.* religione *f.*

religious /rɪ'lɪdʒəs/ *a.* religioso.

relinquish /rɪ'lɪnkwɪʃ/ *v.t.* abbandonare.

relish /'relɪʃ/ *n.* gusto *m.*; (*culin.*) salsa *f.* —*v.t.* gustare; (*fig.*) apprezzare.

relocate /riːləʊ'keɪt/ *v.t.* ricollocare.

reluctan|t /rɪ'lʌktənt/ *a.* riluttante. ~**ce** *n.* riluttanza *f.* ~**tly** *adv.* a malincuore.

rely /rɪ'laɪ/ *v.i.* ~ **on** contare su; (*trust*) fidarsi di; (*depend*) dipendere da.

remain /rɪ'meɪn/ *v.i.* rimanere. ~**s** *n.pl.* resti *m.pl.*; (*dead body*) spoglie *f.pl.*

remainder /rɪ'meɪndə(r)/ *n.* resto *m.*; (*comm.*) rimanenza *f.*

remand /rɪ'mɑːnd/ *v.t.* ~ **in custody**

rinviare con detenzione provvisoria. —*n.* on ~ in detenzione preventiva.

remark /rɪ'mɑːk/ *n.* osservazione *f.* —*v.t.* osservare. ~**able** *a.* notevole.

remarry /riː'mærɪ/ *v.i.* risposarsi.

remed|y /'remədɪ/ *n.* rimedio *m.* —*v.t.* rimediare. ~**ial** /rɪ'miːdɪəl/ *a.* correttivo.

rememb|er /rɪ'membə(r)/ *v.t./i.* ricordare, ricordarsi. ~**rance** *n.* ricordo *m.*

remind /rɪ'maɪnd/ *v.t.* (far) ricordare. ~**er** *n.* promemoria *m.*; (*letter*) lettera di sollecito *f.*

reminisce /remɪ'nɪs/ *v.i.* rievocare il passato. ~**nces** *n.pl.* memorie *f.pl.*

reminiscent /remɪ'nɪsnt/ *a.* ~ **of** che richiama alla mente.

remiss /rɪ'mɪs/ *a.* negligente.

remission /rɪ'mɪʃn/ *n.* remissione *f.*; (*of sentence*) condono *m.*

remit /rɪ'mɪt/ *v.t.* (*p.t.* **remitted**) perdonare; (*money*) rimettere; (*mitigate*) diminuire. ~**tance** *n.* rimessa *f.*

remnant /'remnənt/ *n.* resto *m.*; (*of cloth*) scampolo *m.*; (*trace*) traccia *f.*

remonstrate /'remənstreɪt/ *v.i.* fare rimostranze.

remorse /rɪ'mɔːs/ *n.* rimorso *m.* ~**ful** *a.* pieno di rimorso. ~**less** *a.* spietato.

remote /rɪ'məʊt/ *a.* remoto; (*slight*) minimo. ~ **control** *n.* telecomando *m.* ~**ly** *adv.* lontanamente. ~**ness** *n.* lontananza *f.*

removable /rɪ'muːvəbl/ *a.* rimovibile.

remov|e /rɪ'muːv/ *v.t.* levare; (*dismiss*) licenziare; (*get rid of*) eliminare. ~**al** *n.* eliminazione *f.*; (*from house*) trasloco *m.*

remunerat|e /rɪ'mjuːnəreɪt/ *v.t.* rimunerare. ~**ion** /-'reɪʃn/ *n.* rimunerazione *f.* ~**ive** *a.* rimunerativo.

Renaissance /rə'neɪsəns/ *n.* Rinascimento *m.*

rend /rend/ *v.t.* (*p.t.* **rent**) lacerare.

render /'rendə(r)/ *v.t.* rendere; (*comm.*) presentare; (*fat*) sciogliere; (*mus.*) interpretare. ~**ing** *n.* (*mus.*) interpretazione *f.*

rendezvous /'rɒndɪvuː/ *n.* (*pl.* -**vous** /-vuːz/) convegno *m.*

renegade /'renɪgeɪd/ *n.* rinnegato, a *m.,f.*

renew /rɪ'njuː/ *v.t.* rinnovare. ~**able** *a.* rinnovabile. ~**al** *n.* rinnovo *m.*

renounce /rɪ'naʊns/ *v.t.* rinunciare a; (*disown*) ripudiare.

renovat|e /'renəveɪt/ *v.t.* rinnovare. ~**ion** /-'veɪʃn/ *n.* rinnovamento *m.*

renown /rɪ'naʊn/ *n.* fama *f.* ~**ed** *a.* rinomato.

rent¹ /rent/ *see* **rend.**

rent² /rent/ *n.* affitto *m.* —*v.t.* affittare. (**fair**) ~ **act** *n.* equo canone *m.* ~**al** *n.* affitto *m.*

renunciation /rɪnʌnsɪ'eɪʃn/ *n.* rinunzia *f.*

reopen /riː'əʊpən/ *v.t./i.* riaprire. ~**ing** *n.* riapertura *f.*

reorganize /riː'ɔːgənaɪz/ *v.t.* riorganizzare.

rep /rep/ *n.* (*comm., fam.*) rappresentante *m./f.*; (*theatr., fam.*) teatro di repertorio *m.*

repair /rɪ'peə(r)/ *v.t.* riparare. —*n.* riparazione *f.* **in good** ~ in buono stato.

repartee /repɑː'tiː/ *n.* risposta pronta *f.*

repatriat|e /riː'pætrɪeɪt/ *v.t.* rimpatriare. ~**ion** /-'eɪʃn/ *n.* rimpatrio *m.*

repay /riː'peɪ/ *v.t.* (*p.t.* **repaid**) ripagare; (*reward*) ricompensare. ~**ment** *n.* rimborso *m.*

repeal /rɪ'piːl/ *v.t.* abrogare. —*n.* abrogazione *f.*

repeat /rɪ'piːt/ *v.t./i.* ripetere. —*n.* ripetizione *f.*; (*mus.*) ripresa *f.*

repeatedly /rɪ'piːtɪdlɪ/ *adv.* ripetutamente.

repel /rɪ'pel/ *v.t.* (*p.t.* **repelled**) ripugnare. ~**lent** *a.* ripulsivo.

repent /rɪ'pent/ *v.i.* pentirsi. ~**ance** *n.* pentimento *m.* ~**ant** *a.* pentito.

repercussion /riːpə'kʌʃn/ *n.* ripercussione *f.*

repertoire /'repətwɑː(r)/ *n.* repertorio *m.*

repertory /'repətrɪ/ *n.* ~ **company** compagnia stabile *f.*

repetit|ion /repɪ'tɪʃn/ *n.* ripetizione *f.* ~**ious** /-'tɪʃəs/, ~**ive** /rɪ'petətɪv/ *adjs.* che si ripete; (*dull*) monotono.

replace /rɪ'pleɪs/ *v.t.* rimettere; (*take the place of*) sostituire. ~**ment** *n.* sostituzione *f.*; (*person*) sostituto, a *m.,f.* ~**ment part** *n.* pezzo di ricambio *m.*

replay /'riːpleɪ/ *n.* (*sport*) partita ripetuta *f.*

replenish /rɪ'plenɪʃ/ *v.t.* rifornire; (*refill*) riempire di nuovo.

replete /rɪ'pliːt/ *a.* ~ **with** pieno di.

replica /'replɪkə/ *n.* copia *f.*

reply /rɪ'plaɪ/ *v.t./i.* rispondere. —*n.* risposta *f.*

report /rɪ'pɔːt/ v.t./i. riportare; (present o.s.) presentarsi; (denounce) denunciare. **~ on** (news item) fare la cronaca di. —n. rapporto m.; (schol.) pagella f.; (rumour) diceria f.; (newspaper) cronaca f. **~age** /repɔː'tɑːʒ/ n. reportage m. **~edly** adv. secondo quanto si dice.

reporter /rɪ'pɔːtə(r)/ n. cronista m./f.

repose /rɪ'pəʊz/ n. riposo m.

repository /rɪ'pɒzɪtrɪ/ n. deposito m.

repossess /riːpə'zes/ v.t. ripossedere.

reprehen|d /reprɪ'hend/ v.t. rimproverare. **~sible** /-səbl/ a. biasimevole.

represent /reprɪ'zent/ v.t. rappresentare. **~ation** /-'teɪʃn/ n. rappresentazione f.

representative /reprɪ'zentətɪv/ a. rappresentativo. —n. rappresentante m./f.

repress /rɪ'pres/ v.t. reprimere. **~ion** /-ʃn/ n. repressione f. **~ive** a. repressivo.

reprieve /rɪ'priːv/ n. sospensione di pena capitale f.; (fig.) tregua f. —v.t. sospendere la sentenza di; (fig.) dar tregua.

reprimand /'reprɪmɑːnd/ v.t. sgridare. —n. sgridata f.

reprint[1] /'riːprɪnt/ n. ristampa f.

reprint[2] /riː'prɪnt/ v.t. ristampare.

reprisal /rɪ'praɪzl/ n. rappresaglia f.

reproach /rɪ'prəʊtʃ/ v.t. rimproverare. —n. rimprovero m. **~ful** a. riprovevole. **~fully** adv. con aria di rimprovero.

reprobate /'reprəbeɪt/ n. reprobo, a m., f.

reproduc|e /riːprə'djuːs/ v.t./i. riprodurre, riprodursi. **~tion** /-'dʌkʃn/ n. riproduzione f. **~tive** /-'dʌktɪv/ a. riproduttivo.

reprove /rɪ'pruːv/ v.t. biasimare.

reptile /'reptaɪl/ n. rettile m.

republic /rɪ'pʌblɪk/ n. repubblica f. **~an** a. & n. repubblicano, a m., f.

repudiate /rɪ'pjuːdɪeɪt/ v.t. ripudiare.

repugnan|t /rɪ'pʌgnənt/ a. ripugnante. **~ce** n. ripugnanza f.

repuls|e /rɪ'pʌls/ v.t. respingere. **~ion** /-ʃn/ n. repulsione f. **~ive** a. ripugnante.

reputable /'repjʊtəbl/ a. rispettabile.

reputation /repjʊ'teɪʃn/ n. reputazione f.

repute /rɪ'pjuːt/ n. reputazione f. **~d** /-ɪd/ a. reputato. **~dly** adv. presumibilmente.

request /rɪ'kwest/ n. richiesta f. —v.t. richiedere. **~ stop** n. fermata facoltativa f.

require /rɪ'kwaɪə(r)/ v.t. richiedere; (need) aver bisogno di; (demand) esigere. **~d** a. richiesto. **~ment** n. esigenza f.

requisite /'rekwɪzɪt/ a. necessario. —n. requisito m.

requisition /rekwɪ'zɪʃn/ n. requisizione f. —v.t. requisire.

resale /'riːseɪl/ n. rivendita f.

rescind /rɪ'sɪnd/ v.t. rescindere.

rescue /'reskjuː/ v.t. salvare. —n. soccorso m. **~r** /-ə(r)/ n. salva|tore, -trice m., f.

research /rɪ'sɜːtʃ/ n. ricerca f. —v.t. fare ricerche su. **~er** n. ricerca|tore, -trice m., f.

resembl|e /rɪ'zembl/ v.t. rassomigliare. **~ance** n. rassomiglianza f.

resent /rɪ'zent/ v.t. risentirsi (di). **~ful** a. pieno di risentimento. **~ment** n. risentimento m.

reservation /rezə'veɪʃn/ n. riserva f.; (booking) prenotazione f.; (doubt) dubbio m.

reserve /rɪ'zɜːv/ v.t. riservare. —n. riserva f.; (self-restraint) riserbo m. **~d** a. riservato.

reservist /rɪ'zɜːvɪst/ n. riservista m.

reservoir /'rezəvwɑː(r)/ n. bacino idrico m; (container) serbatoio m.

reshape /riː'ʃeɪp/ v.t. rifoggiare.

reshuffle /riː'ʃʌfl/ v.t. (pol.) rimaneggiare. —n. (pol.) rimaneggiamento m.

reside /rɪ'zaɪd/ v.i. risiedere.

residen|t /'rezɪdənt/ a. & n. residente m./f. **~ce** n. residenza f. **be in ~ce** essere in sede. **~ce permit** n. permesso di soggiorno m.

residential /rezɪ'denʃl/ a. residenziale.

residue /'rezɪdjuː/ n. residuo m.

resign /rɪ'zaɪn/ v.t. dimettersi da. —v.i. dare le dimissioni. **~ o.s. to** rassegnarsi a. **~ation** /rezɪg'neɪʃn/ n. rassegnazione f.; (from job) dimissioni f.pl. **~ed** a. rassegnato.

resilien|t /rɪ'zɪlɪənt/ a. resiliente. **~ce** n. capacità di recupero f.

resin /'rezɪn/ n. resina f.

resist /rɪ'zɪst/ v.t./i. resistere (a). **~ance** n. resistenza f. **~ant** a. resistente.

resolut|e /'rezəluːt/ a. risoluto. **~ion** /-'luːʃn/ n. risoluzione f.

resolve /rɪ'zɒlv/ *v.t.* ~ **to do** decidere di fare. —*n.* risoluzione *f.* ~**d** *a.* risoluto.

resonan|t /'rezənənt/ *a.* risonante. ~**ce** *n.* risonanza *f.*

resort /rɪ'zɔːt/ *v.i.* ~ **to** ricorrere a. —*n.* ricorso *m.*; (*place*) stazione climatica *f.* **in the last** ~ come ultima risorsa.

resound /rɪ'zaʊnd/ *v.i.* risonare (**with**, di). ~**ing** *a.* risonante.

resource /rɪ'sɔːs/ *n.* risorse *f.pl.* ~**ful** *a.* ingegnoso. ~**fulness** *n.* ingegnosità *f.*

respect /rɪ'spekt/ *n.* rispetto *m.*; (*aspect*) aspetto *m.* —*v.t.* rispettare. **with** ~ **to** in quanto a. ~**ful** *a.* rispettoso.

respectab|le /rɪ'spektəbl/ *a.* rispettabile. ~**ility** /-'bɪlətɪ/ *n.* rispettabilità *f.* ~**ly** *adv.* rispettabilmente.

respective /rɪ'spektɪv/ *a.* rispettivo. ~**ly** *adv.* rispettivamente.

respiration /respə'reɪʃn/ *n.* respirazione *f.*

respite /'respaɪt/ *n.* respiro *m.*

resplendent /rɪ'splendənt/ *a.* risplendente.

respond /rɪ'spɒnd/ *v.i.* rispondere. ~ **to** (*react*) reagire a.

response /rɪ'spɒns/ *n.* risposta *f.*

responsib|le /rɪ'spɒnsəbl/ *a.* responsabile; (*job*) impegnativo. ~**ility** /-'bɪlətɪ/ *n.* responsabilità *f.* ~**ly** *adv.* in modo responsabile.

responsive /rɪ'spɒnsɪv/ *a.* sensibile.

rest¹ /rest/ *v.t./i.* riposare, riposarsi; (*lean*) appoggiare, appoggiarsi; (*place*) posare, posarsi. —*n.* riposo *m.*; appoggio *m.*; (*mus.*) pausa *f.*

rest² /rest/ *v.i.* (*remain*) restare. —*n.* (*remainder*) (il) resto *m.*; (*people*) gli altri *m.pl.*

restaurant /'restrɒnt/ *n.* ristorante *m.*

restful /'restfl/ *a.* riposante.

restitution /restɪ'tjuːʃn/ *n.* restituzione *f.*

restive /'restɪv/ *a.* irrequieto.

restless /'restlɪs/ *a.* inquieto. ~**ly** *adv.* agitatamente. ~**ness** *n.* inquietudine *f.*

restor|e /rɪ'stɔː(r)/ *v.t.* ristabilire; (*building*) restaurare; (*put back in position*) rimettere (a posto). ~**ation** /restə'reɪʃn/ *n.* restituzione *f.*; (*of building*) restauro *m.*

restrain /rɪ'streɪn/ *v.t.* trattenere. ~ **o.s.** controllarsi. ~**ed** *a.* trattenuto; controllato. ~**t** *n.* restrizione *f.*; (*moderation*) ritegno *m.*

restrict /rɪ'strɪkt/ *v.t.* restringere. ~**ion** /-ʃn/ *n.* restrizione *f.*

restrictive /rɪ'strɪktɪv/ *a.* restrittivo.

result /rɪ'zʌlt/ *n.* risultato *m.* —*v.i.* ~ **from** risultare da. ~ **in** concludersi con.

resum|e /rɪ'zjuːm/ *v.t./i.* riprendere. ~**ption** /rɪ'zʌmpʃn/ *n.* ripresa *f.*

résumé /'reʒjuːmeɪ/ *n.* riassunto *m.*

resurgence /rɪ'sɜːdʒəns/ *n.* rinascita *f.*

resurrect /rezə'rekt/ *v.t.* far risorgere. ~**ion** /-ʃn/ *n.* risurrezione *f.*

resuscitat|e /rɪ'sʌsɪteɪt/ *v.t.* risuscitare. ~**ion** /-'teɪʃn/ *n.* rianimazione *f.*

retail /'riːteɪl/ *n.* vendita al minuto *f.* —*a.* & *adv.* al minuto. —*v.t./i.* vendere, vendersi al minuto. ~**er** *n.* rivendi|tore, -trice *m.*, *f.*

retain /rɪ'teɪn/ *v.t.* ritenere; (*keep*) conservare.

retainer /rɪ'teɪnə(r)/ *n.* (*fee*) onorario *m.*; (*person*) dipendente *m./f.*

retaliat|e /rɪ'tælɪeɪt/ *v.i.* ricambiare (offesa, insulto). ~**ion** /-'eɪʃn/ *n.* rappresaglia *f.*

retarded /rɪ'tɑːdɪd/ *a.* ritardato.

retentive /rɪ'tentɪv/ *a.* (*memory*) che ritiene.

rethink /riː'θɪŋk/ *v.t.* (*p.t.* **rethought**) ripensare.

reticen|t /'retɪsnt/ *a.* reticente. ~**ce** *n.* reticenza *f.*

retina /'retɪnə/ *n.* retina *f.*

retinue /'retɪnjuː/ *n.* seguito *m.*

retire /rɪ'taɪə(r)/ *v.i.* ritirarsi. —*v.t.* (far) ritirare. ~**d** *a.* a riposo. ~**ment** *n.* ritiro *m.*

retiring /rɪ'taɪərɪŋ/ *a.* riservato.

retort /rɪ'tɔːt/ *v.t./i.* ribattere. —*n.* rimbeccata *f.*

retrace /riː'treɪs/ *v.t.* rintracciare. ~ **one's steps** ritornare sui propri passi.

retract /rɪ'trækt/ *v.t.* ritirare. —*v.i.* ritrarsi.

retrain /riː'treɪn/ *v.t.* riaddestrare.

retreat /rɪ'triːt/ *v.i.* ritirarsi; (*mil.*) battere in ritirata. —*n.* ritirata *f.*

retrial /riː'traɪəl/ *n.* nuovo processo *m.*

retribution /retrɪ'bjuːʃn/ *n.* castigo *m.*

retriev|e /rɪ'triːv/ *v.t.* salvare; (*recover*) ricuperare. ~**al** *n.* ricupero *m.* ~**er** *n.* (*dog*) cane da riporto *m.*

retrograde /'retrəgreɪd/ *a.* retrogrado.

retrospect /'retrəspekt/ *n.* **in** ~ guardando indietro. ~**ive** /-'spektɪv/ *a.* retrospettivo.

return /rɪ'tɜ:n/ v.i. ritornare; (go home) rientrare. —v.t. (give back) restituire; (put back) rimettere; (send back) mandare indietro; (comm.) rendere. —n. ritorno m.; (comm.) profitto m.; (restitution) restituzione f. **in ∼ for** in cambio di. **∼ match** n. rivincita f. **∼ of income** n. dichiarazione dei redditi f. **∼ ticket** n. biglietto di andata e ritorno m. **∼s** n.pl. (comm.) incassi m.pl. **many happy ∼s!** tanti auguri!

returning /rɪ'tɜ:nɪŋ/ a. **∼ officer** (at elections) scrutatore m.

reunion /ri:'ju:nɪən/ n. riunione f.

reunite /ri:ju:'naɪt/ v.t. riunire.

rev /rev/ n. (auto., fam.) giro (di motore) m. —v.t./i. **∼ (up)** (p.t. **revved**) (auto., fam.) andare su di giri.

revamp /ri:'væmp/ v.t. rimettere a nuovo.

reveal /rɪ'vi:l/ v.t. rivelare. **∼ing** a. rivelatore; (dress) trasparente.

revel /'revl/ v.i. **∼ in** (p.t. **revelled**) godere di. **∼s** n.pl. festeggiamenti m.pl. **∼ry** n. baldoria f.

revelation /revə'leɪʃn/ n. rivelazione f.

revenge /rɪ'vendʒ/ n. vendetta f.; (sport) rivincita f. —v.t. vendicare. **take ∼** vendicarsi. **∼ful** a. vendicativo.

revenue /'revənju:/ n. reddito m.

reverberate /rɪ'vɜ:bəreɪt/ v.i. riverberare.

revere /rɪ'vɪə(r)/ v.t. riverire. **∼nce** /'revərəns/ n. reverenza f.

reverend /'revərənd/ a. venerando.

reverent /'revərənt/ a. reverente.

reverie /'revərɪ/ n. sogno ad occhi aperti m.

revers /rɪ'vɪə/ n. (pl. **revers** /rɪ'vɪəz/) n. risvolto m.

revers|e /rɪ'vɜ:s/ a. inverso. —n. contrario m.; (back) rovescio m.; (auto.) marcia indietro f. —v.t. invertire; (turn inside out) rivoltare. —v.i. (auto.) far marcia indietro. **∼al** n. rovesciamento m.

revert /rɪ'vɜ:t/ v.i. **∼ to** tornare a.

review /rɪ'vju:/ n. rassegna f.; (mil.) rivista f.; (of book, play, etc.) recensione f. —v.t. (situation) riesaminare; (book, play, etc.) recensire. **∼er** n. recensore, a m., f.

revile /rɪ'vaɪl/ v.t. ingiuriare.

revis|e /rɪ'vaɪz/ v.t. rivedere. **∼ion** /-ɪʒn/ n. revisione f.

reviv|e /rɪ'vaɪv/ v.t./i. ravvivare, ravvi-

varsi; (person) rianimare, rianimarsi. **∼al** n. rinascita f.; (of faith) risveglio m.

revoke /rɪ'vəʊk/ v.t. revocare.

revolt /rɪ'vəʊlt/ v.i. ribellarsi. —v.t. rivoltare. —n. rivolta f.

revolting /rɪ'vəʊltɪŋ/ a. ripugnante.

revolution /revə'lu:ʃn/ n. rivoluzione f. **∼ary** a. & n. rivoluzionario, a m., f. **∼ize** v.t. rivoluzionare.

revolv|e /rɪ'vɒlv/ v.i. rotare. **∼ing** a. rotante.

revolver /rɪ'vɒlvə(r)/ n. rivoltella f.

revue /rɪ'vju:/ n. rivista f.

revulsion /rɪ'vʌlʃn/ n. ripugnanza f.

reward /rɪ'wɔ:d/ n. ricompensa f. —v.t. ricompensare. **∼ing** a. gratificante.

rewrite /ri:'raɪt/ v.t. (p.t. **rewrote**, p.p. **rewritten**) riscrivere.

rhapsody /'ræpsədɪ/ n. rapsodia f.

rhetoric /'retərɪk/ n. retorica f. **∼al** /rɪ'tɒrɪkl/ a. retorico.

rheumati|c /ru:'mætɪk/ a. reumatico. **∼sm** /'ru:mətɪzəm/ n. reumatismo m.

rhinestone /'raɪnstəʊn/ n. strass m.

rhinoceros /raɪ'nɒsərəs/ n. (pl. **-oses**) rinoceronte m.

rhubarb /'ru:bɑ:b/ n. rabarbaro m.

rhyme /raɪm/ n. rima f.; (poem) verso m. —v.t./i. (far) rimare.

rhythm /'rɪðəm/ n. ritmo m. **∼ic(al)** /'rɪðmɪk(l)/ a. ritmico.

rib /rɪb/ n. costola f. —v.t. (p.t. **ribbed**) (fam.) prendere in giro.

ribald /'rɪbld/ a. osceno.

ribbon /'rɪbən/ n. nastro m.

rice /raɪs/ n. riso m.

rich /rɪtʃ/ a. (-er, -est) ricco. **∼es** n.pl. ricchezze f.pl. **∼ly** adv. riccamente. **∼ness** n. ricchezza f.

rickety /'rɪkətɪ/ a. (shaky) malfermo.

ricochet /'rɪkəʃeɪ/ n. rimbalzo m. —v.i. rimbalzare.

rid /rɪd/ v.t. (p.t. **rid**, pres. p. **ridding**) sbarazzare (of, di). **get ∼ of** liberarsi di.

riddance /'rɪdns/ n. **good ∼!** che liberazione!

ridden /'rɪdn/ see **ride**. —a. **∼ by** pieno di; (fear etc.) tormentato da.

riddle[1] /'rɪdl/ n. enigma m.

riddle[2] /'rɪdl/ v.t. **∼ with** crivellare di.

ride /raɪd/ v.i. (p.t. **rode**, p.p. **ridden**) andare a cavallo or in bicicletta; (sport) cavalcare; (in car) viaggiare; —v.t. (horse) montare. —n. (on horse) cavalcata f.; (in car) giro m., corsa f. **take s.o. for a ∼** (fam.)

prendere qcno. in giro. ~r /-ə(r)/ n.
cavalca|tore, -trice m., f.; (in race)
fantino m.; (in document) codicillo m.
ridge /rɪdʒ/ n. spigolo m.; (of mountain) cresta f.
ridicule /'rɪdɪkjuːl/ n. ridicolo m.
—v.t. mettere in ridicolo; (make fun
of) canzonare.
ridiculous /rɪ'dɪkjʊləs/ a. ridicolo.
riding /'raɪdɪŋ/ n. equitazione f.
rife /raɪf/ a. diffuso. ~ with pieno di.
riff-raff /'rɪfræf/ n. marmaglia f.
rifle /'raɪfl/ n. fucile m. —v.t. depre-
dare. ~-range n. tiro al bersaglio m.
rift /rɪft/ n. fessura f.; (fig.) screzio m.
rig[1] /rɪg/ v.t. (p.t. rigged) equipaggiare. —n. equipaggiamento m.; (at
sea) piattaforma per trivellazioni subacquee f. ~-out n. (fam.) tenuta f. ~
out v.t. attrezzare. ~ up v.t. allestire.
rig[2] /rɪg/ v.t. (p.t. rigged) (pej.) manovrare.
right /raɪt/ a. (correct, fair) corretto,
giusto; (not left) destro; (suitable) appropriato. —n. giusto m.; (not left)
destra f.; (not evil) bene m.; (what is
due) diritto m. —v.t. raddrizzare; (fig.)
riparare. —adv. a destra; (directly)
diritto; (completely) per tutto,
completamente. **be in the** ~ essere
nel giusto. **on the** ~ a destra. **put** ~
rettificare. ~ **angle** n. angolo retto
m. ~ **away** adv. immediatamente. ~-
hand man n. braccio destro m. ~ **of
way** n. (auto.) precedenza f. ~ **wing**
a. (pol.) di destra; n. (sport) ala destra
f. ~**ly** adv. giustamente.
righteous /'raɪtʃəs/ a. retto; (cause)
giusto.
rightful /'raɪtfl/ a. legittimo. ~**ly** adv.
legittimamente.
rigid /'rɪdʒɪd/ a. rigido. ~**ity** /-'dʒɪdətɪ/
n. rigidità f.
rigmarole /'rɪgmərəʊl/ n. tiritera f.
rig|our /'rɪgə(r)/ n. rigore m. ~**orous**
a. rigoroso; (of weather) rigido.
rile /raɪl/ v.t. (fam.) irritare.
rim /rɪm/ n. bordo m.; (of wheel) cer-
chione m. ~**med** a. bordato.
rind /raɪnd/ n. scorza f.; (on cheese)
crosta f.; (on bacon) cotenna f.
ring[1] /rɪŋ/ n. (circle) cerchio m.; (on
finger) anello m.; (boxing) ring m.;
(arena) arena f.; (for circus) circo m.
—v.t. accerchiare. ~ **road** n. raccordo
anulare m.
ring[2] /rɪŋ/ v.t./i. (p.t. rang, p.p. rung)
suonare. —n. suono m.; (fam., phone)

colpo di telefono m. ~ **back** v.t./i.
richiamare. ~ **off** v.i. riattaccare il
ricevitore. ~ **the changes** (fig.) fare
variazioni. ~ **up** v.t. telefonare a.
ringleader /'rɪŋliːdə(r)/ n. capobanda
m.
rink /rɪŋk/ n. pista di pattinaggio f.
rinse /rɪns/ v.t. sciacquare. —n. riscia-
cquo m.; (for hair) cachet m.
riot /'raɪət/ n. rivolta f.; (of colours)
profusione f. —v.i. insorgere. **run** ~
abbandonarsi ad eccessi. ~**er** n. di-
mostrante m./f. ~**ous** a. tumultuante.
rip /rɪp/ v.t./i. (p.t. ripped) strappare,
strapparsi. —n. strappo m. **let** ~ (fig.)
lasciar perdere. ~**-cord** n. (of parachute) cavo di spiegamento m. ~ **off**
v.t. (sl.) defraudare. ~**-off** n. (sl.) frode
f.
ripe /raɪp/ a. (-er, -est) maturo. ~**ness**
n. maturità f.
ripen /'raɪpən/ v.t./i. (far) maturare.
ripple /'rɪpl/ n. increspatura f.; (sound)
mormorio m. —v.t./i. increspare, incresparsi.
rise /raɪz/ v.i. (p.t. rose, p.p. risen)
levarsi, alzarsi; (rebel) insorgere; (of
river) crescere; (of prices) aumentare. —n. levata f.; (land) altura f.;
(increase) aumento m.; (to power)
ascesa f. **give** ~ **to** far sorgere.
~r /-ə(r)/ n. **early** ~r persona matti-
niera f.
rising /'raɪzɪŋ/ n. (revolt) insurrezione
f. —a. (sun) levante. ~ **generation**
nuova generazione f.
risk /rɪsk/ n. rischio m. —v.t. rischiare. ~**y** a. (-ier, -iest) rischioso.
risqué /'riːskeɪ/ a. spinto.
rissole /'rɪsəʊl/ n. polpetta f.
rite /raɪt/ n. rito m.
ritual /'rɪtʃʊəl/ a. & n. rituale m.
rival /'raɪvl/ a. n. rivale m./f. —v.t.
(p.t. rivalled) rivaleggiare. ~**ry** n.
rivalità f.
river /'rɪvə(r)/ n. fiume m.
rivet /'rɪvɪt/ n. rivetto m. —v.t. inchiodare.
Riviera /rɪvɪ'erə/ n. **the (French)** ~
la Costa Azzurra f. **the (Italian)** ~ la
Riviera Ligure f.
rivulet /'rɪvjʊlɪt/ n. ruscelletto m.
road /rəʊd/ n. strada, via f. **on the** ~
in cammino. ~**-hog** n. pirata della
strada m. ~**-house** n. trattoria f. ~-
map n. carta stradale f. ~ **sign** n.
cartello stradale m. ~**-works** n.pl.
lavori stradali m.pl.

roadside /'rəʊdsaɪd/ *n.* bordo della strada *m.*

roadway /'rəʊdweɪ/ *n.* carreggiata *f.*

roadworthy /'rəʊdwɜːðɪ/ *a.* (*of vehicle*) sicuro.

roam /rəʊm/ *v.i.* girovagare.

roar /rɔː(r)/ *n.* ruggito *m.*; (*laughter*) scroscio *m.* —*v.t.*/*i.* ruggire; (*with pain*) urlare; (*of lorry, thunder*) rombare. ~ **with laughter** ridere fragorosamente.

roaring /'rɔːrɪŋ/ *a.* (*trade etc.*) fiorente.

roast /rəʊst/ *v.t.*/*i.* arrostire, arrostirsi. —*n.* arrosto *m.* —*a.* arrostito. ~ **beef** *n.* manzo arrosto *m.*

rob /rɒb/ *v.t.* (*p.t.* **robbed**) rubare; (*bank*) svaligiare. **be** ~**bed** essere derubato. ~ **of** privare. ~**ber** *n.* rapinatore *m.* ~**bery** *n.* rapina *f.*

robe /rəʊb/ *n.* abito lungo *m.* **bath-**~ *n.* accappatoio *m.*

robin /'rɒbɪn/ *n.* pettirosso *m.*

robot /'rəʊbɒt/ *n.* robot *m. invar.*

robust /rəʊ'bʌst/ *a.* robusto.

rock[1] /rɒk/ *n.* roccia *f.*; (*boulder*) macigno *m.*; (*in sea*) scoglio *m.*; (*sweet*) zucchero candito *m.* **on the** ~**s** (*drink*) con ghiaccio; (*ship*) sugli scogli; (*marriage*) in crisi. ~**-bottom** *a.* (*fam.*) bassissimo.

rock[2] /rɒk/ *v.t.*/*i.* dondolare, dondolarsi; (*baby*) cullare; (*shake*) scuotere. —*n.* (*mus.*) rock *m.* ~**ing-chair** *n.* sedia a dondolo *f.* ~**ing-horse** *n.* cavallo a dondolo *m.*

rockery /'rɒkərɪ/ *n.* giardino roccioso *m.*

rocket /'rɒkɪt/ *n.* razzo *m.*; (*sl.*) cicchetto *m.*

rocky /'rɒkɪ/ *a.* (**-ier, -iest**) roccioso; (*fig.*) traballante.

rod /rɒd/ *n.* verga *f.*; (*for fishing*) canna *f.*; (*wooden*) bacchetta *f.*

rode /rəʊd/ *see* **ride.**

rodent /'rəʊdnt/ *n.* roditore *m.*

rodeo /rəʊ'deɪəʊ/ *n.* (*pl.* **-os**) rodeo *m.*

roe[1] /rəʊ/ *n.* uova di pesce *f.pl.*

roe[2] /rəʊ/ *n.* (*pl.* **roe** *or* **roes**) (*deer*) capriolo *m.*

rogu|e /rəʊg/ *n.* farabutto *m.* ~**ish** *a.* furfantesco.

role /rəʊl/ *n.* ruolo *m.*

roll /rəʊl/ *v.t.*/*i.* rotolare; (*rock*) rollare; (*flatten lawn, pastry*) spianare. —*n.* rotolo *m.*; (*of ship, drum*) rullio *m.*; (*bread*) panino *m.*; (*list*) lista *f.* **be** ~**ing** (**in money**) (*fam.*) guazzare (nell'oro). ~**-call** *n.* appello

m. ~ **over** *v.i.* rigirarsi. ~ **up** *v.i.* (*fam.*) giungere.

roller /'rəʊlə(r)/ *n.* rullo *m.*; (*wheel*) rotella *f.* ~ **blind** *n.* persiana avvolgibile *f.* ~**-coaster** *n.* montagne russe *f.pl.* ~**-skate** *n.* pattino a rotelle *m.*

rollicking /'rɒlɪkɪŋ/ *a.* allegro.

rolling /'rəʊlɪŋ/ *a.* ondulato. ~**-pin** *n.* mattarello *m.*

romance /rəʊ'mæns/ *n.* racconto fantastico *or* sentimentale *m.*; (*love affair*) idillio *m.*

Romania /rə'meɪnɪə/ *n.* Rumania *f.* ~**n** *a.* & *n.* rumeno, a *m.*, *f.*

romantic /rəʊ'mæntɪk/ *a.* romantico. ~**ism** *n.* romanticismo *m.*

Rom|e /'rəʊm/ Roma *f.* ~**an** *a.* & *n.* romano, a *m.*, *f.* ~**an Catholic** *a.* & *n.* cattolico, a *m.*, *f.*

romp /rɒmp/ *v.i.* giocare rumorosamente. —*n.* gioco rumoroso *m.*

rompers /'rɒmpəz/ *n.pl.* pagliaccetto *m.s.*

roof /ruːf/ *n.* tetto *m.*; (*of mouth*) palato *m.* —*v.t.* ricoprire con tetto. ~**garden** *n.* giardino pensile *m.* ~**rack** *n.* portabagagli *m. invar.* ~**-top** *n.* tetto *m.*

rook[1] /rʊk/ *n.* cornacchia *f.* —*v.t.* barare.

rook[2] /rʊk/ *n.* (*chess*) torre *f.*

room /ruːm/ *n.* stanza *f.*; (*bedroom*) camera *f.*; (*space*) spazio *m.*; (*large hall*) sala *f.* ~**y** *a.* spazioso; (*clothes*) ampio.

roost /ruːst/ *n.* posatoio *m.* —*v.i.* appollaiarsi.

root[1] /ruːt/ *n.* radice *f.*; (*fig.*) fonte *f.* —*v.t.*/*i.* metter radice. ~ **out** *v.t.* estirpare. ~**less** *a.* senza radice.

root[2] /ruːt/ *v.i.* ~ **about** grufolare. —*v.t.* ~ **for** (*Amer. sl*) parteggiare per.

rope /rəʊp/ *n.* corda *f.* —*v.t.* legare con corda. **know the** ~**s** sapere il fatto proprio. ~ **in** *v.t.* coinvolgere.

rosary /'rəʊzərɪ/ *n.* (*relig.*) rosario *m.*

rose[1] /rəʊz/ *n.* rosa *f.*; (*nozzle*) rosetta *f.*

rose[2] /rəʊz/ *see* **rise.**

rosé /'rəʊzeɪ/ *n.* (*vino*) rosato *m.*

rosette /rəʊ'zet/ *n.* rosetta *f.*

roster /'rɒstə(r)/ *n.* elenco (di servizio) *m.*

rostrum /'rɒstrəm/ *n.* rostro *m.*

rosy /'rəʊzɪ/ *a.* (**-ier, -iest**) roseo.

rot /rɒt/ *v.t.*/*i.* (*p.t.* **rotted**) marcire.

—*n.* marciume *m.*; (*sl.*) sciocchezze *f.pl.*

rota /'rəʊtə/ *n.* orario dei turni *m.*

rotary /'rəʊtərɪ/ *a.* rotante.

rotat|e /rəʊ'teɪt/ *v.t./i.* (far) ruotare; (*change round*) succedersi. ~**ion** /-ʃn/ *n.* rotazione *f.*

rote /rəʊt/ *n.* **by** ~ meccanicamente.

rotten /'rɒtn/ *a.* marcio; (*fam.*) sgradevole.

rotund /rəʊ'tʌnd/ *a.* paffuto.

rouge /ruːʒ/ *n.* rossetto (per le guance) *m.*

rough /rʌf/ *a.* (**-er, -est**) ruvido; (*person*) rozzo; (*bad*) cattivo; (*ground*) accidentato; (*sound*) aspro; (*estimate*) approssimativo. —*adv.* rudemente; (*play*) grossolanamente. —*n.* stato grezzo *m.*; (*ruffian*) giovinastro *m.*; (*golf*) macchia *f.* —*v.t.* ~ **it** vivere primitivamente. ~**-and-ready** *a.* improvvisato. ~**-and-tumble** *n.* mischia *f.* ~ **copy** *n.* brutta copia *f.* ~ **draft** *n.* abbozzo *m.* ~ **out** *v.t.* abbozzare. ~**ly** *adv.* rudemente; (*more or less*) pressappoco. ~**ness** *n.* ruvidità *f.*; rudezza *f.*

roughage /'rʌfɪdʒ/ *n.* fibre *f.pl.*

roulette /ruː'let/ *n.* roulette *f.*

round /raʊnd/ *a.* (**-er, -est**) rotondo. —*n.* tondo *m.*; (*slice*) fetta *f.*; (*of visits, drinks*) giro *m.*; (*of competition*) partita *f.*; (*boxing*) ripresa *f.* —*prep.* intorno a. —*adv.* intorno. —*v.t.* arrotondare; (*corner*) girare. **go** *or* **come** ~ **to** (*a friend etc.*) passare da. ~ **about** (*approximately*) all'incirca. ~ **off** *v.t.* completare. ~ **trip** *n.* gita di andata e ritorno *f.* ~ **up** *v.t.* radunare; (*of police*) fare una retata; (*price*) arrotondare. ~**-up** *n.* raduno *m.*; retata *f.*

roundabout /'raʊndəbaʊt/ *n.* giostra *f.*; (*for traffic*) rotonda *f.* —*a.* indiretto.

rous|e /raʊz/ *v.t.* svegliare; (*incite*) incitare. ~**ing** *a.* eccitante.

rout /raʊt/ *n.* disfatta *f.* —*v.t.* sbaragliare.

route /ruːt/ *n.* itinerario *m.*; (*naut., aeron.*) rotta *f.*; (*of bus*) percorso *m.*

routine /ruː'tiːn/ *n.* routine *f.*; (*theatr.*) numero *m.* —*a.* di routine.

rov|e /rəʊv/ *v.t./i.* vagare. ~**ing** *a.* itinerante.

row[1] /rəʊ/ *n.* fila *f.*

row[2] /rəʊ/ *v.i.* remare. —*n.* remata *f.* ~**ing** *n.* canottaggio *m.* ~**ing-boat** *n.* barca a remi *f.*

row[3] /raʊ/ *n.* (*fam., noise*) baccano *m.*; (*quarrel*) lite *f.* —*v.i.* (*fam.*) litigare.

rowdy /'raʊdɪ/ *a.* (**-ier, -iest**) chiassoso. —*n.* attaccabrighe *m.*

royal /'rɔɪəl/ *a.* reale. ~**ist** *a.* & *n.* realista *m.*/*f.* ~**ly** *adv.* regalmente.

royalty /'rɔɪəltɪ/ *n.* i reali *m.pl.*; (*payment*) diritti d'autore *m.pl.*

rub /rʌb/ *v.t.* (*p.t.* **rubbed**) fregare. —*n.* strofinata *f.* ~ **it in** insistere su qcsa. ~ **off** *v.i.* andar via. ~ **off on** trasferirsi su. ~ **out** *v.t.* cancellare.

rubber /'rʌbə(r)/ *n.* gomma *f.* ~ **band** *n.* elastico *m.* ~ **stamp** *n.* timbro di gomma *m.* ~**-stamp** *v.t.* (*fig.*) approvare a occhi chiusi. ~**y** *a.* gommoso.

rubbish /'rʌbɪʃ/ *n.* immondizie *f.pl.*; (*junk*) robaccia *f.*; (*fig.*) sciocchezze *f.pl.* ~**y** *a.* senza valore.

rubble /'rʌbl/ *n.* macerie *f.pl.*; (*small*) pietrisco *m.*

ruby /'ruːbɪ/ *n.* rubino *m.*

rucksack /'rʌksæk/ *n.* sacco da montagna *m.*

rudder /'rʌdə(r)/ *n.* timone *m.*

ruddy /'rʌdɪ/ *a.* (**-ier, -iest**) rubicondo; (*sl.*) dannato.

rude /ruːd/ *a.* (**-er, -est**) sgarbato; (*improper*) osceno; (*brusque*) brusco. ~**ly** *adv.* scortesemente. ~**ness** *n.* scortesia *f.*

rudiment /'ruːdɪmənt/ *n.* rudimento *m.* ~**ary** /-'mentrɪ/ *a.* rudimentale.

rueful /'ruːfl/ *a.* mesto.

ruffian /'rʌfɪən/ *n.* farabutto *m.*

ruffle /'rʌfl/ *v.t.* (*hair*) arruffare; (*clothes*) scompigliare. —*n.* ruche *f.*

rug /rʌg/ *n.* tappeto *m.*; (*plaid*) coperta *f.*

Rugby /'rʌgbɪ/ *n.* ~ (**football**) rugby *m.*

rugged /'rʌgɪd/ *a.* ruvido; (*landscape*) accidentato; (*fig.*) rozzo.

ruin /'ruːɪn/ *n.* rovina *f.* —*v.t.* rovinare. ~**ous** *a.* rovinoso.

rule /ruːl/ *n.* regola *f.*; (*regulation*) regolamento *m.*; (*custom*) consuetudine *f.* —*v.t.* governare; (*control*) reggere; (*master*) dominare; (*jurid.*) decretare. **as a** ~ generalmente. ~ **out** *v.t.* scartare. ~**d paper** *n.* carta rigata *f.* ~**r** /-ə(r)/ *n.* (*sovereign*) sovrano, a *m.*, *f.*; (*leader*) capo (dello Stato) *m.*; (*measure*) regolo *m.* **ruling** *a.* (*class*) dirigente; (*pol.*) al potere; *n.* decisione *f.*

rum /rʌm/ *n.* rum *m.*

rumble /'rʌmbl/ *v.i.* rintronare; (*of*

stomach) brontolare. —*n.* rombo *m.*; brontolio *m.*

ruminant /'ru:mɪnənt/ *a.* & *n.* ruminante *m.*

rummage /'rʌmɪdʒ/ *v.i.* rovistare.

rumour /'ru:mə(r)/ *n.* diceria *f.* —*v.t.* it is ~ed that si dice che.

rump /rʌmp/ *n.* natiche *f.pl.* ~ **steak** bistecca di girello *f.*

rumpus /'rʌmpəs/ *n.* (*fam.*) baccano *m.*

run /rʌn/ *v.i.* (*p.t.* ran, *p.p.* run, *pres. p.* running) correre; (*flow*) scorrere; (*pass*) passare; (*function*) funzionare; (*melt*) liquefarsi; (*of bus etc.*) fare servizio; (*of play*) durare; (*of colours*) sbiadire; (*in election*) presentarsi (come candidato). —*v.t.* (*house*) tenere; (*control*) dirigere; (*drive*) condurre. —*n.* corsa *f.*; (*journey*) percorso *m.*; (*ladder*) smagliatura *f.*; (*ski*) pista *f.*; (*outing*) giro *m.* **at a** ~ di corsa. **have the** ~ **of** usare liberamente. **in the long** ~ a lungo andare. **on the** ~ in movimento. ~ **a temperature** avere la febbre. ~ **across/into** *v.t.* (*friend*) imbattersi in. ~ **away** *v.i.* scappar via. ~ **down** *v.i.* (*clock*) scaricarsi; *v.t.* (*belittle*) denigrare. ~**down** *n.* analisi *f.* ~ **down** *a.* (*person*) esaurito. ~ **in** *v.t.* (*vehicle*) fare il rodaggio. ~ **into** *v.i.* (*knock against*) urtare. ~ **off** *v.t.* (*copies etc.*) stampare. ~**-of-the-mill** *a.* solito. ~ **out** *v.i.* (*liquid*) colare; (*fig.*) esaurirsi. ~ **out of** rimanere senza. ~ **over** *v.t.* (*auto*) investire. ~ **through** *v.t.* scorrere. ~ **up** *v.t.* (*bill*) far salire. ~ **up against** (*difficulties*) incontrare. **the** ~**-up to** il periodo che precede.

runaway /'rʌnəweɪ/ *a.* & *n.* fuggitivo, a *m.*, *f.* —*a.* (*success*) decisivo; (*inflation*) galoppante.

rung[1] /rʌŋ/ *n.* (*of ladder*) gradino *m.*

rung[2] /rʌŋ/ *see* **ring**[2].

runner /'rʌnə(r)/ *n.* podista *m.|f.*; (*in race*) corridore *m.*; (*carpet*) guida *f.*; (*on sledge*) pattino *m.* ~ **bean** *n.* fagiolo (rampicante) *m.* ~**-up** *n.* secondo, a in classifica *m.*, *f.*

running /'rʌnɪŋ/ *n.* corsa *f.* —*a.* in corsa; (*water*) corrente. **be in the** ~ avere probabilità di vincere. **four times** ~ quattro volte di seguito. ~ **commentary** *n.* radiocronaca *f.*

runny /'rʌnɪ/ *a.* semiliquido. ~ **nose** naso che cola.

runway /'rʌnweɪ/ *n.* pista *f.*

rupture /'rʌptʃə(r)/ *n.* rottura *f.*; (*med.*) ernia *f.* —*v.t.|i.* rompere, rompersi.

rural /'rʊərəl/ *a.* rurale.

ruse /ru:z/ *n.* inganno *m.*

rush[1] /rʌʃ/ *n.* (*plant*) giunco *m.*

rush[2] /rʌʃ/ *v.i.* precipitarsi. —*v.t.* far premura; (*mil.*) irrompere in. —*n.* fretta *f.*; (*run*) gran corsa *f.* ~**-hour** *n.* ora di punta *f.*

rusk /rʌsk/ *n.* biscotto *m.*

russet /'rʌsɪt/ *a.* rossiccio. —*n.* (*apple*) mela ruggine *f.*

Russia /'rʌʃə/ *n.* Russia *f.* ~**n** *a.* & *n.* russo, a *m.*, *f.*; (*lang.*) russo *m.*

rust /rʌst/ *n.* ruggine *f.* —*v.t.|i.* arrugginire, arrugginirsi. ~**-proof** *a.* inossidabile. ~**y** *a.* (-ier, -iest) arrugginito.

rustic /'rʌstɪk/ *a.* rustico.

rustle /'rʌsl/ *v.t.|i.* (far) frusciare; (*Amer.*) rubare (bestiame). ~ **up** (*fam.*) racimolare.

rut /rʌt/ *n.* solco *m.* **in a** ~ nella solita routine.

ruthless /'ru:θlɪs/ *a.* spietato. ~**ness** *n.* inesorabilità *f.*

rye /raɪ/ *n.* segala *f.*

S

sabbath /'sæbəθ/ *n.* giorno di riposo *m.*

sabbatical /sə'bætɪkl/ *a.* sabatico; (*univ.*) di congedo.

sabot|age /'sæbətɑːʒ/ *n.* sabotaggio *m.* —*v.t.* sabotare. ~**eur** /-'tɜː(r)/ *n.* sabota|tore, -trice *m., f.*

saccharin /'sækərɪn/ *n.* saccarina *f.*

sachet /'sæʃeɪ/ *n.* sacchetto profumato *m.*

sack[1] /sæk/ *n.* sacco *m.* —*v.t.* (*fam.*) licenziare. **get the** ~ (*fam.*) essere licenziato. ~**ing** *n.* tela da sacchi *f.*; (*fam.*) licenziamento *m.*

sack[2] /sæk/ *v.t.* (*plunder*) saccheggiare.

sacrament /'sækrəmənt/ *n.* sacramento *m.*

sacred /'seɪkrɪd/ *a.* sacro.

sacrifice /'sækrɪfaɪs/ *n.* sacrificio *m.* —*v.t.* sacrificare.

sacrileg|e /'sækrɪlɪdʒ/ *n.* sacrilegio *m.* ~**ious** /-'lɪdʒəs/ *a.* sacrilego.

sacrosanct /'sækrəʊsæŋkt/ *a.* sacrosanto.

sad /sæd/ *a.* (**sadder, saddest**) triste. ~**ly** *adv.* tristemente; (*fig.*) sfortunatamente. ~**ness** *n.* tristezza *f.*

sadden /'sædn/ *v.t.* rattristare.

saddle /'sædl/ *n.* sella *f.* —*v.t.* sellare. **be** ~**d with** (*fig.*) avere il peso di. **in the** ~ (*fig.*) al comando. ~**-bag** *n.* bisaccia *f.*

sadis|t /'seɪdɪst/ *n.* sadico, a *m., f.* ~**m** /-zəm/ *n.* sadismo *m.* ~**tic** /sə'dɪstɪk/ *a.* sadico.

safari /sə'fɑːrɪ/ *n.* safari *m.*

safe /seɪf/ *a.* (**-er, -est**) sicuro; (*out of danger*) salvo; (*cautious*) prudente. —*n.* cassaforte *f.* ~ **and sound** sano e salvo. ~ **deposit** *n.* cassetta di sicurezza *f.* ~**ly** *adv.* in modo sicuro.

safeguard /'seɪfɡɑːd/ *n.* salvaguardia *f.* —*v.t.* salvaguardare.

safety /'seɪftɪ/ *n.* sicurezza *f.* ~**-pin** *n.* spilla di sicurezza *f.* ~**-valve** *n.* valvola di sicurezza *f.*

saffron /'sæfrən/ *n.* zafferano *m.*

sag /sæg/ *v.i.* (*p.t.* **sagged**) abbassarsi; (*give*) afflosciarsi. ~**ging** *n.* abbassamento *m.*

saga /'sɑːɡə/ *n.* saga *f.*

sage[1] /seɪdʒ/ *n.* (*herb*) salvia *f.*

sage[2] /seɪdʒ/ *a.* & *n.* saggio *m.*

Sagittarius /sædʒɪ'teərɪəs/ *n.* (*astr.*) Sagittario *m.*

sago /'seɪɡəʊ/ *n.* sago *m.*

sail /seɪl/ *n.* vela *f.*; (*trip*) giro in barca a vela *m.* —*v.i.* veleggiare; (*leave*) salpare; (*sport*) praticare la vela; (*fig.*) scivolare. —*v.t.* (*boat*) manovrare. ~**ing** *n.* (*sport*) vela *f.* ~**ing-boat** *n.* barca a vela *f.* ~**ing-ship** *n.* veliero *m.*

sailor /'seɪlə(r)/ *n.* marinaio *m.*

saint /seɪnt/ *n.* santo, a *m., f.* ~**ly** *a.* da santo.

sake /seɪk/ *n.* **for the** ~ **of** per amor di.

salacious /sə'leɪʃəs/ *a.* salace.

salad /'sæləd/ *n.* insalata *f.* ~ **bowl** *n.* insalatiera *f.*

salar|y /'sælərɪ/ *n.* stipendio *m.* ~**ied** *a.* stipendiato.

sale /seɪl/ *n.* vendita *f.*; (*at reduced prices*) svendita *f.* **for/on** ~ in vendita.

saleable /'seɪləbl/ *a.* vendibile.

sales|man /'seɪlzmən/ *n.* (*pl.* **-men**) venditore *m.*; (*in shop*) commesso *m.*; (*traveller*) rappresentante *m.* ~**woman** *n.* (*pl.* **-women**) commessa *f.*; rappresentante *f.*

salient /'seɪlɪənt/ *a.* saliente.

saliva /sə'laɪvə/ *n.* saliva *f.*

sallow /'sæləʊ/ *a.* (**-er, -est**) giallastro.

sally /'sælɪ/ *n.* (*mil.*) sortita *f.*; (*witty remark*) facezia *f.* —*v.t.* ~ **forth/out** balzar fuori.

salmon /'sæmən/ *n. invar.* salmone *m.*

salon /'sælɒn/ *n.* salone *m.*

saloon /sə'luːn/ *n.* (*on ship*) sala *f.*; (*Amer.*) bar *m.*; (*auto*) berlina *f.*

salt /sɔːlt/ *n.* sale *m.* —*a.* salato. —*v.t.* salare. ~**-cellar** *n.* saliera *f.* ~**y** *a.* salato.

salutary /'sæljʊtrɪ/ *a.* salutare.

salute /sə'luːt/ *n.* saluto *m.* —*v.t.* salutare. —*v.i.* fare il saluto.

salvage /'sælvɪdʒ/ *n.* salvataggio *m.*; (*of waste*) merce recuperata *f.* —*v.t.* salvare; recuperare.

salvation /sæl'veɪʃn/ *n.* salvezza *f.*

salve /sɑːv/ *n.* pomata *f.*

salver /'sælvə(r)/ *n.* vassoio *m.*

salvo /'sælvəʊ/ *n.* (*pl.* **-os**) salva *f.*

same /seɪm/ a. stesso (**as**, di). —pron. **the ~** lo stesso. —adv. **the ~** nello stesso modo. **all the ~** nondimeno. **do the ~ as** fare come.

sample /'sɑːmpl/ n. campione m. —v.t. (food) assaggiare.

sanatorium /sænə'tɔːrɪəm/ n. (pl. -ums) sanatorio m.

sanctify /'sæŋktɪfaɪ/ v.t. santificare.

sanctimonious /sæŋktɪ'məʊnɪəs/ a. bigotto.

sanction /'sæŋkʃn/ n. autorizzazione f.; (penalty) sanzione f. —v.t. autorizzare.

sanctity /'sæŋktətɪ/ n. santità f.

sanctuary /'sæŋktʃʊərɪ/ n. (relig.) santuario m.; (for wildlife) riserva f.; (refuge) asilo m.

sand /sænd/ n. sabbia f. **~s** n.pl. spiaggia f.s. —v.t. insabbiare.

sandal /'sændl/ n. sandalo m.

sandpaper /'sændpeɪpə(r)/ n. carta vetrata f. —v.t. levigare.

sandstorm /'sændstɔːm/ n. tempesta di sabbia f.

sandwich /'sænwɪdʒ/ n. tramezzino, sandwich m. —v.t. **~ed between** serrato tra.

sandy /'sændɪ/ a. sabbioso.

sane /seɪn/ a. (**-er**, **-est**) (person) equilibrato; (judgement, policy) sensato. **~ly** adv. sensatamente.

sang /sæŋ/ see **sing**.

sanitary /'sænɪtrɪ/ a. igienico; (system etc.) sanitario.

sanitation /sænɪ'teɪʃn/ n. igiene f.; (drainage) sistema sanitario m.

sanity /'sænətɪ/ n. sanità di mente f.; (fig.) buon senso m.

sank /sæŋk/ see **sink**.

sap /sæp/ n. (in plants) succo m. —v.t. (p.t. **sapped**) indebolire.

sapling /'sæplɪŋ/ n. alberello m.

sapphire /'sæfaɪə(r)/ n. zaffiro m.

sarcas|m /'sɑːkæzəm/ n. sarcasmo m. **~tic** /-'kæstɪk/ a. sarcastico.

sardine /sɑː'diːn/ n. sardina f.

Sardinia /sɑː'dɪnɪə/ n. Sardegna f. **~n** a. & n. sardo, a m., f.

sardonic /sɑː'dɒnɪk/ a. sardonico.

sash /sæʃ/ n. fascia f. **~-window** n. finestra a ghigliottina f.

sat /sæt/ see **sit**.

satanic /sə'tænɪk/ a. satanico.

satchel /'sætʃl/ n. cartella f.

satellite /'sætəlaɪt/ n. & a. satellite m.

satiate /'seɪʃɪeɪt/ v.t. saziare.

satin /'sætɪn/ n. raso m. —a. di raso.

satir|e /'sætaɪə(r)/ n. satira f. **~ical** /sə'tɪrɪkl/ a. satirico.

satiri|ze /'sætəraɪz/ v.t. satireggiare. **~st** /-ɪst/ n. autore di satire m.

satisfactor|y /sætɪs'fæktərɪ/ a. soddisfacente. **~ily** adv. in modo soddisfacente.

satisf|y /'sætɪsfaɪ/ v.t. soddisfare; (convince) convincere. **~action** /-'fækʃn/ n. soddisfazione f. **~ying** a. soddisfacente.

saturat|e /'sætʃəreɪt/ v.t. impregnare. **~ed** a. saturo. **~ion** /-'reɪʃn/ n. saturazione f.

Saturday /'sætədɪ/ n. sabato m.

sauce /sɔːs/ n. salsa f.; (cheek) impertinenza f.

saucepan /'sɔːspən/ n. pentola f.

saucer /'sɔːsə(r)/ n. piattino m.

saucy /'sɔːsɪ/ a. (**-ier**, **-iest**) impertinente.

Saudi Arabia /saʊdɪə'reɪbɪə/ n. Arabia Saudita f.

sauna /'sɔːnə/ n. sauna f.

saunter /'sɔːntə(r)/ v.i. andare a zonzo.

sausage /'sɒsɪdʒ/ n. salsiccia f.

savage /'sævɪdʒ/ a. selvaggio; (fierce) feroce; (fam., furious) furibondo. —n. selvaggio, a m.,f. —v.t. attaccare. **~ry** n. ferocia f.

sav|e /seɪv/ v.t. salvare; (money, time) risparmiare; (prevent) evitare. —n. (football) salvataggio m. —prep. salvo. **~r** n. risparmia|tore, -trice m., f. **~ing** n. economia f. **~ings** n.pl. risparmi m.pl.

saviour /'seɪvɪə(r)/ n. salvatore m.

savour /'seɪvə(r)/ n. sapore m. —v.t. assaporare. **~y** a. saporito; n. salatino m.

saw[1] /sɔː/ see **see**[1].

saw[2] /sɔː/ n. sega f. —v.t./i. (p.t. **sawed**, p.p. **sawn**) segare.

sawdust /'sɔːdʌst/ n. segatura f.

sawn /sɔːn/ see **saw**[2].

saxophone /'sæksəfəʊn/ n. sassofono m.

say /seɪ/ v.t./i. (p.t. **said** /sed/) dire. —n. **have a ~** esprimere un'opinione; (in decision) aver voce in capitolo. **I ~!** davvero!

saying /'seɪɪŋ/ n. proverbio m.

scab /skæb/ n. crosta f.; (fam., pej.) crumiro m.

scaffold /'skæfəʊld/ n. patibolo m.

scaffolding /'skæfəldɪŋ/ n. impalcatura f.

scald /skɔːld/ *v.t.* scottare; (*milk etc.*) scaldare. —*n.* scottatura *f.*

scale[1] /skeɪl/ *n.* (*of fish*) scaglia *f.*

scale[2] /skeɪl/ *n.* scala *f.* —*v.t.* (*climb*) scalare. ∼ **down** *v.t.* diminuire.

scales /skeɪlz/ *n.pl.* (*for weighing*) bilancia *f.s.*

scallop /'skɒləp/ *n.* conchiglia *f.*; (*on dress*) smerlo *m.*

scalp /skælp/ *n.* cuoio capelluto *m.* —*v.t.* scalpare.

scalpel /'skælpəl/ *n.* scalpello *m.*

scamp /skæmp/ *n.* bricconcello, a *m.*, *f.* —*v.t.* lavorare con svogliatezza.

scamper /'skæmpə(r)/ *v.i.* ∼ **away** darsela a gambe.

scampi /'skæmpɪ/ *n.pl.* gamberoni *m.pl.*

scan /skæn/ *v.t.* (*p.t.* **scanned**) scrutare; (*quickly*) scorrere in fretta; (*poetry*) scandire; (*radar*) esplorare.

scandal /'skændl/ *n.* scandalo *m.*; (*gossip*) maldicenza *f.* ∼**ous** *a.* scandaloso.

scandalize /'skændəlaɪz/ *v.t.* scandalizzare.

Scandinavia /skændɪ'neɪvɪə/ *n.* Scandinavia *f.* ∼**n** *a.* & *n.* scandinavo, a *m.*, *f.*

scant /skænt/ *a.* scarso.

scant|y /'skæntɪ/ *a.* (-ier, -iest) scarso; (*clothing*) succinto. ∼**ily** *adv.* scarsamente; succintamente.

scapegoat /'skeɪpgəʊt/ *n.* capro espiatorio *m.*

scar /skɑː(r)/ *n.* cicatrice *f.* —*v.t./i.* (*p.t.* **scarred**) cicatrizzare, cicatrizzarsi.

scarc|e /skeəs/ *a.* (-er, -est) scarso. **make o.s.** ∼**e** (*fam.*) svignarsela. ∼**ity** *n.* scarsezza *f.*

scarcely /'skeəslɪ/ *adv.* appena.

scare /'skeə(r)/ *v.t.* spaventare. —*n.* spavento *m.* **be** ∼**d** aver paura.

scarecrow /'skeəkrəʊ/ *n.* spaventapasseri *m. invar.*

scaremonger /'skeəmʌŋgə(r)/ *n.* allarmista *m./f.*

scarf /skɑːf/ *n.* (*pl.* **scarves**) sciarpa *f.*

scarlet /'skɑːlət/ *a.* scarlatto. ∼ **fever** *n.* scarlattina *f.*

scary /'skeərɪ/ *a.* (-ier, -iest) allarmante.

scathing /'skeɪðɪŋ/ *a.* mordace.

scatter /'skætə(r)/ *v.t.* spargere. —*v.t./i.* (*disperse*) disperdere, dispersersi. ∼**-brained** *a.* scervellato. ∼**ed** *a.* sparso.

scatty /'skætɪ/ *a.* (-ier, -iest) (*sl.*) svitato.

scavenge /'skævɪndʒ/ *v.i.* frugare nella spazzatura. ∼**r** /-ə(r)/ *n.* spazzino *m.*

scenario /sɪ'nɑːrɪəʊ/ *n.* (*pl.* -os) sceneggiatura *f.*

scene /siːn/ *n.* scena *f.*; (*sight*) veduta *f.*; (*quarrel*) scenata *f.* **behind the** ∼**s** dietro le quinte.

scenery /'siːnərɪ/ *n.* paesaggio *m.*; (*theatr.*) scenario *m.*

scenic /'siːnɪk/ *a.* panoramico.

scent /sent/ *n.* profumo *m.*; (*trail*) traccia *f.* —*v.t.* fiutare; (*make fragrant*) profumare.

sceptic /'skeptɪk/ *n.* scettico, a *m.*, *f.* ∼**al** *a.* scettico. ∼**ism** /-sɪzəm/ *n.* scetticismo *m.*

sceptre /'septə(r)/ *n.* scettro *m.*

schedule /'ʃedjuːl/ *n.* piano, programma *m.* —*v.t.* mettere in programma. **behind** ∼ in ritardo. **on** ∼ in orario.

scheme /skiːm/ *n.* piano *m.*; (*plot*) complotto *m.* —*v.i.* progettare; (*pej.*) macchinare. ∼**r** *n.* intrigante *m./f.*

schism /'sɪzəm/ *n.* scisma *m.*

schizophrenic /skɪtsəʊ'frenɪk/ *a.* & *n.* schizofrenico, a *m.*, *f.*

scholar /'skɒlə(r)/ *n.* letterato, a *m.*, *f.* ∼**ly** *a.* erudito. ∼**ship** *n.* erudizione *f.*; (*grant*) borsa di studio *f.*

scholastic /skə'læstɪk/ *a.* scolastico.

school /skuːl/ *n.* scuola *f.*; (*of univ.*) facoltà *f.* —*v.t.* istruire; (*discipline*) disciplinare. ∼**ing** *n.* istruzione *f.*

school|boy /'skuːlbɔɪ/ *n.* scolaro *m.* ∼**girl** /-gəːl/ *n.* scolara *f.*

school|master /'skuːlmɑːstə(r)/ *n.* (*primary*) maestro *m.*; (*secondary*) insegnante *m.* ∼**mistress** *n.* maestra *f.*; insegnante *f.* ∼**teacher** *n.* insegnante *m./f.*

schooner /'skuːnə(r)/ *n.* goletta *f.*

sciatica /saɪ'ætɪkə/ *n.* sciatica *f.*

scien|ce /'saɪəns/ *n.* scienza *f.* ∼**ce fiction** *n.* fantascienza *f.* ∼**tific** /-'tɪfɪk/ *a.* scientifico.

scientist /'saɪəntɪst/ *n.* scienziato, a *m.*, *f.*

scintillate /'sɪntɪleɪt/ *v.i.* scintillare.

scissors /'sɪzəz/ *n.pl.* forbici *f.pl.*

sclerosis /sklə'rəʊsɪs/ *n.* sclerosi *f.*

scoff[1] /skɒf/ *v.i.* ∼ **at** schernire.

scoff[2] /skɒf/ *v.t.* (*sl.*) divorare.

scold /skəʊld/ *v.t.* sgridare. ∼**ing** *n.* sgridata *f.*

scone /skɒn/ *n.* focaccina da tè *f.*

scoop /sku:p/ *n.* mestolo *m.*; (*news*) articolo esclusivo *m.* —*v.t.* ~ **out** scavare. ~ **up** tirar su.

scoot /sku:t/ *v.i.* correr via.

scooter /'sku:tə(r)/ *n.* motoretta *f.*; (*for child*) monopattino *m.*

scope /skəʊp/ *n.* portata *f.*; (*opportunity*) opportunità *f.*

scorch /skɔ:tʃ/ *v.t.* bruciare. ~**er** *n.* (*fam.*) giornata torrida *f.* ~**ing** *a.* (*fam.*) bruciante.

score /skɔ:(r)/ *n.* punteggio *m.*; (*mus.*) partitura *f.* —*v.t.* intaccare; (*success*) riportare. —*v.i.* far punti; (*keep score*) segnare il punteggio. **a** ~ **of** una ventina di. **on that** ~ su quel punto. ~ **over s.o.** aver la meglio su qcno. ~**r** /-ə(r)/ *n.* segnapunti *m. invar.*

scorn /skɔ:n/ *n.* sprezzo *m.* —*v.t.* sprezzare. ~**ful** *a.* sprezzante. ~**fully** *adv.* sdegnosamente.

Scorpio /'skɔ:pɪəʊ/ *n.* (*astr.*) Scorpione *m.*

scorpion /'skɔ:pɪən/ *n.* scorpione *m.*

Scot /skɒt/ *n.* scozzese *m.*/*f.* ~**s** *a.* scozzese. ~**sman**, ~**swoman** *ns.* scozzese *m.*, *f.* ~**tish** *a.* scozzese.

Scotch /skɒtʃ/ *a.* scozzese. —*n.* whisky *m.*

scotch /skɒtʃ/ *v.t.* sopprimere.

scot-free /skɒt'fri:/ *a.* impunito; (*gratis*) senza pagare.

Scotland /'skɒtlənd/ *n.* Scozia *f.*

scoundrel /'skaʊndrəl/ *n.* mascalzone *m.*

scour[1] /'skaʊə(r)/ *v.t.* strofinare. ~**er** *n.* paglietta *f.*; (*detergent*) smacchiatore *m.*

scour[2] /'skaʊə(r)/ *v.t.* (*search*) perlustrare.

scourge /skɜ:dʒ/ *n.* flagello *m.*

scout /skaʊt/ *n.* esploratore *m.* —*v.i.* ~ (**for**) andare in cerca di.

Scout /skaʊt/ *n.* **Boy**/**Girl** ~ giovane esplora|tore, -trice *m.*, *f.*

scowl /skaʊl/ *n.* sguardo torvo *m.* —*v.i.* guardare torvo.

scraggy /'skrægɪ/ *a.* (-ier, -iest) scarno.

scram /skræm/ *v.i.* (*sl.*) filar via.

scramble /'skræmbl/ *v.i.* (*clamber*) arrampicarsi. —*v.t.* (*eggs*) strapazzare. —*n.* scalata *f.*; (*struggle*) mischia *f.* ~ **for** azzuffarsi per.

scrap[1] /skræp/ *n.* pezzetto *m.* ~**s** *n.pl.* rimasugli *m.pl.*; (*of food*) avanzi *m.pl.* —*v.t.* (*p.t.* **scrapped**) scartare. ~**-book** *n.* album *m.* ~**-iron** *n.* rottami di ferro *m.pl.* ~**py** *a.* frammentario.

scrap[2] /skræp/ *n.* (*fight*, *fam.*) litigio *m.*

scrape /skreɪp/ *v.t.* fregare; (*graze*) scorticare; (*rub*) raschiare. —*v.i.* strisciare. —*n.* raschiatura *f.*; (*fig.*) guaio *m.* ~ **through** cavarsela. ~ **together** racimolare. ~**r** /-ə(r)/ *n.* raschietto *m.*

scratch /skrætʃ/ *v.t.*/*i.* graffiare; (*with nails*) grattare, grattarsi. —*n.* graffio *m.*; grattata *f.* **start from** ~ partire da zero. **up to** ~ all'altezza della situazione.

scrawl /skrɔ:l/ *n.* scarabocchio *m.* —*v.t.*/*i.* scarabocchiare.

scrawny /'skrɔ:nɪ/ *a.* (-ier, -iest) stecchito.

scream /skri:m/ *v.t.*/*i.* strillare. —*n.* strillo *m.*

screech /skri:tʃ/ *v.i.* stridere. —*n.* stridore *m.*

screen /skri:n/ *n.* paravento *m.*; (*cinema*, *TV*) schermo *m.* —*v.t.* proteggere; (*film*) proiettare; (*candidates*) selezionare. ~**ing** *n.* (*med.*) dépistage *m. invar.*

screw /skru:/ *n.* vite *f.* —*v.t.* avvitare; (*sl.*, *money*) spremere. ~ **up** (*eyes*) strizzare; (*face*) storcere.

screwdriver /'skru:draɪvə(r)/ *n.* cacciavite *m.*

screwy /'skru:ɪ/ *a.* (-ier, -iest) (*sl.*) svitato.

scribble /'skrɪbl/ *v.t.*/*i.* scarabocchiare. —*n.* scarabocchio *m.*

scribe /skraɪb/ *n.* copista *m.*/*f.*

script /skrɪpt/ *n.* scrittura (a mano) *f.*; (*of film etc.*) copione *m.* ~**-writer** *n.* sceneggia|tore, -trice *m.*, *f.*

Scriptures /'skrɪptʃəz/ *n.pl.* Sacre Scritture *f.pl.*

scroll /skrəʊl/ *n.* rotolo (di pergamena) *m.*

scrounge /skraʊndʒ/ *v.t.*/*i.* scroccare. ~**r** /-ə(r)/ *n.* scroccone, a *m.*, *f.*

scrub[1] /skrʌb/ *n.* (*land*) boscaglia *f.*

scrub[2] /skrʌb/ *v.t.*/*i.* (*p.t.* **scrubbed**) strofinare. —*n.* strofinata *f.*

scruff /skrʌf/ *n.* **the** ~ **of the neck** la collottola *f.*

scruffy /'skrʌfɪ/ *a.* (-ier, -iest) trasandato.

scrummage /'skrʌmɪdʒ/ *n.* (*Rugby*) mischia *f.*

scruple /'skru:pl/ *n.* scrupolo *m.*

scrupulous /'skru:pjʊləs/ *a.* scrupoloso. ~**ly** *adv.* scrupolosamente.

scrutin|y /'skru:tını/ *n.* esame minuzioso *m.* **~ize** *v.t.* scrutinare.

scuff /skʌf/ *v.t./i.* strascicare (i piedi).

scuffle /'skʌfl/ *n.* tafferuglio *m.*

scullery /'skʌlərı/ *n.* retrocucina *f.*

sculpt /skʌlpt/ *v.t./i.* (*fam.*) scolpire. **~or** *n.* scultore *m.* **~ure** /-tʃə(r)/ *n.* scultura *f.*; *v.t./i.* scolpire.

scum /skʌm/ *n.* schiuma *f.*; (*people, pej.*) feccia *f.*

scurf /skɜːf/ *n.* scaglia *f.*

scurrilous /'skʌrıləs/ *a.* scurrile.

scurry /'skʌrı/ *v.i.* affrettarsi.

scurvy /'skɜːvı/ *n.* scorbuto *m.*

scuttle[1] /'skʌtl/ *n.* secchio (per il carbone) *m.*

scuttle[2] /'skʌtl/ *v.t.* (*ship*) autoaffondare.

scuttle[3] /'skʌtl/ *v.i.* **~ away** svignarsela.

scythe /saıð/ *n.* falce *f.*

sea /si:/ *n.* mare *m.* **at ~** in mare; (*fig.*) confuso. **by ~** via mare. **~-horse** *n.* cavalluccio marino *m.* **~-urchin** *n.* riccio di mare *m.*

seaboard /'si:bɔ:d/ *n.* costiera *f.*

seafarer /'si:feərə(r)/ *n.* uomo di mare *m.*

seafood /'si:fu:d/ *n.* frutti di mare *m.pl.*

seagull /'si:gʌl/ *n.* gabbiano *m.*

seal[1] /si:l/ *n.* (*animal*) foca *f.*

seal[2] /si:l/ *n.* sigillo *m.* —*v.t.* sigillare. **~ off** (*area*) bloccare. **~ing-wax** *n.* ceralacca *f.*

seam /si:m/ *n.* cucitura *f.*; (*of coal*) strato *m.*

seaman /'si:mən/ *n.* (*pl.* -men) marinaio *m.*

seamy /'si:mı/ *a.* **the ~ side** il lato squallido.

seance /'seıɑ:ns/ *n.* seduta spiritica *f.*

seaplane /'si:pleın/ *n.* idrovolante *m.*

seaport /'si:pɔ:t/ *n.* porto di mare *m.*

search /sɜːtʃ/ *v.t./i.* cercare. —*n.* ricerca *f.*; (*official*) perquisizione *f.* **in ~ of** alla ricerca di. **~-party** *n.* squadra di ricerca *f.* **~ through** *v.t.* frugare. **~ing** *a.* penetrante.

searchlight /'sɜːtʃlaıt/ *n.* riflettore *m.*

seascape /'si:skeıp/ *n.* paesaggio marino *m.*

seasick /'si:sık/ *a.* **be ~** avere il mal di mare.

seaside /'si:saıd/ *n.* spiaggia *f.* **~ resort** *n.* stazione balneare *f.* **~ town** *n.* città di mare *f.*

season /'si:zn/ *n.* stagione *f.* —*v.t.* (*flavour*) condire; (*treat wood*) stagionare. **~able, ~al** *adjs.* di stagione. **~ticket** *n.* abbonamento *m.* **~ing** *n.* condimento *m.*

seasoned /'si:znd/ *a.* (*fig.*) esperto.

seat /si:t/ *n.* sedile *m.*; (*place*) posto *m.*; (*of trousers*) fondo *m.*; (*bottom*) didietro *m.* —*v.t.* mettere a sedere; (*have seats for*) aver posti (a sedere) per. **~-belt** *n.* cintura di sicurezza *f.* **take a ~** prendere posto a sedere.

seaweed /'si:wi:d/ *n.* alga marina *f.*

seaworthy /'si:wɜːðı/ *a.* atto a tenere il mare.

secateurs /'sekətɜːz/ *n.pl.* cesoie *f.pl.*

sece|de /sı'si:d/ *v.i.* staccarsi. **~ssion** /-eʃn/ *n.* secessione *f.*

seclu|de /sı'klu:d/ *v.t.* isolare. **~ded** *a.* appartato. **~sion** /-ʒn/ *n.* isolamento *m.*

second[1] /'sekənd/ *a.* & *n.* secondo *m.* **~s** *n.pl.* (*goods*) merce di seconda scelta *f.s.* **have ~s** (*fam., meal*) fare il bis. —*adv.* (*in race etc.*) al secondo posto. —*v.t.* assecondare; (*proposal*) appoggiare. **~-best** *a.* di seconda scelta. **~-class** *a.* di seconda classe. **~-hand** *a.* di seconda mano; *adv.* per sentito dire. **~-rate** *a.* di categoria inferiore. **on ~ thoughts** ripensandoci meglio. **~ly** *adv.* in secondo luogo.

second[2] /sı'kɒnd/ *v.t.* (*transfer*) distaccare.

secondary /'sekəndrı/ *a.* secondario. **~ school** *n.* scuola media *f.*

secrecy /'si:krəsı/ *n.* segretezza *f.*

secret /'si:krıt/ *a.* & *n.* segreto *m.* **~ly** *adv.* segretamente.

secretaire /sekrə'teə(r)/ *n.* scrittoio *m.*

secretariat /sekrə'teərıət/ *n.* segretariato *m.*

secretar|y /'sekrətrı/ *n.* segretario, a *m.*, *f.* **Home S~y** Ministro degli Interni *m.* **~ial** /-'teərıəl/ *a.* di segretario.

secret|e /sı'kri:t/ *v.t.* segregare; (*of person*) secernere. **~ion** /-ʃn/ *n.* occultamento *m.*; secrezione *f.*

secretive /'si:krətıv/ *a.* reticente.

sect /sekt/ *n.* setta *f.* **~arian** /-'teərıən/ *a.* settario.

section /'sekʃn/ *n.* sezione *f.*; (*surgical*) taglio *m.*

sector /'sektə(r)/ *n.* settore *m.*

secular /'sekjulə(r)/ *a.* secolare.

secure /sı'kjuə(r)/ *a.* sicuro; (*fixed*) assicurato. —*v.t.* assicurare; (*obtain*) procurare. **~ly** *adv.* saldamente.

security /sɪ'kjʊərətɪ/ *n.* sicurezza *f.*;
(*for loan*) garanzia *f.*
sedate /sɪ'deɪt/ *a.* posato.
sedation /sɪ'deɪʃn/ *n.* **under** ~ sotto
l'effetto di sedativi.
sedative /'sedətɪv/ *a.* & *n.* sedativo *m.*
sedentary /'sedntrɪ/ *a.* sedentario.
sediment /'sedɪmənt/ *n.* sedimento *m.*
seduce /sɪ'djuːs/ *v.t.* sedurre. ~r /-ə(r)/
n. sedut|tore, -trice *m.*, *f.*
seduct|ion /sɪ'dʌkʃn/ *n.* seduzione *f.*
~ive /-tɪv/ *a.* seducente.

see[1] /siː/ *v.t./i.* (*p.t.* **saw**, *p.p.* **seen**)
vedere; (*understand*) capire; (*notice*)
notare; (*escort*) accompagnare. ~
about *or* **to** occuparsi di. ~ **off** veder
partire. ~ **through** portare a buon
fine; (*person*) leggere dentro. ~ing
that visto che. ~ **you later!** a più
tardi!
see[2] /siː/ *n.* diocesi *f.*
seed /siːd/ *n.* seme *m.*; (*fig.*) germe
m.; (*tennis*) testa di serie *f.* **go to** ~
sciuparsi. ~ling *n.* pianticella *f.*
seedy /'siːdɪ/ *a.* (**-ier**, **-iest**) squallido.
feel ~ (*fam.*) sentirsi giù.
seek /siːk/ *v.t.* (*p.t.* **sought**) cercare. ~
out scovare.
seem /siːm/ *v.i.* sembrare. ~ingly *adv.*
apparentemente.
seemly /'siːmlɪ/ *a.* (**-ier**, **-iest**) corretto.
seen /siːn/ *see* **see**[1].
seep /siːp/ *v.i.* filtrare. ~age *n.* infiltra-
zione *f.*
see-saw /'siːsɔː/ *n.* altalena *f.*
seethe /siːð/ *v.i.* ~ **with** (*anger*) bollire
di.
see-through /'siːθruː/ *a.* trasparente.
segment /'segmənt/ *n.* segmento *m.*;
(*of orange*) spicchio *m.*
segregat|e /'segrɪgeɪt/ *v.t.* segregare.
~ion /-'geɪʃn/ *n.* segregazione *f.*
seize /siːz/ *v.t.* afferrare; (*jurid.*) confiscare. ~ **on** *v.i.* prendere al volo. ~
up *v.i.* (*techn.*) bloccarsi.
seizure /'siːʒə(r)/ *n.* (*med.*) attacco
(apoplettico) *m.*
seldom /'seldəm/ *adv.* raramente.
select /sɪ'lekt/ *v.t.* scegliere; (*sport*)
selezionare. —*a.* scelto; (*exclusive*)
esclusivo. ~ion /-ʃn/ *n.* selezione *f.*
~ive *a.* selettivo.
self /self/ *n.* (*pl.* **selves**) sé, se stesso.
payable to ~ (*comm.*) pagabile al
firmatario.
self- /self/ *pref.* ~**-addressed** *a.* con
il proprio indirizzo. ~**-assurance** *n.*
sicurezza di sé *f.* ~**-assured** *a.* sicuro

di sé. ~**-centred** *a.* egocentrico. ~
confidence *n.* fiducia in se stesso
f. ~**-confident** *a.* sicuro di sé. ~
conscious *a.* impacciato. ~**-con-
tained** *a.* (*person*) autosufficiente;
(*flat*) indipendente. ~**-control** *n.* padronanza di sé *f.* ~**-denial** *n.* rinuncia
f. ~**-employed** *a.* che lavora in proprio. ~**-evident** *a.* ovvio ~
important *a.* borioso. ~**-indulgent**
a. indulgente verso se stesso. ~
interest *n.* interesse personale *m.*
~**-made** *a.* che si è fatto da sé. ~
opinionated *a.* pieno di sé. ~**-pity** *n.*
autocommiserazione *f.* ~**-portrait** *n.*
autoritratto *m.* ~**-possessed** *a.* padrone di sé. ~**-respect** *n.* amor proprio *m.* ~**-righteous** *a.* presuntuoso.
~**-sacrifice** *n.* abnegazione *f.* ~
satisfied *a.* compiaciuto di sé. ~
seeking *a.* egoista. ~**-service** *a.* & *n.*
selfservice *m.* ~**-styled** *a.* sedicente.
~**-sufficient** *a.* autosufficiente. ~
willed *a.* ostinato.
selfish /'selfɪʃ/ *a.* egoista. ~ness *n.*
egoismo *m.*
selfless /'selflɪs/ *a.* disinteressato.
sell /sel/ *v.t./i.* (*p.t.* **sold**) vendere, vendersi. **be sold on** (*fam.*) credere in.
be sold out essere esaurito. ~ **off** *v.t.*
liquidare. ~**-out** *n.* vendita totale *f.*;
(*fam.*, *betrayal*) tradimento *m.* ~ **up**
v.t. mettere in liquidazione. ~er *n.*
vendi|tore, -trice *m.*, *f.*
sellotape /'seləʊteɪp/ *n.* (*P.*) nastro
adesivo *m.*
semantic /sɪ'mæntɪk/ *a.* semantico.
~s *n.* semantica *f.*
semaphore /'seməfɔː(r)/ *n.* semaforo
m.
semblance /'sembləns/ *n.* parvenza *f.*
semen /'siːmən/ *n.* liquido seminale *m.*
semester /sɪ'mestə(r)/ *n.* (*Amer.*) seme-
stre *m.*
semi- /'semɪ/ *pref.* semi-.
semibreve /'semɪbriːv/ *n.* semibreve
m.
semicirc|le /'semɪsɜːkl/ *n.* semicerchio
m. ~**ular** /-'sɜːkjʊlə(r)/ *a.* semicircola-
re.
semicolon /semɪ'kəʊlən/ *n.* punto e
virgola *m.*
semi-detached /semɪdɪ'tætʃt/ *a.*
(*house*) gemella.
semifinal /semɪ'faɪnl/ *n.* semifinale *f.*
seminar /'semɪnɑː(r)/ *n.* seminario *m.*
~y *n.* (*college*) seminario *m.*

semiquaver /'semɪkweɪvə(r)/ *n.* (*mus.*) semicroma *f.*

Semit|e /'si:maɪt/ *n.* semita *m.|f.* ~**ic** /sɪ'mɪtɪk/ *a.* semitico.

semolina /semə'li:nə/ *n.* semolino *m.*

senat|e /'senɪt/ *n.* senato *m.* ~**or** /-ətə(r)/ *n.* senatore *m.*

send /send/ *v.t.|i.* (*p.t.* **sent**) mandare. ~ **for** *v.t.* (*person*) mandare a chiamare; (*thing*) far venire. ~-**off** *n.* commiato *m.* ~ **up** *v.t.* (*fam.*) parodiare. ~**er** *n.* mittente *m.|f.*

senil|e /'si:naɪl/ *a.* senile. ~**ity** /sɪ'nɪlətɪ/ *n.* senilità *f.*

senior /'si:nɪə(r)/ *a.* più vecchio (**to**, di); (*in rank*) superiore. —*n.* anziano, a *m., f.* ~ **citizen** *n.* pensionato, a *m., f.* ~**ity** /-'ɒrətɪ/ *n.* maggior età *f.*; (*in service*) anzianità *f.*

sensation /sen'seɪʃn/ *n.* sensazione *f.* ~**al** *a.* sensazionale.

sense /sens/ *n.* senso *m.*; (*common sense*) buon senso *m.* **make** ~ aver senso. —*v.t.* intuire. ~**less** *a.* insensato; (*med.*) privo di sensi.

sensibilit|y /sensə'bɪlətɪ/ *n.* sensibilità *f.* ~**ies** *n.pl.* suscettibilità *f.s.*

sensible /'sensəbl/ *a.* assennato, saggio.

sensitiv|e /'sensətɪv/ *a.* sensibile; (*touchy*) suscettibile. ~**ity** /-'tɪvətɪ/ *n.* sensibilità *f.*

sensory /'sensərɪ/ *a.* sensoriale.

sensual /'senʃʊəl/ *a.* sensuale. ~**ity** /-'ælətɪ/ *n.* sensualità *f.*

sensuous /'senʃʊəs/ *a.* voluttuoso.

sent /sent/ *see* **send.**

sentence /'sentəns/ *n.* frase *f.*; (*jurid.*) sentenza *f.*; (*punishment*) condanna *f.* —*v.t.* ~ **to** condannare a.

sentiment /'sentɪmənt/ *n.* sentimento *m.*

sentimental /sentɪ'mentl/ *a.* sentimentale ~**ity** *n.* /-'tælətɪ/ sentimentalità *f.*

sentry /'sentrɪ/ *n.* sentinella *f.*

separable /'sepərəbl/ *a.* separabile.

separate[1] /'sepərət/ *a.* separato. ~**s** *n.pl.* (indumenti) coordinati *m.pl.* ~**ly** *adv.* separatamente.

separat|e[2] /'sepəreɪt/ *v.t.|i.* separare, separarsi. ~**ion** /-'reɪʃn/ *n.* separazione *f.* ~**ist** *n.* separatista *m.|f.*

September /sep'tembə(r)/ *n.* settembre *m.*

septic /'septɪk/ *a.* settico. ~ **tank** *n.* fossa biologica *f.*

sequel /'si:kwəl/ *n.* seguito *m.*

sequence /'si:kwəns/ *n.* sequela *f.*; (*of film*) sequenza *f.*

sequin /'si:kwɪn/ *n.* lustrino *m.*

serenade /serə'neɪd/ *n.* serenata *f.* —*v.t.* fare una serenata (a).

seren|e /sɪ'ri:n/ *a.* sereno. ~**ity** /-enətɪ/ *n.* serenità *f.*

sergeant /'sɑ:dʒənt/ *n.* sergente *m.*

serial /'sɪərɪəl/ *n.* racconto a puntate *m.*; (*TV*) teleromanzo a puntate *m.* —*a.* di serie. ~**ize** *v.t.* pubblicare; trasmettere a puntate.

series /'sɪəri:z/ *n.* serie *f. invar.*

serious /'sɪərɪəs/ *a.* serio. ~**ly** *adv.* seriamente; (*ill*) gravemente. **take** ~**ly** prendere sul serio. ~**ness** *n.* serietà *f.*; gravità *f.*

sermon /'sɜ:mən/ *n.* sermone *m.*

serpent /'sɜ:pənt/ *n.* serpente *m.*

serrated /sɪ'reɪtɪd/ *a.* dentellato.

serum /'sɪərəm/ *n.* (*pl.* -**a**) siero *m.*

servant /'sɜ:vənt/ *n.* domestico, a *m., f.*

serve /sɜ:v/ *v.t.|i.* servire; (*in the army etc.*) prestare servizio (militare); (*sentence*) scontare. **it** ~**s you right** ben ti sta. ~ **as** servire da. ~ **its purpose** servire al proprio scopo.

service /'sɜ:vɪs/ *n.* servizio *m.*; (*maintenance*) revisione *f.* ~**s** *n.pl.* forze armate *f.pl.* —*v.t.* (*car etc.*) revisionare. **of** ~ **to** utile *a.* ~ **charge** *n.* servizio *m.* ~ **flat** *n.* appartamento ammobiliato con servizio incluso *m.* ~ **station** *n.* stazione di servizio *f.*

serviceable /'sɜ:vɪsəbl/ *a.* pratico; (*durable*) resistente.

serviceman /'sɜ:vɪsmən/ *n.* (*pl.* -**men**) militare *m.*

serviette /sɜ:vɪ'et/ *n.* tovagliolo *m.*

servile /'sɜ:vaɪl/ *a.* servile.

session /'seʃn/ *n.* sessione *f.*; (*univ.*) anno accademico *m.*

set /set/ *v.t.* (*p.t.* **set**, *pres. p.* **setting**) mettere, porre; (*clock etc.*) regolare; (*limit etc.*) fissare; (*typ.*) comporre. —*v.i.* (*of sun*) tramontare; (*of jelly*) solidificarsi. —*n.* serie *f.*; (*of cutlery etc.*) servizio *m.*; (*tennis*) partita *f.*; (*TV, radio*) apparecchio *m.*; (*of hair*) messa in piega *f.*; (*theatr.*) scenario *m.*; (*of people*) circolo *m.* —*a.* fisso. **be** ~ **on** essere risoluto *a.* ~ **about** *v.i.* incominciare *a.* ~ **back** *v.t.* mettere indietro; (*sl.*) costare. ~-**back** *n.* rovescio *m.* ~ **fire to** dare fuoco *a.* ~ **free** *v.t.* liberare. ~ **off** *v.i.* partire; *v.t.* (*make start*) avviare;

(*bomb*) fare esplodere. ∼ **out** *v.i.* (*declare*) dichiarare; (*leave*) partire. ∼ **square** *n.* squadra *f.* ∼ **the table** apparecchiare la tavola. ∼ **to** *v.i.* mettersi all'opera. ∼-**to** *n.* zuffa *f.* ∼-**up** *n.* (*fam.*) sistema *m.* ∼ **up** *v.t.* fondare.

settee /se'ti:/ *n.* divano *m.*

setting /'setɪŋ/ *n.* (*of sun*) tramonto *m.*; (*of jewel*) montatura; (*theatr.*) scenario *m.*; (*typ.*) composizione *f.* ∼-**lotion** *n.* fissatore *m.*

settle /'setl/ *v.t.* sistemare; (*date*) fissare; (*nerves*) calmare; (*bill*) saldare. —*v.i.* (*come to rest*) posarsi; (*live*) stabilirsi. ∼ **down** sistemarsi; calmarsi. ∼ **for** accettare. ∼ **up** regolare i conti. ∼**r** /-ə(r)/ *n.* colonizza|tore, -trice *m.*, *f.*

settlement /'setlmənt/ *n.* sistemazione *f.*; (*agreement*) accordo *m.*; (*comm.*) liquidazione *f.*; (*place*) colonia *f.*

seven /'sevn/ *a.* & *n.* sette *m.* ∼**th** *a.* & *n.* settimo, a *m.*, *f.*

seventeen /sevn'ti:n/ *a.* & *n.* diciassette *m.* ∼**th** *a.* & *n.* diciassettesimo, a *m.*, *f.*

sevent|y /'sevntɪ/ *a.* & *n.* settanta *m.* ∼**ieth** *a.* & *n.* settantesimo, a *m.*, *f.*

sever /'sevə(r)/ *v.t.* troncare. ∼**ance** *n.* rottura *f.*

several /'sevrəl/ *a.* & *pron.* parecchi.

sever|e /sɪ'vɪə(r)/ *a.* (-er, -est) severo; (*pain*) violento; (*illness*) grave; (*winter*) rigido. ∼**ely** *adv.* severamente; gravemente. ∼**ity** /-'verətɪ/ *n.* severità *f.*; violenza *f.*; gravità *f.*

sew /səʊ/ *v.t./i.* (*p.t.* sewed, *p.p.* sewn or sewed) cucire. ∼**ing** *n.* cucito *m.* ∼**ing-machine** *n.* macchina da cucire *f.*

sewage /'sju:ɪdʒ/ *n.* acqua di scolo *f.*

sewer /'sju:ə(r)/ *n.* fogna *f.*

sewn /səʊn/ *see* sew.

sex /seks/ *n.* sesso *m.* —*a.* sessuale. have ∼ avere rapporti sessuali. ∼**y** *a.* (-ier, -iest) sexy.

sexist /'seksɪst/ *a.* & *n.* maschilista *m.*

sextet /seks'tet/ *n.* sestetto *m.*

sexual /'sekʃʊəl/ *a.* sessuale. ∼ **intercourse** *n.* rapporti sessuali *m.pl.* ∼**ity** /-'ælətɪ/ *n.* sessualità *f.*

shabb|y /'ʃæbɪ/ *a.* (-ier, -iest) trasandato; (*mean*) meschino. ∼**ily** *adv.* miseramente. ∼**iness** *n.* trasandatezza *f.*; meschineria *f.*

shack /ʃæk/ *n.* baracca *f.*

shackles /'ʃæklz/ *n.pl.* ferri *m.pl.*

shade /ʃeɪd/ *n.* ombra *f.*; (*of colour*) tonalità *f.*; (*for lamp*) paralume *m.* **a** ∼ **better** un tantino meglio. —*v.t.* ombreggiare.

shadow /'ʃædəʊ/ *n.* ombra *f.* —*v.t.* fare ombra; (*follow*) pedinare. **S**∼ **Cabinet** *n.* governo ombra *m.* ∼**y** *a.* ombroso; (*fig.*) indistinto.

shady /'ʃeɪdɪ/ *a.* (-ier, -iest) ombroso; (*fig.*) losco.

shaft /ʃɑ:ft/ *n.* freccia *f.*; (*mech.*) asse *f.*; (*of light*) raggio *m.*; (*of lift*) tromba *f.*; (*of mine*) pozzo *m.*

shaggy /'ʃægɪ/ *a.* (-ier, -iest) irsuto; (*animal*) peloso.

shake /ʃeɪk/ *v.t.* (*p.t.* shook, *p.p.* shaken) scuotere; (*bottle*) agitare; (*shock*) sconvolgere. —*v.i.* tremare. —*n.* scrollata *f.* milk ∼ *n.* frappé di latte *m.* ∼ **hands with** stringere la mano a. ∼ **off** *v.i.* scrollarsi di dosso. ∼-**up** *n.* riorganizzazione *f.*

shaky /'ʃeɪkɪ/ *a.* (-ier, -iest) tremante; (*table etc.*) traballante; (*unreliable*) incerto.

shall /ʃæl/ *v. aux.* (*first person in future tense*) I ∼ **go** (io) andrò. **we** ∼ **see** (noi) vedremo.

shallot /ʃə'lɒt/ *n.* scalogna *f.*

shallow /'ʃæləʊ/ *a.* (-er, -est) basso, poco profondo; (*fig.*) superficiale.

sham /ʃæm/ *n.* finzione *f.* —*a.* falso. —*v.t.* (*p.t.* shammed) simulare.

shambles /'ʃæmblz/ *n.pl.* baraonda *f.s.*

shame /ʃeɪm/ *n.* vergogna *f.* —*v.t.* svergognare. **what a** ∼! che peccato! ∼**ful** *a.* vergognoso. ∼**fully** *adv.* vergognosamente. ∼**less** *a.* spudorato.

shamefaced /'ʃeɪmfeɪst/ *a.* vergognoso.

shampoo /ʃæm'pu:/ *n.* shampoo *m. invar.* —*v.t.* lavare (i capelli, tappeti, ecc.).

shandy /'ʃændɪ/ *n.* miscela di birra e gassosa *f.*

shan't /ʃɑ:nt/ = shall not.

shanty /'ʃæntɪ/ *n.* capanna *f.* ∼ **town** *n.* bidonville *f. invar.*

shape /ʃeɪp/ *n.* forma *f.* —*v.t.* formare. —*v.i.* ∼ (**up**) fare progressi. ∼**less** *a.* informe.

shapely /'ʃeɪplɪ/ *a.* (-ier, -iest) ben fatto.

share /ʃeə(r)/ *n.* porzione *f.*; (*comm.*) azione *f.* —*v.t./i.* dividere. **go** ∼**s** dividere equamente. ∼ **in** prendere parte a. ∼-**out** *n.* distribuzione *f.*

shareholder /'ʃeəhəʊldə(r)/ *n.* azionista *m.*|*f.*

shark /ʃɑːk/ *n.* squalo *m.*; (*fig.*) truffa- |tore, -trice *m., f.*

sharp /ʃɑːp/ *a.* (-er, -est) (*knife etc.*) tagliente; (*pin etc.*) appuntito; (*pain, sound*) acuto; (*taste*) piccante; (*sudden, harsh*) brusco; (*well defined*) marcato; (*person*) scaltro. —*adv.* in punto. **seven o'clock** ∼ le sette in punto. —*n.* (*mus.*) diesis *m. invar.* ∼**ly** *adv.* bruscamente.

sharpen /ʃɑːpn/ *v.t.* affilare. ∼**er** (*mech.*) affilatoio *m.*

shatter /ʃætə(r)/ *v.t./i.* frantumare, frantumarsi; (*upset*) sconvolgere.

shav|e /ʃeɪv/ *v.t./i.* radere, radersi. *n.* **have a** ∼**e** farsi la barba. ∼**en** *a.* rasato. ∼**er** *n.* rasoio elettrico *m.* ∼**ing-brush** *n.* pennello da barba *m.*

shawl /ʃɔːl/ *n.* scialle *m.*

she /ʃiː/ *pron.* ella, lei, essa. —*n.* fem- mina *f.*

sheaf /ʃiːf/ *n.* (*pl.* **sheaves**) fascio *m.*

shear /ʃɪə(r)/ *v.t.* (*p.p.* **shorn** or **sheared**) tosare.

shears /ʃɪəz/ *n.pl.* cesoie *f.pl.*

sheath /ʃiːθ/ *n.* (*pl.* -s /ʃiːðz/) fodero *m.*

sheathe /ʃiːð/ *v.t.* rinfoderare.

shed[1] /ʃed/ *n.* baracca *f.*

shed[2] /ʃed/ *v.t.* (*p.t.* **shed, *pres. p.* shedding**) perdere; (*tears*) versare; (*clothes*) togliersi. ∼ **light on** far luce su.

sheen /ʃiːn/ *n.* lucentezza *f.*

sheep /ʃiːp/ *n. invar.* pecora *f.* ∼**-dog** *n.* cane da pastore *m.*

sheepish /ʃiːpɪʃ/ *a.* impacciato. ∼**ly** *adv.* timidamente.

sheepskin /ʃiːpskɪn/ *n.* pelle di mon- tone *f.*

sheer /ʃɪə(r)/ *a.* vero e proprio; (*steep*) perpendicolare; (*fabric*) sottile. —*adv.* a picco.

sheet /ʃiːt/ *n.* lenzuolo *m.*; (*of paper*) foglio *m.*; (*of glass, ice*) lastra *f.*

sheikh /ʃeɪk/ *n.* sceicco *m.*

shelf /ʃelf/ *n.* (*pl.* **shelves**) scaffale *m.* **on the** ∼ in disparte.

shell /ʃel/ *n.* conchiglia *f.*; (*of egg*) guscio *m.*; (*of building*) struttura *f.*; (*explosive*) proiettile *m.* —*v.t.* (*peas etc.*) sgusciare; (*mil.*) bombardare. ∼ **out** (*fam.*) sborsare.

shellfish /ʃelfɪʃ/ *n. invar.* mollusco *m.*

shelter /ʃeltə(r)/ *n.* rifugio *m.* —*v.t./i.* rifugiare, rifugiarsi; (*protect*) proteg- gere; (*give lodging to*) dare asilo a. ∼**ed** *a.* (*spot*) riparato; (*life*) ritirato.

shelve /ʃelv/ *v.t.* mettere su uno scaffale; (*fig.*) rinviare.

shelving /ʃelvɪŋ/ *n.* scaffali *m.pl.*

shepherd /ʃepəd/ *n.* pastore *m.* —*v.t.* guidare. ∼**ess** /-ˈdes/ *n.* pastorella *f.* ∼'**s pie** *n.* pasticcio di carne tritata e patate *m.*

sherbet /ʃɜːbət/ *n.* bevanda ghiacciata a base di succo di frutta *f.*

sheriff /ʃerɪf/ *n.* sceriffo *m.*

sherry /ʃerɪ/ *n.* sherry *m.*

shield /ʃiːld/ *n.* scudo *m.* —*v.t.* pro- teggere.

shift /ʃɪft/ *v.t./i.* cambiare; (*furniture etc.*) spostare; (*blame etc.*) river- sare. —*n.* cambiamento *m.*; (*of wor- kers*) turno *m.* **make** ∼ arrangiarsi.

shiftless /ʃɪftlɪs/ *a.* privo di risorse.

shifty /ʃɪftɪ/ *a.* (-ier, -iest) disonesto; (*eyes*) sfuggente.

shilling /ʃɪlɪŋ/ *n.* scellino *m.*

shilly-shally /ʃɪlɪʃælɪ/ *v.i.* titubare.

shimmer /ʃɪmə(r)/ *v.i.* brillare. —*n.* scintillio *m.*

shin /ʃɪn/ *n.* stinco *m.*

shine /ʃaɪn/ *v.i.* (*p.t.* **shone**) splen- dere. —*v.t.* lucidare. ∼ **on** (*torch*) puntare verso. —*n.* splendore *m.*; lu- centezza *f.*

shingle /ʃɪŋgl/ *n.* (*pebbles*) ghiaia *f.*

shingles /ʃɪŋglz/ *n.pl.* (*med.*) erpete *m.s.*

shiny /ʃaɪnɪ/ *a.* (-ier, -iest) lucido.

ship /ʃɪp/ *n.* nave *f.* —*v.t.* (*p.t.* **shipped**) trasportare (via mare); (*send*) spedire (via mare). ∼**ment** *n.* spedizione *f.*; (*consignment*) carico *m.* ∼**per** *n.* spe- dizioniere *m.* ∼**ping** *n.* spedizione *f.*; (*ships*) navi *f.pl.*

shipbuilding /ʃɪpbɪldɪŋ/ *n.* co- struzione di navi *f.*

shipshape /ʃɪpʃeɪp/ *adv. & a.* in per- fetto ordine.

shipwreck /ʃɪprek/ *n.* naufragio *m.* ∼**ed** *a.* naufragato. **be** ∼**ed** far nau- fragio.

shipyard /ʃɪpjɑːd/ *n.* cantiere navale *m.*

shirk /ʃɜːk/ *v.t.* scansare. ∼**er** *n.* scan- safatiche *m./f. invar.*

shirt /ʃɜːt/ *n.* camicia *f.*; (*for woman*) camicetta *f.* **in** ∼-**sleeves** in maniche di camicia.

shirty /ʃɜːtɪ/ *a.* (*sl.*) irritabile.

shiver /ʃɪvə(r)/ *v.i.* rabbrividire. —*n.* brivido *m.*

shoal /ʃəʊl/ *n.* (*of fish*) banco *m.*

shock /ʃɒk/ *n.* urto *m.*; (*fig.*) colpo *m.*;

(*electr.*) scossa (elettrica) *f.*; (*med.*) shock *m.* —*v.t.* scioccare; colpire. ~ing *a.* scioccante; (*fam.*) orribile. ~ingly *adv.* terribilmente.

shod /ʃɒd/ *see* **shoe.**

shodd|y /'ʃɒdɪ/ *a.* (-**ier, -iest**) scadente. ~ily *adv.* in modo scadente.

shoe /ʃuː/ *n.* scarpa *f.*; (*of horse*) ferro di cavallo *m.* —*v.t.* (*p.t.* **shod, pres. p. shoeing**) (*horse*) ferrare. **be well shod** essere ben calzato. **on a ~ string** con poco denaro. ~-**lace** *n.* laccio da scarpe *m.* ~-**tree** *n.* forma da scarpa *f.*

shoehorn /'ʃuːhɔːn/ *n.* corno (da scarpe) *m.*

shoemaker /'ʃuːmeɪkə(r)/ *n.* calzolaio *m.*

shone /ʃɒn/ *see* **shine.**

shoo /ʃuː/ *v.t.* cacciar via.

shook /ʃʊk/ *see* **shake.**

shoot /ʃuːt/ *v.t./i.* (*p.t.* **shot**) sparare; (*hunt*) andare a caccia; (*film*) girare. —*n.* germoglio *m.*; (*hunt*) spedizione di caccia *f.* ~ **down** *v.t.* abbattere. ~ **out** *v.i.* (*rush*) balzar fuori. ~ **up** *v.i.* (*of prices*) salire di colpo; *v.i.* (*grow*) crescere in fretta. ~ing-**range** *n.* poligono di tiro *m.*

shop /ʃɒp/ *n.* negozio *m.*; (*workshop*) officina *f.* —*v.i.* (*p.t.* **shopping**) far compere. ~ **around** paragonare i prezzi. ~ **assistant** *n.* commesso, a *m., f.* ~-**lifter** *n.* taccheggia|tore, -trice *m., f.* ~-**lifting** *n.* taccheggio *m.* ~ **steward** *n.* rappresentante sindacale *m.|f.* ~-**window** *n.* vetrina *f.* **talk** ~ parlare di affari. ~per *n.* compra| tore, -trice *m., f.*

shopkeeper /'ʃɒpkiːpə(r)/ *n.* negoziante *m.|f.*

shopping /'ʃɒpɪŋ/ *n.* compere *f.pl.* **go** ~ far compere. ~ **bag** *n.* borsa per la spesa *f.* ~ **centre** *n.* centro commerciale *m.*

shore /ʃɔː(r)/ *n.* riva *f.*

shorn /ʃɔːn/ *see* **shear.**

short /ʃɔːt/ *a.* (-**er, -est**) corto; (*not lasting*) breve; (*person*) basso; (*curt*) brusco. —*adv.* improvvisamente. ~s *n.pl.* calzoncini corti *m.pl.* **a** ~ **time ago** poco tempo fa. **be** ~ **of** essere a corto di. **in** ~ in breve. **Mick is** ~ **for Michael** Mick è il diminutivo di Michael. ~-**change** *v.t.* truffare. ~ **circuit** *n.* corto circuito *m.* ~ **cut** *n.* accorciatoia *f.* ~-**lived** *a.* di breve durata. ~ **of doing** a meno che non

si faccia. ~-**sighted** *a.* miope. ~-**tempered** *a.* irascibile.

shortage /'ʃɔːtɪdʒ/ *n.* mancanza *f.*

shortbread /'ʃɔːtbred/ *n.* biscotto di pasta frolla *m.*

shortcoming /'ʃɔːtkʌmɪŋ/ *n.* difetto *m.*

shorten /'ʃɔːtn/ *v.t.* abbreviare; (*dress*) accorciare.

shorthand /'ʃɔːthænd/ *n.* stenografia *f.* ~ **typist** stenodattilografo, a *m., f.*

shortly /'ʃɔːtlɪ/ *adv.* presto.

shot /ʃɒt/ *see* **shoot.** —*n.* colpo *m.*; (*person*) tiratore *m.*; (*photo*) foto *f.*; (*injection*) iniezione *f.* **like a** ~ come un razzo. ~-**gun** *n.* fucile da caccia *m.*

should /ʃʊd, ʃəd/ *v. aux.* **I** ~ **go** dovrei andare. **I** ~ **have seen him** avrei dovuto vederlo. **I** ~ **like** mi piacerebbe. (*possible future event*) **if he** ~ **come** se dovesse venire.

shoulder /'ʃəʊldə(r)/ *n.* spalla *f.* —*v.t.* accollarsi. ~-**blade** *n.* scapola *f.* ~-**strap** *n.* spallina *f.*

shout /ʃaʊt/ *n.* grido *m.* —*v.t./i.* gridare. ~ **at** alzar la voce con. ~ **down** far tacere gridando.

shove /ʃʌv/ *n.* spintone *m.* —*v.t./i.* spingere; (*put, fam.*) ficcare. ~ **off** *v.i.* (*fam.*) andarsene.

shovel /'ʃʌvl/ *n.* pala *f.* —*v.t.* (*p.t.* **shovelled**) spalare.

show /ʃəʊ/ *v.t.* (*p.t.* **showed,** *p.p.* **shown**) mostrare; (*put on display*) esporre; (*film*) proiettare. —*n.* dimostrazione *f.*; (*exhibition*) mostra *f.*; (*ostentation*) pompa *f.*; (*theatr.*) spettacolo (teatrale) *m.*; (*cinema*) proiezione *f.* **on** ~ in mostra. ~-**down** *n.* resa dei conti *f.* ~-**jumping** *n.* concorso ippico *m.* ~ **off** *v.t.* ostentare; *v.i.* farsi notare. ~-**off** *n.* esibizionista *m.|f.* ~-**place** *n.* luogo d'interesse turistico *m.* ~ **up** *v.i.* risaltare; (*be present*) farsi vedere; *v.t.* (*unmask*) smascherare.

shower /'ʃaʊə(r)/ *n.* acquazzone *m.*; (*of blows etc.*) scarica *f.*; (*for washing*) doccia *f.* —*v.t.* ~ **with** coprire di. —*v.i.* fare la doccia. ~y *a.* da acquazzoni.

showerproof /'ʃaʊəpruːf/ *a.* impermeabile.

showmanship /'ʃəʊmənʃɪp/ *n.* arte di presentare *f.*

shown /ʃəʊn/ *see* **show.**

showroom /'ʃəʊruːm/ *n.* salone per esposizioni *m.*

showy /'ʃəʊɪ/ a. (-ier, -iest) appariscente.

shrank /ʃræŋk/ see **shrink.**

shrapnel /'ʃræpnəl/ n. schegge di granata f.pl.

shred /ʃred/ n. brandello m.; (fig.) briciolo m. —v.t. (p.t. **shredded**) fare a brandelli; (culin.) tagliuzzare. ∼**der** n. (culin.) tagliaverdura m. invar.

shrew /ʃru:/ n. (woman) bisbetica f.

shrewd /ʃru:d/ a. (-er, -est) accorto. ∼**ness** n. accortezza f.

shriek /ʃri:k/ n. strillo m. —v.t./i. strillare.

shrift /ʃrɪft/ n. **give s.o. short** ∼ liquidare qcno. bruscamente.

shrill /ʃrɪl/ a. stridulo.

shrimp /ʃrɪmp/ n. gamberetto m.

shrine /ʃraɪn/ n. reliquiario m.

shrink /ʃrɪŋk/ v.t./i. (p.t. **shrank,** p.p. **shrunk**) restringere, restringersi; (draw back) ritrarsi. ∼**age** n. restringimento m.

shrivel /'ʃrɪvl/ v.t./i. (p.t. **shrivelled**) raggrinzare.

shroud /ʃraʊd/ n. sudario m.; (fig.) manto m. —v.t. avvolgere.

Shrove /ʃrəʊv/ n. ∼ **Tuesday** martedì grasso m.

shrub /ʃrʌb/ n. arbusto m.

shrug /ʃrʌg/ v.t. (p.t. **shrugged**) scrollare le spalle. —n. scrollata di spalle f.

shrunk /ʃrʌŋk/ see **shrink.** ∼**en** a. rimpicciolito.

shudder /'ʃʌdə(r)/ v.i. fremere. —n. fremito m.

shuffle /'ʃʌfl/ v.i. (feet) strascicare. —v.t. (cards) mescolare. —n. strascicamento m.; mescolata f.

shun /ʃʌn/ v.t. (p.t. **shunned**) rifuggire.

shunt /ʃʌnt/ v.t. smistare.

shush /ʃʊʃ/ int. zitto!

shut /ʃʌt/ v.t./i. (p.t. **shut,** pres. p. **shutting**) chiudere, chiudersi. ∼ **down** or **up** chiudere. ∼**-down** n. chiusura f. ∼ **up** (fam.) (far) tacere.

shutter /'ʃʌtə(r)/ n. imposta f.; (photo) otturatore m.

shuttle /'ʃʌtl/ n. navetta f. —v.i. far la spola. ∼ **service** n. servizio pendolare m.

shuttlecock /'ʃʌtlkɒk/ n. volano m.

shy /ʃaɪ/ a. (-er, -est) timido. —v.i. (p.t. **shied**) (of horse) impennarsi. ∼ **away from** rifuggire da. ∼ **off** schivare. ∼**ness** n. timidezza f.

Siamese /saɪə'mi:z/ a. siamese.

sibling /'sɪblɪŋ/ n. fratello m., sorella f.

Sicil|y /'sɪsɪlɪ/ n. Sicilia f. ∼**ian** /-'sɪljən/ a. & n. siciliano, a m., f.

sick /sɪk/ a. ammalato; (humour) macabro; (fam., fed up) stufo. **be** ∼ (vomit) vomitare. **feel** ∼ aver la nausea. ∼**-room** n. camera d'ammalato f.

sicken /'sɪkən/ v.t. disgustare. —v.i. **be** ∼**ing for** stare per ammalarsi di.

sickle /'sɪkl/ n. falce f.

sickly /'sɪklɪ/ a. (-ier, -iest) malaticcio.

sickness /'sɪknɪs/ n. malattia f.

side /saɪd/ n. lato, fianco m.; (of road) orlo m.; (of river) sponda f.; (fig.) parte f. —a. laterale. —v.i. ∼ **with** parteggiare per. **on the** ∼ (sideline) come attività secondaria; (pej.) di straforo. ∼ **by** ∼ fianco a fianco. ∼-**car** n. side-car m. ∼**-effect** n. effetto collaterale m. ∼**-saddle** n. sella femminile f. ∼**-show** n. attrazione f. ∼**-step** v.t. schivare. ∼**-track** v.t. sviare. ∼**-whiskers,** ∼**burns** ns.pl. basette f.pl.

sideboard /'saɪdbɔ:d/ n. credenza f. ∼**s** n.pl. (sl.) fedine f.pl.

sidelight /'saɪdlaɪt/ n. luce laterale f.

sideline /'saɪdlaɪn/ n. attività secondaria f.

sidewalk /'saɪdwɔ:k/ n. (Amer.) marciapiede m.

side|ways /'saɪdweɪz/, ∼**long** /-lɒŋ/ advs. & adjs. di traverso.

siding /'saɪdɪŋ/ n. binario di raccordo m.

sidle /'saɪdl/ v.i. camminare furtivamente (up to, verso).

siege /si:dʒ/ n. assedio m.

siesta /sɪ'estə/ n. siesta f.

sieve /sɪv/ n. setaccio m. —v.t. setacciare.

sift /sɪft/ v.t. setacciare. —v.i. ∼ **through** esaminare.

sigh /saɪ/ n. sospiro m. —v.i. sospirare.

sight /saɪt/ n. vista f.; (spectacle) veduta f.; (on gun) mira f. —v.t. avvistare. **at** or **on** ∼ a prima vista. **catch** ∼ **of** intravedere. **lose** ∼ **of** perdere di vista. **within** ∼ **of** vicino a.

sightsee|ing /'saɪtsi:ɪŋ/ n. visita turistica f. ∼**r** /-ə(r)/ n. turista m./f.

sign /saɪn/ n. segno m.; (notice) insegna f. —v.t. firmare. ∼ **on** or **up** v.t./i. arruolare, arruolarsi; (register) firmare.

signal /'sɪgnəl/ n. segnale m. —v.t./i.

(*p.t.* **signalled**) segnalare; (*person*)
far segno a. ∼-**box** *n.* cabina di segna-
lazione *f.*

signalman /'sɪɡnəlmən/ *n.* (*pl.* -**men**)
segnalatore *m.*

signatory /'sɪɡnətrɪ/ *n.* firmatario, a
m., *f.*

signature /'sɪɡnətʃə(r)/ *n.* firma *f.* ∼
tune *n.* sigla musicale *f.*

signet-ring /'sɪɡnɪtrɪŋ/ *n.* anello con
sigillo *m.*

significan|t /sɪɡ'nɪfɪkənt/ *a.* significa-
tivo; (*important*) importante. ∼**ce** *n.*
significato *m.*; importanza *f.* ∼**tly**
adv. in modo significativo.

signify /'sɪɡnɪfaɪ/ *v.t.* denotare;
(*matter*) importare.

signpost /'saɪnpəʊst/ *n.* indicatore
stradale *m.*

silence /'saɪləns/ *n.* silenzio *m.* —*v.t.*
far tacere. ∼**r** /-ə(r)/ *n.* silenziatore
m.

silent /'saɪlənt/ *a.* silenzioso; (*film*)
muto. ∼**ly** *adv.* silenziosamente.

silhouette /sɪluː'et/ *n.* siluetta *f.* —*v.t.*
be ∼**d** profilarsi.

silicon /'sɪlɪkən/ *n.* silicio *m.* ∼ **chip**
n. piastrina di silicio *f.*

silk /sɪlk/ *n.* seta *f.* ∼**en**, ∼**y** *adjs.* di
seta, come la seta. ∼**worm** *n.* baco
da seta *m.*

sill /sɪl/ *n.* davanzale *m.*

silly /'sɪlɪ/ *a.* (-**ier**, -**iest**) sciocco. —*n.*
∼-**billy** (*fam.*) sciocchino, a *m.*, *f.*

silo /'saɪləʊ/ *n.* (*pl.* -**os**) silo *m.*

silt /sɪlt/ *n.* melma *f.*

silver /'sɪlvə(r)/ *n.* argento *m.*; (*silverware*) argenteria *f.* —*a.* d'argento. ∼
plate *n.* metallo argentato *m.* ∼ **wedding** *n.* nozze d'argento *f.pl.* ∼**y** *a.*
argenteo; (*sound*) argentino.

silverside /'sɪlvəsaɪd/ *n.* (*culin.*) girello
m.

silversmith /'sɪlvəsmɪθ/ *n.* argentiere
m.

silverware /'sɪlvəweə(r)/ *n.* argenteria
f.

similar /'sɪmɪlə(r)/ *a.* simile. ∼**ity**
/-ə'lærətɪ/ *n.* somiglianza *f.* ∼**ly** *adv.*
similmente.

simile /'sɪmɪlɪ/ *n.* similitudine *f.*

simmer /'sɪmə(r)/ *v.t./i.* (far) bollire
lentamente; (*fig.*) ribollire. ∼ **down**
calmarsi.

simpl|e /'sɪmpl/ *a.* (-**er**, -**est**) semplice;
(*person*) ingenuo. ∼**e-minded** *a.* credulone. ∼**icity** /-'plɪsetɪ/ *n.* semplicità

f. ∼**y** *adv.* semplicemente; (*absolutely*) assolutamente.

simpleton /'sɪmpltən/ *n.* sempliciotto,
a *m.*, *f.*

simplif|y /'sɪmplɪfaɪ/ *v.t.* semplificare.
∼**ication** /-ɪ'keɪʃn/ *n.* semplificazione
f.

simulat|e /'sɪmjʊleɪt/ *v.t.* simulare.
∼**ion** /-'leɪʃn/ *n.* simulazione *f.*

simultaneous /sɪml'teɪnɪəs/ *a.* simul-
taneo. ∼**ly** *adv.* simultaneamente.

sin /sɪn/ *n.* peccato *m.* —*v.i.* (*p.t.*
sinned) peccare.

since /sɪns/ *prep.* da, da quando. —*adv.*
da allora. —*conj.* da che; (*because*)
poiché.

sincer|e /sɪn'sɪə(r)/ *a.* sincero. ∼**ely**
adv. sinceramente. ∼**ity** /-'serətɪ/ *n.*
sincerità *f.*

sinew /'sɪnjuː/ *n.* tendine *m.* ∼**s** *n.pl.*
muscoli *m.pl.*

sinful /'sɪnfl/ *a.* peccaminoso.

sing /sɪŋ/ *v.t./i.* (*p.t.* **sang**, *p.p.* **sung**)
cantare. ∼**er** *n.* cantante *m.*/*f.*

singe /sɪndʒ/ *v.t.* (*pres. p.* **singeing**)
bruciacchiare.

single /'sɪŋgl/ *a.* unico; (*not double*)
semplice; (*unmarried man*) celibe;
(*unmarried woman*) nubile; (*room*)
singolo; (*bed*) a una piazza. —*n.* (*tennis*) singolo *m.*; (*ticket*) biglietto di
sola andata *m.* —*v.t.* ∼ **out** scegliere;
(*distinguish*) distinguere. ∼-
breasted *a.* a un petto. ∼-**handed**
a. & *adv.* senza aiuto. ∼-**minded** *a.*
risoluto. **singly** *adv.* a uno a uno.

singlet /'sɪŋglɪt/ *n.* canottiera *f.*

singsong /'sɪŋsɒŋ/ *n.* cantilena *f.*

singular /'sɪŋgjʊlə(r)/ *n.* singolare
m. —*a.* singolare; (*uncommon*)
eccezionale. ∼**ly** *adv.* singolarmente.

sinister /'sɪnɪstə(r)/ *a.* sinistro.

sink /sɪŋk/ *v.t./i.* (*p.t.* **sank**, *p.p.* **sunk**)
affondare; (*of ground*) cedere; (*pati-
ent*) peggiorare; (*well*) scavare;
(*money*) investire. —*n.* lavandino *m.*
∼ **in** *v.i.* penetrare.

sinner /'sɪnə(r)/ *n.* pecca|tore, -trice
m., *f.*

sinuous /'sɪnjʊəs/ *a.* sinuoso.

sinus /'saɪnəs/ *n.* (*pl.* -**uses**) seno *m.*

sip /sɪp/ *n.* sorso. *m.* —*v.t.* (*p.t.* **sipped**)
sorseggiare.

siphon /'saɪfən/ *n.* sifone *m.* —*v.t.* ∼
out travasare.

sir /sɜː(r)/ *n.* signore *m.* **S**∼ *n.* (*title*)
Sir *m.*

siren /'saɪərən/ *n.* sirena *f.*

sirloin /'sɜːlɔɪn/ n. lombo di manzo m.

sirocco /sɪ'rɒkəʊ/ n. scirocco m.

sissy /'sɪsɪ/ n. uomo effeminato m.

sister /'sɪstə(r)/ n. sorella f.; (nurse) infermiera-capo f.; (nun) suora f. **~-in-law** n. (pl. **~s-in-law**) cognata f. **~ly** a. di sorella.

sit /sɪt/ v.t./i. (p.t. **sat**, pres. p. **sitting**) sedere, sedersi; (of committee etc.) riunirsi. **~ back** v.i. (fig.) rilassarsi. **~ down** v.i. mettersi a sedere. **~ for** v.i. (exam) dare un esame; (portrait) posare (per). **~-in** n. occupazione (di azienda ecc.) f. **~ up** v.i. alzarsi a sedere. **~ting** n. sessione f.; (in restaurant) turno m. **~ting-room** n. soggiorno m.

site /saɪt/ n. posto m. **building ~** n. cantiere m. −v.t. situare.

situat|e /'sɪtʃʊeɪt/ v.t. situare. **~ed** a. situato. **~ion** /-'eɪʃn/ n. situazione f.

six /sɪks/ a. & n. sei m. **~th** a. & n. sesto, a m., f.

sixteen /sɪk'stiːn/ a. & n. sedici m. **~th** a. & n. sedicesimo, a m., f.

sixt|y /'sɪkstɪ/ a. & n. sessanta m. **~ieth** a. & n. sessantesimo, a m., f.

size /saɪz/ n. misura f.; (of clothes) taglia f.; (extent) dimensione f. −v.t. **~ up** (fam.) valutare. **~able** a. piuttosto grande.

sizzle /'sɪzl/ v.i. sfrigolare.

skate[1] /skeɪt/ n. invar. (fish) razza f.

skat|e[2] /skeɪt/ n. pattino m. −v.i. pattinare. **~er** n. pattina|tore, -trice m.,f. **~ing** n. pattinaggio m. **~ing-rink** n. pista di pattinaggio f.

skateboard /'skeɪtbɔːd/ n. skateboard m.

skein /skeɪn/ n. matassa f.

skelet|on /'skelɪtn/ n. scheletro m. **~al** a. scheletrico. **~on staff** n. personale ridotto m.

sketch /sketʃ/ n. schizzo m.; (theatr.) sketch m. −v.t. schizzare. **~ out** delineare.

sketchy /'sketʃɪ/ a. (-ier, -iest) incompleto.

skew /skjuː/ n. **on the ~** di traverso.

skewer /'skjʊə(r)/ n. spiedo m.

ski /skiː/ n. (pl. **-is**) sci m. invar. −v.i. (p.t. **skied**, pres. p. **skiing**) sciare. **go ~ing** andare a sciare. **~er** n. scia|tore, -trice m., f. **~ing** n. lo sci m. **~-lift** n. sciovia f.

skid /skɪd/ v.i. (p.t. **skidded**) slittare. −n. slittata f.

skilful /'skɪlfl/ a. abile.

skill /skɪl/ n. abilità f. **~ed** a. esperto; (worker) specializzato.

skim /skɪm/ v.t. (p.t. **skimmed**) schiumare; (milk) scremare. **~ over** v.t. rasentare. **~ through** v.i. scorrere.

skimp /skɪmp/ v.t. lesinare.

skimpy /'skɪmpɪ/ a. (-ier, -iest) (clothes) succinto.

skin /skɪn/ n. pelle f. −v.t. (p.t. **skinned**) spellare; (fruit) sbucciare. **~-deep** a. superficiale. **~-diving** n. nuoto subacqueo m.

skinflint /'skɪnflɪnt/ n. miserabile m./f.

skinny /'skɪnɪ/ a. (-ier, -iest) ossuto.

skint /skɪnt/ a. (sl.) senza una lira.

skip[1] /skɪp/ v.i. (p.t. **skipped**) saltare. −v.t. omettere. −n. salto m. **~ping-rope** n. corda per saltare f.

skip[2] /skɪp/ n. (container) benna f.

skipper /'skɪpə(r)/ n. capitano m.

skirmish /'skɜːmɪʃ/ n. scaramuccia f.

skirt /skɜːt/ n. gonna f. −v.t. confinare. **~ing-board** n. zoccolo m.

skit /skɪt/ n. bozzetto comico m.

skittish /'skɪtɪʃ/ a. frivolo.

skittle /'skɪtl/ n. birillo m.

skive /skaɪv/ v.i. (sl.) fare lo scansafatiche.

skivvy /'skɪvɪ/ n. (fam.) serva f.

skulk /skʌlk/ v.i. muoversi furtivamente.

skull /skʌl/ n. cranio m. **~-cap** n. papalina f.

skunk /skʌŋk/ n. moffetta f.; (person) farabutto m.

sky /skaɪ/ n. cielo m. **~-blue** a. & n. azzurro cielo m.

skyjack /'skaɪdʒæk/ n. dirottamento aereo m. **~er** n. dirottatore m.

skylight /'skaɪlaɪt/ n. lucernario m.

skyscraper /'skaɪskreɪpə(r)/ n. grattacielo m.

slab /slæb/ n. lastra f.

slack /slæk/ a. (-er, -est) (person) fiacco; (not tight) lento. −n. (of rope) imbando m. −v.i. **~ off** (fam.) rilassarsi.

slacken /'slækən/ v.i. **~ (off)** diminuire. −v.t. allentare.

slacks /slæks/ n.pl. pantaloni m.pl.

slag /slæg/ n. scorie f.pl.

slain /sleɪn/ see **slay**.

slake /sleɪk/ v.t. appagare.

slam /slæm/ v.t./i. (p.t. **slammed**) sbattere; (throw) scaraventare; (sl.) criticare. −n. rumore forte m.

slander /'slɑːndə(r)/ n. diffamazione

f. —*v.t.* diffamare. ~**ous** *a.* diffamatorio.

slang /slæŋ/ *n.* gergo *m.* ~**y** *a.* popolaresco.

slant /slɑ:nt/ *v.t./i.* pendere; (*news*) distorcere. —*n.* pendenza *f.*; (*point of view*) punto di vista *m.*

slap /slæp/ *v.t.* (*p.t.* **slapped**) schiaffeggiare; (*put*) sbattere. —*n.* schiaffo *m.* —*adv.* in pieno. ~**-happy** *a.* (*fam.*) spensierato. ~**-up** *a.* (*sl.*) di prim'ordine.

slapdash /'slæpdæʃ/ *a.* avventato.

slapstick /'slæpstɪk/ *n.* farsa grossolana *f.*

slash /slæʃ/ *v.t.* sfregiare; (*fig.*) stroncare; (*prices etc.*) ridurre fortemente. —*n.* taglio *m.*

slat /slæt/ *n.* stecca *f.*

slate /sleɪt/ *n.* ardesia *f.* —*v.t.* (*fam.*) criticare severamente.

slattern /'slætən/ *n.* sciattona *f.*

slaughter /'slɔ:tə(r)/ *v.t.* macellare; (*massacre*) massacrare. —*n.* macello *m.*; massacro *m.*

slaughterhouse /'slɔ:təhaʊs/ *n.* macello *m.*

Slav /slɑ:v/ *a. & n.* slavo, a *m.,f.* ~**onic** /slə'vɒnɪk/ *a.* (*lang.*) slavo.

slave /sleɪv/ *n.* schiavo, a *m., f.* —*v.i.* lavorare come uno schiavo. ~**-driver** *n.* aguzzino, a *m., f.* ~**ry** /-ərɪ/ *n.* schiavitù *f.*

slavish /'sleɪvɪʃ/ *a.* servile.

slay /sleɪ/ *v.t.* (*p.t.* **slew**, *p.p.* **slain**) ammazzare.

sleazy /'sli:zɪ/ *a.* (-ier, -iest) (*fam.*) sordido.

sledge /sledʒ/ *n.* slitta *f.* ~**-hammer** *n.* martello da fabbro *m.*

sleek /sli:k/ *a.* (-er, -est) liscio, lucente; (*manner*) sdolcinato; (*car etc.*) slanciato.

sleep /sli:p/ *n.* sonno *m.* —*v.i.* (*p.t.* **slept**) dormire. —*v.t.* dar da dormire a. **go to** ~ addormentarsi. ~**er** *n.* dormiente *m./f.*; (*on track*) traversina *f.*; (*berth*) vagone letto *m.* ~**ing-bag** *n.* sacco a pelo *m.* ~**ing-pill** *n.* sonnifero *m.* ~**less** *a.* insonne. ~**lessness** *n.* insonnia *f.* ~**-walker** *n.* sonnambulo, a *m.,f.*

sleep|y /'sli:pɪ/ *a.* (-ier, -iest) assonnato. **be** ~**y** aver sonno. ~**ily** *adv.* con aria addormentata.

sleet /sli:t/ *n.* nevischio *m.* —*v.i.* venir giù nevischio.

sleeve /sli:v/ *n.* manica *f.*; (*for record*) copertina *f.* **up one's** ~ nascosto. ~**less** *a.* senza maniche.

sleigh /sleɪ/ *n.* slitta *f.*

sleight /slaɪt/ *n.* ~ **of hand** gioco di prestigio *m.*

slender /'slendə(r)/ *a.* esile; (*fig.*) scarso.

slept /slept/ *see* **sleep.**

sleuth /slu:θ/ *n.* investigatore *m.*

slew[1] /slu:/ *v.i.* girare.

slew[2] /slu:/ *see* **slay.**

slice /slaɪs/ *n.* fetta *f.*; (*implement*) paletta *f.* —*v.t.* affettare.

slick /slɪk/ *a.* liscio; (*cunning*) astuto. —*n.* (oil) ~ macchia di petrolio *f.*

slide /slaɪd/ *v.t./i.* (*p.t.* **slid**) (far) scivolare. —*n.* scivolata *f.*; (*in playground*) scivolo *m.*; (*for hair*) fermaglio (per capelli) *m.*; (*photo*) diapositiva *f.* ~ **out of** sgusciare fuori da. ~ **over** sorvolare su. ~**-rule** *n.* regolo calcolatore *m.* **sliding** *a.* scorrevole. **sliding scale** *n.* scala mobile *f.*

slight /slaɪt/ *a.* (-er, -est) sottile, leggero. —*v.t.* offendere. —*n.* affronto *m.* ~**est** *a.* minimo. **not in the** ~**est** affatto. ~**ly** *adv.* leggermente.

slim /slɪm/ *a.* (**slimmer, slimmest**) snello. —*v.i.* (*p.t.* **slimmed**) dimagrire. ~**ness** *n.* snellezza *f.*

slim|e /slaɪm/ *n.* melma *f.* ~**y** *a.* melmoso; (*fig.*) untuoso.

sling /slɪŋ/ *n.* benda al collo *f.* —*v.t.* (*p.t.* **slung**) lanciare.

slip /slɪp/ *v.t./i.* (*p.t.* **slipped**) (far) scivolare. —*n.* scivolata *f.*; (*mistake*) lieve errore *m.*; (*petticoat*) sottana *f.*; (*paper*) scontrino *m.* **give the** ~ **to** sbarazzarsi di. ~ **away** *v.i.* sgusciar via. ~ **into** *v.i.* (*clothes*) infilarsi. ~ **of the tongue** *n.* lapsus linguae *m.* ~**-road** *n.* bretella *f.* ~ **s.o.'s mind** sfuggire dalla mente di qcno. ~ **up** *v.i.* (*fam.*) sbagliare. ~**-up** *n.* (*fam.*) papera *f.*

slipper /'slɪpə(r)/ *n.* pantofola *f.*

slippery /'slɪpərɪ/ *a.* scivoloso.

slipshod /'slɪpʃɒd/ *a.* sciatto.

slit /slɪt/ *n.* fessura *f.* —*v.t.* (*p.t.* **slitted**) tagliare, fendere.

slither /'slɪðə(r)/ *v.i.* sdrucciolare.

sliver /'slɪvə(r)/ *n.* scheggia *f.*

slobber /'slɒbə(r)/ *v.i.* sbavarsi.

slog /slɒg/ *v.t.* (*p.t.* **slogged**) colpire fortemente. —*v.i.* sgobbare. —*n.* sgobbata *f.*

slogan /'sləʊgən/ *n.* slogan *m. invar.*

slop /slɒp/ *v.t./i.* ~ **(over)** (*p.t.* **slopped**) traboccare. ~s *n.pl.* acqua sporca *f.*; (*fam.*) brodaglia *f.*

slop|e /sləʊp/ *v.i.* essere·inclinato, inclinarsi. —*v.t.* declinare. —*n.* pendenza *f.* ~ing *a.* in pendenza.

sloppy /'slɒpɪ/ *a.* (**-ier, -iest**) acquoso; (*work*) fatto male; (*person*) sciatto; (*fig.*) sdolcinato.

slosh /slɒʃ/ *v.i.* (*fam.*) sguazzare. —*v.t.* (*hit, sl.*) picchiare.

slot /slɒt/ *n.* fessura *f.* —*v.t.* (*p.t.* **slotted**) infilare. ~-**machine** *n.* distributore automatico *m.*

sloth /sləʊθ/ *n.* pigrizia *f.*

slouch /slaʊtʃ/ *v.i.* camminare pigramente.

slovenl|y /'slʌvnlɪ/ *a.* sciatto. ~iness *n.* sciatteria *f.*

slow /sləʊ/ *a.* (**-er, -est**) lento. —*adv.* lentamente. —*v.t./i.* ~ (**down/up**) rallentare. **be** ~ (*of clock*) essere indietro. **in** ~ **motion** al rallentatore. ~ly *adv.* lentamente. ~ness *n.* lentezza *f.*

slowcoach /'sləʊkəʊtʃ/ *n.* pigrone, a *m., f.*

sludge /slʌdʒ/ *n.* fanghiglia *f.*

slug /slʌg/ *n.* lumaca *f.*; (*bullet*) pallottola *f.*

sluggish /'slʌgɪʃ/ *a.* lento.

sluice /sluːs/ *n.* chiusa *f.*; (*channel*) canale di scarico *m.*

slum /slʌm/ *n.* catapecchia *f.* ~s *n.pl.* bassibondi *m.pl.*

slumber /'slʌmbə(r)/ *n.* sonnellino *m.*

slump /slʌmp/ *n.* crollo *m.*; (*in business*) depressione *f.* —*v.i.* crollare; (*flop down*) cadere pesantemente.

slung /slʌŋ/ *see* **sling.**

slur /slɜː(r)/ *v.t./i.* (*p.t.* **slurred**) pronunciare difettosamente. —*n.* dizione difettosa *f.*; (*discredit*) affronto *m.*

slush /slʌʃ/ *n.* fanghiglia *f.*; (*fig.*) sdolcinatezza *f.* ~ **money** *n.* bustarella *f.* ~y *a.* fangoso.

slut /slʌt/ *n.* sgualdrina *f.*

sly /slaɪ/ *a.* (**slyer, slyest**) (*crafty*) scaltro; (*mischievous*) birichino *m.* **on the** ~ alla chetichella. ~ly *adv.* astutamente.

smack[1] /smæk/ *n.* colpo *m.*; (*on face*) schiaffo *m.* —*v.t.* sbattere; schiaffeggiare. —*adv.* (*fam.*) direttamente.

smack[2] /smæk/ *v.i.* ~ **of** sapere di.

small /smɔːl/ *a.* (**-er, -est**) piccolo. —*n.* **the** ~ **of the back** le reni *f.pl.* ~ **ads** *n.pl.* piccola pubblicità *f.s. f.*

~ **change** *n.* spiccioli *m.pl.* ~ **talk** *n.* chiacchiere *f.pl.* ~ **time** *a.* (*fam.*) da poco.

smallholding /'smɔːlhəʊldɪŋ/ *n.* piccola fattoria *f.*

smallpox /'smɔːlpɒks/ *n.* vaiolo *m.*

smarmy /'smɑːmɪ/ *a.* (**-ier, -iest**) (*fam.*) untuoso.

smart /smɑːt/ *a.* (**-er, -est**) elegante; (*clever*) intelligente; (*brisk*) svelto. —*v.i.* bruciare. ~ly *adv.* elegantemente. ~ness *n.* eleganza *f.*

smarten /'smɑːtn/ *v.t./i.* abbellire, abbellirsi. ~ **up** *v.i.* farsi bello.

smash /smæʃ/ *v.t./i.* frantumare, frantumarsi; (*crash*) andare in pezzi; (*door*) sfondare; (*opponent*) annientare. —*n.* urto violento *m.*; (*collision*) scontro *m.*; (*ruin*) crollo *m.*

smashing /'smæʃɪŋ/ *a.* (*fam.*) fantastico.

smattering /'smætərɪŋ/ *n.* infarinatura *f.*

smear /smɪə(r)/ *v.t.* imbrattare; (*coat*) spalmare; (*fig.*) denigrare. —*n.* macchia *f.*; (*med.*) striscio *m.*

smell /smel/ *n.* odore *m.*; (*sense*) odorato *m.* —*v.t./i.* (*p.t.* **smelt**) odorare. ~y *a.* puzzolente.

smelt[1] /smelt/ *see* **smell.**

smelt[2] /smelt/ *v.t.* fondere.

smile /smaɪl/ *n.* sorriso *m.* —*v.i.* sorridere.

smirk /smɜːk/ *n.* sorriso compiaciuto *m.*

smite /smaɪt/ *v.t.* (*p.t.* **smote,** *p.p.* **smitten**) colpire.

smith /smɪθ/ *n.* fabbro *m.*

smithereens /smɪðə'riːnz/ *n.pl.* **to** *or* **in** ~ in mille pezzi.

smitten /'smɪtn/ *see* **smite.** —*a.* tutto preso (**with,** da).

smock /smɒk/ *n.* grembiule *m.*

smog /smɒg/ *n.* smog *m.*

smoke /sməʊk/ *n.* fumo *m.* —*v.t./i.* fumare. ~less *a.* senza fumo. ~r /-ə(r)/ *n.* fuma|tore, -trice *m., f.* ~-**screen** *n.* cortina di fumo *f.*

smoky *a.* fumoso.

smooth /smuːð/ *a.* (**-er, -est**) liscio; (*sound*) dolce; (*movement*) scorrevole; (*sea*) calmo; (*manners*) mellifluo. —*v.t.* lisciare; (*fig.*) facilitare. ~ly *adv.* dolcemente; scorrevolmente.

smote /sməʊt/ *see* **smite.**

smother /'smʌðə(r)/ *v.t.* soffocare.

smoulder /'sməʊldə(r)/ *v.i.* covare.

smudge /smʌdʒ/ n. macchia f. —v.t./i. imbrattare.

smug /smʌg/ a. (**smugger, smuggest**) soddisfatto di sé. ~**ly** adv. con aria di sufficienza. ~**ness** n. (auto)compiacimento m.

smuggl\|e /'smʌgl/ v.t. contrabbandare ~**er** n. contrabbandiere, a m.,f. ~**ing** n. contrabbando m.

smut /smʌt/ n. macchia di fuliggine f. ~**ty** a. (**-ier, -iest**) fuligginoso; (fig.) sconcio.

snack /snæk/ n. spuntino m. ~**-bar** n. tavola calda f.

snag /snæg/ n. intoppo m.; (in cloth) filo tirato m.

snail /sneɪl/ n. lumaca f. ~'**s pace** passo di lumaca m.

snake /sneɪk/ n. serpente m.

snap /snæp/ v.t./i. (p.t. **snapped**) (far) schioccare; (break) spezzare, spezzarsi; (bite) addentare; (say) parlare aspramente. —n. colpo secco m.; (photo) istantanea f. —a. improvviso. ~ **at** v.t. (bite) azzannare; (fig.) investire. ~ **up** v.t. afferrare.

snappy /'snæpɪ/ a. (**-ier, -iest**) (fam.) stizzoso. **make it** ~! (fam.) sbrigati!

snap\shot /'snæpʃɒt/ n. istantanea f.

snare /sneə(r)/ n. trappola f.

snarl /snɑːl/ v.i. ringhiare. —n. ringhio m.

snatch /snætʃ/ v.t. strappare (di mano); (steal) rubare. —n. strappo m.; (short part) brano m.; (theft) scippo m.

sneak /sniːk/ v.i. ~ **in/out** entrare/ uscire furtivamente —n. (schol. sl.) spia m.\|f.; (coward) persona abietta f. ~**y** a. abietto.

sneakers /'sniːkəz/ n.pl. scarpe da ginnastica f.pl.

sneaking /'sniːkɪŋ/ a. furtivo.

sneer /snɪə(r)/ n. ghigno m. —v.i. sogghignare.

sneeze /sniːz/ n. sternuto m. —v.i. sternutire.

snide /snaɪd/ a. (fam.) malizioso.

sniff /snɪf/ v.t./i. annusare. —n. annusata f.

snigger /'snɪgə(r)/ n. risatina repressa f. —v.i. ridacchiare.

snip /snɪp/ v.t. (p.t. **snipped**) tagliuzzare. —n. taglio m.; (sl., bargain) affare m.

snipe /snaɪp/ v.i. sparare da un nascondiglio. ~**r** /ə(r)/ n. cecchino m.

snippet /'snɪpɪt/ n. pezzetto m.

snivel /'snɪvl/ v.i. (p.t. **snivelled**) piagnucolare. ~**ling** a. piagnucoloso.

snob /snɒb/ n. snob m.\|f. ~**bery** n. snobismo m. ~**bish** a. snob.

snooker /'snuːkə(r)/ n. (tipo di) biliardo m.

snoop /snuːp/ v.i. (fam.) curiosare.

snooty /'snuːtɪ/ a. (fam.) sdegnoso.

snooze /snuːz/ n. sonnellino m. —v.i. fare un sonnellino.

snore /snɔː(r)/ v.i. russare.

snorkel /'snɔːkl/ n. respiratore a tubo m.

snort /snɔːt/ n. sbuffo m. —v.i. sbuffare.

snout /snaʊt/ n. grugno m.

snow /snəʊ/ n. neve f. —v.i. nevicare. **be** ~**ed under with** essere sommerso da. ~**-drift** n. cumulo di neve m. ~**-plough** n. spazzaneve m. ~**y** a. nevoso.

snowball /'snəʊbɔːl/ n. palla di neve f.

snowdrop /'snəʊdrɒp/ n. bucaneve m.

snowfall /'snəʊfɔːl/ n. nevicata f.

snowflake /'snəʊfleɪk/ n. fiocco di neve m.

snowman /'snəʊmæn/ n. (pl. **-men**) pupazzo di neve m.

snowstorm /'snəʊstɔːm/ n. tormenta f.

snub /snʌb/ v.t. (p.t. **snubbed**) snobbare. —n. sgarbo m.

snub-nosed /'snʌbnəʊzd/ a. dal naso camuso.

snuff[1] /snʌf/ n. tabacco da fiuto m.

snuff[2] /snʌf/ v.t. (candle) spegnere.

snuffle /'snʌfl/ v.i. aspirare rumorosamente.

snug /snʌg/ a. (**snugger, snuggest**) comodo; (tight) aderente.

snuggle /'snʌgl/ v.i. rannicchiarsi.

so /səʊ/ adv. così, tanto. —conj. però. —a. & pron. tanto. **and** ~ **forth** or **on** e così via. **I think** ~ credo di sì. **if** ~ se è così. **or** ~ pressappoco. ~ **am I** anch'io. ~**-and-**~ n. un, una tale m., f. ~ **as to** in modo da. ~**-called** a. cosiddetto. ~ **far** adv. finora. ~ **far as** per quanto. ~ **long!** (fam.) a presto! ~ **much** tanto. ~~ a. & adv. così così. ~ **that** conj. affinché.

soak /səʊk/ v.t./i. immergere, immergersi; (of liquid) penetrare; (sl.) estorcere (soldi da). —n. (sl.) ubriacone m. ~ **up** v.t. assorbire. ~**ing** a. inzuppato; n. ammollo m.

soap /səʊp/ n. sapone m. —v.t. insaponare. ~ **powder** *n.* sapone in polvere *m.* ~y *a.* insaponato.

soar /sɔ:(r)/ *v.i.* elevarsi.

sob /sɒb/ *n.* singhiozzo *m.* —*v.i.* (*p.t.* **sobbed**) singhiozzare.

sober /'səʊbə(r)/ *a.* equilibrato; (*abstemious*) parco; (*colour, style*) sobrio.

soccer /'sɒkə(r)/ *n.* (*fam.*) (gioco del) calcio *m.*

sociable /'səʊʃəbl/ *a.* socievole.

social /'səʊʃl/ *a.* sociale; (*sociable*) socievole. —*n.* serata *f.* ~ly *adv.* socialmente. ~ **security** *n.* assistenza sociale *f.* ~ **worker** *n.* assistente sociale *m.*/*f.*

socialis|t /'səʊʃəlɪst/ *a.* & *n.* socialista *m.*/*f.* ~m /-zəm/ *n.* socialismo *m.*

socialize /'səʊʃəlaɪz/ *v.t.* socializzare.

society /sə'saɪətɪ/ *n.* società *f.*

sociolog|y /səʊsɪ'ɒlədʒɪ/ *n.* sociologia *f.* ~**ical** /-ə'lɒdʒɪkl/ *a.* sociologico. ~**ist** *n.* sociologo, a *m.*, *f.*

sock[1] /sɒk/ *n.* calzino *m.*

sock[2] /sɒk/ *v.t.* (*sl.*) picchiare. —*n.* (*sl.*) pugno *m.*

socket /'sɒkɪt/ *n.* cavità *f.*; (*of eye*) orbita *f.*; (*wall plug*) presa di corrente *f.*; (*for bulb*) portalampada *m. invar.*

soda /'səʊdə/ *n.* soda *f.* ~**-water** *n.* acqua di seltz *f.*

sodden /'sɒdn/ *a.* inzuppato.

sodium /'səʊdɪəm/ *n.* sodio *m.*

sofa /'səʊfə/ *n.* divano *m.*

soft /sɒft/ *a.* (-**er**, -**est**) morbido, soffice; (*of sound*) sommesso; (*of light, colour*) tenue; (*gentle*) tenero; (*silly*) stupido. ~ **drink** *n.* bevanda non alcoolica *f.* ~ **spot** *n.* debole *m.* ~ly *adv.* dolcemente. ~**ness** *n.* morbidezza *f.*; dolcezza *f.*

soften /'sɒfn/ *v.t.*/*i.* ammorbidire, ammorbidirsi; (*tone down*) mitigare; mitigarsi. ~**er** *n.* depuratore *m.*

software /'sɒftweə(r)/ *n.* software *m.*

soggy /'sɒgɪ/ *a.* (-**ier**, -**iest**) zuppo d'acqua.

soh /səʊ/ *n.* (*mus.*) sol *m.*

soil[1] /sɔɪl/ *n.* suolo *m.*

soil[2] /sɔɪl/ *v.t.*/*i.* macchiare, macchiarsi.

solace /'sɒləs/ *n.* sollievo *m.*

solar /'səʊlə(r)/ *a.* solare.

solarium /səʊ'leərɪəm/ *n.* (*pl.* -**a**) solarium *m.*

sold /səʊld/ *see* sell.

solder /'sɒldə(r)/ *n.* lega *f.* —*v.t.* saldare.

soldier /'səʊldʒə(r)/ *n.* soldato *m.* —*v.i.*

~ **on** (*fam.*) perseverare tenacemente.

sole[1] /səʊl/ *n.* (*of foot*) pianta *f.*; (*of shoe*) suola *f.*

sole[2] /səʊl/ *n.* (*fish*) sogliola *f.*

sole[3] /səʊl/ *a.* unico, solo. ~ly *adv.* unicamente.

solemn /'sɒləm/ *a.* solenne. ~**ity** /sə'lemnətɪ/ *n.* solennità *f.* ~ly *adv.* solennemente.

solicit /sə'lɪsɪt/ *v.t.* sollecitare. —*v.i.* importunare.

solicitor /sə'lɪsɪtə(r)/ *n.* avvocato *m.*

solicitous /sə'lɪsɪtəs/ *a.* sollecito.

solid /'sɒlɪd/ *a.* solido; (*not hollow*) pieno; (*gold*) massiccio; (*unanimous*) solidale; (*meal*) sostanzioso. —*n.* solido *m.* ~**ity** /sə'lɪdətɪ/ *n.* solidità *f.* ~ly *adv.* solidamente.

solidarity /sɒlɪ'dærətɪ/ *n.* solidarietà *f.*

solidify /sə'lɪdɪfaɪ/ *v.t.*/*i.* solidificare, solidificarsi.

soliloquy /sə'lɪləkwɪ/ *n.* soliloquio *m.*

solitaire /sɒlɪ'teə(r)/ *n.* solitario *m.*

solitary /'sɒlɪtrɪ/ *a.* solitario.

solitude /'sɒlɪtjuːd/ *n.* solitudine *f.*

solo /'səʊləʊ/ *n.* (*pl.* -**os**) (*mus.*) assolo *m.*; (*aeron.*) (volo) da solo *m.* ~**ist** *n.* solista *m.*/*f.*

solstice /'sɒlstɪs/ *n.* solstizio *m.*

soluble /'sɒljʊbl/ *a.* solubile.

solution /sə'luːʃn/ *n.* soluzione *f.*

solv|e /sɒlv/ *v.t.* risolvere. ~**able** *a.* risolvibile.

solvent /'sɒlvənt/ *a.* solvente. —*n.* (dis) solvente *m.*

sombre /'sɒmbə(r)/ *a.* tetro; (*of clothes*) scuro.

some /sʌm/ *a.* (*quantity, number*) del, un po' di; (*unspecified*) qualche, (*pl.*) alcuni. —*pron.* alcuni, e; (*certain quantity*) ne; (*a little*) un po'. —*adv.* circa. **I want** ~ ne voglio. **will you have** ~ **wine?** vuoi del vino? ~ **day** qualche giorno. ~ **of us** alcuni di noi. ~ **two hours** circa due ore.

somebody /'sʌmbədɪ/ *pron.* & *n.* qualcuno *m.*

somehow /'sʌmhaʊ/ *adv.* in qualche modo. ~ **or other** in un modo o nell'altro.

someone /'sʌmwʌn/ *pron.* & *n.* = **somebody.**

somersault /'sʌməsɔːlt/ *n.* capriola *f.* —*v.i.* fare una capriola.

something /'sʌmθɪŋ/ *pron.* qualche

cosa. ~ **like** un po' come; (*approximately*) circa.

sometime /'sʌmtaɪm/ *adv.* un giorno o l'altro; (*in past*) ~ **last summer** durante l'estate scorsa. —*a.* ex.

sometimes /'sʌmtaɪmz/ *adv.* qualche volta.

somewhat /'sʌmwɒt/ *adv.* piuttosto.

somewhere /'sʌmweə(r)/ *adv.* da qualche parte.

son /sʌn/ *n.* figlio *m.* ~**-in-law** *n.* (*pl.* ~**s-in-law**) genero *m.*

sonata /sə'nɑːtə/ *n.* sonata *f.*

song /sɒŋ/ *n.* canzone *f.* **sell for a** ~ vendere per quattro soldi. ~**-book** *n.* canzoniere *m.*

sonic /'sɒnɪk/ *a.* sonico.

sonnet /'sɒnɪt/ *n.* sonetto *m.*

sonny /'sʌnɪ/ *n.* (*fam.*) figliolo *m.*

soon /suːn/ *adv.* (-**er**, -**est**) presto; (*in a short time*) tra poco. **as** ~ **as** (non) appena. **as** ~ **as possible** il più presto possibile. **I would** ~**er go** preferirei andare. ~ **after** subito dopo. ~**er or later** presto o tardi.

soot /sʊt/ *n.* fuliggine *f.* ~**y** *a.* fuligginoso.

sooth|e /suːð/ *v.t.* calmare. ~**ing** *a.* calmante.

sop /sɒp/ *n.* **throw a** ~ **to** corrompere.

sophisticated /sə'fɪstɪkeɪtɪd/ *a.* raffinato; (*complex*) sofisticato.

soporific /sɒpə'rɪfɪk/ *a.* soporifero.

sopping /'sɒpɪŋ/ *a.* ~ (**wet**) bagnato fradicio.

soppy /'sɒpɪ/ *a.* (-**ier**, -**iest**) (*fam.*) svenevole.

soprano /sə'prɑːnəʊ/ *n.* (*pl.* -**os**) soprano *m./f.*

sorcerer /'sɔːsərə(r)/ *n.* stregone *m.*

sordid /'sɔːdɪd/ *a.* sordido.

sore /'sɔː(r)/ *a.* (-**er**, -**est**) dolorante; (*distressed*) dolente; (*vexed*) irritato. —*n.* piaga *f.* ~ **throat** *n.* mal di gola *m.*

sorely /'sɔːlɪ/ *adv.* gravemente.

sorrow /'sɒrəʊ/ *n.* afflizione *f.* ~**ful** *a.* triste.

sorry /'sɒrɪ/ *a.* (-**ier**, -**ier**) spiacente; (*wretched*) pietoso. **be** ~ (*repent*) pentirsi. **be** ~ **for** (*pity*) essere addolorato per. ~! scusa!, scusi!, scusate!

sort /sɔːt/ *n.* specie, genere *m.*; (*person, fam.*) tipo *m.* —*v.t.* classificare. ~ **out** (*choose*) scegliere; (*problem*) risolvere. **be out of** ~**s** essere giù di corda.

soufflé /'suːfleɪ/ *n.* soufflé *m. invar.*

sought /sɔːt/ *see* **seek**.

soul /səʊl/ *n.* anima *f.*

soulful /'səʊlfl/ *a.* sentimentale.

sound[1] /saʊnd/ *n.* suono *m.* —*v.t./i.* suonare; (*seem*) sembrare (**as if**, che). ~ **barrier** *n.* muro del suono *m.* ~**proof** *a.* impenetrabile al suono. ~**track** *n.* colonna sonora *f.*

sound[2] /saʊnd/ *a.* (-**er**, -**est**) sano; (*sensible*) saggio; (*secure*) solido. ~ **asleep** profondamente addormentato. ~**ly** *adv.* sanamente.

sound[3] /saʊnd/ *v.t.* (*test*) sondare.

sound[4] /saʊnd/ *n.* (*strait*) stretto *m.*

soup /suːp/ *n.* minestra *f.* **in the** ~ (*sl.*) nei guai.

sour /'saʊə(r)/ *a.* (-**er**, -**est**) agro; (*not fresh*) acido; (*fig.*) acrimonioso. —*v.t./i.* inacidire, inacidirsi.

source /sɔːs/ *n.* fonte *f.*

south /saʊθ/ *n.* sud *m.* —*a.* del sud, meridionale. —*adv.* a sud. **S~ Africa/America** *ns.* Africa/ America del Sud *f.* **S~ American** *a.* & *n.* sud-americano, a *m.*, *f.* ~**-east** *n.* sud-est *m.* ~**erly** /'sʌðəlɪ/ *a.* del sud. ~**ward** *a.* & *adv.* verso sud. ~**wards** *adv.* verso sud. ~**-west** *n.* sud-ovest *m.*

southern /'sʌðən/ *a.* del sud, meridionale. ~ **Italy** il Mezzogiorno *m.* ~**er** *n.* meridionale *m./f.*

souvenir /suːvə'nɪə(r)/ *n.* ricordo *m.*

sovereign /'sɒvrɪn/ *n.* & *a.* sovrano, a *m.*, *f.* ~**ty** *n.* sovranità *f.*

Soviet /'səʊvɪət/ *a.* sovietico. **the** ~ **Union** *n.* l'Unione Sovietica *f.*

sow[1] /səʊ/ *v.t.* (*p.t.* **sowed**, *p.p.* **sowed** *or* **sown**) seminare.

sow[2] /saʊ/ *n.* scrofa *f.*

soya /'sɔɪə/ *n.* ~ **bean** soia *f.*

spa /spɑː/ *n.* stazione termale *f.*

space /speɪs/ *n.* spazio *m.* —*a.* (*research etc.*) spaziale. —*v.t.* spaziare. ~ **out** distanziare.

space|craft /'speɪskrɑːft/ *n.* veicolo spaziale *m.* ~**ship** *n.* astronave *f.* ~**suit** *n.* tuta spaziale *f.*

spacious /'speɪʃəs/ *a.* spazioso.

spade /speɪd/ *n.* vanga *f.*; (*for child*) paletta *f.* ~**s** *n.pl.* (*cards*) picche *f.pl.*

spadework /'speɪdwɜːk/ *n.* lavoro preparatorio *m.*

Spa|in /speɪn/ *n.* Spagna *f.* ~**niard** /'spænɪəd/ *n.* Spagnolo, a *m.*, *f.* ~**nish** /'spænɪʃ/ *a.* spagnolo; *n.* (*lang.*) spagnolo *m.*

span[1] /spæn/ *n.* spanna *f.*; (*of arch*) luce *f.*; (*of time*) spazio *m.*; (*of wings*) apertura f. —v.t. (p.t. **spanned**) estendersi (attraverso).

span² /spæn/ see **spick**.

spaniel /'spænɪəl/ n. spaniel m. invar.

spank /spæŋk/ v.t. sculacciare. ~**ing** n. sculacciata f.

spanner /'spænə(r)/ n. chiave inglese f.

spar /spɑ:(r)/ v.i. (p.t. **sparred**) esercitarsi al pugilato; (argue) disputare.

spare /speə(r)/ v.t. risparmiare; (do without) fare a meno di; (afford to give) dare. —a. di riserva; (of person) smilzo; (meal etc.) frugale. ~ (**part**) n. pezzo di ricambio m. ~ **time** n. tempo libero m.

sparing /'speərɪŋ/ a. parco. ~**ly** adv. frugalmente.

spark /spɑ:k/ n. scintilla f. —v.t. ~ **off** far esplodere. ~**ing-plug** n. (auto.) candela f.

sparkl|e /'spɑ:kl/ v.i. scintillare. —n. scintillio m. ~**ing** a. scintillante; (wine) spumante.

sparrow /'spærəʊ/ n. passero m.

sparse /spɑ:s/ a. rado. ~**ly** adv. scarsamente.

spartan /'spɑ:tn/ a. spartano.

spasm /'spæzəm/ n. spasimo m.; (of cough) accesso m.

spasmodic /spæz'mɒdɪk/ a. spasmodico.

spastic /'spæstɪk/ a. & n. spastico, a m., f.

spat /spæt/ see **spit¹**.

spate /speɪt/ n. piena f.

spatial /'speɪʃl/ a. spaziale.

spatter /'spætə(r)/ v.t./i. schizzare. —n. schizzo m.

spatula /'spætjʊlə/ n. spatola f.

spawn /spɔ:n/ n. uova (di pesci) f.pl. —v.t./i. deporre uova; (generate) generare.

speak /spi:k/ v.t./i. (p.t. **spoke**, p.p. **spoken**) parlare. ~ **for** v.i. parlare a nome di. ~ **up** v.i. parlare più forte.

speaker /'spi:kə(r)/ n. (in public) oratore m.; (loudspeaker) altoparlante m. **be an Italian** ~ parlare italiano.

spear /spɪə(r)/ n. lancia f.

spearhead /'spɪəhed/ n. gruppo d'assalto m. —v.t. condurre.

spearmint /'spɪəmɪnt/ n. menta romana f.

spec /spek/ n. **on** ~ (fam.) senza certezza.

special /'speʃl/ a. speciale. ~**ity** /-ɪ'ælətɪ/ n. specialità f. ~**ly** adv.

specialmente; (particularly) particolarmente.

specialist /'speʃəlɪst/ n. specialista m./f.

specializ|e /'speʃəlaɪz/ v.t./i. specializzare, specializzarsi. ~**ation** /-'zeɪʃn/ n. specializzazione f.

species /'spi:ʃi:z/ n. specie f. invar.

specific /spə'sɪfɪk/ a. specifico. ~**ally** adv. specificamente.

specif|y /'spesɪfaɪ/ v.t. specificare. ~**ication** /-ɪ'keɪʃn/ n. specificazione f.; (details) descrizione f.

specimen /'spesɪmɪn/ n. campione m.

speck /spek/ n. macchiolina f.; (particle) granello m.

speckled /'spekld/ a. picchiettato.

specs /speks/ n.pl. (fam.) occhiali m.pl.

spectacle /'spektəkl/ n. spettacolo m. ~**s** n.pl. occhiali m.pl.

spectacular /spek'tækjʊlə(r)/ a. spettacolare.

spectator /spek'teɪtə(r)/ n. spetta|tore, -trice m., f.

spectre /'spektə(r)/ n. spettro m.

spectrum /'spektrəm/ n. (pl. -**tra**) spettro m.; (of ideas) gamma f.

speculat|e /'spekjʊleɪt/ v.i. speculare. ~**ion** /-'leɪʃn/ n. speculazione f. ~**ive** /-lətɪv/ a. speculativo. ~**or** n. specula|tore, -trice m., f.

sped /sped/ see **speed**.

speech /spi:tʃ/ n. (faculty) parola f.; (address) discorso m. ~**less** a. senza parola.

speed /spi:d/ n. velocità f.; (rapidity) fretta f. —v.i. (p.t. **sped**) affrettarsi; (p.t. **speeded**) andare a velocità eccessiva. ~ **up** v.t./i. accelerare. ~**ing** n. eccesso di velocità m.

speedboat /'spi:dbəʊt/ n. fuoribordo m.

speedometer /spi:'dɒmɪtə(r)/ n. tachimetro m.

speedway /'spi:dweɪ/ n. pista f.; (Amer.) autostrada f.

speed|y /'spi:dɪ/ a. (-**ier**, -**iest**) rapido. ~**ily** adv. rapidamente.

spell¹ /spel/ n. (magic) incantesimo m.; (attraction) fascino m.

spell² /spel/ v.t./i. (p.t. **spelled** or **spelt**) scrivere/pronunciare lettera per lettera; (mean) significare. ~ **out** v.t. compitare; (fig.) spiegare. ~**ing** n. ortografia f.

spell³ /spel/ n. periodo m.

spellbound /'spelbaʊnd/ a. affascinato.

spelt /spelt/ *see* **spell**[2].

spend /spend/ *v.t./i.* (*p.t.* **spent**) spendere; (*time etc.*) passare; (*care etc.*) dedicare.

spendthrift /'spendθrɪft/ *n.* spendaccione, a *m.*, *f.*

spent /spent/ *see* **spend.**

sperm /spɜːm/ *n.* (*pl.* **sperms** or **sperm**) sperma *m.*

spew /spjuː/ *v.t./i.* vomitare.

sphere /sfɪə(r)/ *n.* sfera *f.*

spherical /'sferɪkl/ *a.* sferico.

sphinx /sfɪŋks/ *n.* sfinge *f.*

spic|e /spaɪs/ *n.* spezie *f.*; (*fig.*) sapore *m.* **~y** *a.* piccante.

spick /spɪk/ *a.* **~ and span** lindo.

spider /'spaɪdə(r)/ *n.* ragno *m.*

spik|e /spaɪk/ *n.* punta *f.* **~y** *a.* appuntito; (*person*) stizzoso.

spill /spɪl/ *v.t.* (*p.t.* **spilled** or **spilt**) versare. *—v.i.* spandersi.

spin /spɪn/ *v.t./i.* (*p.t.* **spun**, *pres. p.* **spinning**) (far) girare; (*wool etc.*) filare. *—n.* rotazione *f.*; (*short drive*) giretto *m.* **~-drier** *n.* centrifuga *f.* **~-off** *n.* vantaggio secondario *m.*

spinach /'spɪnɪdʒ/ *n.* spinaci *m.pl.*

spinal /'spaɪnl/ *a.* spinale. **~ cord** *n.* midollo spinale *m.*

spindl|e /'spɪndl/ *n.* fuso *m.* **~y** *a.* affusolato.

spine /spaɪn/ *n.* spina dorsale *f.*; (*of book*) dorso *m.* **~less** *a.* (*fig.*) senza carattere; (*fam.*) smidollato.

spinning /'spɪnɪŋ/ *n.* filatura *f.* **~-top** *n.* trottola *f.* **~-wheel** *n.* filatoio *m.*

spinster /'spɪnstə(r)/ *n.* donna nubile *f.*; (*old maid, fam.*) zitella *f.*

spiral /'spaɪərəl/ *a.* a spirale. **~ staircase** *n.* scala a chiocciola *f.* *—n.* spirale *f.* *—v.i.* (*p.t.* **spiralled**) salire a spirale.

spire /'spaɪə(r)/ *n.* guglia *f.*

spirit /'spɪrɪt/ *n.* spirito *m.* **~s** *n.pl.* (*drinks*) liquori alcoolici *m.pl.* **in low ~s** abbattuto. *—v.t.* **~ away** portar via. **~-lamp** *n.* lampada a spirito *f.* **~-level** *n.* livella a bolla d'aria *f.*

spirited /'spɪrɪtɪd/ *a.* vivace.

spiritual /'spɪrɪtʃʊəl/ *a.* spirituale. *—n.* (*Amer.*) spiritual *m.*

spiritualis|t /'spɪrɪtʃʊəlɪst/ *n.* spiritista *m.|f.* **~m** /-zəm/ *n.* spiritismo *m.*

spit[1] /spɪt/ *v.t./i.* (*p.t.* **spat** or **spit**, *pres. p.* **spitting**) sputare; (*of rain*) piovigginare. *—n.* sputo *m.* **the ~ting image of** il ritratto di.

spit[2] /spɪt/ *n.* (*for roasting*) spiedo *m.*

spite /spaɪt/ *n.* dispetto *m.* *—v.t.* far dispetto a. **in ~ of** malgrado. **~ful** *a.* dispettoso. **~fully** *adv.* dispettosamente.

spittle /'spɪtl/ *n.* saliva *f.*

spiv /spɪv/ *n.* (*sl.*) trafficante *m.*

splash /splæʃ/ *v.t.* spruzzare. *—v.i.* schizzare. *—n.* spruzzo *m.*; (*of colour*) macchia *f.*; (*fam.*, *drop*) goccio *m.* **~ about** *v.i.* sguazzare. **~ down** *v.i.* (*of spacecraft etc.*) ammarare.

spleen /spliːn/ *n.* milza *f.*

splendid /'splendɪd/ *a.* splendido.

splendour /'splendə(r)/ *n.* splendore *m.*

splint /splɪnt/ *n.* assicella *f.*

splinter /'splɪntə(r)/ *n.* scheggia *f.* *—v.i.* scheggiarsi. **~ group** *n.* ala scissionista *f.*

split /splɪt/ *v.t./i.* (*p.t.* **split**, *pres. p.* **splitting**) spaccare, spaccarsi; (*tear*) strappare, strapparsi; (*divide*) dividere, dividersi. *—n.* fessura *f.*; (*tear*) strappo *m.*; (*quarrel*) rottura *f.*; (*pol.*) scissione *f.* **a ~ second** un attimo. **~ on s.o.** (*sl.*) tradire qcno. **~ one's sides** sbellicarsi dalle risa. **~ up** *v.i.* separarsi.

splurge /splɜːdʒ/ *v.i.* fare sfoggio di.

splutter /'splʌtə(r)/ *v.i.* farfugliare. *—n.* farfuglio *m.*

spoil /spɔɪl/ *v.t.* (*p.t.* **spoilt** or **spoiled**) guastare; (*indulge*) viziare. *—n.* (*pl.*) **~(s)** bottino *m.s.* **~-sport** *n.* guastafeste *m.|f. invar.*

spoke[1] /spəʊk/ *n.* (*of wheel*) raggio *m.*

spoke[2], **spoken** /spəʊk, spəʊkən/ *see* **speak.**

spokesman /'spəʊksmən/ *n.* (*pl.* -men) portavoce *m. invar.*

sponge /spʌndʒ/ *n.* spugna *f.* *—v.t.* pulire (con la spugna). *—v.i.* **~ on** scroccare a. **~-cake** *n.* pan di Spagna *m.* **~r** /-ə(r)/ *n.* scroccone, a *m.*, *f.*

spongy *a.* spugnoso.

sponsor /'spɒnsə(r)/ *n.* garante *m.*; (*radio*, *TV*) finanzia|tore, -trice *m.*, *f.* *—v.t.* sponsorizzare. **~ship** *n.* patrocinio *m.*; finanziamento *m.*

spontaneous /spɒn'teɪnjəs/ *a.* spontaneo. **~ly** *adv.* spontaneamente.

spoof /spuːf/ *n.* (*sl.*) burla *f.*

spooky /'spuːkɪ/ *a.* (-ier, -iest) (*fam.*) sinistro.

spool /spuːl/ *n.* bobina *f.*

spoon /spuːn/ *n.* cucchiaio *m.* **~-feed** *v.t.* (*p.t.* -fed) imboccare. **~ful** *n.* (*pl.* -fuls) cucchiaiata *f.*

spoonerism /'spu:nərɪzəm/ n. papera f.

sporadic /spə'rædɪk/ a. sporadico.

sporran /'spɒrən/ n. borsa (di pelo) f.

sport /spɔːt/ n. sport m.; (amusement) passatempo m.; (person, fam.) persona di spirito f. —v.t. sfoggiare. ~s car n. automobile sportiva f. ~s coat n. giacca sportiva f. ~ing a. sportivo. ~ing chance n. probabilità di successo f.

sportsman, sportswoman /'spɔːtsmən, 'spɔːtswumən/ ns. (pl. -men, -women) sportivo, a m., f.

spot /spɒt/ n. macchia f.; (pimple) brufolo m.; (place) posto m.; (in pattern) pallino m.; (drop) goccia f.; (fam., a little) un po' m. —v.t./i. (p.t. spotted) macchiare, macchiarsi; (notice, fam.) individuare. **in a** ~ (fam.) in difficoltà. **on the** ~ sul posto. ~ **check** n. controllo saltuario m. ~**less** a. immacolato. ~**ted** a. a pallini. ~**ted with** punteggiato di. ~**ty** a. (-ier, -iest) macchiato.

spotlight /'spɒtlaɪt/ n. riflettore m.

spouse /spaʊz/ n. sposo, a m., f.

spout /spaʊt/ n. beccuccio m.; (jet) getto m. —v.i. zampillare. **up the** ~ distrutto.

sprain /spreɪn/ v.t. slogare. —n. slogatura f.

sprang /spræŋ/ see **spring**[2].

sprat /spræt/ n. spratto m.

sprawl /sprɔːl/ v.i. (of person) stravaccarsi; (of city etc.) estendersi.

spray[1] /spreɪ/ n. (shoot) ramoscello m.

spray[2] /spreɪ/ n. spruzzo m.; (device) spruzzatore m. —v.t. spruzzare. ~**gun** n. pistola a spruzzo f.

spread /spred/ v.t./i. (p.t. spread) spargere, spargersi; (cloth, arms) stendere; (jam etc.) spalmare; (disease) diffondersi; (newspaper) spiegare; (distribute) distribuire. —n. estensione f.; (paste) pasta f.; (of disease) diffusione f.; (fam., feast) banchetto m. ~**eagled** a. disteso.

spree /spriː/ n. (fam.) baldoria f. **go on a** ~ far festa.

sprig /sprɪg/ n. rametto m.

sprightly /'spraɪtlɪ/ a. (-ier, -iest) vivace.

spring[1] /sprɪŋ/ n. primavera f. —a. di primavera. ~**time** n. stagione primaverile f.

spring[2] /sprɪŋ/ v.t./i. (p.t. sprang, p.p. sprung) balzare; (issue) spun-

tare. —n. balzo m.; (device) molla f.; (elasticity) elasticità f.; (water) fonte f. ~**board** n. trampolino m. ~ **from** v.i. provenire da. ~ **up** v.i. presentarsi. ~**y** a. (-ier, -iest) elastico.

sprinkle /'sprɪŋkl/ v.t. spruzzare. —n. spruzzatina f. ~**d with** cosparso di. ~**r** /-ə(r)/ n. spruzzatore m.

sprinkling /'sprɪŋklɪŋ/ n. spruzzatina f.; (fig.) infarinatura f.

sprint /sprɪnt/ n. scatto m. —v.i. percorrere a tutta velocità. ~**er** n. velocista m./f.

sprite /spraɪt/ n. folletto m.

sprout /spraʊt/ v.i. germogliare. —n. germoglio m. **(Brussels)** ~**s** n.pl. cavolini di Bruxelles m.pl.

spruce /spruːs/ a. elegante.

sprung /sprʌŋ/ see **spring**[2]. —a. molleggiato.

spry /spraɪ/ a. (**spryer, spryest**) arzillo.

spud /spʌd/ n. (sl.) patata f.

spume /spjuːm/ n. spuma f.

spun /spʌn/ see **spin**.

spunk /spʌŋk/ n. (fam.) fegato m.

spur /spɜː(r)/ n. sperone m.; (stimulus) stimolo m.; (of road) svincolo m. —v.t. ~ **(on)** (p.t. spurred) spronare. **on the** ~ **of the moment** lì per lì.

spurious /'spjʊərɪəs/ a. falso. ~**ly** adv. falsamente.

spurn /spɜːn/ v.t. sdegnare.

spurt /spɜːt/ v.t./i. sprizzare; (increase speed) scattare. —n. scatto m.

spy /spaɪ/ n. spia f. —v.t./i. spiare. ~ **out** esplorare. ~**ing** n. spionaggio m.

squabble /'skwɒbl/ n. alterco m. —v.i. altercare.

squad /skwɒd/ n. squadra f.

squadron /'skwɒdrən/ n. squadrone di cavalleria m.; (naut., aeron.) squadriglia f.

squalid /'skwɒlɪd/ a. squallido. ~**ly** adv. squallidamente.

squall /skwɔːl/ n. strillo m.; (storm) bufera f. —v.i. strillare. ~**y** a. burrascoso.

squalor /'skwɒlə(r)/ n. squallore m.

squander /'skwɒndə(r)/ v.t. sperperare.

square /skweə(r)/ n. quadrato m.; (area) piazza f.; (for drawing) squadra f. —a. quadrato; (not owing) pari; (precise) netto; (meal) sostanzioso; (build) tozzo; (sl.) antiquato. —v.t. (settle) regolare; (math.) elevare al quadrato. —v.i. (agree) accordarsi. **all**

~ pari. ~ **up to** affrontare. ~**ly** *adv.*
direttamente.
squash /skwɒʃ/ *v.t.* schiacciare; (*suppress*) sopprimere. —*n.* calca *f.*;
(*drink*) spremuta *f.*; (*sport*) squash *m.*
~**y** *a.* floscio.
squat /skwɒt/ *v.t./i.* (*p.t.* **squatted**)
accovacciarsi; (*occupy illegally*) occupare abusivamente. —*n.* casa occupata (abusivamente) *f.* —*a.* (*dumpy*)
tarchiato. ~**ter** /-ə(r)/ *n.* occupante
abusivo, a *m.*, *f.*
squawk /skwɔːk/ *n.* stridio *m.* —*v.i.*
stridere.
squeak /skwiːk/ *n.* scricchiolio *m.*
—*v.t./i.* scricchiolare.
squeal /skwiːl/ *n.* strillo *m.* —*v.t./i.*
strillare; (*sl.*) fare la spia.
squeamish /'skwiːmɪʃ/ *a.* schifiltoso;
(*scrupulous*) scrupoloso.
squeegee /'skwiːdʒiː/ *n.* tergivetro *m.*
squeeze /skwiːz/ *v.t./i.* premere;
(*lemon etc.*) spremere; (*hand*) stringere; (*extort*) estorcere (**from,** da).
—*n.* stretta *f.* **credit** ~ *n.* restrizioni
di credito *f.pl.*
squelch /skweltʃ/ *v.i.* spiaccicare.
—*n.* spiaccichio *m.*
squib /skwɪb/ *n.* petardo *m.*
squid /skwɪd/ *n.* calamaro *m.*
squiggle /'skwɪgl/ *n.* scarabocchio *m.*
squint /skwɪnt/ *v.i.* essere strabico;
(*look sideways*) guardare di traverso. —*n.* strabismo *m.*
squire /'skwaɪə(r)/ *n.* signorotto di
campagna *m.*
squirm /skwɜːm/ *v.i.* contorcersi; (*feel
embarrassed*) stare sulle spine.
squirrel /'skwɪrəl/ *n.* scoiattolo *m.*
squirt /skwɜːt/ *v.t./i.* spruzzare. —*n.*
spruzzo *m.*; (*person, fam.*) presuntuoso *m.*
St *abbr.* (*of* **saint, street**).
stab /stæb/ *v.t.* (*p.t.* **stabbed**) pugnalare. —*n.* pugnalata *f.*; (*sensation*) fitta
f.; (*attempt, fam.*) tentativo *m.*
stabilize /'steɪbəlaɪz/ *v.t.* stabilizzare.
~**r** /-ə(r)/ *n.* stabilizzatore *m.*
stab|le[1] /'steɪbl/ *a.* (**-er, -est**) stabile.
~**ility** /stə'bɪlətɪ/ *n.* stabilità *f.*
stable[2] /'steɪbl/ *n.* stalla *f.*; (*establishment*) scuderia *f.* —*v.t.* mettere in
stalla. ~**-boy** *n.* mozzo di stalla *m.*
stack /stæk/ *n.* catasta *f.*; (*fam., large
quantity*) montagna *f.* —*v.t.* accatastare.
stadium /'steɪdjəm/ *n.* stadio *m.*
staff /stɑːf/ *n.* (*stick*) bastone *m.*; (*em-*

ployees) personale *m.*; (*mil.*) stato
maggiore *m.*; (*in school*) corpo degli
insegnanti *m.* —*v.t.* fornire di personale.
stag /stæg/ *n.* cervo *m.* ~**-party** *n.*
riunione per soli uomini *f.*
stage /steɪdʒ/ *n.* palcoscenico *m.*;
(*theatre*) teatro *m.*; (*phase*) fase *f.*
—*v.t.* rappresentare; (*arrange*) organizzare. **by easy** ~**s** a piccole tappe.
go on the ~ darsi al teatro. ~**-coach**
n. (*old use*) diligenza *f.* ~ **fright** *n.*
paura del pubblico *f.* ~**-manager** *n.*
direttore di scena *m.* ~ **whisper** *n.*
sussurro udibile *m.*
stager /'steɪdʒə(r)/ *n.* **old** ~ vecchia
volpe *f.*
stagger /'stægə(r)/ *v.i.* barcollare.
—*v.t.* sbalordire; (*holidays etc.*)
scaglionare. —*n.* vacillamento *m.*
~**ing** *a.* sbalorditivo.
stagnant /'stægnənt/ *a.* stagnante.
stagnat|e /stæg'neɪt/ *v.i.* (ri)stagnare.
~**ion** /-ʃn/ *n.* ristagno *m.*; (*fig.*) inattività *f.*
staid /steɪd/ *a.* posato.
stain /steɪn/ *v.t.* macchiare; (*colour*)
tingere. —*n.* macchia *f.*; (*liquid*) colorante *m.* ~ **remover** *n.* smacchiatore
m. ~**ed glass window** *n.* vetrata a
colori *f.*
stainless /'steɪnlɪs/ *a.* senza macchia.
~ **steel** acciaio inossidabile *m.*
stair /steə(r)/ *n.* gradino *m.* ~**s** *n.pl.*
scale *f.pl.* **flight of** ~**s** *n.* rampa di
scale *f.*
stair|case /'steəkeɪs/ *n.* scale *f.pl.*
~**way** *n.* scala *f.*
stake /steɪk/ *n.* palo *m.*; (*for execution*)
rogo *m.*; (*wager*) scommessa *f.*;
(*comm.*) interessi *m.pl.* —*v.t.* puntellare; (*wager*) scommettere. **at** ~ in
gioco. ~ **a claim** reclamare.
stalactite /'stæləktaɪt/ *n.* stalattite *f.*
stalagmite /'stæləgmaɪt/ *n.* stalagmite
f.
stale /steɪl/ *a.* (**-er, -est**) stantio;
(*uninteresting*) trito.
stalemate /'steɪlmeɪt/ *n.* (*chess*) stallo
m.; (*deadlock*) vicolo cieco *m.*
stalk[1] /stɔːk/ *n.* stelo *m.*
stalk[2] /stɔːk/ *v.i.* camminare impettito. —*v.t.* inseguire.
stall /stɔːl/ *n.* stalla *f.*; (*theatr.*) poltrona *f.*; (*in market*) bancarella *f.*;
(*kiosk*) chiosco *m.* —*v.t./i.* (*of engine*)
fermare, fermarsi; (*stave off*) tenere
lontano.

stallion /'stæljən/ *n.* stallone *m.*

stalwart /'stɔːlwət/ *n.* membro fidato *m.*

stamina /'stæmmə/ *n.* (capacità di) resistenza *f.*

stammer /'stæmə(r)/ *v.i.* balbettare. —*n.* balbettio *m.*

stamp /stæmp/ *v.t./i.* (*feet*) battere (con forza); (*press*) imprimere; (*envelope*) affrancare; (*fig.*) caratterizzare. —*n.* impronta *f.*; (*instrument, fig.*) stampo *m.*; (*mark*) timbro *m.*; (*postage*) francobollo *m.* ~ **out** (*fig.*) soffocare.

stampede /stæm'piːd/ *n.* fuga precipitosa *f.*; (*fam.*) fuggi-fuggi *m.* —*v.i.* fuggire precipitosamente.

stance /stæns/ *n.* posizione *f.*

stand /stænd/ *v.i.* (*p.t.* **stood**) stare in piedi; (*rise*) alzarsi in piedi; (*be*) trovarsi; (*stay firm*) restare. —*v.t.* (*endure*) sopportare; (*place*) mettere; (*offer*) offrire. —*n.* posizione *f.*; (*rack*) appoggio *m.*; (*for goods*) banco *m.*; (*booth*) chiosco *m.*; (*sport*) tribuna *f.*; (*for vehicles*) posteggio *m.* ~ **a chance** avere probabilità di riuscita. ~ **by** *v.i.* stare a guardare; *v.t.* (*support*) appoggiare. ~**-by** *n.* (*person*) riserva *f.*; (*at airport*) lista d'attesa *f.* ~ **down** *v.i.* ritirarsi. ~ **for** *v.t.* rappresentare. ~ **in for** sostituire. ~**-in** *n.* controfigura *f.* ~**-offish** *a.* (*fam.*) scostante. ~ **one's ground** non cedere. ~ **to reason** essere logico. ~ **up** *v.i.* alzarsi in piedi. ~ **up for** prendere le difese di. ~ **up to** *v.t.* affrontare.

standard /'stændəd/ *n.* standard *m.invar.*; (*level*) livello *m.*; (*quality*) qualità *f.*; (*flag*) stendardo *m.*; (*shrub*) arbusto *m.* ~**s** *n.pl.* principi *m.pl.* —*a.* standard. ~ **lamp** *n.* lampada a stelo *f.* ~**ize** *v.t.* uniformare.

standing /'stændɪŋ/ *a.* in piedi. —*n.* posizione *f.*; (*duration*) durata *f.*

standpoint /'stændpɔɪnt/ *n.* punto di vista *m.*

standstill /'stændstɪl/ *n.* at a ~ inattivo. **come to a** ~ fermarsi.

stank /stæŋk/ *see* **stink.**

staple[1] /steɪpl/ *n.* graffa *f.* —*v.t.* fissare con graffa. ~**r** /-ə(r)/ *n.* cucitrice *f.*

staple[2] /steɪpl/ *a.* principale.

star /stɑː/ *n.* stella *f.*; (*asterisk*) asterisco *m.*; (*cinema, theatr.*) divo, a *m., f.* —*v.i.* (*p.t.* **starred**) essere l'interprete principale. ~**-gazer** *n.* (*hum.*) astronomo, a *m., f.* ~**dom** *n.* celebrità *f.* ~**light** *n.* chiarore delle stelle *m.*

~**ry** *a.* stellato. ~**ry-eyed** *a.* (*fam.*) ingenuo.

starboard /'stɑːbəd/ *n.* tribordo *m.*

starch /stɑːtʃ/ *n.* amido *m.*; (*fig.*) formalismo *m.* —*v.t.* inamidare. ~**y** *a.* (*fig.*) formale.

stare /steə(r)/ *v.i.* ~ **at** fissare. —*n.* sguardo fisso *m.*

starfish /'stɑːfɪʃ/ *n.* stella di mare *f.*

stark /stɑːk/ *a.* (-**er**, -**est**) rigido; (*utter*) completo. —*adv.* completamente.

starling /'stɑːlɪŋ/ *n.* storno *m.*

start /stɑːt/ *v.t./i.* (in)cominciare; (*jump*) trasalire; (*leave*) avviarsi. —*n.* principio *m.*; (*leaving*) partenza *f.*; (*sport*) vantaggio *m.*; (*jump*) sobbalzo *m.* ~**er** *n.* (*sport*) partente *m./f.*; (*auto.*) motorino d'avviamento *m.*; (*culin.*) primo piatto *m.* ~**ing-point** *n.* punto di partenza *m.*

startle /'stɑːtl/ *v.t.* far trasalire.

starv|**e** /stɑːv/ *v.i./t.* (far) morire di fame. ~**ation** /-'veɪʃn/ *n.* fame *f.*

stash /stæʃ/ *v.t.* (*sl.*) tenere nascosto.

state /steɪt/ *n.* stato *m.*; (*grand style*) pompa *f.* **S**~ *n.* Stato *m.* —*v.t.* dichiarare; (*fix*) stabilire. **be in a** ~ essere agitato. **lie in** ~ essere esposto nella camera ardente. —*a.* di Stato; (*schol.*) pubblico; (*with ceremony*) di gala. ~**less** *a.* senza nazionalità. ~**ly** *a.* (-**ier**, -**iest**) maestoso.

statement /'steɪtmənt/ *n.* dichiarazione *f.*; (*account*) rapporto *m.* **bank** ~ *n.* estratto conto *m.*

stateroom /'steɪtruːm/ *n.* (*on ship*) cabina di lusso *f.*

statesman /'steɪtsmən/ *n.* (*pl.* -**men**) statista *m.*

static /'stætɪk/ *a.* statico. ~**s** *n.* disturbi atmosferici *m.pl.*

station /'steɪʃn/ *n.* stazione *f.*; (*mil.*) base *f.*; (*status*) condizione sociale *f.* —*v.t.* collocare; (*mil.*) postare. ~**-wagon** *n.* giardinetta *f.*

stationary /'steɪʃnəri/ *a.* stazionario, fermo.

stationer /'steɪʃnə(r)/ *n.* cartolaio, a *m., f.* ~**y** *n.* cartoleria *f.*

statistic|**s** /stə'tɪstɪks/ *n.* statistica *f.* ~**al** *a.* statistico.

statue /'stætʃuː/ *n.* statua *f.* ~**sque** /-ʊ'esk/ *a.* statuario. ~**tte** /-ʊ'et/ *n.* statuetta *f.*

stature /'stætʃə(r)/ *n.* statura *f.*

status /'steɪtəs/ *n.* condizione sociale *f.*

statut|**e** /'stætʃuːt/ *n.* statuto *m.* ~**ory** /-ʊtrɪ/ *a.* statutario.

staunch /stɔːnʃ/ *a.* (**-er, -est**) fedele. **~ly** *adv.* fedelmente.

stave /'steɪv/ *n.* (*mus.*) rigo *m.* —*v.t.* **~ off** tenere lontano.

stay[1] /steɪ/ *n.* sostegno *m.* **~s** *n.pl.* (*old use*) busto *m.s.*

stay[2] /steɪ/ *v.i.* stare, restare; (*spend time*) trattenersi. —*n.* soggiorno *m.*; (*jurid.*) sospensione *f.* **~ put** rimanere fermo. **~ the course** resistere fino alla fine. **~ing-power** *n.* resistenza *f.*

stead /sted/ *n.* vece *f.* **in s.o.'s ~** in sostituzione di qcno. **stand s.o. in good ~** essere utile a qcno.

steadfast /'stedfɑːst/ *a.* fermo.

stead|y /'stedɪ/ *a.* (**-ier, -iest**) saldo, fermo; (*regular*) regolare; (*dependable*) serio. **~ily** *adv.* fermamente; regolarmente.

steak /steɪk/ *n.* bistecca *f.*

steal /stiːl/ *v.t.* (*p.t.* **stole**, *p.p.* **stolen**) rubare. **~ in/out** *v.i.* entrare/uscire furtivamente. **~ the show** essere il centro d'attenzione.

stealth /stelθ/ *n.* **by ~** di nascosto. **~y** *a.* furtivo.

steam /stiːm/ *n.* vapore *m.*; (*energy*) energia *f.* —*v.t.* trattare con vapore; (*cook*) cucinare a vapore. —*v.i.* fumare. **~ ahead** (*fam.*) fare grandi progressi. **~-engine** *n.* locomotiva *f.* **~ up** *v.i.* (*of glass*) appannarsi. **~y** *a.* appannato.

steamer /'stiːmə(r)/ *n.* piroscafo *m.*; (*saucepan*) pentola a vapore *f.*

steamroller /'stiːmrəʊlə(r)/ *n.* compressore stradale *m.*

steel /stiːl/ *n.* acciaio *m.* —*v.t.* **~ o.s.** temprarsi. **~ wool** *n.* lana d'acciaio *f.* **~y** *a.* d'acciaio.

steep[1] /stiːp/ *v.t.* immergere; (*soak*) macerare. —*v.i.* imbevere.

steep[2] /stiːp/ *a.* (**-er, -est**) ripido; (*price, fam.*) esorbitante. **~ly** *adv.* ripidamente. **~ness** *n.* ripidità *f.*

steeple /'stiːpl/ *n.* guglia *f.*

steeplechase /'stiːpltʃeɪs/ *n.* corsa ippica a ostacoli *f.*

steer /stɪə(r)/ *v.t./i.* guidare. **~ clear of** scansare. **~age** *n.* (*naut.*) governo del timone *m.* **~ing** *n.* (*auto*) sterzo *m.* **~ing-wheel** *n.* volante *m.*

stem[1] /stem/ *n.* stelo *m.*; (*of glass*) gambo *m.*; (*of word*) radice; (*of ship*) prua *f.* —*v.i.* (*p.t.* **stemmed**) **~ from** derivare da.

stem[2] /stem/ *v.t.* (*p.t.* **stemmed**) arginare; (*fig.*) arrestare.

stench /stentʃ/ *n.* puzzo *m.*

stencil /'stensl/ *n.* stampino *m.* —*v.t.* (*p.t.* **stencilled**) stampinare.

step /step/ *v.i.* (*p.t.* **stepped**) camminare, andare. —*n.* passo *m.*; (*surface*) gradino *m.*; (*fig.*) misura *f.* **in ~** al passo. **out of ~** fuori passo. **~ in** intervenire. **~-ladder** *n.* scala (portatile) *f.* **~ up** *v.t.* aumentare.

step|brother /'stepbrʌðə(r)/ *n.* fratellastro *m.* **~daughter** *n.* figliastra *f.* **~father** *n.* patrigno *m.* **~mother** *n.* matrigna *f.* **~sister** *n.* sorellastra *f.* **~son** *n.* figliastro *m.*

stepping-stone /'stepɪŋstəʊn/ *n.* pietra per guadare *f.*; (*fig.*) passo *m.*

stereo /'sterɪəʊ/ *n.* (*pl.* **-os**) stereo *m.*

stereophonic /sterɪə'fɒnɪk/ *a.* stereofonico.

stereotype /'sterɪətaɪp/ *n.* stereotipo *m.* **~d** *a.* stereotipato.

steril|e /'steraɪl/ *a.* sterile. **~ity** /stə'rɪlətɪ/ *n.* sterilità *f.*

steriliz|e /'sterɪlaɪz/ *v.t.* sterilizzare. **~ation** /-'zeɪʃn/ *n.* sterilizzazione *f.*

sterling /'stɜːlɪŋ/ *n.* sterlina *f.* —*a.* genuino. **~ silver** *n.* argento puro *m.*

stern[1] /stɜːn/ *a.* (**-er, -est**) rigido. **~ly** *adv.* rigidamente.

stern[2] /stɜːn/ *n.* (*of boat*) poppa *f.*

stethoscope /'steθəskəʊp/ *n.* stetoscopio *m.*

stew /stjuː/ *v.t./i.* (far) cuocere in umido. —*n.* stufato *m.* **in a ~** (*fam.*) agitato.

steward /stjʊəd/ *n.* amministratore *m.*; (*on ship, aircraft*) steward *m.* **~ess** /-'des/ *n.* hostess *f.*

stick[1] /stɪk/ *n.* bastone *m.*; (*of chalk*) pezzo *m.*; (*of celery etc.*) gambo *m.*; (*mus.*) bacchetta *f.*

stick[2] /stɪk/ *v.t./i.* (*p.t.* **stuck**) (con) ficcare; (*glue*) incollare; (*put, fam.*) mettere; (*jam*) bloccarsi; (*endure, sl.*) sopportare. **~ at** (*fam.*) perseverare in. **~-in-the-mud** *n.* persona senza iniziativa *f.* **~ out** sporgere; (*fam., catch the eye*) risaltare. **~ to** restare fedele a. **~ up for** (*fam.*) difendere. **~ing-plaster** *n.* cerotto *m.*

sticker /'stɪkə(r)/ *n.* etichetta adesiva *f.*

stickler /'stɪklə(r)/ *n.* **be a ~ for** tenere molto a.

sticky /'stɪkɪ/ *a.* (**-ier, -iest**) appiccicoso; (*label*) adesivo; (*sl.*) difficile.

stiff /stɪf/ *a.* (**-er, -est**) rigido; (*difficult*) difficile; (*formal*) contenuto; (*drink*) forte; (*price*) alto. ~ **neck** *n.* torcicollo *m.* ~**ly** *adv.* rigidamente. ~**ness** *n.* rigidezza *f.*

stiffen /'stɪfn/ *v.t.* irrigidire.

stifl|e /'staɪfl/ *v.t.* soffocare. ~**ing** *a.* soffocante.

stigma /'stɪgmə/ *n.* (*pl.* **-as**) marchio *m.*; (*pl.* **stigmata** /'stɪgmətə/) (*relig.*) stimmate *f.pl.* ~**tize** *v.t.* stigmatizzare.

stile /staɪl/ *n.* scaletta *f.*

stiletto /stɪ'letəʊ/ *n.* (*pl.* **-os**) stiletto *m.* ~ **heels** tacchi a spillo *m.pl.*

still[1] /stɪl/ *a.* fermo; (*of drink*) non frizzante. —*n.* calma *f.*; (*photo*) posa *f.* —*adv.* ancora; (*nevertheless*) nondimeno, comunque. ~**born** *a.* nato morto. ~ **life** *n.* (*pl.* **-s**) natura morta *f.* ~**ness** *n.* calma *f.*

still[2] /stɪl/ *n.* (*apparatus*) alambicco *m.*

stilted /'stɪltɪd/ *a.* artificioso.

stilts /stɪlts/ *n.pl.* trampoli *m.pl.*

stimula|te /'stɪmjʊleɪt/ *v.t.* stimolare. ~**nt** *n.* sostanza stimolante *f.* ~**tion** /-'leɪʃn/ *n.* stimolo *m.*

stimulus /'stɪmjʊləs/ *n.* (*pl.* **-li** /-laɪ/) stimolo *m.*

sting /stɪŋ/ *n.* puntura *f.*; (*organ*) pungiglione *m.* —*v.t./i.* (*p.t.* **stung**) pungere.

sting|y /'stɪndʒɪ/ *a.* (**-ier, -iest**) avaro. ~**iness** *n.* avarizia *f.*

stink /stɪŋk/ *n.* puzza *f.* —*v.t./i.* (*p.t.* **stank** *or* **stunk**, *p.p.* **stunk**) puzzare. ~**er** /-ə(r)/ *n.* (*sl.*) cosa *or* persona sgradevole *f.*

stint /stɪnt/ *v.i.* ~ **on** lesinare su. —*n.* (*work*) lavoro *m.*

stipple /'stɪpl/ *v.t.* punteggiare.

stipulat|e /'stɪpjʊleɪt/ *v.t./i.* stipulare. ~**ion** /-'leɪʃn/ *n.* stipulazione *f.*

stir /stɜː(r)/ *v.t./i.* (*p.t.* **stirred**) muovere, muoversi; (*mix*) rimescolare; (*stimulate*) stimolare. —*n.* rimescolata *f.*; (*commotion*) trambusto *m.*

stirrup /'stɪrəp/ *n.* staffa *f.* ~**pump** *n.* pompa antincendio *f.*

stitch /stɪtʃ/ *n.* punto *m.*; (*pain*) fitta *f.* —*v.t./i.* cucire. **in** ~**es** (*fam.*) ridendo a crepapelle.

stoat /stəʊt/ *n.* ermellino *m.*

stock /stɒk/ *n.* (*for use or selling*) rifornimento *m.*; (*livestock*) bestiame *m.*; (*lineage*) stirpe *f.*; (*finance*) titoli *m.pl.*; (*culin.*) brodo *m.*; (*plant*) violacciocca

f. —*a.* comune. —*v.t.* approvvigionare. —*v.i.* ~ **up** far provvista (**with**, di). **out of** ~ esaurito. **S~ Exchange** *n.* Borsa Valori *f.* ~**in-trade** *n.* ferri del mestiere *m.pl.* ~ **phrase** *n.* cliché *m. invar.* ~**still** *a.* immobile. ~**taking** *n.* (*comm.*) inventario *m.* **take** ~ (*fig.*) studiare la situazione. **well-** ~**ed** *a.* ben fornito.

stockbroker /'stɒkbrəʊkə(r)/ *n.* agente di cambio *m.*

stocking /'stɒkɪŋ/ *n.* calza *f.*

stockist /'stɒkɪst/ *n.* grossista *m./f.*

stockpile /'stɒkpaɪl/ *n.* riserva *f.* —*v.t.* fare scorta.

stocky /'stɒkɪ/ *a.* (**-ier, -iest**) tarchiato.

stodg|e /stɒdʒ/ *n.* (*fam.*) cibo pesante *m.* ~**y** *a.* pesante.

stoic /'stəʊɪk/ *n.* stoico, a *m., f.* ~**al** *a.* stoico. ~**ally** *adv.* stoicamente. ~**ism** /-sɪzəm/ *n.* stoicismo *m.*

stoke /stəʊk/ *v.t.* alimentare. ~**r** /'stəʊkə(r)/ *n.* fuochista *m.*

stole[1] /stəʊl/ *n.* stola *f.*

stole[2], **stolen** /stəʊl, 'stəʊlən/ *see* **steal.**

stolid /'stɒlɪd/ *a.* stolido. ~**ly** *adv.* stolidamente.

stomach /'stʌmək/ *n.* stomaco *m.* —*v.t.* sopportare. ~**ache** *n.* mal di stomaco *m.*

stomp /stɒmp/ *v.i.* battere il piede.

ston|e /stəʊn/ *n.* pietra *f.*; (*med.*) calcolo *m.*; (*in fruit*) nocciolo *m.*; (*weight, pl.* **stone**) pietra *f.* (= 6.348 *kg.*) —*a.* di pietra. —*v.t.* lapidare; (*fruit*) snocciolare. ~**e-deaf** *a.* sordo come una campana. ~**y** *a.* pietroso.

stonemason /'stəʊnmeɪsn/ *n.* scalpellino *m.*

stonework /'stəʊnwɜːk/ *n.* lavoro in muratura *m.*

stood /stʊd/ *see* **stand.**

stooge /stuːdʒ/ *n.* (*theatr.*) spalla *f.*; (*underling*) tirapiedi *m./f. invar.*

stool /stuːl/ *n.* sgabello *m.*

stoop /stuːp/ *v.t./i.* piegare, piegarsi; (*fig.*) abbassarsi. —*n.* curvatura *f.*

stop /stɒp/ *v.t./i.* (*p.t.* **stopped**) fermare, fermarsi; (*cease*) smettere; (*a leak etc.*) otturare; (*prevent*) impedire. —*n.* (*bus etc.*) fermata *f.*; (*gram.*) punto *m.*; (*mech.*) fermo *m.*; (*photo*) apertura *f.* ~ **dead** *v.i.* fermarsi di colpo. ~**(-over)** *n.* sosta *f.* ~**press** *n.* ultimissime *f.pl.* ~**watch** *n.* cronometro (a scatto) *m.*

stopcock /'stɒpkɒk/ *n.* rubinetto di arresto *m.*

stopgap /'stɒpgæp/ n. rimedio temporaneo m.

stoppage /'stɒpɪdʒ/ n. ostruzione f.; (interruption) interruzione f.

stopper /'stɒpə(r)/ n. turacciolo m.

storage /'stɔ:rɪdʒ/ n. deposito m.; (computer) memoria f. **in cold ~** a freddo.

store /stɔ:(r)/ n. provvista f.; (shop) grande magazzino m.; (depot) deposito m.; (in computer) memoria f. —v.t. (in warehouse) immagazzinare. **in ~** da parte. **set ~ by** tenere in gran conto. **~ up** v.t. conservare. **~room** n. magazzino m.

storey /'stɔ:rɪ/ n. (pl. **-eys**) piano m.

stork /stɔ:k/ n. cicogna f.

storm /stɔ:m/ n. temporale m.; (mil.) assalto m. —v.i. infuriare. —v.t. (mil.) prendere d'assalto. **~y** a. tempestoso.

story /'stɔ:rɪ/ n. racconto m.; (in newspaper) articolo m.; (fam.) frottola f. **~-teller** n. narra|tore, -trice m., f.

stout /staʊt/ a. (-er, -est) robusto; (fat) grosso; (brave) coraggioso. —n. birra scura f. **~ly** adv. fortemente.

stove /stəʊv/ n. stufa f.

stow /stəʊ/ v.t. metter via. —v.i. **~ away** imbarcarsi clandestinamente.

stowaway /'stəʊəweɪ/ n. passeggero, a clandestino, a m., f.

straddle /'strædl/ v.t./i. stare a cavalcioni.

straggl|e /'strægl/ v.i. crescere disordinatamente. **~y** a. sparpagliato.

straight /streɪt/ a. (-er, -est) diritto; (tidy) in ordine; (frank) franco; (drink, hair) liscio. —adv. diritto; (direct) direttamente; (without delay) subito. —n. posizione diritta f. **go ~** vivere onestamente. **~ away** immediatamente. **~ on** sempre diritto. **~ out** senza esitare. **~ness** n. rettitudine f.

straighten /'streɪtn/ v.t./i. raddrizzare, raddrizzarsi.

straightforward /streɪt'fɔ:wəd/ a. franco; (easy) semplice. **~ly** adv. francamente.

strain¹ /streɪn/ n. (lineage) stirpe f.; (streak) tendenza f.

strain² /streɪn/ v.t./i. tirare; (tire) stancare; (injure) sforzare; (sieve) scolare. —n. tensione f.; sforzo m. **~s** n.pl. (mus.) versi m.pl. **~ed** a. sforzato. **~er** /-ə(r)/ n. colino m.

strait /streɪt/ n. stretto m. **~s** n.pl. difficoltà f. **~-jacket** n. camicia di forza f. **~-laced** a. puritano.

strand¹ /strænd/ n. filo m.

strand² /strænd/ n. sponda f. —v.i. arenarsi. **be ~ed** essere in difficoltà.

strange /streɪndʒ/ a. (-er, -est) strano; (not known) sconosciuto; (unaccustomed) nuovo. **~ly** adv. stranamente. **~ness** n. stranezza f.

stranger /'streɪndʒə(r)/ n. estraneo, a m., f.

strangle /'stræŋgl/ v.t. strangolare; (fig.) reprimere. **~r** /-ə(r)/ n. strangola|tore, -trice m., f.

stranglehold /'stræŋglhəʊld/ n. stretta mortale f.

strangulation /stræŋgjʊ'leɪʃn/ n. strangolamento m.

strap /stræp/ n. (leather) cinghia f.; (on bus etc.) maniglia f.; (of watch) cinturino m.; (of garment) bretella f. —v.t. (p.t. **strapped**) legare; (flog) frustare.

strapping /'stræpɪŋ/ a. robusto.

strata /'strɑ:tə/ see **stratum**.

stratagem /'strætədʒəm/ n. stratagemma m.

strategic /strə'ti:dʒɪk/ a. strategico. **~ally** adv. strategicamente.

strateg|y /'strætədʒɪ/ n. strategia f. **~ist** n. stratega m.

stratum /'strɑ:təm/ n. (pl. **strata**) strato m.

straw /strɔ:/ n. paglia f.; (single piece) fuscello m.; (for drinking) cannuccia f. **the last ~** il colmo.

strawberry /'strɔ:brɪ/ n. fragola f. **~-mark** n. voglia di fragola f.

stray /streɪ/ v.i. vagare; (deviate) deviare (**from**, da). —a. (animal) randagio; (isolated) raro. —n. derelitto m.

streak /stri:k/ n. striscia f.; (element) traccia f. —v.t. striare. —v.i. muoversi come un lampo. **~y** a. (-ier, -iest) striato; (bacon) lardellato.

stream /stri:m/ n. ruscello m.; (current) corrente f.; (of people) fiumana f.; (schol.) corso m. —v.i. scorrere; (sweat) grondare. —v.t. (schol.) classificare. **~ out** v.i. uscire a fiotti.

streamer /'stri:mə(r)/ n. pennone m.; (paper) stella filante f.

streamline /'stri:mlaɪn/ v.t. dare linea aerodinamica (a); (simplify) semplificare. **~d** a. aerodinamico.

street /stri:t/ n. strada f. **~ lamp** n. lampione m. **~-wise** a. scaltro.

streetcar /'stri:tkɑ:/ n. (Amer.) tram m.

strength /streŋθ/ n. forza f.; (of wall

etc.) solidità *f*. **on the** ∼ **of** tenendo conto di.

strengthen /'streŋθn/ *v.t.* rinforzare.

strenuous /'strenjʊəs/ *a*. strenuo. ∼**ly** *adv*. strenuamente.

stress /stres/ *n*. enfasi *f*.; (*gram*.) accento *m*.; (*mech*.) tensione *f*.; (*strain*) stress *m*. −*v.t.* insistere su.

stretch /stretʃ/ *v.t./i.* tirare; (*extend*) allungarsi, allungare; (*exaggerate*) esagerare. −*n*. stiramento *m*.; (*of period*) periodo di tempo *m*.; (*of road*) estensione *f*. **at a** ∼ tutto di seguito. ∼ **a point** fare uno strappo alla regola.

stretcher /'stretʃə(r)/ *n*. barella *f*.; (*device*) stenditore *m*.

strew /struː/ *v.t.* (*p.t.* **strewed**, *p.p.* **strewn** *or* **strewed**) spargere.

stricken /'strɪkən/ *a*. colpito.

strict /strɪkt/ *a*. (**-er, -est**) severo; (*precise*) preciso. ∼**ly** *adv*. severamente. ∼**ly speaking** in senso stretto.

stricture /'strɪktʃə(r)/ *n*. critica *f*.; (*constriction*) restringimento *m*.

stride /straɪd/ *v.i.* (*p.t.* **strode**, *p.p.* **stridden**) andare a gran passi. −*n*. (*lungo*) passo *m*. ∼ **over** scavalcare. **take sth. in one's** ∼ fare qcsa. con facilità.

strident /'straɪdnt/ *a*. stridente.

strife /straɪf/ *n*. conflitto *m*.

strike /straɪk/ *v.t.* (*p.t.* **struck**) colpire; (*match*) accendere; (*gold etc.*) trovare. −*v.i.* (*go on strike*) scioperare; (*attack*) attaccare; (*clock*) suonare. −*n*. sciopero *m*. **on** ∼ in sciopero. ∼ **off** *or* **out** tagliare. ∼ **up a friendship** fare amicizia. ∼**r** /'straɪkə(r)/ *n*. scioperante *m*./*f*.

striking /'straɪkɪŋ/ *a*. impressionante; (*attractive*) attraente.

string /strɪŋ/ *n*. spago *m*., corda *f*.; (*mus.*) corda *f*.; (*of lies*) serie *f*.; (*of pearls*) filo *m*. −*v.t.* (*p.t.* **strung**) (*thread*) infilare; (*beans*) togliere il filo. **pull** ∼**s** agire dietro le quinte. ∼ **along** (*fam.*) ingannare. ∼ **out** disporre in fila. ∼**ed** *a*. (*mus.*) a corda. ∼**y** *a*. filaccioso.

stringen|t /'strɪndʒənt/ *a*. rigido. ∼**cy** *n*. rigore *m*.

strip[1] /strɪp/ *v.t./i.* (*p.t.* **stripped**) svestire, svestirsi; (*tear away*) strappare; (*machine*) smontare; (*deprive*) privare. ∼**-tease** *n*. spogliarello *m*. ∼**per** /-ə(r)/ *n*. spogliarellista *f*.; (*solvent*) sverniciatore *m*.

strip[2] /strɪp/ *n*. striscia *f*. ∼ **cartoon**

n. racconto a fumetti *m*. ∼ **light** *n*. tubo al neon *m*.

stripe /straɪp/ *n*. striscia *f*.; (*mil.*) gallone *m*. ∼**d** *a*. a strisce.

strive /straɪv/ *v.i.* (*p.t.* **strove**, *p.p.* **striven**) ∼ **to** sforzarsi a.

strode /strəʊd/ *see* **stride**.

stroke[1] /strəʊk/ *n*. colpo *m*.; (*in swimming*) bracciata *f*.; (*oarsman*) primo vogatore *m*.; (*of pen etc.*) tratto *m*.; (*of clock*) tocco *m*.

stroke[2] /strəʊk/ *v.t.* accarezzare. −*n*. carezza *f*.

stroll /strəʊl/ *v.i.* passeggiare. −*n*. passeggiata *f*.

strong /strɒŋ/ *a*. (**-er, -est**) forte. ∼**-box** *n*. cassaforte *f*. ∼ **language** imprecazioni *f.pl.* ∼ **measures** misure energiche *f.pl.* ∼**-minded** *a*. risoluto. ∼**-room** *n*. camera blindata *f*. ∼**ly** *adv*. fortemente.

stronghold /'strɒŋhəʊld/ *n*. roccaforte *f*.

stroppy /'strɒpɪ/ *a*. (*sl.*) irascibile.

strove /strəʊv/ *see* **strive**.

struck /strʌk/ *see* **strike**. ∼ **on** (*sl.*) entusiasta di.

structur|e /'strʌktʃə(r)/ *n*. struttura *f*. ∼**al** *a*. strutturale.

struggle /'strʌgl/ *v.i.* lottare. −*n*. lotta *f*. ∼ **to one's feet** alzarsi con fatica. ∼ **through** procedere a fatica.

strum /strʌm/ *v.t./i.* (*p.t.* **strummed**) strimpellare.

strung /strʌŋ/ *see* **string**. −*a*. ∼ **up** teso.

strut /strʌt/ *n*. puntello *m*.; (*walk*) andatura solenne *f*. −*v.i.* (*p.t.* **strutted**) camminare impettito.

stub /stʌb/ *n*. mozzicone *m*.; (*counterfoil*) matrice *f*. −*v.t.* (*p.t.* **stubbed**) ∼ **out** schiacciare.

stubble /'stʌbl/ *n*. barba ispida *f*.

stubborn /'stʌbən/ *a*. ostinato. ∼**ly** *adv*. ostinatamente. ∼**ness** *n*. ostinazione *f*.

stubby /'stʌbɪ/ *a*. (**-ier, -iest**) tozzo.

stucco /'stʌkəʊ/ *n*. (*pl.* **-oes**) stucco *m*.

stuck /stʌk/ *see* **stick**[2]. −*a*. ∼ **on** (*sl.*) attratto da. ∼**-up** *a*. (*sl.*) borioso.

stud[1] /stʌd/ *n*. chiodo a capocchia larga *m*.; (*for collar*) bottoncino *m*. −*v.t.* (*p.t.* **studded**) ornare. ∼**ded with** tempestato di.

stud[2] /stʌd/ *n*. (*of horses*) scuderia *f*.

student /'stjuːdənt/ *n*. studente *m*., studentessa *f*.

studied /'stʌdɪd/ *a*. deliberato.

studio /'stju:dɪəʊ/ *n.* (*pl.* **-os**) studio *m.*; (*radio*) auditorio *m.* ~ **couch** *n.* divano letto *m.*

studious /'stju:djəs/ *a.* studioso; (*studied*) studiato. ~**ly** *adv.* studiosamente; (*carefully*) attentamente.

study /'stʌdɪ/ *n.* studio *m.*; (*investigation*) indagine *f.* —*v.t./i.* studiare.

stuff /stʌf/ *n.* materiale *m.*; (*unnamed*) roba *f.* —*v.t.* riempire; (*with padding*) imbottire; (*culin.*) farcire. ~**ing** *n.* (*padding*) imbottitura *f.*; (*culin.*) ripieno *m.*

stuffy /'stʌfɪ/ *a.* (**-ier, -iest**) che sa di chiuso; (*old-fashioned*) antiquato.

stumbl|e /'stʌmbl/ *v.i.* inciampare; (*falter*) impappinarsi. —*n.* passo falso *m.* ~**e across** *or* **on** imbattersi in. ~**ing-block** *n.* ostacolo *m.*

stump /stʌmp/ *n.* tronco *m.*; (*of limb*) moncherino *m.*; (*of cigar etc.*) mozziconе *m.*

stumped /stʌmpt/ *a.* (*fam.*) perplesso.

stumpy /'stʌmpɪ/ *a.* (**-ier, -iest**) tozzo.

stun /stʌn/ *v.t.* (*p.t.* **stunned**) stordire; (*astonish*) sbalordire. ~**ning** *a.* assordante; (*fabulous*) favoloso.

stung /stʌŋ/ *see* **sting.**

stunk /stʌŋk/ *see* **stink.**

stunt[1] /stʌnt/ *v.t.* arrestare lo sviluppo (di). ~**ed** *a.* stentato.

stunt[2] /stʌnt/ *n.* (*fam.*) trovata pubblicitaria *f.* ~ **man** *n.* cascatore *m.*

stupefy /'stju:pɪfaɪ/ *v.t.* istupidire.

stupendous /stju:'pendəs/ *a.* stupendo. ~**ly** *adv.* stupendamente.

stupid /'stju:pɪd/ *a.* stupido. ~**ly** *adv.* stupidamente. ~**ity** /-'pɪdətɪ/ *n.* stupidità *f.*

stupor /'stju:pə(r)/ *n.* torpore *m.*

sturd|y /'stɜ:dɪ/ *a.* (**-ier, -iest**) robusto. ~**iness** *n.* robustezza *f.*

sturgeon /'stɜ:dʒən/ *n.* (*pl.* **sturgeon**) storione *m.*

stutter /'stʌtə(r)/ *v.i.* balbettare. —*n.* balbuzie *f.*

sty[1] /staɪ/ *n.* (*pl.* **sties**) porcile *m.*

sty[2] /staɪ/ *n.* (*med.*) orzaiolo *m.*

style /staɪl/ *n.* stile *m.*; (*fashion*) moda *f.* —*v.t.* disegnare. **in** ~ con stile.

stylish /'staɪlɪʃ/ *a.* elegante. ~**ly** con eleganza.

stylist /'staɪlɪst/ *n.* stilista *m./f.* **hair** ~ *n.* parrucchiere, a *m., f.*

stylized /'staɪlaɪzd/ *a.* stilizzato.

stylus /'staɪləs/ *n.* (*pl.* **-uses**) puntina *f.*

suave /swɑːv/ *a.* (*pej.*) mellifluo.

sub- /sʌb/ *pref.* sotto.

subaquatic /sʌbə'kwætɪk/ *a.* subacqueo.

subconscious /sʌb'kɒnʃəs/ *a.* & *n.* subcosciente *m.* ~**ly** *adv.* subcoscientemente.

subcontinent /sʌb'kɒntɪnənt/ *n.* sottocontinente *m.*

subcontract /sʌbkən'trækt/ *v.t./i.* subappaltare. ~**or** /-ə(r)/ *n.* subappaltatore *m.*

subdivide /sʌbdɪ'vaɪd/ *v.t.* suddividere.

subdue /səb'dju:/ *v.t.* assoggettare; (*make quieter*) attenuare. ~**d** *a.* sottomesso.

subhuman /sʌb'hju:mən/ *a.* disumano.

subject[1] /'sʌbdʒɪkt/ *a.* soggetto. —*n.* suddito, a *m., f.*; (*theme*) soggetto *m.* ~ **to** soggetto a; (*depending*) salvo.

subject[2] /səb'dʒekt/ *v.t.* assoggettare; (*submit*) sottoporre. ~**ion** /-ʃn/ *n.* assoggettamento *m.*

subjective /səb'dʒektɪv/ *a.* soggettivo. ~**ly** *adv.* soggettivamente.

subjugate /'sʌbdʒʊgeɪt/ *v.t.* soggiogare.

subjunctive /səb'dʒʌŋktɪv/ *a.* & *n.* congiuntivo *m.*

sublet /sʌb'let/ *v.t.* (*p.t.* **sublet**, *pres. p.* **subletting**) subaffittare.

sublimat|e /'sʌblɪmeɪt/ *v.t.* sublimare. ~**ion** /-'meɪʃn/ *n.* sublimazione *f.*

sublime /sə'blaɪm/ *a.* sublime. ~**ly** *adv.* sublimamente.

submarine /sʌbmə'ri:n/ *n.* sommergibile *m.*

submerge /səb'mɜ:dʒ/ *v.t./i.* immergere, immergersi.

submi|t /səb'mɪt/ *v.t./i.* (*p.t.* **submitted**) sottomettere, sottomettersi. ~**ssion** /-ʃn/ *n.* sottomissione *f.* ~**ssive** /-sɪv/ *a.* sottomesso.

subordinate[1] /sə'bɔ:dɪnət/ *a.* & *n.* subordinato, a *m., f.*

subordinat|e[2] /sə'bɔ:dɪneɪt/ *v.t.* subordinare. ~**ion** /-'neɪʃn/ *n.* subordinazione *f.*

subpoena /sʌb'pi:nə/ *n.* (*pl.* **-as**) citazione *f.* —*v.t.* (*p.t.* **subpoenaed**) citare.

subscri|be /səb'skraɪb/ *v.i.* contribuire. ~**be to** (*fund*) sottoscrivere; (*agree*) aderire a; (*newspaper*) abbonarsi a. ~**ber** /-ə(r)/ abbonato, a *m., f.* ~**ption** /-rɪpʃn/ *n.* abbonamento *m.*; sottoscrizione *f.*

subsequent /'sʌbsɪkwənt/ *a.* susseguente. ~**ly** *adv.* in seguito.

subservient /səb'sɜːvjənt/ *a.* ossequioso. ~**ly** *adv.* ossequiosamente.

subside /səb'saɪd/ *v.i.* sprofondare; (*of storm*) quietarsi.

subsidiary /səb'sɪdɪərɪ/ *a.* sussidiario. —*n.* filiale *f.*

subsid|y /'sʌbsədɪ/ *n.* sovvenzione *f.* ~**ize** /-ɪdaɪz/ *v.t.* sovvenzionare.

subsist /səb'sɪst/ *v.i.* sussistere. ~**ence** *n.* sussistenza *f.*

subsoil /'sʌbsɔɪl/ *n.* sottosuolo *m.*

subsonic /sʌb'sɒnɪk/ *a.* subsonico.

substance /'sʌbstəns/ *n.* sostanza *f.*

substandard /sʌb'stændəd/ *a.* di qualità inferiore.

substantial /səb'stænʃl/ *a.* solido; (*meal*) sostanzioso; (*considerable*) notevole. ~**ly** *adv.* notevolmente.

substantiate /səb'stænʃɪeɪt/ *v.t.* convalidare.

substitut|e /'sʌbstɪtjuːt/ *n.* sostituto *m.* —*v.t./i.* sostituire. ~**ion** /-'tjuːʃn/ *n.* sostituzione *f.*

subterfuge /'sʌbtəfjuːdʒ/ *n.* sotterfugio *m.*

subterranean /sʌbtə'reɪnjən/ *a.* sotterraneo.

subtitle /'sʌbtaɪtl/ *n.* sottotitolo *m.*

subtle /'sʌtl/ *a.* (-**er**, -**est**) indefinibile; (*person*) acuto. ~**ty** *n.* sottigliezza *f.*

subtract /səb'trækt/ *v.t.* sottrarre. ~**ion** /-ʃn/ *n.* sottrazione *f.*

suburb /'sʌbɜːb/ *n.* sobborgo *m.* ~**an** /sə'bɜːbən/ *a.* suburbano; (*person*) ristretto. ~**ia** /sə'bɜːbɪə/ *n.* i sobborghi *m.pl.* **the** ~**s** la periferia *f.*

subvention /səb'venʃn/ *n.* sovvenzione *f.*

subversive /səb'vɜːsɪv/ *a.* sovversivo.

subver|t /səb'vɜːt/ *v.t.* sovvertire. ~**sion** /səb'vɜːʃn/ *n.* sovversione *f.*

subway /'sʌbweɪ/ *n.* sottopassaggio *m.*; (*Amer.*) ferrovia sotterranea *f.*

succeed /sək'siːd/ *v.i.* aver successo. —*v.t.* succedere a. ~ **in doing** riuscire a fare. ~**ing** *a.* successivo.

success /sək'ses/ *n.* successo *m.* ~**ful** *a.* riuscito.

succession /sək'seʃn/ *n.* successione *f.* **in** ~ di seguito.

successive /sək'sesɪv/ *a.* successivo. ~**ly** *adv.* successivamente.

successor /sək'sesə(r)/ *n.* successore *m.*

succinct /sək'sɪŋkt/ *a.* succinto.

succour /'sʌkə(r)/ *v.t.* soccorrere. —*n.* soccorso *m.*

succulent /'sʌkjʊlənt/ *a.* succulento.

succumb /sə'kʌm/ *v.i.* soccombere.

such /sʌtʃ/ *a.* tale. —*pron.* tale, questo; (*so much*) tanto. **and** ~ e simili. ~ **as it is** così com'è. ~**like** *a.* (*fam.*) di tal genere.

suck /sʌk/ *v.t.* succhiare. ~ **up** assorbire. ~ **up to** (*sl.*) fare il leccapiedi di.

sucker /'sʌkə(r)/ *n.* (*plant*) pollone *m.*; (*fig.*) parassita *m./f.*; (*person, fam.*) credulone, a *m., f.*

suckle /'sʌkl/ *v.t.* allattare.

suction /'sʌkʃn/ *n.* succhiamento *m.*

sudden /'sʌdn/ *a.* improvviso. **all of a** ~ all'improvviso. ~**ly** *adv.* improvvisamente. ~**ness** *n.* subitaneità *f.*

suds /sʌds/ *n.pl.* saponata *f.s.*

sue /sjuː/ *v.t.* (*pres. p.* **suing**) far causa.

suede /sweɪd/ *n.* pelle scamosciata *f.*

suet /'suːɪt/ *n.* strutto *m.*

suffer /'sʌfə(r)/ *v.t./i.* soffrire; (*loss etc.*) subire. ~**ing** *n.* sofferenza *f.*

sufferance /'sʌfərəns/ *n.* **on** ~ appena tollerato.

suffice /sə'faɪs/ *v.i.* bastare.

sufficien|t /sə'fɪʃnt/ *a.* sufficiente; (*enough*) abbastanza. ~**cy** *n.* sufficienza *f.* ~**tly** *adv.* sufficientemente.

suffix /'sʌfɪks/ *n.* (*pl.* -**ixes**) suffisso *m.*

suffocat|e /'sʌfəkeɪt/ *v.t./i.* soffocare. ~**ion** /-'keɪʃn/ *n.* soffocazione *f.*

sugar /'ʃʊgə(r)/ *n.* zucchero *m.* —*v.t.* zuccherare. ~-**bowl** *n.* zuccheriera *f.* ~**y** *a.* zuccheroso.

suggest /sə'dʒest/ *v.t.* suggerire. ~**ion** /-tʃən/ *n.* suggerimento *m.*; (*trace*) sfumatura *f.*

suggestible /sə'dʒestɪbl/ *a.* suggestionabile.

suggestive /sə'dʒestɪv/ *a.* suggestivo. ~**ly** *adv.* suggestivamente.

suicid|e /'sjuːɪsaɪd/ *n.* suicidio *m.*; (*person*) suicida *m.f.* **commit** ~**e** suicidarsi. ~**al** /-'saɪdl/ *a.* suicida.

suit /suːt/ *n.* vestito *m.*; (*woman's*) due pezzi *m.*; (*cards*) seme *m.*; (*jurid.*) causa *f.* —*v.t.* andar bene a; (*adapt*) adattare. **be** ~**ed for** essere adatto a. ~**able** *a.* adatto. ~**ably** *adv.* convenientemente.

suitcase /'suːtkeɪs/ *n.* valigia *f.*

suite /swiːt/ *n.* (*of furniture*) mobilia *f.*; (*of rooms*) appartamento *m.*; (*retinue*) corteo *m.*

suitor /'suːtə(r)/ *n.* pretendente *m.*

sulk /sʌlk/ v.i. fare il broncio. ~s n.pl. broncio m.s. ~y a. imbronciato.

sullen /'sʌlən/ a. accigliato; (dark) tetro. ~ly adv. con astio.

sully /'sʌlɪ/ v.t. (fig.) macchiare.

sulphur /'sʌlfə(r)/ n. zolfo m. ~ic /-'fjʊərɪk/ a. ~ic acid acido solforico.

sultan /'sʌltən/ n. sultano m.

sultana /səl'tɑːnə/ n. uva sultanina f.

sultry /'sʌltrɪ/ a. (-ier, -iest) (weather) afoso; (fig.) sensuale.

sum /sʌm/ n. somma f. —v.t. (p.t. summed) ~ up (situation) riassumere.

summar|y /'sʌmərɪ/ a. & n. sommario m. ~ily adv. sommariamente. ~ize v.t. riassumere.

summer /'sʌmə(r)/ n. estate f. ~house n. padiglione m. ~-time n. estate f. ~ time n. ora legale (estiva) f. ~y a. estivo.

summit /'sʌmɪt/ n. cima f. ~ conference n. conferenza al vertice f.

summon /'sʌmən/ v.t. convocare; (jurid.) citare. ~ up raccogliere.

summons /'sʌmənz/ n. chiamata f.; (jurid.) citazione f. —v.t. citare in giudizio.

sump /sʌmp/ n. (mech.) coppa dell'olio f.

sumptuous /'sʌmptʃʊəs/ a. sontuoso. ~ly adv. sontuosamente.

sun /sʌn/ n. sole m. —v.t. (p.t. sunned) ~ o.s. prendere il sole. ~-tan n. abbronzatura f. ~-tanned a. abbronzato. ~ny a. (-ier, -iest) assolato.

sunbathe /'sʌnbeɪð/ v.i. far bagni di sole.

sunbeam /'sʌnbiːm/ n. raggio di sole m.

sunburn /'sʌnbɜːn/ n. scottatura (solare) f. ~t a. scottato (dal sole).

sundae /'sʌndeɪ/ n. gelato con frutta m.

Sunday /'sʌndɪ/ n. domenica f. ~ school n. scuola di catechismo f.

sundial /'sʌndaɪl/ n. meridiana f.

sundown /'sʌndaʊn/ n. tramonto m.

sundry /'sʌndrɪ/ a. parecchi. all and ~ tutti quanti. sundries n.pl. cianfrusaglie f.pl.

sunflower /'sʌnflaʊə(r)/ n. girasole m.

sung /sʌŋ/ see sing.

sunk, sunken /sʌŋk, 'sʌŋkən/ see sink. —adjs. incavato.

sunlight /'sʌnlaɪt/ n. luce del sole f.

sunrise /'sʌnraɪz/ n. alba f.

sunset /'sʌnset/ n. tramonto m.

sunshade /'sʌnʃeɪd/ n. parasole m.; (awning) tendone m.

sunshine /'sʌnʃaɪn/ n. luce del sole f. ~ roof n. (auto) tetto scorrevole m.

sunspot /'sʌnspɒt/ n. macchia solare f.

sunstroke /'sʌnstrəʊk/ n. insolazione f.

sup /sʌp/ v.t./i. (p.t. supped) sorseggiare.

super /'suːpə(r)/ a. (fam.) fantastico.

superannuation /suːpərænjʊ'eɪʃn/ n. pensione per vecchiaia f.

superb /suː'pɜːb/ a. superbo. ~ly adv. splendidamente.

supercilious /suːpə'sɪlɪəs/ a. sdegnoso.

superficial /suːpə'fɪʃl/ a. superficiale. ~ly adv. superficialmente.

superfluous /suː'pɜːflʊəs/ a. superfluo.

superhuman /suːpə'hjuːmən/ a. sovrumano.

superimpose /suːpərɪm'pəʊz/ v.t. sovrapporre.

superintend /suːpərɪn'tend/ v.t. sorvegliare. ~ence n. direzione f. ~ent n. sorvegliante m.|f.; (of police) commissario m.

superior /suː'pɪərɪə(r)/ a. & n. superiore, a m., f. ~ity /-'ɒrətɪ/ n. superiorità f.

superlative /suː'pɜːlətɪv/ a. & n. superlativo m.

superman /'suːpəmæn/ n. (pl. -men) superuomo m.

supermarket /'suːpəmɑːkɪt/ n. supermercato m.

supernatural /suːpə'nætʃrəl/ a. soprannaturale.

superpower /'suːpəpaʊə(r)/ n. superpotenza f.

supersede /suːpə'siːd/ v.t. rimpiazzare. be ~d essere superato.

supersonic /suːpə'sɒnɪk/ a. supersonico.

superstitio|n /suːpə'stɪʃn/ n. superstizione f. ~us a. superstizioso.

superstructure /'suːpəstrʌktʃə(r)/ n. sovrastruttura f.

supervene /suːpə'viːn/ v.i. sopravvenire.

supervis|e /'suːpəvaɪz/ v.t. sorvegliare. ~ion /-'vɪʒn/ n. sorveglianza. f. ~or /-ə(r)/ n. sorvegliante m.|f.

supper /'sʌpə(r)/ n. cena f.

supplant /sə'plɑːnt/ v.t. soppiantare.

supple /sʌpl/ *a.* flessibile. **~ness** *n.* flessibilità *f.*

supplement /'sʌplɪmənt/ *n.* supplemento *m.* —*v.t.* integrare. **~ary** /-'mentri/ *a.* supplementare.

supplier /sə'plaɪə(r)/ *n.* forni|tore, -trice *m., f.*

supply /sə'plaɪ/ *v.t.* fornire; (*a need*) soddisfare. **~ with** approvvigionare di. —*n.* provvista *f.*; (*techn.*) alimentazione *f.*

support /sə'pɔːt/ *v.t.* sostenere; (*strengthen*) rafforzare; (*keep*) mantenere; (*tolerate*) sopportare; (*sport*) fare il tifo per. —*n.* sostegno *m.*; (*mech.*) supporto *m.*; (*keep*) mantenimento *m.* **~er** /-ə(r)/ *n.* sosteni|tore, -trice *m., f.*; (*sport*) tifoso, a *m., f.* **~ive** *a.* incoraggiante.

suppos|e /sə'pəʊz/ *v.t./i.* supporre; (*think*) pensare. **be ~ed to** essere tenuto a. **not be ~ed to** (*fam.*) non avere il permesso di. **~edly** *adv.* presumibilmente. **~ition** /sʌpə'zɪʃn/ *n.* supposizione *f.*

suppository /sə'pɒzɪtrɪ/ *n.* supposta *f.*

suppress /sə'pres/ *v.t.* sopprimere. **~ion** *n.* soppressione *f.* **~or** /-ə(r)/ *n.* soppressore *m.*

suprem|e /suː'priːm/ *a.* supremo. **~acy** /sʊ'preməsɪ/ *n.* supremazia *f.*

surcharge /'sɜːtʃɑːdʒ/ *n.* supplemento *m.*; (*tax*) soprattassa *f.*

sure /ʃʊə(r)/ *a.* (-er, -est) sicuro, certo. —*adv.* (*Amer., fam.*) certamente. **make ~** assicurarsi. **~ enough** infatti. **~-footed** *a.* dal piede fermo. **~ly** *adv.* certamente.

surety /'ʃʊərətɪ/ *n.* garanzia *f.*

surf /sɜːf/ *n.* frangente *m.* **~board** *n.* tavola da surfing *f.* **~ing, ~-riding** *ns.* surfing *m.*

surface /'sɜːfɪs/ *n.* superficie *f.*; (*fig.*) apparenza *f.* —*a.* superficiale. —*v.t./i.* ricoprire la superficie (**with**, di); (*emerge*) emergere. **~ mail** *n.* posta normale *f.*

surfeit /'sɜːfɪt/ *n.* eccesso *m.*

surge /sɜːdʒ/ *v.i.* riversarsi; (*increase*) montare. —*n.* impeto *m.*

surgeon /'sɜːdʒən/ *n.* chirurgo *m.*

surg|ery /'sɜːdʒərɪ/ *n.* chirurgia *f.*; (*consulting room*) gabinetto medico *m.*; (*consulting hours*) ore di visita *f.pl.* **~ical** /-dʒɪkl/ *a.* chirurgico.

surl|y /'sɜːlɪ/ *a.* (-ier, -iest) sgarbato. **~iness** *n.* malagrazia *f.*

surmise /sə'maɪz/ *v.t./i.* supporre.

surmount /sə'maʊnt/ *v.t.* sormontare.

surname /'sɜːneɪm/ *n.* cognome *m.*

surpass /sə'pɑːs/ *v.t.* sorpassare.

surplus /'sɜːpləs/ *n.* soprappiù *m.* —*a.* d'avanzo.

surpris|e /sə'praɪz/ *n.* sorpresa *f.* —*v.t.* sorprendere. **~ing** *a.* sorprendente.

surrealis|m /sə'rɪəlɪzəm/ *n.* surrealismo *m.* **~t** *n.* surrealista *m.|f.*

surrender /sə'rendə(r)/ *v.t.* cedere. —*v.i.* arrendersi. —*n.* resa *f.*; (*comm.*) riscatto *m.*

surreptitious /sʌrəp'tɪʃəs/ *a.* clandestino.

surrogate /'sʌrəgeɪt/ *n.* sostituto *m.*

surround /sə'raʊnd/ *v.t.* circondare. —*n.* bordo *m.* **~ing** *a.* circostante. **~ings** *n.pl.* dintorni *m.pl.*

surveillance /sɜː'veɪləns/ *n.* sorveglianza *f.*

survey[1] /sə'veɪ/ *v.t.* esaminare; (*property*) fare una perizia. **~or** *n.* perito *m.*

survey[2] /'sɜːveɪ/ *n.* quadro generale *m.*; (*report*) perizia *f.*

survival /sə'vaɪvl/ *n.* sopravvivenza *f.*; (*relic*) reliquia *f.*

surviv|e /sə'vaɪv/ *v.t./i.* sopravvivere. **~or** /-ə(r)/ *n.* superstite *m.|f.*; (*hardy*) persona piena di risorse *f.*

susceptib|le /sə'septəbl/ *a.* influenzabile. **~le to** sensibile a. **~ility** /-'bɪlətɪ/ *n.* sensibilità *f.*

suspect[1] /sə'spekt/ *v.t.* sospettare; (*assume*) supporre.

suspect[2] /'sʌspekt/ *n.* persona sospetta *f.* —*a.* sospetto.

suspen|d /sə'spend/ *v.t.* appendere; (*stop*) sospendere. **~sion** *n.* sospensione *f.* **~sion bridge** *n.* ponte sospeso *m.*

suspender /səs'pendə(r)/ *n.* giarrettiera *f.* **~ belt** *n.* reggicalze *m.*

suspense /sə'spens/ *n.* sospensione d'animo *f.*; (*in book etc.*) suspense *m.*

suspicio|n /sə'spɪʃn/ *n.* sospetto *m.*; (*trace*) pizzico *m.* **~us** *a.* sospettoso; (*causing suspicion*) sospetto.

sustain /sə'steɪn/ *v.t.* sostenere; (*suffer*) subire; (*jurid.*) appoggiare.

sustenance /'sʌstɪnəns/ *n.* sostentamento *m.*; (*nourishment*) nutrimento *m.*

svelte /svelt/ *a.* slanciato.

swab /swɒb/ *n.* (*med.*) tampone *m.*

swagger /'swægə(r)/ *v.i.* pavoneggiarsi.

swallow¹ /'swɒləʊ/ v.t./i. inghiottire. ∼ **up** esaurire.

swallow² /'swɒləʊ/ n. rondine f. ∼-**dive** n. tuffo a rondine m.

swam /swæm/ see **swim**.

swamp /swɒmp/ n. palude f. —v.t. inondare; (fig.) travolgere. ∼**y** a. paludoso.

swan /swɒn/ n. cigno m.

swank /swæŋk/ n. (fam.) ostentazione f. —v.i. (fam.) darsi arie.

swap /swɒp/ v.t./i. (p.t. **swapped**) (fam.) scambiare. —n. (fam.) scambio m.

swarm /swɔːm/ n. sciame m. —v.i. sciamare; (of place) brulicare.

swarthy /'swɔːðɪ/ a. (-ier, -iest) bruno.

swastika /'swɒstɪkə/ n. svastica f.

swat /swɒt/ v.t. (p.t. **swatted**) colpire.

sway /sweɪ/ v.i. oscillare; (person) barcollare. —v.t. (influence) influenzare. —n. oscillazione f.

swear /sweə(r)/ v.t./i. (p.t. **swore**, p.p. **sworn**) giurare; (curse) bestemmiare. ∼ **by** (fam.) credere ciecamente in. ∼-**word** n. parolaccia f.

sweat /swet/ n. sudore m.; (fam.) fatica f. —v.i. sudare; (fam.) faticare.

sweater /'swetə(r)/ n. maglione m.

swede /swiːd/ n. rapa svedese f.

Swed|e /swiːd/ n. svedese m./f. ∼**en** n. Svezia f. ∼**ish** a. & n. svedese m.

sweep /swiːp/ v.t./i. (p.t. **swept**) scopare; (go swiftly) andare rapidamente; (of road) stendersi; (fig.) scorrere. —n. scopata f.; (curve) curva f.; (slope) declivio m.; (movement) gesto m. ∼ **away** v.t. portar via. ∼ **the board** vincere tutto. ∼**ing** a. (gesture) largo; (changes etc.) completo. ∼**ing statement** affermazione generica f.

sweepstake /'swiːpsteɪk/ n. lotteria f.

sweet /swiːt/ a. (-er, -est) dolce; (fragrant) fragrante; (pleasant) piacevole. —n. (toffee etc.) caramella f.; (dish) dolce m. **have a** ∼ **tooth** avere un debole per i dolci. ∼ **pea** n. pisello odoroso m. ∼**ly** adv. dolcemente. ∼**ness** n. dolcezza f.

sweetbread /'swiːtbred/ n. animella f.

sweeten /'swiːtn/ v.t. addolcire. ∼**er** /-ə(r)/ n. dolcificante m.

sweetheart /'swiːthɑːt/ n. innamorato, a m., f.

swell /swel/ v.t./i. (p.t. **swelled**, p.p. **swollen** or **swelled**) gonfiare, gonfiarsi; (of prices etc.) (far) salire. —a.

(fam.) eccellente. —n. (of sea) risacca f. ∼**ing** n. gonfiore m.

swelter /'sweltə(r)/ v.i. essere oppresso dal caldo.

swept /swept/ see **sweep**.

swerve /swɜːv/ v.i. deviare.

swift /swɪft/ a. (-er, -est) rapido. —n. (bird) rondone m. ∼**ly** adv. rapidamente. ∼**ness** n. rapidità f.

swig /swɪg/ v.t. (p.t. **swigged**) (fam.) tracannare. —n. (fam.) sorso m.

swill /swɪl/ v.t./i. risciacquare; (drink) bere avidamente. —n. risciacquatura f.; (food for pigs) brodaglia f.

swim /swɪm/ v.i. (p.t. **swam**, p.p. **swum**) nuotare; (room, head) girare. —n. nuotata f. ∼**mer** n. nuota|tore, -trice m., f. ∼**ming-bath**, ∼**ming-pool** ns. piscina f. ∼-**suit** n. costume da bagno m.

swimmingly /'swɪmɪŋlɪ/ adv. a gonfie vele.

swindle /'swɪndl/ v.t. truffare. —n. truffa f. ∼**r** /-ə(r)/ n. truffa|tore, -trice m., f.

swine /swaɪn/ n.pl. maiali m.pl. —n. (pl. **swine**) (person, fam.) porco m.

swing /swɪŋ/ v.t./i. (p.t. **swung**) oscillare; (hang) penzolare; (turn) girare; (sway) dondolare. —n. oscillazione f.; (see-saw) altalena f.; (mus.) swing m. **in full** ∼ in piena attività. ∼ **bridge** n. ponte girevole m.

swingeing /'swɪndʒɪŋ/ a. forte.

swipe /swaɪp/ v.t. colpire; (snatch, sl.) rubare. —n. (fam.) botta f.

swirl /swɜːl/ v.t./i. (far) girare. —n. vortice m.

swish /swɪʃ/ v.t. frusciare. —a. (fam.) chic.

Swiss /swɪs/ a. & n. svizzero, a m., f. ∼ **roll** n. rotolo di pan di Spagna m.

switch /swɪtʃ/ n. (electr.) interruttore m.; (rail.) scambio m.; (change) cambiamento m. —v.t. (deviate) deviare; (change) cambiare. ∼ **off** (electr.) spegnere. ∼ **on** (electr.) accendere; (engine) mettere in moto.

switchback /'swɪtʃbæk/ n. montagne russe f.pl.

switchboard /'swɪtʃbɔːd/ n. centralino m.

Switzerland /'swɪtsələnd/ n. Svizzera f.

swivel /'swɪvl/ n. perno m. —v.i. (p.t. **swivelled**) girare.

swollen /'swəʊln/ see **swell**. —a. gonfio. ∼-**headed** a. presuntuoso.

swoon /swu:n/ *v.i.* svenire.

swoop /swu:p/ *v.i.* piombare. —*n.* (*by police*) incursione *f.*

sword /sɔ:d/ *n.* spada *f.*

swordfish /'sɔ:dfiʃ/ *n.* pescespada *m.*

swore /swɔ:(r)/ *see* **swear.**

sworn /swɔ:n/ *see* **swear.** —*a.* (*enemy*) acerrimo; (*friend*) fidato.

swot /swɒt/ *v.t./i.* (*p.t.* **swotted**) (*schol.*, *sl.*) sgobbare. —*n.* (*schol.*, *sl.*) studio intenso; (*person*, *sl.*) sgobbone, a *m.*, *f.*

swum /swʌm/ *see* **swim.**

swung /swʌŋ/ *see* **swing.**

sycamore /'sɪkəmɔ:(r)/ *n.* sicomoro *m.*

syllable /'sɪləbl/ *n.* sillaba *f.*

syllabus /'sɪləbəs/ *n.* (*pl.* -**buses**) programma (dei corsi) *m.*

sylph /sɪlf/ *n.* silfide *f.*

symbol /'sɪmbl/ *n.* simbolo *m.* ∼**ic(al)** /-'bɒlɪk(l)/ *a.* simbolico. ∼**ism** *n.* simbolismo *m.* ∼**ize** *v.t.* simboleggiare.

symmetr|y /'sɪmətrɪ/ *n.* simmetria *f.* ∼**ical** /-'metrɪkl/ *a.* simmetrico.

sympathetic /sɪmpə'θetɪk/ *a.* comprensivo; (*showing pity*) compassionevole.

sympath|y /'sɪmpəθɪ/ *n.* comprensione *f.*; (*pity*) compassione *f.*; (*condolences*) condoglianze *f.pl.* **be in** ∼**y with** essere d'accordo con. ∼**ize** /-aɪz/ *v.i.* provare comprensione (**with,** per). ∼**izer** *n.* (*pol.*) simpatizzante *m.*/*f.*

symphon|y /'sɪmfənɪ/ *n.* sinfonia *f.* ∼**ic** /-'fɒnɪk/ *a.* sinfonico.

symposium /sɪm'pəʊzɪəm/ *n.* (*pl.* -**ia**) simposio *m.*

symptom /'sɪmptəm/ *n.* sintomo *m.* ∼**atic** /-'mætɪk/ *a.* sintomatico.

synagogue /'sɪnəgɒg/ *n.* sinagoga *f.*

synchroniz|e /'sɪŋkrənaɪz/ *v.t.* sincronizzare. ∼**ation** /-'zeɪʃn/ *n.* sincronizzazione *f.*

syncopat|e /'sɪŋkəpeɪt/ *v.t.* sincopare. ∼**ion** /-'peɪʃn/ *n.* sincopatura *f.*

syndicate /'sɪndɪkət/ *n.* sindacato *m.*

syndrome /'sɪndrəʊm/ *n.* sindrome *f.*

synod /'sɪnəd/ *n.* sinodo *m.*

synonym /'sɪnənɪm/ *n.* sinonimo *m.* ∼**ous** /-'nɒnɪməs/ *a.* sinonimo.

synopsis /sɪ'nɒpsɪs/ *n.* (*pl.* -**opses** /-si:z/) sinossi *f.* invar.

synta|x /'sɪntæks/ *n.* sintassi *f.* invar.

synthesi|s /'sɪnθəsɪs/ *n.* (*pl.* -**theses** /-si:z/) sintesi *f.* invar. ∼**ze** *v.t.* sintetizzare.

synthetic /sɪn'θetɪk/ *a.* sintetico.

syphilis /'sɪfɪlɪs/ *n.* sifilide *f.*

Syria /'sɪrɪə/ *n.* Siria *f.* ∼**n** *a.* & *n.* siriano, a *m.*, *f.*

syringe /'sɪrɪndʒ/ *n.* siringa *f.* —*v.t.* siringare.

syrup /'sɪrəp/ *n.* sciroppo *m.*; (*treacle*) melassa *f.* ∼**y** *a.* sciropposo.

system /'sɪstəm/ *n.* sistema *m.*; (*mech.*) impianto *m.* ∼**s analyst** *n.* analista programmatore *m.* ∼**atic** /-ə'mætɪk/ *a.* sistematico. ∼**atically** /-ə'mætɪklɪ/ *adv.* sistematicamente.

T

tab /tæb/ n. etichetta f. **keep ~s on** (fam.) sorvegliare.

tabby /'tæbɪ/ n. gatto tigrato m.

tabernacle /'tæbənækl/ n. tabernacolo m.

table /'teɪbl/ n. tavolo m., tavola f.; (list) elenco m. —v.t. proporre. **~-cloth** n. tovaglia f. **~ tennis** n. tennis da tavola m.

tablespoon /'teɪblspuːn/ n. cucchiaio m. **~ful** n. (pl. -fuls) cucchiaiata f.

tablet /'tæblɪt/ n. targa f.; (pill) pastiglia f.; (of soap etc.) tavoletta f.

tabloid /'tæblɔɪd/ n. giornale di formato ridotto m.

taboo /tə'buː/ a. & n. tabù m.

tabulator /'tæbjʊleɪtə(r)/ n. tabulatore m.

tacit /'tæsɪt/ a. tacito.

taciturn /'tæsɪtɜːn/ a. taciturno.

tack /tæk/ n. chiodino m.; (stitch) imbastitura f.; (naut.) virata f.; (fig.) linea di condotta f. —v.t. inchiodare; imbastire. —v.i. virare. **~ on** aggiungere a.

tackle /'tækl/ n. (equipment) attrezzatura f.; (football) tackle m. —v.t. affrontare.

tacky /'tækɪ/ a. appiccicoso.

tact /tækt/ n. tatto m. **~ful** a. pieno di tatto. **~fully** adv. con tatto. **~less** a. privo di tatto. **~lessly** adv. senza tatto.

tactic|s /'tæktɪks/ n.pl. tattica f.s. **~al** a. tattico.

tactile /'tæktaɪl/ a. tattile.

tadpole /'tædpəʊl/ n. girino m.

tag /tæg/ n. (on shoe-lace) punta f.; (label) etichetta f. —v.t. (p.t. tagged) attaccare. —v.i. **~ along** (fam.) seguire.

tail /teɪl/ n. coda f. **~s** n.pl. (tailcoat) frac m.; (of coin) croce f. —v.t. (sl.) seguire. —v.i. **~ off** diminuire. **~-end** n. parte finale f.; (of train etc.) coda f.

tailor /'teɪlə(r)/ n. sarto m. —v.t. confezionare. **~-made** n. fatto su misura. **~ess** n. sarta f.

tailplane /'teɪlpleɪn/ n. stabilizzatore m.

taint /teɪnt/ n. tara f. —v.t. contaminare.

take /teɪk/ v.t./i. (p.t. took, p.p. taken) prendere; (passengers etc.) contenere; (capture) catturare; (endure) sopportare; (require) occorrere; (walk, bath, etc.) fare; (carry) portare; (accompany) accompagnare. —n. presa f.; (photo, cinema, TV) ripresa f. **be ~n ill** ammalarsi. **~ advantage of** approfittare di. **~ after** assomigliare a. **~ back** (statement etc.) ritirare. **~ in** (garment) riprendere; (understand) capire; (deceive) ingannare. **~ off** (clothes) togliere; (mimic) imitare; (aeron.) decollare. **~ o.s. off** andarsene. **~-off** n. decollo m. **~ on** (undertake) impegnarsi; (employee) assumere. **~ out** (remove) levare. **~ over** assumere il controllo di. **~-over** n. rilevamento m. **~ part** partecipare. **~ to** darsi a; (like) affezionarsi a. **~ up** (hobby) dedicarsi a; (occupy) occupare; (dress) accorciare. **~ up with** legarsi con.

takings /'teɪkɪŋz/ n.pl. incassi m.pl.

talcum /'tælkəm/ n. **~ powder** boro talco m.

tale /teɪl/ n. storia f.; (pej.) fandonia f.

talent /'tælənt/ n. talento m. **~ed** a. dotato.

talisman /'tælɪzmən/ n. talismano m.

talk /tɔːk/ v.t./i. parlare. —n. conversazione f.; (lecture) conferenza f. **small ~** chiacchiere f.pl. **~ about** parlare di. **~ over** discutere. **~ative** a. loquace. **~er** n. parla|tore, -trice m., f.; (chatterbox) ciarlone, a m., f. **~ing-to** n. sgridata f.

tall /tɔːl/ a. (-er, -est) alto. **~ order** n. (fam.) impresa difficile f. **~ story** n. (fam.) panzana f.

tallboy /'tɔːlbɔɪ/ n. cassettone m.

tally /'tælɪ/ n. conteggio m. —v.i. corrispondere (with, a).

talon /'tælən/ n. artiglio m.

tambourine /tæmbə'riːn/ n. tamburello m.

tame /teɪm/ a. (-er, -est) (of animal) domestico; (of person) docile; (dull) insipido. —v.t. domare. **~ly** adv. docilmente. **~r** /-ə(r)/ n. doma|tore, -trice m., f.

tamper /'tæmpə(r)/ v.i. **~ with** manomettere.

tampon /'tæmpən/ *n.* tampone *m.*

tan /tæn/ *v.t./i.* (*p.t.* **tanned**) (*hide*) conciare; (*become brown*) abbronzare, abbronzarsi. —*n.* abbronzatura *f.* —*a.* (*colour*) marrone rossiccio.

tandem /'tændəm/ *n.* tandem *m. invar.*

tang /tæŋ/ *n.* sapore *or* odore forte *m.* ~**y** *a.* piccante; (*smell*) pungente.

tangent /'tændʒənt/ *n.* tangente *f.*

tangerine /tændʒə'riːn/ *n.* mandarino *m.*

tangibl|e /'tændʒəbl/ *a.* tangibile. ~**y** *adv.* tangibilmente.

tangle /'tæŋgl/ *v.t./i.* aggrovigliare, aggrovigliarsi. —*n.* groviglio *m.*

tango /'tæŋgəʊ/ *n.* (*pl.* **-os**) tango *m.*

tank /tæŋk/ *n.* contenitore *m.*; (*for petrol*) serbatoio *m.*; (*mil.*) carro armato *m.*

tankard /'tæŋkəd/ *n.* boccale *m.*

tanker /'tæŋkə(r)/ *n.* nave cisterna *f.*; (*truck*) autobotte *f.*

tantaliz|e /'tæntəlaɪz/ *v.t.* tormentare. ~**ing** *a.* allettante.

tantamount /'tæntəmaʊnt/ *a.* ~ **to** equivalente a.

tantrum /'tæntrəm/ *n.* scoppio d'ira *m.*

tap /tæp/ *n.* rubinetto *m.* —*v.t.* (*p.t.* **tapped**) dare un colpetto; (*resources*) sfruttare; (*phone*) intercettare. **on** ~ a disposizione. ~**-dance** *n.* tip tap *m.*

tape /teɪp/ *n.* fettuccia *f.*, nastro *m.* —*v.t.* legare con nastro; (*record*) registrare. **have sthg.** ~**d** (*sl.*) capire perfettamente. ~ **deck** *n.* impianto (di riproduzione) *m.* ~**-measure** *n.* metro *m.* ~ **recorder** *n.* registratore *m.* ~ **recording** *n.* registrazione *f.*

taper /'teɪpə(r)/ *n.* candela sottile *f.* —*v.t./i.* affusolare, affusolarsi. ~ **off** assottigliarsi.

tapestry /'tæpɪstrɪ/ *n.* arazzo *m.*

tapioca /tæpɪ'əʊkə/ *n.* tapioca *f.*

tar /tɑː(r)/ *n.* pece *f.* —*v.t.* (*p.t.* **tarred**) incatramare. ~**ry** *a.* catramoso.

tard|y /'tɑːdɪ/ *a.* (**-ier, -iest**) tardo. ~**ily** *adv.* lentamente.

target /'tɑːgɪt/ *n.* bersaglio *m.*; (*fig.*) obiettivo *m.*

tariff /'tærɪf/ *n.* tariffa *f.*

Tarmac /'tɑːmæk/ *n.* (*P.*) macadam al catrame *m.* **tarmac** *n.* pista di decollo *f.*

tarnish /'tɑːnɪʃ/ *v.t./i.* ossidare, ossidarsi; (*fig.*) macchiare, macchiarsi.

tarpaulin /tɑː'pɔːlɪn/ *n.* telone impermeabile *m.*

tarragon /'tærəgən/ *n.* dragoncello *m.*

tart¹ /tɑːt/ *a.* (**-er, -est**) aspro.

tart² /tɑːt/ *n.* crostata *f.*; (*sl., woman*) sgualdrina *f.* —*v.t.* ~ **o.s. up** (*fam.*) farsi bello.

tartan /'tɑːtn/ *n.* tessuto scozzese *m.*

tartar /'tɑːtə(r)/ *n.* tartaro *m.*

task /tɑːsk/ *n.* compito *m.* **take to** ~ riprendere. ~ **force** *n.* gruppo d'assalto in missione speciale *m.*

tassel /'tæsl/ *n.* fiocco *m.*

taste /teɪst/ *n.* gusto *m.*; (*small quantity*) assaggio *m.* —*v.t.* gustare; assaggiare. —*v.i.* ~ **of** sapere di. ~**ful** *a.* di buon gusto. ~**less** *a.* senza gusto.

tasty *a.* (**-ier, -iest**) gustoso.

tat /tæt/ *see* **tit**².

tattered /'tætəd/ *a.* cencioso.

tatters /'tætəz/ *n.pl.* brandelli *m.pl.*

tattle /'tætl/ *v.i.* parlare a vanvera. —*n.* discorso a vanvera *m.*

tattoo¹ /tə'tuː/ *n.* (*mil.*) ritirata *f.*

tattoo² /tə'tuː/ *v.t.* tatuare. —*n.* tatuaggio *m.*

tatt|y /'tætɪ/ *a.* (**-ier, -iest**) trasandato. ~**ily** *adv.* in modo trasandato.

taught /tɔːt/ *see* **teach.**

taunt /tɔːnt/ *v.t.* schernire. —*n.* scherno *m.*

Taurus /'tɔːrəs/ *n.* (*astr.*) Toro *m.*

taut /tɔːt/ *a.* teso.

tavern /'tævən/ *n.* taverna *f.*

tawdry /'tɔːdrɪ/ *a.* (**-ier, -iest**) appariscente.

tawny /'tɔːnɪ/ *a.* bronzeo.

tax /tæks/ *n.* tassa *f.*; (*on income*) imposte *f.pl.* —*v.t.* tassare; (*fig.*) mettere alla prova. ~**able** *a.* tassabile. ~**ation** /-'seɪʃn/ *n.* tasse *f.pl.* ~**-collector** *n.* esattore delle imposte *m.* ~**-free** *a.* esente da imposte. ~**payer** *n.* contribuente *m./f.*

taxi /'tæksɪ/ *n.* (*pl.* **-is**) tassì *m.* —*v.i.* (*v.t.* **taxied**, *pres.p.* **taxiing**) (*of aircraft*) rullare. ~ **rank** *n.* posteggio per tassì *m.*

te /tiː/ *n.* (*mus.*) si *m.*

tea /tiː/ *n.* tè *m. invar.* ~**-bag** *n.* bustina di tè *f.* ~**-break** *n.* intervallo per il tè *m.* ~**-leaf** *n.* fogliolina di tè *f.* ~**-set** *n.* servizio da tè *m.* ~**-towel** *n.* asciugapiatti *m. invar.*

teach /tiːtʃ/ *v.t./i.* (*p.t.* **taught**) insegnare. ~**er** *n.* insegnante *m./f.*; (*primary*) maestro, a *m.*, *f.* ~**-in** *n.* dibattito di protesta *m.* ~**ing** *n.* insegnamento *m.*

teacup /'tiːkʌp/ *n.* tazza da tè *f.*

teak /tiːk/ n. tek m.

team /tiːm/ n. squadra f.; (of animals) tiro m. —v.i. ~ up unirsi. ~-work n. lavoro di squadra m.

teapot /'tiːpɒt/ n. teiera f.

tear[1] /teə(r)/ v.t./i. (p.t. **tore**, p.p. **torn**) strappare, strapparsi; (run) precipitarsi. —n. strappo m. ~ **apart** (fig.) straziare. ~ **o.s. away** staccarsi.

tear[2] /tɪə(r)/ n. lacrima f. ~-**gas** n. gas lacrimogeno m. ~**ful** a. lacrimoso.

tearaway /'teərəweɪ/ n. giovinastro m.

tease /tiːz/ v.t. prendere in giro; (cloth etc.) cardare. —n. burlone, a m., f. ~**r** /-ə(r)/ n. (fam.) dilemma m.

teaspoon /'tiːspuːn/ n. cucchiaino (da tè) m. ~**ful** n. (pl. -**fuls**) (amount) cucchiaino m.

teat /tiːt/ n. capezzolo m.; (of rubber) tettarella f.

technical /'teknɪkl/ a. tecnico. ~**ity** n. /-'kælətɪ/ n. tecnicismo m. ~**ly** adv. tecnicamente.

technician /tek'nɪʃn/ n. tecnico, a m., f.

technique /tek'niːk/ n. tecnica f.

technolog|**y** /tek'nɒlədʒɪ/ n. tecnologia f. ~**ist** n. tecnologo, a m., f.

teddy bear /'tedɪbeə(r)/ n. orsacchiotto m.

tedious /'tiːdɪəs/ a. noioso. ~**ly** adv. noiosamente.

tedium /'tiːdɪəm/ n. tedio m.

tee /tiː/ n. (golf) tee m. invar.

teem /tiːm/ v.i. abbondare. **be** ~**ing with** pullulare di.

teenage /'tiːneɪdʒ/ a. per giovani. ~**r** /-ə(r)/ n. adolescente m./f.

teens /tiːnz/ n.pl. **the** ~ l'adolescenza f.s.

teeny /'tiːnɪ/ a. (-**ier**, -**iest**) (fam.) piccolissimo.

teeter /'tiːtə(r)/ v.i. ondeggiare.

teeth /tiːθ/ see **tooth**.

teeth|**e** /tiːð/ v.i. mettere i (primi) denti. ~**ing troubles** n.pl. (fig.) difficoltà iniziali f.pl.

teetotaller /tiː'təʊtlə(r)/ n. astemio, a m., f.

telecommunications /telɪkəmjuːnɪ'keɪʃnz/ n.pl. telecomunicazioni f.pl.

telegram /'telɪgræm/ n. telegramma m.

telegraph /'telɪgrɑːf/ n. telegrafo m. —v.t. telegrafare. ~**ic** /-'græfɪk/ a. telegrafico.

telepath|**y** /tɪ'lepəθɪ/ n. telepatia f. ~**ic** /telɪ'pæθɪk/ a. telepatico.

telephon|**e** /'telɪfəʊn/ n. telefono m. —v.t. telefonare. ~**e booth** n. cabina telefonica f. ~**e directory** n. elenco telefonico m. ~**e exchange** n. centralino m. ~**ic** /-'fɒnɪk/ a. telefonico. ~**ist** /tɪ'lefənɪst/ n. telefonista m./f.

telephoto /telɪ'fəʊtəʊ/ a. ~ **lens** teleobiettivo.

teleprinter /'telɪprɪntə(r)/ n. telescrivente f.

telescop|**e** /'telɪskəʊp/ n. telescopio m. ~**ic** /-'kɒpɪk/ a. telescopico.

televis|**ion** /'telɪvɪʒn/ n. televisione f. ~**e** /-vaɪz/ v.t. trasmettere per televisione. ~**ion set** n. televisore m.

telex /'teleks/ n. telex m. invar. —v.t. inviare per telex.

tell /tel/ v.t. (p.t. **told**) dire; (story) raccontare; (distinguish) distinguere. —v.i. (produce an effect) fare effetto. ~ **off** v.t. sgridare. ~-**tale** n. spione, a m., f.

teller /'telə(r)/ n. (in bank) cassiere, a m., f.

telling /'telɪŋ/ a. efficace.

telly /'telɪ/ n. (fam.) televisione f.

temerity /tɪ'merətɪ/ n. temerarietà f.

temp /temp/ n. (fam.) impiegato, a non di ruolo m., f.

temper /'tempə(r)/ n. (disposition) carattere m.; (mood) umore m.; (fit of anger) collera f.; (of metal) tempra f. —v.t. (metal) temprare. **be in a** ~ essere in collera. **keep one's** ~ mantenersi calmo. **lose one's** ~ arrabbiarsi.

temperament /'temprəmənt/ n. temperamento m. ~**al** /-'mentl/ a. capriccioso.

temperance /'tempərəns/ n. temperanza f.

temperate /'tempərət/ a. moderato; (of climate) temperato.

temperature /'temprətʃə(r)/ n. temperatura f. **have a** ~ avere la febbre.

tempest /'tempɪst/ n. tempesta f. ~**uous** /-'pestʃʊəs/ a. tempestoso.

temple[1] /'templ/ n. tempio m.

temple[2] /'templ/ n. (anat.) tempia f.

tempo /'tempəʊ/ n. (pl -**os**) ritmo m.

temporar|**y** /'tempərərɪ/ a. temporaneo. ~**ily** adv. temporaneamente.

temporize /'tempəraɪz/ v.i. temporeggiare.

tempt /tempt/ v.t. tentare. ~ **s.o. to**

ten

436 that

indurre qcno. a. **~ation** /-'teɪʃn/ n. tentazione f. **~ing** a. allettante.

ten /ten/ a. & n. dieci m. **~th** a. & n. decimo, a m., f.

tenable /'tenəbl/ a. sostenibile.

tenaci|ous /tɪ'neɪʃəs/ a. tenace. **~ty** /-æsətɪ/ n. tenacia f.

tenancy /'tenənsɪ/ n. affitto m.

tenant /'tenənt/ n. inquilino, a m., f.

tend[1] /tend/ v.t. prendersi cura di.

tend[2] /tend/ v.i. **~ to** tendere a.

tendency /'tendənsɪ/ n. tendenza f.

tender[1] /'tendə(r)/ a. tenero; (painful) dolorante. **~ly** adv. teneramente. **~ness** n. tenerezza f.

tender[2] /'tendə(r)/ v.t. offrire, presentare. —n. (comm.) offerta f. **legal ~** n. valuta legale f.

tendon /'tendən/ n. tendine m.

tenement /'tenəmənt/ n. casamento m.

tenet /'tenɪt/ n. principio m.

tenfold /'tenfəʊld/ a. decuplo. —adv. al decuplo.

tenner /'tenə(r)/ n. (fam.) (biglietto da) dieci sterline m.

tennis /'tenɪs/ n. tennis m.

tenor /'tenə(r)/ n. tenore m.

tense[1] /tens/ n. (gram.) tempo m.

tense[2] /tens/ a. (-er, -est) teso. —v.i. **~ up** tendersi. **~ness** n. tensione f.

tension /'tenʃn/ n. tensione f.

tent /tent/ n. tenda f.

tentacle /'tentəkl/ n. tentacolo m.

tentative /'tentətɪv/ a. a titolo di prova; (hesitant) esitante. **~ly** adv. timidamente.

tenterhooks /'tentəhʊks/ n.pl. **on ~** sulle spine.

tenuous /'tenjʊəs/ a. tenue.

tenure /'tenjʊə(r)/ n. possesso m.

tepid /'tepɪd/ a. tiepido.

term /tɜːm/ n. (of time) periodo m.; (schol.) trimestre m.; (word etc.) termine m. **~s** n.pl. (comm.) condizioni f.pl. —v.t. chiamare. **on good/bad ~s** in buoni/cattivi rapporti.

terminal /'tɜːmɪnl/ a. finale; (med.) terminale. —n. (rail.) stazione di testa f.; (electr.) morsetto m. **(air) ~** n. terminal m. invar.

terminat|e /'tɜːmɪneɪt/ v.t. terminare. —v.i. **~e in** finire in. **~ion** /-'neɪʃn/ n. termine m.

terminology /tɜːmɪ'nɒlədʒɪ/ n. terminologia f.

terrace /'terəs/ n. terrazza f., terrazzo m.; (houses) fila di case f. **~d** a. (garden) a terrazze.

terrain /tə'reɪn/ n. terreno m.

terrestrial /tɪ'restrɪəl/ a. terrestre.

terribl|e /'terəbl/ a. terribile. **~y** adv. terribilmente.

terrier /'terɪə(r)/ n. terrier m. invar.

terrific /tə'rɪfɪk/ a. (excellent, fam.) fantastico; (huge, fam.) enorme. **~ally** adv. (fam.) terribilmente.

terrify /'terɪfaɪ/ v.t. atterrire. **~ing** a. terrificante.

territorial /terɪ'tɔːrɪəl/ a. territoriale.

territory /'terɪtrɪ/ n. territorio m.

terror /'terə(r)/ n. terrore m.

terroris|t /'terərɪst/ n. terrorista m./f. **~m** /-zəm/ n. terrorismo m.

terrorize /'terəraɪz/ v.t. terrorizzare.

terse /tɜːs/ a. incisivo. **~ly** incisivamente.

test /test/ n. prova f., esperimento m.; (exam) esame m. —v.t. provare; esaminare. **~ match** n. partita di campionato f. **~-tube** n. provetta f.

testament /'testəmənt/ n. testamento m. **Old/New T~** Antico/ Nuovo Testamento m.

testicle /'testɪkl/ n. testicolo m.

testify /'testɪfaɪ/ v.t./i. testimoniare.

testimonial /testɪ'məʊnɪəl/ n. certificato di servizio m.

testimony /'testɪmənɪ/ n. testimonianza f.

testy /'testɪ/ a. irascibile.

tetanus /'tetənəs/ n. tetano m.

tetchy /'tetʃɪ/ a. stizzoso.

tether /'teðə(r)/ v.t. legare. —n. **at the end of one's ~** estenuato.

text /tekst/ n. testo m. **~book** n. manuale m.

textile /'tekstaɪl/ n. stoffa f. —a. tessile.

texture /'tekstʃə(r)/ n. grana f.

Thai /taɪ/ a. & n. tailandese m./f. **~land** n. Tailandia f.

Thames /temz/ n. Tamigi m.

than /ðæn, ðən/ conj. che; (with numbers, names) di.

thank /θæŋk/ v.t. ringraziare. **~s** n.pl. ringraziamenti m.pl. **~ you** grazie. **~s!** (fam.) grazie! **~s to** grazie a.

thankful /'θæŋkfl/ a. grato. **~ly** adv. con gratitudine; (happily) fortunatamente.

thankless /'θæŋklɪs/ a. ingrato.

that /ðæt, ðət/ a. & pron. (pl. **those**) quel, quello, quella. —adv. così, tanto. —rel. pron. che, il quale. —conj. che. **is ~ you?** sei tu? **like ~** in questo modo, così. **~ is** cioè. **~'s it!** proprio così! **~ is why** ecco perché.

thatch /θætʃ/ *n.* copertura di paglia *f.*
~**ed** *a.* coperto di paglia.

thaw /θɔ:/ *v.t./i.* sgelare, sgelarsi. —*n.*
disgelo *m.*

the /ðə, ði:/ *def. art.* il, lo, la, i, gli, le.
—*adv.* **all** ~ **better** tanto meglio. **at**
~, **to** ~ al. **from** ~ dal.

theatr|e /ˈθɪətə(r)/ *n.* teatro *m.* ~**ical**
/-ˈætrɪkl/ *a.* teatrale.

theft /θeft/ *n.* furto *m.*

their /ðeə(r)/ *a.* (il) loro, (la) loro.

theirs /ðeəz/ *poss. pron.* il loro.

them /ðem, ðəm/ *pron.* li, le; (*after
prep.*) loro.

theme /θi:m/ *n.* tema *m.* ~ **song** *n.*
motivo principale *m.*

then /ðen/ *adv.* allora; (*next*) poi. —*a.*
di quel tempo. **by** ~ ormai. **now and**
~ ogni tanto. **since** ~ sin da allora.

theolog|y /θɪˈɒlədʒɪ/ *n.* teologia *f.* ~**ian**
/θɪəˈlaʊdʒən/ *n.* teologo, a *m.,f.*

theorem /ˈθɪərəm/ *n.* teorema *m.*

theoretical /θɪəˈretɪkl/ *a.* teorico.

theory /ˈθɪərɪ/ *n.* teoria *f.*

therap|y /ˈθerəpɪ/ *n.* terapia *f.* ~**eutic**
/-ˈpju:tɪk/ *a.* terapeutico. ~**ist** *n.* terapeutico, a *m.,f.*

there /ðeə(r)/ *adv.* là, lì. —*int.* via, su!
down ~ laggiù. ~ **is**, ~ **are** c'è, ci
sono. ~ **he/it is** eccolo. **up** ~ lassù.
~**abouts** *adv.* all'incirca. ~**after**
adv. dopo di che. ~**by** *adv.* in tal
modo.

therefore /ˈðeəfɔ:(r)/ *adv.* perciò.

thermal /ˈθɜ:ml/ *a.* termale.

thermometer /θəˈmɒmɪtə(r)/ *n.* termo-
metro *m.*

thermonuclear /θɜ:məʊˈnju:klɪə(r)/ *a.*
termonucleare.

Thermos /ˈθɜ:məs/ *n.* (*P.*) termos *m.
invar.*

thermostat /ˈθɜ:məstæt/ *n.* termostato
m.

thesaurus /θɪˈsɔ:rəs/ *n.* (*pl.* **-ri** /-raɪ/)
lessico *m.*

these /ði:z/ *see* **this.**

thesis /ˈθi:sɪs/ *n.* (*pl.* **theses** /-si:z/) tesi
f. invar.

they /ðeɪ/ *pron.* essi, loro; (*unspecified*)
si. ~ **say that** si dice che.

thick /θɪk/ *a.* (-er, -est) spesso; (*dense*)
denso; (*hoarse*) rauco; (*hair*) folto;
(*stupid, fam.*) ottuso; (*close, fam.*)
molto unito. —*adv.* = **thickly.** —*n.*
in the ~ **of** nel mezzo di. ~**ly** *adv.*
densamente. ~**ness** *n.* spessore *m.*
~**-skinned** *a.* insensibile.

thicken /ˈθɪkən/ *v.t./i.* ispessire, ispes-
sirsi.

thicket /ˈθɪkɪt/ *n.* boschetto *m.*

thickset /θɪkˈset/ *a.* tozzo.

thief /θi:f/ *n.* (*pl.* **thieves**) ladro, a *m.,
f.*

thiev|e /θi:v/ *v.t./i.* rubare. ~**ing** *a.*
ladro.

thigh /θaɪ/ *n.* coscia *f.*

thimble /ˈθɪmbl/ *n.* ditale *m.*

thin /θɪn/ *a.* (**thinner, thinnest**) sottile; (*person*) magro; (*weak*) leggero;
(*fine*) fine. —*adv.* = **thinly.** —*v.t./i.*
(*p.t.* **thinned**) assottigliare, assottigliarsi; (*hair*) sfoltire. ~ **out** diradarsi.
~**ly** *adv.* (*clothed etc.*) leggermente;
(*disguised, populated*) scarsamente.
~**ness** *n.* magrezza *f.*; leggerezza *f.*

thing /θɪŋ/ *n.* cosa *f.* ~**s** *n.pl.* (*belongings*) roba *f.s.* **for one** ~ in primo
luogo. **just the** ~ proprio quel che ci
vuole. **poor** ~! povera creatura!

think /θɪŋk/ *v.t./i.* (*p.t.* **thought**) pensare (**about, of** a); (*deem*) credere. **I**
~ **so** credo di sì. ~ **better of it**
ripensarci. ~ **over** *v.t.* riflettere su.
~**-tank** *n.* gruppo di esperti *m.* ~ **up**
v.t. escogitare. ~**er** *n.* pensa|tore,
-trice *m.,f.*

third /θɜ:d/ *a. & n.* terzo, a *m., f.* ~
degree *n.* (interrogatorio di) terzo
grado *m.* ~**-rate** *a.* scadente. **T~
World** *n.* Terzo Mondo *m.*

thirst /θɜ:st/ *n.* sete *f.* ~**ily** *adv.* con
sete. ~**y** *a.* assetato. **be** ~**y** aver sete.

thirteen /θɜ:ˈti:n/ *a. & n.* tredici *m.*
~**th** *a. & n.* tredicesimo, a *m.,f.*

thirt|y /ˈθɜ:tɪ/ *a. & n.* trenta *m.* ~**ieth**
a. & n. trentesimo, a *m.,f.*

this /ðɪs/ *a. & pron.* (*pl.* **these**) questo,
questa. **like** ~ così. ~ **one** questo
(qui).

thistle /ˈθɪsl/ *n.* cardo *m.*

thong /θɒŋ/ *n.* cinghia *f.*

thorn /θɔ:n/ *n.* spina *f.* ~**y** *a.* spinoso.

thorough /ˈθʌrə/ *a.* completo; (*deep*)
profondo; (*cleaning etc.*) a fondo; (*person*) scrupoloso. ~**ly** *adv.* completamente; a fondo.

thoroughbred /ˈθʌrəbred/ *n.* purosan-
gue *m. invar.*

thoroughfare /ˈθʌrəfeə(r)/ *n.* via principale *f.*

those /ðəʊz/ *see* **that.**

though /ðəʊ/ *conj.* sebbene. —*adv.* tuttavia. **as** ~ come se.

thought /θɔ:t/ *see* **think.** —*n.* pensiero
m.; (*idea*) idea *f.*

thoughtful /'θɔ:tfl/ *a.* pensieroso; (*considerate*) premuroso. ~**ly** *adv.* pensierosamente; premurosamente.

thoughtless /'θɔ:tlɪs/ *a.* sbadato; (*inconsiderate*) sconsiderato.

thousand /'θaʊznd/ *a.* & *n.* mille *m.* *invar.* ~**s** *n.pl.* migliaia *f.pl.* ~**th** *a.* & *n.* millesimo, a *m.*, *f.*

thrash /θræʃ/ *v.t.* sferzare; (*defeat*) sconfiggere. ~ **out** discutere a fondo.

thread /θred/ *n.* filo *m.*; (*of screw*) filetto *m.* —*v.t.* infilare. ~ **one's way** farsi strada.

threadbare /'θredbeə(r)/ *a.* logoro.

threat /θret/ *n.* minaccia *f.*

threaten /'θretn/ *v.t./i.* minacciare. ~**ing** *a.* minaccioso. ~**ingly** *adv.* minacciosamente.

three /θri:/ *a.* & *n.* tre *m.* ~**fold** *a.* & *adv.* triplo.

threesome /'θri:səm/ *n.* trio *m.*

thresh /θreʃ/ *v.t.* battere.

threshold /'θreʃhəʊld/ *n.* soglia *f.*

threw /θru:/ *see* **throw**.

thrift /θrɪft/ *n.* economia *f.* ~**y** *a.* frugale.

thrill /θrɪl/ *n.* fremito *m.*; (*excitement*) emozione *f.* —*v.t./i.* (far) fremere. **be** ~**ed with** essere entusiasta di. ~**ing** *a.* eccitante.

thriller /'θrɪlə(r)/ *n.* romanzo *or* film giallo *m.*

thriv|e /θraɪv/ *v.i.* (*p.t.* **throve**, *p.p.* **thrived**) prosperare. ~**ing** *a.* fiorente.

throat /θrəʊt/ *n.* gola *f.* **sore** ~ mal di gola *m.*

throb /θrɒb/ *v.i.* (*p.t.* **throbbed**) pulsare; (*of heart*) battere. —*n.* pulsazione *f.*; battito *m.* ~**bing** *a.* (*pain*) acuto.

throes /θrəʊz/ *n.pl.* **in the** ~ **of** alle prese con.

thrombosis /θrɒm'bəʊsɪs/ *n.* trombosi *f.*

throne /θrəʊn/ *n.* trono *m.*

throng /θrɒŋ/ *n.* calca *f.*

throttle /'θrɒtl/ *n.* valvola a farfalla *f.* —*v.t.* strozzare.

through /θru:/ *prep.* attraverso; (*during*) durante; (*by means of*) tramite; (*thanks to*) grazie a. —*adv.* attraverso; (*entirely*) completamente. —*a.* (*train etc.*) diretto. **be** ~ (*finished*) aver finito; (*phone*) avere la comunicazione.

throughout /θru:'aʊt/ *prep.* per tutto. —*adv.* completamente.

throve /θrəʊv/ *see* **thrive**.

throw /θrəʊ/ *v.t.* (*p.t.* **threw**, *p.p.* **thrown**) gettare, buttare; (*baffle etc.*) disorientare. —*n.* tiro *m.* ~ **a party** (*fam.*) dare un ricevimento. ~ **away** buttar via. ~**-away** *a.* disponibile. ~ **over** abbandonare. ~ **up** alzare; *v.i.* (*vomit*) rigettare.

thrush /θrʌʃ/ *n.* tordo *m.*

thrust /θrʌst/ *v.t.* (*p.t.* **thrust**) spingere; (*push in*) conficcare. —*n.* spinta *f.* ~ (**up**)**on** imporre a.

thud /θʌd/ *n.* tonfo *m.*

thug /θʌg/ *n.* malvivente *m.*

thumb /θʌm/ *n.* pollice *m.* —*v.t.* (*book*) sfogliare. ~ **a lift** chiedere un passaggio. ~**-index** *n.* indice a rubrica *m.* **under the** ~ **of** dominato da.

thump /θʌmp/ *v.t.* battere su. —*v.i.* picchiare. —*n.* colpo *m.*

thunder /'θʌndə(r)/ *n.* tuono *m.* —*v.i.* tuonare; (*make loud noise*) rimbombare. ~**y** *a.* temporalesco.

thunderbolt /'θʌndəbəʊlt/ *n.* fulmine *m.*

thunderclap /'θʌndəklæp/ *n.* scoppio di tuono *m.*; (*fig.*) fulmine a ciel sereno *m.*

thunderstorm /'θʌndəstɔ:m/ *n.* temporale *m.*

Thursday /'θɜ:zdɪ/ *n.* giovedì *m.*

thus /ðʌs/ *adv.* così.

thwart /θwɔ:t/ *v.t.* frustrare.

thyme /taɪm/ *n.* timo *m.*

thyroid /'θaɪrɔɪd/ *n.* tiroide *f.*

tiara /tɪ'ɑːrə/ *n.* tiara *f.*

Tiber /'taɪbə(r)/ *n.* **the** ~ il Tevere *m.*

tic /tɪk/ *n.* tic (nervoso) *m.*

tick[1] /tɪk/ *n.* ticchettio *m.*; (*mark*) segno *m.*; (*fam., instant*) attimo *m.* —*v.i.* ticchettare. —*v.t.* ~ (**off**) spuntare. ~ **off** *v.t.* (*sl.*) rimproverare. ~ **over** *v.i.* (*of engine*) andare al minimo.

tick[2] /tɪk/ *n.* (*insect*) zecca *f.*

tick[3] /tɪk/ *n.* **on** ~ (*fam.*) a credito.

ticket /'tɪkɪt/ *n.* biglietto *m.*; (*label*) cartellino *m.*; (*fine*) multa *f.* ~**-collector** *n.* controllore *m.* ~**-office** *n.* biglietteria *f.*

tickle /'tɪkl/ *v.t.* solleticare; (*amuse*) divertire. —*n.* solletico *m.*

ticklish /'tɪklɪʃ/ *a.* che soffre il solletico; (*problem*) delicato.

tidal /'taɪdl/ *a.* di marea.

tiddly-winks /'tɪdlɪwɪŋks/ *n.* gioco delle pulci *m.*

tide /taɪd/ *n.* marea *f.*; (*of events*) corrente *f.* —*v.t.* ~ **over** aiutare a superare.

tidings /'taɪdɪŋz/ *n.pl.* notizie *f.pl.*

tid|y /'taɪdɪ/ *a.* (-**ier**, -**iest**) ordinato; (*amount*, *fam.*) considerevole. —*v.t.*/*i.* ~**y** (**up**) ordinare. ~**y o.s. up** mettersi in ordine. ~**ily** *adv.* ordinatamente. ~**iness** *n.* ordine *m.*

tie /taɪ/ *v.t.*/*i.* (*pres. p.* **tying**) legare; (*a knot*) fare; (*link*) unire; (*sport*) pareggiare. —*n.* legame *m.*; (*necktie*) cravatta *f.*; (*sport*) pareggio *m.* **be** ~**d up** (*busy*) essere occupato. ~ **in with** avere un legame con. ~ **up** (*comm.*) vincolare. ~-**up** *n.* connessione *f.*

tier /tɪə(r)/ *n.* fila *f.*; (*in stadium etc.*) gradino *m.*; (*of cake*) strato *m.*

tiff /tɪf/ *n.* bisticcio *m.*

tiger /'taɪgə(r)/ *n.* tigre *f.*

tight /taɪt/ *a.* (-**er**, -**est**) (*clothes*) stretto; (*firm*) saldo; (*control etc.*) rigido; (*drunk*, *fam.*) sbronzo. —*adv.* forte; (*shut*) ermeticamente. ~ **corner** situazione difficile *f.* ~-**fisted** *a.* tirchio. ~**ly** *adv.* strettamente. ~**ness** *n.* strettezza *f.*

tighten /'taɪtn/ *v.t.*/*i.* stringere, stringersi; (*a screw*) avvitare; (*control*, *etc.*) rinforzare.

tightrope /'taɪtrəʊp/ *n.* fune (da funamboli) *f.*

tights /taɪts/ *n.pl.* collant *m. invar.*

tile /taɪl/ *n.* mattonella *f.*; (*on roof*) tegola *f.* —*v.t.* coprire con mattonelle *or* tegole.

till[1] /tɪl/ *v.t.* coltivare.

till[2] /tɪl/ *prep.* & *conj.* = **until.**

till[3] /tɪl/ *n.* cassa *f.*

tilt /tɪlt/ *v.t.*/*i.* inclinare, inclinarsi. —*n.* inclinazione *f.* **at full** ~ a piena velocità.

timber /'tɪmbə(r)/ *n.* legname *m.*; (*trees*) alberi da legname *m.pl.*

time /taɪm/ *n.* tempo *m.*; (*moment*) momento *m.*; (*occasion*) volta *f.*; (*by clock*) ora *f.* —*v.t.* scegliere il momento (per); (*race*) cronometrare. **behind** ~ in ritardo. **behind the** ~**s** antiquato. **for the** ~ **being** per il momento. **from** ~ **to** ~, **at** ~**s** ogni tanto. **in a year's** ~ fra un anno. ~ **in tempo; (*eventually*) col tempo. **on** ~ in orario. ~ **bomb** *n.* bomba a orologeria *f.* ~-**honoured** *a.* venerando. ~-**lag** *n.* intervallo di tempo *m.* ~ **zone** *n.* fuso orario *m.*

timeless /'taɪmlɪs/ *a.* eterno.

timely /'taɪmlɪ/ *a.* tempestivo.

timer /'taɪmə(r)/ *n.* (*mech.*) sincronizzatore *m.*

timetable /'taɪmteɪbl/ *n.* orario *m.*

timid /'tɪmɪd/ *a.* timido; (*fearful*) spaurito. ~**ly** *adv.* timidamente.

timing /'taɪmɪŋ/ *n.* calcolo del tempo *m.*; (*sport*) cronometraggio *m.*

timorous /'tɪmərəs/ *a.* timoroso. ~**ly** *adv.* timorosamente.

tin /tɪn/ *n.* stagno *m.*; (*container*) scatola *f.*—*v.t.* (*p.t.* **tinned**) conservare in scatola. ~ **foil** *n.* (carta) stagnola *f.* ~-**opener** *n.* apriscatole *m. invar.* ~ **plate** latta *f.* ~**ned** *a.* in scatola. ~**ny** *a.* metallico.

tinge /tɪndʒ/ *v.t.* dare una sfumatura. —*n.* sfumatura *f.* ~**d with** (*fig.*) misto a.

tingle /'tɪŋgl/ *v.i.* pizzicare.

tinker /'tɪŋkə(r)/ *n.* stagnino *m.* —*v.i.* ~ (**with**) armeggiare (con).

tinkle /'tɪŋkl/ *n.* tintinnio *m.*; (*phone call*, *fam.*) colpo di telefono *m.*

tinpot /'tɪnpɒt/ *a.* (*pej.*) da due soldi.

tinsel /'tɪnsl/ *n.* filo d'argento *m.*

tint /tɪnt/ *n.* tinta *f.*

tiny /'taɪnɪ/ *a.* (-**ier**, -**iest**) minuscolo.

tip[1] /tɪp/ *n.* punta *f.* ~**ped** *a.* (*cigarette*) col filtro.

tip[2] /tɪp/ *v.t.*/*i.* (*p.t.* **tipped**) (*tilt*) inclinare, inclinarsi; (*overturn*) capovolgere, capovolgersi; (*pour*) versare; (*reward*) dare una mancia. —*n.* (*reward*) mancia *f.*; (*advice*) consiglio *m.*; (*for rubbish*) deposito di rifiuti *m.* ~ **off** mettere sull'avviso. ~-**off** *n.* avvertimento *m.* ~ **out** scaricare.

tipple /'tɪpl/ *v.i.* bere (bevande alcooliche). —*n.* **have a** ~ prendere un bicchierino.

tipsy /'tɪpsɪ/ *a.* brillo.

tiptoe /'tɪptəʊ/ *n.* **on** ~ in punta di piedi.

tiptop /'tɪptɒp/ *a.* (*fam.*) di prim'ordine.

tirade /tɪ'reɪd/ *n.* tirata *f.*

tir|e /'taɪə(r)/ *v.t.*/*i.* stancare, stancarsi. ~**eless** *a.* instancabile. ~**ing** *a.* stancante.

tired /'taɪəd/ *a.* stanco. ~ **of** stufo di. ~ **out** stanco morto.

tiresome /'taɪəsəm/ *a.* fastidioso.

tissue /'tɪʃuː/ *n.* tessuto *m.*; (*handkerchief*) velina *f.* ~-**paper** *n.* carta velina *f.*

tit[1] /tɪt/ *n.* (*bird*) cincia *f.*

tit[2] /tɪt/ *n.* ~ **for tat** pan per focaccia.

titbit /'tɪtbɪt/ *n.* leccornia *f.*

titillate /'tɪtɪleɪt/ *v.t.* titillare.

title /'taɪtl/ *n.* titolo *m.* ~-**deed** *n.* atto di proprietà *m.* ~-**role** *n.* parte principale *f.* ~**d** *a.* titolato.

tittle-tattle /'tɪtltætl/ *n.* pettegolezzi *m.pl.*

titular /'tɪtjʊlə(r)/ *a.* nominale.

tizzy /'tɪzɪ/ *n.* (*sl.*) **in a** ~ in grande agitazione.

to /tuː/ *prep. before verb as sign of infinitive;* a, da, in; (*towards*) verso. —*adv.* **push** *or* **pull** ~ chiudere. **come** ~ **me** vieni da me. **give it** ~ **me** dammelo. **go** ~ **Italy** andare in Italia. **go** ~ **the market** andare al mercato. ~ **and fro** *adv.* avanti e indietro. **twenty** ~ **seven** (*by clock*) le sette meno venti. ~**-be** *a.* futuro. ~**-do** *n.* trambusto *m.*

toad /təʊd/ *n.* rospo *m.*

toadstool /'təʊdstuːl/ *n.* fungo a ombrello *m.*

toast /təʊst/ *n.* pane tostato *m.*; (*drink*) brindisi *m.* —*v.t.* tostare; brindare (a). ~**er** *n.* tostapane *m. invar.*

tobacco /tə'bækəʊ/ *n.* tabacco *m.* ~**n-ist** *n.* tabaccaio *m.* ~**nist's shop** *n.* tabaccheria *f.*

toboggan /tə'bɒgən/ *n.* toboga *m.*

today /tə'deɪ/ *n. & adv.* oggi *m.* ~ **week** oggi a otto.

toddler /'tɒdlə(r)/ *n.* bambino, a ai primi passi *m.*, *f.*

toddy /'tɒdɪ/ *n.* grog *m. invar.*

toe /təʊ/ *n.* dito del piede *m.*; (*of shoe*) punta *f.* —*v.t.* ~ **the line** rigar dritto. **big** ~ alluce *m.* **on one's** ~**s** (*fig.*) pronto ad agire. ~**-hold** *n.* punto d'appoggio *m.*

toff /tɒf/ *n.* (*sl.*) elegantone *m.*

toffee /'tɒfɪ/ *n.* caramella *f.*

together /tə'geðə(r)/ *adv.* insieme; (*at same time*) allo stesso tempo. ~ **with** unitamente a. ~**ness** *n.* solidarietà *f.*

toil /tɔɪl/ *v.i.* faticare. —*n.* fatica *f.*

toilet /'tɔɪlɪt/ *n.* toletta *f.*; (*lavatory*) gabinetto *m.* ~**-paper** *n.* carta igienica *f.* ~ **water** *n.* acqua di colonia *f.*

toiletries /'tɔɪlɪtrɪz/ *n.pl.* articoli da toletta *m.pl.*

token /'təʊkən/ *n.* segno *m.*; (*voucher*) buono *m.*; (*coin*) gettone *m.* —*a.* simbolico.

told /təʊld/ *see* **tell.** —*a.* **all** ~ in tutto.

tolerabl|e /'tɒlərəbl/ *a.* tollerabile; (*not bad*) discreto. ~**y** *adv.* discretamente.

toleran|t /'tɒlərənt/ *a.* tollerante. ~**ce** *n.* tolleranza *f.* ~**tly** *adv.* con tolleranza.

tolerate /'tɒləreɪt/ *v.t.* tollerare.

toll[1] /təʊl/ *n.* pedaggio *m.* **death** ~ numero di morti *m.* **take a heavy** ~ costare gravi perdite.

toll[2] /təʊl/ *v.i.* suonare.

tom /tɒm/, ~**-cat** *ns.* gatto maschio *m.*

tomato /tə'mɑːtəʊ/ *n.* (*pl.* ~**oes**) pomodoro *m.*

tomb /tuːm/ *n.* tomba *f.*

tomboy /'tɒmbɔɪ/ *n.* maschiaccio *m.*

tombstone /'tuːmstəʊn/ *n.* pietra tombale *f.*

tome /təʊm/ *n.* tomo *m.*

tomfoolery /tɒm'fuːlərɪ/ *n.* stupidaggine *f.*

tomorrow /tə'mɒrəʊ/ *n. & adv.* domani *m.* **see you** ~! a domani!

ton /tʌn/ *n.* tonnellata *f.* (= *1,016 kg.*). **metric** ~ (= *1,000 kg.*) tonnellata metrica *f.* ~**s of** (*fam.*) un sacco di.

tone /təʊn/ *n.* tono *m.*; (*colour*) tonalità *f.* —*v.t.* ~ **down** attenuare. —*v.i.* ~ **in** intonarsi. ~**-deaf** *a.* che non ha orecchio. ~ **up** *v.t.* (*muscles*) tonificare.

tongs /tɒŋz/ *n.pl.* pinze *f.pl.*

tongue /tʌŋ/ *n.* lingua *f.* ~ **in cheek** *adv.* ironicamente. ~**-tied** *a.* senza parola. ~**-twister** *n.* scioglilingua *m. invar.*

tonic /'tɒnɪk/ *a. & n.* tonico *m.* ~ **water** *n.* acqua tonica *f.*

tonight /tə'naɪt/ *adv.* stanotte; (*evening*) stasera. —*n.* questa notte *f.*; questa sera *f.*

tonne /tʌn/ *n.* tonnellata metrica *f.*

tonsil /'tɒnsl/ *n.* tonsilla *f.* ~**litis** /-'laɪtɪs/ *n.* tonsillite *f.*

too /tuː/ *adv.* troppo; (*also*) anche. ~ **many** *a.* troppi. ~ **much** *a.* troppo.

took /tʊk/ *see* **take.**

tool /tuːl/ *n.* arnese *m.* ~**-bag** *n.* borsa attrezzi *f.*

toot /tuːt/ *n.* suono di clacson *m.* —*v.i.* suonare il clacson.

tooth /tuːθ/ *n.* (*pl.* **teeth**) dente *m.* ~**less** *a.* sdentato.

toothache /'tuːθeɪk/ *n.* mal di denti *m.*

toothbrush /'tuːθbrʌʃ/ *n.* spazzolino da denti *m.*

toothcomb /'tuːθkəʊm/ *n.* pettine fitto *m.*

toothpaste /'tuːθpeɪst/ *n.* dentifricio *m.*

toothpick /'tuːθpɪk/ *n.* stuzzicadenti *m. invar.*

top[1] /tɒp/ *n.* cima *f.*; (*upper part*) sopra *m.*; (*upper surface*) superficie *f.*; (*lid*) coperchio *m.*; (*of bottle*) tappo *m.*; (*of* list) testa *f.* —*a.* in alto; (*in rank*) superiore; (*maximum*) massimo. —*v.t.* (*p.t.* **topped**) coprire; (*exceed*) sorpassare. **from ~ to bottom** da cima a fondo. **on ~ (of)** sopra; (*besides*) inoltre. **~ floor** *n.* ultimo piano *m.* **~ hat** *n.* cilindro *m.* **~-heavy** *a.* sovraccarico. **~-notch** *a.* (*fam.*) eccellente. **~ secret** segretissimo. **~ up** *v.t.* riempire.

top² /tɒp/ *n.* (*toy*) trottola *f.*

topic /'tɒpɪk/ *n.* soggetto *m.*

topical /'tɒpɪkl/ *a.* d'attualità.

topless /'tɒplɪs/ *a.* (*bather*) topless.

topmost /'tɒpməʊst/ *a.* (il) più alto.

topography /tə'pɒɡrəfɪ/ *n.* topografia *f.*

topple /'tɒpl/ *v.i.* rovesciarsi.

topsy-turvy /tɒpsɪ'tɜːvɪ/ *adv.* & *a.* sottosopra.

torch /tɔːtʃ/ *n.* lampadina tascabile *f.*; (*flaming*) fiaccola *f.*

tore /tɔː(r)/ *see* **tear**¹.

toreador /'tɒrɪədɔː(r)/ *n.* torero *m.*

torment¹ /'tɔːment/ *n.* tormento *m.*

torment² /tɔː'ment/ *v.t.* tormentare.

torn /tɔːn/ *see* **tear**¹.

tornado /tɔː'neɪdəʊ/ *n.* (*pl.* **-oes**) tromba d'aria *f.*

torpedo /tɔː'piːdəʊ/ *n.* (*pl.* **-oes**) siluro *m.* —*v.t.* silurare.

torpor /'tɔːpə(r)/ *n.* torpore *m.*

torrent /'tɒrənt/ *n.* torrente *m.* **~ial** /tə'renʃl/ *a.* torrenziale.

torrid /'tɒrɪd/ *a.* torrido.

torso /'tɔːsəʊ/ *n.* (*pl.* **-os**) torso *m.*

tortoise /'tɔːtəs/ *n.* tartaruga *f.* **~shell** *n.* tartaruga *f.*

tortuous /'tɔːtʃʊəs/ *a.* tortuoso.

torture /'tɔːtʃə(r)/ *n.* tortura *f.* —*v.t.* torturare. **~r** /-ə(r)/ *n.* tortura|tore, -trice *m.*, *f.*

Tory /'tɔːrɪ/ *a.* & *n.* (*fam.*) Tory *m.*|*f.*

toss /tɒs/ *v.t.* gettare; (*shake*) scrollare. **~ and turn** (*in bed*) rigirarsi. **~ up** tirare a sorte.

tot¹ /tɒt/ *n.* bimbetto, *a m.*,*f.*; (*of liquor*, *fam.*) sorso *m.*

tot² /tɒt/ *v.t.* (*p.t.* **totted**) **~ up** (*fam.*) addizionare.

total /'təʊtl/ *a.* & *n.* totale *m.* —*v.t.* (*p.t.* **totalled**) ammontare (a). **~ity** /-'tælətɪ/ *n.* totalità *f.* **~ly** *adv.* totalmente.

totalitarian /təʊtælɪ'teərɪən/ *a.* totalitario.

totter /'tɒtə(r)/ *v.i.* barcollare. **~y** *a.* malfermo.

touch /tʌtʃ/ *v.t.* toccare; (*reach*) arrivare a; (*move*) commuovere. —*n.* tocco *m.*; (*sense*) tatto *m.*; (*contact*) contatto *m.*; (*trace*) traccia *f.* **get in ~ with** mettersi in contatto con. **~-and-go** *a.* incerto. **~ down** (*of aircraft*) atterrare. **~ off** (*gun*) scaricare; (*fig.*) scatenare. **~ on** trattare brevemente. **~ up** ritoccare.

touching /'tʌtʃɪŋ/ *a.* commovente.

touchstone /'tʌtʃstəʊn/ *n.* (*fig.*) pietra di paragone *f.*

touchy /'tʌtʃɪ/ *a.* permaloso.

tough /tʌf/ *a.* (**-er**, **-est**) duro; (*strong*) resistente. **~ness** *n.* durezza *f.*; resistenza *f.*

toughen /'tʌfn/ *v.t.* rinforzare; (*person*) indurire.

toupee /'tuːpeɪ/ *n.* toupet *m.*

tour /tʊə(r)/ *n.* giro *m.*; (*by team etc.*) tournée *f.* —*v.t.* visitare.

tourism /'tʊərɪzəm/ *n.* turismo *m.*

tourist /'tʊərɪst/ *n.* turista *m.*|*f.* —*a.* turistico. **~ office** *n.* agenzia turistica *f.*

tournament /'tɔːnəmənt/ *n.* torneo *m.*

tousle /'taʊzl/ *v.t.* scompigliare.

tout /taʊt/ *v.i.* **~ (for)** sollecitare. —*n.* sollecita|tore, -trice *m.*,*f.*; (*horse-racing*) informatore *m.*

tow /təʊ/ *v.t.* rimorchiare. —*n.* rimorchio *m.* **in ~** (*fam.*) al seguito. **~-path** *n.* strada alzaia *f.*

toward(s) /tə'wɔːd(z)/ *prep.* verso.

towel /'taʊəl/ *n.* asciugamano *m.* **~ling** *n.* (*fabric*) spugna *f.*

tower /'taʊə(r)/ *n.* torre *f.* —*v.i.* **~ above** dominare. **~ block** *n.* grattacielo *m.* **~ing** *a.* torreggiante; (*rage*) violento.

town /taʊn/ *n.* città *f.* **go to ~** (*fam.*) far le cose in grande. **~ hall** *n.* municipio *m.* **~ planning** *n.* urbanistica *f.*

toxic /'tɒksɪk/ *a.* tossico.

toxin /'tɒksɪn/ *n.* tossina *f.*

toy /tɔɪ/ *n.* giocattolo *m.* —*v.i.* **~ with** trastullarsi con. **~shop** *n.* negozio di giocattoli *m.*

trace /treɪs/ *n.* traccia *f.* —*v.t.* seguire le tracce (di); (*draw*) tracciare; (*with tracing-paper*) ricalcare; (*track down*) rintracciare.

tracing /'treɪsɪŋ/ *n.* ricalco *m.* **~-paper** *n.* carta da ricalco *f.*

track /træk/ *n.* traccia *f.*; (*path*, *sport*) pista *f.*; (*of rocket etc.*) traiettoria *f.*; (*rail.*) binario *m.* —*v.t.* seguire le tracce di. **keep ~ of** tenere d'occhio.

make ~s for (sl.) avviarsi verso. one-
~ mind una mente a senso unico. ~
down v.t. scovare. ~ suit n. tuta
sportiva f.
tract¹ /trækt/ n. (land) distesa f.;
(anat.) apparato m.
tract² /trækt/ n. (pamphlet) opuscolo
m.
tractable /'træktəbl/ a. trattabile; (docile) maneggevole.
traction /'trækʃn/ n. trazione f.
tractor /'træktə(r)/ n. trattore m.
trade /treɪd/ n. commercio m.; (occupation) mestiere m.; (people) commer-
cianti m.pl. —v.t./i. commerciare. ~
in (give in part-exchange) dare in
cambio. ~ mark n. marchio di fabbrica m. ~ on approfittare di. ~
union n. sindacato m. ~ wind n.
(vento) aliseo m. ~r /-ə(r)/ n. commer-
ciante m.|f.
tradesman /'treɪdzmən/ n. (pl. -men)
commerciante m.
trading /'treɪdɪŋ/ n. commercio m. ~
estate n. zona industriale f.
tradition /trə'dɪʃn/ n. tradizione f. ~al
a. tradizionale. ~alist n. tradiziona-
lista m.|f. ~ally adv. tradizionalmen-
te.
traffic /'træfɪk/ n. traffico m.; (trading) commercio m. —v.t./i. (p.t.
trafficked) commerciare. ~-lights
n.pl. semaforo m.s. ~ warden vigile
urbano m.
tragedy /'trædʒədɪ/ n. tragedia f.
tragic /'trædʒɪk/ a. tragico. ~ally adv.
tragicamente.
trail /treɪl/ v.i. strisciare; (lag) trascinarsi; (of plant) arrampicarsi. —v.t.
trascinare. —n. traccia f.; (track)
orma f.; (path) sentiero m.
trailer /'treɪlə(r)/ n. rimorchio m.;
(film) presentazione f.
train /treɪn/ n. treno m.; (procession)
corteo m.; (of dress) strascico m.
—v.t. esercitare; (sport) allenare;
(child) educare; (plant) far crescere;
(animal) ammaestrare. ~ee n.
apprendista m.|f. ~er n. allena|tore,
-trice m., f.; (of animals) domatore m.
~ing n. esercitazione f.; allenamento
m.
traipse /treɪps/ v.i. (fam.) trascinarsi.
trait /treɪt/ n. caratteristica f.
traitor /'treɪtə(r)/ n. tradi|tore, -trice
m., f.
tram /træm/ n. tram m. ~-lines n.pl.
linee tramviarie f.pl.

tramp /træmp/ v.t. percorrere. —v.i.
camminare (con passo pesante).
—n. calpestio m.; (hike) camminata f.;
(vagrant) vagabondo, a m., f.
trample /'træmpl/ v.t./i. ~ (on) calpestare.
trampoline /'træmpəli:n/ n. trampolino m.
trance /trɑ:ns/ n. trance f.
tranquil /'træŋkwɪl/ a. tranquillo. ~-
lity /-'kwɪlətɪ/ n. tranquillità f.
tranquillize /'træŋkwɪlaɪz/ v.t.
tranquillizzare. ~r /-ə(r)/ n. calmante
m.
transact /træn'zækt/ v.t. negoziare.
~ion /-ʃn/ n. trattativa f.
transatlantic /trænzət'læntɪk/ a.
transatlantico.
transcend /træn'send/ v.t. tra-
scendere. ~ent a. trascendente.
transcendental /trænsen'dentl/ a.
trascendentale.
transcri|be /træns'kraɪb/ v.t. trascri-
vere; (recorded sound) registrare.
~ption /-ɪpʃn/ n. trascrizione f.;
registrazione f.
transcript /'trænskrɪpt/ n. trascrizione f.
transfer¹ /træns'fɜ:(r)/ v.t./i. (p.t.
transferred) trasferire, trasferirsi;
(drawing) ricalcare. ~able a. trasfe-
ribile.
transfer² /'trænsfɜ:(r)/ n. trasferimento m.; (paper) ricalco m.
transfigur|e /træns'fɪgə(r)/ v.t. trasfi-
gurare. ~ation /-gjʊ'reɪʃn/ n. trasfigu-
razione f.
transfix /træns'fɪks/ v.t. trafiggere;
(fig.) immobilizzare.
transform /træns'fɔ:m/ v.t. trasfor-
mare. ~ation /-ə'meɪʃn/ n. trasforma-
zione f. ~er /-ə(r)/ n. trasformatore
m.
transfusion /træns'fju:ʒn/ n. trasfu-
sione f.
transgress /træns'gres/ v.t./i. oltrepassare. ~ion /-ʃn/ n. trasgressione
f.
transient /'trænzɪənt/ a. passeggero.
transistor /træn'zɪstə(r)/ n. transistor
m. invar.; (radio) radiolina a transistor f.
transit /'trænsɪt/ n. transito m.
transition /træn'zɪʒn/ n. transizione f.
transitive /'trænsətɪv/ a. transitivo.
transitory /'trænsɪtrɪ/ a. transitorio.
translat|e /trænz'leɪt/ v.t. tradurre.

~ion /-ʃn/ *n.* traduzione *f.* **~or** /-ə(r) / *n.* tradut|tore, -trice *m.*, *f.*

translucen|t /trænz'luːsnt/ *a.* traslucido. **~ce** *n.* traslucidità *f.*

transmi|t /trænz'mɪt/ *v.t.* (*p.t.* **transmitted**) trasmettere. **~ssion** /-ʃn/ *n.* trasmissione *f.* **~tter** /-ə(r)/ *n.* trasmittente *m.*

transparen|t /træns'pærənt/ *a.* trasparente. **~cy** *n.* trasparenza *f.*; (*photo*) diapositiva *f.*

transpire /træn'spaɪə(r)/ *v.i.* trapelare; (*happen*, *fam.*) accadere.

transplant[1] /træns'plɑːnt/*v.t.*trapiantare.

transplant[2] /'trænsplɑːnt/ *n.* trapianto *m.*

transport[1] /træn'spɔːt/ *v.t.* trasportare.

transport[2] /'trænspɔːt/ *n.* trasporto *m.* **~ation** /-'teɪʃn/ *n.* trasportazione *f.*

transpos|e /træn'spəʊz/ *v.t.* trasporre. **~ition** /-pə'zɪʃn/ *n.* trasposizione *f.*

transverse /'trænzvɜːs/ *a.* trasversale.

transvestite /trænz'vestaɪt/ *n.* travestito, a *m.*, *f.*

trap /træp/ *n.* trappola *f.*; (*carriage*) calesse *m.* —*v.t.* (*p.t.* **trapped**) intrappolare; (*jam*) schiacciare.

trapdoor /'træpdɔː(r)/ *n.* botola *f.*

trapeze /trə'piːz/ *n.* trapezio *m.*

trappings /'træpɪŋz/ *n.pl.* ornamenti *m.pl.*

trash /træʃ/ *n.* robaccia *f.*; (*nonsense*) sciocchezze *f.pl.* —*a.* senza valore.

trauma /'trɔːmə/ *n.* trauma *m.* **~tic** /-'mætɪk/ *a.* traumatico.

travel /'trævl/ *v.i.* (*p.t.* **travelled**) viaggiare. —*v.t.* percorrere. —*n.* viaggio *m.*; viaggi *m.pl.* **~ler** /-ə(r)/ *n.* viaggia-|tore, -trice *m.*, *f.* **~ler's cheque** *n.* assegno turistico *m.* **~ling** *n.* viaggi *m.pl.*

traverse /træ'vɜːs/ *v.t.* traversare.

travesty /'trævəstɪ/ *n.* parodia *f.*

trawler /'trɔːlə(r)/ *n.* motopeschereccio *m.*

tray /treɪ/ *n.* vassoio *m.*; (*on desk*) contenitore (da scrivania) *m.*

treacher|y /'tretʃərɪ/ *n.* tradimento *m.* **~ous** *a.* traditore; (*deceptive*) ingannevole.

treacle /'triːkl/ *n.* melassa *f.*

tread /tred/ *v.i.* (*p.t.* **trod**, *p.p.* **trodden**) camminare. —*v.t.* **~ on** calpestare. —*n.* andatura *f.*; (*step*) gradino *m.*; (*of tyre*) battistrada *m.*

treadle /'tredl/ *n.* pedale *m.*

treadmill /'tredmɪl/ *n.* macina di mulino *f.*; (*fig.*) lavoro monotono *m.*

treason /'triːzn/ *n.* tradimento *m.*

treasure /'treʒə(r)/ *n.* tesoro *m.* —*v.t.* tenere in gran conto. **~r** *n.* tesoriere, a *m.*, *f.*

treasury /'treʒərɪ/ *n.* tesoreria *f.* **the T~** il Tesoro *m.*

treat /triːt/ *v.t.* trattare; (*med.*) curare. —*n.* piacere *m.*; (*present*) regalo *m.*

treatise /'triːtɪz/ *n.* trattato *m.*

treatment /'triːtmənt/ *n.* trattamento *m.*; (*med.*) cura *f.*

treaty /'triːtɪ/ *n.* trattato *m.*

treble /'trebl/ *a.* triplo. —*v.t./i.* triplicare, triplicarsi. —*n.* il triplo *m.*

tree /triː/ *n.* albero *m.*

trek /trek/ *n.* viaggio (faticoso) *m.* —*v.i.* (*p.t.* **trekked**) viaggiare (faticosamente).

trellis /'trelɪs/ *n.* traliccio *m.*

tremble /'trembl/ *v.i.* tremare.

tremendous /trɪ'mendəs/ *a.* tremendo; (*fam.*, *huge*) enorme. **~ly** *adv.* tremendamente.

tremor /'tremə(r)/ *n.* tremore *m.*; (*earth*) **~** scossa (sismica) *f.*

tremulous /'tremjʊləs/ *a.* tremulo.

trench /trentʃ/ *n.* fosso *m.*; (*mil.*) trincea *f.* **~ coat** *n.* trench *m.*

trend /trend/ *n.* tendenza *f.* **~-setter** *n.* persona che lancia la moda *f.* **~y** *a.* (-ier, -iest) (*fam.*) di *or* alla moda.

trepidation /trepɪ'deɪʃn/ *n.* trepidazione *f.*

trespass /'trespəs/ *v.i.* **~ on** introdursi abusivamente in; (*fig.*) abusare di. **~er** /-ə(r)/ *n.* intruso, a *m.*, *f.*

tress /tres/ *n.* treccia *f.*

trestle /'tresl/ *n.* cavalletto *m.* **~-table** *n.* tavolo a cavalletto *m.*

trews /truːz/ *n.pl.* calzoni stretti *m.pl.*

trial /'traɪəl/ *n.* prova *f.*; (*jurid.*) processo *m.*; (*ordeal*) tribolazione *f.* **on ~** in prova; (*jurid.*) in giudizio.

triang|le /'traɪæŋgl/ *n.* triangolo *m.* **~ular** /-'æŋgjʊlə(r)/ *a.* triangolare.

trib|e /traɪb/ *n.* tribù *f.* **~al** *a.* tribale.

tribulation /trɪbjʊ'leɪʃn/ *n.* tribolazione *f.*

tribunal /traɪ'bjuːnl/ *n.* tribunale *m.*

tributary /'trɪbjʊtrɪ/ *a. & n.* (*stream*) affluente *m.*

tribute /'trɪbjuːt/ *n.* tributo *m.* **pay ~ to** rendere omaggio a.

trice /traɪs/ *n.* **in a ~** in un attimo.

tricholog|y /trɪ'kɒlədʒɪ/ n. tricologia f. **~ist** n. tricologo, a m., f.

trick /trɪk/ n. trucco m.; (*stratagem*) stratagemma m.; (*joke*) scherzo m.; (*at cards*) presa f. —v.t. truffare. **do the ~** fare al caso. **play a ~ on** giocare un tiro a.

trickery /'trɪkərɪ/ n. inganno m.

trickle /'trɪkl/ v.t./i. (far) colare. **~ out/in** (*fig.*) uscire/entrare a poco a poco.

trickster /'trɪkstə(r)/ n. imbroglione, a m., f.

tricky /'trɪkɪ/ a. (*problem*) complesso.

tricolour /'trɪkələ(r)/ n. tricolore m.

tricot /'trɪkəʊ/ n. tricot m. invar.

tricycle /'traɪsɪkl/ n. triciclo m.

trident /'traɪdənt/ n. tridente m.

tried /traɪd/ see **try**.

trifl|e /'traɪfl/ n. inezia f.; (*culin.*) zuppa inglese f. —v.i. frivoleggiare. **~ing** a. insignificante.

trigger /'trɪgə(r)/ n. grilletto m. —v.t. **~ (off)** generare.

trigonometry /trɪgə'nɒmɪtrɪ/ n. trigonometria f.

trilby /'trɪlbɪ/ n. feltro m.

trilogy /'trɪlədʒɪ/ n. trilogia f.

trim /trɪm/ a. (**trimmer, trimmest**) ordinato, lindo; (*figure*) snello. —v.t. (*p.t.* **trimmed**) rifilare; (*hair etc.*) spuntare; (*adorn*) ornare. —n. (*cut*) taglio m.; (*decoration*) rifinitura f. **~ly** adv. ordinatamente. **~ming** n. ornamento m. **~mings** n.pl. ritagli m.pl.; (*decorations*) guarnizioni f.pl.

trinity /'trɪnətɪ/ n. trinità f. **the T~** la Trinità f.

trinket /'trɪŋkɪt/ n. ninnolo m.

trio /'triːəʊ/ n. (*pl.* **-os**) trio m.

trip /trɪp/ v.t. (*p.t.* **tripped**) far inciampare. —v.i. saltellare. —n. gita f.; (*stumble*) passo falso m. **~ up** v.i. inciampare; v.t. fare lo sgambetto a.

tripe /traɪp/ n. trippa f.; (*nonsense, sl.*) fesserie f.pl.

triple /'trɪpl/ a. triplo. —v.t./i. triplicare, triplicarsi.

triplets /'trɪplɪts/ n.pl. bambini, e trigemini, e m., f.

triplicate /'trɪplɪkət/ a. **in ~** in triplice copia.

tripod /'traɪpɒd/ n. treppiedi m. invar.

tripper /'trɪpə(r)/ n. gitante m./f.

triptych /'trɪptɪk/ n. trittico m.

trite /traɪt/ a. banale.

triumph /'traɪʌmf/ n. trionfo m. —v.i.

~ (over) trionfare (su). **~al** /-'ʌmfl/ a. trionfale. **~ant** /-'ʌmfnt/ a. trionfante.

trivial /'trɪvɪəl/ a. insignificante. **~ity** /-'ælətɪ/ n. banalità f.

trod, trodden /trɒd, trɒdn/ see **tread**.

trolley /'trɒlɪ/ n. (*pl.* **-eys**) carrello m. **~bus** n. filobus m. invar.

trollop /'trɒləp/ n. donnaccia f.

trombone /trɒm'bəʊn/ n. trombone m.

troop /truːp/ n. gruppo m. **~s** n.pl. (*mil.*) truppe f.pl. —v.i. **~ in/out** entrare/uscire a frotte. **~er** n. soldato di cavalleria m. **~ing the colour** sfilata della bandiera f.

trophy /'trəʊfɪ/ n. trofeo m.

tropic /'trɒpɪk/ n. tropico m. **~s** n.pl. tropici m.pl. **~al** a. tropicale.

trot /trɒt/ n. trotto m. —v.i. (*p.t.* **trotted**) trottare. **on the ~** (*fam.*) indaffarato. **~ out** (*fam., produce*) produrre.

trotter /'trɒtə(r)/ n. (*culin.*) piedino di maiale m.

trouble /'trʌbl/ n. guaio m.; (*inconvenience*) incomodo m.; (*conflict*) conflitto m.; (*med.*) disturbo m.; (*mech.*) guasto m. —v.t./i. turbare; incomodare. **be in ~** essere nei guai. **be ~d about** preoccuparsi di. **be ~d with** essere tormentato da. **make ~** combinare guai. **take ~** darsi da fare. **~maker** n. agita|tore, -trice m., f. **~some** a. fastidioso.

trough /trɒf/ n. truogolo m.; (*of wave*) cavo dell'onda m.; (*atmospheric*) depressione f.

trounce /traʊns/ v.t. sconfiggere.

troupe /truːp/ n. compagnia di attori f.

trousers /'traʊzəz/ n.pl. pantaloni m.pl.

trousseau /'truːsəʊ/ n. (*pl.* **-s** /-əʊz/) corredo m.

trout /traʊt/ n. (*pl.* **trout**) trota f.

trowel /'traʊəl/ n. paletta f.

truant /'truːənt/ n. **play ~** marinare la scuola.

truce /truːs/ n. tregua f.

truck /trʌk/ n. carrello m.; (*rail.*) carro merci m.; (*lorry*) camion m.

truculent /'trʌkjʊlənt/ a. truculento.

trudge /trʌdʒ/ v.i. arrancare. —n. camminata faticosa f.

true /truː/ a. (**-er, -est**) vero; (*loyal*) leale; (*genuine*) genuino. **come ~** avverarsi.

truffle /'trʌfl/ n. tartufo m.

truism /'truːɪzəm/ n. truismo m.

truly /'truːlɪ/ adv. in verità; (*sincerely*)

sinceramente. **yours** ~ distinti saluti.

trump /trʌmp/ n. (cards) atout m.; (person, fam.) tesoro m. —v.t. ~ **up** escogitare.

trumpet /'trʌmpɪt/ n. tromba f. ~**er** /-ə(r)/ n. trombettiere m.

truncated /trʌn'keɪtɪd/ a. tronco.

truncheon /'trʌntʃən/ n. manganello m.

trundle /'trʌndl/ v.t./i. (far) rotolare.

trunk /trʌŋk/ n. tronco m.; (body) torso m.; (box) baule m.; (of elephant) proboscide f. ~**s** n.pl. calzoncini m.pl. ~**-call** n. chiamata interurbana f. ~**road** n. strada maestra f.

truss /trʌs/ n. (med.) cinto erniario m. ~ **up** v.t. (culin.) legare.

trust /trʌst/ n. fiducia f.; (association) trust m. —v.i. fidarsi di. —v.t. aver fiducia (in); (hope) augurarsi. **on** ~ sulla parola. ~ **to** affidare a. ~**ed** a. fidato. ~**ful** a. fiducioso. ~**fully** adv. fiduciosamente. ~**worthy**, ~**y** adjs. degno di fiducia.

trustee /trʌ'stiː/ n. amministra|tore, -trice (fiduciario, a) m., f.

truth /truːθ/ n. (pl. -s /truːðz/) verità f. ~**ful** a. veritiero. ~**fully** adv. sinceramente.

try /traɪ/ v.t./i. (p.t. **tried**) provare; (be a strain on) mettere a dura prova; (jurid.) processare. —n. prova f.; (rugby) meta f. ~ **for** v.i. cercare d'ottenere. ~ **on** v.t. (garment) misurare. ~ **out** v.t. sperimentare. ~**-out** n. esperimento m. ~**ing** a. difficile; (annoying) fastidioso.

tryst /trɪst/ n. appuntamento m.

T-shirt /'tiːʃɜːt/ n. maglietta f.

tub /tʌb/ n. tino m.; (bath) vasca da bagno f.

tubby /'tʌbɪ/ a. (-ier, -iest) tozzo.

tub|e /tjuːb/ n. tubo m.; (rail., fam.) ferrovia sotterranea f. **inner** ~**e** n. camera d'aria f. ~**ing** n. tubi m.pl. ~**ular** a. tubolare.

tuber /'tjuːbə(r)/ n. tubero m.

tuberculosis /tjuːbɜːkjʊ'ləʊsɪs/ n. tubercolosi f.

tuck /tʌk/ n. piega f. —v.t. piegare; (put) mettere; (put away) riporre. —v.i. ~ **in** or **into** (eat, sl.) mangiare avidamente. ~**-shop** n. pasticceria (vicino a una scuola) f. ~ **up** v.t. (child) rimboccare.

Tuesday /'tjuːzd(e)ɪ/ n. martedì m.

tuft /tʌft/ n. ciuffo m.

tug /tʌg/ v.t./i. (p.t. **tugged**) tirare; (tow) rimorchiare. —n. strattone m.; (naut.) rimorchiatore m. ~**-of-war** n. tiro alla fune m.

tuition /tjuː'ɪʃn/ n. istruzione f.

tulip /'tjuːlɪp/ n. tulipano m.

tumble /'tʌmbl/ v.i. ruzzolare. —n. ruzzolone m. ~**-drier** n. centrifuga f. ~ **to** (fam.) capire.

tumbledown /'tʌmbldaʊn/ a. cadente.

tumbler /'tʌmblə(r)/ n. bicchiere (senza stelo) m.

tummy /'tʌmɪ/ n. (fam.) stomaco m.

tumour /'tjuːmə(r)/ n. tumore m.

tumult /'tjuːmʌlt/ n. tumulto m. ~**uous** /-'mʌltʃʊəs/ a. tumultuoso.

tuna /'tjuːnə/ n. (pl. **tuna**) tonno m.

tune /tjuːn/ n. motivo m. —v.t. accordare; (radio, TV) sintonizzare; (mech.) mettere a punto. —v.i. ~ **in** (to) (radio, TV) sintonizzarsi. **be in** ~/**out of** ~ essere intonato/stonato. ~ **up** mettersi in tono. ~**ful** a. melodioso. ~**r** /-ə(r)/ n. accorda|tore, -trice m., f.; (radio, TV) sintonizzatore m.

tunic /'tjuːnɪk/ n. tunica f.

tuning-fork /'tjuːnɪŋfɔːk/ n. diapason m. invar.

tunnel /'tʌnl/ n. tunnel m. —v.i. (p.t. **tunnelled**) costruire una galleria.

Tunisia /tjuː'nɪzɪə/ n. Tunisia f. ~**n** a. & n. tunisino, a m., f.

turban /'tɜːbən/ n. turbante m.

turbid /'tɜːbɪd/ a. torbido.

turbine /'tɜːbaɪn/ n. turbina f.

turbo-jet /'tɜːbəʊdʒet/ n. turboreattore m.

turbot /'tɜːbət/ n. rombo m.

turbulen|t /'tɜːbjʊlənt/ a. turbolento. ~**ce** n. turbolenza f.

tureen /tjʊ'riːn/ n. zuppiera f.

turf /tɜːf/ n. (pl. **turfs** or **turves**) tappeto erboso m.; (segment) zolla f. —v.t. ~ **out** (sl.) buttar fuori. **the** ~ n. l'ippica f. ~ **accountant** n. allibratore m.

turgid /'tɜːdʒɪd/ a. (of language) pomposo.

Turk /tɜːk/ n. turco, a m., f. ~**ey** n. Turchia f. ~**ish** a. & n. turco m.

turkey /'tɜːkɪ/ n. (pl. -eys) tacchino m.

turmoil /'tɜːmɔɪl/ n. tumulto m.

turn /tɜːn/ v.t./i. girare, girarsi; (direction, page, etc.) voltare; (of hour, age) (sor)passare; (change) mutare; (become) diventare. —n. giro m.; (in road) svolta m.; (change) cambiamento m.; (sequence) turno m.; (service) azione *f.*; (*theatr.*) numero *m.*; (*of illness, fam.*) indisposizione *f.* **in** ~ a turno. **out of** ~ fuori tempo. **to a** ~ (*culin.*) a puntino. ~ **against** *v.t.* mettere contro. ~ **down** *v.t.* (*fold*) piegare; (*reduce*) abbassare; (*reject*) respingere. ~ **in** *v.t.* restituire; *v.i.* (*go to bed, fam.*) andare a letto. ~ **off** *v.t.* (*tap*) chiudere; (*light, TV, etc.*) spegnere. ~ **on** *v.t.* (*tap*) aprire; (*light etc.*) accendere; (*attack*) attaccare; (*attract, fam.*) eccitare. ~ **out** *v.t.* espellere; (*light etc.*) spegnere; (*produce*) produrre; (*empty*) svuotare; (*result*) risultare. ~**-out** *n.* (*of room etc.*) ordinata *f.*; (*of people*) assembramento *m.*; (*of goods*) produzione *f.* ~ **round** *v.i.* voltarsi. ~ **the tables** rovesciare la situazione. ~ **up** *v.i.* apparire; *v.t.* (*gas*) alzare. ~**-up** *n.* (*of trousers*) risvolto *m.* ~**ed-up** *a.* (*nose*) all'insù.

turning /'tɜːnɪŋ/ *n.* svolta *f.* ~**-point** *n.* svolta decisiva *f.*

turnip /'tɜːnɪp/ *n.* rapa *f.*

turnover /'tɜːnəʊvə(r)/ *n.* (*culin.*) pasticcio *m.*; (*comm.*) giro d'affari *m.*; (*of staff*) rotazione *f.*

turnpike /'tɜːnpaɪk/ *n.* (*Amer.*) autostrada *f.*

turnstile /'tɜːnstaɪl/ *n.* cancelletto girevole *m.*

turntable /'tɜːnteɪbl/ *n.* piattaforma girevole *f.*; (*on record-player*) piatto (di giradischi) *m.*

turpentine /'tɜːpəntaɪn/ *n.* trementina *f.*

turquoise /'tɜːkwɔɪz/ *a.* & *n.* turchese *m.*

turret /'tʌrɪt/ *n.* torretta *f.*

turtle /'tɜːtl/ *n.* tartaruga *f.* ~**-neck** *n.* collo alla ciclista *m.*

tusk /tʌsk/ *n.* zanna *f.*

tussle /'tʌsl/ *v.i.* ~ (**with**) rissare. —*n.* rissa *f.*

tussock /'tʌsək/ *n.* ciuffo d'erba *m.*

tutor /'tjuːtə(r)/ *n.* istitutore; (*univ.*) insegnante universitario *m.*

tutorial /tjuːˈtɔːrɪəl/ *n.* ora di istruzione individuale *f.*

tuxedo /tʌkˈsiːdəʊ/ *n.* (*pl.* **-os**) (*Amer.*) smoking *m. invar.*

TV /tiːˈviː/ *n.* televisione *f.*

twaddle /'twɒdl/ *n.* frottole *f.pl.*

twang /twæŋ/ *n.* vibrazione metallica *f.*; (*in voice*) suono nasale *m.* —*v.t./i.* (far) vibrare.

tweed /twiːd/ *n.* tweed *m. invar.*

tweet /twiːt/ *n.* cinguettio *m.* —*v.i.* cinguettare.

tweezers /'twiːzəz/ *n.pl.* pinzetta *f.s.*

twel∥ve /twelv/ *a.* & *n.* dodici *m.* ~**fth** *a.* & *n.* dodicesimo, a *m.*, *f.*

twent∥y /'twentɪ/ *a.* & *n.* venti *m.* ~**ieth** *a.* & *n.* ventesimo, a *m.*, *f.*

twerp /twɜːp/ *n.* (*sl.*) stupido, a *m.*, *f.*

twice /twaɪs/ *adv.* due volte.

twiddle /'twɪdl/ *v.t.* giocherellare. ~ **one's thumbs** girarsi i pollici.

twig[1] /twɪg/ *n.* ramoscello *m.*

twig[2] /twɪg/ *v.t./i.* (*p.t.* **twigged**) (*fam.*) intuire.

twilight /'twaɪlaɪt/ *n.* crepuscolo *m.*

twin /twɪn/ *a.* & *n.* gemello, a *m.*, *f.*

twine /twaɪn/ *n.* spago *m.* —*v.t./i.* intrecciare, intrecciarsi.

twinge /twɪndʒ/ *n.* fitta *f.*

twinkle /'twɪŋkl/ *v.i.* scintillare. —*n.* scintillio *m.*

twirl /twɜːl/ *v.t./i.* attorcigliare, attorcigliarsi. —*n.* piroetta *f.*

twist /twɪst/ *v.t./i.* intrecciare, intrecciarsi; (*wring*) torcere; (*wind*) attorcigliare; (*distort*) distorcere; (*swindle, fam.*) abbindolare. —*n.* torsione *f.*; (*curve*) svolta *f.*; (*of character*) inclinazione *f.* ~**er** /-ə(r)/ *n.* (*swindler*) imbroglione, a *m.*, *f.*

twit[1] /twɪt/ *v.t.* (*p.t.* **twitted**) stuzzicare.

twit[2] /twɪt/ *n.* (*sl.*) fesso, a *m.*, *f.*

twitch /twɪtʃ/ *v.t./i.* contrarre, contrarsi. —*n.* tic *m.*; (*jerk*) strattone *m.*

twitter /'twɪtə(r)/ *v.i.* cinguettare; (*person*) cianciare. —*n.* cinguettio *m.* **in a** ~ (*fam.*) agitato.

two /tuː/ *a.* & *n.* due *m.* **in** ~ **minds** indeciso. ~**-faced** *a.* insincero. ~**piece** (**suit**) *n.* due pezzi *m. invar.* ~**way** *a.* (*traffic*) a due sensi.

twosome /'tuːsəm/ *n.* coppia *f.*

tycoon /taɪˈkuːn/ *n.* magnate *m.*

tying /'taɪɪŋ/ *see* **tie.**

typ∥e /taɪp/ *n.* tipo *m.*; (*typ.*) carattere (tipografico) *m.* —*v.t./i.* scrivere a macchina. ~**e-cast** *a.* (*actor*) a ruolo fisso.

typescript /'taɪpskrɪpt/ *n.* dattiloscritto *m.*

typewrit∥er /'taɪpraɪtə(r)/ *n.* macchina per scrivere *f.* ~**ten** /-ɪtn/ *a.* scritto a macchina.

typhoid /'taɪfɔɪd/ *n.* ~ **fever** tifo *m.*

typhoon /taɪˈfuːn/ *n.* tifone *m.*

typical /'tɪpɪkl/ *a.* tipico. ~**ly** *adv.* tipicamente.

typify /'tɪpɪfaɪ/ v.t. tipicizzare.
typi|ng /'taɪpɪŋ/ n. dattilografia f. ~**st** n. dattilografo, a m., f.
typography /taɪˈpɒɡrəfɪ/ n. tipografia f.

tyrann|y /'tɪrənɪ/ n. tirannia f. ~**ical** /-'rænɪkl/ a. tirannico. ~**ize** v.i. tiranneggiare.
tyrant /'taɪərənt/ n. tiranno, a m., f.
tyre /'taɪə(r)/ n. gomma f.

U

ubiquitous /juːˈbɪkwɪtəs/ a. onnipresente.

udder /ˈʌdə(r)/ n. mammella di vacca f.

ugl|y /ˈʌglɪ/ a. (-ier, -iest) brutto. ~iness n. bruttezza f.

UK n. abbr. see unite.

ulcer /ˈʌlsə(r)/ n. ulcera f. ~ous a. ulceroso.

ulterior /ʌlˈtɪərɪə(r)/ a. ulteriore. ~ motive n. secondo fine m.

ultimate /ˈʌltɪmət/ a. definitivo; (cause etc.) fondamentale. ~ly adv. alla fine.

ultimatum /ʌltɪˈmeɪtəm/ n. (pl. -ums) ultimatum m. invar.

ultra- /ˈʌltrə/ pref. ultra-.

ultramarine /ʌltrəməˈriːn/ a. oltremarino. —n. azzurro oltremare m.

ultrasonic /ʌltrəˈsɒnɪk/ a. ultrasonico.

ultraviolet /ʌltrəˈvaɪəlɪt/ a. ultravioletto.

umbilical /ʌmˈbɪlɪkl/ a. ombelicale. ~ cord n. cordone ombelicale m.

umbrage /ˈʌmbrɪdʒ/ n. risentimento m. take ~ offendersi.

umbrella /ʌmˈbrelə/ n. ombrello m.

umpire /ˈʌmpaɪə(r)/ n. arbitro m. —v.t. arbitrare.

umpteen /ˈʌmptiːn/ a. (sl.) innumerevole. ~th a. (sl.) ennesimo.

UN abbr. see unite.

un- /ʌn/ pref. in, non.

unable /ʌnˈeɪbl/ a. incapace (to di). be ~ to non potere.

unabridged /ʌnəˈbrɪdʒd/ a. integrale.

unaccountabl|e /ʌnəˈkaʊntəbl/ a. inspiegabile. ~y adv. inspiegabilmente.

unaccustomed /ʌnəˈkʌstəmd/ a. insolito. be ~ to non essere abituato a.

unadopted /ʌnəˈdɒptɪd/ a. (of road) privata.

unadulterated /ʌnəˈdʌltəreɪtɪd/ a. puro.

unaffected /ʌnəˈfektɪd/ a. senza affettazione.

unaided /ʌnˈeɪdɪd/ a. da solo.

unalloyed /ʌnəˈlɔɪd/ a. genuino.

unanimous /juːˈnænɪməs/ a. unanime. ~ly adv. unanimemente.

unannounced /ʌnəˈnaʊnst/ a. inaspettato.

unarmed /ʌnˈɑːmd/ a. disarmato.

unassuming /ʌnəˈsjuːmɪŋ/ a. senza pretese.

unattached /ʌnəˈtætʃt/ a. senza legami.

unattended /ʌnəˈtendɪd/ a. (car etc.) incustodito.

unattractive /ʌnəˈtræktɪv/ a. poco attraente.

unavoidabl|e /ʌnəˈvɔɪdəbl/ a. inevitabile. ~y adv. inevitabilmente.

unaware /ʌnəˈweə(r)/ a. ignaro. ~s /-eəz/ adv. inaspettatamente.

unbalanced /ʌnˈbælənst/ a. squilibrato.

unbearabl|e /ʌnˈbeərəbl/ a. insopportabile. ~y adv. insopportabilmente.

unbeat|able /ʌnˈbiːtəbl/ a. imbattibile. ~en a. non battuto.

unbeknown /ʌnbɪˈnəʊn/ a. (fam.) ~ to all'insaputa di.

unbelievable /ʌnbɪˈliːvəbl/ a. incredibile.

unbend /ʌnˈbend/ v.t. (p.t. unbent) raddrizzare. —v.i. (relax) distendersi. ~ing a. inflessibile.

unbiased /ʌnˈbaɪəst/ a. obiettivo.

unbidden /ʌnˈbɪdn/ a. spontaneo.

unblock /ʌnˈblɒk/ v.t. sbloccare.

unbolt /ʌnˈbəʊlt/ v.t. togliere il chiavistello.

unborn /ʌnˈbɔːn/ a. non ancora nato.

unbounded /ʌnˈbaʊndɪd/ a. illimitato.

unbreakable /ʌnˈbreɪkəbl/ a. infrangibile.

unbridled /ʌnˈbraɪdld/ a. sfrenato.

unburden /ʌnˈbɜːdn/ v.t. ~ o.s. sfogarsi.

unbutton /ʌnˈbʌtn/ v.t. sbottonare.

uncalled-for /ʌnˈkɔːldfɔː(r)/ a. fuori luogo.

uncanny /ʌnˈkænɪ/ a. (-ier, -iest) misterioso.

unceasing /ʌnˈsiːsɪŋ/ a. incessante.

unceremonious /ʌnserɪˈməʊnjəs/ a. privo di cerimonie.

uncertain /ʌnˈsɜːtn/ a. incerto; (of weather) instabile. ~ty n. incertezza f.

unchanged /ʌnˈtʃeɪndʒd/ a. invariato.

uncharitable /ʌnˈtʃærɪtəbl/ a. severo.

uncle /ˈʌŋkl/ n. zio m.

unclean /ʌnˈkliːn/ a. sporco.

unclear /ʌnˈklɪə(r)/ *a.* poco chiaro.

uncomfortable /ʌnˈkʌmfətəbl/ *a.* scomodo; (*unpleasant*) spiacevole. **feel** ~ sentirsi a disagio.

uncommon /ʌnˈkɒmən/ *a.* insolito.

uncompromising/ʌnˈkɒmprəmaɪzɪŋ/ *a.* intransigente.

unconditional /ʌnkənˈdɪʃənl/ *a.* incondizionato. ~**ly** *adv.* incondizionatamente.

unconscionable /ʌnˈkɒnʃənəbl/ *a.* senza scrupoli; (*fig.*) irragionevole.

unconscious /ʌnˈkɒnʃəs/ *a.* incosciente; (*unaware*) ignaro. ~**ly** *adv.* inconsciamente.

unconventional /ʌnkənˈvenʃənl/ *a.* non convenzionale.

uncooperative /ʌnkəʊˈɒpərətɪv/ *a.* non cooperativo.

uncork /ʌnˈkɔːk/ *v.t.* sturare.

uncouth /ʌnˈkuːθ/ *a.* zotico.

uncover /ʌnˈkʌvə(r)/ *v.t.* scoperchiare; (*expose*) esporre.

uncrushable /ʌnˈkrʌʃəbl/ *a.* ingualcibile.

unctious /ˈʌŋktʃʊəs/ *a.* untuoso.

undecided /ʌndɪˈsaɪdɪd/ *a.* indeciso.

undeniabl|e /ʌndɪˈnaɪəbl/ *a.* innegabile. ~**y** *adv.* innegabilmente.

under /ˈʌndə(r)/ *prep.* sotto; (*less than*) al di sotto di; (*in the course of*) in. *—adv.* sotto. ~ **age** *a.* minorenne. ~ **way** *adv.* in corso di realizzazione.

under- /ˈʌndə(r)/ *pref.* sotto-.

undercarriage /ˈʌndəkærɪdʒ/ *n.* (*aeron.*) carrello *m.*

underclothes /ˈʌndəkləʊðz/ *n.pl.* biancheria intima *f.s.*

undercoat /ˈʌndəkəʊt/ *n.* (*of paint*) prima mano *f.*

undercover /ʌndəˈkʌvə(r)/ *a.* segreto.

undercurrent /ˈʌndəkʌrənt/ *n.* corrente sottomarina *f.*; (*fig.*) tendenza nascosta *f.*

undercut /ˈʌndəkʌt/ *v.t.* (*p.t.* **undercut**) (*comm.*) vendere a minor prezzo di.

underdog /ˈʌndədɒg/ *n.* perdente *m.*

underdone /ʌndəˈdʌn/ *a.* (*meat*) al sangue.

underestimate /ʌndərˈestɪmeɪt/ *v.t.* sottovalutare.

underfed /ʌndəˈfed/ *a.* denutrito.

underfoot /ʌndəˈfʊt/ *adv.* sotto i piedi.

undergo /ˈʌndəgəʊ/ *v.t.* (*p.t.* **-went**, *p.p.* **-gone**) subire.

undergraduate /ʌndəˈgrædʒʊət/ *n.*

studen|te, **-tessa** (universitario, a) *m.*, *f.*

underground[1] /ʌndəˈgraʊnd/ *adv.* sottoterra; (*in secret*) in segreto.

underground[2] /ˈʌndəgraʊnd/ *a.* sotterraneo; (*secret*) segreto. *—n.* metropolitana *f.*

undergrowth /ˈʌndəgrəʊθ/ *n.* sottobosco *m.*

underhand[1] /ˈʌndəhænd/ *a.* clandestino.

underhand[2] /ʌndəˈhænd/ *adv.* sottomano.

underlay /ˈʌndəleɪ/ *n.* carta impermeabile *f.*

underl|ie /ʌndəˈlaɪ/ *v.t.* (*p.t.* **-lay**, *p.p.* **-lain**, *pres.p.* **-lying**) stare sotto; (*fig.*) essere alla base di. ~**ying** *a.* fondamentale.

underline /ʌndəˈlaɪn/ *v.t.* sottolineare.

underling /ˈʌndəlɪŋ/ *n.* subalterno, a *m.*, *f.*

undermine /ʌndəˈmaɪn/ *v.t.* minare; (*fig.*) insidiare.

underneath /ʌndəˈniːθ/ *prep.* & *adv.* sotto.

underpaid /ʌndəˈpeɪd/ *a.* mal pagato.

underpants /ˈʌndəpænts/ *n.pl.* mutande *f.pl.*

underpass /ˈʌndəpaːs/ *n.* sottopassaggio *m.*

underprivileged /ʌndəˈprɪvəlɪdʒd/ *a.* non abbiente.

underrate /ʌndəˈreɪt/ *v.t.* sottovalutare.

undersell /ʌndəˈsel/ *v.t.* (*p.t.* **-sold**) vendere a minor prezzo di.

undersigned /ˈʌndəsaɪnd/ *a.* sottoscritto.

undersized /ʌndəˈsaɪzd/ *a.* di misura inferiore.

understand /ʌndəˈstænd/ *v.t./i.* (*p.t.* **-stood**) capire; (*realize*) rendersi conto. ~**able** *a.* comprensibile. ~**ably** *adv.* comprensibilmente.

understanding /ʌndəˈstændɪŋ/ *a.* comprensivo. *—n.* comprensione *f.*; (*agreement*) accordo *m.*

understatement /ʌndəˈsteɪtmənt/ *n.* understatement *m. invar.*

understudy /ˈʌndəstʌdɪ/ *n.* sostituto, a *m.*, *f.*

undertake /ʌndəˈteɪk/ *v.t.* (*p.t.* **-took**, *p.p.* **-taken**) impegnarsi (a); (*engage in*) intraprendere.

undertaker /ˈʌndəteɪkə(r)/ *n.* imprenditore di pompe funebri *m.*

undertaking   450   unhook

undertaking /ʌndə'teɪkɪŋ/ n. impegno m.; (*promise*) promessa f.

undertone /'ʌndətəʊn/ n. tono sommesso m.; (*fig.*) sottofondo m.

undertow /'ʌndətəʊ/ n. risacca f.

undervalue /ʌndə'væljuː/ v.t. sottovalutare.

underwater /ʌndə'wɔːtə(r)/ a. subacqueo. —adv. sott'acqua.

underwear /'ʌndəweə(r)/ n. biancheria (intima) f.

underweight /'ʌndəweɪt/ a. sotto peso.

underwent /ʌndə'went/ see **undergo.**

underworld /'ʌndəwɜːld/ n. (*criminals*) malavita f.

underwrite /ʌndə'raɪt/ v.t. (*p.t.* -**wrote**, *p.p.* -**written**) sottoscrivere; (*comm*) assicurare. ~**r** /-ə(r)/ n. assicuratore m.

undeserved /ʌndɪ'zɜːvd/ a. immeritato.

undesirable /ʌndɪ'zaɪərəbl/ a. indesiderabile.

undeveloped /ʌndɪ'veləpt/ a. non sviluppato; (*land*) non sfruttato.

undies /'ʌndɪz/ n.pl. (*fam.*) biancheria intima (da donna) f.s.

undignified /ʌn'dɪgnɪfaɪd/ a. non dignitoso.

undo /ʌn'duː/ v.t. (*p.t.* -**did**, *p.p.* -**done**) disfare; (*ruin*) distruggere. **leave** ~**ne** tralasciare.

undoubted /ʌn'daʊtɪd/ a. indubitato. ~**ly** adv. senza dubbio.

undress /ʌn'dres/ v.t./i. svestire, svestirsi.

undu|e /ʌn'djuː/ a. eccessivo. ~**ly** adv. eccessivamente.

undulat|e /'ʌndjʊleɪt/ v.i. ondulare. ~**ion** /-'leɪʃn/ n. ondulazione f.

undying /ʌn'daɪɪŋ/ a. eterno.

unearth /ʌn'ɜːθ/ v.t. dissotterrare; (*fig.*) scovare.

unearthly /ʌn'ɜːθlɪ/ a. soprannaturale; (*fam., impossible*) assurdo.

uneas|y /ʌn'iːzɪ/ a. a disagio; (*worrying*) inquieto. ~**ily** adv. a disagio; con inquietudine.

uneconomic /ʌniːkə'nɒmɪk/ a. poco rimunerativo.

unemploy|ed /ʌnɪm'plɔɪd/ a. disoccupato; (*not in use*) inutilizzato. ~**ment** n. disoccupazione f.

unending /ʌn'endɪŋ/ a. senza fine.

unequal /ʌn'iːkwəl/ a. disuguale.

unequivocal /ʌnɪ'kwɪvəkl/ a. inequivocabile.

unerring /ʌn'ɜːrɪŋ/ a. infallibile.

unethical /ʌn'eθɪkl/ a. contro l'etica.

uneven /ʌn'iːvn/ a. irregolare.

unexceptional /ʌnɪk'sepʃənl/ a. comune.

unexpected /ʌnɪk'spektɪd/ a. inaspettato.

unfailing /ʌn'feɪlɪŋ/ a. infallibile.

unfair /ʌn'feə(r)/ a. ingiusto. ~**ly** adv. ingiustamente. ~**ness** n. ingiustizia f.

unfaithful /ʌn'feɪθfl/ a. infedele. ~**ness** n. infedeltà f.

unfamiliar /ʌnfə'mɪlɪə(r)/ a. inconsueto. **be** ~ **with** non conoscere.

unfasten /ʌn'fɑːsn/ v.t. slacciare.

unfavourable /ʌn'feɪvərəbl/ a. sfavorevole.

unfeeling /ʌn'fiːlɪŋ/ a. insensibile.

unfit /ʌn'fɪt/ a. inadatto; (*unwell*) in cattiva salute.

unflinching /ʌn'flɪntʃɪŋ/ a. risoluto.

unfold /ʌn'fəʊld/ v.t. spiegare; (*fig.*) rivelare. —v.i. (*view etc.*) distendersi.

unforeseen /ʌnfɔː'siːn/ a. imprevisto.

unforgettable /ʌnfə'getəbl/ a. indimenticabile.

unforgivable /ʌnfə'gɪvəbl/ a. imperdonabile.

unfortunate /ʌn'fɔːtʃʊnət/ a. sfortunato; (*regrettable*) spiacevole. ~**ly** adv. sfortunatamente, purtroppo.

unfounded /ʌn'faʊndɪd/ a. infondato.

unfriendly /ʌn'frendlɪ/ a. poco amichevole.

unfurl /ʌn'fɜːl/ v.t./i. spiegare, spiegarsi.

ungainly /ʌn'geɪnlɪ/ a. sgraziato.

ungodly /ʌn'gɒdlɪ/ a. empio. ~ **hour** (*fam.*) ora impossibile.

ungrateful /ʌn'greɪtfl/ a. ingrato.

unguarded /ʌn'gɑːdɪd/ a. indifeso; (*incautious*) incauto.

unhapp|y /ʌn'hæpɪ/ a. (-**ier**, -**iest**) infelice; (*unsuitable*) inopportuno. ~**y with** (*plans etc.*) insoddisfatto di. ~**ily** adv. infelicemente; (*unfortunately*) purtroppo. ~**iness** n. infelicità f.

unharmed /ʌn'hɑːmd/ a. incolume.

unhealth|y /ʌn'helθɪ/ a. (-**ier**, -**iest**) poco sano; (*insanitary*) malsano. ~**ily** adv. in modo insalubre.

unhinge /ʌn'hɪndʒ/ v.t. scardinare; (*fig.*) sconvolgere.

unholy /ʌn'həʊlɪ/ a. (-**ier**, -**iest**) empio; (*terrible, fam.*) spaventoso.

unhook /ʌn'hʊk/ v.t. sganciare.

unhurt /ʌn'hɜːt/ *a.* illeso.

unicorn /'juːnɪkɔːn/ *n.* unicorno *m.*

uniform /'juːnɪfɔːm/ *a.* & *n.* uniforme *f.* **~ly** *adv.* uniformemente. **~ity** /-'fɔːmətɪ/ *n.* uniformità *f.*

unif|y /'juːnɪfaɪ/ *v.t.* unificare. **~ica- tion** /-ɪ'keɪʃn/ *n.* unificazione *f.*

unilateral /juːnɪ'lætrəl/ *a.* unilaterale.

unimpeachable /ʌnɪm'piːtʃəbl/ *a.* ir- reprensibile.

unintentional /ʌnɪn'tenʃənl/ *a.* invo- lontario.

union /'juːnjən/ *n.* unione *f.*; (*trade union*) sindacato *m.* **U~ Jack** *n.* ban- diera britannica *f.* **~ist** *n.* sindacali- sta *m./f.*

unique /juː'niːk/ *a.* unico. **~ly** *adv.* unicamente.

unisex /'juːnɪseks/ *a.* unisex.

unison /'juːnɪsn/ *n.* **in ~** all'unisono.

unit /'juːnɪt/ *n.* unità *f.*; (*of furniture etc.*) elemento *m.* **~ trust** *n.* fondo comune d'investimento *m.*

unite /juː'naɪt/ *v.t./i.* unire, unirsi. **U~d Kingdom (UK)** *n.* Regno Unito *m.* **U~d Nations (Organization) (UNO)** *n.* (Organizzazione delle) Na- zioni Unite *f.pl.* **U~d States (of America) (USA)** *n.* Stati Uniti (d'America) *m.pl.*

unity /'juːnətɪ/ *n.* unità *f.*; (*fig.*) accordo *m.*

universal /juːnɪ'vɜːsl/ *a.* universale.

universe /'juːnɪvɜːs/ *n.* universo *m.*

university /juːnɪ'vɜːsətɪ/ *n.* università *f.*

unjust /ʌn'dʒʌst/ *a.* ingiusto.

unkempt /ʌn'kempt/ *a.* trasandato.

unkind /ʌn'kaɪnd/ *a.* scortese. **~ly** *adv.* scortesemente. **~ness** *n.* catti- veria *f.*

unknown /ʌn'nəʊn/ *a.* sconosciuto. **U~ Soldier** *n.* Milite Ignoto *m.*

unlawful /ʌn'lɔːfl/ *a.* illecito.

unleash /ʌn'liːʃ/ *v.t.* sguinzagliare; (*fig.*) scatenare.

unless /ʌn'les/ *conj.* a meno che.

unlike /ʌn'laɪk/ *a.* dissimile (da); (*not typical*) non tipico. **—prep.** a diffe- renza di.

unlikel|y /ʌn'laɪklɪ/ *a.* improbabile. **~ihood** *n.* improbabilità *f.*

unlimited /ʌn'lɪmɪtɪd/ *a.* illimitato.

unload /ʌn'ləʊd/ *v.t.* scaricare.

unlock /ʌn'lɒk/ *v.t.* aprire (con chia- ve).

unluck|y /ʌn'lʌkɪ/ *a.* (**-ier, -iest**) sfor-

tunato; (*number*) che porta sfortuna. **~ily** *adv.* sfortunatamente.

unmanly /ʌn'mænlɪ/ *a.* poco virile.

unmanned /ʌn'mænd/ *a.* senza equi- paggio.

unmarried /ʌn'mærɪd/ *a.* non sposato. **~ mother** *n.* ragazza madre *f.*

unmask /ʌn'mɑːsk/ *v.t./i.* sma- scherare, smascherarsi.

unmentionable /ʌn'menʃənəbl/ *a.* in- nominabile.

unmistakabl|e /ʌnmɪ'steɪkəbl/ *a.* in- confondibile. **~y** *adv.* chiaramente.

unmitigated /ʌn'mɪtɪgeɪtɪd/ *a.* assolu- to.

unmoved /ʌn'muːvd/ *a.* fermo; (*fig.*) impassibile.

unnatural /ʌn'nætʃrəl/ *a.* innaturale; (*not normal*) anormale.

unnecessar|y /ʌn'nesəsrɪ/ *a.* inutile. **~ily** *adv.* inutilmente.

unnerve /ʌn'nɜːv/ *v.t.* snervare.

unnoticed /ʌn'nəʊtɪst/ *a.* inosservato.

unobtainable /ʌnəb'teɪnəbl/ *a.* non ot- tenibile.

unobtrusive /ʌnəb'truːsɪv/ *a.* riserva- to.

unofficial /ʌnə'fɪʃl/ *a.* non ufficiale. **~ly** *adv.* ufficiosamente.

unpack /ʌn'pæk/ *v.t./i.* disfare le vali- gie; (*parcel*) spacchettare.

unpalatable /ʌn'pælətəbl/ *a.* sgrade- vole.

unparalleled /ʌn'pærəleld/ *a.* senza pari.

unpick /ʌn'pɪk/ *v.t.* scucire.

unpleasant /ʌn'pleznt/ *a.* spiacevole. **~ness** *n.* spiacevolezza *f.*

unplug /ʌn'plʌg/ *v.t.* staccare.

unpopular /ʌn'pɒpjʊlə(r)/ *a.* im- popolare.

unprecedented /ʌn'presɪdentɪd/ *a.* senza precedenti.

unpredictable /ʌnprɪ'dɪktəbl/ *a.* im- prevedibile.

unpremeditated /ʌnprɪ'medɪteɪtɪd/ *a.* involontario.

unprepared /ʌnprɪ'peəd/ *a.* im- preparato.

unprepossessing /ʌnpriːpə'zesɪŋ/ *a.* poco attraente.

unpretentious /ʌnprɪ'tenʃəs/ *a.* senza pretese.

unprincipled /ʌn'prɪnsəpld/ *a.* senza principi.

unprofessional /ʌnprə'feʃnəl/ *a.* con- trario alle regole professionali.

unqualified /ʌn'kwɒlɪfaɪd/ *a.* non qualificato; (*fig.*) assoluto.

unquestionable /ʌn'kwestʃənəbl/ *a.* incontestabile.

unquote /ʌn'kwəʊt/ *v.i.* chiudere le virgolette.

unravel /ʌn'rævl/ *v.t./i.* (*p.t.* **unravelled**) districare, districarsi; (*knitting etc.*) disfare.

unreal /ʌn'rɪəl/ *a.* irreale.

unreasonable /ʌn'riːznəbl/ *a.* irragionevole.

unrelated /ʌnrɪ'leɪtɪd/ *a.* (*facts*) senza rapporto; (*person*) non imparentato.

unreliable /ʌnrɪ'laɪəbl/ *a.* inattendibile; (*person*) che non dà affidamento.

unrelieved /ʌnrɪ'liːvd/ *a.* non alleviato.

unremitting /ʌnrɪ'mɪtɪŋ/ *a.* incessante.

unrepentant /ʌnrɪ'pentənt/ *a.* impenitente.

unrequited /ʌnrɪ'kwaɪtɪd/ *a.* non corrisposto.

unreservedly /ʌnrɪ'zɜːvɪdlɪ/ *adv.* senza riserve.

unrest /ʌn'rest/ *n.* fermento *m.*

unrivalled /ʌn'raɪvld/ *a.* ineguagliato.

unroll /ʌn'rəʊl/ *v.t./i.* svolgere, svolgersi.

unruly /ʌn'ruːlɪ/ *a.* indisciplinato.

unsafe /ʌn'seɪf/ *a.* pericoloso; (*person*) in pericolo.

unsaid /ʌn'sed/ *a.* inespresso.

unsatisfactory /ʌnsætɪs'fæktərɪ/ *a.* poco soddisfacente.

unsavoury /ʌn'seɪvərɪ/ *a.* disgustoso.

unscathed /ʌn'skeɪðd/ *a.* illeso.

unscramble /ʌn'skræmbl/ *v.t.* decifrare.

unscrew /ʌn'skruː/ *v.t.* svitare.

unscrupulous /ʌn'skruːpjʊləs/ *a.* senza scrupoli.

unseat /ʌn'siːt/ *v.t.* (*pol.*) privare del seggio.

unseemly /ʌn'siːmlɪ/ *a.* indecoroso.

unseen /ʌn'siːn/ *a.* inosservato. —*n.* traduzione a prima vista *f.*

unselfish /ʌn'selfɪʃ/ *a.* disinteressato.

unsettle /ʌn'setl/ *v.t.* turbare. **~d** *a.* turbato; (*weather*) instabile; (*bill*) non saldato.

unshakeable /ʌn'ʃeɪkəbl/ *a.* irremovibile.

unsightly /ʌn'saɪtlɪ/ *a.* sgraziato.

unskilled /ʌn'skɪld/ *a.* inesperto. **~ worker** *n.* manovale *m.*

unsociable /ʌn'səʊʃəbl/ *a.* scontroso.

unsolicited /ʌnsə'lɪsɪtɪd/ *a.* non richiesto.

unsophisticated /ʌnsə'fɪstɪkeɪtɪd/ *a.* naturale.

unsound /ʌn'saʊnd/ *a.* difettoso. **of ~ mind** malato di mente.

unsparing /ʌn'speərɪŋ/ *a.* prodigo.

unspeakable /ʌn'spiːkəbl/ *a.* indicibile.

unstable /ʌn'steɪbl/ *a.* instabile.

unsteady /ʌn'stedɪ/ *a.* instabile; (*hand*) malfermo.

unstinted /ʌn'stɪntɪd/ *a.* abbondante.

unstuck /ʌn'stʌk/ *a.* scollato. **come ~** (*fam., fail*) andare a monte.

unstudied /ʌn'stʌdɪd/ *a.* spontaneo.

unsuccessful /ʌnsək'sesfl/ *a.* non riuscito. **be ~** non aver successo.

unsuitable /ʌn'sjuːtəbl/ *a.* inadatto; (*inconvenient*) sconveniente.

unsuspecting /ʌnsə'spektɪŋ/ *a.* fiducioso.

unthinkable /ʌn'θɪŋkəbl/ *a.* impensabile.

untidy /ʌn'taɪdɪ/ *a.* (**-ier, -iest**) disordinato. **~ily** *adv.* disordinatamente. **~iness** *n.* disordine *m.*

untie /ʌn'taɪ/ *v.t.* slegare.

until /ʌn'tɪl/ *prep. & conj.* fino a.

untimely /ʌn'taɪmlɪ/ *a.* inopportuno; (*premature*) prematuro.

untiring /ʌn'taɪərɪŋ/ *a.* instancabile.

untold /ʌn'təʊld/ *a.* incalcolabile.

untoward /ʌntə'wɔːd/ *a.* sconveniente.

untraceable /ʌn'treɪsəbl/ *a.* introvabile.

untried /ʌn'traɪd/ *a.* non provato.

untrue /ʌn'truː/ *a.* falso.

unused /ʌn'juːzd/ *a.* non (ancora) usato. **~ to** non essere abituato a.

unusual /ʌn'juːʒʊəl/ *a.* insolito. **~ly** *adv.* eccezionalmente.

unutterable /ʌn'ʌtərəbl/ *a.* indicibile.

unveil /ʌn'veɪl/ *v.t./i.* scoprire; (*disclose*) svelare.

unversed /ʌn'vɜːst/ *a.* inesperto.

unwanted /ʌn'wɒntɪd/ *a.* indesiderato.

unwarranted /ʌn'wɒrəntɪd/ *a.* ingiustificato.

unwelcome /ʌn'welkəm/ *a.* male accolto; (*guest*) sgradito.

unwell /ʌn'wel/ *a.* indisposto.

unwieldy /ʌn'wiːldɪ/ *a.* ingombrante.

unwilling /ʌn'wɪlɪŋ/ *a.* contrario. **~ly** *adv.* mal volentieri.

unwind /ʌn'waɪnd/ *v.t./i.* (*p.t.* **un-**

wound) svolgere, svolgersi; (*relax*, *fam.*) rilassarsi.

unwise /ʌnˈwaɪz/ *a.* imprudente.

unwitting /ʌnˈwɪtɪŋ/ *a.* inconsapevole; (*involuntary*) involontario. **~ly** *adv.* involontariamente.

unworthy /ʌnˈwɜːðɪ/ *a.* indegno.

unwrap /ʌnˈræp/ *v.t.* (*p.t.* **unwrapped**) svolgere; (*a present*) scartare.

unwritten /ʌnˈrɪtn/ *a.* (*agreement*) tacito.

up /ʌp/ *adv.* su, in su; (*out of bed*) alzato. *—prep.* su, per su. *—v.t.* (*p.t.* **upped**) aumentare. **be ~ to** (*plot*) tramare; (*one's turn*) toccare a; (*task*) essere all'altezza di; (*reach*) arrivare a. **be one ~ on** essere in vantaggio su. **feel ~ to it** sentirsela. **~ against** alle prese con. **~ here** quassù. **~ in** (*fam.*) bene informato su. **~ there** lassù. **~ to** fino a. **ups and downs** *n.pl.* alti e bassi *m.pl.* **~-market** *a.* di qualità. **~-to-date** *a.* aggiornato; (*news*) recente. **what is ~?** cosa succede?

upbraid /ʌpˈbreɪd/ *v.t.* rimproverare.

upbringing /ˈʌpbrɪŋɪŋ/ *n.* educazione *f.*

update /ʌpˈdeɪt/ *v.t.* aggiornare.

upgrade /ʌpˈɡreɪd/ *v.t.* promuovere.

upheaval /ʌpˈhiːvl/ *n.* sconvolgimento *m.*

uphill /ʌpˈhɪl/ *a. & adv.* in salita.

uphold /ʌpˈhəʊld/ *v.t.* (*p.t.* **upheld**) sostenere.

upholster /ʌpˈhəʊlstə(r)/ *v.t.* tappezzare. **~er** /-rə(r)/ *n.* tappezziere, a *m.*, *f.* **~y** *n.* tappezzeria *f.*

upkeep /ˈʌpkiːp/ *n.* mantenimento *m.*

upon /əˈpɒn/ *prep.* su. **once ~ a time** (c'era) una volta.

upper /ˈʌpə(r)/ *a.* superiore. *—n.* (*of shoe*) tomaia *f.* **~ class** *n.* alta borghesia *f.* **~ hand** *n.* predominio *m.* **~most** *a.* il più alto.

uppish /ˈʌpɪʃ/ *a.* presuntuoso.

upright /ˈʌpraɪt/ *a.* dritto; (*of piano*) verticale. *—n.* montante *m.*

uprising /ˈʌpraɪzɪŋ/ *n.* rivolta *f.*

uproar /ˈʌprɔː(r)/ *n.* tumulto *m.* **~ious** /-ˈrɔːrɪəs/ *a.* tumultuante.

uproot /ʌpˈruːt/ *v.t.* sradicare.

upset[1] /ʌpˈset/ *v.t.* (*p.t.* **upset, pres.p.** **upsetting**) rovesciare; (*plan etc.*) sconvolgere; (*distress*) turbare.

upset[2] /ˈʌpset/ *n.* sconvolgimento *m.*; (*of stomach*) disturbo *m.*

upshot /ˈʌpʃɒt/ *n.* risultato *m.*

upside-down /ʌpsaɪdˈdaʊn/ *adv.* sottosopra. **turn ~** capovolgere.

upstairs[1] /ʌpˈsteəz/ *adv.* (al piano) di sopra.

upstairs[2] /ˈʌpsteəz/ *a.* del piano superiore.

upstart /ˈʌpstɑːt/ *n.* arrivato, a *m.*, *f.*

upstream /ʌpˈstriːm/ *adv.* controcorrente.

upsurge /ˈʌpsɜːdʒ/ *n.* insorgenza *f.*

uptake /ˈʌpteɪk/ *n.* **quick on the ~** veloce di comprendonio.

uptight /ˈʌptaɪt/ *a.* (*fam.*) teso.

upturn /ˈʌptɜːn/ *n.* ripresa *f.*

upward /ˈʌpwəd/ *a. & adv.*, **~s** *adv.* verso l'alto.

uranium /jʊˈreɪnɪəm/ *n.* uranio *m.*

urban /ˈɜːbən/ *a.* urbano. **~ize** *v.t.* urbanizzare.

urbane /ɜːˈbeɪn/ *a.* cortese.

urchin /ˈɜːtʃɪn/ *n.* monello *m.*

urge /ɜːdʒ/ *v.t.* esortare (**to**, a). *—n.* forte desiderio *m.* **~ on** spronare.

urgen|t /ˈɜːdʒənt/ *a.* urgente. **~cy** *n.* urgenza *f.* **~tly** *adv.* urgentemente.

urin|e /ˈjʊərɪn/ *n.* urina *f.* **~ate** *v.i.* urinare.

urn /ɜːn/ *n.* urna *f.*

us /ʌs/ *pron.* ci; (*after prep.*) noi.

US, USA *abbr. see* **unite.**

usage /ˈjuːzɪdʒ/ *n.* uso *m.*

use[1] /juːz/ *v.t.* usare. **~ up** consumare. **~r** /-ə(r)/ utente *m.*/*f.* **~d** *a.* (*clothes*) smesso.

use[2] /juːs/ *n.* uso *m.* **be of ~** essere utile. **it is no ~** è inutile. **make ~ of** adoperare. **~less** *a.* inutile; (*person*) incapace.

used /juːst/ *p.t.* **he ~ to say** diceva. *—a.* **~ to** abituato a.

useful /ˈjuːsfl/ *a.* utile. **~ly** *adv.* utilmente.

usher /ˈʌʃə(r)/ *n.* usciere *m.* *—v.t.* **~ in** fare entrare. **~ette** *n.* maschera *f.*

USSR *abbr.* (*of* **Union of Soviet Socialist Republics**) URSS *f.*

usual /ˈjuːʒʊəl/ *a.* usuale. **as ~** come al solito. **~ly** *adv.* di solito.

usur|er /ˈjuːʒərə(r)/ *n.* usuraio, a *m.*, *f.* **~y** *n.* usura *f.*

usurp /juːˈzɜːp/ *v.t.* usurpare. **~er** /-ə(r)/ *n.* usurpa|tore, -trice *m.*, *f.*

utensil /juːˈtensl/ *n.* utensile *m.*

uterus /ˈjuːtərəs/ *n.* utero *m.*

utilitarian /juːtɪlɪˈteərɪən/ *a.* utilitario.

utility /juːˈtɪlətɪ/ *n.* utilità *f.* —*a.* utilitario. **public** ∼ *n.* servizio pubblico *m.*

utilize /ˈjuːtɪlaɪz/ *v.t.* utilizzare.

utmost /ˈʌtməʊst/ *a.* estremo. —*n.* **one's** ∼ il massimo *m.*

utter[1] /ˈʌtə(r)/ *a.* completo. ∼**ly** *adv.* completamente.

utter[2] /ˈʌtə(r)/ *v.t.* (*sound*) emettere; (*speak*) proferire. ∼**ance** *n.* espressione *f.*

U-turn /ˈjuːtɜːn/ *n.* inversione a U *f.*

V

vacan|cy /'veɪkənsɪ/ *n.* posto vacante *m.*; (*room*) stanza disponibile *f.* ~**t** *a.* vuoto; (*person*) assente.

vacate /və'keɪt/ *v.t.* lasciare libero.

vacation /və'keɪʃn/ *n.* (*Amer.*) vacanza *f.*

vaccinat|e /'væksɪ:neɪt/ *v.t.* vaccinare. ~**ion** /-'neɪʃn/ *n.* vaccinazione *f.*

vaccine /'væksi:n/ *n.* vaccino *m.*

vacuum /'vækjʊəm/ *n.* (*pl.* **-cua** *or* **-cuums**) vuoto *m.* ~ **cleaner** *n.* aspirapolvere *m. invar.* ~ **flask** *n.* thermos *m. invar.* (P.).

vagabond /'vægəbɒnd/ *n.* vagabondo, a *m., f.*

vagary /'veɪgərɪ/ *n.* capriccio *m.*

vagina /və'dʒaɪnə/ *n.* vagina *f.*

vagrant /'veɪgrənt/ *n.* accattone, a *m., f.*

vague /veɪg/ *a.* (**-er, -est**) vago; (*outline*) impreciso. ~**ly** *adv.* vagamente.

vain /veɪn/ *a.* (**-er, -est**) vanitoso; (*useless*) vano. **in** ~ invano. ~**ly** *adv.* vanamente.

valance /'væləns/ *n.* balza *f.*

vale /veɪl/ *n.* valle *f.*

valentine /'væləntaɪn/ *n.* (*card*) cartolina di San Valentino *f.*

valet /'vælɪt *or* 'væleɪ/ *n.* valletto *m.*

valiant /'vælɪənt/ *a.* valoroso.

valid /'vælɪd/ *a.* valido. ~**ate** *v.t.* convalidare. ~**ity** /-'i:dətɪ/ *n.* validità *f.*

valley /'vælɪ/ *n.* (*pl.* **-eys**) valle *f.*

valour /'vælə(r)/ *n.* valore *m.*

valuable /'væljʊəbl/ *a.* di valore; (*fig.*) prezioso. ~**s** *n. pl.* oggetti preziosi *m. pl.*

valuation /væljʊ'eɪʃn/ *n.* valutazione *f.*

value /'vælju:/ *n.* valore *m.*; (*usefulness*) utilità *f.* —*v.t.* valutare; (*cherish*) apprezzare. **face** ~ *n.* valore nominale *m.* ~ **added tax** (**VAT**) *n.* imposta sul valore aggiunto (IVA) *f.* ~**d** *a.* (*appreciated*) apprezzato. ~**r** /-ə(r)/ *n.* stima|tore, -trice *m., f.*

valve /vælv/ *n.* valvola *f.*

vamp /væmp/ *n.* (*fam.*) donna fatale *f.*

vampire /'væmpaɪə(r)/ *n.* vampiro *m.*

van /væn/ *n.* furgone *m.*; (*rail.*) bagagliaio *m.*

vandal /'vændl/ *n.* vandalo, a *m., f.* ~**ism** /-əlɪzəm/ *n.* vandalismo *m.*

~**ize** *v.t.* danneggiare intenzionalmente.

vane /veɪn/ *n.* banderuola *f.*; (*naut., aeron.*) manica a vento *f.*

vanguard /'vænɡɑ:d/ *n.* avanguardia *f.*

vanilla /və'nɪlə/ *n.* vaniglia *f.*

vanish /'vænɪʃ/ *v.i.* svanire.

vanity /'vænətɪ/ *n.* vanità *f.* ~ **bag** *or* **case** *n.* borsetta per il trucco *f.*

vantage /'vɑ:ntɪdʒ/ *n.* vantaggio *m.* ~-**point** *n.* punto favorevole *m.*

vapour /'veɪpə(r)/ *n.* vapore *m.*

vari|able /'veərɪəbl/ *a.* variabile. ~**ation** /-'eɪʃn/ *n.* variazione *f.* ~**ed** *a.* vario.

variance /'veərɪəns/ *n.* **at** ~ in disaccordo.

variant /'veərɪənt/ *a.* differente. —*n.* variante *f.*

varicoloured /'veərɪkʌləd/ *a.* variopinto.

varicose /'værɪkəʊs/ *a.* ~ **veins** *n.pl.* vene varicose *f.pl.*

variety /və'raɪətɪ/ *n.* varietà *f.*; (*quantity*) gran numero *m.* ~ **show** *n.* (*theatr.*) varietà *m.*

various /'veərɪəs/ *a.* vario. ~**ly** *adv.* variamente.

varnish /'vɑ:nɪʃ/ *n.* vernice *f.*; (*fig.*) aspetto esteriore *m.* —*v.t.* verniciare.

vary /'veərɪ/ *v.t./i.* variare. ~**ing** *a.* variabile.

vase /vɑ:z/ *n.* vaso *m.*

vasectomy /və'sektəmɪ/ *n.* vasectomia *f.*

vast /vɑ:st/ *a.* vasto. ~**ly** *adv.* di gran lunga. ~**ness** *n.* vastità *f.*

vat /væt/ *n.* tino *m.*

VAT *abbr. see* **value**.

vault[1] /vɔ:lt/ *n.* (*roof*) volta *f.*; (*in bank*) camera di sicurezza *f.*; (*tomb*) cripta *f.*

vault[2] /vɔ:lt/ *n.* volteggio *m.* —*v.t./i.* volteggiare.

vaunt /vɔ:nt/ *v.t.* vantare.

veal /vi:l/ *n.* carne di vitello *f.*

veer /vɪə(r)/ *v.i.* cambiare direzione; (*naut.*) virare.

vegetable /'vedʒtəbl/ *a.* & *n.* vegetale *m.* ~**s** *n.pl.* verdura *f.s.*

vegetarian /vedʒɪ'teərɪən/ *a.* & *n.* vegetariano, a *m., f.*

vegetate /'vedʒɪteɪt/ v.i. vegetare.
vegetation /vedʒɪ'teɪʃn/ n. vegetazione f.
vehemen|t /'viːəmənt/ a. veemente. ~ce n. veemenza f. ~tly adv. impetuosamente.
vehicle /'viːɪkl/ n. veicolo m.
veil /veɪl/ n. velo m. —v.t. velare. **take the** ~ farsi suora.
vein /veɪn/ n. vena f.; (mood) umore m. ~ed a. venato.
velocity /vɪ'lɒsətɪ/ n. velocità f.
velvet /'velvɪt/ n. velluto m. ~y a. vellutato.
venal /'viːnl/ a. venale. ~ity /-'nælətɪ/ n. venalità f.
vendetta /ven'detə/ n. vendetta f.
vending-machine /'vendɪŋməʃiːn/ n. distributore automatico m.
vendor /'vendə(r)/ n. vendi|tore, trice m., f.
veneer /və'nɪə(r)/ n. impiallacciatura f.; (fig.) vernice f.
venerable /'venərəbl/ a. venerabile.
venereal /və'nɪərɪəl/ a. venereo.
Venetian /və'niːʃn/ a. & n. veneziano, a m., f. **v**~ **blind** n. persiana alla veneziana f.
vengeance /'vendʒəns/ n. vendetta f. **with a** ~ (fig.) in modo straordinario.
Venice /'venɪs/ n. Venezia f.
venison /'venɪzn/ n. carne di cervo f.
venom /'venəm/ n. veleno m. ~ous a. velenoso.
vent /vent/ n. apertura f.; (in jacket etc.) spacco m.; (mech.) sfiatatoio m. —v.t. aprire un foro; (fig.) scaricare. **give** ~ **to** dar sfogo a.
ventilat|e /'ventɪleɪt/ v.t. ventilare. ~ion /-'leɪʃn/ n. ventilazione f. ~or /-ə(r)/ n. ventilatore m.
ventriloquist /ven'trɪləkwɪst/ n. ventriloquo, a m., f.
venture /'ventʃə(r)/ n. impresa f. —v.t./i. arrischiare, arrischiarsi. **at a** ~ alla ventura.
venue /'venjuː/ n. luogo di convegno m.
veranda /və'rændə/ n. veranda f.
verb /vɜːb/ n. verbo m.
verbal /'vɜːbl/ a. verbale. ~ly adv. verbalmente.
verbatim /vɜː'beɪtɪm/ a. letterale. —adv. parola per parola.
verbose /vɜː'bəʊs/ a. prolisso.
verdant /'vɜːdənt/ a. verdeggiante.
verdict /'vɜːdɪkt/ n. verdetto m.; (opinion) parere m.

verge /vɜːdʒ/ n. orlo m. —v.t. ~ **on** essere vicino a.
verger /'vɜːdʒə(r)/ n. sagrestano m.
verif|y /'verɪfaɪ/ v.t. verificare. ~ication /-ɪ'keɪʃn/ n. verifica f.
veritable /'verɪtəbl/ a. vero.
vermin /'vɜːmɪn/ n. insetti nocivi m.pl. ~ous a. verminoso.
vermouth /'vɜːməθ/ n. vermut m.
vernacular /və'nækjʊlə(r)/ n. vernacolo m.
versatil|e /'vɜːsətaɪl/ a. versatile. ~ity /-'tɪlətɪ/ n. versatilità f.
verse /vɜːs/ n. verso m.; (poetry) versi m.pl.; (of Bible) versetto m.
versed /vɜːst/ a. ~ **in** versato in.
version /'vɜːʃn/ n. versione f.; (translation) traduzione f.
versus /'vɜːsəs/ prep. contro.
vertebra /'vɜːtɪbrə/ n. (pl. -brae /-briː/) vertebra f.
vertical /'vɜːtɪkl/ a. & n. verticale f. ~ly adv. verticalmente.
vertigo /'vɜːtɪgəʊ/ n. vertigine f.
verve /vɜːv/ n. verve f.
very /'verɪ/ adv. molto, assai. —a. vero, proprio. **the** ~ **first** il primissimo. **the** ~ **thing** proprio ciò che ci vuole. ~ **well** benissimo.
vespers /'vespəz/ n.pl. vespri m.pl.
vessel /'vesl/ n. bastimento m.; (receptacle) recipiente m.; (anat.) vaso m.
vest /vest/ n. maglia f.; (Amer.) panciotto m. —v.t. conferire. ~ed **interest** n. interesse acquisito m.
vestige /'vestɪdʒ/ n. vestigio m.
vestment /'vestmənt/ n. (relig.) paramento m.
vestry /'vestrɪ/ n. sagrestia f.
vet /vet/ n. (fam.) veterinario, a m., f. —v.t. (p.t. vetted) esaminare.
veteran /'vetərən/ n. veterano, a m., f. ~ **car** n. auto d'epoca f.
veterinary /'vetrɪnrɪ/ a. veterinario. ~ **surgeon** n. medico veterinario m.
veto /'viːtəʊ/ n. (pl. -oes) proibizione f. —v.t. proibire.
vex /veks/ v.t. irritare. ~ation /-'seɪʃn/ n. vessazione f. ~ed **question** n. questione controversa f. ~ing a. fastidioso.
via /'vaɪə/ prep. via, per.
viab|le /'vaɪəbl/ a. vitale; (practicable) fattibile. ~ility /-'bɪlətɪ/ n. vitalità f.
viaduct /'vaɪədʌkt/ n. viadotto m.
vibrant /'vaɪbrənt/ a. vibrante.
vibrat|e /vaɪ'breɪt/ v.t./i. (far) vibrare. ~ion /-ʃn/ n. vibrazione f.

vicar /'vɪkə(r)/ *n.* parroco *m.* ~age /-rɪdʒ/ *n.* casa parrocchiale *f.*

vicarious /vɪ'keərɪəs/ *a.* sostituto.

vice¹ /vaɪs/ *n.* vizio *m.*

vice² /vaɪs/ *n.* (*techn.*) morsa *f.*

vice- /vaɪs/ *pref.* vice-.

vice versa /vaɪsɪ'vɜːsə/ *adv.* viceversa.

vicinity /vɪ'sɪnətɪ/ *n.* vicinanza *f.* **in the ~ of** vicino a.

vicious /'vɪʃəs/ *a.* maligno. **~ circle** *n.* circolo vizioso *m.* **~ly** *adv.* con malignità.

vicissitudes /vɪ'sɪsɪtjuːdz/ *n.pl.* vicissitudini *f.pl.*

victim /'vɪktɪm/ *n.* vittima *f.* **~ization** /-aɪ'zeɪʃn/ *n.* persecuzione *f.* **~ize** *v.t.* vittimizzare.

victor /'vɪktə(r)/ *n.* vincitore *m.*

Victorian /vɪk'tɔːrɪən/ *a.* vittoriano.

victor|y /'vɪktərɪ/ *n.* vittoria *f.* **~ious** /-'tɔːrɪəs/ *a.* vittorioso.

video /'vɪdɪəʊ/ *a.* video. **~ (-recorder)** *n.* videoregistratore *m.* **~tape** *n.* videocassetta *f.*

vie /vaɪ/ *v.i.* (*pres.p.* **vying**) rivaleggiare.

view /vjuː/ *n.* vista *f.*; (*mental survey*) visione *f.*; (*opinion*) opinione *f.* —*v.t.* visitare; (*consider*) considerare. **in my ~** secondo me. **in ~ of** in considerazione di. **on ~** in mostra. **with a ~ to** allo scopo di. **~er** /-ə(r)/ *n.* spetta|tore, -trice *m.*, *f.*; (*TV*) telespetta|tore, -trice *m.*, *f.*

viewfinder /'vjuːfaɪndə(r)/ *n.* mirino *m.*

viewpoint /'vjuːpɔɪnt/ *n.* punto di vista *m.*

vigil /'vɪdʒɪl/ *n.* veglia *f.* **~ance** *n.* vigilanza *f.* **~ant** *a.* vigile.

vignette /vɪ'njet/ *n.* illustrazione *f.*; (*description*) breve profilo *m.*

vigo|ur /'vɪgə(r)/ *n.* vigore *m.* **~rous** *a.* vigoroso.

vile /vaɪl/ *a.* abietto; (*bad*) orribile; (*temper*) pessimo.

vilif|y /'vɪlɪfaɪ/ *v.t.* diffamare. **~ication** /-ɪ'keɪʃn/ *n.* diffamazione *f.*

village /'vɪlɪdʒ/ *n.* villaggio *m.* **~r** /-ə(r)/ *n.* abitante (di un villaggio) *m.*/*f.*

villain /'vɪlən/ *n.* furfante *m.*; (*in story etc.*) cattivo *m.* **~ous** *a.* infame. **~y** *n.* furfanteria *f.*

vim /vɪm/ *n.* (*fam.*) energia *f.*

vinaigrette /vɪnɪ'gret/ *n.* **~ sauce** *n.* salsa di olio e aceto *f.*

vindicat|e /'vɪndɪkeɪt/ *v.t.* rivendicare. **~ion** /-'keɪʃn/ *n.* rivendicazione *f.*

vindictive /vɪn'dɪktɪv/ *a.* vendicativo. **~ness** *n.* spirito vendicativo *m.*

vine /vaɪn/ *n.* vite *f.*

vinegar /'vɪnɪgə(r)/ *n.* aceto *m.* **~y** *a.* agro.

vineyard /'vɪnjəd/ *n.* vigneto *m.*

vintage /'vɪntɪdʒ/ *n.* (*year*) annata *f.* —*a.* (*wine*) pregiato; (*car*) di vecchio modello.

vinyl /'vaɪnɪl/ *n.* vinile *m.*

viola /vɪ'əʊlə/ *n.* (*mus.*) viola *f.*

violat|e /'vaɪəleɪt/ *v.t.* violare. **~ion** /-'leɪʃn/ *n.* violazione *f.*

violen|t /'vaɪələnt/ *a.* violento. **~ce** *n.* violenza *f.* **~tly** *adv.* violentemente.

violet /'vaɪələt/ *n.* viola *m.*; (*flower*) violetta *f.* —*a.* violetto.

violin /'vaɪəlɪn/ *n.* violino *m.* **~ist** *n.* violinsta *m.*/*f.*

VIP /viːaɪ'piː/ *n. abbr.* (*of* **very important person**) personaggio importante *m.*

viper /'vaɪpə(r)/ *n.* vipera *f.*

virgin /'vɜːdʒɪn/ *a.* & *n.* vergine *f.* **~al** *a.* verginale. **~ity** /və'dʒɪnətɪ/ *n.* verginità *f.*

Virgo /'vɜːgəʊ/ *n.* (*astr.*) Vergine *f.*

viril|e /'vɪraɪl/ *a.* virile. **~ity** /-'rɪlətɪ/ *n.* virilità *f.*

virtual /'vɜːtʃʊəl/ *a.* effettivo. **~ly** *adv.* praticamente.

virtu|e /'vɜːtʃuː/ *n.* virtù *f.* **by** *or* **in ~e of** a causa di. **~ous** *a.* virtuoso.

virtuoso /vɜːtʃʊ'əʊzəʊ/ *n.* (*pl.* **-si** /-ziː/) virtuoso *m.*

virulent /'vɪrʊlənt/ *a.* virulento.

virus /'vaɪərəs/ *n.* (*pl.* **-uses**) virus *m. invar.*

visa /'viːzə/ *n.* visto *m.*

vis-à-vis /viːzɑː'viː/ *adv.* di fronte. —*prep.* in rapporto a.

viscount /'vaɪkaʊnt/ *n.* visconte *m.* **~ess** *n.* viscontessa *f.*

viscous /'vɪskəs/ *a.* viscoso.

visib|le /'vɪzəbl/ *a.* visibile. **~ility** /-'bɪlətɪ/ *n.* visibilità *f.* **~ly** *adv.* visibilmente.

vision /'vɪʒn/ *n.* visione *f.*; (*sight*) vista *f.*

visionary /'vɪʒənrɪ/ *a.* & *n.* visionario, a *m.*, *f.*

visit /'vɪzɪt/ *v.t.* visitare; (*inspect*) ispezionare. —*n.* visita *f.* **~or** *n.* visita|tore, -trice *m.*, *f.*; (*guest*) ospite *m.*, *f.*; (*in hotel*) cliente *m.*, *f.*

visor /'vaɪzə(r)/ *n.* visiera *f.*; (*on vehicle*) parasole *m.*

vista /'vɪstə/ *n.* prospettiva *f.*

visual /'vɪʒʊəl/ *a.* visuale. ~**ly** *adv.* visualmente.

visualize /'vɪʒʊəlaɪz/ *v.t.* visualizzare.

vital /'vaɪtl/ *a.* vitale; (*essential*) essenziale. ~ **statistics** *n.pl.* (*fam.*) misure *f.pl.* ~**s** *n.pl.* organi vitali *m.pl.*

vitality /vaɪ'tælətɪ/ *n.* vitalità *f.*

vitally /'vaɪtəlɪ/ *adv.* estremamente.

vitamin /'vɪtəmɪn/ *n.* vitamina *f.*

vitiate /'vɪʃɪeɪt/ *v.t.* guastare.

vitreous /'vɪtrɪəs/ *a.* vitreo.

vituperat|e /vɪ'tju:pəreɪt/ *v.t.* vituperare. ~**ion** /-'reɪʃn/ *n.* vituperio *m.*

vivaci|ous /vɪ'veɪʃəs/ *a.* vivace. ~**ously** *adv.* vivacemente. ~**ty** /-'væsətɪ/ *n.* vivacità *f.*

vivid /'vɪvɪd/ *a.* vivido. ~**ly** *adv.* vividamente. ~**ness** *n.* vivezza *f.*

vivisection /vɪvɪ'sekʃn/ *n.* vivisezione *f.*

vixen /'vɪksn/ *n.* volpe femmina *f.*

vocabulary /və'kæbjʊlərɪ/ *n.* vocabolario *m.*

vocal /'vəʊkl/ *a.* vocale; (*fig.*) eloquente. ~**ist** *n.* vocalista *m.*|*f.*

vocation /vəʊ'keɪʃn/ *n.* vocazione *f.* ~**al** *a.* professionale.

vocifer|ate /və'sɪfəreɪt/ *v.t.*|*i.* vociferare. ~**ous** *a.* vociferante.

vogue /vəʊg/ *n.* voga *f.* **in** ~ di moda.

voice /vɔɪs/ *n.* voce *f.* —*v.t.* esprimere.

void /vɔɪd/ *a.* vuoto; (*not valid*) nullo. —*n.* vuoto *m.* —*v.t.* annullare. ~ **of** privo di.

volatile /'vɒlətaɪl/ *a.* volatile; (*of person*) volubile.

volcan|o /vɒl'keɪnəʊ/ *n.* (*pl.* **-oes**) vulcano *m.* ~**ic** /-'kænɪk/ *a.* vulcanico.

volition /və'lɪʃn/ *n.* **of one's own** ~ di propria volontà.

volley /'vɒlɪ/ *n.* (*pl.* **-eys**) (*of blows* etc.) raffica *f.*; (*of gunfire*) salva *f.*

volt /vəʊlt/ *n.* volt *m. invar.* ~**age** *n.* voltaggio *m.*

voluble /'vɒljʊbl/ *a.* loquace.

volume /'vɒlju:m/ *n.* volume *m.*; (*radio, TV*) regolatore *m.*

voluminous /və'lju:mɪnəs/ *a.* voluminoso.

voluntar|y /'vɒləntrɪ/ *a.* volontario; (*unpaid*) non retribuito. ~**ily** *adv.* volontariamente.

volunteer /vɒlən'tɪə(r)/ *n.* volontario, a *m.*,*f.* —*v.t.*|*i.* offrire, offrirsi volontariamente; (*mil.*) arruolarsi volontario.

voluptuous /və'lʌptʃʊəs/ *a.* voluttuoso.

vomit /'vɒmɪt/ *v.t.*|*i.* vomitare. —*n.* vomito *m.*

voracious /və'reɪʃəs/ *a.* vorace.

vot|e /vəʊt/ *n.* voto *m.*; (*right*) diritto di voto *m.* —*v.i.* votare. ~**er** /-ə(r)/ *n.* elet|tore, -trice *m.*, *f.* ~**ing** *n.* votazione *f.*; (*process*) scrutinio *m.*

vouch /vaʊtʃ/ *v.i.* ~ **for** garantire.

voucher /'vaʊtʃə(r)/ *n.* buono *m.*

vow /vaʊ/ *n.* voto *m.* —*v.i.* giurare.

vowel /'vaʊəl/ *n.* vocale *f.*

voyage /'vɔɪdʒ/ *n.* viaggio (per mare) *m.*

vulgar /'vʌlgə(r)/ *a.* volgare. ~**ity** /-'gærətɪ/ *n.* volgarità *f.* ~**ize** *v.t.* volgarizzare.

vulnerab|le /'vʌlnərəbl/ *a.* vulnerabile. ~**ity** /-'bɪlətɪ/ *n.* vulnerabilità *f.*

vulture /'vʌltʃə(r)/ *n.* avvoltoio *m.*

vying /'vaɪɪŋ/ *see* **vie**.

W

wad /wɒd/ n. batuffolo m.; (bundle) rotolo m.

wadding /'wɒdɪŋ/ n. ovatta f.

waddle /'wɒdl/ v.i. camminare ondeggiando.

wade /weɪd/ v.t. guadare. —v.i. ~ **through** procedere faticosamente.

wafer /'weɪfə(r)/ n. wafer m. invar.; (relig.) ostia f.

waffle[1] /'wɒfl/ n. (fam.) discorso a vanvera m. —v.i. (fam.) parlare a vanvera.

waffle[2] /'wɒfl/ n. (culin.) cialda f.

waft /wɒft/ v.t./i. diffondere, diffondersi.

wag /wæg/ v.t./i. (p.t. **wagged**) agitare, agitarsi.

wage[1] /weɪdʒ/ v.t. ~ **war** far guerra.

wage[2] /weɪdʒ/ n., ~**s** n.pl. salario m.s.

wager /'weɪdʒə(r)/ n. scommessa f. —v.t. scommettere.

waggle /'wægl/ v.t./i. dimenare.

wagon /'wægən/ n. carro m.; (rail.) vagone merci m. **on the** ~ (sl.) astemio.

waif /weɪf/ n. trovatello, a m., f.

wail /weɪl/ v.i. lamentarsi. —n. lamento m.

wainscot /'weɪnskət/ n. zoccolo m.

waist /weɪst/ n. vita f. ~**band** n. cintura f. ~**line** n. linea (della cintura) f.

waistcoat /'weɪstkəʊt/ n. gilè m.invar.

wait /weɪt/ v.t./i. aspettare, (at table) servire. —n. attesa f. **lie in** ~ stare in agguato. ~ **for** attendere. ~ **on** servire; (visit) fare visita a. ~**ing-list** n. lista d'attesa f. ~**ing-room** n. sala d'aspetto f.

wait|er /'weɪtə(r)/ n. cameriere m. ~**ress** n. cameriera f.

waive /weɪv/ v.t. rinunciare a.

wake[1] /weɪk/ v.t./i. (p.t. **woke**, p.p. **woken**) ~ (**up**) svegliare, svegliarsi; (evoke) rievocare. —n. veglia (funebre) f. ~**ful** a. sveglio.

wake[2] /weɪk/ n. (naut.) scia f. **in the** ~ **of** in seguito a.

waken /'weɪkən/ v.t./i. risvegliare, risvegliarsi.

Wales /weɪlz/ n. Galles m.

walk /wɔːk/ v.i. camminare; (not ride) andare a piedi. —v.t. (streets) percor-

rere; (dog) far camminare. —n. passeggiata f.; (gait) andatura f.; (path) sentiero m. ~ **of life** livello sociale m. ~ **out** uscire; (of workers) scioperare. ~**-out** n. sciopero m. ~ **out on** abbandonare. ~**-over** n. vittoria facile f. ~**er** /-ə(r)/ n. cammina|tore, -trice m., f.

walkabout /'wɔːkəbaʊt/ n. (of royalty) incontro con la folla m.

walkie-talkie /wɔːkɪ'tɔːkɪ/ n. walkie-talkie m. invar.

walking /'wɔːkɪŋ/ n. camminare m. ~**stick** n. bastone da passeggio m.

Walkman /'wɔːkmæn/ n. (P.) Walkman f.

walkway /'wɔːkweɪ/ n. corsia pedonale f.

wall /wɔːl/ n. muro m.; (of mountain etc.) parete f. —v.t. murare. **go to the** ~ (of firm) soccombere. **up the** ~ (fam.) fuori di sé.

wallet /'wɒlɪt/ n. portafoglio m.

wallflower /'wɔːlflaʊə(r)/ n. violaciocca f.

wallop /'wɒləp/ v.t. (p.t. **walloped**) (sl.) picchiare. —n. (sl.) percossa f.

wallow /'wɒləʊ/ v.i. sguazzare.

wallpaper /'wɔːlpeɪpə(r)/ n. carta da parati f.

walnut /'wɔːlnʌt/ n. noce f.; (tree) noce m.

walrus /'wɔːlrəs/ n. tricheco m.

waltz /wɔːls/ n. valzer m. —v.i. ballare il valzer. ~ **through** superare facilmente.

wan /wɒn/ a. esangue. ~**ly** adv. debolmente.

wand /wɒnd/ n. bacchetta f.

wander /'wɒndə(r)/ v.i. girovagare; (of road, river) serpeggiare; (fig.) divagare. —n. passeggiata senza meta f. ~**er** /-ə(r)/ n. vagabondo, a m., f.

wanderlust /'wɒndəlʌst/ n. spirito vagabondo m.

wane /weɪn/ —v.i. decrescere; (of moon) calare. —n. **on the** ~ in declino.

wangle /wæŋgl/ v.t. (sl.) brigare. —n. (sl.) raggiro m.

want /wɒnt/ v.t. volere; (need) aver bisogno (di). —v.i. ~ **for** mancare di. —n. bisogno m.; mancanza f. ~**ed**

a. (*of criminal*) ricercato. **~ing** *a.* (*lacking*) mancante.

wanton /'wɒntən/ *a.* sventato.

war /wɔː(r)/ *n.* guerra *f.* **at ~ in** guerra. **on the ~-path** sul sentiero di guerra. **~ on want** *n.* lotta contro la povertà *f.*

warble /'wɔːbl/ *v.t./i.* trillare. —*n.* trillo *m.* **~r** /-ə(r)/ *n.* uccello canoro *m.*

ward /wɔːd/ *n.* (*in hospital*) corsia *f.*; (*of town*) rione *m.*; (*child*) bimbo, a sotto tutela *m.*, *f.* —*v.t.* **~ off** parare.

warden /'wɔːdn/ *n.* sovrintendente *m./f.*; (*of park*) guardiano, a *m.*, *f.*

warder /'wɔːdə(r)/ *n.* carceriere *m.*

wardrobe /'wɔːdrəʊb/ *n.* guardaroba *m.*

wardroom /'wɔːdrʊm/ *n.* quadrato degli ufficiali *m.*

wares /weəz/ *n.pl.* merci *m.pl.*

warehouse /'weəhaʊs/ *n.* deposito *m.*

warfare /'wɔːfeə(r)/ *n.* guerra *f.*

warhead /'wɔːhed/ *n.* testata esplosiva *f.*

warlike /'wɔːlaɪk/ *a.* bellicoso; (*of war*) di guerra.

warm /wɔːm/ *a.* (**-er, -est**) caldo; (*hearty*) caloroso. **~ (up)** *v.t./i.* scaldare, scaldarsi; (*fig.*) animarsi. **be ~** aver caldo. **it is ~** fa caldo. **~-blooded** *a.* dal sangue caldo. **~-hearted** *a.* espansivo. **~ to** (*person*) aver simpatia per; (*task etc.*) appassionarsi a. **~ly** *adv.* caldamente. **~th** *n.* calore *m.*

warmonger /'wɔːmʌŋgə(r)/ *n.* guerrafondaio *m.*

warn /wɔːn/ *v.t.* avvertire. **~ off** intimare di allontanarsi. **~ing** *n.* avvertimento *m.*; (*notice*) preavviso *m.*

warp /wɔːp/ *v.t./i.* deformare, deformarsi; (*fig.*) corrompere.

warrant /'wɒrənt/ *n.* (*for arrest*) mandato (d'arresto) *m.* —*v.t.* giustificare. **~-officer** *n.* sottufficiale *m.*

warranty /'wɒrəntɪ/ *n.* garanzia *f.*

warring /'wɔːrɪŋ/ *a.* guerreggiante.

warrior /'wɒrɪə(r)/ *n.* guerriero, a *m.*, *f.*

warship /'wɔːʃɪp/ *n.* nave da guerra *f.*

wart /wɔːt/ *n.* porro *m.*

wartime /'wɔːtaɪm/ *n.* tempo di guerra *m.*

war|y /'weərɪ/ *a.* (**-ier, -iest**) circospetto; (*cautious*) cauto. **~ily** *adv.* cautamente.

was /wəz, wɒz/ *see* **be.**

wash /wɒʃ/ *v.t./i.* lavare, lavarsi; (*flow over*) bagnare. —*n.* lavata *f.*; (*clothes*) bucato *m.*; (*of ship*) scia *f.* **~-basin** *n.* lavandino *m.* **~ out** *v.t.* lavar via; (*fig.*) cancellare. **~-out** *n.* (*sl.*) fiasco *m.* **~-room** *n.* (*Amer.*) gabinetto *m.* **~-stand** *n.* lavabo *m.* **~-tub** *n.* tinozza *f.* **~ up** *v.i.* lavare i piatti. **~able** *a.* lavabile. **~ed-out** *a.* (*person*) stremato.

washer /'wɒʃə(r)/ *n.* guarnizione *f.*

washing /'wɒʃɪŋ/ *n.* bucato *m.* **~-machine** *n.* lavatrice *f.* **~-powder** *n.* detersivo *m.* **~-up** *n.* rigovernatura *f.*

wasp /wɒsp/ *n.* vespa *f.*

waspish /'wɒspɪʃ/ *a.* pungente.

wastage /'weɪstɪdʒ/ *n.* spreco *m.*

waste /weɪst/ *v.t.* sprecare. —*v.i.* **~ away** deperire. —*a.* di scarto; (*of land*) incolto. —*n.* spreco *m.*; (*rubbish*) rifiuto *m.*; (*of time*) perdita *f.* **~s** *n.pl.* distesa desolata *f.s.* **~-disposal unit** *n.* eliminatore di rifiuti *m.* **~ful** *a.* dispendioso; (*person*) sprecone. **~-paper basket** *n.* cestino per la carta straccia *m.*

watch /wɒtʃ/ *v.t./i.* guardare; (*keep an eye on*) tener d'occhio; (*take heed*) stare attento. —*n.* guardia *f.*; (*period of duty*) turno di guardia *m.*; (*timepiece*) orologio *m.* **on the ~** all'erta. **~-dog** *n.* cane da guardia *m.* **~ out** *v.i.* stare attento. **~-tower** *n.* torre di guardia *f.* **~ful** *a.* attento.

watchmaker /'wɒtʃmeɪkə(r)/ *n.* orologiaio, a *m.*, *f.*

watchman /'wɒtʃmən/ *n.* (*pl.* **-men**) guardiano *m.*

watchword /'wɒtʃwɜːd/ *n.* parola d'ordine *f.*

water /'wɔːtə(r)/ *n.* acqua *f.* —*v.t.* (*plants etc.*) innaffiare; (*dilute*) annacquare. —*v.i.* (*of eyes*) lacrimare. **by ~** (*of travel*) per via d'acqua. **in hot ~** (*fam.*) nei guai. **make s.o.'s mouth ~** far venir l'acquolina in bocca a qcno. **~-biscuit** *n.* cracker *m.* **~-closet** *n.* gabinetto *m.* **~-colour** *n.* acquarello *m.* **~ down** *v.t.* diluire; (*fig.*) attenuare. **~-ice** *n.* sorbetto *m.* **~-lily** *n.* ninfea *f.* **~-line** *n.* linea di galleggiamento *f.* **~-main** *n.* conduttura dell'acqua *f.* **~-melon** *n.* cocomero *m.*; **~-mill** *n.* mulino ad acqua *m.* **~ polo** *n.* pallanuoto *f.* **~-power** *n.* energia idraulica *f.* **~-skiing** *n.* sci nautico *m.* **~-softener** *n.* depuratore dell'acqua *m.* **~way** *n.* canale navigabile *m*. ~**-wheel** *n*. ruota idraulica *f*. ~**-wings** *n.pl.* salvagente *m.s.*

watercourse /'wɔːtəkɔːs/ *n*. corso d'acqua *m*.

watercress /'wɔːtəkres/ *n*. crescione *m*.

waterfall /'wɔːtəfɔːl/ *n*. cascata *f*.

waterfront /'wɔːtəfrʌnt/ *n*. (*of sea*) lungomare *m*.; (*of river*) lungofiume *m*.

watering-can /'wɔːtəriŋkæn/ *n*. innaffiatoio *m*.

watering-place /'wɔːtəriŋpleis/ *n*. (*for animals*) abbeveratoio *m*.; (*spa*) stazione termale *f*.

waterlogged /'wɔːtəlɒgd/ *a*. impregnato d'acqua.

waterproof /'wɔːtəpruːf/ *a*. & *n*. impermeabile *m*.

watershed /'wɔːtəʃed/ *n*. spartiacque *m*. *invar*.

watertight /'wɔːtətait/ *a*. a tenuta d'acqua; (*fig*.) inconfutabile.

waterworks /'wɔːtəwɜːks/ *n*. impianto idrico *m*.

watery /'wɔːtəri/ *a*. acquoso; (*of colour*) slavato; (*of eyes*) lacrimoso.

watt /wɒt/ *n*. watt *m*. *invar*.

wav|e /weiv/ *n*. onda *f*.; (*of hand*) cenno *m*.; (*fig*.) ondata *f*. —*v.t.* agitare; (*hair*) ondulare. —*v.i.* (*signal*) far segno; (*flag*) sventolare. ~**y** *a*. (**-ier, -iest**) ondulato.

waveband /'weivbænd/ *n*. gamma d'onda *f*.

wavelength /'weivleŋθ/ *n*. lunghezza d'onda *f*.

waver /'weivə(r)/ *v.i.* vacillare; (*hesitate*) esitare.

wax[1] /wæks/ *n*. cera *f*. —*v.t.* dare la cera (a). ~**en**, ~**y** *adjs*. cereo.

wax[2] /wæks/ *v.i.* (*of moon*) crescere.

waxwork /'wækswɜːk/ *n*. modello in cera *m*.

way /wei/ *n*. via *f*.; (*distance*) distanza *f*.; (*manner*) modo *m*.; (*direction*) direzione *f*. ~**s** *n.pl.* usanze *f.pl.* **be in the** ~ essere tra i piedi. **by the** ~ a proposito. **by** ~ **of** a titolo di. **either** ~ in un modo o nell'altro. **in a** ~ in un certo senso. **in some** ~**s** sotto certi aspetti. **lead the** ~ far strada. **make** ~ far posto. **on the** ~ strada facendo; (*coming*) in viaggio. **out of the** ~ fuori mano. **under** ~ in corso. ~**-bill** *n*. lista di passeggeri *or* merci *f*. ~ **in** *n*. entrata *f*. ~ **out** *n*. uscita *f*. ~**-out** *a*. insolito.

wayfarer /'weifeərə(r)/ *n*. viaggia|tore, -trice *m*., *f*.

waylay /wei'lei/ *v.t.* (*p.t.* **-laid**) aspettare al varco.

wayside /'weisaid/ *n*. margine *m*.

wayward /'weiwəd/ *a*. cocciuto. ~**ness** *n*. cocciutaggine *f*.

we /wiː/ *pron*. noi.

weak /wiːk/ *a*. (**-er, -est**) debole; (*of liquid*) leggero. ~**-kneed** *a*. fiacco. ~**en** *v.t.* indebolire. ~**ly** *adv*. debolmente; *a*. gracile. ~**ness** *n*. debolezza *f*.; (*liking*) debole *m*.

weakling /'wiːkliŋ/ *n*. persona debole *f*.

weal /wiːl/ *n*. vescica *f*.

wealth /welθ/ *n*. ricchezza *f*.; (*plenty*) gran quantità *f*. ~**y** *a*. (**-ier, -iest**) ricco.

wean /wiːn/ *v.t.* svezzare.

weapon /'wepən/ *n*. arma *f*.

wear /weə(r)/ *v.t.* (*p.t.* **wore,** *p.p.* **worn**) portare; (*damage*) consumare. —*v.i.* consumarsi; (*last*) durare. —*n*. uso *m*.; (*endurance*) resistenza *f*.; (*clothing*) indumenti *m.pl.* ~ **and tear** logorio *m*. ~ **down** *v.t.* consumare; (*opposition etc.*) estenuare. ~ **off** *v.i.* svanire. ~ **on** *v.i.* (*of time*) passare lentamente. ~ **out** *v.t.* consumare; (*tire*) stancare. ~**able** *a*. portabile.

wearisome /'wiərisəm/ *a*. stancante.

wear|y /'wiəri/ *a*. (**-ier, -iest**) affaticato. —*v.t.* affaticare. —*v.i.* ~**y of** stancarsi di. ~**ily** *adv*. stancamente. ~**iness** *n*. stanchezza *f*.

weasel /'wiːzl/ *n*. donnola *f*.

weather /'weðə(r)/ *n*. tempo *m*. —*a*. meteorologico. —*v.t.* (*wood*) stagionare; (*survive*) superare. **under the** ~ (*fam*.) giù di corda. ~**-beaten** *a*. ruvido. ~**-vane** *n*. banderuola *f*.

weathercock /'weðəkɒk/ *n*. segnavento *m*.

weave /wiːv/ *v.t.* (*p.t.* **wove,** *p.p.* **woven**) tessere; (*story etc.*) intessere; (*flowers etc.*) intrecciare. —*n*. tessuto *m*. ~**r** /-ə(r)/ *n*. tessi|tore, -trice *m*., *f*.

web /web/ *n*. rete *f*.; (*of spider*) ragnatela *f*.; (*on foot*) palma *f*. ~**bing** *n*. tessuto ritorto *m*.

wed /wed/ *v.t./i.* (*p.t.* **wedded**) sposare, sposarsi. ~**ded to** (*fig*.) attaccato a.

wedding /'wediŋ/ *n*. matrimonio *m*. ~**cake** *n*. torta nuziale *f*. ~**-ring** *n*. fede *f*.

wedge /wedʒ/ *n*. cuneo *m*.; (*space filler*)

triangolo *m.* —*v.t.* incuneare; (*fix*) fissare.

wedlock /'wedlɒk/ *n.* stato coniugale *m.*

Wednesday /'wenzdɪ/ *n.* mercoledì *m.*

wee /wiː/ *a.* (*fam.*) piccolissimo.

weed /wiːd/ *n.* erbaccia *f.*; (*person*) persona debole *f.* —*v.t.* sarchiare. ∼**killer** *n.* erbicida *m.* ∼ **out** eliminare. ∼**y** *a.* ricoperto di erbacce; (*person*) sparuto.

week /wiːk/ *n.* settimana *f.* ∼**end** *n.* fine settimana *m.*

weekday /'wiːkdeɪ/ *n.* giorno feriale *m.*

weekly /'wiːklɪ/ *a.* & *n.* settimanale *m.* —*adv.* settimanalmente.

weep /wiːp/ *v.i.* (*p.t.* **wept**) piangere; (*of eyes*) lacrimare. —*n.* pianto *m.* ∼**ing willow** *n.* salice piangente *m.*

weevil /'wiːvɪl/ *n.* curculione *m.*

weigh /weɪ/ *v.t./i.* pesare. ∼ **anchor** levare l'ancora. ∼ **down** *v.t.* (*fig.*) opprimere. ∼ **up** *v.t.* (*fig.*) considerare.

weight /weɪt/ *n.* peso *m.* ∼**-lifting** *n.* sollevamento pesi *m.* ∼**less** *a.* senza peso. ∼**lessness** *n.* perdita di gravità *f.* ∼**y** *a.* (**-ier, -iest**) pesante; (*influential*) influente.

weir /wɪə(r)/ *n.* chiusa *f.*

weird /wɪəd/ *a.* (**-er, -est**) misterioso; (*bizarre*) bizzarro.

welcom|e /'welkəm/ *a.* benvenuto. —*n.* accoglienza *f.* —*v.t.* dare il benvenuto (a); (*appreciate*) gradire. ∼**e to do** libero di fare. ∼**ing** *a.* accogliente.

weld /weld/ *v.t.* saldare. —*n.* saldatura *f.* ∼**er** *n.* saldatore *m.*

welfare /'welfeə(r)/ *n.* benessere *m.* (*aid*) assistenza *f.* **W**∼ **State** *n.* Stato assistenziale *m.* ∼ **work** *n.* opera assistenziale *f.*

well[1] /wel/ *n.* pozzo *m.*; (*of staircase*) tromba *f.*

well[2] /wel/ *adv.* (**better, best**) bene; (*with good reason*) ben. —*a.* bene. —*int.* beh! **as** ∼ anche. **as** ∼ **as** in aggiunta a. **be** ∼ **star** bene. **very** ∼ benissimo. ∼**-being** *n.* benessere *m.* ∼**-bred** *a.* educato. ∼**-disposed** *a.* benevolo. ∼ **done!** bravo! ∼**groomed** *a.* curato. ∼**-heeled** *a.* (*fam.*) ricco. ∼ **I never!** ma no! ∼**knit** *a.* ben piantato. ∼**-meaning** *a.* bene intenzionato. ∼ **meant** *a.* inteso a fin di bene. ∼ **off** *a.* benestante. ∼**read** *a.* colto. ∼**-spoken** *a.* raffinato

nel parlare. ∼**-to-do** *a.* ricco. ∼**wisher** *n.* sosteni|tore, -trice *m.*, *f.*

wellington /'welɳtən/ *n.* stivale di gomma *m.*

Welsh /welʃ/ *a.* & *n.* gallese *m.* ∼ **rabbit** *n.* pane tostato con formaggio *m.*

wench /wentʃ/ *n.* (*old use*) fanciulla *f.*

wend /wend/ *v.t.* ∼ **one's way** incamminarsi.

went /went/ *see* **go.**

wept /wept/ *see* **weep.**

were /wɜː(r), wə(r)/ *see* **be.**

west /west/ *n.* ovest *m.* **the** ∼ l'occidente *m.* —*a.* occidentale. —*adv.* verso occidente. **go** ∼ (*sl.*) crepare. **W**∼ **Germany** Germania Occidentale *f.* ∼**erly** *a.* verso ovest; (*wind*) occidentale. ∼**ern** *a.* occidentale; (*film*) western *m.* ∼**erner** /-ənə(r)/ *n.* occidentale *m.*/*f.* ∼**ward** *a.* ∼**ward(s)** *adv.* a ponente.

wet /wet/ *a.* (**wetter, wettest**) bagnato; (*rainy*) piovoso; (*person, sl.*) fiacco. —*v.t.* (*p.t.* **wetted**) bagnare. **get** ∼ bagnarsi. ∼ **blanket** *n.* guastafeste *m.*/*f. invar.* ∼ **paint** pittura fresca *f.* ∼ **suit** *n.* tuta da sub *f.*

whack /wæk/ *v.t.* (*fam.*) percuotere. —*n.* (*fam.*) bastonata *f.* **do one's** ∼ (*sl.*) fare la propria parte. ∼**ing** *a.* (*sl., huge*) enorme; *n.* bastonatura *f.*

whacked /wækt/ *a.* (*fam.*) stanco morto.

whale /weɪl/ *n.* balena *f.* **a** ∼ **of a** (*fam.*) formidabile.

wham /wæm/ *int.* bam.

wharf /wɔːf/ *n.* (*pl.* **wharfs**) banchina *f.*

what /wɒt/ *a.* quale, che; (*any that*) quel, quello (che). —*pron.* che, (che) cosa. ∼ **about** (*news of*) cosa si dice di; (*opinion about*) che ne dici di. ∼ **for?** perché? ∼ **if** cosa succederebbe se. ∼ **is it?** cos'è?

whatever /wɒt'evə(r)/ *a.* qualunque. —*pron.* qualsiasi cosa.

whatnot /'wɒtnɒt/ *n.* nonnulla *m.*; (*stand*) scaffaletto *m.*

whatsoever /wɒtsəʊ'evə(r)/ *a.* & *pron.* = **whatever.**

wheat /wiːt/ *n.* frumento *m.* ∼**en** *a.* di frumento. ∼**-meal** *n.* farina di frumento *f.*

wheedle /'wiːdl/ *v.t.* ottenere con lusinghe.

wheel /wiːl/ *n.* ruota *f.* (**steering-**) ∼ *n.* volante *m.* —*v.t.* spingere (una bicicletta ecc.) —*v.i.* ~ (**round**) ruotare. **at the** ~ al volante.

wheelbarrow /'wi:lbærəʊ/ *n.* carriola *f.*

wheelchair /'wi:ltʃeə(r)/ *n.* sedia a rotelle *f.*

wheeze /wi:z/ *v.i.* ansare. —*n.* affanno *m.*

when /wen/ *adv.* & *conj.* quando; (*although*) sebbene.

whence /wens/ *adv.* donde.

whenever /wen'evə(r)/ *adv.* in qualsiasi momento; (*every time that*) ogni volta che.

where /weə(r)/ *adv.* & *conj.* dove; (*in which place*) in cui. ~**by** *adv.* per cui. ~**upon** *adv.* dopo di che.

whereabouts /'weərəbaʊts/ *adv.* (pressappoco) dove. —*n.* paraggi *m.pl.*

whereas /weər'æz/ *conj.* poiché; (*in contrast*) mentre.

wherever /weər'evə(r)/ *adv.* (*in whatever place*) dove. —*conj.* dovunque.

whet /wet/ *v.t.* (*p.t.* **whetted**) affilare; (*fig.*) aguzzare.

whether /'weðə(r)/ *conj.* se. **I don't know** ~ **she will like it** non so se le piacerà. ~ **you like it or not** che ti piaccia o no.

which /wɪtʃ/ *a.* & *pron.* quale, chi, che. —*rel. pron.* (*object*) il quale, la quale. ~ **one** quale. ~ **one of you** chi di voi. ~ **way** da che parte; (*how*) in che modo.

whichever /wɪtʃ'evə(r)/ *a.* & *pron.* qualunque; (*person*) chiunque.

whiff /wɪf/ *n.* soffio *m.*

while /waɪl/ *n.* tempo *m.* —*conj.* mentre; (*although*) sebbene; (*as long as*) finché. —*v.t.* ~ **away** passare (il tempo).

whilst /waɪlst/ *conj.* mentre.

whim /wɪm/ *n.* capriccio *m.*

whimper /'wɪmpə(r)/ *v.i.* piagnucolare. —*n.* piagnucolio *m.*

whimsical /'wɪmzɪkl/ *a.* capriccioso; (*fanciful*) fantasioso.

whine /waɪn/ *v.i.* lamentarsi. —*n.* lamento *m.* ~**r** /-ə(r)/ *n.* piagnucolone, a *m.*, *f.*

whip /wɪp/ *n.* frusta *f.*; (*pol.*) capogruppo parlamentare *m.* —*v.t.* (*p.t.* **whipped**) frustare; (*culin.*) frullare; (*seize*) afferrare. ~**cord** *n.* (*fabric*) tessuto a costine *m.* ~**ped cream** *n.* panna montata *f.* ~**round** *n.* colletta *f.* ~ **up** (*incite*) stimolare.

whipper-snapper /'wɪpəsnæpə(r)/ *n.* sfrontatello *m.*

whipping-boy /'wɪpɪŋbɔɪ/ *n.* capro espiatorio *m.*

whirl /wɜ:l/ *v.t./i.* (far) girare rapidamente. —*n.* turbine *m.*; (*confused state*) tumulto *m.*

whirlpool /'wɜ:lpu:l/ *n.* vortice *m.*

whirlwind /'wɜ:lwɪnd/ *n.* turbine *m.*

whirr /wɜ:(r)/ *n.* ronzio *m.* —*v.i.* ronzare.

whisk /wɪsk/ *v.t.* (*culin.*) frullare. ~ **away** portare via. —*n.* (*culin.*) frullino *m.*

whisker /'wɪskə(r)/ *n.* baffo *m.* ~**s** *n.pl.* basette *f.pl.*

whisky /'wɪskɪ/ *n.* whisky *m.*

whisper /'wɪspə(r)/ *v.t./i.* sussurrare; (*of leaves etc.*) frusciare. —*n.* sussurro *m.*; (*rumour*) diceria *f.*

whistle /'wɪsl/ *n.* fischio *m.*; (*instrument*) fischietto *m.* —*v.i.* fischiare. ~-**stop** *n.* (*pol.*) giro elettorale *m.*

white /waɪt/ *a.* (-**er**, -**est**) bianco. —*n.* bianco *m.*; (*person*) uomo, donna di razza bianca *m.*, *f.*; (*of egg*) albume *m.* **go** ~ impallidire. ~ **coffee** *n.* caffellatte *m.* ~-**collar worker** *n.* impiegato *m.* ~ **elephant** *n.* oggetto inutile *m.* ~ **horses** *n.* cavalloni *m.pl.* ~-**hot** *a.* (*of metal*) arroventato. ~ **lie** *n.* bugia pietosa *f.* **W**~ **Paper** *n.* resoconto governativo *m.* ~**n** *v.t.* imbiancare; *v.i.* impallidire. ~**ness** *n.* bianchezza *f.*

whitebait /'waɪtbeɪt/ *n.* (*pl.* **whitebait**) bianchetti *m.pl.*

Whitehall /'waɪthɔ:l/ *n.* il governo britannico *m.*

whitewash /'waɪtwɒʃ/ *n.* calce *f.*; (*fig.*) copertura *f.* —*v.t.* dare una mano di calce; (*fig.*) coprire.

whiting /'waɪtɪŋ/ *n.* (*pl.* **whiting**) (*fish*) merlano *m.*

whitlow /'wɪtləʊ/ *n.* patereccio *m.*

Whitsun /'wɪtsn/ *n.* Pentecoste *f.*

whittle /'wɪtl/ *v.t.* ~ (**down**) tagliuzzare; (*fig.*) ridurre.

whiz /wɪz/ *v.t./i.* (*p.t.* **whizzed**) sibilare. ~-**kid** *n.* (*fam.*) giovane brillante *m.*

who /hu:/ *pron.* chi; (*particular person*) il quale, la quale, che.

whodunit /hu:'dʌnɪt/ *n.* (*fam.*) giallo *m.*

whoever /hu:'evə(r)/ *pron.* chiunque.

whole /həʊl/ *a.* intero; (*not broken*) intatto. —*n.* il tutto *m.* **as a** ~ nell'insieme. **on the ~** tutto considerato. **~-hearted** *a.* di tutto cuore; (*person*) devoto. **~meal** *a.* integrale.

wholesale /'həʊlseɪl/ *n.* vendita all'ingrosso *f.* —*a.* & *adv.* all'ingrosso. **~r** /-ə(r)/ *n.* grossista *m.*|*f.*

wholesome /'həʊlsəm/ *a.* salutare.

wholly /'həʊlɪ/ *adv.* completamente.

whom /huːm/ *pron.* che, il quale; (*inter.*) chi.

whooping cough /'huːpɪŋkɒf/ *n.* pertosse *f.*

whoops /'wuːps/ *int.* (*fam.*) oh.

whore /hɔː(r)/ *n.* puttana *f.*

whose /huːz/ *pron.* di chi, di cui; (*rel.*) il cui.

why /waɪ/ *adv.* (*inter.*) perché; (*on account of*) per cui. —*int.* diamine.

wick /wɪk/ *n.* lucignolo *m.*

wicked /'wɪkɪd/ *a.* cattivo; (*severe*) brutto; (*mischievous*) birichino. **~ness** *n.* cattiveria *f.*

wicker /'wɪkə(r)/ *n.* vimine *m.* —*a.* di vimini. **~work** *n.* lavoro in vimini *m.*

wicket /'wɪkɪt/ *n.* (*cricket*) porta *f.*

wide /waɪd/ *a.* (**-er, -est**) largo; (*fully opened*) spalancato; (*far from target*) lontano. —*adv.* largamente. **far and ~** in lungo e in largo. **~ awake** *a.* del tutto sveglio. **~ly** *adv.* largamente; (*believed*) generalmente; (*different*) molto. **~n** *v.t.* allargare.

widespread /'waɪdspred/ *a.* diffuso.

widow /'wɪdəʊ/ *n.* vedova *f.* **~ed** *a.* vedovo. **~er** *n.* vedovo *m.* **~hood** *n.* vedovanza *f.*

width /wɪdθ/ *n.* larghezza *f.*; (*of material*) altezza *f.*

wield /wiːld/ *v.t.* maneggiare; (*power*) esercitare.

wife /waɪf/ *n.* (*pl.* **wives**) moglie *f.*

wig /wɪg/ *n.* parrucca *f.*

wiggle /'wɪgl/ *v.t.* dimenare. —*v.i.* traballare.

wild /waɪld/ *a.* (**-er, -est**) selvaggio; (*enraged*) furibondo; (*idea*) folle; (*with joy*) pazzo; (*random*) avventato. —*adv.* a casaccio. **~s** *n.pl.* zona selvaggia *f.s.* **run ~** crescere senza controllo. **~-goose chase** *n.* impresa inutile *f.* **~ly** *adv.* selvaggiamente; (*fig.*) follemente.

wildcat /'waɪldkæt/ *a.* **~ strike** sciopero irregolare *m.*

wilderness /'wɪldənɪs/ *n.* deserto *m.*

wildfire /'waɪldfaɪə(r)/ *n.* **spread like ~** diffondersi rapidamente.

wildlife /'waɪldlaɪf/ *n.* natura *f.*

wilful /'wɪlfʊl/ *a.* intenzionale; (*self-willed*) ostinato. **~ly** *adv.* intenzionalmente; ostinatamente.

will[1] /wɪl/ *v. aux.* **he ~ be** (lui) sarà. **~ you have some wine?** vuoi del vino? **you ~ be back soon, won't you?** tornerai presto, no?

will[2] /wɪl/ *n.* volontà *f.*; (*document*) testamento *m.* **~-power** *n.* forza di volontà *f.*

willies /'wɪlɪz/ *n.pl.* (*sl.*) **give one the ~** far venire i brividi a qcno.

willing /'wɪlɪŋ/ *a.* disposto; (*eager*) volonteroso. **~ly** *adv.* volentieri. **~ness** *n.* buona volontà *f.*

willow /'wɪləʊ/ *n.* salice *m.*

willy-nilly /wɪlɪ'nɪlɪ/ *adv.* volente o nolente.

wilt /wɪlt/ *v.i.* appassire.

wily /'waɪlɪ/ *a.* (**-ier, -iest**) astuto.

win /wɪn/ *v.t.*|*i.* (*p.t.* **won**, *pres. p.* **winning**) vincere; (*fame etc.*) conquistare. —*n.* vittoria *f.* **~ back** *v.t.* riconquistare. **~ over** *v.t.* convincere. **~ner** /-ə(r)/ *n.* vinci|tore, -trice *m.*, *f.* **~ning-post** *n.* punto d'arrivo *m.* **~ning smile** sorriso simpatico *m.* **~nings** *n.pl.* vincite *f.pl.*

wince /wɪns/ *v.i.* sussultare. —*n.* sussulto *m.*

winch /wɪntʃ/ *n.* argano *m.* —*v.t.* sollevare con l'argano.

wind[1] /wɪnd/ *n.* vento *m.*; (*in stomach*) flatulenza *f.*; (*fig.*) sentore *m.* —*v.t.* (*smell*) fiutare. **get** *or* **have the ~ up** (*sl.*) aver fifa. **get ~ of** aver sentore di. **in the ~** nell'aria. **~-cheater** *n.* giacca a vento *f.* **~ instrument** *n.* strumento a fiato *m.* **~-swept** *a.* esposto al vento. **~y** *a.* (**-ier, -iest**) ventoso.

wind[2] /waɪnd/ *v.t.* (*p.t.* **wound**) (*wrap around*) avvolgere; (*move by turning*) (*far*) girare; (*clock etc.*) caricare. —*v.i.* (*road*) serpeggiare. **~ up** *v.t.* (*fig.*) concludere; (*end*) terminare. **~er** /-ə(r)/ *n.* chiave (per l'orologio) *f.* **~ing** *a.* serpeggiante.

windbag /'wɪndbæg/ *n.* chiacchierone, a *m.*, *f.*

windfall /'wɪndfɔːl/ *n.* frutta abbattuta dal vento *f.*; (*fig.*) fortuna inaspettata *f.*

windmill /'wɪndmɪl/ *n.* mulino a vento *m.*

window /'wɪndəʊ/ *n.* finestra *f.*; (*in shop*) vetrina *f.* **~-box** *n.* cassetta per

i fiori *f.* ~**-dresser** *n.* vetrinista *m./f.*
~**-dressing** *n.* arredamento di
vetrina *m.* ~**-shopping** *n.* (il) comprare con gli occhi *m.*

windpipe /'wɪndpaɪp/ *n.* trachea *f.*

windscreen /'wɪndskriːn/ *n.* parabrezza *m. invar.* ~ **wiper** *n.* tergicristallo *m.*

wine /waɪn/ *n.* vino *m.* ~**glass** *n.*
bicchiere da vino *m.*

wing /wɪŋ/ *n.* ala *f.*; (*auto*) parafango
m.; (*mil. unit*) squadriglia *f.* ~**s** *n.pl.*
(*theatr.*) quinte *f.pl.* **under one's** ~
sotto la protezione di qcno. ~**ed** *a.*
alato. ~**er** /-ə(r)/ *n.* (*sport*) ala *f.*

wink /wɪŋk/ *v.i.* strizzare l'occhio; (*of
light etc.*) lampeggiare. —*n.* strizzata
d'occhio *f.* **not to sleep a** ~ non
chiudere occhio.

winkle /'wɪŋkl/ *v.t.* ~ **out** estrarre.

winsome /'wɪnsəm/ *a.* attraente.

wint|er /'wɪntə(r)/ *n.* inverno *m.* —*v.i.*
svernare. ~**ry** *a.* invernale.

wipe /waɪp/ *v.t.* strofinare; (*dry*) asciugare. —*n.* strofinata *f.* ~ **out** (*cancel*)
eliminare; (*destroy*) distruggere. ~
up asciugare.

wir|e /'waɪə(r)/ *n.* filo *m.*; (*fam.*, *telegram*) telegramma *m.* ~**e netting** *n.*
rete metallica *f.* ~**ing** *n.* impianto
elettrico *m.*

wireless /'waɪəlɪs/ *n.* radio *f.*

wiry /'waɪərɪ/ *a.* (-ier, -iest) (*of person*)
instancabile.

wisdom /'wɪzdəm/ *n.* saggezza *f.* ~
tooth *n.* dente del giudizio *m.*

wise /waɪz/ *a.* (-er, -est) saggio; (*scholarly*) dotto. ~**ly** *adv.* saggiamente.

wisecrack /'waɪzkræk/ *n.* (*fam.*) battuta arguta *f.* —*v.i.* (*fam.*) dire spiritosaggini.

wish /wɪʃ/ *n.* desiderio *m.*; (*greeting*)
augurio *m.* —*v.t.* desiderare; augurare. ~ **on** (*fam.*) affibbiare a. ~ **s.o.**
well augurare bene a qcno. **with best**
~**es** con i migliori saluti.

wishbone /'wɪʃbəʊn/ *n.* forcella (di
pollo) *f.*

wishful /'wɪʃfl/ *a.* desideroso. ~
thinking pensieró illusorio *m.*

wishy-washy /'wɪʃɪwɒʃɪ/ *a.* insipido.

wisp /wɪsp/ *n.* ciuffo *m.*; (*of smoke*) filo
m.

wistaria /wɪs'teərɪə/ *n.* glicine *m.*

wistful /'wɪstfl/ *a.* languido. ~**ly** *adv.*
languidamente.

wit /wɪt/ *n.* spirito *m.*; (*person*) persona
spiritosa *f.*; (*intelligence*) ingegno *m.*

be at one's ~**s' end** non saper più
cosa fare. **live by one's** ~**s** vivere di
espedienti.

witch /wɪtʃ/ *n.* strega *f.* ~**craft** *n.*
magia *f.* ~**-doctor** *n.* stregone *m.*

with /wɪð/ *prep.* con; (*having*) di;
(*cause*) per. **be** ~ **it** (*fam.*) essere
aggiornato.

withdraw /wɪð'drɔː/ *v.t.* (*p.t.* **withdrew**, *p.p.* **withdrawn**) ritirare;
(*money*) prelevare. —*v.i.* appartarsi.
~**al** *n.* ritiro *m.*; prelevamento *m.*;
(*med.*) stato di privazione *m.*

withdrawn /wɪð'drɔːn/ *see* **withdraw**. —*a.* (*of person*) poco socievole.

wither /'wɪðə(r)/ *v.i.* appassire. —*v.t.*
(*fig.*) agghiacciare.

withhold /wɪð'həʊld/ *v.t.* (*p.t.* **withheld**) trattenere. ~ **from** rifiutare
(a); (*hide*) nascondere (a).

within /wɪð'ɪn/ *prep.* dentro, entro.
—*adv.* all'interno, (dal di) dentro.

without /wɪð'aʊt/ *prep.* senza.

withstand /wɪð'stænd/ *v.t.* (*p.t.* **withstood**) resistere a.

witness /'wɪtnɪs/ *n.* testimone *m./f.*;
(*proof*) testimonianza *f.* —*v.t.* testimoniare. ~**-box** *n.* banco dei testimoni *m.*

witticism /'wɪtɪsɪzəm/ *n.* spiritosaggine *f.*

wittingly /'wɪtɪŋlɪ/ *adv.* consapevolmente.

witty /'wɪtɪ/ *a.* (-ier, -iest) spiritoso.

wives /waɪvz/ *see* **wife**.

wizard /'wɪzəd/ *n.* mago *m.* ~**ry** *n.*
magia *f.*

wizened /'wɪznd/ *a.* raggrinzito.

wobbl|e /'wɒbl/ *v.i.* traballare. ~**y** *a.*
traballante.

wodge /wɒdʒ/ *n.* (*fam.*) mucchio *m.*

woe /wəʊ/ *n.* afflizione *f.* ~**ful** *a.* doloroso.

woebegone /'wəʊbɪgɒn/ *a.* desolato.

woke, woken /wəʊk, 'wəʊkən/ *see*
wake[1].

wolf /wʊlf/ *n.* (*pl.* **wolves**) lupo *m.*;
(*womanizer, sl.*) donnaiolo *m.* —*v.t.*
divorare. **cry** ~ dare falsi allarmi. ~**-
whistle** *n.* fischio del pappagallo *m.*

woman /'wʊmən/ *n.* (*pl.* **women**)
donna *f.* **single** ~ donna nubile *f.*
~**ly** *a.* femminile. **women's lib** *n.*
movimento femminista *m.*

womanize /'wʊmənaɪz/ *v.i.* correre
dietro alle donne.

womb /wuːm/ *n.* utero *m.*

women /'wɪmɪn/ *n.pl. see* **woman**.

womenfolk /'wɪmɪnfəʊk/ *n.pl.* le donne *f.pl.*

won /wʌn/ *see* **win.**

wonder /'wʌndə(r)/ *n.* meraviglia *f.*; (*bewilderment*) stupore *m.* —*v.i.* meravigliarsi; (*reflect*) chiedersi. **no ~** non fa meraviglia che.

wonderful /'wʌndəfl/ *a.* meraviglioso. **~ly** *adv.* meravigliosamente.

wonderland /'wʌndəlænd/ *n.* paese delle meraviglie *m.*

wonky /'wɒŋkɪ/ *a.* (**-ier, -iest**) (*sl.*) malfermo; (*of person*) debole.

won't /wəʊnt/ = **will not.**

woo /wuː/ *v.t.* corteggiare.

wood /wʊd/ *n.* legno *m.*; (*for burning*) legna *f.*; (*area*) bosco *m.*; (*in bowls*) boccino *m.*; (*in golf*) bastone *m.* **out of the ~** (*fig.*) fuori dai guai. **~ed** *a.* boscoso. **~en** *a.* di legno. **~land** *n.* terreno boscoso *m.* **~y** *a.* legnoso.

woodbine /'wʊdbaɪn/ *n.* caprifoglio *m.*

woodcutter /'wʊdkʌtə(r)/ *n.* boscaiolo *m.*

woodpecker /'wʊdpekə(r)/ *n.* picchio *m.*

woodwind /'wʊdwɪnd/ *n.* strumenti a fiato *m.pl.*

woodwork /'wʊdwɜːk/ *n.* ebanisteria *f.*; (*in room etc.*) rivestiture in legno *f.pl.*

woodworm /'wʊdwɜːm/ *n.* tarlo *m.*

wool /wʊl/ *n.* lana *f.* **pull the ~ over s.o.'s eyes** ingannare qcno. **~-gathering** *n.* fantasticheria *f.* **~len** *a.* di lana. **~lens** *n.pl.* indumenti di lana *m.pl.* **~ly** *a.* (**-ier, -iest**) di lana; (*fig.*) confuso; *n.* indumento di lana *m.*

word /wɜːd/ *n.* parola *f.*; (*news*) notizie *f.pl.* —*v.t.* esprimere. **by ~ of mouth** a voce. **have ~s with** bisticciare con. **in one ~** brevemente. **in other ~s** in altri termini. **the last ~** l'ultima novità *f.* **~-perfect** *a.* che sa a memoria. **~ing** *n.* espressione *f.* **~y** *a.* prolisso.

wore /wɔː(r)/ *see* **wear.**

work /wɜːk/ *n.* lavoro *m.*; (*art, lit.*) opera *f.* **~s** *n.pl.* (*building*) fabbrica *f.s.*; (*mech.*) meccanismo *m.s.* —*v.t./i.* (*far*) lavorare; (*of machine*) (*far*) funzionare; (*have effect*) fare effetto; (*of student*) (*far*) studiare. **~ in** infiltrare. **~ off** dare sfogo a. **~ out** risolvere; (*plan*) progettare; (*succeed*) riuscire. **~-out** *n.* allenamento *m.*

~to-rule *n.* sciopero bianco *m.* **~ up** sviluppare. **~ed up** agitato.

workable /'wɜːkəbl/ *a.* (*project*) fattibile.

workaholic /wɜːkə'hɒlɪk/ *n.* lavora|tore, -trice inguaribile *m.*, *f.*

worker /'wɜːkə(r)/ *n.* lavora|tore, -trice *m.*, *f.*; (*manual*) operaio, a *m.*, *f.*

workhouse /'wɜːkhaʊs/ *n.* ospizio di mendicità *m.*

working /'wɜːkɪŋ/ *a.* (*day*) lavorativo; (*clothes etc.*) di lavoro. —*n.* (*mech.*) funzionamento *m.* **in ~ order** funzionante. **~ class** *n.* classe operaia *f.* **~-class** *a.* operaio.

workman /'wɜːkmən/ *n.* (*pl.* **-men**) operaio *m.* **~ship** *n.* lavorazione *f.*

workmanlike /'wɜːkmənlaɪk/ *a.* fatto con competenza.

workshop /'wɜːkʃɒp/ *n.* officina *f.*

world /wɜːld/ *n.* mondo *m.*; (*people*) gente *f.* —*a.* mondiale. **a ~ of** un sacco di. **out of this ~** meraviglioso. **~-wide** *a.* mondiale. **~ly** *a.* terreno; (*fig.*) mondano.

worm /wɜːm/ *n.* verme *m.* —*v.i.* **~ one's way** insinuarsi. **~eaten** *a.* tarlato.

worn /wɔːn/ *see* **wear.** —*a.* sciupato. **~-out** *a.* consumato; (*person*) sfinito.

worr|y /'wʌrɪ/ *v.t.* infastidire. —*v.t./i.* preoccupare, preoccuparsi. —*n.* preoccupazione *f.* **~ied** *a.* preoccupato. **~ier** /-ə(r)/ *n.* ansioso, a *m.*, *f.* **~ying** *a.* preoccupante.

worse /wɜːs/ *a.* peggiore. —*adv.* peggio. —*n.* (il) peggio *m.* **~n** *v.t./i.* (*far*) peggiorare.

worship /'wɜːʃɪp/ *n.* culto *m.*; (*title*) signoria *f.* —*v.t.* (*p.t.* **worshipped**) venerare. —*v.i.* andare in chiesa.

worst /wɜːst/ *a.* (il) peggiore. —*adv.* peggio (di tutti). —*n.* (il) peggio *m.* **get the ~ of it** avere la peggio.

worsted /'wʊstɪd/ *n.* lana pettinata *f.*

worth /wɜːθ/ *n.* valore *m.* —*a.* **be ~** valere. **it is ~ trying** vale la pena di provare. **it was ~ my while** ne valeva la pena. **~less** *a.* senza valore.

worthwhile /'wɜːθwaɪl/ *a.* meritevole; (*cause*) lodevole.

worthy /'wɜːðɪ/ *a.* degno; (*motive*) lodevole.

would /wʊd/ *v. aux.* **he ~ come if he could** verrebbe se potesse. **I ~ do it** lo farei. **~ you go?** andresti? **~-be** *a.* aspirante.

wound[1] /wu:nd/ *n.* ferita *f.* —*v.t.* ferire.

wound[2] /waʊnd/ *see* **wind**[2].

wove, woven /wəʊv, 'wəʊvn/ *see* **weave.**

wow /waʊ/ *int.* perbacco. —*n.* (*sl.*) successo strepitoso *m.*

wrangle /'ræŋgl/ *v.i.* azzuffarsi. —*n.* zuffa *f.*

wrap /ræp/ *v.t.* (*p.t.* **wrapped**) avvolgere; (*parcel*) incartare. —*n.* mantello *m.*; (*shawl*) scialle *m.* **be ~ped up in** (*fig.*) essere completamente preso da. **~per** /-ə(r)/ *n.* copertina *f.* **~ping** *n.* materiale da imballaggio *m.*

wrath /rɒθ/ *n.* ira *f.* **~ful** *a.* iroso.

wreath /ri:θ/ *n.* (*pl.* **-ths** /-ðz/) ghirlanda *f.*

wreck /rek/ *n.* rovina *f.*; (*of ship*) naufragio *m.*; (*remains*) relitto *m.*; (*person*) rudere *m.* —*v.t.* demolire; far naufragare. **be a nervous ~** avere i nervi a pezzi. **~age** *n.* rottami *m.pl.*

wren /ren/ *n.* scricciolo *m.*

wrench /rentʃ/ *v.t.* strappare; (*wrist etc.*) slogare. —*n.* strappo *m.*; (*tool*) chiave inglese *f.*

wrest /rest/ *v.t.* strappare (**from** a).

wrestl|e /'resl/ *v.i.* lottare. **~er** /-ə(r)/ *n.* lotta|tore, -trice *m.,f.* **~ing** *n.* lotta *f.*

wretch /retʃ/ *n.* persona disgraziata *f.*; (*rascal*) briccone, a *m.,f.* **~ed** *a.* infelice; (*weather*) orribile; (*dog etc.*) detestabile.

wriggle /'rɪgl/ *v.i.* contorcersi. —*n.* contorsione *f.*

wring /rɪŋ/ *v.t.* (*p.t.* **wrung**) torcere; (*clothes*) strizzare. **~ out of** (*obtain from*) estorcere a. **~ing wet** inzuppato.

wrinkle /'rɪŋkl/ *n.* grinza *f.*; (*on skin*) ruga *f.* —*v.t./i.* increspare, incresparsi.

wrist /rɪst/ *n.* polso *m.* **~-watch** *n.* orologio da polso *m.*

wristlet /'rɪstlɪt/ *n.* braccialetto *m.*

writ /rɪt/ *n.* mandato *m.* **Holy W~** *n.* Sacra Scrittura *f.*

write /raɪt/ *v.t./i.* (*p.t.* **wrote**, *p.p.* **written**, *pres.p.* **writing**) scrivere. **~ down** *v.t.* annotare. **~ off** *v.t.* cancellare. **~-off** *n.* rottame *m.* **~ up** *v.t.* fare un resoconto. **~-up** *n.* resoconto scritto *m.*; (*review*) recensione *f.* **~r** /-ə(r)/ *n.* scrit|tore, -trice *m., f.*; (*author*) au|tore, -trice *m.,f.*

writhe /raɪð/ *v.i.* contorcersi.

writing /'raɪtɪŋ/ *n.* (lo) scrivere *m.*; (*handwriting*) scrittura *f.* **~s** *n.pl.* scritti *m.pl.* **in ~** per iscritto. **~-paper** *n.* carta da lettere *f.*

written /'rɪtn/ *see* **write.**

wrong /rɒŋ/ *a.* scorretto; (*not just*) ingiusto; (*mistaken*) sbagliato. —*adv.* in modo sbagliato; ingiustamente; (*badly*) male. —*n.* ingiustizia *f.*; (*evil*) male *m.* —*v.t.* fare un torto (a). **be ~** (*of person*) aver torto; (*be mistaken*) sbagliare. **go ~** (*err*) sbagliar strada; (*plan*) fallire; (*of car etc.*) guastarsi. **in the ~** dalla parte del torto. **~ful** *a.* ingiusto. **~ly** *adv.* male; ingiustamente.

wrote /rəʊt/ *see* **write.**

wrought /rɔːt/ *a.* **~ iron** ferro battuto *m.*

wrung /rʌŋ/ *see* **wring.**

wry /raɪ/ *a.* (**wryer, wryest**) storto; (*of smile*) sforzato.

wych-hazel /wɪtʃ'heɪzl/ *n.* amamelide *m.*

X

xenophobia /zenə'fəʊbɪə/ *n.* xenofobia *f.*

Xerox /'zɪərɒks/ *n.* (*P.*) macchina xerografica *f.* **xerox** *n.* xerocopia *f.*

Xmas /'krɪsməs/ *n. abbr.* (*of* **Christmas**) Natale *m.*

X-ray /'eksreɪ/ *n.* radiografia *f.* **~s** *n.pl.* raggi *m.pl.* —*v.t.* radiografare.

xylophone /'zaɪləfəʊn/ *n.* xilofono *m.*

Y

yacht /jɒt/ n. yacht m. ~ing n. sport nautico m.

yam /jæm/ n. patata dolce f.

yank /jæŋk/ v.t. (fam.) strappar (via).

Yankee /'jæŋkɪ/ n. (fam.) americano, a m., f.

yap /jæp/ v.i. (p.t. yapped) (dog) guaire.

yard¹ /jɑːd/ n. iarda f. (= 0.9144 metre). ~age n. metraggio m.

yard² /jɑːd/ n. cortile m. the Y~ (fam.) la polizia londinese f.

yardstick /'jɑːdstɪk/ n. (fig.) pietra di paragone f.

yarn /jɑːn/ n. filo m.; (tale, fam.) storia f.

yashmak /'jæʃmæk/ n. velo (delle donne mussulmane) m.

yawn /jɔːn/ v.i. sbadigliare. —n. sbadiglio m.

year /jɪə(r)/ n. anno m.; (of wine) annata f. ~-book n. annuario m. ~ly a. annuale; adv. annualmente.

yearling /'jɜːlɪŋ/ n. animale di un anno m.

yearn /'jɜːn/ v.i. struggersi. ~ing n. desiderio m.

yeast /jiːst/ n. lievito m.

yell /jel/ v.i. urlare. —n. urlo m.

yellow /'jeləʊ/ a. & n. giallo m. ~ish a. giallastro.

yelp /jelp/ n. guaito m. —v.i. guaire.

yen /jen/ n. forte desiderio m.

yeoman /'jəʊmən/ n. (pl. -men) Y~ of the Guard guardia del corpo reale f.

yes /jes/ adv. & n. sì m. invar. ~-man n. (fam.) tirapiedi m. invar.

yesterday /'jestədeɪ/ adv. & n. ieri m. invar. the day before ~ avantieri.

yet /jet/ adv. ancora; (already) già. —conj. tuttavia; (in spite of that) eppure. as ~ fino ad ora.

yew /juː/ n. tasso m.

Yiddish /'jɪdɪʃ/ n. yiddish m.

yield /jiːld/ v.t. produrre. —v.i. cedere. —n. frutto m.; (comm.) reddito m.

yodel /'jəʊdl/ v.t./i. (p.t. yodelled) jodellare. —n. jodel m.

yoga /'jəʊgə/ n. yoga m.

yoghurt /'jɒgət/ n. yogurt m. invar.

yoke /jəʊk/ n. giogo m.; (of garment) sprone m.

yokel /'jəʊkl/ n. burino m.

yolk /jəʊk/ n. tuorlo m.

yonder /'jɒndə(r)/ adv. laggiù. —a. quello (là).

you /juː/ pron. tu, (pl.) voi; (formal) Lei, (pl.) Loro; (object) ti, (pl.) vi; (after prep.) te, (pl.) voi.

young /jʌŋ/ a. (-er, -est) giovane. the ~ n.pl. i giovani m.pl.; (of animals) i piccoli m.pl. ~ lady n. signorina f. ~ man n. giovanotto m. her ~ man (boyfriend) il suo ragazzo m.

youngster /'jʌŋstə(r)/ n. giovincello, a m., f.

your /jɔː(r)/ a., yours /jɔːz/ poss. prons. tuo, vostro; (formal) Suo, Loro. a book of ~s un tuo libro. Y~s faithfully distinti saluti. Y~s sincerely cordiali saluti.

yourself /jɔː'self/ pron. (pl. yourselves) ti, vi; (emphatic) tu stesso, voi stessi. by ~ da solo.

youth /juːθ/ n. (pl. youths /juːðz/) gioventù f.; (boy) giovanetto m.; (young people) i giovani m.pl. ~ hostel n. ostello della gioventù m. ~ful a. giovanile.

yowl /jaʊl/ v.i. ululare. —n. ululato m.

yule, yule-tide /juːl, 'juːltaɪd/ ns. (old use) feste natalizie f.pl.

Yugoslav /'juːgəʊslɑːv/ a. & n. jugoslavo, a m., f. ~ia /-'slɑːvɪə/ n. Jugoslavia f.

Z

zany /'zeɪnɪ/ *a.* (-ier, -iest) da buffone.
zeal /ziːl/ *n.* zelo *m.* ~ous /'zeləs/ *a.* zelante. ~ously /'zeləslɪ/ *adv.* zelantemente.
zealot /'zelət/ *n.* fanatico, a *m.,f.*
zebra /'ziːbrə/ *n.* zebra *f.* ~ crossing *n.* passaggio pedonale a strisce *m.*
zenith /'zenɪθ/ *n.* zenit *m.*
zero /'zɪərəʊ/ *n.* (*pl.* -os) zero *m.*
zest /zest/ *n.* gusto *m.*; (*peel*) scorza (di arancio *or* limone) *f.*
zigzag /'zɪgzæg/ *n.* zigzag *m. invar.* —*v.i.* (*p.t.* **zigzagged**) andare a zigzag.
zinc /zɪŋk/ *n.* zinco *m.*
Zionis|m /'zaɪənɪzəm/ *n.* sionismo *m.* ~t *n.* sionista *m.|f.*
zip /zɪp/ *n.* ~ (**fastener**) *n.* cerniera lampo *f.* —*v.t.* ~ (**up**) chiudere con la cerniera lampo. **Zip code** *n.* (*Amer.*) codice postale *m.*
zircon /'zɜːkn/ *n.* zircone *m.*
zither /'zɪðə(r)/ *n.* cetra *f.*
zodiac /'zəʊdɪæk/ *n.* zodiaco *m.*
zombie /'zɒmbɪ/ *n.* (*fam.*) morto, a vivente *m.,f.*
zone /zəʊn/ *n.* zona *f.*
zoo /zuː/ *n.* (*fam.*) zoo *m. invar.*
zoolog|y /zəʊˈɒlədʒɪ/ *n.* zoologia *f.* ~ical /-əˈlɒdʒɪkl/ *a.* zoologico. ~ist *n.* zoologo, a *m.,f.*
zoom /zuːm/ *v.i.* sfrecciare rumorosamente; (*photo*) zumare. ~ lens *n.* obiettivo trasfocatore *m.*
Zulu /'zuːluː/ *n.* zulù *m.*

Italian Verb Tables

Notes: The three forms of the imperative are like the corresponding forms of the present for the second and third conjugation. In the first conjugation all forms are also the same except for the second person singular: present *compri*, imperative *compra*. The negative form of the second person singular is formed by putting *non* before the infinitive: *non comprare*. For the other two forms, place *non* before the verb: *non compriamo*. In polite forms the third person of the present subjunctive is used instead: *compri, comprino*. The singular form of the imperative is used regularly, whereas the first person plural is very formal and in daily usage is replaced by the second person plural: *comprate*.

Regular verbs:

1. in *-are* (e.g. **compr|are**)

> *Present.* ∼o, ∼i, ∼a, ∼iamo, ∼ate, ∼ano.
> *Imperfect.* ∼avo, ∼avi, ∼ava, ∼avamo, ∼avate, ∼avano.
> *Past historic.* ∼ai, ∼asti, ∼ò, ∼ammo, ∼aste, ∼arono.
> *Future.* ∼erò, ∼erai, ∼erà, ∼eremo, ∼erete, ∼eranno.
> *Present subjunctive.* ∼i, ∼i, ∼i, ∼iamo, ∼iate, ∼ino.
> *Past subjunctive.* ∼assi, ∼assi, ∼asse, ∼assimo, ∼aste, ∼assero.
> *Present participle.* ∼ando.
> *Past participle.* ∼ato.
> *Imperative.* ∼a, ∼iamo, ∼ate.
> *Conditional.* ∼erei, ∼eresti, ∼erebbe, ∼eremmo, ∼ereste, ∼erebbero.

2. in *-ere* (e.g. **vend|ere**)

> *Pres.* ∼o, ∼i, ∼e, ∼iamo, ∼ete, ∼ono.
> *Impf.* ∼evo, ∼evi, ∼eva, ∼evamo, ∼evate, ∼evano.
> *Past hist.* ∼ei or ∼etti, ∼esti, ∼è or ∼ette, ∼emmo, ∼este, ∼erono or ∼ettero.
> *Fut.* ∼erò, ∼erai, ∼erà, ∼eremo, ∼erete, ∼eranno.
> *Pres. sub.* ∼a, ∼a, ∼a, ∼iamo, ∼iate, ∼ano.
> *Past sub.* ∼essi, ∼essi, ∼esse, ∼essimo, ∼este, ∼essero.
> *Pres. part.* ∼endo.
> *Past part.* ∼uto.
> *Imp.* ∼i, ∼iamo, ∼ete.
> *Cond.* ∼erei, ∼eresti, ∼erebbe, ∼eremmo, ∼ereste, ∼erebbero.

3. in *-ire* (e.g. **dorm|ire**)

> *Pres.* ∼o, ∼i, ∼e, ∼iamo, ∼ite, ∼ono.
> *Impf.* ∼ivo, ∼ivi, ∼iva, ∼ivamo, ∼ivate, ∼ivano.
> *Past hist.* ∼ii, ∼isti, ∼ì, ∼immo, ∼iste, ∼irono.
> *Fut.* ∼irò, ∼irai, ∼irà, ∼iremo, ∼irete, ∼iranno.
> *Pres. sub.* ∼a, ∼a, ∼a, ∼iamo, ∼iate, ∼ano.
> *Past sub.* ∼issi, ∼issi, ∼isse, ∼issimo, ∼iste, ∼issero.
> *Pres. part.* ∼endo.
> *Past part.* ∼ito.
> *Imp.* ∼i, ∼iamo, ∼ite.
> *Cond.* ∼irei, ∼iresti, ∼irebbe, ∼iremmo, ∼ireste, ∼irebbero.

Note: Many verbs in the third conjugation take *isc* between the stem and the ending in the first, second, and third person singular and in the third person plural of the present, the present subjunctive, and the imperative: **fin|ire** *Pres.* ∼isco, ∼isci, ∼isce, ∼iscono. *Pres. sub.* ∼isca, ∼iscano. *Imp.* ∼isci.

Irregular verbs:

Certain forms of all irregular verbs are regular (except *essere*). These are: the second person plural of the present, the past subjunctive, and the present participle. All forms not listed below are regular and can be derived from the parts given. Only those irregular verbs considered to be the most useful are shown in the tables.

accadere	*as* CADERE.
accendere	• *Past hist.* accesi, accendesti. • *Past part.* acceso.
affliggere	• *Past hist.* afflissi, affliggesti. • *Past part.* afflitto.
ammettere	*as* METTERE.
andare	• *Pres.* vado, vai, va, andiamo, andate, vanno. • *Fut.* andrò *etc.* • *Pres. sub.* vada, vadano. • *Imp.* và, vada, vadano.
apparire	• *Pres.* appaio, appari *or* apparisci, appare *or* apparisce, appaiono *or* appariscono. • *Past hist.* apparvi *or* apparsi, apparisti, apparve *or* apparì *or* apparse, apparvero *or* apparirono *or* apparsero. • *Pres. sub.* appaia *or* apparisca.
aprire	• *Pres.* apro. • *Past hist.* aprii, apristi. • *Pres. sub.* apra. • *Past part.* aperto.
avere	• *Pres.* ho, hai, ha, abbiamo, hanno. • *Past hist.* ebbi, avesti, ebbe, avemmo, aveste, ebbero. • *Fut.* avrò *etc.* • *Pres. sub.* abbia *etc.* • *Imp.* abbi, abbia, abbiate, abbiano.
bere	• *Pres.* bevo *etc.* • *Impf.* bevevo *etc.* • *Past hist.* bevvi *or* bevetti, bevesti. • *Fut.* berrò *etc.* • *Pres. sub.* beva *etc.* • *Past sub.* bevessi *etc.* • *Pres. part.* bevendo. • *Cond.* berrei *etc.*
cadere	• *Past hist.* caddi, cadesti. • *Fut.* cadrò *etc.*
chiedere	• *Past hist.* chiesi, chiedesti. • *Pres. sub.* chieda *etc.* • *Past part.* chiesto *etc.*
chiudere	• *Past hist.* chiusi, chiudesti. • *Past part.* chiuso.
cogliere	• *Pres.* colgo, colgono. • *Past hist.* colsi, cogliesti. • *Pres. sub.* colga. • *Past part.* colto.
correre	• *Past hist.* corsi, corresti. • *Past part.* corso.
crescere	• *Past hist.* crebbi. • *Past part.* cresciuto.
cuocere	• *Pres.* cuocio, cuociamo, cuociono. • *Past hist.* cossi, cocesti. • *Past part.* cotto.
dare	• *Pres.* do, dai, da, diamo, danno. • *Past hist.* diedi *or* detti, desti. • *Fut.* darò *etc.* • *Pres. sub.* dia *etc.* • *Past sub.* dessi *etc.* • *Imp.* da', dia, diate, diano.
dire	• *Pres.* dico, dici, dice, diciamo, dicono. • *Impf.* dicevo *etc.* • *Past hist.* dissi, dicesti. • *Fut.* dirò *etc.* • *Pres. sub.* dica, diciamo, diciate, dicano. • *Past sub.* dicessi *etc.* • *Pres. part.* dicendo. • *Past part.* detto. • *Imp.* di', dica, dite, dicano.
dovere	• *Pres.* devo *or* debbo, devi, deve, dobbiamo, devono *or* debbono. • *Fut.* dovrò *etc.* • *Pres. sub.* debba, dobbiamo, dobbiate, devano *or* debbano. • *Cond.* dovrei *etc.*
essere	• *Pres.* sono, sei, è, siamo, siete, sono. • *Impf.* ero, eri, era, eravamo, eravate, erano. • *Past hist.* fui, fosti, fu, fummo, foste, furono. • *Fut.* sarò *etc.* • *Pres. sub.* sia *etc.* • *Past sub.* fossi, fossi, fosse, fossimo, foste, fossero. • *Past part.* stato. • *Imp.* sii, sia, siate, siano. • *Cond.* sarei *etc.*
fare	• *Pres.* faccio, fai, fa, facciamo, fanno. • *Impf.* facevo *etc.* • *Past hist.* feci, facesti. • *Fut.* farò *etc.* • *Pres. sub.* faccia *etc.* • *Past sub.* facessi *etc.* • *Pres. part.* facendo. • *Past part.* fatto. • *Imp.* fa', faccia. • *Cond.* farei *etc.*
fingere	• *Past hist.* finsi, fingesti, finsero. • *Past part.* finto.
giungere	• *Past hist.* giunsi, giungesti, giunsero. • *Past part.* giunto.
leggere	• *Past hist.* lessi, leggesti. • *Past part.* letto.

mettere	● *Past hist.* misi, mettesti. ● *Past part.* messo.
morire	● *Pres.* muoio, muori, muore, muoiono. ● *Fut.* morirò *or* morrò *etc.* ● *Pres. sub.* muoia. ● *Past part.* morto.
muovere	● *Past hist.* mossi, movesti. ● *Past part.* mosso.
nascere	● *Past hist.* nacqui, nascesti. ● *Past part.* nato.
offrire	● *Past hist.* offersi *or* offrii, offristi. ● *Pres. sub.* offra. ● *Past part.* offerto.
parere	● *Pres.* paio, pari, pare, pariamo, paiono. ● *Past hist.* parvi *or* parsi, paresti. ● *Fut.* parrò *etc.* ● *Pres. sub.* paia, paiamo *or* pariamo, pariate, paiano. ● *Past part.* parso.
piacere	● *Pres.* piaccio, piaci, piace, piacciamo, piacciono. ● *Past hist.* piacqui, piacesti, piacque, piacemmo, piaceste, piacquero. ● *Pres. sub.* piaccia *etc.* ● *Past part.* piaciuto.
porre	● *Pres.* pongo, poni, pone, poniamo, ponete, pongono. ● *Impf.* ponevo *etc.* ● *Past hist.* posi, ponesti. ● *Fut.* porrò *etc.* ● *Pres. sub.* ponga, poniamo, poniate, pongano. ● *Past sub.* ponessi *etc.*
potere	● *Pres.* posso, puoi, può, possiamo, possono. ● *Fut.* potrò *etc.* ● *Pres. sub.* possa, possiamo, possiate, possano. ● *Cond.* potrei *etc.*
prendere	● *Past hist.* presi, prendesti. ● *Past part.* preso.
ridere	● *Past hist.* risi, ridesti. ● *Past part.* riso.
rimanere	● *Pres.* rimango, rimani, rimane, rimaniamo, rimangono. ● *Past hist.* rimasi, rimanesti. ● *Fut.* rimarrò *etc.* ● *Pres. sub.* rimanga. ● *Past part.* rimasto. ● *Cond.* rimarrei.
salire	● *Pres.* salgo, sali, sale, saliamo, salgono. ● *Pres. sub.* salga, saliate, salgano.
sapere	● *Pres.* so, sai, sa, sappiamo, sanno. ● *Past hist.* seppi, sapesti. ● *Fut.* saprò *etc.* ● *Pres. sub.* sappia *etc.* ● *Imp.* sappi, sappia, sappiate, sappiano. ● *Cond.* saprei *etc.*
scegliere	● *Pres.* scelgo, scegli, sceglie, scegliamo, scelgono. ● *Past hist.* scelsi, scegliesti *etc.* ● *Past part.* scelto.
scrivere	● *Past hist.* scrissi, scrivesti *etc.* ● *Past part.* scritto.
sedere	● *Pres.* siedo *or* seggo, siedi, siede, siedono. ● *Pres. sub.* sieda *or* segga.
spegnere	● *Pres.* spengo, spengono. ● *Past hist.* spensi, spegnesti. ● *Past part.* spento.
stare	● *Pres.* sto, stai, sta, stiamo, stanno. ● *Past hist.* stetti, stesti. ● *Fut.* starò *etc.* ● *Pres. sub.* stia *etc.* ● *Past sub.* stessi *etc.* ● *Past part.* stato. ● *Imp.* sta', stia, stiano.
tacere	● *Pres.* taccio, tacciono. ● *Past hist.* tacqui, tacque, tacquero. ● *Pres. sub.* taccia.
tendere	● *Past hist.* tesi. ● *Past part.* teso.
tenere	● *Pres.* tengo, tieni, tiene, tengono. ● *Past hist.* tenni, tenesti. ● *Fut.* terrò *etc.* ● *Pres. sub.* tenga.
trarre	● *Pres.* traggo, trai, trae, traiamo, traete, traggono. ● *Past hist.* trassi, traesti. ● *Fut.* trarrò *etc.* ● *Pres. sub.* tragga. ● *Past sub.* traessi *etc.* ● *Past part.* tratto.
udire	● *Pres.* odo, odi, ode, odono. ● *Pres. sub.* oda. ● *Imp.* odi.
uscire	● *Pres.* esco, esci, esce, escono. ● *Pres. sub.* esca. ● *Imp.* esci, esca, escano.
valere	● *Pres.* valgo, valgono. ● *Past hist.* valsi, valesti. ● *Fut.* varrò *etc.* ● *Pres. sub.* valga, valgano. ● *Past part.* valso. ● *Cond.* varrei *etc.*
vedere	● *Past hist.* vidi, vedesti. ● *Fut.* vedrò *etc.* ● *Past part.* visto *or* veduto. ● *Cond.* vedrei *etc.*
venire	● *Pres.* vengo, vieni, viene, vengono. ● *Past hist.* venni, venisti. ● *Fut.* verrò *etc.*
vivere	● *Past hist.* vissi, vivesti. ● *Fut.* vivrò *etc.* ● *Past part.* vissuto. ● *Cond.* vivrei *etc.*

volere ● *Pres.* voglio, vuoi, vuole, vogliamo, volete, vogliono. ● *Past hist.* volli, volesti. ● *Fut.* vorrò *etc.* ● *Pres. sub.* voglia *etc.* ● *Imp.* vogli, voglia, vogliate, vogliano. ● *Cond.* vorrei *etc.*

Numbers · Numeri

one (first)	1	uno (primo)
two (second)	2	due (secondo)
three (third)	3	tre (terzo)
four (fourth)	4	quattro (quarto)
five (fifth)	5	cinque (quinto)
six (sixth)	6	sei (sesto)
seven (seventh)	7	sette (settimo)
eight (eighth)	8	otto (ottavo)
nine (ninth)	9	nove (nono)
ten (tenth)	10	dieci (decimo)
eleven (eleventh)	11	undici (undicesimo)
twelve (twelfth)	12	dodici (dodicesimo)
thirteen (thirteenth)	13	tredici (tredicesimo)
fourteen (fourteenth)	14	quattordici (quattordicesimo)
fifteen (fifteenth)	15	quindici (quindicesimo)
sixteen (sixteenth)	16	sedici (sedicesimo)
seventeen (seventeenth)	17	diciassette (diciassettesimo)
eighteen (eighteenth)	18	diciotto (diciottesimo)
nineteen (nineteenth)	19	diciannove (diciannovesimo)
twenty (twentieth)	20	venti (ventesimo)
twenty-one (twenty-first)	21	ventuno (ventunesimo)
twenty-two (twenty-second)	22	ventidue (ventiduesimo)
twenty-three (twenty-third)	23	ventitré (ventitreesimo)
twenty-four (twenty-fourth)	24	ventiquattro (ventiquattresimo)
thirty (thirtieth)	30	trenta (trentesimo)
forty (fortieth)	40	quaranta (quarantesimo)
fifty (fiftieth)	50	cinquanta (cinquantesimo)
sixty (sixtieth)	60	sessanta (sessantesimo)
seventy (seventieth)	70	settanta (settantesimo)
eighty (eightieth)	80	ottanta (ottantesimo)
ninety (ninetieth)	90	novanta (novantesimo)
a *or* one hundred, (a *or* one hundredth)	100	cento (centesimo)
a hundred and one (hundred and first)	101	cento uno (centunesimo)
two hundred (two hundredth)	200	duecento (duecentesimo)
a *or* one thousand (one thousandth)	1,000	mille (millesimo)
two thousand (two thousandth)	2,000	duemila (duemillesimo)
ten thousand (ten thousandth)	10,000	diecimila (diecimillesimo)
a *or* one million (millionth)	1,000,000	un milione (milionesimo)